HENRY VIII
and the
Art of Majesty

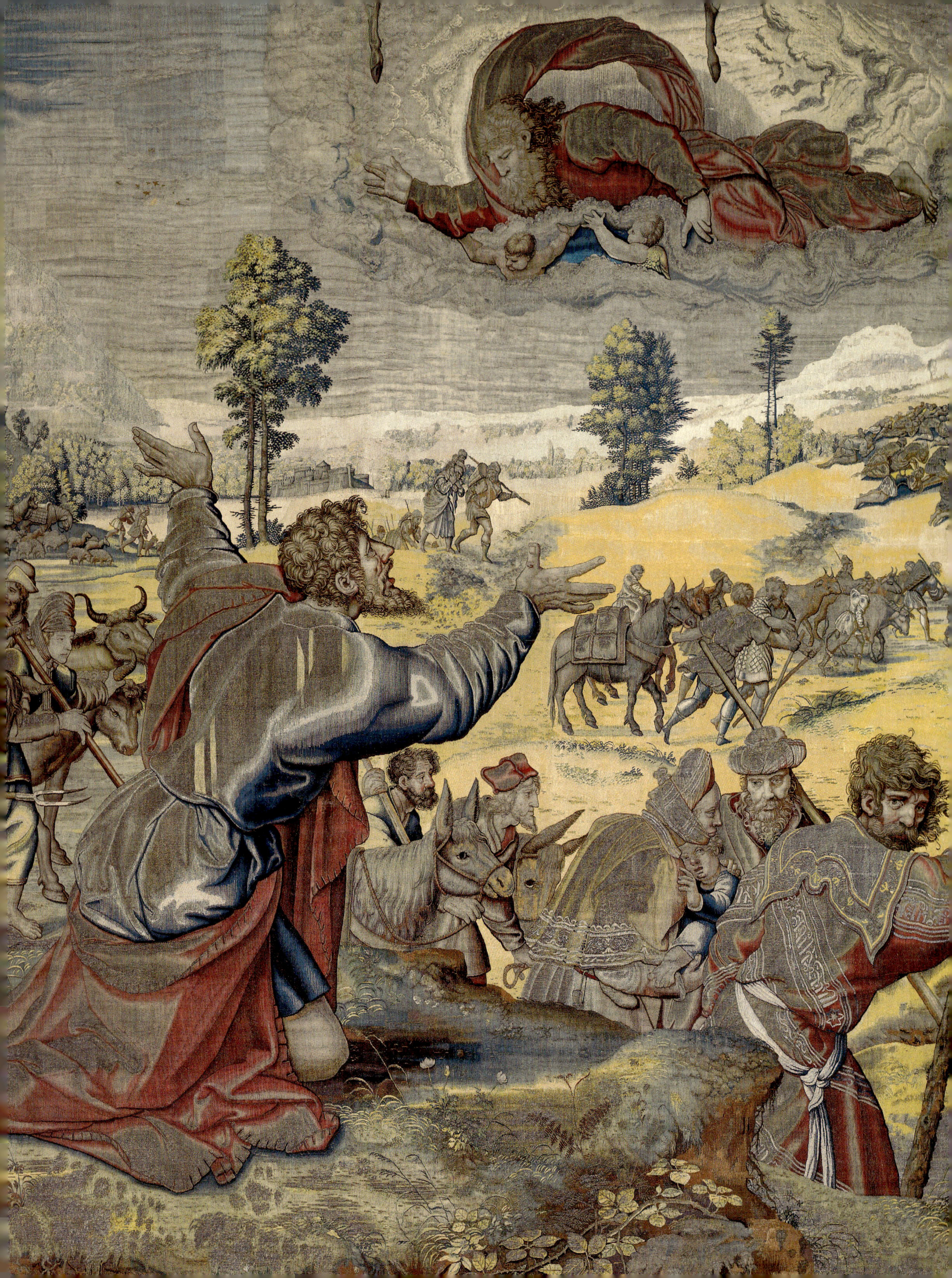

HENRY VIII
and the Art of Majesty

TAPESTRIES AT THE TUDOR COURT

Thomas P. Campbell

PUBLISHED FOR
The Paul Mellon Centre for Studies in British Art
BY YALE UNIVERSITY PRESS
New Haven and London

Designed by Bruce Campbell
Set in Centaur and Centaur Swash by Aardvark Type
Printed in Singapore by C S Graphics

Library of Congress Cataloging-in-Publication Data
Campbell, Thomas P.
Henry VIII and the art of majesty : tapestries at the Tudor Court / Thomas P. Campbell.
p. cm.
Includes bibliographical references and index.
ISBN 978-0-300-12234-3 (clothbound : alk. paper)
1. Tapestry, Flemish. 2. Tapestry, Renaissance—Flanders. 3. Henry VIII, King of England, 1491–1547—Art collections. 4. Henry VIII, King of England, 1491–1547—Art patronage. 5. Tapestry—Private collections—England. I. Paul Mellon Centre for Studies in British Art. II. Title.
NK3055.A1C36 2007
746.3942'09031--DC22

2007016895

A catalogue record for this book is available from the British Library.

The paper in this book meets the guidelines for permanence and durability of the Committee on Production Guidelines for Book Longevity of the Council on Library Resources.
10 9 8 7 6 5 4 3 2 1

Frontispiece: detail of fig. 14.4
Endleaves: *The Unicorn in Captivity* (details of front and back), Southern Netherlands, 1495–1505. Wool, warp, silk and gilt-metal wrapped threads, 368 x 252 cm. The Metropolitan Museum of Art, Gift of John D. Rockefeller, Jr., 1937 (37.80.6)
Jacket illustration: detail of fig. 10.2

Contents

Acknowledgments

It is twenty years since I first became interested in the formation of the English royal tapestry collection, and over this period I have incurred debts of gratitude to many friends and scholars. First and foremost, I thank John Newman, supervisor of my Courtauld Institute Ph.D. thesis, on which this book is largely based. Lorne Campbell and Scot McKendrick were the examiners of that thesis, and I benefited considerably from their criticisms, as also from the content and example of their own minutely researched studies. Between 1987 and 1994 I was fortunate to work as founder and archivist of the Franses Tapestry Archive, and I enjoyed many discussions on issues of tapestry connoisseurship with Simon and David Franses. During these years I also came to know the group of dedicated tapestry historians around the world whose hard-won discoveries provided the foundations on which my own work was based. For their achievement in the field, as well as the encouragement and friendship they gave me, I would particularly like to acknowledge Rotraud Bauer, Pascal Bertrand, Iain Buchanan, Dus Cavallo, Guy Delmarcel, Nello Forti Grazzini, Wendy Hefford, Concha Herrero Carretero, and Isabelle van Tichelen. Above all, I am indebted to the late Edith Standen, whose scholarly generosity remains a constant source of inspiration to me. Over the years I have also benefited immeasurably from discussions with colleagues working in the field of Tudor studies, especially Simon Thurley, whose enthusiasm for all things Tudor helped determine my own nascent career as an art historian. I am also indebted to the work of David Starkey and the scholars who are contributing to the Henry VIII inventory project. With a significant number of Henry VIII's tapestries still at Hampton Court, I have been a regular visitor to that palace, and colleagues at the Historic Royal Palaces Agency and the Textile Conservation Studio have been most helpful in responding to requests for access, information, and photography. Sir Hugh Roberts and the staff of the Royal Collection have always been graciously supportive of my work, and the sumptuous visual character of this book owes much to the generous terms under which I have been allowed to reproduce works of art from the Royal Collection. Following my move to the department of European sculpture and decorative arts at The Metropolitan Museum of Art in 1995, Olga Raggio, chair of the department until 2001, was unfailingly supportive of my research on Henry VIII. Her successor, Ian Wardropper, has been equally encouraging. The final version of this book has been written over the course of the past three years, during which time I have benefited immensely from the aid of Ken Soehner and the staff of the Watson Library at the Metropolitan Museum. A number of friends and colleagues have read the text in whole or in part, and for their perceptive comments and suggestions I am especially grateful to Percy Campbell, Elizabeth Cleland, Guy Delmarcel, John Guy, Maria Hayward, Maurice Howard, Edmée Reit, Kay Staniland, Hilary Turner, and Greg Walker. Production of such a lavish book is, of course, a complex and expensive process. I would like to thank Patricia Fidler and Kristin Swan at Yale University Press for their guidance and help, Laura Jones Dooley for her painstaking and judicious work in editing the text, Bruce Campbell for the design and layout, Kay Banning and Pippa Letsky for indexing and proofreading the text, and Mary Mayer and John Long for the production. Financial support for the illustrations has been most generously provided by the Paul Mellon Foundation, Mrs. Hester Diamond, and The Metropolitan

Museum of Art. For the last of these I thank Philippe de Montebello, Doralynn Pines, and Ian Wardropper. The immense task of collating the illustrations has been undertaken by Elizabeth Cleland, assisted by Giovanna Fiorino-Iannace, Emily Silber, and Sarah Thein. Bruce White made the excellent new photographs of some of the Hampton Court tapestries and various pieces in Spain and France, while Yvan Maes and Thierry Crépin-Leblond have generously allowed me to use photography undertaken at the Royal Tapestry Manufactory in Mechelen of the *Story of David* tapestries from the Musée de la Renaissance, Écouen. Many other colleagues have also contributed to the visual richness of this book. In particular, I would like to thank Santiago Samaniego for helping to coordinate photography in Spain, Barbara Bridgers and the staff of The Metropolitan Museum's photography studio, and Deanna Cross and Julie Zeftel of the Image Library. Finally, I would like to thank my parents, Jean and Percy Campbell, my wife, Phoebe, and our children, Charles and Honor, for their support and patience with this project over the years.

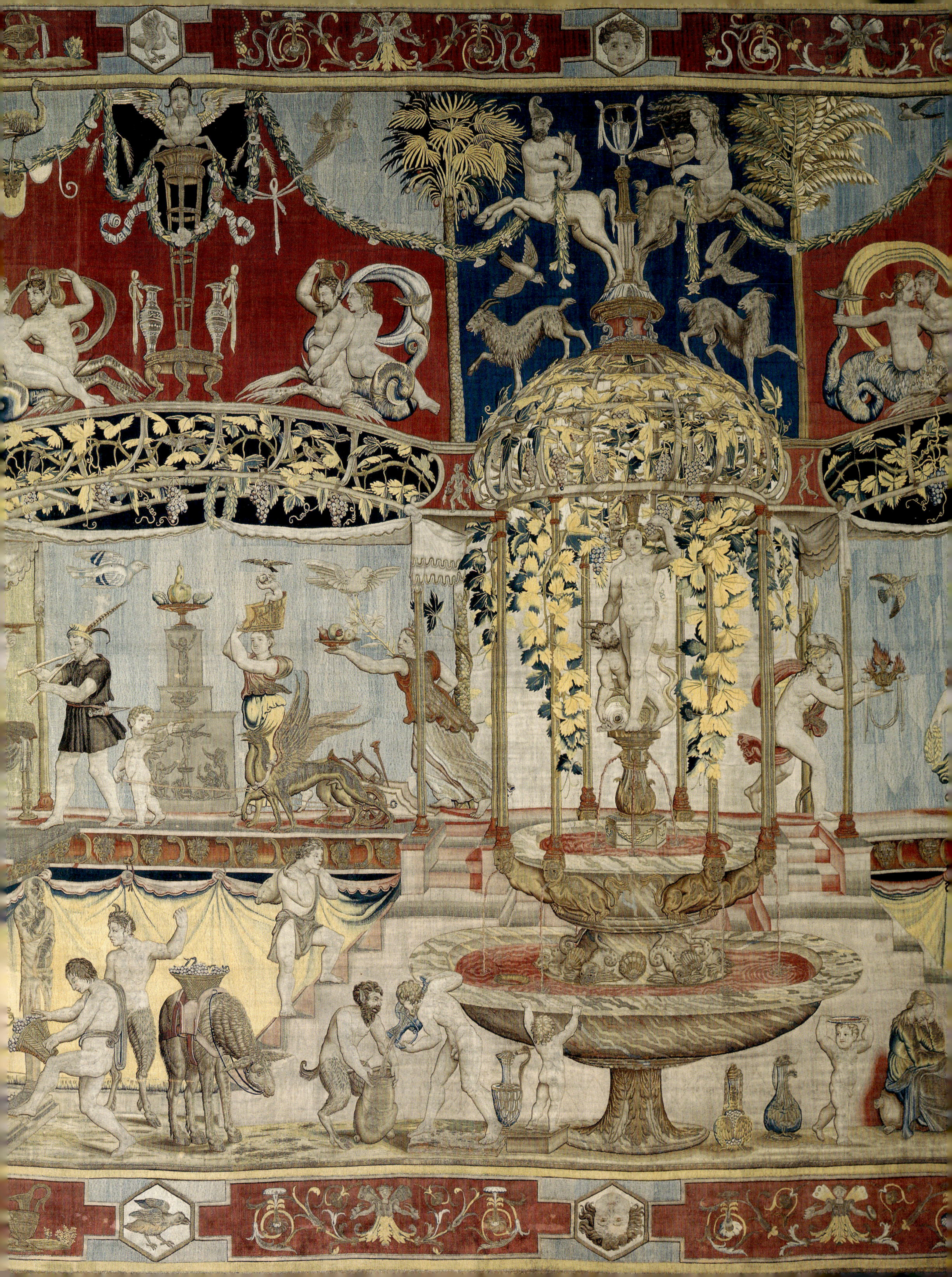

Introduction

"More tapestries, or at least as many, as any Christian king"

For most of the sixteenth century Brussels was the center of high-quality tapestry manufacture in the Low Countries, and rich patrons all over Europe keenly sought its goods. Quality was strictly controlled by the tapestry guild, whose headquarters was located in the Grand Place, facing the town hall. In 1539 this guild prosecuted four of its richest and most powerful members on the grounds that they had allowed their workshops to paint certain details of the tapestries they made, rather than weaving them in entirety as guild regulations stipulated. In their defense the four merchants obtained a deposition exonerating them from this charge by a man whose opinion was evidently expected to carry weight. His name was Jan Mostinck, and for the preceding twelve years he had been the officer responsible for the tapestries belonging to King Henry VIII of England. According to Mostinck's deposition, Henry owned more tapestries, or at least as many, as any Christian king.[1] Mostinck continued that in his career he had never encountered the fraudulent practices of which the merchants were charged.

Jan Mostinck's work for Henry and his role in sourcing tapestries for the English crown will be the subject of later discussion. The notable aspect of his deposition here is his emphatic, even boastful statement regarding the number of tapestries that Henry already owned in 1539. Confirmation of the size of Henry's collection is provided by the two-volume inventory of royal possessions taken eight years later, following the king's death on January 27, 1547.[2] Leaving aside other hangings of embroidery and precious materials, this inventory records approximately 2,450 tapestry wall hangings, comprising over three hundred sets of three or more pieces, sixty-five pairs of tapestry, and about 160 individual tapestry hangings. In addition, the inventory also lists more than three hundred miscellaneous furnishing tapestries, for a combined total of more than 2,770 tapestry items.

This enormous assemblage was not a collection in the modern sense of the word, a carefully composed selection of objects undertaken by one individual. Rather, these hangings had been acquired for all sorts of purposes—practical, aesthetic, and political—over the previous two centuries. The diverse origins of the collection were reflected by the disposition and descriptions of the tapestries recorded by the 1547 inventory. They were divided among the "standing wardrobes" of fourteen palaces and lesser residences and four "removing wardrobes." Although several hundred pieces were relatively small, made as altar frontals, counterpanes, and window pieces, and while some sets were also of modest dimensions, many others were much larger, covering hundreds, even thousands of square feet (fig. i.1). The tapestries embraced every conceivable subject: allegorical, chivalric, decorative, genre (fig. i.2), heraldic, mythological (fig. i.3), and religious. Many at the older palaces like Richmond and Windsor were antique and Henry had evidently inherited them, but large numbers at residences like Hampton Court and Westminster were described as "newe." Similarly, while certain sets were said to be coarse, many others were described as "riche" or "with gold," including a large number that can be related to purchases made by Henry himself. No complete inventories for the tapestry collections of Henry's contemporaries, Francis I, king of France, and Charles V, king of Spain and Holy Roman Emperor, have survived, but the extant lists and purchase documentation leave little doubt that,

Detail of fig. 13.19

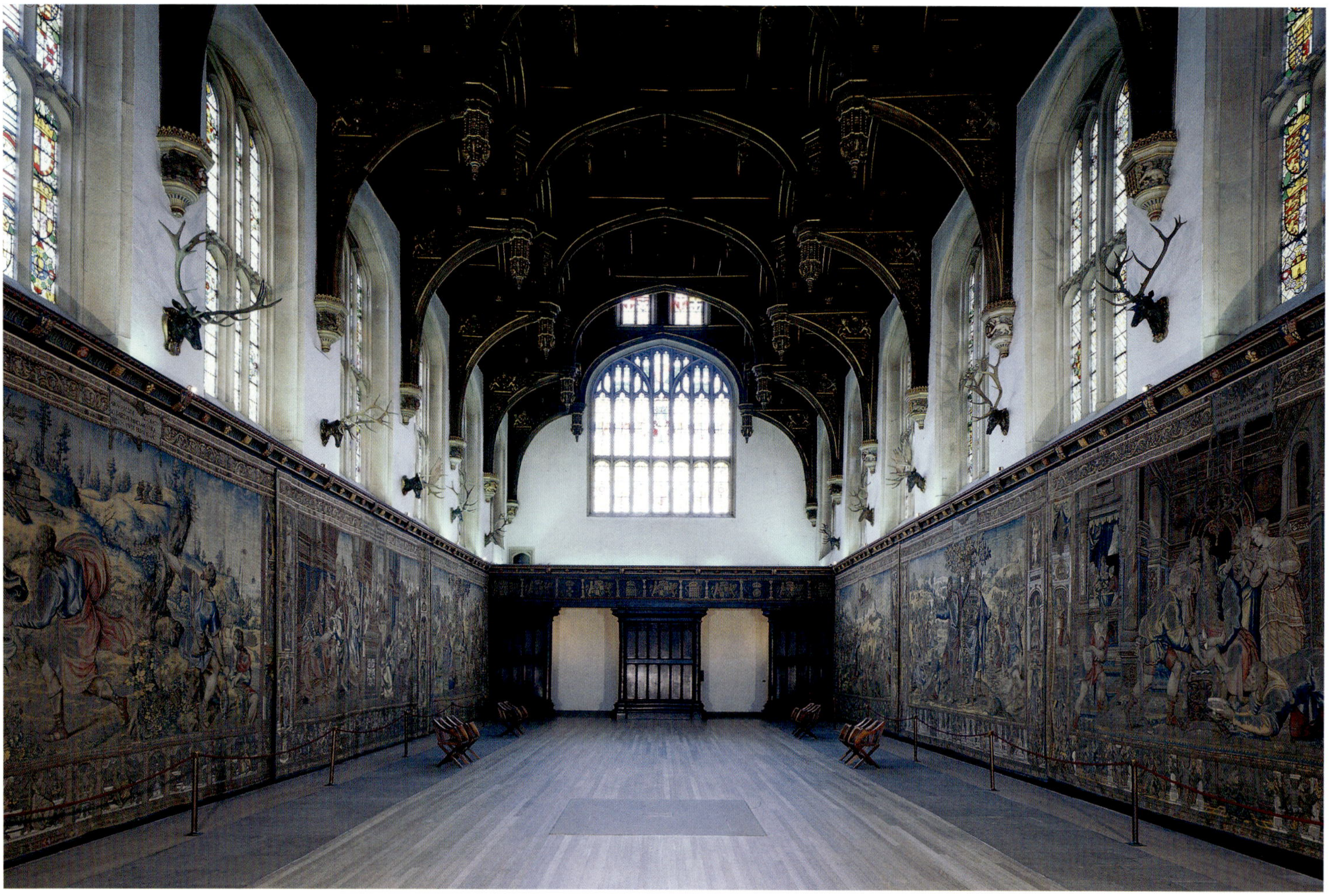

i.1 View of the great hall at Hampton Court hung with part of the *Story of Abraham* set

by the end of his reign, Henry's collection was much larger than either. It also greatly exceeded the size of any other papal or secular collections of the day. Indeed, so far as we know, it was the largest collection ever amassed, with the exception of that formed 150 years later by Louis XIV, king of France.[3]

The Subsequent History and Perception of the Tudor Tapestry Collection

Despite the gigantic number of tapestries dispersed around the royal palaces and documentary evidence of the enormous sums that Henry spent on key sets, the royal tapestry collection has received scant attention in studies of the Tudor kings or of English art and patronage. Various factors have contributed to this neglect of which the most obvious is the destruction and dispersal of more than 95 percent of the collection between 1547 and the early nineteenth century. Although the royal tapestries continued to play a central role in court decoration and ceremony in the century after Henry's death, the collection was depleted in size by about 50 percent during the early 1650s when the royal collection was put up for sale by the Commonwealth government. A number of the finest and most valuable sets did survive in the collection at the time of the Restoration because they had been reserved from sale for the use of Oliver Cromwell. These antique hangings, many richly woven with gold, continued to provide the key figurative decoration in the state apartments at the royal palaces for much of the eighteenth century. But as the decades passed, long-term exposure led to fading and damage, which in turn led to growing indifference. With the rise of interest in Old Master paintings during the eighteenth and early nineteenth centuries, the antique hangings were increasingly overlooked in favor of the canvasses that now crowded the palace walls, often directly on top of the tapestries. The majority of the tapestries that survived in the royal collection were removed and discarded during the first third of the nineteenth century, and by the time that respect for the tapestry medium recovered in the mid- to late nineteenth century, only about thirty items from the Tudor era remained in the collection. These pieces survive today at Hampton Court.[4]

Scholarly and public interest in the surviving royal tapestries began to develop from the mid-nineteenth century, largely through the attention they received by association with Hampton Court, which was opened as a showcase for the royal picture collection in 1839. Attention was further stimulated during the last quarter of the century by contemporary interest in the arts and crafts, particularly those of the medieval era. Initial archival research was undertaken in the 1890s on the tapestry collections of Henry VIII and Cardinal Wolsey, but it was not until 1906 that W. G. Thomson's *History of Tapestry from the Earliest Times to the Present Day* provided the first extensive discussion of the royal tapestry collection.[5] This wide-ranging study incorporated substantial sections on the formation of the English royal collection and the manufacture and patronage of tapestry in Britain. Eight years later these portions were expanded and revised for a second book, titled *Tapestry Weaving in England from the Earliest Times to the End of the Eighteenth Century* (1914). Although both books were largely based on secondary texts, they were significant for synthesizing many of the archival references revealed by late-nineteenth-century calendars of state and royal papers. One of the most significant documents to which Thomson drew attention was the 1547 inventory of Henry VIII's possessions, of which he published the tapestry entries, in synopsis and without dimensions.[6] Recognizing the extraordinary scale of the collection it listed, Thomson commented that Henry "had a perfect mania for acquiring tapestries by any means that presented itself," but although he surmised that the "royal palaces were plentifully adorned with the richest tapestries the world could furnish," the sheer size of the collection appears to have forestalled any more detailed analysis.[7] Apart from recognizing that some of the Hampton Court tapestries once belonged to Henry, his work provided little further information about the content or use of the collection.

Despite its limitations, Thomson's *History of Tapestry* has remained the primary text on English tapestry patronage since its first publication. Although it was reissued in 1930 and 1973, the revisions add little information on Henry's collection, and this has been a major factor in the continuing neglect of the subject.[8] Another has been the entrenchment of the bias in favor of "fine arts" at the expense of

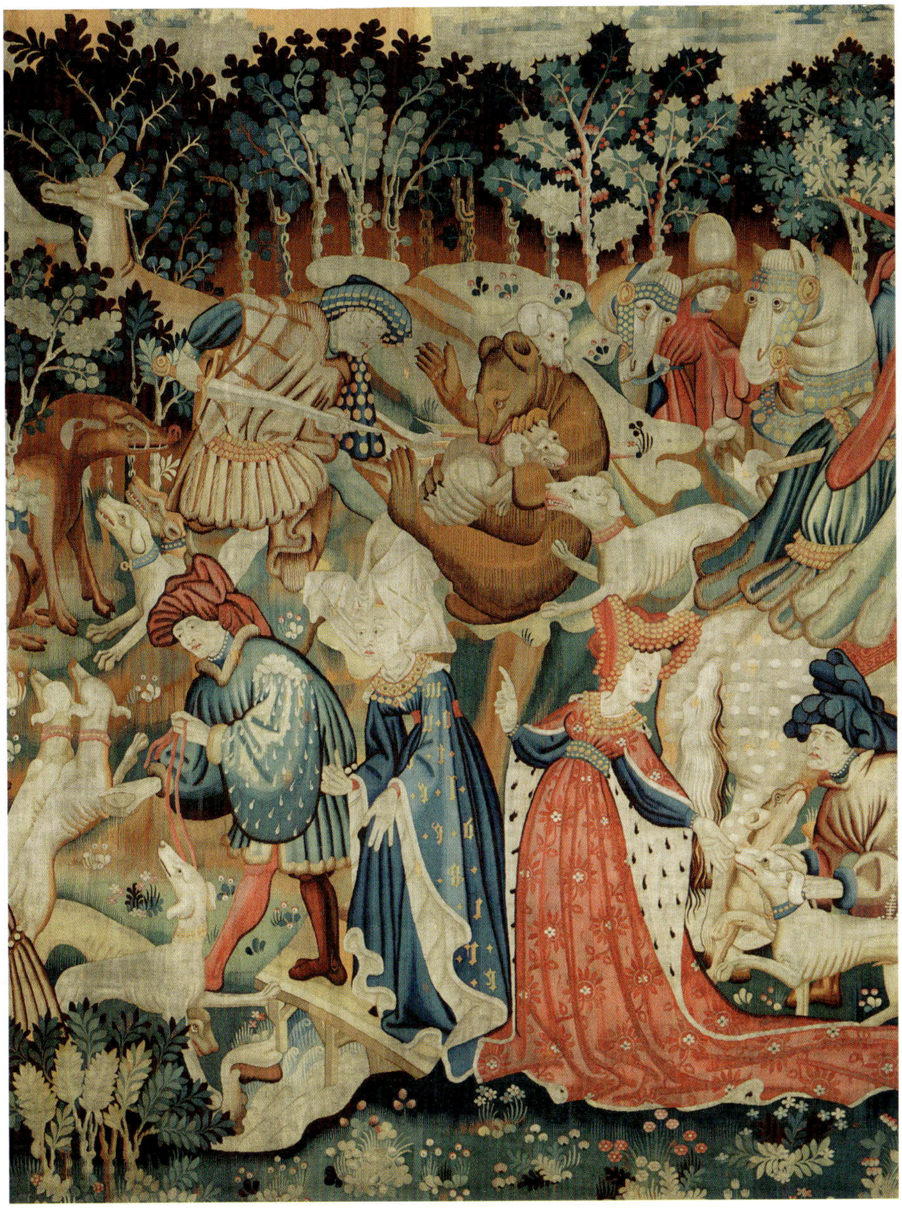

i.2 Detail of fig. 2.11. The *Devonshire Hunts*, now in the Victoria and Albert Museum, London, typify the sort of medieval hunting tapestries Henry VIII would have inherited.

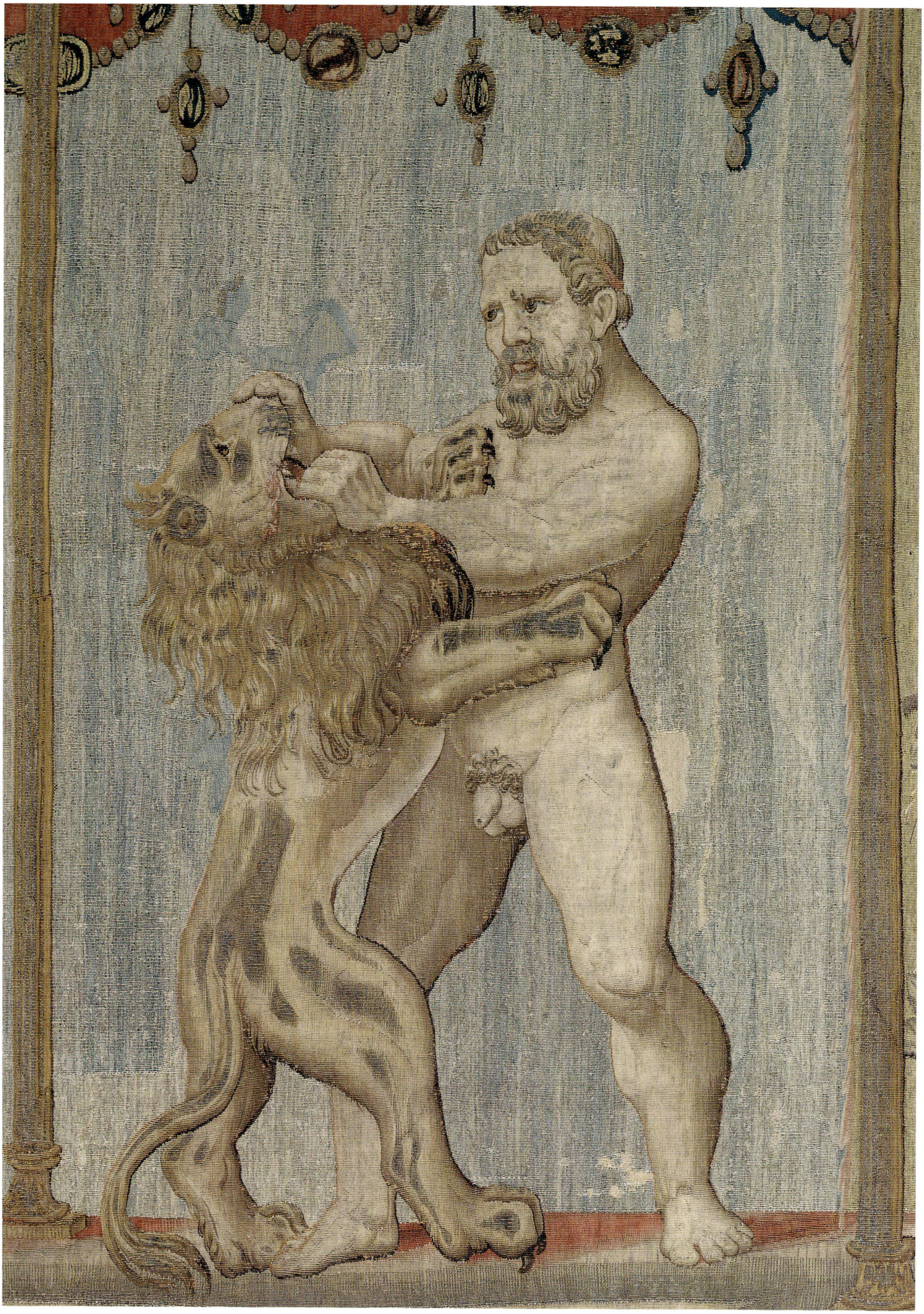

i.3 Detail of fig. 13.18

"decorative arts" that came about with the foundation of the Courtauld Institute in 1931, and the proliferation of its connoisseur-based methodology as the guiding principle of the English-speaking art world during the second third of the century. Indeed, the royal tapestry collection is barely mentioned in analyses of Tudor art produced before the 1970s. This neglect is typified by Erna Auerbach's influential survey, *Tudor Artists* (1954), which only makes one reference to Cardinal Wolsey's tapestry collection and does not mention that of Henry VIII at all.[9] A similar picture emerges from architectural studies of the period and the sizeable literature devoted to Tudor painters and miniaturists published over the past forty years.[10] The overriding impression provided by these medium-specific studies is that the figurative art of the Tudor court was essentially a matter of painted portraits and miniatures and, to a lesser extent, fresco decorations.

The royal tapestry collection fared little better in works devoted to the "decorative arts" during the mid-twentieth century. Although a catalogue of the Hampton Court tapestries was published in 1932 by H. C. Marillier, and revised and reissued in 1951 and 1962, this gave only a superficial analysis of the tapestries.[11] On a more general level, the continuing neglect of the subject was reflected and propagated by the *Connoisseur Period Guide* (1956) and works such as Margaret Wood's *English Mediaeval House* (1965), which added little information to that provided by Thomson.[12] The paucity of detailed information on the royal tapestry collection ensured that it was overlooked by the more scholarly, interdisciplinary studies that began to appear in the late 1960s, as exemplified by J. J. Scarisbrick's history of Henry VIII's reign (1968) and Sidney Anglo's ground-breaking study of the spectacle and pageantry of the Tudor court (1969).

A new direction was anticipated by Joyceline Russell's study of the Field of Cloth of Gold, the famous meeting that took place between Henry VIII and Francis I in France in June 1520. Based on a close reading of contemporary documentation, Russell's work (1969) reflected the important role that tapestry played in the magnificence of the Tudor court.[13] This theme was developed by Gordon Kipling, whose studies of the influence of Burgundian culture on the early Tudor court and Henry VII's artistic patronage (1977, 1981) were the first to consider the strong link between Continental and Tudor tastes and the first to place the royal tapestry collection in the broader context of Henry VII's artistic patronage.[14] During the 1980s, the context of Tudor tapestry patronage was greatly enriched by Scot McKendrick's dissertation (1988) on the representation of classical myth and history in fifteenth-century art and the ground-breaking research articles that resulted from this work.[15] These were notable for the wealth of archival sources that they brought to light and the rigorous analysis they provided of native tapestry patronage in the light of Continental practice. My debt to McKendrick's work is readily evident in the introductory chapters of this book.

The Purpose of This Study

Although these various studies reflect an increasing awareness of the central role that tapestry played in the culture of the Tudor court, there remained a lack of substance regarding the collections of Henry VII and Henry VIII, and it was this gap in scholarship that spurred my interest as a student at the Courtauld Institute.[16] The reason for the continuing neglect of the subject is not difficult to detect. In view of the loss of more than 95 percent of the Tudor tapestry collection, the information provided by contemporary documents and the 1547 inventory is frequently impenetrable. How does one begin to interpret the long lists of set names or dimensions that they provide? Can such information be used for anything but the most basic thematic analysis?

In the course of the late 1980s and 1990s my research suggested a variety of techniques through which the information could, indeed, be broken down and interpreted. Scrutiny of contemporary terminology demonstrated that from the 1510s many court documents use the term *arras* to identify tapestries woven with gold thread—that is, a gilt-metallic filament wrapped round a silk core.[17] Use of this term in documents such as the 1547 inventory therefore provides us with a means to focus on those sets that were the most valuable and important in the collection. Moreover, although the contemporary purchase documentation is very incomplete, extant accounts from various departments of the royal household provide some information about the dates at which various key sets were purchased. In addition, because tapestries were copied from full-scale designs that were often rewoven for several patrons, visual evidence regarding some of Henry's tapestries can be deduced by comparison between the subjects and dimensions of pieces listed in the 1547 inventory and those of tapestries in the collections of other contemporary patrons that have survived elsewhere. Taken as a whole, these sources and methodology allow us to identify the design and date of acquisition for a substantial number of Henry's most important tapestries. On this basis, we are finally in a position to assess the contribution that the collection made to the art and magnificence of the Tudor court.

This consideration formed the subject of my doctoral dissertation, "The English Royal Tapestry Collection, 1485–1547" (1999). In this I argued that study of Henry's tapestry collection provided a revolutionary new understanding of the visual culture of the Tudor court, because it revealed the extent to which tapestry was the preeminent figurative art form in this venue, valued both as a medium of artistry and as a medium of suggestion and magnificence. The use of tapestry as a tool of suggestion was especially significant during the 1530s and 1540s because of the English Reformation and the efforts that Henry was making to influence the opinions of key sections of society.

This book covers much of the same ground but in a different fashion. The thesis provided a synthesis of the evidence and a thematic consideration of such topics as the circumstances in which the collection was formed, how it was used, the criteria by which it was appreciated, and a long catalogue of possible identifications. In contrast, the material presented in this book has been rewritten in a more chronological form so that the development of the collection is more closely related to the personalities and events that shaped its formation. The book is divided into seven parts. When Henry VIII

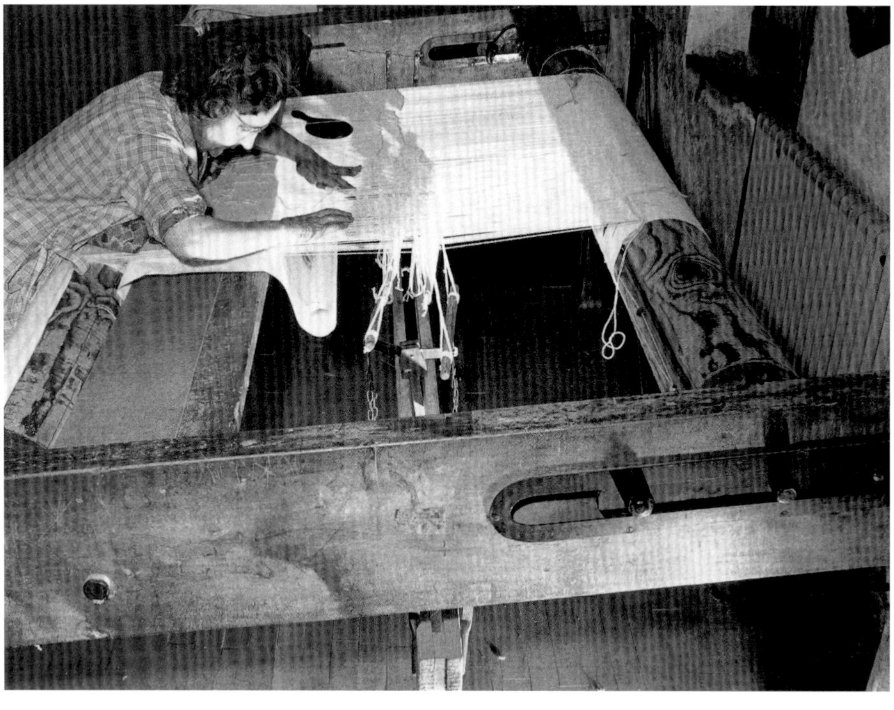

i.4 View of a weaver working on a low-warp loom

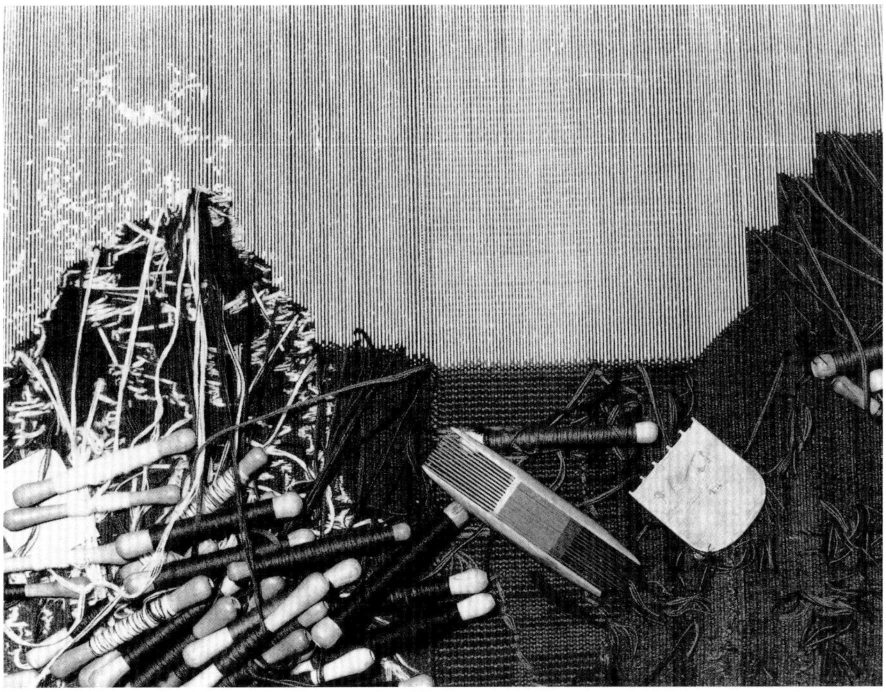

i.5 View of the back of a tapestry being woven on a low-warp loom

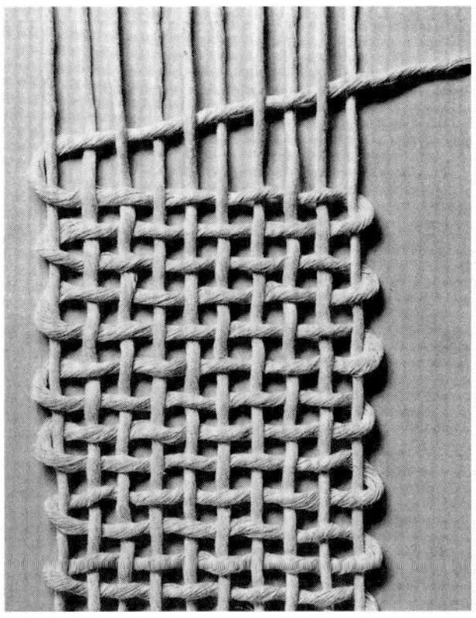

i.6 Model of plain weave

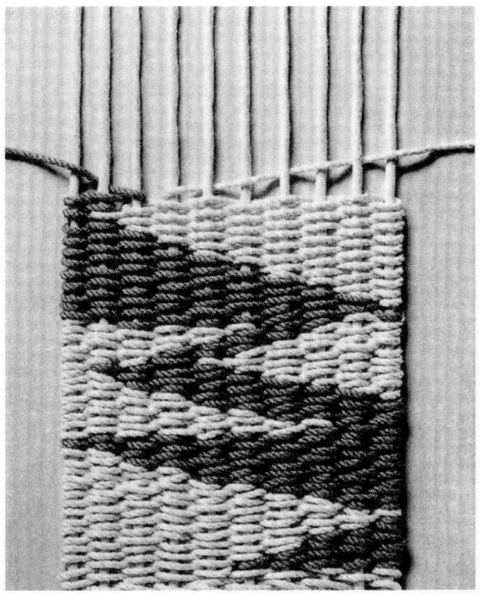

i.7 Model of weft-faced tapestry weave

became king in 1509, tapestry had been one of the principal forms of display for the English crown for more than one hundred years and many practices of usage were well established. The first part of the book (Chapters 1 to 3) therefore considers the formation and use of the collection before the Tudor accession. Part II (Chapters 4 and 5) addresses the years of Henry VII's reign and the extent to which the first Tudor king followed and adapted existing practices. Part III (Chapters 6 to 10) considers the development of the royal tapestry collection between Henry VIII's accession and the late 1520s. Attention is paid also to Cardinal Wolsey's tapestry patronage both because he was so closely linked with the king in this period and because his sizeable collection was appropriated by the Crown following his fall in 1529. Part IV (Chapters 11 and 12) analyzes how Henry's patronage developed during the 1530s as he sought to use tapestry as a tool of suggestion during the turbulent years of the English Reformation. Part V (Chapters 13 to 15) considers the highly expensive and rich tapestries that Henry purchased in the years following the birth of Prince Edward, when the dissolution of the monasteries provided him with unprecedented resources for new commissions. Part VI (Chapters 16 and 17) provides an analysis of the character and disposition of the royal tapestry collection as it was documented by the inventory taken after Henry's death in 1547 and draws together various conclusions regarding the contribution that the collection made to the culture of the Tudor court. Finally, Part VII (Chapters 18 and 19) surveys the subsequent history of the Tudor tapestry collection and the circumstances that depleted the size and status of the collection so radically between 1547 and the present.

Although many individual identifications and theories presented in the following pages remain conjectural, the overwhelming conclusion that emerges—the significance of tapestry as a medium of art, magnificence, and propaganda at the Tudor court—seems unassailable. Much remains to be discovered about relationships among Tudor courtiers, Antwerp merchants, and Flemish artists and the circumstances in which some of the more important commissions were conceived. Many individual tapestry series deserve monographic treatment in this new light. In a related field, much remains to be said about the relationship of the iconography of the Tudor tapestry collection and the influence it may have exerted on contemporary writing, in both the political and literary spheres. I hope that the material presented here may form the platform for future, more detailed studies of different aspects of this fascinating and little-known subject.

How Tapestries Are Made

Many issues relating to the character and aesthetic of the tapestry medium are addressed in the course of this book, but for those readers unfamiliar with the medium, some brief introductory remarks are in order. The word *tapestry* is loosely applied in the modern world to describe both a range of machine-made textured fabrics and a type of hand-stitched needlepoint. Before the advent of mechanization, however, it designated a particular kind of textile that was woven by hand on a loom, and it is in this sense that the term is used here. In European practice, the loom consists of two

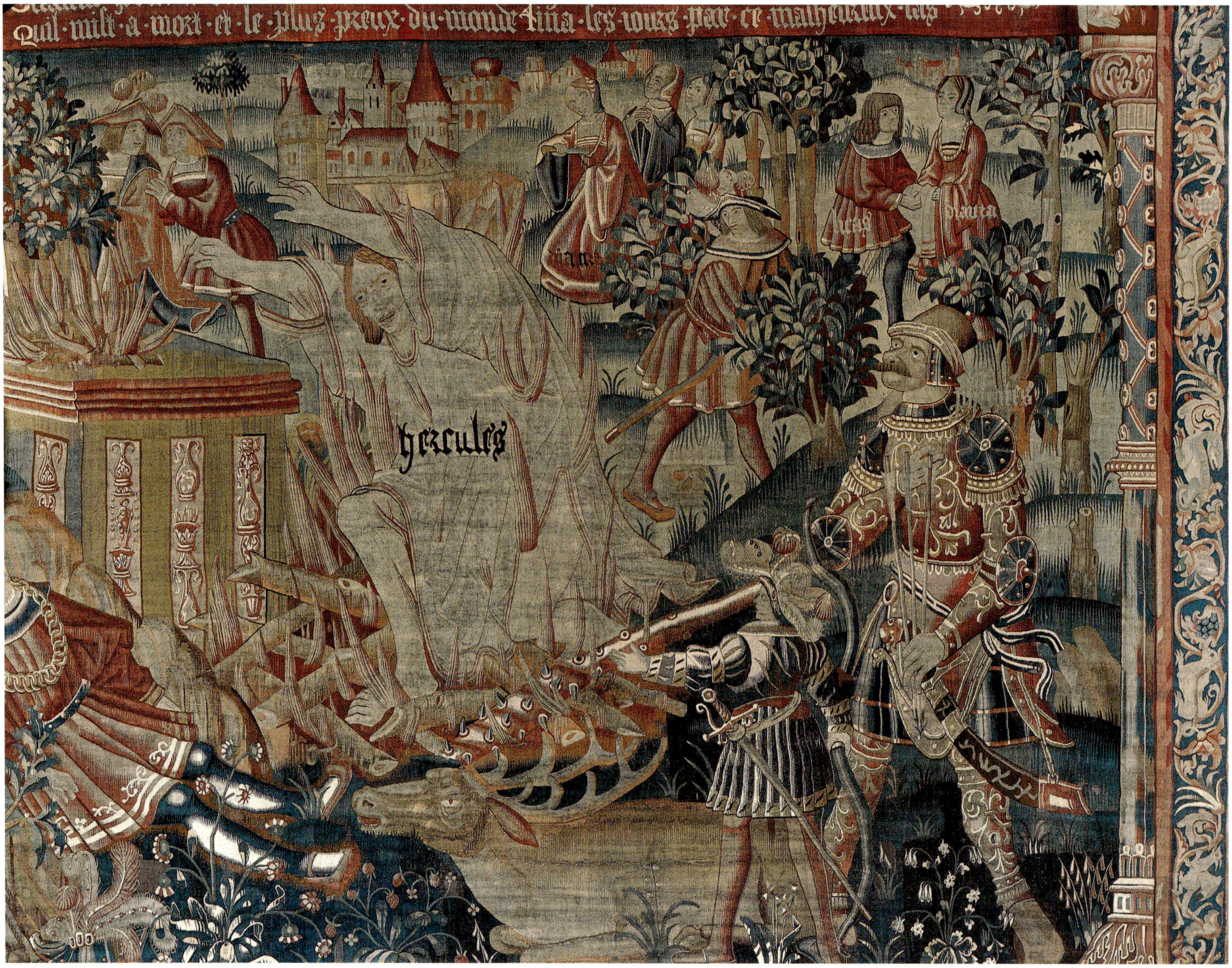

i.8 *The Death of Hercules* (detail of fragment) from a set of the *Story of Hercules*. Tapestry woven in the Southern Netherlands, ca. 1515. Wool, 396 x 518 cm. Hampton Court Palace

Opposite:
i.9 Detail of fig. 10.17

rollers between which the plain warp threads, generally of wool, are stretched.[18] The warps are arranged horizontally on a low-warp loom (fig. i.4) or vertically on a high-warp loom. In both cases the warps are arranged so that a small space, called the shed, exists between the even and odd warps. The weaver passes the colored weft thread, wrapped on a handheld shuttle, through this space. Alternate warps are attached to drawstrings with which the weaver can pull them forward or backward to create a second shed, through which the weft is passed back. The weaver works from the reverse side of the tapestry (fig. i.5). By passing the weft back and forth through the two sheds, the weaver effectively inserts the weft over one warp and under the next in one direction and then back in the opposite direction around the other side of each warp (figs. i.6, i.7). Periodically the weaver tamps down the developing web so that the warps are completely covered by the weft. By varying the colors of the weft, the weaver creates a pattern or figurative image. Between 1400 and 1530 Netherlandish weavers developed the ability to reproduce a broad range of textures and painterly effects through the use of fine interlocking areas of color (hachures), the juxtaposition of different materials, and the use of different techniques to link the weft threads.

Tapestries are copied from a full-scale version of the intended design known as the cartoon, which was generally based on a smaller design known as the *modello*. The artist

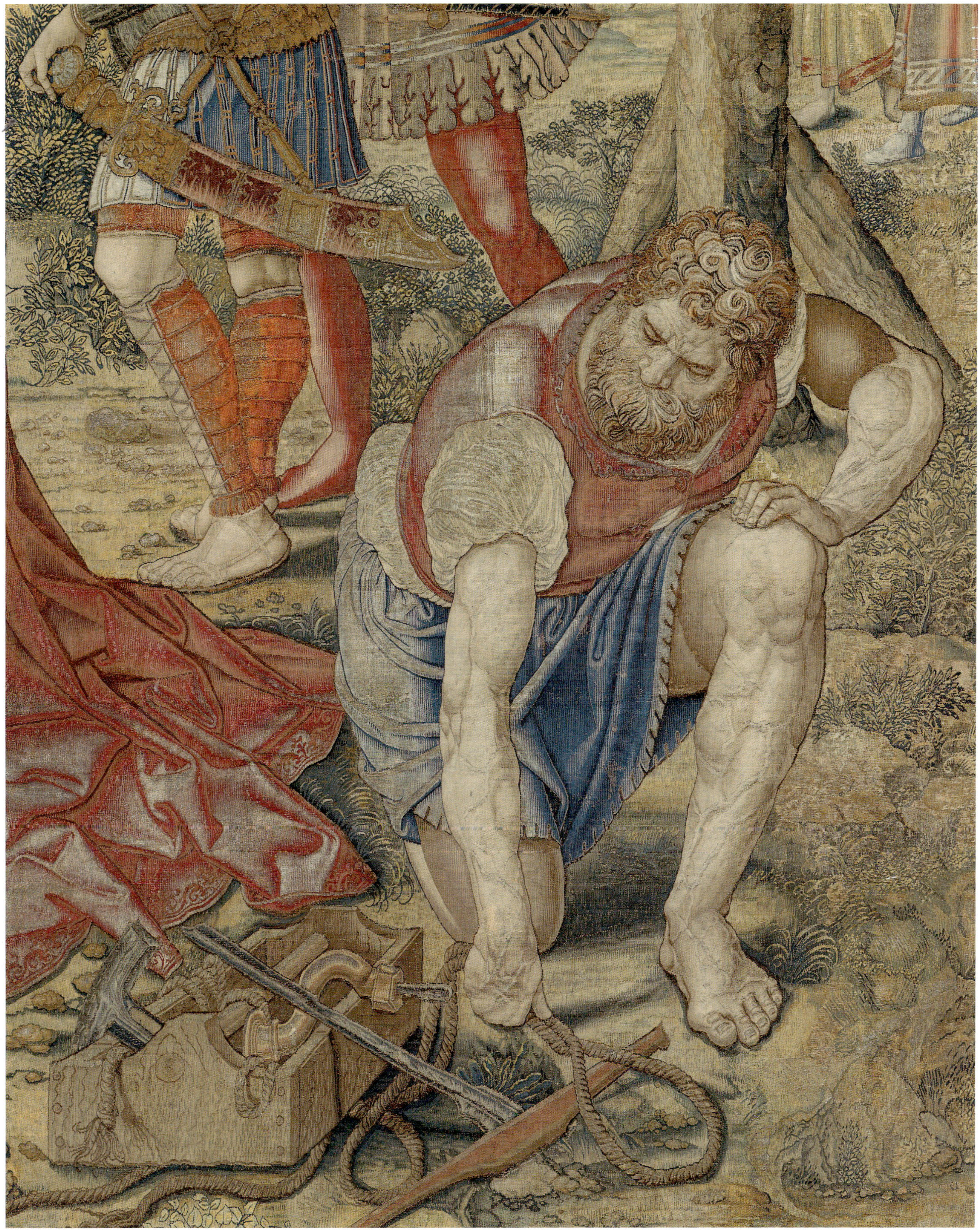

responsible for painting the cartoon was not necessarily the same as the artist who created the initial modello.[19] During the fifteenth century the cartoon was generally painted on linen, but from the early sixteenth century paper became the more common medium. Before starting work the weaver traces the cartoon onto the bare warps. With the high-warp loom the cartoon is then hung on the wall behind the weaver. In the case of the low-warp loom the cartoon is folded or cut into strips and placed directly beneath the warp threads, a proximity that is especially useful in the case of complex designs. An additional advantage of the low-warp loom is that the drawstrings used by the weaver to create the sheds are controlled by foot pedals, leaving both of the weaver's hands free to pass the weft. For these reasons, the low-warp technique was the predominant mode of production during the medieval and Renaissance periods. The disadvantage of the low-warp technique is that it reverses the orientation of the cartoon because the weaver is copying the front of the cartoon from the back of the tapestry. The designer therefore needs to create the cartoon for the low-warp technique in the direction opposite to that intended for the completed tapestry.

Another issue that should be emphasized right at the start is the extreme variation in the quality and cost of the tapestries that were being made during the era with which this study is concerned. Tapestry quality depends on the artistic quality of the cartoon, the skill of the weavers at translating that cartoon into woven form, the fineness of the weave—the number of warps per inch and the grade of the weft—and the physical quality and richness of the materials. The difference between low- and high-grade tapestry is considerable both in material richness and illusionistic possibilities (figs. i.8, i.9). In the late medieval and Renaissance eras, the cost rose steeply with the quality of the tapestry. One key factor was manpower. The execution of large tapestries required the participation of many skilled weavers over long periods. It is generally estimated that a weaver can produce about one square yard of medium-quality pictorial tapestry each month. Higher-quality production, with a finer warp and weft count, is much slower, yielding perhaps half a square yard per month.[20] An even more significant factor in determining cost was material. During the medieval era and Renaissance period, wool was used principally for the warps and for most of the weft, providing the weavers with the means to produce strong, bold designs. Finer-quality pieces also incorporated silk, which introduced a broader palette of colors and a lustrous texture, both of which allowed the weavers to produce more subtle highlights and illusionistic effects. The finest and most expensive works included "gold thread," which was actually silk thread wrapped in a thin gilt-metal filament. Use of such thread provided an almost enamel-like richness to the surface of the tapestry. Contemporary documents demonstrate that during Henry VIII's reign, tapestry woven with silk cost about four times more than that woven with wool alone. The inclusion of gilt-metal-wrapped thread increased the cost by a factor of about fifty.[21] Only the richest members of society could afford large high-quality sets of gold-woven tapestries, and it was for this reason that tapestry became a fundamental part of court display during the medieval era.

PART I

The Medieval Precedents

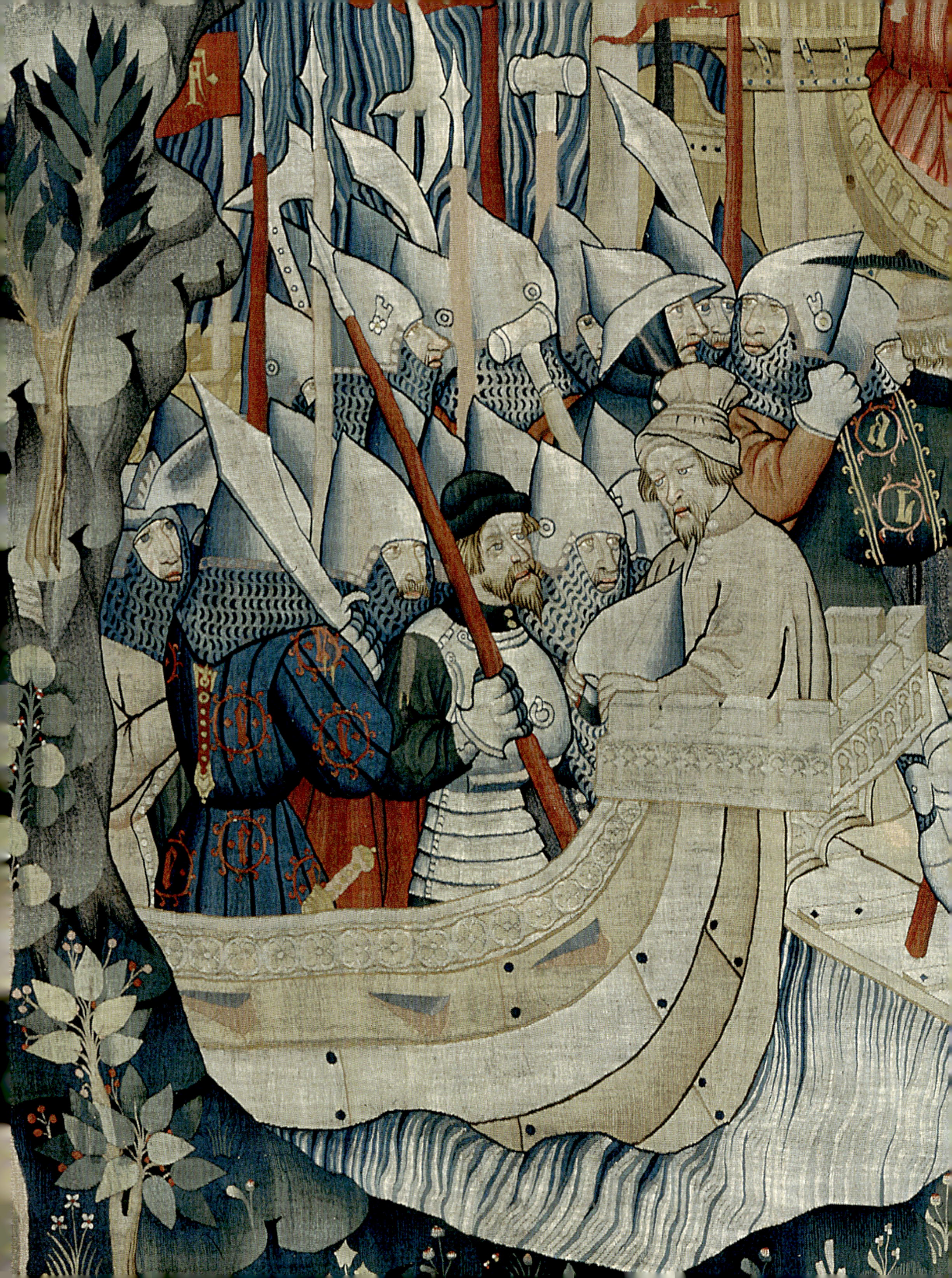

CHAPTER 1

The Royal Tapestry Collection before 1399

Early Origins

The period when figurative tapestry began to play a significant role in the English royal household is uncertain. Large figurative textiles made in the tapestry technique and a related knotted technique, dating from the late twelfth and early thirteenth centuries, survive at Quedlinberg and Halberstadt Cathedrals in Germany (fig. 1.1), demonstrating that workshops capable of producing such goods were in operation in northern Europe by this time.[1] Considering the scale of trade between the Continent and England, it is possible that similar products might have been imported at this period, long before any distinct records survive. The presence of tapestries in both Continental and English collections is better documented from the early fourteenth century. Although the evidence is often ambiguous and the terminology obscure, from around 1300 textiles that can be identified as tapestries begin to appear with greater frequency in contemporary descriptions and inventories.

The appeal and importance of tapestry and other luxury textiles at this time are easy to understand for they humanized the huge and drafty interiors of medieval castles, providing insulation and color. The furniture of the period consisted of wooden frames over which padding and textiles were draped and tied, and tapestry provided a durable medium for this purpose. Indeed, many of the earliest tapestry ensembles included throne or ceremonial bed hangings and even bench covers as well as wall hangings. While tapestries and textiles provided warmth, comfort, and decoration, they were also portable, a key advantage in an age when powerful households were constantly on the move. Woven primarily of wool, with thick, tightly packed yarns, medieval tapestries were more robust than other luxury textiles like silk damask and velvet, and they could easily be rolled up and dispatched on carts to be hung in advance of the arrival of the main party. Many castle chambers were equipped with hooks fixed permanently into the walls beneath the vaults, so the plainest rooms could be transformed into bright, colorful interiors in the time it took to unroll and hang the tapestries.

Quite apart from the practical value, the tapestry medium had a further attraction: every colored thread was placed by hand, which allowed the weavers to create complex designs that were impossible to achieve on the semi-

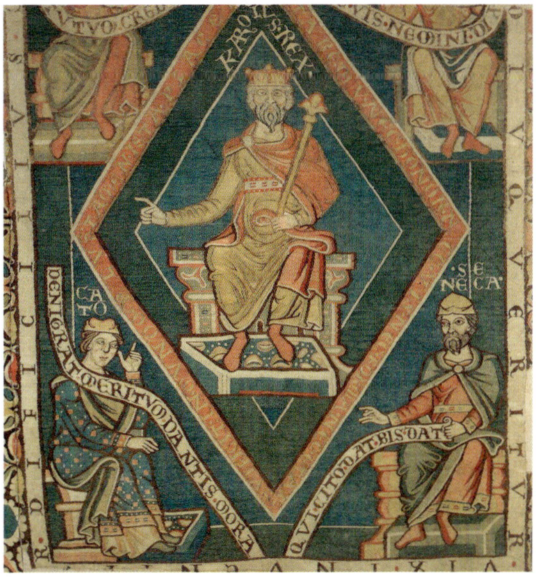

1.1 *The Charlemagne Tapestry*. Tapestry made by an unidentified workshop in Halberstadt, ca. 1230–40. Wool, 240 x 187 cm. Cathedral Treasury, Halberstadt

Detail of fig. 1.11

mechanized looms used to produce other luxury textiles such as silk and velvet. Tapestry was thus eminently suitable for the production of individualized designs, whether figurative, decorative, or heraldic. And in contrast to other woven textiles, in which the technology generally limited the fabric to widths of under a yard, a tapestry loom could be several yards wide, facilitating the production of much larger hangings.

The origins of these hangings were various. While our knowledge of the antecedents of the European tapestry industry is hampered by the paucity of surviving examples and the vague terminology used in contemporary documents, it is evident that organized workshops of tapestry weavers were active in northern France and the Low Countries by the beginning of the fourteenth century and that this nascent industry was of a scale and sophistication unlike that of previous eras or contemporary production elsewhere in Europe.[2] During the following decades increasing numbers of references to "tapissiers" and "haute lisse" weavers in contemporary records, combined with larger numbers of tapestry ensembles listed in contemporary inventories, point to an expanding production in these regions. Much of this activity was focused in Paris and Arras, although "tapissiers" are also mentioned from an early date in other towns in the Low Countries such as Brussels, Lille, and Tournai. The majority of this production comprised hangings with repeating heraldic and decorative motifs, with a lesser quantity of figurative work. Given the volume of raw wool exported to the Low Countries from England during this period, it seems likely that many of these tapestries were being woven with English wool.

Origins of the Royal Tapestry Collection under the Plantagenet Kings

Evidence of the use of large textile hangings in the English royal household begins to come into clearer focus from the reign of King Edward II (r. 1307–1327). Wardrobe accounts relating to his residence in Amiens in July 1320 include payment for the removal of diverse hangings ("tenta") from the rooms of his residence and for their transport by river to a place where they could be repaired.[3] The same accounts also include payments for various types of precious fabrics including silks and cloth of gold and what appear to have been tapestries. In 1317–18 Edward paid a London merchant £26 13s. 6d. for fifteen tapestries with diverse coats of arms as a gift to his sister, Mary, on her departure from court for the nunnery at Amesbury.[4] And during the same year, he paid £30 to Thomas de Hebenhirth, a mercer of London, for a great hanging of wool ("dorsorium lanae") woven with figures of the king and an earl upon it, for the king's service in his hall on solemn occasions. The earl in question must have been Edward's cousin Thomas, earl of Lancaster, who held sway over the king during the second half of the 1310s. A Thomas de Varley was then reimbursed 6s. 3d. for the costs of making and attaching a border of green cloth to save damage in fixing the hanging up.[5] Although it is possible that this hanging was a large embroidery, the development of the Continental tapestry industry at this time supports the supposition that it was a tapestry. Either way, the reference provides an early example of the English royal household acquiring a large precious textile with figurative imagery that emphasized the monarch's status for use on important ceremonies. This would have formed a focal point among the numbers of less expensive cloths that were also used on such occasions, as for example, Edward III's coronation feast in Westminster Hall in 1327, when the walls were hung with brightly colored woolen hangings.[6]

The earliest textiles that can certainly be identified as tapestries in the possession of the English royal family belonged to Queen Isabella, mother of Edward III. Among the goods returned to the Exchequer in 1358–59 after her death were a variety of rich textiles, including at least ten large textile ensembles that included tapestry wall hangings ("tapetis"). About half of these included bed and wall hangings in a variety of colors. Others were described as chambers ("aulum"), one with a dorser (a hanging to go behind a throne) and four costers (wall hangings), decorated with leopards; another with a dorser and four tapestries decorated with dolphins; and another with a dorser and two long costers illustrating the *Story of the Apocalypse*. A fourth group included a dorser with white roses and four blue tapestries decorated with fishes. There were also at least two dorsers described as "de Aras," along with various other ensembles of precious textiles.[7] Since the town of Arras was one of the first centers in which a sizeable tapestry industry developed, it seems likely that, in this context, the term is an indication of origin. The en suite character of these ensembles, both heraldic and figurative, is typical of much early Continental tapestry production.

The long reign of Isabella's son, Edward III (r. 1327–1377), coincided with a period of growth in the Continental tapestry industry, and W. G. Thomson, the first historian of English tapestry production, suggested that Edward was responsible for encouraging the production of tapestries in England.[8] Evidence of a budding industry is provided by an ordinance of 1331 regarding London "tapicers" that stipulated that armorial tapestries must be woven with good English or Spanish wool. In 1370 this ordinance was extended to all forms of tapestry.[9] However, judging by the terms used in the ordinance, it seems that the majority of this production actually comprised lengths of plain or striped weft-faced cloth, rather than more elaborately patterned tapestry, and there is no evidence of any sizeable figurative industry in England at this date.[10] Instead, the English and Low Country tapestry weavers active in London during the second half of the fourteenth century appear to have specialized in the production of decorative and heraldic tapestries. Large but relatively simple tapestries with repeating armorial devices were certainly being made in London in the last quarter of the century. For example, the will of Richard Fitzalan, earl of Arundel, drawn up in 1392, mentions a large tapestry chamber of blue with red roses and coats of arms "lately made in London."

1.2 Arms of the Scrope Family of Masham (fragment). Tapestry, possibly woven in England, ca. 1400. Wool, 81 x 98 cm. York Minster

Fragments of heraldic tapestries made for the Scrope family of Bolton, probably of English origin and dating from around 1400, survive at York Minster (fig. 1.2).[11] As we will see, Richard II also sourced heraldic tapestries from a John Dykes, "tapicer" of London, during the 1390s.

Although the evidence regarding Edward's support of a native tapestry industry is ambiguous, Edward was certainly responsible for appointing a member of the court to care for his tapestries and textile hangings. This royal office was to survive in various guises until the eighteenth century. Edward was also responsible for the construction of custom-built premises for the Great Wardrobe at a site near Baynard's Castle in the Parish of Saint Andrew's in the City of London that was purchased in 1360. Just north of Puddle Wharf, this warehouse provided a conveniently located depository from which goods might be quickly shipped up or down the Thames. Besides storage for the large volumes of precious and commonplace textiles required by the royal household, the premises also provided offices for the key staff and space for various tailors and embroiderers who worked for the Wardrobe. The Great Wardrobe moved into the new building on October 1, 1361, and continued at this site until the Great Fire of London in 1666. The space formerly occupied by the building survives today as Wardrobe Place.[12]

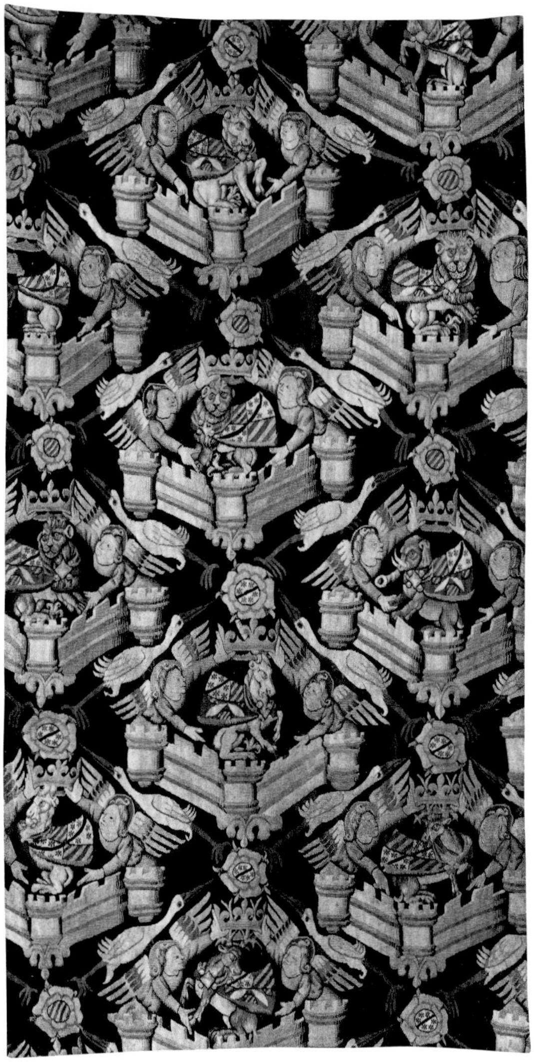

1.3 Heraldic Composition with the Arms of Beaufort, Turenne, and Comminges. Tapestry woven in the Southern Netherlands, ca. 1350–75. Wool, 231 x 116 cm. The Metropolitan Museum of Art, New York

For all this, little is known of Edward's tapestry patronage. His will bequeathed a "large and noble" set of hangings for his hall, possibly the great hall at Westminster, to Richard II.[13] A Wardrobe account taken in the year Edward died records seven miscellaneous "arras" wall hangings of which one included gold thread. Three were identified by subject, one of *Fame,* one of *David and Goliath,* and one of "regibus exulatis [?]."[14]

The 1377 Wardrobe document gives no indication of the sizes of the royal tapestries, but evidence that sets of considerable scale were in use by this date is provided by the 1376 will of Edward, the Black Prince, eldest son of Edward III. This lists several large ensembles, including one for a hall, decorated with heraldic devices of ostrich feathers and swans with ladies' heads, which he bequeathed to his son Richard—subsequently Richard II—and another with eagles and griffins that he left to his wife. A third, described as a "halling" of black tapestry with ostrich feathers and a red border of swans with ladies' heads, was bequeathed to Canterbury Cathedral, where Edward was to be buried. The scale of this set is suggested by the direction that it was to be cut to provide hangings for the high altar, that of Saint Thomas à Becket, two other altars, and the area around the prince's tomb, while the eight costers were to be hung above the choir stalls in memory of the prince on feast days.[15] None of these Plantagenet armorial tapestries have survived, but fragments of a set dating from the third quarter of the century, bearing the arms of a French noble, Guillaume III Rogier, comte de Beaufort, and his family demonstrate the effect of these repeating patterns (fig. 1.3).[16] In summary, the Black Prince's will shows that by the third quarter of the fourteenth century, mechanisms existed whereby English patrons could obtain large armorial suites woven in tapestry and that these were sufficiently esteemed to warrant specific assignation in contemporary wills. It also suggests the continuing rarity of figurative tapestries in England in the 1360s, as the prince only appears to have owned one such set worthy of note, a chamber of "arras" of the "pas de Saladyn," presumably a visualization of the legendary exploits of Richard the Lionheart and Saladin during the Third Crusade.[17]

Continental Developments

The last years of Edward's reign coincided with a period of extraordinary development in the tapestry industry of northern Europe. Indeed, from the middle of the fourteenth century, both the volume and the character of Continental production changed markedly. Whereas in the first half of the century the

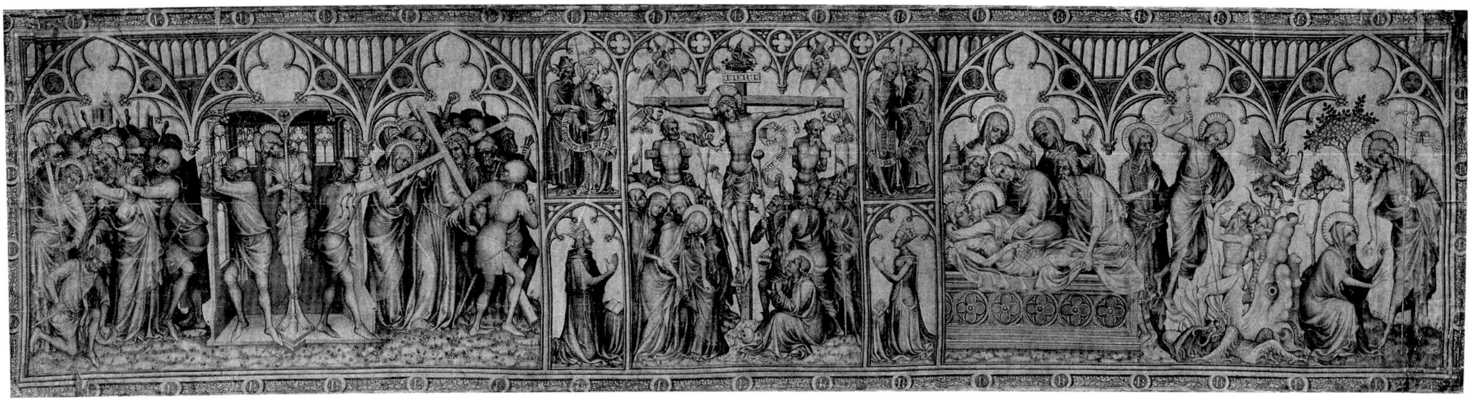

1.4 *Parement de Narbonne,* Paris, ca. 1375. Black ink on white silk, 77.5 x 28.6 cm. Musée du Louvre, Paris

inventories of the leading Continental nobility frequently mention two or three tapestry chambers and a handful of tapestry wall hangings, mostly with decorative or heraldic designs, inventories compiled during the 1360s, 1370s, and 1380s reveal a significant increase in the number of tapestries with narrative subjects. Although we know too little about the previous era to make definitive assumptions, there seems little question that the larger numbers reflect a new appreciation among the European nobility of the potential of tapestry as a medium of figurative decoration.

Nowhere is this phenomenon more pronounced than in the patronage of the sons of John II, the Valois king of France (r. 1350–1364). Well known as sophisticated patrons of architecture and the arts, these four brothers all committed huge sums to the purchase of tapestries during the second half of the fourteenth century. For example, by the time of his death, Charles V, king of France (r. 1364–1380), had amassed more than two hundred tapestries, as well as other luxury textiles of which the sole surviving piece today is the so-called *Parement de Narbonne* (fig. 1.4).[18] His younger brother, Louis, duke of Anjou from 1360 and king of Naples and Sicily from 1382, was equally drawn to the richness and splendor of the tapestry medium. An inventory taken in 1364 shows that by the age of twenty-five he already owned more than seventy tapestries, and during the 1370s and 1380s he made many other purchases.[19] The inventory taken at the death of Philip, duke of Burgundy (r. 1363–1404), lists more than one hundred tapestries, a number that includes purchases from Louis's estate.[20] The 1416 inventory of John, duke of Berry (r. 1360–1416), documents a collection of more than thirty large figurative panels and several large tapestry chambers.[21] Although some of these were woven in wool alone, others were executed in precious materials at a cost of thousands of francs. Quite apart from their richness, significant numbers were of enormous dimensions.

Motivating this patronage was a new awareness of the contribution that tapestries could make to the patron's "magnificence." This concept, which can be characterized as the public demonstration of power and wealth through lavish and tasteful expenditure and generosity, ultimately derived from Aristotle's *Nicomachean Ethics,* although it had been propagated in medieval court culture in the guise of the "largesse" required of a nobleman. The concept received renewed attention from the late fourteenth century through contemporary translations of Aristotle, including one of about 1370–77 by Nicolas Oresme, a councillor and chaplain to Charles V of France. Tapestry was the perfect medium of ostentation. Far more than any number of paintings or sculptures, the scale and richness of tapestry provided a dramatic physical demonstration of the wealth of the patron, and as such, it was more highly valued as a material possession. Tapestry also provided a monumental medium on which the patron could parade images of ancestors, of military conquests, or of the historical and mythological heroes with whom he wished to be associated. In an age when pictorial images of any kind were, of necessity, handmade and therefore rare, an extensive display of high-quality tapestries must have been truly extraordinary, and it is not surprising that, again and again, contemporary documents record the amazement with which eyewitnesses reacted to such spectacles.

The majority of tapestries acquired by the Valois princes were purchased or commissioned through a small number of rich merchants, mostly based in Paris and Arras, who acted as middlemen between the patrons and the workshops, many of which were also located in Paris and Arras.[22] Inevitably, the subject matter of these tapestries reflected the religious character of contemporary life, with a significant portion devoted to Old and New Testament subjects, saints' lives, and religious allegories. But there was also an abundance of secular narrative. Writing in the thirteenth century, Jean Bodel, a romance author and native of Arras, defined the three great matters of contemporary literature as those of ancient Rome, France, and Britain. The first comprised stories relating to the heroes of the classical world, which included Troy, Macedonia, and Rome; the stories relating to Charlemagne and his paladins, the matter of France; and stories about King Arthur and his knights, the matter of Britain. All were the subject of long and complex romances, many originating in the twelfth and thirteenth centuries, that were subsequently retold and translated into a variety of European languages during the fourteenth and fifteenth centuries.[23] Apart from the martial prowess and chivalric values that these tales frequently celebrate, another common theme is the resistance of Christian heroes to the infidel. In this respect, the engagements between Charlemagne and his vassals and the Saracen army provided particularly rich material for embellishment, as evidenced by the many visual cycles on these characters. The heroes of all three great narrative traditions evidently had widespread appeal and formed the subject of an expanding number of tapestry series from the late fourteenth century.

The circumstances in which most designs were conceived are unclear. Armorials were obviously created as specific commissions, and with their repetitive heraldic and decorative elements they were relatively inexpensive to design. Less certain are the circumstances governing the order for large figurative subjects, but the accounts of the duke of Burgundy suggest that in many cases tapestries were purchased from the merchant's stock or were commissioned from cartoons already in the merchant's possession. Equally, procedures existed for custom-made commissions when the patrons were prepared to spend the necessary money. For example, the most remarkable of Louis of Anjou's acquisitions was a six-piece set of the *Apocalypse of Saint John* that was designed for him by Jan Boudolf (fl. 1368–1381), one of the leading artists at the court of his brother, Charles V. Arrangements for the production of this set were made with the Parisian merchant, Nicolas Bataille, who had supplied Louis with tapestries since 1363 and who supplied him with many more during the 1370s and 1380s. Woven between 1373 and 1380 at a cost of 6,000 francs, the set comprised six panels, each over six yards high and about twenty-six yards long, which survive in part at the château of Angers (figs. 1.5, 1.6).[24] The scale was unprecedented and must reflect a conscious decision by Louis to commission a work of art of a monumentality that had never been seen before.

While Louis's patronage is of note for the scale and grandeur of some of his acquisitions, the patronage of his brother Philip, duke of Burgundy, reflects an even more sophisticated vision of the potential of the tapestry medium. From the mid-1380s, Philip committed considerable sums of money to tapestry acquisitions, both for his own use and as gifts for family, friends, and allies, including leading members of the English court.[25] In part, this investment seems to have been intended to stimulate the portion of the industry that fell within the dominions of Flanders and Artois, which he had inherited at the death of his father-in-law, Louis II de Male, in 1384. But above all, these extravagant gifts were meant to demonstrate

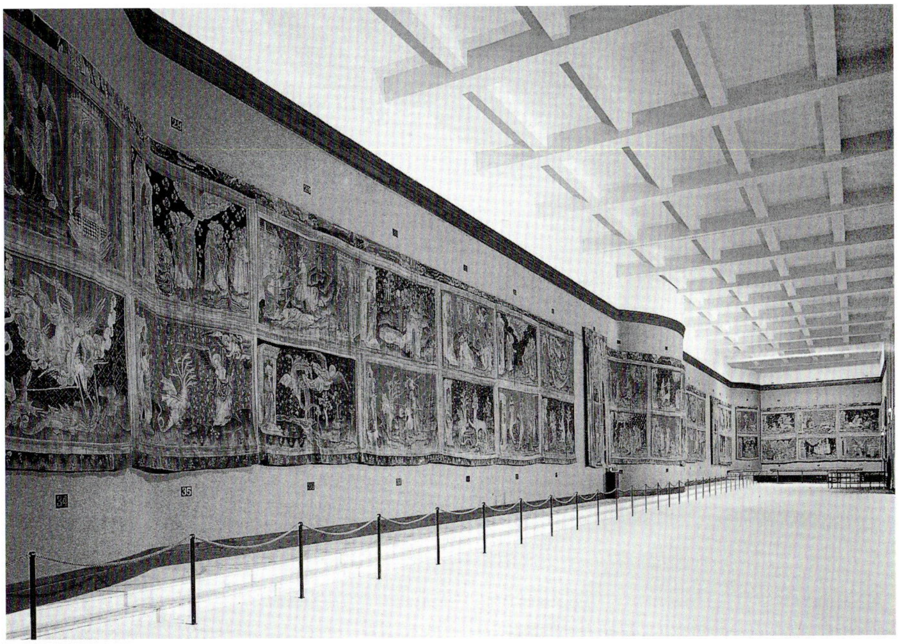

1.5 *The Story of the Apocalypse.* Tapestries designed by Jan Boudolf, woven in the workshop of Robert Poinçon, Paris, ca. 1373–80. Wool. Château, Angers

Burgundian magnificence. Philip's patronage was also groundbreaking in terms of the subjects he acquired, and he was the first of the Valois princes to commission designs depicting events in his own reign. The most dramatic exercise in this respect was the *Battle of Roosebeke,* which commemorated the victory of his forces over the rebellious towns of Ghent, Bruges, and Ypres in November 1382. Commissioned in 1384 through an Arras merchant, Michel Bernard, the tapestry was delivered two years later at a total cost of 3,600 gold francs, of which 300 was for the cartoon, the price of a lavish illuminated manuscript.[26] The tapestry was gigantic, measuring more than five yards in height and over forty yards in length, one of the most ambitious works of political art of the Middle Ages.

The Impact of Continental Developments on English Patronage

The close political and trade ties that existed between England, France, and the Low Countries during the fourteenth century must have ensured that word of the Valois princes' extravagant commissions rapidly reached the English court, and events such as the Jousts of Saint Ingelvert, held near Calais in 1389–90, provided members of the English nobility with firsthand experience of Continental splendor. The jousts

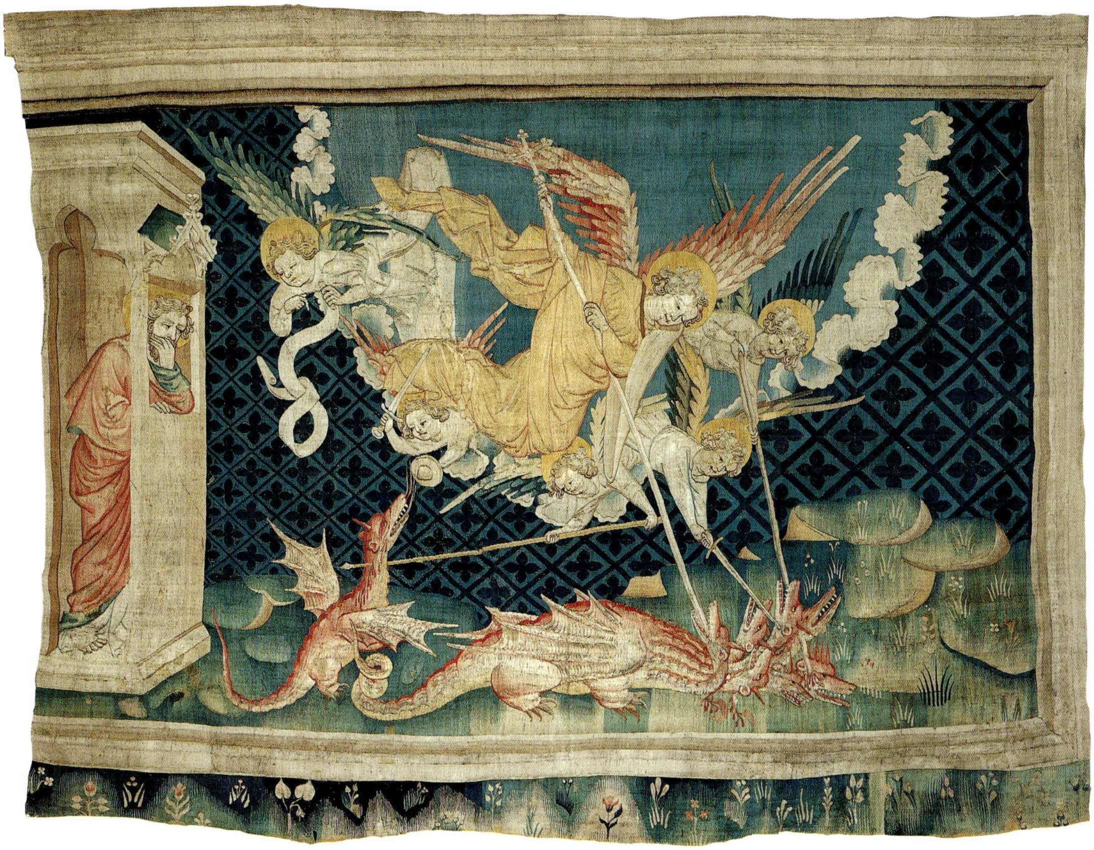

1.6 *Saint Michael Killing the Dragon of the Apocalypse* (detail) from the *Story of the Apocalypse.* Tapestry designed by Jan Boudolf, woven in the workshop of Robert Poinçon, Paris, ca. 1373–80. Wool. Château, Angers

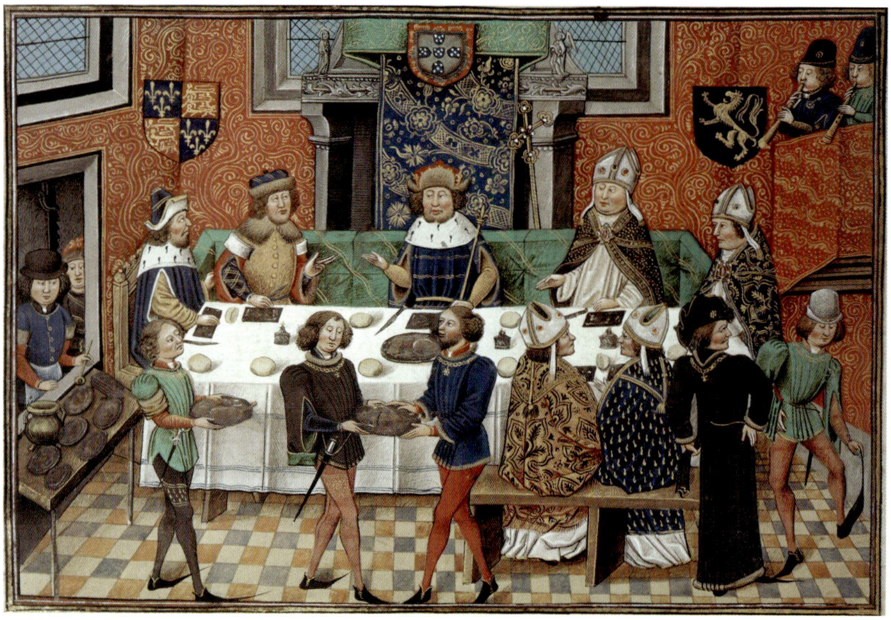

1.7 *John I of Portugal Entertaining John of Gaunt.* Miniature painting from Jean de Wavrin's *Chroniques d'Angleterre,* 14 x 20 cm. British Library, London (Royal Ms 14 E IV, fol. 244v)

themselves were subsequently commemorated in a lavish set of tapestries woven for the French king Charles VI.[27] Inventories of possessions of the leading English nobility compiled during the 1390s reflect a marked increase in the number of narrative tapestries. Since Richard II inherited the throne at the age of ten, the initial impact of this new fashion was first reflected in the patronage of his surviving uncles, John of Gaunt, duke of Lancaster, Edmund of Langley, duke of York, and Thomas of Woodstock, duke of Gloucester, respectively the fourth, fifth, and sixth sons of Edward III. All three had accumulated a number of significant tapestries by the late 1390s, of which key pieces were to be absorbed into the royal collection in the last years of Richard's reign. Complete inventories of the collections of Lancaster and York have not survived, but anecdotal evidence of the splendor of Lancaster's tapestries by the mid-1380s is provided by Jean Froissart's account of the duke's meeting with the king of Portugal in 1386 near Monção (fig. 1.7). The duke's temporary lodgings were hung with tapestries emblazoned with his arms, and the furnishings were so splendid that the Portuguese commented that it was as if they were being received at one of his residences in England.[28] Whether these hangings were actually tapestries or embroideries is uncertain, but greater insight to the size, richness, and variety of the ducal tapestry collections is provided by the inventory of the goods of the duke of Gloucester, taken at Pleshey in 1397. This lists approximately twenty-five pieces of "arras," ten of which were over ten yards in length and five of which contained gold thread, besides other tapestry and textile hangings.[29] The majority of these tapestries depicted the warrior heroes of the chansons de geste, including *Charlemagne,* the Arthurian hero *Lancelot,* and *Godfrey of Bouillon,* one of the leaders of the First Crusade and the first ruler of Jerusalem after it was captured in 1099. Another large panel depicted *Saint George,* patron saint of the chivalric Order of the Garter founded by Edward III in 1348. There was also a set of hangings with the arms of Edward III and his sons, with borders in alternating stripes of red and black, decorated with swans, the Bohun badge, and the arms of Hereford.[30]

Even though evidence is lacking for the dates and means by which these tapestries were obtained, it seems likely that Gloucester and his brothers were acquiring tapestries from Continental sources during the 1370s and 1380s. The extent to which these "arras" tapestries were actually made in Arras is uncertain. While many of them, perhaps a majority, no doubt were, from the late fourteenth century the term also seems to have become increasingly synonymous with high-quality production, irrespective of the place of origin. In contrast, coarser weavings were sometimes described in Continental inventories as made in "gros fil" or "fil délye" of Paris.[31] Most of the subjects listed in Gloucester's inventory also appear in the collections of Continental nobles and were probably woven from preexisting designs, but the *Saint George* tapestry may have been custom-designed. That it was custom-made is certain, for it was described as carrying Gloucester's arms when it was listed in a more detailed inventory of the royal tapestries compiled in 1422.

Although Richard was first exposed to the splendor of contemporary Continental tapestry production through the patronage of his uncles, the face-to-face meetings that took place during the early 1390s between members of the English royal family and the duke of Burgundy can only have stimulated his sense that tapestry was a crucial component of kingly magnificence. For example, a contemporary account of 1393 records the splendor of the preparations made at Calais for the meeting between the duke of Lancaster and the dukes of Berry and Burgundy and relates that, at the first meeting, Lancaster objected to the display by his Continental hosts of tapestries depicting battle scenes, because these provided an inappropriate background to peace negotiations. The tapestries were duly replaced with others depicting the *Passion of Christ,* of which the duke approved.[32] Lancaster's objections may have been formulaic, but the anecdote reveals the extent to which these large figurative tapestries were the subject of considerable attention and of the way they contributed to the stagecraft of contemporary state affairs.

The diplomatic exchanges between the Burgundian and English courts during the early 1390s also generated significant tapestry gifts for the king and his uncles.[33] In 1390, Philip purchased tapestries of the *Story of Percival the Gaul* and the *Story of Octavian,* both measuring just under eleven yards in length, from Andrieu de Monchy and Michel Bernard, two leading Arras tapestry merchants, that were sent to England as gifts for the duke of York.[34] Judging by the prices paid, these panels did not include gold thread. The *Percival* panel must have been a narrative of the Arthurian hero of Chrétien de Troye's *Conte du Graal* (c. 1182), which recounts how Percival's experience at the court of the Fisher King initiated the quest for the Holy Grail, a story in which chivalric values are blended with Christian mysticism. Octavian was the subject of a popular romance that originated in the Paris region in the mid-thirteenth century and focuses on the convoluted tale of Octavian's twin boys. Expelled from their home as babies, one of them, Florent, is suckled by a lion. As a young man he becomes a hero in the combat between the French and the Saracens, killing the giant Arageous, but also falling in love with the sultan's daughter. The story involves treachery, mistaken identities, martial prowess, loyalty, and, ultimately, victory over the Saracens.

Three years later, in January 1394, Philip purchased three tapestries from the Paris-based merchant Jaquet Dourdin, this time to be sent to Richard. Richly woven with gold, these represented the *Crucifixion,* a "mont de Calvaire," presumably a Lamentation scene, and a *Death of the Virgin,* with a total of 195 Arras ells for the three pieces—that is, approximately 110 square yards.[35] Four months later, further tapestry purchases were made from the Arras merchants Michel Bernard, Pierre Le Conte, and Andrieu de Monchy for Richard's uncles; the duke of Lancaster received a panel of *Clovis,* the first Christian king of France, measuring twenty-four yards in length, and a panel of *Pharaoh and the Nation of Moses,* containing ninety-two square yards; the duke of Gloucester received a gold-woven *Story of the Virgin,* fifteen yards in length, and an allegory of *Sport and Pleasantry,* containing about seventy square yards; and the duke of York received a gold-woven tapestry of the romance of *Amis and Amiles,* companions in arms to Charlemagne, containing just under one hundred square yards.[36] Finally, in 1396, Philip presented Richard with a gold-woven tapestry of the *Trinity* when Richard was at Calais to marry Isabella, the six-year-old French princess. This, too, was purchased from Andrieu de Monchy.[37]

Tapestries Belonging to the English Crown in 1399

With the examples of Philip the Bold and his own uncles before him, Richard developed a keen appreciation for tapestry for himself. Written sources regarding his patronage are minimal, but the number of tapestries belonging to the English king increased markedly during his reign.[38] The main evidence for this growth is provided by an indenture drawn up in April 1399 for the release of a large number of tapestries from the Great Wardrobe. This may have been occasioned by preparations for the decoration of Windsor Castle for the Garter Feast, which was celebrated with especial splendor that year.[39] The 1399 indenture lists more than forty tapestries, indicating the extent to which, at this date, many of the finest tapestries were concentrated at the Great Wardrobe. A later inventory of 1422 demonstrates that some of these were as much as thirty yards in length.[40] Equally, the true numbers were probably already somewhat larger than this, as the list omits items that we know of from other sources. Judging by later practice, it is probable that there were already deposits of precious textiles and tapestries in standing wardrobes at the Tower and at Windsor.

The numerical growth of the assemblage reflected by the 1399 list was matched by an increase in the quality of the tapestries. Where evidence relating to Edward III's tapestries indicates only one piece with gold, more than twenty tapestries listed in 1399 included gold thread. Gifts and appropriations certainly accounted for a significant portion of the additions. Five pieces of the *Story of the Greeks and the Trojans* listed in 1399 bore the arms of Sir John Beaumont, the former constable of Dover Castle and lord warden of the Cinque Ports, who had died in 1396.[41] The duke of Lancaster's will of February 1398 also directed that Richard was to have the piece of "arras" that the duke of Burgundy had given to him at Calais.[42] Other pieces came from appropriations made from the Appellant Lords, who had usurped Richard's power between 1387 and 1389 and on whom he took revenge in 1397, chief of whom was the duke of Gloucester. Although none of the tapestries listed in the duke's inventory taken at Pleshey in 1397 can be identified with certainty in the 1399 list, a Great Wardrobe list of 1405–6 records three heraldic pieces woven with Gloucester's arms, and the inventory of royal tapestries taken after Henry V's death in 1422 records the gold-woven tapestry of *Saint George* with Gloucester's arms. It was said to measure four by eleven yards.[43] The 1422 list also includes two very large gold-woven tapestries of *Charlemagne,* one of which may correspond to a gold-woven piece with similar dimensions listed at Pleshey.[44] In the same year as Gloucester's discomfiture, tapestries were also forfeit to the Crown from the goods of other lords who had supported the revolt of 1387. These included an "arras" bed and a dorser from the collection of the earl of Arundel.[45] The 1406 Wardrobe document that mentions the three Gloucester armorials also mentions four tapestries with Arundel's arms.[46] Even richer pickings devolved to the Crown from the collection of Thomas de Beauchamp, earl of Warwick. Among a range of precious textiles, the inventories of his goods drawn up by the king's commissioners list a dorser and four costers of the *Story of Alexander,* two tapestries of the *Story of Ferumbras,* a dorser and four costers of the *Story of Guy of Warwick,* a coster of *John the Baptist,* and several sets of armorial tapestries.[47]

With the exception of the last of these figurative panels, the subjects of the larger ensembles were all drawn from contemporary romances. Alexander was one of the most popular subjects of medieval mythology, his legend disseminated through works such as Walter de Châtillon's ten-book epic, the *Alexandreis* (1178–82). In this and subsequent medieval works, the hero's exploits were elaborated into a fanciful pageant where historic events are largely indistinguishable from encounters with monsters and mythological personages. It seems likely that this fantastical matter featured in Warwick's tapestries, just as it was to characterize *Alexander* tapestries made for the duke of Burgundy more than sixty years later. Ferumbras was the hero of a chanson de geste written around 1170, according to which the eponymous hero was a king of Alexandria who, after initial battle with Charlemagne's forces, converted to Christianity and became ruler of part of Spain. Guy of Warwick was a hero of English legend, rendered into French romance during the twelfth century, who, returning from a pilgrimage to the Holy Land, helped defend Winchester against invading northern kings by killing the giant Coibrand.

There is some uncertainty as to how many of the earl of Warwick's tapestries were absorbed into the royal collection because much of his property and possessions were granted to Thomas Holland, duke of Surrey, and then returned to Warwick on the accession of Henry IV. The restituted goods included the *Guy of Warwick* tapestries, which were sufficiently esteemed to be mentioned by name at this time. They were also subsequently mentioned in Warwick's will.[48] But it seems that at least three of Warwick's *Alexander* tapestries were received by the Crown in February 1398 and are probably to be identified with the three gold-woven tapestries of this subject listed in the 1399 indenture relating to Richard's tapestries.[49]

Richard II's Purchases

The foregoing items reflect the increase in the number of tapestries belonging to the Crown through bequest and appropriation, but evidence that Richard himself took an active role in purchasing tapestries is provided by a brief reference in the Great Wardrobe accounts to twenty-four gold-woven tapestries that he acquired between 1394 and 1398.[50] The purchase roll of the keeper of the Great Wardrobe for 1392–94 records payment for one of these pieces, a dorser of "arras" including gold thread, subject unspecified, with a width of four and a half ells and a length of twenty-five ells. The price of £85 is an indication of the high cost of such acquisitions.[51] No information is provided regarding the subjects of these twenty-four gold-woven tapestries, but we can deduce some of the principal pieces on the basis of the 1399 list.[52] Although several of the entries can be related to the Burgundian gifts or appropriations listed above, a number of gold-woven tapestries cannot be accounted for in this way. The subject matter of these precious hangings was heavily weighted toward the medieval romances, including three of *Octavian,* one of which measured thirty-one by five and a half yards, a panel of the *Story of Percival,* and another of "filie Regis Tiry." The *Octavian* and *Percival* tapestries were probably rich reweavings of the designs of these subjects already discussed. The last panel may have been a rendition of the antique story of *Apollonius of Tyre,* whose wife and daughter are lost at sea and then rediscovered. This romance enjoyed great popularity from the twelfth century onward and was among the courtly tales that John Gower included in his *Confessio amantis,* written for Richard II between 1386 and 1390.

In addition to these romances, other gold-woven figurative tapestries that Richard may have purchased included two panels depicting *Kings of England,* another of *King Saul,* another of *Saint Anne,* and four other allegorical tapestries of the *God of Love, Love, Vices and Virtues,* and the *Virtues.* There were also a number of tapestries without gold of which no earlier mention has appeared. These included allegorical panels of *Fortuna* and the *God of Love;* narrative panels of *King David,* unless this was the piece formerly in Edward III's collection; two pieces of *King Richard;* and one piece of the *King of Cyprus,* possibly the crusader Peter of Lusignan, who captured Alexandria in 1365 and was celebrated in Froissart's *Chronicles.*[53]

The majority of these tapestries are described in the list as "opere d'arras" and although we lack specific evidence of their place of manufacture, there can be little doubt of their Continental origin, with the proviso made above that works cited as "arras" were not necessarily made in that town. The origin of the pieces received from Philip the Bold is indisputable, and the subjects of many of the other hangings correspond to tapestries listed in contemporary Continental collections.[54] For example, gold-woven tapestries of *Alexander* were among the treasures that Philip the Bold sent to Sultan Bayezid I as part of the ransom for his son, John, captured by the Turks at Nicopolis in 1396, while another tapestry of this subject is listed in the posthumous inventory of Philip's wife, Marguerite of Flanders, in 1405.[55] Similarly, panels of *Percival,* the *God of Love, Fortuna,* the *Vices and Virtues,* and *Saint Anne* are also recorded in the inventory of Philip's collection drawn up in 1404.[56] Most of Richard's tapestries therefore appear to have been made from cartoons that had been conceived at the behest of the Valois princes or as speculative ventures by the merchants who were supplying them, in itself an interesting reflection of how extensively Richard was appropriating the visual arts of the Burgundian and Valois courts to his use. Nonetheless, the subjects of a number of Richard's tapestries invite comment in the context of his own preoccupations and tastes.

Following his return to power in 1389, Richard had taken a range of initiatives to enhance his authority and regal image, in terms of both material splendor and protocol; subjects were required to address him as "Majesty" and were not allowed to look him in the eye.[57] Great Wardrobe expenses—which at this date accounted for many of the royal household's most significant outgoings—increased by an enormous factor; according to one estimate, they had averaged just over £3,000 per year during the first ten years of his reign and now rose to approximately £10,000 per year.[58] As early as 1385 Richard was employing a silk weaver from Lucca to weave designs created by the court painter Gilbert Prince, and the accounts of the Great Wardrobe reflect that his clothes were made from the most opulent materials, with rich embroidery featuring heraldic and religious motifs and royal insignia.[59] Richard's keen interest in the cult of saints and in his royal lineage resulted in architectural projects that stressed his legitimacy and sacral role, for example, in the development of the sanctuary of Edward the Confessor in Westminster Abbey and the tomb of his father at Canterbury Cathedral.[60] Most splendid of all was the enlargement of the great hall at Westminster, where the new ceiling combined his own white hart motif and the arms of Edward the Confessor (fig. 1.8). It hardly needs to be said that the enormous bare walls of the hall were an ideal space for the display of large tapestries.[61] The decorative scheme of the hall was to be completed with a cycle of sculptures of his forebears, culminating in a statue of Richard himself. This stress on his image also extended to the field of painting. Richard is the first king of whom good contemporary portrayals survive. In the finest of these, the Wilton Diptych (fig. 1.9), dated between 1395 and 1399, Richard's sense of his exalted status is conflated with his interest in the cults of the Virgin and the royal saints, in an allegory of his role as the anointed king of Albion, the dower of the Virgin.[62]

In view of the expenditure that Richard lavished on self-aggrandizement and the sophistication of at least some of this image making, the question arises as to whether any of the tapestry acquisitions may have been custom-made for him. Armorial tapestries and woolen hangings were obviously made to order, and evidence of one such commission is provided by the Great Wardrobe accounts. The keeper's expenses roll for 1385–87 records payment to Richard's painter, Gilbert Prince, for "three patterns made by him for three circles of ostrich plumes and crowns of which two have the coat of arms of our Lord King and one with the helm of the King in the middle" for the use of the tapicer as his model for a woolen tapestry.[63] The Wardrobe's purchase records for 1392–94 duly record payment of £64 6s. 8d. for a large set of woolen hangings and bench covers, with comparable patterns, that had been woven to order by John Dykes, "tapicer" of London. This ensemble comprised fifteen hangings of which eight measured four by eight ells and seven of them, four by six ells. Each featured a central roundel with Richard's arms and a shield with his arms in each corner. The cost of weaving the armorials was higher than that of the plain surround. There were also three bench covers, each measuring two and a half by eight ells. The complete ensemble measured 106 ells in length and was intended for the "camera Regis," presumably the king's audience chamber.[64]

So far as figurative tapestries are concerned, the evidence is more ambiguous. Although it is tempting to think that Richard II may have commissioned the *King Richard* panels, they may actually have been the residue of the chamber of the "pas de Saladyn" formerly in his father's collection. Circumstantial evidence that the tapestries depicted Richard the Lionheart rather than Richard II is provided by the presence of a tapestry of the same subject in the 1416

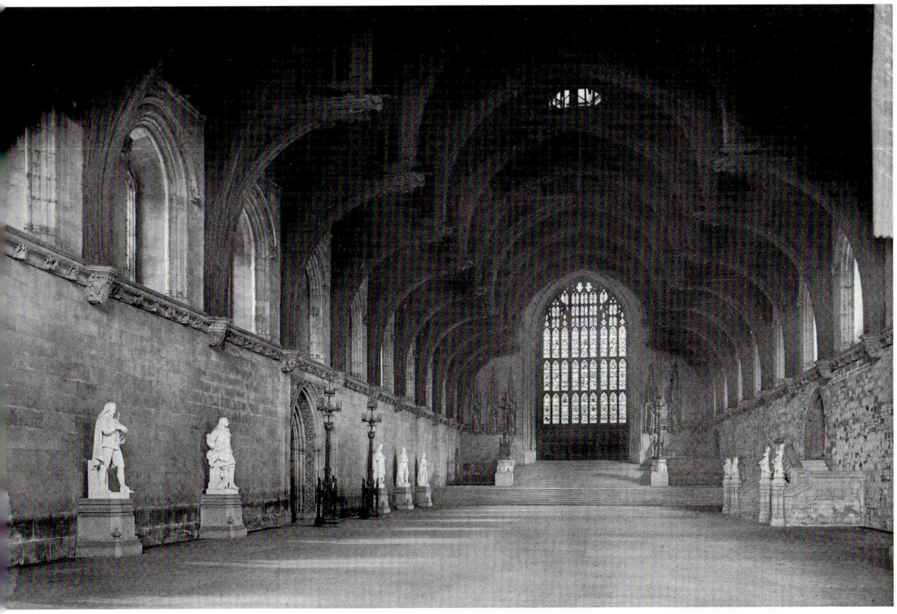

.8 Westminster Hall (1097–99; remodeled 1394–1401)

inventory of the duke of Berry, who, one imagines, would have had more interest in Richard I than Richard II.[65] Evidence regarding other tapestries in the 1399 list is similarly inconclusive. For example, the acquisition of a gold-woven tapestry of *Saint Anne,* mother of the Virgin Mary, reflects Richard's interest in the cult of the Virgin. Pope Urban VI extended the Feast of Saint Anne to England in 1378, at the king's request, and she was the namesake of his first wife, Anne of Bohemia, queen from 1382 until her death of the plague in 1394. Richard was devoted to Anne, so the presence of a tapestry depicting her patron saint is intriguing, although again, assumptions regarding the circumstances in which this design was conceived must be cautious because, as already noted, the duke of Burgundy also owned a tapestry of *Saint Anne* by 1404 and it is uncertain which was the earlier weaving. The tapestries of *King Saul* and *King David* provide other interesting cases. Richard is known to have encouraged identifications between himself and role models who exemplified wisdom, and David, as the first of the anointed kings of Israel, was an especially flattering comparison. It might therefore be suggested that these tapestries may have been commissioned or acquired with such parallels in mind. Again, however, it is possible that the *David* tapestry, at least, is to be identified with the panel formerly in Edward III's collection, and even if Richard did acquire it, there is nothing distinctive about either subject to support the supposition that the designs were conceived for the English court.

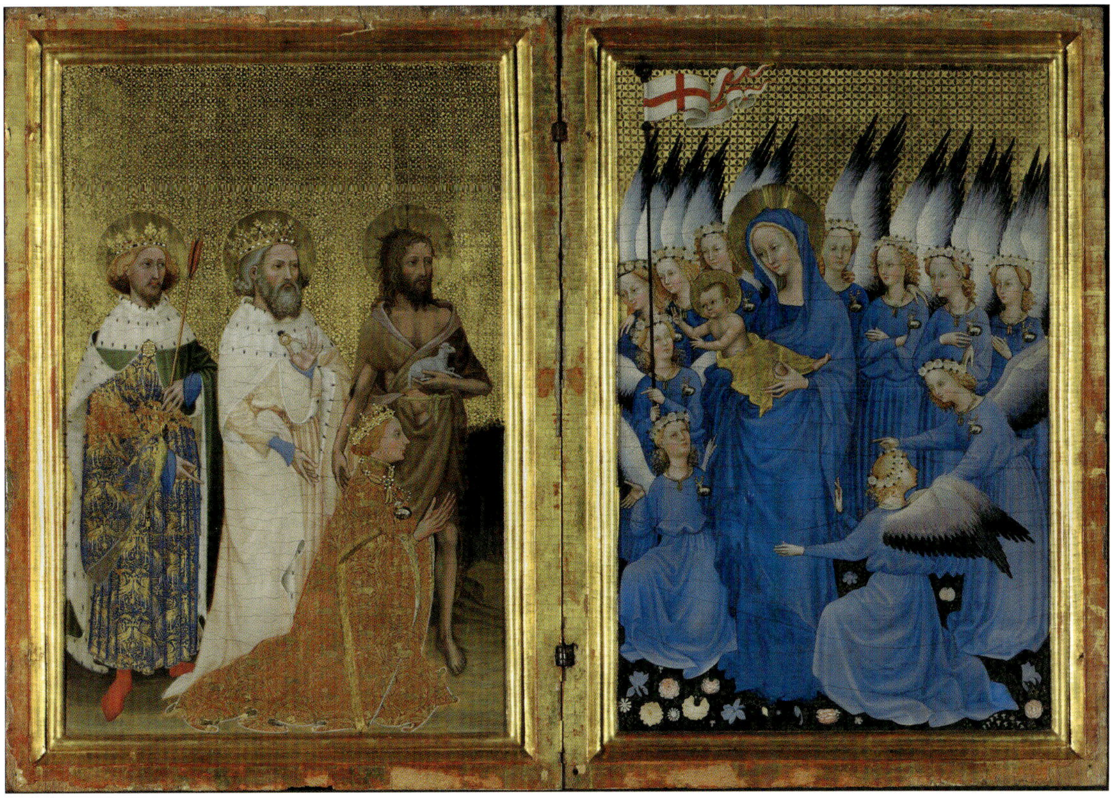

.9 *Richard II Presented to the Virgin and Child by His Patron Saint John the Baptist and Saints Edward and Edmund* (The Wilton Diptych) by an unidentified artist, ca. 1395–99. Tempera on panel, 57 x 29.2 cm (each panel). The National Gallery, London

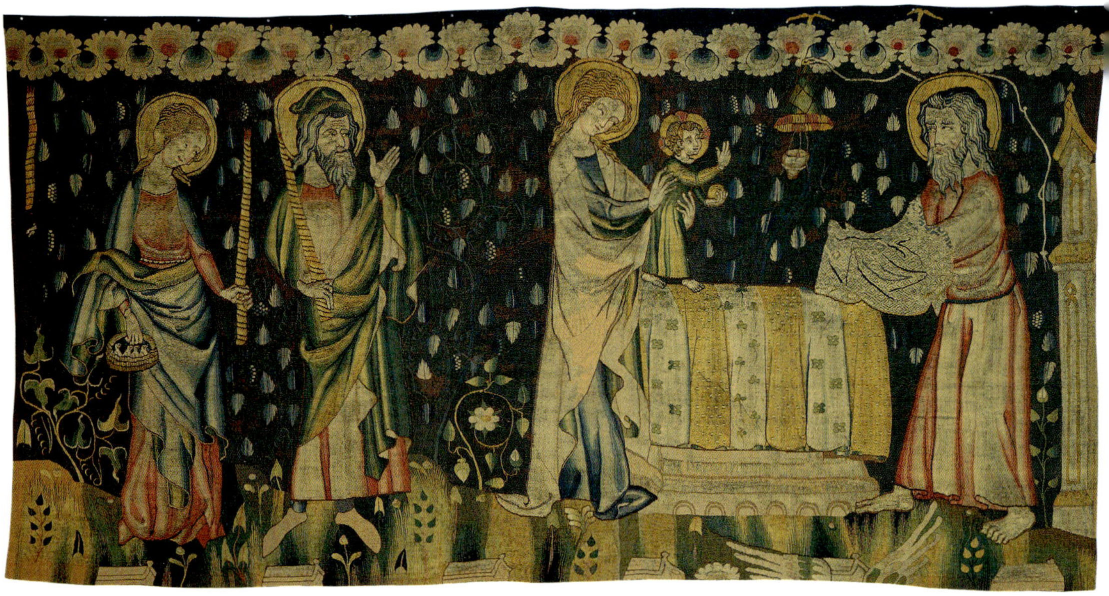

1.10 *Presentation of the Infant Christ in the Temple* (fragment). Tapestry woven in northern France or the Southern Netherlands, ca. 1380. Wool, 153 x 285 cm. Musées Royaux d'Art et d'Histoire, Brussels

Nonetheless, evidence that at least one figurative ensemble was custom-made for Richard is provided by the reference to two gold-woven tapestries of "Kings of England" in the 1399 list. More information is provided by the inventory of royal possessions compiled in 1422 when one piece, measuring five and a half by fifteen yards, was described as depicting Saint Lucius, and another, measuring five and a half by fourteen yards, was said to portray Saint Oswaldus.[66] According to legend popularized by Geoffrey of Monmouth's *Historia regum Britanniae,* completed in 1138, Lucius was the first Christian king of Britain, who lived in the second century at the time of Pope Eleutherus, while Saint Oswald, king of the Northumbrians ca. 605–642, was thought to have unified British territories to a greater degree than any of his predecessors. On the strength of these descriptions it seems likely that these two large tapestries illustrated a cycle of English kings, Richard's forebears, analogous to the sculptures intended for Westminster Hall. Since no comparable tapestries appear in Continental inventories of the day, it is probable that this pair, at least, were custom-made.

What did these tapestries look like? No designs corresponding to those in the 1399 list can certainly be identified, but a general idea of their appearance can be surmised from the small number of tapestries now extant from the late fourteenth and early fifteenth centuries, such as the aforementioned Angers *Apocalypse* and the *Presentation of the Infant Christ in the Temple* in the Musées Royaux, Brussels (fig. 1.10), the first certainly and the second probably woven in Paris, ca. 1380; the *Story of Jourdain de Blaye* at the Museo Civico in Padua (fig. 1.11 and detail opposite p. 3), probably woven in Paris or Arras, ca. 1385–1400; and the *Story of Saint Piat and Saint Eleuthère* in Tournai Cathedral (fig. 1.12), woven in Arras in 1402.[67] Although the number of surviving tapestries is too small to allow definitive statements regarding the stylistic trends of contemporary production, such pieces and fragments suggest that some of the grandest designs of the third quarter of the century were characterized by monumental figures represented against patterned grounds and that during the 1390s this style was increasingly displaced by a compositional formula in which the narrative was articulated in terms of alternating landscape and architectural settings. The extent to which the two styles may have existed in parallel during earlier periods is uncertain.

The foregoing examples all came from workshops in Paris and Arras. Another structural model that may also have been followed by at least some of the fourteenth-century tapestries in the English royal collection is reflected by a tapestry depicting the Goddess

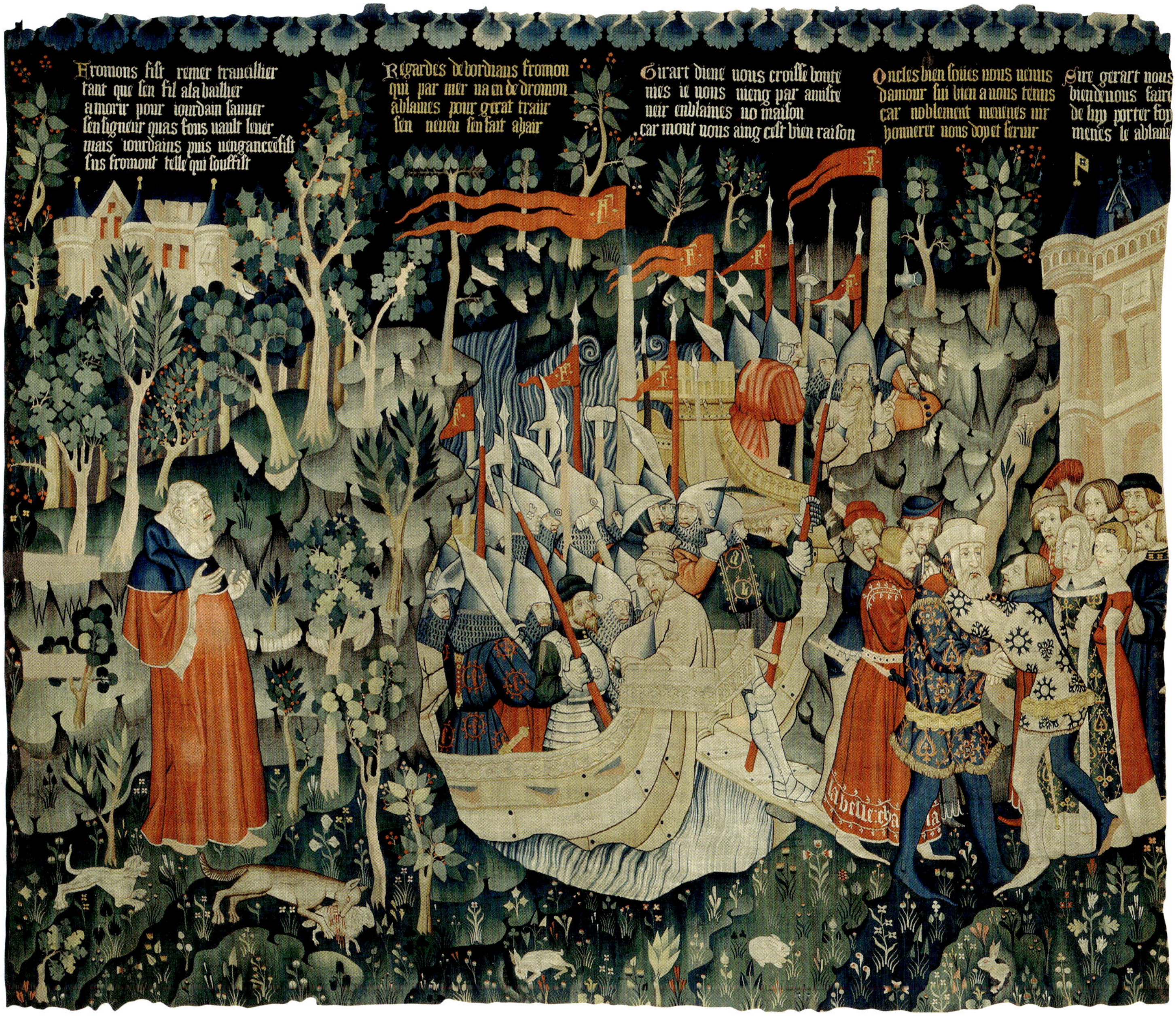

1.11 *The Meeting of Fromont and Gérard* (fragment) from a set of the *Story of Jourdain de Blaye*. Tapestry woven in northern France or the Southern Netherlands, ca. 1385–1400. Wool, 328 x 380 cm. Museo Civico, Padua

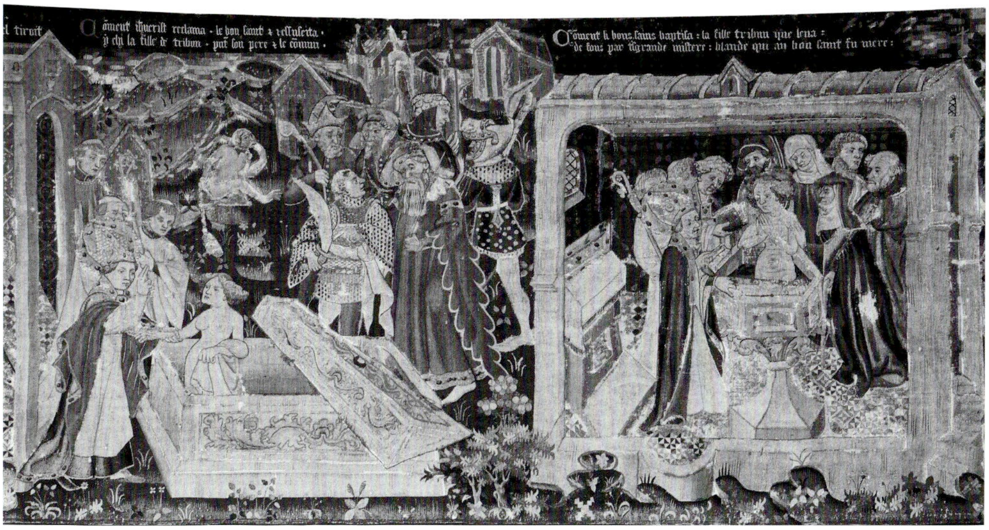

1.12 *Scenes from the Story of Saint Piat and Saint Eleuthère* (detail). Tapestry woven in the workshop of Pierre Feré, Arras, 1402. Wool and silk, 186 x 615 cm. Cathedral, Tournai

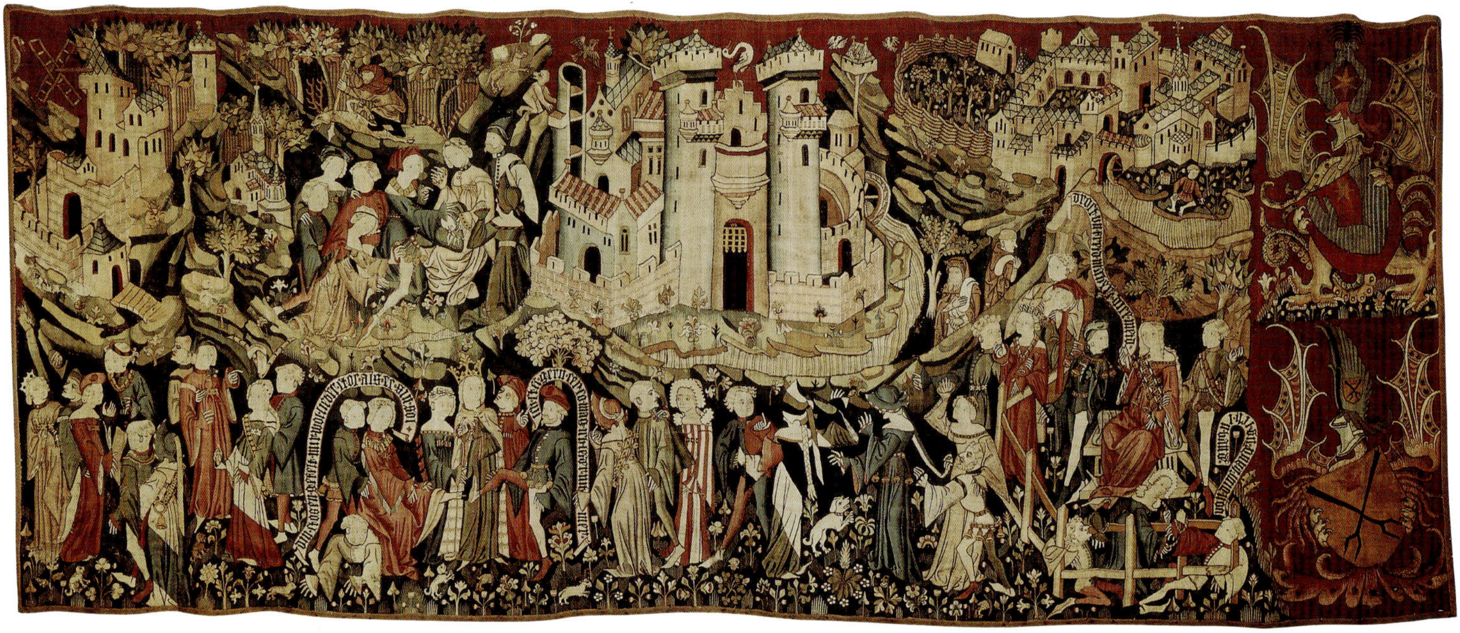

1.13 *Courtly Games.* Tapestry woven in Alsace, ca. 1385. Wool and silk, 160 x 394 cm. Germanisches Nationalmuseum, Nuremberg

of Love adjudicating courtly games (fig. 1.13), thought to have been made in the Alsace region sometime around 1385.[68] The narrative is arranged in two tiers, each composed of a frieze-like arrangement of small figures, some with banderoles of text, interspersed with architectural and landscape elements. Those spaces not occupied by figures or architectural elements are filled by decorative floral and landscape elements. This compositional formula would certainly have been well suited to the complex narratives of the chansons de geste that featured in so many of the late-fourteenth-century tapestries.

Generally speaking, all of these tapestries share a common emphasis on line and pattern rather than volumetric illusion. In part this reflects the linear character of contemporary

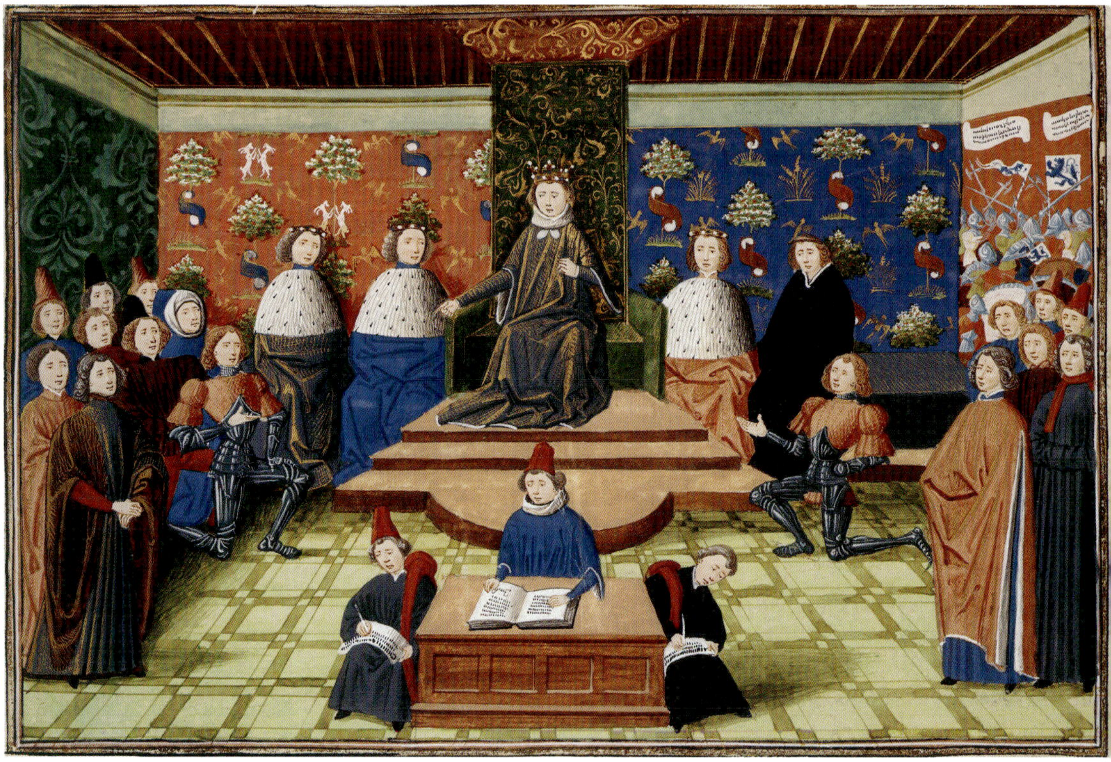

1.14 *Richard Exiles Henry Bolingroke, Earl of Derby, and Thomas Mowbray, Duke of Norfolk.* Miniature painting in a copy of Froissart's *Chronicles*, France, ca. 1470. 13.5 x 19.5 cm. British Library, London (Harl. Ms 4380, fol. 148)

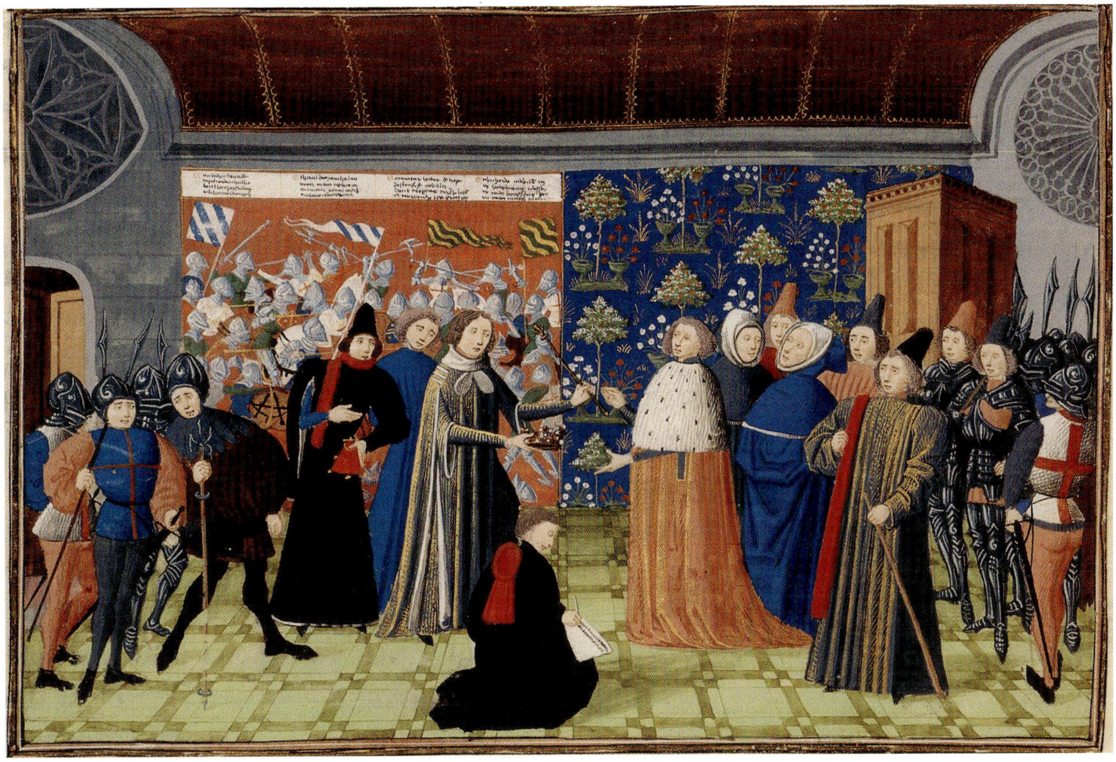

1.15 *Richard II Surrenders His Crown to Henry Bolingbroke, Earl of Derby.* Miniature painting in a copy of Froissart's *Chronicles,* France, ca. 1470. 13.5 x 19.5 cm. British Library, London (Harl. Ms 4380, fol. 184v)

design, as evidenced by the manuscripts and paintings of the day, but it is also a reflection of the state of development of the tapestry industry at this date. Technically, it was more practical for the weavers to depict figures reduced to profiles and flat shapes because the suggestion of three-dimensional form and perspectival depth required painstaking gradations of color that were slow and exacting to reproduce in tapestry and thus more expensive to make.

Considering the number of tapestries with subjects drawn from contemporary romances recorded in the collections of Richard and his uncles, the *Jourdain* fragment now at Padua is especially interesting. Approximately four yards wide, it is only the left-side fragment of a larger tapestry, or sequence of tapestries, that depicted a story of murder and retribution in the family of Amis, companion in arms to Charlemagne and grandfather to Jourdain de Blaye.[69] The duke of Burgundy is known to have purchased a gold-woven hanging of *Jourdain de Blaye* from the Paris-based tapestry merchant Jehan Dourdin in 1386–87, so the Padua fragment can be tentatively dated to ca. 1385–1400, although the relationship of this design to the *Amis and Amiles* tapestries documented in the collections of the duke of York and Richard II is uncertain. Structurally, the extended narrative is reduced into discrete episodes in which crowded pockets of figures, depicted in profile or semiprofile, enact key events of the story. These episodes are divided one from another by stylized rocks, foliage, and buildings that add decorative richness to the design. A text at the top of the tapestry summarizes the narrative. This structural formula probably typifies the appearance of many of the romance tapestries recorded in the royal collection during the reigns of Richard II and Henry IV. A hint of the splendor of Richard's court is provided by the illuminations accompanying an edition of Froissart's *Chronicles* now in the British Library (figs. 1.14, 1.15). Although the illuminations were executed some seventy years after Richard's death, the bright colors and archaic style of the tapestries represented in them provide a suggestive impression of the contribution that the tapestry collection must have made to the appearance of the English court during his reign.

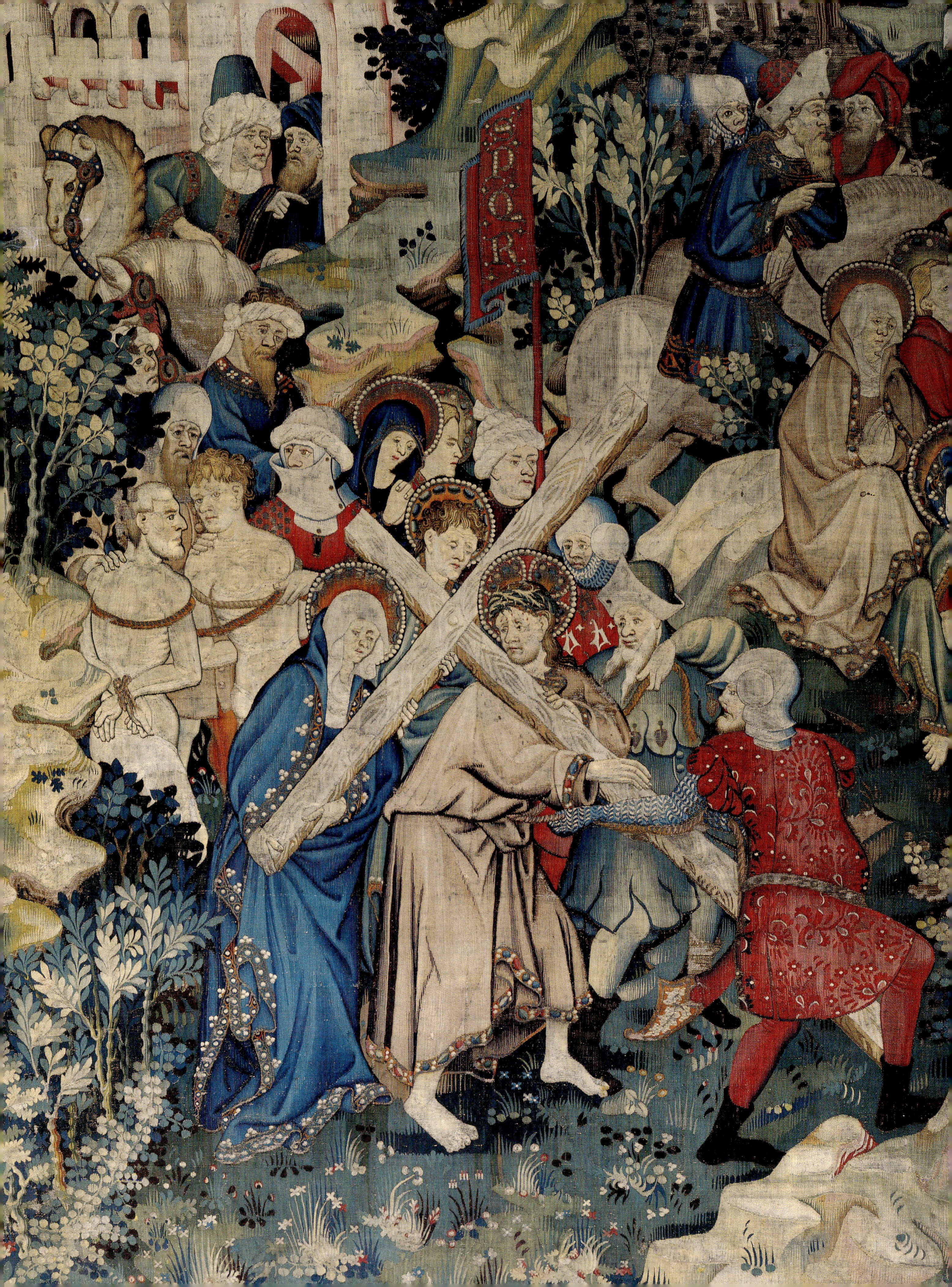
SPQR

CHAPTER 2

The Royal Tapestry Collection under the Lancastrian Kings, 1399–1461

The Royal Tapestry Collection under Henry IV

English efforts to emulate the magnificence of the Burgundian and French courts were abruptly curtailed by the events of 1399. That February, Richard II took steps to confiscate the Lancastrian estates after the death of John of Gaunt, duke of Lancaster, because the duke's son, Henry Bolingbroke, had been banished for ten years in 1398. In response, Henry invaded England while Richard was absent in Ireland. Richard was subsequently caught, imprisoned, and eventually murdered, and Henry was crowned as Henry IV (r. 1399–1413). The extensive military campaigns in which Henry engaged during the following thirteen years were not conducive to artistic patronage, and the tapestry collection does not appear to have been expanded significantly during his reign. Indeed, of the tapestries that did enter the collection during this period, the majority may have come from Lancaster's collection. As already noted, although no inventory of Lancaster's tapestries has survived, he evidently owned a significant collection. His will, drawn up in 1398, bequeathed one of the tapestries that he had been given by the duke of Burgundy to Richard II and also directed that a grand bed of cloth of gold and thirteen tapestries were to be given to the altar of Saint Paul's Cathedral. With these exceptions, he left his two other best pieces of "arras" to his son Henry, "one of which was given me by my lord and nephew the king, and the other by my dear brother the Duke of Gloucester."[1] Thus the three finest pieces of Lancaster's collection evidently entered the royal collection after Henry's accession.

A clue to the identity of some of these pieces is provided by the Wardrobe accounts drawn up in the first year of the reign of Henry V, which include two closely related lists of royal tapestries. The first details those in the Great Wardrobe, and the second describes tapestries entrusted to the keeping of John Stout as keeper of the same during that year.[2] Although they omit a number of items mentioned in 1399, probably because these were stored elsewhere at the time, the 1413 lists provide evidence of the current state of the collection and the basis for the identification of individual tapestries with more detailed descriptions of the same pieces in an inventory taken in 1422, the first year of Henry VI's reign. It is from this later inventory that the dimensions of individual tapestries, cited below, are drawn. Tapestries that appear for the first time in 1413 include three gold-woven panels that all measured over twenty yards in length. One of these featured the *Seven Ages of Man*. A second described as the *Twelve Peers* was presumably a representation of the twelve peers of France, a college of dignitaries that played a privileged role in French state affairs, particularly in the coronation of the king.[3] The tapestry in the English royal collection almost certainly duplicated a design owned by Philip the Bold that, in turn, is probably to be identified with a tapestry depicting *Charles VI and the Twelve Peers of France* that survived at the royal palace in Brussels in the early eighteenth century. An engraving made at this time (fig. 2.1) shows that it depicted the French king flanked to the left by

Detail of fig. 2.8

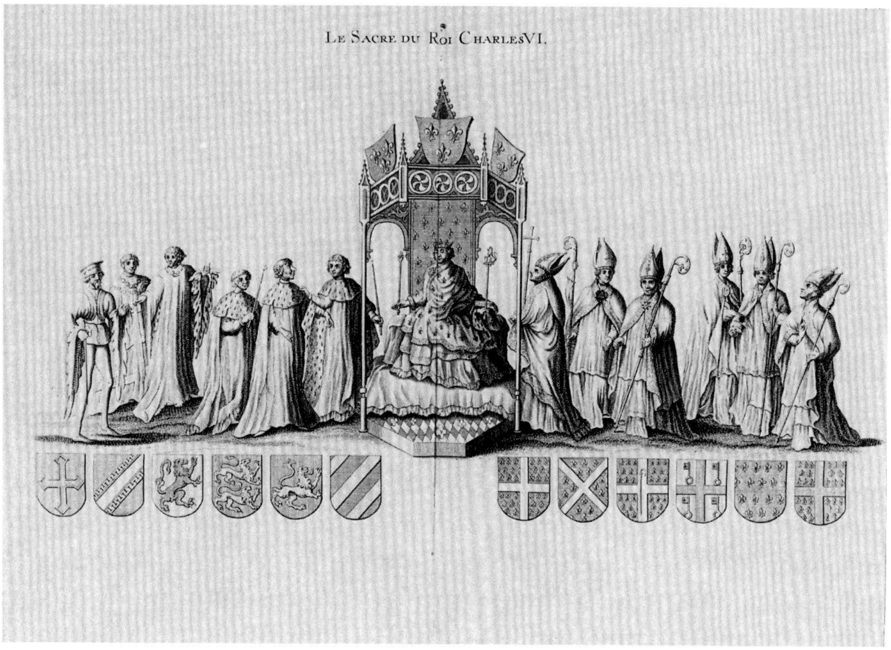

2.1 *Charles VI and the Twelve Peers of France.* 18th-c. engraving of a tapestry woven ca. 1400 in an unidentified workshop in the Southern Netherlands. Reproduced from Bernard de Montfaucon, *Les monuments de la monarchie françoise,* vol. 3 (1731).

the six secular peers, including Philip the Bold and his stepfather, Louis II de Male, and to the right by the six ecclesiastic peers, each identified by his coat of arms.[4]

The third very wide gold-woven tapestry mentioned for the first time in the 1413 lists was described as "Bayard" and must have depicted the *Story of Renaud of Montauban,* one of Charlemagne's vassals. Bayard was the name of Renaud's horse, and evidence that Renaud was the subject of the tapestry in the 1413 lists is provided by the 1422 inventory, which cites a gold-woven panel with an inscription beginning, "Coment Reynaut . . . ."[5] Renaud was celebrated in medieval legend for his heroic defiance of Charlemagne from his seat at Montauban. After reconciliation with Charlemagne, Renaud made a pilgrimage to the Holy Land before returning to Cologne, where, devoting himself to Christ, he worked as a mason on the church of Saint Peter. The tale was elaborated in a thirteenth-century chanson de geste that was widely disseminated in verse and prose during the following century. The story of a virtuous vassal resisting his tyrannous lord would have had special significance for the Appellant Lords during the 1390s, and it is conceivable that this was the tapestry that Lancaster's will described as a gift from his brother, the duke of Gloucester.

In addition to these very wide panels, other rich pieces that may have been additions to the royal collection since 1399 included a gold-woven tapestry of *Tournaments;* another of *Helcanus,* measuring four by sixteen yards;[6] and another of the "*ix conquests,*" measuring four by thirteen yards. Helcanus was the hero of a thirteenth-century French romance who traveled from the court of his father, Cassidorus, to Britain, where he met the heroes of King Arthur's court. The "ix conquests" can probably be identified as a depiction of the Nine Worthies, the idealized selection of heroes that was to form the subject of numerous visual cycles in subsequent years. The sequence represented three heroes from pagan antiquity, Hector, Alexander, and Caesar; three from biblical history, David, Joshua, and Judas Maccabeus; and three from Christian history, King Arthur, Charlemagne, and Godfrey of Bouillon.

The 1413 lists also mention a number of tapestries without gold that are not identifiable in the 1399 list. These included one of *King Priam,* presumably representing episodes of the Trojan War; one of the *Siege of Jerusalem,* perhaps a depiction of Godfrey of Bouillon's campaign of 1099, and if this was the case, it may have been the large *Godfrey of Bouillon* tapestry from Gloucester's collection that had been confiscated at Pleshey; and the enigmatically titled "King Gyngebras," measuring five by nineteen yards, whose subject is uncertain. There were also two panels of *Bevis of Hampton,* which were subsequently described as old in the 1422 inventory.[7] Bevis was a popular romance that recounted the story of the son of Guy of Hampton, who was sold to merchants by his mother and eventually arrived at the Armenian court. There, despite refusing to convert to Islam, he earned the respect of the Armenian king before engaging in adventures involving epic battles, extraordinary coincidences, betrayals, and dragons.

Duplicates of most of the subjects that first appear in the 1413 lists also appear in Continental inventories. For example, Nicolas Bataille sold a tapestry of *Bevis of Hampton* to the duke of Orleans in 1396 and another of the

Children of Renaud of Montaubon to the duke of Burgundy in the same year. While the pieces in the English royal collection were not necessarily woven from the same cartoons, none of the subjects that first appear in the 1413 lists can be identified as having been commissioned for Henry IV. Whether any had been acquired because of the significance they held for the king is also open to discussion. None were overtly related to his attempts to assert his claim to the throne, although the presence of the *Twelve Peers* panel in the collection would have chimed with his dynastic interest in France. On becoming king of England, Henry considered that he had inherited the Plantagenet claim to the French throne, which had been in abeyance since the truce established by Richard II in 1396.

Whatever the origin of these various tapestries, the chivalric and exemplary character of the hangings acquired between 1399 and 1413 is readily evident, reflecting the martial aspirations of Lancaster and his son. The *Nine Worthies* tapestry is of note as being the earliest representation of this theme documented in an English collection. The dimensions of the panel, as specified by the 1422 inventory, are of a similar magnitude to those that can be estimated for an ensemble of this subject, probably made for the duke of Berry sometime around 1400, that survives in fragmentary form at the Metropolitan Museum, New York (fig. 2.2). While this might be purely coincidental—the Metropolitan Museum ensemble appears to have been created as three pieces, whereas the panel in the English royal

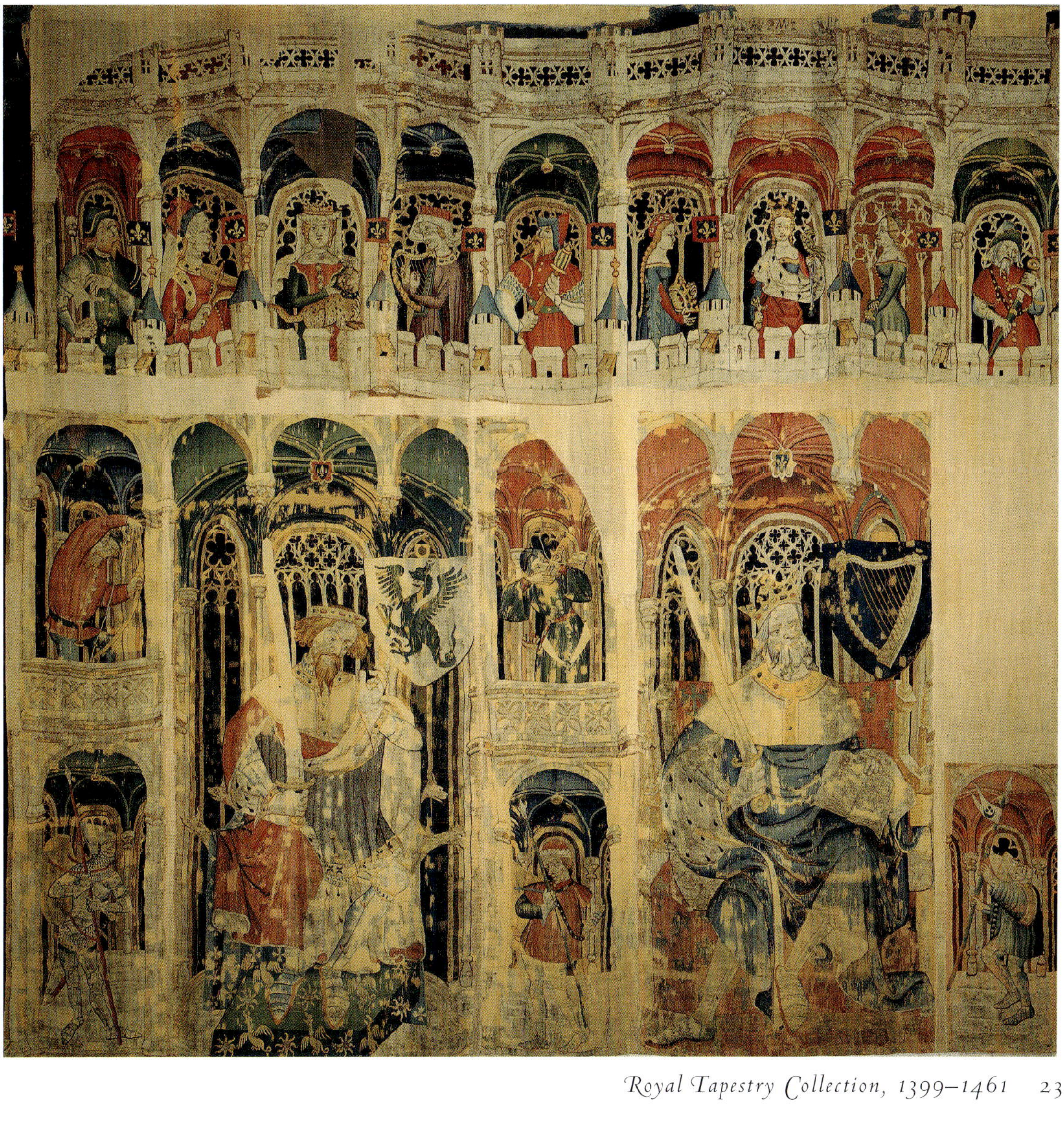

2.2 *Joshua and David* (detail of fragment) from a set of the *Nine Worthies*. Tapestry woven in the Southern Netherlands, ca. 1400. Wool, 429 x 635 cm. The Metropolitan Museum of Art, New York

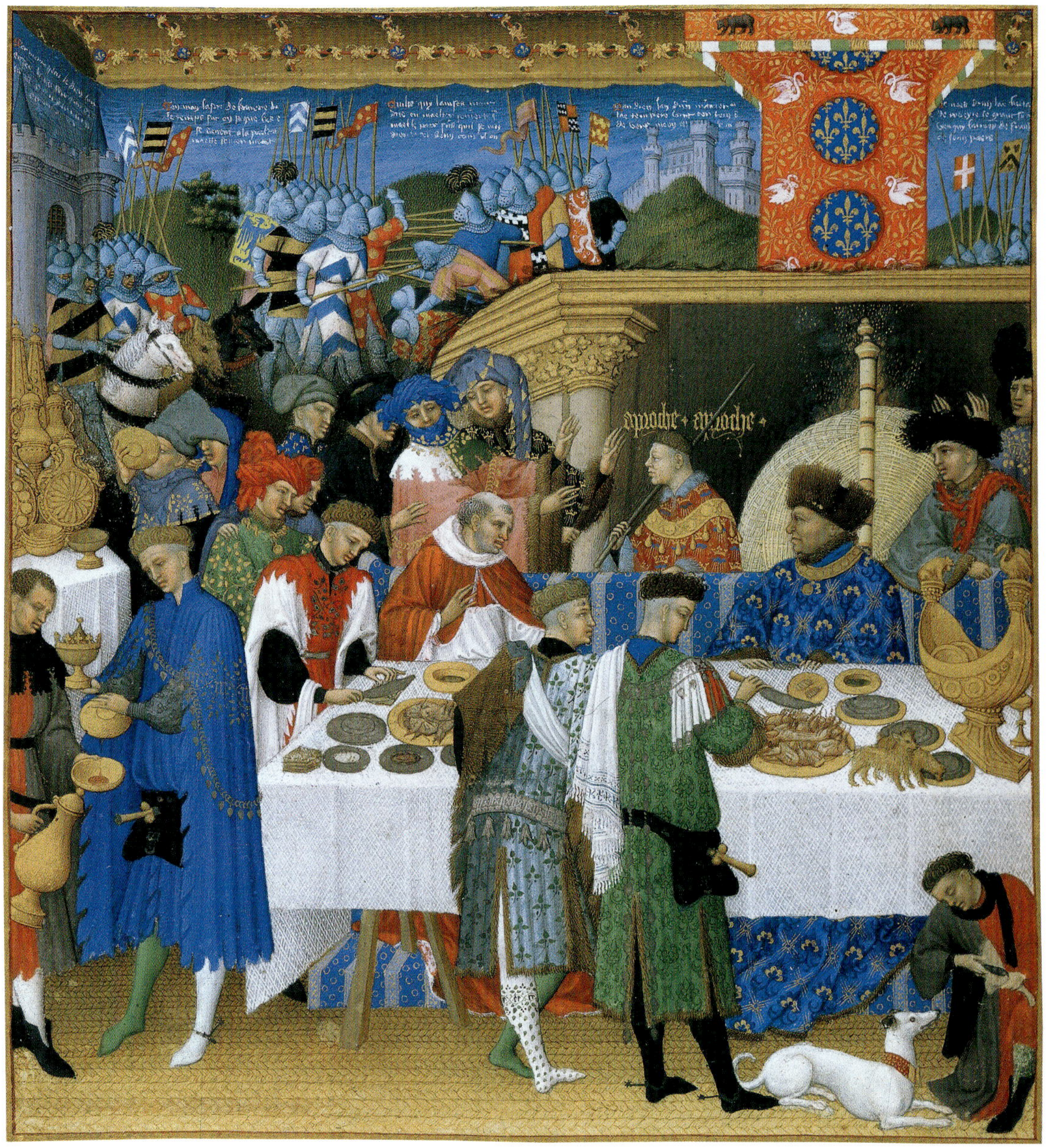

2.3 *January* (detail). Miniature painting by the Limbourg brothers in the *Très riches heures of Jean, duke of Berry,* ca. 1410. Musée Condé, Chantilly (Ms 65, fol. 1v)

collection was a single piece—it is conceivable that the Cloisters fragments may thus provide an idea of the appearance of the panel once in the English royal collection.[8] Whether or not this is the case, the duke of Berry's court certainly produced one of the most telling visualizations of contemporary tapestry usage. This is the famous illumination in the Limbourg brothers' *Très riches heures* (fig. 2.3), which shows the duke being served dinner on a textile-covered dais, with an elaborate battle tapestry on the wall behind him. The coats of arms of the protagonists are prominently displayed, and inscriptions in the top border explain the images below. It has been suggested that the words "de tro(?)yes le grant" are legible in one of these inscriptions, and it is therefore conceivable that the fictive tapestry reproduces the appearance of a real Trojan War tapestry, perhaps even one that was duplicated in the English royal collection.[9] At any rate, the illustration gives an idea of the striking contribution that such tapestries made as the predominant figurative decoration in the grand courts of the day.

The Berry illumination is also interesting for the circumstantial evidence it provides regarding the compositional structure of such tapestries. Generally speaking, the structural model of the Pavia *Jourdain de Blaye* fragment, in

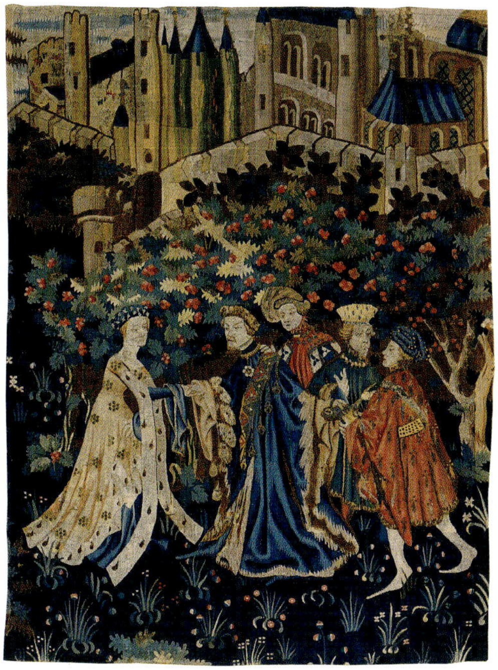

2.4 Scene from an unidentified romance. Tapestry woven in the Southern Netherlands or northern France, ca. 1400. Wool and silk, 204 x 151 cm. Musée des Arts Décoratifs, Paris

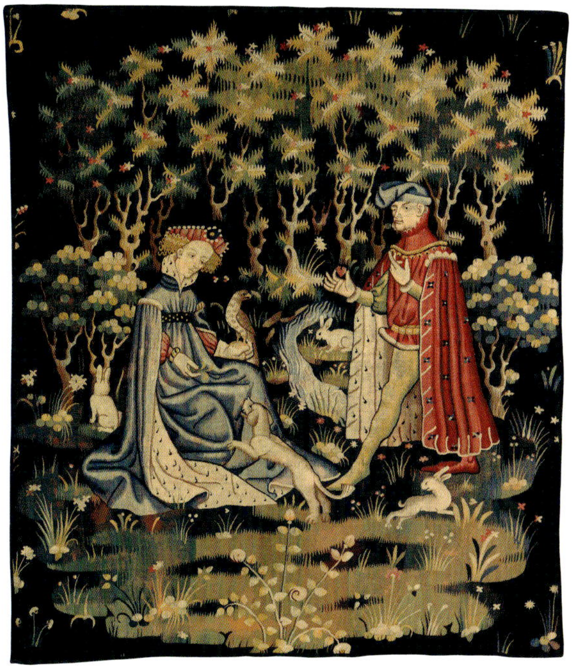

2.5 *The Gift of the Heart.* Tapestry woven in the Southern Netherlands or northern France, ca. 1400–1410 (with later restorations). Wool, 247 x 209 cm. Musée du Louvre, Paris

which pockets of narrative episode were embedded within architectural and landscape components, evidently became the typical format for tapestries made in the Low Countries by the turn of the century, in place of the more repetitive frame structure employed in the *Apocalypse* series.[10] However, where the rocks and vegetation of the *Jourdain* scene were relatively simple in form, those in tapestries of the early 1400s were depicted with increasing linear complexity and density of pattern. The effect of richness was also enhanced by how weavers used small parallel lines of color, often within larger lozenge shapes, to provide life and variety in the clouds, rocks, and architectural elements. These stylistic tendencies are demonstrated by tapestries such as the scenes from an unidentified romance at the Musée des Arts Décoratifs, Paris (fig. 2.4), the heavily restored *Gift of the Heart* at the Louvre (fig. 2.5), the scenes of the *Passion* at the Victoria and Albert Museum (fig. 2.6), the *Annunciation* at the Metropolitan

2.6 *Scenes from the Passion of Christ.* Tapestry woven in an unidentified workshop in the Southern Netherlands, possibly Arras, ca. 1400–1420. Wool, silk, and gilt-metal-wrapped thread, 112 x 302 cm. Victoria and Albert Museum, London

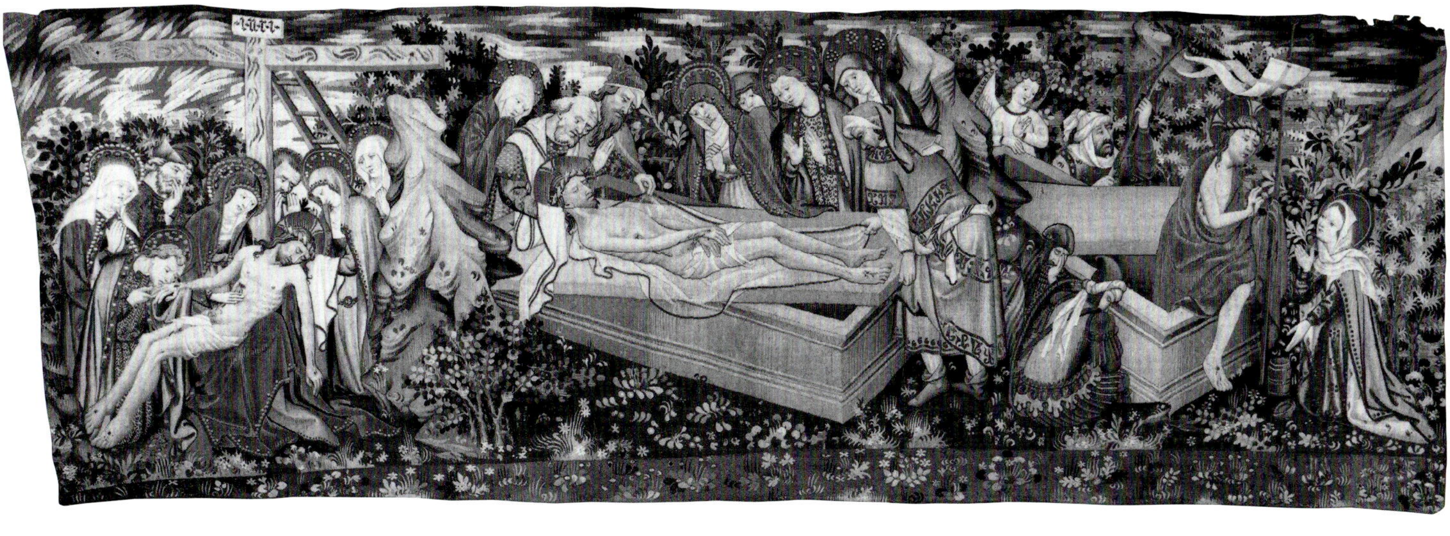

Museum (fig. 2.7), and the two large and magnificent *Passion* tapestries at La Seo Cathedral, Saragossa (fig. 2.8 and detail opposite p. 21). These designs, if not necessarily the weavings themselves, date between 1400 and about 1415. All are characterized by compositions in which the figures are embedded in dense groves of trees and/or elaborate architecture and rocks. The floral and vegetal details are rendered with similar scale and complexity to the features, gestures, and costume patterns of the figures so that the narrative seems to be suspended in a shimmering, almost febrile, surface.

Expansion of the Collection under Henry V

Evidence about the tapestry collection under Henry IV indicates that he had little time or inclination to make significant additions, but the pace of acquisition seems to have increased again under his son, Henry V, who acceded to the throne in 1413 (fig. 2.9). Henry V's diplomatic and military activities were to provide him with extensive exposure to Continental tastes. During the early years of the reign, it was the Burgundian example that remained in the fore. Although the current duke, John the Fearless (r. 1404–1419), was not as innovative in his tapestry patronage as his father, he continued to make numerous purchases from the Arras workshops, demonstrating a particular liking for scenes of courtly life and hunting. In addition, he augmented the Burgundian collection with one major commission, a six-piece set of gold-woven tapestries depicting the *Battle of Liège,* in commemoration of his victory over the rebels of that town in 1408. This set was completed by 1411 and was among the decorations used at Arras that October when Thomas Fitzalan, earl of Arundel, brought a force of English soldiers to aid the duke in his war against the Armagnacs.[11] Following his father's example, John also marked the major diplomatic negotiations of his reign with generous tapestry gifts, such as those distributed to an English embassy in 1411, when Francis de Court received a tapestry depicting beautiful women, perhaps a scene of the Virtues or the Beatitudes, and John Cadryk and Henry Chichele, bishop of Saint David's, also received tapestries.[12] Similar rich gifts were distributed in 1416 to the English and Hungarian ambassadors when they met with the duke at Lille to conclude the treaty against France. On this occasion, Richard Beauchamp, earl of Warwick, received a large tapestry representing people and birds, of which nothing more is known.[13]

During the second half of Henry V's reign, the conquest of northern France exposed the king and his nobles, many of whom accompanied him to the Continent, to another aspect of the Valois tapestry heritage, the treasures of the French royal collection. As the campaign unfolded, the English advances provided unprecedented opportunities for plunder, culminating with the capitulation of the French king and the Treaty of Troyes, which was signed on May 8, 1420. According to this treaty, the French dauphin was disinherited in favor of Henry, who was to marry the French princess Katherine, and Henry was to act as regent in France

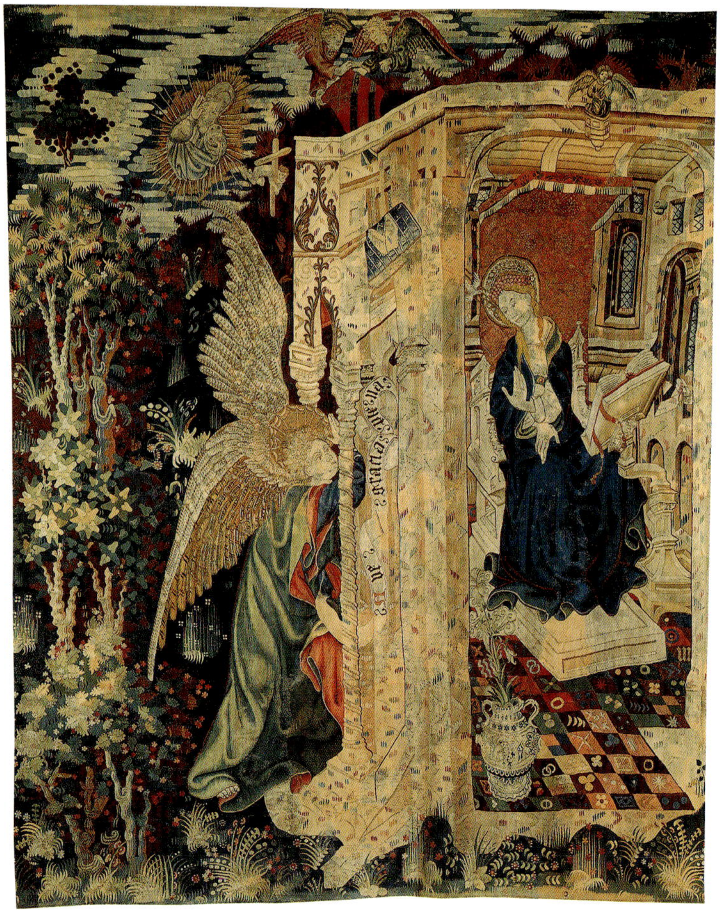

2.7 *The Annunciation.* Tapestry woven in the Southern Netherlands, possibly Arras, ca. 1410–20. Wool and gilt-metal-wrapped thread, 351 x 297 cm. The Metropolitan Museum of Art, New York

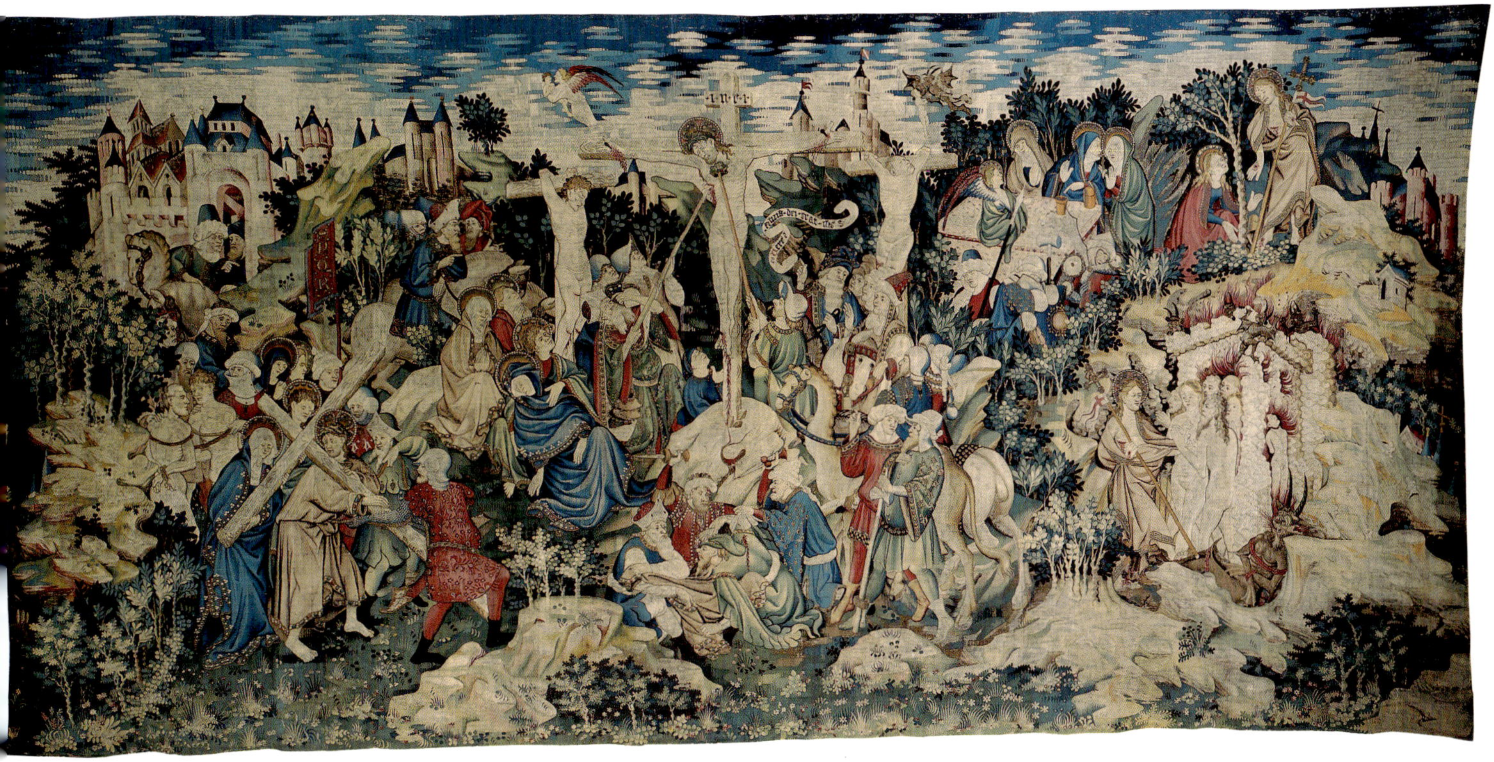

2.8 *Scenes from the Passion* from a pair of tapestries of the *Passion of Christ*. Tapestry woven in the Southern Netherlands, probably Arras, ca. 1420. Wool, silk, and gilt-metal-wrapped thread, 420 x 825 cm. Cathedral Museum of La Seo, Saragossa

during the life of the enfeebled Charles VI. The marriage was celebrated the same day with the duke of Burgundy in attendance. Although we have no documentary evidence of the formal appropriation of French royal tapestries by the English before Henry's death in 1422, it seems probable that the king was already using some part of the collection after his triumphal entry to Paris. Contemporary accounts mention the splendor of the household that he and Katherine maintained at the Louvre and the contrast this provided to the impoverished conditions of Charles VI and his wife, Isabeau, at the Hôtel Saint Pol.

The 1422 Inventory

The growth of the English royal collection during the previous decade, and before any documented influx of French plunder, can be gauged by the detailed probate inventory drawn up in the months following Henry V's unexpected death on August 31, 1422. Henry VI was then an infant of six months, and this is the probable explanation for the compilation of such a comprehensive inventory by Henry V's

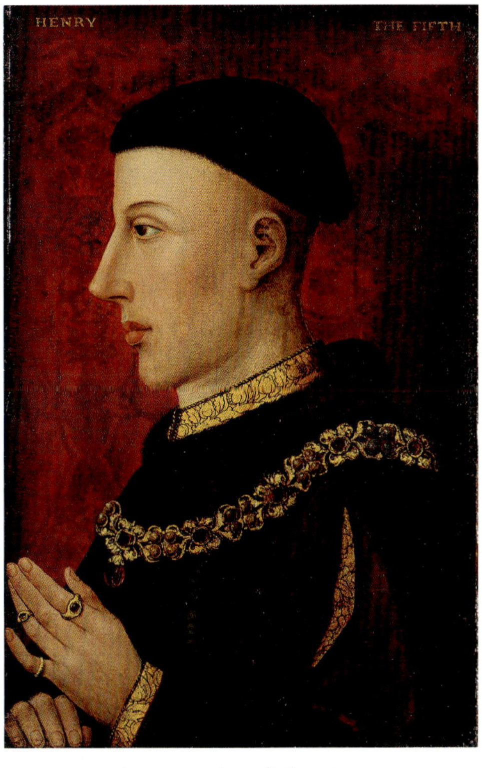

2.9 *Henry V* by an unidentified artist, ca. 1520. Oil on panel, 56.5 x 36.2 cm. The Royal Collection

executors at this date. Because the 1422 inventory is the last detailed account of the royal tapestry collection until a century later, and because many of the tapestries listed in 1422 survived in the royal collection in the 1530s and 1540s, it deserves special attention at this point.

In total, the inventory itemizes more than 170 tapestry hangings and furnishing pieces in the English palaces and royal wardrobes.[14] Thirty-five of these were specified as including gold thread, of which twenty-six were wall hangings, many over ten yards in length, and the other nine were components for three bedchambers. In addition, another sixty-four "arras" tapestries were listed, comprising nine sets or bedchamber ensembles and nineteen independent wall hangings. The majority of the tapestries that appeared in the lists of Richard II and Henry IV's collections are identifiable, while others almost certainly survived, disguised by inadequate descriptions. The most valuable items that had not appeared in the earlier lists were two gold-woven pieces of *Charlemagne* measuring, respectively, four and a half by fourteen and a quarter yards, and four and a half by twenty-eight yards; two of the *Apostles' Creed,* measuring five by fourteen yards and five by eighteen and a half yards; one of *Abraham and Isaac,* measuring four and a quarter by fifteen yards; and one of the *Five Joys of the Virgin,* measuring four and a half by eighteen yards.[15] The 1422 inventory also records for the first time at least ten other large pieces only identified by the opening words of the inscriptions. Six of these depicted courtly and allegorical subjects.[16] Others included a gold-woven panel of *Duke Gloriant,* probably the noble Saracen celebrated in one of the Charlemagne legends, measuring four and a half by fourteen and a quarter yards long; and another of "Farman, first king of France"—that is, *Faramund,* the semilegendary Frankish leader who was claimed as the first king of France—measuring four by ten yards.[17]

The extent to which these additions represented items that had been omitted from earlier lists or new acquisitions by Henry is uncertain. As already noted, the two valuable *Charlemagne* tapestries were of a comparable scale to those recorded in the collection of the duke of Gloucester at Pleshey in 1397 although both were said to contain gold thread, whereas only one of Gloucester's tapestries was specified as such. The large panel of the *Five Joys of the Virgin* listed in the 1422 inventory may also be identical with the *Life of the Virgin* presented to Gloucester by the duke of Burgundy in 1394. One panel, that of *Abraham and Isaac,* certainly stands out as a potential Lancastrian acquisition. As the first of the great biblical patriarchs and traditional founder of the Hebrew nation, Abraham was an attractive comparison for any ruler. Considering the circumstances in which Henry IV came to the throne, and the possibility that his son's accession may have been contested, the subject of the continuation of God's covenant between Abraham and God in the person of his son, Isaac, would have held appealing resonance for the Lancastrian court. More than 130 years later, Henry VIII chose the same subject to celebrate the future succession of his own son and heir, Prince Edward. Other panels, such as that of *Faramund,* may have been appropriations, although it is to be noted that Geoffrey of Monmouth identified this Frankish ruler as an ancestor of the English kings, a claim that was subsequently taken up by Plantagenet genealogies. So it is conceivable that this piece may also have been made for the English royal household.

Besides these large single panels, many of the other hangings that first appear in the 1422 inventory were components for chambers that incorporated bed and furnishing pieces in addition to wall hangings. Four such sets represented allegorical or courtly subjects with, respectively, figures of lovers and "Plesaunce"; women playing the harp; courtly figures with the "noble Vierge Plesance"; and scenes of "Youth."[18] An impression of the appearance of some of these subjects may perhaps be gleaned from a fragmentary tapestry dating from ca. 1420, now at the Cloisters, which represents Honor making a chaplet of roses for her children (fig. 2.10).[19] Although this is a patchwork of fragments from a larger tapestry, the com-

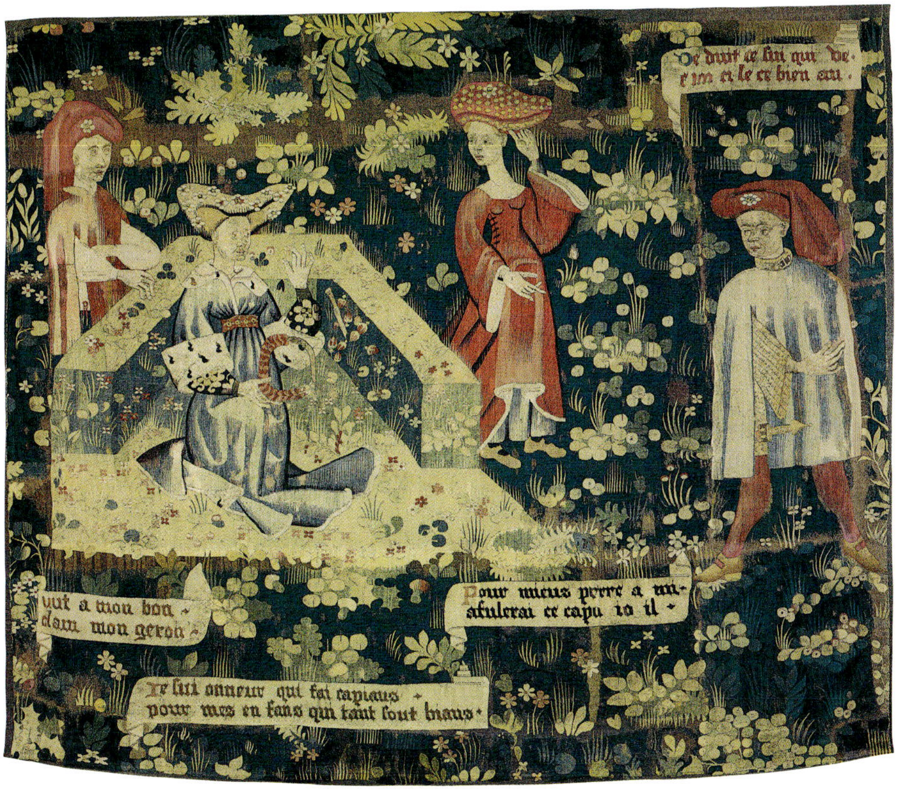

2.10 *Honor Making a Chaplet of Roses* (fragment with extensive modern reweaving). Tapestry made in the Southern Netherlands, ca. 1410–20. Wool, 236 x 274 cm. The Metropolitan Museum of Art, New York

bination of richly costumed figures, a floral ground, and banderoles with allegorical texts, probably typifies the appearance of at least some of the lost bed and wall hangings listed in the 1422 inventory, with the proviso that where the Cloisters fragment is woven in wool alone, several of those in the English royal collection evidently included gilt-metal-wrapped thread.

Four other suites listed in the 1422 inventory featured scenes of hawking and hunting. Three were woven with gold, including one said to have been appropriated from Henry, Lord Scrope of Masham, a former favorite of Henry's who had been executed in 1415 for his involvement in the plot to assassinate the king in Southampton on the eve of his departure for France.[20] In all likelihood, Henry was responsible for buying the other three rich sets himself, since he was a passionate hunter, in recognition of which his cousin, Edward, duke of York, dedicated to him a translation of Gaston Fébus's *Livre de chasse*. In acquiring such tapestries, Henry was following the example of John the Fearless, who purchased a number of large hunting sets for himself and as diplomatic gifts during the 1410s, many from the Arras merchant Jehan Walois.[21] Four large hunting tapestries dating from between 1420 and 1440 survive at the Victoria and Albert Museum, the so-called *Devonshire Hunts* (fig. 2.11, see also fig. i.2). Although there is no evidence that these were from the Walois workshop, they almost certainly provide an idea of the style of allover design and subject matter that characterized the *Hunt* tapestries acquired by Henry V and his courtiers in the late 1410s.[22] The compositions of the *Devonshire Hunt* tapestries are less condensed than those of earlier designs like the La Seo *Passion* tapestries, and this seems to have been a trend in Netherlandish tapestry design from the early 1420s. Although the narrative pockets are still framed by landscape and architectural components, the figures are proportionally larger in respect to the surrounding landscape elements than those in designs of the first two decades of the century. They are arranged in two tiers, and although those above are smaller than those below, little effort is made to represent spatial recession. Instead the figures tend to appear frontally or in three-quarter profile in elaborately folded and boldly patterned costumes. The cumulative effect keeps the eye moving smoothly around the entire surface of the tapestry.

The 1422 inventory is also notable for the number of armorial sets it records, although several of these had evidently been in the collection for some years. Eight sets are listed, including two ensembles with the royal arms "for the chapel," one with a white ground, the second on a red ground.[23] Most of the other sets may have been from appropriations. One set depicted the duke of Gloucester's arms while another single panel bore those of Lord Scrope.[24] One set featured yellow crowns; another had a red-and-black ground scattered with roses; another, a blue ground with roses.[25] The last may have been the set of armorials listed in the earl of Arundel's collection in 1397 and subsequently in the royal collection in 1406.

The 1422 inventory also provides interesting information about the disposition of the royal tapestries. A significant portion were at

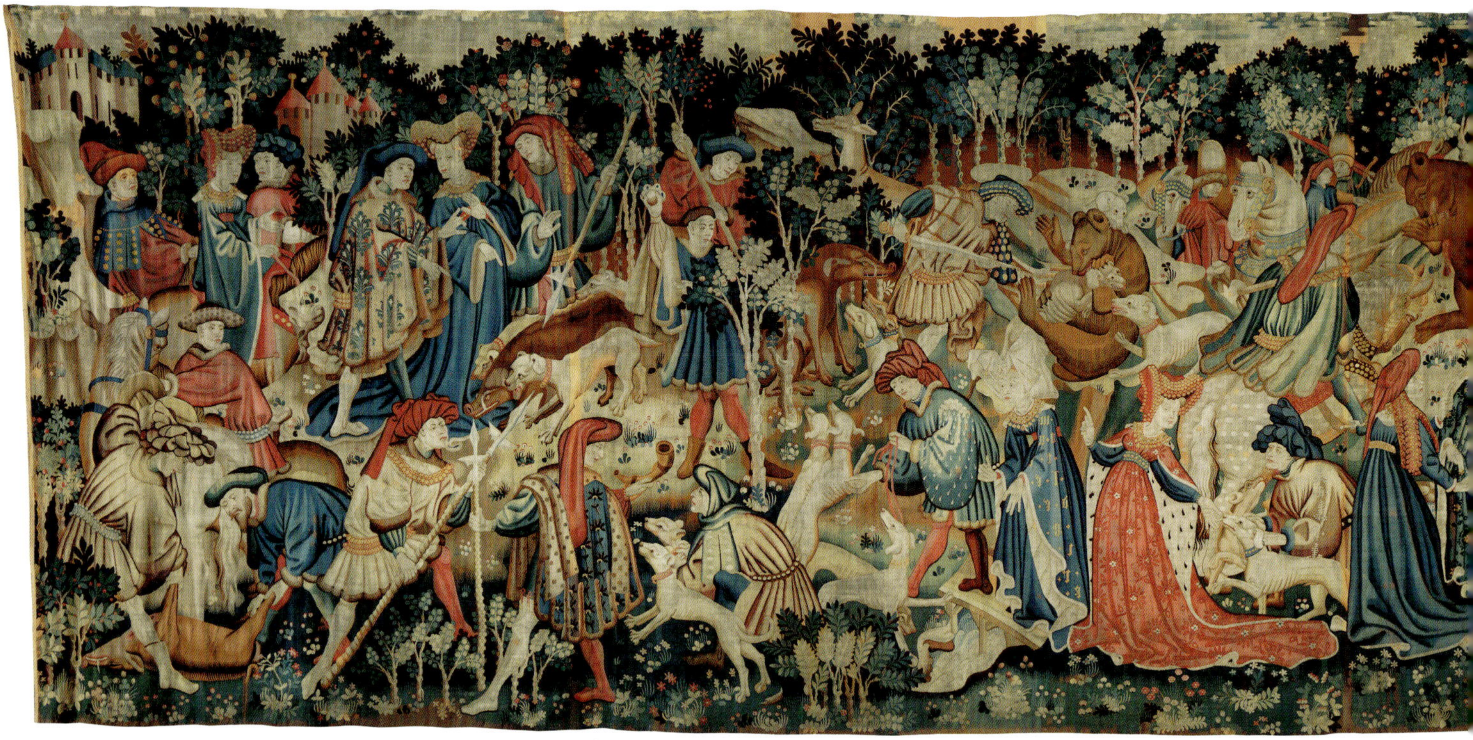

2.11 *The Boar and Bear Hunt* from the *Devonshire Hunts*. Tapestry woven in the Southern Netherlands, possibly Arras, ca. 1430. Wool, 407 x 1021 cm. Victoria and Albert Museum, London

Westminster Palace under the jurisdiction of Robert Rolleston, keeper of the Great Wardrobe; other important pieces were at Windsor in the care of Roger Assent, keeper of the king's beds at that location, including the *Saint George* tapestry with Gloucester's arms and the valuable tapestries of *Charlemagne* and *Renaud of Montauban*.[26] Several of the associations documented in 1422 between particular tapestries and locations endured into the sixteenth century and, in a few cases, into the seventeenth. Some precious textiles were also listed in the wardrobe of the prince (that is, the young Henry VI), including two pieces of the *Story of King Priam*.[27]

The Infancy of Henry VI and the Duke of Bedford's Regency in France

With Henry V's sudden death in 1422, circumstances once again ran counter to the steady growth of the royal tapestry collection. Henry VI was only six months old, and Henry's will divided the responsibilities of government between his brothers, Humphrey, duke of Gloucester, responsible for England, and John, duke of Bedford, responsible for the English rule in France. The existing tapestry collection survived this turn of events relatively unscathed. A number of Henry V's precious textiles were the object of specific bequests, such as the two beds he left to the duke of Bedford; one, of "arras," of *Children*, the second of red velvet.[28] Apart from this and despite the Crown's debts, comparison between the probate inventory compiled by Henry V's executors in 1422 and a list of the goods that were purchased for Henry VI in 1426 demonstrates that about half of Henry V's possessions were transferred to his son, with "arras" forming the bulk of the inheritance. The sum of £1,500 paid for the goods did not reflect their true worth.[29]

Although the integrity of the inherited collection was largely respected, the situation was inevitably different with regard to the privileges of appropriation that had traditionally been the Crown's prerogative. The second quarter of the fifteenth century offered unprecedented opportunities in this respect because of the occupation of northern France, but with the minority of the king it was his guardians, particularly Bedford, who first benefited from this situation. Bedford was no stranger to regal magnificence. Third son of Henry IV, he had received grants and offices during the early years

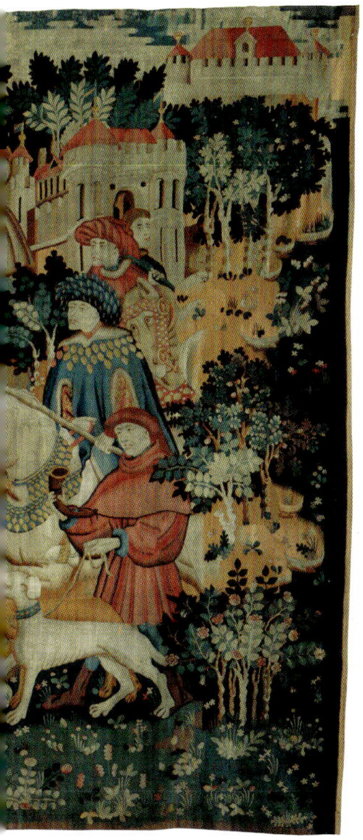

of Henry V's reign that made him one of the richest nobles in the country. During the second half of the 1410s he served as lieutenant of England while Henry was campaigning in France, and following the death of the duke of Clarence in battle in March 1421, he became heir to the throne of England. Bedford assumed the role of regent of France by November 1422. Shortly thereafter, on December 12, he contracted to marry Anne of Burgundy, sister of the young Duke Philip, to ensure Burgundian support for the English occupation. The marriage was celebrated at Troyes the next May. During the following two years, he consolidated the English grip on northern France, culminating in the Battle of Verneuil, when many French nobles were captured, including Jean II, duke of Alençon, for whom Bedford demanded a huge ransom of 200,000 *écus d'or*. The first installment was paid in jewels, plate, vestments, and at least one valuable set of tapestries.[30]

As regent, Bedford acquired extensive territories and property in France, but the greatest spoils were those of the Valois heritage, including Charles V's library of more than eight hundred books and some thirty sets of precious chapel vestments.[31] The most visible and valuable appropriations of all were the Valois tapestries. Mention has already been made of the tapestry collection amassed by Charles V, and this had been augmented by Charles VI, who reigned from 1380 until 1422 (fig. 2.12). Despite the bouts of insanity with which Charles VI was debilitated from 1392, he and his circle had instituted a number of major commissions such as the *Jousts of Saint Ingelvert*, cited above. Even more ambitious was the set of the *Jousts of Saint Denis*, arranged in 1397 through the Paris merchants Nicolas Bataille and Jacques Dourdin. This thirteen-piece chamber of gold-woven tapestries depicted the festivities held in 1389 to celebrate the knighthood of Louis, duke of Orléans, and his cousin, Louis II, duke of Anjou. Measuring 285 square French ells (about 490 square yards), the ensemble cost 2,743 livres.[32]

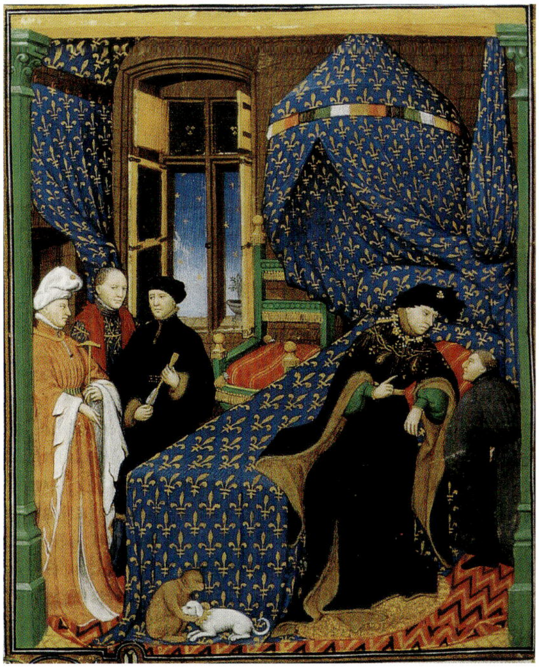

.12 *Charles VI with the Author and Three Nobles*. Miniature painting y the Boucicaut Master, in ierre Salmon's *Réponses de Pierre almon*, after 1411. 26.5 x 19.5 cm. ibliothèque Publique et Univeritaire, Geneva (Ms fr. 165, fol. 4r)

The size and splendor of the French royal tapestry collection is demonstrated by an inventory drawn up in 1422, which lists several hundred tapestries, many including gold thread.[33] The same inventory attests to Bedford's appropriations, which were carefully recorded by Jean Duval, the officer responsible for the French royal tapestries. Between 1422 and 1433 John Brigge, Bedford's valet of the wardrobe, took receipt of more than two hundred tapestries with an aggregate value of 9,000 *livres tournois*.[34] These included the gold-woven sets of the *Jousts of Saint Ingelvert* and the *Jousts of Saint Denis*; an eleven-piece set richly woven with Charles's heraldic devices and mottoes; large panels of the *Story of Octavian*; the *Twelve Peers*; the *Conquest of England by William the Conqueror*; the *Battle of the Thirty Knights*, a much fabled encounter between thirty Bretons and thirty English knights in 1351; the *Story of Bertrand Duguesclin*, the fourteenth-century French hero; and chambers of allegorical subjects such as *Plaisance*, also called the *Chamber of Honor*; *Good Renown*, featuring sages such as Solomon, Jason, and Absalom; *Fortune*; *Love*; and *Youth*. As will be apparent from the titles and subjects, a number of these may have been duplicates of sets and tapestries already in the English royal collection.

Although Bedford undoubtedly enriched himself enormously by these appropriations,

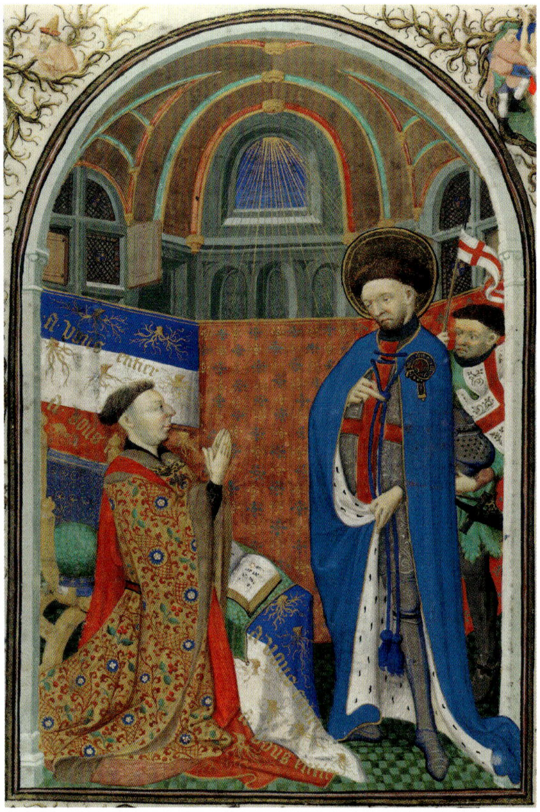

2.13 *John, Duke of Bedford, Kneeling before Saint George.* Miniature painting from the *Bedford Book of Hours.* Paris, 1423–30. 26 x 18 cm. British Library, London (Add. Ms 18850, fol. 256v)

he was not motivated solely by greed and opportunism. In the absence of the English king, Bedford embodied his presence, and his court needed to be suitably magnificent.[35] Additionally, Bedford now had a crucial political task in strengthening the English hold on France. Accordingly, he took a range of steps to bind the conquered French subjects to their new English king and to denigrate the usurped dynasty, including pointedly denying a royal style of address to Charles, "who calls himself the dauphin," in public ordinances, enlisting the University of Paris to issue proclamations in favor of the Anglo-Burgundian claims to the French crown, commissioning genealogies that demonstrated Henry VI's descent in the line of Saint Louis, and distributing crude verses that smeared the dauphin.[36] As one of the most eye-catching components of French royal regalia, the appropriation of the Valois tapestries for the ceremonial use of the English court was thus a logical part of efforts to consolidate the Lancastrian claim to the French throne.

The early successes of the English occupation were reversed in the late 1420s with the collapse of the Burgundian alliance in April 1428, the failure of the siege of Orléans in May 1428, the defeat of the English army by Joan of Arc at Patay in June, and the coronation of the dauphin at Reims in July. It was in response to this situation that plans were initiated for the long-delayed coronation of Henry VI in London and France. The eight-year-old king was crowned with great pomp and ceremony at Westminster in November 1429. The following April, he crossed the channel with an entourage of three hundred, arriving in late July in Rouen where he remained for more than a year. With the capture of Joan and the English victories of 1431, the safety of the route was ensured for his onward journey, and Henry eventually traveled to Paris in December 1431. Before his arrival in the city he was greeted by mounted figures representing the God of Fame and the nine male and nine female Worthies, a reminder of the extent to which the exemplary characters represented in contemporary tapestries also provided the main themes of courtly pageantry. During his progress into the city, pageants were also mounted at key junctures on stages that were hung with tapestries and precious cloths.[37] Henry was crowned at Notre Dame on December 16. It seems safe to assume that these grandiose events took place against a backdrop of the Valois tapestries.

The subsequent fate of the Valois textiles is a mystery. Bedford died on September 14, 1435 and his enormous estates in England and France were the subject of protracted legal proceedings, some of which dragged on for more than two decades.[38] The extant inventories of his goods were drawn up between 1447 and 1449 for his executors, but it is clear that these give only a partial record of his possessions. Most notably, in contrast to the detailed listing of liturgical vestments contained therein, there is little information about the tapestries. A brief entry in one list refers to a large amount of precious objects and textiles at Bedford's London residence, including vestments, "arras," tapestry, and beds of cloth of gold and silk but no details are given. In fact, the only tapestries and textile hangings from Bedford's collection that are described are seven sets of hangings, one of embroidery and six of tapestry, that were sent from Bedford's wardrobe to Cardinal Beaufort, second son of John of Gaunt and the principal executor of Bedford's estate between 1438 and 1447, and another unfinished set of heraldic embroideries that was left in the wardrobe.[39] Of the sets sent to Beaufort, at least four had been custom-made for Bedford. The embroidered chamber was described as having Bedford's root badges and inscriptions on fields of red, white, and blue. Valued at £80 10s., it probably resembled the hanging illustrated in the *Bedford Hours* (fig. 2.13). The second, unfinished set, left in Bedford's wardrobe was similarly described. Two of the tapestry sets sent to Beaufort also appear to have been woven with Bedford's devices, one with eagles and roots, the other with ostrich feathers. Few details are given on the four figurative tapestry sets that are listed. One, comprising a celure (canopy) and dorser, with a surface area of 112 square yards and said to be of silk and "wrought as aras richely," had formerly belonged to the duke of Clarence. No subject is given. The others sets also constituted chambers of en suite hangings. The first, comprising a celure, tester, and counterpoint alone, depicted "jousting." The second, with bed components and six costers, was called the "bed of the gardens." The third was called the "bed of the Boscherons" (woodcutters) and had formed part of the ransom that Bedford received in September 1427 for Jean II, duke of Alençon. Although the *Jousting* and *Gardens* ensembles may have originated in the French royal collection, the brief descriptions are inadequate to allow certain identification. The possibility remains that, like the heraldic ensembles, they may all have been purchased by Bedford himself. At his death Bedford owed money to Richard Worsley, a rich London mercer and merchant of Bruges who played a major role in supplying tapestries to Henry VI and his courtiers during the 1440s.[40] An idea of the appearance of Bedford's *Gardens* tapestries may be suggested by extant fragments like the Metropolitan Museum's *Courtiers in a Rose Garden* (fig. 2.14) or the modello for a courtly garden scene now in Dresden (fig. 2.15).[41] Like the *Devonshire Hunts,* these extant fragments indicate the stylistic shift that was taking place in tapestry design during the 1430s and 1440s, as the small figures and dense surface pattern of compositions like the La Seo *Passion* tapestries gave way to designs in which the figures occupied a larger proportion of the picture space and in which the vegetation and costume patterns became more rounded and harmonious.

Since the few tapestry sets described in Bedford's collection probably resulted from purchases that he made, the question arises as to the fate of the many other Valois hangings that he appropriated during the 1420s. Some had certainly been given to members of his court in France, and others may have succumbed to the rigors of use.[42] And if any remained in Bedford's properties in Paris and other regions regained by the French in spring 1436, they would have been repossessed by the French.[43] But since Bedford took large quantities of the Valois treasures back to England in 1433, including twenty-seven of the Valois sets of liturgical vestments, it seems likely that he would also have taken the most valuable tapestries and that these constituted the rich textiles briefly mentioned at his London residence.[44]

If that was the case, it would help to explain the subsequent appearance of a small portion of the French royal tapestry collection in the hands of the Crown. No inventories for the royal collection survive between that taken in 1426 and those compiled a century later for Henry VIII, so evidence for this transfer depends largely on deductions drawn from a handful of fifteenth- and sixteenth-century documents. The earliest of these is a description of the room at Westminster Palace in which Henry VI received the important French embassy in July 1445. On this occasion, the decorations included the gold-woven heraldic tapestry set depicting a diaper of fleur de lis, "broomcods," and Charles VI's motto, "Jamais," that Bedford appropriated from the French royal collection before 1432. A gold-woven dorser that depicted the *Clovis* legend was also

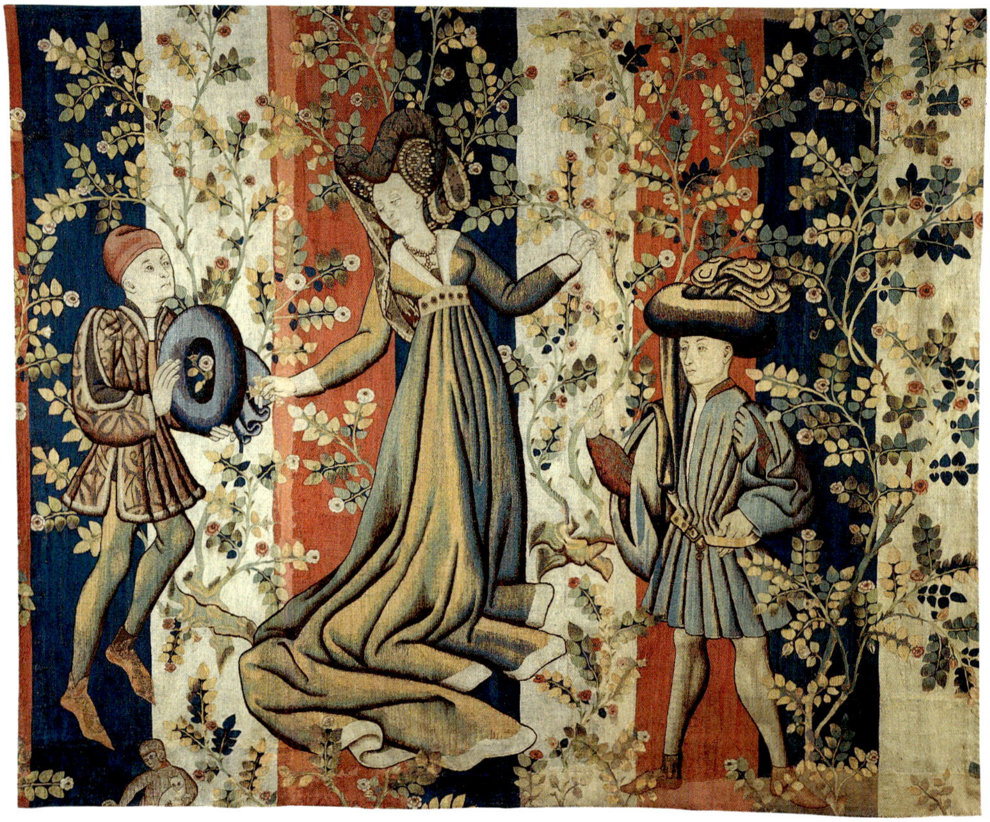

2.14 *Courtiers in a Rose Garden.* Tapestry (fragment) made in the Southern Netherlands, ca. 1440–50. Wool, silk, and gilt-metal-wrapped thread, 289 x 325 cm. The Metropolitan Museum of Art, New York

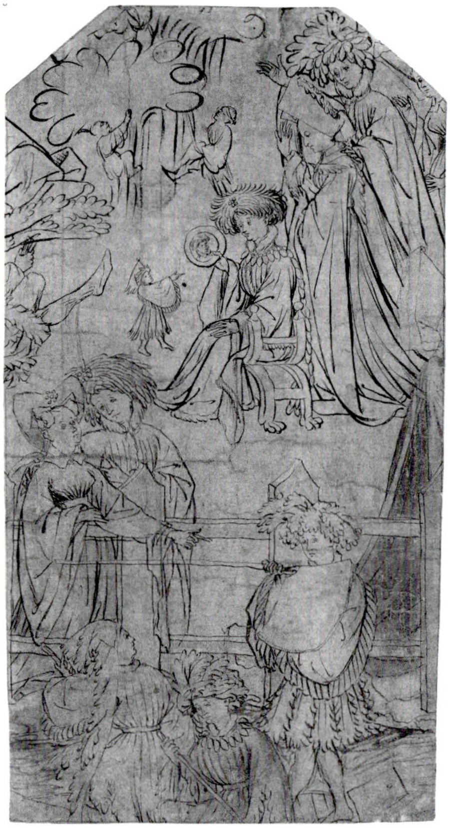

2.15 *Courtly Figures in a Garden* (fragment). Design for a tapestry? by an unidentified Southern Netherlandish artist, ca. 1440–50. Pen, brown and black ink, 32.9 x 17.2 cm. Kupferstich-Kabinett, Dresden

hung above the throne. This, too, can be identified in the inventories of Charles VI's goods and was taken by Bedford before 1423.[45] Both these ensembles survived in the English royal collection during the reign of Henry VIII, the heraldic ensemble at Hampton Court and the *Clovis* canopy at Windsor.[46] The *Clovis* canopy was to survive at Windsor until the sale of the goods of Charles I in 1650, a prized relic of the English conquest of France. Given the paucity of information about the appearance of the Valois tapestries, the *Clovis* tapestry is unusual in that it was described by several tourists who visited Windsor in the late sixteenth and seventeenth centuries. The most detailed record was made in 1599 by the Swiss tourist Thomas Platter, who stated that the first scene showed an angel dropping three lilies from heaven into the hut of a hermit. The next showed the hermit giving the lilies to King Clovis's consort and instructing her in the Christian faith. In turn, she was shown giving them to her husband and persuading him to convert to Christianity. The tapestry also incorporated a thirty-line inscription that explained the moral significance of the story and concluded with an account of Clovis's anointment at Reims with an ampoule of holy oil and a statement of the continuity of that ceremony in modern times.[47] The tapestry was thus an explicit celebration of the quasi-divine status of the French monarch and the continuing role in the coronation ceremony of the sacred oil preserved at Reims.

Quite apart from confirming the transition of some of the French royal tapestry collection into that of the English crown, the use of these tapestries in 1445 for the reception of an embassy of great potential significance for the continuing presence of England in northern France indicates that they had been chosen for this occasion specifically to emphasize Henry's claims to the French throne.[48] As such, this is the earliest documented example of tapestry being used at the English court for a political purpose.

Were these Valois ensembles just two of many that had entered the royal collection? Following Henry VII's coronation in 1485 John de Vere received various perquisites in his capacity as lord chamberlain, including a bed of satin that closely resembled one of those listed in Bedford's inventories, along with hangings for an "arras" bed depicting a tournament. It has been suggested that these hangings may have been the remnants of one of the French *Joust* sets.[49] Another larger jousting set from the French royal collection may have survived in the English royal collection for even longer, as evidenced by the presence of six large "arras" hangings of "Attorney" (that is, A tournament?) at Windsor Castle a few years later. These panels were removed from Windsor for repair at the Great Wardrobe in 1502–3 and were subsequently listed in the 1547 inventory of Windsor goods.[50] Although these examples suggest that a number of tapestries from the Valois collection did survive among the antique textiles that the Tudor kings inherited, the fact that so few can be identified even tentatively suggests that a significant portion may have been burned or otherwise dismembered during the mid- to late fifteenth century in order to extract the precious metals with which they were woven. This fate befell many of the sixteenth-century gold-woven tapestries in the French royal collection after the 1789 revolution, and circumstantial evidence that this practice had a long antecedence is provided by the fate of a dorser from a set of liturgical vestments in the Valois collection known as the "chapelle Saint-Denis." Richly embroidered in gold and silver, the vestments were looted in 1420 when they were on loan to Saint-Germain l'Auxerrois, and subsequent inquiry revealed that they had been burned to extract the gilt-metal thread.[51] Of all the rich textiles listed in the French royal inventory of 1422 and subsequently taken by Bedford, the only piece known to survive is the so-called *Parement de Narbonne,* an ink drawing on silk (see fig. 1.4). Although the materials in which this panel is worked were of minimal value in comparison to those of many of the royal tapestries and embroideries, which may account for its survival, this exquisitely drawn altar frontal provides a hint of the artistic quality of many of the items that Bedford brought back to England.

The Earl of Suffolk

Following Bedford's death, the young Henry VI fell under the control of a court faction headed first by Cardinal Beaufort and subsequently by William de la Pole, fourth earl of Suffolk. It was Suffolk who traveled to France to negotiate for a marriage with the French princess in 1444. Margaret of Anjou eventually traveled to England the following April and was crowned in Westminster Abbey on May 30, 1445. Suffolk was evidently a tapestry patron of some standing in his own right, and the collection he amassed is worthy of note, especially since some pieces appear to have entered the royal collection after his death. He sourced at least part of his collection through the London mercer Robert Worsley, already mentioned in connection with the duke of Bedford. Contemporary documents record that in 1440 Worsley imported, on Suffolk's behalf, tapestries, carpets, beds, and other furnishings, all purchased in Flanders and shipped via Sandwich.[52] Worsley had extensive dealings in Bruges, and this may have been where he obtained the tapestries he supplied. Bruges was then a flourishing international port and one of the most important hubs of the tapestry trade. In 1438 the Spanish traveler Pero Tafur had compared it favorably with Venice, noting tapestry among the luxury commodities that were traded there.[53] The sources of the tapestries sold in Bruges were various. Arras continued to be the center of high-quality production throughout the second quarter of the century, although there was also increasing competition from such towns as Tournai, Lille, and Brussels from the 1430s.[54] Tafur described Arras as a

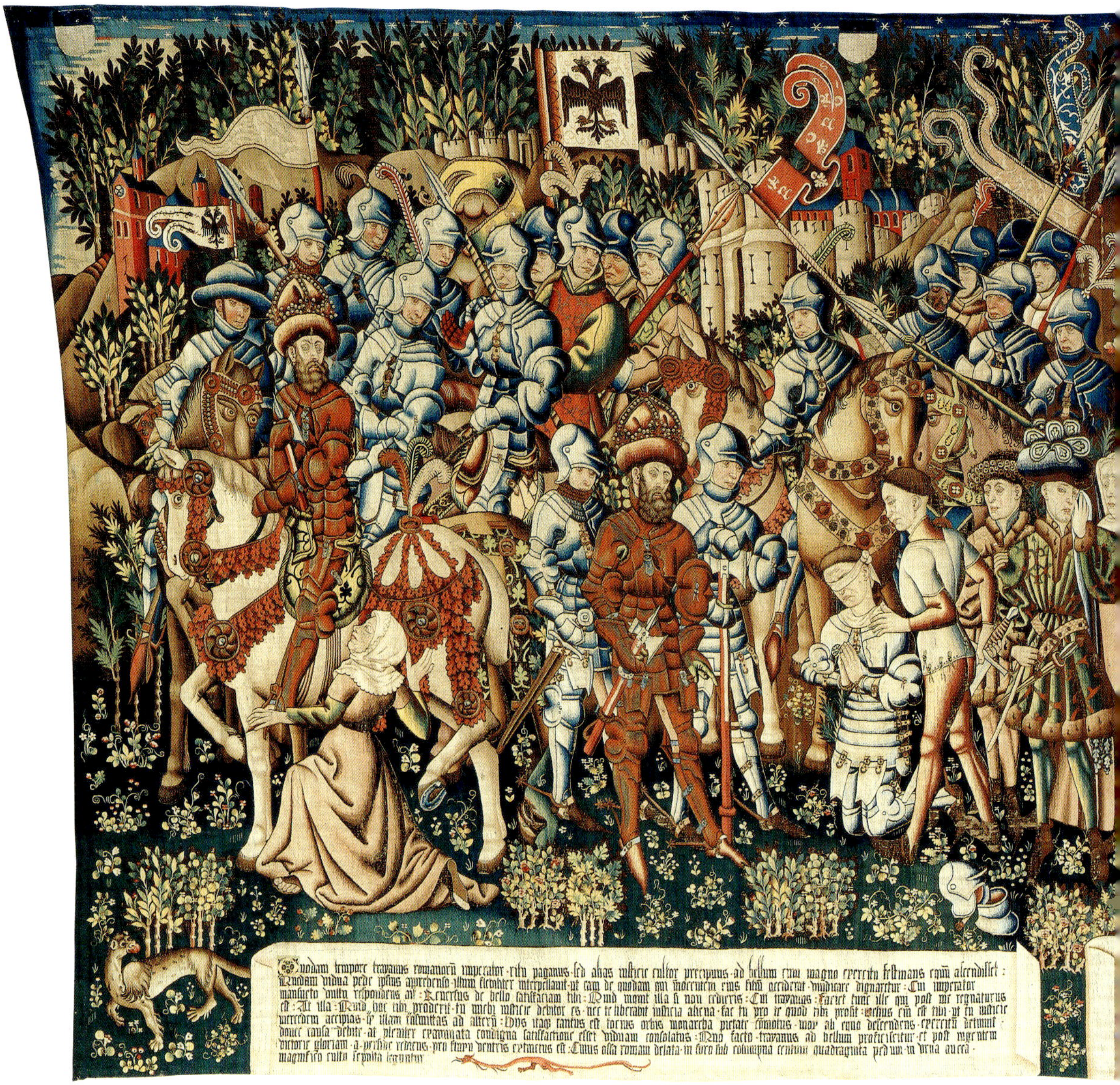

2.16 *The Justice of Trajan and the Justice of Herkinbald.* Tapestry woven in the Southern Netherlands, ca. 1460. Wool and silk, 461 x 1053 cm. Historisches Museum, Bern

very rich town, "especially by reason of its woven cloths and all kinds of tapestries, and although they are also made in other places, yet it well appears that those which are made in Arras have the preference."[55]

The tapestries that Worsley imported in 1440 were presumably among those listed in Suffolk's residence at Ewelme in an inventory taken some years later in 1464.[56] This records about twenty large tapestries, including two silk-woven "arras" hangings of the *Seven Sciences,* another with gold of *Tigers,* a large gold-woven panel of *King Herkinbald,* and others, presumably without gold, of the *City of Peace, Dame Honor, Hercules' Tournament,* the *Fifteen Signs of the Doom,* and *Saint Anne.* Though long since lost, the dimensions of the *Herkinbald* panel suggest that it was almost certainly woven from the same cartoon as a large tapestry of the *Justice of Trajan and Herkinbald* now in Bern (figs. 2.16, 2.17). The design of this tapestry is based, in part, on the four large paintings that Rogier van der Weyden executed ca. 1436–40 for the town hall of Brussels.[57] These paintings, now also lost, depicted events in the lives of Trajan and Herkinbald that exemplified the highest judicial integrity. Although the tapestry design reworked the figures, interiors, and landscapes into more two-dimensional forms than those that must have characterized Van der Weyden's

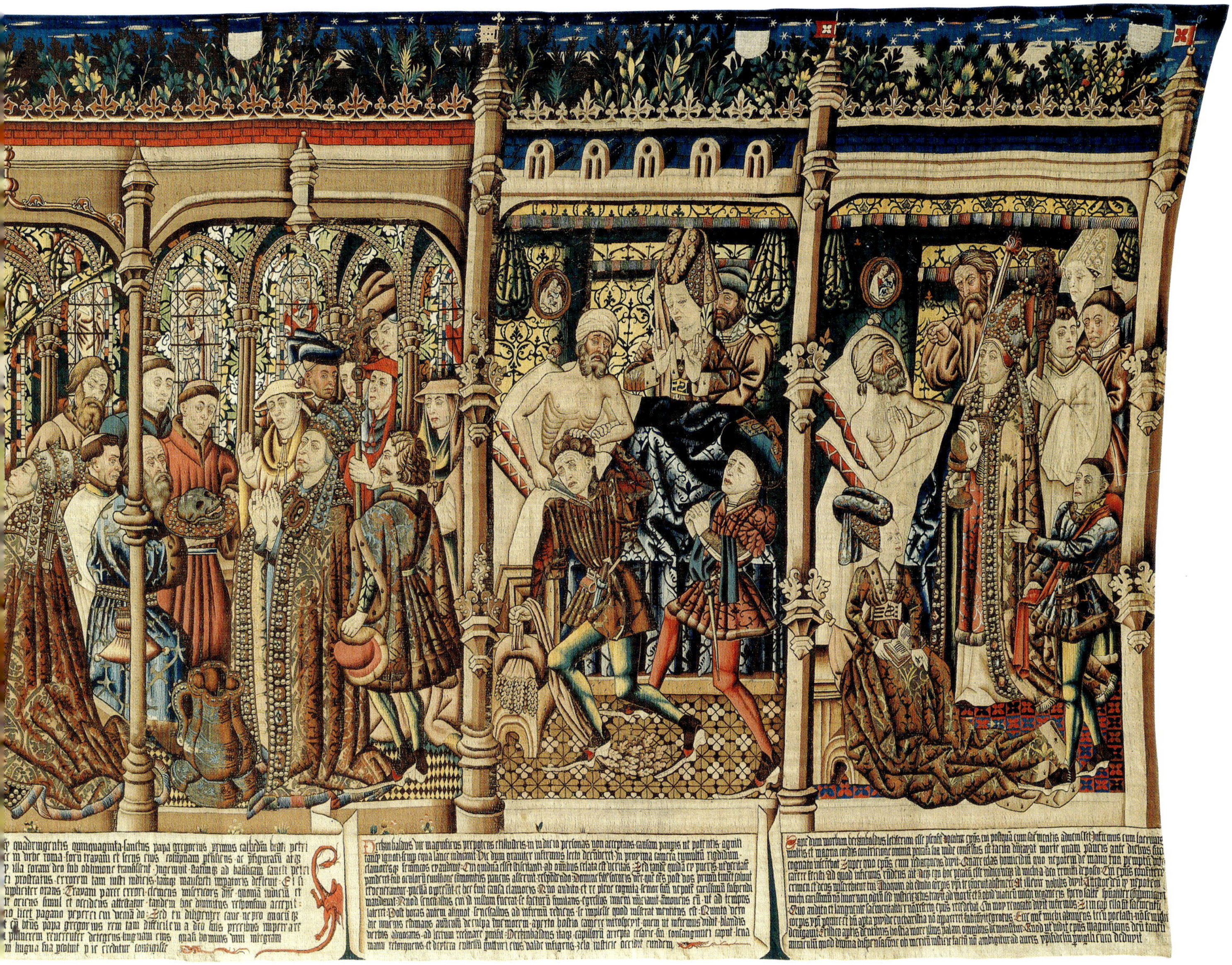

paintings, with a concomitant emphasis on the pattern of costumes and the decorative details of the architectural settings, the overall compositions appear to have followed those of the original paintings fairly closely. The presence of a woven reproduction of these paintings in an English courtier's collection so soon after the completion of the originals is an interesting reflection of the role that tapestry played in transmitting artistic ideas and motifs around Europe. We can only guess whether Suffolk acquired this tapestry to promote his own status as a figure of judgment. At the time the inventory was taken, it was displayed in a room with another tapestry of the *City of Peace,* which suggests that the hangings had been selected as models of good governance.[58]

Suffolk's tapestries also included components for several bed ensembles depicting genre and hunting scenes. One, however, located in the great chamber, was described as "Orchia." This unusual subject allows us to be fairly certain that it was a weaving from the same cartoon as a tapestry now in Boston that depicts Orchia, queen of the Amazons, presiding over the preparation of her daughters, Hippolyte and Menalippe, for a joust (fig. 2.18). In turn, the Orchia panel may have been en suite with another tapestry described in Suffolk's inventory as "Hercules tournament," which was

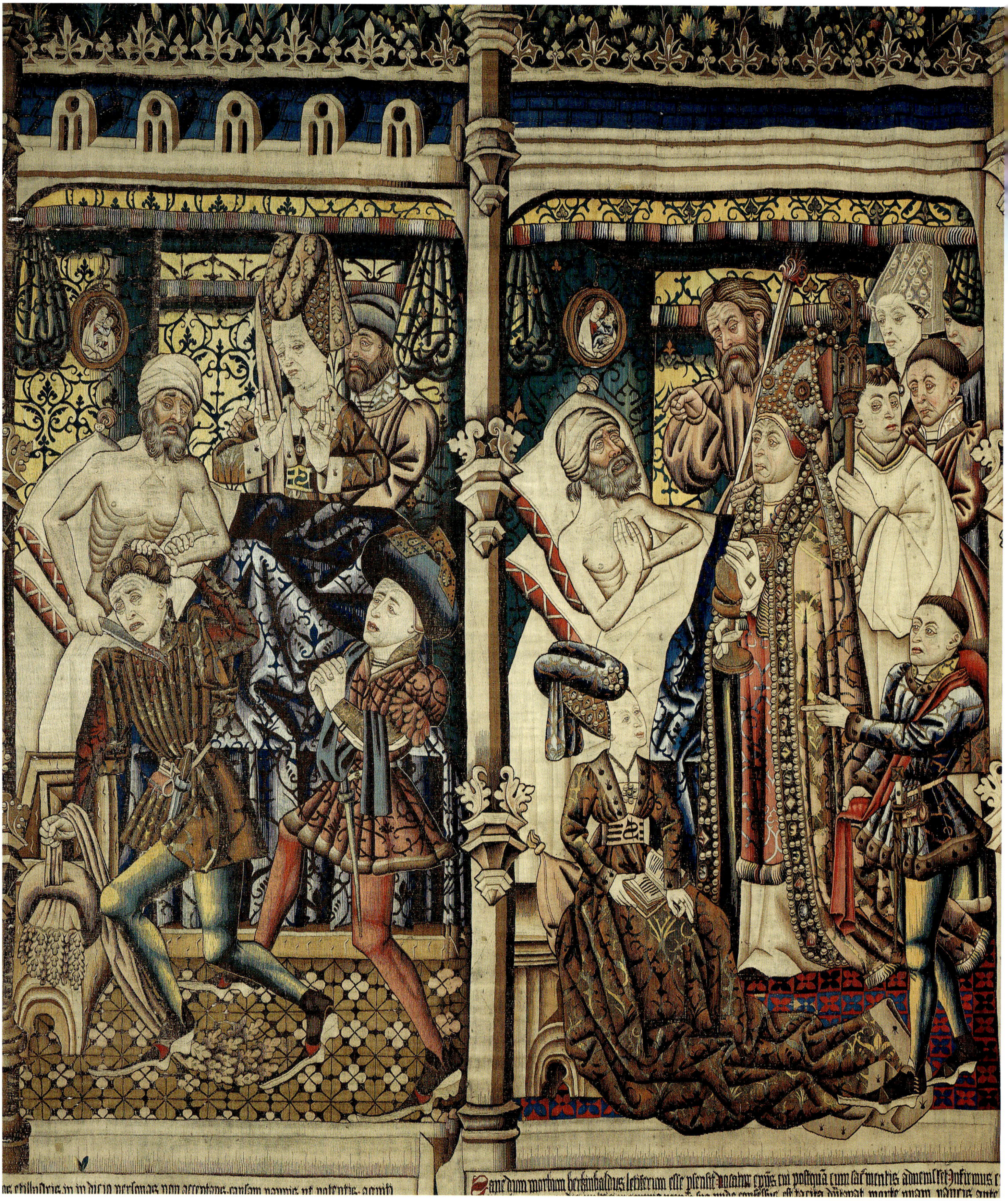

2.17 Detail of fig. 2.16

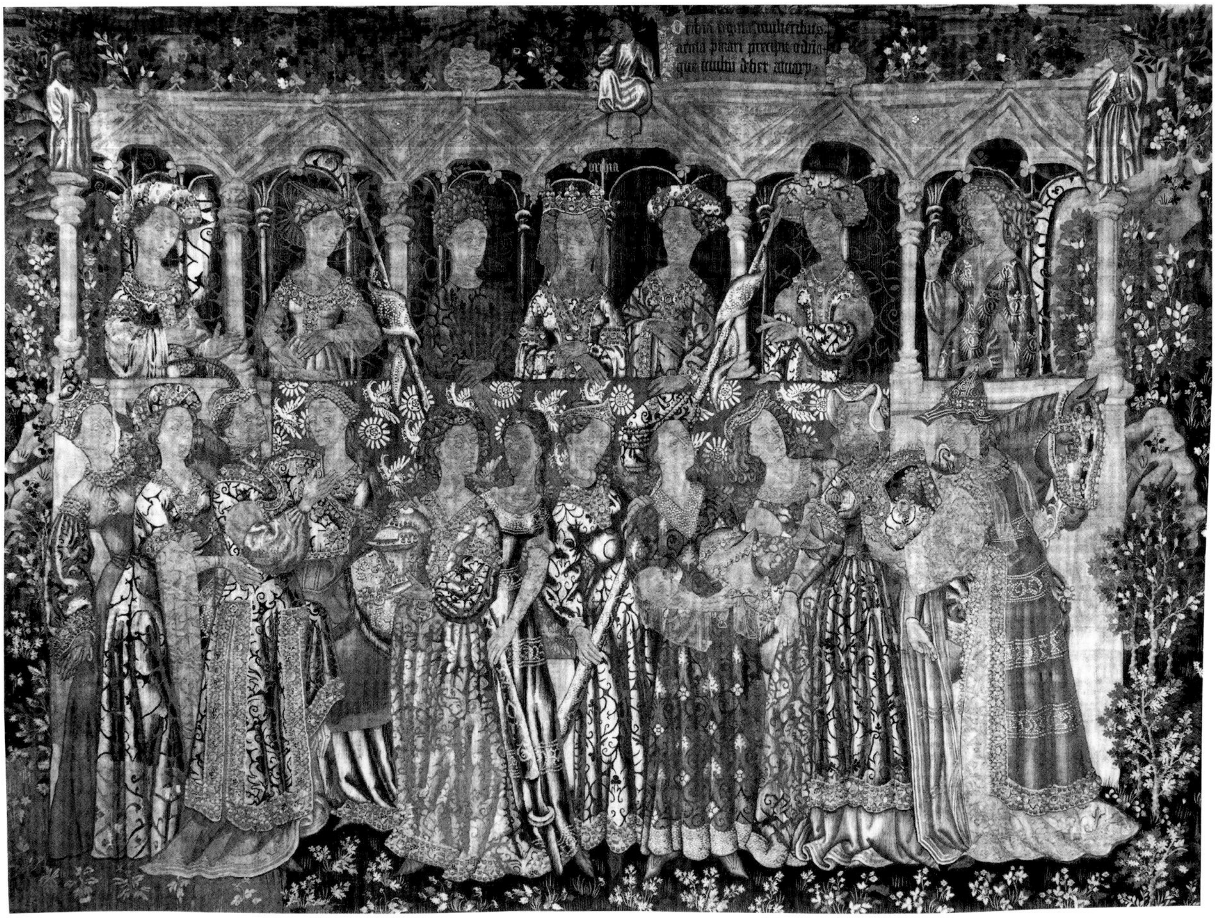

2.18 *Joust of the Amazons*. Tapestry woven in the Southern Netherlands, ca. 1440–50. Wool and silk, 398 x 497 cm. Isabella Stewart Gardner Museum, Boston

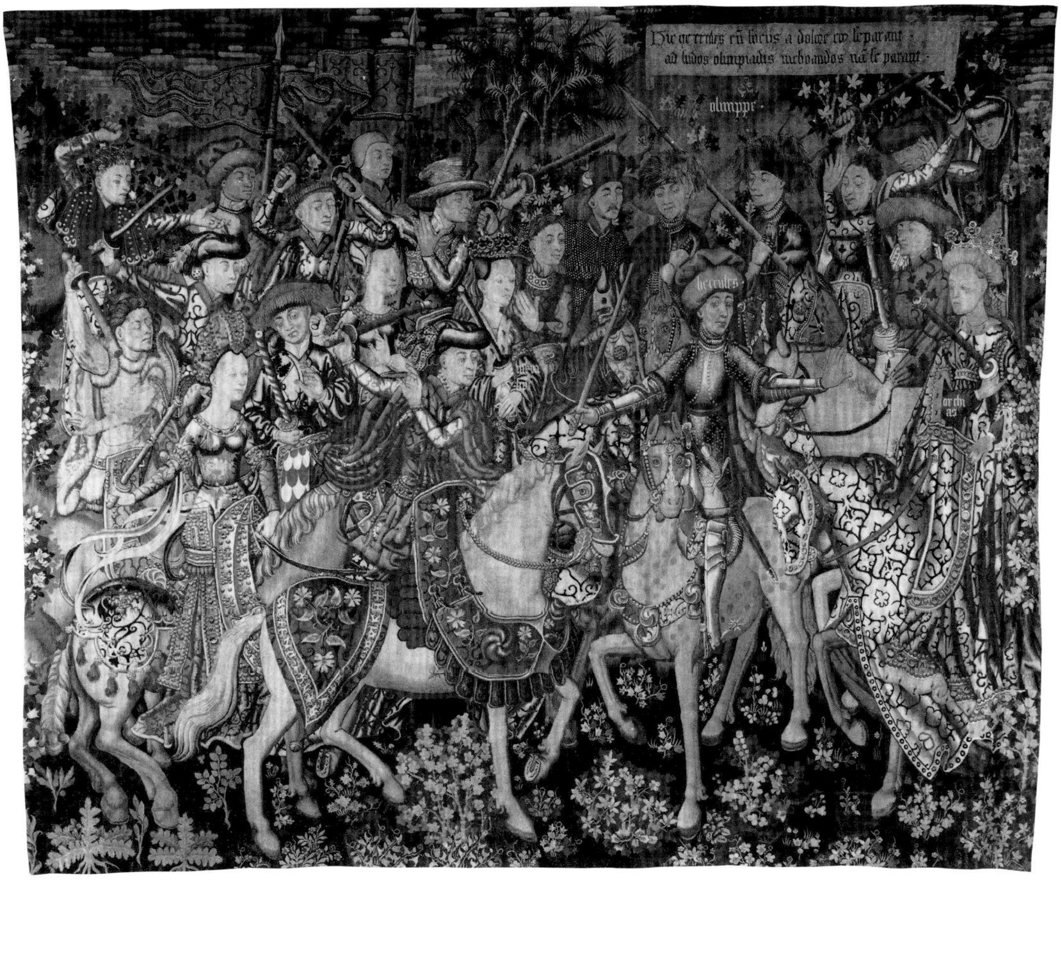

2.19 *Hercules Founding the Olympic Games on Mount Olympus* (fragment). Tapestry woven in the Southern Netherlands, ca. 1440–50. Wool and silk, 386 x 478 cm. The Burrell Collection, Glasgow

probably a weaving from the same cartoon used to make a tapestry of this subject now at the Burrell Collection in Glasgow (fig. 2.19).[59] This depicts Hercules initiating the Olympic Games, in the company of Theseus, Menalippe, Hippolyte, and Orchia. The subject matter of these tapestries derived from Christine de Pisan's *City of Women*, where the episodes were included as demonstrations of the martial prowess of women. A similar ensemble comprising tapestries of Orchia and Hercules was acquired before 1450 by Leonello d'Este.[60] Because the *Orchia* bed and *Hercules* tapestry at Ewelme were displayed with another panel of *Dame Honor* in the great chamber of the dowager duchess, it has been suggested that the three other tapestries in the room, depicting "locus Perfectionis," may also have represented an idealized female world and that this assemblage provides a rare documented example of the thematic selection of tapestries for a patron, in this case Suffolk's widow, Alice Chaucer, granddaughter of the poet.[61] Stylistically, the flat and rounded forms of the figures in the *Orchia* and *Hercules* panels, the richly patterned damasks and silks in which they are depicted, and the encompassing foliage, typify tapestry design of the 1440s.

Suffolk was impeached and murdered in 1450, and at some point after 1464 the Crown appears to have acquired part of his collection. A very wide panel of *Herkinbald* with dimensions similar to those of Suffolk's panel is listed in the inventory of Cardinal Wolsey's collection in the early 1520s, along with various other tapestries that Wolsey had probably received as perquisites from the king.[62] After Wolsey's fall these all returned to the Crown collection.

Tapestry Acquisitions by Henry VI

With the example of English nobles like Bedford and Suffolk before him, Henry VI is unlikely to have been insensitive to the tapestry medium, but evidence regarding his patronage is limited. In 1444, in anticipation of the arrival of the French princess Margaret of Anjou, the tapicer John Bonauntre was paid for the production of five "tapets" of tapestry, each with the princess's escutcheons and arms, which were copied from a pattern made by John Stratford, the king's painter.[63] During the same year, and presumably also in preparation for Margaret's arrival, Henry or courtiers acting on his behalf purchased a gold-woven tapestry of the *Vices and the Virtues* and another of *Saint George* from the merchant Robert Worsley for £210 and £230, respectively.[64] Considering the central role that Saint George played in the imagery of the Order of the Garter and the frequency with which he was invoked as the patron saint of England during Henry VI's reign, it seems likely that this was a custom-made design. The fact that these tapestries were sourced through Worsley indicates the extent to which upscale production continued to be concentrated in the hands of a small number of merchants with international connections, a situation that was to prevail well into the sixteenth century.

The scale of the sums involved in the 1444 purchase indicate that the tapestries in question were large and impressive, and it is tempting to speculate that this reflects broader interest by Henry VI and his advisers in the tapestry medium. But the only other documented acquisition dates from 1450, when Henry purchased secondhand tapestries from the estate of William Ayscough, bishop of Salisbury, for 40 marks.[65] Beyond this, all we have to go on are hints. Evidence that Henry VI or someone close to him commissioned a history or portrait series is provided by the will of Sir David Tudor, son of Owen Tudor and Henry V's widow, Katherine. This mentions five hangings depicting Henry V, Henry VI, the duke of Clarence, John, duke of Bedford, and Humphrey, duke of Gloucester—second, third, and fourth sons of Henry IV—along with other great men of the period.[66] Another tantalizing reference is provided by an eighteenth-century French author who records seeing a tapestry representing the Marriage of Henry V and Katherine of France.[67] If the subject was correctly identified, we might surmise that this tapestry was commissioned after

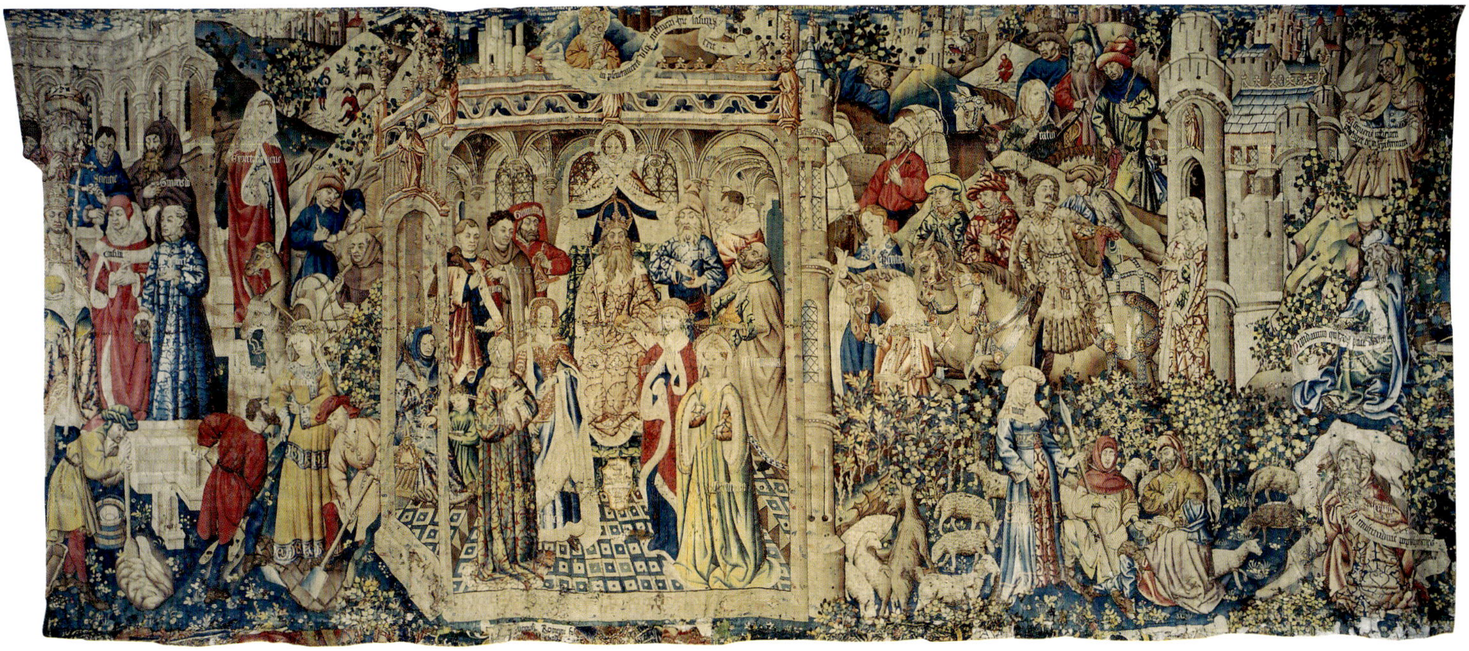

2.20 *The Story of the Good Life.* Tapestry woven in the Southern Netherlands, ca. 1440–50. Wool, 465 x 1065 cm. Museo Diocesano, Tarragona

Henry V's death as part of the English efforts to establish their hold in France. Another documented set in whose acquisition Henry VI may have been involved, at least peripherally, was the provision of a set of tapestries for Eton College, founded by Henry in 1440, which were confiscated under Edward IV but subsequently returned.[68]

Circumstantial evidence of other possible acquisitions by or on behalf of Henry VI is provided by the inventory taken after Henry VIII's death in 1547. This lists a number of large individual tapestries and rich ensembles that correspond to designs that can be dated to the 1440s. Although some of these may have entered the royal collection from other sources, the scale and richness of others indicates that they may have been royal purchases. For example, the 1547 inventory of Richmond Palace cites a tapestry with "the Busshope of Rome [the pope] and the Themperor," which measured just under seventeen yards in length and five and a half in height.[69] A panel of similar dimension and subject survives at Tarragona Cathedral (fig. 2.20). Traditionally known as "The Good Life" after one of the inscriptions on the tapestry, it depicts an allegory of temporal power and the Three Estates.[70] The left section of the tapestry, now damaged, represents the Church, embodied by the Pope, who is surrounded by the Seven Gifts of the Holy Ghost: Wisdom, Understanding, Good Counsel, Fortitude, Knowledge, Piety, and Fear. The center of the tapestry is dominated by a figure of an emperor, surrounded by the Seven Liberal Arts and the Cardinal Virtues. The right third of the tapestry represents the Nobility and the Peasants. The figures are separated by architectural and landscape elements. While the scale of the figures in proportion to the landscape and decorative elements are similar to those of series like the *Devonshire Hunts* and the *Courtiers in a Rose Garden,* the figures and decorative details are more densely massed than in those earlier designs, a trend that was to become more pronounced in the following two decades. The date of the design can be ascribed to the late 1430s on the grounds that Philip the Good presented a tapestry of similar subject to Pope Eugenius IV in 1440.[71] How and when a tapestry of this design entered the English royal collection remains a matter of conjecture.

Another ensemble recorded in 1547 that may have been an acquisition of the 1440s comprised three large pieces of "olde Arras" of *Charlemagne,* at Windsor.[72] The 1547 inventory lists a number of *Charlemagne* tapestries, some of which can be tentatively identified with pieces that entered the collection between 1390 and 1422; thus the very old fragments of "Charlemagne of Amys & Amilis" itemized at Nottingham Castle were probably those first listed in 1399,[73] while the large "arras" panels listed at Woodstock and The More can perhaps be identified as the remains of the two large "arras" panels listed in the 1422 inventory.[74] But the origin of the three "arras" pieces at Windsor is uncertain, as also is that of five pieces of the same subject listed in the King's Removing Wardrobe. The dimensions and quality of the pieces in the wardrobe are not specified. Those of the pieces at Windsor certainly indicate an origin in the second quarter of the fifteenth century. An idea of the character, perhaps even the identity of the ensemble, is suggested by various fragments of the late 1440s or early 1450s that represent the *Battle of Roncevaux,* at which Charlemagne's ally Roland faced overwhelming odds before dying heroically. Fragments from this series survive in Brussels (fig. 2.21), Stockholm, Florence, and London, and it has been suggested that they were probably part of a larger *Charlemagne* cycle.[75] The design represents a mass of struggling figures that occupy the foreground of the tapestry to the exclusion of any other landscape details, a style of composition that was to become increasingly fashionable in the 1450s and 1460s. The confusion and gruesome details of these scenes provide a vivid reminder of the brutality of contemporary armored conflict, an experience with which many of the English nobles were all too familiar by the end of Henry VI's reign.

The turbulent circumstances of the last ten years of Henry's reign ended any thought of tapestry acquisitions. Following Suffolk's murder, the king fell under the sway of his wife, Queen Margaret, and Edmund Beaufort, second duke of Somerset. In 1453 he suffered his first bout of insanity, which effectively prostrated him for the next seventeen months, and thenceforth, control of the realm was contested between the queen and royal council, on one hand, and Richard, duke of York, on the other. York defeated the Lancastrians in battle in 1455 and controlled the council for one year, after which Margaret was able to reassert herself, relocating the Lancastrian court to Coventry, where it remained for the next four years, thus establishing an association between Henry VI and the town that was to be celebrated in a tapestry, discussed below (p. 83), that was woven during the reign of Henry VII. York's forces were defeated again, and York himself was killed at the Battle of Wakefield in December 1460, but on February 2, 1461, his son, Edward, earl of March, defeated the Lancastrians at Mortimer's Cross and shortly thereafter was proclaimed king in London. Henry fled to Scotland, where he remained until 1465, when he was captured in Lancashire and imprisoned in the Tower. The restoration in 1470 of the enfeebled king, a puppet in the hands of Richard Neville, earl of Warwick, was short-lived. With Edward's return to England in March 1471, the capture of Henry VI in London, the Yorkist victories at Barnet and Tewkesbury, and Henry's subsequent death in the Tower, the Lancastrian era was at an end. Given the impoverished and fugitive circumstances in which Henry VI lived for much of the last decade of his life, it is not surprising that he made no contribution to the development of the royal tapestry collection during his later years.

Tapestry Disposition and Usage under Henry VI

As in previous reigns, the royal tapestries remained under the supervision of an assigned officer. Following John Stout's death, a William Jenkins received a grant of this office for life on December 12, 1450, with a wage of 6d. a day, along with an annual allocation from the Great Wardrobe of a livery of the yeoman of the chamber.[76] Little evidence has come down to us relating to the disposition of tapestry at the English court during the mid-fifteenth century, but analogy with contemporary and subsequent usage, both in England and on the Continent, suggests that the large, high-quality narrative and heraldic tapestries were displayed on special occasions in the great halls and

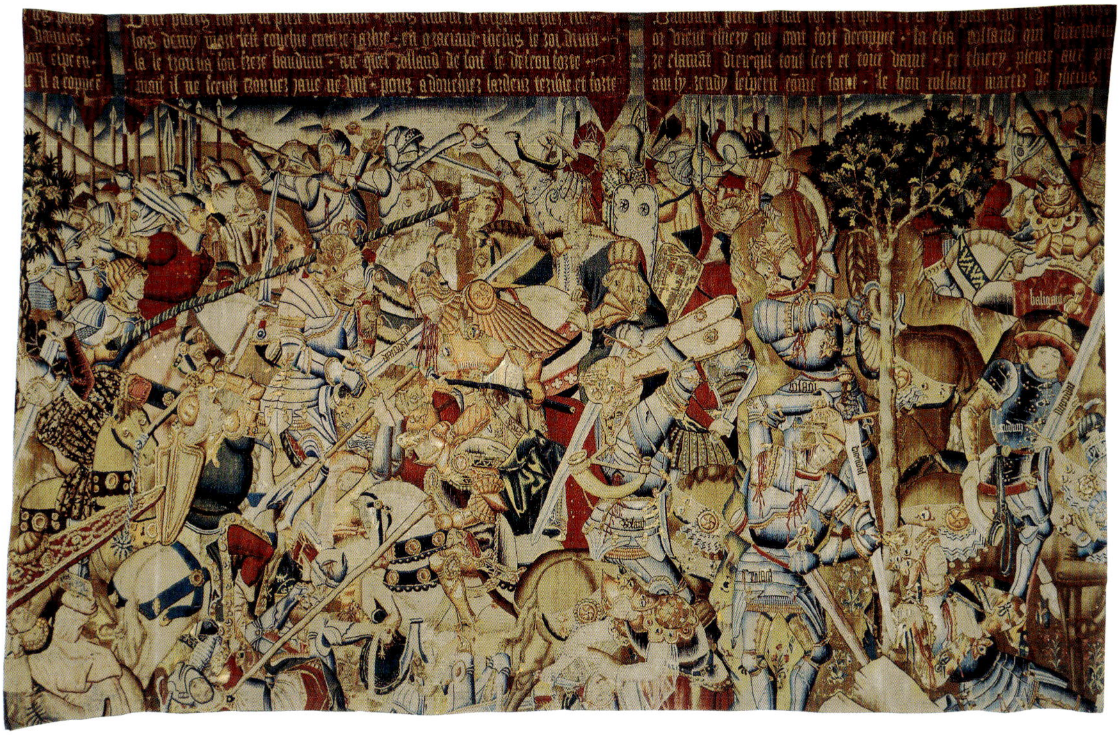

2.21 *The Battle of Roncevaux* (fragment) from a set of the *Story of Charlemagne*. Tapestry woven in the Southern Netherlands, ca. 1450. Wool, 378 x 569 cm. Musées Royaux d'Art et d'Histoire, Brussels

chambers of presence, as for example during the French embassy in July 1445, while hangings with decorative and lighthearted subject matter were generally employed in more private chambers. In both settings, the quality of tapestries would have reflected the significance of the room, with the finest pieces used in the most important rooms.

The relationship between the location, subject matter, and quality of tapestry hangings was touched on in the context of the tapestries belonging to the de la Poles at Ewelme in 1464. Another interesting demonstration of usage is provided by the inventory of the collection of Sir John Fastolf, master of the household of the duke of Bedford, taken at Caister Castle in 1459.[77] In the absence of any large, high-quality ensembles in Fastolf's collection, the display in the great hall depended on a mix of historical and allegorical subjects, including a large panel depicting the Siege of "Faleys" or "Phalist" (the variant spellings appear in two contemporary inventories). Fastolf had served in the 1417 campaign in northern France during which Henry V's forces had besieged Falaise, and it has long been thought that this was probably a custom-made commemoration of this campaign, although more recently it has been suggested that the panel may, in fact, have depicted the siege of Falerii in 395 BC by the Roman commander Furius Camillus, an exemplum of justice that may have had some relevance to Fastolf's attempts to restore his reputation during the 1430s.[78] Either way, the display of this panel in the main hall was evidently intended to project a message about Fastolf to those he entertained at Caister. In contrast, the main chambers in which Fastolf and his family lived were hung with tapestries and bed hangings depicting genre and hunting scenes. Although none of these tapestries can be identified with surviving pieces, the subjects and character are all consistent with contemporary descriptions of other tapestries produced in the Low Countries. The mix of one or two custom-made figurative and armorial panels or sets, along with a larger number that appear to have been made from popular, commercially available designs, probably typifies the tapestry collections of the leading English nobility during the mid-fifteenth century. The Fastolf inventory thus provides a useful measure of comparison for the much larger and richer collection of the Crown.

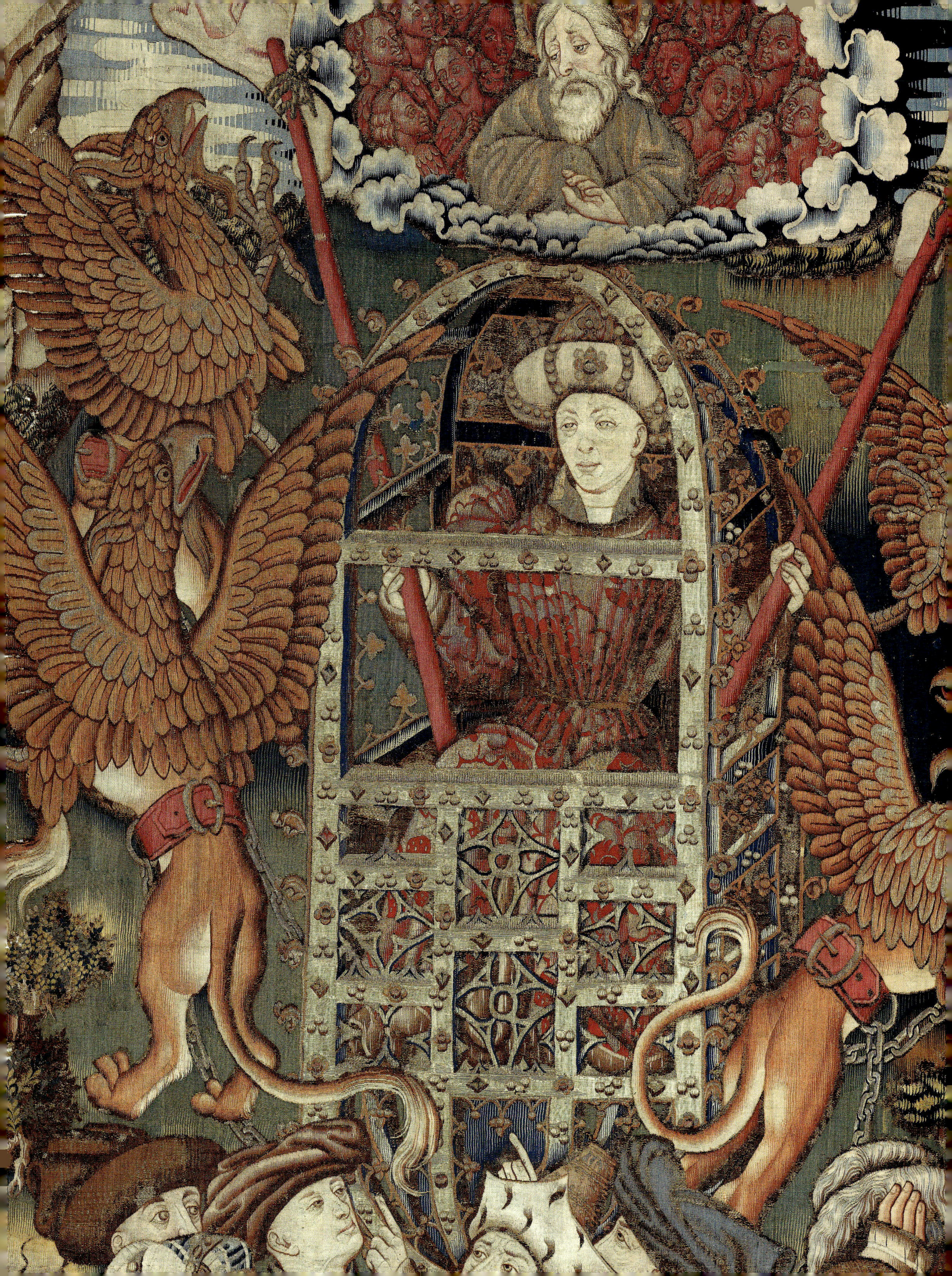

CHAPTER 3

The Royal Tapestry Collection under Edward IV, 1461–1483

Detail of fig. 3.2

Philip the Good and the Burgundian Example

Edward's accession coincided with the apogee of magnificence at the Burgundian court. In view of the close links that were to develop between Burgundy and England during the ensuing years, it is useful to introduce Edward's tapestry patronage with a brief review of that of Duke Philip (fig. 3.1), who is renowned as one of the greatest patrons of his age. Following his accession in 1419, Philip spent much of his early reign in territorial disputes with rebellious districts in his own domains and with the French king, Charles VII, who had been responsible for the assassination of Philip's father in 1419. These experiences undoubtedly contributed to the use he subsequently made of public spectacles and major artworks to promote the stature of the Burgundian house. The most significant demonstration of this was his establishment in 1430 of the Order of the Golden Fleece, a chivalric brotherhood of European rulers and nobles whose regular meetings were intended to strengthen their ties to Philip's sovereignty. During the following decades Philip undertook extensive building programs at his properties in Bruges, Lille, and Brussels and commissioned numerous works of art and tapestries to decorate them.[1]

At his accession in 1419, Philip had inherited a sizeable collection of tapestries purchased by his father and grandfather. An inventory of 1430–32 records over sixty tapestry ensembles in the ducal collection, including such large and valuable pieces as the *Battle of Roosebeke* and the *Battle of Liège*, and these continued to play a key role in the spectacles and diplomacy of the day.[2] For example, during negotiations with England and France in 1435, the Abbey of Saint Vaast was hung with the *Battle of Liège* tapestries as a somber reminder of what lay at stake. Like his father and grandfather, Philip also used tapestry as a form of diplomatic gift. Following the treaty of 1435 he rewarded his supporters with tapestries purchased from the Arras-based merchant Jehan Walois, and each of the popes elected during his reign were similarly favored with gifts of tapestry.[3]

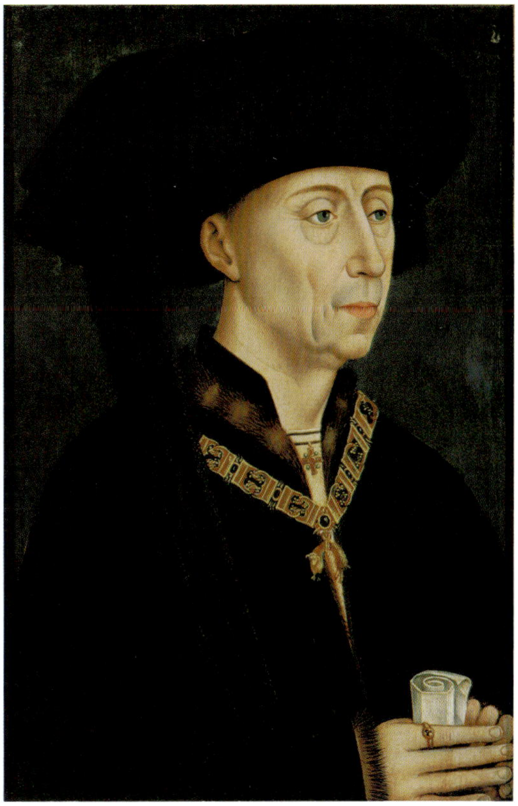

3.1 *Philip the Good*. Rogier van der Weyden, after 1450. Oil on panel, 31 x 23 cm. Kunsthistorisches Museum, Vienna

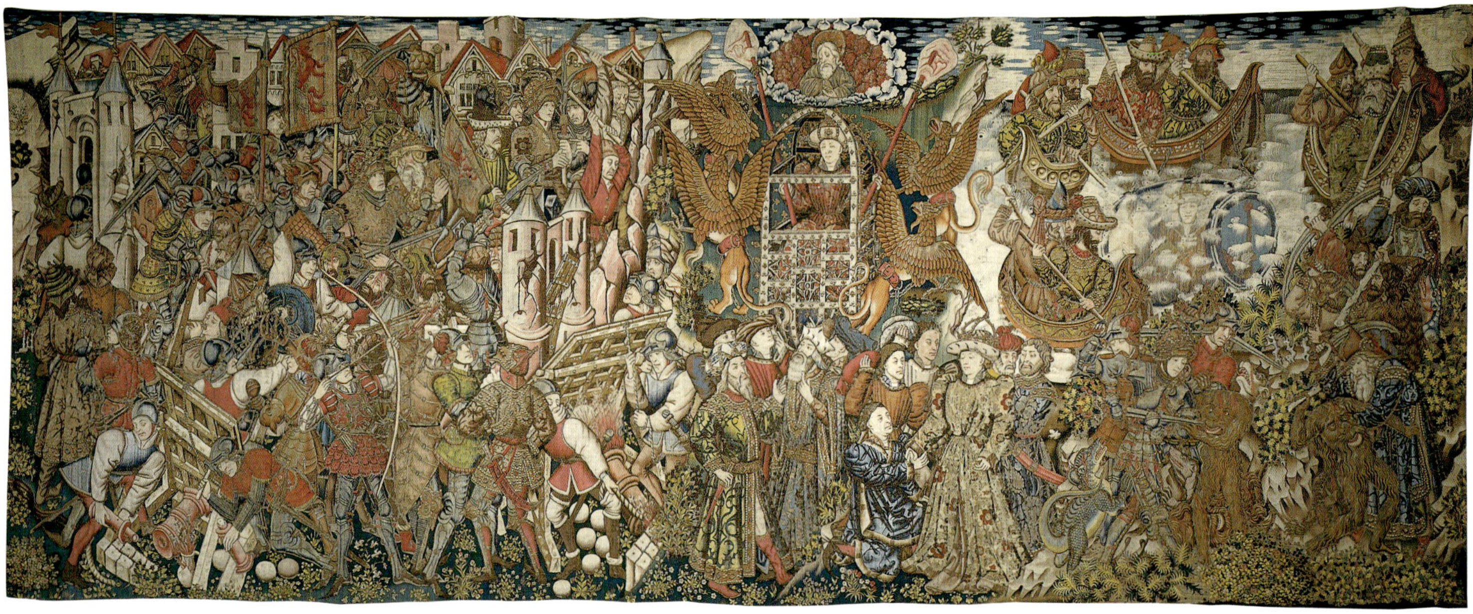

3.2 *The Military Exploits and Fabulous Deeds of Alexander* from the *Story of Alexander*. Tapestry woven in the Southern Netherlands, possibly Tournai, ca. 1455–60. Wool, silk, and gilt-metal-wrapped thread, 415 x 985 cm. Palazzo Doria, Genoa

But it was in new acquisitions that Philip's interest in tapestry was most notably manifested. By the time of his death, Philip had increased the ducal tapestry collection to almost one hundred sets. Although some were intended purely for decorative use, many of the more valuable related to dynastic claims and political aspirations. The grandest was a set of the *Story of Gideon* that Philip commissioned in 1449 to provide a backdrop to ceremonies of the Order of the Golden Fleece.[4] Nominal patron of the order, Gideon, with his victory over the Mideonites, provided a resonant model for Philip and his much-vaunted ambition to liberate the Holy Land from the Turks. The design was provided by Bauduin de Bailleul, the leading artist in Arras, at a cost of 300 *écus d'or,* and the production was arranged by two Tournai-based master weavers, Robert Dary and Jehan de l'Ortie. The set comprised eight pieces with a height of about six yards and a total length of more than a hundred yards and was completed by 1453. It was richly woven in silver- and gilt-metal-wrapped thread, wool, and silk and cost the enormous sum of 8,960 *écus d'or*. Philip took a close personal interest in the project, paying Bailleul to bring the completed cartoons to Bruges in 1449 for his inspection and subsequently taking the unusual step of purchasing the cartoons to prevent duplication of the design. The set appears to have been truly outstanding and drew universal admiration. It was exhibited at all the meetings of the brotherhood and at a number of other ducal ceremonies, such as Philip's visit to Paris following the coronation of Louis XI at Reims in 1461.[5] The *Gideon* tapestries survived in Brussels until the end of the eighteenth century; they were transported to Vienna in 1794, after which they disappeared.

While Philip's use of tapestry as a demonstration of wealth and iconographic suggestion provided an important model for courts throughout Europe, he was also influential in the choice of subject matter. Like his grandfather and great-uncles, he was a keen bibliophile, commissioning many illuminated manuscripts and prose translations of medieval "classical" texts for his library, which expanded from some two hundred volumes to more than a thousand during his reign.[6] Philip's interest in these "classics" was also reflected in the subjects of the tapestries produced for him, such as a *Story of Alexander* set that he purchased in 1459 from a Tournai-based merchant named Pasquier Grenier, of whom more will be said shortly. This set comprised six wall hangings and matching bed furnishings and was displayed in Paris in 1461 along with the *Gideon* set. An idea of the appearance of Philip's *Alexander* set may be obtained from two tapestries of this subject that survive in Genoa in the Doria collection (fig. 3.2 and detail opposite p. 45).[7] Whatever their provenance, the Doria tapestries typify the style of high-quality tapestries produced in the Burgundian Netherlands during the 1450s. Landscape and architectural elements have been largely displaced by a dense mass of overlapping narrative episodes in which historic personages and incidents mingle with monsters and fabulous deeds. This is not the Alexander of classical texts but the legend as it had been reinterpreted by medieval romance. In this case, one of the principal sources for the narrative was Jean Wauquelin's *Le livre des conquestes et faits d'Alexandre,* written for Philip before 1440.

The cumulative effect of this burgeoning interest in classical texts at the Burgundian court was that from the 1450s the heroes of Greek and Roman mythology and history gradually displaced those of the Charlemagne and Arthurian cycles in new tapestry designs, a shift that was also to be reflected in the acquisitions by the English monarchy.[8] The transliteration of these classical sources via medieval verse romance was matched by how the subjects were visualized, with the figures generally represented in elaborate contemporary costume or a stylized notion of classical costume. The current taste for opulence was satisfied by the visual richness of the designs and the abundance of decorative detail and pattern on every surface.

Although the tapestries of the Burgundian court were the most splendid in Europe, this was also a period in which the French court began to regain its former magnificence following the reconquest of northern France. The

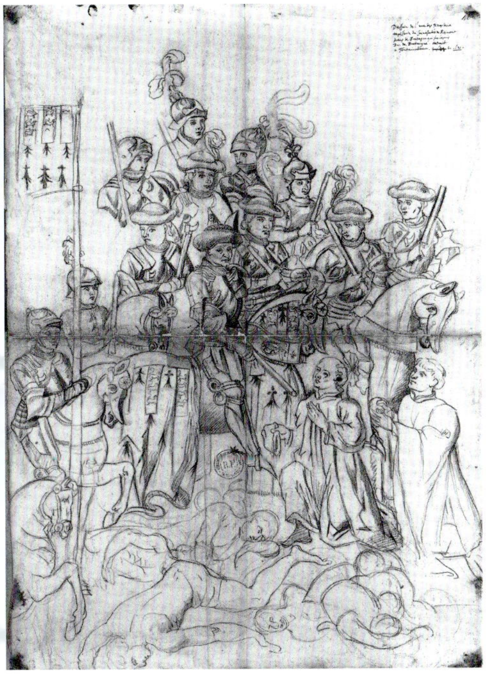

3.3 *The Constable of Richemont Paying the Clerics to Bury the Dead.* Drawing by Jean Gobert, 1621, of one of a lost set of 15th-c. tapestries depicting the Battle of Formigny. Bibliothèque Nationale de France, Paris

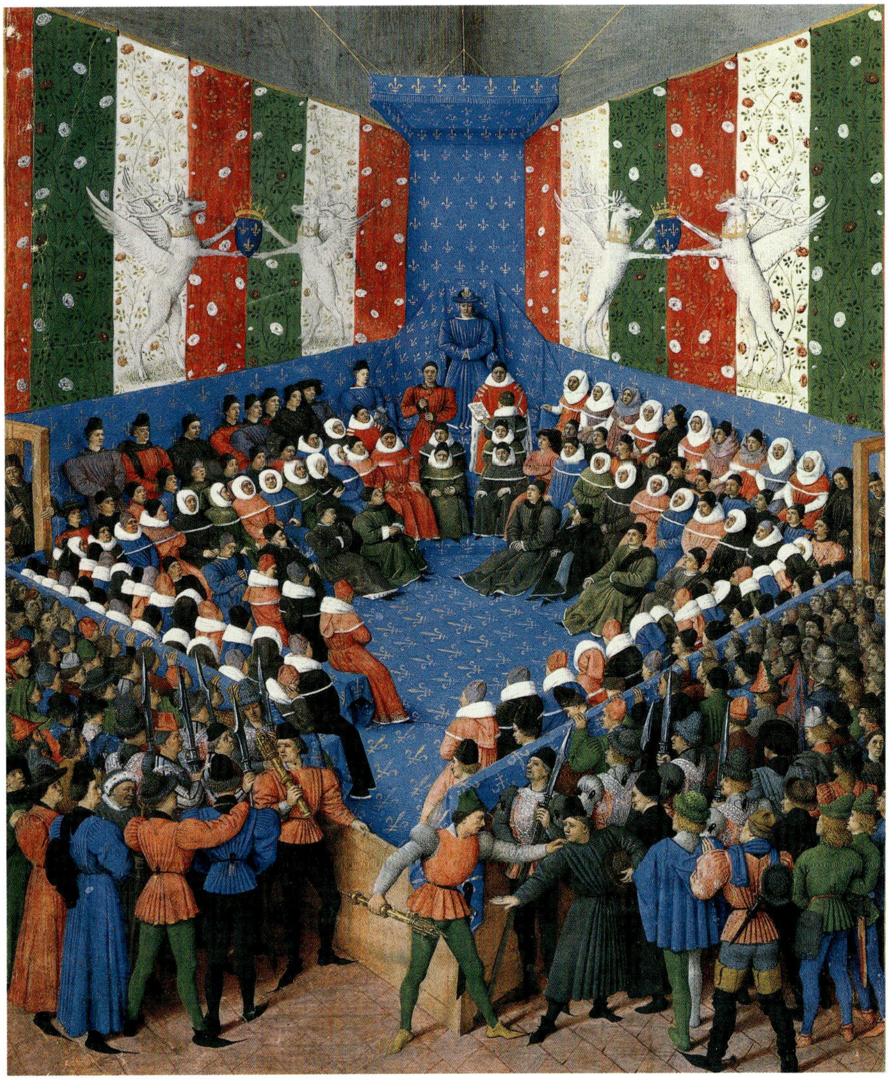

3.4 *The Trial of Jean, Duke of Alençon.* Miniature painting attributed to Jean Fouquet in Laurent Girard's French edition of Giovanni Boccaccio's *De casibus virorum illustrium,* 1458. 34 x 28 cm. Bayerisches Staatsbibliothek, Munich (Cod. gall. 369, fol. 2v)

bloody victory over the English at Formigny in 1450 was commemorated in a six-piece set of tapestries, possibly after designs by Jean Fouquet. Although the set is long since lost, the appearance of two sections, one depicting the surrender of English clerics to the Constable of Richemont (fig. 3.3), is recorded by two eighteenth-century drawings.[9] A rare visual impression of Charles VII's court is provided by an illumination of the king sitting in judgment at the trial of the duke of Alençon in 1458 surrounded by tapestries depicting heraldic beasts and coats of arms (fig. 3.4).[10] Descriptions of court festivals and triumphal entries during the reigns of Louis XI and Charles VIII confirm that the tapestry medium played an important part in French court pageantry during the second half of the fifteenth century.[11]

Edward IV's Tapestry Patronage, 1461–1470

With the constant political traffic between the northern courts, Edward may well have heard of the splendid tapestries in Burgundy and France during his teenage years. His exposure to people with firsthand experience of the Burgundian court increased after the death of his father, Richard, duke of York, at the Battle of Wakefield on December 30, 1460. Following this defeat, Edward's younger brothers, George and Richard, spent five months in exile at the Burgundian court. Further evidence of the close links between Edward's circle and the Burgundian court is provided by the proposal, made within months of Edward's accession, that he should marry one of Philip's nieces. Although Edward's marriage to Elizabeth Woodville forestalled that scheme, it did nothing to interrupt the dialogue between the two courts, culminating with negotiations in May 1467 for the marriage of Edward's sister Margaret to Philip's son Charles, then count of Charolais. The negotiations were followed by an elaborate tournament at Smithfield. Inspired by the spectacles of the Burgundian court, this was conceived as a feat of arms between Philip's bastard son, Anthony, count of La Roche, the paragon of knightly virtue at the Burgundian court, and Edward's brother-in-law Antony Woodville, Lord Scales. In the event, the celebrations were cut short by Philip's death on June 15, 1467. The marriage eventually took place in July of the following year.

How did this exposure to Burgundian culture manifest itself at Edward's court? From the start of his reign, Edward was keenly aware of the importance of material display. He spent lavishly on his coronation, and during the following years he manifested a pronounced taste for fine clothes and jewels.[12] The impoverished circumstances of the Crown in the early 1460s prevented ambitious artistic patronage, but when opportunity arose he began to spend considerable sums on tapestries, sourcing them from the Tournai merchant Pasquier Grenier. An initial payment of £1,400 is recorded to Grenier in 1467 for unidentified tapestries, and then in 1468 Grenier was paid £984 for a bulk delivery comprising a four-piece "arras" set of the *Story of Nebuchadnezzar;* a nine-piece "arras" set of the *Story of Alexander,* with three valances for a bed; a six-piece "arras" set of the *Passion;* a single piece of "arras" of the *Last Judgment;* twenty-eight verdures, a type of tapestry in which the ground was largely taken up with floral and plant motifs, often known today as millefleur; fifteen valences for a verdure bed; and a number of verdure cushions.[13] The commission had presumably been made some time before, and comparison with the cost of similarly rich tapestries supplied to Philip the Good in the previous years suggests that the payment of 1467 was an advance for these sets.[14]

The cost of the tapestries for which Grenier was paid in 1467 and 1468 was enormous, and combined with the fact that all but the verdure pieces are described as "arras," it seems probable that the figurative sets were woven with gold. To put this expenditure in perspective, the Black Book, the register of household ordinances compiled at Edward's direction in 1471–72, estimates the annual expense of a knight's household at £100, that of a baron at £500, and that of a viscount at £1,000.[15] Contemporary documents indicate that expenditure by the royal household during the 1460s ran at approximately £10,000 to £12,000 per year, of which the chancellor received a fee of £420. As these figures suggest, the financial value of the Grenier tapestries was exceptional, reflecting a quality of production that only the elite European nobility and richest merchants could afford.

In the event, the payment to Grenier in 1468 was not met from royal coffers but drawn from a fine imposed that year on Thomas Cook, lord mayor of London. Cook had been accused of treason, and during his imprisonment Sir John Fogge, treasurer of the royal household, looted his house of its wine and valuables. These included an expensive tapestry of the *Last Judgment*, said by Cook's steward to have a value of £800, that the queen's mother, Jacquetta, duchess of Bedford, desired. According to the steward, the duchess is said to have borne a grudge against Cook because she had not been able to buy this tapestry "at her pleasure and price." Whether true or not, the anecdote reflects how strongly contemporary patrons valued high-quality tapestries.[16] The charges against Cook were baseless, and eventually he was convicted only of misprision and condemned to pay a large fine to the Crown. It was from this fine that the second Grenier payment was financed.

In purchasing tapestries from Grenier, Edward was dealing with Europe's leading tapestry merchant, who exerted a control over high-quality production akin to the influence that Nicholas Bataille and Jean Cosset exercised in Paris and Arras in the late fourteenth century.[17] A patrician of Tournai, Grenier was the principal wine importer to the town. The first mention of his independent activity as a tapestry merchant dates from 1449, when as a "marcheteur" he was selling tapestries through agents in Le Puy (in the Auvergne) and Lyon, and in later transactions he employed an agent in Reims.[18] He also had depots in Antwerp and Bruges. Grenier's involvement with the Burgundian court is documented from the late 1450s. As already noted, he sold Philip the Good a suite of the *Story of Alexander* in 1459, and in following years he supplied Philip with additional sets of the *Passion* and *Shepherds* (1461), the *Story of Esther and Ahasuerus* and the *Story of the Swan Knight* (1462), and chambers of pastoral scenes and woodcutters (1466).[19] Grenier's activity was not limited to the Burgundian court. Eight months before he sold the *Alexander* set to Philip, Melchior and Guillaume Grenier, his son and nephew, had transported the *Alexander* designs along with various unnamed tapestries to Milan at the request of Duke Francesco Sforza, and it is conceivable that the two *Alexander* panels now in the Doria collection resulted from this initiative.[20] From the late 1460s the Greniers were in regular contact with many other leading courts of Europe. The wealth and status that this international trade brought to Grenier is reflected by the high civic offices he occupied in Tournai and by the donation he made to the church of Saint Quentin for the construction of an ambulatory and family funerary chapel in 1474, followed in 1475 by a further gift of a tapestry set of the *Seven Sacraments*.[21]

The circumstances in which Grenier's design series were conceived is undocumented, but it seems almost certain that like the powerful merchants of the late fourteenth century, he was active in commissioning new cartoons that would appeal to the richest patrons. When he died, he left "tous mes patrons" to be divided among his sons, a clear indication of their importance.[22] So far as we know, Grenier owned no workshops himself. Rather, when he received an order he presumably subcontracted with a workshop for the production of the set, advancing funds for material costs and wages. Where the Grenier tapestries were woven has been debated, but in view of the status that Grenier enjoyed as a patrician of Tournai and the scale of the local industry at this date, a majority of his products were probably made locally. Tournai had supplanted Arras as the main center of high-quality production from the late 1440s.[23]

Although none of Edward's purchases of 1468 have survived, they were presumably woven from the same cartoons as tapestries of those subjects that had been supplied to Continental

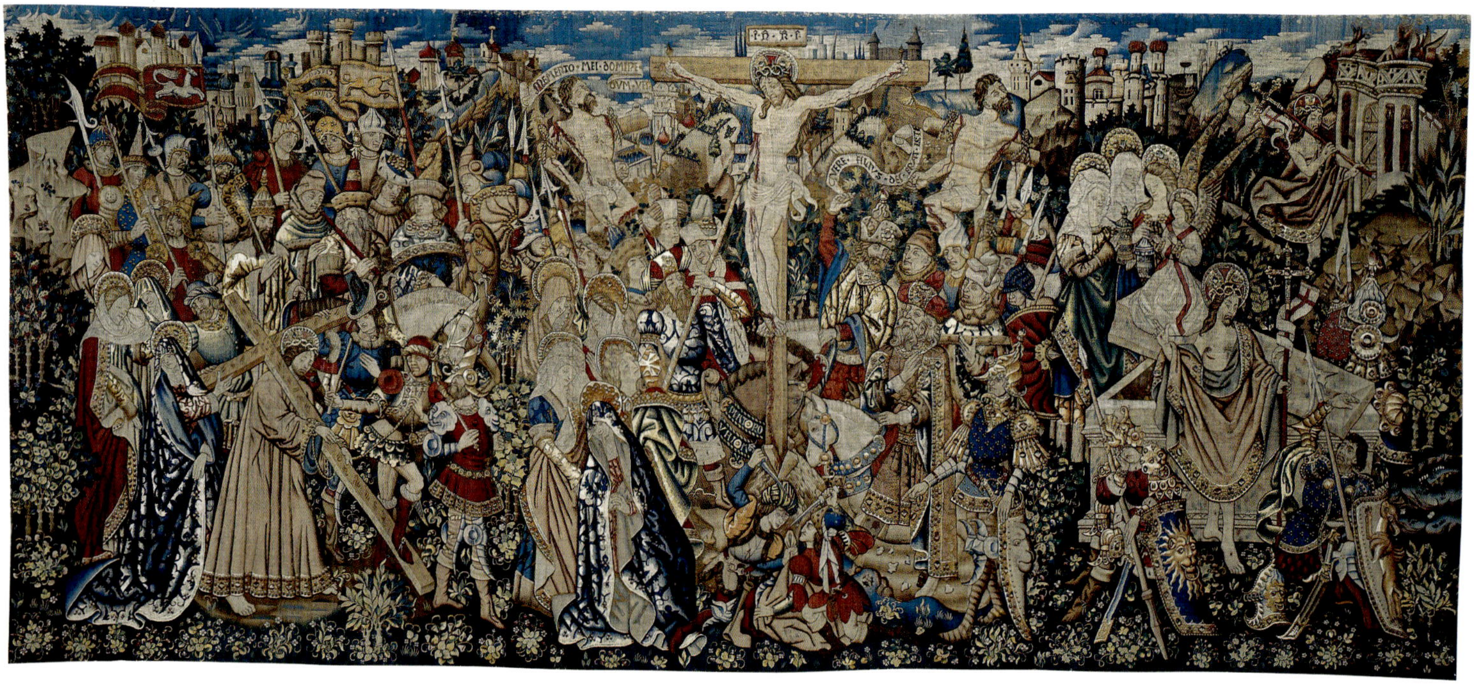

3.5 *Scenes of the Passion* from a set of the *Passion*. Tapestry woven in the Southern Netherlands, probably Tournai, ca. 1460. Wool and silk, 424 x 911 cm. Musées Royaux d'Art et d'Histoire, Brussels

patrons in recent years. A probable identification for the *Alexander* series has already been mentioned, and the *Nebuchadnezzar* set may have been woven from the same designs as a four-piece set purchased by Alfonso V of Aragon from a Catalan merchant, Andreu Pol, in 1453–54. The *Passion* set was probably a reweaving of a design supplied by Grenier to Philip in 1461.[24] An idea of the character and perhaps even of the appearance of the *Passion* series may be obtained from two large related tapestries of this subject now in Rome and Brussels that date from the late 1450s or early 1460s (fig. 3.5).[25]

Finally, it is tempting to speculate that a model, or close analogy, for Edward's verdure bed ensemble may also survive in the form of another notable Burgundian commission. In the final year of his life, Duke Philip purchased an extremely fine set of millefleur tapestries that incorporated his cipher and heraldic devices, which, on account of the rich symbolic potential of the numerous flowers depicted, is generally assumed to have embodied an allegory of the benefits of his rule. It was purchased from the Lille-based merchant Jehan de Haze, and a large fragment is extant in Bern (fig. 3.6).[26] A number of other contemporary millefleur tapestries also incorporate the insignia or arms of the patrons for whom they were made. Given the cost of the tapestries supplied to Edward by Grenier and the forethought that presumably went into the supply of so many high-grade tapestries at once, it is tempting to think that some of these verdure tapestries, particularly those of the bed, may have also incorporated Edward's heraldic devices. Evidence that Edward acquired at least one bed ensemble of high-quality heraldic tapestries is provided by a description in Cardinal Wolsey's inventory (ca. 1522) of four pieces of "rich arras" of "the Bedde called the Sonne, Wherof oon pece having the Sonne with his splayed Beames." The motif of the golden sun of York was said to have its origins in a meteorological phenomenon, three suns in a clear sky, that appeared before the decisive battle of Mortimer's Cross on February 2–3, 1461. Yorkist propagandists interpreted the suns as the crowns of England, France, and Spain to which Edward laid claim. Wolsey had presumably acquired this bed as a perquisite from the royal collection, and it returned there after Wolsey's fall.[27] The 1540 and 1547 inventories of objects at the Tower also describe a "pece of arras wrought with Rooses and Sonnes made in kynge Edwardes tyme," which measured four and three-quarter by ten yards.[28]

Payment for the Grenier tapestries coincided with one of the grandest events of Edward's reign, albeit one at which he was not present, the marriage of his sister to the new Burgundian duke, Charles the Bold, as his third wife. Contemporary descriptions indicate that the wedding celebrations in Bruges were among the most magnificent of the century.[29] It was the first great court event of Charles's reign, following his accession in 1467, and it gave him an opportunity to match up to the splendor of his father's court in front of an international audience. Although the tapestries used on this occasion were all drawn from the Burgundian wardrobes, the accounts of Margaret's journey and reception are of interest because they reveal the careful selection of visual models, including tapestries, in relation to the events. This usage provides important evidence of a practice that, in all likelihood, the English court was also following.

Margaret was conveyed to the Netherlands on a boat called the *New Ellen* (that is, Helen), probably a reference to the medieval notion that the English monarchy traced its roots to Brutus, the great-grandson of the Trojan warrior Aeneas. According to this legend, popularized by works such as Geoffrey of Monmouth's *Brut,* the eponymous hero traveled to Albion, renamed Britain after him, where he founded a new Troy, subsequently known as London. Following her arrival in Bruges, Margaret watched various pageants that included one of the Old Testament king Ahasuerus and his consort, Esther.[30] Conventional wisdom identified Esther as the epitome of the wise consort whose advice helped save her husband's people from destruction. In this case there was an additional resonance for Margaret because, like Esther, she was a foreigner. The tapestries decorating the ducal residence for the wedding festivities made similar flattering analogies for Charles and Margaret.[31] According to the eyewitness account of Jean de Haynin, never before had so many rich tapestries been displayed together; the great hall was hung with Philip's *Story of Gideon,* and behind the high table, a rich cloth of gold embroidered with the duke's arms. The *Battle of Liège* set was displayed in the hall behind the sideboard, and the hall of the chamberlains was hung with tapestry of the *Coronation of King Clovis,* described with enough details to identify it as a weaving of a design series of which a partial set has survived in Reims.[32] The hall in front of the chapel was decorated with tapestries depicting the romance of *Begue and Garin of Lorraine,* but before the wedding this set was changed for another of *Ahasuerus and Esther,* identifiable with a design series of which fragments survive today in Nancy, Minneapolis,

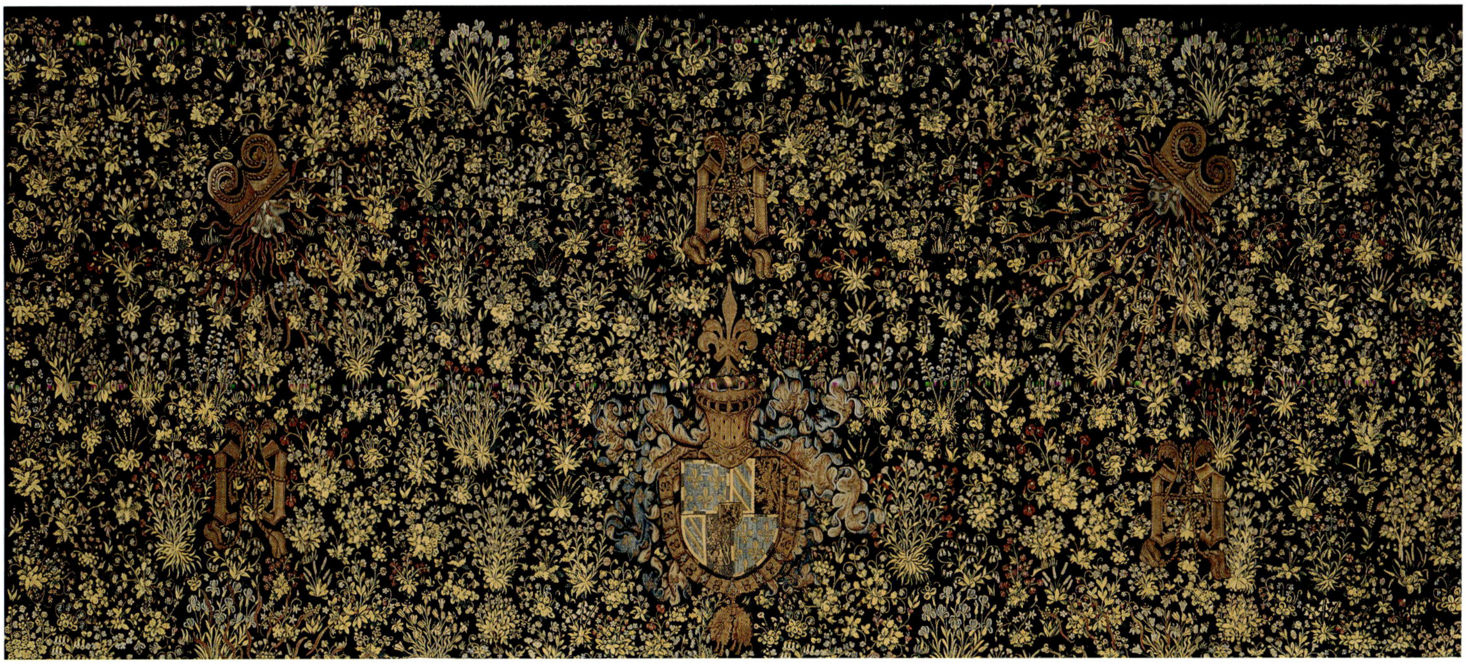

3.6 Millefleurs with the Arms of Philip the Good. Tapestry woven in the Southern Netherlands in the workshop of Jehan de Haze, before 1466. Wool, silk, and gilt-metal-wrapped thread, 306 x 687 cm. Historisches Museum, Bern

and Paris.[33] Similarly, the first installation in the chapel, a tapestry of the *Pilgrimage of Life,* was replaced by another set showing the *Passion.* Margaret's dressing room was hung with a suite of textiles "chequered throughoute with white, red and green squares, the colors of the marguerite," and with tapestries of the *Story of Lucretia,* the Roman heroine who epitomized the virtuous wife because, having been raped by Sextus Tarquinus, son of the king of Rome, she took her own life to save her family from dishonor. In contrast, Mary of Burgundy's room featured tapestry of trees and personages in antique fashion. Antony of Burgundy's chambers were decorated with tapestry of his arms and, in his dressing room, a suite of "ancient histories."

The description reveals the self-conscious way that the tapestries were selected to celebrate the legendary and historic origins of the Burgundian dynasty and the quasi-religious stature of the duke himself. Similarly, it provides an unusually explicit example of the use of tapestries depicting virtuous prototypes, Esther and Lucretia, in reference to the duke's bride, Margaret. Although such analogies were formulaic, they must have contributed significantly to the solemnity of the marriage ceremony and also to the audience's perception of the level of commitment and self-sacrifice expected of the young English princess.

Edward's decision to marry his sister to Charles the Bold and the alliance this entailed with Burgundy rather than France brought the long-standing tensions at the English court to a head. The earl of Warwick, who resented the elevation of members of the queen's family to prominence at court and who had favored an alliance with France, now sought to return the deposed Henry VI to the throne. With the backing of Louis XI of France, he and his forces landed in Devonshire in September 1470, stimulating outbreaks of rebellion across the country. Unable to rally sufficient force to meet the rebels, Edward fled, taking temporary exile between October 1470 and March 1471 with Charles the Bold's governor of Holland, Louis de Bruges, lord of Gruthuyse. After stalling to see which way the wind was blowing, Charles met with Edward late in December and early January, secretly supplying him with 50,000 florins (£20,000) to fund his return to England. Edward's invasion force of thirty-six ships set sail on March 11, 1471.

The practical details of Edward's return to the throne are incidental to our story, but in passing it is worth noting one event that stands out in contemporary accounts. During Edward's advance on London, Archbishop Nevill paraded Henry VI through the city streets in an attempt to rouse the London populace in his support. The effort backfired, however, because it merely demonstrated the impoverished state of the former monarch. According to the description of the *Great Chronicle of London,* Henry was dressed "in a long blue gown of velvet as though he had no more to change with." The poverty of his attire and the small size of his retinue was "more like a play than the showing of a prince to win men's hearts" and undermined the cause.[34] Although this account was written by someone sympathetic to the Yorkist cause, it serves as a reminder of the contemporary perception of the significance of material trappings of power.[35] The degree to which the concept of magnificence was an issue of discussion in England at this date is reflected by the commentary that Sir John Fortescue included in his *Governance of England.* This treatise on the art of kingship, probably written shortly after Edward's return to power, details the necessary expenditure that the king should make on buildings, hospitality, and "rich hangings and other apparel." Without these, states Fortescue, a king lived not according to his rank but "rather in miserie and in more subgeccion than doth a private person."[36]

Edward IV's Tapestry Patronage, 1471–1483

Following the recovery of the crown in 1471, Edward (fig. 3.7) was more secure than hitherto, leading to a period of greater peace and, in time, prosperity for him and the country. His recent sojourn in Burgundy manifested itself in various ways. The example of the Burgundian court stimulated him to reorganize the royal household along the lines defined by the Black Book of the Household (1471–72), which sought to wed magnificence to order and economy, although, as recent research has demonstrated, Edward was as much indebted to existing court ceremony and structures as to the Burgundian model.[37] Subsequently, in 1473–74, Olivier de la Marche, master of ceremonies for Charles the Bold and the man responsible for the arrangements of Charles's marriage to Margaret, drew up an account of the organization of the ducal household in response to an English request.[38]

From an artistic point of view, the time Edward spent in the Low Countries provided him with firsthand experience of contemporary Burgundian taste. His host, Louis de Gruthuyse, was a distinguished bibliophile, and through him, Edward would have learned of Charles the Bold's tastes in literature, manuscripts, and tapestries. Olivier de la Marche records that Charles would spend his evening hours reading from the *Faits des Romains,* and his predilection for classical subject matter is reflected by the manuscripts and tapestries he acquired.[39] In 1468 he purchased a set of *Hannibal and Scipio* tapestries, and in the same year the Portuguese writer Vasco da Lucena dedicated to Charles his translation of Quintus Curtius Rufus's *Historiae Alexandri Magni.* Two years later, Charles commissioned Lucena to produce a French translation of Xenophon's *Life of Cyrus.* It was presumably in response to Charles's known taste for classical subjects that in 1472 the magistrates and Franc of Bruges presented him with the first weaving of an enormous tapestry series of the *Story of Troy,* one of the most ambitious design series of the age (see below).

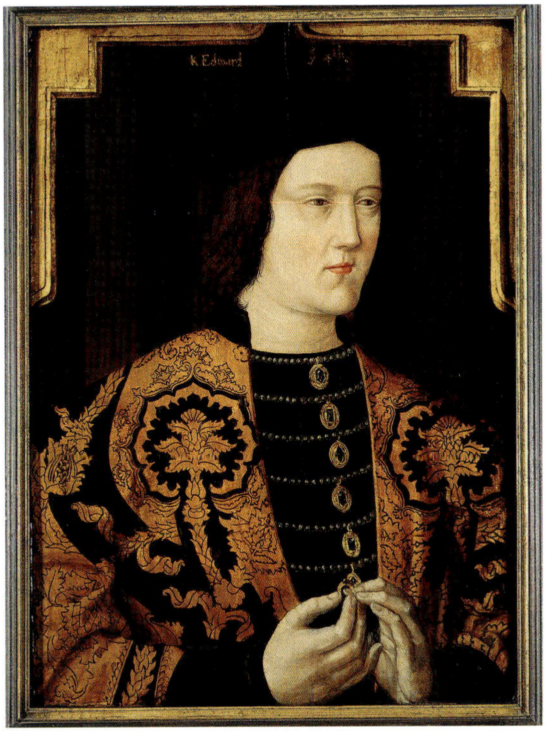

3.7 *Edward IV* by an unidentified artist. Oil on panel, 67.9 x 47.9 cm. The Royal Collection

Even though the erudite interests of the Burgundian court evidently made a significant impression on Edward, it was nonetheless some years before this manifested itself in any notable projects because of the continuing financial problems of the early 1470s. During this period Edward was also much occupied with Continental politics, leading to the invasion of France in 1475. The bloodless outcome of this campaign and the resulting Treaty of Picquigny on August 29 did much to improve his finances. Edward agreed to withdraw his troops in exchange for a French payment of 75,000 crowns and an annual pension of 50,000 gold crowns thereafter. The security of Edward's position was further strengthened in 1477 when he finally accused his troublesome brother George, duke of Clarence, of treason. George was executed at the Tower in February 1478.

With the immediate threats to his reign in abeyance and with financial resources at a level that he had not previously enjoyed, Edward began to invest considerable sums in architectural projects, most notably the highly ambitious scheme at Saint George's Chapel in Windsor Castle (fig. 3.8). Extensive building projects were also initiated at a number of palaces along the Thames, including Westminster, where a great chamber was constructed for the queen; Eltham, where a magnificent hall was constructed; and Greenwich.[40] Little evidence of further tapestry purchases survives before 1478, but whether this reflects the full facts of the situation is uncertain. Edward certainly acquired some new tapestries during this period because in 1475 he received a gift of

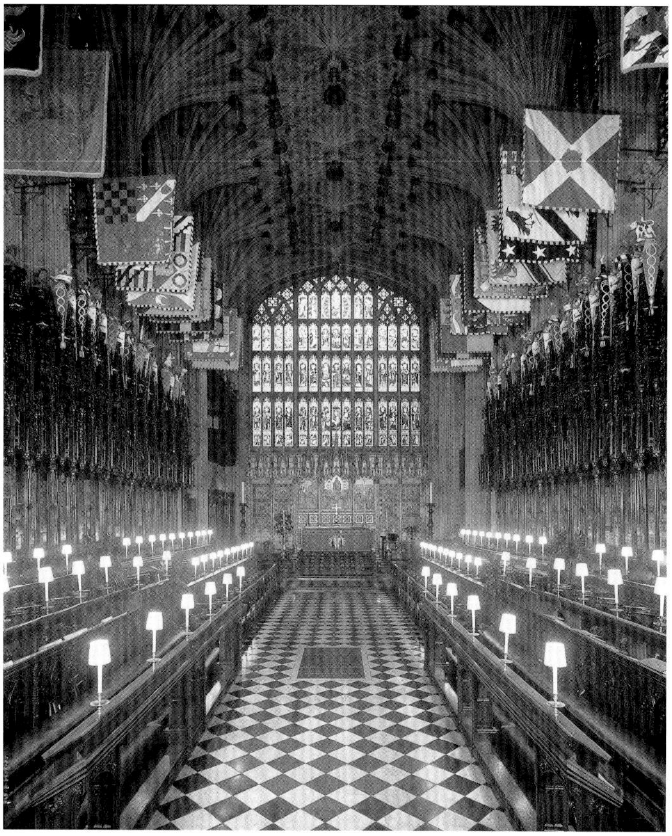

3.8 Saint George's Chapel, Windsor. Built in present form between 1475 and 1511 by Edward IV

Brussels tapestries, subject unspecified, from his sister Margaret when they met at Calais at the start of the English campaign in France.[41] The following year he paid 100 marks to purchase tapestries from the estate of Walter Lyhert, bishop of Norwich.[42]

Documentary evidence makes clear that Edward started to spend much larger sums on tapestries, as well as on Flemish manuscripts, from about 1478. The main stimulus to this activity must have been the need to provide new or redecorated apartments at the various palaces with suitable tapestries. To a lesser extent, it may also reflect the influence of renewed contacts with the Burgundian court. Following the death in battle of Charles the Bold in 1477 and the opportunistic campaign that Louis XI launched into Burgundy and Picardy—resulting in the capture of Arras—Margaret of Burgundy and her stepdaughter, Mary of Burgundy, made concerted efforts to reestablish the favored relationship that had previously existed between England and Burgundy. During 1478 there was constant traffic between the two courts, and William Lord Hastings, Edward's great chamberlain and close friend, spent much time there. During these visits, he took the opportunity to commission illuminated manuscripts for himself, at least one of which, the second book of Froissart, he seems to have passed on to Edward.[43] That tapestry was also a subject of mutual discussion is suggested by a valuable gift sent to Hastings in 1478 by Mary of Burgundy and her new husband, Maximilian of Austria. This consisted of an altar hanging of the *Adoration of the Three Kings,* another unidentified piece of tapestry worked with gold, a panel of the *Story of Absalom,* and two tapestries of the *Story of the Emperor*. It is not at all certain that this last pair embodied a representation of Maximilian himself, as has sometimes been suggested. These tapestries had been purchased in October 1478 for just over 1,000 Flemish pounds from a Tournai merchant, resident in Bruges, called Philippe Scellier (d. 1483).[44] Whether all of these tapestries were intended for Hastings alone or whether some were destined for Edward is uncertain, but given the close relationship between the two, the latter seems more likely. One way or another, it is probable that some pieces from this delivery would have entered the royal collection because Richard III executed Hastings in 1483, when his possessions would have been forfeit to the Crown.

The gift to Hastings coincided with a period of intense collecting activity by Edward. From 1478 he spent considerable sums on large, elaborately illuminated manuscripts purchased in the Netherlands, laying the foundations of what was to become the royal library.[45] Of the thirty or so surviving manuscripts that can be associated with Edward, twenty-one can be identified as having been made especially for him, with his coat of arms and heraldic devices incorporated into the illuminations.[46] Eleven also incorporated the arms of his sons, Edward, Prince of Wales, and Richard, duke of York. Five of these are dated 1479 and one to 1480. Other manuscripts that have not survived are also mentioned in the Great Wardrobe accounts for 1480. As analysis of Edward's manuscript acquisitions has revealed, he appears to have had a marked preference for history of the classical world, in line with the choices of his Burgundian peers.[47] Fifteen of the volumes distinguished by Edward's arms have historical texts, and others contain texts with historical exemplum. Notable works in his library included Raoul Le Fèvre's *Receuil des histoires de Troie,* the anonymous *Grande histoire Cesar* (fig. 3.9), and translations of Quintus Curtius Rufus's *Historiae Alexandri Magni* and Benvenuto da Imola's *Romuléon* (fig. 3.12). General histories included William of Tyre's *History of the Crusades,* portions of Froissart's *Chronicles,* and two of Jean de Wavrin's seven-part *Anchiennes et nouvelles chronicques d'Angleterre.* There were also a number of didactic and moralistic works, such as the *IX malheureux et les IX malheureuses* and Boccaccio's *De cas des nobles hommes et femmes malheureux.* As noted, several of these incorporated the arms of Edward and his sons, and it seems that at least one motivation underlying this spate of acquisition was the provision of appropriate educational and exemplary material for the young princes. In 1475, when a separate household was established for the Prince of Wales, the king directed that his governors were to read "such noble stories as it behooveth a prince to understand and know" while the prince was at dinner, and some of these manuscripts may have been intended for that purpose. Certainly, books of this size must have been intended for public reading from a lectern.[48]

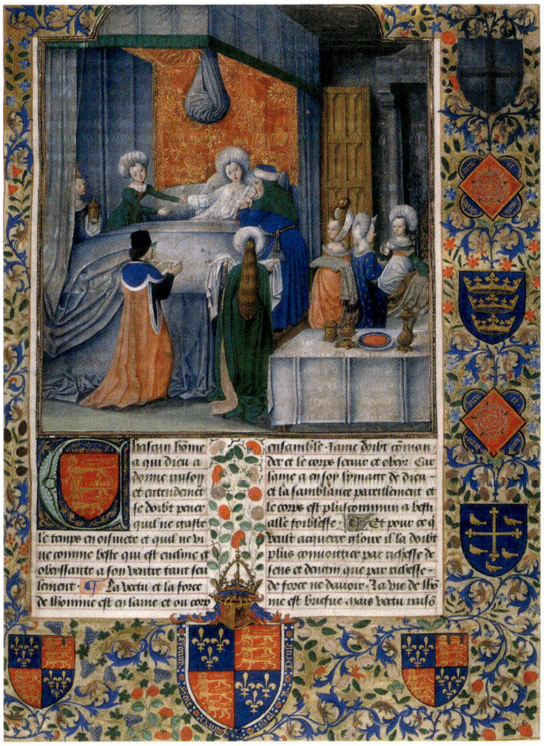

3.9 *The Birth of Caesar* with foliate border including arms of Edward IV, his sons, and Brutus. Miniature painting from *Le fait de Julius Cesar, Grande Histoire Cesar,* ca. 1479. 48 x 33 cm. British Library, London (Royal Ms 17 F II, fol. 9)

That a portion of these acquisitions resulted from a deliberate decision is suggested by the stylistic consistency of the text and illuminations and by that of the heraldic components with which they are decorated, indicating that the heraldic designs were executed from patterns supplied by Edward. Further evidence of a concerted effort is provided by a payment made on February 14, 1478, to "Philip Maisertuell merchant stranger" toward £240 due him, "for certaine bokes by the said Philip to be provided to the kyngs use in the parties beyond the see as in an endentur made betwene the kyngs highnes and the said Philip more plainly it may appier."[49]

In tandem with this spate of manuscript acquisitions a steady stream of tapestry purchases is also documented. A hint that these might also have been part of an orchestrated campaign is suggested by the fact that the majority of the purchases were made through two men. The first was John Pickering, a London mercer and at this time governor of the English merchants in the Netherlands, the second Edmund Rigon, a London draper.[50] The payments begin in August 1478, when Pickering was paid £242 15s. 2d. for "certaine verdures grene and white and other stuffe" and Rigon was paid £152 12d. for "certaine clothes of contrefetaras of silk" and other furnishing textiles. In September, Pickering received a further £51 2s. 10d. for a silk-woven, four-piece set of the *Story of Noah,* with an unspecified number of valances, and four silk-woven verdures. In November, he received a further payment of £60 in partial payment of £175 10s. for "dyverse hanginges of tapestry work verdoures and paving tyles." Two weeks later, on December 4, Rigon received £100 in partial payment of £265 12s. 8d. for "certaine arras, verdour & fetherbeddes." The following February, Pickering received a further £175 10s. for "certaine clothes of tapestrie werk, verdours and other stuff," while Rigon received £165 12s. 8d. for a consignment of "certain clothes of Aras, federbeddes, tykes and othre stuff."[51]

With the exception of the *Noah* tapestries and the white and green verdures, the subjects of these tapestries are not specified. That some were specifically commissioned for the king is suggested by the apparent correspondence between one of the Pickering deliveries and a tapestry described in an inventory of Katherine of Aragon's possessions taken in 1535.[52] According to this, the tapestry was of white and green verdure with falcons and "feterlockis as also with rooses and Sonnes"—that is, Edward's heraldic devices. Further evidence of heraldic commissions, possibly to be identified with the tapestries delivered by Pickering and Rigon in 1478 and 1479, comes from the description of a set of tapestries at the Wardrobe in 1480. This was "paled red and blue [Edward's heraldic colors] with roses sonnes and crownes in every pane."

If the verdures were custom-made for Edward, could the *Noah* series also have been custom-made or at least purchased from an existing design with a specific intent? Noah was among the ancient forebears that the English genealogists, emulating Continental example, had claimed for the Lancastrian kings.[53] Following Edward's accession, the descent was adapted to Yorkist purposes, and Noah featured in a number of genealogical rolls produced during his reign. But the choice of this subject may also have been intended to make an impact in another way. One of these rolls, made for Edward during the mid-1460s, is prefaced with five scenes of Edward's life interspersed with scenes of biblical history, an adaptation of religious typological programs in which Old Testament scenes prophesy or anticipate scenes from the life of Christ. Thus a scene of Joshua at the Battle of Jericho is paired with a scene of Edward at battle, David's vision of three men anticipates Edward's vision of three suns, and Moses floating on the Nile prefigures Edward escaping across the Channel.[54] In the context of this typological roll, it therefore seems reasonable to propose that the set of *Noah* tapestries may have been purchased to draw a direct parallel between Noah and Edward, the pilot who had steered the nation through the deluge of the Wars of the Roses.

The source of the tapestries supplied by Pickering and Rigon is unknown, but in all likelihood they were purchased or commissioned at the annual fairs held in the Low Countries. Certainly in June 1480, the Wardrobe paid a subsidy of £18 13s. due to the Port of London by John Pickering for "three standerds with verdeurs and othre hangings" along with paving tiles, purchased at the "bowmis" market in November 1478 and for verdures and other hangings also purchased there in February and October 1479.[55] An idea of the relative ease with which merchants could commission new designs or have existing designs customized for their clients at these markets, is suggested by evidence relating to transactions by the London merchant, Jan Pasmer, at Bergen op Zoom in 1477.[56] On this occasion, Pasmer commissioned the Brussels weaver Gielis van de Putte (ca. 1420–1503), to weave a tapestry measuring approximately four and a quarter by sixteen and a half yards according to a design in which the central scene of the *Last Supper* was to be replaced by Saint Gregory delivering the Mass to the doctors and bishops of the Church. Two years later Van de Putte received a further order from Pasmer and an associate for two tapestries measuring approximately three and a half yards by, respectively, thirteen and two-thirds and fourteen and a half yards in length, in this case to be woven from cartoons supplied by the patrons. Presumably, the tapestries for which Pickering and Rigon were paid in 1478 and 1479 may have been commissioned in similar circumstances.

The sole surviving volume of Great Wardrobe accounts for Edward's reign dates from April 18 to September 29, 1480. This records the delivery of a number of miscellaneous tapestries, some of which may have come from Pickering and Rigon, including the set of red and blue heraldic tapestries already mentioned and five counterpoints, or counterpanes. Two were woven with figurative imagery, one with green verdures and trees, one with white verdure and "scripture," and one in plain white. The Wardrobe staff was paid for lining these panels with buckram, a coarse cotton fabric. During the same period, the Wardrobe also took delivery of two pieces of "arras" of the *Story of Paris and Helen*. These were among a group of textiles subsequently delivered in July 1480 to Greenwich and Coldharbour, a riverside house in the City of London, as part of the provisions for Edward's sister Margaret during her extended embassy to England in 1480.[57] Edward thus seems to have been furthering the Trojan conceit first raised at Margaret's departure for Bruges fourteen years before. The topicality and interest of this subject to Margaret is suggested by the testimony of William Caxton, governor of the Merchant Adventurers in Bruges from 1462, who had entered Margaret's service before March 1471. According to the inscription in his translation of Raoul Le Fèvre's *Recueil des histoires de Troie* (ca. 1475), it was Margaret who encouraged him to undertake the translation, and she even helped with some corrections.[58] The design of the panels acquired in 1480 is unknown, but it is possible that they were a part of the larger design series of the *Story of Troy* of which the first weaving had been purchased in 1472 from Pasquier Grenier by the town and Franc of Bruges as a gift for Margaret's husband, Charles the Bold. Henry VII was to acquire a complete set of this eleven-piece series in 1486.

More sizeable purchases followed. In September 1480 Rigon received a payment of £163 12s., further to an earlier payment of £100, for a seven-piece set of the *Story of Tullus Hostilius* containing 659 Flemish ells (370 square yards).[59] Tullus was the third legendary king of Rome who defeated the Albans and expanded the Roman domain, but it is doubtful that the set was entirely devoted to this hero because no other examples of this subject are recorded in Continental inventories. It has therefore been suggested that the set may have been identical with one of *Roman Histories* bought in September 1478 by an English merchant from the estate of Charles the Bold's former chancellor, Guillaume Hugonet, following Hugonet's execution in Ghent in 1477. Edward's sister Mary also acquired tapestries from this sale.[60] Although no tapestries illustrating the story of Tullus Hostilius are extant, a single piece illustrating scenes from the life of Tarquinius Priscus, the seventh king of Rome, famed for defeating the Sabines, has survived at Zamora Cathedral (fig. 3.10).[61] Thought to date from the 1470s, it may have belonged to a larger ensemble of the *Story of Rome*, thus providing a possible clue as to the appearance of the set purchased by Edward.

Two years later, in 1482, the merchant John Pickering was paid for providing Edward with an eight-piece set of the *Story of Thebes*, purchased at the Easter fair in Bergen op Zoom.[62] It had a total surface area of 472 square yards, and Pickering received a payment of £300. Whether this was payment in full or a partial payment is unrecorded. Three pieces of tapestry with Theban subjects are extant from this period, two of them being small fragments depicting scenes from the life of Oedipus. The third, a large tapestry now at Madrid Town Hall, depicts a scene from the *Story of Tydeus* (fig. 3.11). The dimensions of the Madrid piece are similar to those recorded for panels in the *Thebes* set in the 1547 inventory,[63] and the angular figures, crowded compositions, and richly patterned costumes common to all three surviving pieces must provide an idea of the style and content of Edward IV's lost set.

Whether these figurative sets were purchased from available stock or were specially commissioned is uncertain, but given the cost and how closely Edward was involved in all aspects of his administration, the decisions underlying these acquisitions were probably his. Similarly, in view of the evidence that Edward's manuscript purchases reflect a consistent preference for subjects drawn from history, especially classical history, and considering the character of the staggered payments to Pickering and Rigon, suggestive of the delivery of sets that had been ordered in advance, it seems

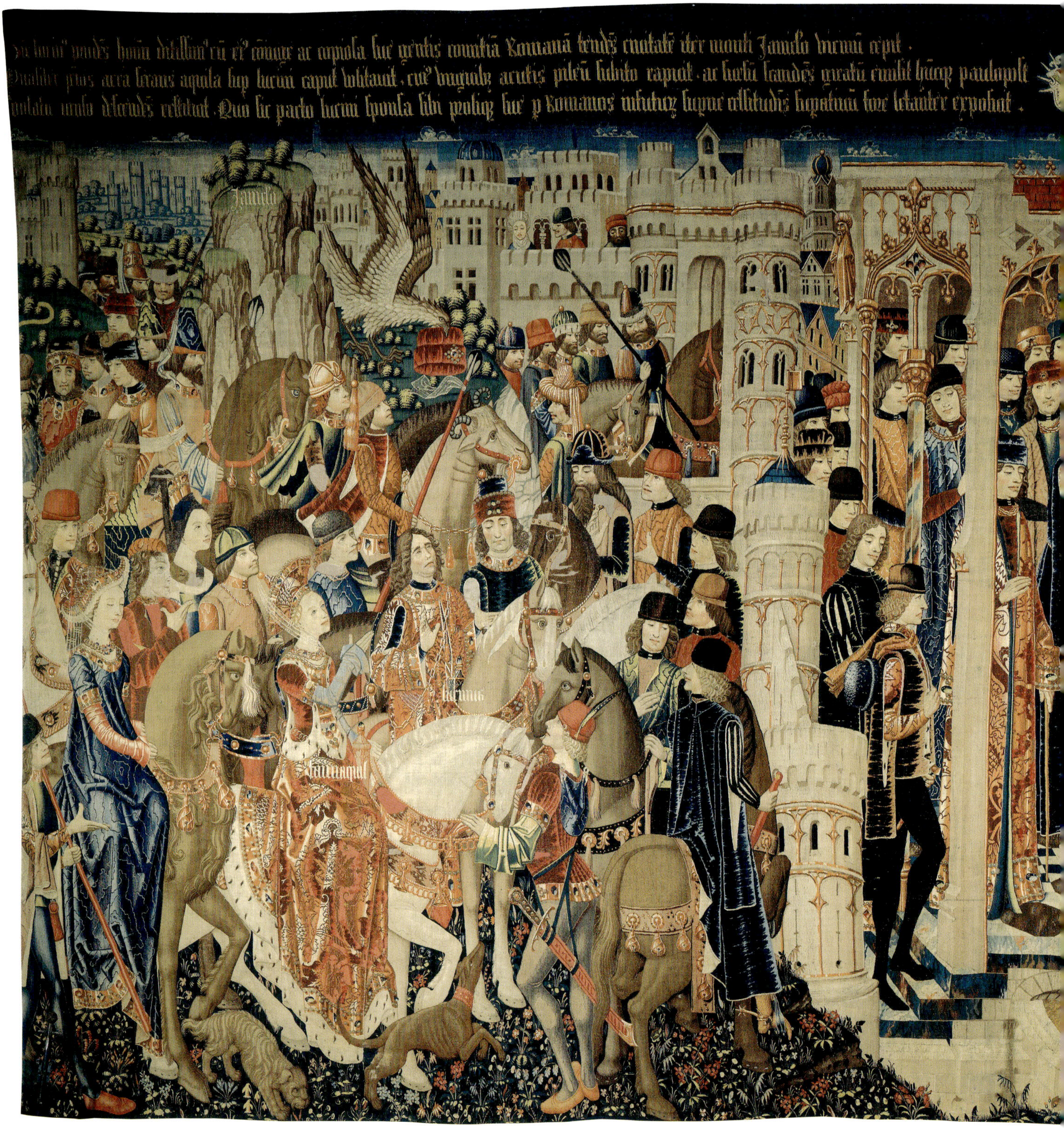

3.10 *Scenes from the Life of Tarquinius Priscus*, probably from a set of the *Story of Rome*. Tapestry woven in the Southern Netherlands, ca. 1470. Wool and silk, 425 x 850 cm. Museo Catedralicio, Zamora

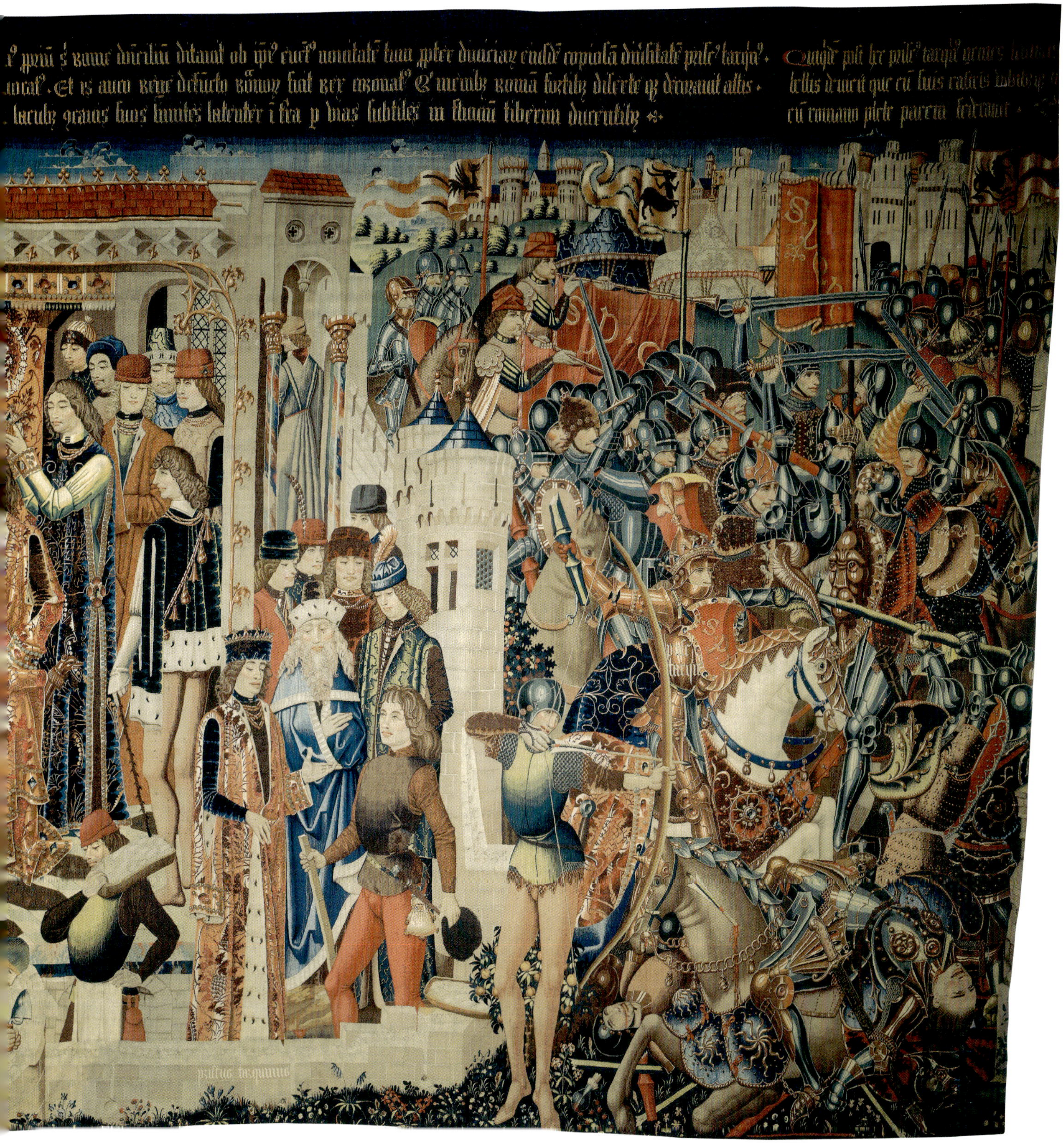

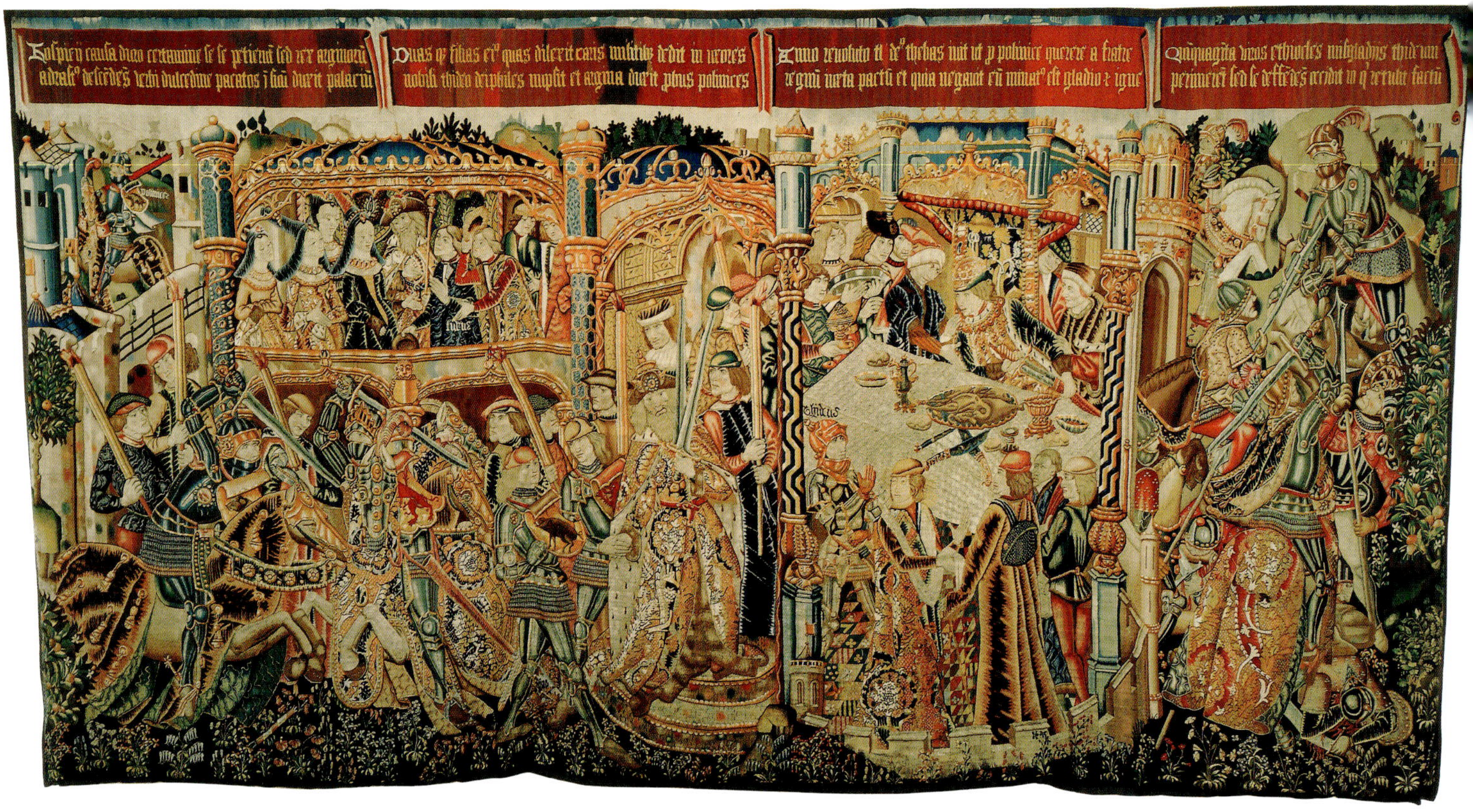

3.11 *The Story of Tydeus* from a set of the *Story of Thebes*. Tapestry woven in the Southern Netherlands, ca. 1480. Wool, silk, and gilt-metal-wrapped thread, 430 x 790 cm. Town Hall, Madrid

reasonable to propose that at least some of these acquisitions may, indeed, have been woven to order, albeit from existing designs. Whatever the case, the choice of subjects so similar to those of Edward's manuscripts suggests that from the late 1470s he was explicitly interested in works of art depicting classical rulers and heroes in preference to other models. In his tapestries as in his manuscripts—such as the French translation of Benvenuto da Imola's *Romuléon* (fig. 3.12)—the heroes of ancient Thebes and Rome provided resonant and fitting amplifications of Edward's own deeds of martial prowess and leadership, serving also as a reminder of the putative ancestral links between the emperors of the classical world and their modern successor.

No further purchases of figurative tapestries by Edward are documented, but those we know of were likely just part of his acquisitions. A set of three "Bussheron" (woodcutter) tapestries that John Wilde, the king's tapicer, repaired in 1471, may have been woven from the same cartoons as sets of this subject previously supplied by Pasquier Grenier to the Burgundian court in 1461 and 1466. An idea of their appearance may be provided by a tapestry of exactly this subject that bears the arms of Nicholas Rolin, chancellor of Burgundy, who died in 1461 (fig. 3.13).[64] The descriptions of a number of other tapestries listed in the 1547 inventory also suggest that they can be identified with design series produced in the late fifteenth century. Although Henry VII may have acquired some, Edward almost certainly purchased others. The most notable of these was a four-piece set of the *Story of Brutus* that was located at Richmond Palace in 1547.[65] As a considerable number of the fifteenth-century tapestries were deposited there by that date, the location suggests that this may have been one of the sets that Henry VIII inherited, and the large dimensions of the tapestries in the documented set are of the same order as those of a large example now at La Seo Cathedral in Saragossa, which can be dated to the late 1460s or early 1470s on stylistic grounds (fig. 3.14 and detail opposite p. 329).[66] Evidently one of a larger series, the extant tapestry depicts part of the Brutus legend as narrated

3.12 *Hadrian Kneeling before Trajan.* Miniature painting by a Netherlandish artist from Edward IV's copy of Roberto della Porta's *Romuléon.* 13.5 x 18.5 cm. British Library, London (Royal Ms 19 E V, fol. 367v)

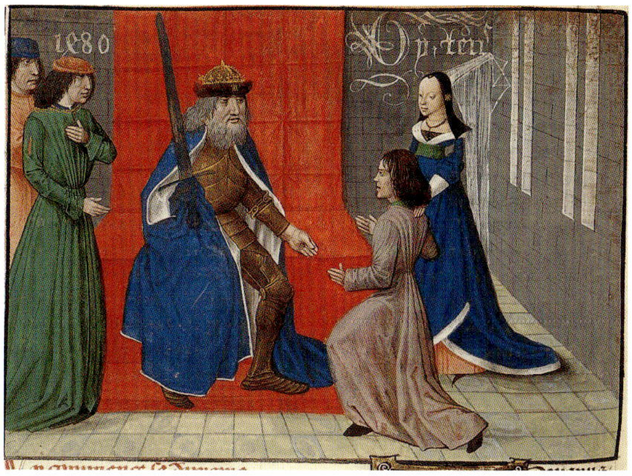

by Geoffrey of Monmouth's *Historia regum Britanniae,* from the departure of Brutus and his troops from Greece, and their journey through the Mediterranean, to their arrival in Britain and the ensuing battle with King Gofaria and the giants who then inhabited the land. As already mentioned, following this victory, Brutus became king of Britain whereupon he founded a new Troy (London), and we can assume that these events were featured in another of the lost royal set. The circumstances in which this series was conceived are unknown, but whatever the origin of the design, the appeal of the subject to Edward is readily evident.[67] Brutus was a figure of significance for any English king, and quite apart from the qualities of heroism and leadership he embodied, his defeat of King Gofaria provided a resonant analogy for Edward's defeat of Henry VI's forces in 1461 and 1471.[68] As such, Brutus figured in a number of genealogical rolls created for Edward during the course of his reign, including the elaborate example now in the Free Library of Philadelphia. In this, the horse trapper of the equestrian portrait of Edward at the top of the genealogy has a central escutcheon that features the heraldic device attributed to Brutus by medieval heraldry (three gold crowns on a blue ground), and the same arms appear on one of the escutcheons that are given pride of place below (fig. 3.15).[69] Given the style and probable

3.13 *Woodcutters with Arms of Nicolas Rolin* (fragment). Tapestry woven in the Southern Netherlands, probably Tournai, before 1462. Wool and silk, 315 x 495 cm. Musée des Arts Décoratifs, Paris

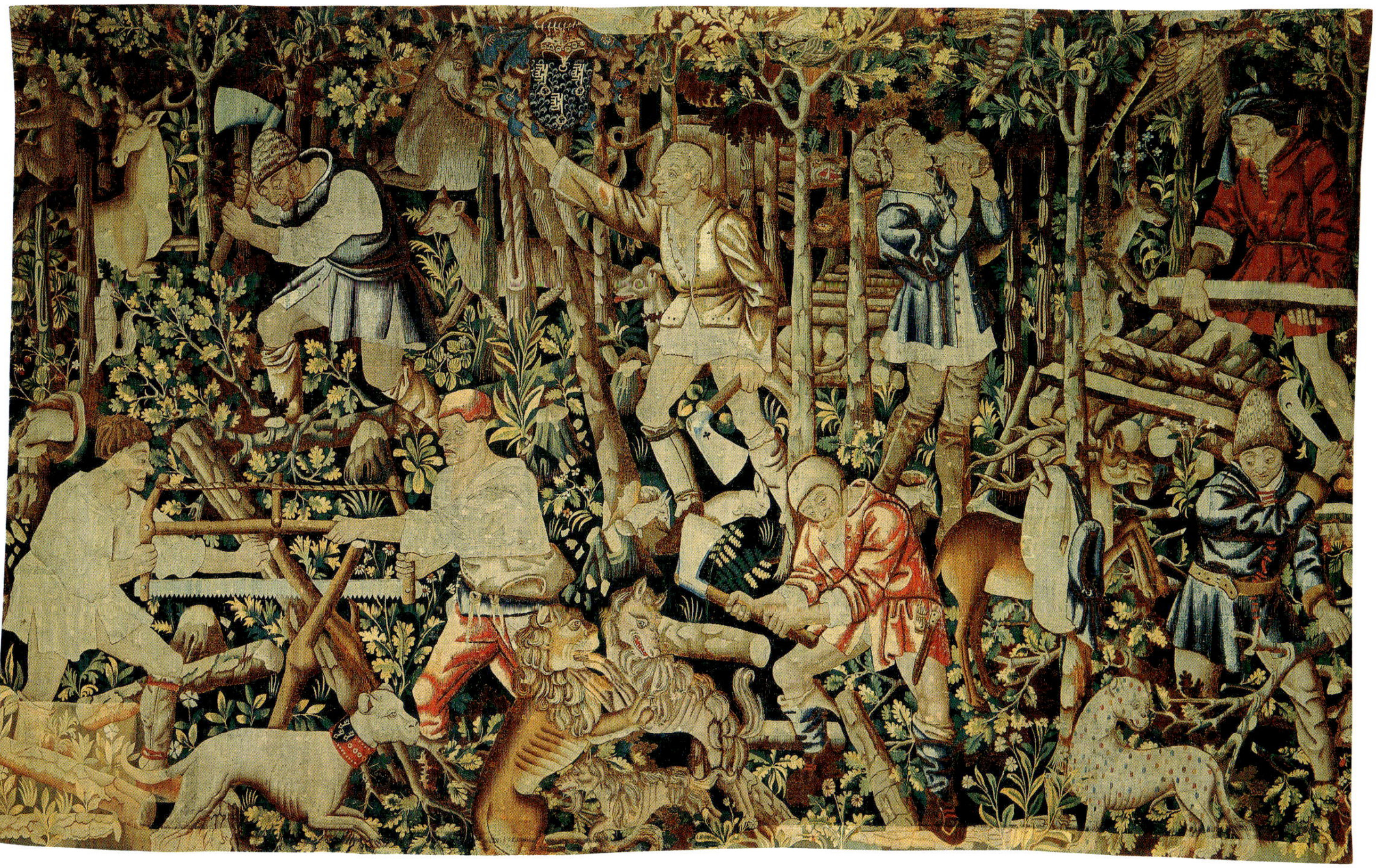

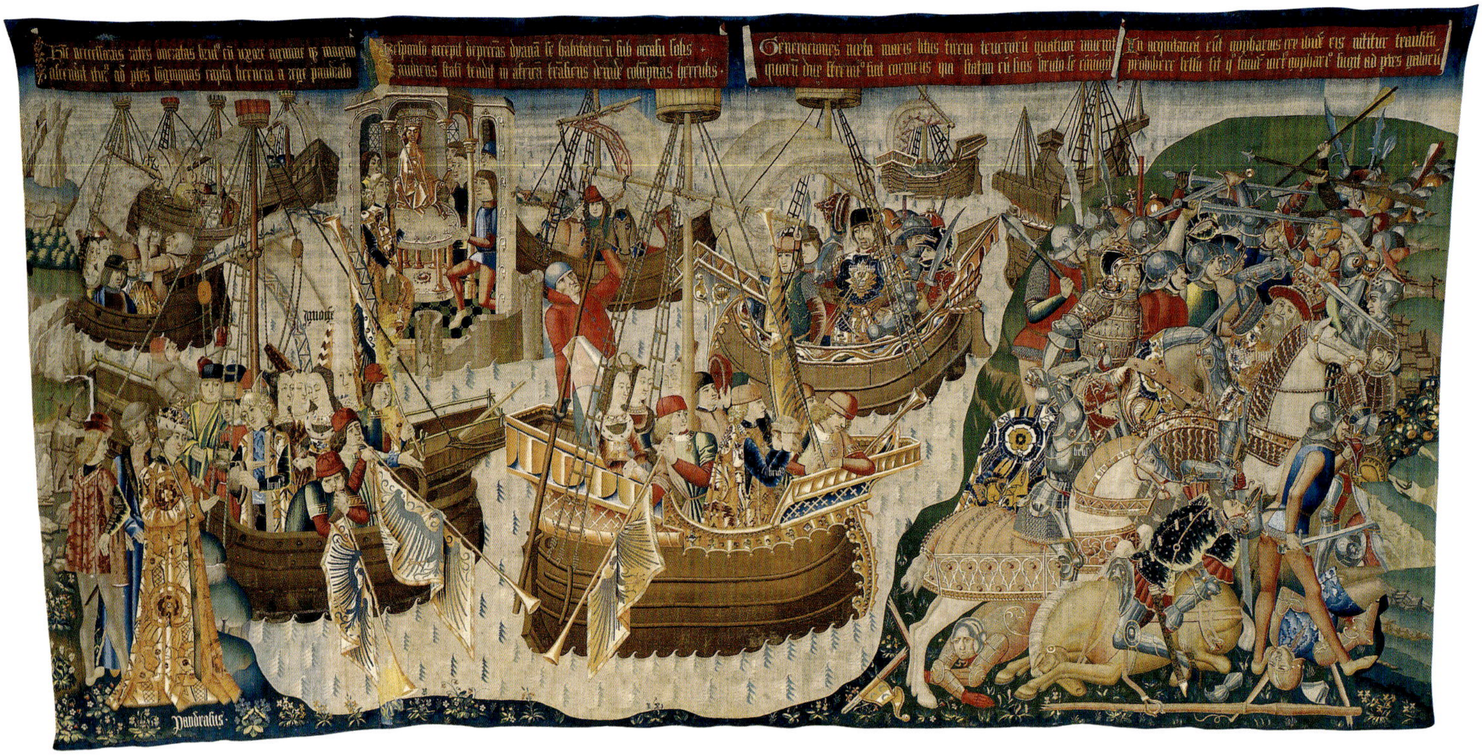

3.14 *The Invasion of England* from a set of the *Story of Brutus*. Tapestry woven in the Southern Netherlands, ca. 1470–80. Wool and silk, 410 x 790 cm. Cathedral Museum of La Seo, Saragossa

date of the *Brutus* design, together with Edward's known interest in classical subject matter, it seems likely that he was the patron of this tapestry.

The Use and Perception of Tapestry at Edward's Court

Whereas some of Edward's tapestry purchases were probably intended for specific locations, others would have been part of the king's Removing Wardrobe that was transported from one palace to another, as necessary. The household regulations that Edward instigated during the early 1470s reflect efforts to codify the activities of the king's household, albeit along the lines of usage already in existence at the Lancastrian court, including those for the provision of furnishings and hangings.[70] The Black Book stipulated that the chamberlain was to ensure that appropriate furnishings were always provided for the king and defines the duties of the king's Wardrobes of Robes and Beds. It also spells out the privileges, rewards, and relationships of the ushers, grooms, and pages of the chamber. The ten grooms were instructed to daily "make fyres to set up trestyls and bourds, with yomen of chambre, and to helpe dresse the beddes of sylke and arras uppon the usshers apoyntment." They were also to "help hang the chambre, and to kepe hem clene from dogges and other unclennes." The grooms and pages of both wardrobes were enjoined to gather "swete flowers, herbis, toez, to make amonges them othyr swete fumes, thinges to make them brethe most holesomly and delectable: and all thinges to be preciously and dylygently for mothese and all other unclennesse attended.[71]

Like the Wardrobe of Robes, the Wardrobe of Beds had a cart and at least twelve pack-horses for the carriage of the king's possessions. Beside carts, the Great Wardrobe had a boat for transporting furnishings by water, many of the royal palaces being situated along the Thames.[72] When the royal household was on the move, as it frequently was—the household accounts for the period from September 1478 to September 1479, for example, show that the king changed lodging about sixty times—the Wardrobe activities must have been an enormous undertaking.[73] When Edward campaigned in France

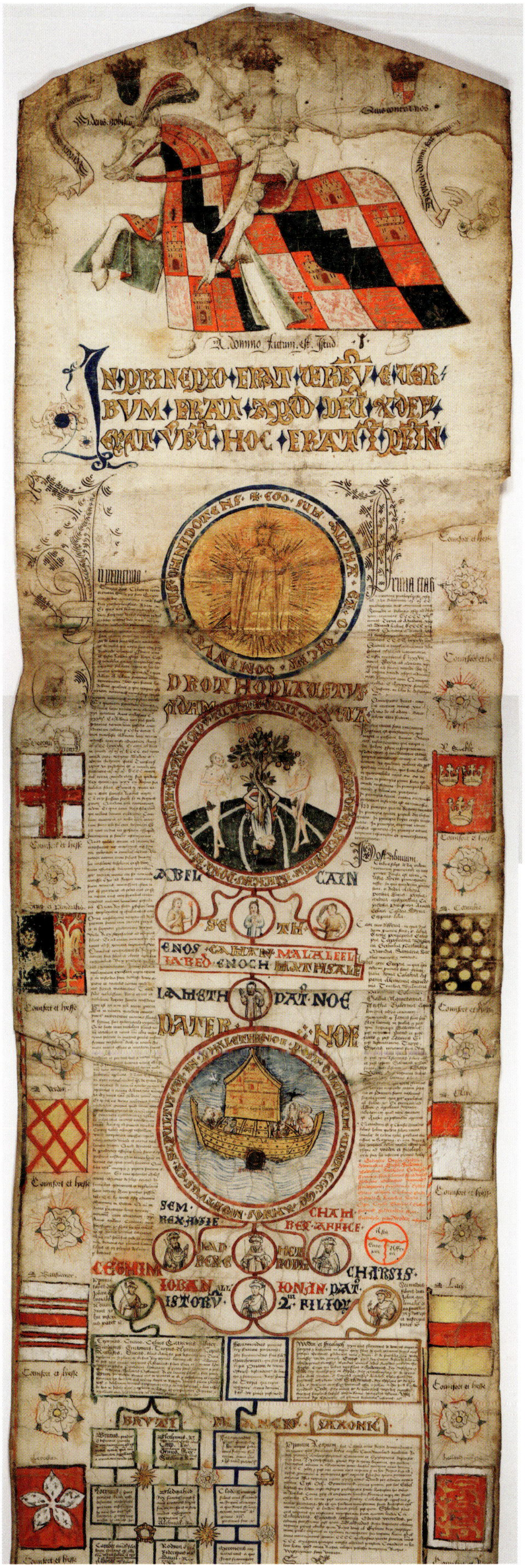

3.15 *The Edward IV Roll* (detail). England, after June 1461. Vellum, 477.8 x 46 cm (dimensions of whole). The Free Library of Philadelphia, Rare Book Department (Lewis E 201)

in 1475, his entourage also included Wardrobe workers responsible for repairing his tapestries.[74] During Edward's reign, the officer responsible for the care of the king's tapestries was a John Wilde, who was presumably assisted by various other weavers, like his successors under Henry VII and Henry VIII.

It would be fascinating to know how Edward and his circle looked at and thought about the tapestries by which they were surrounded, but as with the painting and literature of the day, there is scant reference to such matters in contemporary writing. Considering the minimal furnishings of the grand chambers and reception rooms of the court, the figurative tapestries must have been the principal feature of note in most of the grand interiors. And if we take into account the long periods that people were often required to wait before an audience with the king, the tapestries must have been the object of extensive contemplation. Although the more learned members of the court may have been able to pick their way through the narratives with the aid of the inscriptions, it seems unlikely that the majority would have been up to this task, even allowing for the greater familiarity of a contemporary audience with the legends and heroes that the tapestries depicted. One can only surmise that leading courtiers, palace servants, and Wardrobe officers may, on occasion, have been called on to provide ad hoc commentaries and explanations. The scale and clarity of the narrative components of late medieval tapestries certainly lend themselves to verbal exposition, and it would have been in this sort of forum that the analogies between the monarch and the heroes of old could have been explored and elaborated.

One rare description of Edward's court as it had been prepared for a grand event is provided by the record published by the royal herald Bluemantle Pursuivant of the festivities associated with Lord Gruthuyse's visit to England in 1472 on the occasion of his elevation to the Order of the Garter. On the evening of his arrival at Windsor, Gruthuyse dined with Lord Hastings in two chambers provided for him, which, at the king's order, had been "richly hanged with cloths of arras and beds of estate."[75] We can conjecture that the provisions included the tapestries supplied by Grenier three years previously. Although this is the only eyewitness account that specifically mentions Edward's tapestries, other testimonies leave no doubt that his court conveyed an impression of magnificence, even during the earlier years of his reign. When Gabriel Tetzel visited England in 1465 in the entourage of the Bohemian ambassador, Leo of Rozmital, he judged it "the most splendid Court that could be found in all Christendom."[76] Given that he had just visited the Burgundian court, this was high praise. Evidence that Edward's contemporaries considered tapestry to be a key ingredient of the royal image that he projected, a self-conscious contrast to the inadequacy of his predecessor, is confirmed by the description in the *Croyland Chronicle* of Edward's later years, written in about 1486 by an anonymous writer who had been a member of Edward's council: "for collecting vessels of gold and silver, tapestries and decorations of the most precious nature, both for his palaces and for various churches, and for building castles, colleges and other distinguished places . . . not one of his predecessors was at all able to equal his remarkable achievements."[77]

PART II

The Founding of a Dynasty

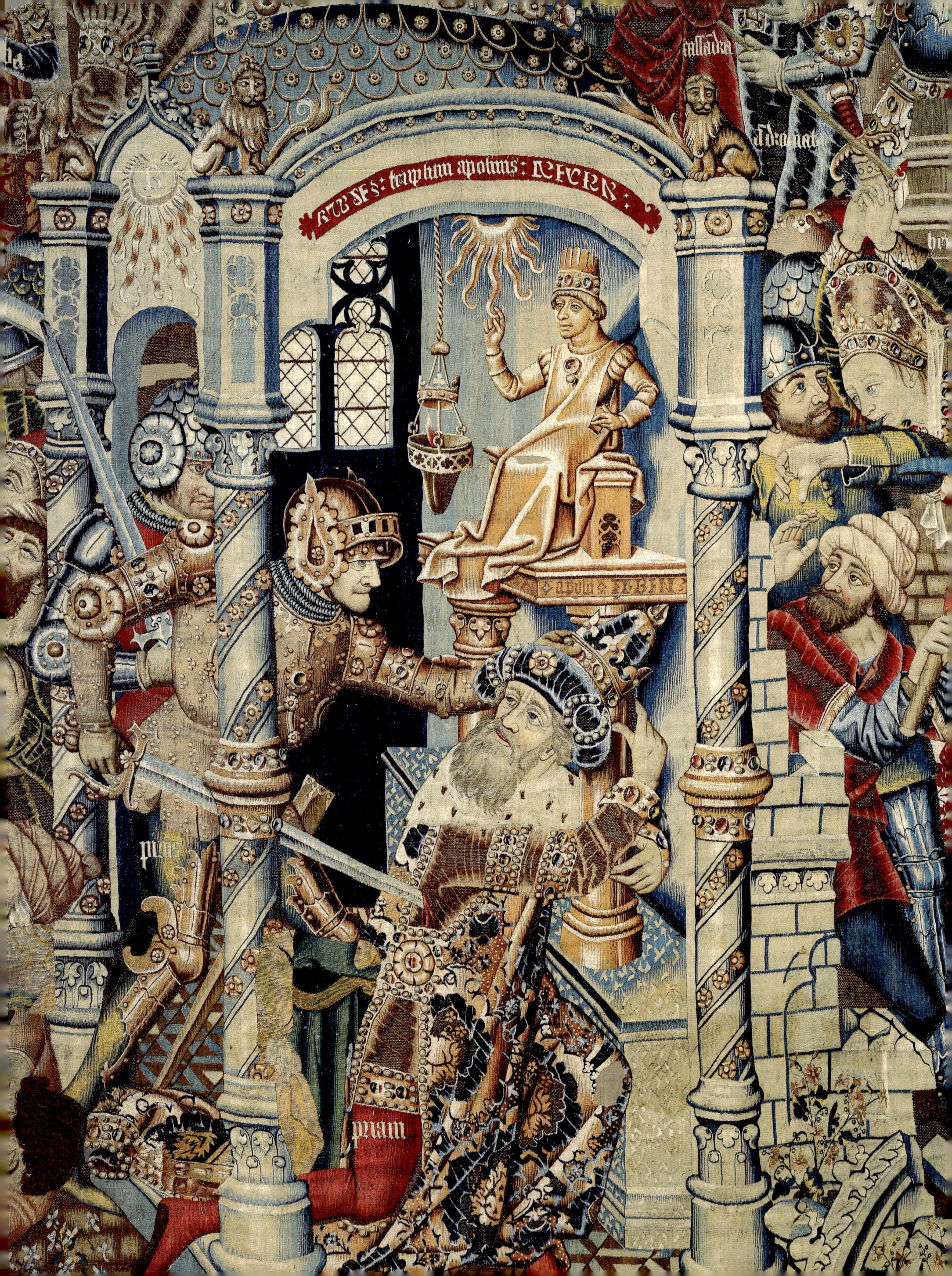
templum apolinis
priam

CHAPTER 4

Tapestry Acquisitions under Henry VII

Detail of fig. 4.3

Edward IV died on April 9, 1483, plunging the kingdom into another period of dynastic struggle in which the throne was usurped from the rightful heir, the twelve-year-old Edward V, by his uncle Richard III. Two years later, Richard was in turn challenged and defeated in battle by Henry Tudor (fig. 4.1). No inventories for the royal tapestry collection survive between those taken in the 1420s and those of the late 1530s and 1540s, but many of Edward IV's tapestries, along with others that can be identified from Richard II and Henry IV's collections, are recognizable in the 1547 inventory. It therefore seems that as in 1399, 1461, and 1471, the very abruptness of the change of dynasty protected the collection from dispersal by legacy or courtly perquisite. As Henry Tudor advanced through the English countryside from his victory at Bosworth, the royal palaces that awaited him were already hung with a sumptuous array of antique and modern tapestries that, in the custody of previously appointed Wardrobe officers and palace staff, were subject to well-established procedures of use and storage.

Both the royal residences and their contents would have been unfamiliar to the twenty-nine-year-old king, who had spent most of his life in exile at the court of Francis II, duke of Brittany, where he and his uncle, Jasper Tudor, had been diplomatic pawns between the English and French courts. Little is known of Francis's tapestry collection, but his ancestors had purchased tapestries from the leading Paris merchants in the late fourteenth century, and more recently, Francis had established his own tapestry workshops in Rennes and Nantes in 1477, of which nothing more is known.[1] Following the accession of Richard III and his renewed attempts to persuade Francis to extradite Henry Tudor into his custody, Henry sought protection at the court of the fifteen-year-old French king, Charles VIII. Henry spent the autumn of 1484 in the Loire Valley, and over the winter he was resident in Paris. During this time he would have seen some of the fine tapestries of the French royal collection, perhaps including such sets as the *Battle of Formigny* and the rich armorial tapestries made

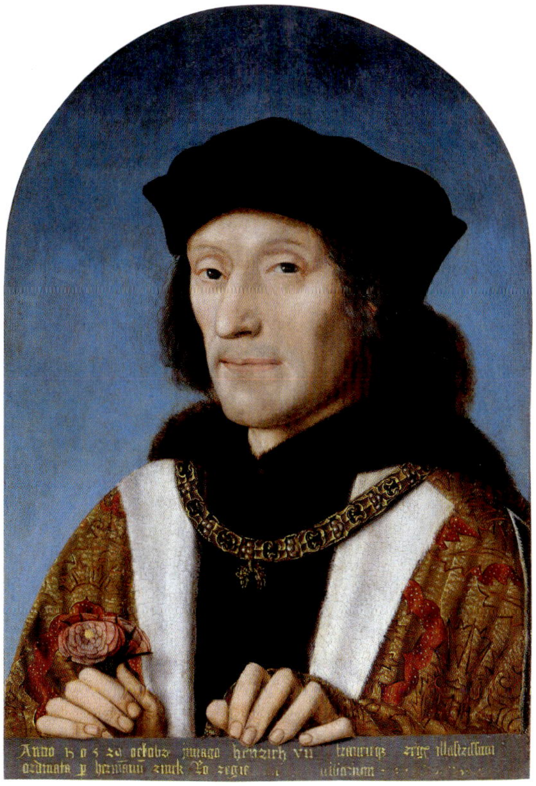

4.1 *Henry VII*, attributed to Michael Sittow. Oil on panel, 42.5 x 30.5 cm. National Portrait Gallery, London

for Charles VII.[2] By the end of the fifteenth century it had also become a tradition in France for leading officers of the cathedrals and richer churches to commission sets of tapestry depicting their patron saints for display in their choirs or naves on feast days, like that of the *Life of Saint Peter* that Bishop Guillaume de Hellande donated to Beauvais Cathedral in 1460.[3] Henry would almost certainly have seen examples of such choir sets in use. Thus, even though he was a stranger to the English palaces and collections, the new Tudor king would have had some experience of Continental tapestry usage and a familiarity with at least some of the major design series of the day.

Henry came to the throne when a high premium was placed on regal magnificence. Given the tenuous nature of his claim to the Crown and the ambivalent attitude adopted by many of the nobility to his cause in the days leading up to the Battle of Bosworth, he cannot have been under any illusions about the necessity of maintaining the appearance of a strong and prosperous court that could reward its adherents well and move swiftly to quell opposition. In the event, Henry appears to have adopted the mantle of regal magnificence with ease, aided no doubt by the procedures put in place by Edward IV. Accounts relating to his coronation include payments for the transportation of Wardrobe stuff from one palace to another, for hanging "arras" at Westminster and elsewhere, for guarding the precious Wardrobe textiles overnight to protect them from looting, and for taking them down again afterward.[4] On the occasion of Prince Arthur's christening in 1486 at Winchester, "The Body of all the Cathedral Chyrche of Wynchester was hanged with Clothes of Arras," with a "Travers hanged with cloth of arras" on the north side, presumably for the royal party.[5] And when the queen made her ceremonial procession through the city before her coronation the following year, "Al the strets ther wich she shulde passe by, were clenly dressed and besene with Clothes of Tappestrye and Arras. And some Strets, as Cheape, hangyed with riche Clothes of gold Velvets and Silks."[6] Following the death of Alvered Corneburgh, keeper of the Great Wardrobe during the first two years of Henry's reign, his widow received payment for her late husband's transportation costs as he attended the king from London to Westminster, Greenwich, Sheen, and other palaces with the state robes and "divers finely wrought cloths and cloth of gold."[7] Cloth of gold was a generic term that appears with greater frequency from the late fifteenth century. It referred to a type of especially sumptuous velvet that was heavily brocaded with gilt-metal-wrapped thread. In the most sumptuous examples, the surface of the textile is almost entirely covered with gold thread.

Early Purchases and the Grenier Trojan War *Series*

No evidence survives of artistic patronage during the first year or so of Henry's reign, but when he did turn his attention to such matters, tapestry commissions were among the first orders he made.[8] The link that Edward IV had established with the Grenier family of Tournai has already been discussed, and the tapestries they provided, such as the *Alexander* and *Passion* sets, must have been among the most striking that now passed into Henry's hands. We do not have any evidence of the relationship that Pasquier Grenier maintained with Edward's court after 1469, but he and his sons evidently moved with relative ease between the European courts during the 1470s and 1480s. It is of little surprise then, that when Henry first purchased tapestries on his own account he turned to the Greniers. On September 22, 1486, safe conduct and protection were granted to Pasquier Grenier and his son Jean, with permission for them and their servants to import cloths of arras, tapestry, and carpets to England.[9] We can conjecture that, before this date, a representative of the family must have traveled to the English court to meet the new king and to demonstrate available designs, much as Melchior and Guillaume Grenier had traveled to the Sforza court in 1459.

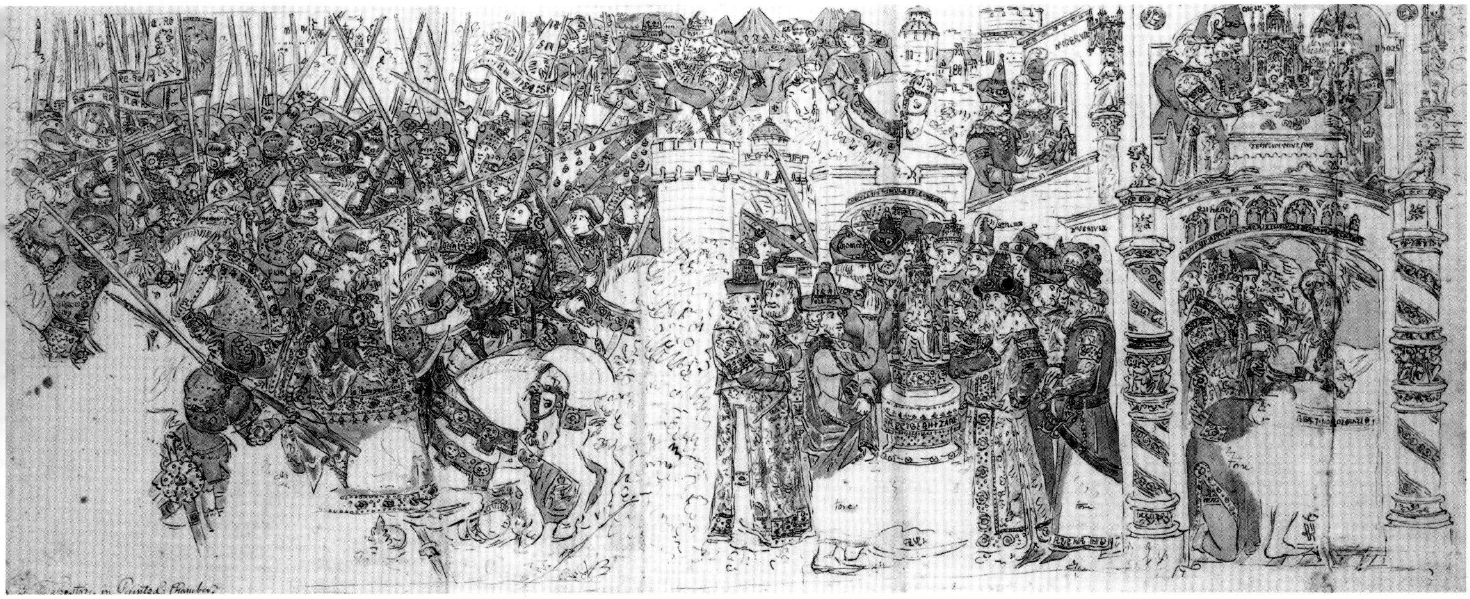

4.2 *The Greeks Capture the City of Tenedon and Other Subjects* by John Carter (1748–1817), 1799. Drawing after a set of *Trojan War* tapestries then hanging in the Painted Chamber at Westminster Palace. Pen and ink and watercolor. Victoria and Albert Museum, London

The resulting order came to fruition one and a half years later with the delivery by Jean Grenier of two tapestry altar cloths and eleven "clothes of Arras of thistorye of Trojan Ware." A royal warrant of March 13, 1488, instructed Richard Fox, bishop of Exeter and keeper of the Privy Seal, to discharge Jean Grenier from paying customs on these objects.[10] Subsequently, the accounts of Peter Curteis, keeper of the Great Wardrobe, for the eighteen months to Michaelmas 1488 include notice of the receipt of 1,142½ ells of "arras of Flanders."[11] This is equivalent to 642½ square yards of tapestry, the approximate surface area of an eleven-piece set of the *Story of the Trojan War* recorded in the 1547 Windsor inventory, and it is therefore probable that this was the set concerned.[12]

The identity of this *Trojan War* set can be established more firmly than any tapestries yet discussed in this study because several pieces can be traced in royal inventories for the next two hundred years.[13] At the end of the eighteenth century, five large fragments still hung in the Painted Chamber at the Palace of Westminster, where they were sketched by antiquarians shortly before being sold (fig. 4.2).[14] These drawings reveal that Henry VII's *Trojan War* tapestries were woven from a set of designs of which a number of fragmentary sets survive today (figs. 4.3, 5.4, 17.1, and detail opposite p. 67).[15] In addition, nine highly finished preparatory drawings for the series, which may also have served as demonstration pieces for prospective clients, have also survived (fig. 4.4).[16] Although Henry VII's set is now lost and probably destroyed, the combination of drawings and extant tapestries allows reconstruction of the appearance of the entire eleven-piece series, which, when complete, measured over one hundred yards in length. The series epitomized the grandest large-scale tapestry production in the Low Countries during the third quarter of the fifteenth century in terms of its design, its dense complex narrative, and its subject matter, a classical myth reinterpreted in terms of medieval romance.

The exact origin of the series is uncertain.[17] The earliest documented set was delivered to Charles the Bold between September 1471 and September 1472, the cost being paid at the duke's request by the town and Franc of Bruges, perhaps as part of the reparations made to Charles following the destruction of the Castle of Mâle near Bruges in April 1472. The short time that elapsed between Charles's request and the start of payments for a set already delivered suggests that it was not made to order for Charles but, rather, that it may have been woven, at least in part, as a speculative venture by Pasquier Grenier. These circumstances, taken in conjunction with the design, whose character relates closely to the work of the

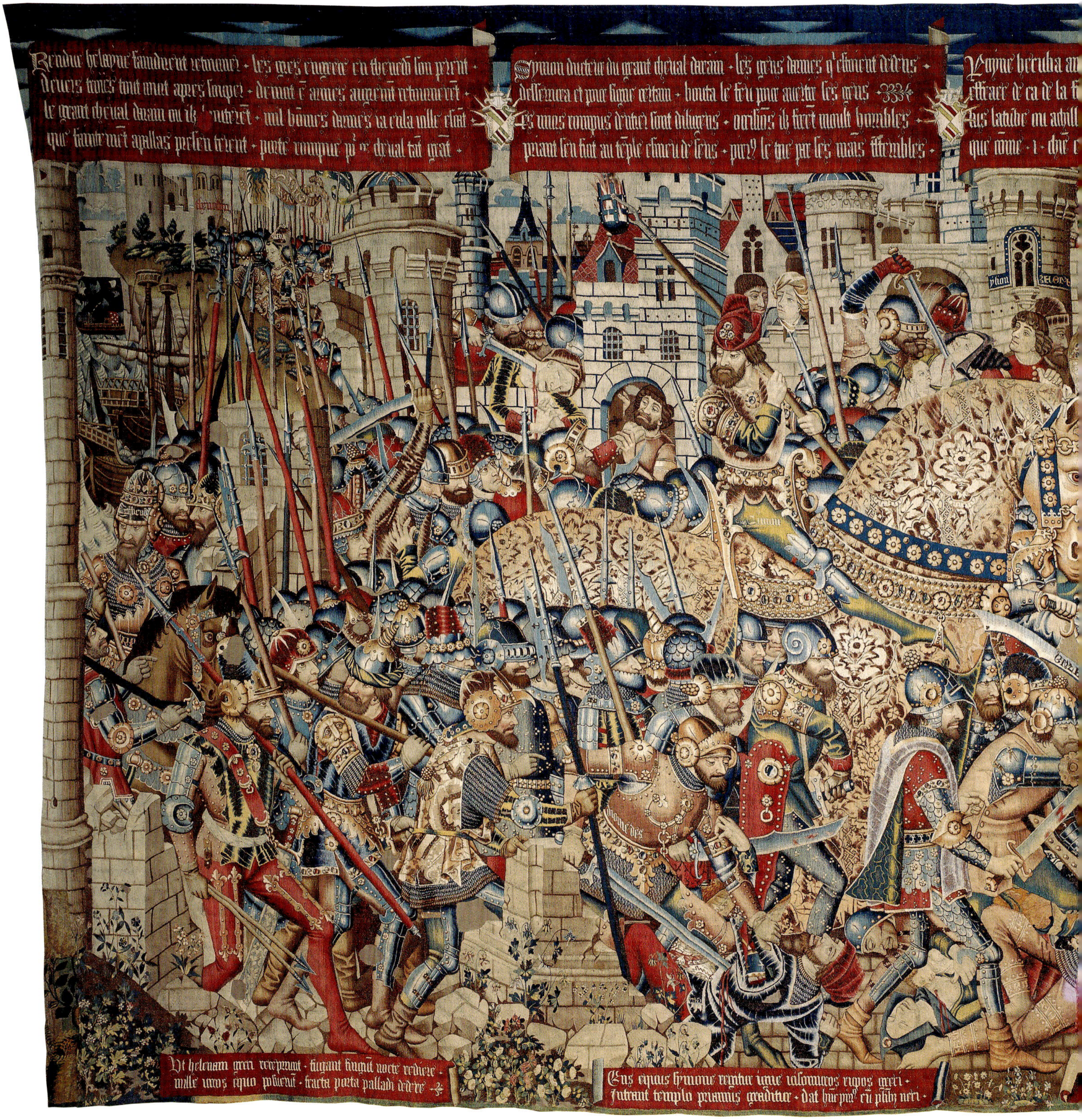

4.3 *The Sack of Troy* from an eleven-piece set of the *Story of the Trojan War*. Tapestry woven in the Southern Netherlands, probably Tournai, ca. 1480–90. Wool and silk, 477 x 942 cm. Museo Catedralicio, Zamora

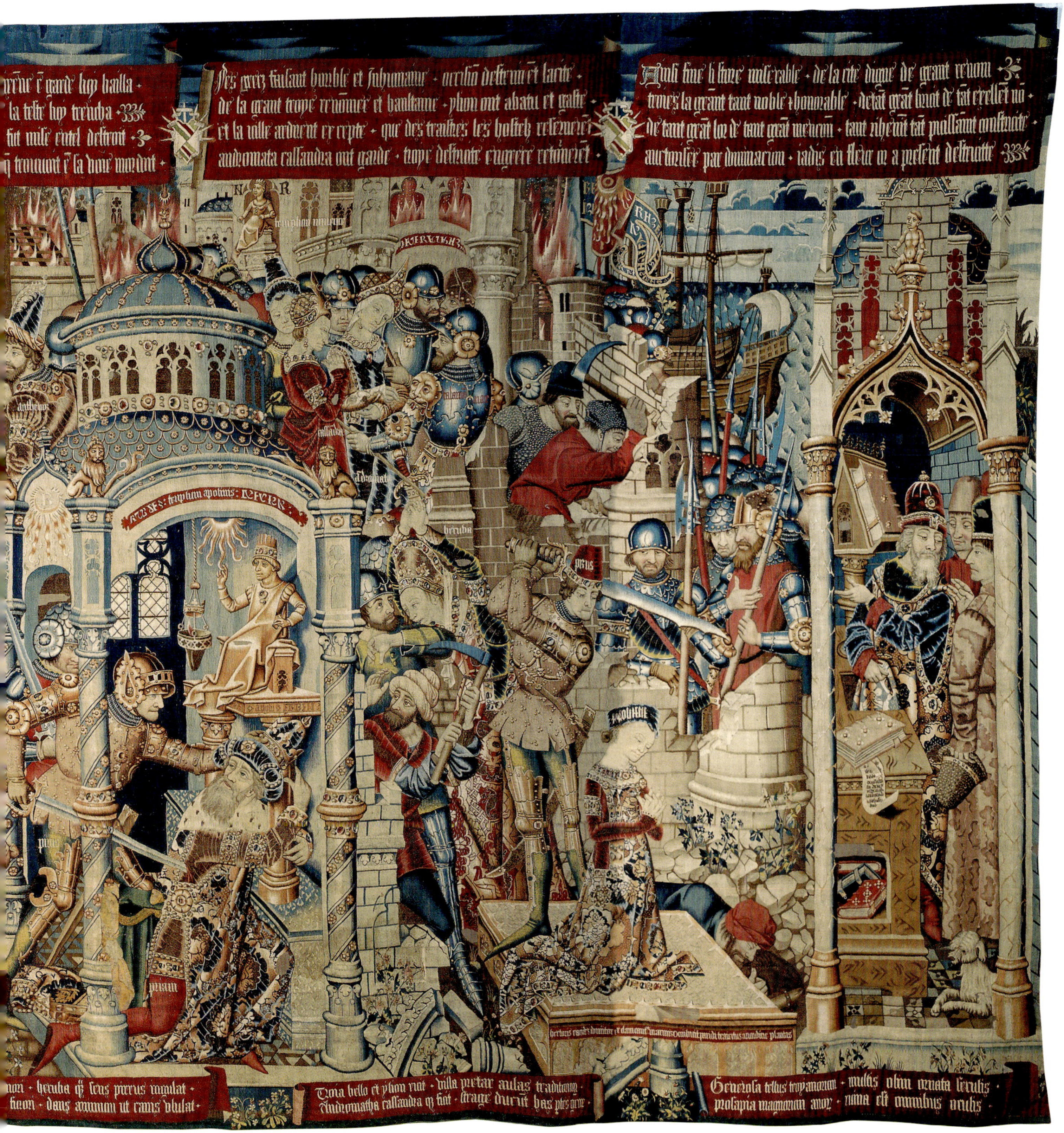

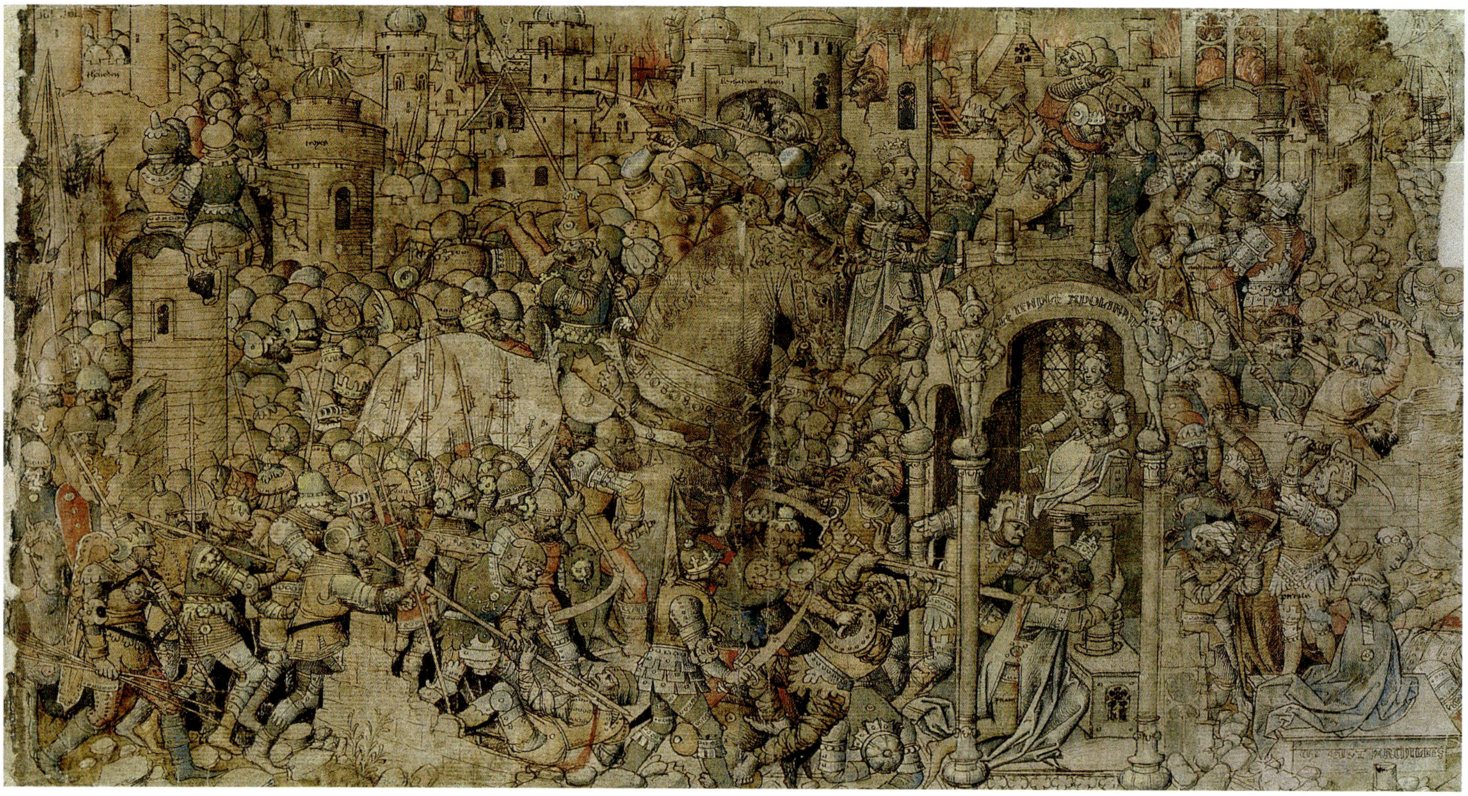

4.4 *The Destruction of Troy* by the Coëtivy Master (or circle), ca. 1465–70. Modello for eleventh tapestry in the *Trojan War* series. Brown ink and colored wash on paper, 31 x 57.5 cm. Musée du Louvre, Paris

Coëtivy Master, an unidentified artist working for the French court between 1461 and 1481, have led to the suggestion that the design may actually have been conceived for a French court patron sometime in the mid-1460s and that this may have been Charles of France, favorite son of Charles VII and brother of Louis XI.[18] Circumstantial support for this proposal comes from the presence of an eleven-piece set of the *Trojan War* in the French royal collection by 1494 and the fact that in 1495–96 Charles VIII paid for changes to the heraldic devices, indicating that it had previously belonged to someone else. A single piece from this set, with Charles's device of the sun woven in the upper section, survives at the Victoria and Albert Museum.[19] In placing an order for a *Trojan War* set with Grenier, Henry may therefore have been acquiring a design that he had first seen at the French court during his exile.

The author of the complex program was dependent on two late-twelfth-century texts, the *Roman de Troie* by Benoît de Sainte-Maure and the *Historia destructionis Troiae* by Guido delle Colonne, which in turn were based on the sixth-century accounts of Dares the Phrygian and Dictys the Cretan, both of whom claimed to be eyewitnesses of the war.[20] The Trojan War had been depicted in tapestry from the late fourteenth century and sets of this subject are recorded in the collections of, among others, Louis of Anjou, Philip the Bold, and, as we have already seen in England, Sir John Beaumont and Richard II. The development of the Grenier series followed a renewed interest in the Trojan legends that developed during the 1450s and 1460s at the French-speaking courts. Philip the Good owned seventeen manuscripts relating to Troy and he commissioned Raoul Le Fèvre to edit a *Recueil des histoires de Troie,* the first two books of which were produced in 1464.[21] This interest may have been stimulated by a renewed focus on the eastern Mediterranean following the fall of Constantinople in 1453.

If the *Trojan War* series did result from a commission from a member of the French court, rather than from an entrepreneurial exercise by Pasquier Grenier, the cartoons were probably executed from the Coëtivy Master's preparatory drawings under the direction of Grenier, because they subsequently remained Grenier's property. This seems to have been standard practice. For example, in 1454, when Giovanni de' Medici was planning to send designs from Florence that were to be made into cartoons in the Low Countries, his agent explained that it was normal for the cartoons to stay in the possession of the merchant unless the patron paid an additional sum.[22] The *Trojan War* cartoons gave Grenier a design that was to enjoy as much popularity as the *Story of Alexander* series had done during the late 1450s and 1460s. Assuming that Charles the Bold's set had been completed by 1472, it seems likely that another speculative set was begun shortly afterward because in 1476 Grenier supplied one to Federigo da Montefeltro, duke of Urbino. Thereafter, the cartoons must have been in constant production during the 1470s and 1480s. Besides the set listed in the French royal collection by 1494, others are recorded in the Hungarian royal collection in 1495, said to have been acquired by King Matthias Corvinus, who died in 1490, and in that of Ludovico Sforza of Milan. Finally, another set is listed in the collection of James IV of Scotland by 1503.[23] On the basis of comparison between the extant duplicate fragments and the documentary evidence, it has been estimated that there may have been as many as nine different weavings of this design series.[24] As noted above, where the tapestries were woven has been debated, but on the grounds that the *Trojan War* tapestries were so large, the sets produced with such speed, and the weaving and materials so consistent, it seems probable that they were produced in a number of sizeable workshops working near the Grenier family's base of operation. Combined with the nature of guild regulations at this time and Grenier's influential role in Tournai, it is logical to assume that these workshops were either in Tournai or in its environs.[25]

In summary, in purchasing a set of the *Trojan War* in 1488, Henry was acquiring one of the most elaborate tapestry series available, developed in response to the taste for classical subject matter then prevalent at the French courts. It hardly needs to be said that the violent scenes of hand-to-hand combat depicted in the tapestries were more familiar to Henry and his nobles than they are to a modern audience. Most of Henry's senior courtiers had served on one or other of the battlefields of the Wars of the Roses, and force of arms continued to be the principal factor in Henry's grip on the throne. The loyalty, bravery, and sacrifice of the classical heroes were therefore values that were of immediate relevance to the new Tudor king as he sought to face down the challenges to his rule fermenting at the Burgundian court of Margaret of York and elsewhere and which had already produced one pretender to the throne, Lambert Simnel, whose supporters were defeated at the Battle of Stoke Field in June 1487.

The *Trojan War* tapestries were very likely just the first of a sequence of commissions that Henry placed with the Greniers. One other major set that he probably acquired in the late 1480s or early 1490s, but for which no documentation is extant, requires special mention. In 1501 a set of tapestries of "Jerusalem" was recorded at Richmond Palace (see below), and the following year a set of the *Siege of Jerusalem* was repaired and relined at the Great Wardrobe.[26] In turn, this set can be identified with a gold-woven, seven-piece set of this subject recorded at Windsor in 1547.[27] Approximately one hundred years later it was one of the sets reserved from the sale of the royal goods for the use of the Protector, and fragments were still at Windsor in the 1670s.[28] Its subsequent fate is unknown. Fortunately, the idiosyncratic title allows us to identify it as a representation of the *Vengeance of Our Lord* legend, which dealt with the punishment of the Jews for the murder of Jesus, as enacted in the siege of Jerusalem by Vespasian and Titus in A.D. 66. Inspired by the *Jewish Antiquities* of Flavius Josephus, especially the apocryphal *Acta Pilati,* this story had been the subject of a twelfth-century verse chronicle and several fifteenth-century dramatizations before it was printed in Paris in 1491. Fragments from at least three tapestry design series survive, created during the second third of the fifteenth century.[29] One of these series, apparently dating

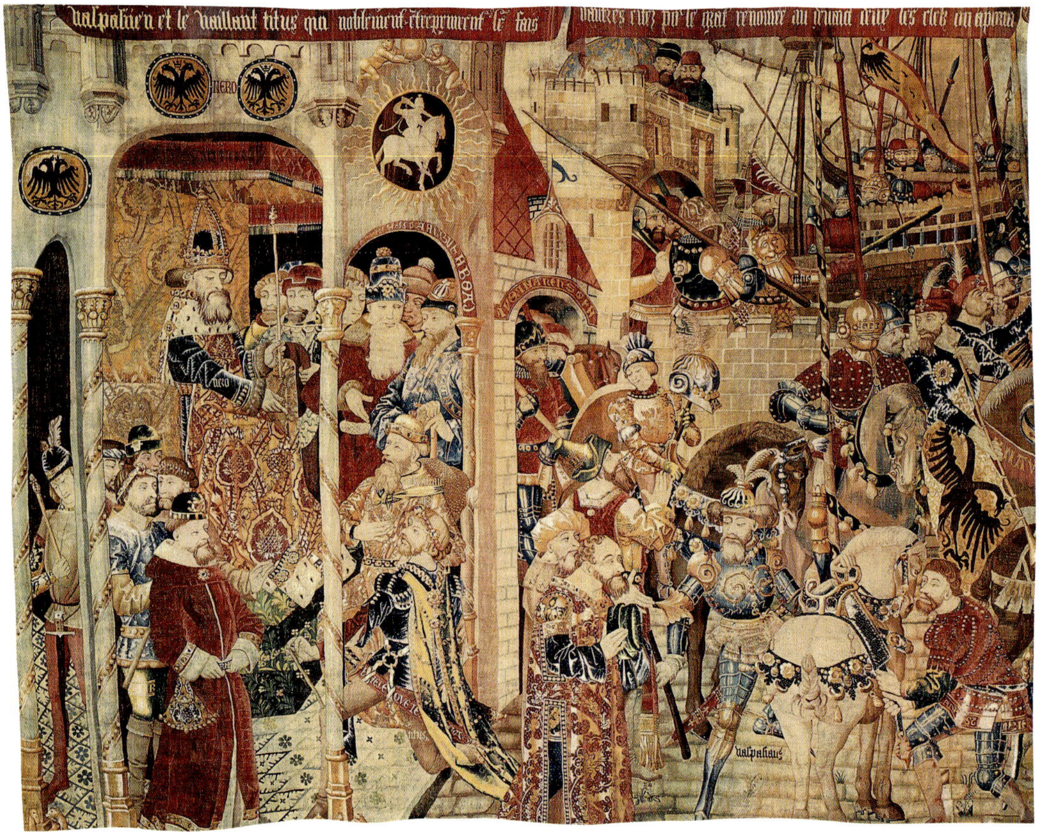

4.5 *Nero Sends Vespasian and Titus to Judaea* (fragment) from a set of the *Vengeance of Our Lord*. Tapestry made in the Southern Netherlands, probably Tournai, ca. 1475–95. Wool and silk, 380 x 470 cm. Musée des Arts Décoratifs, Lyon

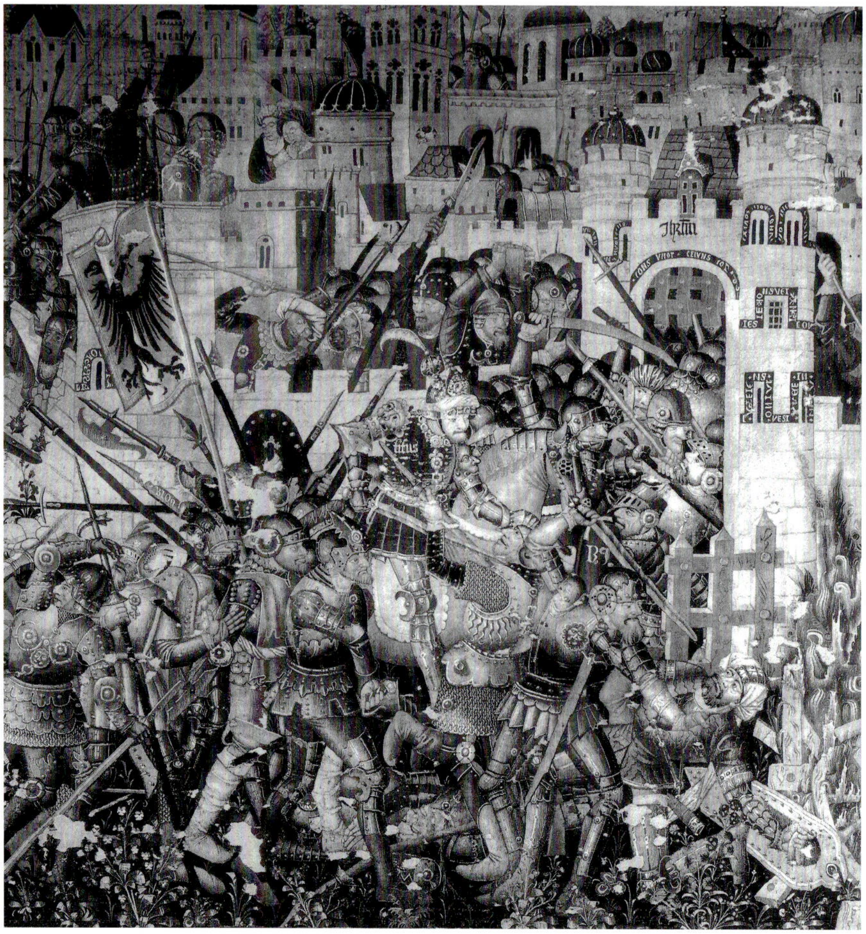

4.6 *The Sack of Jerusalem* (fragment) from a set of the *Vengeance of Our Lord*. Tapestry made in the Southern Netherlands, probably Tournai, ca. 1475–95. Wool and silk, 430 x 380 cm. Museo Nazionale del Bargello, Florence

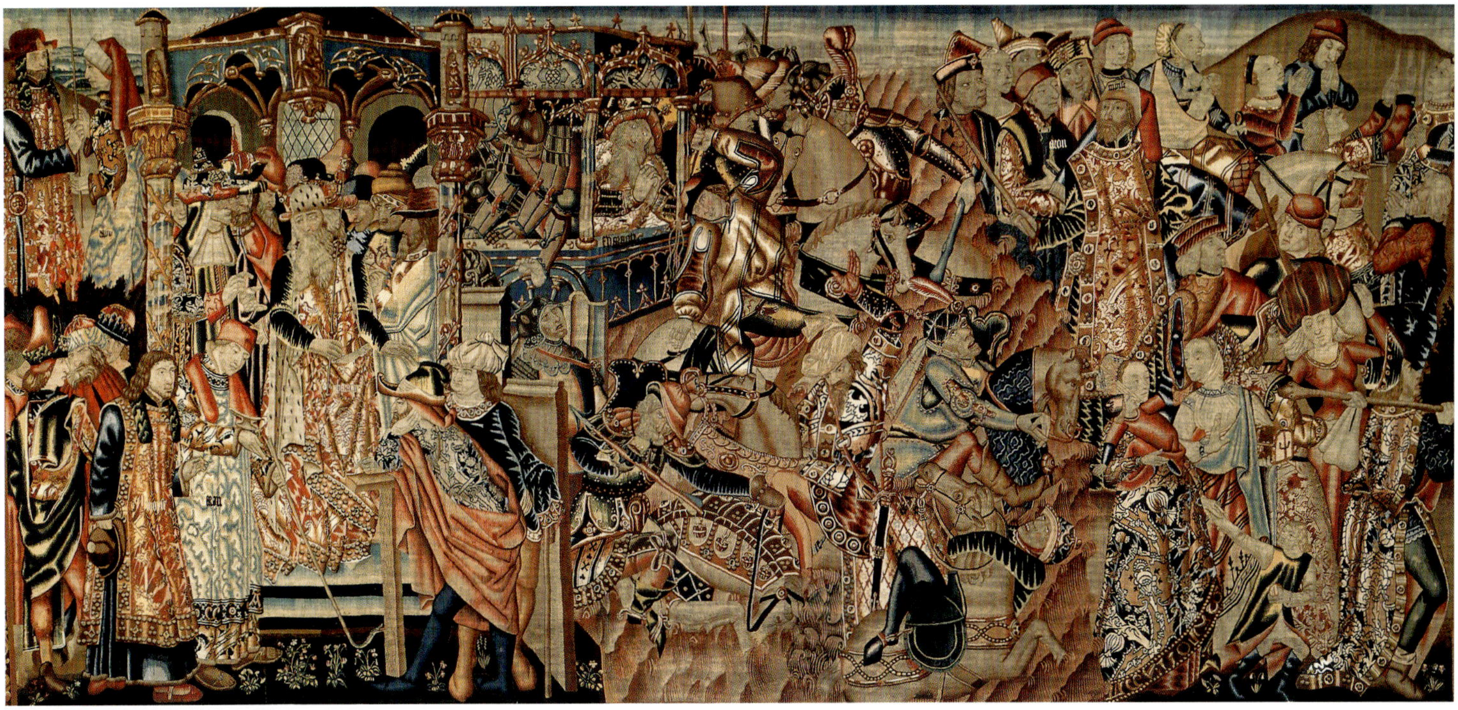

4.7 *The Crossing of the Red Sea* from a set of the *Story of Moses.* Tapestry woven in the Southern Netherlands, ca. 1490–1500. Wool and silk, 408 x 772 cm. Town Hall, Madrid

from the late 1470s, is so close in style to the Grenier *Trojan War* series that it seems likely that the modelli may also have been produced by the workshop of the Coëtivy Master and that the cartoons may have been made in the same cartoon workshop as those of the *Trojan War* series.[30] As such, it is tempting to conjecture that Henry's set may have been a weaving of this design obtained via the Grenier enterprise. Surviving fragments of the series depict Nero sending Vespasian and Titus to Judaea, their arrival in Palestine, the coronation of Vespasian, and the brutal sack of Jerusalem (figs. 4.5, 4.6). Quite apart from any frisson that the *Siege of Jerusalem* may have imparted to the Tudor audience as a clarion call for a modern crusade, the series may have been acquired with a more immediate comparison in mind. Vespasian was revered as the emperor who ended a phase of civil war within the Roman Empire and introduced a period of reform and consolidation. As such, he was an appealing role model for Henry VII, the monarch who had ended the Wars of the Roses.

Although the Grenier enterprise may have been Henry's principal tapestry supplier during the 1480s and early 1490s, it was not his exclusive source. In February 1489, for example, a warrant was issued to pay £40 3s. 6d. to William Horwell, a London merchant, for four pieces of "arras of the Storye of Moyses."[31] A single panel from a *Moses* series that dates from the late fifteenth century has survived in Spain (fig. 4.7).[32] It may well give an idea of the style and appearance of Henry's lost set. As the patriarch, who at God's direction and with his aid, led the chosen people out of Israel, confounded the army of the pharaoh, and delivered the Ten Commandments, Moses was obviously a resonant model for Henry. As such, this purchase suggests that like Edward before him, Henry may have employed tapestries depicting Old Testament patriarchs to emphasize his consecrated role as God's chosen ruler. Circumstantial evidence that he purchased other sets depicting biblical heroes comes from the mention of a gold-woven set of the *Story of Joshua* at Sheen Palace eight years later (see below). And in 1500, a set of "riche clothe of arras" of the *Story of Esther and Ahasuerus* was among the textiles provided from the English royal wardrobe for the meeting between Henry VII and Philip the Handsome at Calais. This set can be identified with a five-piece "arras" set recorded at Windsor Castle in the 1547 inventory.[33] The dimensions of the Windsor set

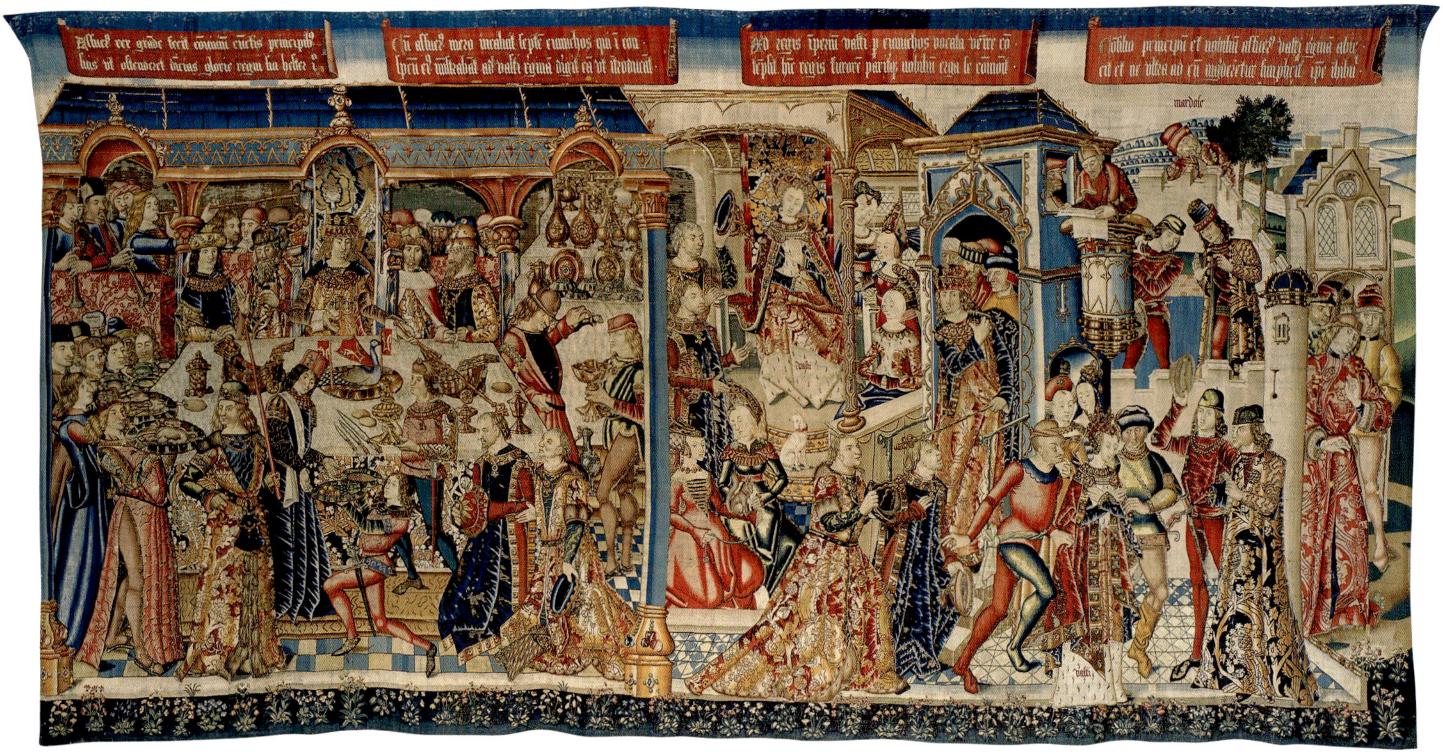

4.8 *Episodes from the Story of Esther* from a set of the *Story of Esther*. Tapestry woven in the Southern Netherlands, probably Tournai, ca. 1480–1500. Wool and silk, 430 x 770 cm. Cathedral Museum of La Seo, Saragossa

suggest that it may have been woven from the same cartoons as three large panels of this subject that survive at the La Seo Cathedral in Saragossa (figs. 4.8, 5.3) whose design can be dated around 1490 on stylistic grounds.[34] Although the composition is less crowded than that of the *Trojan War* series, the quality of material and weave are similar to that of extant fragments of that series, and it is quite possible that production of the *Esther* series was also controlled by Pasquier Grenier. The protagonists are represented in modish contemporary costumes, and little effort is made to suggest the antique character of the narrative. Rather, the story is represented in terms of late-fifteenth-century court etiquette and splendor. The attraction of Ahasuerus and Esther as models of wisdom, justice, and virtue for Henry VII and his queen, Elizabeth of York, is readily evident.

Other than these examples, the documentary evidence relating to purchases for the early years of Henry VII's reign is partial. The only other known acquisition before the late 1490s is that of July 4, 1494, when a George Ardeson, merchant of Genoa, was paid £90 for "certain stuf and countrefait arraies of hym bought."[35]

Tapestry Provisions for Richmond Palace and the Marriage of Prince Arthur

Where written records are patchy regarding the early years of Henry's reign, documentation is more complete for the years between 1498 and 1502, and a significant number of tapestry purchases are listed. This spending spree was probably initiated in response to the fire that devastated Sheen Palace at Christmas 1497. Besides the damage caused to the buildings, the *Chronicle of London* states, "much more harm [was] done upon Costryngis & hangyng beddis of cloth of gold & silk & much othir Rich apparayll wyth plate & other manyfold Joyallis."[36] That these losses included tapestries is evidenced by a reference in the 1547 Tower inventory to an "arras" tapestry of *Joshua* that was "saved at Shene where the residue were brent."[37] To replace Sheen, Henry immediately began work on a new palace that was christened Richmond. Using the original stone donjon of Sheen as the new palace's core, construction proceeded rapidly, and the *Chronicle of London* states that it was almost complete by January of 1501 (fig. 4.9).[38] According to a description of the castle written in that year, the chapel

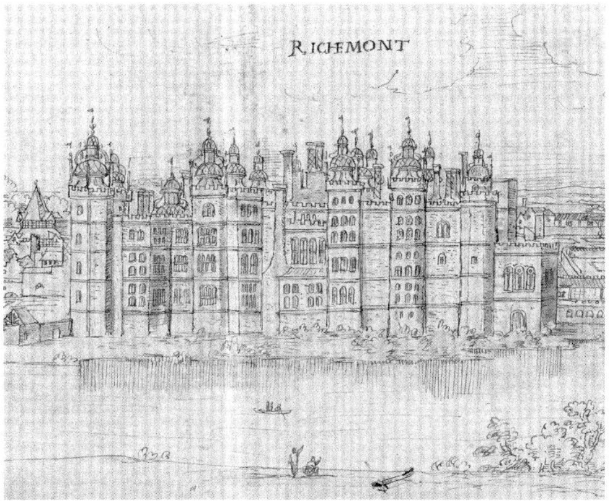

4.9 *Richmond Palace from across the Thames* (detail) by A. van den Wyngaerde, ca. 1558–62. Pen and brown ink and watercolor over black chalk, 20.1 x 89.7 cm. Ashmolean Museum, Oxford

was hung with "arras" tapestry, as were the king's chambers: "the first, the secunde, the thirde enhaugyd all thre with riche and costely clothes of Arras."[39]

Many of the tapestry purchases made during the late 1490s must have been related to the provisions for this new palace. On May 15, 1498, a sum of £122 4s. 4d. was disbursed to an unidentified Flemish merchant as partial payment of £245 6s. 8d. for ninety-two ells of "arras" (fifty-two square yards).[40] The high price of 53s. 4d. per ell suggests that this was an especially fine and rich weaving. That the new furnishing also included more mundane weavings is reflected by a warrant issued one month later on June 13 to reimburse "Jossendus de Marinie," merchant of Genoa, for the customs he had been charged on seven counterpoints of "arras" comprising 140 ells (seventy-nine square yards) with a value of £5 16s. 8d.[41] Another large payment was made to the Grenier enterprise. Pasquier had died in 1493, but his sons maintained the business for the next two decades, and on May 31, 1499, Antony Grenier received the substantial payment of £405 3s. for "divers peces of hangings."[42] Three months later, on August 20, a payment of £73 6s. 8d. was issued to a "merchaunt of fraunce . . . the third partt [installment] upon his bills for tappestry."[43] The other tapestry merchants with whom Henry was involved at this date were either Italian or Flemish, so it seems likely that the August payment was also to the Greniers, Tournai then being in French territory.

Although Henry continued to source large tapestries from the Grenier enterprise during 1498–99, he also started to purchase tapestries from a Brussels merchant called Pieter d'Enghien van Aelst (or Pieter van Edinghen), known as Van Aelst. The appearance of Van Aelst at this time is an indication of changes in the Netherlandish tapestry industry. Where the economies of Arras and Tournai were profoundly affected by the French invasion of 1477—indeed, this event more or less ended production in Arras—Brussels had benefited from its uninterrupted role as the administrative capital of the Burgundian Netherlands, and during the late fifteenth century its tapestry industry expanded and prospered.[44] Van Aelst was the leading merchant of this flourishing industry from the late 1490s, and he was to maintain this preeminence for the first three decades of the sixteenth century, consecutively supplier of tapestries to the Burgundian dukes, the Habsburg court, and the papal court, as well as to the Crown and other important patrons.[45] Born at Waterloos near Aalst in about 1450, he became a freeman of Brussels in 1493, a distinction that would have given him the right to sell tapestries in the town. Perhaps benefiting from Pasquier Grenier's recent death, he developed a relationship with the young duke, Philip the Handsome, and his wife, Joanna of Castile, akin to that which Grenier had enjoyed with Philip's grandfather. The earliest documentation of his activity is provided by a sale in 1497 to Philip of two chambers of verdures, one with *Shepherds and Shepherdesses,* the other with *Woodcutters.* Subsequently, in July 1502, Van Aelst was appointed as Philip's "valet de chambre et tapissier du roy," and he traveled to Spain with Philip in both 1502 and 1506, selling him several sets of tapestry before the second trip and subsequently lending him 22,000 guilders. When Philip died on September 25, 1506, Van Aelst was instrumental in resolving the dispute that developed between Philip's Spanish and Burgundian courtiers for the control of his moveable possessions, a task that took him two years, including a spell in prison because of his loyalty to the Burgundian faction,

4.10 *Arthur, Prince of Wales* by an unidentified artist, ca. 1500. Oil on panel, 39.1 x 28 cm. The Royal Collection

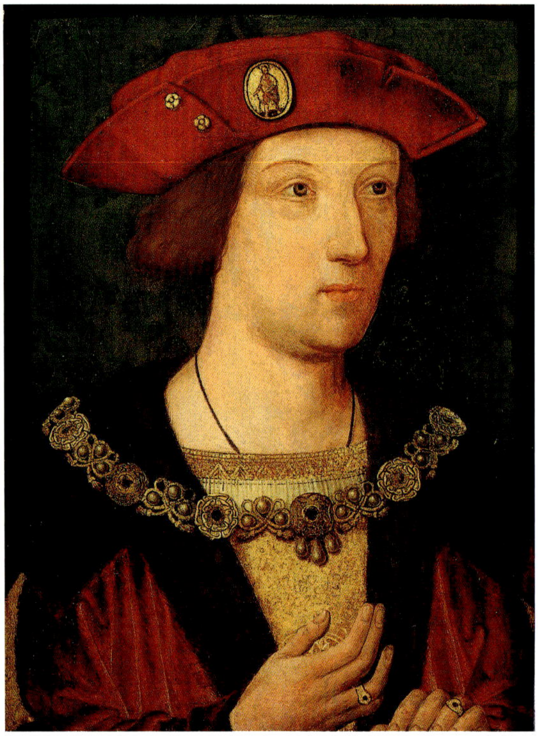

and that involved an advance of 3,285 Flemish pounds for which he was eventually repaid in 1509. Like Bataille and Grenier before him, Van Aelst was evidently a man of substantial means. In contrast, however, he appears to have held a controlling interest in a sizeable workshop. That he certainly played a key role in commissioning new cartoons is suggested by the inscription of his name in various designs.[46] Van Aelst first appears in the English royal Treasurer's accounts in April and May 1498, when he received a sequence of payments for two sets of tapestry, of which one was especially large, comprising some 332 square yards, a set of verdure hangings, and a number of counterpoint tapestries.[47] These sets were valued at between 3 and 5 shillings per ell, indicating that they were woven with wool and silk, but not gold thread. The subjects and intended locations are uncertain, but those made in 1498 probably related to the furnishing of Richmond.

A further stimulus to Henry's patronage at this time were the preparations associated with the impending marriage of Prince Arthur (fig. 4.10) to Katherine of Aragon, youngest daughter of the Spanish king and queen, Ferdinand of Aragon and Isabella of Castile. This had been agreed by treaty in July 1497, was celebrated by proxy in May 1499, and finally took place in November 1501. Before this, Henry must have commissioned a particularly expensive set or sets of tapestry, because in November 1500 Van Aelst received a payment of £791 8s. 1d., of which £600 was "lent him by the king's grace."[48] Whether this was literally a loan or an advance against tapestry costs is uncertain. The following June another recognizance for £274 11s. 3d. was drawn up between the king on one part and Van Aelst, Ludovica de la Fava, and Lorenzo Barduce, merchants of Florence, whereby Van Aelst undertook to fulfill all the articles in a "pair of indentures" made between him and Sir Charles Somerset for the bringing and delivering of certain pieces of "arras" and tapestry for the king's use.[49] Somerset was Henry's lord chamberlain and thus the man responsible for overseeing all aspects of the operation and staging of the "domus magnificie," the household above stairs, as opposed to the "domus providencie," the below-stairs operations, which fell under the jurisdiction of the lord steward. The transactions suggest that Van Aelst was receiving enormous advances for valuable tapestries that were being woven to order. The possibility that these included tapestries celebrating the Tudor accession and dynasty will be discussed shortly.[50] The relationships between Van Aelst and his Florentine sponsors were typical of those he used throughout his career in order to fund the projects for which he was to become famous, but such arrangements were not trouble-free. In 1509 the exorbitant demands placed on him by a partnership with the Frescobaldi led Van Aelst to appeal to Archduke Charles for the nomination of an independent arbitrator to settle their differences.[51]

Also in June 1501, a payment of £12 5s. 7d. is recorded to a certain John Atkinson for "pet Engham"—that is, Van Aelst—along with another payment of £20 to the same for "certain stuff."[52] Eight months later, a warrant was issued on February 7, 1502, to the customs officers at Sandwich to waive customs on "oon

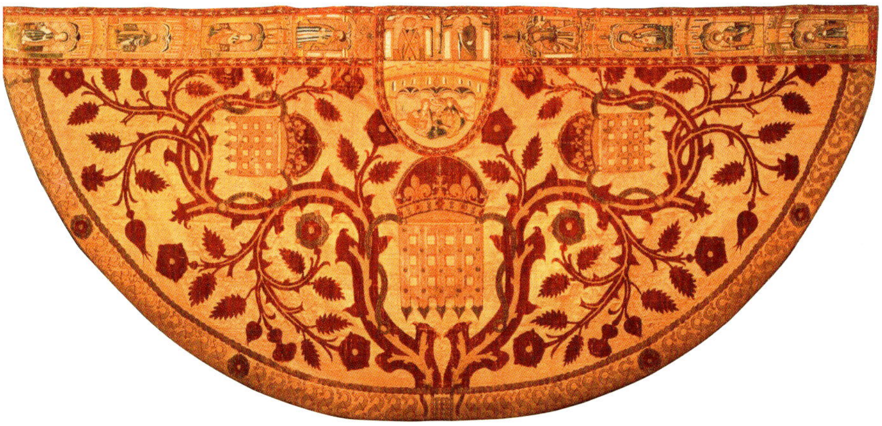

4.11 Cope with Tudor devices (detail) by an unidentified English workshop (?) from Italian materials, ca. 1485–1509. Ground: cloth of gold with pattern in cut and uncut velvet on voided silver-gilt ground with additional gilt metallic loops; orphrey: linen embroidered in silks and gilt-metal-wrapped threads; 148.5 x 314.9 cm. Stonyhurst College, Lancashire

4.12 Tapestry with the English Royal Arms. Woven in the Southern Netherlands or England, ca. 1500–1520. Wool and silk; 102 x 208 cm. Hever Castle, Kent

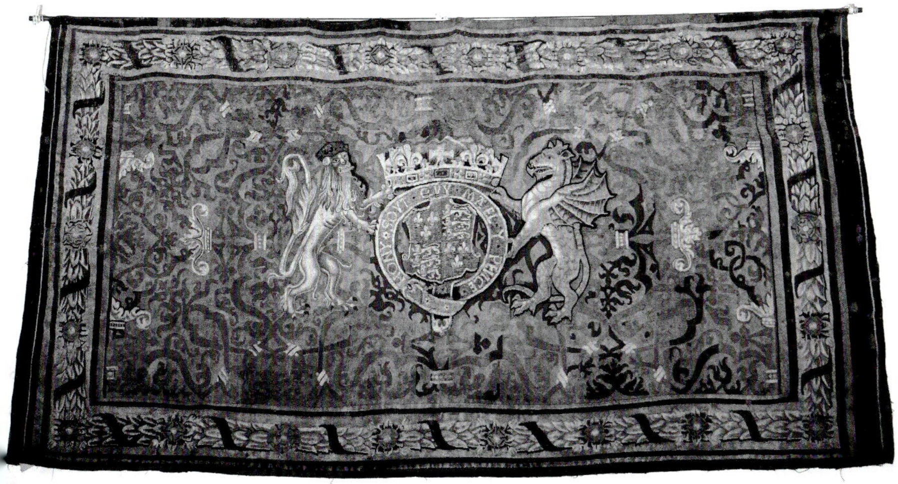

pece of arras of tholde lawe and newe and nyne bordoures of the same wrought with fyne golde broughte from the parties of beyonde the see by Peter Enghem arras maker of Bruxelles." The fee of £16 13d. due on these tapestries was to be paid to the customs officers from the Exchequer.[53] The size of the fee suggests that the ensemble involved was very large. Its identity will be discussed below (pp. 85–87). These are the last payments to Van Aelst for which documents have survived, but in all likelihood he continued to supply tapestries to Henry VII throughout his reign. In passing, it is to be noted that Van Aelst's involvement with the English court at such an early date in his career suggests that English royal patronage as much as any other helped establish the success of his business.

Circumstantial evidence that the king continued to obtain tapestries as opportunity arose is provided by a record of 1507 relating to the purchase of secondhand tapestries from the executors of Thomas Savage, archbishop of York, for £232 20d. The transaction included "all the arras, as well as the fyne arras as counterfait arras, with silloures, testours, and counterpoyntes of arras."[54]

Tapestry Commissions with Tudor Imagery

The foregoing evidence reflects a considerable volume of tapestry purchases by Henry VII during the late 1490s and early 1500s with some of the finest sets purchased for Richmond Palace and others for the marriage of Prince Arthur and Katherine of Aragon. The documents impart little information of the subjects and appearance of these tapestries, but various identifications can be made on the basis of surviving tapestries, contemporary descriptions, and later inventories. Taken as a whole, these sources provide insight into how Henry VII sought to use tapestry as a tool of suggestion. They also indicate how the style of design evolved during Henry's reign and the artistic contribution that the tapestry collection made to the early Tudor court.

Among the tapestries that can be linked to Henry VII by means other than written sources, the most obvious are those with heraldic and armorial devices. As modern studies have revealed, Henry applied his coat of arms and heraldic devices widely in the architectural moldings, painted decorations, and stained glass incorporated in his palaces.[55] Such devices also figured prominently in the embroidered and woven textiles supplied to him, such as the sumptuous cloth-of-gold vestments that were made for him in Italy sometime in the early 1500s and of which several pieces have survived at Stonyhurst College (fig. 4.11).[56] In the same spirit, and like Edward before him, he commissioned sets of tapestries that also incorporated his armorials and heraldic devices. A number of these are extant. The simplest and coarsest is represented by a small panel, now at Hever Castle (fig. 4.12). Probably dating from about 1500, it depicts the English royal arms within the Order of the Garter, surmounted by a crown and supported by a lion and a dragon, on a faux damask ground, framed by a leaf and ribbon border interspersed with Tudor roses. The small size suggests that it was intended to hang above a chimney, as part of a larger en suite chamber of heraldic hangings. A second type of armorial, represented by a single tapestry now at Haddon Hall, depicts the royal arms framed by the Order of the Garter on a millefleur ground, with the arms repeated in the four corners (fig. 4.13). This piece is dated to the 1490s or early 1500s on stylistic grounds.[57] It is conceivable that it may be related to a set of tapestries and counterpoints of verdure with "our arms" that were lined by the royal tailors in 1503 (see below).[58]

4.13 Millefleurs with the English Royal Arms. Tapestry woven in the Southern Netherlands, ca. 1485–1509. Wool and silk, 391 x 266 cm. Haddon Hall, Derbyshire

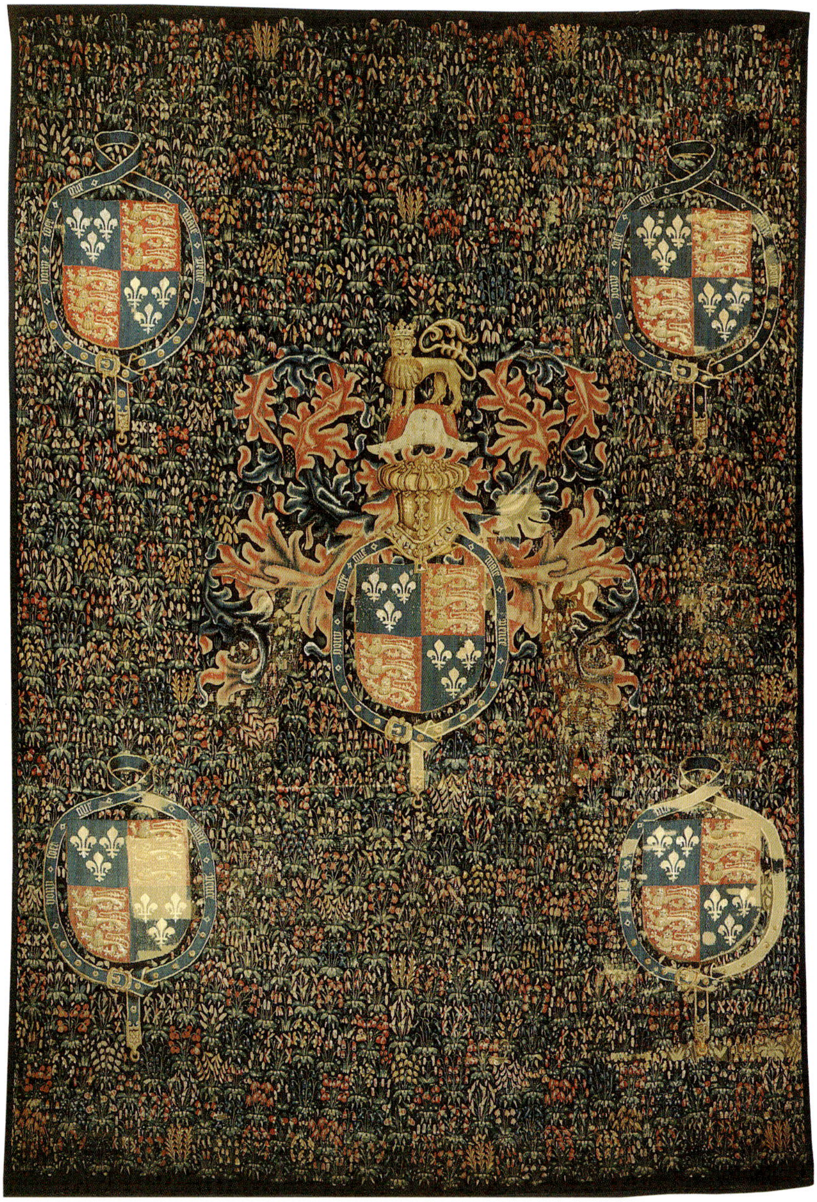

A third group of armorial fragments, now at Winchester College, is more intriguing from an iconographic point of view (fig. 4.14).[59] The ground imitates the effect of stripes of red and blue Italian damask with a repeating vase and pomegranate pattern. Superimposed on this ground are motifs of the sacred monogram "IHS," red and white Tudor roses, and a heraldic shield bearing three crowns of gold on a blue ground, one above another. This shield has been variously interpreted as that of King Arthur, of the ancient kings of England, and of Belinus, a legendary king of Britain, from whom the Tudors also claimed descent.[60] Given the fact that this series was probably commissioned to celebrate the birth of Prince Arthur, it seems most likely that the device is here intended to evoke his namesake, King Arthur, rather than a narrower identification with Belimawr or Belinus. Another of the fragments, presumably the focal point of the larger piece from which it came, represents the Lamb of God lying on a red Lancastrian rose. Although later restoration and reconstruction have obscured the original arrangement of the motifs, the basic concept must have been to celebrate the union of the houses of York and Lancaster in the person of Prince Arthur, successor to his legendary namesake and the ancient kings of England, under the divine sanction of Christ the Redeemer (fig. 4.15). The fragments probably come from one large tapestry that was part of a set commissioned for Arthur sometime during the late 1490s. No comparable group is identifiable in the 1547 inventory, but the collection of Henry's mother, Lady Margaret Beaufort, included ten pieces of "verdors with Jhs the redde rose and the white."[61] We can conjecture that following the death of Prince Arthur in 1502, this set passed into his grandmother's possession, and it was among the goods sold following her death. Margaret Beaufort's collection included three other sets decorated with Tudor roses and portcullises that were also likely to have been purchased by Henry, rather than Margaret herself. Taken as a

4.14 *The Sacred Monogram, Tudor Devices, and the Arms of Arthur, Legendary King of Britain* (two fragments). Tapestry woven in the Southern Netherlands, ca. 1500. Wool and silk, the larger, 258 x 155 cm; the smaller, 50.5 x 48 cm. Winchester College, Winchester

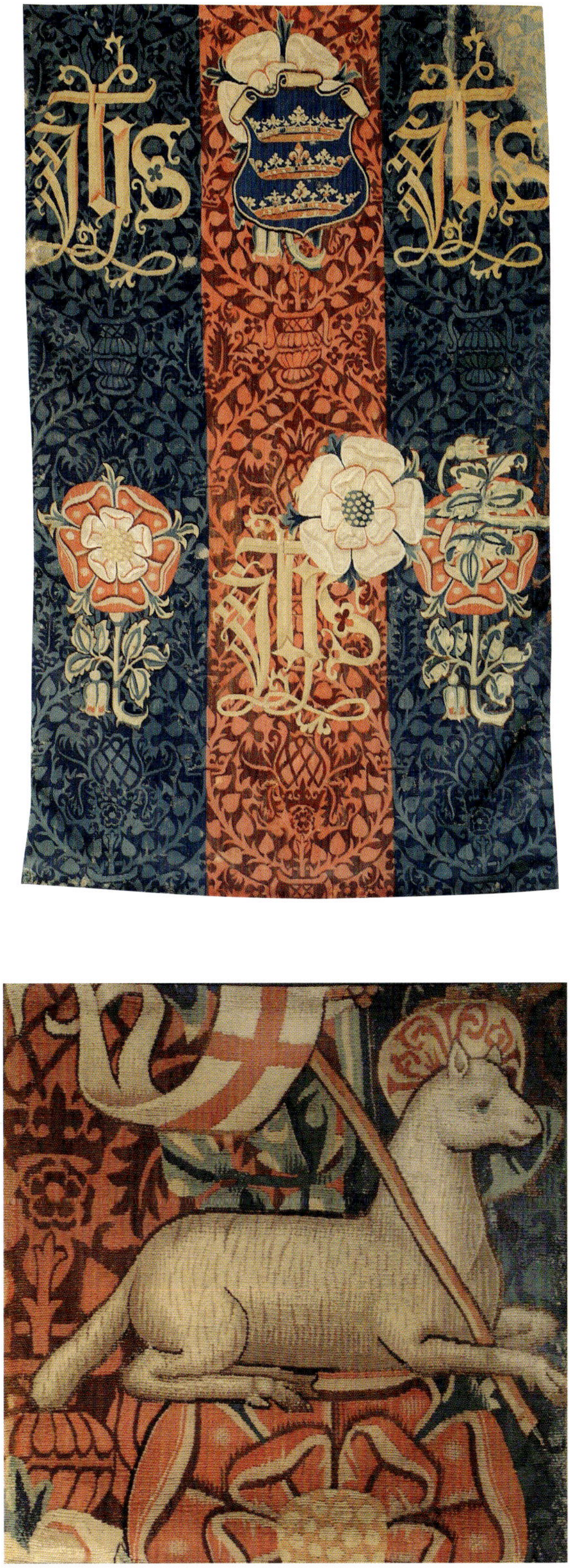

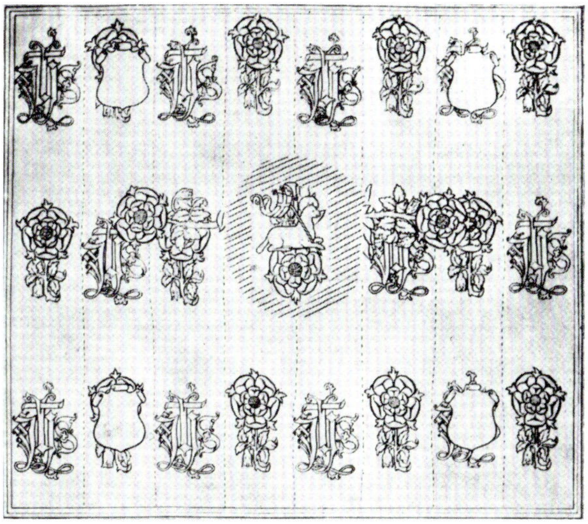

4.15 Reconstruction of Winchester armorials from W. G. Thomson, *History of Tapestry from the Earliest Times to the Present Day* (1906)

whole, these fragmentary survivals provide an indication of the type of heraldic tapestries used daily by Henry's court.

Thus far, Henry's patronage differs little from that of many of his predecessors and Continental peers, but there is also evidence that he placed commissions with subjects that incorporated a more overt celebration of the Tudor accession. The 1547 Hampton Court inventory included two tapestries described as follows: "one pece of Arras of the Comyng into Englonde of king henry vijth takinge with thone hande the crowne from king Richard the thurde usurper of the same, & with thother hand holding a roose crowned, lined with blewe buckeram given by the Mr of thorse"; and "one pece of Arras of the mariage of a kinge & a Quene lyned with blewe buckeram by the Mr of the horse Sir Anthonie browne."[62] Both remained in the royal collection until the sale of royal possessions held by the Commonwealth government between 1649 and 1654, when they were sold for £58 10s. and £54, respectively. At this time the second piece was described, perhaps incorrectly, as "ye Marrage of Prince Arthurr & ye Ladye. Katherine."[63] According to the dimensions provided by one of the Commonwealth sale inventories, these panels measured, respectively, thirty-nine and thirty-six square yards.[64] Assuming a height of about four and a half yards, we can conjecture that each would have been approximately eight yards in length.

No evidence survives of the date or place of origin of these tapestries, and the fact that they were stated to have been "given" by Sir Anthony Brown, master of the horse, is perplexing. Brown was appointed to this position only in 1539, and though it could be argued that he had commissioned the pair as a gift to Henry VIII, the subjects would hardly have been appropriate at this date. The most logical explanation is that they were Crown pieces that had passed to Brown or his father as a perquisite and that he then returned them to the king at a later date, much as a number of royal tapestries passed from the royal collection to Cardinal Wolsey and Thomas Cromwell and then back again. Although it could be suggested that the marriage scene may have been commissioned by Henry VIII in the late 1520s as part of his campaign to advertise the invalidity of his marriage to Katherine, the fact that it was associated with a panel of Henry VII defeating Richard III weakens that argument. On balance, it seems much more probable that the two panels were commissioned by Henry VII, and it is tempting to speculate that they were the subject of the "pair of indentures" between Van Aelst and Sir Charles Somerset in June 1501. If that was the case, it is possible that the marriage tapestry actually celebrated the union of Henry Tudor and Elizabeth of York, as it seems unlikely that an image of Arthur's wedding would have been commissioned in advance of the event. Considering how soon Arthur died after his wedding, it also seems unlikely that an image of his wedding would ever have been completed. Given the dynastic import of Henry's marriage to Elizabeth and the closure this brought to the Wars of the Roses, Henry's marriage was certainly the more significant subject. The subsequent fate of the dynastic tapestries is unknown, but the marriage tapestry, or a fragment of it, is probably to be identified with a panel that was sold from the royal collection during the Commonwealth sale and subsequently listed in the 1661 inventory of Cardinal Mazarin's goods.[65] If we are to visualize the lost dynastic tapestries, we should perhaps envisage a combination of the dynastic portrait of Henry VII's family and Saint George now at Hampton Court (fig. 4.16) and the high-quality tapestries that Van Aelst delivered to the Spanish crown during the opening years of the sixteenth century.[66]

In conjunction with the Winchester armorial fragments, the two dynastic pieces provide evidence of an innovative approach by Henry to the tapestry medium to celebrate the Tudor dynasty. It is conceivable that some of the other sets listed in the 1547 inventory may also have been purchased by Henry VII because of their relevance to dynastic claims that were made for the Tudor house. One would particularly like to know more about the *Story of Arthur* set listed at The More in 1547. In view of Henry's evident intention to invest the Tudor dynasty with associations of the Arthurian court via the choice of his oldest son's name, it is tempting to think that this set may have been commissioned as a celebration of his son's namesake. Unfortunately, nothing more is known of that ensemble.

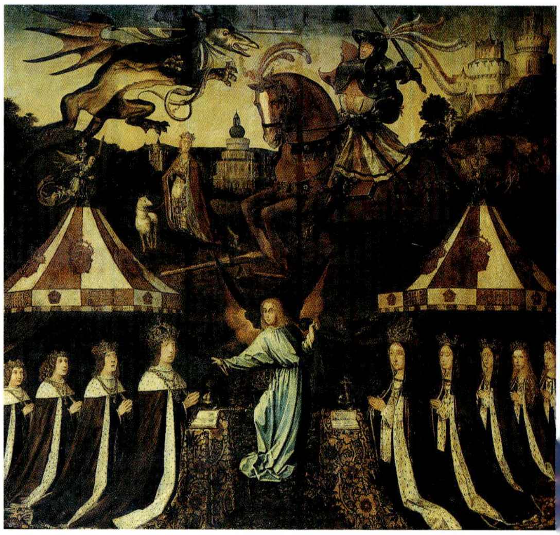

4.16 *The Family of Henry VII with Saint George and the Dragon* by an unidentified Netherlandish artist, ca. 1505–9. Oil on panel, 142.2 x 146.1 cm. The Royal Collection

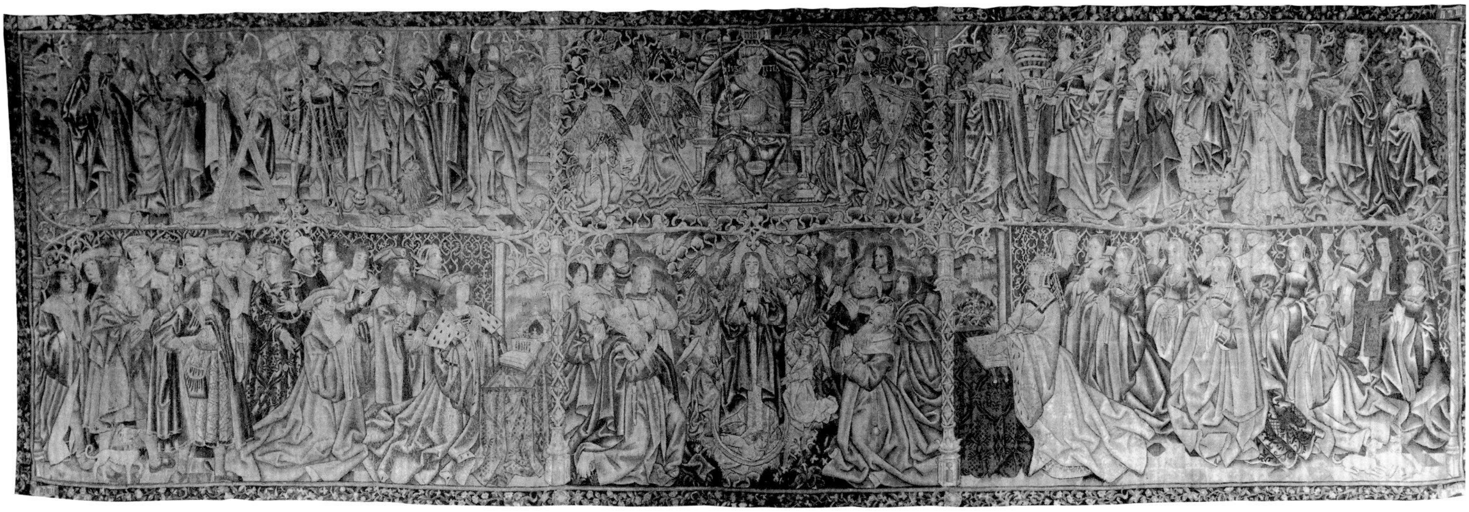

4.17 *The Glorification of the Virgin with Attendant Saints and the Family and Court of Henry VI.* Tapestry woven in the Southern Netherlands, ca. 1490–1500. Wool, 305 x 914 cm. Saint Mary's Hall, Coventry

In this context, it is to be noted that a large tapestry depicting Henry VI, his wife, Margaret, their children, and senior courtiers, has survived at Saint Mary's Hall in Coventry (fig. 4.17).[67] The male and female figures are arranged in supplication on either side of an image of the Ascension of the Virgin. Originally, the Ascension was probably crowned by an image of Christ in Glory but this has been replaced at some unknown date with a figure of Justice. The tapestry is relatively coarse and can be dated to ca. 1500 on stylistic grounds. It fits exactly in the space at the dais end of Saint Mary's Hall and appears to have been made for this location. In the absence of any evidence that this panel was a gift from Henry VII, it has been suggested that the tapestry was commissioned by the town of Coventry during the late 1490s. As mentioned above, Henry VI's court had been located at Coventry between 1456 and 1459, and the town had received many benefits from his reign.[68] Civic gratitude may have been stimulated by the cult of Henry VI, which was encouraged during Henry VII's reign. At Henry VII's request, Pope Alexander VI had established a commission in 1494 to investigate Henry VI's suitability for canonization, which resulted in a tract detailing the 174 "wonders" attributed to this saintly forebear of the Tudor dynasty. Henry VII intended to transfer the body from Windsor to Westminster Abbey and built an elaborate chapel for that purpose, but the translation never took place. By 1500, the cult of Henry VI was rivaling that of Thomas à Becket, and it was probably against this background that the Coventry tapestry was commissioned.[69]

The Rise of Brussels and the Pre-Renaissance Style

In addition to the aforementioned heraldic and dynastic tapestries, Henry VII was responsible for acquiring significant numbers of figurative and verdure tapestries. His reign coincided with a period of marked development in the style and refinement of high-quality tapestry production in the Southern Netherlands, particularly in Brussels, and Van Aelst seems to have played a pivotal role in this process. Indeed, if Van Aelst enjoyed a privileged role in relation to the Burgundian and English courts at the turn of the century, this must, in part, have been because of the quality of the cartoons at his disposal and the skill of the weavers working for him.

The origin of these stylistic and technical developments lay in the 1470s. With the presence of artists like Rogier van der Weyden (d. 1464), Vranke van der Stockt (c. 1420–c. 1495), and Colijn de Coter (c. 1446–1538), the Brussels tapestry workshops had access to skilled painters, or artists in their circles, from the second third of the fifteenth century. The role of Brussels artists in local production gained special significance from the late 1470s

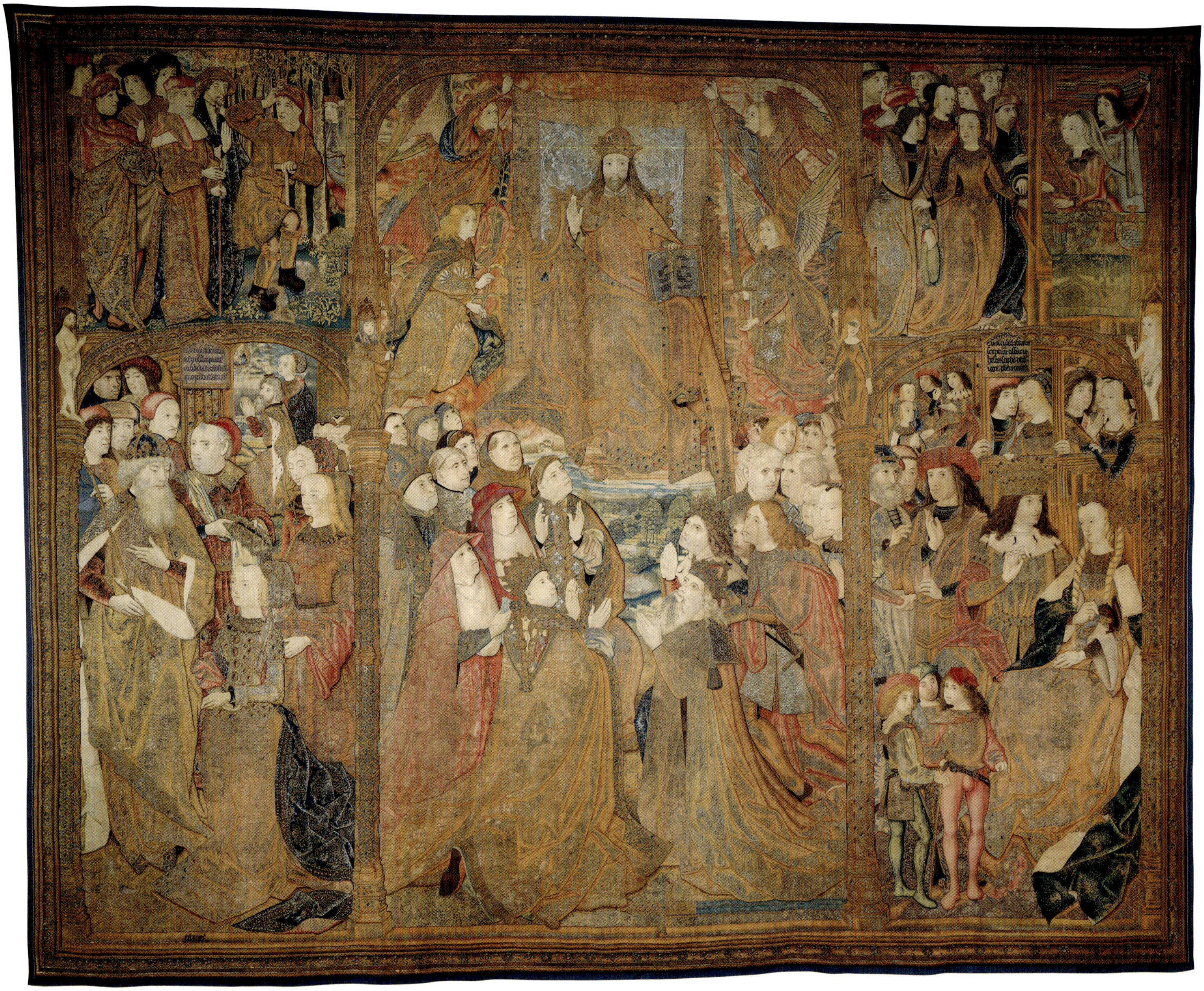

4.18 *The Glorification of Christ.* Tapestry woven in the Southern Netherlands, probably Brussels, ca. 1500. Wool, silk, and gilt-metal-wrapped thread, 343 x 416 cm. National Gallery of Art, Washington

because of a conflict that had developed between the painters' guild and the tapestry guild regarding who had the right to make tapestry cartoons. According to the agreement that was established between the two guilds in 1476, the weavers were allowed to add only flowers, shrubs, birds, and animals to verdure designs. Furthermore, they were allowed only to adapt existing cartoons with charcoal, crayon, and ink, which presumably meant they could color only in black, white, and red. Taken as a whole, the implication of this agreement was that any other work was the domain of the painters, who thereby effectively gained a monopoly over the drawing of all new figurative designs.[70] This arrangement had a twofold impact on the tapestry industry. First, it guaranteed the pictorial quality of Brussels tapestry design by ensuring that the tapestries were woven from good cartoons. Second, it stimulated a considerable development in the technical quality of Brussels weaving as the workshops refined their techniques in order to reproduce the illusionistic effects created by artists who were used to the tonal potential of oil paint. From the 1470s surviving tapestries, particularly smaller, high-quality panels, reflect a new attention to the reproduction of tactile and visual values such as the textures of skin, hair, damask silk, velvet pile and fur, the play of light on water, the mottled effect of marbling, and the appearance of flames and smoke. Carefully re-created through the use of a broader spectrum of colors, woven in finer and finer "hachures," the small triangles of interlocking color by which volume is suggested, and exploiting the different visual properties of wool, silk, and metallic thread, these effects appear with increasing refinement between about 1480 and 1500 in tapestries whose probable origin was Brussels.

Although a small number of tapestries made in the 1480s and 1490s went so far as to imitate the appearance of contemporary oil paintings, the aerial and spatial effects that could be achieved with relative ease in oil paint were time-consuming and difficult to effect in tapestry. In tandem with this technical development, the tapestry cartoonists therefore developed an array of devices that allowed them to concentrate such illusionistic passages at the focal point of compositions that were largely made up of more two-dimensional decoration and pattern. From the mid-1490s, Brussels designs typically become crowded with richly clad figures arranged close to the picture plane, framed by elaborately ornamented architecture or millefleur grounds. The formula of illusionistic focal points and decorative grounds was to dominate high-quality production for the next twenty years and is often generically described as the "pre-Renaissance" style. These developments are typified by the tapestries that Van Aelst provided to Philip the Handsome and Joanna of Castile between 1502 and 1506, such as the *Devotion of the Virgin* and the *Mass of Saint Gregory* panel, which survive in the Spanish royal collection.[71]

Although all but one of Van Aelst's deliveries to Henry is unidentified, it is reasonable to suppose that they might have included tapestries of this style. One possible identification is a panel known as the *Glorification of Christ,* now in the National Gallery of Art in Washington (fig. 4.18 and detail opposite p. 89).[72] Conceived as a trompe-l'oeil retable, this includes a central image of Christ in Glory, flanked by secondary scenes from the Old Testament, within an elaborately decorated Gothic frame. The faces of the figures and certain tactile effects are reproduced with extraordinary skill, but little attempt is made to represent space or movement. Instead, the emphasis is on visual complexity and decoration, from the jewels on the pilasters to the rich patterns and complex folds of the clothes and gowns. A tentative link between this panel and Henry VII's collection can be established through its provenance. During the seventeenth century, it was owned by Cardinal Mazarin, a great collector of tapestries, who acquired many items from the sale of royal goods held after Charles I's execution.[73] Many of Mazarin's tapestries, including this one, were described as "fabrique d'Angleterre" in the inventory of his possessions, because the officers responsible for inventorying his goods mistakenly assumed that early Netherlandish tapestries from the English royal collection were of English manufacture. Netherlandish tapestries were not required to carry marks of origin until the second quarter of the century, and this mistake may have been compounded because many of the tapestries from the English royal collection probably carried English inscriptions on their canvas linings regarding the subjects, dimensions, and palace wardrobe of origin (see below, p. 359).[74] Whatever the case, the Washington tapestry provides a fine example of the kind of high-quality product that the Van Aelst workshop was producing ca. 1500 and, as such, an idea of the type of goods that Henry was sourcing from this merchant.

Another significant set that Van Aelst may have supplied to Henry was made from one of the most ambitious cartoon series undertaken in this pre-Renaissance style. The series is now known as the *Redemption of Man,* but during the sixteenth century it was commonly known as the *Old and the New Law.* Its conception can be dated to around 1500 on the basis of the style of design. As we have seen, Henry acquired a gold-woven tapestry and nine "borders" from Van Aelst of exactly this title in 1502. Whether this was a single dorser with related borders or whether the "borders" were actually other

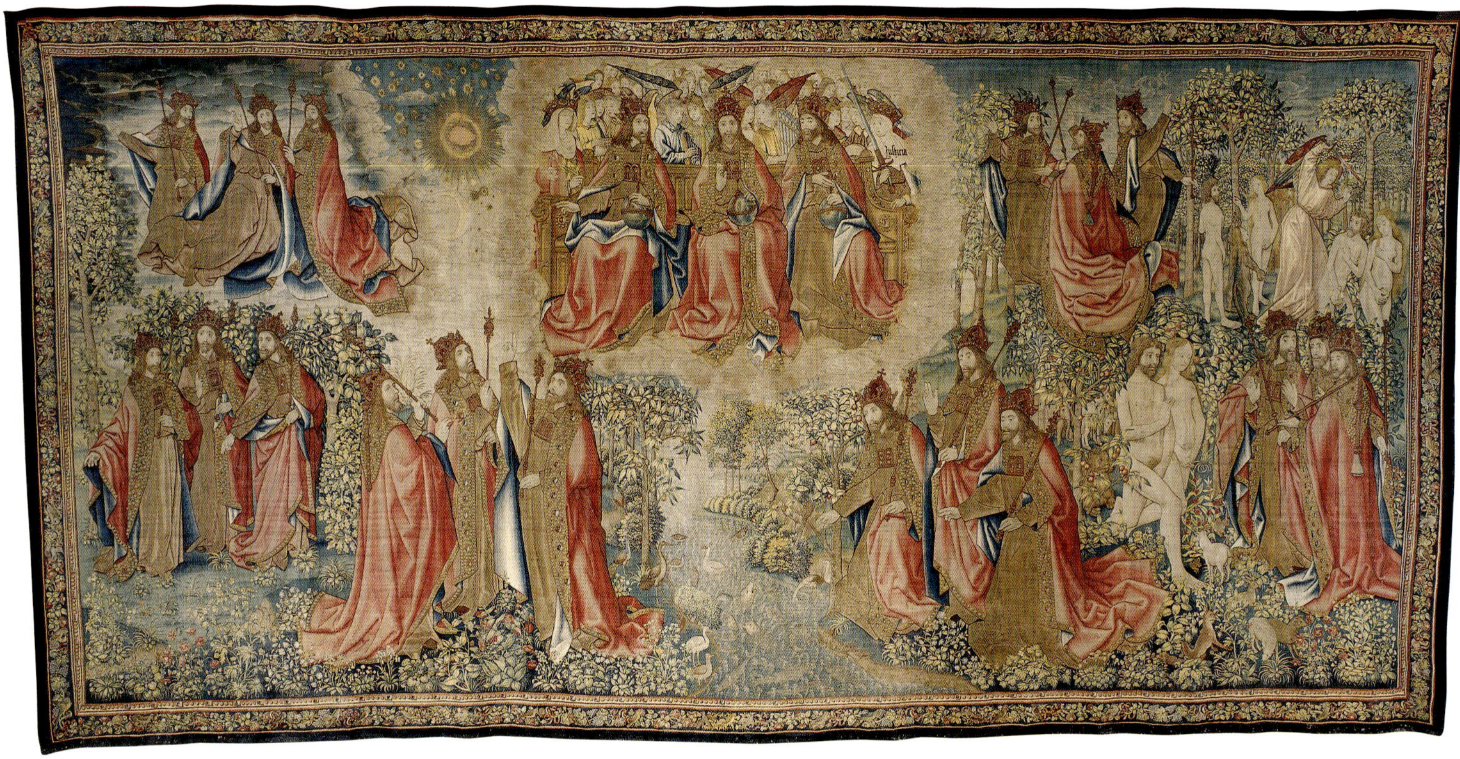

4.19 *The Creation* from a set now known as the *Redemption of Man.* Tapestry woven in the Southern Netherlands, probably Brussels, ca. 1500–1502. Wool, silk, and gilt-metal-wrapped thread, 420 x 785 cm. Cathédral Saint-Just, Narbonne

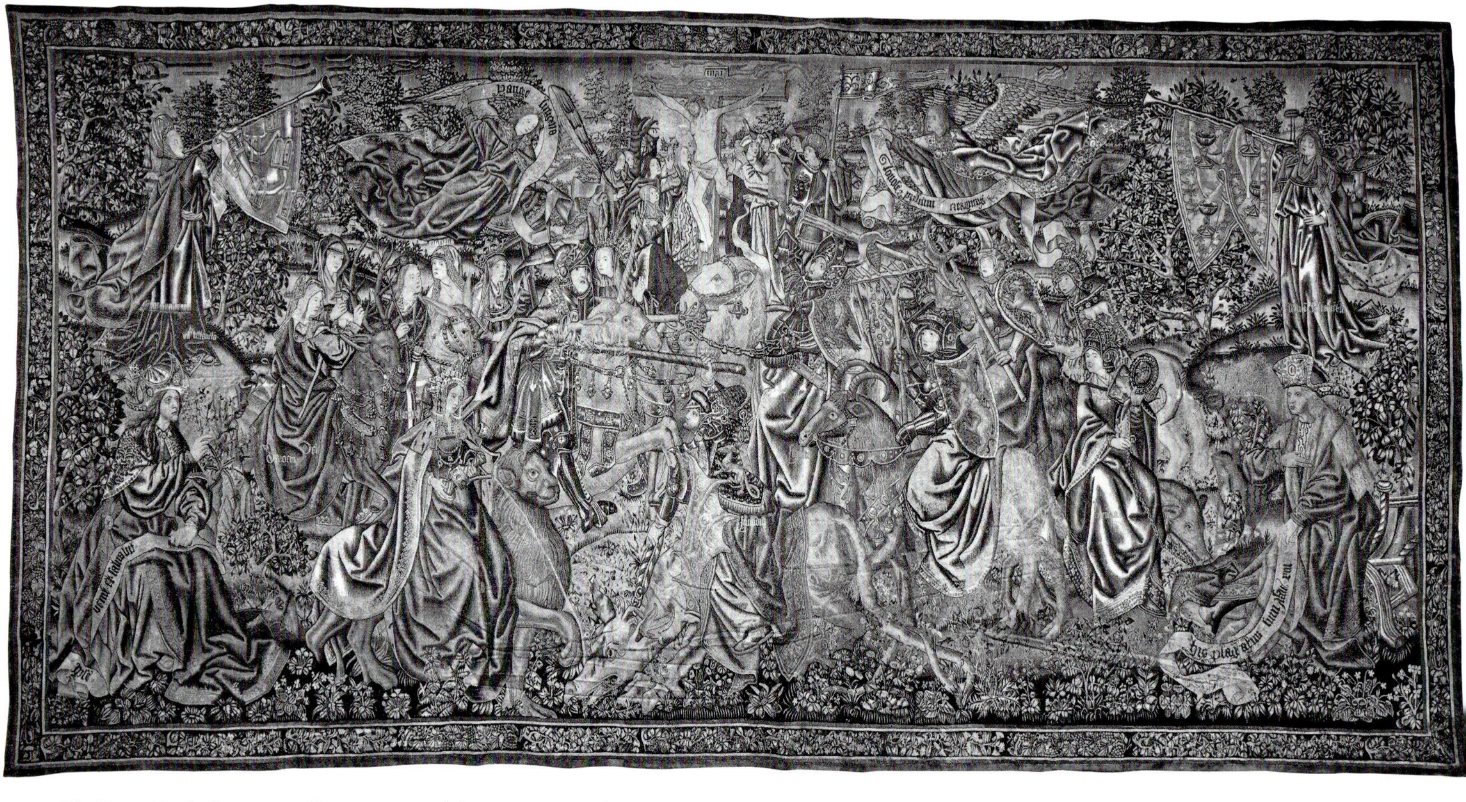

4.20 *The Virtues Battle the Vices as Christ Is Crucified* from a set now known as the *Redemption of Man.* Tapestry woven in the Southern Netherlands, probably Brussels, ca. 1520. Wool and silk, 417 x 798 cm. The Fine Arts Museums of San Francisco

tapestries in a set is unclear, but the large customs duty due on the ensemble suggests that the latter may have been the case. At any rate, circumstantial evidence that Henry VII or his son Henry VIII did indeed acquire an especially fine set of this series is provided by descriptions of a gold-woven set of this design that was displayed at the Field of Cloth of Gold celebrations at Guines in 1520 and listed in the 1547 inventory, when it was said to have an attached border with the king's arms.[75] Described at Hampton Court in the early seventeenth century, the set survived in the royal collection until the Commonwealth sale, when it was recorded at Richmond, with the high valuation of £1,817 10s.[76] Sold in 1651, its subsequent fate is unrecorded, but it can be tentatively identified with a ten-piece, gold-woven set that appeared some years later in the collection of François Fouquet, archbishop of Narbonne. François presented it to the Chapter of Saint-Just in Narbonne in 1673, and one piece survives today at Narbonne Cathedral (fig. 4.19; see also fig. 5.2).[77] Significantly, of all the extant versions of the design—tapestries from as many as fifteen sets survive—that from which the Narbonne panel comes is the only weaving known to have included metallic thread. It therefore seems probable that the tapestry surviving at Narbonne is the sole survivor of a set once in the English royal collection.

The subject matter of the *Redemption* series reflects the profound spirituality of the age, embodying a complex religious and moral narrative that is closely related to the Miracle cycles performed on feast days in some of the main European cathedral towns.[78] The series opens with a panel depicting the story of the Creation and the Fall of Man, with the Holy Trinity represented as three identical crowned and bearded men. This scene is followed by others in which the Vices and Virtues contend for control over Mankind. Unable to defend Mankind on the basis of his innate virtues, Mercy pleads to Christ for intervention, which introduces a narrative of the story of Christ's life. This culminates in a depiction of the Passion that takes place above a violent battle between the Vices and the Virtues. The Crucifixion scene is flanked by figures representing the Old and the New Law (fig. 4.20), and it was from this detail that the series received its sixteenth-century title. The series concludes with a Last Judgment. The foreground of each scene is populated by Old Testament prophets and patriarchs whose words foretold the coming of Christ. Although the narrative content of the series is complex, the visual effect is highly decorative, thanks to the rich floral grounds by which the narrative elements are subdivided and the gloriously folded and patterned robes worn by the figures.

It should be emphasized that the *Glorification of Christ* tapestry and *Redemption of Man* series represented the finest-quality products of the day and that most of Henry's acquisitions would have been of a coarser, cheaper grade, intended for daily use. The Wardrobe accounts relating to repairs undertaken on the royal tapestries indicate the presence of sizeable numbers of verdure tapestries in the collection by the early sixteenth century, and although some of these may have been purchased by Edward IV, many others were likely to have been acquired by Henry. Where the verdures of the early fifteenth century had typically featured small islands with rooted trees and flowers against plain grounds dotted with plants and animals,[79] those of the last third of the fifteenth century depicted grounds covered with a mass of wild flowers, in consequence of which they have come in modern times to be known as millefleurs. During Tudor times they were generally known as "verdures." Cheap types repeated a small number of basic flower patterns, but more expensive designs often represented highly naturalistic flowers.[80] In both cases, the designs were often enlivened with animals, birds, and sometimes figures engaged in genre or hunting activities. The inventory of Princess Mary taken in 1547 included a set of thirteen tapestries of hunting and hawking with borders containing the royal arms and the letters "HE" (presumably for Henry VII and his wife, Elizabeth of York).[81]

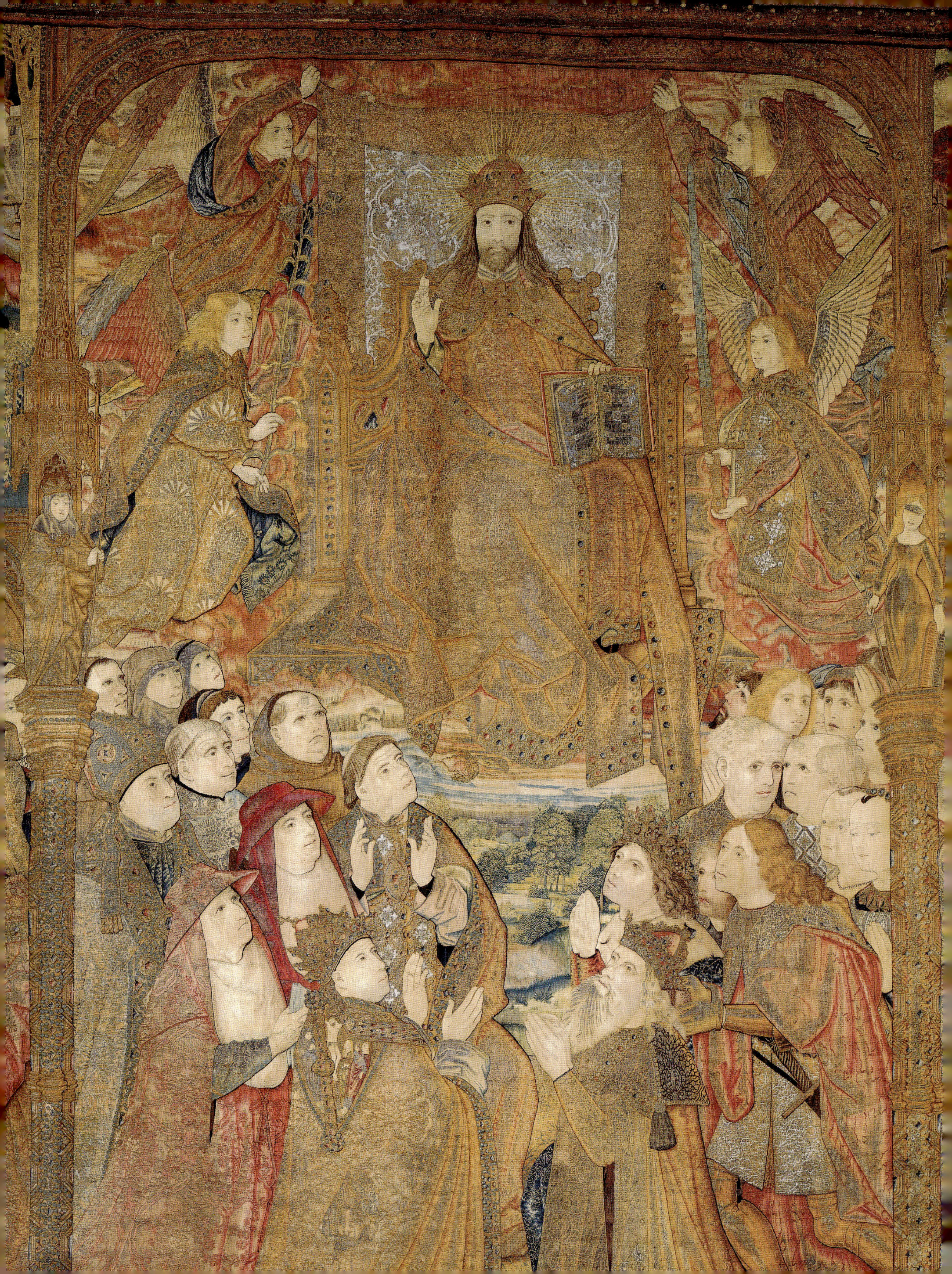

CHAPTER 5

Tapestry Usage under Henry VII

Storage and Maintenance

As we have seen, in becoming king of England in 1485, Henry VII took possession of a sizeable collection of precious textiles that he augmented with substantial purchases. The question remains as to how these tapestries were used and the extent to which traditional practices were continued or modified during his reign. Although the textiles were under the control of the Great Wardrobe, whose officers remained at the City of London site purchased by Edward III in 1360, they were largely distributed among "standing wardrobes" at the main royal palaces according to tradition and practical requirements. By the end of his reign, Henry owned twelve palaces and residences, of which four seem to have had such permanent wardrobes: Windsor, Richmond, Westminster, and the Tower. There may also have been one at Nottingham Castle.[1] Only a small stock of tapestry and verdure counterpoints were maintained at the Great Wardrobe, and these were dispensed ad hoc, as needed.[2] Evidence that the existing distribution among the palaces remained largely undisturbed by the accession of Henry VII, and subsequently that of Henry VIII, is suggested by the fact that several of the large tapestries recorded in the 1420s at the Tower and Windsor survived at these locations in 1547. No details have survived of the wardship arrangements for the collection during Henry VII's reign, but analogy with earlier and later practice suggests that the textiles deposited at each palace were charged to the care of the resident keeper by indenture. This officer was required to maintain an accurate inventory of the goods in his care and to answer for anything lost or damaged at the end of his tenure unless otherwise exempted by royal warrant.

In addition to the "standing wardrobes" at the palaces, "removing wardrobes" were maintained for principal members of the royal family, as revealed by payments to the Office of Works for building work at a wardrobe in the City of London for three years from March 1488. This was described as the wardrobe in which Elizabeth of York's possessions were kept and in which the goods of the prince—that is, Prince Arthur—were to be kept in due course.[3] The contents of this princely wardrobe are undocumented, and the only evidence we have relates to the legacy of Cecily, duchess of York and mother of Edward IV. To Arthur she bequeathed an "arras" tapestry of the pope, a counterpoint of "arras," and a bed of "arras" of the *Wheel of Fortune* with en suite tester (canopy); while to the young Henry, then duke of York, she left three "tappettes of arres," one of the *Life of Saint John the Baptist,* another of *Mary Magdalene,* and the third of the *Passion of Our Lord and Saint George.*[4]

The Royal Arras Maker

Repair of the tapestries was undertaken by an appointed officer who supervised a workshop located at the Great Wardrobe.[5] During the first part of Henry's reign this office was occupied by John Bakes, as documented by a grant of January 24, 1486, whereby he was to receive the office for life, "of maker and mender of the

Detail of fig. 4.18

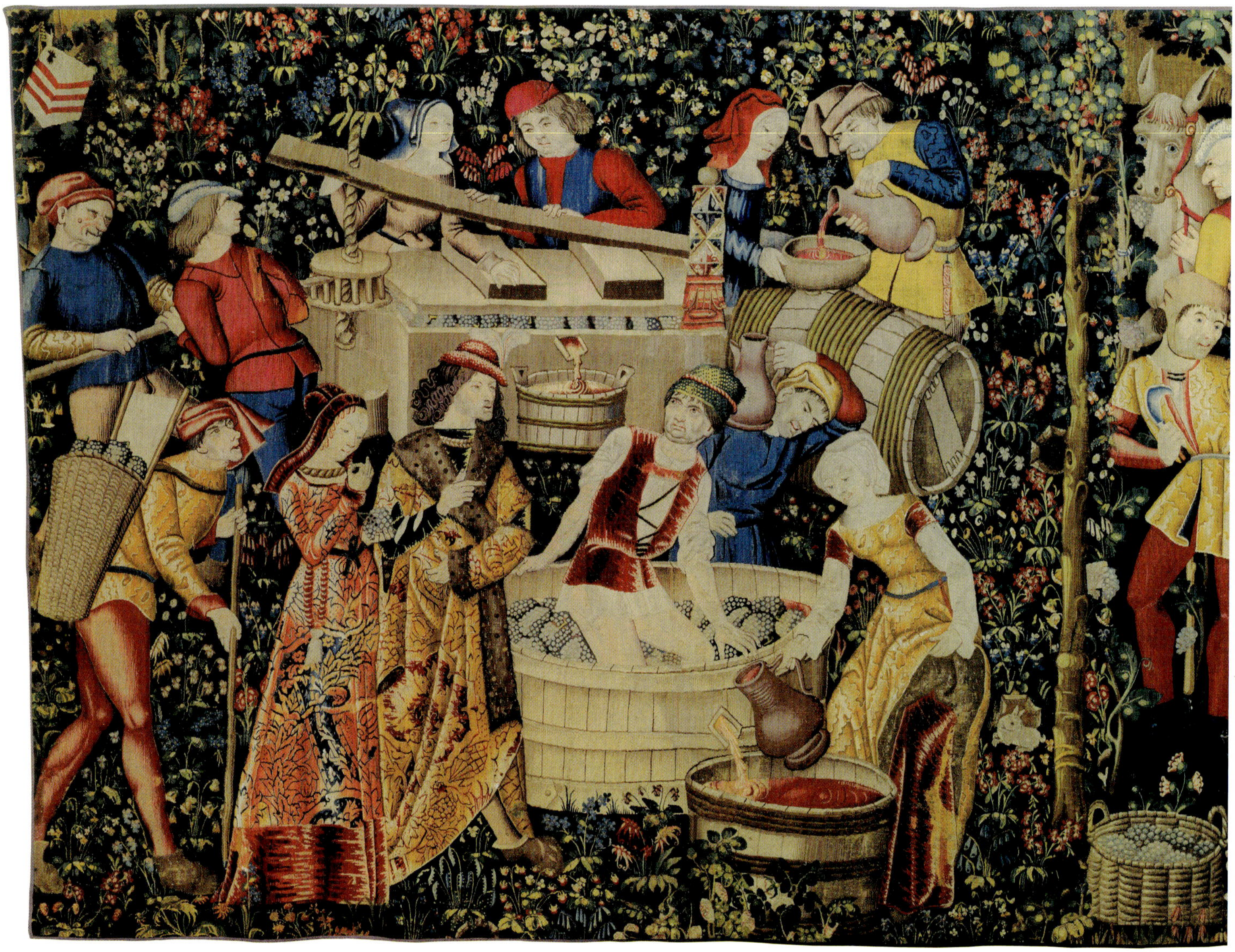

5.1 *Scenes of Winemaking* (detail). Tapestry woven in the Southern Netherlands, ca. 1490–1520. Wool and silk, 245 x 490 cm. Musée de Cluny, Paris

king's cloths and pieces of arras and tapestry," with 12d. a day (£18 5s. per year) for wages for himself and 4d. a day (£6 1s. 8d. per year) for a boy, a livery from the Wardrobe, and all benefits such as John Bullock and John Wylde had in the same office.[6] This wage is comparable to that issued to the king's sergeant tailor, George Lovekyn.[7] The wording of the grant to Bakes indicates that this role, like so many arrangements associated with the court, was subject to long-standing tradition; while John Wylde held the position from 1461 to 1486, Bullock had served as keeper of the king's tapestry in 1364–67.[8] Bakes was succeeded on January 17, 1502, by Cornelius van der Strete, whose name indicates that he was of Netherlandish origin and who may therefore have been employed because he was an experienced weaver.[9] During Henry VIII's reign, Van der Strete took an active role in purchasing tapestries on the king's behalf in the Low Countries, and it is possible that he began this function under Henry VII.

Most of the royal arras maker's work was undertaken in response to warrants issued by the lord chamberlain to the keeper of the Great Wardrobe, indicating that the decisions to repair antique tapestries and prepare new ones were made at the most senior level by an officer who was closely associated with the king. A summary of the arras maker's activity was provided by the keeper of the Great Wardrobe as part of the detailed accounts he prepared each year for auditing purposes.[10] The scale and character of ongoing activity is revealed by warrants and accounts for the years 1502–5. On June 20, 1502, a warrant was issued to the keeper, Sir Robert Lytton, to have certain tapestries mended and lined with strips of canvas.[11] This was standard Wardrobe practice, for the linings both strengthened the tapestries and provided the base for the hooks or ropes by which the tapestries were suspended. In order to minimize costs and weight, many tapestries were lined only with strips of canvas, and this was the case in this particular instance, where the tapestries were to be lined "above [with] canvas brede [broad] and beneth half canvas brede and at the ends of the same oon quarter brede and striped thorowe out with canvas oon quarter brede and bounde with lior." The tapestries treated on this occasion included three pieces of the *Story of Judith and Holofernes,* the set of the *Siege of Jerusalem,* five "paled verdures"—that is, tapestries in which the ground comprised stripes of color, like those with Prince Arthur's devices—twelve verdures of "hawking and hunting," and a bed of verdure with en suite celure and tester. Because of the partial nature of the written records, it is difficult to ascertain which of these tapestries were older pieces being repaired and relined and which were new tapestries being lined for the first time. One year later a similar warrant was issued on June 14, 1503, to have more than fifty tapestries treated or repaired.[12] The tapestries included "arras" panels of the *Seven Ages of Man, Saint George,* and the *Trinity and Assumption of the Virgin,* which probably can be identified with antique pieces acquired by Richard II and Henry VI. Such repairs suggest the role that the older tapestries continued to play in certain settings or on particular occasions.

Other work undertaken during the summer of 1503 may have related to preparations for the marriage of Henry's daughter, Margaret, to King James IV of Scotland on August 8, 1503. Among the tapestries lined and repaired in this period were a seven-piece set of the *Story of the Ladies;* two sets of the *Passion,* one of twelve pieces and one of four; six pieces of verdure with the king's arms and two matching counterpoints; a piece of tapestry of *Nebuchadnezzar,* perhaps one of the set purchased by Edward IV; and nine pieces depicting *Vineyards,* perhaps akin to the piece that survives at the Cluny Museum (fig. 5.1).[13] The *Story of the Ladies* was possibly a representation of Christine de Pisan's *City of Women,* the famous discourse on the great women of history. This allegorical subject was selected, presumably, as being especially appropriate for the trousseau of Princess Margaret, but whether it was a new acquisition or an older set is unspecified.

The preparations for Margaret's wedding reveal other aspects of Van der Strete's activity. Besides the foregoing repairs, he was also paid for setting red roses and heraldic devices in the borders of the verdures.[14] In addition, he was also paid for seventy-four Flemish ells (approximately forty-one and a half square yards) of "arras," lined with canvas, that he "hath by our comandement made and delyvered for thuse of our derrest doughter the Quene of Scottes . . . the price of every stikke [ell] so lyned two shillings."[15] This is the first evidence of tapestry production by the royal arras maker during the Tudor era, but such work seems to have been a long-standing tradition. During Henry VI's reign, John Stout, the royal tapicer and keeper of the king's arras and tapestries, had been paid for the production of tapestry cushions and bench covers for the Star Chamber.[16] Given the ready availability of figurative tapestry from the Low Countries and the time-consuming nature of such production, it seems probable that the tapestries made by Van der Strete's workshop would have been fairly simple, featuring heraldic and armorial devices along the lines of the Hever Castle tapestry discussed in the previous chapter, rather than figurative designs. Alternatively, the work may have comprised armorial borders designed to be attached to tapestries in Margaret's trousseau.[17] Quite apart from demonstrating that Van der Strete had workers capable of weaving such tapestry, the warrant suggests that this was a well-established practice, since the price of two shillings per ell was said to be "like as he hath ratably [?] had heretofore for our Arras."

Lytton was succeeded as keeper of the Great Wardrobe by Andrew Windsor, whose account for the period from Michaelmas 1504 to Michaelmas 1506 included charges for the arras makers and tailors repairing and relining more than forty identified tapestries, many of them verdures. About fifty workers are listed, and they were paid per diem.[18] Although fragmentary, these accounts indicate the character and scale of activity of the royal arras maker and his assistants, repairing antique tapestries, inserting heraldic devices in the borders, and, in all probability, weaving new armorial borders to attach to new acquisitions.

Disposition and Usage under Henry VII

Where the documentation for tapestry usage up to and including the reign of Edward IV is extremely limited, that for Henry VII's reign, though fragmentary, is more informative. Household ordinances and descriptions of contemporary events allow us to characterize a number of existing procedures and how they were refined during the reign. Little evidence has survived of the type of tapestries used in more private and informal rooms, but analogy with earlier and later practice, as well as that of contemporary Continental courts, suggests that these would have been hung with sets of decorative and pastoral subjects, such as the verdure, *Vineyard,* and *Hunt* tapestries cited above. As already noted, large numbers of verdure tapestries are listed in the records relating to the hangings that the royal tailors lined and repaired during the years 1502–6.

Although no written records survive regarding the private spaces of the palaces, more information survives in relation to the areas where display was an important factor. We can identify two different types of space in which the material, quality, and subject matter of tapestry would have been especially significant. The first, during regular court activity, was any room in which the king conducted business, devotion, or entertainment in public, particularly the watching chamber, the privy chamber, and the chapel, and any room in which official business was conducted on his behalf. The second space in which relevant iconography might be displayed to advantage were the streets, courtyards, and great halls through which processions passed on state occasions. It was in these larger arenas that the enormous tapestry cycles of the day came into their own, when they could be seen in entirety and when onlookers would have had little to do but consider the images around them as they waited for the royal entourage to appear. Judging by the care paid to the selection of tapestries for grand events during Henry VII's reign, this was a potential that he sought to exploit in a range of ways and with a greater sophistication than his predecessors.

The household ordinances promulgated during Edward's reign indicated the responsibilities of the household officers in respect to the provision of furnishings and hangings. During the early 1490s, further directives were issued regarding the provisions for major court events, sometimes erroneously attributed to Henry VII's mother, Margaret Beaufort.[19] These include detailed instructions for the use of the bedding and hangings in exactly the arenas where major court events were staged. For example, the ordinances stipulate that for the momentous event of the queen's lying-in, the chamber must "be hanged with riche Clothe of Arras, Sydes, rowffe, Windowes and all, excepte One Windowe, which muste be hanged so as she may have Light when it pleasethe her." Carpets and cupboards are to be "covered with the same Suyte as the Chamber is hanged withall." The great chamber was also to be hung with "riche Arras."[20] For the royal christening, the doorway and font of the church were to be hung with cloth of gold, and "the chirche muste be hangid all about the sides with arras; and the highe aecter [altar] must be araid in the recheste wise." In addition, "Westminster halle and the Whit-halle [must be] hangid with arras for the prince to be borne throughe the palis to the churche, and home agayne the same way, when he is cristenyde."[21] To an extent, these ordinances may have codified practices that the Wardrobe had developed under Edward IV and carried over into Henry VII's reign, as is indicated by comparison between the regulation just cited and the description of Prince Arthur's christening at Winchester in 1486 described above. Nonetheless, the codification of such practices reflects the self-conscious manner in which the household was manipulating the tapestries as part of the staging and appearance of the Tudor court.

Subsequent descriptions of the birth and christening of other royal children confirm the extent to which these stipulations were applied. They also provide hints of practices and codes of decorum that are otherwise undocumented. For example, a description of the confinement of the queen before the birth of Princess Margaret in 1489 states that she departed "to her inner Chambre, which was hanged and seyled with rich Clothe of blew Arras, with Flour delissis of Golde, without any ouder Clothe of Arras of Ymagerye, which is not convenient aboute Wymen in such Cas."[22] The hanging in question was evidently the heraldic set made for Charles VI that the duke of Bedford appropriated during the 1420s. The selection of a suite deemed to be restful on the eyes and mind echoes a situation recorded at the French court some decades earlier in 1453, when hangings depicting "figures, animals and birds" were thought inappropriate in the bedchamber of Yolande of France, third daughter of Charles VII, during a feverish childbirth. On this occasion, the tapestries in question were replaced with plain blue textiles.[23]

The description of the subsequent christening ceremony in 1489 provides another interesting insight. The royal party progressed from the chapel into Westminster, "wiche Hallis and alsoo all the kyngs Chambres wer that Day as richely beseen and hangyed as ever I saw them. The riche Bed called Hewdykes Bed was hanged in the Kyngs Chambre."[24] Hugh Dyke was a rich mercer, active during the second quarter of the fifteenth century, who supplied luxury textiles to Henry V, the duke of Bedford, and Henry VI and lent considerable sums of money to the Crown during the 1430s.[25] The use of this sumptuous bed, presumably supplied by Dyke to Henry VI some sixty years or so earlier, again demonstrates how the Tudor court was consciously presenting itself in historic trappings. While this may seem an obvious expedient and was paralleled by the use that the Burgundian court made of antique tapestries and textiles dating from Philip the Bold's day, it is nonetheless worthy of remark, especially in the context of the efforts that Henry VII took to stress his Lancastrian heritage and the encouragement he gave to the cult of Henry VI during the 1490s.

Progressions of Splendor

Although the ordinances reflect how extensively tapestry usage was formalized for ceremonial occasions by the 1480s and 1490s, a new development is apparent from the early 1500s. From this point, written descriptions start to reveal heightened sensitivity to different qualities of tapestry. Products of a range of quality had obviously been imported to England long before this, but the new sensitivity reflected by contemporary nomenclature was probably symptomatic of the increasing volumes of such products, a greater familiarity with various grades and values, and thus a need to define them. An insight to the significance and availability of these gradations of quality is provided by the Port Book of Rates issued in July 1507, an official index of values that was compiled to aid customs officers calculate the appropriate levy for imported goods, at the rate of 1s. in the pound of the total cost.[26] Although the true price of commodities would have varied depending on a variety of economic factors, the valuations given by this list demonstrate the contemporary perception of the proportional difference of cost between different types and grades of object. The book lists three different grades of tapestry, along with their nominal unit cost in square Flemish ells. The cheapest, "Tapestry or verders withowt sylke," was valued at 5d. per ell. "Tapestry or verders with cades [worsted thread]" was more

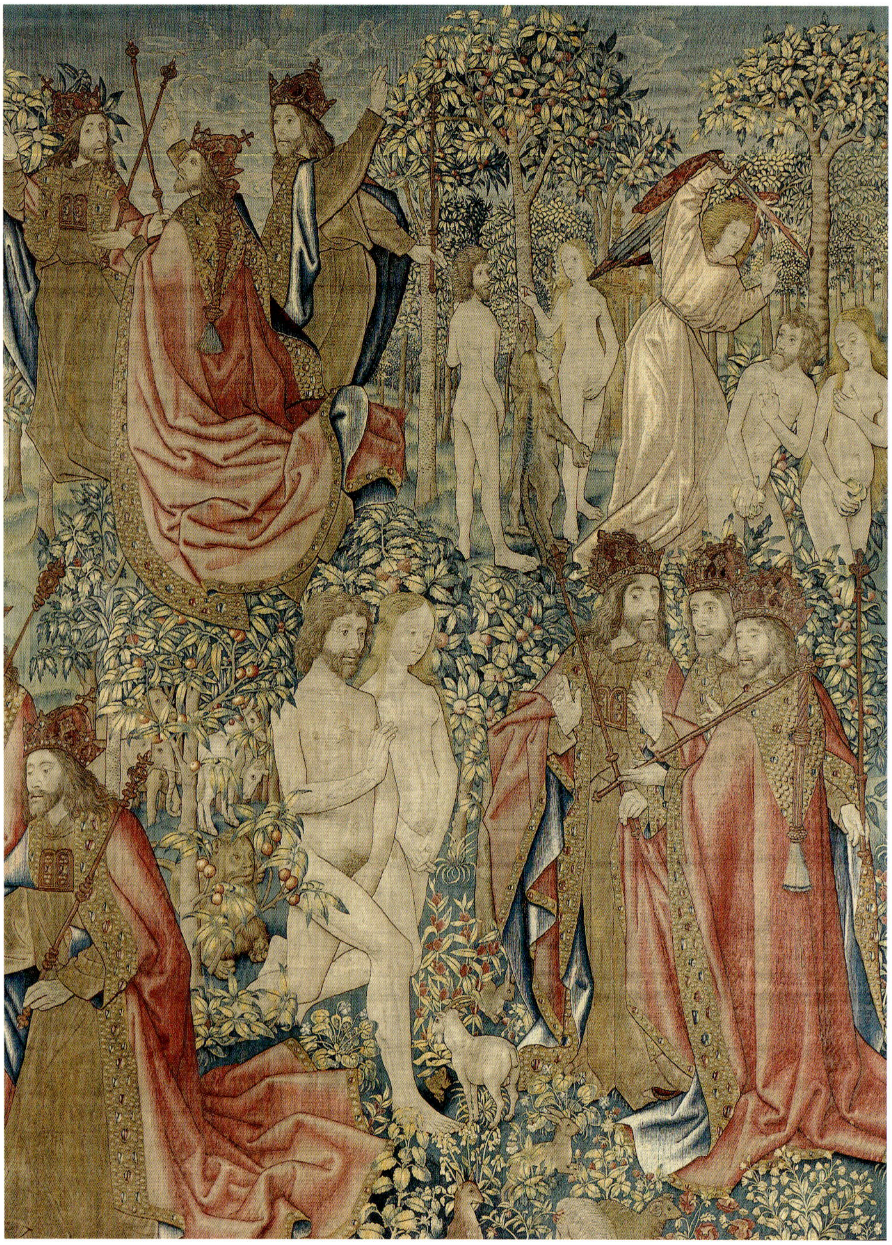

5.2 Detail of fig. 4.19

valuable at 1s. per ell, and the most expensive type listed was "Tapestrye or verderes with sylke," which was valued at 1s. 8d. per ell.[27] No mention is made of tapestry with gilt-metal thread. Henry VII's purchases of such material would have been exempted from import tax, and it is possible that at this date imports of tapestry of this quality and cost for other clients were sufficiently rare as to not warrant inclusion in the list or, alternatively, that it was taxed ad hoc.[28] Indeed, "arras" is not mentioned as a specific category until the Port Book of Rates was updated and reissued in 1558, when it was specifically described as tapestry woven with gold thread and valued at 40 shillings per ell. Nonetheless, documents relating to tapestry purchases by Henry VII and Henry VIII during the first two decades of the sixteenth century confirm that tapestry with gilt-thread cost between 20 and 40 shillings per ell, long before this figure was codified in the updated 1558 Book of Rates.[29]

Based on the evidence of the 1507 Port Book of Rates and documented purchases from this period, we can therefore identify the proportional variation of cost among tapestries woven with coarse wool, those with finer wool, those with wool and silk, and those with gilt-metal-wrapped thread as a ratio of 1 : 2.5 : 4 : 50, the cheapest wool tapestry being valued at about 5d. per ell and the most expensive gold-woven tapestry being valued at upward of 20s. per ell (see, for example, detail opposite p. 89 and fig. 5.2). In response to this wide variation of quality and cost, the terminology used to describe tapestries became increasingly specialized in the early sixteenth century, at least when used by court officers. Analysis of contemporary documents suggests that in this period court warrants and inventories increasingly use "arras" to distinguish tapestries woven with gilt-metal-wrapped thread (this usage is less consistent in documents other than inventories, where the term is also, on occasion, used to describe old tapestries).[30] Similarly, "counterfeit arras," which appears with relative frequency in written records between 1500 and 1530, was probably used to describe high-quality tapestries in which silk rather than metallic thread was used for the highlights.[31]

The heightened sensitivity to distinctions of quality is reflected by the tapestries' deployment at court. From the early 1500s we find increasing evidence of the use of different qualities of tapestry and rich embroideries to dramatize the hierarchic importance of state chamber sequences. For example, when Philip the Fair and Joanna of Castile were forced to land in England en route to Spain in 1506, Henry received them with great ceremony at Windsor. An anonymous narrative of this reception vividly describes how the qualitative progression of the furnishings provided not only the stage set but also the subject matter of the royal performance. Following their arrival, the royal entourages ascended to the great chamber:

> which was richly hanged with cloth of aras and a great rich bed, where remained the knights and esquires; and from thence [they progressed] to the second chamber which was also richly hanged, where remained the barons and bannerets. From thence to the third chamber, which was hanged with very rich arras, in the which there was a cloth of estate and as rich a bed as I have ever seen; where remained the bishops, earls and officers that attended upon him. And from thence [Henry] would have conveyed the king of Castile to the fourth chamber, which was all hanged with rich cloth of gold, the border of crimson velvet and embroidered with the king's arms, with other the king's devices, as roses, portcullises, &c. but the king of Castile excused him, and said that the king should not take the pains to convey him to his lodging. Then the king [Henry] showed him that all that he had passed through was and should be his lodgings . . . when the king of Castile perceived that that great lodgings was made for him he thanked the king bareheaded and said that he was sorry that the king had taken so much labor and pains for him.[32]

Evidence that this progression was not just the creation of the chronicler's imagination is provided by another document that shows the level of attention underlying the creation of such a hierarchic sequence. Dating from late 1508, this document relates to the betrothal ceremony that Henry VII then planned between his daughter, Princess Mary, and the young archduke Charles, an event that never actually took place.[33] It details the arrangements to be made for the princess's rooms and those of the Emperor Maximilian and Margaret of Austria, and annotations appear to have been made by Henry VII himself. The outermost of the princess's four rooms was to be hung with "a story of good and fyne tapicery . . . with a bordour of her armys and bagies" with a unit value of 4s. per square ell. The provision for the next room was originally stipulated as "Aras, not so fyne as is the seconde chamber [the next in sequence toward the bedchamber]," but this was amended to "a hangynge of fyne tapessherye with bagies and armys [badges and coats of arms] in the bordour." The antechamber to her bedroom was to be hung with "a rich story of Aras golde and silk with a bordor of her armys and bagies" at a unit price of 20s. per ell. A marginal annotation stipulates that this set "muste be provided in Flaundres." Finally, the bedchamber itself was to be hung with cloth of gold. A similar equipage was stipulated for the emperor's lodging, the progression running from fine tapestry in the outermost of his three rooms to "riche aras of golde and silke" in the middle chamber to cloth of gold for his bedchamber. In contrast, that for Margaret was less grand, the third chamber hung with "fyne tapestry" and the second chamber and bedchamber hung with "riche aras," but no cloth of gold.[34] As will be apparent, the detail reflects the degree of consideration that underlay the tapestry displays for important occasions and the extent to which tapestry hangings were used to dramatize the hierarchy of the audience chambers, with a progression from tapestries woven in wool alone to those woven in wool and silk to those woven with wool, silk, and gold and, finally, cloth of gold embroidered with royal devices for the richest and most important focal points.

How rare and valuable would these gold-woven tapestries have appeared to the early Tudor audience? Although conclusions are impeded by the imprecision of contemporary terminology, analysis of contemporary collections does confirm that nobody but the king owned gold-woven tapestries in any quantity. An inventory taken in 1509 of the possessions of Edmund Dudley, Henry's unpopular minister of finance, indicates that the main rooms at his London property were decorated with hangings

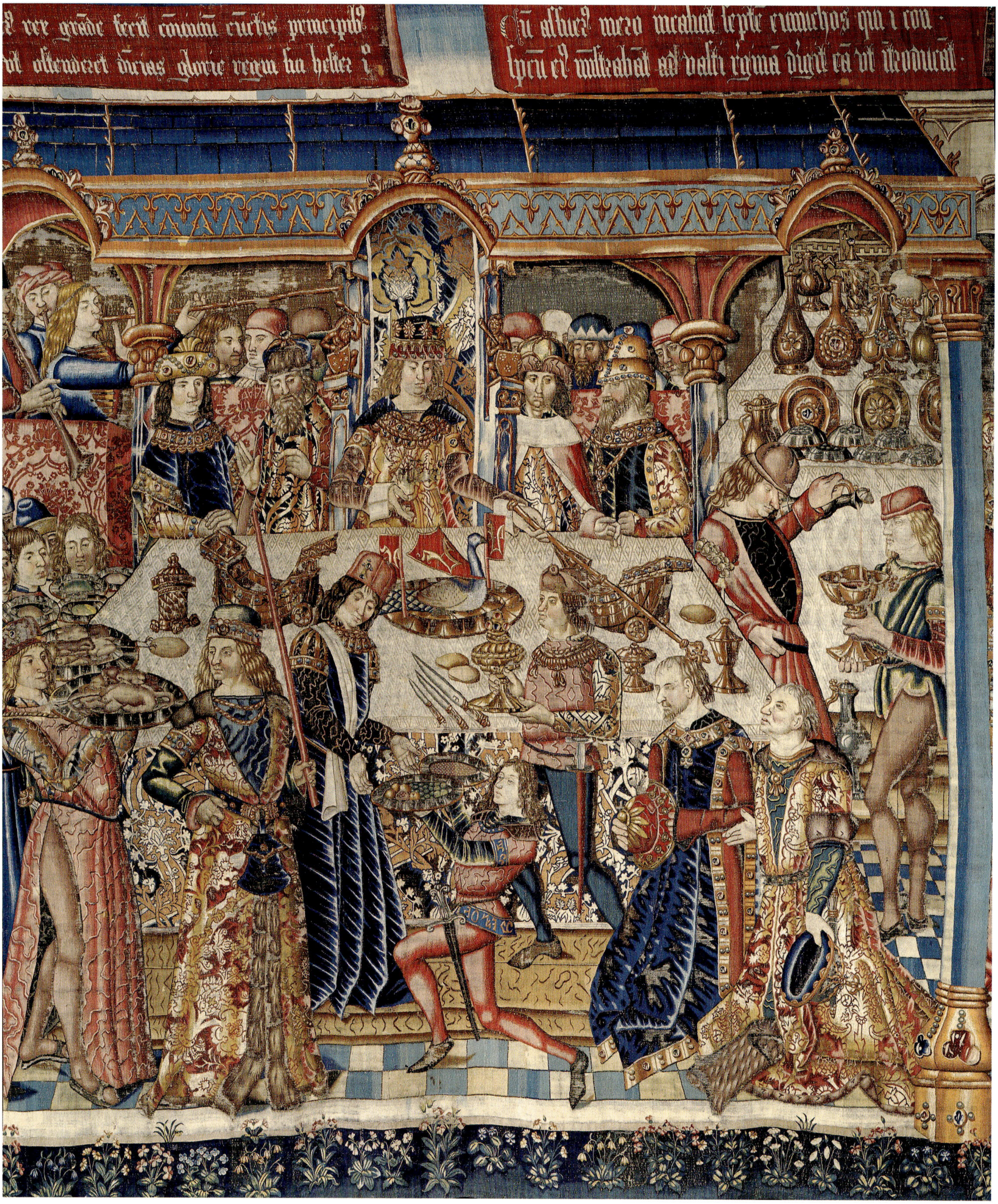

5.3 Detail of fig. 4.8

of colored buckram, but the inventory also lists ten pieces of "arras." Of those, five were described as old and two as "rich" counterpoints. Dudley may well have received the older pieces as perquisites from the royal collection. There were also one piece of fine "counterfeit arras," twelve pieces of tapestry, two beds of tapestry, and several verdure counterpoints.[35] The inventory taken in 1513 of the goods of John de Vere, thirteenth earl of Oxford, the lord high admiral and lord great chamberlain, lists about ten pieces of tapestry defined as "arras," but most of these pieces appear to have been of considerable age and may also have been acquired as perquisites in a collection whose finest pieces are generally defined as "counterfeit arras."[36] The duke of Buckingham is known to have purchased gold-woven tapestries in 1512, and we can assume that these entered the royal collection after his execution, but only two gold-woven pieces with his arms are listed in the 1547 royal inventory.[37] Some years later, the duke of Norfolk's collection at Framlingham in 1524 was composed entirely of "counterfeit arras," tapestry, and verdure.[38] In short, gold-woven tapestries of any size appear to have been extremely rare in any collection but that of the Crown, a rarity that we can all too easily overlook today because of the disproportionate survival of high-quality tapestries over lower-quality pieces.

Iconography and Suggestion

That the material quality of the tapestries was so carefully considered, at least for important state occasions, leads to the question whether equivalent attention was paid to the subject matter when tapestries were chosen for a specific event and how much Henry VII followed or developed existing practice. Analogy with the use of literary and artistic models in the public spectacles of the day suggests that the educated Tudor audience was highly sensitive to both overt comparisons and a range of more subtle analogies. The pageantry and triumphal entries performed in the early years of Henry's reign include exhaustive references to heroes of the classical and biblical worlds, those of ancient British history, and more recent heroes.[39] For example, during his triumphal entry to York on April 20, 1486, Henry was addressed by figures representing King Ebrancus, the supposed founder of York, Solomon, King David, and the Virgin. At Worcester, similar pageants had been prepared, although it is not certain that Henry witnessed them. According to the herald's account, Henry was first to be addressed by Henry VI and then Janitor (the gatekeeper) who rhetorically demanded to whom he was speaking, whether Noah, Jason, Julius, Abraham, Isaac, Jacob, Joseph, David, Scipio, Arthur, or the "Fulfiller of the Profecye." At Hereford, Henry was greeted by Saint George, King Ethelbert, and the Virgin; and at Bristol, by King Brennius, the supposed founder of Bristol, Prudentia, and Justicia.[40] Similar imagery informs the political and popular literature of the day.[41] For example, Bernard André's *Twelve Triumphs of Henry VII* compares Henry to Hercules and Margaret, duchess of Burgundy and sponsor of two pretenders against Henry, to Juno and Menalippe, queen of the Amazons.[42]

The royal tapestry collection provided a ready palette of such subjects, and it seems logical to suppose that comparisons like these would have been an implicit element of the tapestry displays used in more formal settings or on state occasions, whether the display was intended to impute virtues to Henry by association, such as the valor of Hercules or the wisdom of Solomon, or to promote more subtle comparisons. Documenting such usage is, however, more difficult, because of the lack of any formal or personal accounts or, indeed, of any literary tradition that might have encouraged such records. As we have seen, a sense of decorum certainly appears to have dictated the hangings provided for Elizabeth of York's confinement for the birth of Princess Margaret, and following the christening, the reception was decorated with a bed dating from Henry VI's reign, suggesting an intention to present this dynastic event in the context of the Tudors' Lancastrian ancestry. Similarly, the tapestries lined in the months before Margaret Tudor's marriage to James IV of Scotland included the protofeminist *Story of the Ladies,* again suggesting a selection specific to the princess. But beyond this we are dependent on a handful of contemporary descriptions that are rarely informative.

The most detailed is that of the meeting of Henry and Philip the Fair at Calais in 1500. In advance, a Richard Maner was paid £4 for transporting "rich arras" to Calais for the event.[43] These hangings were used to divide the church in which they were lodging into apartments for the duke and his entourage. The Lady Chapel was equipped as a bedchamber for the duke and was hung with a "riche clothe of arras" of the *Story of Esther and Ahasuerus.* The altar was adapted as a "secret place" with hangings embroidered with Henry's arms and crest. The lower part of the aisle was equipped as the duke's great chamber, hung with "arras" of the *Siege of Troy,* and the choir was hung with "blew clothe of arras with floredeluce perssis, and written in gold 'Jamais.'" The south side of the church was prepared in equally rich materials for the use of the duke's wife, while the vestry was equipped as a council chamber.[44]

The most obvious point that emerges from this selection is that here again we see older tapestries being used to provide weight and authority to the Tudor king. In particular, the use of Charles VI's rich heraldic tapestries may have been intended as a reminder of the ancient English claim to the French throne and of the Lancastrian victories under Henry V. The intention underlying the choice of the *Esther and Ahasuerus* set (see figs. 4.8, 5.3) and *Trojan War* set (see figs. 4.3, 5.4) is more ambiguous. With selective reading, both might be seen as the source of flattering analogies for Philip and Henry VII, but beyond this one cannot help but suspect that the selection also reflected an element of expediency. The Royal Wardrobe was inevitably restricted by the subjects available among the large rich sets.

A similar ambiguous impression emerges from contemporary descriptions of the festivities associated with the wedding of Prince Arthur and Katherine of Aragon in November 1501. For the wedding, we learn that the choir of Saint Paul's Cathedral was hung with "clothis of Aras," while the nave was hung, "with costely and riche clothis of Arras, whoes works and texturys represented the noble and valiaunt acts, storis, and gests, that for the moost partie poets and oratours writt and remembre in their comments, boks and scripture; as well the besegyng of noble cities as other batalls, turneis, their horsis, and persons, after the moost goodly paintinge, shapp, and fachyon, with th' endevor and practis of the maker his reason and imaginacon."[45] The description is evidently designed to evoke a chivalric, elegiac tone, and considering the number of late-fourteenth and early-fifteenth-century tapestries that survived in the royal collection at this time, it is quite plausible that the selection of tapestries hung at Saint Paul's may have been selected with a similar intent. For example, the tournament tapestries cited in the description may have been from one of Charles VI's *Tournament* sets, appropriated by the duke of Bedford during the 1420s, in themselves the record of events that sought to re-create a romanticized, chivalric ideal. After the service, the royal party proceeded to Westminster Palace for the marriage feast, where a great chamber was hung with "hangyngs of Rialte."[46] Here, it is tempting to read this phrase as an indication of the use of tapestries with a specific dynastic import, whether the panels depicting Henry's invasion and defeat of Richard III, if those had yet been delivered, or perhaps the venerable panels of the ancient English kings made for Richard II in the 1390s.

Following the ceremonies in London, the court repaired to Richmond Palace, which gave the chronicler an opportunity to describe this new and magnificent building. The walls of the great hall were hung "with riche clothes of Arras, ther werkys representing many noble batalls and seagees, as of Jerusalem, Troye, Alba and many other."[47] The named sets are

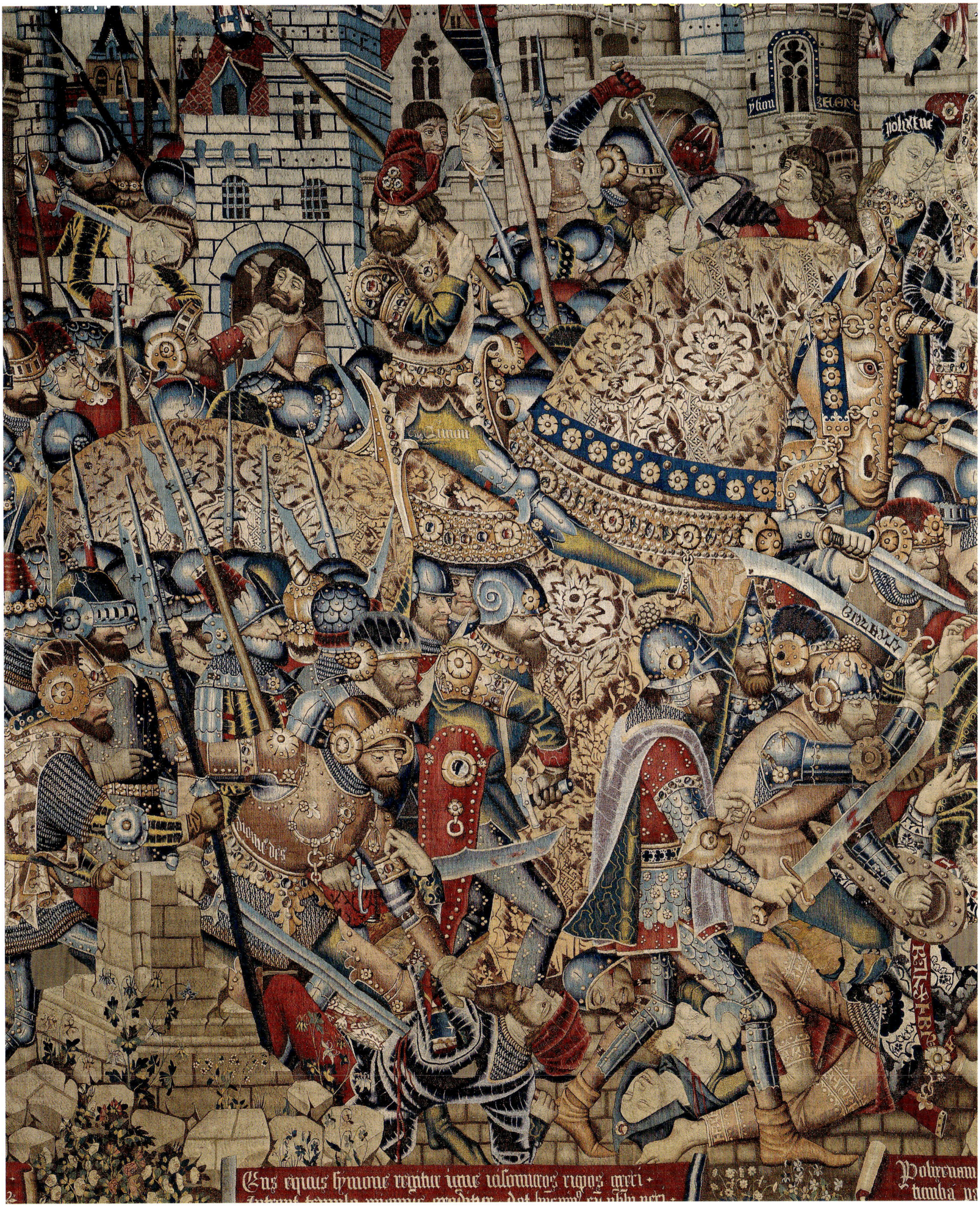

5.4 Detail of fig. 4.3

readily identifiable from those known to have been in the collection at this time. The *Jerusalem* and *Trojan War* sets have both been discussed in the context of Henry's purchases from Grenier, while the *Alba* set can probably be identified with the *Roman Histories* purchased in 1480 by Edward because Mont Alba was the site of Alba Longa, ancient city of Latium, destroyed during Tullus Hostilius's reign. It has been suggested that the tapestries used on this occasion were devoted to images of chivalric conquest to promote the presentation of Henry as a chivalric conqueror.[48] Given the evidence of Henry's acquisition of tapestries with other kinds of subject matter such as those of Old Testament patriarchs and the possibility that such analogies may also have been evoked on this occasion, this may be something of an overstatement. Nonetheless, the description confirms that the tapestries on display at Richmond had a pronounced martial and chivalric flavor. Support for this notion is provided by evidence that the pictures between the windows in the great hall at Richmond featured English kings such as Brutus, Hengest, William Rufus, King Arthur, King Henry, King Richard, King Edward, and Henry VII himself, who achieved fame as conquerors, rather than just Henry VII's ancestors.[49] In a related vein, the chapel, also hung with arras, had paintings of English kings who had been sanctified, such as Saint Edward, King Cadwaladr, and Saint Edmund.[50]

Although the foregoing documents fall short of providing us with detailed evidence of the degree of care underlying the selection of subjects for particular occasions, they support the notion that Henry made extensive use of the inherited tapestries to lend an atmosphere of antique grandeur, heritage, and authority to his public appearances. And if the selection of some of the larger sets may have involved an element of expediency, the descriptions hint at a level of discrimination in the decision to use particular sets on particular occasions, whether for reasons of historic or chivalric associations or specific analogy. In tandem with the evidence regarding the large investment that Henry made in specific purchases and commissions, it seems reasonable to conclude that the king was keenly aware of the suggestive potential of the tapestry medium and that it was a crucial component of the range of literary and visual devices with which the new Tudor dynasty asserted its validity in the minds of its subjects. Indeed, Henry's close involvement with the Brussels merchant Pieter van Aelst at such an early stage of that merchant's career and the considerable sums paid to him provide a tantalizing hint that Henry may have been a more sophisticated patron of narrative tapestry than the surviving evidence records and that his example may have provided the model for some of the more elaborate tapestry usage subsequently practiced by Cardinal Wolsey and Henry VIII during the 1520s and 1530s.

PART III

Henry VIII and Cardinal Wolsey

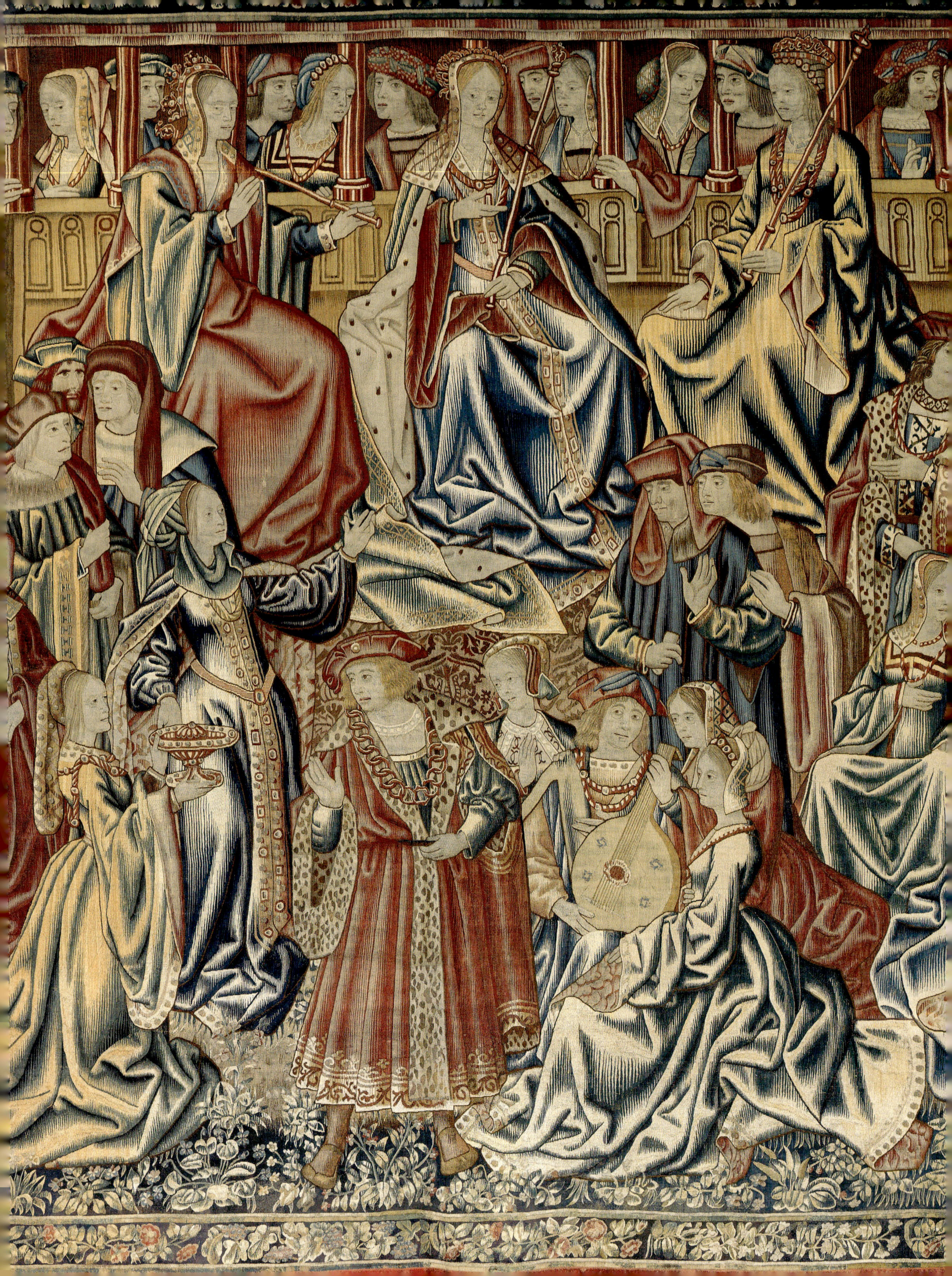

CHAPTER 6

Henry VIII

Purchases and Use of Tapestry, 1509–1519

Detail of fig. 6.6

Henry VIII came to the throne at the age of seventeen (fig. 6.1). He had been surrounded by tapestries from the moment of his birth, and the collection he inherited, perhaps numbering as many as four to five hundred pieces divided among the most important royal palaces and removing wardrobes, had been a constant backdrop to his youth. Indeed, the wealth of subject matter embodied by the tapestries may have made a significant contribution to the breadth of learning for which he was widely eulogized on his accession. In the coming decades he was to become one of the most active tapestry patrons of his age, using the medium as a means of iconographic suggestion and self-aggrandizement on a scale and grandeur equaled only by Francis I of France and Charles V, Holy Roman Emperor. But because his accession was more secure than that of any English monarch since Edward III, he had no immediate motivation to use the visual arts as a tool of propaganda beyond the way they were already an institutionalized component of court splendor. From the late 1510s he also manifested a marked appreciation of tapestry as an art form in its own right. Whether this began in the early years of his reign is less clear because of the partial nature of the documentation, but Henry's romantic and youthful tastes almost certainly influenced the subject matter of the tapestries purchased and used during these years.

Irrespective of his inclinations or maturity as a patron, Henry was now the center of a court that, under the influence of Continental example, had developed magnificence into an art form, and tapestry was a central component of that splendor. The dominant personality of the royal household following his father's death was his indomitable grandmother Margaret Beaufort (fig. 6.2). It must have been she who supervised the arrangements for Henry's coronation, aided by the lord great chamberlain, John de Vere, thirteenth earl of Oxford, and Henry's appointed guardians, the lord chancellor, Archbishop Warham, the treasurer, Thomas Howard (first earl of Surrey and second duke of Norfolk), and the lord privy seal,

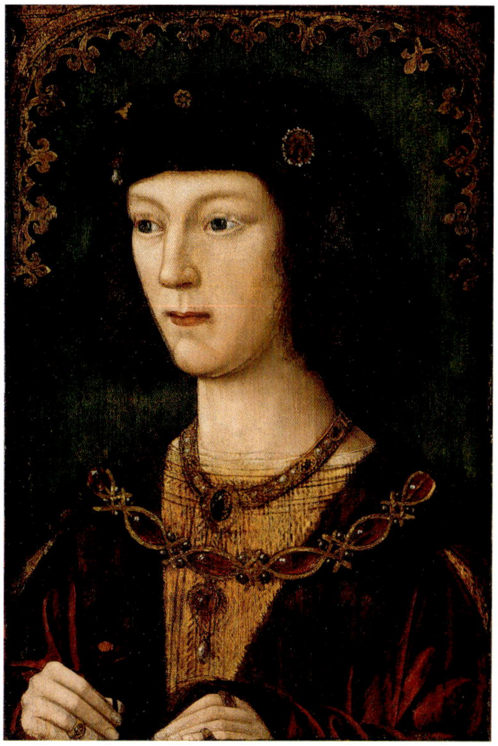

6.1 *Henry VIII*, ca. 1509, by an unidentified artist. Oil on panel, 39 x 25 cm. Denver Art Museum, Denver

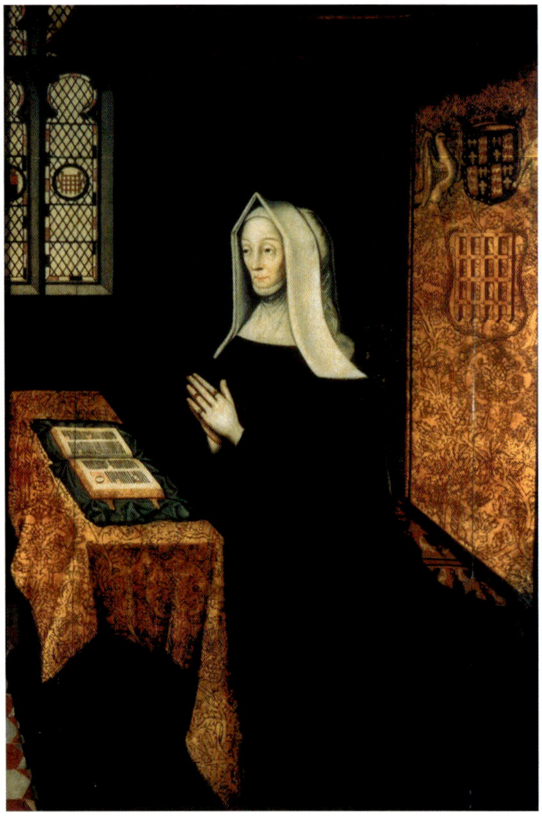

6.2 *Lady Margaret Beaufort* by Rowland Lockey, ca. 1598. Oil on panel, 177.8 x 114.3 cm. Saint John's College, Cambridge

Richard Fox. All of these personalities, in fact, are known to have owned interesting tapestry collections in their own right.[1] As was traditional, Westminster Abbey and Palace were draped with black hangings for Henry VII's funeral obsequies, providing a doleful contrast to the splendor of the decorations attendant on the festivities of the following weeks. The character and appearance of these events and Henry VIII's court in general are better documented than those of his predecessors thanks to a number of contemporary accounts, especially Edward Hall's *Triumphant Reigne of Kyng Henry the VIII,* published in 1542 but apparently based on notes made shortly after the events described. Further detail is provided by the descriptions of foreign correspondents, particularly those of the Venetian ambassadors.

The Use and Purchase of Tapestry at Court, 1509–1513

Henry VIII's first significant decision as king was to marry the pious and learned Katherine of Aragon, his brother's widow. The wedding took place at Greenwich on June 11, 1509, following which Henry and Katherine progressed from the Tower through the City of London on their way to Westminster. As on such progresses during Henry VII's reign, they were presented with a sequence of pageants, and focal points of the journey were decorated with precious textiles and tapestries. The route along Cornhill was hung with "cloth of Sundry colours as scarlettys, Cremesynys, Sangwynys, murreyes lygth and brown . . . and upon that othir side alle wyth Rych tapettis & clothis of aras, and as far as Chepe was Garnysshid wyth Clothis of Gold, of velvet & of sylk."[2] In all likelihood, many of these hangings were provided by the City guilds, most of whom owned tapestries and luxury textiles that hung in their halls on feast days.[3] Two weeks later, on June 24, similar decorations were in place for the procession after the double coronation.[4] The ensuing festivities at Westminster Palace also took place against a sumptuous array of hangings. According to Hall, the royal party was entertained with jousts and tournaments that they viewed from a "fare house covered with Tapistrie, and hanged wyth riche clothes of Arras."[5]

These festivities and tapestry's role therein set the tone for the next decade of court life. Henry was surrounded by a group of young noblemen with whom he had been educated, and their heads were full of chivalric and courtly ambitions. Much of the first years of Henry's reign passed in a round of tournaments, pageants, parties, and flirtation, in which the king and his confidants often assumed allegorical or symbolic roles. Reading Hall's descriptions, it is clear that tapestry continued to be the ubiquitous setting against which these events took place, even on occasion intimately involved in their staging. For example, in anticipation of Katherine's second child—the first, a girl, had been stillborn in June 1510—the royal household prepared a tournament and elaborate celebrations. On January 1, 1511, Katherine gave birth to a son who was christened Henry and who was also to die just seven weeks later. After the initial thanksgivings, the king and queen repaired to

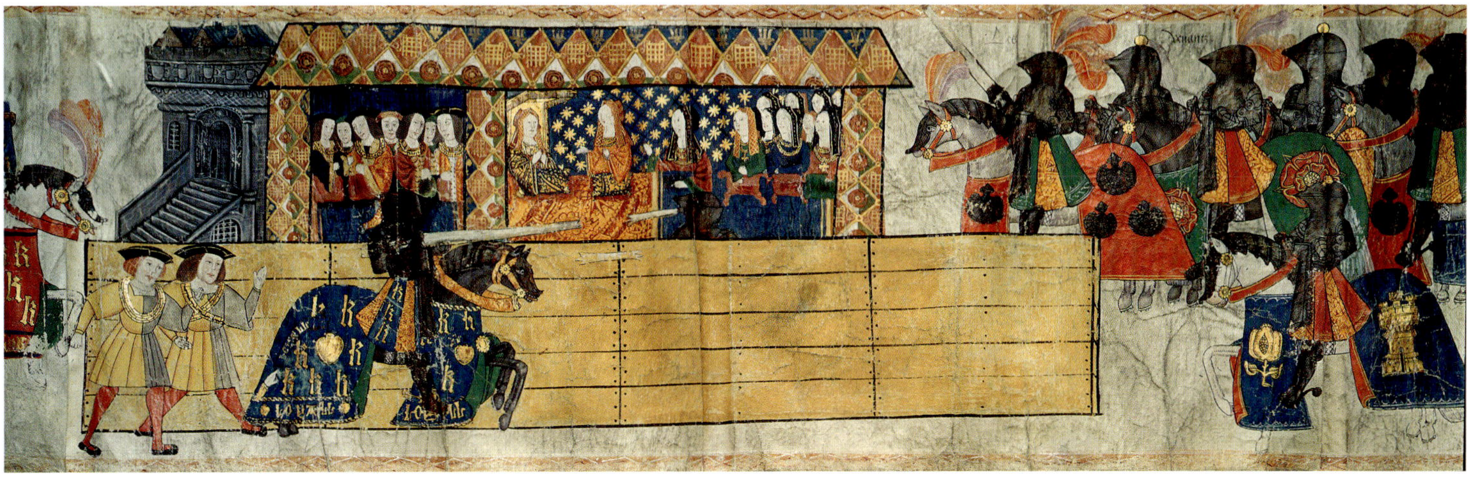

6.3 *Henry VIII Tilting at the Westminster Tournament of February 1511* (detail) from the *Westminster Tournament Roll*, 1511. Body color on vellum, 37.5 x 1,798 cm (dimensions of whole). The College of Arms, London

Richmond, where a "place in the Pallayce was prepared for the Kynge, and also the Quene, rychely hanged, the inner parte with clothe of golde, and the utter with ryche clothe of Arras," from which the royal party could watch the jousts (fig. 6.3).[6] Following these, a banquet was held for the court and the ambassadors. Hall describes the arrangements as follows: "After supper, his grace with the Quene, Lordes and Ladies came into the white Hal, within the sayed Pallays, which was hanged rychely." At some point during the following dance, the king disappeared and a pageant was rolled in on wheels. Next, "a greate clothe of Arras that did hang before the pageaunt was taken awaye, and the pageant bought more nere," revealing the king and other courtiers in fancy dress and masks on the pageant.[7] Although no subject is given for the tapestry in question, we can conjecture that it may have been chosen in accordance with the theme of the pageant, which was a Garden of Love, populated by allegorical personages such as "Cuer loyall," "Bone espoire," and "Amour loyall." As a coda to this event, it is to be noted that when the pageant was moved to the end of the hall, "sodainly the rude people ranne to the pageant, and rent tare and spoyled the pagent, so that the Lord Stuard nor the head officers could not cause them to abstaine, excepte they should have foughten and drawn bloud."[8] The incident provides a vivid reminder of the high value of the materials used in such a display and also of the extent to which these events were, in many respects, a genuine theater, which took place in front of an audience whose character varied depending on the location and occasion.

The play on illusion and reality embodied by the theatrical use of a tapestry to conceal the tableau of the pageant points to another interesting issue that emerges from these descriptions. This is the correlation between courtly activities and the imagery in various contemporary tapestries. In some cases the link is so marked as to suggest that certain festivities may have been inspired by the iconography of the tapestries or, alternatively, that the designs may have been inspired by descriptions of these courtly events. For example, in the jousts of February 1511, Henry appeared in the guise of "Couer Loyal," the earl of Devon as "Bon Valois," Thomas Knyvet as "Bon Espoir," and Edward Neville as "Bon Valoir."[9] A visual correlation can be found in a tapestry depicting a tournament scene dating from ca. 1510–15 formerly at Knole House, Sevenoaks (fig. 6.4).[10] The tapestry depicts two knights saluting a king who is seated above in a crowded stand. The helm and trappings of one knight are decorated with a crowned heart and a crowned heart in a vice, while those of the other knight represent a colander and water drops. A second tapestry, evidently woven from the same design series, depicts the same knights in combat with broadswords; one is inscribed "cor" (coeur, or heart) and the other "vis" (vice).[11] Circumstantial evidence that the tapestry once at Knole

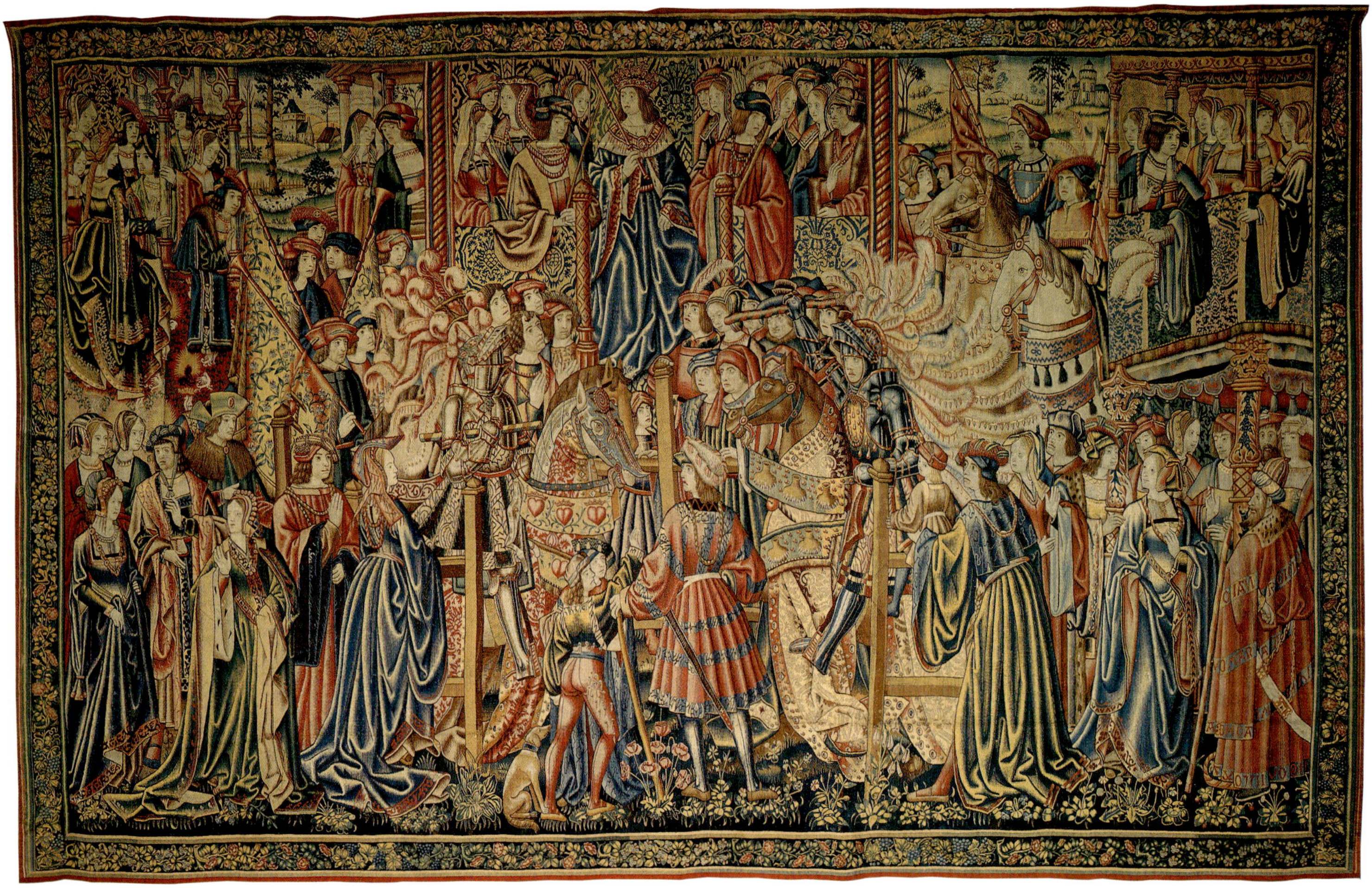

6.4 *The Salute before the Tournament* from a set of the *Tournament of Vice and Virtue*. Tapestry woven in the Southern Netherlands, probably Brussels, ca. 1510–20. Wool and silk, 438 x 701 cm. Bass Museum of Art, Miami Beach

may come from a set acquired by Henry comes from the fact that many of the sixteenth- and seventeenth-century tapestries and furnishings there entered the Sackville collection in the late seventeenth century as perquisites to the sixth earl of Dorset in his capacity as lord chamberlain from 1689 to 1697.[12]

Another case where court life and tapestry imagery are closely related is provided by the festivities at Greenwich on New Year's Eve 1511. This included a pageant in which the king and his closest friends besieged a castle defended by the leading women of the court, using oranges and cotton balls as their weapons. This calls to mind the imagery of one of a set of tapestries depicting the *Romance of the Rose* now in the Hermitage Museum (fig. 6.5), which depicts a similar assault where the women use roses as their weapons. Again, the style of the tapestry indicates that it must have been designed sometime between 1510 and 1515. The set from which this piece originates is made from very high-quality materials, but the original owner has never been identified.[13]

The correspondence between the courtly and chivalric subject matter of the festivities held at the Tudor court during the opening years of Henry's reign and the imagery of various contemporary tapestries raises the question whether he was buying similar pieces. Unfortunately, the evidence is scant. One problem is the variety of ways in which Henry paid for tapestries during these years. The official source for purchases of all kinds at the time of his accession was the Treasury of the Chamber. During the first half of the fifteenth century this had been the repository for the king's private funds, but during the reigns of Edward IV and Henry VII it had developed into the most important revenue department of the court, funding everything from gambling debts and minor rewards to significant public expenditure such as building works and the equipment of armies. As such, it

6.5 *Assault on the Castle of Love* from a set known as the *Romance of the Rose*. Tapestry woven in the Southern Netherlands, probably Brussels, ca. 1510–20. Wool, silk, and gilt-metal-wrapped thread, 425 x 407 cm. The State Hermitage Museum, Saint Petersburg

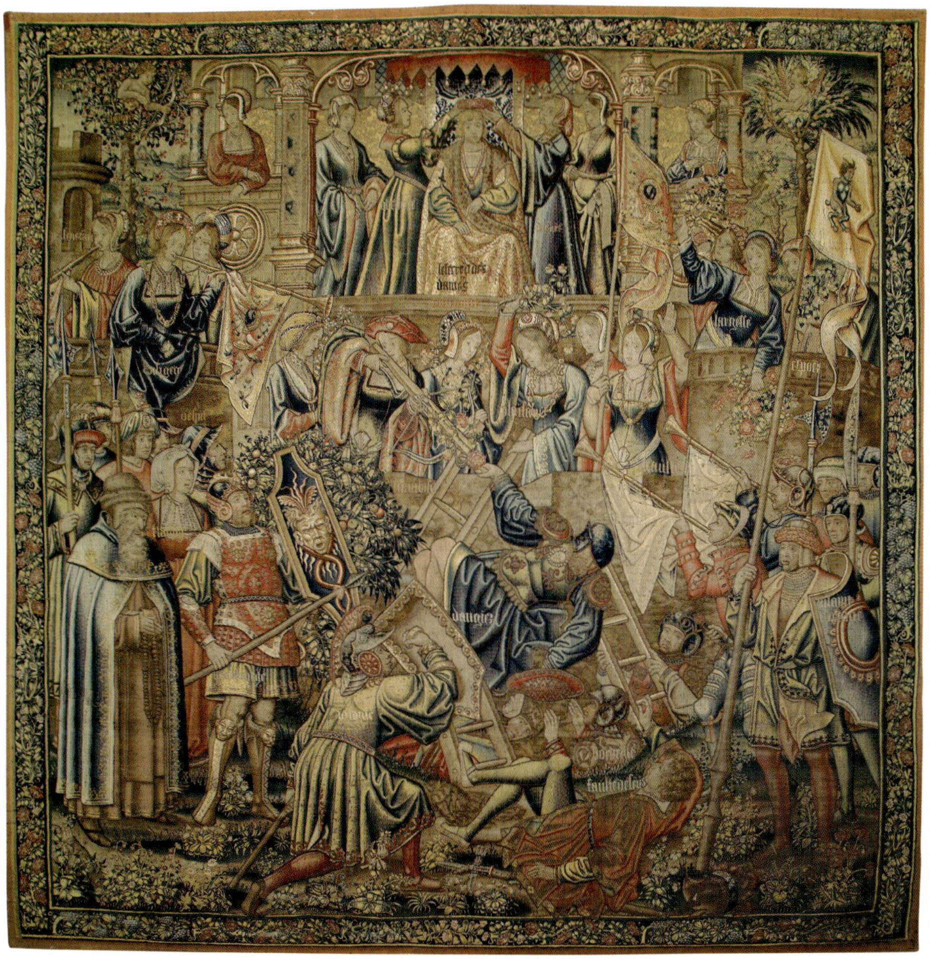

continued to be one of the most important funds for a variety of luxury goods during the first twenty years of Henry's reign, and details of disbursements made from this source are listed in the so-called King's Book of Payments.[14] Between April 1509 and May 1520 this series of accounts records expenditures of just under £200,000 (approximately £18,000 a year). The main items were cloth and fur for the Great Wardrobe (just under £50,000), the revels and jousts (£22,000), and jewelry and plate (just under £46,000).[15] In total, twelve payments for tapestry are cited in this list of accounts, which ranged from sums of a few shillings for cheap window covers to hundreds of pounds in the mid- to late 1510s for immense gold-woven tapestries.

The Treasury of the Chamber was one important and relatively well-documented source of royal expenditure, but there was also a second, the so-called Privy Purse, for which written records are lacking. The Privy Purse came into being because disbursements from the Treasury of the Chamber were cumbersome, requiring written warrants for all payments. Shortly after his coronation Henry therefore began to withdraw large sums from the chamber for use as occasion demanded, which he confided to Sir William Compton, a groom of the chamber, and groom of the stool from 1510. In 1516, for example, £18,000 was withdrawn in this way, and Henry was clearly using this fund to pay substantial bills. Compton's accounts were not subject to the usual public audit, so any records he maintained have not survived, if they were ever written down. Perhaps for this reason, the only tapestry purchases documented during the first two years of Henry's reign are minor furnishing pieces acquired through the Great Wardrobe.[16] Yet evidence that this was just part of the story is provided by the fact that the inventory taken after Henry's death in 1547 includes many allegorical and courtly subjects of the kind that

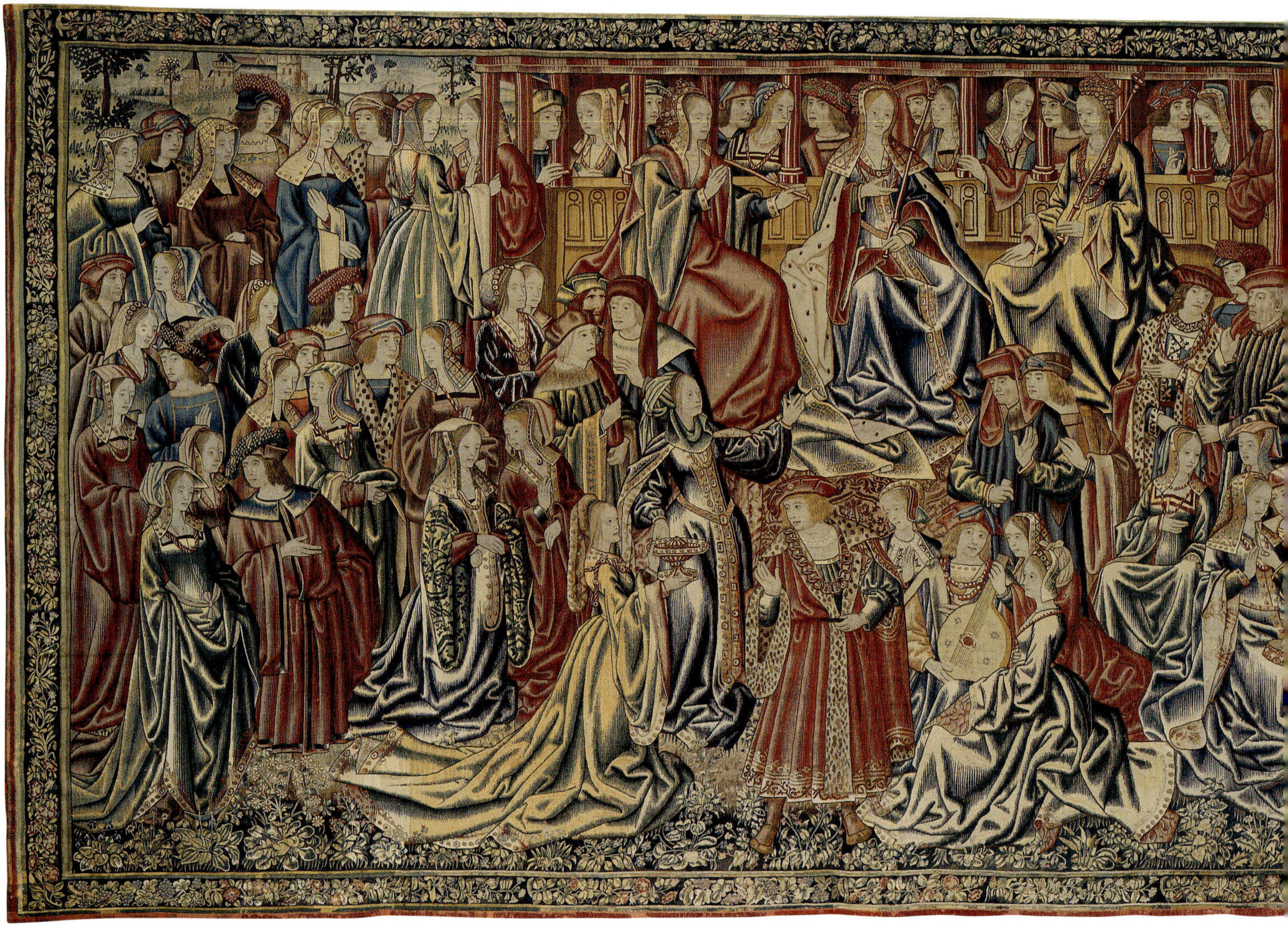

6.6 *Allegorical Court Scene.* Tapestry woven in the Southern Netherlands, ca. 1510–20. Wool and silk, 396 x 746 cm. Hampton Court Palace

were produced during the 1510s but not thereafter. In addition, eight months after his accession Henry renewed the privileged status of Pieter d'Enghien van Aelst with a grant whereby he was accepted as the king's "Arrasmaker" to import "cloths of tapestry and arras" into England for sale.[17] No purchases are documented from Van Aelst during the next seven years, but it seems unlikely that Henry would have gone to the lengths of awarding Van Aelst this exclusive role if he did not plan to use his services.

In summary, although there is no firm evidence to confirm that sets such as the *Allegorical Joust* and *Romance of the Rose* originate from the English royal collection, they probably give an idea of the sort of acquisitions that Henry was making from Van Aelst during the early years of his reign. The only allegorical tapestry of this type and date with a certain royal provenance is a panel at Hampton Court that depicts three women sitting in judgment among a large group of courtly figures, with a kneeling woman offering a covered cup to a man standing in the foreground (fig. 6.6 and detail opposite p. 103).[18] The subject has not been identified, but it may be part of a sequence depicting an allegory such as the early-fifteenth-century poem the *Court of Love.* The design typifies the style of contemporary Brussels production, which continued to emphasize pattern and ornamentation. Much of the decorative effect comes from the tightly packed figures who fill most of the picture plane. Such figures were often drawn from a stock of models easily adapted from one tapestry design to another, giving tapestry merchants

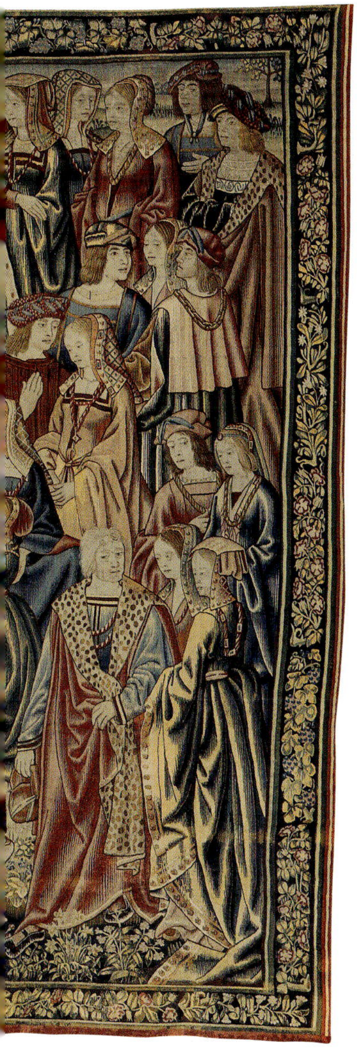

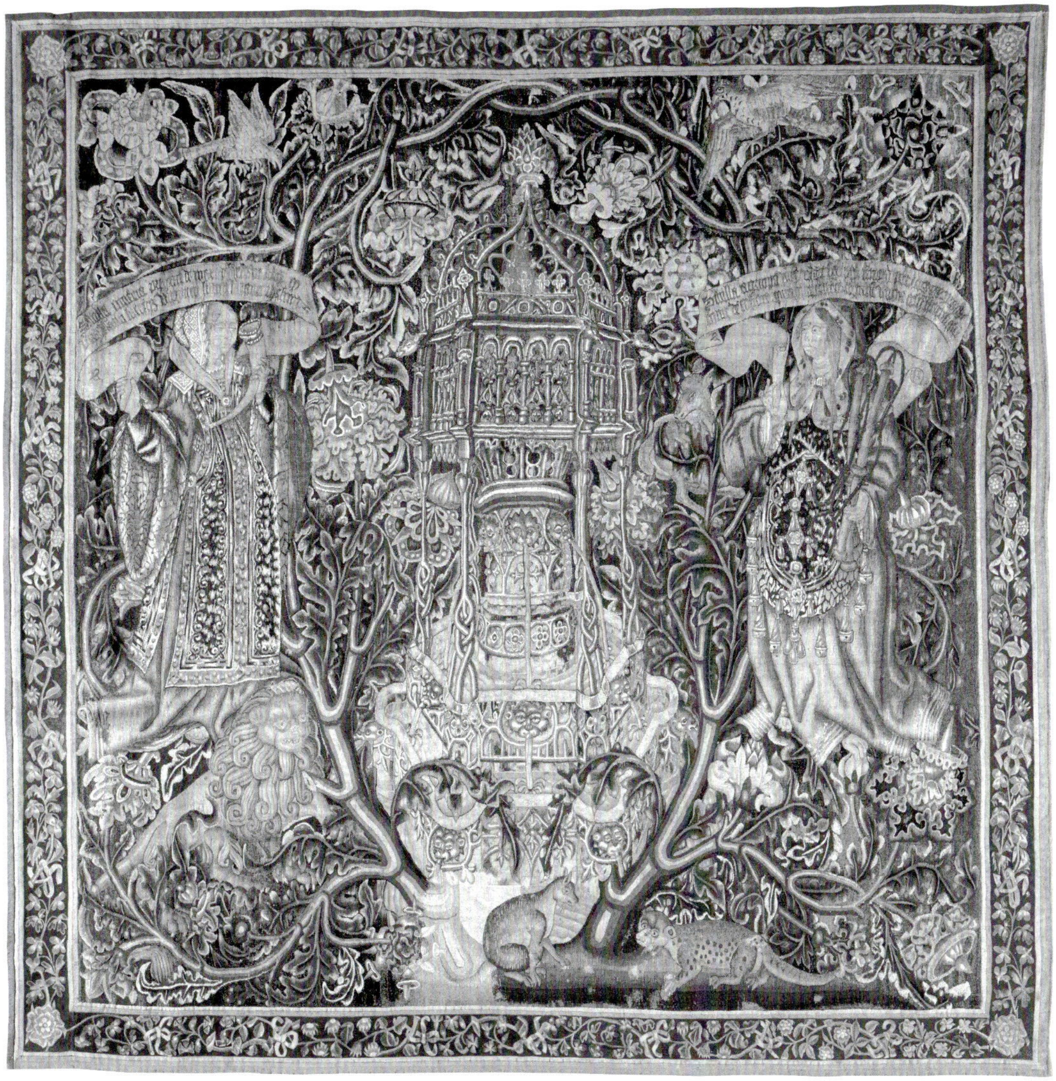

6.7 *Verdure with Roses and Sibyls.* Tapestry woven in the Southern Netherlands, ca. 1510–20. Wool and silk, 330 x 314 cm. The Burrell Collection, Glasgow

a convenient means to expand or reduce designs to widths specified by their patrons. Although a number of early-sixteenth-century Brussels tapestries do incorporate Renaissance motifs, these elements are generally used for little more than decorative effect.

Although there is nothing about the Hampton Court allegorical scene to suggest that it was specifically designed for the Tudor court, evidence of some custom orders in the early years of Henry's reign is suggested by a distinctive group of verdure tapestries, now dispersed, that depict the sibyls with Tudor roses woven in the corners of the borders. These roses probably typify the sort of insertions undertaken by Van der Strete's workshop in the early sixteenth century. Each panel has a ground formed by two branches, one representing roses, the Tudor badge, the other stylized pomegranates, Katherine of Aragon's symbol, which form an enclosure around a fountain. At either side there is a sibyl, with an inscription, while below there are fabulous beasts, such as unicorns, griffins, and lions. A number of pieces of this design are extant, of which the largest group, numbering six pieces, is now in the Burrell Collection (fig. 6.7).[19] The style of design suggests a production date in the early sixteenth century, ca. 1510. Because these tapestries feature the rose and the pomegranate so prominently, in conjunction with other elements evoking the *hortus conclusus* and symbolic of the Passion of Christ, it is conceivable that this series was conceived as a symbolic celebration of the holy union of Henry and Katherine following their marriage in 1509. Equally, it is also possible that this series was commissioned by Henry VII eight years before, at the time of the marriage of Prince Arthur to Katherine.

The Great Wardrobe and the 1513 Campaign in France

Henry's accession had no immediate impact on the structure of the Great Wardrobe, and this department continued to function as it had under his father. Surviving accounts for the early years of his reign provide a glimpse of the efforts that were being made by the lord chamberlain and the Great Wardrobe to ensure that appropriate furnishings and decorations were provided in the various royal palaces. Cornelius van der Strete, whose appointment as "arras maker to the king" had been renewed by a grant issued in October 1509, was also kept busy repairing tapestries in the collection.[20] For example, in 1511 he was paid for traveling to Nottingham Castle with about ten men to repair diverse tapestries, verdures, and counterpoints in situ, in advance of Henry's progress to Nottingham that summer.[21] The same account records a payment to John Harvill, the royal tailor, for 2,000 ells (1,125 square yards) of canvas for lining tapestries at Nottingham.

The royal arras maker certainly had a challenging task. In 1512, we find him being paid for repairs to pieces of "arras" of *Saint George* and *Nebuchadnezzar*, the same tapestries he had repaired in 1503, suggesting that these two pieces played a particularly important role in various court events.[22] The *Saint George* tapestry presumably featured in the celebrations associated with the Order of the Garter and the feast of Saint George, celebrated every April 23, the anniversary of Henry's accession and his official birthday. Part of the problem may simply have been keeping the tapestries clean. Most of the rooms in the palaces had fireplaces that must have generated enormous amounts of smoke and soot. Evidence that contemporary patrons were aware of the damage this caused to their precious hangings comes from the household accounts of Henry Percy, fifth earl of Northumberland. During 1512, the earl's accounts include a payment for twenty "chowders" of sea coal and twenty quarters of charcoal. The charcoal was for use at Christmas, the season when the earl's best arras was displayed, because the sea coal was so detrimental to the hangings.[23] How the royal tapestries were cleaned during Henry VIII's reign is uncertain. During the seventeenth century, the royal arras maker and his staff swept damp breadcrumbs across the surface of the tapestries with brooms, a process that extracted some dirt by a process of absorption but which was obviously detrimental to the weft threads, particularly the silk and gilt surface of the metallic filaments. At that date, when a significant portion of the historic hangings was constantly displayed, many of the more important tapestries were cleaned about once every twenty to thirty years.[24] Whether the same technique was used in the sixteenth century is uncertain, but considering how many court activities were the subject of long-standing tradition, it is likely that it was.

Wardrobe accounts give a glimpse of the ongoing efforts that were undertaken by the court officers and the "arras makers" in respect to domestic arrangements in the royal palaces, but more extreme measures were called for when Henry mounted his first campaign to the Continent. Henry VII had pursued a strategy of peace, but his son was altogether more belligerent and hungry for glory. As the Venetian ambassador reported in 1509, "The new king is magnificent, liberal and a great enemy of the French." In Thomas Wolsey Henry found a minister who could promote his martial agenda in opposition to the opinions of his older advisers, and from 1511 he began to steer a course that was to reopen the time-honored tradition of animosity with France. Under the banner of the "Holy League" formed in 1511, whereby England, Spain, and the Holy Roman Empire agreed to help drive France out of northern Italy, an expeditionary force of twelve thousand men was dispatched in 1512 to combine forces with Ferdinand of Aragon in taking Bayonne. This plan foundered when

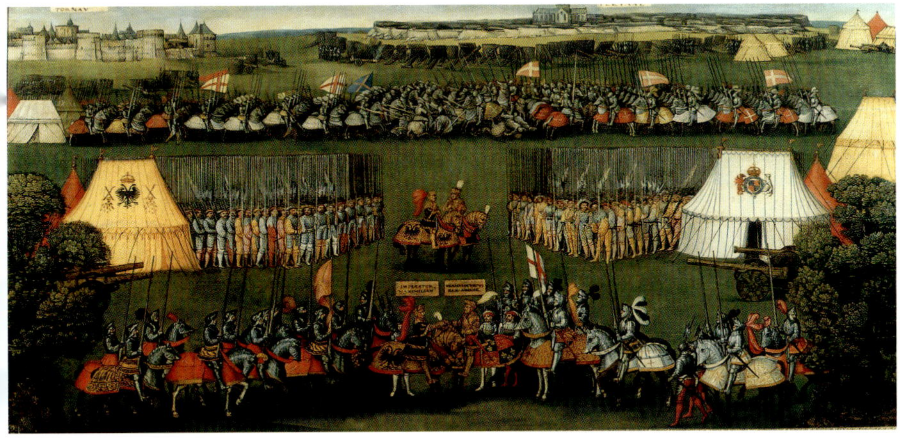

6.8 *The Meeting of Henry VIII and the Emperor Maximilian* by an unidentified artist, ca. 1545. Oil on panel, 99.1 x 205.7 cm. The Royal Collection

Ferdinand's forces attacked Navarre instead. Determined to make up for this humiliation, Henry instigated a second assault into France that he would lead in person.

The second campaign was launched in the late summer of 1513. Much of the organization was entrusted to Wolsey, and precious textiles were necessarily a key component of regal splendor. The expenses for the campaign included charges for wagons to transport the goods of the Wardrobe of the Robes and the Wardrobe of the Beds to France, and the English tapestries were in use quite literally from the moment Henry disembarked at Calais, because he was conveyed to shore by a "bote covered with arras, and so was set on londe."[25] Henry's campaign lodgings consisted of a timber house with an iron chimney, and large tents, striped in white and yellow, with the royal beasts on the pinnacles, subdivided internally into a sequence of chambers. In total the ensemble measured 125 feet in length. The interiors of the tents were painted throughout with images of the rising sun, and they were presumably hung with precious textiles and tapestries.[26] When the Emperor Maximilian visited Henry's field camp on August 13 (fig. 6.8), he was "broughte to a tente of cloth of gold all ready apparaled accordynge to his estate, for all the tente within was syled wyth clothe of golde and blewe velvet, and all the blewe velvet was embrowdered with H.K. [for Henry and Katherine] of fyne golde, and hys cupboard was rychely furnyshed."[27]

Hall's account does not detail tapestries from the royal collection, but presumably they also figured in the splendor of Henry's temporary residences. And they would certainly have featured in the decorations of the ducal residence in Lille, where Henry was received in September 1513 by Margaret of Savoy, regent of the Netherlands, the emperor Maximilian, and the young archduke Charles. Indeed, the tapestries at Margaret's disposal may have made a strong impression on the young English king, because they would have included part of the Burgundian heritage that had been such a formative influence in the development of the English tapestry collection under Edward IV and Henry VII. Margaret herself was a keen amateur of tapestry. She had been appointed regent of the Netherlands in 1506 by Maximilian, her father, following the death of her brother, Philip the Fair, whose son and heir, Charles, was still a minor. Charles achieved his majority in 1515, but because of the size of his kingdom he confirmed Margaret in her post and she maintained this role until her death in 1530. Although Margaret lacked the scale of funds that her ancestors had enjoyed, she ensured the careful preservation of the Burgundian collection during her reign, and in time she developed a small but interesting collection of her own. In 1509 she purchased armorial tapestries from a workshop in Bruges, and in 1511 she presented Maximilian with the design for a tapestry genealogy of the kings of Portugal that she had obtained from Pieter van Aelst. During the mid- and late 1510s, she commissioned important religious and allegorical tapestry designs from her court artist, Bernaert van Orley.[28]

Henry made his entry into Lille on September 11, and the streets were hung with tapestries for the occasion.[29] He was received at the town hall by Margaret and Prince Charles and then taken to Margaret's palace, where according to the Milanese ambassador, he was presented with a suite of gold-woven tapestries that hung in four rooms. Although this report is unconfirmed, the king subsequently made a gift of £13 6s. 8d. to Margaret's tapissiers, which indicates that he had reason to be grateful to them.[30] After three days of partying and dancing

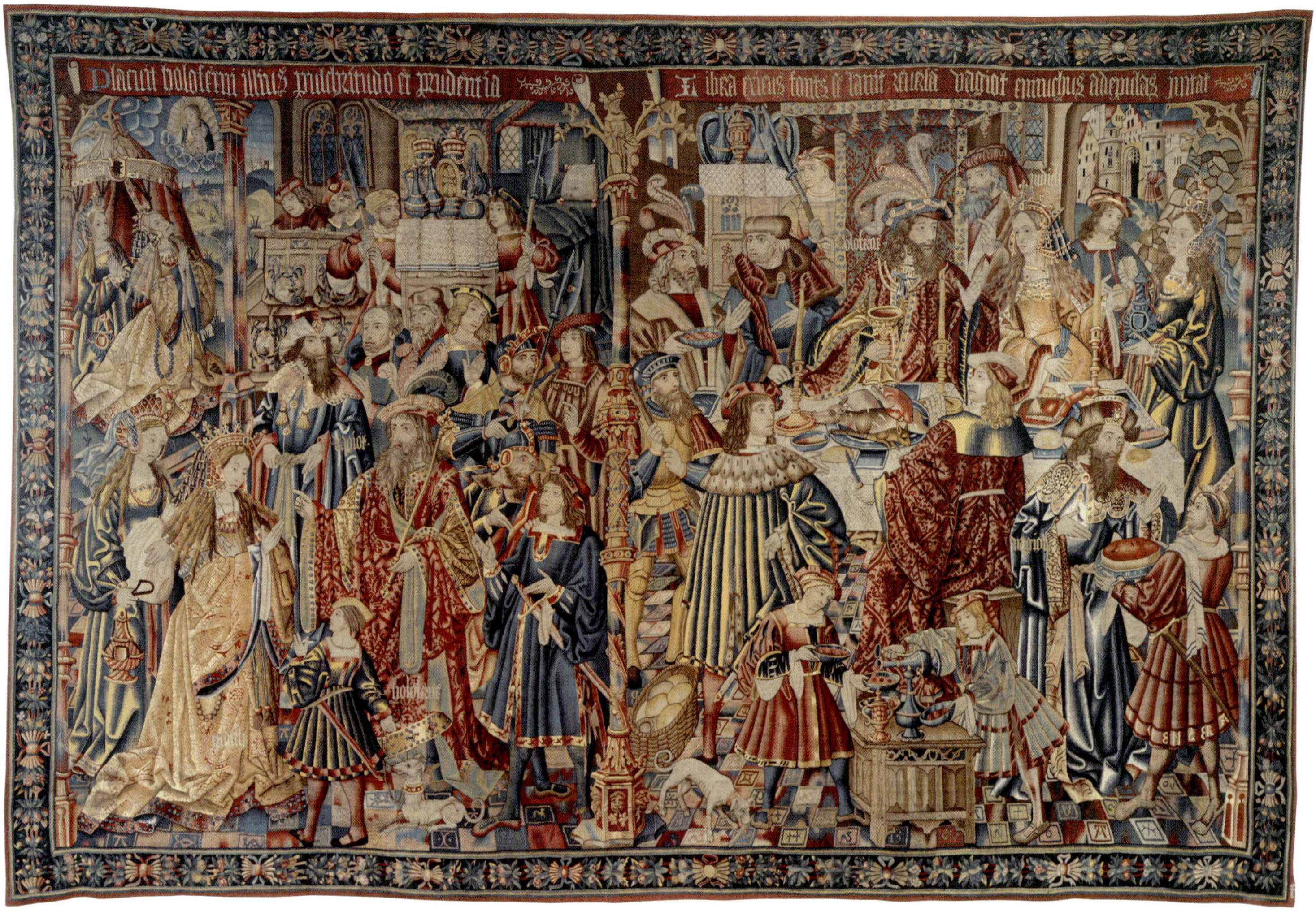

6.9 *Scene from the Story of Judith and Holofernes*. Tapestry woven in the Southern Netherlands, probably Tournai, ca. 1515. Wool and silk, 438 x 614 cm. Musées Royaux d'Art et d'Histoire, Brussels

at Margaret's court in Lille, Henry hastened back to Tournai, which the English cannons had been bombarding mercilessly. The city finally capitulated on September 23, accepting Henry as its king in place of Louis XII, and Henry made his triumphal entry on Sunday, September 25, where a sullen citizenry greeted him.

As we have seen, Tournai had been one of the leading centers of high-quality tapestry production during the second half of the fifteenth century, and many of the greatest sets in the English royal collection had been purchased from merchants based there. Although Brussels had now become the focus of high-quality production, Tournai seems to have established a niche producing tapestries of moderate quality with simple, bold figures executed in a limited palette of colors.[31] Products from the town workshops must have figured among the tapestries lining the streets for Henry VIII's triumphal entry on September 25, 1513.[32] The next day, during Margaret's state visit to the English king, the civic authorities presented her with a set of tapestries illustrating the *City of Women,* perhaps a visualization of the Christine de Pisan treatise of this name.[33] In the following days and months, several leading English courtiers were also given, or promised, sets of tapestry. The king was presented with an unnamed set purchased from the leading Tournai tapestry merchant Arnould Poissonier, Thomas Wolsey received a set of the *Twelve Months,* and Sir Edward Poynings, the new town governor, received a chamber of tapestries of the *Story of Hercules*. Poissonier also provided a set of the "Voyage de Caluce," depicting European explorers in Calcutta, that was presented to Sir Robert Wingfield, while a set of the *Story of Judith* was promised to Charles Brandon, duke of Suffolk, that was eventually delivered to him in 1517 (see below).[34] The character of these gifts is suggested by the contract that the Tournai authorities drew up with the weaver Clement Sarrasin for the set of *Hercules* intended for Edward Poynings. This stipulated that the tapestries were to be woven in the best wool and that the garments of all the principal figures were to be woven in silk, with yellow silk being used to depict the highlights in gowns of cloth of gold, and green and blue silk for the highlights in gowns of velvet or damask "to make them stand out against the others." The weaver also contracted to use silk in the pillars, carpets, and tabernacles depicted, as also in the border.[35] Although the exact identity of these sets is unknown, a number of Tournai tapestries of this period and subject have survived, giving a clear idea of the sort of character and quality of the tapestries involved in these gifts (fig. 6.9). These displays and gifts were not without effect and clearly promoted the town's products to the new English rulers, as evidenced by a letter that Brian Tuke, clerk of the signet, addressed to Richard Pace, Wolsey's secretary: the town "manufactures excellent carpets and table covers, and will prove useful for the king, as the Burgundian and Rhenish wines can conveniently be brought from thence to England."[36]

The success of the Tournai campaign ensured Wolsey's rapid promotion during the following months, and one of the new appointments he received was the bishopric of Tournai. A keen aficionado of tapestries, Wolsey was to make good use of his Tournai connections to augment his collection with both antique and modern tapestries, as will be discussed in the next chapter.

Royal Tapestry Usage and Purchases, 1513–1519

After the spate of descriptions associated with the first years of Henry's reign, evidence is less abundant regarding tapestry usage at court during the years immediately following the Tournai campaign. Nonetheless, surviving accounts reveal that tapestries and precious textiles continued to play an uninterrupted role. The character of this usage is suggested by the account that Sebastian Giustinian, the Venetian ambassador, gave of his reception at court in April 1515: "Though it was before Mass they made us breakfast, for fear we should faint, after which, we were conducted to the presence through sundry chambers all hung with the most beautiful tapestry, passing down the ranks of the bodyguard. We were ushered into a stately hall. At one extremity was His Majesty, standing under a canopy of gold embroidered at Florence, the most costly thing I ever witnessed. He was leaning against his gilt throne, on which was a large gold brocade cushion, where lay the long gold sword of state." The king was magnificently outfitted for the occasion, wearing the costume and jewelry of the Order of the Garter. He was accompanied by eight knights of the Garter to his left, various prelates to his right, six officers of the Household bearing their rods of office, ten heralds outfitted in tabards of cloth of gold, and a "crowd of nobility, all arrayed in cloth of gold and silk." Henry was evidently already a master of the grandest ceremony. Fresh from his journey, Giustinian was duly impressed with the Tudor court, which "glittered with jewels, gold and silver, the pomp being unprecedented."[37]

Giustinian's description provides a vivid impression of an ambassadorial reception at Henry's court, the sort of event that was staged with the greatest care. A handful of references in Hall's account also reflect the extensive preparations that underlay other grand events of the day, several of which evidently followed the provisions laid down by Henry VII's ordinances of 1493. For example, preparations for the christening of Princess Mary on February 21, 1516, followed the prescriptions closely: "From the court gate [Westminster Palace] to the church door of the Friars [Austin Friars] was railed and hung with arras . . . at the church door was set a house well formed of timber, covered with arras."[38] The following May, when the king attended Westminster Hall to give judgment on the ringleaders of the anti-alien riots, it was equipped for the occasion with a cloth of estate and "hanged with Arras."[39] Fifteen months later, in August 1518, when the king held a banquet in honor of Cardinal Campeggio and Cardinal Wolsey, the dining room was "hung with arras, having a cloth of estate, chair and cushions for the king of riche cloth of gold of tissue . . . also two chairs of cloth of gold were set for the Legates on the king's right."[40] Although brief, these vignettes hint at the ongoing activity of the Great Wardrobe and the continuing use of gradations of textile quality in direct relation to the importance of personages and events.

Tapestry Purchases Made on Henry's Behalf

If the use of tapestry and precious textiles was constant during this period, changes can be detected in the volume of purchases and the channels through which they were made. As before, the Great Wardrobe handled much of the more quotidian furnishings. For example, in 1514, Ralph Jenet, yeoman of the Wardrobe, was reimbursed by the Treasury of the Chamber for £18 18s. for "diverse peces of new tappestrye by hym bought for the king for Eltham."[41] According to a warrant in a file of subsidiary documents, the purchase involved fifty-six pieces of new tapestry, "with Imagerye every pece conteyning ix flemys elles [just under five square yards] at ix d. the ell," which Jenet had bought of "dyvers persons."[42]

A more ambitious purchase was undertaken during the same year as part of the dowry of Henry's sister Mary. Mary had been betrothed to Charles of Spain, but this alliance was abruptly curtailed when Henry's erstwhile allies, King Ferdinand of Spain and Emperor Maximilian, signed a treaty with Louis XII in March 1514. After frantic behind-the-scenes negotiations by Wolsey, Henry established his own treaty with Louis on July 30, 1514, sealed with the promise of the hand of his sister in marriage. Mary traveled to France to marry Louis in October 1514. In his typically laconic way, Hall tells us that "Great was the ryches in plate, juels, money apparel, and hanginges that this lady brought into Fraunce," but in this instance, the provisions are relatively well documented.[43] In advance of the marriage Cornelius van der Strete, the royal arras maker, traveled to Bruges to purchase the tapestries in question. A bill in the State Papers details his expenses, which included £520 3s. 4d. for an unidentified six-piece "arras" set containing 390¼ ells (219½ square yards) at 26s. 8d. per ell; £63 for three "borders" comprising sixty-three ells (thirty-three square yards) at 20s. per ell; and £151 24s. for a seven-piece *Story of Hercules,* measuring 552 ells (305 square yards) at 3s. 8d. per ell. Van der Strete's bill also included £4 14s. 8d. for transporting the tapestry from Bruges to London via Calais, £3 for his own costs, and £6 for exchange charges. The document is accompanied by a certificate from John Lord Berners stating that he had received these tapestries for the French queen's use on September 15, 1514.[44] In a subsequent bill, Van der Strete stated that the tapestries had been purchased in Flanders from a man called Philip Calthorpe, possibly to be identified with a rich Norfolk merchant of this name. The document also identifies Calthorpe's factor, a Florentine merchant called Giovanni Cavalcanti.[45] Cavalcanti was subsequently to figure in a number of major tapestry purchases in the late 1510s. First recorded in London in June 1509 as an exporter of sizeable quantities of wool, he had probably moved there because of the difficult political and social climate in Florence at the time.[46] Scion of a rich Florentine family, he evidently played a key role in the Italian community in London and in November 1511 acted as a guarantor, along with Leonardo Frescobaldi, for Pietro Torrigiano's contract for Lady Margaret Beaufort's tomb. In October 1512 he was granted "Safe conduct and protection to trade in England for the next ten years," and the King's Book of Payments evidences numerous purchases from him during the next two decades. He was responsible for supplying many of the munitions and equipment required for the war against France, and Henry rewarded his services in February 1513 with a grant to retain for five years the customs on all his imports and exports. In April of the same year, he received

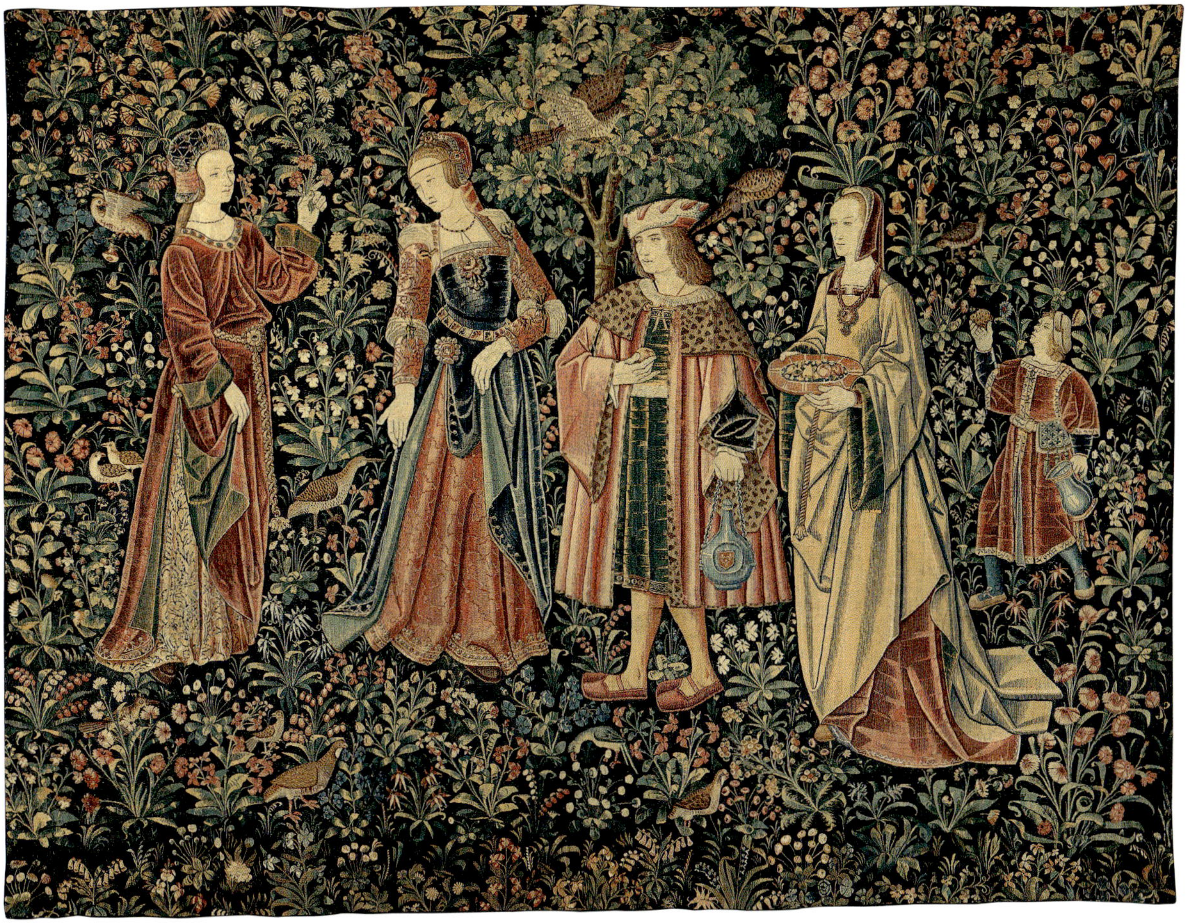

6.10 *Millefleurs with Courtly Figures* (fragment) from a set known as *La vie seigneuriale*. Tapestry woven in the Southern Netherlands, ca. 1510–20. Wool and silk, 284 x 360 cm. Musée de Cluny, Paris

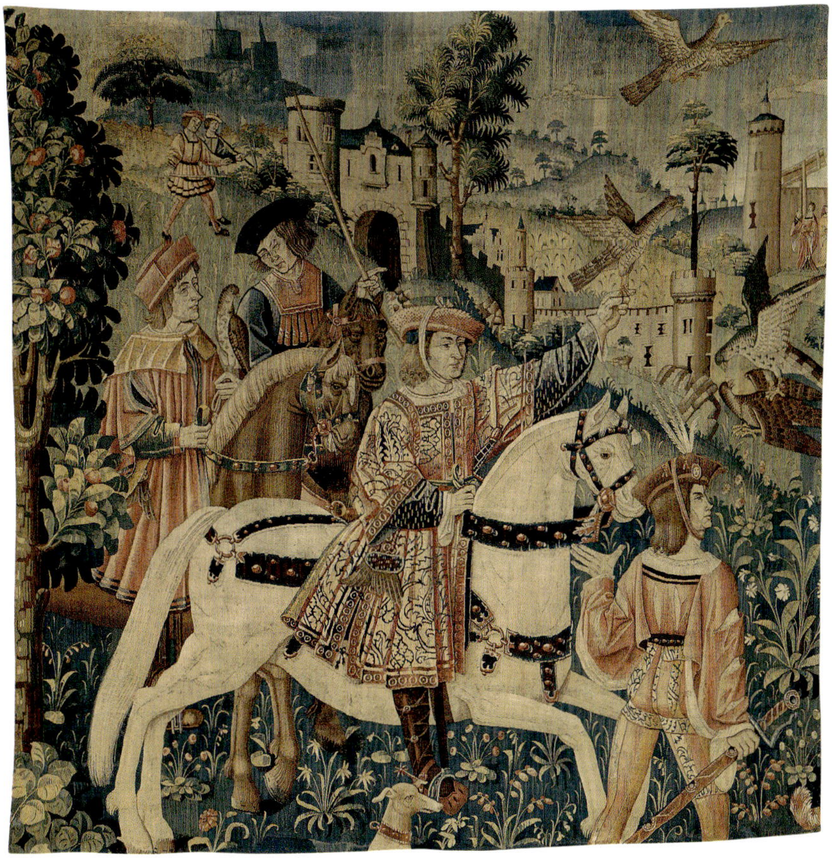

6.11 *Hawking* (fragment). Tapestry woven in the Southern Netherlands, ca. 1510–20. Wool and silk, 250 x 250 cm. Musée de Cluny, Paris

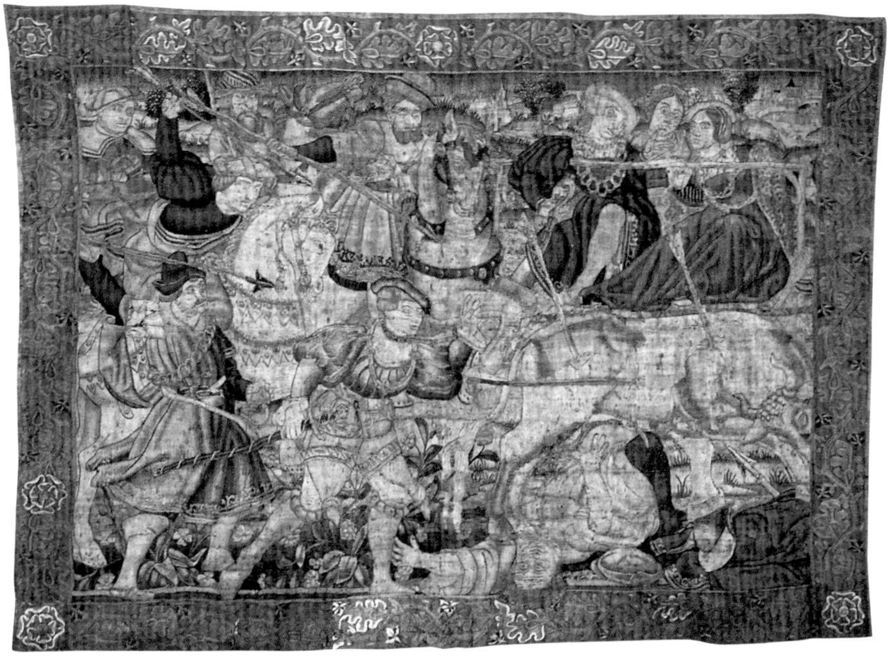

6.12 *The Bull Hunt* with border featuring Tudor Roses (fragment with reduced borders). Tapestry woven in the Southern Netherlands, ca. 1510–30. Wool and silk, 255 x 360 cm. Location unidentified (Sotheby's, London, May 22, 1987, lot 16)

a grant of denization for life. He evidently traveled regularly between London and Italy and enjoyed a close relationship with the new Medici pope, Leo X, who had been elected in March 1513. Subsequent documents indicate that he held the role of gentleman usher at the papal court.

An inventory of goods delivered by Andrew Windsor to Louis XII's officers at Abbeville in October provides further details of Mary's dowry. Besides the tapestries already listed, it included a thirteen-piece set with figures of *Shepherds and Shepherdesses* and twelve counterpoints of verdure.[47] In view of the short period that elapsed between the cancellation of Mary's engagement to Charles of Spain, her engagement to Louis XII, and this delivery, it seems most probable that most of these tapestries were purchased from existing stocks rather than specifically commissioned. Although this is the only documented instance of Van der Strete purchasing tapestries on behalf of the Crown, the sizeable sums that he dispensed on this occasion suggest that he was relatively familiar with this responsibility. One of his successors, Jan Mostinck, appears to have played an analogous role during the 1530s, evidently enjoying close contacts with leading Netherlandish tapestry merchants. In passing, it is to be noted that the liberality displayed in equipping Mary's trousseau was a component of the magnificence expected of a great ruler. A comparable example is provided three years later when Margaret, Henry's other sister, returned to Scotland on May 18, 1517, after staying at Baynard's Castle for one year at Henry's charge. Hall tells us that she was "richely appoynted of all things mete to her estate, both of Jewells, plate, tapissry, Arras, Coyne, Horsses, and all other thinges of the kynges gift and liberalitie."[48]

A large purchase of a different kind was handled in 1516 by the Great Wardrobe for the Manor of Beaulieu, subsequently known as Newhall, which Henry had acquired from Sir Thomas Boleyn for £1,000 and on which building work began that January.[49] Information is provided by a declaration submitted by James Chapell of the Wardrobe to the general surveyors of the Exchequer, regarding the advance of £1,100 he had received from John Heron, treasurer of the Chamber, in September 1516.[50] The declaration states that having traveled to Beaulieu to take necessary measurements, Chapell traveled with three servants and four horses to Flanders, where he remained thirty-nine days. In that time, he purchased 108 tapestries, with a total surface area of 3,238 Flemish ells (1,818 square yards), at a cost of £402 13s. 10d. Eleven grades of tapestry are cited, presumably corresponding to eleven sets, which ranged in price from 14d. to 8s. per ell.[51] Chapell also purchased twenty-three "lyke verdures and Tappestry called Tappettes for Chymneyes" containing 177 ells, four "carpetes" of fine verdure and tapestry "to lay upon tables," thirty-nine counterpoints of verdures and tapestry, again of a range of qualities, and a variety of other materials, sheets, and bedding.[52] Though no subjects are given, we can speculate that these tapestries would have comprised the sort of verdure, genre, courtly, and hunting scenes that have survived in considerable numbers from the 1510s, some woven on millefleur grounds, others with landscape grounds (figs. 6.10–6.12). Many of the surviving examples are fairly schematic, incorporating different combinations of the same figures from one set to another, a reflection of the formulaic manner in which such cartoons were created.[53]

Henry as a Tapestry Patron in His Own Right during the 1510s

The scale of expenditure on Beaulieu was considerable, but a Wardrobe officer handled it. From the mid-1510s, however, we find evidence that Henry was directly involved in purchases. In this period Wolsey, his leading administrator and constant companion, was also expending considerable effort and funds to acquire tapestries for his properties at Hampton Court and York Place (see below), so the medium was a logical subject of common interest and discussion between them. Part of the motivation for this heightened expenditure may have been Henry and Wolsey's efforts to assert a greater role for Henry in the Continental arena, as manifested, for example, by Wolsey's negotiations to secure the imperial title for Henry in succession to Maximilian. From 1515 the King's Book of Payments records a number of large disbursals from the Treasury to leading Continental tapestry merchants or to English merchants who specialized in trade with the Low Countries. In view of the scale of the sums involved, it seems almost certain that the king must have been instrumental in these transactions, particularly as he seems to have been highly attentive to the details of the construction and appearance of his palaces, and indeed, to the details of his administration in general. As the Milanese envoy noted, "He wants to have his feet in a thousand shoes."[54]

The first such purchase for which evidence survives was made from a Hanse merchant called Gerard Smytting (also called Smyth or Smything) in March 1515. Smytting received £673 6s. 8d. for 202 ells (113½ square yards) of "arras," at a cost of £3 6s. 8d. per ell.[55] The subject of the set is unrecorded, but it must have been an extremely fine and rich set. The location for which it was intended is also unknown, but it may have been Bridewell Palace, which Henry took over from Wolsey in 1515 and which he was to expand considerably in following years to replace the central London residence he had lost in April 1512 to a fire that extensively damaged the old palace of Westminster.[56] That the most expensive purchases of these years were related to current building projects is suggested by purchases that Henry made two years later in 1517. The King's Book of Payments records a payment of £1,481 16s. 3d. that December to the son of Pieter van Aelst for "arras" bought from him by the earl of Worcester, the lord chamberlain, "of the story of king David and Saint John the Baptist."[57] In view of the payment, the sets must have been extremely fine.[58] They appear to have been made in conjunction with refurbishment at Greenwich (fig. 6.13), Henry's birthplace and favorite palace during the first two decades of his reign, because "arras" sets corresponding to these subjects are listed there in the 1547 inventory. Other luxury textiles were also being acquired for the palace at this time, as documented

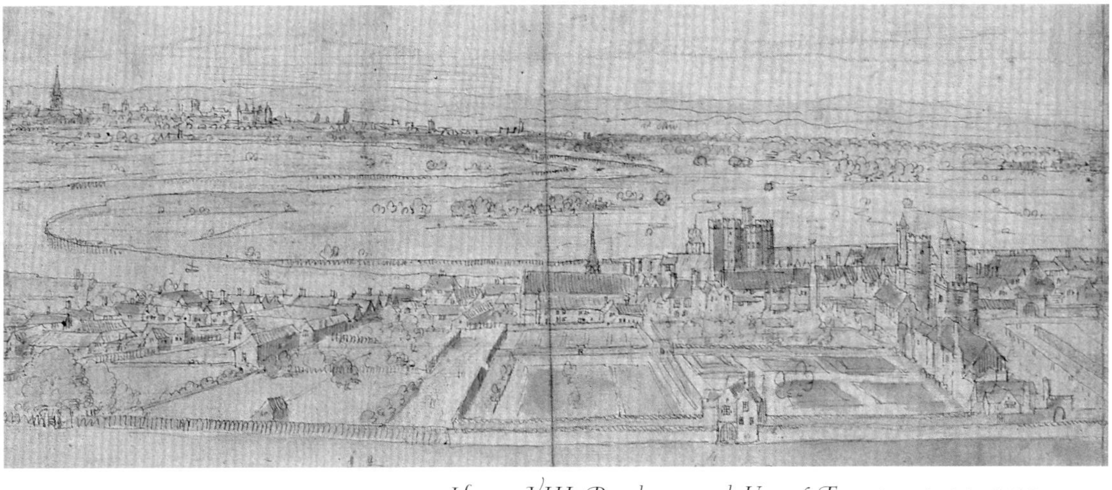

6.13 *Greenwich Palace from the South* (detail) by A. van den Wyngaerde, ca. 1558. Pen and brown ink and watercolor over black chalk, 28.8 x 121.5 cm. Ashmolean Museum, Oxford

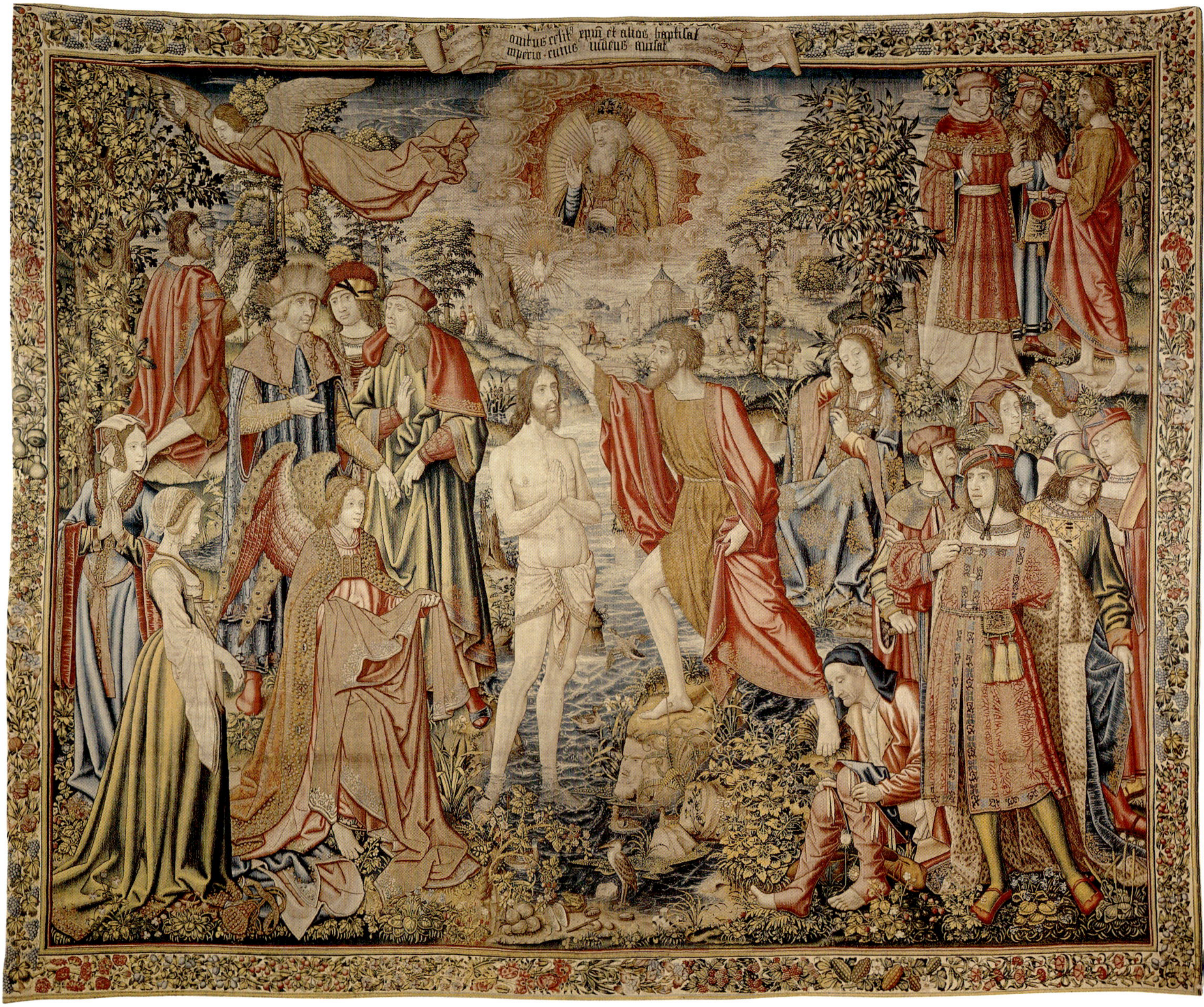

6.14 *The Baptism of Christ* from a set of the *Story of Saint John*. Tapestry woven in the Southern Netherlands, probably Brussels, ca. 1510–20. Wool, silk, and gilt-metal-wrapped thread, 355 x 405 cm. Patrimonio Nacional, Madrid

by a payment of £120 to Robert Hanforde, a tailor of London, in August 1517, "for certain clothes of arras bought of hym for the hangyng of the kinges gallery at Grenewyche."[59]

A probable identification for the *John* series can be established on the basis of the dimensions. The 1547 inventory records a six-piece set of this subject at Greenwich, which was still there a hundred years later at the time of the Commonwealth sale, when it was said to be composed of six large and two small pieces, the latter perhaps cut from a larger panel to accommodate the set to the dimensions of a particular room, with a total surface area of 180 square ells.[60] On the basis of these dimensions, it is tempting to suppose that the set was a duplicate weaving of a high-quality design series dating from the mid-1510s, of which one partial set survives in the Spanish royal collection (fig. 6.14). This now comprises four panels, but since several significant episodes from the story are omitted, such as the *Beheading of Saint John,* it is reasonable to suppose that it originally contained more. The dimensions of the surviving panels are regular (approximately three and two-thirds by just over four yards),

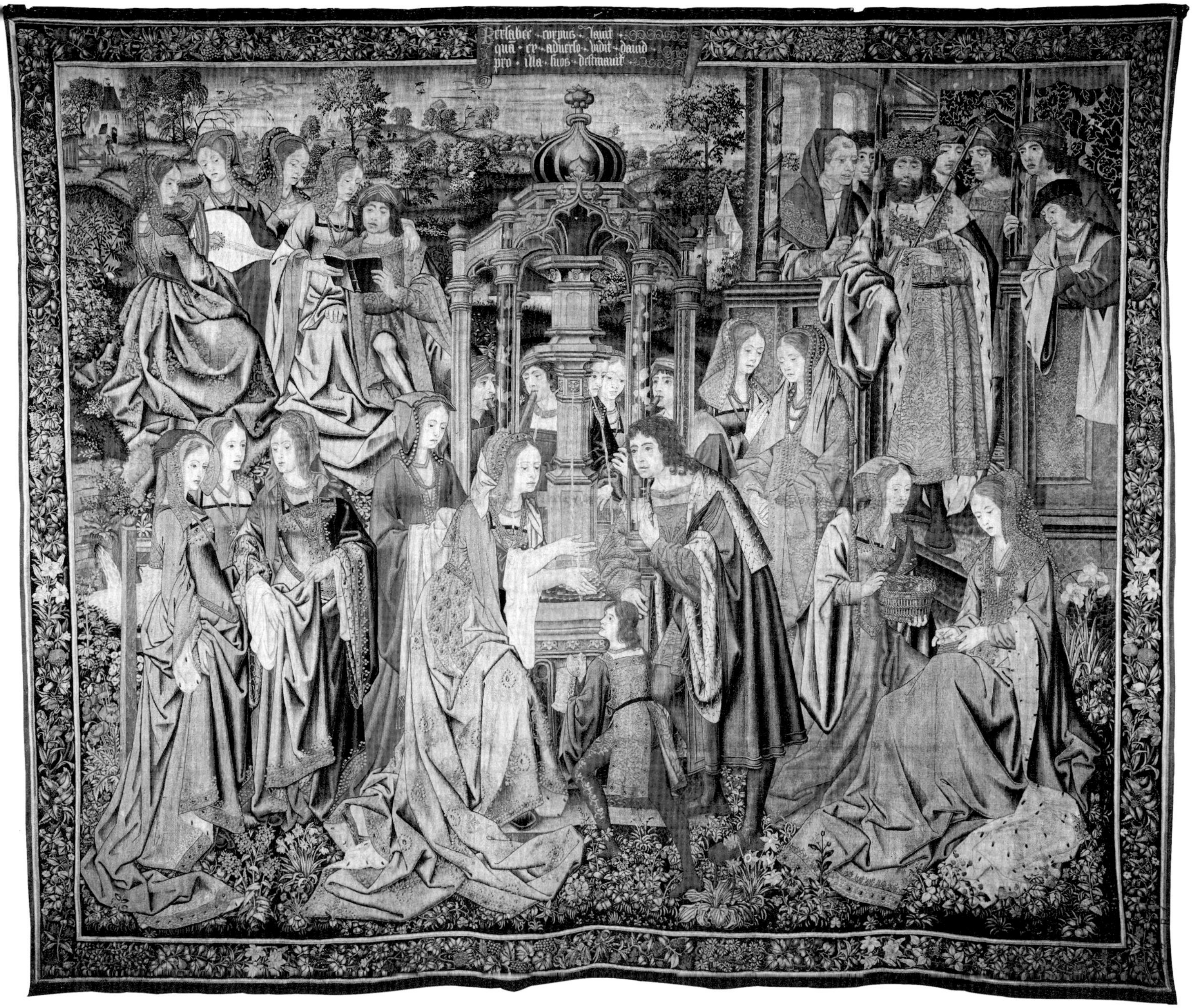

6.15 *Bathsheba at the Fountain* from a set of the *Story of David*. Tapestry woven in the Southern Netherlands, probably Brussels, ca. 1510–20. Wool, silk, and gilt-metal-wrapped thread, 350 x 415 cm. Patrimonio Nacional, Madrid

and if we speculate that the set originally contained six pieces of the same size, then it would have had a surface area equivalent to the set recorded in the English royal collection by the Commonwealth inventory.

The tentative identification of the *John* set raises the question of the *David* set. The Spanish royal collection preserves three panels from a high-quality *David* set that are close in date and style to the *John* tapestries, and it is possible that Henry's set was a weaving of this series (fig. 6.15). The problem with this identification is that, like the *John* tapestries, the *David* tapestries are of relatively modest dimensions, and even if Henry's set numbered several more pieces than survive in the Spanish set, it seems that this design series would have been inadequate in dimension to account for the balance of the large sum paid to Van Aelst in 1517. One possibility is that Henry's set was woven from the same designs as the Spanish set, but with additional figures at either side of the main scenes, like the single tapestry of *David Watching Bathsheba at the Fountain,* now at Brussels Hôtel de Ville (fig. 6.16).[61] A second possible identification is provided by a fragmentary set of

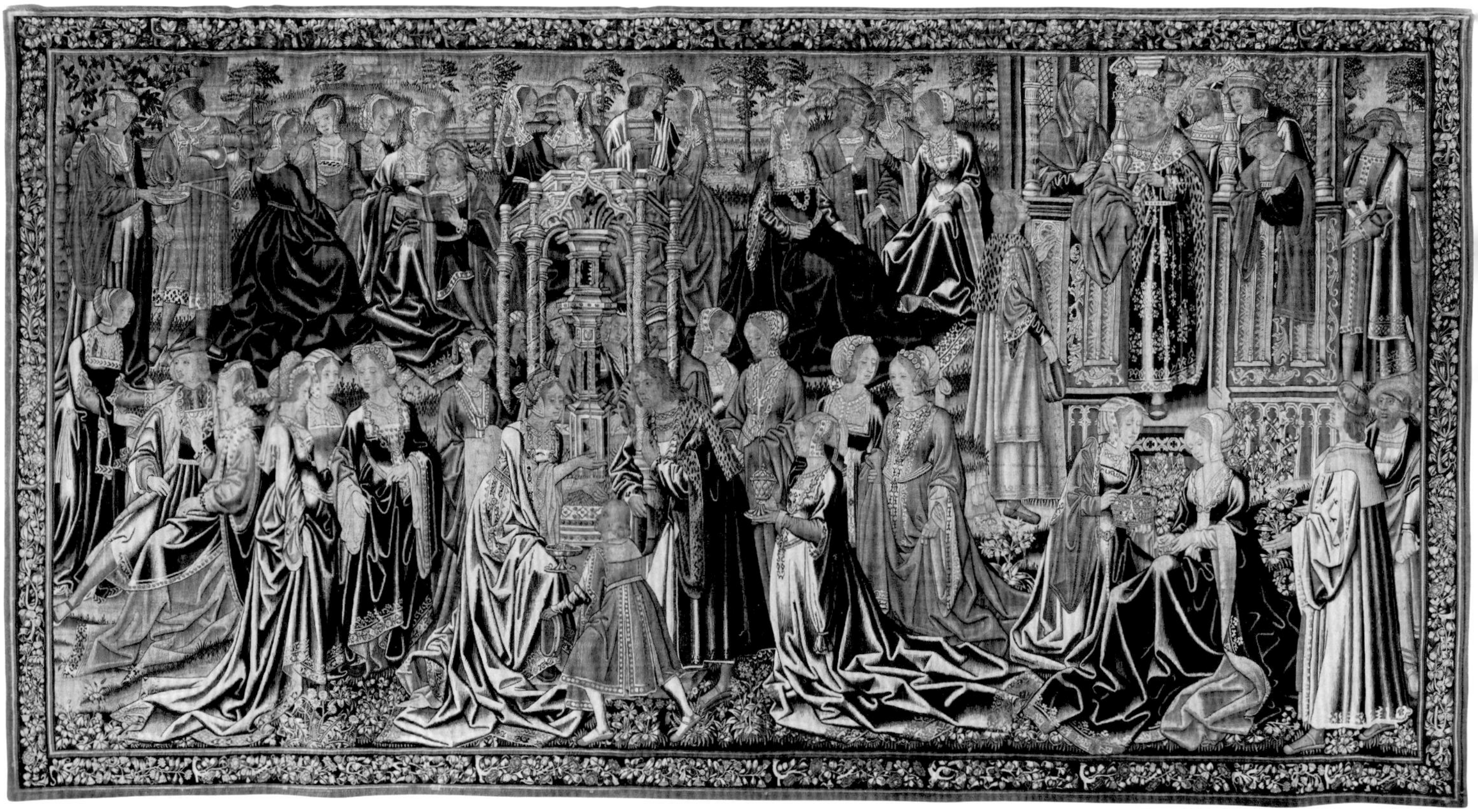

6.16 *Bathsheba at the Fountain* from a set of the *Story of David*. Tapestry woven in the Southern Netherlands, probably Brussels, ca. 1510–20. Wool and silk, 360 x 650 cm. Hôtel de Ville, Brussels

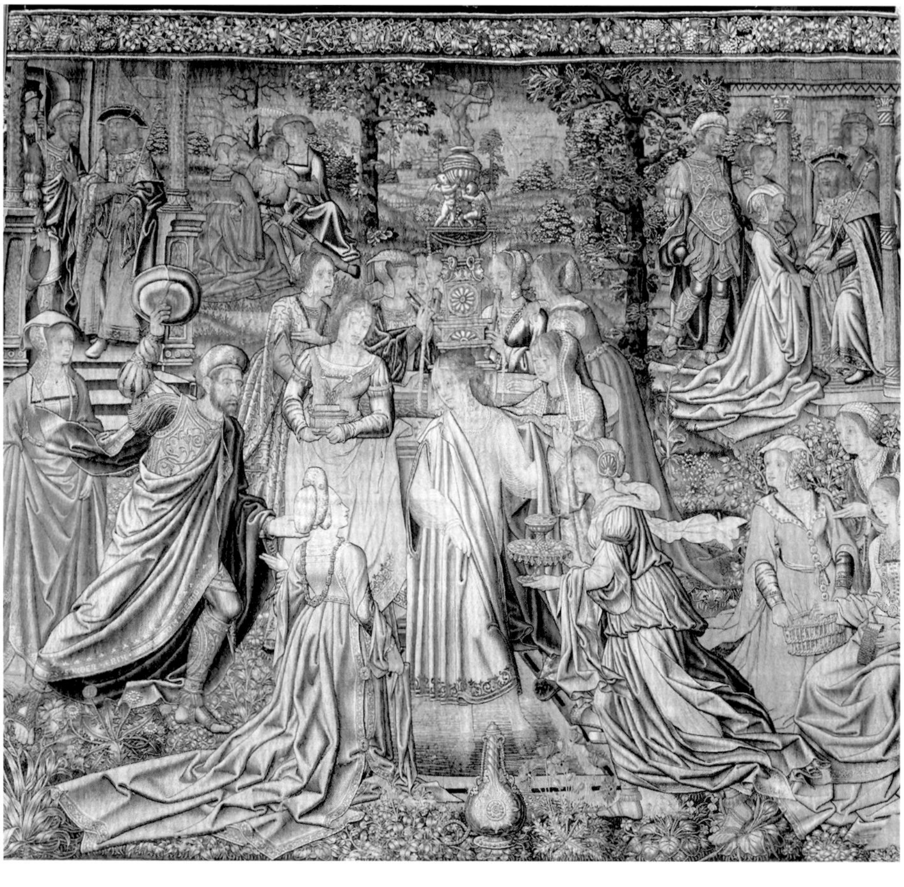

6.17 *Bathsheba at the Fountain* (fragment) from a set of the *Story of David*. Tapestry woven in the Brussels workshop of Pieter Enghien van Aelst, ca. 1515–20. Wool and silk, 330 x 340 cm. Schloss Sigmaringen

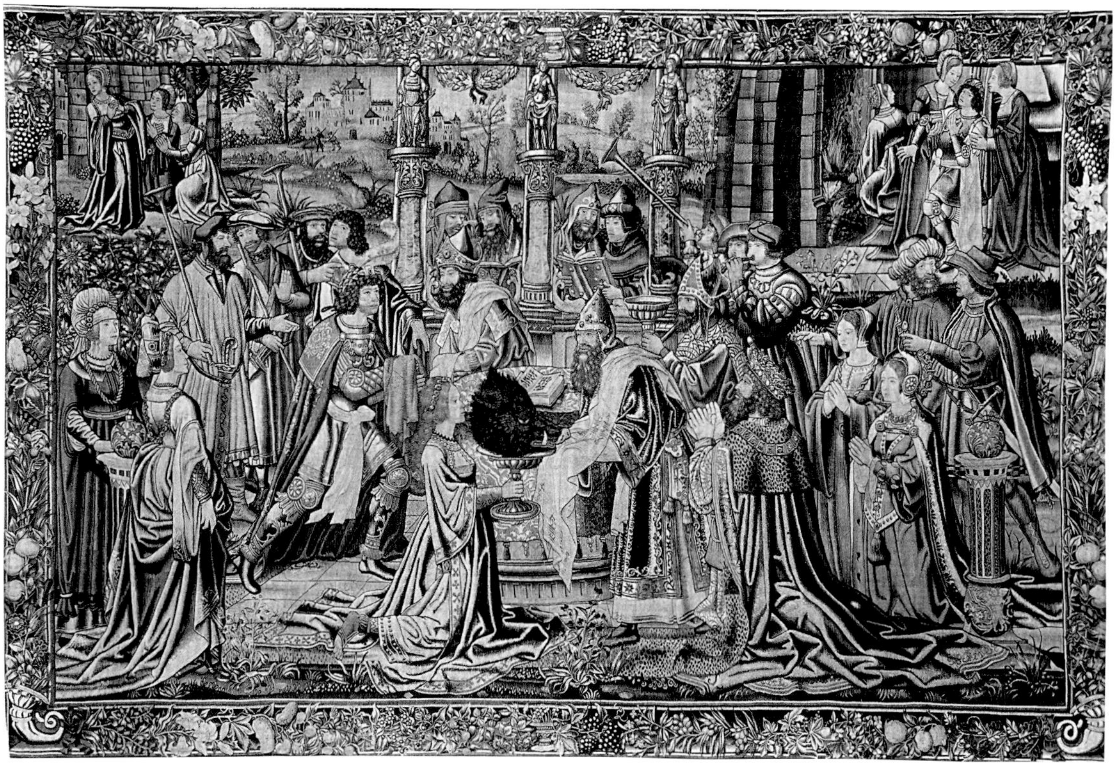

.18 *Atalanta Presenting the Boar's Head to the High Priest* from a set of the *Story of Meleager*. Tapestry by an unidentified Brussels workshop, ca. 1510–25. Wool and silk, 345 x 513 cm. Museum of Art, Toledo

David tapestries, now at Schloss Sigmaringen, one of which carries an inscription indicating that the cartoons belonged to Pieter van Aelst (fig. 6.17).[62] Stylistically, the design of the Sigmaringen set appears to date from the mid- to late 1510s, which would be appropriate, but here, too, the dimensions of the surviving panels are relatively small, even allowing for their fragmentary form.

Identification of the *David* set purchased in 1517 is complicated by the fact that it was the first of three large payments that Henry made for *David* tapestries in an eleven-year period. The other two purchases were made in 1520, also from the Van Aelst enterprise, and 1528. Although the design of the 1520 set is equally uncertain, the set purchased in 1528 can be identified as a weaving from a large, high-quality design series of which a complete ten-piece set survives at the Musée de la Renaissance in Écouen (see figs. 10.1, 10.2, 10.5–10.10). However, since the design of the Écouen set appears to date from the late 1510s, and since the 1547 and Commonwealth inventories provide evidence that Henry may, conceivably, have owned two sets of this design, it is also possible that either the 1517 or 1520 purchase, or both together, related to an earlier weaving of the same design. The evidence is complex and will be considered as a separate issue below.

Van Aelst appears next in documents for January 1519, when a payment was made to John Buller, "factor to Pieter van halst upon a warrant by hande of John Cavalcant for certan Arras of hym bought."[63] Again, no subject or intended location is given, but we can speculate that this purchase may have been related to extensive building work taking place at Eltham or Bridewell.[64] In the same month, Smytting appears again in the King's Book of Payments, receiving a payment of £75 for twenty-five ells (fourteen square yards) of "arras" at 60s. per ell.[65]

Although the foregoing records provide only partial evidence about the subject matter of the tapestries that Henry purchased from Smytting and Van Aelst, one point that does emerge clearly is the enormous scale of his expenditure on tapestry, even by comparison with the richest peers of the realm. The duke of Buckingham's annual income has been estimated at just over £6,000 during the height of his power in the 1510s, and his estate was valued at just under £5,000 in 1521. Wolsey's annual income is estimated at about £7,000 from 1518,

6.19 *The Crucifixion* from a set known as the *Square Passion*. Tapestry designed by Bernaert van Orley, woven in the workshop of Pieter de Pannemaker, Brussels, ca. 1518–20. Wool, silk, and gilt-metal-wrapped thread, 345 x 345 cm. Patrimonio Nacional, Madrid

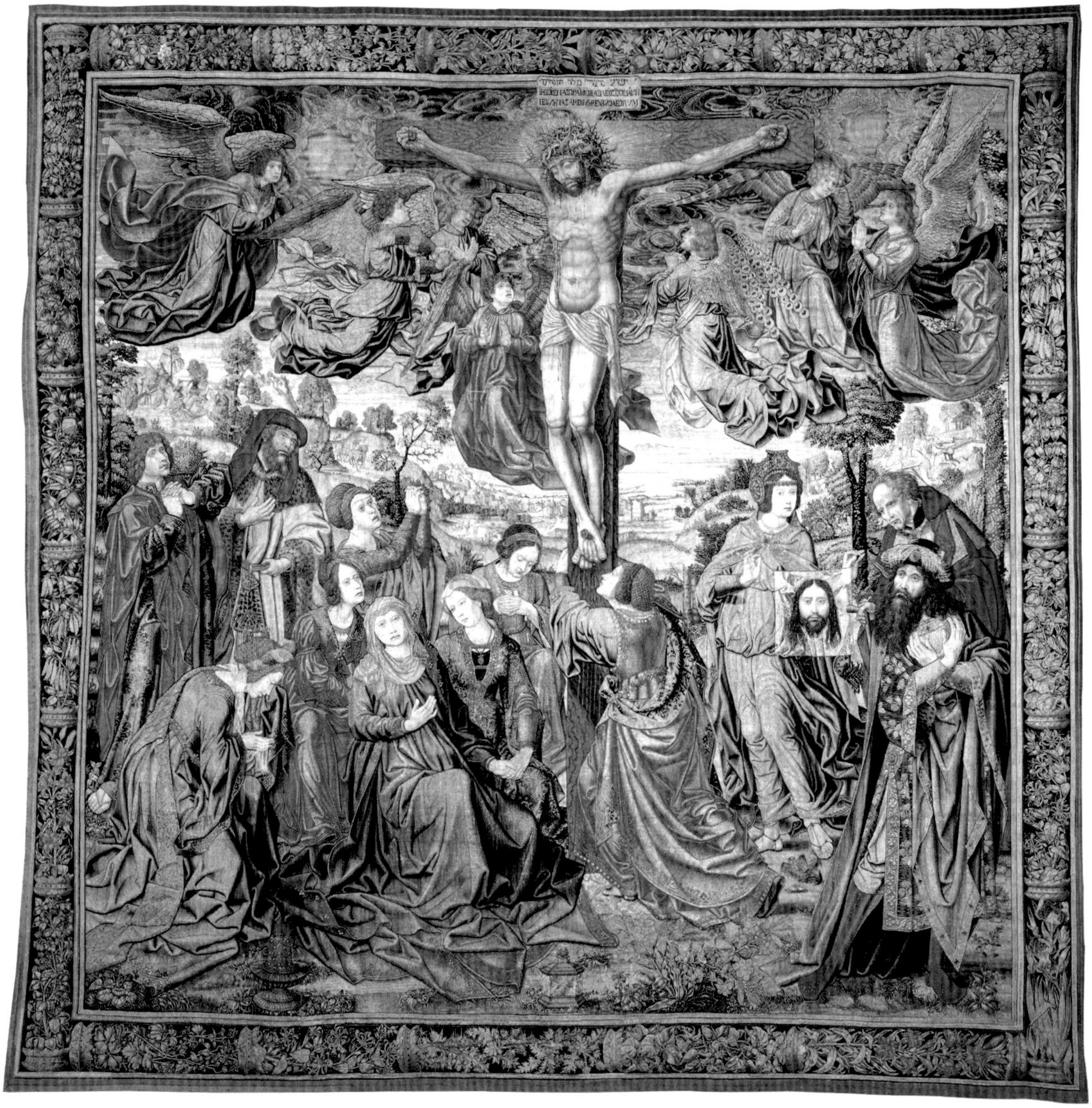

and the duke of Norfolk was taxed on an estate of £4,000 in 1524.[66] Below these rich figures, income levels dropped away sharply. The subsidy rolls of 1523–24 show that of the thirty-four noble families assessed, only eleven had annual incomes of more than £1,000, while seven had less than £300. The highest income was that of Henry Percy, fifth earl of Northumberland, assessed at £2,920, but the median income was £801.[67] The cost of the "arras" sets that Henry purchased in the mid- to late 1510s was equally significant in proportion to real estate and building expenses, as demonstrated by comparison with the sum of £1,000 that Henry paid for Beaulieu manor in 1516.[68] The enormous gilt-woven tapestry sets were thus among the most expensive commodities of the day, a prerogative of the king simply by virtue of their inordinate cost.

The paucity of information regarding the subject matter of the tapestries that Henry purchased during these years is especially frustrating because he was the center of a nascent but already dazzling intellectual circle, enjoying the close company of such humanists as William Blount, Lord Mountjoy, and Thomas More and the correspondence of such internationally renowned men as Desiderius Erasmus. Yet the extent to which the scholarship of such men may have influenced his tapestry purchases is undocumented. The 1547 inventory certainly lists a number of tapestry sets with classical subjects whose dimensions and subjects correspond to design series produced

6.20 *The Deposition* from a set known as the *Square Passion.* Tapestry designed by Bernaert van Orley, woven in the workshop of Pieter de Pannemaker, Brussels, ca. 1518–20. Wool, silk, and gilt-metal-wrapped thread, 345 x 345 cm. Patrimonio Nacional, Madrid

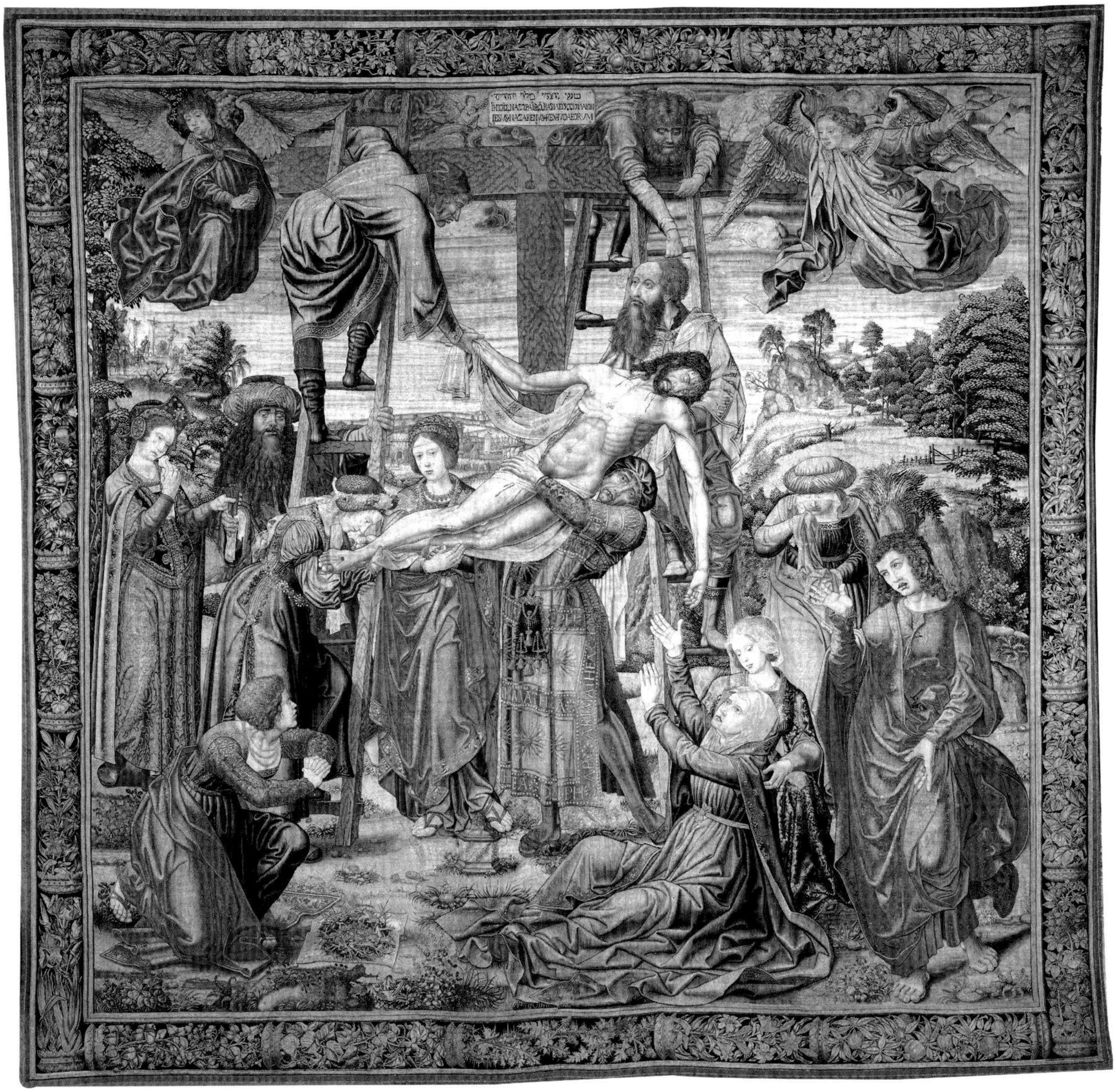

during the late 1510s and early 1520s. For example, in view of the fact that Henry was evidently purchasing high-grade tapestries to decorate Greenwich Palace in the late 1510s and early 1520s, it is tempting to identify a six-piece "arras" set of the *Story of Meleager* listed at this palace in 1547 with a high-quality design series dating from around 1520, of which a single panel survives at the Toledo Museum of Art (fig. 6.18). Unfortunately, this hypothesis cannot be tested because the 1547 Greenwich inventory does not provide dimensions.[69] Similarly, the sheer number of tapestries depicting the *Story of Hercules* listed in 1547 also suggests that Henry must have purchased sets of this subject during the same period.[70] But with the exception of a customized set of the allegorical subject of the *Triumphs of Petrarch,* probably completed for Cardinal Wolsey in 1520 (see below), there is little evidence to suggest that the English king or his courtiers were commissioning new designs stimulated by such humanist leanings, as yet. Rather, the acquisitions that can be tentatively identified at this date indicate that Henry was purchasing sets with "classical" subjects that were available in the marketplace.[71] As in preceding decades, the protagonists of these designs were represented in a stylized version of contemporary—that is, sixteenth-century—costume, with little attention to the distinctive characteristics of the antique world.

The one fact that can be asserted is that during this period Henry must have also continued to purchase significant numbers of high-quality devotional tapestries.[72] The 1547 inventory records a large number of devotional panels of a kind that were designed and produced during the first two decades of the sixteenth century. Although a portion of these certainly came from Cardinal Wolsey's collection, appropriated by the Crown in 1530, and others may have derived from the dissolution of the monasteries during the 1530s, the number of high-quality and thus high-cost panels, indicates that some at least must have been Crown purchases. This is entirely logical in the light of both Henry's and Katherine's profound faith and devotion to a traditional form of worship at this time of increasing challenge to the Catholic Church. No certain identifications can be made with extant tapestries, but it is tempting to speculate that the large payment to Smytting in 1519 for a single, very rich tapestry of fourteen square yards—equivalent to a panel approximately three and three-quarter yards square—may have been one of these. Circumstantial evidence for a possible identification is provided by the fact that ten years later, an Edward Smytting was to sell Henry a set of four *Passion* tapestries that were woven from designs by the Brussels artist Bernaert van Orley (see below for discussion). While two of this later set were woven from cartoons designed ca. 1525, the other two appear to have been duplicates of panels designed by Van Orley for Margaret of Austria between 1520 and 1522 and woven at the workshop of a leading Brussels merchant weaver called Pieter de Pannemaker. In turn, Margaret's two new designs were paired in her collection with scenes of the *Crucifixion* (fig. 6.19) and *Deposition* (fig. 6.20) that had been made between 1518 and 1520 from preexisting designs.[73] Given the likelihood that Edward Smytting may have been a son or relation of Gerard and that there may

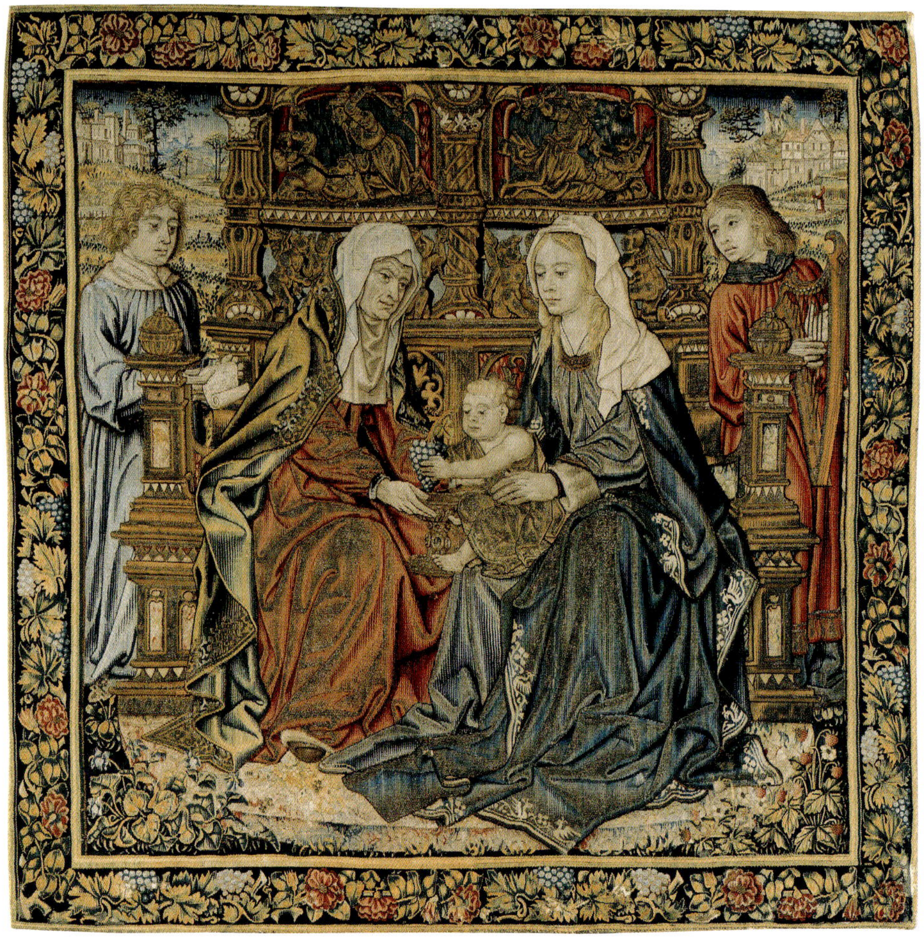

6.21 *The Virgin, Saint Anne, and the Infant Christ.* Tapestry woven in the Southern Netherlands, probably Brussels, ca. 1515. Wool, silk, and gilt-metal-wrapped thread, 105 x 105 cm. Musées Royaux d'Art et d'Histoire, Brussels

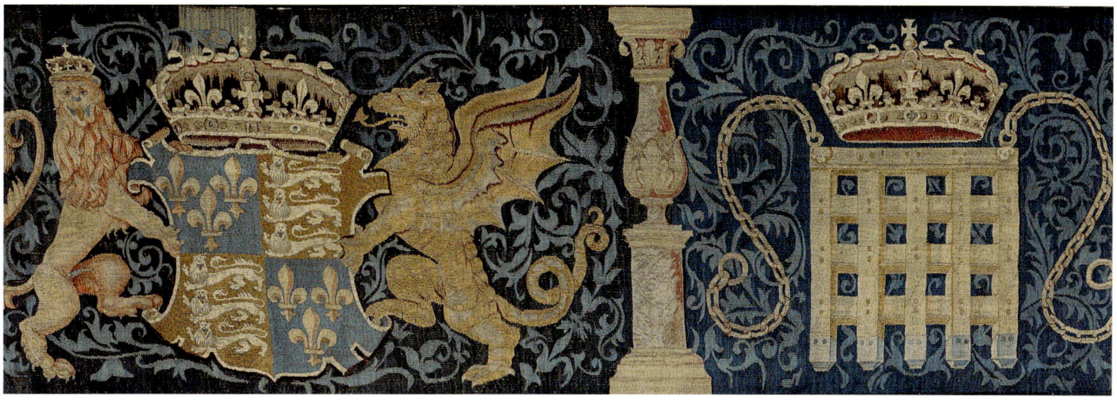

6.22 Border with the English Royal Arms and Tudor Devices (fragment). Tapestry woven in the Southern Netherlands or England, ca. 1500–1520. Wool and silk, 94 x 213 cm. Hampton Court Palace

have been some sort of familial link between this merchant family and the Pannemaker–Van Orley group of *Passion* designs, it is possible that Henry's 1519 purchase may therefore have been a weaving of one of these earlier designs. Although such speculation is tenuous, these earlier *Passion* designs certainly give an impression of the sort of high-quality devotional subjects with which the Chapel Royal would have been decorated by the late 1510s.

In this context, it is to be noted that the 1547 inventory also records "one lytle pece of Arras of Christ in our Ladies armes cont. one yarde one naile square by tharrisman [the royal arras maker]" and "one square pece of Arras of Christe and one geving him grapes & our Ladie standing by iij qrt of a yarde square by tharrise man."[74] The dimensions and subjects of these tapestries sound similar to those of a group of small devotional tapestries that date from the first decade of the sixteenth century (fig. 6.21), so it is likely that these two small pieces were made by Van der Strete rather than by his successor.[75] Similar pieces are recorded in a number of late-fifteenth and sixteenth-century Continental collections, in particular in those of female members of the Spanish and Burgundian courts. It is therefore possible that the taste for such pieces was brought to the English court by Katherine of Aragon and that Van der Strete may have been copying an example or pattern acquired by Katherine or one of her circle.[76] Whatever the case, it is clear that this style of devotional tapestry enjoyed a vogue at a number of courts during this period and that the royal arras maker, or weavers he employed, were capable of making pieces of this nature quite apart from the heraldic borders and devices that they seem regularly to have produced (fig. 6.22). Equally, it is unlikely that this was a major part of his activity. On the contrary, the origin of these tapestries may well have been indicated in the 1547 inventory because of their novelty. The small size and high quality of the panels suggests that they may have been made as New Year's Day gifts for the king or the queen. It was traditional for leading courtiers and court artisans to present the king with gifts on New Year's Day in the presence of the court. In return, the king rewarded them with gifts that ranged in value according to the recipient's status and office. For leading artisans and artists, this ceremony provided a perfect opportunity to display their abilities, and one can well imagine that the two small devotional panels listed in the 1547 inventory may have been conceived by the royal arras maker with this intent.[77]

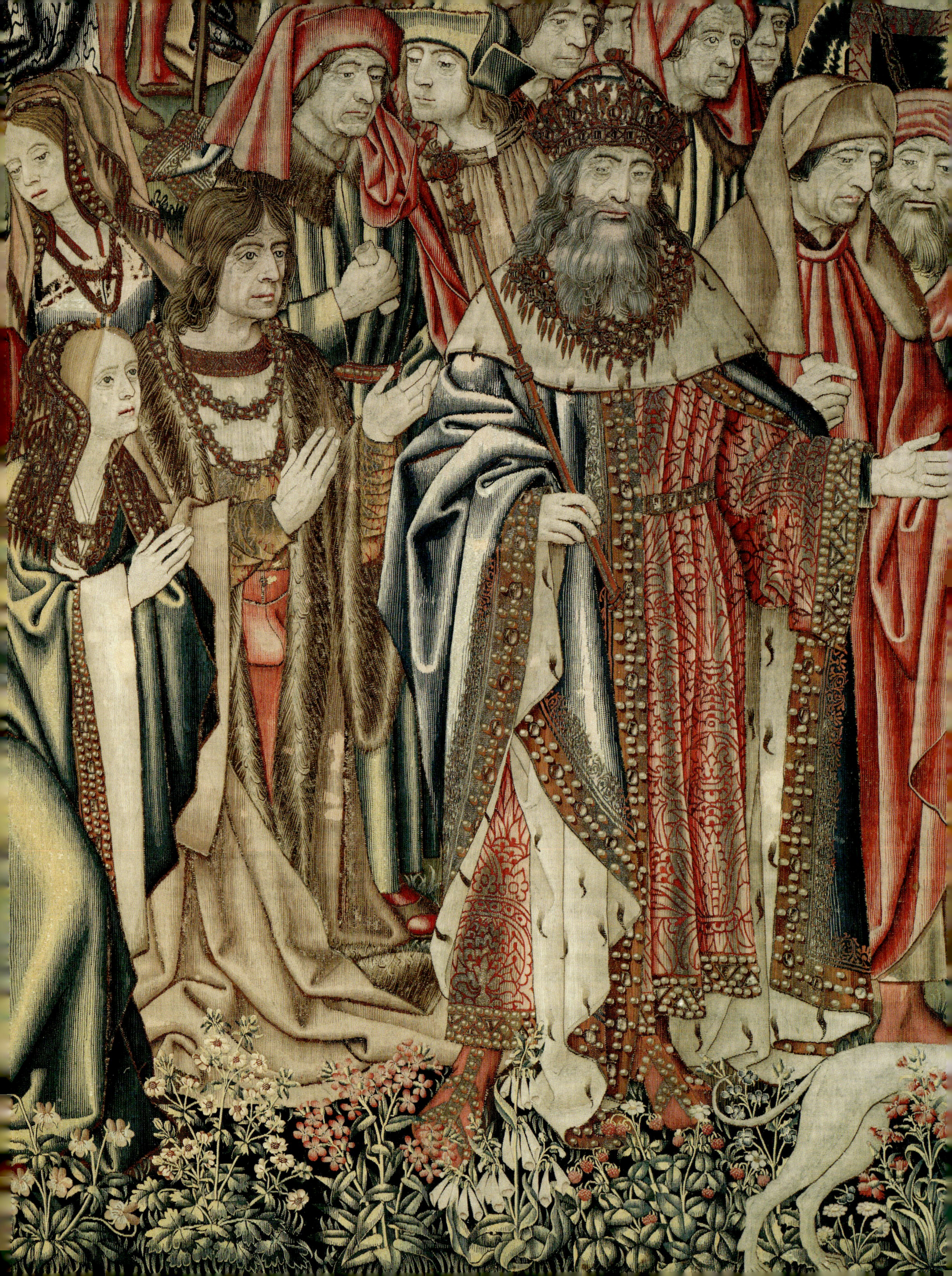

CHAPTER 7

Cardinal Wolsey's Tapestry Patronage, 1509–1519

Detail of fig. 7.13

Paralleling the large sums that Henry was allocating to tapestry purchases during the 1510s were the efforts of his friend and adviser Thomas Wolsey. Wolsey had come to prominence at the Tudor court during the reign of Henry VII. Hard-working and extremely competent, he quickly demonstrated his abilities as an administrator, and after Henry VIII's accession he proved an able ally to the young king against his older advisers. From 1511 he played a key role in promoting Henry's agenda for renewed confrontation with France, and he was responsible for organizing many of the arrangements for the campaign of 1513. The success of that expedition, combined with the friendship that he developed with Henry, guaranteed his rapid promotion thereafter. Henry was only too happy to have someone as driven and efficient as Wolsey to manage his affairs of state, so long as Wolsey kept him in touch with what was going on, and during the following decade Wolsey effectively ran many aspects of the administration on the king's behalf. In reward, Henry showered him with lucrative ecclesiastic and secular appointments. Between 1517 and 1525, Wolsey invested huge sums in the development of his three major properties, Hampton Court, York Place in central London, and The More (Hertfordshire), and to furnish them he acquired large numbers of tapestries, amassing a collection of more than six hundred pieces by the mid-1520s.[1] The story of the development of this enormous collection in such a short period has a twofold relevance to that of the royal collection. First, as Henry VIII's right-hand man between the early 1510s and the late 1520s, Wolsey's obsession with tapestries and the material trappings of power in general illuminates the values and priorities of the minister who was closest to the young king. This insight is of special relevance because of the relative lack of information about the king's tapestry patronage at this time. Second, the story of the development of Wolsey's collection is, in effect, part of the story of the royal tapestry collection because following Wolsey's disgrace in autumn 1529, the Crown appropriated all his possessions.

The Early Formation of Wolsey's Tapestry Collection

Wolsey's modest origins and early career would have provided few of the trappings that his wealthy contemporaries at the Tudor court inherited as a matter of course. It was in the years following Henry VIII's accession that Wolsey's personal wealth began to accrue through promotions and ecclesiastical preferment. In February 1509 he was appointed dean of Lincoln, and in May he received the office of royal almoner. The following April he was appointed registrar of the Order of the Garter, and he acquired an independent London residence the same year when Henry granted him a lease of the rectory house of Saint Bride's and the neighboring land. Wolsey begun construction of a new lodging for himself, and it is to be assumed that he would have acquired hangings to decorate this building.[2] The grant of the goods of "felones de se" that he enjoyed

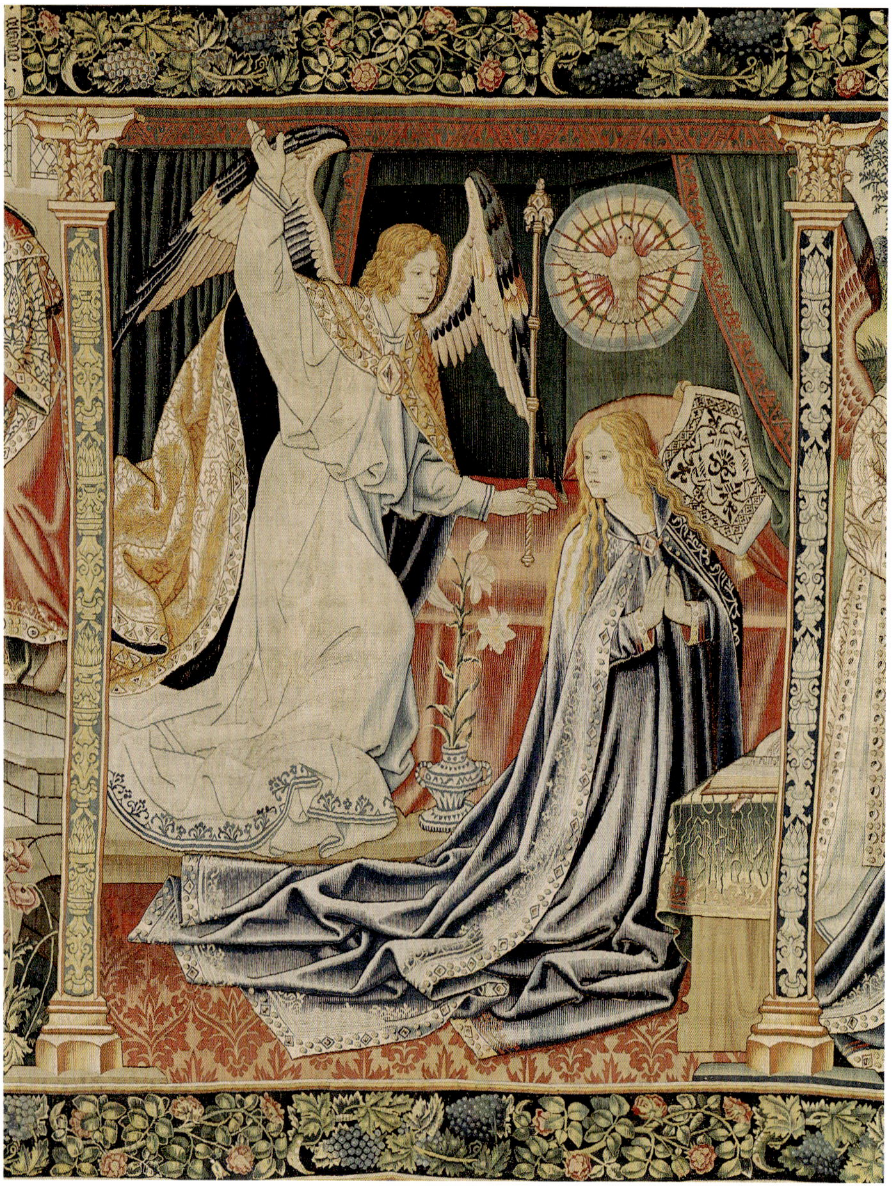

7.1 *The Annunciation* (detail) from a set of the *Life of Christ and the Virgin*. Tapestry woven in the Southern Netherlands, probably Brussels, ca. 1510–13. Wool and silk, 190 x 139 cm (dimensions of detail). Formerly Canterbury Cathedral, now Cathédral Saint Sauveur, Aix-en-Provence

as royal almoner may have enabled him to acquire some furnishings and tapestries at second hand, but at this stage, his income and status would have supported only a limited expenditure on tapestry because of the cost of even fairly coarse forms of the material. Surviving inventories indicate that painted cloths and hangings of colored say—fine woolen cloth—were still the prevalent form of decoration for even quite senior court officers.[3] Whatever his financial means, Wolsey's taste for opulent surroundings and his awareness of the impressiveness of valuable tapestry displays must have been engendered during this period. With his increasing involvement in court affairs from 1507, Wolsey would have seen the best hangings in the royal collection in use for religious and state occasions, as well as those of other leading courtiers and nobles. His journeys to the courts of Maximilian and Margaret of Austria to conduct business for Henry VII may also have given him a glimpse of part of the Burgundian tapestry collection.

Another forum in which tapestry played a significant role at this period, and to which Wolsey would have been exposed through his professional office, was the Church. Although, in contrast to France, there was no widely established precedent for English ecclesiastics to donate tapestry sets to their churches, tapestry displays were an important feature in some of the richer cathedrals.[4] One ensemble of which Wolsey would probably have heard was the large six-piece set depicting twenty-six scenes of the *Life of Christ and the Virgin* that was donated to Canterbury Cathedral in 1511 by the prior Thomas Goldstone and the cellarer Richard Dering (fig. 7.1).[5] In addition, many leading English ecclesiastics had important personal tapestry collections. Papers relating to the goods of Thomas Savage, archbishop of York, record that after his death in 1507, Henry VII acquired tapestries worth £232 from his estate.[6] William Warham, archbishop of Canterbury, and Richard Fox, bishop of Winchester, both made specific mention of tapestries in their wills, and an inventory of the goods of Nicholas West, bishop of Ely, taken after his death in 1533 lists more than fifteen sets of tapestry totaling about seventy pieces.[7] The evidence that Wolsey's own collection was founded largely on appropriations made from the effects of William Smith, bishop of Lincoln, and Cardinal Bainbridge, archbishop of York, and that subsequently it was expanded with acquisitions from the collections of Richard Fitzjames, bishop of London, and Thomas Ruthal, bishop of Durham, will be considered below.

A further stimulus to Wolsey's interest in tapestry must have been provided by the campaign to France in 1513. Following the capitulation of Tournai, the civic authorities presented Wolsey with a set of tapestries of the *Twelve Months* purchased from the merchant Jean Devenins, and as already noted, Henry subsequently rewarded him with the bishopric of the city.[8] Later evidence reveals that during the short stay of the English court in the town Wolsey found time to make a number of tapestry purchases. His early disposition to extravagant display was exemplified by the tents that he took with him on the campaign, said to have been half as large again as those of Lord de L'Isle, the second in command of the English forces.[9] However, he still lacked many of the accoutrements of wealth that his contemporaries at court could take for granted. In view of the cost of new tapestry, the acquisition of second-hand sets was one route to the formation of an impressive collection, and later evidence indicates that many of the older tapestries in Wolsey's collection were acquired in this way. The opportunity to make appropriations on a grand scale came with the ecclesiastical preferment that Wolsey received in 1514. That March he was made bishop of Lincoln following the death of the incumbent, William Smith, and in August he was translated to the archbishopric of York after the death of Cardinal Bainbridge in Rome. In the biography of Wolsey that he wrote in the 1550s, his gentleman usher, George Cavendish, noted that after Wolsey's consecration as bishop of Lincoln, he "found the means to gett the possession of all his predicessors goodes into his handes wherof I have seen dyvers tymes some part therof furnyshe his housse," and one of the charges against Wolsey in 1529 was that he "had the more part of the goods of Dr. Smyth," as well as of other bishops whom he succeeded, "contrary to their wills and to law and justice."[10] Evidence of the eagerness with which Wolsey sought to acquire Bainbridge's possessions is provided by correspondence with Richard Pace, who was acting as executor of the deceased in Rome in 1514. Wolsey must have given instructions that any valuable textiles should be reserved for his use, and in September Pace wrote to inform him that he had found "certayne ryche vestments and an altare cloithe of golde whyche stuff dide cost my late lord Vc duc [that is, 500 ducats] of golde; and oon odre ryche cloithe of arrace," which he was instructing Mr. Burbank to present to Wolsey.[11] A later undated draft instructs Silvestro Gigli, bishop of Worcester, to send Bainbridge's "alter cloths, vestments and tapestry [to] me into England by ship or otherwise as ye [think] most best."[12]

The inventory of Wolsey's goods taken sometime around 1522 provides little detail regarding the origin of the older tapestries that it lists, and only two sets can be identified from these earlier collections with certainty, one "with losinges of diverse coloures with bishop Smythes armes" and another "for the hanging of the olde halle at Westmynster [that is, York Place]."[13] It is likely that many others shared a similar provenance, however. The inventory divides the collection into seven categories of quality ranging from old and worn hangings to "newe arras," which, in this context, unquestionably designates gold-woven tapestry. The sheer number of tapestries that the inventory classes as "old" or "somewhat worne" within only fifteen years of the date from which Wolsey can have been acquiring them, confirms that the collections of his ecclesiastic predecessors must have formed the basis of his own collection, and the miscellaneous subject matter of the tapestries recorded in these categories was consistent with such ad hoc acquisition.

Wolsey's status reached new heights with his election as a cardinal in September 1515, and a contemporary witness recorded the richness of the hangings at his residence during the ceremony at which he received the hat on 18 November.[14] In December Henry appointed Wolsey as his lord chancellor. This position gave Wolsey access to large sources of capital, and it has been estimated that, thereafter, his annual income can never have been much less than £7,000. This new liquidity is reflected by the ambitious building projects in which he immediately engaged. As archbishop of York he had taken possession in 1514 of the see's London residences, including York Place, the principal palace in central London since the

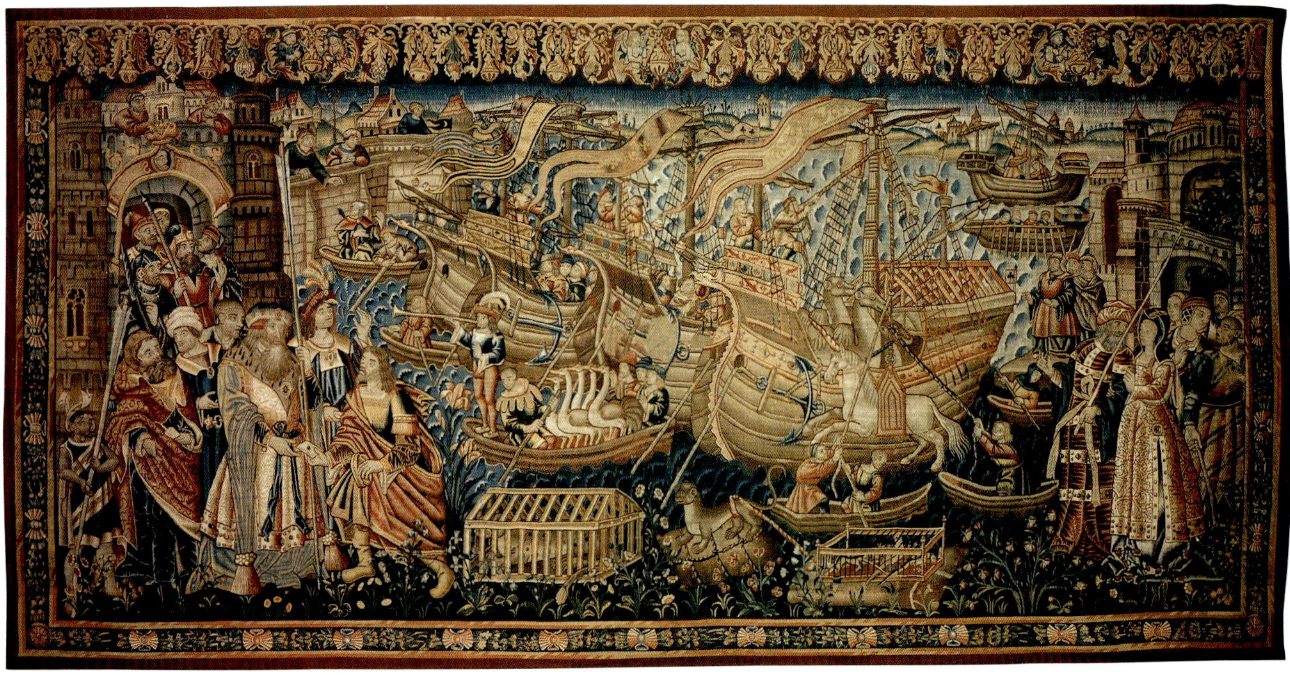

7.2 *Embarking Exotic Animals* from a set of *European Explorers in the Indies*. Tapestry woven in the Southern Netherlands, probably Tournai, ca. 1510. Wool, 400 x 760 cm. Caixa Geral de Depósitos, Lisbon

destruction by fire of Westminster Palace in 1512, and in the same year he acquired the lease of the property of Hampton Court to provide him with a country residence. There were no tapestries among the furnishings at this time.[15] Expansion and embellishment of these two residences had begun in late 1514, the nature of the work being dictated by the function of the buildings.[16] York Place was Wolsey's town house where he held audience; the work there concentrated on the provision of new reception rooms beyond the great hall, which were completed by 1517.[17] In contrast, Hampton Court was envisaged as a palace for ambassadorial and royal entertainment; the building there focused on improving and expanding the accommodation. The principal rooms were on the first floor around a central courtyard, and during 1515 and 1516 these were overhauled to provide grand apartments for the king, with the addition of a long gallery that ran out over the garden, completed by May 1517. A series of four parlors below was fitted for Wolsey's own use. Subsequently, work commenced on the construction of extensive accommodation around a new courtyard, Base Court, which was completed by late 1521 or early 1522 (see fig. 9.1). This included thirty double lodgings. The external decorations included terra-cotta roundels depicting Roman emperors by Giovanni da Maiano.[18]

Evidence regarding the decorative arrangements that Wolsey made for his new residences is incomplete, but in view of his links with Tournai it was natural that he should turn to this source for tapestries, and surviving correspondence confirms that this was the case. His affairs in Tournai were represented by his vicar general, Dr. Richard Sampson, whose awareness of Wolsey's interest in tapestry is reflected by the gift he sent him in April 1515 of a tapestry of *Saint George*.[19] That Wolsey made a more substantial purchase some time before August 1515 is indicated by a letter of August 25, from Guillermus Bernaert, canon of Tournai, which requested payment for certain tapestries that Wolsey had purchased from his mother at Tournai and for which prompt payment had been promised. This had not been forthcoming, and Bernaert now pleaded that since his mother had suffered much loss by the war, both before and since the coming of Wolsey, he would see satisfaction made according to the tenor of the bill that he, Wolsey, had signed himself.[20]

Although no evidence of these earlier purchases survives, the category of "somewhat worn" hangings in Wolsey's 1522 inventory in-

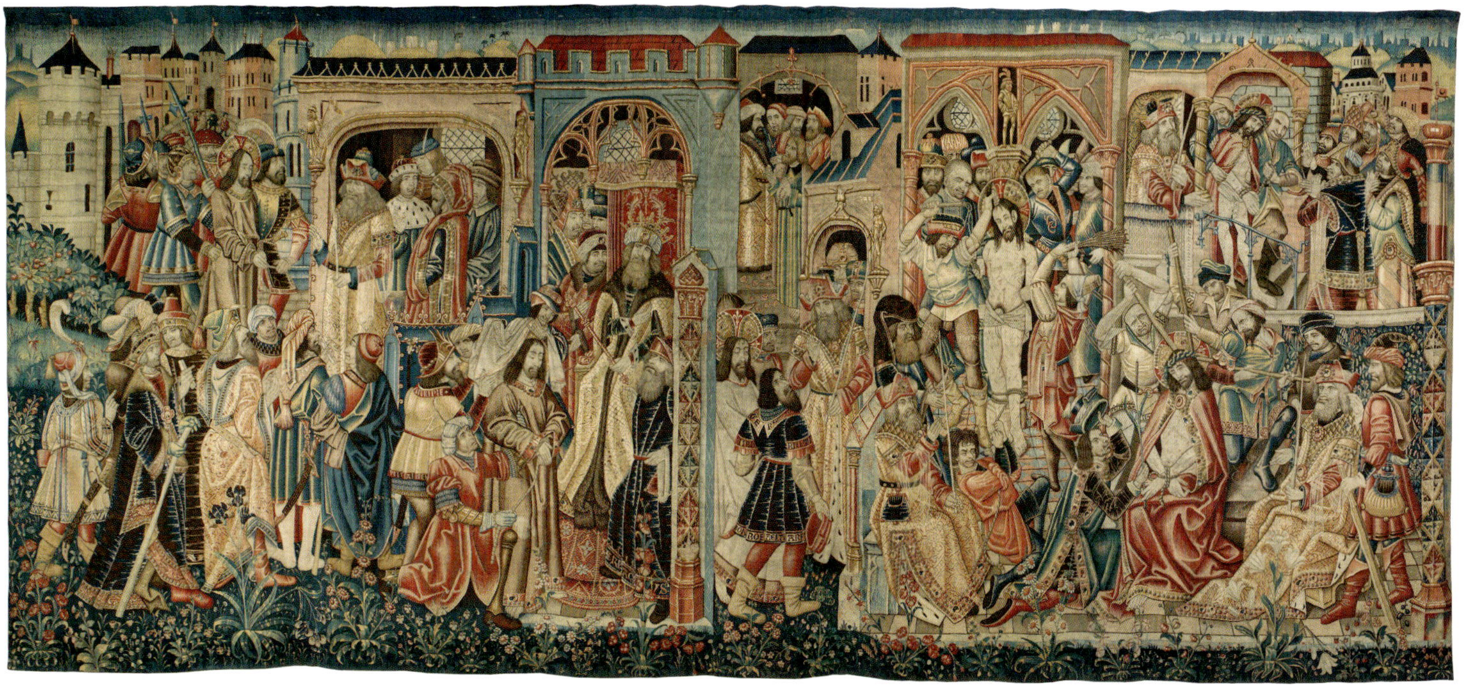

7.3 *Scenes from the Passion* from a set of the *Passion*. Tapestry woven in the Southern Netherlands, probably Tournai, ca. 1510. Wool and silk, 417 x 890 cm. Museum of Fine Arts, Boston

cluded a number of sets that can be identified with subjects known to have been produced in Tournai during the first two decades of the 1500s, and the set of *Months* presented to him by the Tournai authorities in 1513 was also listed in this category.[21] For example, a ten-piece set of "Calycoto" (Calcutta) was almost certainly of the type that depicted a mixture of European explorers, exotic beasts, and wild men of which examples are documented as having been woven and traded by Tournai manufactories in the first two decades of the period (fig. 7.2).[22] Similarly, the subject and dimension of a set of "Bankette" invite association with a series of which an example survives in Nancy.[23] This depicts the fifteenth-century narrative of *The Condemnation of Banquet*, published in 1508 by Nicole de la Chesnaye, an allegory on the theme of self-governance and temptation, embodied in the figures of Banquet, Supper, Experience, Gluttony, and their compatriots.

Not all of the subjects were secular. A six-piece set of the *Passion of Christ* can probably be identified on the basis of dimensions and subsequent descriptions with a design series of which one piece survived at Knole in the early twentieth century (fig. 7.3).[24] Dating from ca. 1500 and woven in a style that traditionally has been associated with the Tournai ateliers, this series shows the continuing vitality of the fifteenth-century design idiom in which an extended and complex composition is spread across the whole surface of the tapestry, with individual narrative scenes separated by architectural and landscape features. As already noted, a portion of the sixteenth- and seventeenth-century tapestries formerly at Knole came from the royal collection, so it is possible that this tapestry once belonged to Wolsey.

Jehan Scellier and New Tapestry Provisions for York Place and Hampton Court

The foregoing examples typify the style and quality of the tapestries that Wolsey acquired somewhat haphazardly during the early 1510s. From around 1517 he seems to have developed a more ambitious approach. Public awareness of his interest in the medium is reflected by a letter of that August from the Venetian ambassadorial secretary Gasparo Spinelli to Brian Tuke asking if Wolsey would like a fair mule or a tapestry as a gift.[25] Tuke was Wolsey's secretary, but in 1517 he was also appointed "governor of the king's posts," in which capacity he established England's postal system. He was friendly with Francisco de Tassis (later known as Franz von Thurn und Taxis), the imperial postmaster, and through this connection news may have passed to the English court of the set of tapestries that Taxis commissioned sometime before his death in 1517 for the church of Notre-Dame du Sablon in Brussels. In these tapestries, ostensibly a history of the legendary statue of the Virgin housed by the church, many of the historical figures are actually portraits of the imperial dynasty, and Taxis himself was also portrayed in each tapestry, along with members of his own family (fig. 7.4).[26] The inclusion of hidden and explicit portraits in this work may have inspired the inclusion of portraits of Henry VIII and Wolsey in a set of the *Triumphs of Petrarch* probably made for Wolsey in 1520 (see below).

Explicit evidence of the scale on which Wolsey was now planning his tapestry acquisitions is provided by a letter that he received in May 1517 from Jehan Scellier, the provost of Tournai.[27] Scellier was the most senior Tournaisien to collaborate with the occupying English force, and in early 1514 he was one of the deputies selected to represent the town at Westminster. Subsequently he was appointed as one of the two supervisors of the king's building works in Tournai.[28] He was also one of the principal witnesses in the contract between the town authorities and the weaver Clement Sarrasin for the set of *Hercules* tapestries made for Sir Edward Poynings, and he was probably related to the tapestry merchant family of the same name. A Philippe le Scellier provided Maximilian with the tapestries that were given to Lord Hastings in 1478, and in the early sixteenth century a "Jan Saillie" was paid for armorial tapestries for the corporate buildings of the Bruges Franc.[29] Scellier had been in England in late January 1517, when one of the tasks with which he had been entrusted was the delivery of tapestries promised to the duke of Suffolk by the Tournai town authorities in 1513.[30] It is clear from Scellier's subsequent letter that during his visit he and Wolsey must have discussed the commission of a large number of tapestries for the newly furnished rooms at Hampton Court and York Place.

Scellier's letter starts by referring to this previous discussion when Wolsey had expressed a desire to acquire tapestries of moderate price to decorate his houses in England and indicates that, subsequently, Richard Sampson had communicated Wolsey's wish to procure more tapestries similar to those he had already

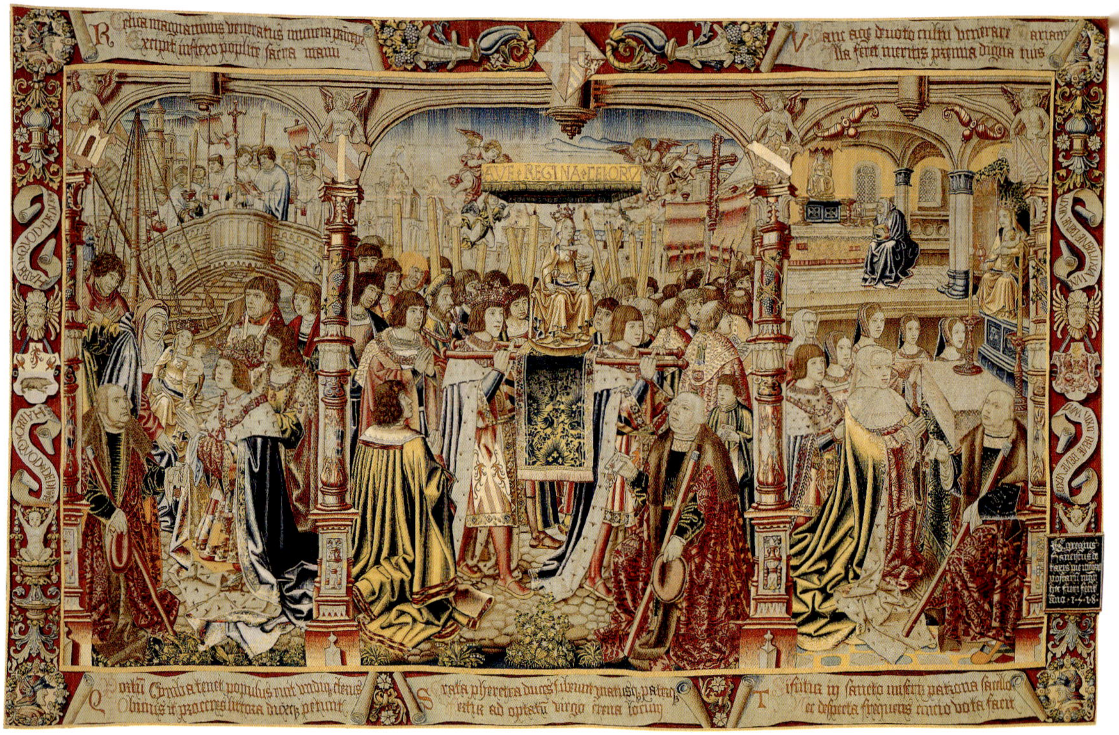

7.4 *The Statue of the Virgin Arrives in Brussels* from a set of the *Legend of Notre-Dame du Sablon* from a design attributed to Bernaert van Orley. Probably woven in Brussels, ca. 1518. Wool and silk, 341 x 528 cm. Musées Royaux d'Art et d'Histoire, Brussels

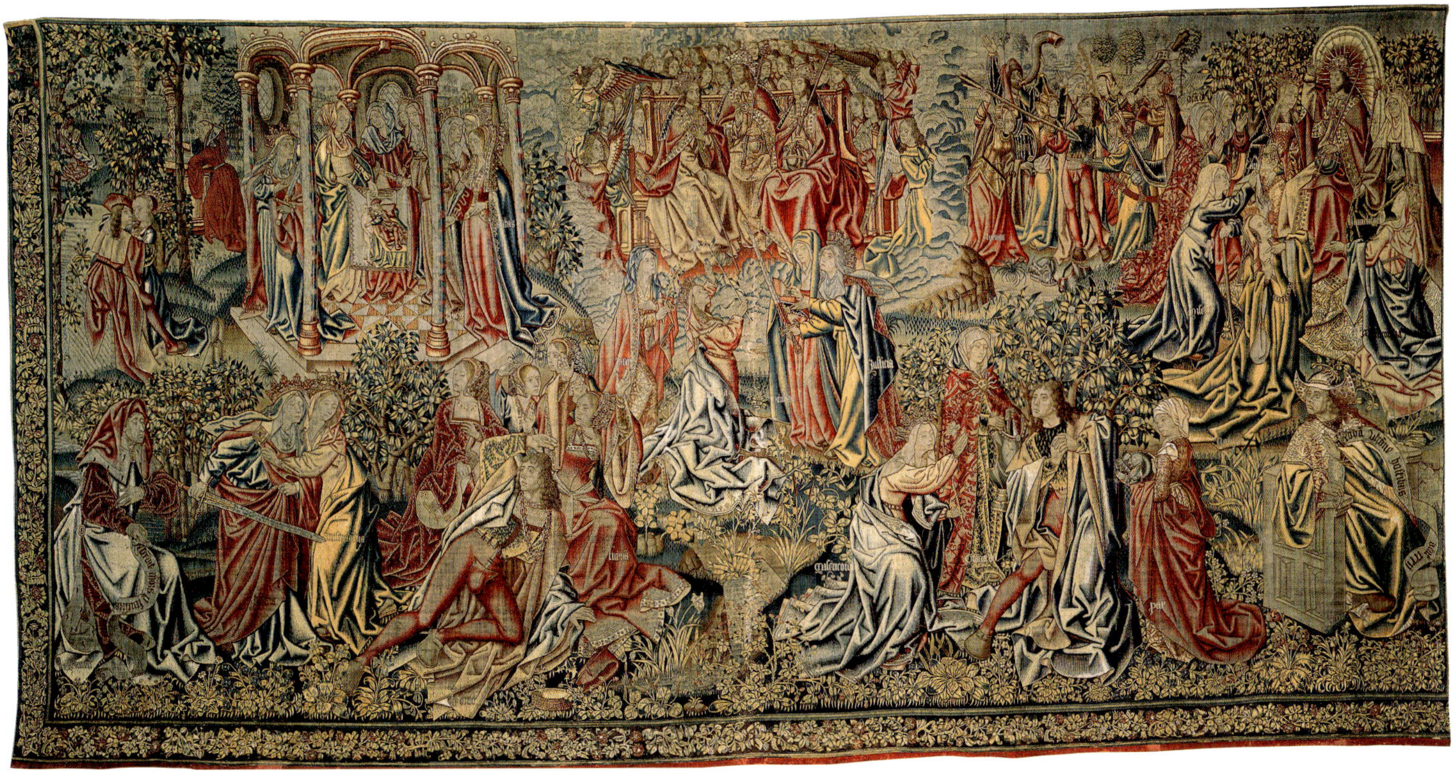

7.5 *Peace and Mercy Win the Promise of Redemption for Man* from a set now known as the *Redemption of Man*. Tapestry woven in the Southern Netherlands, probably Brussels, ca. 1517–21. Wool and silk, 397 x 755 cm. Hampton Court Palace

bought in Tournai from an old woman "qui estoit la mere de votre hoste," in all likelihood the mother of Bernaert mentioned above. Scellier informs Wolsey that he could not obtain such tapestry with as good material and color for less than 5s. 6d. per Flemish ell, even though that was more than double its cost, because it was thirty years since such stuff had been made—that is, the 1480s, when the Tournai workshops were producing series like the Grenier *Trojan War* series. In a partly destroyed section of the letter he then appears to refer to the set of tapestries presented to Margaret of Austria by the town authorities in 1513, perhaps as an example of the quality of work that was available. He continues that at Whitsuntide the great fair will be held at Antwerp, which will be attended by all the tapestry dealers, and he will see what he can purchase for Wolsey on that occasion, as well as other forms of textiles for which he had inquired.[31] He wishes to know the required heights of tapestry for hall, chamber, and gallery, the sorts and the price range, from 8 or 9 "gross sterling" for the least valuable tapestry with figures, to whatever price Wolsey was prepared to pay. In a further partly destroyed section he appears to be informing Wolsey about an attractive design with wild beasts that was then available. The letter also appears to indicate that Wolsey could dictate the Latin text that was to go in the border of the tapestries. Finally he begs Wolsey to inform him of his wishes before Whitsuntide and the commencement of the fair.

Aside from its interest regarding contemporary trading practice the letter reflects a significant involvement and level of discrimination by Wolsey in the commission. Two points are of especial note. First, the fact that Wolsey was interested in a type of tapestry that had not been produced for thirty years indicates that he was trying to obtain a style or quality of product that the king and many of his rivals in power would have inherited. The second point of interest is the scale on which Wolsey was now thinking, seeking to buy several chambers' worth of tapestry at once for the most important rooms in his palaces. Scellier died between August and October 1517, but since this was some months after the fair at which this order would have been given, it seems unlikely to have affected the arrange-

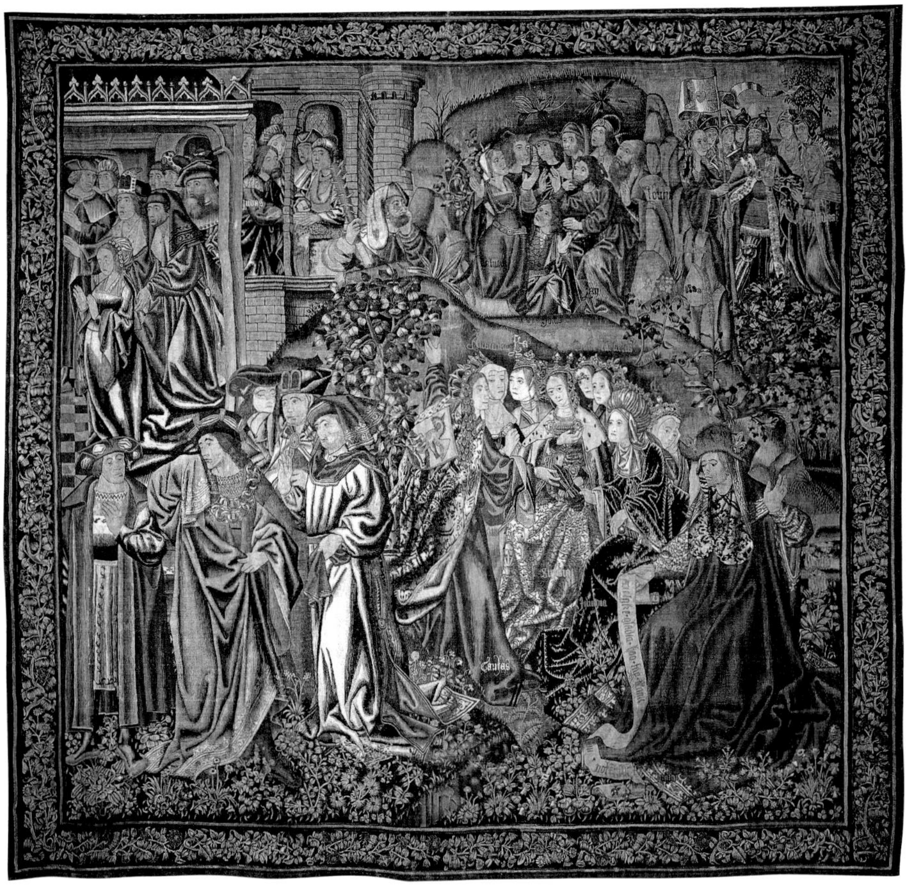

7.6 *The Virtues Challenge the Vices as Christ Begins His Ministry* from a set now known as the *Redemption of Man*. Tapestry woven in the Southern Netherlands, probably Brussels, ca. 1517–21. Wool and silk, 408 x 422 cm. Hampton Court Palace

ments.[32] Circumstantial evidence that the commission was fulfilled is provided by the "new counterfeit arras and tapestry" category in the 1522 inventory of Wolsey's possessions.[33] This includes twenty sets of good-quality tapestry of which about half were listed with window pieces and widely varying dimensions indicating that they had been woven for specific locations. Furthermore, almost all of these sets had biblical subjects, the majority being drawn from the Old Testament. In view of a subsequent large commission that Richard Gresham, a London merchant, made for Wolsey in 1520, also for sets with predominantly biblical subject matter, and the fact that none of the later commissions were for the hall, one of the rooms specifically alluded to in Scellier's letter, there are grounds for assuming that a significant portion of the sets in this category of the inventory resulted from the Scellier commission.

The largest of the sets with idiosyncratic dimensions was called the *Old and New Law*. As discussed in the context of Henry VII's collection, this subject can be identified with a design series now known as the *Redemption of Man*. Six of Wolsey's set "whiche were firste bought" had regular dimensions, but the other six had irregular widths, indicating that they may have been custom-made to adapt the series for a specific location. In view of the vast size of this set, whose total width came to around ninety yards, this could only have been a large hall, possibly that at Hampton Court. The tapestries were made even more impressive by the addition of Wolsey's arms to the top border. One complete and one fragmentary piece from that set survive today at Hampton Court (figs. 7.5, 7.6).[34] The tapestries are finely woven but, in contrast to those of the same subject in the royal collection by this date, lack gold thread.

The suggestion that the *Old and New Law* set may have been intended for use in a particular location at Hampton Court or York Place is supported by the nature of the following sets. Seven of the next eight listed in the inventory had window pieces and/or irregular dimen-

Opposite, top:
7.7 *Scenes from the Story of Judith and Holofernes,* with a border of Cardinal Wolsey's arms attached, from a set of the *Story of Judith and Holofernes*. Tapestry woven in the Southern Netherlands, ca. 1520–21. Wool and silk, 325 x 590 cm. Sens, Musées de Sens

Opposite, bottom:
7.8 *The Nativity and Youth of Saint John the Baptist* from a set of the *Story of Saint John the Baptist*. Tapestry woven in the Southern Netherlands, ca. 1517–19. Wool and silk, 300 x 533 cm. Musée Antoine Lécuyer, Saint Quentin

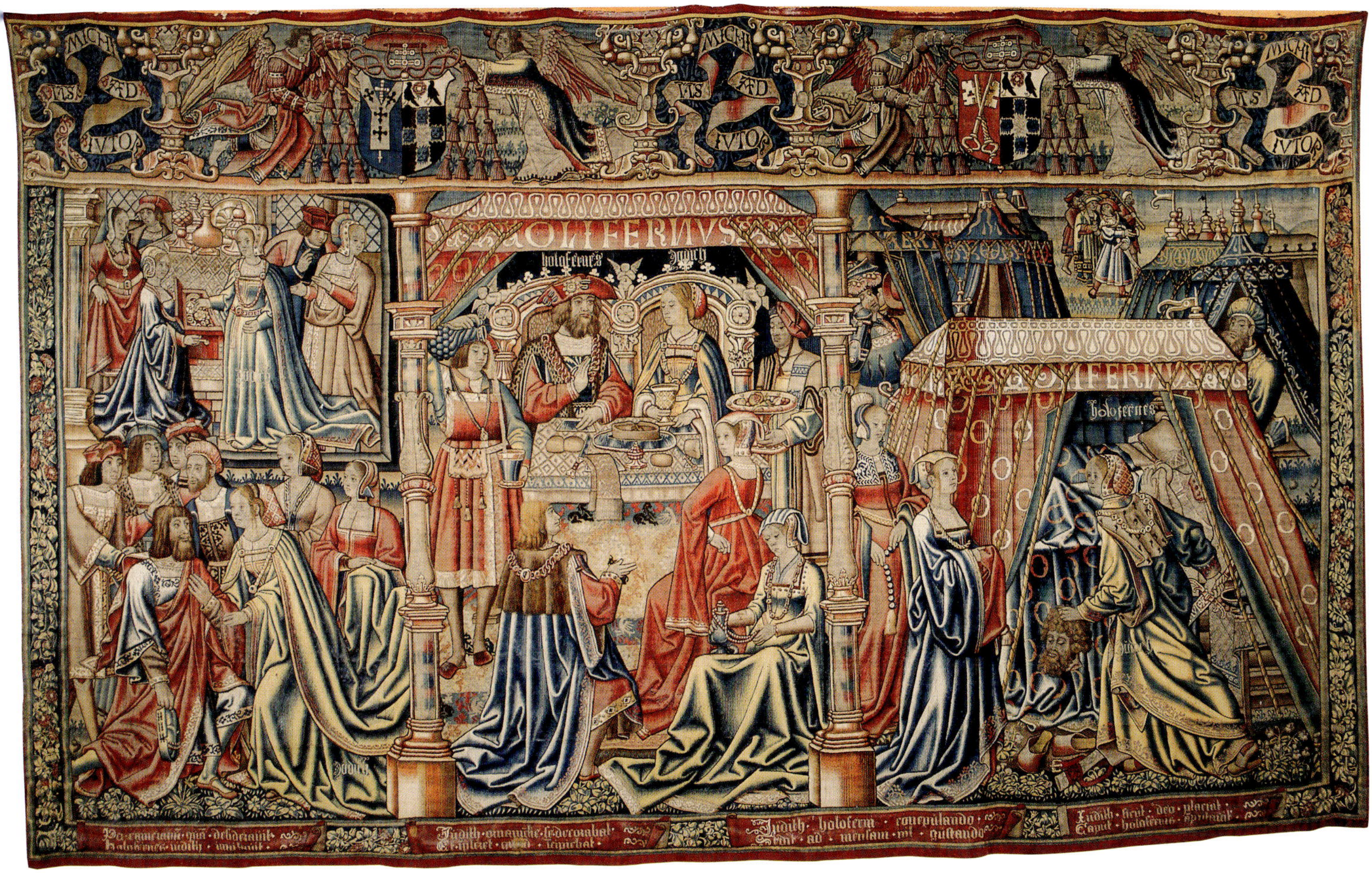

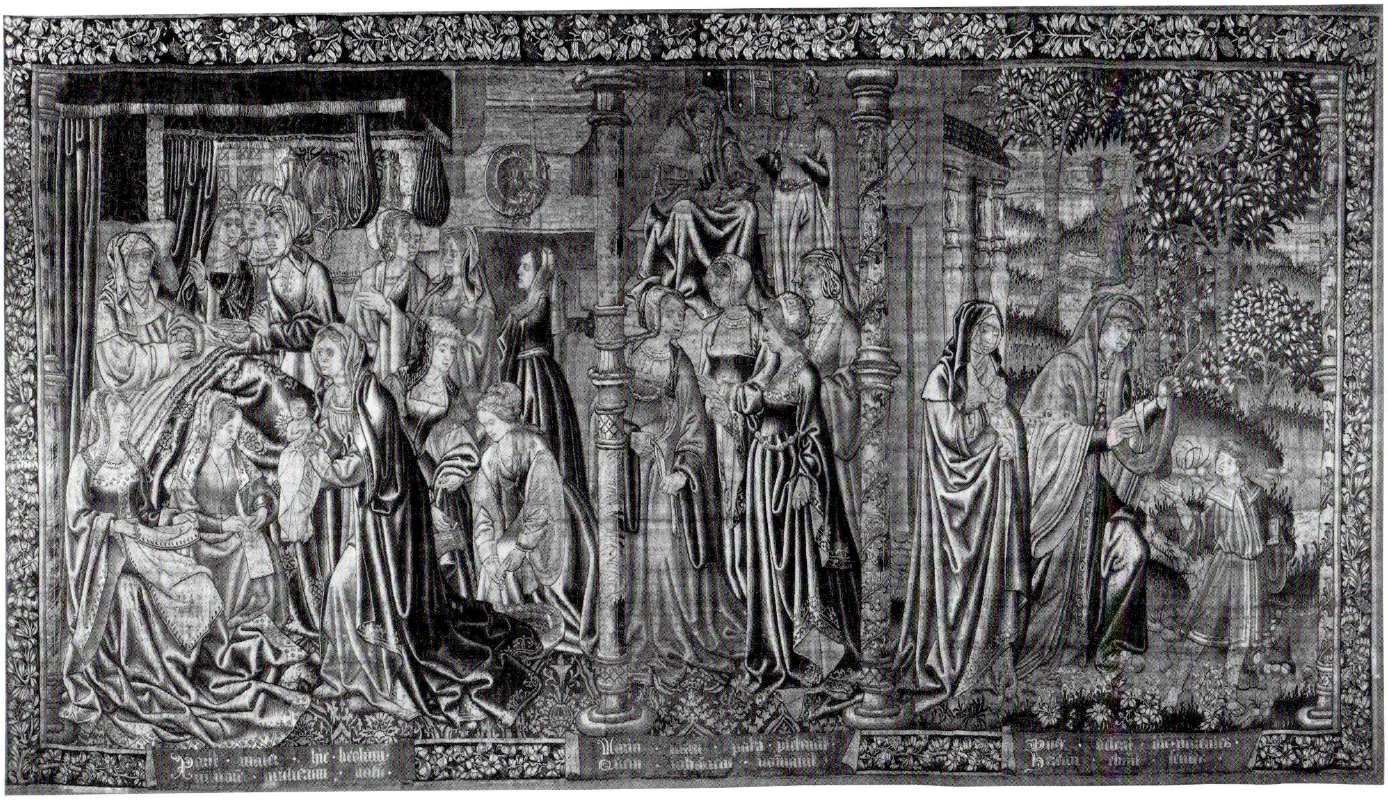

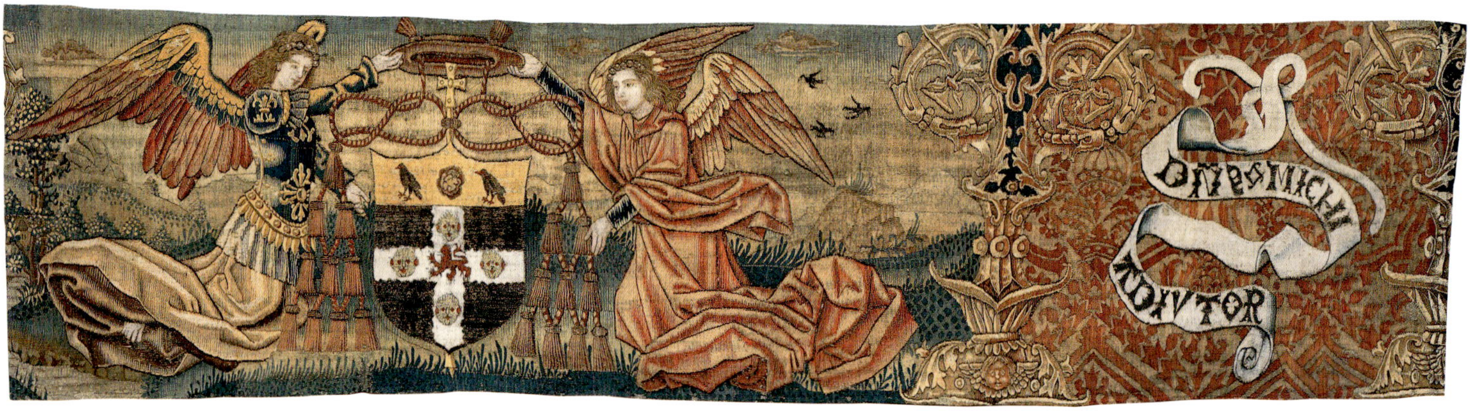

7.9 Arms of Cardinal Wolsey with Cardinal's Hat, Archiepiscopal Cross, and Wolsey's Motto. Tapestry woven in the Southern Netherlands or England, ca. 1517–21. Wool and silk, 60 x 292 cm. Hampton Court Palace

sions, suggesting that they had been woven for specific rooms, and all had upper borders with Wolsey's arms.[35] Subjects included *Samson, Solomon, Susanna, Jacob, Judith and Holofernes, Joseph,* and *John the Baptist*. The *Joseph* set was of twenty-three pieces including eleven window pieces, which suggests that it was for a gallery, possibly that completed at Hampton Court in 1517. Although none of these tapestries have survived in the royal collection, a single panel of *Judith and Holofernes,* still carrying Wolsey's arms, is now in the treasury at Sens Cathedral (fig. 7.7).[36] The dimensions of this piece correspond to those given for the second piece listed in Wolsey's set of this subject.[37]

Another probable identification from the Scellier commission is a panel from a set of the life of *John the Baptist* that survives along with a second panel of *Tobias* at the Musée Lécuyer at Saint Quentin (fig. 7.8).[38] The *Tobias* panel carries Wolsey's arms and can be identified with a set delivered by Richard Gresham for Hampton Court in 1522 (see below). The *John* panel does not carry the arms but corresponds in dimension with the second piece of the set of this subject described in Wolsey's inventory as "the nativitie of Seinte John."[39] Fragments of three other border sections with Wolsey's arms survive at Hampton Court (figs. 7.9–7.11).

The single-minded concentration on religious subjects within the group of tapestries tentatively identified with those ordered through Scellier is as remarkable as the scale of this commission. Wolsey's religious stature was enhanced on May 17, 1518, when he was appointed as papal legate, and the possibility of having himself elected as the next pope in succession to Leo X may already have been in his mind. By this date he was certainly encouraging the notion that he was the *alter papa* in England, just as in Italy he was the *alter rex*.[40] The subjects of the tapestries ordered for Hampton Court and York Place in 1517–18 were evidently intended to reinforce his ecclesiastical status. Although there was a long-standing tradition for the use of tapestry as a means of suggestion, and both Edward IV and Henry VII purchased tapestries with religious and historical

7.10 Arms of Cardinal Wolsey and the See of York, with Cardinal's Hat, Archiepiscopal Cross, and Wolsey's Motto. Tapestry woven in the Southern Netherlands or England, ca. 1517–21. Wool and silk, 60 x 216 cm. Hampton Court Palace

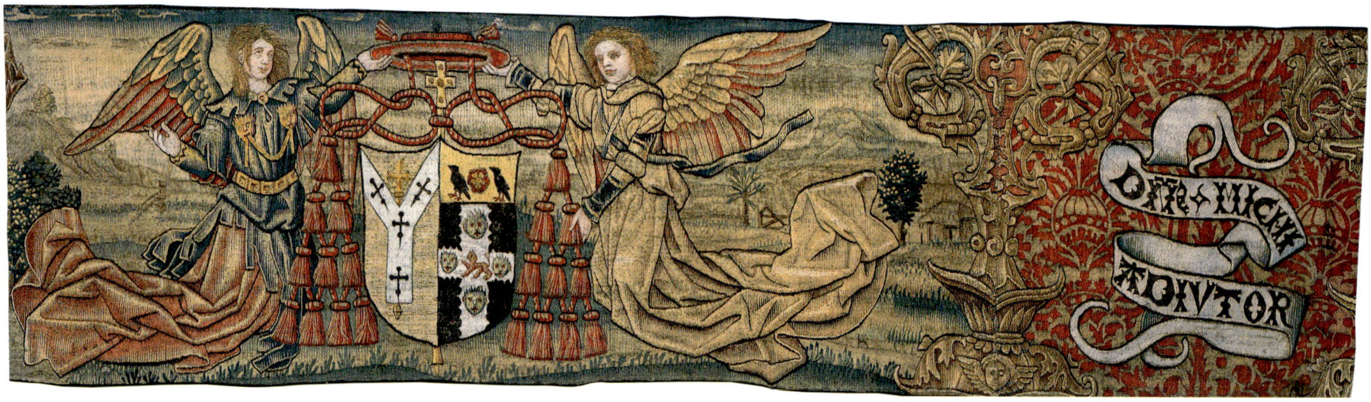

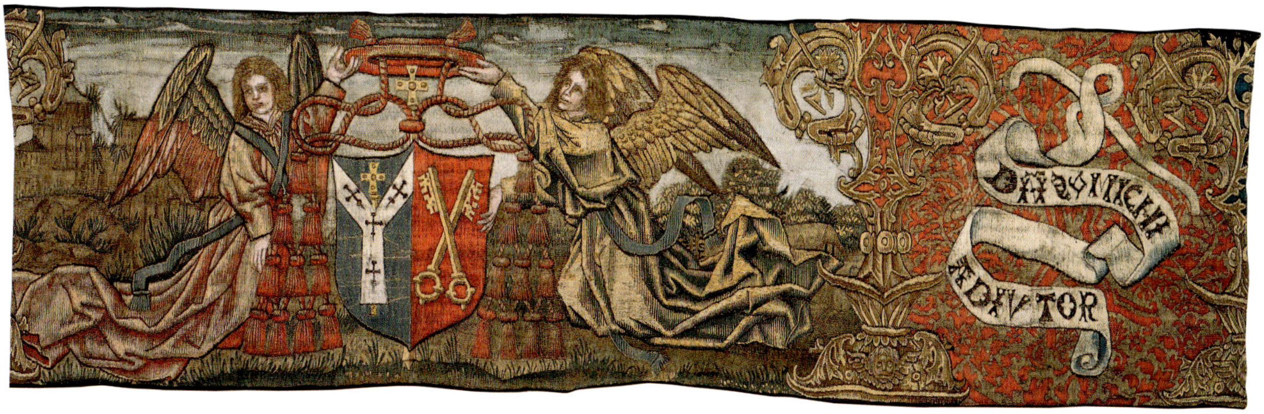

7.11 Arms of the See of York with Wolsey's Cardinal's Hat, Archiepiscopal Cross, and Wolsey's Motto. Tapestry woven in the Southern Netherlands or England, ca. 1517–21. Wool and silk, 60 x 239 cm. Hampton Court Palace

subjects to evoke parallels with particular role models, the bulk purchase of so many religious tapestries appears to have been unprecedented at this date.

Various influences probably played a part in this ambitious program. One of these may have been Paulo Cortesi's treatise *De Cardinalatu,* published in 1510 in San Gimignano. Written for the edification of contemporary princes of the church, this was divided into three books, the first addressing the cardinal's educational needs, the second his mode of life, and the third his political and ecclesiastical duties. It is the second that is especially interesting in this context because it includes extensive discussion of the ideal cardinal's palace, including prescriptions for its decoration. Cortesi drew on a wide range of classic sources, particularly Vitruvius, along with more recent humanist works. Following a venerable tradition that was rooted in Aristotelian thought and that had been propounded more recently by Leon Battista Alberti, Cortesi advocated the use of history paintings as a means of moral persuasion and propaganda.[41] Accordingly, for the decoration of the palace courtyard, he advised images of emperors performing Christian deeds; for the loggias and passages, scenes depicting the teaching of the prophets and Old Testament stories, but emphatically not mythological scenes; for the great hall, scenes of justice and punishment of those who opposed the Church; for the chapel, scenes of the Virgin and the saints; for the audience chamber, scenes of the different ways that princes give audiences; for the bedrooms, scenes of virtue; and for the "summer rooms," images of subtle inventions and scientific curiosities.[42] In view of the close links that existed between Wolsey's household and papal Rome at this time, not least because of his employment of several men who formerly worked for Cardinal Bainbridge, it is certainly conceivable that an awareness of Cortesi's work may have underpinned Wolsey's selection of didactic tapestries for so many chambers in the late 1510s and early 1520s.

Cortesi's work suggested the use of wall frescoes as the medium of decoration. In choosing tapestry over fresco, Wolsey was both following native precedent and blending didacticism with the notion of magnificence. But in choosing tapestry he also had a recent and striking Italian precedent, from no less a figure than the pope himself. In 1515 Leo X had commissioned Raphael to design a set of tapestries depicting the lives of Saint Peter and Saint Paul for the Sistine Chapel in Rome. The cartoons were prepared by Raphael and his assistants and then dispatched to Brussels in the course of 1516, where the tapestries were made in the workshop of Pieter van Aelst between 1517 and 1521 (see below, pp. 188–89). In view of Van Aelst's close links to the English court through Giovanni Cavalcanti, it seems quite likely that news of the papal commission would have reached Wolsey by the time he was commissioning tapestries for York Place and Hampton Court, although it was to be more than a decade before the novel style of Raphael's designs was to be reflected in tapestries made for English patrons.

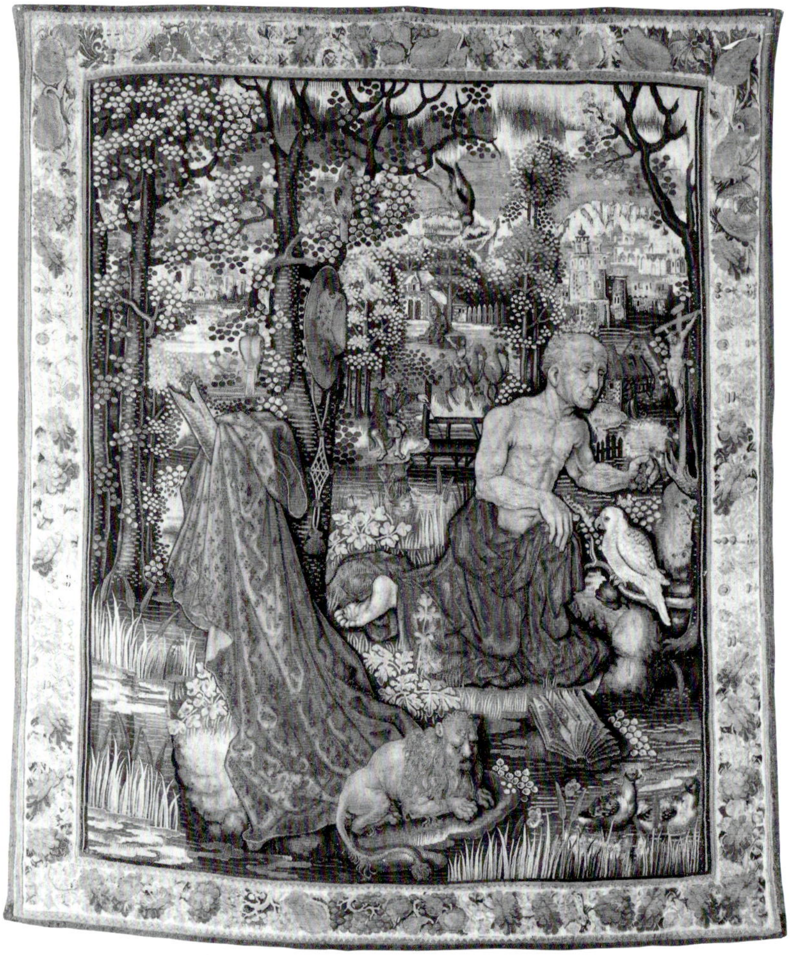

7.12 *Saint Jerome.* Tapestry woven in the Southern Netherlands, ca. 1510–20. Wool, silk, and gilt-metal-wrapped thread, 163 x 132 cm

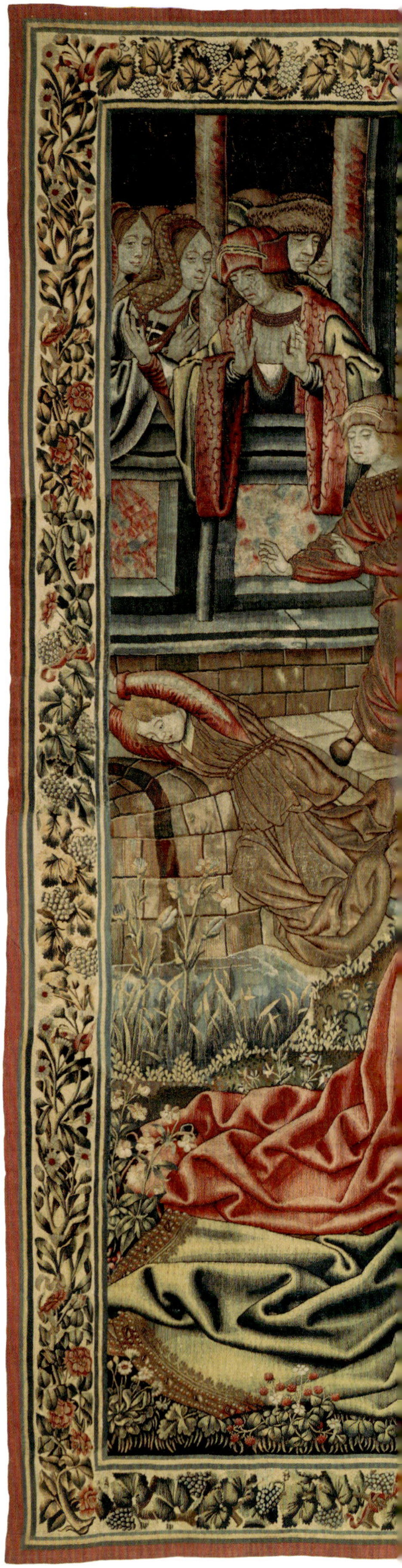

7.13 *The Justice of Trajan.* Tapestry woven in the Southern Netherlands, probably Brussels, ca. 1510–20. Wool, silk, and gilt-metal-wrapped thread, 327 x 364 cm. Museum of Fine Arts, Boston

Whatever the practical and programmatic influences that played a part in the decision regarding the subjects of Wolsey's new tapestries, the wholesale acquisition of so many complementary religious sets appears to have been exceptional at the time, even if it is assumed that they were of moderate quality and woven from available designs. The destruction of almost all of the collection precludes any detailed analysis of an underlying iconographic program, but in view of the subjects listed and the disposition in the rooms of York Place and Hampton Court, it is quite probable that this was no more sophisticated than to associate Wolsey generally with a large number of religious role models. The fact that he did not attempt to commission any of the specific subjects advocated by Cortesi certainly indicates that he was not following that treatise in an especially prescriptive fashion.[43]

Assuming that the tapestries ordered by Scellier would have been woven to specific

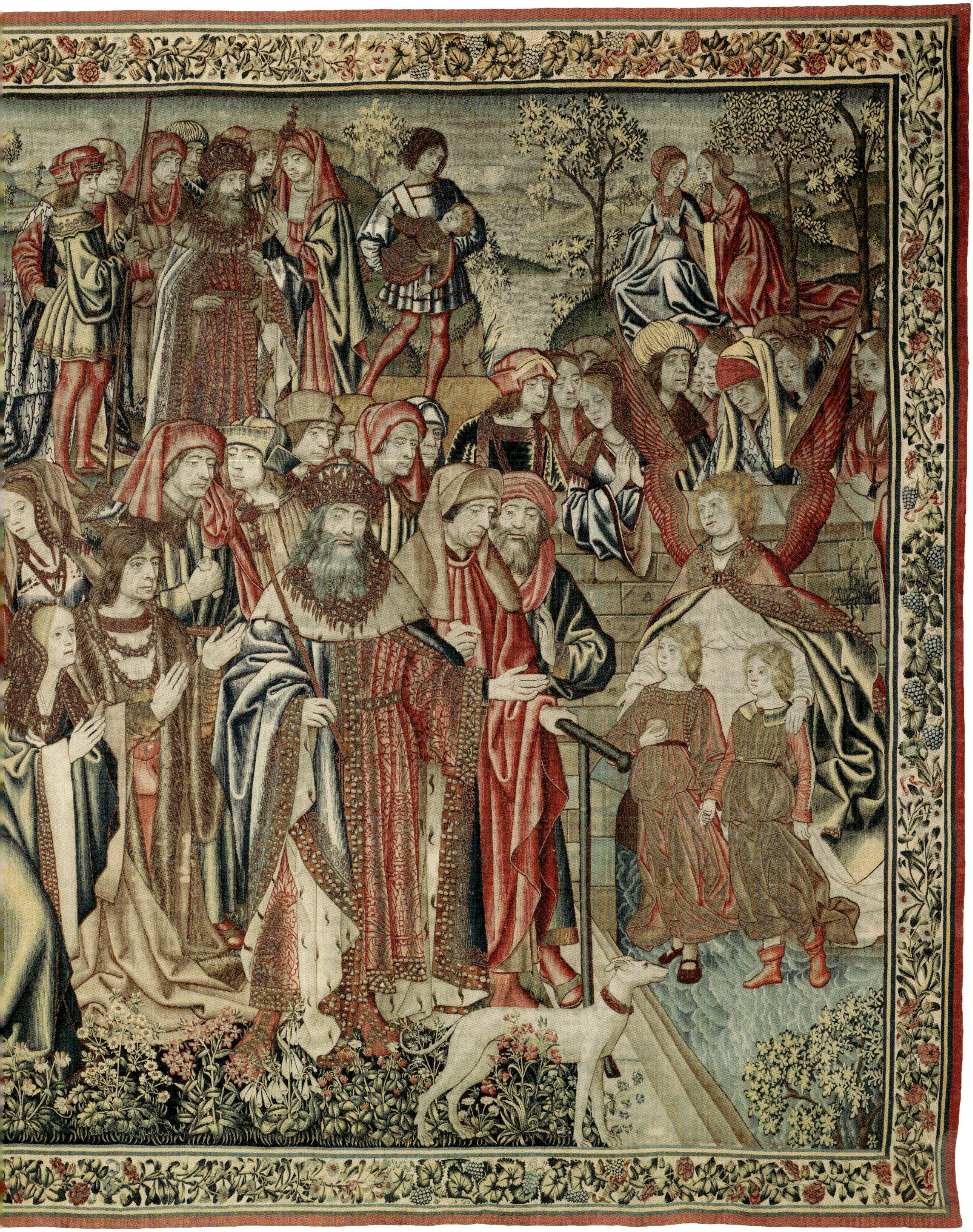

requirements like those ordered later from Gresham, they may have taken twelve to eighteen months to weave, and they would not have been delivered until late 1518 or early 1519. We can conjecture that some at least may have been among the tapestries that so impressed Sebastian Giustinian, the Venetian ambassador, in October 1519. Giustinian reported to the Signory that Wolsey "had a very fine palace, where one traverses eight rooms before reaching his audience chamber and they are all hung with tapestry, which is changed once a week."[44] Although there are no further accounts to confirm the accuracy of this claim, such theatrical deployment would be consistent with other steps taken to demonstrate Wolsey's wealth and power, from the scale of his building to the pomp and ceremony surrounding his movements. Indeed, Giustinian's words may provide an echo of the sort of comments with which Wolsey's officers may have bragged of their master's wealth. An analogy is to be found in the ostentatious display of sideboards of gold plate that remained untouched even while the guests were served on similarly elaborate plate during great banquets such as that given at Hampton Court for the French embassy in 1527.[45]

Where the numerical majority of Wolsey's collection comprised tapestries made from wool or wool and silk, the finest included gold thread and were listed in his inventory as "arras."[46] By the early 1520s, Wolsey owned about forty "arras" pieces, mostly of relatively small dimensions, which were divided into categories of old and new, and we can assume that some of these pieces must have been acquired during the 1510s. The group of old "arras" included nineteen items of which ten were components for three sets of bed hangings. One ensemble was described as the "bedde called infantilage Wherof oon pece hath birdes and fowles in it fleying in the ayre." The second depicted "Beastes and fowles having Banyers abought their nekkes and in the Banyers the armes of England," and the third was the bed called "the Sonne Wherof oon pece having the Sonne with his splayed Beames" (probably Edward IV's emblem). Evidently, these were ensembles from the royal collection that Wolsey must have received as perquisites. The same may have been the case with some of the wall hangings, which included *Dame Pleasaunce*, the *Story of the Duke of Bry and the Gyaunte Orible* (sic), and one piece "sore worn" of the *Story of King Charles*. All sound like pieces dating from the late fourteenth or early fifteenth century discussed above in the context of the early development of the royal collection. Another panel that may have come to Wolsey as a perquisite was an especially wide tapestry of "Seinte Gregory and the Emperor Traian," whose subject and dimensions indicate that it was woven from the same cartoon as the large tapestry of this subject that survives in Bern (see figs. 2.16, 2.17).[47] As discussed above, a duplicate weaving of this design had been recorded in the posthumous inventory of the collection of the earl of Suffolk (1464), and it has recently been shown that Suffolk's panel was probably appropriated by the Crown and had subsequently passed to Wolsey as a perquisite.[48]

Where the "old arras" category reflects a mix of subject matter, indicating that it was made up of pieces that Wolsey had received as perquisites or at second hand, it is likely that those in the "new arras" category comprised new purchases.[49] The majority were of religious subjects, and with the exception of a four-piece set of the *Passion*, most of the others were single panels for use as altarpieces or devotional purposes. Although analogies for several of the religious pieces survive, only one small panel of *Saint Jerome* is of idiosyncratic and close-enough dimension for a probable identification with one of the lost Wolsey panels (fig. 7.12).[50] However, the unusual description of one of the secular panels, that of "ii children saved from drowning by an Aungell," allows it to be identified with a tapestry that survived at Knole in the early twentieth century and is now in Boston (fig. 7.13 and detail opposite p. 127).[51] The tapestry depicts a scene from the legend of Trajan, as described by a Flemish translation of Jacques de Cessole's medieval treatise, the *Ludus scaccorum*, which was printed in Delft in 1483. According to this text, Trajan had decreed that anyone guilty of murder should be killed in the same fashion as the victim. Learning that his own son had accidentally drowned a boy from a poor family, Trajan instructed the father of the dead boy to throw Trajan's son into the Tiber in fulfillment of this law. When the punishment was completed, an angel miraculously restored the two boys to life, divine recompense to Trajan for his action. The scene thus exemplified Justice, and it was paired in Wolsey's collection with a second Trajan panel of similar dimensions, probably a scene of the legend wherein Trajan commanded the execution of a soldier for having accidentally killed a woman's son.[52] The Boston tapestry contains gold thread, as we know Wolsey's did from its inclusion in the "arras" category of his inventory. In view of the cost and rarity of tapestries of this quality and the fact that a number of items at Knole are known to have been acquired from the royal collection at the end of the seventeenth century, there is therefore a possibility that Wolsey's panel and the panel at Boston are one and the same.

The presence of three Trajan panels, one antique and two modern, in Wolsey's collection cannot have been coincidental. Wolsey's involvement in the judicial system is well documented. As judge in the Court of Chancery he encouraged and presided over a boom in chancery litigation and he was also responsible for developing the judicial role of the Star Chamber.[53] As an exemplum of evenhanded justice Trajan was thus an appropriate role model for Wolsey, and we can conjecture that these panels would have been used to draw attention to this parallel.

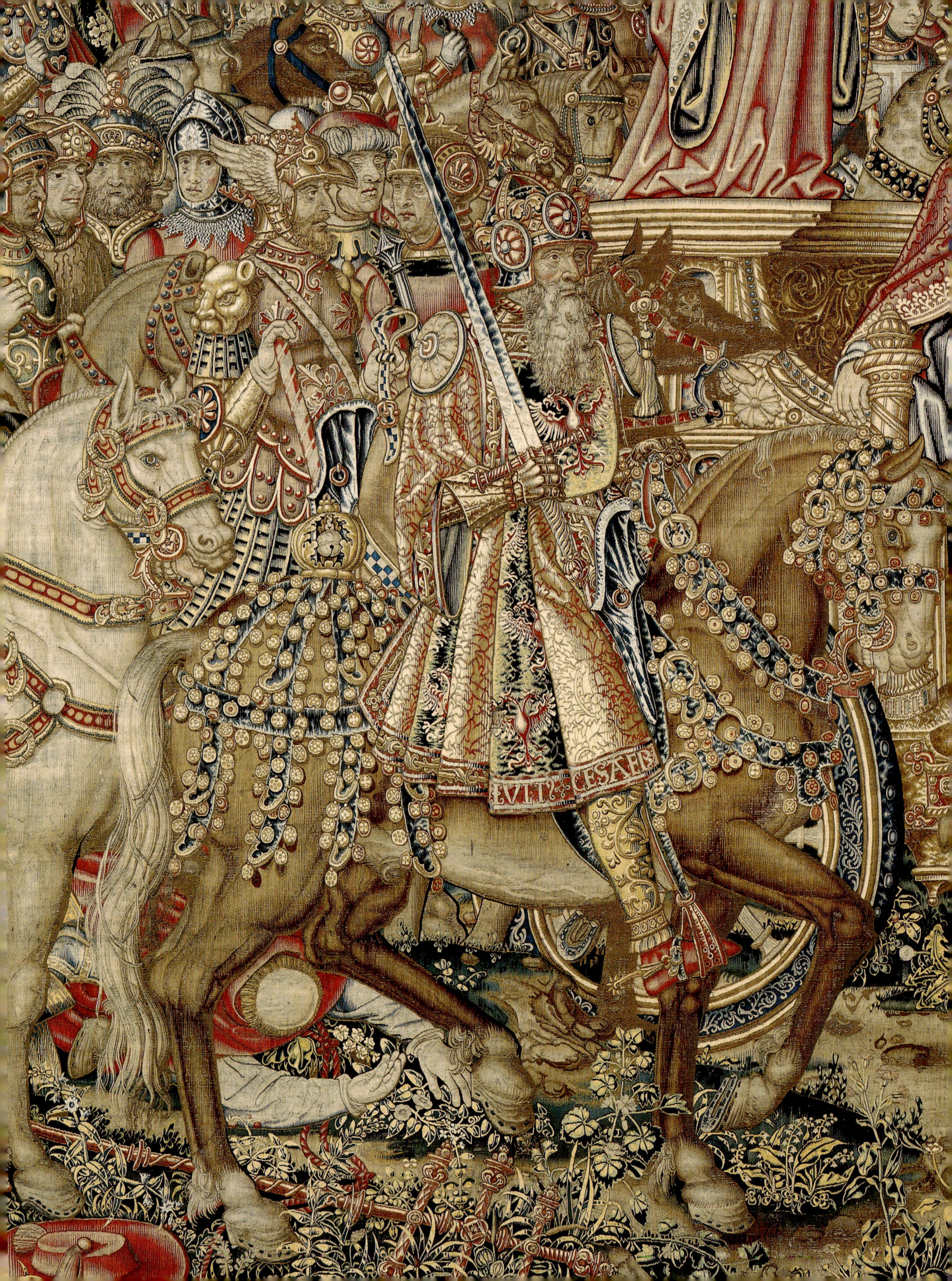

CHAPTER 8

The Field of Cloth of Gold

The conspiracies, negotiations, and treaties that Wolsey was initiating on behalf of Henry during the late 1510s ensured a constant stream of information to London on every aspect of the Continental courts. One effect of this exposure was that it stimulated Henry's personal rivalry with his peers, particularly his near contemporary, Francis I, king of France, and also the slightly younger Charles, king of Spain and, as of 1519, Holy Roman Emperor. This spirit of rivalry was a major factor in Henry's lavish expenditure on precious textiles from the late 1510s. As the previous chapters have revealed, both Henry and Wolsey committed increasing sums of money to tapestry purchases during this period, setting new standards of grandeur and magnificence at the English court.

Wolsey's maneuvers to establish Henry as the arbiter in the balance of power between Spain and France climaxed with the summit meetings between Henry and Charles, Henry and Francis, and then Henry and Charles again in the summer of 1520. Plans for the meeting with Francis were finalized in February of that year, and the meeting was scheduled to take place in June at Guines in the Pale of Calais on the border between English and French territory.[1] Fueled by the spirit of competition between the two courts, each deployed the greatest displays of magnificence of which they were capable, and as the leading medium of portable grandeur, tapestry inevitably played a central role in the arrangements.

Detail of fig. 8.8

Preparations for the Guines Meeting

Preparations for the meeting began several months in advance. A memorandum drawn up early in 1520 stipulated that "all the kynges rich stuff aswell of arras as clothis of tissue and goolde with also the best and fynest tapissery, & other honorable stuff convenient for garnysshyng of such howsis & lodgings, shalbe transported and conveyed to the kynges towne of Calais, the charge whereof is comitted to the said Lord Chamberlayn [that is, Charles Somerset, first earl of Worcester], he, with the mistress of the warderobe [of the Robes], and such other as he shall thinke convenient to devise and appoynt for the preparing & furnisshyng of the kynges lodgynges in moost honorable manner." At the same time, the dean of the king's chapel was to arrange for all necessaries, books, rich vestments, and hangings to be put in readiness for the same purpose, and for the vestments given to the monastery of Westminster by Henry VII (that is, the Stonyhurst vestments, see fig. 4.11) to be borrowed.[2] Meanwhile, the clerk of the closet was responsible for ensuring that the closet in the chapel should be decorated with the best hangings, jewels, images, and plate.[3] Somerset was instructed to travel to France at least forty days in advance of the meeting to oversee preparations, and the scale of the ensuing removals is suggested by a payment to Thomas Betberd for carriage of fifty-two loads of the king's wardrobe stuff in Calais.[4]

During the months preceding the meeting, a series of payments also was made for a number

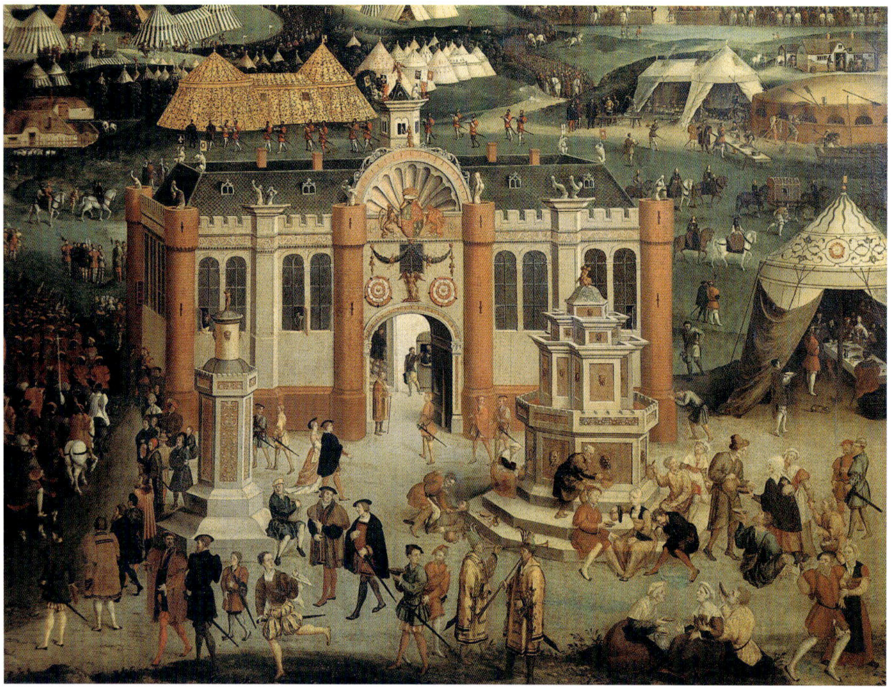

8.1 *The Field of the Cloth of Gold* (detail) by an unidentified artist, ca. 1545. Oil on canvas, 168.9 x 347.3 cm. The Royal Collection

of highly expensive tapestries. In April Giovanni Cavalcanti was paid £410 5s. 9d. from the Treasury of the Chamber for "tapestry with the story of David."[5] Subsequently, in May a payment of £971 5d. was made from the Treasury of the Chamber to Pieter van Aelst for 484 ells (272 square yards) of "arras," subject unspecified, "by thandes of John Cavalcannte."[6] During the same period, Cavalcanti also received further disbursements for cloth of gold and other luxury materials. In the circumstances, it seems certain that these tapestries and textiles were among those that were used at Guines in June. The meeting with Francis had been envisioned for almost two years by this date, so it is possible that the tapestries had been ordered with this occasion in mind.

The role that Cavalcanti played in the transactions between the English court and Van Aelst suggests how intimately Cavalcanti was involved in Van Aelst's business. Given the scale of the orders that Leo X was giving to the Van Aelst workshops and the close relationship between Cavalcanti and Leo, it is even possible that the Florentine was involved in financing the papal commissions. At any rate, he may well have been a conduit of information through which the English court learned about current papal orders and perhaps a spur to those placed by Wolsey and Henry at this period. Cavalcanti was among those who accompanied Henry to Guines, so he would have been able to judge the effect of his work in situ.

By late May everything was ready for the arrival of the English court at Guines, and Henry began his progress to France, via Canterbury, where he first met with and feted Charles V, as Wolsey had arranged. No details have survived of the decorations, but it is to be noted that during this meeting Charles indicated to Wolsey that he might support his candidacy in the next papal election, a hope that probably determined the character of Wolsey's tapestry acquisitions later in the year. With the meeting with Charles out of the way, Henry proceeded to Calais.

Tapestries in the English Temporary Palace

As instructed, the lord chamberlain had arrived in France some weeks earlier, and under his supervision, an army of carpenters and court craftsmen had assembled a temporary palace built for the use of Henry and the most senior members of his court. Others were housed in the nearby castle of Guines or in an army of tents erected for the occasion. Several descriptions and a later, somewhat stylized painting record the exterior and interior appearance of the temporary palace (fig. 8.1). Constructed of wood and canvas, the palace was approximately one hundred yards square, with suites of rooms for the king, his wife, his sister, and Cardinal Wolsey arranged around a central courtyard.[7] Given how quickly the palace had been constructed, the splendor of the interiors inevitably depended on portable furnishings and sumptuous fabrics, including the lavish brocaded velvets, known as cloth of gold (fig. 8.2), with which the whole event is forever linked in popular imagination. Several descriptions mention the tapestries, providing a vivid impression of the contribution that they made to the aesthetics and atmosphere of the proceedings. The interior of the palace was constructed so that the rooms were lit by a row of clerestory windows, below which there was an elaborate cornice decorated with heraldic devices. The space below this was specifically intended for tapestries.[8] Edward Hall describes the effect as follows: "[below the cornice] hanged riche and marveilous clothes of Arras wroughte of golde and silke, compassed of many auncient stories, with which clothes of Arras, every wall and chamber were hanged, and all the wyndowes so richely covered, that it passed all other sightes before seen. In every chamber in place convenient were clothes of estate, greate and large of clothe of golde, of Tissue, and riche embroudery, with Chaiers covered with like cloth, with pomelles of fine gold: and great Cushyns of riche woorke of the Turkey makynge, nothynge lacked of honourable furnishement." The chapel was similarly hung with "Tappettes embraudered with riche worke fret with pearles and stones."[9]

Many visitors were struck by the quality of the tapestries. Marino Sanuto, the Venetian ambassador, recorded that the figures really seemed alive, while Count Alexandro Donado stated that they were "wove with figures and horses represented to the life."[10] Further information about the tapestries in the great hall is provided by an account published by Jacques Dubois in Paris later in the year. According to this, the great hall was decorated with "tapestries woven with gold and silk depicting the Creation of Man, all the Old and New Testaments, and on the other side how David envied Uriah and took Bathsheba, which [were so lifelike they] appeared to be living."[11] The first of these ensembles can be tentatively identified with the valuable *Redemption of Man* set that, as suggested above, may have been purchased by Henry VII from Pieter van Aelst and of which a single piece survives in Narbonne (see figs. 4.19, 5.2). We can conjecture that this set was selected because of its great richness and because it provided a moral and religious framework for the proceedings.

Identification of the *David* series is more problematic. It seems reasonable to suppose that the set was that for which Cavalcanti had been paid earlier in the year. Like the *David* tapestries purchased in 1517, it originated from the workshop of Pieter van Aelst, and it was evidently of exceptionally fine quality. Seven years later, it was displayed again in the temporary banqueting house created at Greenwich for the visit of the French embassy. On this occasion it was described as the "most costly" in England, which suggests that the sum of just over £400 paid to Cavalcanti in April 1520 for a *David* set may have been a partial payment.[12] As already noted, several different *David* design series are extant from the 1510s. In view of the reported quality and the lifelike character of the figures and horses in the set displayed at Guines, it is tempting to identify it as a weaving of the finest of these, the ten-piece design series that survives at the Renaissance Museum in Écouen (see figs. 10.1, 10.2, 10.5–10.10). This depicts David's affair with Bathsheba, the betrayal and death of Uriah, Nathan's denunciation of David, God's punishment of David through the death of his first child, David's repentance and reconciliation with God, and

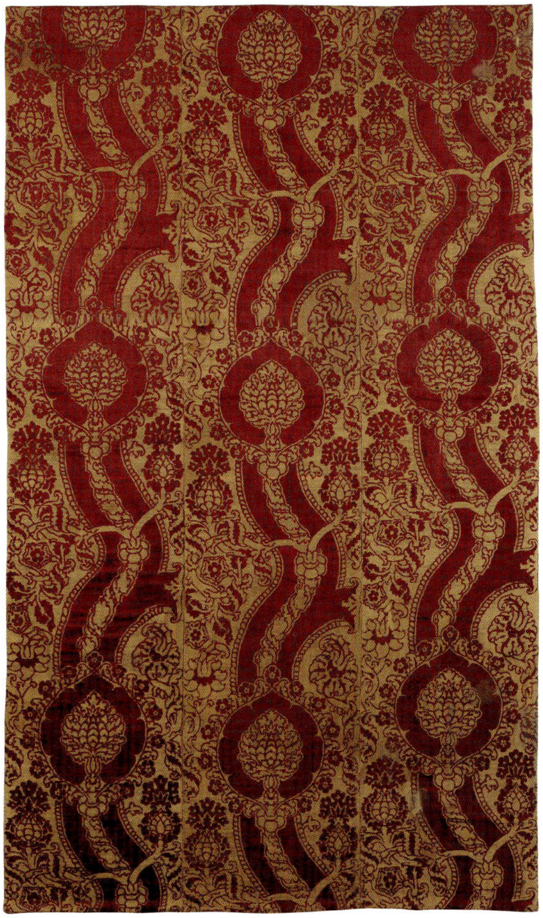

8.2 Cloth of Gold with Pattern of Pomegranates and Roses. Florence, ca. 1515–20. Cut pile velvet brocaded with gilt-metal-wrapped thread, 279.5 x 167.5 cm. The Metropolitan Museum of Art, New York

the eventual victory of David's forces over the Ammonites. The subject of the Écouen set certainly conforms to that described by Dubois, and it also includes life-size figures and horses of extraordinary detail and realism. Further support for this identification between the Écouen series and that purchased in 1520 comes from the style of design, which appears to date from the late 1510s. Indeed, the armor depicted in the Écouen tapestries, that of both the warriors and the horses, is extremely close in appearance to that being made for Henry from the mid-1515s at the armory he established at Greenwich.[13]

The problem with this identification is that the Écouen set has idiosyncratic dimensions that correspond exactly to another, high-quality set of *David* tapestries that Henry purchased in October 1528 for the enormous sum of £1,500. This later purchase coincided with the period in which Henry was seeking to divorce Katherine of Aragon on the basis that he had contravened religious law in marrying her and that this was why she had failed to produce a male heir. Without anticipating discussion of that later purchase in entirety, it is to be noted that the details of David's life, as illustrated in the Écouen set, provided a resonant parallel for Henry's situation as he then perceived it, because God had punished David for his sins with the death of his firstborn son. The rationale for the 1528 purchase may therefore have been to justify Henry's divorce in the arena of the Tudor court by analogy with David's repentance and eventual reconciliation with God.

The evidence that Henry acquired a set of the Écouen design in 1528, probably the Écouen set itself, is incontrovertible, so the suggestion that the set exhibited at Guines in 1520 was also a version of this design would indicate that the later purchase was a duplicate, possibly with some alterations, of a design that he had first acquired some eight years before. Although such duplication might seem surprising, it would certainly not be unique. For example, as will be discussed below, during the early 1520s Wolsey was to acquire two sets of a series depicting the *Triumphs of Petrarch,* while in the late 1530s and early 1540s, Henry acquired duplicate sets of the *Story of Saint Paul,* one of exceptionally high quality. Circumstantial evidence that Henry may indeed have owned two gold-woven, ten-piece sets of *David* of extremely similar dimensions is provided by the 1547 and Commonwealth inventories. The 1547 inventory lists a ten-piece "arras" *David* set at the Tower that can be certainly identified with the 1528 purchase because of its dimensions.[14] In addition, five "arras" tapestries of *David,* described as "tholder Storye of king David" and said to be lined with blue buckram, were at Greenwich (as also were the *Saint John* tapestries purchased in 1517).[15] Five other "arras" tapestries of *David,* also lined with blue buckram, were at Whitehall.[16] No dimensions for the tapestries at Greenwich are provided. Those at Whitehall were of a similar order to those of the large panels in the Tower set. One hundred years later, when the royal tapestries were inventoried for the Commonwealth sale, the ten-piece set formerly at the Tower had been divided into three separate groups, but all were purchased as one lot at the high price of £4 per ell.[17] The two five-piece groups of *David* were now both at Denmark House, where both were valued at £3 per ell.[18] Although the separate listing for the two groups at Denmark House may indicate that they were separate sets purchased in 1517 and 1520, the tapestries were remarkably large, and if these two groups of five are considered as a single group, then the dimensions of the ten component tapestries, as provided by the Commonwealth inventory, also correspond closely to those of the Écouen set.[19] Although this may be coincidental, the unusual size and quality of the tapestries raises the possibility that these two groups originally formed a single set that, for unknown reasons, had been divided by the time of the 1547 inventory and remained divided thereafter. If the set supplied to Henry in 1520 was indeed a first weaving of the Écouen design, then the payment of £410 made to Cavalcanti that April could not have reflected the full cost of the set, since the set supplied in 1528 cost just over

£1,500. It is therefore possible that the payment of £971 to Pieter van Aelst, via Cavalcanti, in May 1520 may have been the balance of the payment. Alternatively, it is conceivable that the large sum paid in 1517 to Van Aelst for tapestries of *David* may have been an advance for this set and that the 1520 payment related to the balance due on delivery.

The tentative identification of the *David* set exhibited at Guines in 1520 as an early weaving of the Écouen design raises an interesting question. By this date it was eleven years since Henry had married Katherine, and he was evidently growing frustrated with her inability to produce a male heir. Since the birth of Mary, Katherine had suffered a series of miscarriages. Most recently, she had produced another female child who had died shortly after birth in November 1518. In contrast, Henry's current mistress, Elizabeth Blount, had recently produced a son, Henry Fitzroy, in June 1519. In making this purchase, was Henry already manifesting a self-identification with David and an uneasiness about the legality of his marriage to Katherine that was to become a pronounced feature of his self-image during the mid-1520s? At the least, the purchase would shed light on the cultural milieu in which he was to develop the conviction that his lack of a male heir resulted from an unholy alliance. Whether thought had yet matured into the notion of divorce is a matter of conjecture, but Henry would not have been the first man to fantasize about divorce long before taking active steps to accomplish it.

The *Redemption of Man* and *David* tapestries were just two of the splendid sets on display in the English palace. Others were located in the suites provided for Queen Katherine, Queen Mary of Scotland (Henry's sister), and Wolsey, where the tapestries, heraldic embroideries, and cloth of gold were arranged in the customary progression of value to dramatize the hierarchy of the chambers. Information about the tapestries in Katherine's suite is provided by the Venetian ambassador Sanuto: "The chambers of Queen Katherine were hung with tapestry of silk and gold representing the most minute foliage, the most beautiful that the eye of man ever beheld; and it cost seven ducats per

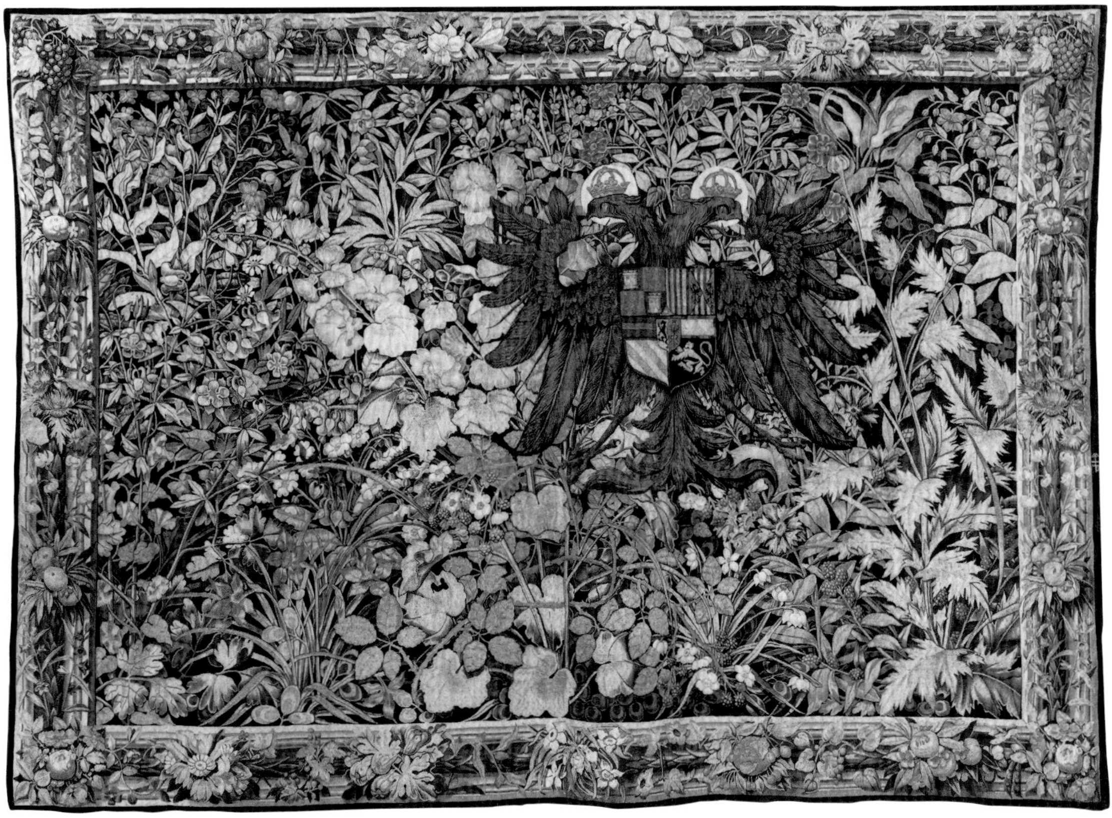

8.3 *Verdure with the Arms of Charles V.* Tapestry woven in the workshop of Willem de Pannemaker, Brussels, ca. 1540. Wool, silk, and gilt-metal-wrapped thread, 200 x 272 cm. Kunsthistorisches Museum, Vienna

yard."[20] This description allows us to identify the ensemble with a high-quality set of verdures listed at the Tower in the 1547 inventory that were probably among the tapestries purchased from Van Aelst during the late 1510s or in spring 1520.[21] Evidently of great magnificence and cost, the set featured at several significant events during the following years and survived in the royal collection until the Commonwealth sale, when it was described as "nine peeces of rich verdours the ground or field of gold."[22] Acquired for £2,292 by a consortium led by a merchant named Robert Houghton, it was subsequently sold to Philip IV's ambassador, Don Alonso de Cárdenas, from whom it passed into the Spanish royal collection. The later fate of the set is unclear, but it is thought to have been lost in a fire at the Alcázar.[23] Although its appearance is unknown, we can conjecture that the design embodied the new spirit of realism and detail that was developing in verdure design during the 1510s. It is conceivable that a detail of one piece of the set may be represented by the verdure tapestry that appears in the background of Hans Holbein's painting of Henry VIII granting the charter to the Barber-Surgeons' Company (see fig. 12.9).[24] A comparable high-quality verdure series with the armorials of Charles V, but without the gold ground that made Henry's set so sumptuous, survives in Vienna (fig. 8.3).[25] In view of the documented quality of Henry's lost set, it is unlikely that it was woven as a speculative venture and more probable that it was commissioned.

Information about the suites provided for Mary and Wolsey comes from Soardino, the Mantuan ambassador to the French court. The decorations of Mary's apartments emphasized her recent marriage to Francis's predecessor: "The first hall was hung with very exquisite tapestry of gold and silk as above; the other with crimson velvet and gold tissue, the velvet being embroidered with the letters M.L. [Mary and Louis] within a gold knot; and in certain other places were embroidered sundry porcupines, the hangings having been made when she was the wife of King Louis XII. In the chamber was a bedstead with canopy and curtains of gold brocade; the hangings like those of the halls being of gold and silk."[26] In passing it is interesting to note that although some of these heraldic hangings may still have belonged to Mary, their quality and significance marked them out as items that would eventually come into the royal collection. According to an indenture made between Henry VIII on one hand and Mary and Sir Charles Brandon on the other, Henry agreed to discharge Mary's debts at her death, but any French royal goods remaining in her possession were to come to the Crown. An ensemble of eight rich embroideries with Mary and Louis's arms is duly listed in the 1547 inventory.[27]

Wolsey's suite was described as follows: "the first [room] very large hung with silken tapestry, without gold, of astounding beauty; the second tapestried in the same fashion. In the chamber are most beautiful tapestries of gold and silk, and a very large bedstead with gilt posts and a canopy of cloth of gold." It is conceivable that the wool and silk tapestries displayed in Wolsey's outer chamber are to be identified with a set of the *Triumphs of Petrarch* that appears to have been made for him in 1520, an issue that will be discussed below.

Besides the role that tapestry played inside the English palace, it also formed the staging for many open-air events. When Henry and Francis met at the Vale of Ardres on June 7, the tent in which they convened was decorated externally "all of clothe of gold, and riche embroudery of the kyng of Englandes." Inside it was "hanged of the richest Arras, newly contrived and made, that ever before was seen," along with the inevitable cloths of estate and thrones.[28] Similarly, the stage on which Wolsey celebrated Mass before the two kings on June 23 was decorated with rich embroideries, and the enclosure in which the royal parties sat was hung with tapestries.[29]

Although incomplete, the foregoing evidence suggests that the tapestries displayed at Guines featured a mixture of old and new tapestries, many of which Pieter van Aelst had supplied to Henry or his father. Indeed, the whole event provided an incomparable advertisement for Van Aelst's business. Although the underlying choices may have been dictated largely by the richness and magnificence of the sets, it is possible that, with the *David* set at least, we see an early example of Henry identifying himself with an Old Testament role model, a process that became increasingly marked in the following years. Irrespective of the iconographic associations of the English tapestries, the eyewitness accounts provide no room for doubt that the display was truly remarkable. As such, it seems to have raised the bar for European court splendor and must have played a key part in fueling the enormous expenditure that Henry, Francis I, and Charles V were all to commit to tapestry patronage during the following two decades.

Considering the prominence of tapestries in the decorations of the English residence, it is interesting that none of the contemporary descriptions refer to tapestries in the French tents where, if the accounts are reliable, the effect of richness was achieved with hangings of cloth of gold. Francis was to become a significant tapestry patron in his own right during the late 1520s and 1530s, but little evidence of his activity in this sphere has survived from the 1510s, so the lack of reference to tapestries in his tents may be accurate. The caveat to this assumption is that he purchased a woven copy of Leonardo da Vinci's famous *Last Supper* fresco sometime during the 1510s (see fig. 11.6).[30] This tapestry, presumably woven in Brussels, survives today in the Vatican collections because Francis presented it to Clement VII in 1533 on the occasion of the marriage of the dauphin to Catherine de' Medici, Clement's niece. Whether it was exhibited at Guines is a matter of conjecture; there is no mention of it in any of the accounts or evidence of subsequent awareness of this design by members of the English court.

Wolsey's Triumphs of Petrarch

None of the descriptions mention the subjects of the tapestries in Wolsey's rooms, but there is one notable possibility. The 1522 inventory of Wolsey's possessions shows that by this date he had acquired a splendid set of the *Triumphs of Petrarch,* and circumstantial evidence, discussed below, indicates that this can be identified with a partial set of this subject that survives at the Victoria and Albert Museum.[31] As we shall see, one of these designs, *The Triumph of Fame over Death* (see fig. 8.8), appears to have been specifically adapted for Wolsey. If the "1520" inscription in one of the other tapestries of the Victoria and Albert Museum set, *The Triumph of Chastity over Love* (fig. 8.4), indicates the date of its execution, this set could conceivably have been completed in time for display at Guines. Whether or not this was the case, the adapted set must have been conceived in or shortly before 1520, and it reveals much about the current taste at the English court and how extensively Wolsey was engaged in his tapestry commissions.

The designs for this series, one of the most ambitious of the early 1500s, appear to have been created for the French king Louis XII on the basis of an illuminated manuscript of the *Triumphs of Petrarch* (figs. 8.5, 8.6) presented to him by Georges d'Amboise, archbishop of Rouen, in about 1503.[32] The gift reflected the interest in Italian culture that had been stimulated by Louis's capture of Milan in 1498 and the ensuing importation to France of many Italian works of art and literature. The cartoons were probably created in 1507, a second date that appears on the *Triumph of Chastity over Love* in the Victoria and Albert Museum set. Like the manuscript, each scene features chariots carrying, in succession, the triumphal figures described in Petrarch's visionary poem: Love, Chastity, Death, Fame, Time, and Religion. Petrarch's poem gave a chariot only to the first of these, but from the mid-fifteenth century Italian artists began to portray all the triumphs in this way, and this model was disseminated through prints. The Rouen manuscript was the most ambitious realization of this formula undertaken by a northern European artist up until that time, with double-page confronted illustrations, akin to the structure of a diptych,

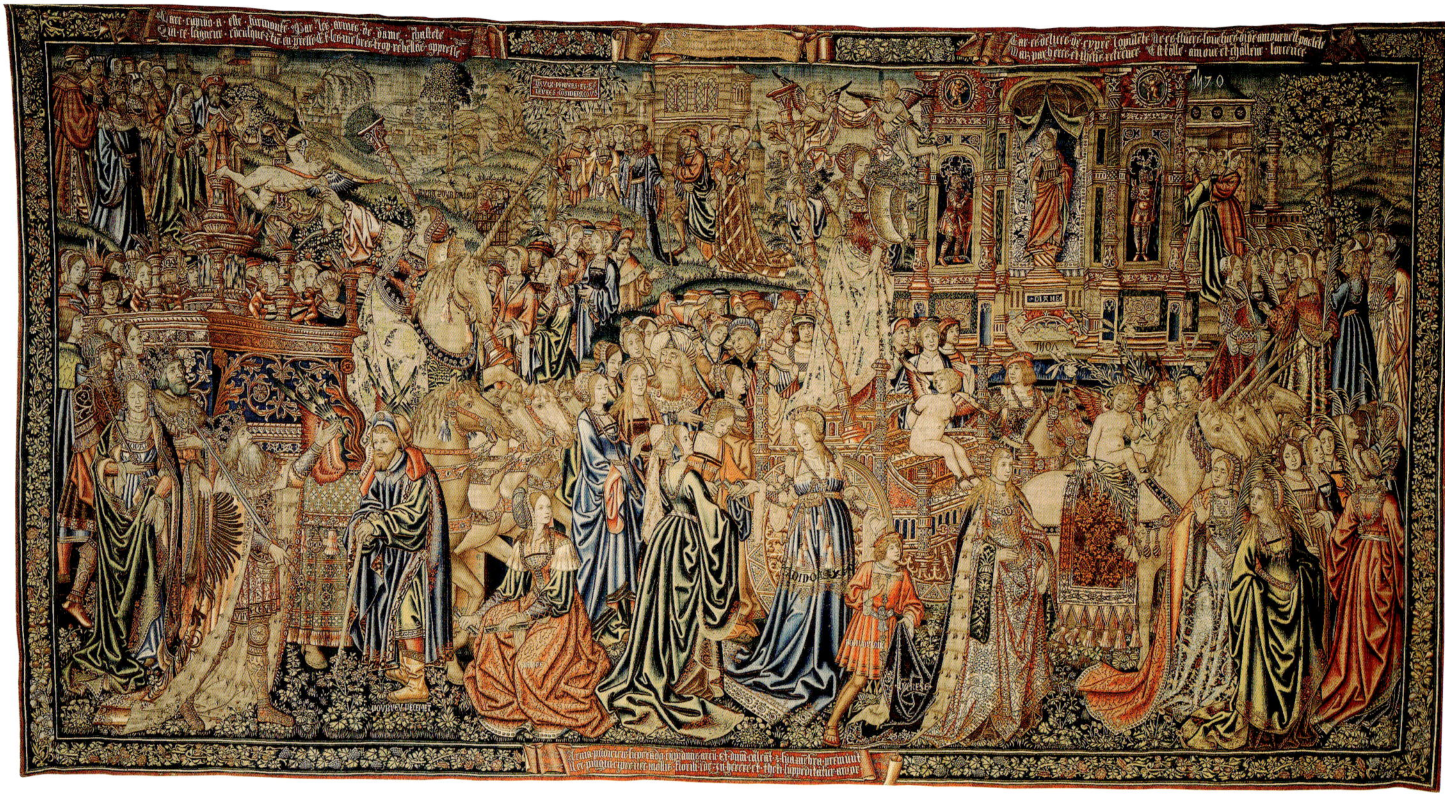

8.4 *The Triumph of Chastity over Love* from a set of the *Triumphs of Petrarch*. Tapestry woven in the Southern Netherlands, probably Brussels, ca. 1520. Wool and silk, 447 x 823 cm. Victoria and Albert Museum, London

in which the first showed the ascendant power defeating his or her predecessor and the second the triumph of the victorious power. The tapestries are equally innovative, both in scale and in the elaborate visualization of the scenes. In each, the confronted images of the manuscript are conflated into a single scene depicting two triumphal cars, the first of the waning power at the moment of defeat, the second of the ascendant power. As in the manuscript, each chariot is surrounded by a crowd of figures who exemplify the ascendant power, providing a

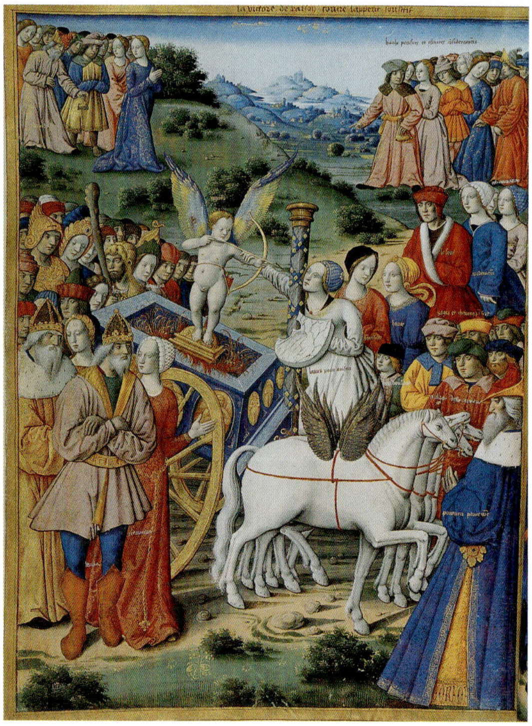

8.5 *The Triumph of Chastity over Love*. Miniature painting by an unidentified artist from *Les triumphes du poethe messire Françoys Petrarche* . . . (Rouen, ca. 1503). Watercolor on parchment, 37 x 26 cm. Bibliothèque Nationale de France, Paris (Ms fr. 594, fol. 101v)

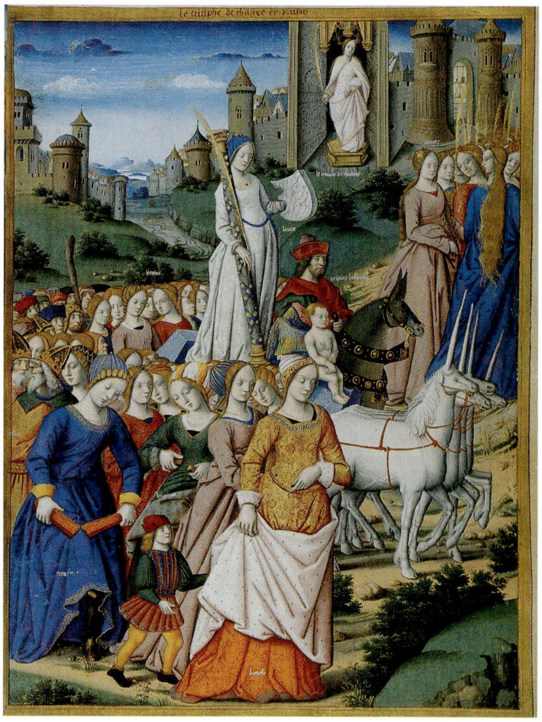

8.6 *The Triumph of Chastity*. Miniature painting by an unidentified artist from *Les triumphes du poethe messire Françoys Petrarche* . . . (Rouen, ca. 1503). Watercolor on parchment, 37 x 26 cm. Bibliothèque Nationale de France, Paris (Ms fr. 594, fol. 102r)

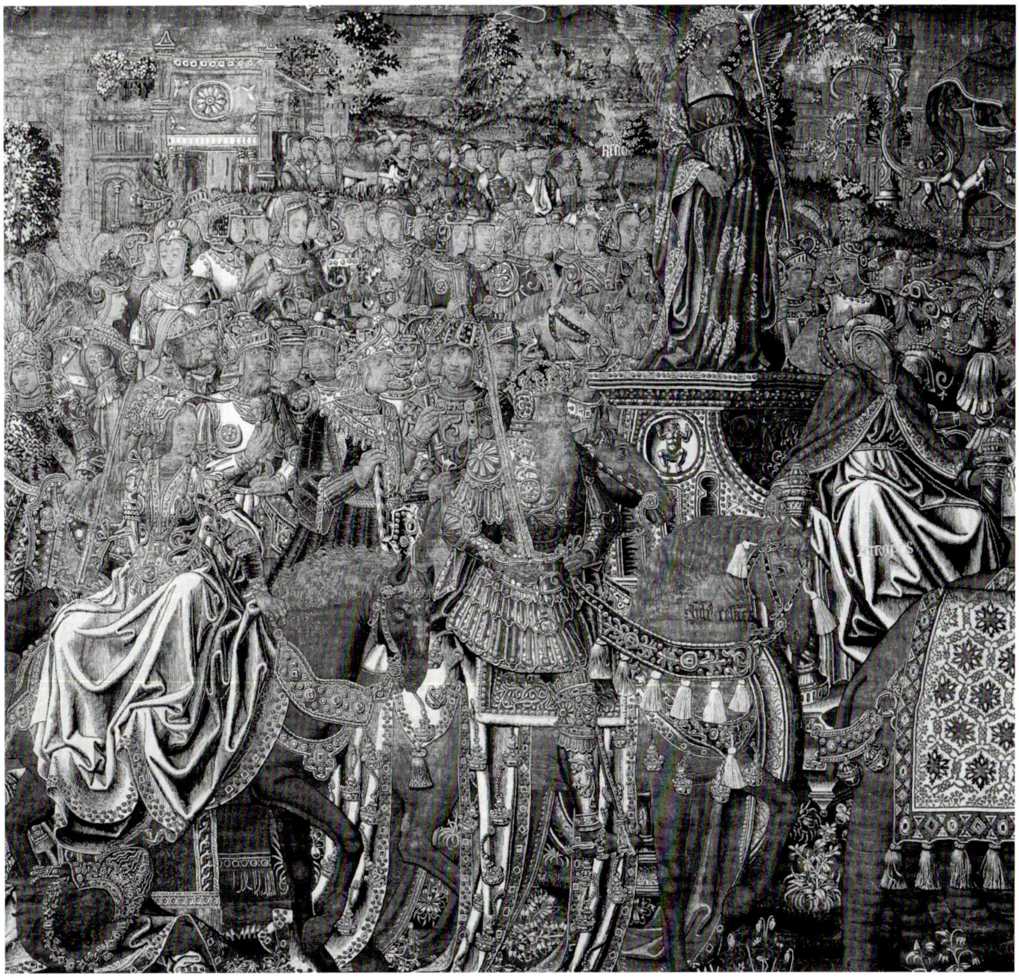

8.7 *The Triumph of Fame over Death* (detail) from a set of the *Triumphs of Petrarch.* Tapestry woven in the Southern Netherlands, probably Brussels, ca. 1515–20. Wool and silk, 406 x 810 cm. Hampton Court Palace

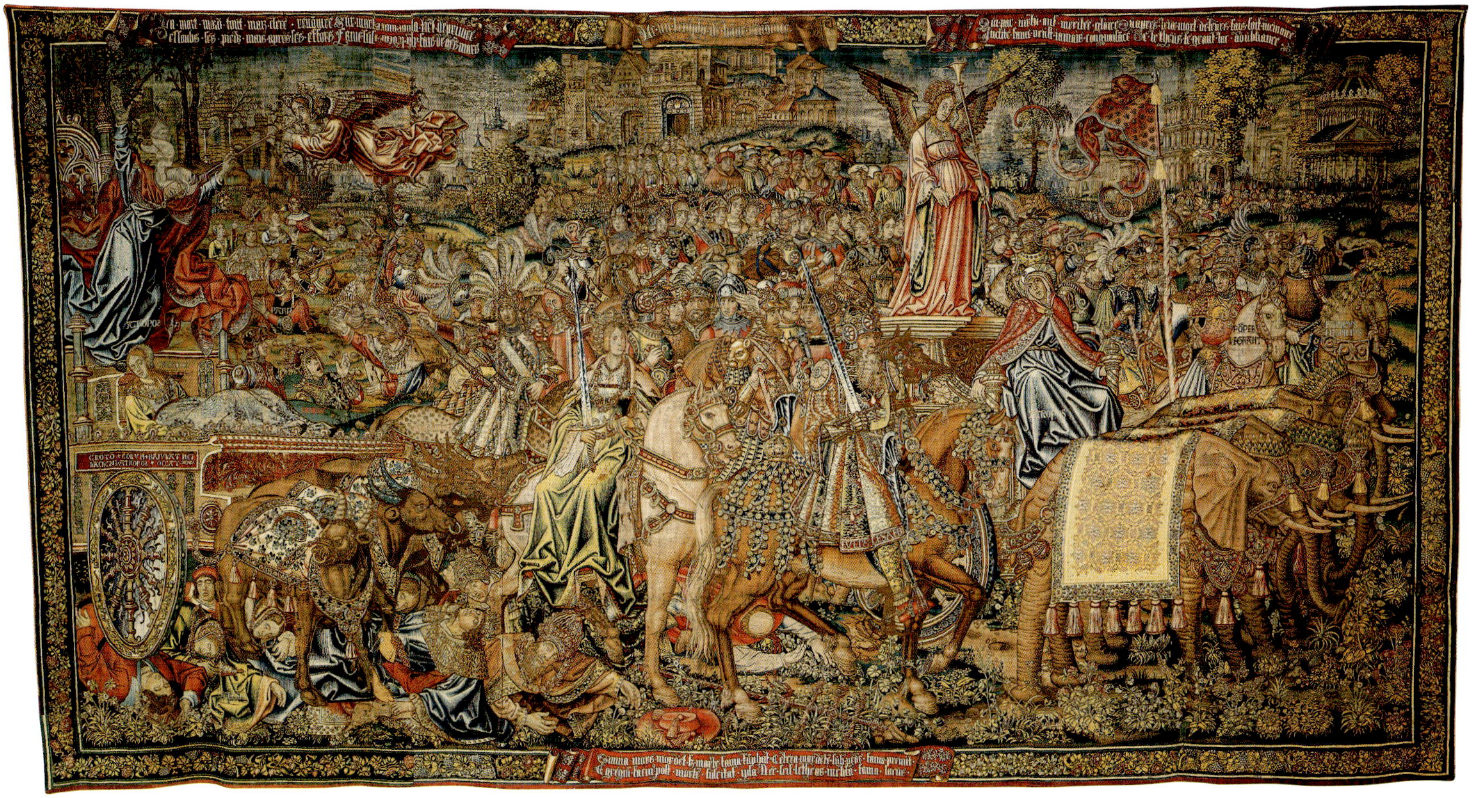

8.8 *The Triumph of Fame over Death* from a set of the *Triumphs of Petrarch.* Tapestry woven in the Southern Netherlands, probably Brussels, 1520. Wool and silk, 439 x 821 cm. Victoria and Albert Museum, London

rich synthesis of the visual and interpretative traditions that had developed in association with the theme of Petrarch's *Triumphs* over the previous fifty years.[33]

Louis XII's set of this design can probably be identified with one that was listed in the French royal inventory in the mid-sixteenth century and again in the late seventeenth century but that disappeared thereafter and is presumed destroyed.[34] During the late 1510s, this design enjoyed popularity among English patrons, stimulated no doubt by the renewed contact between the French and English courts after 1514. The earliest weaving appears to have been that made for Thomas Ruthal, bishop of Durham, which Wolsey purchased from Durham's executors following his death in February 1523. According to an addendum to Wolsey's 1522 inventory in which it is listed, the Ruthal group included eight tapestries of which two were duplicates.[35] Ruthal had been one of the most Francophile members of the English court, serving as ambassador for Henry VII to Louis XII in 1499, being present at the marriage of Henry's sister Mary to Louis in 1514, and acting as one of the commissioners when Henry's daughter, Mary, was betrothed to the French dauphin in 1518. It is therefore possible that Ruthal's acquisition was precipitated by acquaintance with the set in the French royal collection, which he may have seen during his visit to Paris in 1514. In turn, Ruthal's example may have been the spur to Wolsey's acquisition. At any rate, at some point before the 1522 inventory was compiled, Wolsey acquired an especially rich weaving of the design on his own account, which is listed first in the category of his largest and richest tapestries in the inventory.[36] According to the description provided by this document, this had been enlarged with borders that depicted the arms of England and Spain and Tudor roses on a ground of daisies. As the longitudinal dimensions of the borders did not correspond to those of the tapestries it seems unlikely that they were made for this set.

The subsequent history of Wolsey's two *Petrarch* sets is somewhat uncertain, but in all likelihood four of the set that Wolsey acquired from Ruthal can be identified with the tapestries of this design that survive at Hampton Court (fig. 8.7; see also fig. 17.2).[37] That this set predates the manufacture of the set at the Victoria and Albert Museum is revealed by adaptations that have been made to the design of the latter. The fate of the high-quality set listed in the 1522 inventory is harder to trace because this set is not readily identifiable in the inventory made at the time of the Commonwealth sale in 1649 and may already have left the royal collection by this date. Nonetheless, circumstantial evidence that the tapestries now at the Victoria and Albert Museum may originate from Wolsey's high-quality set is provided by the known provenance of that group, which is first documented in Genoa in 1658—that is, just a few years after the Commonwealth sale, when other tapestries from the royal collection were being disseminated across the Continent by merchants and collectors.[38] In addition, certain idiosyncratic changes incorporated into the design suggest that the Victoria and Albert Museum tapestries come from a set whose design had been customized for Wolsey in 1520—the second of the two dates that appear on one of the museum's tapestries.[39]

The most significant of these adaptations occurs in the panel of the *Triumph of Fame over Death,* which incorporates a number of figures in the train of heroes following Fame's chariot that do not appear in the earlier version of the design at Hampton Court (figs. 8.8–8.10). Two figures are especially striking. The first, wearing a cardinal's scarlet biretta, appears at the top of the tapestry in the center of an additional register of clergy. The second appears directly below, about two-thirds from the bottom of the tapestry, and shows the face of a bearded warrior staring out of the tapestry at the viewer. Although these additional figures may be anonymous types, added to repair a damaged section of the cartoon, their idiosyncratic features and costume and placement exactly on the central axis of the design seem considered rather than coincidental, raising the possibility

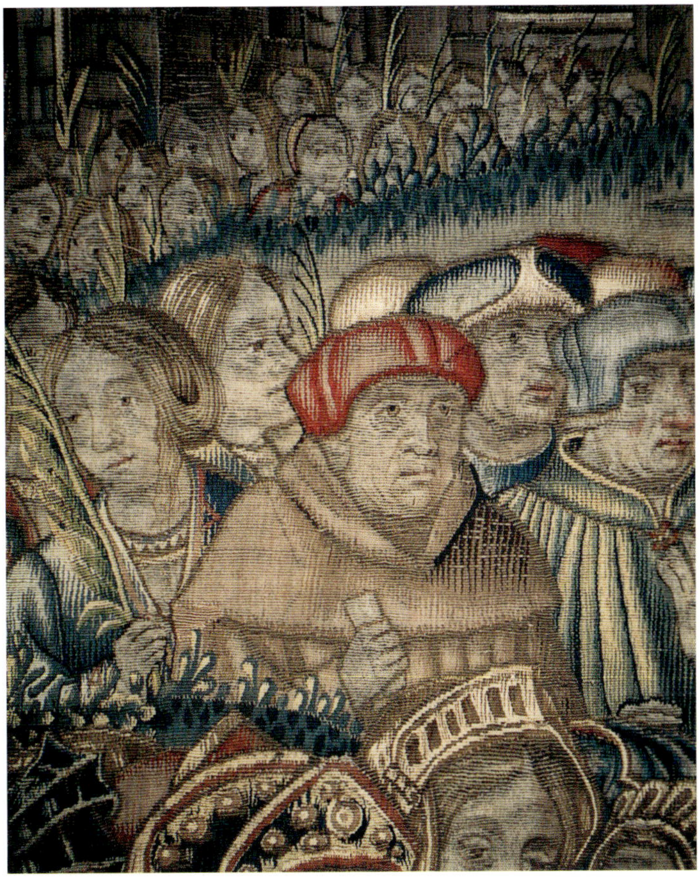

8.9 Detail of fig. 8.8 showing Cardinal Wolsey

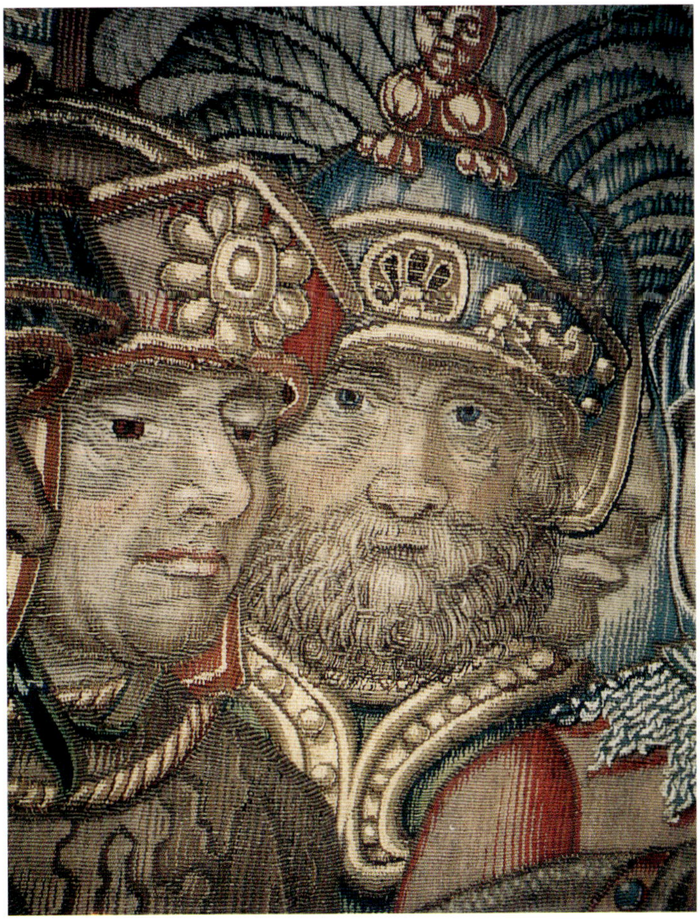

8.10 Detail of fig. 8.8 showing Henry VIII

that they are portraits. They lack the clarity of portraits executed in pencil or oil paint, but there can be little doubt that they share common features with images of Wolsey and Henry. No contemporary likeness of Wolsey survives, and our knowledge of his appearance depends on the famous, but somewhat coarse, profile in the National Portrait Gallery (fig. 8.11), probably part of a sequence executed some years after his death, and a mid-sixteenth-century drawing attributed to Jacques Le Boucq (fig. 8.12). Although the drawing also dates from some thirty years after Wolsey's death, it is presumably based on a lost original. The face in the tapestry is more corpulent that that of the drawing but slimmer than that represented in the National Portrait Gallery painting. Yet the heavy jowls, double chin, arched eyebrows, and strong nose of the ecclesiastic in the tapestry are common to all three portraits, and if we allow for the imprecision introduced to the three depictions by the vagaries of the weaving process and the stylization inherent in the later reproduction of lost images, there seems little doubt that the tapestry depiction may well portray the same figure as the painting and drawing.

Identification of the bearded face (see fig. 8.10) with Henry is also problematic because of the paucity of reliable likenesses of the king before Holbein's famous works of the mid-1530s. Nor is it helped by the stylized manner in which the weaver has interpreted the beard. We know that Henry was clean-shaven during the 1510s but that he intermittently sported a beard from the late 1510s and early 1520s as he appears in a miniature of ca. 1525–27 (fig. 8.13), attributed to Lucas Horenbout, now in the royal collection. The beard was originally grown in 1519 in anticipation of the meeting that was planned that year with Francis I, then, when the meeting was delayed, removed at Katherine of Aragon's insistence. Finally, Henry regrew the beard in time for the eventual meeting with Francis at Guines in June 1520.[40] If, as suggested above, the second date that appears in the Victoria and Albert Museum *Triumph of Chastity over Love*

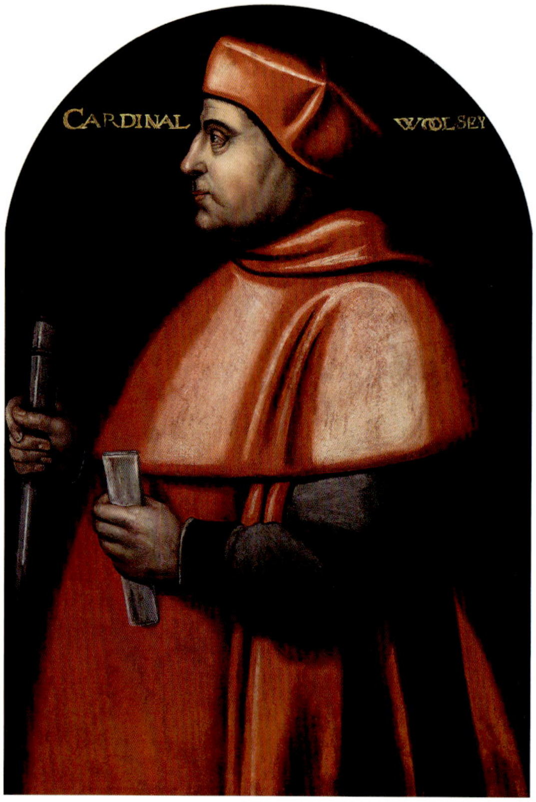

8.11 *Cardinal Wolsey* by an unidentified artist, ca. 1550. Oil on panel, 83.8 x 55.9 cm. National Portrait Gallery, London

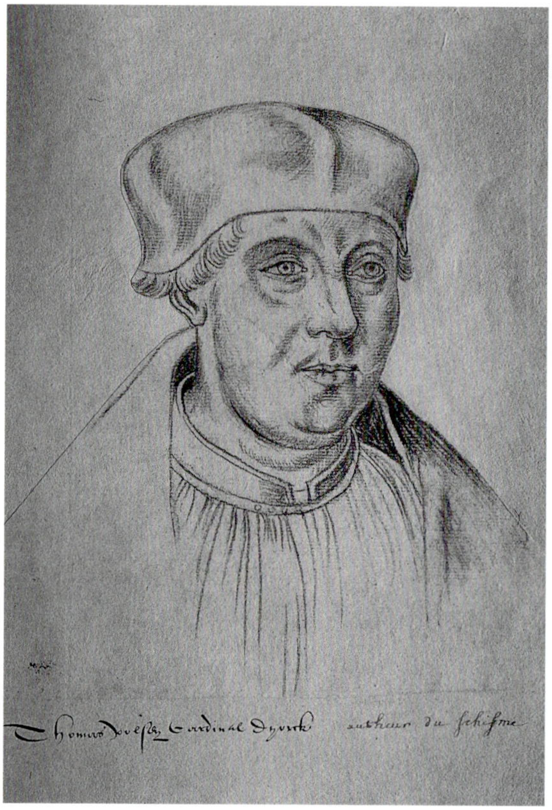

8.12 *Cardinal Wolsey* by Jacques Le Boucq, ca. 1565. Chalk on paper, 41 x 26 cm. Bibliothèque Municipale, Arras (Ms 266, fol. 257)

is read as 1520, and if we assume that this was also the date of the adaptations to the cartoon from which the museum's *Triumph of Fame over Death* was woven, then this bearded face fits appropriately with what we might expect for a portrayal of Henry in 1520 at the age of about thirty. The wide, flat cheeks, strong nose, and relatively small mouth certainly conform with the regal physiognomy familiar from the royal collection miniature and from Holbein's later portrayals. And taking the argument from a different direction, if these two additional figures are indeed portraits, one a cardinal, the other a layperson of importance, no individuals at the other courts of the day conform to the pair of men depicted so closely as Wolsey and Henry.

If the cartoon used to make the Victoria and Albert Museum's *Triumph of Fame over Death* was indeed adapted to incorporate portraits of Wolsey and Henry in 1520, which of them commissioned the adapted set? This year was obviously a glorious one for both, and as we have seen, several very large payments for tapestries were disbursed from the king's treasury for tapestries during that year. It is conceivable that these acquisitions included the *Triumphs of Petrarch*, and this would provide one explanation why the set recorded in Wolsey's inventory two years later had an attached border of the king's arms. Given the central role Wolsey played in planning the Field of Cloth of Gold celebrations and the fact that he had a suite of rooms in the temporary palace, alongside those of Henry VIII, Katherine of Aragon, and Henry's sister Mary, it is possible that he received the tapestries as a perquisite after the event.

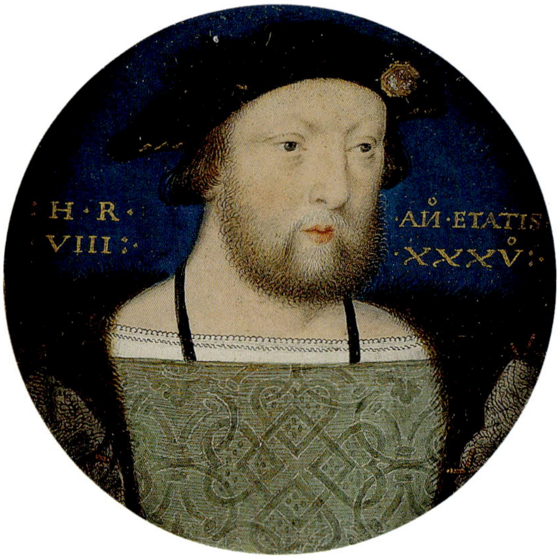

8.13 *Henry VIII with a Beard* attributed to Lucas Horenbout, ca. 1525. Watercolor on vellum, 4.7 x 4.7 cm. The Royal Collection

An alternative explanation for the presence of borders with the royal arms on the set listed in Wolsey's inventory is that Wolsey had commissioned the set and that these borders were provided to him from the Great Wardrobe either in anticipation of the Field of Cloth of Gold meeting or when he traveled to France as Henry's ambassador in 1522 to negotiate peace between France and Spain. An analogous dispensation occurred in 1512 when the Great Wardrobe was ordered to provide the earl of Surrey with various banners and four tapestry borders with the royal arms for his tapestries, in advance of his journey to Scotland at the head of the English army.[41] This second theory is especially attractive because it would explain why the borders detailed in Wolsey's inventory did not match the dimensions of the *Triumphs* tapestries to which they were affixed.

From a psychological viewpoint, the theory that the designs were adapted for Wolsey is also more compelling. Had they been altered for Henry, we might expect to see other additional figures, such as Katherine of Aragon. But if the design was altered for Wolsey, it makes sense that the only figures who mattered were the cardinal himself and his royal patron. Furthermore, the overweening egotism that would have been required to conceive of this self-portrayal in this context fits in well with what we know of Wolsey's character. Given the close relationship between Ruthal and Wolsey—Giustinian described Ruthal as "singing treble to the cardinal's bass"—it is possible that Wolsey first encountered the *Triumphs* design through Ruthal's set, which, as we have seen, predated the Victoria and Albert Museum tapestries, and then took the necessary steps to commission his own, adapted version, presumably through an intermediary like Giovanni Cavalcanti or Richard Gresham.

Although the foregoing evidence is conjectural, and though the presence of the *Triumphs* set at the Field of Cloth of Gold remains a matter of speculation, the fact remains that Wolsey evidently owned a very high-quality set of this design and that the Victoria and Albert Museum set appears to have been woven from cartoons that had been adapted in or before 1520 to incorporate portraits of Wolsey and Henry. Assuming that they are likely to be one and the same, the set provides a remarkable demonstration of Wolsey's interest in the tapestry medium and of how he appropriated a humanist theme in pursuit of his own aggrandizement.

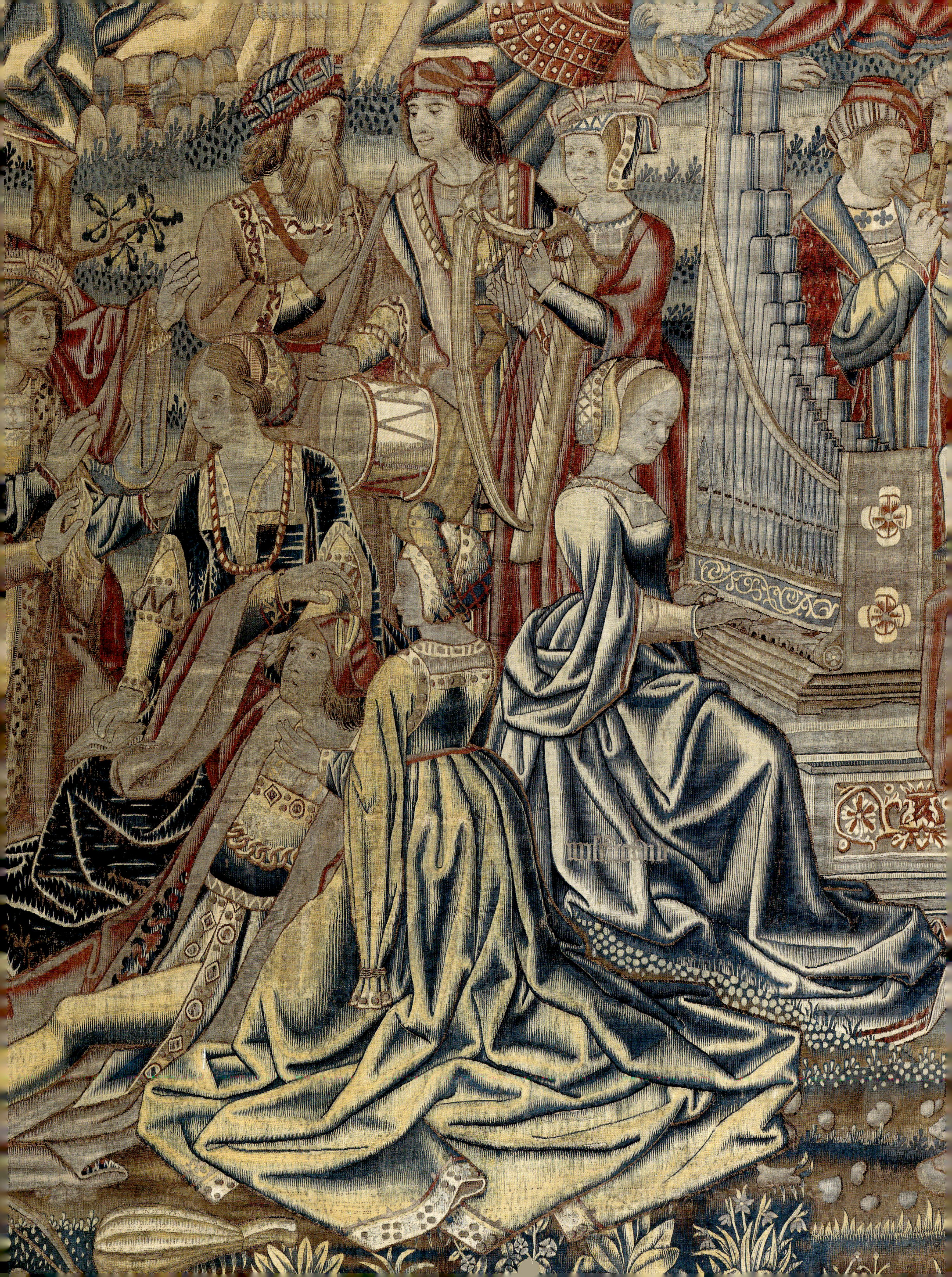

CHAPTER 9

The Patronage of Cardinal Wolsey and Henry VIII in the Early 1520s

Richard Gresham and Further Tapestry Commissions for Hampton Court and York Place

The circumstances in which Wolsey acquired a customized set of the *Triumphs of Petrarch* remain a matter of speculation, but we are on firmer ground with the other tapestry commissions he initiated during the months following the Field of Cloth of Gold meeting. In the summer and autumn of 1520 Wolsey was at the apogee of his power. Buoyed by the apparent success of his international policy, and with ambitions to secure the next papal election, or at least to control its outcome, his position appeared to be unassailable. During the months following the Guines summit, and presumably under the influence of the fabulous displays of textiles and tapestries that this event had featured, he initiated another enormous tapestry commission that was evidently intended to promote his ecclesiastic stature. The tapestries in question were largely intended for Hampton Court, where the building around the Base Court was nearing completion (fig. 9.1).

The arrangements were delegated to the wealthy London merchant Richard Gresham, whose commercial activity centered on the Netherlands.[1] Gresham had been lending money and supplying luxury items to the Crown since the early 1510s and had hired ships to, and from, Henry, for the transport of merchandise as far afield as the Strait of Gibraltar. He had been appointed a gentleman usher extraordinary in 1516 and, along with his brothers William and John, was involved in substantial trade and financial transactions with the Crown in the following years, at one time owing the Crown more than £3,438. In about 1517 he obtained a license to import goods with a custom duty up to £2,000, the duty to be paid over a series of years. Subsequently in 1521 he applied to Wolsey to request a similar license for himself and his brother to export and import goods, with a custom duty value of £2,600, to be paid at the rate of 300 marks per year. In return, he offered to cancel a debt of £280 that Wolsey owed him.

Details of Gresham's work for Wolsey in 1520 are given in a letter addressed to the cardinal on October 14 of that year. Gresham informed

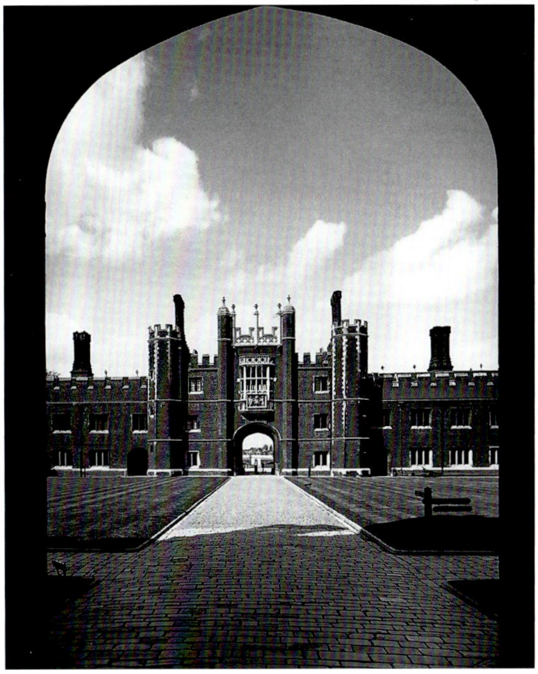

9.1 The gatehouse in Base Court, Hampton Court, built for Wolsey between 1518 and 1521. Originally the Gatehouse had two more stories, but these were removed during the 1770s.

Detail of fig. 9.5

Wolsey that he had taken the measurements of eighteen rooms at Hampton Court and "made a boke of them that your Grace shulld sette your hande." Because Wolsey had been so busy and the market had nearly ended, he could not afford to wait any longer, so he was embarking for "the parties of beyonde the See" and on his arrival would give order for the hangings. The cost of these would amount to 1,000 marks or more. He was commissioning sets with specific measurements for particular locations, rather than buying from stock, for he describes how he will have to provide advances for materials to the weavers as they "be but power men and must have monye to fore hand for proveycion of ther stuffe."[2]

The result of this commission is recorded in considerable detail in the first inventory of Wolsey's possessions drawn up sometime in 1522. Two large deliveries were received in December 1521 and April 1522, comprising twenty-two en suite chambers with a total of 178 tapestries of which forty-three were window pieces. These tapestries were recorded in the inventory in two separate groups corresponding to the two deliveries.[3] This separation, and the fact that the dimensions of the tapestries are still given in Flemish ells rather than in Imperial measurements like all the other hangings listed in the inventory, indicates the proximity of the deliveries to the time at which the inventory was made.

The sets are listed in order of the chambers for which they were intended. The first group, "bought" of Gresham on December 22, 1521, consisted of seven chambers of tapestry for the rooms running around the inner courtyard at Hampton Court. Old Testament sets of *Jacob, Susanna,* and *Judith and Holofernes* were provided for three parlors, followed by a set of the *Seven Deadly Sins* for the "legates chamber"—that is, Wolsey's bedchamber. In addition sets of *Solomon, Samson,* and the *Nine Worthies* were provided for the chamber over the ewery, the next chamber over the porter's lodge, and the great chamber over the gate to the Base Court. Of the sets listed in the second group, "bought" of Gresham on April 2, 1522, all but one were for the new apartments in or connected to the tower over the porter's lodge in the Base Court. Again, most were of Old Testament subjects, *Esther, Samuel, Tobias, Moses, David, Joseph,* and *Emelyke* [Ruth]. The exceptions were sets of *Our Lady,* the *Prodigal Son,* and the unidentified subject of *Estrogeas* (perhaps a corruption of the opening words of the inscription on one of the tapestries). The only tapestries not intended for Hampton Court in this second delivery were those of a large twenty-one-piece set of the story of *Jacob and Joseph* provided for the gallery at York Place that was accompanied by fourteen window pieces.

None of these hangings survive in the rooms for which they were provided at Hampton Court, but enough can be identified at this palace and elsewhere for it to be clear that Gresham's deliveries included tapestries of moderate rather than exceptional quality. The Musée Lécuyer *Tobias* fragment with Wolsey's arms has already been mentioned (fig. 9.2). Since the only tapestries of this subject in the collection were those provided by Gresham for the third and fifth chambers on the south side of the gatehouse at Hampton Court, the correspondence between the two is certain.[4] The fragment is woven from a fairly rudimentary cartoon in a restricted palette of wool with some highlights executed in silk. The quality is close to that of another fragment illustrating the *Story of Ruth* (fig. 9.3) that was formerly attached to the Sens *Judith and Holofernes* panel. Again, the only set of which this could have been part was that of *Emelyke* (sic) delivered by Gresham for the inner chamber to the fifth chamber over the porter's lodge in the Base Court.[5]

More complete are the two *Vices and Virtues* panels that survive at Hampton Court (figs. 9.4, 9.5, and detail opposite p. 157). They come from the *Seven Deadly Sins* set delivered by Gresham for Wolsey's bedchamber.[6] Woven from a series known in modern times as the *Triumph of the Virtues over the Vices,* the appearance of the entire design is documented by a complete four-piece set now in Brussels (fig. 9.6).[7] As comparison between the Brussels set and

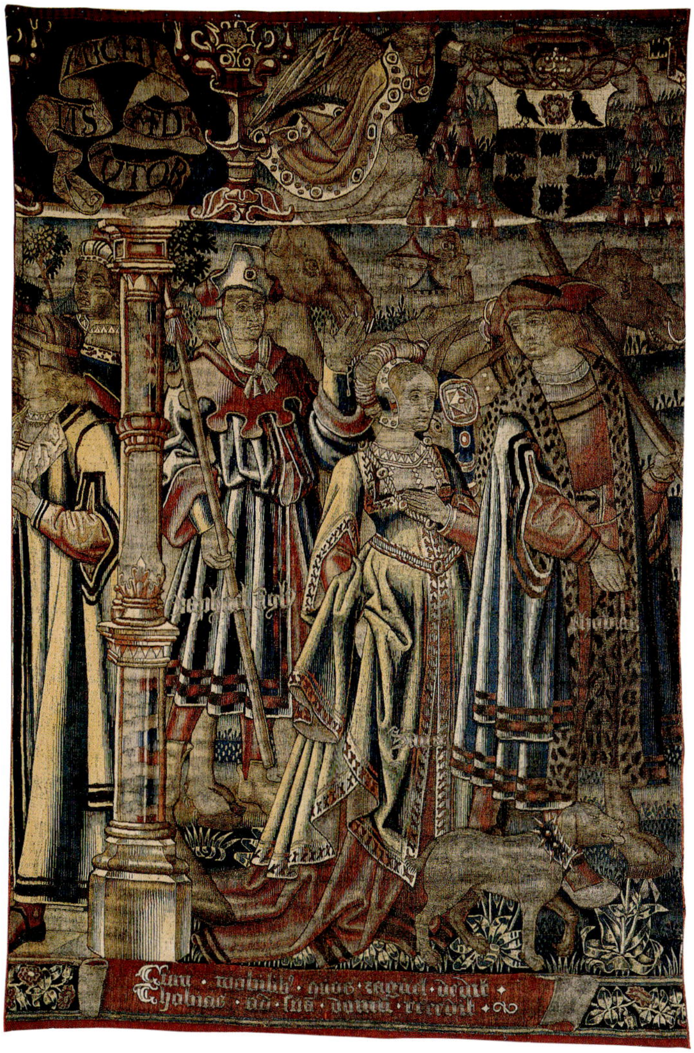

9.2 *The Return of Tobias and His Wife to Ninevah* (fragment), with a border of Cardinal Wolsey's arms attached, from a set of the *Story of Tobias.* Tapestry woven in the Southern Netherlands, ca. 1520–22. Wool and silk, 276 x 171 cm. Musée Antoine Lécuyer, Saint Quentin

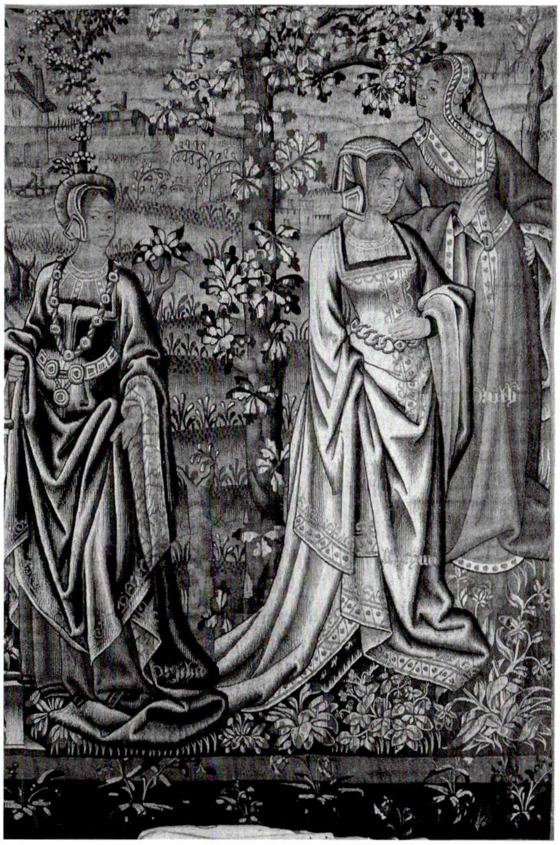

9.3 *Scene from the Story of Ruth* (after removal of upper border with Cardinal Wolsey's arms and lower border with inscription), fragment, from a set of the *Story of Ruth.* Tapestry woven in the Southern Netherlands, ca. 1520–22. Wool and silk, 240 x 138 cm. Sens, Musée de Sens

the pieces at Hampton Court reveals, for the weaving of Wolsey's set the cartoons of the series were divided into smaller sections in accordance with the dimensions of the rooms for which they were intended. The complete series depicts a sequence of scenes in which hapless courtly figures are beset by scheming Sins and vengeful Virtues. In one panel, the figures include a number of lissome women who dance in front of the advancing figure of Lust (this set was, after all, commissioned for Wolsey's bedchamber). The postures and exposed legs of these women appear to be inspired by an Andrea Mantegna engraving, but this Italianate component is absorbed within a traditional "pre-Renaissance" style, in which the folds and patterns of the gowns and costumes provide the principal decorative effect.

The sheer number of tapestries commissioned by Gresham for Hampton Court in 1520, when Wolsey's collection already numbered more than four hundred pieces, must have been designed to impress, and there is no question that the scale of Wolsey's tapestry acquisition was unparalleled in England in the Tudor period. Surviving inventories suggest that for the wealthy nobility it was not uncommon to own at least fifty tapestries, the collections of the wealthier magnates inevitably reflecting a higher proportion of antique or high-quality pieces.[8] For the very rich this figure might have been considerably higher. For example, as already noted, an inventory of the goods of John de Vere, thirteenth earl of Oxford, taken posthumously in 1513, records around one hundred tapestries of which about one quarter were described as "arras" or

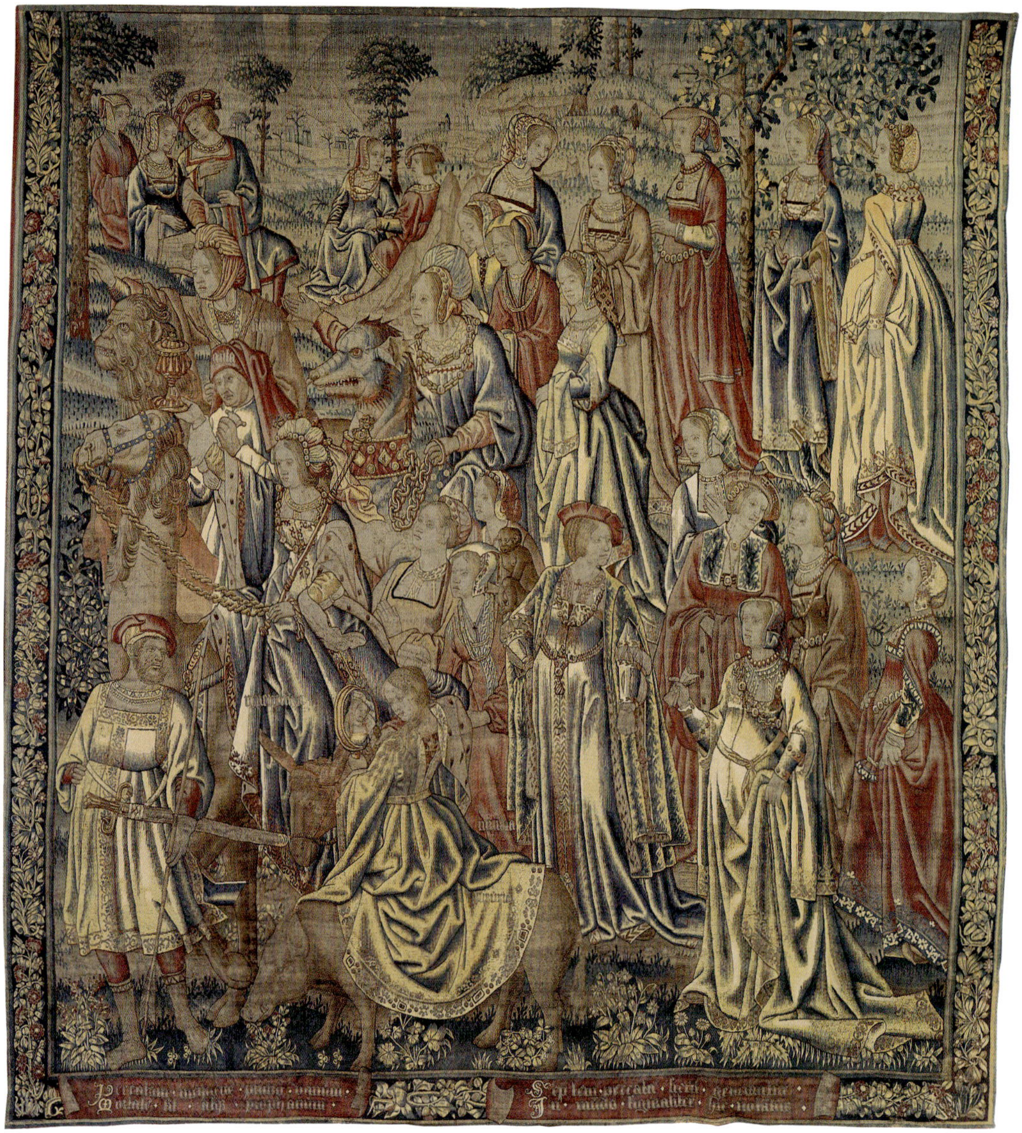

9.4 *The Vices Beset Sinful Man* (right portion of design only) from a set now known as the *Triumph of the Virtues over the Vices*. Tapestry woven in the Southern Netherlands, probably Brussels, ca. 1520–21. Wool and silk, 399 x 353 cm. Hampton Court Palace

"counterfeit arras," while the inventory of Thomas Howard, second duke of Norfolk, taken at Framlingham after his death in 1524 records about ninety tapestries of which about a third appear to have been better-quality tapestry.[9] Such comparisons highlight the enormous scale of Wolsey's collection and the high proportion of silk-woven tapestries it contained.

Not only was the scale of the commissions coordinated by Gresham unprecedented, but the choice of subject matter, like that of the earlier commission from Scellier, was also remarkable for its homogeneity. Of the twenty-two sets enumerated by the inventory, seventeen were of Old Testament subjects, two of New Testament subjects, and two, the *Seven Deadly Sins* and another set of the *Nine Worthies*, of exemplary subject matter. The accumulation of so many complementary sets appears to have been unique at this date, even if it is assumed that they were woven from available designs in moderate quality. The loss of almost all of the collection precludes any detailed analysis of an underlying iconographic program, but in view of the subjects listed and the disposition in the rooms of York Place and Hampton Court, both recorded and deduced, it is quite probable that this was no more sophisticated than to associate Wolsey generally with a large number of religious prototypes. Nonetheless, iconographic propaganda on this scale was remarkable and must have provided the example for Henry VIII's use of tapestries depicting Old Testament patriarchs from the late 1520s.

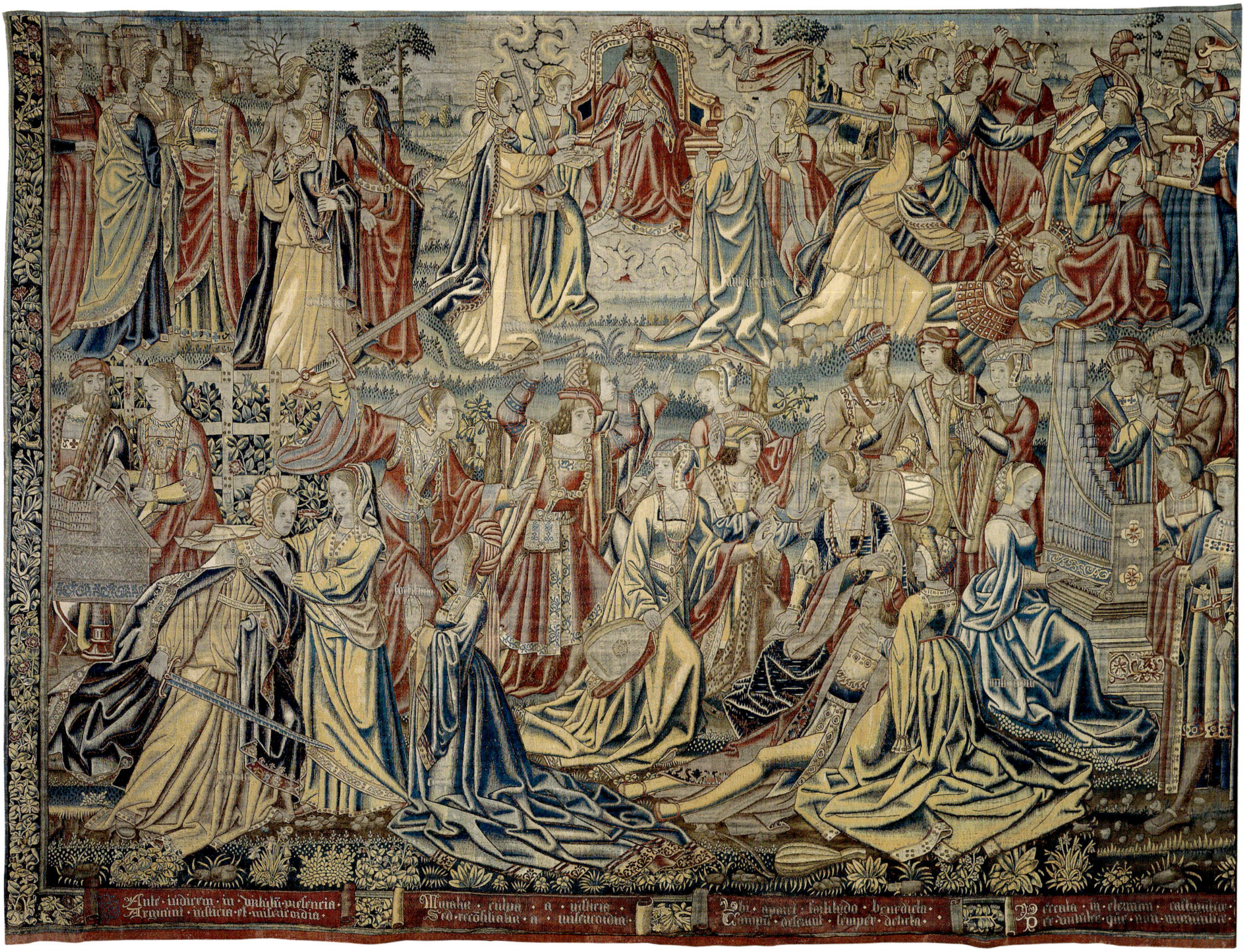

9.5 *Justice Disarmed by Mercy* from a set now known as the *Triumph of the Virtues over the Vices*. Tapestry woven in the Southern Netherlands, probably Brussels, ca. 1520–21. Wool and silk, 400 x 535 cm. Hampton Court Palace

The second Gresham delivery arrived shortly before Wolsey entertained Charles V at Hampton Court in April 1522, and we can imagine that the impending visit must have provided an urgent deadline for the Flemish weavers to complete and deliver this second commission. The resulting display must have been stupendous, with room after room of brightly colored and richly patterned tapestry, with a wealth of iconographic reference. Wolsey's extravagant building and patronage had earned him huge notoriety during the late 1510s, and he was widely reviled by the senior members of the Tudor court, many of whom resented his influence over the king. This resentment seems to have come to a head in 1521, no doubt compounded by the extravagance of the ongoing work at Hampton Court and York Place. It was given vivid form by the satirical poems of the poet John Skelton, some of which may have been written with the encouragement of patrons whose antipathy to Wolsey ran deep. One of these, *Colyn Clout*, was written in late 1521 and early 1522, while Skelton was living in the sanctuary of Westminster Abbey to evade the persecution that he feared from Wolsey in response to an earlier attack titled "Speke Parrot." Framed in the guise of a complaint about the behavior of the modern clergy, *Colyn Clout* gleefully describes the worldly subject matter of Wolsey's tapestries as a means of satirizing the cardinal's expenditure, which might have been better used in the repair of dilapidated cathedrals:

Hangynge about the walles
Clothes of golde and paules,
Arayse of ryche aray,
Fresshe as floures in May;
With Dame Dyana naked;
Howe lusty Venus quaked,
And howe Cupide shaked
His dart, and bent his bowe
For to shote a crowe
At her tyrly trylowe;
And howe Parys of Troy
Danced a lege moy,
Made lusty sporte and joy
With Dame Helyn the quene.
With suche storyes bydene
Theyr chambres well sene,
With tryumphes of Cesar
And of his Pompeyus warre,
Of renowne and of fame
By them to gette a name.
Howe all the worlde stares
Howe they ryde in goodly chares,
Conveyde by olyfauntes
With laryat garlantes,
And by unycornes
With theyr semely hornes;
Upon these beestes rydinge,
Naked boyes strydynge,
With wanton wenches wynking!
Nowe trewely, to my thynkyng,
That is a speculacyon
And a mete meditacyon
For prelates of estate
Theyr courage to abate
From worldly wantones,
Theyr chambre thus to dresse
With suche perfytenesse
And all suche holynesse.
Howebeit they let downe fall
Theyr churches cathedral.[10]

Although somewhat generalized, the descriptions appear to be inspired by the figures of Wolsey's *Triumphs of Petrarch* tapestries. Whatever the case, the poem provides a rare and vivid glimpse of the impression that, for better or worse, Wolsey's tapestry acquisitions made on his contemporaries and how his enemies were attempting to turn his extravagance against him.

Wolsey's Later Tapestry Acquisitions

The delivery of the tapestries commissioned through Gresham appears to have coincided with the compilation of the earlier inventory of Wolsey's possessions. This is undated, and several previous commentators have confused it with the one that Wolsey is said to have compiled by his own hand after his fall in 1529.[11] Internal evidence, however, shows that it was drawn up sometime between late 1521 and early 1523 because the Gresham deliveries of tapestries for Hampton Court made in December 1521 and April 1522 are recorded as self-standing groups.[12] It is not clear whether this was because the inventory was being compiled when the Gresham deliveries were being anticipated and space was left for their later addition or whether it was because it was simplest to treat them as distinct groups because of their recent arrival. Either way, a *terminus ante quem* is provided by the acquisitions from the estate of the bishops of Durham and London, made before the end of 1523, which appear in the inventory as later interpolations. It is possible that the accession of the large number of tapestries commissioned by Gresham may have provided the occasion for the compilation of the inventory. Whatever the case, by the time the inventory was compiled Wolsey's collection already numbered about 440 tapestries, and with the addition of the Gresham tapestries this figure rose to more than six hundred (including window pieces). Later additions were noted at the end of appropriate categories, providing us with evidence of the development of the collection during the 1520s.

No mention is made of further large-scale purchases for Wolsey's existing properties or for the two he acquired in 1522 as titular abbot of Saint Albans, The More and Tyttenhanger, and these must have been decorated from the tapestries surplus to requirements at York Place and Hampton Court.[13] Nonetheless, he continued to expand his collection as and when opportunity arose. Between the compilation of the inventory and his fall in 1529 the collection was increased by another sixty or so tapestries.

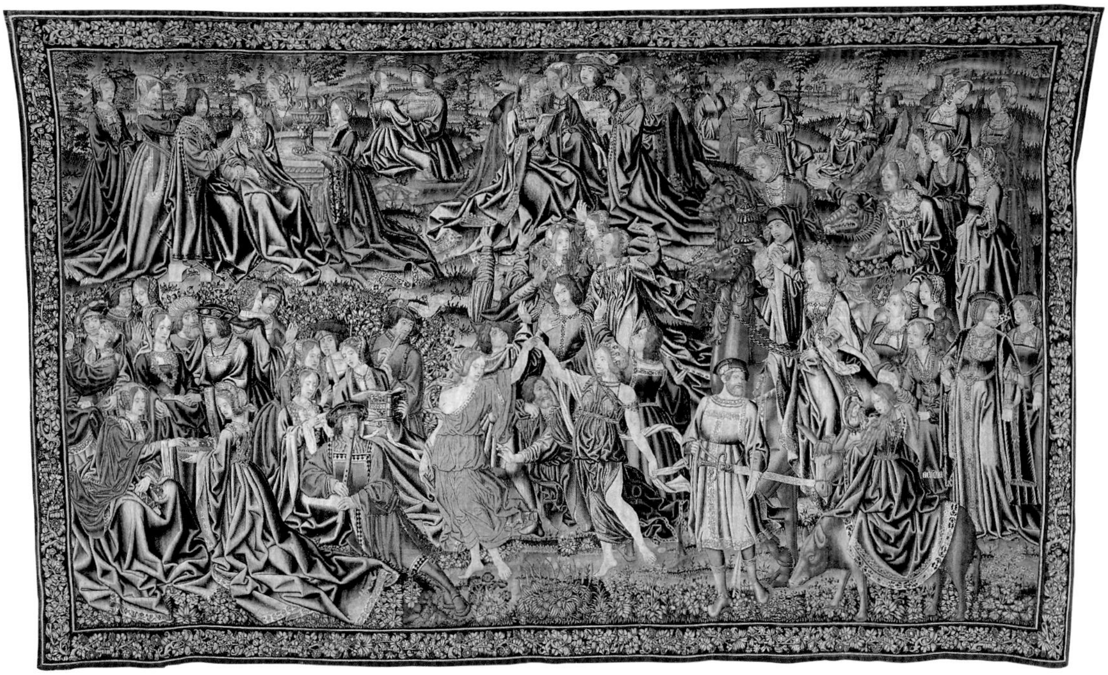

9.6 *The Vices Beset Sinful Man* from a set of the *Triumphs of the Virtues over the Vices*. Tapestry woven in the Southern Netherlands, probably Brussels, ca. 1520. Wool and silk, 411 x 650 cm. Musées Royaux d'Art et d'Histoire, Brussels

Most were acquired from the executors of several ecclesiastical estates. In 1523 Wolsey was granted the see of Durham after the death of the incumbent, Thomas Ruthal, and the inventory records twenty-nine tapestries that he purchased from Ruthal's executors. These included an unidentified six-piece set of "counterfeit arras" with a border of the arms of Ruthal and Saint Cuthbert; eight pieces of the *Triumphs of Petrarch;* five pieces of the *Prodigal Son;* two old pieces of mythology figuring *Priam, Paris, and Achilles,* and *Jupiter, Pluto, and Ceres;* and six pieces of various subjects that had been used in Durham hall on "inferior days"—namely, three pieces of *Hannibal,* one of *Virtue,* and two of *Hunting*. In addition to the

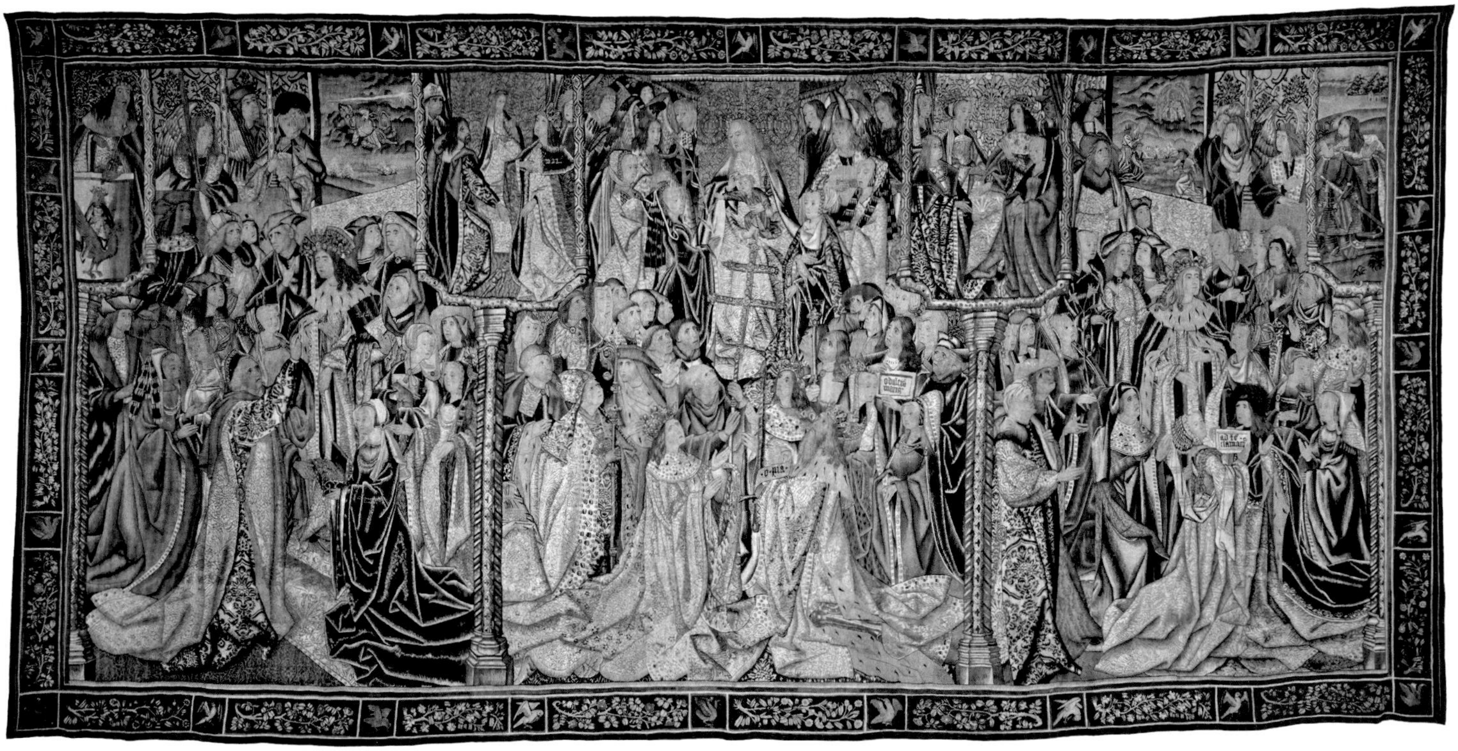

9.7 *The Triumph of the Virgin*. Tapestry woven in the Southern Netherlands, ca. 1500–1515. Wool and silk, 464 x 817 cm. The Burrell Collection, Glasgow

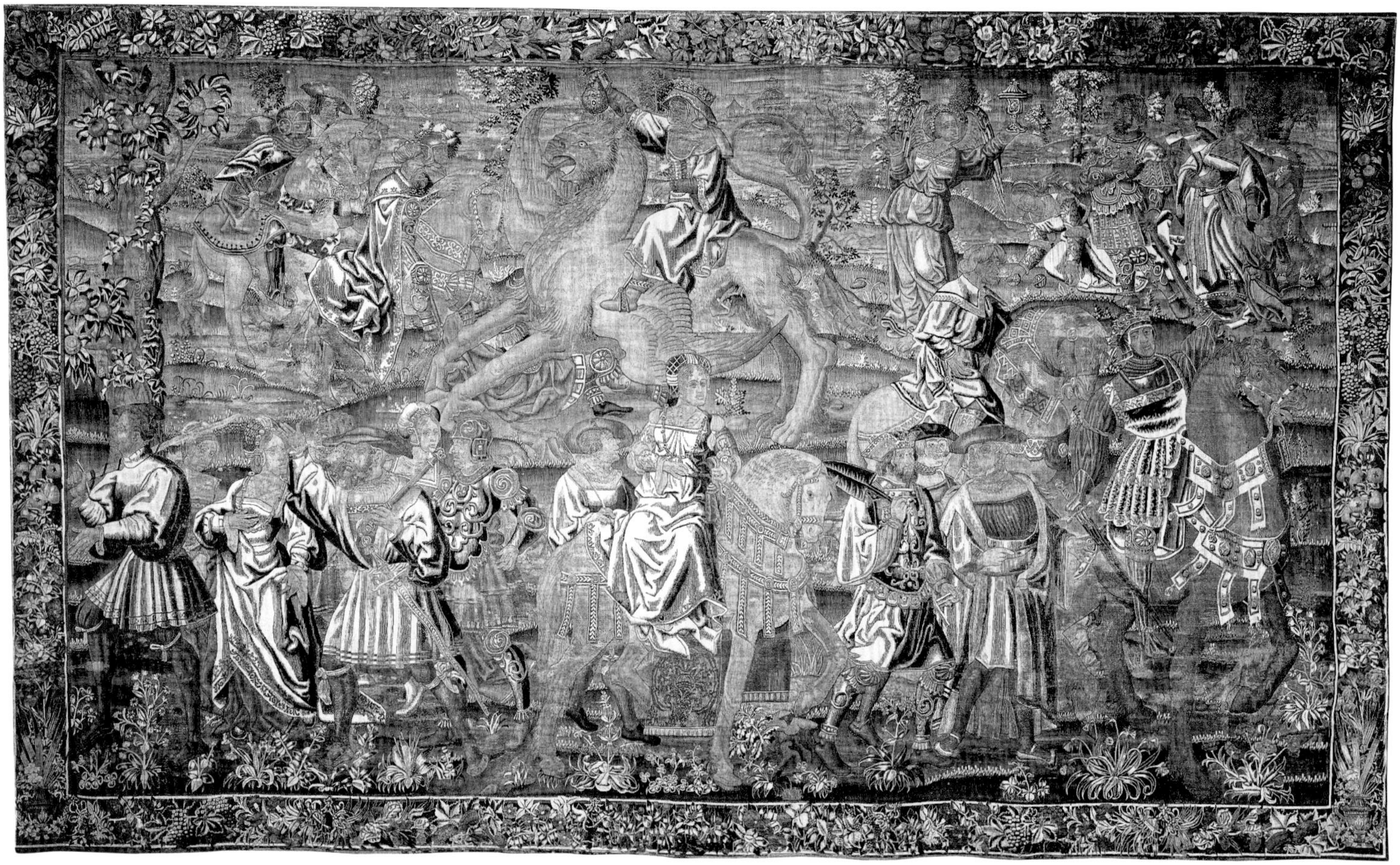

9.8 *The Triumph of Avarice* (also known as the *Griffin Allegory*) possibly from a set of *The Path to Honor*. Tapestry woven in the Southern Netherlands, probably Brussels, ca. 1520–25. Wool and silk, 426 x 670 cm. Hampton Court Palace

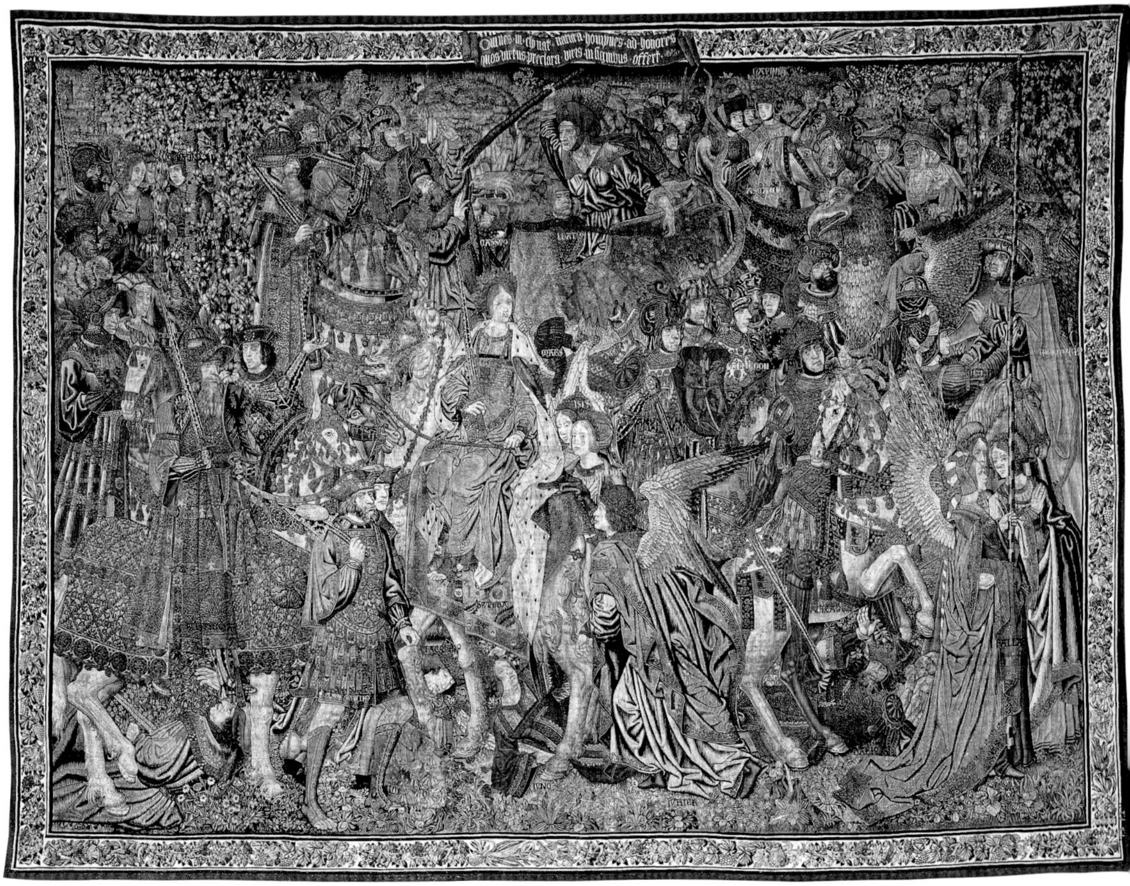

9.9 *The Triumph of Justice* from a three-piece set of the *Moralities* (also known as *The Path to Honor*). Tapestry woven in the Southern Netherlands, probably Brussels, ca. 1510–20. Wool, silk, and gilt-metal-wrapped thread, 422 x 540 cm. Patrimonio Nacional, Madrid

tapestries the inventory records twenty-two pieces of velvet and cloth of gold hangings for three chambers.[14] Other accessions were made from the possessions of John Young, former master of the rolls (seven tapestries of miscellaneous subjects),[15] Richard Fitzjames, bishop of London (four pieces),[16] and Robert Tonyes, registrar of the Joint-Prerogative Court (one tapestry of hawking and hunting and four of coarse verdures).[17] The idiosyncratic description of two of those acquired from Fitzjames's estate, one with the inscription "O pia, O clemens, O dulcis maria" and the other with "king David harping," allows an identification to be made with the design of a devotional series of which examples survive in the Burrell Collection (fig. 9.7) and the Warsaw Museum.[18] The terms under which these acquisitions entered Wolsey's collection are unclear. In the inventory, the later interpolations were said to have been "bought of the executors" of each of the deceased, but the 1529 list of ecclesiastical figures whose goods Wolsey was accused of appropriating included Ruthal and Tonyes.[19]

Most of the acquisitions recorded by the inventory resulted from appropriations, but there were also a handful of purchases, some of which may have been related to the expansions Wolsey undertook on his private apartments at Hampton Court during the mid-1520s.[20] These included a six-piece set of "counterfeit arras" of *Triumphs* purchased from Richard Gresham in December 1525, all measuring just under five by eight yards.[21] It is conceivable that a panel at Hampton Court, now known as the *Griffin Allegory* (fig. 9.8), may originate from that set.[22] The style of the figures and the rich floral border would all be consistent with a production of the early to mid-1520s. The tapestry evidently belonged to a set of moderate pictorial and material quality, which depicted a psychomachia in the form of two processions of allegorical figures passing in opposite directions. Key figures in the design are copied from a more complex allegorical series, dating from about 1510, of which one high-quality set known as the *Moralities* or *The Path to Honor* survives in the Spanish royal collection (fig. 9.9).[23] But where the protagonists of the Spanish set are richly costumed and surrounded by subsidiary figures, those in the Hampton Court panel have been simplified and placed in a schematic landscape.

Wolsey's tapestry purchases tail off after 1525, possibly in reaction to the volume of criticism that he was now receiving for his ostentatious lifestyle, and it may be significant that in this year he made a symbolic gift of Hampton Court to Henry to offset some of these attacks, although he continued to live at the palace until his fall. But the more probable explanation may simply be that having spent so much money on furnishing his palaces with appropriate tapestries, he had little need to make further purchases. The last acquisition interpolated in the 1522 inventory was a purchase of June 1527, described as a "pece of riche arrais of Cryste nyled on the crosse."[24]

Deployment of Wolsey's Tapestries

Given the paucity of evidence about the physical disposition of royal tapestries at this time, information relating to Wolsey's household, which was evidently based on the royal household, is illuminating. Even though size may have been the most impressive aspect of Wolsey's collection, the deployment of the tapestries was also calculated to impress. Along with the other furnishings listed in the inventory, the tapestries and hangings were in the keeping of a wardrobe department that Cavendish informs us was staffed by a master, two yeomen, and ten other persons.[25] The 1522 inventory shows that with the exception of the tapestries recently ordered through Gresham, which were listed in discrete groups according to the date of delivery and the location for which they were intended, the rest of Wolsey's tapestries were divided into six categories, according to quality. In ascending order of value, these were titled "hangings of veerdors," "Olde hanginges of Counterfette Arrais and Tappestry," "hanginges of Counterfette Arrais and of tapstry somewhat worne," "new hanginges of counterfette arras and tapestrye," "olde hangynges of Arrais," and "hangings of Newe and riche Arrais." Blank pages were left after each section on which later acquisitions such as those from the collection of the bishop of Durham were entered.

The purpose of such careful categorization, a reflection of Wolsey's almost obsessive attention to detail, must have been directly related to the use to which the tapestries were put. The logic of grouping the verdure tapestries together reflects that they were traditionally used in more informal, private, or less important settings. Similarly, the older hangings, of which about half depicted hunting or genre subjects, were evidently deemed to have a lower display value. The general tenor of their usage is suggested by the description of six tapestries bought from Durham's executors as serving "for the hanging of Durhams halle of inferior days," and it is to be assumed that many of the tapestries recorded in this category were in everyday use in the less important areas of the palaces.[26] A seven-piece set of *Moses* tapestries had been made up with four of "newe Tappestry course stuff,"[27] while an annotation against the entry for thirteen verdure tapestries with the arms of Bishop Smith set in lozenges indicates that these had been "shorne and newe dressed on the wronge side and made mete for the hanging of the halle at hampton Courte."[28] In other words, the loose ends at the back of the tapestry had been cut off and tidied up so that the tapestry could be reversed, substituting the back of the tapestry for the front, which had presumably become faded through exposure to light. Although this is the only recorded instance of this practice, it may have been common with coarse forms of tapestry. Unfortunately, it was also a process that would have hastened the destruction of the tapestry as a whole.

The use of these older hangings in rooms of lesser importance contrasted markedly with the new tapestries that Wolsey had ordered for the more important apartments of his palaces. The finest tapestries were evidently kept in reserve for special occasions. George Cavendish, Wolsey's gentleman usher, vividly describes the preparations for the banquet given for the French ambassadors at Hampton Court in 1527, when the yeomen and grooms of the Wardrobe were occupied for several days "in hangyng of the Chambers with costly hangings, and furnyssyng the same with Beddes of sylke and other furnyture apt for the same in every degree."[29] On such occasions and in Wolsey's immediate vicinity on a more everyday basis, there is evidence that varying qualities of tapestry were used to dramatize the hierarchic importance of the rooms that Wolsey occupied, the practice we have already observed in court usage. Cavendish records that for the 1527 reception the first chamber was hung with "fine arras," "and so was all the rest, one better than another," up to the chamber of presence which was hung with "very rich arras, wherin was a gorgeous and a precious cloth of estate hanged up."[30] The logical conclusion of such a progression was a room hung entirely with cloth of gold, and this format appears to have been standard court practice for special occasions. Evidence that Wolsey's progression of audience rooms also concluded with cloth of gold hangings, at least from the early 1520s, is provided by the postscript in a letter addressed to him by Richard Gresham in March 1521, which reports that "Your Grace spake unto me for serteyn cloths of golde for to hange your Closset at Hampton Cortte: I have nowe cum viii. peces. wyche I shall brynge to your Grace the next Weke God wyllynge."[31]

The evidence for Wolsey's use of tapestry as a means of self-aggrandizement and iconographic suggestion is overwhelming, but his taste seems to have been relatively conservative. Apart from the correspondence from Scellier in 1517 indicating that Wolsey was interested in acquiring more of a sort of antique tapestry that had not been made for thirty years, as suggestive of Wolsey's social aspirations as of his aesthetic awareness, and his obvious predilection for tapestries designed in the "pre-Renaissance" style, we find no evidence of any pursuit of designs conceived in the new style that was to develop in Brussels in the early 1520s under the influence of the Raphael school cartoons.

Equally, this perception must be tempered by recognition of the partial nature of the records. He certainly did acquire a small number of tapestries in the mid-1520s, and these may well have reflected new stylistic developments.

Whatever the sophistication of Wolsey's taste in regard to tapestry, analysis of his patronage reveals the extent to which he saw the medium as a central prop to buttress his rise to fame and fortune. Indeed, the rapid formation of Wolsey's collection is one of the most impressive examples of the importance of tapestry in England in the Tudor period. In view of the intimate relationship between Wolsey and Henry VIII, it seems reasonable to assume that Henry was fully aware of Wolsey's example. And although certain aspects of Wolsey's patronage merely aped royal practice, others may have set Henry an important example. Most significantly, Wolsey's use of Old Testament subject matter to promote his ecclesiastic stature may have played a significant part in determining the character of Henry's patronage during the late 1520s and 1530s.

Royal Tapestry Patronage during the Early 1520s

Wolsey's tapestry patronage was certainly impressive and innovative, but the outstanding collection of the day nonetheless remained that of the king, by virtue of the size and quality of his inheritance and the sheer spending power of the Crown. Confiscations continued to provide an additional source of growth. As we have seen during the fifteenth century, the royal collection benefited from the appropriation of properties from noble families whose fate placed them on the losing side of the struggle between the houses of Lancaster and York. With the relative stability that prevailed in the kingdom after Edward's return to power in 1471 and the consolidation of this stability under Henry VII, such attainted properties had played a small part in the further development of the collection during the first decade of the sixteenth century. But a vivid reminder of the absolute power of the Crown in this respect had been provided two days after Henry VIII's accession with the arrests of Richard Empson and Edmund Dudley, unpopular instruments of Henry VII's financial policy, both of whom were eventually executed for treason in August 1510. Details of Empson's possessions have not survived, but an inventory of Dudley's goods made at the time states that they were to be taken "to thuse of our seid Soveraign lorde." Most of the rooms at Dudley's London property were decorated with hangings of colored buckram, but the inventory also lists ten pieces of "arras," of which five were described as old and two as "rich" counterpoints, one piece of fine "counterfeit arras," twelve of tapestry, two beds of tapestry, and several verdure counterpoints.[32]

The royal tapestry collection may also have been augmented in 1513 by another traditional source, plunder, after the victory of the English over the Scots at Flodden. The 1547 inventory lists a set of bed hangings with the Scottish arms at Hampton Court.[33] Whether this was part of a larger ensemble of textiles and tapestries taken by the earl of Surrey from James IV's camp is uncertain, but the Scottish kings were certainly keen patrons of tapestry in their own right, and so it seems highly likely that tapestries may have been among the plunder.[34]

Apart from these isolated incidents, appropriations and plunder seem to have played a small part in the growth of the royal collection until the execution in May 1521 of Edward Stafford, third duke of Buckingham, and the forfeiture of his properties to the Crown. Buckingham (fig. 9.10) was the leading peer of the realm in terms of both wealth and heritage; like the Tudors, he traced his descent from John of Gaunt. He had played a key role in the court ceremonies of Henry VII's reign and had acted as lord high constable and lord high steward at the coronation of Henry VIII. His landed estates were the largest of any of Henry's subjects, generating more than £5,000 per year by the mid-1510s, and he enjoyed a lifestyle appropriate to his rank. The gown he wore at the wedding of Prince Arthur and Katherine of Aragon was said to have cost

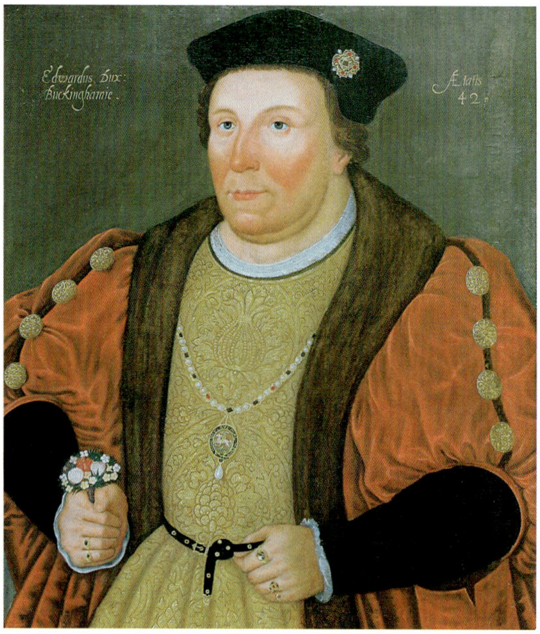

9.10 *Edward Stafford, Third Duke of Buckingham* by an unidentified artist, 1520. Oil on canvas, 74 x 62.5 cm. Magdalene College, Cambridge

£1,500. From 1508, Buckingham undertook extensive building work at Thornbury, his seat in Gloucester, which he rebuilt in a castellated style (fig. 9.11), and he also remodeled his London residence.[35] Although his household accounts are incomplete, evidence of his activity as a tapestry patron is provided by two documents.[36] The first, dating from September 1512 and thus coinciding with completion of the first phase of building at Thornbury, is a contract between Gabriel de Leenere, a Brussels tapestry merchant, and Jan de Buleere, also of Brussels, who was to transport into England 138 ells (77½ square yards) of gold-woven tapestry belonging to the duke.[37] The second is a receipt made in May 1520 by Brian Tuke for £65 received from Thomas Brydges, chaplain to the duke, for four pieces of "arras of hawkyng and huntyng" containing two hundred Flemish ells (112½ square yards).[38] These purchases were evidently part of a larger pattern of acquisition.

Tension between Buckingham and the king had been building since 1519, when, during a visit to Penshurst, Henry rebuked a member of the royal household for appearing before him in Buckingham's livery. Wolsey's advancement at court was a constant point of irritation to the duke, who, as the leading peer of the realm, regarded the cardinal as an common upstart, displacing his rightful place as the senior member of the nobility. The friction between the two is captured by Stow's famous account of the meeting with Charles V at Canterbury in May 1520, when Buckingham, in his capacity as royal sewer, was holding a bowl of water for Henry and the emperor to wash their hands and was humiliated when Wolsey took the liberty of also using the water.[39] Tension reached new heights at Guines in June 1520. Buckingham resented the cost involved in accompanying Henry to Guines and, according to a later account by his son, quarreled with Wolsey on that occasion for a rebuke that Wolsey had given to Queen Katherine. The circumstances in which Henry decided to act are uncertain, but in an undated letter written in his own hand, he instructed Wolsey to maintain careful watch over Buckingham, and the duke was arrested in April 1521. According to the evidence presented against him by a former employee, Buckingham believed that the judicial murder of the earl of Warwick in 1499 had brought a curse on the Tudor family and that this explained Henry's failure to produce a male heir. Further, according to the same witness, Buckingham had been receiving prophecies since 1512 that he would eventually become king, and his advisers had encouraged him to build up his armed retinue and to develop his popularity among the populace. The proceedings were swift. Charged with treason on May 8, Buckingham was brought before a court of

9.11 Thornbury Castle, Avon (south facade)

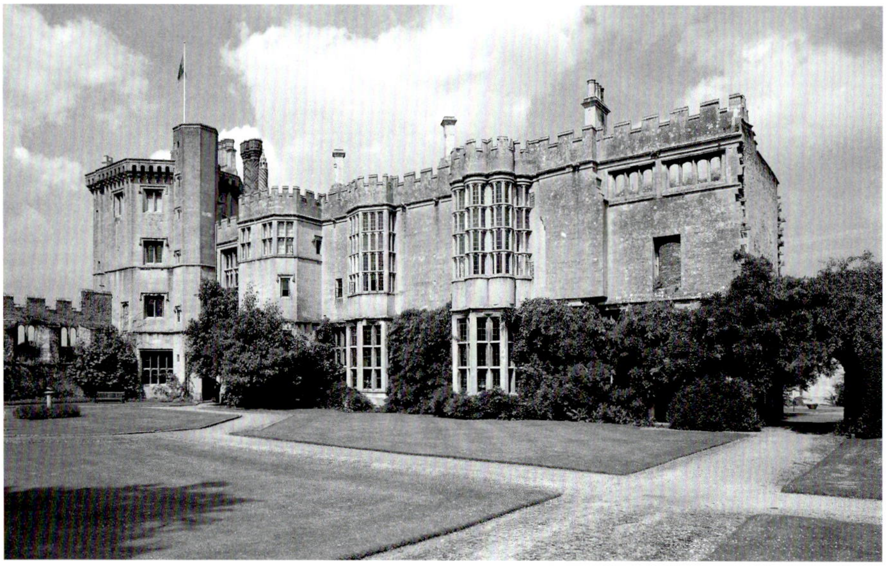

his peers and executed on May 17. His properties were forfeit to the Crown, and on May 20, Humphrey Andrews of the Wardrobe delivered the hangings from Buckingham's London residence to Sir Andrew Windsor.[40] According to a list drawn up at the time, these included five pieces of the *Story of Moses,* each about nine yards by four; three pieces of the *Story of King Medow* (sic) each about seven yards by four; four pieces of Turkey work, a "tapett" of beasts and trees, and five others of imagery; two pieces of silk verdure of imagery lined with canvas, and three others unlined; six pieces of green say; and five counterpoints of imagery, one of Saint George and the others with verdures, beasts, and birds.

Evidence that Buckingham's other properties also provided a rich haul comes from later documents. An inventory of Princess Mary's Wardrobe of Beds taken in 1523 included eight pieces of yellow verdures and eight of "chequered" verdures with the arms of the duke of Buckingham in the borders and a canopy of yellow verdure with the same arms, while the account of expenses submitted by Andrew Windsor for the Great Wardrobe for the year 1543–44 included a charge for the repair of a piece of "arras" with the duke's lineage.[41] Subsequently, the 1547 inventory recorded two "arras" tapestries at the Tower, one of "Macaborne"—presumably Judas Maccabaeus, one of the Nine Worthies—with Buckingham's arms in the border and another of "Godfey bullen and the petygree of the duke of Buck . . . which pece hadd a bordre of the said Dukes Armes."[42] The prominent inclusion of Buckingham's genealogy in one of the *Nine Worthies* tapestries and of his armorials in two other chambers of verdures suggests the extent to which Buckingham was using tapestry as a medium to promote his lineage and proximity to the throne.

Although the appropriation of Buckingham's tapestries was subsidiary to the confiscation of his property as a whole, the assignation of the heraldic verdure chambers to the wardrobe of the infant princess, Henry's only legitimate heir at this date, may have been intended to emphasize his disdain for any pretenders to the Tudor crown. Similarly, although a significant number of the finest royal tapestries were deposited at the Tower by 1547, the allocation of Buckingham's genealogical tapestry in that location may have been more than accidental, considering that this was also the castle in which traitors were customarily housed and executed. That the tapestry was in use during the 1520s, whether at the Tower or another location, is confirmed by its repair in 1533.

Buckingham's abrupt trial and execution provided a vivid demonstration of Henry's sensitivity to the issue of his succession and of how decisively he was now prepared to wield royal power when he felt threatened. The confiscation of Buckingham's goods also provides an intimation of the larger volumes of objects that were to be appropriated by the Crown between 1529 and 1545, including Wolsey's collection.[43] As the Tudor court fractured under the strain of the political and religious divisions of the late 1520s and 1530s, the display of tapestries with the armorials of Buckingham and Cardinal Wolsey must have provided a chilling warning to other members of the nobility who were not in sympathy with the king's policies. In the context of the early 1520s, Buckingham's judicial murder was, nonetheless, a violent but isolated incident.

Court Tapestry Usage and Acquisitions during the 1520s

The continuing role of tapestry in court splendor during the years immediately following the Guines meeting is most effectively illustrated by the provisions made for the visit of Charles V in the early summer of 1522. On May 26 Charles arrived at Dover, where Henry VIII received him. Having celebrated Mass together at Canterbury, the two royal entourages then proceeded together to Greenwich Palace. Hall tells us that the apartments there were "so richely hanged, that the Spanyardes wondered at it, and specially at the rych cloth of estate."[44] During the subsequent progress through the City of London, "all the

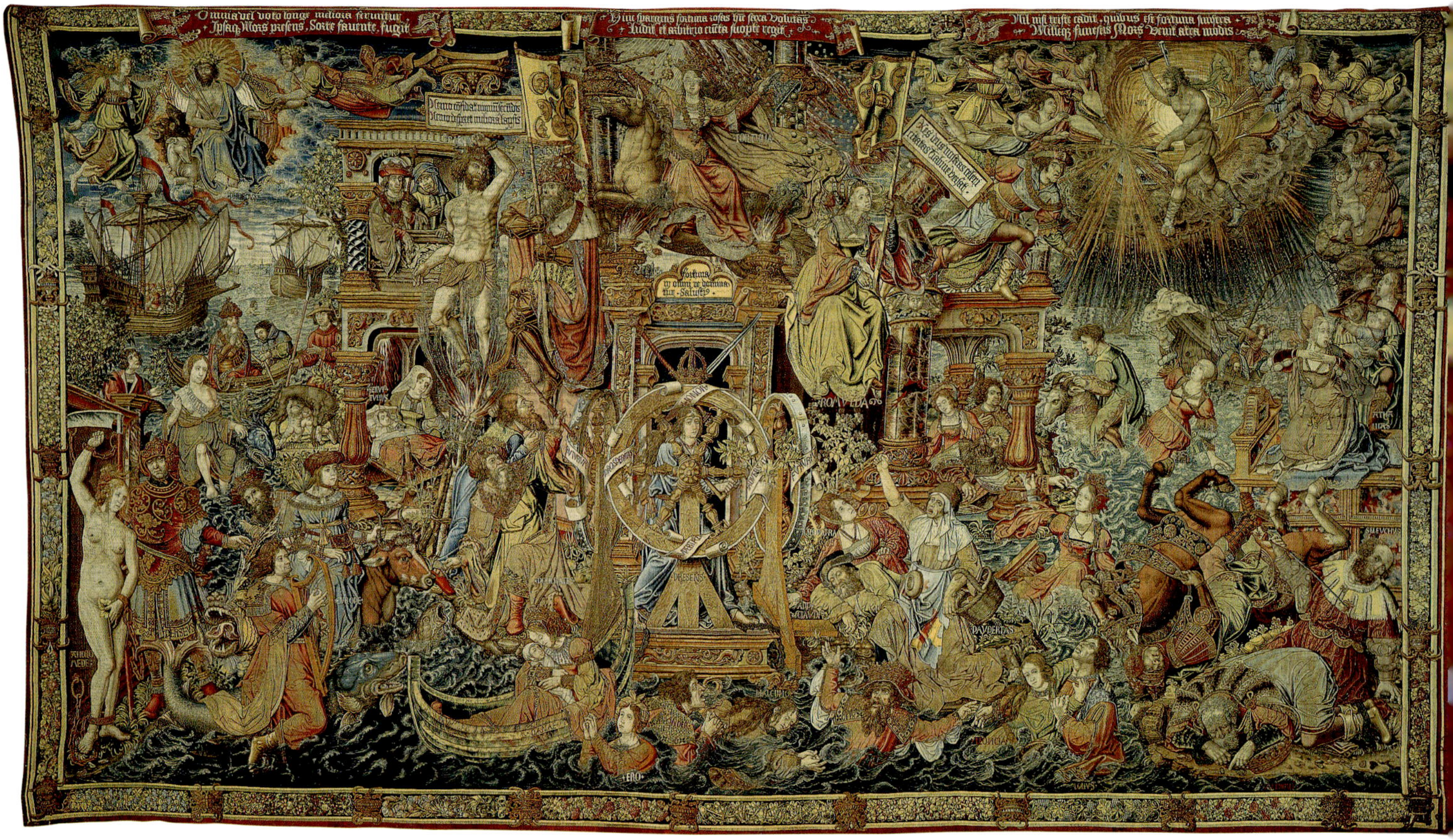

9.12 *Fortuna* from a nine-piece set of the *Honors*. Tapestry designed by Bernaert van Orley and others, woven in the workshop of Pieter Enghien van Aelst, Brussels, ca. 1520. Wool, silk, and gilt-metal-wrapped thread, 496 x 860 cm. Patrimonio Nacional, Madrid

stretes were richely hanged with clothes of golde, silver, velvet and Arras."[45] Following this grand entrance, the emperor was housed at Blackfriars while his nobles were lodged in the new palace at Bridewell. The two were connected by a gallery "whiche was very long, and that gallery and all other galleries ther wer hanged with Arras." The furnishings and hangings of the king's palace were equally sumptuous. Hall took a rhetorical stance with the statement that his "witte is to dull to describe theim."[46]

Assuming that Hall was not exaggerating the Spanish response to the English textiles, the anecdote provides a measure of their impressive character, because Charles and his courtiers must have been among the most sophisticated connoisseurs of such matters at this time. In his capacity as duke of Burgundy, Charles had inherited the Burgundian collection of late-fourteenth- and fifteenth-century tapestries, and at the time of his visit to London, the Brussels workshop of Pieter van Aelst was hard at work for him on one of the largest and most expensive tapestry sets that had ever been undertaken, an allegorical celebration of the Habsburg imperium, known as *Los Honores* (the *Honors*), which was designed by the court artist Bernaert van Orley (fig. 9.12).[47] The circumstances in which the sophisticated program for this series was conceived are uncertain, but the character of the iconography suggests that the design was probably commissioned sometime in the late 1510s by Margaret of Austria and Emperor Maximilian, both of whom are portrayed in the tapestries.[48] Equally, it must have been Charles who gave the order for the actual weaving after the imperial election in 1519. In the event, the set was so costly that Charles was unable to pay for the first seven pieces when they were completed in 1522 and Van Aelst was forced to mortgage them to the Augsburg merchants the Fuggers. Charles eventually purchased these tapestries and the two other pieces in 1526, paying for them out of the dowry that he received from his marriage to Isabel of Portugal. Although it was thus some years before he was to take possession of the tapestries, Charles must have been well aware of the progress of this project when he traveled to London in 1522. Given the ostentatious displays of tapestry on view at the English court, many of which had been woven at the Brussels workshop of Van Aelst, it is even possible that Charles's *Honors* tapestries may have been the subject of discussion between the two kings.

Van Aelst's role as a supplier of high-quality tapestries to both monarchs up to this point raises the question as to why he is absent from English royal records during the following years, the payment to him of May 1520 at the hands of Giovanni Cavalcanti being the last of which record has survived. The explanation may, in part, be Van Aelst's commitment to other major projects. Quite apart from the *Honors* tapestries, his workshop must have been very busy during the early 1520s with a series of commissions that Pope Leo X instigated in the wake of the successful completion of the Raphael *Acts of the Apostles* set. Leo died in December 1521, but his commissions were subsequently completed for Clement VII, who was elected as pope in November 1523. They included an eight-piece set of tapestries depicting mythological gods in whimsical grotesque surrounds, a lavish set of twenty gold-ground tapestries depicting children playing with devices signifying the dawn of a new golden age under Leo X, a throne canopy based on designs after Raphael compositions, and another very rich set of tapestries depicting the *Life and Passion of Christ* (for further discussion of these sets, see below).[49] It is possible that the combination of these commissions occupied Van Aelst's workshop to the exclusion of all others. The precarious financial situation that the combination of the Habsburg and papal commissions caused Van Aelst's business may also have played a part in his lower profile at the English court during these years.

Equally, it is possible that the lack of references to Van Aelst in the early 1520s is simply the result of partial documentation and that he continued to supply the court through the London-based Florentine merchant Giovanni Cavalcanti. Cavalcanti enjoyed a privileged role as a supplier of luxury goods to the English court at this time. In April 1522 he received a new grant to import precious fabrics and cloths of gold on his own behalf. The grant describes Cavalcanti as a gentleman usher of the chamber, but it is uncertain whether this is in reference to the status he enjoyed at the papal court or an honorific role at the English court.[50] Cavalcanti was now at the zenith of his career in London. Quite apart from supplying luxury fabrics to Henry and Wolsey, he was also closely involved with some of the most significant artistic projects involving Italian artists at the English court, including the plan for an elaborate tomb for Henry and Katherine to be made by Pietro Torrigiano, for which Leo had agreed to pay in recognition of Henry's support for the papacy.[51] A further indication of the key role that Cavalcanti played in relations between the English court and the papacy at this time is provided by the fact that he hosted Gregorio da Casale, permanent English resident at the curia, for six months in 1523, when negotiations were taking place regarding a possible alliance with the emperor and the papacy against France.[52] During the early 1520s Cavalcanti received large sums from the Treasury of the Chamber for unspecified luxury goods. Whether these included tapestries is undocumented, but evidence that he maintained a close business relationship with Van Aelst is provided by the goods listed at the residence in Austin Friars that Cavalcanti shared with PierFrancesco de' Bardi and various other Italian merchants. According to an inventory of 1522, this sizeable and well-appointed building, which served as residence, warehouse, and showroom, had eleven "arras" tapestries dispersed among its various chambers. Two were described as "a figure" (that is, figurative) and nine as depicting verdures and animals. One of the verdure and animal hangings was specified as "di conto di Gian van adelst Fiamingo," which suggests that it was an item of stock that Cavalcanti was selling on behalf of the Van Aelst enterprise.[53]

Tapestry Provisions for Other Members of the Royal Household

While Henry was undoubtedly surrounded in his private apartments by new tapestries of the finest quality, it is clear that the court continued to make heavy use of the antique tapestries for both ceremonial and quotidian purposes. The main evidence for this usage is provided by the annual accounts of the royal arras maker. In 1522, for example, Van der Strete received payment for repairs to twenty tapestries in the previous year, including the late-fifteenth-century sets of *Esther and Ahasuerus* and *Brutus,* while in 1524–25 he was paid for repairs to twenty-seven tapestries, including several antique pieces. This work took seven workers a total of 427 days at 6d. per day.[54]

Some of the older tapestries also appear to have been allocated to the wardrobes attendant on members of the royal family. A warrant to provide just such a wardrobe for Princess Mary was issued in the late 1510s, with the stipulation that it was to include a cloth of estate with two cushions of gold and red velvet, a cloth of gold and a velvet chair, and thirty pieces of tapestry, each 3½ yards deep.[55] Two inventories dating from the early 1520s record the tapestries subsequently deposited in the princess's Removing Wardrobe and Wardrobe of Beds. The Removing Wardrobe included six pieces of *Hercules;* four old pieces of the *Story of Alexander,* perhaps part of the set purchased by Edward IV from Grenier in 1468; nine old pieces of "story of vineyards"; eight of "chequered verdures"; and four counterpoints of green verdure.[56] The Wardrobe of Beds included six pieces of the *Siege of Dames;* four pieces of *Ballam and Ballak;* four pieces of "henryke and conrake"; four pieces of the *Passion;* another two of the same; one piece of the *Old Law and New;* one of *Amys and Amylion* "cut in two for tappynges"; eight yellow verdures with the duke of Buckingham's arms in the border; and another eight pieces of "checker verdures" with the same arms.[57] Although the selection appears to have been somewhat arbitrary, combining an intention to provide the princess with suitably grandiose "traditional" tapestries along with an element of expediency, the inclusion of a set of the *Siege of Dames,* probably an allegorical series celebrating female virtues such as the Hermitage *Romance of the Rose* tapestries cited above, suggests that this set was chosen with a didactic intent.

The notion of educating a young noble by exposing him or her to moral examples in word and image, a *speculum principis,* dated from antiquity, but it received fresh impetus in Northern Europe during the Renaissance.[58] In his *Education of a Christian Prince,* Erasmus suggested that a young prince should be educated in virtues through the example of stories and proverbs and that these should "be engraved upon rings, painted in pictures, appended to wreaths of honour."[59] That these ideas enjoyed continuing currency at Henry's court is confirmed by Thomas Elyot's *Boke named the Governour,* published in 1531 at Henry's request, which suggests that the dwelling of a nobleman or man of honor should be decorated with "arras, painted tables and images containing histories, wherein is represented some monument of virtue, most cunningly wrought with the circumstance of the matter briefly declared: whereby other men in beholding it may be instructed, or at least ways, to virtue persuaded."[60]

The didactic intention underlying the choice of tapestries in 1525 for Henry's illegitimate son, Henry Fitzroy, duke of Richmond (fig. 9.13), was even more pronounced. The allocation was made in the year that Henry began to consider Richmond as his heir and the wardrobe items supplied to the newly furbished residence of Durham House on the Strand provide a clear indication of the young child's importance in the king's eyes, just as the size of his retinue indicated his new significance; when Richmond traveled to Yorkshire in July 1525 to escape an outbreak of the plague, his household numbered 254.[61] The list of wardrobe stuff appointed to the young duke includes twenty-four verdure counterpoints of two different grades and size, and tapestry hangings for eight rooms; the hall, chapel,

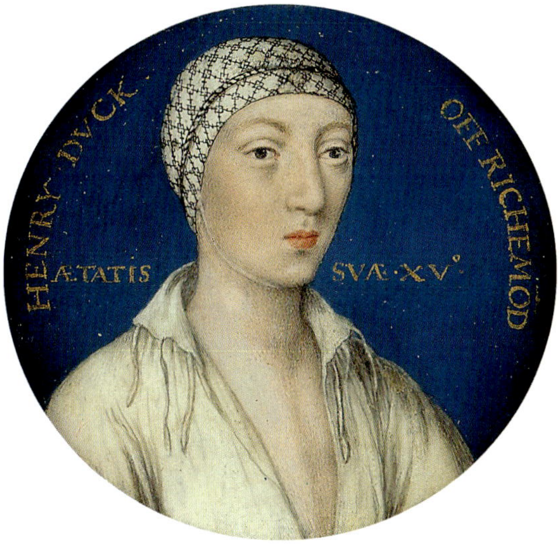

9.13 *Henry Fitzroy, Duke of Richmond,* attributed to Lucas Horenbout. Watercolor on vellum, 4.4 x 4.4 cm. The Royal Collection

closet, great chamber, dining chamber, bed chamber, counsel chamber, a chamber for strangers, and another for a chamber "when he journeys by the way."[62] Some of these sets may have been new purchases, because the 1526 accounts for the duke's wardrobe included a charge of £63 2s. 7d. for miscellaneous hangings.[63] The subjects of the eight sets are not given, but an inventory taken after the duke's death from consumption in July 1536 provides further information. At this date, his chapel stuff included a seven-piece set of the *Passion,* while his Wardrobe of the Beds included a seven-piece set of *Moses,* a large tapestry of "Lady Plesaunce accompanied with many Virtues and assauted with divers Vices," two tapestries of "King Lewes," a riche piece of "arras" of the "Image of Man and of Jessey," another of the *Coronation of Honor* "with divers grete image therin aswell of the olde Testament as also of the newe," four pieces of *Tullus Hostilius,* eight pieces of *Paris and Helen,* ten verdure tapestries, and two other sets of unidentified subject.[64] As with the tapestries supplied to Princess Mary, the subjects and large dimensions of a number of these sets indicate that they dated from the fifteenth century. The *Tullus Hostilius* panels were evidently from the set purchased by Edward IV, while the *Lady Pleasance* tapestry may have been identical with one of the panels of this subject first listed in the collection of Richard II and Henry IV. The same may have been the case with the panel of the *Coronation of Honor,* although it is also conceivable that this may have been a duplicate weaving of one of the designs from Charles V's *Honors* set. This series was reproduced in simplified form for a number of patrons in the 1520s and early 1530s. Five panels of a set formerly belonging to Cardinal Erard de la Marck have survived (fig. 9.14), and given the close contacts that Henry enjoyed with the Van Aelst workshop, he may have acquired duplicate panels of at least part of this set during the mid-1520s.[65] Whether the *Honors* tapestry listed in the 1536 inventory was fifteenth or sixteenth century in origin, there seems little question that the choice was determined by a didactic intent to provide a speculum principis for the young duke.

The continuing validity of such allegorical modes of thinking at the Tudor court is reflected by a pageant held at Wolsey's palace of York Place for the imperial ambassadors in early March 1522. This, the so-called Pageant of the Château Vert, involved a castle defended by ladies bearing the names of Beauty, Honor, Perseverance, Kindness, Constancy, Bounty, Mercy, and Pity. Under attack from more ladies whose names were Danger, Disdain, Jealousy, Unkindness, Scorn, Sharp Tongue, and Strangeness, who were all dressed like "Indian women," the heroines were rescued by a band of gallant knights, Henry VIII among them, titled Love, Devotion, Youth, Loyalty, Pleasure, Gentleness, and Liberty. The group was led by a figure identified as "Ardent Desire."[66] It is as though the figures of the *Honors* tapestries had come to life at the English court.

The Household Ordinances of 1526

The provision of tapestries and luxury textiles for both standing and removing wardrobes for Princess Mary and the duke of Richmond must have been analogous, albeit on a smaller and less grandiose scale, to those already made for Henry and Katherine. A further insight to the daily handling and management of these various wardrobes is provided by the directions for the royal household drawn up in 1526 at the

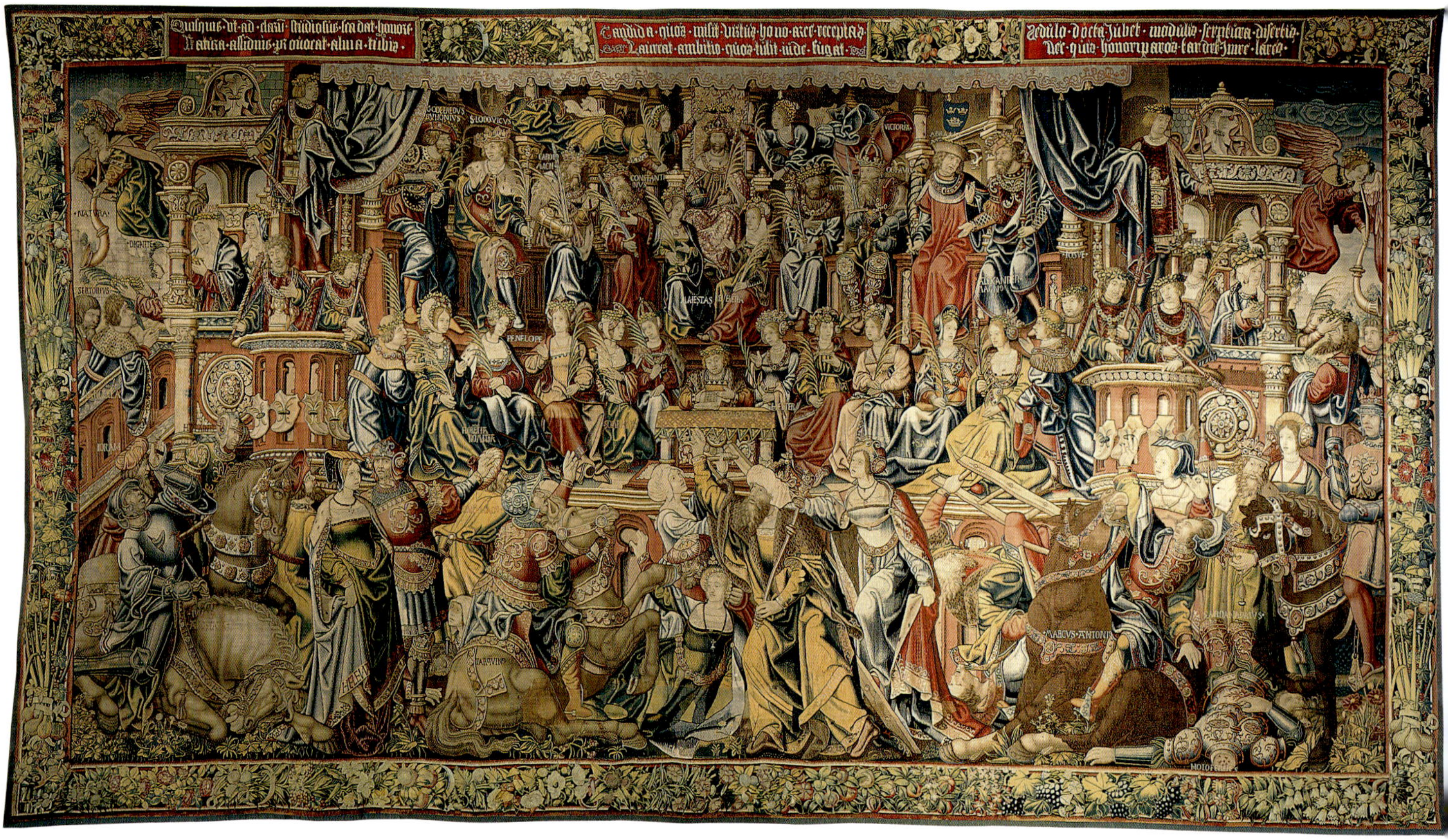

9.14 *The Coronation of Honor* from a set of the *Honors* after a design by Bernaert van Orley and others. Woven in an unidentified Brussels workshop, ca. 1525–30. Wool and silk, 450 x 802 cm. Formerly Wildenstein Collection, New York

king's command by the earl of Arundel, Henry Fitzalan, who served as lord chamberlain from 1526 to 1530.[67] These directives were part of the general reorganization instituted by Wolsey to better regulate and control court activities, the outcome of which was the Eltham Ordinances. An updated version of earlier court ordinances, this provides explicit evidence of provisions made for the use and care of the tapestries by the various court officers.[68] Among the many daily tasks of the gentleman usher was the injunction "to forbidde that no maner man do set any dishe upon the King's bed for feare of hurting the King's riche counterpoyntes that lye thereupon. And that the huisshier take good heede, that no man wipe, or rubbe their handes upon none arras of the King's, wherby thei might be hurted, in the chamber where the King is specially, and in all other."[69] Similarly, among the general attendance duties of the grooms of the king's chamber was the expectation that they would keep watch over the "riche arras, riche beddes, carpets" and other precious textiles in the chamber, "Whefore it hath been seen often tymes past, that there hath ben cut, stolen, and borne away, divers of the said stufs."[70] The grooms of the king's chamber were daily expected to set up and take down the trestle tables used for the meals of the lord chamberlain and the other senior court officers who were privileged to eat separately from the rest of the court staff, the vast majority of whom ate in the great hall. When not in use, these tables were evidently stacked behind the hangings, for the 1526 ordinances stipulated "two groomes to holde upp the King's arras or hangings, and other two to take down the bourdes [that is, trestle tables] of chapleyns, huisshiers, [....] And thei to set aside all fourmes, tressels, and stooles; casting the arras over them, as may be most honest and convenient."[71]

When the king was traveling, the gentleman usher was expected to travel in advance, "well ensured of the King's mynde, and my lorde chamberlayn's," to make the necessary provisions at temporary accommodations to house the king and other members of his entourage with the appropriate "arras, beddes, and what stuf he shall prepare the said Chambers withall." He was to be accompanied by two yeomen, a groom, a page of the chamber, a groom porter, and at least one groom from the Wardrobe of the Beds. Arriving at a destination, he was to call for the keys from the resident keeper, to check all the doors, and to give order for necessary repairs. That done, he was to appoint the chambers at his discretion, giving the king the best and most convenient, then providing chambers for the queen, the king's mother, the prince and the other royal children, and then for other appropriate members of the court.[72] The groom porter was responsible for bringing the necessary ladders for the hanging of the king's chambers, along with all the other necessary forms, trestles, straw for beds, and so on. The tasks of the page of the king's chamber included "to strawe the chambers before thei be hanged for saving of the arras."[73]

Though the ordinances give a glimpse of the formalized way in which the king's staff handled the hangings and precious textiles, little information has survived regarding the disposition of tapestries in the royal household during the mid-1520s. As already noted, however, the way that tapestries were used in Wolsey's household, with different grades being deployed to dramatize the hierarchy of different chambers, presumably echoed usage at the court. Similarly, the effort involved in hanging Wolsey's finest tapestries for events such as the visit of the French embassy in 1527 were certainly mirrored, on an even larger scale, by the provisions for such events in the royal household. For example, in anticipation of the French embassy in May 1527, a temporary banqueting house was constructed at Greenwich and decorated with great elaboration, including a large panel by Holbein depicting Henry's victory at the Battle of Thérouanne and a ceiling painting, also by Holbein, assisted by nineteen other painters, of the heavenly firmament.[74] But these provisions must have been dwarfed in splendor by the main component of the decoration, described by Spinelli, the Venetian ambassador, as "the most costly tapestry in England representing the history of David."[75] This was presumably the *David* set that Henry had purchased in 1520 and that had impressed onlookers so much at Guines. The banqueting house and its furnishings were evidently considered to be a grand demonstration of Tudor magnificence, and Henry ordered that it should be left standing for several days so that people might see the rich decorations, a vivid demonstration of the king's self-conscious display of magnificence.[76] The following year, when a second French embassy visited Greenwich after Henry had been presented with the Order of Saint Michael, the decorations were equally sumptuous, involving the gold-ground verdure first displayed at Guines in 1520.[77] Although brief, these accounts provide a hint of the splendor at the Tudor court in the years immediately preceding those in which Henry initiated divorce proceedings against Queen Katherine, a process that gave new focus to the selection of subject matter for some of his more expensive tapestry commissions.

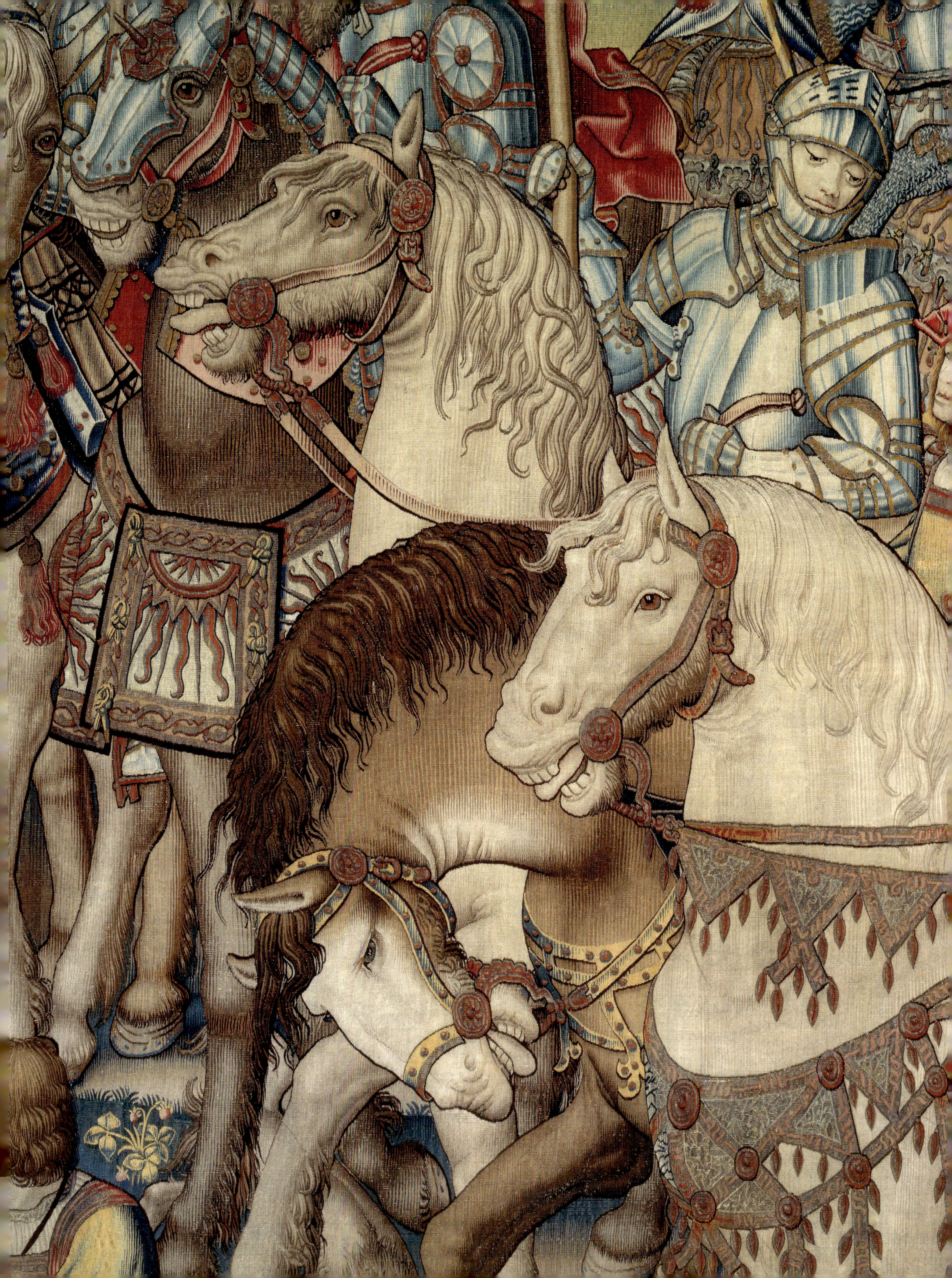

CHAPTER 10

Royal Patronage in the Late 1520s

Style and Iconography

Henry's tapestry patronage during the second half of the 1520s is distinguished from that of previous years by two marked tendencies. First, during this period he made the first of a sequence of purchases, in this case a set of the *Story of David,* whose Old Testament subject matter seems to have been chosen expressly to promote a particular idea about the king himself. While earlier purchases may also have been motivated by the king's identification with certain heroic or religious prototypes, this is the first commission in which his intention to use tapestry as a tool of suggestion to the Tudor court is unambiguous and pointed. The second marked difference is that tapestries acquired in these years begin to reflect the stylistic changes that were taking place in the art of the Southern Netherlands under the influence of the Roman school. Indeed, it was in tapestry, rather than other figurative media, that the Italian Renaissance first made its presence felt in England, albeit through the distorted lens of the Brussels "Romanist" artists. These issues, propagandistic and stylistic, will form the subject of the next chapter.

Henry's "riche historye of king david" and the Royal Divorce

As we have seen, the London merchant Richard Gresham organized Wolsey's 1520 commission for tapestries to decorate Hampton Court and subsequently supplied him with another set of "counterfeit arras" *Triumphs* in 1525. Gresham had also been involved in a variety of transactions with the Crown during the late 1510s and early 1520s, but whether he provided tapestries to Henry at this time is undocumented. He first appears in this capacity in October 1528, when he received the sum of £1,582 10s. for two sets. The first was a ten-piece "arras" set of the *Story of King David,* measuring 743½ ells (418 square yards) at a total cost of £1,548 (41s. 8d. per ell); the second was a twelve-piece tapestry set of the *Twelve Months* containing 345 ells (194 square yards) and costing £34 10s. (2s. per ell).[1] Although the second sum was modest, indicating that the *Months* set was woven in wool alone from a schematic design, the price of the *David* set was staggering and must rank it as the most expensive set that Henry had purchased up until this date. The *David* set must also have been one of the largest of the day, with a surface area of just under 420 square yards. According to the warrant for payment from the lord chamberlain's office, Gresham had delivered the tapestries to the Wardrobe of Beds on October 22, 1528, so it seems clear that this set was not the same as that displayed in the temporary banqueting house for the French embassy in 1527.

The warrant does not detail the dimensions of each tapestry, and no contemporary description has survived, but on the strength of the total surface area the set can be identified with a ten-piece set that was located at the Tower Wardrobe by 1547 and described in the inventory as the "riche historye of king david."[2] A century later, the inventories of the sale held by the Commonwealth government after Charles I's execution list a large number of *David* tapestries of various dimensions and

Detail of fig. 10.2

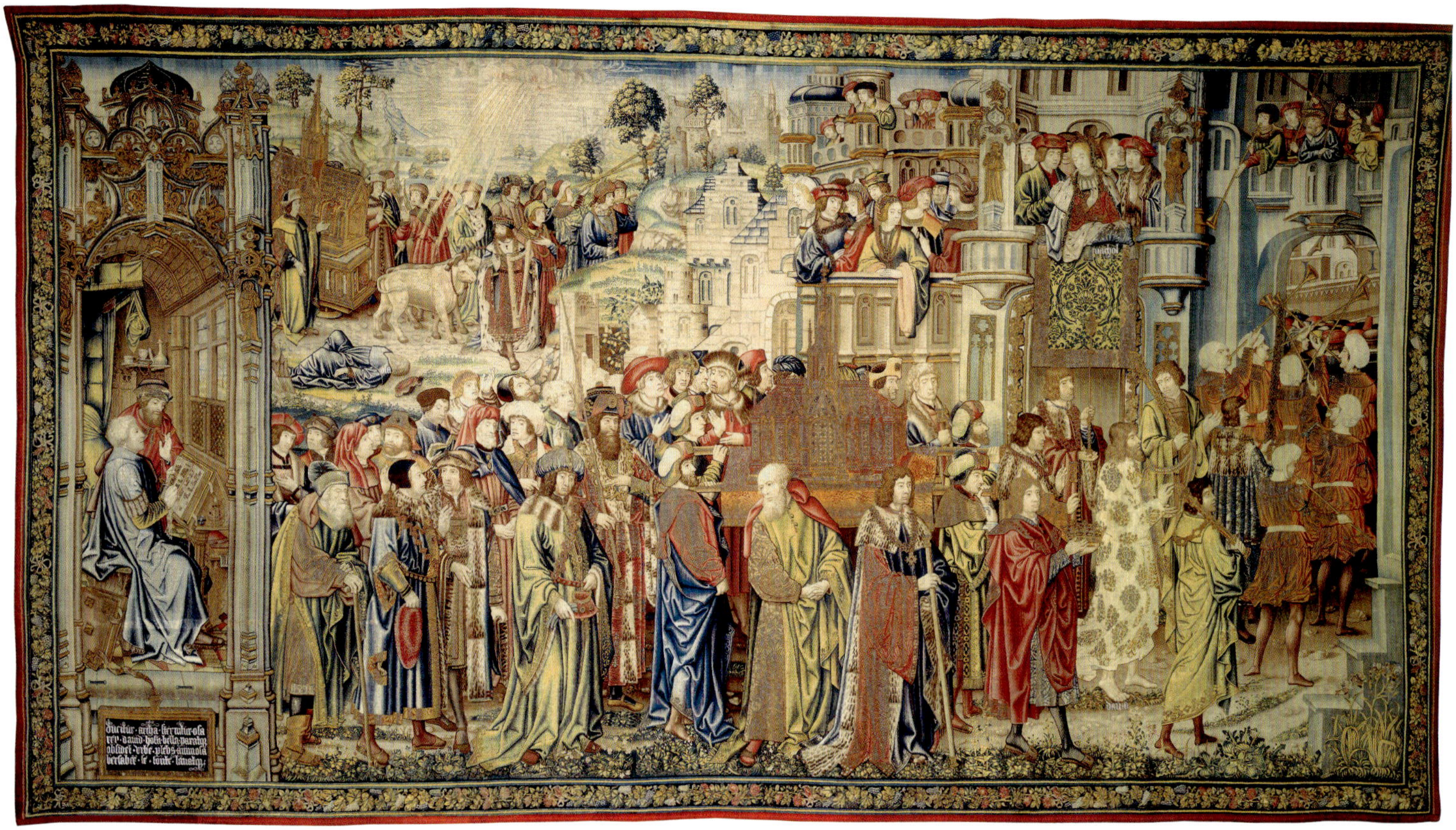

10.1 *The Death of Oza and the Transportation of the Ark into Jerusalem* from a set of the *Story of David*. Tapestry woven in Brussels, ca. 1526–28. Wool, silk, and gilt-metal-wrapped thread, 453 x 814 cm. Musée National de la Renaissance, Écouen

values. No ten-piece set of *David* is recorded, but the Tower Wardrobe included "three pieces of the history of King David" with the very high valuation of £4 per ell, while another four pieces of "Arras of David" of "Tower charge" with the same valuation were recorded at Saint James's. Three other pieces of "Arras of David" also with the same valuation were at the Council of State at Whitehall, as York Place came to be known after Henry took it over following Wolsey's fall in 1529. That these dispersed tapestries were part of the same set is established by documents relating to the sale, which indicate that they were acquired as such by a syndicate run by a Major Bass. In view of the association of seven of these ten pieces with the Tower, where Henry's set had been stored, and as most of Henry's valuable tapestries had remained at the palaces where they were recorded in 1547, it seems reasonable to identify these three groups as dispersed parts of that set.[3]

The subsequent fate of the Bass set is unrecorded, and it may have been sold to a foreign collector like so many of the other royal tapestries. It was not mentioned among the goods repurchased for the Crown after the Restoration, and it cannot be identified with any of the *David* tapestries listed in later royal inventories. Yet as recent research has indicated, there is a strong possibility that the set has survived and that it is to be identified with a high-quality ten-piece set of the *Story of David* at the Musée de la Renaissance at the Château d'Écouen (figs. 10.1, 10.2, 10.5–10.10). This, one of the finest examples in the world of pre-1530 weaving, was purchased in 1846 by the French Ministry of the Interior, having previously belonged to the Serra family of Genoa. Its earlier provenance was undocumented, but according to tradition, it was woven for Louis XII and subsequently given to the English court. From there it was supposed to have passed into the collection of "l'ultimo rampollo dei Duchi d'Jorch" (the last descendant of the duke of York), from whom it is said to have been acquired by a noble of the Spinola family. Assuming, on stylistic grounds, that the set dated from the late 1510s, early-twentieth-century historians ignored this tradition and

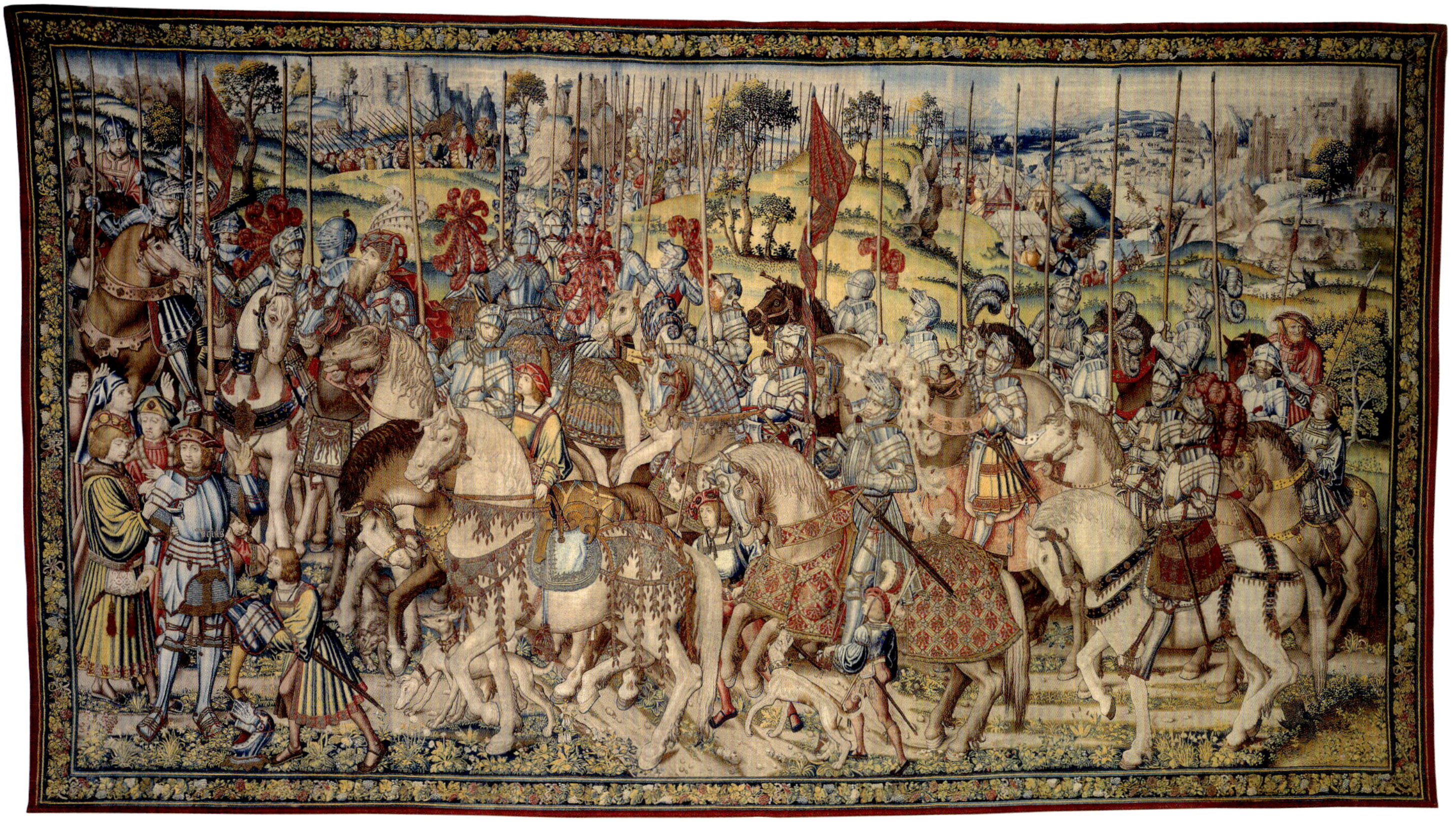

10.2 *The Assembly of the Troops* from a set of the *Story of David*. Tapestry woven in Brussels, ca. 1526–28. Wool, silk, and gilt-metal-wrapped thread, 450 x 815 cm. Musée National de la Renaissance, Écouen

tentatively linked the set with a payment made in 1517 by Emperor Maximilian for four tapestries of *David and Bathsheba*. This assumption must be incorrect, however, because the dimensions of Maximilian's set were much closer to those of the smaller set that survives in the Spanish royal collection today. The suggestion that the Écouen set might be related to the ten-piece set recorded in Henry's 1547 inventory was first made in the 1970s, and careful comparison between the dimensions of that set and those of the Écouen set does demonstrate that the sizes of the individual pieces in the two sets are extremely close. The comparison is additionally notable because the widths of the tapestries in Henry's set varied considerably, just as do those of the Écouen set.[4]

On the basis of this evidence, we can say with absolute certainty that the set that Henry purchased in 1528 was woven from exactly the same cartoons and to the same dimensions as the Écouen set. With the discovery of the purchase document relating to the set and the knowledge that Henry's set was of exceptionally high quality, the link between the two sets becomes even more likely, because few patrons of the day would have been able to afford sets of this size and quality, and no comparable sets are listed in the collections of the French or Habsburg kings or, indeed, in any other known collection. We can therefore conjecture that at some time after the Commonwealth sale the set passed to the Continent and, if the oral tradition of a provenance via the collection of the "last" duke of York has any truth in it, into the collection of one of the Stuart pretenders to the throne. Charles Edward or Henry Benedict Stuart, grandsons of James II and last Stuart claimants to the English throne, died in exile in Rome in 1788 and 1807, respectively. From thence, it would have been a short step to the Spinola family and the subsequent reemergence of the set in Genoa.

The Relevance of the Theme to Henry

Regardless of the provenance of the Écouen set, identification of the design of Henry's 1528 purchase raises the question of how much Henry was involved in the choice and

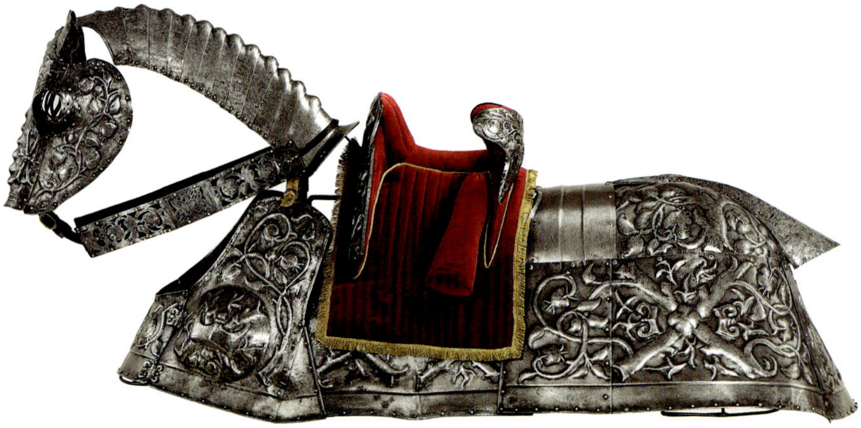

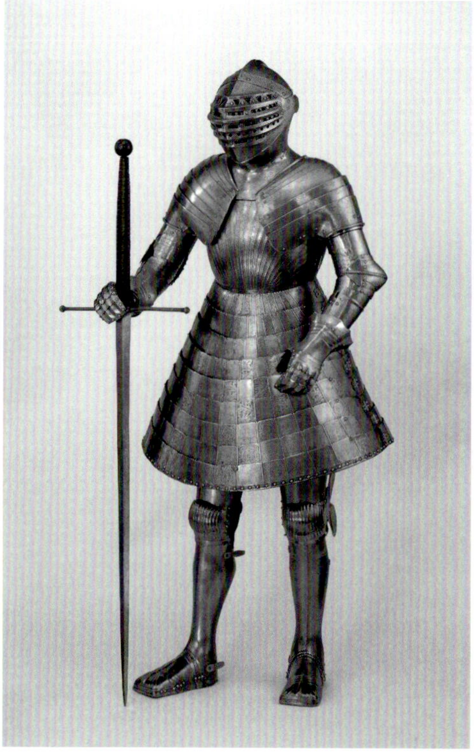

10.3 The *Burgundian Bard* horse armor, probably given by the Emperor Maximilian I to Henry VIII on the occasion of his marriage to Katherine of Aragon in 1509. Steel embossed, engraved, and formerly gilt, 140 x 254 x 990 cm. Royal Armories, Tower of London

10.4 Foot Combat Armor of Henry VIII. Italian or Flemish craftsmen working in England, ca. 1520. Etched steel, 188.5 cm high. Royal Armories, Tower of London

iconography of his set. As God's anointed ruler of the chosen people, David was a flattering comparison for any king and it was a standard component of much fifteenth- and sixteenth-century panegyric on the Continent as well as in England.[5] However, for the Tudor monarchs, whose dynastic claim to the throne was no stronger than the family they had deposed, the notion of a divinely sanctioned king was particularly appealing, and Davidian iconography was an important element in the art and literature generated by the courts of both Henry VII and Henry VIII.[6] Although scholarly studies have long recognized the significance that the analogy with David held for Henry and how it manifested itself in written and painted works, little detailed attention has been given to the possibility that it was also celebrated in tapestry.[7] Yet that was clearly the case. The 1547 inventory lists more than ten whole and partial sets of *David* tapestries, making it the most common storied subject in the collection.[8] Many of these had been inherited or appropriated, but as we have seen, written records reveal that besides the 1528 purchase, Henry was responsible for making large payments on two previous occasions for *David* tapestries, once in 1517 and again in 1520. The appearance of these earlier sets is unknown. They could have been woven to designs commissioned by Henry, but there is no evidence to support such conjecture and it is equally possible that they were made from available cartoons. Similarly, although the presence of high-quality tapestries of this subject in the royal collection must have contributed to associations between Henry and David in the minds of the king and his courtiers, there is no certain evidence to indicate that these earlier acquisitions were acquired to promote a specific agenda other than a general association between Henry VIII and David, although it is possible, as suggested in Chapter 8, that if the 1520 purchase was a duplicate weaving, at least in part, of the Écouen set, then this particular narrative may already have had a special significance for Henry. Whatever the uncertainty about these earlier purchases, analysis of the subject matter of the 1528 purchase, and the political context in which it was acquired, suggest that in this case the choice must have been carefully considered.

The ten panels of the set depict the affair between David and Bathsheba and the Israelites' campaign against the Ammonites, as narrated in 2 Samuel, chapters 6, 11, and 12. The first tapestry in the set (see fig. 10.1) depicts two episodes. In the top left corner, we see the death of Oza, who was struck down for touching the Ark of the Covenant. Below, the main scene depicts David, barefooted and playing his harp, leading the Ark into Jerusalem. Two themes appear to be implicit to this tapestry: the inevitability of divine retribution as illustrated by Oza's death, and the theme of childlessness as a curse, as suggested by the depiction of David's first wife, Michal, who watches his triumphal entry from above. According to the text, Michal angered David by criticizing his humble appearance in the procession, with the consequence that "Michal the daughter of Saul had no children to the day of her death" (2 Sam. 6:23).

After this introduction of the themes of obedience to god and childlessness as a curse, the narrative then jumps to the events related in 2 Samuel, chapters 11 and 12. In the second and third tapestries we see David giving orders for the campaign against Rabbah to commence and the assembly of the troops (see fig. 10.2 and detail opposite p. 177), who wear armor much like that owned by Henry or being made for him in the armory established at Greenwich (figs. 10.3, 10.4). Next the narrative turns to David's adulterous liaison with Bathsheba (fig. 10.5), the betrayal and death of Uriah (fig. 10.6), and Bathsheba appearing before David's court to tell him that she is pregnant. The iconographic pivot of the series is the seventh panel, which depicts Nathan's denunciation of David's behavior and David's subsequent repentance, represented by a sequence of allegorical figures (figs. 10.7, 10.8). At the left of the eighth panel messengers arrive to inform David of the death of Bathsheba's child, an event Nathan had prophesied, and below we see David processing to the temple (fig. 10.9). After this, with David's repentance and punishment complete, the narrative returns to the campaign against Rabbah. At the right of the eighth panel we see David, secure in his reconciliation with God, departing to lead the campaign. The penultimate panel depicts the presentation of the defeated king's insignia to David, and the

10.5 *David Sees Bathsheba Washing and Invites Her to His Palace* from a set of the *Story of David*. Tapestry woven in Brussels, ca. 1526–28. Wool, silk, and gilt-metal-wrapped thread, 452 x 714 cm. Musée National de la Renaissance, Écouen

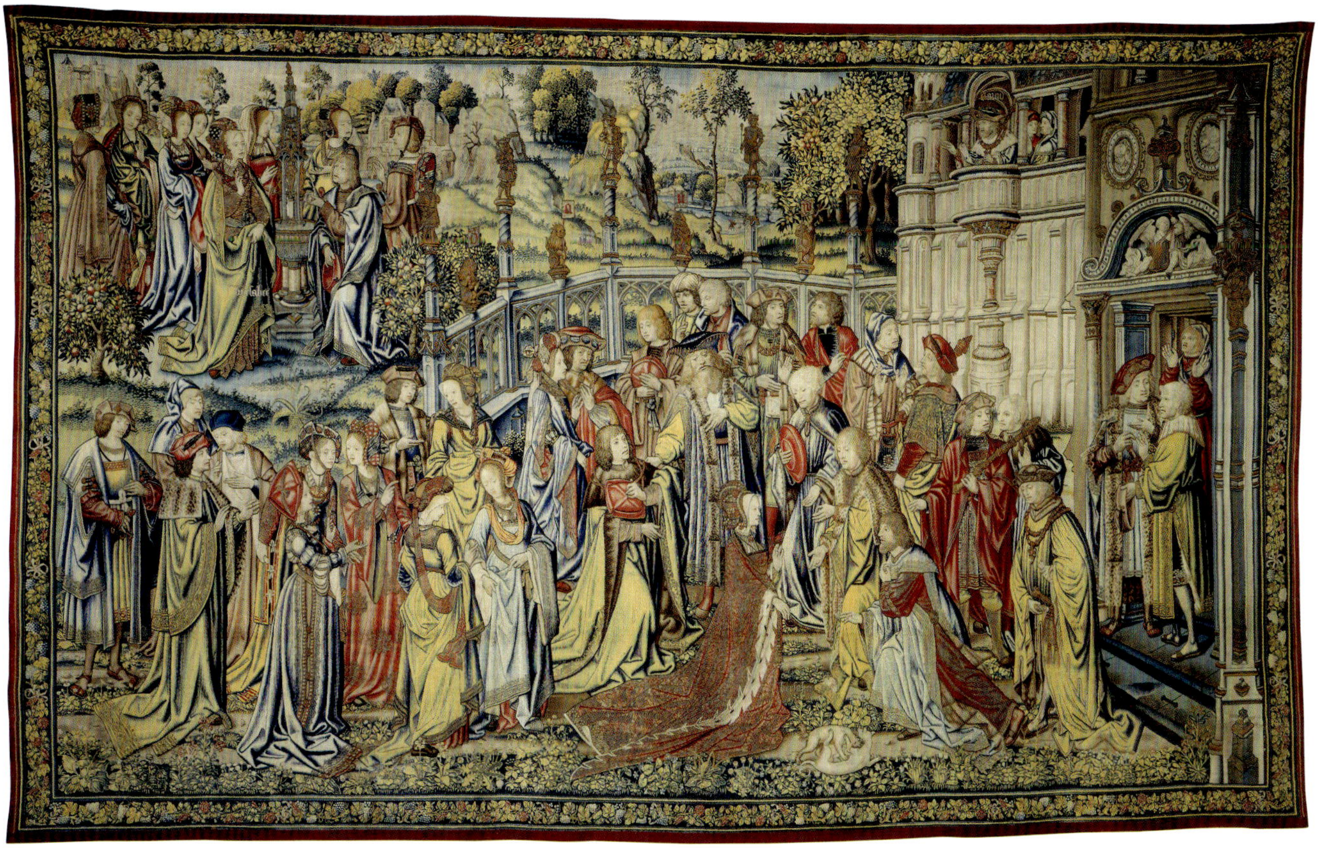

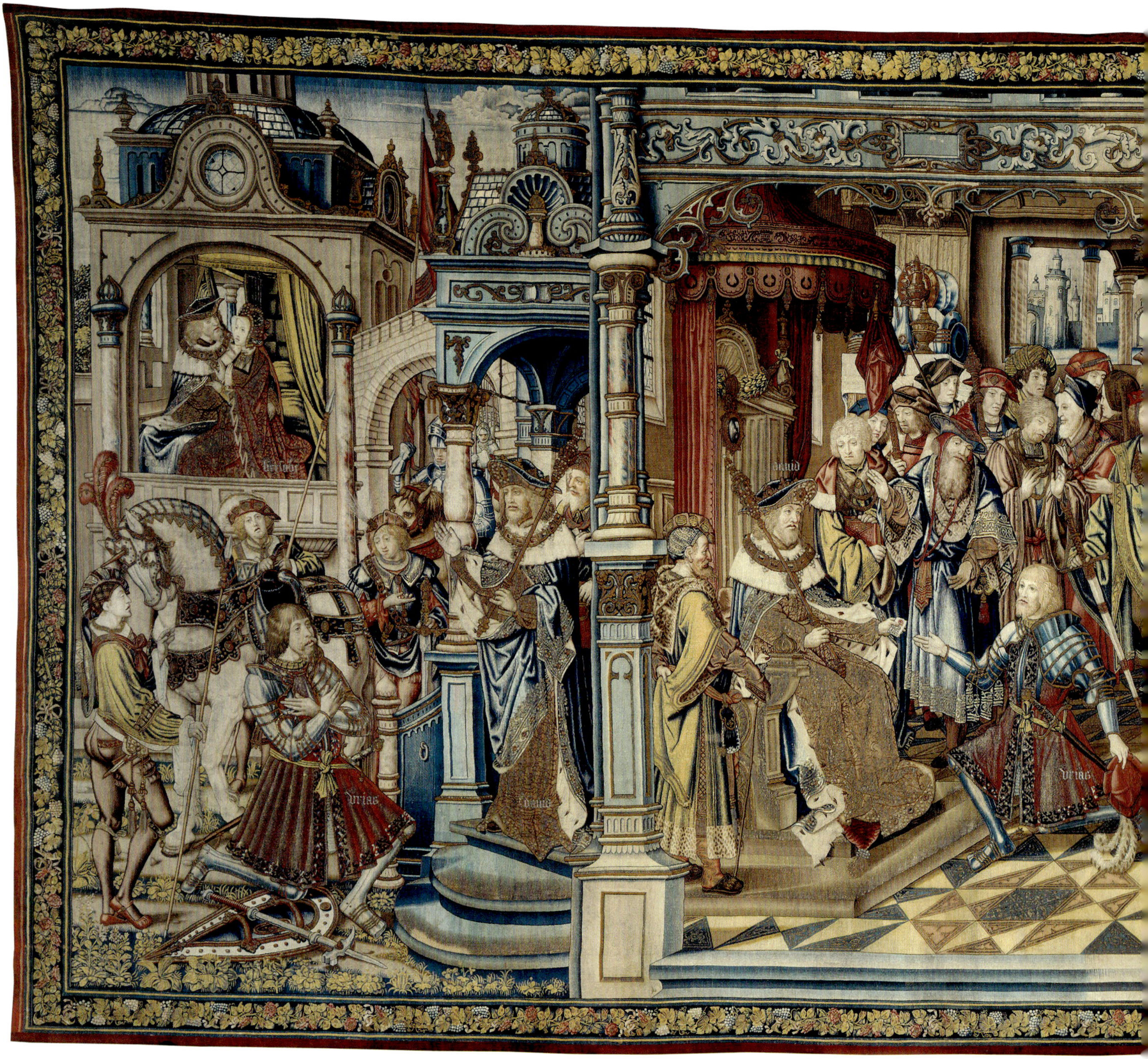

10.6 *The Adultery of David and Bathsheba and the Betrayal of Uriah* from a set of the *Story of David.* Tapestry woven in Brussels, ca. 1526–28. Wool, silk, and gilt-metal-wrapped thread, 454 x 801 cm. Musée National de la Renaissance, Écouen

last, the division of the booty among the troops (fig. 10.10).

As modern historians have recognized, the idiosyncratic choice of narrative scenes in the set yokes the story to a moral rather than a romantic purpose, an intent emphasized by the narrative figures in the first and last panels and the allegorical sequence of the seventh panel.[9] If it were not for the Henrician context, this might be explained as a generic didactic investigation between the personal ethics of a ruler and his public achievement, a recurrent concern in late medieval and Renaissance thought and the staple theme of the speculum principis tradition, as also evidenced in the *Honors* set made for Charles V.[10] But the didactic treatment of the subject is of particular interest in the context of contemporary events at the English court. A set of tapestries of the scale of those at Écouen would have taken about two years to weave.[11] Assuming that this set was woven in response to a commission from the

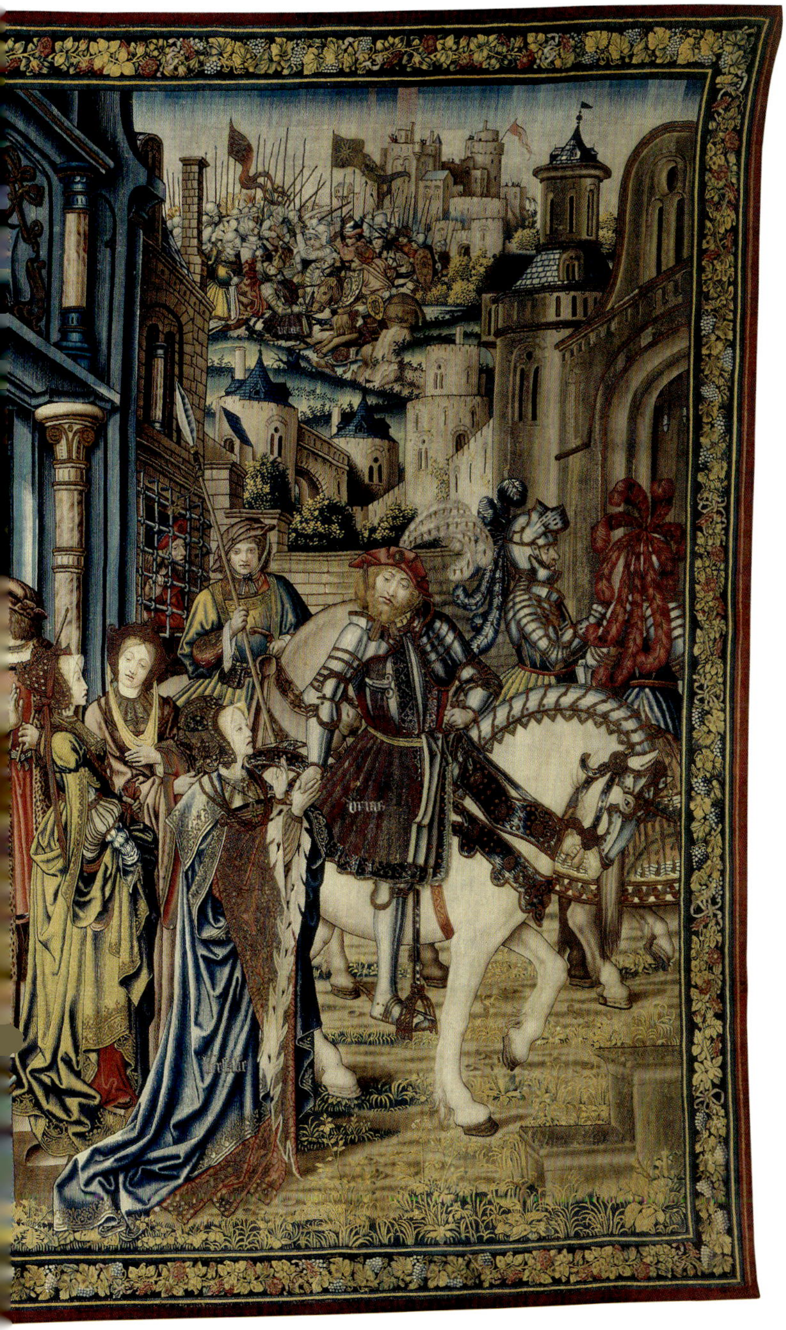

king, a speculative weaving of such a large and expensive set being unlikely, then it seems probable that it was commissioned some time before the end of 1526. This year marked a watershed in Henry's life. His relationship with Katherine of Aragon (fig. 10.11) had been deteriorating for some years, and he had probably stopped having sexual relations with her by 1524. The chances of her producing a male heir were now remote; she was thirty-nine years old and had not conceived in the previous seven years. In June 1525 Henry took steps to have his illegitimate son, Henry Fitzroy, appointed as his heir, and he created him duke of Richmond with precedence over every noble in the land, except any legitimate son the king might have, an action that was widely interpreted as a portent for the future. But at some point in the following year Henry underwent a radical change of direction, deciding that divorce and remarriage was the solution to his problem.

When Henry came to this decision cannot be identified with certainty, but divorce seems to have become his goal in 1526, and it was presumably a wish long before that. In May 1527 Wolsey entered into secret negotiations with the pope to seek a decree of nullity for Henry's marriage to Katherine.[12] The grounds on which the divorce was sought depended on the king's interpretation of canon law. Henry believed that his marriage to Katherine was barren because of her previous contract to Arthur, his older brother. The precedent was biblical. According to Leviticus 20:21, "If a man shall take his brother's wife, it is an unclean thing . . . they shall be childless." Henry had married his brother's wife, and although she had born a number of male children, they had all died. There is no specific evidence as to when Henry developed this conviction.[13] It could have been any time between June 1525 and the winter of 1526–27, but either way, the period coincides with the commissioning of the *Story of David* set.

The coincidence of the thematic subject of the *David* set and the moral discomfort of the king is readily apparent. On one hand, we find Henry arriving at an argument to justify his divorce on the grounds that his marriage had transgressed religious law, and on the other we see him commissioning a tapestry set that pivots on the transgression of David, a figure with whom he felt a strong affinity, and that specifically involves the death of David's first child as a punishment for his transgression.[14] Did Henry buy this set of tapestries simply because the subject struck a resonant chord with his mental state, or was the commission something more, an attempt to substantiate and promote

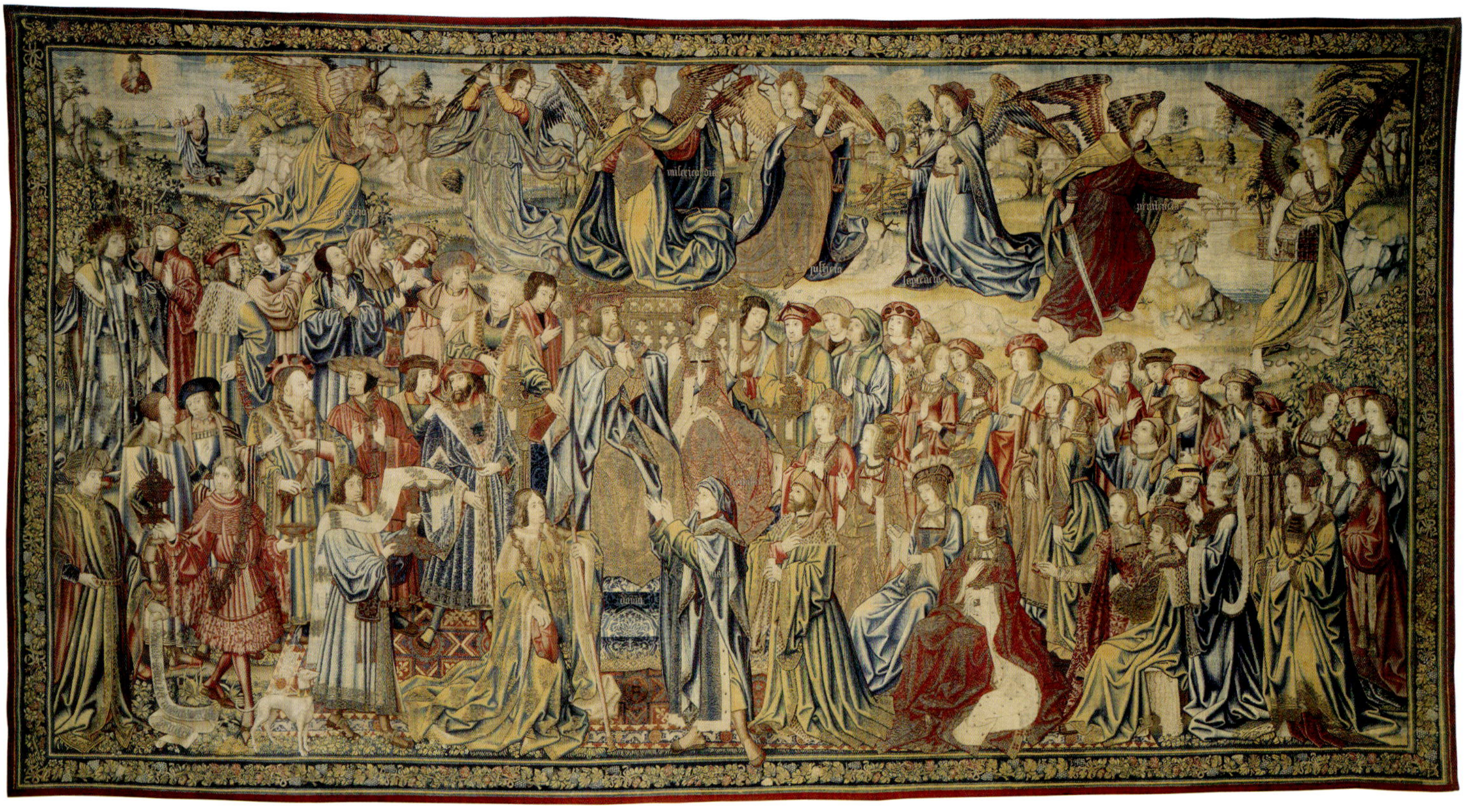

10.7 *The Reproach of Nathan and David's Repentance* from a set of the *Story of David.* Tapestry woven in Brussels, ca. 1526–28. Wool, silk, and gilt-metal-wrapped thread, 453 x 831 cm. Musée National de la Renaissance, Écouen

Opposite:
10.8 Detail of fig. 10.7

his inner convictions in the public arena of the court? The telling factor here must be the richness and scale of the set. At a cost of more than £1,500—equivalent to the price of a battleship—it was one of the most expensive that Henry was ever to acquire. And with a total length of approximately eighty yards, it was not a work of art for private contemplation but a magnificent display set for use at important events. As such it must have been commissioned with the Tudor court in mind as the audience.

Where did the idea for this extravagant exercise in iconographic suggestion originate? In the absence of evidence regarding the terms of the commission, answers to this question must be speculative, but as suggested above, such a self-conscious exercise would not have been without precedent. It was only five years since Wolsey had commissioned more than twenty chambers of biblical tapestry from Gresham in a venture that must have been intended to promote his ecclesiastical stature in the minds of his contemporaries. In view of the close relationship between the king, Wolsey, and, to a lesser extent, Gresham, in the early 1520s, it seems plausible to suggest that the *David* set may have been commissioned with a similarly self-conscious objective: to draw a parallel between Henry's situation and that faced by David in such a way as to imply that the solution to the king's problem would benefit not only the king but also the commonweal, as represented by the division of the booty illustrated in the last tapestry of the sequence. This was, after all, an age in which the cosmic dimension of the Crown's behavior was a matter of faith. A similar argument was presented five years later in the Articles Devised by the Whole Consent of the King's Most Honourable Council, in which the eighth article claimed that God's approval of Henry's marriage to Anne Boleyn was demonstrated by the early issue of the second marriage and the fine weather "with great plenty of corn and cattle."[15] An analogous claim was made by Hall's *Union of the Two Noble and Illustre Famelies of Lancastre and Yorke* (1548), which blamed the "execrable plagues" of the fifteenth century on the subverted lineage of the Crown and assumed that these were cured by the "politike governaunce" of the

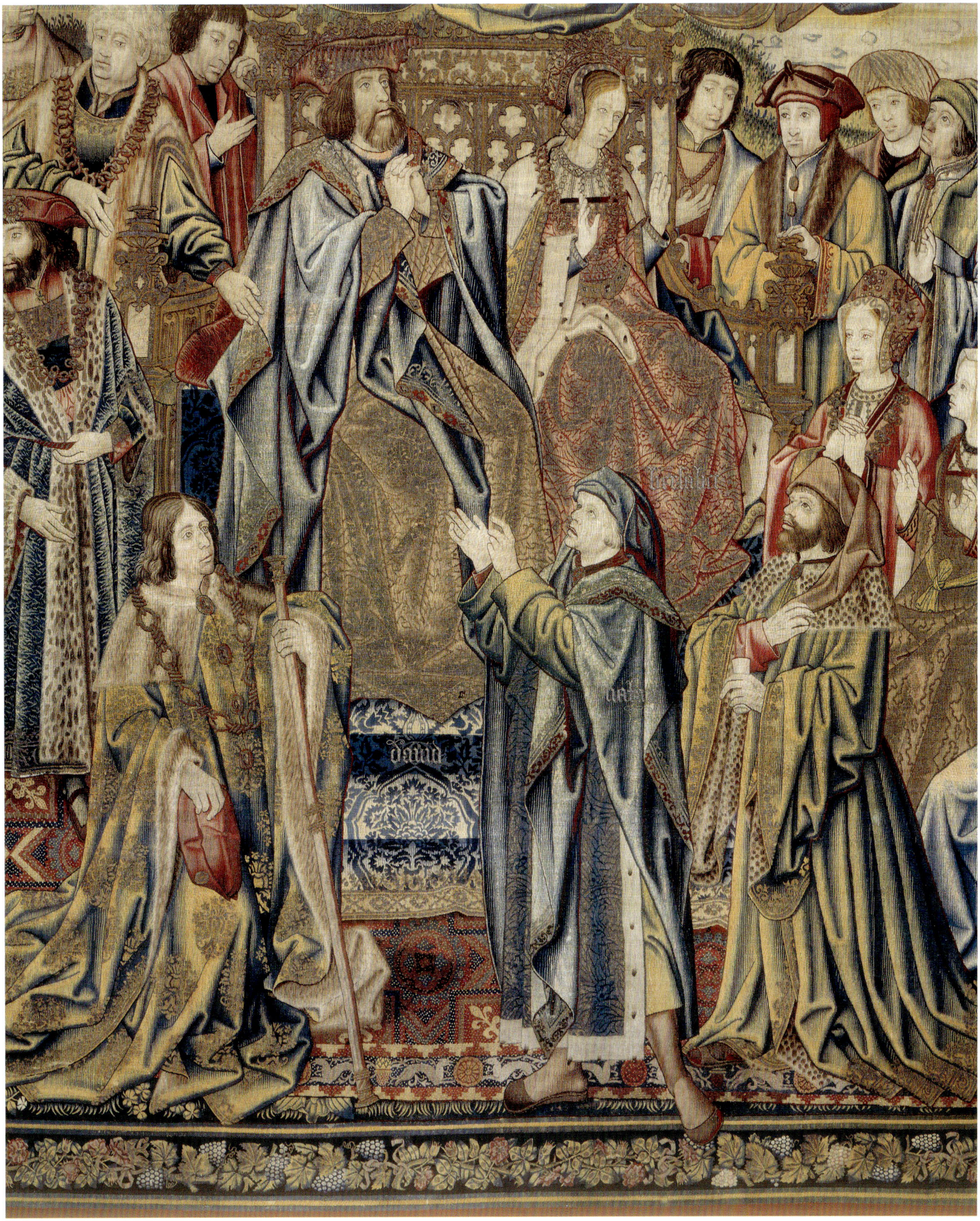
dauid

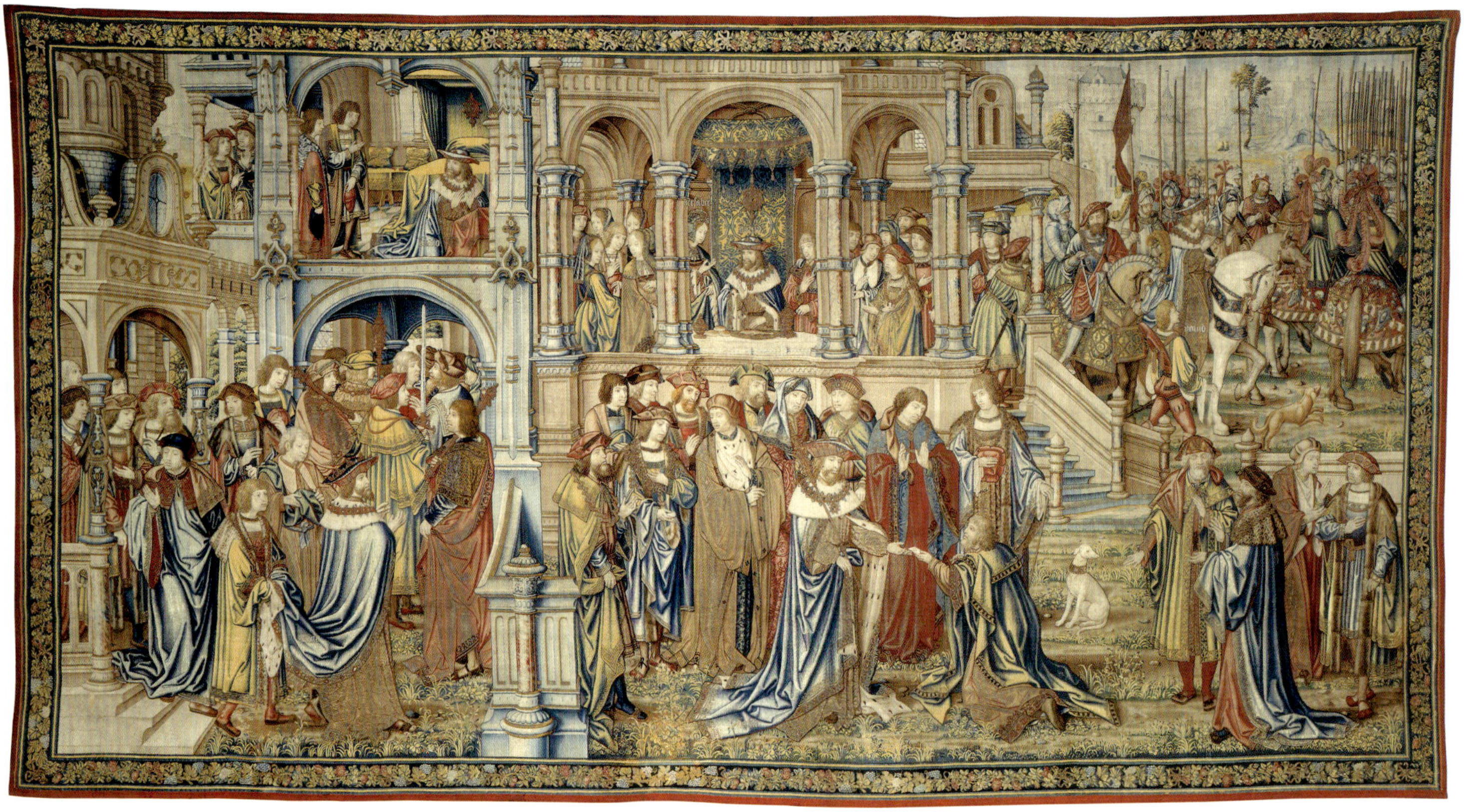

10.9 *Death of David's Son and David's Departure for Rabbah* from a set of the *Story of David*. Tapestry woven in Brussels, ca. 1526–28. Wool, silk, and gilt-metal-wrapped thread, 456 x 828 cm. Musée National de la Renaissance, Écouen

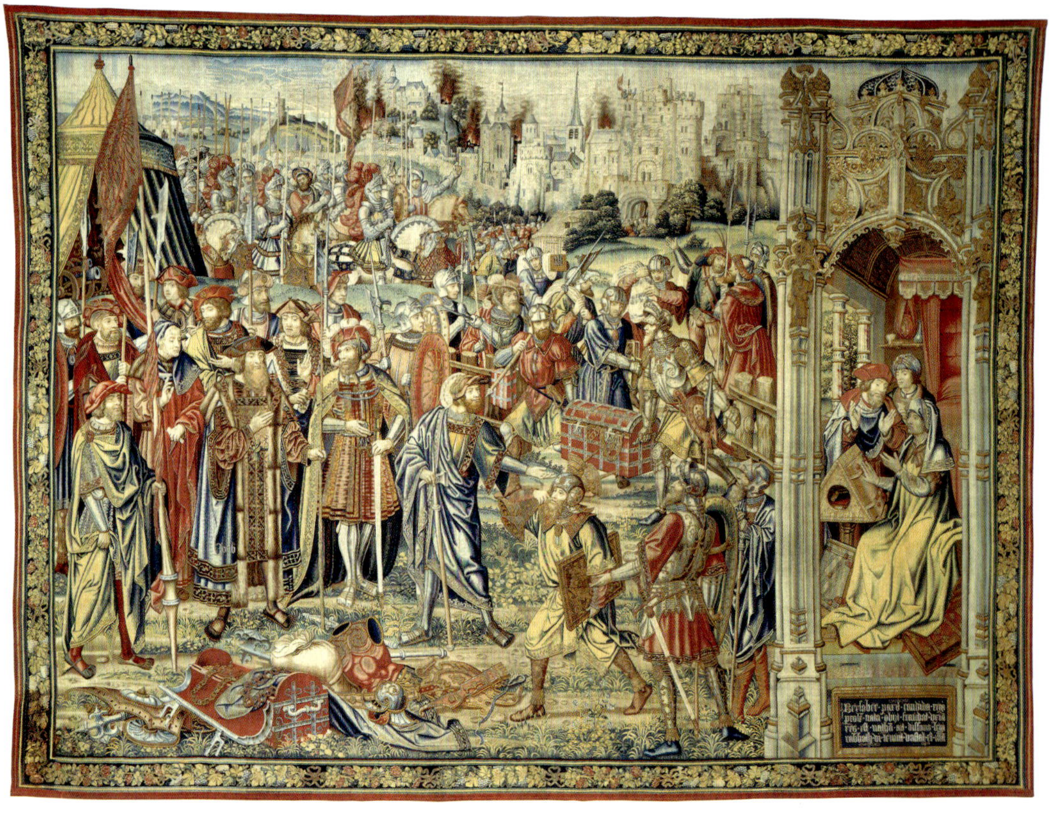

10.10 *The Division of the Booty* from a set of the *Story of David*. Tapestry woven in Brussels, ca. 1526–28. Wool, silk, and gilt-metal-wrapped thread, 455 x 591 cm. Musée National de la Renaissance, Écouen

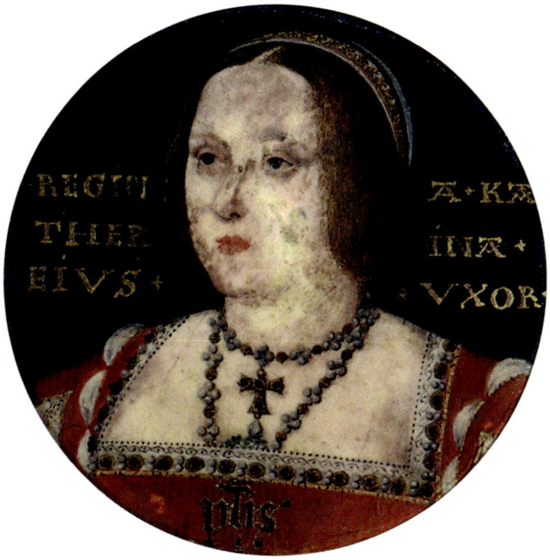

10.11 *Katherine of Aragon,* attributed to Lucas Horenbout, ca. 1525–27. Watercolor on vellum, 3.8 cm x 3.38 cm. National Portrait Gallery, London

Tudors.[16] Although the cost and size of the set indicate that it was intended to promote this viewpoint to a court audience, this is not to suggest that it was in any sense a purely manipulative ploy. On the contrary, Henry evidently believed passionately in his cause. As such, we should probably understand the *David* set as an attempt to project deeply held inner convictions to a wider court audience.

The possibility that the set may have been commissioned to promote a particular point of view in the arena of the Tudor court leads to the question as to whether it was designed for Henry or whether an existing design was appropriated for his use.[17] As already noted, Henry had made two large payments for *David* tapestries in 1517 and 1520, and according to an eyewitness account of the Guines celebrations, the *David* tapestries on display on that occasion depicted very lifelike figures and horses and featured the story of David, Uriah, and Bathsheba, exactly as the Écouen set and, by deduction, the 1528 purchase. It is therefore conceivable, as noted above, that the set purchased in 1520 was an earlier weaving of the same design. With this example before him, we might surmise that, struck by the relevance of this subject to his position in the mid-1520s, Henry may have decided to commission a new, more lavish weaving of the design, perhaps with certain adaptations to emphasize the themes that were of special relevance to him.

Even though the relation between the 1517 and 1520 purchases and that of 1528 remains conjectural, there can be no question that in 1528 Henry purchased and took delivery of a set of *David* tapestries that had the same number of pieces and dimensions as the set at Écouen and that cost the extraordinarily high sum of £1,548. In view of the cost and rarity of such tapestry, it is conceivable that the two sets may have been one and the same. At the least, Henry's set presumably had the same design and was of a comparable richness. As the theme of the *David* set mirrors the preoccupations on which this decision was taken, it seems almost certain that the set was commissioned to draw attention to the parallel between Henry's plight and that of David as a means of sanctioning the divorce that Henry was planning at this date. As such, the commission is the first recognizable example of Henry using tapestry for political purposes and was to set a precedent for much of Henry's most significant tapestry patronage in the following years.

Stylistic Developments in Brussels Tapestry Design, 1515–1530

A central reason for previous historians' overlooking the connection between the *David* set purchased by Henry in October 1528 and that now at Écouen is that the style of the Écouen set is generally perceived to be somewhat old-fashioned in comparison with developments in Brussels tapestry design during the 1520s. The assumption that the Écouen set was woven in a style current in the late 1510s has led to the false conclusion that it must also have been woven in the late 1510s. This argument is wholly erroneous because tapestry cartoons were demonstrably reused over a period of years, old designs remained popular even as new ones were developed, and patrons may have preferred an old-fashioned style for particular commissions. Nonetheless, the conservative style of the Écouen *David* set and the fact that it was probably the set acquired by Henry in 1528 certainly raise the question of stylistic development in tapestry design at this period. When and how

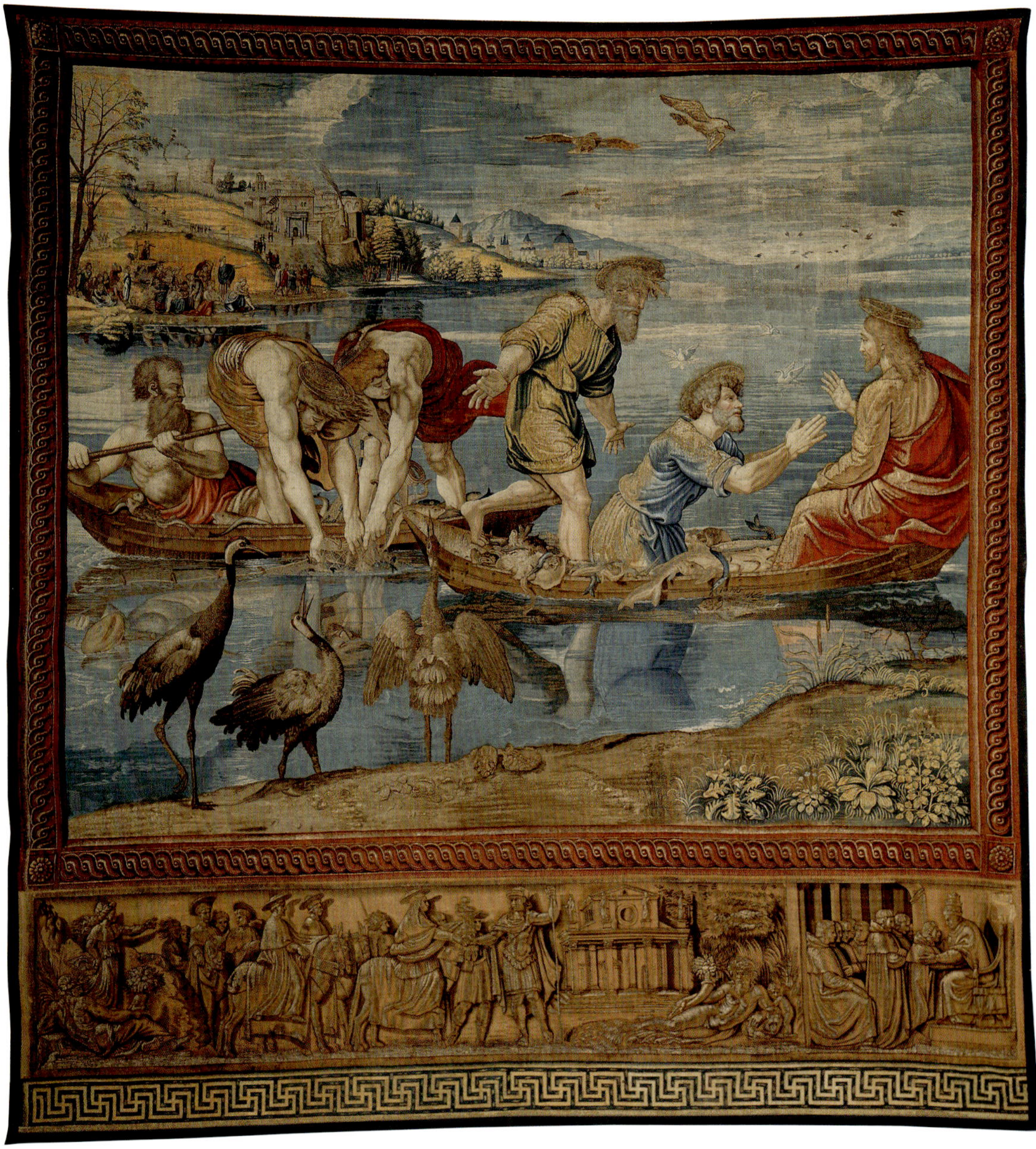

10.12 *The Miraculous Draft of Fishes* from the *Acts of the Apostles*. Tapestry design by Raphael and workshop, woven in the workshop of Pieter Enghien van Aelst, Brussels, ca. 1517–19. Wool, silk, and gilt-metal-wrapped thread, 496 x 440 cm. Vatican Museums, Vatican City

were these changes manifested in the English royal collection? It is to this question that we now turn.

As discussed in previous chapters, despite the technical advances that had been made in high-quality tapestry production toward the end of the fifteenth century, designs of the first two decades of the sixteenth century continued to emphasize line and surface pattern, generally limiting more illusionistic passages to localized focal points. This "pre-Renaissance" style changed drastically during the 1520s as leading Netherlandish artists and weavers responded to the influence of tapestry designs that had been commissioned from Raphael and his workshop by Leo X and Clement VII and sent from Rome to Brussels for execution. The first and most famous of these papal sets was Raphael's *Acts of the Apostles*, commissioned in 1515 and woven between 1517 and 1521 (fig. 10.12).[18] In place of the crowded scenes and "multiple narrative" typical of Netherlandish tapestry design at this date, each panel in this series illustrated a specific moment of intense drama—key events in the lives of Saints Peter and Paul—embodied by large, anatomically correct figures in clearly defined settings that were depicted with a sophisticated understanding of aerial and spatial perspective. Extraneous figures and decorative detail were kept to a minimum. As noted above, the *Acts* cartoons were followed by a succession of other designs from Raphael's workshop that incorporated the full spectrum of Italian Renaissance preoccupations, particularly a fascination with the art of the antique world. This fascination is exemplified by a set of tapestries woven for Leo in the late 1510s and which was known to the sixteenth-century papal court as the *Grotesques of Leo X* and in modern times as the *Triumphs of the Gods*. Although the papal set is now lost, its appearance can be reconstructed on the basis of later weavings, including two pieces that survive from a duplicate set acquired by Henry VIII in 1542 (see figs. 13.18, 13.19). As this reconstruction reveals, the series was conceived as an allegory of a new golden age under Leo X's rule and depicted classical gods in whimsical architectural structures inspired by the antique paintings then being unearthed in Rome's ancient ruins, notably Nero's Golden House. Many of the figures incorporated references to antique statues.[19] Another series conceived in 1520, also as an allegorical celebration of Leo's papacy, was the *Giochi di putti,* which featured putti playing with symbols of the Medici between swags of fruit in shallow niches, a compositional formula inspired by the carvings on the side panels of Roman sarcophagi.[20] Although the original set is lost, its appearance can be reconstructed on the basis of preliminary drawings and later copies (fig. 10.13). The influence was not all one-way. The cartoons for the *Giochi di putti* were executed in Brussels by one of Raphael's collaborators, Tommaso Vincidor, who was dispatched from Rome in 1520 expressly for that purpose. Vincidor was also responsible for painting cartoons for a set of the *Life and Passion of Christ,* after modelli by Raphael's collaborators, Giulio Romano, Giovanni Francesco Penni, and Perino del Vaga, that were woven as tapestries between 1524 and

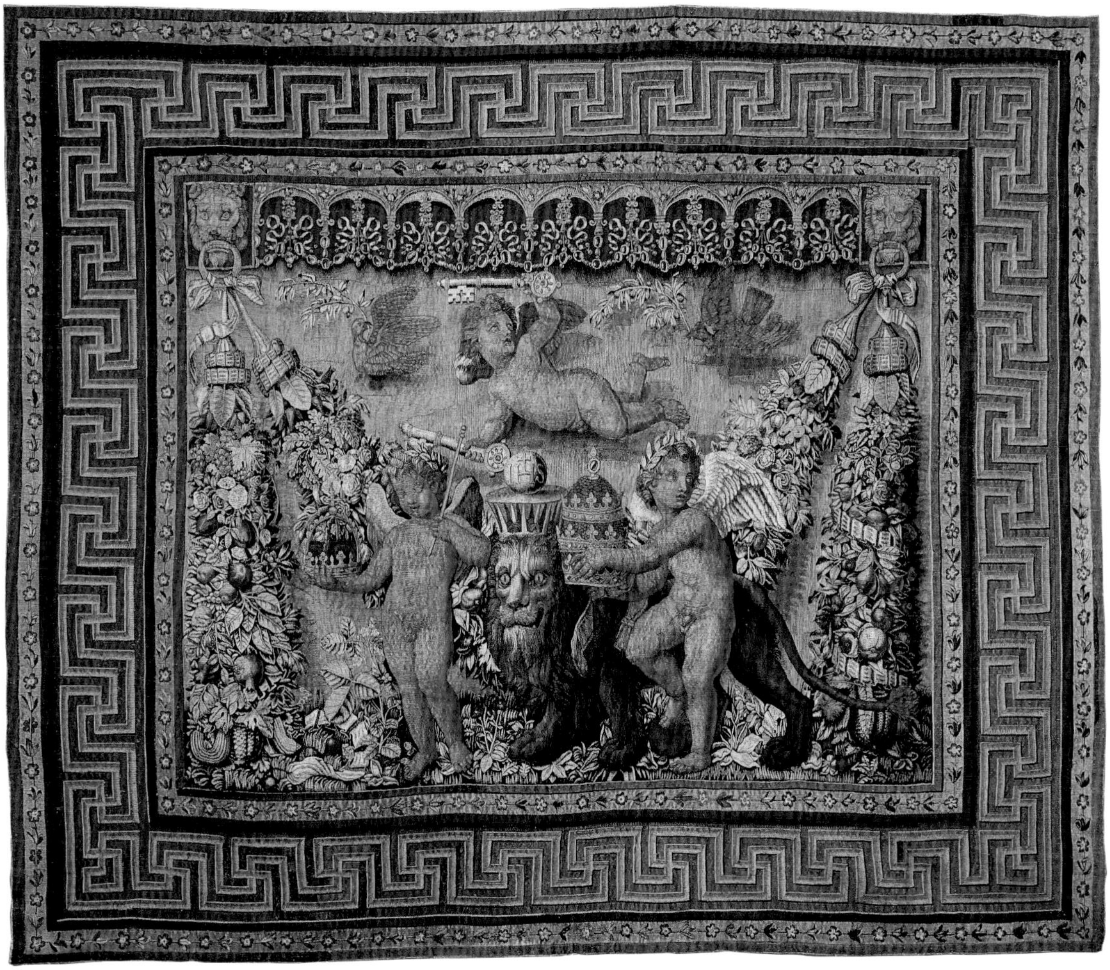

10.13 *Putti with a Lion and Symbols of the Papacy* from the *Giochi di Putti*. Tapestry design by Giovanni da Udine and Tommaso Vincidor, first woven in Brussels in the workshop of Pieter Enghien van Aelst, ca. 1522. This weaving, Rome? ca. 1640? Wool and silk, 310 x 287 cm. Iparművészeti Múzeum, Budapest

1531.[21] In place of the austere monumentality of Raphael's *Acts of the Apostles,* the cartoons for this series were infused with a greater degree of anecdotal, landscape, and genre detail, a reflection of Vincidor's response to the Netherlandish design tradition.

As historians have long recognized, the Raphael school designs revolutionized high-quality tapestry production, although they did not, as is sometimes assumed, lead to the simple rejection of one visual vocabulary in favor of a new one. Instead, Brussels designers took key elements of both native and Italian traditions to produce a new aesthetic that combined the strengths of each. The architect of this style was the court artist to Margaret of Austria, Bernaert van Orley, whose family had been involved in tapestry design since the early years of the century. During the 1520s Van Orley produced several sets of designs in which the drama, anatomical accuracy, and perspectival illusion of Raphael's cartoons were blended with traditional Netherlandish devices, such as multiple narrative, extensive patterning, and attention to landscape and genre detail.[22] The heroic but ornate style that resulted from this fusion was visually engaging, decorative, and monumental.

Although there is nothing to suggest that Henry commissioned designs directly from Van Orley, the evidence relating to Henry's purchases during the late 1520s confirms that he did acquire tapestries from cartoons by this artist and others in his circle. The first of these acquisitions, a rich four-piece set of the *Passion,* was made in circumstances that indicate Henry had little to do with the inception of the weaving. Thereafter, as we shall see, the subject matter and circumstances of other purchases indicate a more direct involvement by Henry and his advisers in the acquisition of designs in the new style.

Henry's "riche historye of the passion"

The *Passion* set in question came to Henry by a rather circuitous route. It had been imported to England sometime in early 1528 by a Hanse merchant called Edward Smytting, probably a relation of the Gerard Smytting who supplied tapestries to Henry, bishop Ruthal, and Cardinal Wolsey in the late 1510s, in the expectation that he would be able to sell it to Wolsey or the king.[23] Acute financial straits forced him to mortgage three of the set before his approach to the cardinal and then to seek protection from his creditors at the Chester home of William Brereton, a groom of the chamber and a rich landowner in his own right. According to a petition Smytting submitted to Brereton, three pieces of the set had been mortgaged and in part wrongfully obtained. The first two were in the hands of an Anthony Duardo, the third in the hands of a Harman Hulseman. A fourth had been delivered to Sir John Gryffith, a priest, for the petitioner's use.[24] Acting on Smytting's behalf, Brereton approached Wolsey, who directed him to discuss matters with his treasurer, but no sale transpired from this meeting. In June Smyttyng informed Brereton that the tapestries had cost him £4 6s. 8d. per ell but accepted that in order to sell them he would have to drop his price to £4 per ell. Subsequently, Brereton approached the king, who, after bargaining, bought the set for 25 percent less than Smyttyng had originally asked.[25] Payment for three pieces was made to Hulseman, the merchant to whom they had been mortgaged, in December 1528.[26] Payment for the fourth was made directly to Smytting in November 1529.[27] The reason for this shift in focus from Wolsey to Henry is unknown, but it almost certainly reflects the changing climate at court. The relationship between king and cardinal had become increasingly strained during the summer of 1528, and that September Henry peremptorily ordered Wolsey to vacate Hampton Court so that he might entertain the papal legate there.[28] During the same period, Brereton became increasingly involved with the Boleyn faction—to the extent that he was eventually executed as one of Anne's supposed lovers—and he was subsequently instrumental in drawing up the 1530 petition to Clement VII regarding the divorce that Henry now desired from Katherine.[29] Against this background, it

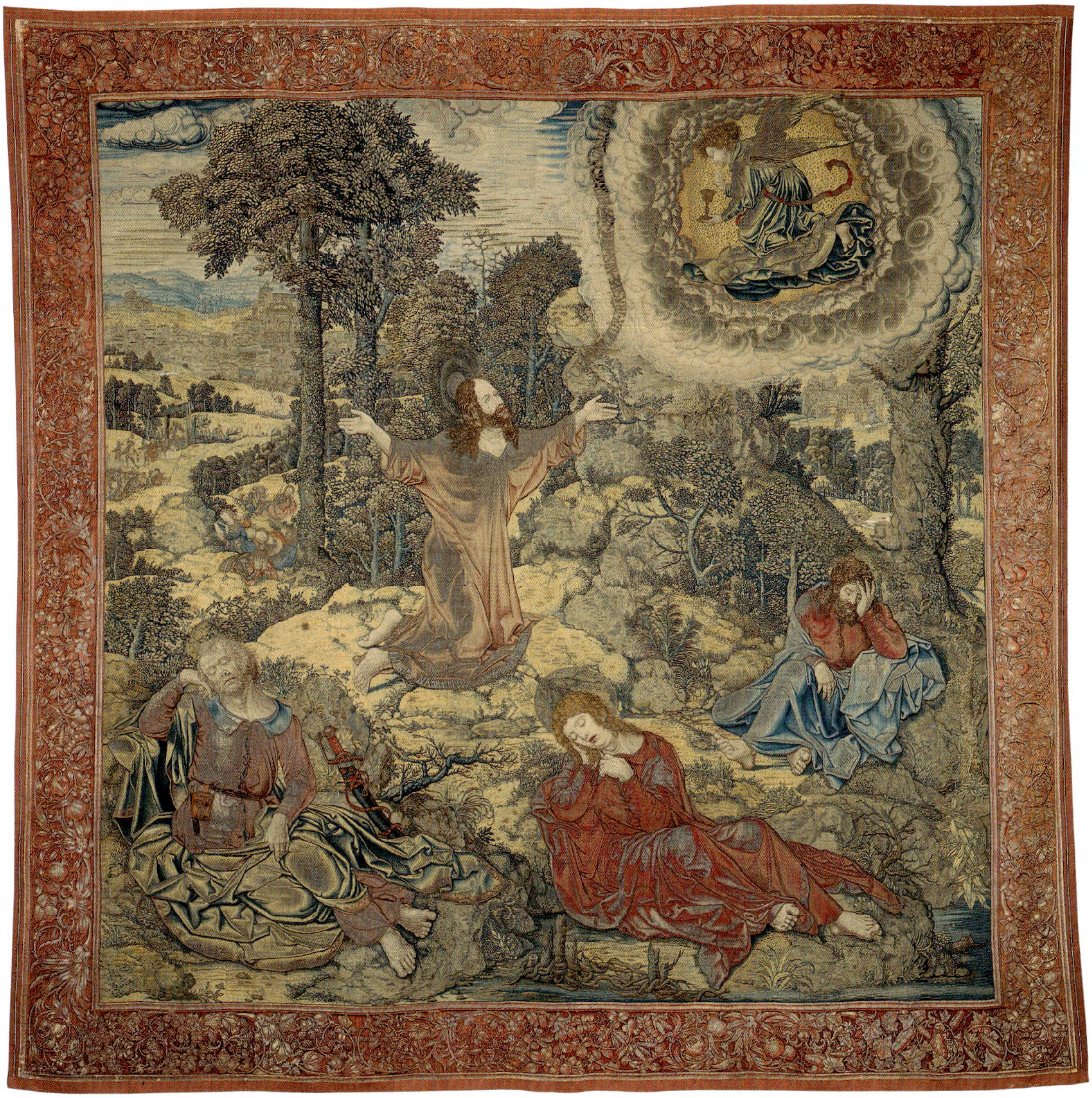

10.14 *Christ in the Garden of Gethsemane* from a set of the *Passion* (known as the *Alba Passion*). Tapestry designed by Bernaert van Orley, probably woven in the workshop of Pieter de Pannemaker, Brussels, ca. 1525–28. Wool, silk, and gilt-metal-wrapped thread, 369 x 358 cm. National Gallery of Art, Washington

may be that once the king grew interested in the tapestries, Wolsey realized that it was expedient to let him have them. Although the circumstances in which Smytting brought the set to England suggest that it was woven as a speculative venture, the fact that he imported it at such personal financial risk, in the expectation of a sale to Wolsey or Henry, is in itself significant. Considering the high cost of the series, it demonstrates the extent to which the Antwerp and Brussels tapestry merchants were aware of the interest in tapestry shared by the cardinal and king and of the likelihood that they would part with large sums to obtain the finest examples, even when they had not been commissioned.

Smytting may have felt especially confident of a sale in light of the high artistic and material quality of this particular set, which can be identified on the basis of his correspondence with Brereton. According to this, the four tapestries depicted the following subjects: "Christe's mawndye," "the praying of hym in the gardeyn," "Jehsus bering the crosse," and "the hanging of our lorde on the crosse." The piece delivered by Smytting in 1529 measured twenty-seven square ells, which allows the set as a whole to be identified with a four-piece set that the 1547 inventory listed in the Tower Wardrobe. This set was described as "the riche historye of the passion," and all four components had surface areas of approximately twenty-seven square ells.[30] The subsequent fate of the set is uncertain, but it can probably be identified with a very high-quality four-piece

10.15 *Christ Carrying the Cross* from a set of the *Passion* (known as the *Alba Passion*). Tapestry designed by Bernaert van Orley, probably woven in the workshop of Pieter de Pannemaker, Brussels, ca. 1525–28. Wool, silk, and gilt-metal-wrapped thread, 345 x 345 cm. Musée Jacquemart-André/Institut de France, Paris

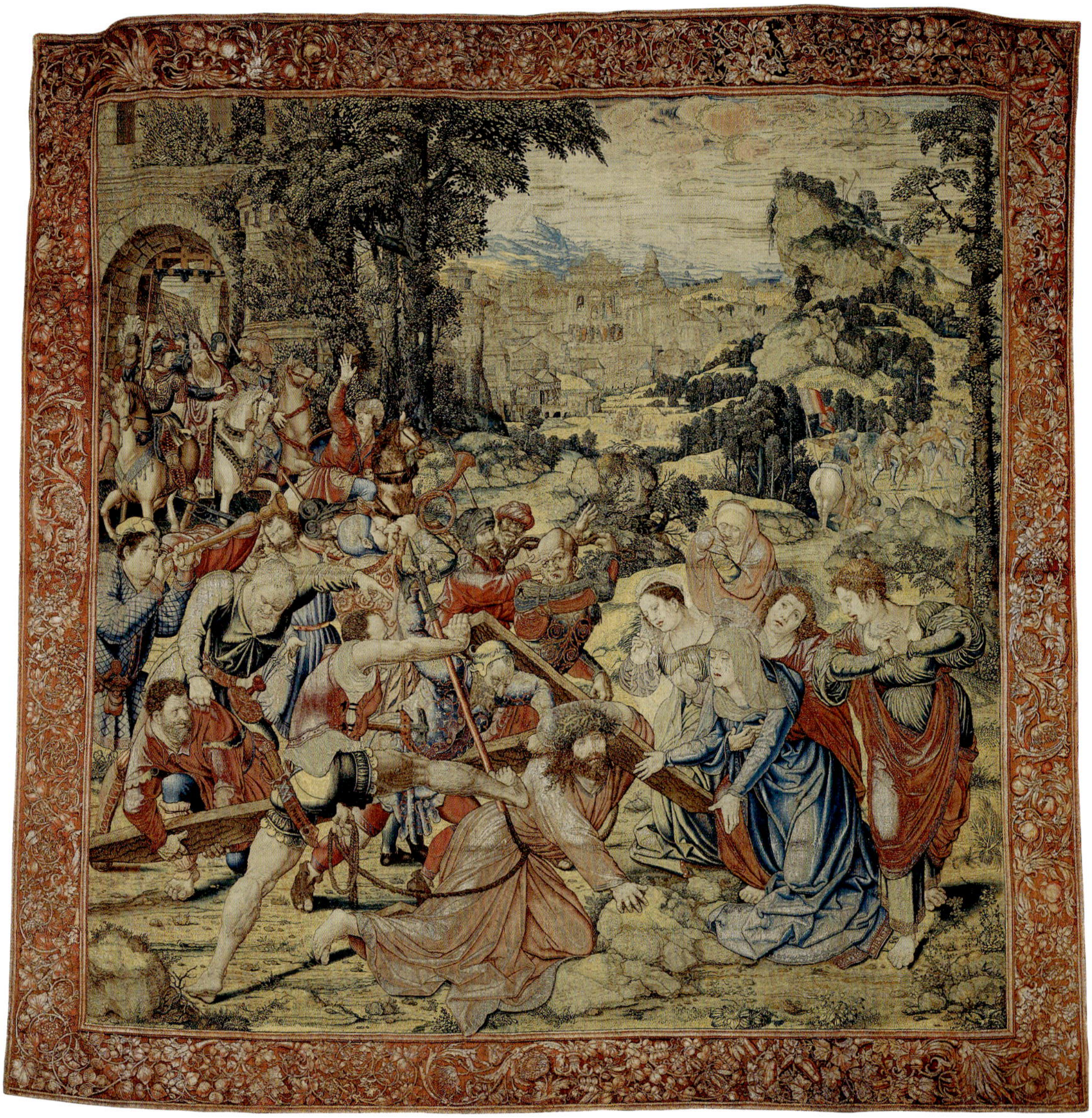

Passion set that was purchased during the early 1650s from the Commonwealth sale by the Spanish ambassador in London, Don Alonso de Cárdenas, on behalf of Don Luis Mendez de Haro, marqués del Carpio.[31] The most valuable sets that Cárdenas purchased at this time were Henry's *Acts of the Apostles* and the gold-ground *Verdure*, but he was also responsible for dispatching many others to Spain, including a four-piece set of the *Passion*. According to a list of goods in a shipment sent before August 1654, the set measured one hundred square ells, close enough to the dimensions of Henry VIII's "rich history of the passion" for us to assume that this was the set in question.[32]

The fate of the set sent to Spain is undocumented, but the key to its later provenance is provided by the subsequent history of Henry's *Acts of the Apostles* set. This was among a group of tapestries and paintings that de Haro left to the estate of the House of El Carpio in his will of 1658.[33] The Carpio dynasty subsequently merged with the House of Alba, with the consequence that the *Acts* set entered the Alba collection, where it remained until the early nineteenth century.[34] De Haro also left other tapestries and paintings to the House of El Carpio, of which the list is now lost, and among a large number of tapestries sold from the Alba collection in 1877 were three panels from a very high-quality *Passion* set, with the same dimensions and subjects as three panels in Henry's lost "riche historye"; respectively, *Christ in the Garden of Gethsemane* (fig. 10.14), *Christ*

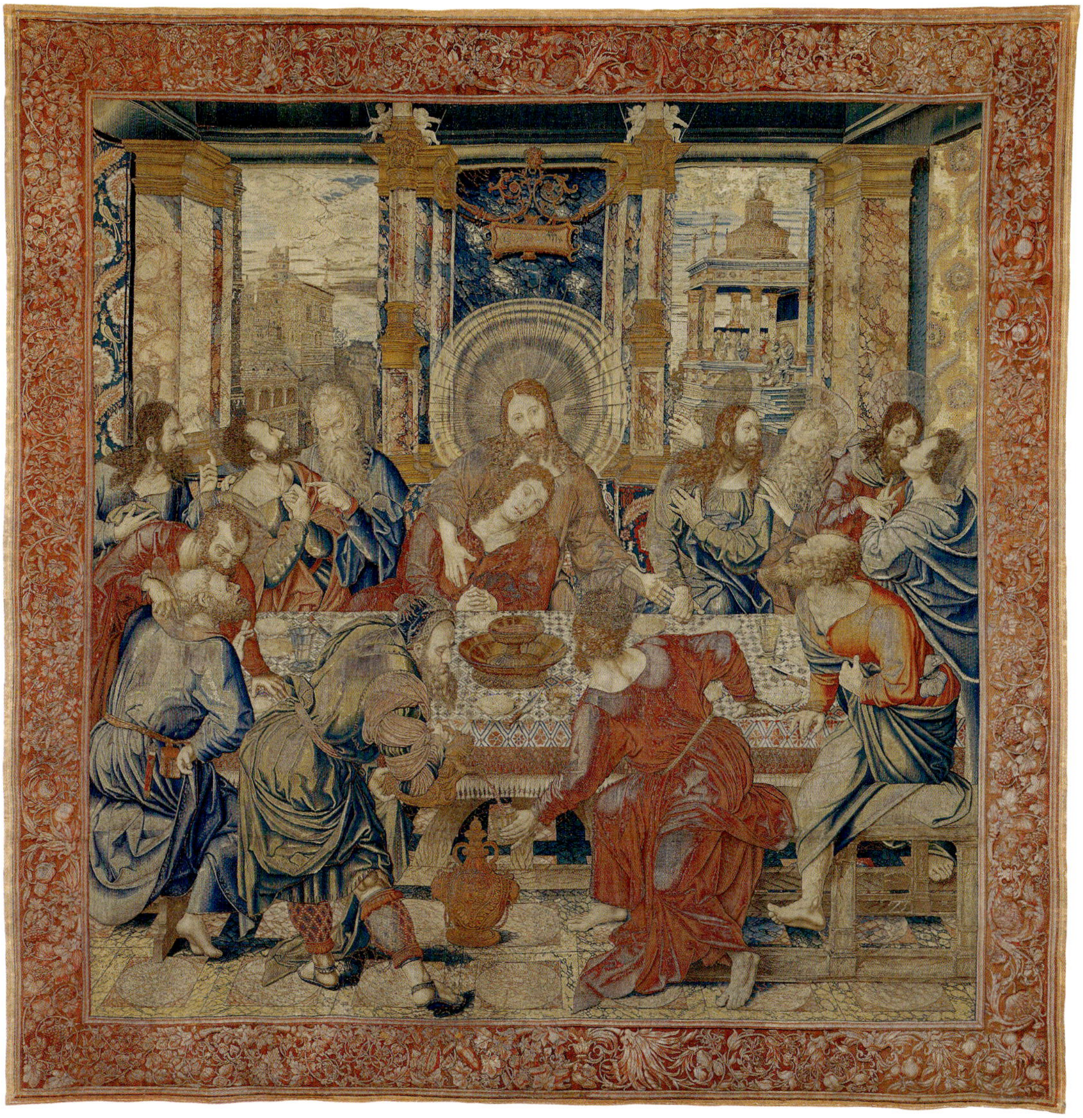

10.16 *The Last Supper* from a set of the *Passion* (known as the *Alba Passion*). Tapestry designed by Bernaert van Orley, probably woven in the workshop of Pieter de Pannemaker, Brussels, ca. 1525–28. Wool, silk, and gilt-metal-wrapped thread, 363 x 351 cm. The Metropolitan Museum of Art, New York

Carrying the Cross (fig. 10.15), and *The Crucifixion* (fig. 10.17, see also fig. 1.9).[35] A fourth piece, evidently from the same set and depicting the *Last Supper* with a scene of Christ washing the disciples' feet in the background, appeared earlier this century in the Lehman Collection (fig. 10.16).[36] Given the high quality of the weaving and the correlation of dimensions and subjects, there is therefore a strong possibility that the Alba ensemble originated from Henry VIII's collection, via Cárdenas and the House of El Carpio.[37] This is significant in the context of Henry VIII's patronage, because the Alba set is a seminal work in the development of the Flemish "Romanist" style. Indeed, it is arguably the design series in which Van Orley's new design style reached maturity.

The genesis of the four designs can be reconstructed with some precision. The Alba set is a partial re-edition of a group of tapestries designed by Van Orley for Margaret of Austria between 1518 and 1523, now in the Spanish royal collection.[38] This earlier set included a *Crucifixion* and a *Deposition* (see figs. 6.19, 6.20) that had been woven before September 1520 and were conceived in the "pre-Renaissance" style. At this time, Margaret contracted with the merchant Pieter de Pannemaker to weave two more panels representing *Christ in the Garden of Gethsemane* and *Christ Carrying the Cross*. These additions combined a new dramatic spirit, stimulated by the Raphael cartoons, with the marked influence of Albrecht Dürer, who had traveled in 1520 to Brussels, where he exchanged

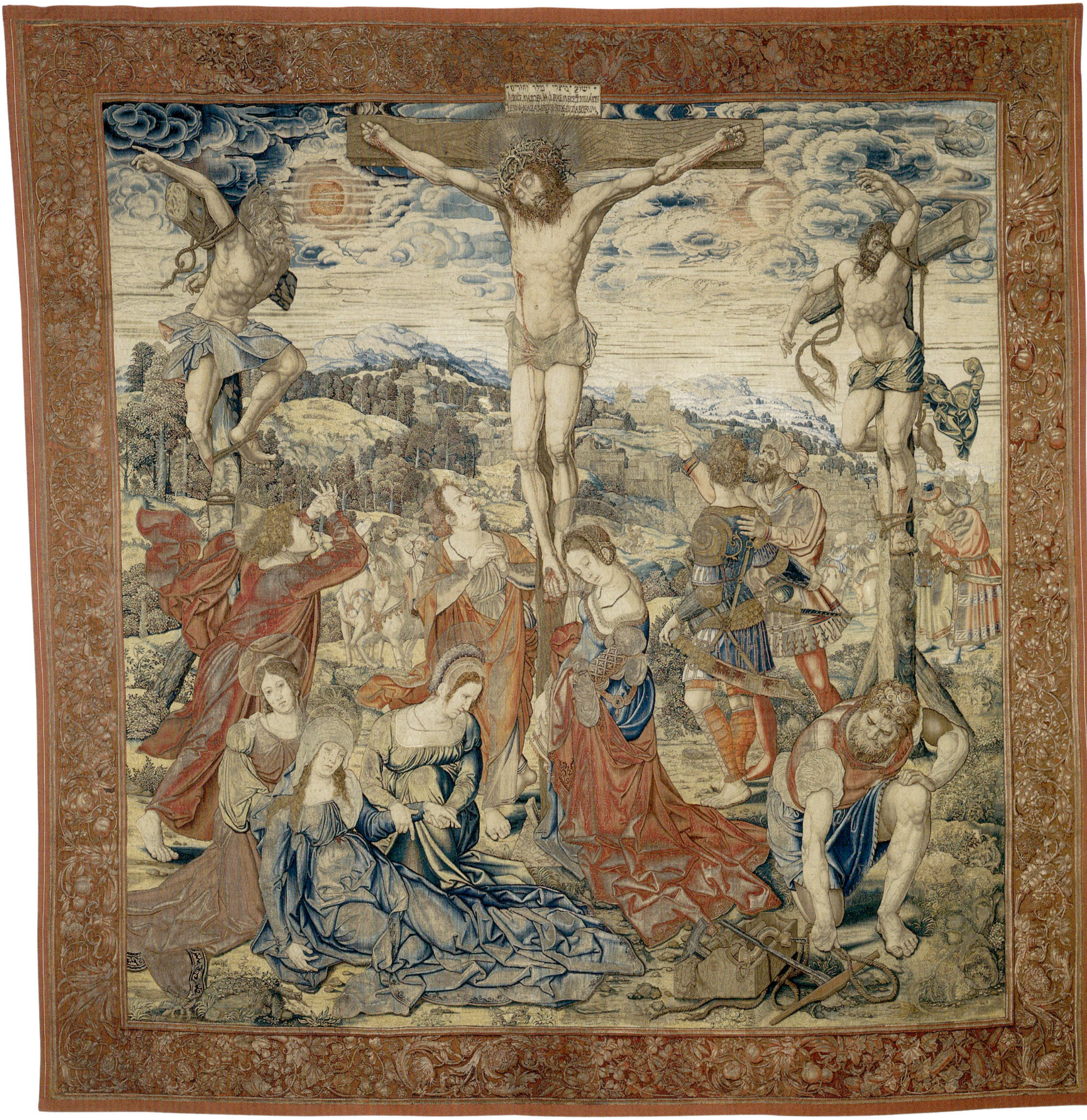

10.17 *The Crucifixion* from a set of the *Passion* (known as the *Alba Passion*). Tapestry designed by Bernaert van Orley, probably woven in the workshop of Pieter de Pannemaker, Brussels, ca. 1525–28. Wool, silk, and gilt-metal-wrapped thread, 364 x 354 cm. National Gallery of Art, Washington

works of art with Van Orley. The additional panels were complete by 1523, when all four pieces were listed in an inventory of Margaret's tapestries.

The success of the new designs appear to have stimulated Van Orley to further innovation, for although the Alba set includes duplicate weavings of the *Christ in the Garden of Gethsemane* and *Christ Carrying the Cross,* first woven for Margaret of Austria between 1520 and 1523, it includes two new scenes in place of the earlier *Crucifixion* and *Deposition:* a new *Crucifixion,* for which a preparatory drawing by Van Orley survives in Stuttgart, and a *Last Supper,* with a subsidiary scene of Christ washing the disciples' feet in the background. The influence of the Raphael school cartoons is even more pronounced in these later designs, which represent dramatic tableaux, enacted by solid life-size figures, in carefully realized perspectival settings. There is also a marked interest in illusionistic effects, particularly in the *Last Supper* design. Indeed, the tapestry is a tour de force of trompe-l'oeil weaving. Pannemaker also supplied a weaving of the *Last Supper* to the Spanish crown, but since he was not paid for that piece until 1531, it is probable that the piece in the Alba set was the first weaving of this striking design.[39] Although it seems unlikely that Henry would have been aware of the complex artistic process underlying the development of this series, the style must have been notably vivid and realistic in comparison to other *Passion* sets in the collection. Given the cost and quality of the set, we can conjecture that it must have been before these images of Christ's suffering that Henry would have celebrated Mass on a number of significant occasions during the following years of his reign. It is also of note that Henry maintained the tradition of washing the feet of the poor on Maundy Thursday, so the *Last Supper* tapestry with its subsidiary scene of the Christ washing the feet of the disciples may have served a particular purpose on these occasions.

The Story of Romulus and Remus

The second "progressive" design that can be firmly documented to this period is a four-piece set of the *Story of Romulus and Remus* that Henry purchased from Richard Gresham in July 1529.[40] In this case, the commission seems to have arisen from a more considered initiative by the king or his advisers. The set

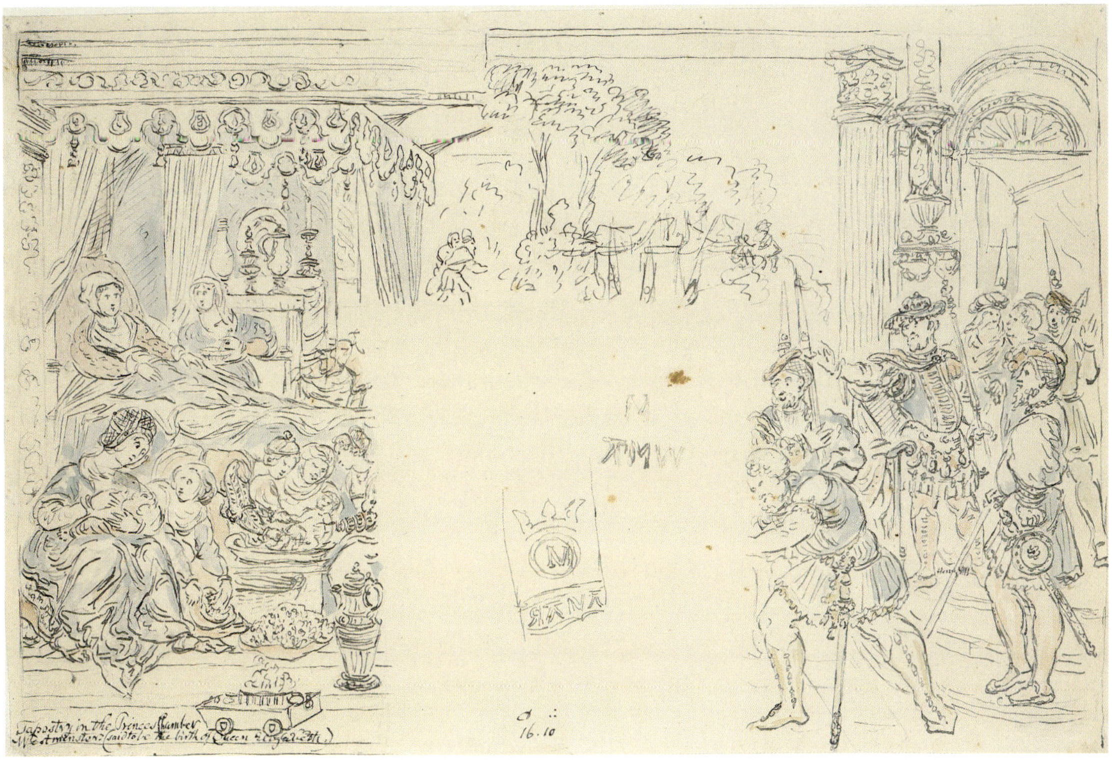

10.18 Drawing by John Carter (1748–1817) of a 16th-c. tapestry of the *Birth of Romulus and Remus and Their Abduction by Amulius* when it hung in the Prince's Chamber, Westminster Palace, ca. 1800. Pen and ink and watercolor on paper, 32.3 x 47.6 cm. Victoria and Albert Museum, London

10.19 *The Abduction of Romulus and Remus by Amulius* (fragment) from a set of the *Story of Romulus and Remus*. Tapestry woven in Brussels, ca. 1527–29. Wool and silk, 333 x 379 cm. Private Collection, London

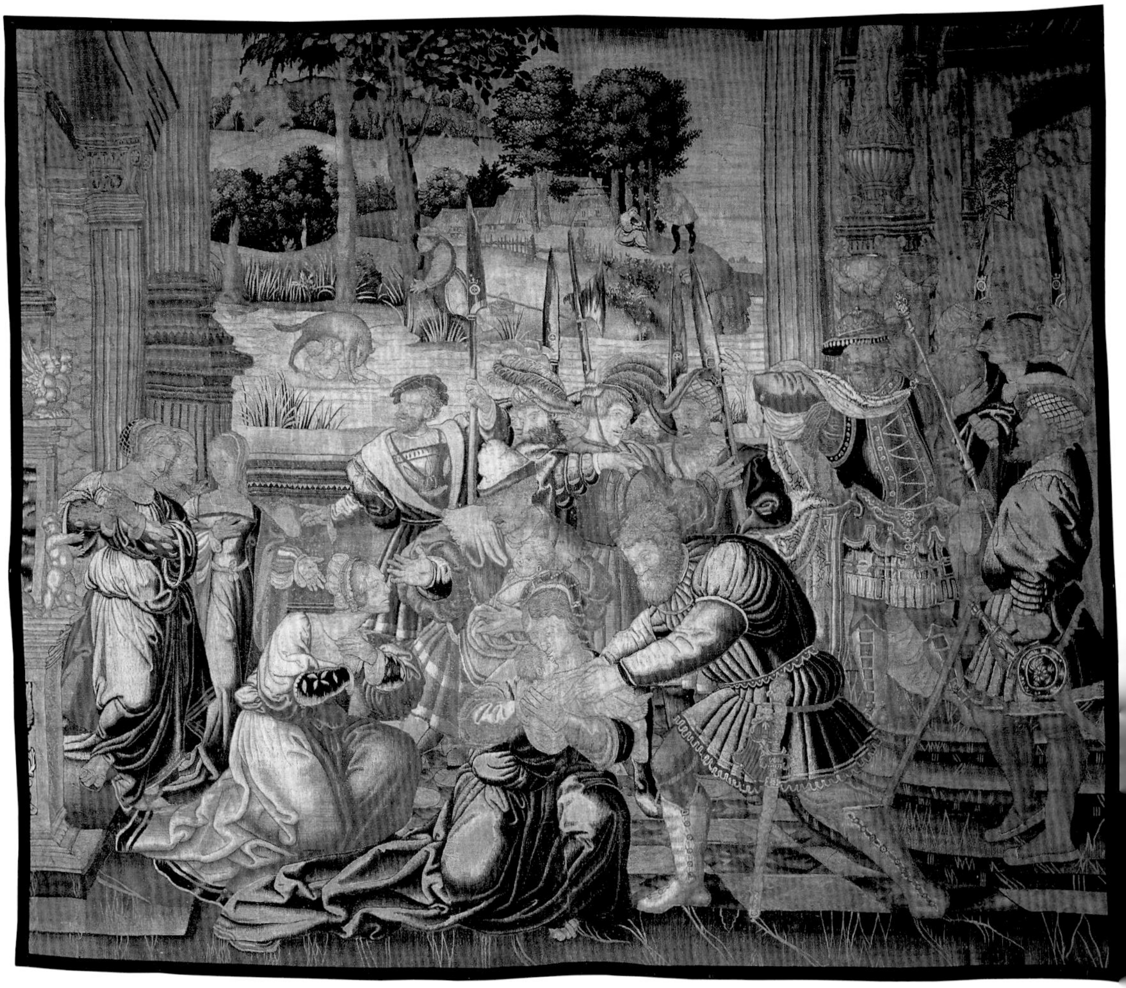

measured 260¾ ells (146½ square yards) and cost £130 7s. 6d., which indicates that it was woven in wool and silk but not gilt-metal-wrapped thread.[41] On the basis of these dimensions, the set can be identified with one that is recorded at Greenwich in the 1547 inventory.[42] It continued to be listed at this location in subsequent royal inventories until the late eighteenth century, at which time it was hanging in the Prince's Chamber at the old palace of Westminster. Before destruction of that chamber and sale of the tapestries, the set was recorded in words and drawings by Richard Carter the antiquary.[43] Although with the exception of a single fragment the tapestries are lost, the drawings, now in the Victoria and Albert Museum, and the extant fragment provide enough information for the subjects of three of the tapestries to be identified as, respectively, the *Birth of Romulus and Remus and Their Abduction by Amulius* (figs. 10.18, 10.19), *Romulus Killing Amulius* (fig. 10.20), and the *Triumphal Return of Numitor to Alba Longa*.

The drawings and fragment also provide enough evidence for it to be clear that the design must have been conceived either by Bernaert van Orley or, more probably, by someone in his circle. Van Orley had certainly created a set of modelli for a *Romulus and Remus* series in 1524, of which four survive today in Munich.[44] These reflect Van Orley's first attempts to assimilate the compositional formula of Raphael's *Acts of the Apostles* to the Flemish multiple-narrative design tradition, depicting volumetric but rather ungainly figures in carefully composed perspectival settings, with subsidiary scenes in the background. Whether these modelli were ever developed into full-scale designs is uncertain. None of the subjects coincide with those of the three tapestries in Henry's set whose designs are known. It is also to be noted that

10.20 Drawing by John Carter (1748–1817) of a 16th-c. tapestry of *Romulus Killing Amulius* as it hung in the Prince's Chamber, Westminster Palace, ca. 1800. Pen and ink and watercolor on paper, 33 x 49.5 cm. Victoria and Albert Museum, London

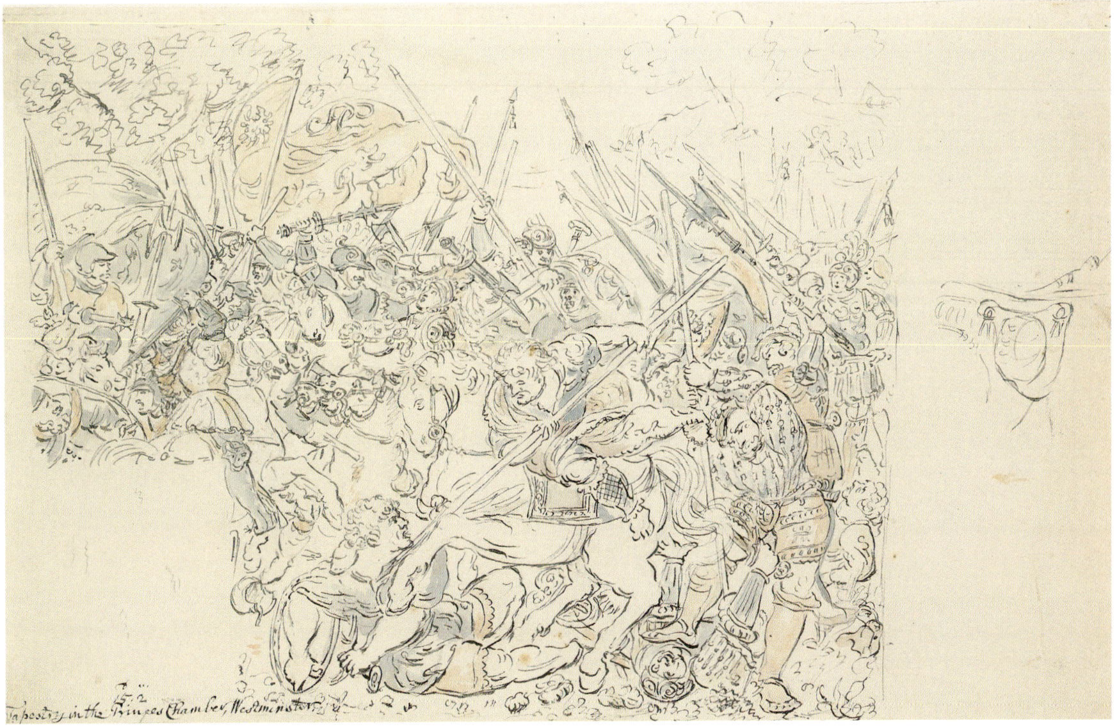

the figures in Henry's set appear to have been designed with greater grace and fluidity of movement than those in Van Orley's modelli. Equally, the style of the figures in Henry's *Romulus* set is so close to those of other designs conceived by Van Orley in the late 1520s, particularly those in the *Battle of Pavia* series, as to suggest a close link between the Romulus master and Van Orley. One possibility is that the cartoons were created by Pieter Coecke van Aelst, a pupil of Van Orley, who is known to have traveled to Rome in the mid-1520s, before establishing himself as a master in Antwerp in 1527. Supportive evidence for this attribution comes from the fact that Coecke's name is inscribed on one of a group of modelli for a *Story of David* set of ca. 1530 (see fig. 11.12) that shares many stylistic traits with Henry's *Romulus* set.[45] The drawing of some of the figures and architectural elements is so close as to suggest that both series were designed by the same artist (see below for further discussion of the *David* series, of which Henry may also have purchased a set before 1531). Attribution of the *Romulus* series to Coecke's Antwerp workshop would also help explain another stylistic feature of the designs. Embodying the pictorial drama, robust figures, and perspectival settings that Van Orley and his circle were then introducing to Netherlandish tapestry, the *Romulus* set also incorporated a number of direct quotations from Italian High Renaissance painting. Most notably, the central horseman in *Romulus Killing Amulius* is based on that of the angelic rider and Heliodorus from Raphael's fresco of the *Expulsion of Heliodorus* painted in the Vatican Stanze in 1512–14.[46] Van Orley and his circle may have encountered these motifs through drawings that Tommaso Vincidor brought with him to Brussels, whether in 1520 or on a subsequent trip, but Coecke's trip to Rome would have given him ample opportunity to study Raphael's frescoes in the original.

Although the attribution of Henry's *Romulus and Remus* set remains a matter of conjecture, the 1529 purchase provides unequivocal evidence of the presence of the most up-to-date style of Netherlandish design, rather than the Italianate style that had inspired this development, at the English court by the late 1520s. In this context it is interesting to note that during the late 1520s or early 1530s Charles V also acquired a set depicting *Romulus and Remus,* which survives today in the Spanish royal collection.[47]

Charles's series contrasts markedly in content to that of Henry, because where Henry's set was essentially a dramatic narrative, featuring key events in the lives of Romulus and Remus, the Habsburg set relegates many of the dramatic incidents to subsidiary scenes in the background, dwelling instead on events that epitomized the heroes' intellectual virtues. The Habsburg set has often been linked to the Van Orley drawings of 1524, with the assumption that the extant tapestries were a further development from that initial stage of design. However, in light of evidence that Henry's set was much closer in character to that of the Van Orley drawings, it seems more likely that the Habsburg set was actually developed some years later, in the early 1530s, possibly by an entirely different artist.

The fact that Henry's *Romulus and Remus* set was purchased from Gresham and that the design may have been supplied by the workshop that Pieter Coecke had recently established in Antwerp raises the question whether it was commissioned or purchased from stock. As founders of Rome and descendants of Aeneas, Romulus and Remus were attractive role models and significant "ancestors" for any Renaissance prince. From early in his reign Henry had nurtured a sense that England was an empire in its own right. An imperial crown had appeared as a decorative motif on his pavilion at the Accession Day tournament in 1511, and in 1513 and 1514 he named two ships the *Henry Imperial* and the *Mary Imperial*. His interest in the concept of imperium can only have been fueled by Maximilian I, who in 1513 offered to resign to him the title of Holy Roman Emperor, a suggestion developed in 1517 when Maximilian offered to adopt Henry to ensure his succession. Henry's belated entry into the imperial election in 1519 was a costly failure, but his lack of success in that contest did not dampen his aspirations to native imperium. In 1521 he referred to his "crown imperial" as derived from the papacy, but in 1525 he ordered a great seal that showed him sitting in majesty with a domed imperial crown, the image that was eventually adopted in the new seal of 1532.[48] Henry's own imperial crown was the first item listed in the 1521 and 1532 jewel house inventories, implying that it was the most valuable and important item. Similarly, it was also the first item listed in the 1547 inventory.[49] It therefore seems plausible to suggest that the subject of the *Romulus and Remus* set purchased in 1529 may have appealed to him because the founders of Rome provided a suitably flattering imperial role model. The comparison with Rome's builders may also have had an additional personal appeal as, by this date, Henry was lavishing large sums of money on his palaces and fortifications. Although this evidence of Henry's interest in the subject falls short of indicating that the *Romulus and Remus* design was conceived at his behest, the fact that it was probably the first weaving of this design and that the design may have been produced by the new Antwerp workshop of Pieter Coecke allows us to entertain this as a possibility. In later years he certainly acquired many designs from the workshop of Pieter Coecke via London merchants who had close links with the English court and the Antwerp community.

PART IV

The Reformation

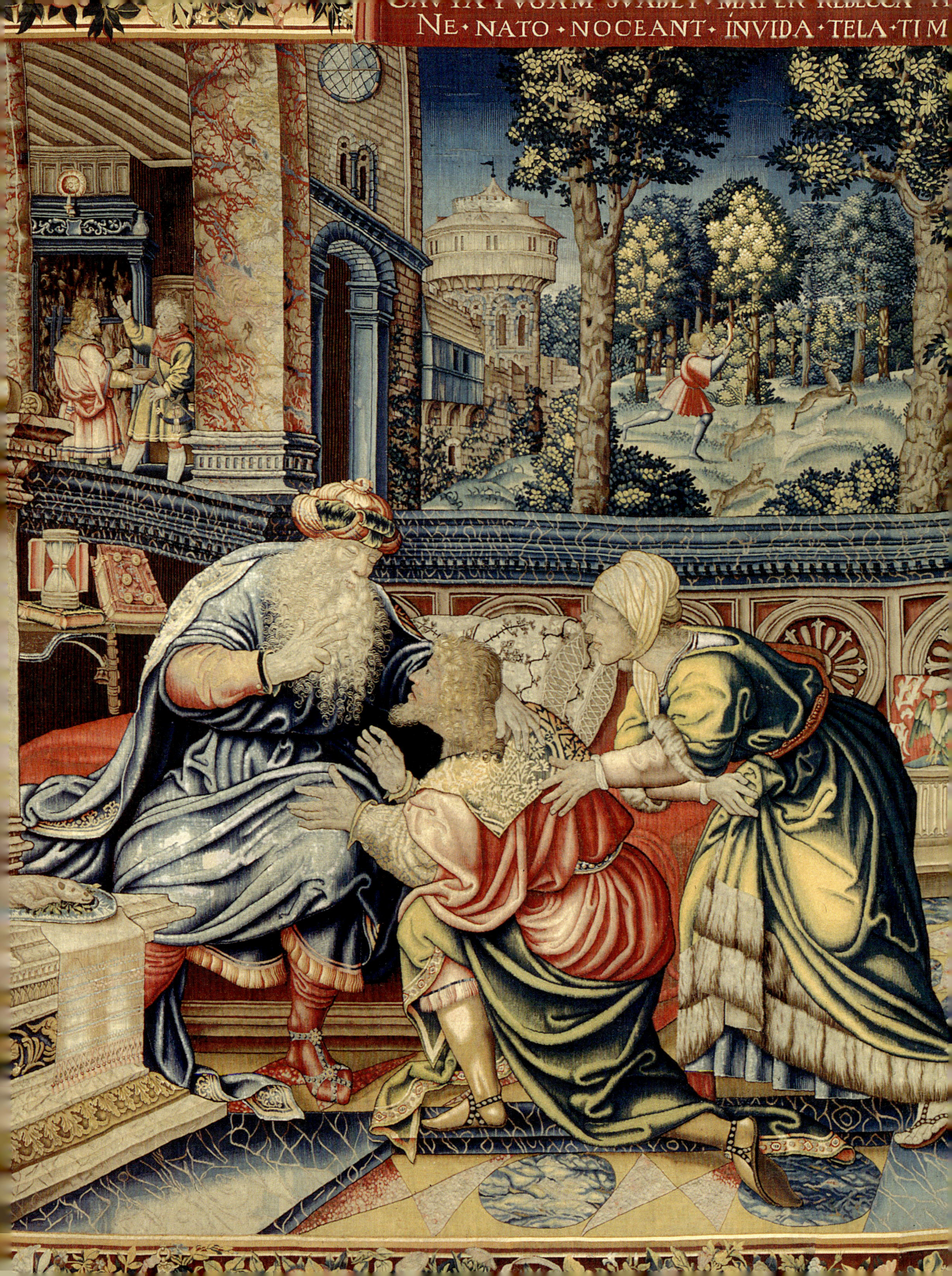
NE · NATO · NOCEANT · ÍNVIDA · TELA · TIM

CHAPTER 11

The Royal Divorce and the Break with Rome

Henry's desire to divorce Katherine of Aragon was, of course, the goal that precipitated the tumultuous events of the break with Rome and the English Reformation. A God-fearing and devout man, Henry's relationship with the papacy had been strong during the 1510s as he joined in various leagues against France. In 1518 he had drafted a response to Martin Luther's recent proclamation, part of which he revised into the *Assertio septem sacramentorum adversus Martinum Lutherum* (Assertion of the Seven Sacraments against Martin Luther), which was published in 1521 and in reward for which Pope Leo X granted him the title Defender of the Faith in October of that year. Even six years later, it should have been a straightforward matter for the new pope, Clement VII, to grant the necessary papal dispensation for Henry to divorce Katherine. But the sack of Rome by Habsburg forces in May 1527 had drastically changed the situation. Clement was now, in effect, the prisoner of Charles V, Katherine's nephew, and Charles was vehemently against divorce. Faced with Henry's demands, Clement procrastinated, eventually dispatching Cardinal Campeggio to London to adjudicate, with Wolsey, whether Henry's marriage to Katherine had ever been valid.

The trial was held at Blackfriars in June 1529. The great hall was furnished for the occasion with tapestry, carpets, and chairs for Wolsey and Campeggio that were covered with cloth of gold. A cloth of estate and chair and cushions of "riche Tyssue" were provided for the king.[1] Given the extraordinary nature of the proceedings, it would be fascinating to know the subjects of the tapestries displayed, but as is so often the case, the records are silent, merely recording the costs involved in the physical labor of installing them. The *Story of David* set purchased in 1528 is certainly a likely candidate.

The collapse of that trial in late July 1529 and the recall of Campeggio to Rome led in turn to Henry's repudiation of papal jurisdiction over the Church of England and opened the door to the influence of religious reformers around Henry. Although Henry himself remained a religious conservative, the succession of religious reforms that he was to introduce during the 1530s laid the foundation for the development of English Protestantism over the following decade. As the main tool of visual suggestion at the Tudor court during these years, tapestry was to play an ever greater part in projecting the religious role models that were important to Henry. A further byproduct of the civic and institutional turmoil of the 1530s and 1540s was that appropriations from attainted courtiers and dissolved religious institutions yielded large numbers of tapestries to the Crown. From a stylistic point of view, these acquisitions, particularly the finer tapestries purchased by the king himself, reflected the continuing evolution of Flemish tapestry design during the 1530s and 1540s. These themes form the subject of the following chapter.

The Surrender of Wolsey's Properties and Collection to the Crown

The close relationship that Wolsey had enjoyed with the king for nearly twenty years had been

Detail of fig. 11.13

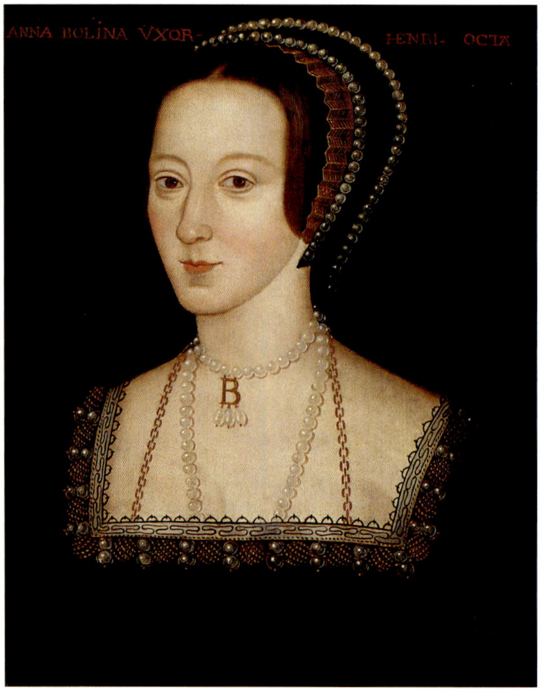

11.1 *Anne Boleyn* by an unidentified artist. Oil on panel, 54.3 x 41.6 cm. National Portrait Gallery, London

undermined by the ascendancy of Anne Boleyn (fig. 11.1) and her entourage during the two years leading up to Katherine's trial. Anne and her supporters had tolerated Wolsey so long as he was useful in respect to the divorce, but his failure to obtain a favorable verdict during those proceedings undermined any standing that he retained with the king. His cause was further weakened by the fact that he was the senior representative of the papal court in England and as such the most obvious target for Henry's frustration with the pope.[2] The ensuing appropriation of Wolsey's properties and collections by the Crown was the largest and most significant of the many that took place during Henry's reign. In total, it added more than six hundred tapestries to the royal collection along with scores of other precious fabrics and furnishings. The process by which the collections were handed over can be reconstructed from contemporary accounts and documents. On October 22, 1529, Wolsey made a formal surrender of his goods to the Crown, and following his indictment for praemunire and the surrender of the Great Seal, he was ordered to leave Hampton Court for his house at Esher. Before his departure he directed that an inventory of his goods be taken (the inventory has not survived). George Cavendish, Wolsey's gentleman usher, describes how Wolsey's most expensive cloths and textiles were hung up for measurement and identification in one of the galleries.[3] During Wolsey's subsequent house arrest at Esher his residence remained unadorned until a cartload of plate, hangings, and other items of furniture were sent to him by the king's order in February 1530.[4] No precise details of the content of this delivery have survived, although the value of the furnishings was put at £3,000. Cavendish noted that the stuffs were not of the finest quality but blamed this on those commissioned to enact the delivery rather than on the king.[5]

The furnishings delivered to Esher presumably formed the bulk of those that accompanied Wolsey to his subsequent exile at Cawood Castle, the residence of the archbishopric of York. Yet Wolsey's hunger for material opulence expressed itself one last time before his departure from London, when he sought to supplement the Esher delivery. Hall records that in advance of his journey, "he made great provision to go Northwarde and appareled his servants newly and bought many costely thinges for his househould."[6] Relatively speaking, however, the tapestry acquisitions cannot have been that grandiose. One of the creditors listed in Wolsey's outstanding debts after his death was Sir John Alen, alderman of London, who was owed £83 12s. for "arras" "sold to my lord at his departure northwards,"[7] and two of the sets listed at Cawood after Wolsey's death were described as new: one of the *Prodigal Son* and the other of *Wilderness*.[8] Given the intention underlying Wolsey's acquisition of religious subjects during the late 1510s and early 1520s, we can conjecture that the *Prodigal Son* set may have been chosen to signal Wolsey's hope that he would also be forgiven and welcomed back to his father's home, in this case, Henry VIII's court.

Few sources chart the decline in Wolsey's fortunes more graphically than the contrast between the inventory taken at the height of his power in the early 1520s and that taken at Cawood Castle after his death.[9] In total, eighty-one tapestries from seventeen sets are listed at Cawood, but they were a motley collection. None of the high-quality pieces from the earlier inventory is mentioned, nor any of those with Wolsey's arms attached, and although about half the tapestries were described as "counterfeit arras," it appears that most were of limited display value. For example, a set of "Certayn storres called Rolles" had been acquired by Wolsey at second hand from John Young, former master of the rolls, and was made up of pieces from different sets, while the "hangyngs of the chappell" were described as "olde and brokyn," as was one of the hunting and one of the verdure sets. Several can be recognized from the 1522 inventory, and without exception they correspond to pieces itemized in the old or worn categories of that listing.[10] It therefore seems that when the cartload of furnishings was sent to Esher, the materials dispatched were taken from one of the standing wardrobes at Hampton Court, which implies that a conscious decision to send only older material had been made by those responsible for the delivery. Considering the extent to which tapestry had been a central component of Wolsey's magnificence, the low caliber of the delivery must have been intended to demonstrate his public humiliation. With Wolsey's death on November 29, 1530, those furnishings and tapestries that remained in his possession were also absorbed into the royal collection. Although the presence of Wolsey's tapestries in the royal palaces during the following years may have given grim satisfaction to some members of the court, their presence would also have provided a constant reminder of the summary power of the monarch and of the roll of Fortune's wheel.

Royal Tapestry Purchases during Henry's Engagement to Anne Boleyn

We know that Henry continued to purchase tapestries throughout the years of the divorce proceedings and the run up to his marriage to Anne, thanks to a brief period in which records for the Treasurer of the Chamber survive (1528–30) and in which detailed accounts were also maintained for the Privy Purse (November 1529–December 1532).[11] As during previous years, acquisitions were evidently being made from a variety of merchants. Although this might be interpreted as evidence that such purchases were opportunistic, selected from pieces that these merchants had imported on a speculative basis, this is not certain. Several of the merchants enjoyed close links to the court and may thus have been responding to commissions or, at the least, a refined sense of what the king might like. One such figure who makes his first appearance during this period is William Lok (or Lock), who in May 1529 was paid £176 12s. for certain pieces of "arras with gold" and cloth of damask.[12] Lok was a successful merchant who had been supplying luxury fabrics both to the court and to such other rich courtiers as the duke of Buckingham since the 1510s. He received a license to import luxury fabrics and jewels for the king on March 7, 1527, and from 1529 was frequently on business in the Netherlands, from where he provided letters of intelligence to Thomas Cromwell, the brilliant lawyer on whose services Henry was increasingly to depend following Wolsey's disgrace and death. Lok shared Cromwell's reformist tendencies, and he subsequently supplied French editions of the Gospels, Epistles, and Psalms to Anne Boleyn, along with luxury goods.[13] Although some of the objects that Lok supplied to Henry may have been specifically ordered through him, he was evidently on the lookout for items that might appeal to the king. This opportunism is reflected by his subsequent purchase of plate from the estate of Cardinal Erard de la Marck because it was "so mete for your Grace and so stately that I cowd nott find it in my harte to suffer it to go to France."[14]

Other merchants who appear as suppliers of tapestry to Henry at this date are less well documented, such as "Roche and Naylinghurst," who were paid £38 5s. from the Privy Purse in July 1530 for 58½ ells (thirty-three square yards) of tapestry.[15]

In all likelihood, several of the acquisitions made between 1529 and 1532 were specifically

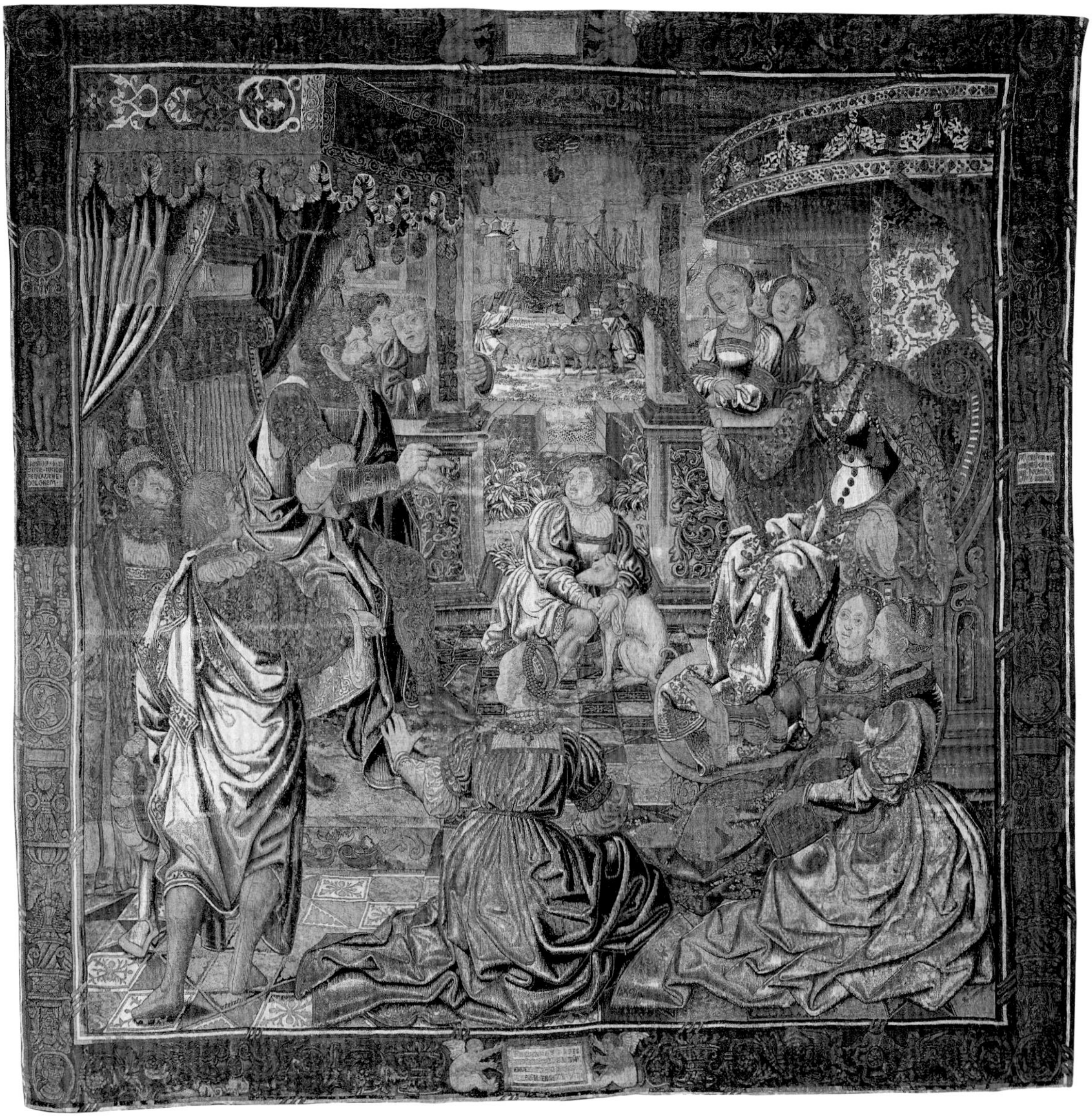

11.2 *Aeneas Relating His Adventures to Dido* from a set of the *Story of Aeneas*. Tapestry woven in Brussels, ca. 1530. Wool, silk, and gilt-metal-wrapped thread, 345 x 330 cm. Hampton Court Palace

for Anne, who from late 1529 was being treated almost as if she was queen already. The Privy Purse expenses reflect the very large sums that Henry spent on jewelry and precious textiles for her during these years, so it seems likely that tapestry would have been among the gifts, although only one such transaction can be documented with certainty. This was in May 1532, when Thomas Assheley, "servant to my lade Anne Rocheford (i.e., Anne Boleyn)," was reimbursed £74 13s. 4d. for thirty-two ells (eighteen square yards) of "golde Aras" at 45s. 8d. per ell, which he had purchased for the "use of Willm Reding."[16] A few months later in August 1532, a payment of £70 was made to a French merchant, Antony Desseforte, for unspecified hangings.[17] Given Anne's close links to the French court, this payment to a French merchant is interesting, but we lack any evidence that might allow us to ascertain whether the tapestries in question had been ordered for Anne.

At least some of the expensive purchases during this period were probably motivated by Henry and Anne's needs at York Place. Henry took this palace from Wolsey in 1529, and thereafter it became his main residence in central London, giving him convenient proximity to Parliament during the Reformation years. The palace was now generally known as Whitehall Palace, in reference to the coloration of one of the buildings built for Wolsey, but in 1536 an Act of Parliament stipulated that the sprawling complex was to be known officially

11.3 *Aeneas Meeting His Mother Venus* from a set of the *Story of Aeneas*. Tapestry woven in Brussels, ca. 1530. Wool, silk, and gilt-metal-wrapped thread, 345 x 264 cm. Hampton Court Palace

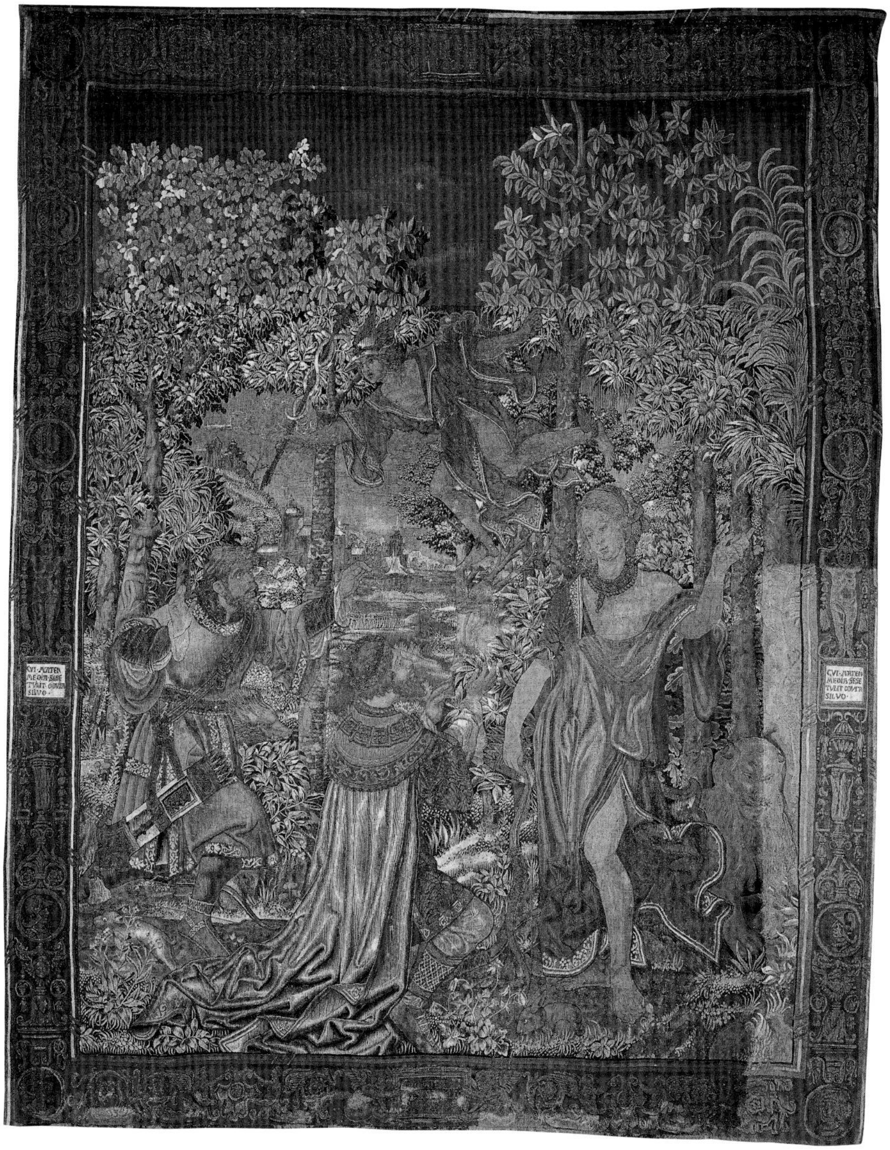

as Westminster Palace, and this is how it is generally named in court documents thereafter, including the 1542 and 1547 palace inventories.[18] Nonetheless, it continued to be called Whitehall in common parlance until much of the complex was destroyed by fire in 1691 and 1698, and it is identified as such here, in accordance with modern practice and to distinguish it from the old palace of Westminster. Thomas Alvard was appointed keeper at the palace in 1530, and during the following year he spent £2,759 13s. 9d. on wardrobe stuff, including beds, pillows, sheets, cushions, cloth of gold, and other luxury textiles.[19] At least part of this provisioning related to new apartments created for Anne Boleyn.

The Story of Aeneas

One purchase that was almost certainly destined for one of the king's private apartments at Whitehall was made in 1533. In May of this year, a warrant was issued to the customers of London requesting them to waive duty on three gold rings set with diamonds and five pieces of "arras" containing fifty-six ells (31½ square yards) that the king had purchased from John Langraunt (sic), his jeweler, of which he had given him the custom and subsidy.[20] Based on the tapestries listed at Whitehall by the 1547 inventory, this ensemble is probably to be identified with a set of five pieces of "fine arras with antique borders."[21] Although the subject was not specified in the inventory, the

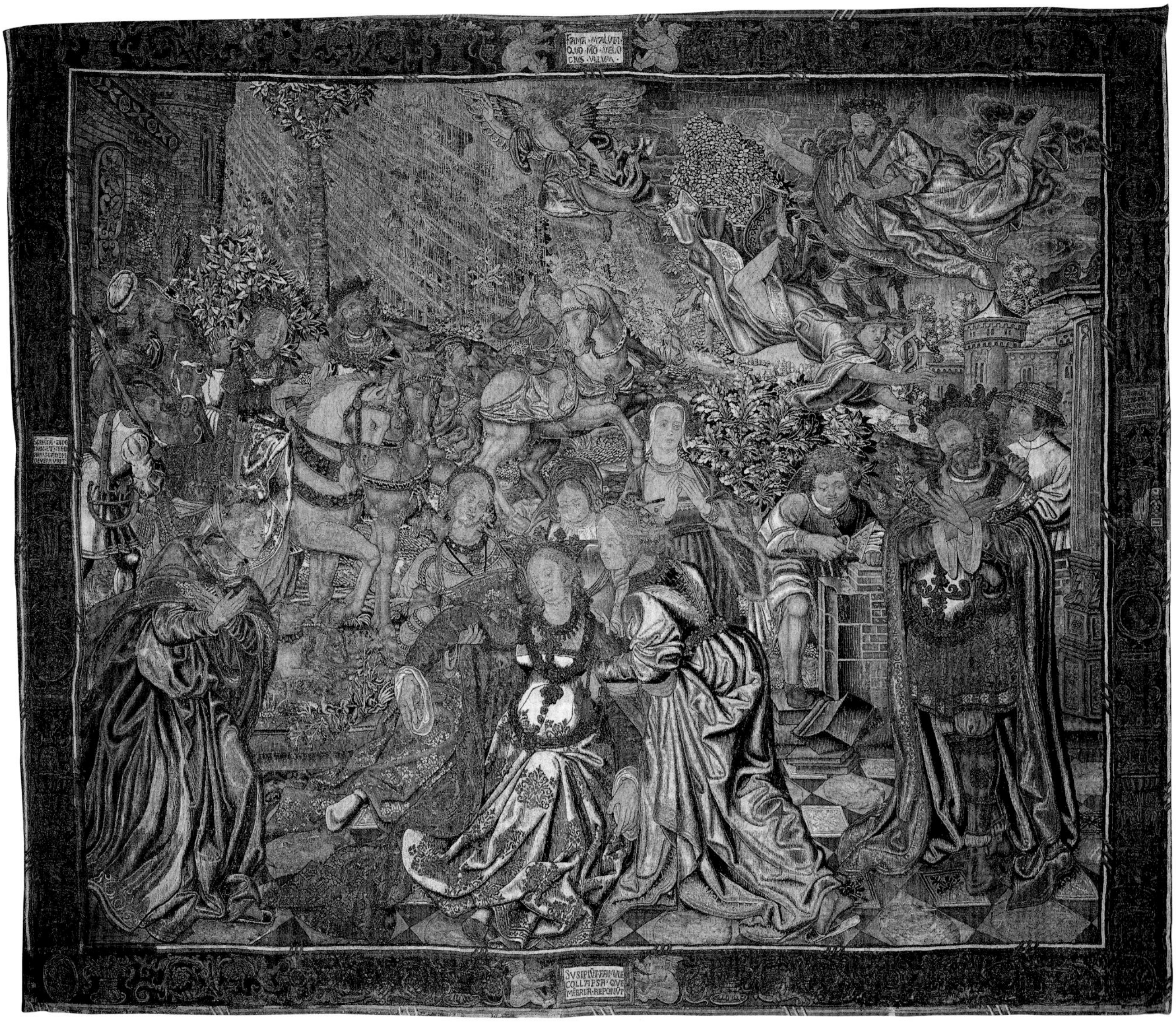

11.4 *Aeneas Departing from Carthage* from a set of the *Story of Aeneas.* Tapestry woven in Brussels, ca. 1530. Wool, silk, and gilt-metal-wrapped thread, 345 x 394 cm. Hampton Court Palace

dimensions of this five-piece set are of a similar order to those of five pieces of the *Story of Aeneas* that remained at Whitehall until the late seventeenth century and are today at Hampton Court (figs. 11.2–11.4). The borders of this set feature a stylized decoration of the kind now generally described as "grotesques" but known as "antiques" in England in the second third of the sixteenth century, hence the description of the set provided by the 1547 inventory. The problem with this identification is that the *Aeneas* set as it survives has a surface area almost twice that listed in the customs discharge to Longraunt. While this might be explained by a variety of arguments—some of the tapestries may have been delivered at a different time—it places a question mark over the relationship of the Longraunt delivery and the surviving *Aeneas* tapestries. Nonetheless, the style of the *Aeneas* tapestries and their long-standing association with Whitehall certainly suggest that they were acquired for this location in the early 1530s.

The first three tapestries of the set depict, respectively, the dispersal by storm of Aeneas's fleet, his arrival at Dido's court, and the lovers' courtship and romance. In the fourth panel, Venus appears to Aeneas to tell him that he must leave Dido and continue his journey, in fulfillment of his destiny to found a new empire. The final scene depicts the departure of Aeneas and the suicide of Dido. Stylistically, the tapestries appear to date from ca. 1530. Although the design continues to place considerable emphasis on decoration and pattern, it embodies the new interest in spatial perspective. The identity of the designer is unknown, but he was presumably a figure in the circle of Van Orley.[22] Although the faded colors of the tapestries now obscure the illusionistic impact of this set, it must have been notably innovative when it arrived at the English court.

The uniform heights of the surviving tapestries result from adaptation made to two pieces in 1703–4 by the royal arras maker John Vanderbank,[23] but the irregular dimensions of the original ensemble suggest that they were made for a specific small chamber. Given the high quality of the panels and the presence of gilt-metal-wrapped thread, we can speculate that this would have been one of the king's private closets. In this context, the choice of subject is intriguing; like the *Romulus and Remus* set purchased in 1529, it appears to have been among a number of classical subjects that Henry acquired during the second half of his reign for use in more private apartments. Whatever the immediate location for which the set was intended, the subject is significant in another respect. Aeneas was celebrated by medieval historians as the link between Troy and Rome and thus as the ancestor of the imperial line. For this reason, various European royal families claimed him as an ancestor during the medieval and Renaissance eras.[24] As we have seen in the context of the *Romulus and Remus* set purchased in 1529, Henry was keenly aware of his "imperial" status, and as we will see below, the notion of "imperium" attained great significance as the debate over the royal divorce developed. Aeneas's role as founder of an imperial line may thus have been one motivation for the acquisition of this set. It is also possible that the subject matter held an additional appeal for Henry. The tapestries dwell on Aeneas's relationship with Dido and, ultimately, the divine intervention that led him to forsake her, in accordance with his destiny. As we have seen, Henry had acquired an expensive set of *David* tapestries in 1528 because he felt an empathy between the story of God's punishment of David with the death of his first son and his belief that he, too, was suffering divine punishment for having married a woman who had been married to his elder brother, in contravention of religious law. By analogy, it is tempting to speculate that the *Story of Aeneas* may have appealed to him because it provided a classical demonstration of the fragility of human bonds in contrast to fate and divine law, and a support to the belief that if his union with Katherine was somehow illegitimate in the eyes of God, then he was destined to abandon her.

Francis I and the Meeting at Boulogne

If the *Aeneas* set was that delivered by Longraunt in May 1533 and if we assume that the design must have been conceived at least eighteen months before that time, we might posit a date of conception in late 1531. That being the case, the style of the set still reflects a somewhat conservative response to the influence of the Raphael school. But shortly thereafter, Henry and Anne were to receive much more direct exposure to Italianate design through the court of Francis I (fig. 11.5). Henry's susceptibility to French taste had been apparent for some years. During the late 1510s he and his minions emu-

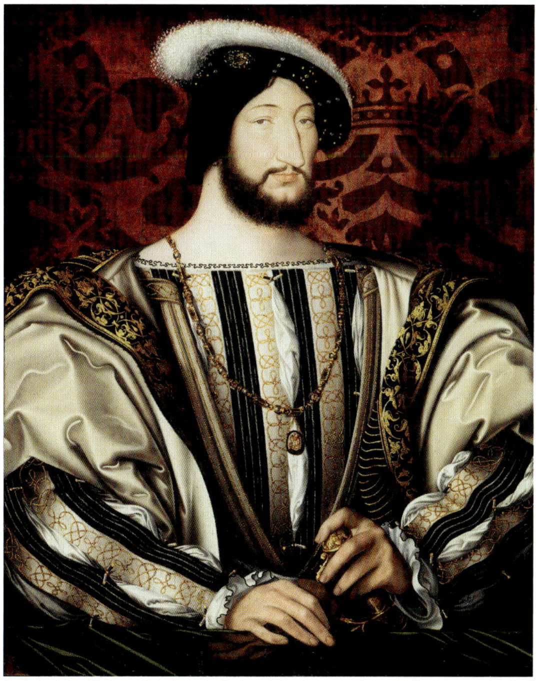

11.5 *Portrait of Francis I* by Jean Clouet. Oil on panel, 96 x 74 cm. Musée du Louvre, Paris

lated French fashion in coiffure and clothing, and the creation of the post of gentleman of the Privy Chamber in 1520 was a direct imitation of an equivalent French position.[25] With Anne at his side, Henry had a new and forceful advocate of Gallic manners.[26] This was potentially significant because during the late 1520s and early 1530s Francis was establishing himself as a tapestry patron to rival Henry and Charles V. Henry and Anne were confronted with the first results of this new trend in October 1532, when they traveled to Boulogne to meet with Francis to ensure his support for the royal divorce.

Francis's precocious interest in tapestry had been demonstrated by the acquisition of a woven version of Leonardo da Vinci's *Last Supper* sometime in the 1510s (fig. 11.6).[27] Further evidence of his use of the textile medium as one in which to acquire Italian designs is provided by the commission he made in 1521 for a rich set of embroidery hangings with imagery inspired by Virgil's *Bucolics* after designs by the Italian artists Barthélemy Guetty and Matteo del Nassaro. This featured ninety-two pastoral scenes and appropriate Virgilian quotations worked in gold and silver on a green velvet ground. The main panel of the set featured a *Charité romaine*.[28] Francis's campaigning activities in Italy during the early 1520s furthered his exposure to Italian influence. The defeat at Pavia and his subsequent imprisonment brought his territorial ambitions to an end, but following his return to France in 1527, he subsumed that passion into a voracious appetite for Italian art and artists, many of whom he encouraged to work for him in France. As the most magnificent figurative medium of the day, tapestry was a central component of this new investment, and during the late 1520s he made a number of expensive purchases.[29] Although none survive, documentary evidence shows the development of Francis's collection and of his taste. Initially his commissions continued to depend on available Flemish designs. For example, in 1528 he purchased sets of *Lot* and of *Constantine* and, in the following year, sets of *Jeroboam* and *Perseus*, all through the Antwerp merchant Georges Vezeleer. In 1529 he also acquired a tapestry of "Leda with certain scenes with satyrs and other characters from poetry" from the Paris merchants Nicolas and Pasquier de Mortaigne. But

11.6 *The Last Supper*. Tapestry design after Leonardo da Vinci, woven in the Southern Netherlands, probably Brussels, ca. 1514. Wool, silk, and gilt-metal-wrapped thread, 490 x 915 cm. Vatican Museums, Vatican City

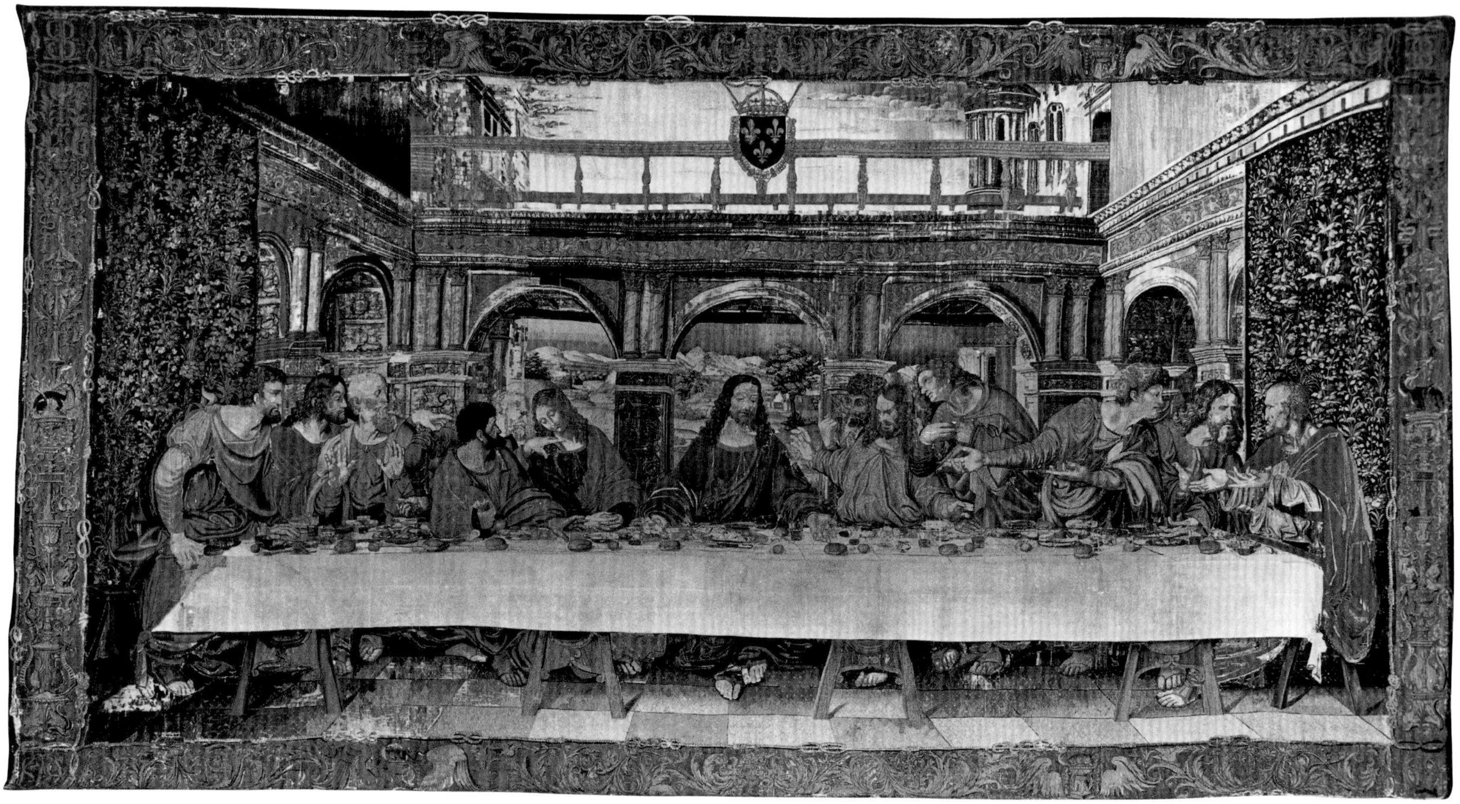

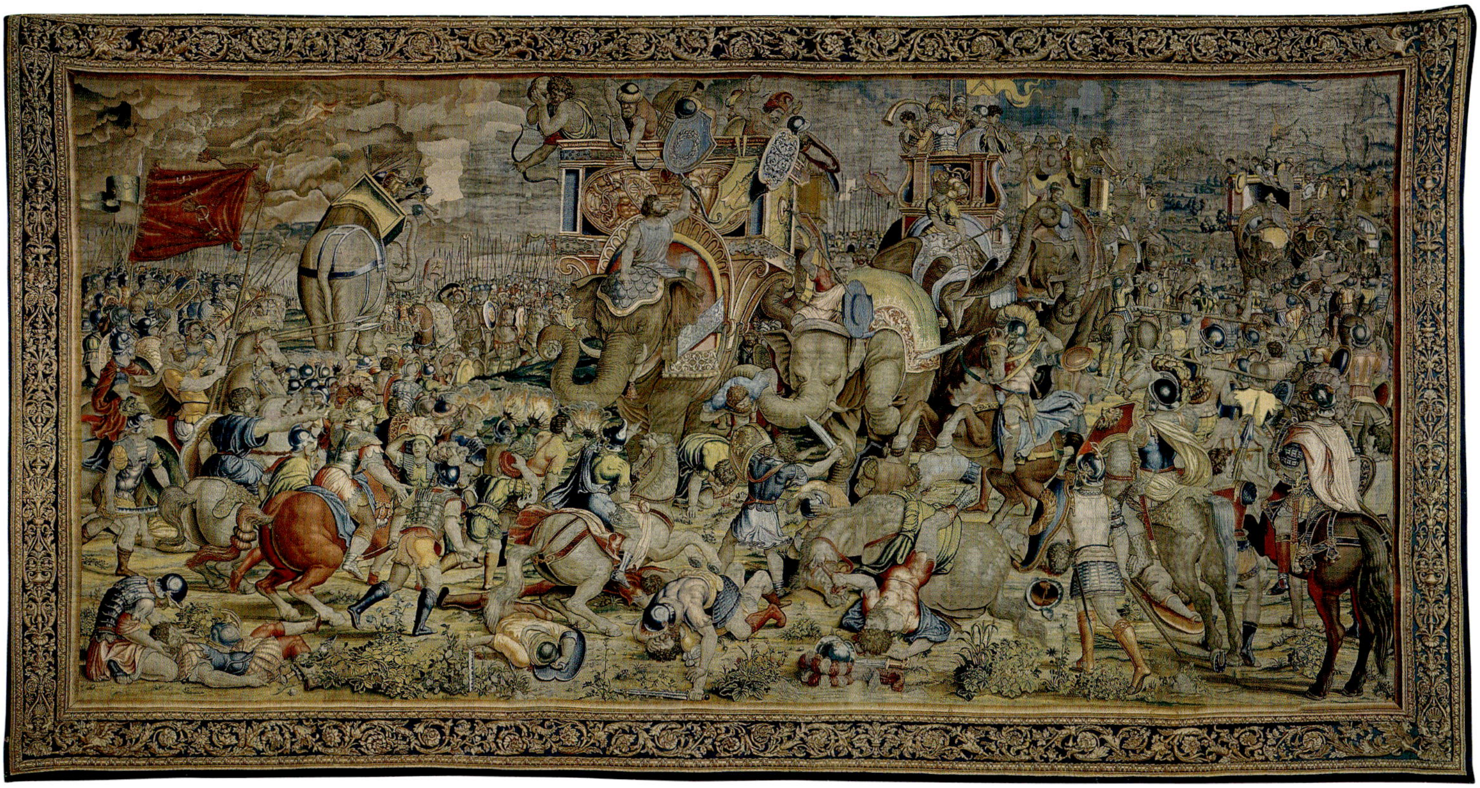

11.7 *The Battle of Zama* from a set of the *Story of Scipio*. Tapestry designed by Giulio Romano, probably woven in the workshop of Balthazar van Vlierden, Brussels, ca. 1544. Wool and silk, 480 x 902 cm. Patrimonio Nacional, Madrid

in 1530 Barthélemy Guetty provided cartoons for two tapestries of "stories of satyrs and nymphs" for the salle du Jeu de Paume at the Louvre and these were just the start of a string of Italian designs that he was to obtain in the following five years.[30]

The most ambitious of these and, indeed, confirmation of the extent to which Francis's territorial ambitions were now being sublimated into artistic projects, was the commission he made in spring 1532 for a twenty-two-piece set of the *Story of Scipio*, woven from designs by Raphael's former collaborators, Giovanni Francesco Penni and Giulio Romano. The circumstances in which this set came to Francis's attention are unclear, but there are grounds to suppose that it was conceived in the hope of a sale to Charles V and that it was then offered to Francis for some unknown reason. At any rate, Francis was shown the first three pieces of the set early in 1532, whereupon he commissioned a further nineteen, an enormous undertaking that was to span the next three years and cost approximately 50,000 livres, making it the most expensive work of art in the French royal collection.[31]

The set was destroyed in 1797, burnt by the French revolutionary government along with Francis's other fine tapestries for the precious metal they contained, but the appearance of the lost ensemble can be reconstructed on the basis of preparatory drawings and later weavings of some of the designs. Taken as a whole, these reveal that the conception of the *Scipio* set was as revolutionary as that of Raphael's *Acts of the Apostles*. It was divided into two parts, the first of which, the *Feats*, had been conceived by Giulio and Penni in the early 1520s and developed into final modelli in the late 1520s.[32] The style of these scenes, with vast illusionistic tableaux of Scipio's battles (fig. 11.7) and deeds, were close to those of the frescoes in the Sala di Costantino in the Vatican, on which Penni and Giulio also collaborated in the early 1520s. The artists paid careful attention to the historical accuracy of the costumes and the character of the action and settings. The second part of the series depicted Scipio's *Triumphs* and was made from designs undertaken by Giulio in the late 1520s or early 1530s (fig. 11.8). These were conceived in the more mannered, two-dimensional, and exuberant style that Giulio developed after

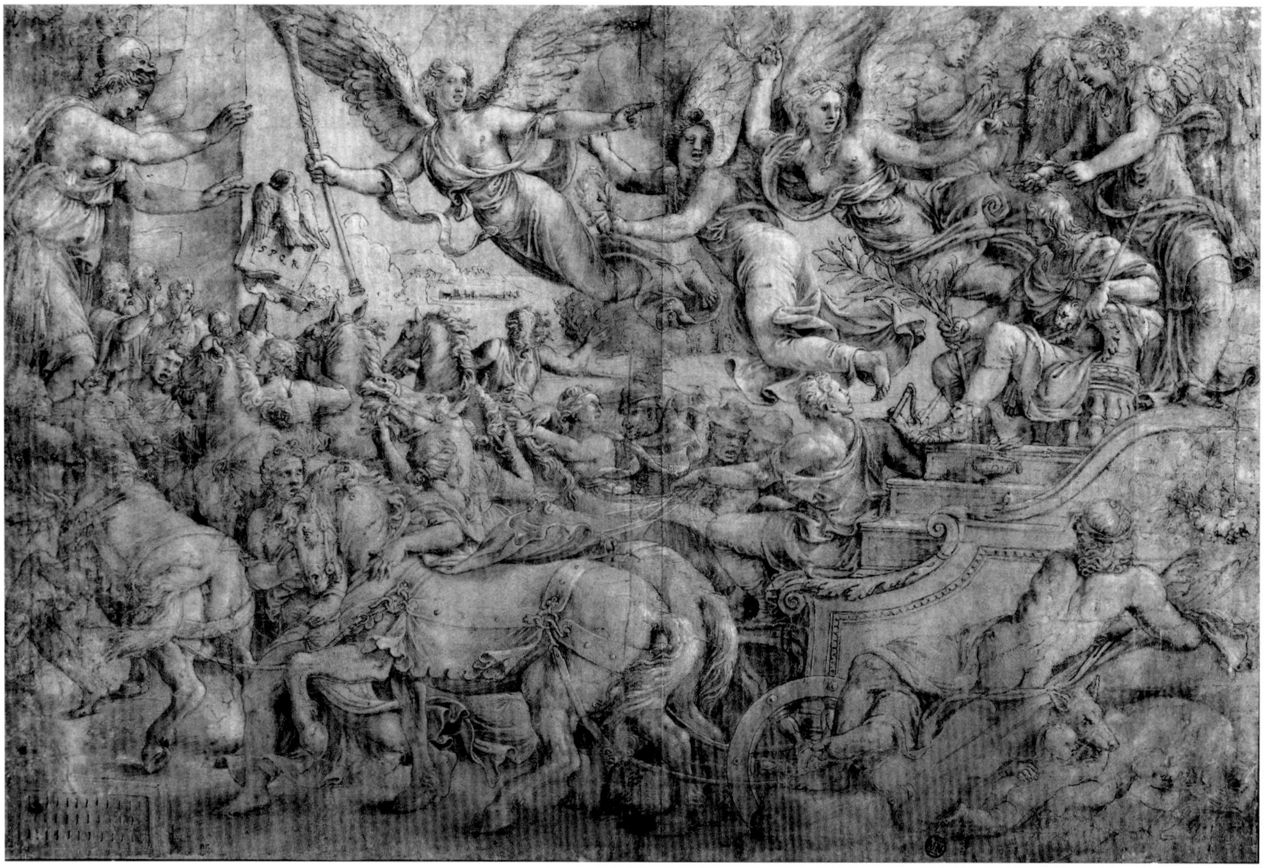

11.8 *The Triumphal Chariot of Scipio* by Giulio Romano, ca. 1530. Modello for the tapestry in Francis I's *Triumphs of Scipio*. Brown ink, brown wash, and white heightening on paper, 41.4 x 60.2 cm. Musée du Louvre, Paris

his move to Mantua in the mid-1520s. Francesco Primaticcio was probably responsible for conveying the designs of the *Triumphs* to the French court from Mantua and subsequently played a role in transporting them on to Brussels, where they were turned into cartoons.

Whatever the exact circumstances by which Francis became involved in this commission, it immediately became a central feature of his artistic arsenal, and the first pieces he received duly formed the main decoration of the Abbey of Notre Dame at Boulogne when it was prepared for the reception of Henry and Anne in October 1532, along with the *Bucolics* embroidery mentioned above. The attention the tapestries commanded on this occasion is reflected in the contemporary description of Martin du Bellay, who noted that the great hall was hung with "four main tapestries, that were of the Victories of Scipio the African, made in high quality, all of gold thread and silk thread, the figures made as well and as natural as it is possible to make them, and no painter in the world could make them better in panel paintings; and it is said that they cost fifty escus per ell."[33] In view of the prominent display of the tapestries, the scale of the commission they presaged, and the competitive character of royal magnificence, it seems inconceivable that they would not have formed the subject of conversation between the kings. An analogous conversation certainly took place two years later when Francis boasted to the Venetian ambassador that his *Scipio* tapestries were finer than the Raphael tapestries owned by the pope. He also claimed that the design was by Raphael.[34] Conversation between Francis and Henry may also have related to two other major commissions that the French king had instigated before October 1532. The first, for which Francis paid in 1532, was a *Story of Saint Paul* set. Although the designs for this series (see figs. 12.12–12.14) were by the Antwerp artist Pieter Coecke, the conception was profoundly influenced by Raphael's *Acts of the Apostles*. It may not be coincidental, then, that the second major commission that Francis seems to have instigated during 1532 was for a set of this Raphael design. The first three pieces were delivered to Francis the following year. This was the first weaving of the Raphael *Acts* since that made for Leo X in the late 1510s. It replicated the original in all respects except the wide lower border, which incorporated new allegorical scenes of good governance, one of which appears to have been a celebration of Francis himself in the guise of Hercules. Francis's set was destroyed at the time of the French Revolution, but its appearance can be ascertained on the basis of duplicate sets woven from the same modified cartoons, now in the Spanish royal collection (see fig. 13.17) and the Palazzo Ducale in Mantua.[35] The Boulogne meeting, therefore, provides the earliest certain date at which Henry was exposed to tapestries designed in the High Renaissance style in a context in which they would almost certainly have been a matter of discussion. There is, however, no evidence that Francis's acquisitions of Italianate tapestry designs had any immediate impact on Henry's tastes. As we will see, for the time being at least, Henry's tapestry purchases continued to be determined by more immediate personal and political considerations.

After the meeting at Boulogne, Henry hosted Francis at Calais. On this occasion the tapestries were provided from the English Great Wardrobe, but the only interiors of which descriptions survive were those prepared for Francis. His outer chamber was decorated with the gold-ground *Verdure* that had been used at Guines in 1520 for Katherine of Aragon's rooms. Considering the purpose of the present meeting between the two kings, Henry's wish to ensure Francis's support for his marriage to Anne, one can only wonder if Francis noted the irony of this choice. The second of Francis's chambers was decorated with cloth of gold and a heraldic cloth of estate embroidered with pearls.[36] The third was hung with even richer cloth of gold, embroidered with branches of flowers of gold bullion and garnished with arms and beasts of bullion, enhanced with pearls and precious stones.[37] In other words, the decorations embodied a traditional hierarchic sequence of increasingly opulent textiles. History does not record whether Francis found this display a trifle dull in comparison to the stylistic novelty of his own textiles.

Preparations for the Coronation of Anne Boleyn

During 1532 and 1533 the Great Wardrobe staff responsible for administering the royal tapestries must have been subjected to extraordinary demands as they hung various palaces and residences for Henry's public appearances to further the goals of his divorce, for the entertainments lavished on Anne, and for the marriage and coronation in 1533. Preparations for these last climactic events were modeled on those used twenty-four years previously for Henry's coronation and marriage to Katherine. A memorandum from the lord chamberlain stipulated that "the mayor, aldermen and crafts of London are to do their service accustomed, and the streets between the Tower and Westminster are to be garnished with tapestry, arras, silk, &c."[38] Contemporary descriptions confirm the rich tapestries and hangings employed: "Cornehill and Gracious strete were hanged with fine Scarlet, Crimosyn and other grayned clothes, and in some places with riche Arras, Tapestry and Carpettes and the moste parte of Chepe was hanged with cloth of Tyssue, Golde, Velvet and many riche hangynges whiche made a goodly shewe."[39] It therefore seems that the majority of the textiles in the streets were provided by the richer guilds, which, as already noted, owned tapestries and hangings that were primarily intended for use in their banqueting halls for feast days. Meanwhile, the reception rooms and public spaces at the Tower, Westminster, and Whitehall were hung with tapestries drawn from the royal wardrobes. Laconic as ever, Hall merely relates that the festivities at Whitehall took place in rooms that were "richely hanged with clothe of Arras and newe glased."[40] The following August, the traditional forms of ceremony and decoration, defined by Henry VII's ordinances of 1493, were also followed for Anne's lying-in and the christening of Princess Elizabeth. Of the latter occasion, Hall recorded that "all the walles betweene the kynges place and the Friars, were hanged with Arras, and all the waye strewed with grene Rushes: the Friars Churche was also hanged with Arras."[41]

Evidence is lacking for the tapestries supplied to Anne in her capacity as queen, but in July 1534 Anne's Wardrobe of the Beds ordered two thousand large hooks, four thousand of medium size, six thousand small hooks, and four hammers, all of which implies that considerable redecorating was being undertaken on her behalf at this time.[42] This was a period in which new apartments were being created for Anne at Hampton Court, so we can assume that some of these Wardrobe provisions would have related to this location.[43]

The splendor of the celebrations of Henry and Anne's wedding, of Anne's coronation, and of the chambers prepared for the couple following their marriage contrasted with the provisions made for Katherine of Aragon at Baynard's Castle, now that Henry had finally divested himself of her presence. An inventory taken after her death in February 1535 records the forty or so tapestries then at the castle.[44] As in the case of the textiles supplied to Wolsey following his disgrace, those provided to Katherine appear to have been of mediocre quality. It is conceivable that some at least had originally constituted part of her dowry. Only three sets are named: a six-piece set of *Jason,* a four-piece set of *Hercules,* and three pieces of the *Old and the New Law*. Another five groups of about fifteen pieces were merely described as "sorting," a term used in the early sixteenth century to describe nondescript pieces of lower value, much as we now use the word "miscellaneous." The single impressive ensemble at Katherine's disposal was a suite of red and green velvet hangings embroidered with the arms of England and Spain, "crowned with a Crowne Imperialle," a poignant testimony to her former status. Given the circumstances of her dismissal from Henry's presence, there was little likelihood that these would be required in Henry's immediate vicinity at this time.

The Royal Arras Maker as an Agent of Tapestry Purchases

The survival of records for the Treasury of the Chamber between 1528 and 1530 and of those for the Privy Purse between 1529 and 1532 reveal the continuing acquisition of tapestries for the Crown by a variety of mechanisms. Although the documentation for the remaining seventeen years of Henry's life is very incomplete, there is no reason to doubt that he continued to purchase a steady stream of tapestries. Indeed, the sheer number of tapestries recorded in the 1547 inventory, whose subjects and dimensions correspond to designs known to have originated during the 1530s and 1540s, suggests that the volume of acquisition increased during these years. The paucity of evidence for these purchases is to be explained by a variety of circumstances. First, with financial reform in the early 1530s the role of the Treasury of the Chamber was diminished, and no further tapestry payments are recorded from this source after 1530.[45] Records for the Privy Purse lapse again after 1532, but since very large sums continued to be paid to Sir Anthony Denny throughout the 1530s both from the Treasury of the Chamber and from various other funds, it seems likely that this continued to be an important source of finance for tapestry purchases. Another explanation for the lack of purchase documents during the 1530s may be how many tapestries were obtained. Circumstantial evidence suggests that during these years the royal arras maker may have played a new role in sourcing tapestries directly from the leading Brussels workshops, and it is to this figure that we now turn our attention.

The office of royal arras maker was held by Cornelius van der Strete from October 1509 until his death in 1528. Although the Great Wardrobe records for these years are not complete, those that survive reflect a constant volume of repair activity by Van der Strete's workshop throughout the 1510s and 1520s. In the year of his death, he was paid for repairs to forty-three tapestries, and a list of "arras makers" under his direction includes the names of twelve workers.[46] In January 1529 a grant was made to a "John Mystyng," that is, Jan Mostinck, to be chief "arras-maker" to the king with a wage of £10. According to the grant, Mostinck had formerly worked for the countess of Richmond and Derby, Henry's grandmother, who had died in June 1509.[47] His whereabouts in the intervening twenty years is unspecified. Like his predecessor, Mostinck was Flemish, and a document of 1539–40 states that he originated from Enghien, well known as a center of tapestry trade and production.[48] He may have been related to the Simon Mostinck who supplied tapestries to Louis of Luxembourg, lord of Enghien, in 1470.[49] His name appears in subsequent documents in various forms: Mostinck, Mostincke, Muscing, and Musting.

At the same time that Mostinck received his appointment as "chief arras maker to the king," Thomas Garton, page of the wardrobe, also received a grant to be the king's "arras maker" at the rate of 6d. a day (that is, £9 2s. 6d. per year).[50] The reason for this dual appointment is not immediately apparent, especially since Garton continued to occupy the position of page of the wardrobe, the title by which he was described when he was paid for preparing the hall at Blackfriars for the trial of Katherine of Aragon in June 1529.[51] Twenty-one months later a further grant was issued to a John Lyson, to be one of the king's "arras makers" with 6d. a day.[52] Lyson must have been replacing Garton, because Garton does not appear in subsequent accounts. The probable partnership of Lyson and Mostinck after January 1529 is supported by a grant issued in April 1535 in which they were described as two of the king's "arras-makers" and allowed to keep in their service as many journeymen or covenanted servants as they thought fit, notwithstanding the Act of Hampton Court of April 18, 1534, which forbade aliens to employ foreign nationals.[53]

Whereas payments for repair materials were made to Van der Strete before 1529, the four Wardrobe accounts that survive from the period 1529–1536/37 all list Lyson as the individual to whom payments were made.[54] Mostinck is not mentioned. During these years Lyson and his men evidently continued the volume of repair work previously undertaken by Van der Strete. For example, in 1531 Lyson was paid for work on eight pieces of tapestry of *King David* and eight pieces of "arras" of the *Story of Job* (the identity of these sets will be discussed below).[55] The following year (Michaelmas 1531–Michaelmas 1532) Lyson and nine workers were paid for repairing thirty tapestries from eight different sets or groups.[56] Two years later, the account for Michaelmas 1533 to Michaelmas 1534 lists sixty-one tapestries for which eight workers were paid for a total of 673 days' work.[57] The year after that, forty-two tapestries were repaired by fourteen men who worked a total of 1,229 days.[58] The documents do not always specify the subjects of the tapestries on which work was undertaken, but many of those named can be identified as dating from the fifteenth century, indicating the important role the antique hangings continued to play in the decoration of the royal palaces. All of these accounts cite Lyson as the individual to whom payments for materials were made, and it seems logical to presume that he was in charge of the workshop during this period.

Lyson must have died in early 1537, because that March a grant was issued to Jan Mostinck of the office "of buying and repairing the King's tapestries," with the usual fees, as enjoyed by Thomas Garton and John Lyson.[59] Subsequently, the Wardrobe accounts for 1537–38 and 1538–39 both name Mostinck as the individual to whom payment was made for repair materials, indicating that he was now fulfilling the supervisory role formerly held by Lyson.[60] The volume of repair work continued undiminished. The account for 1537–38 lists 205 tapestry items, including fifty-eight pieces from Chelsea manor, which Henry acquired in 1536 through land exchanges with Lord Sandys and Westminster Abbey.[61] The 1537–38 account names sixteen "arras workers." The account for the following year records payment for the repair of 114 tapestries by eighteen men who worked a total of 1,163 days.

So what was Mostinck doing between 1529 and 1537? Since his name does not appear in

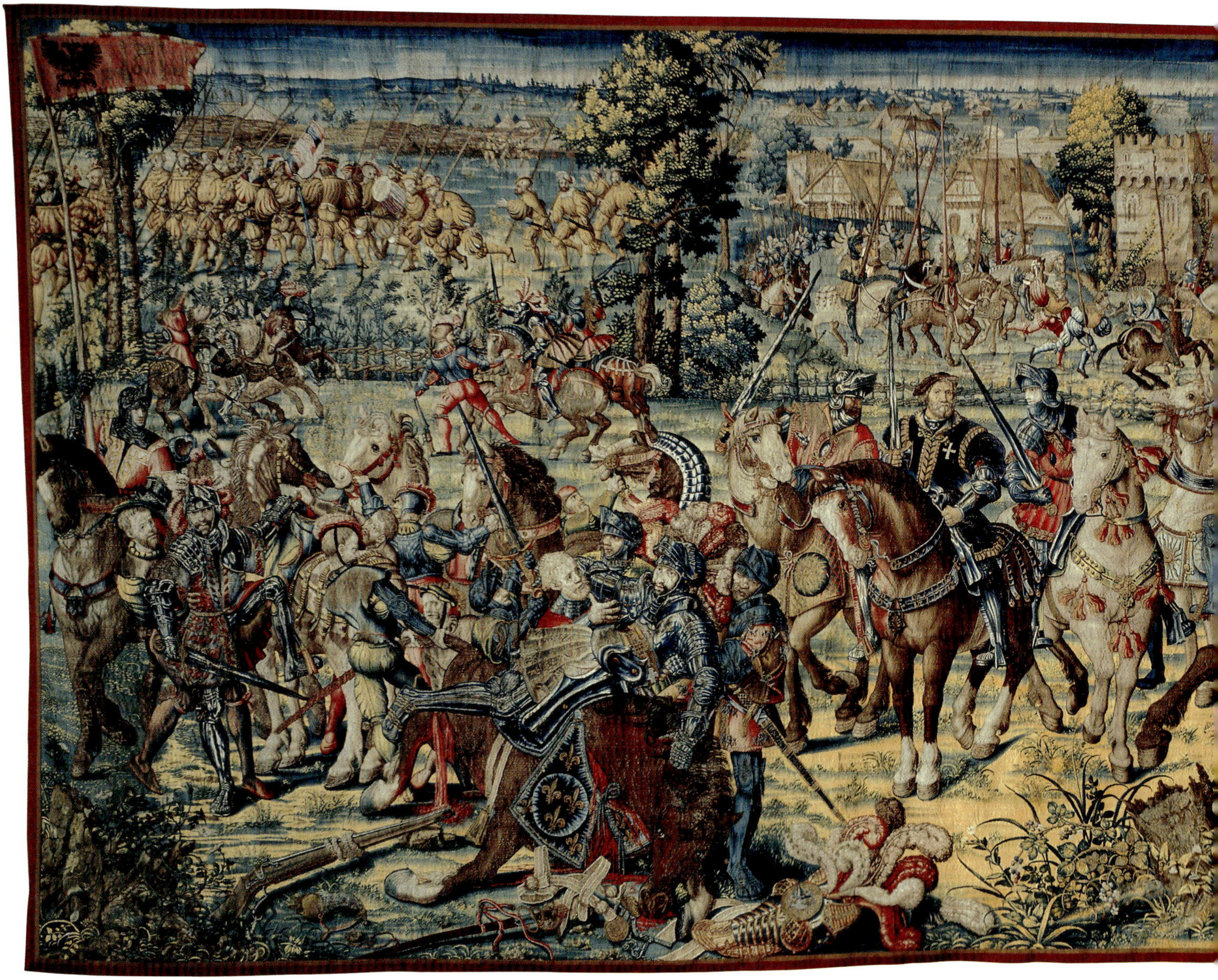

11.9 *The Surrender of King Francis I* from a set of the *Battle of Pavia.* Tapestry designed by Bernaert van Orley, woven in the Dermoyen workshop, Brussels, ca. 1528–31. Wool, silk, and gilt-metal-wrapped thread, 435 x 880 cm. Museo e Gallerie Nazionale di Capodimonte, Naples

documents relating to repair work it might be concluded that the position was a sinecure, the hard work being done by Lyson. However, a clue that this was not the case is provided by the 1537 grant, just cited, which describes Mostinck as occupying the offices of "buying and repairing" the king's tapestries. The detail of "buying" is not specified in grants to other incumbents of this office and suggests therefore that the use of the word in this context was more than mere repetition of a traditional phrase.[62] As we have seen, Van der Strete had purchased tapestries for the dowry of Princess Mary before her marriage to Louis XII in 1514, and although no explicit documentation has survived to show Mostinck performing a similar function, evidence that this may have been exactly what he was up to during the 1530s comes from the deposition, cited in the Introduction, that he gave to the Brussels tapestry guild in 1539.

The issue that occasioned this deposition was the prosecution by the guild of four of the leading Brussels tapestry merchants, Jan de Clerck, Willem de Kempeneer, Willem Dermoyen, and Jan Dermoyen. The defendants were accused of allowing their workshops to use paint to complete certain details of their products, rather than weaving them as guild regulations stipulated. As part of their defense

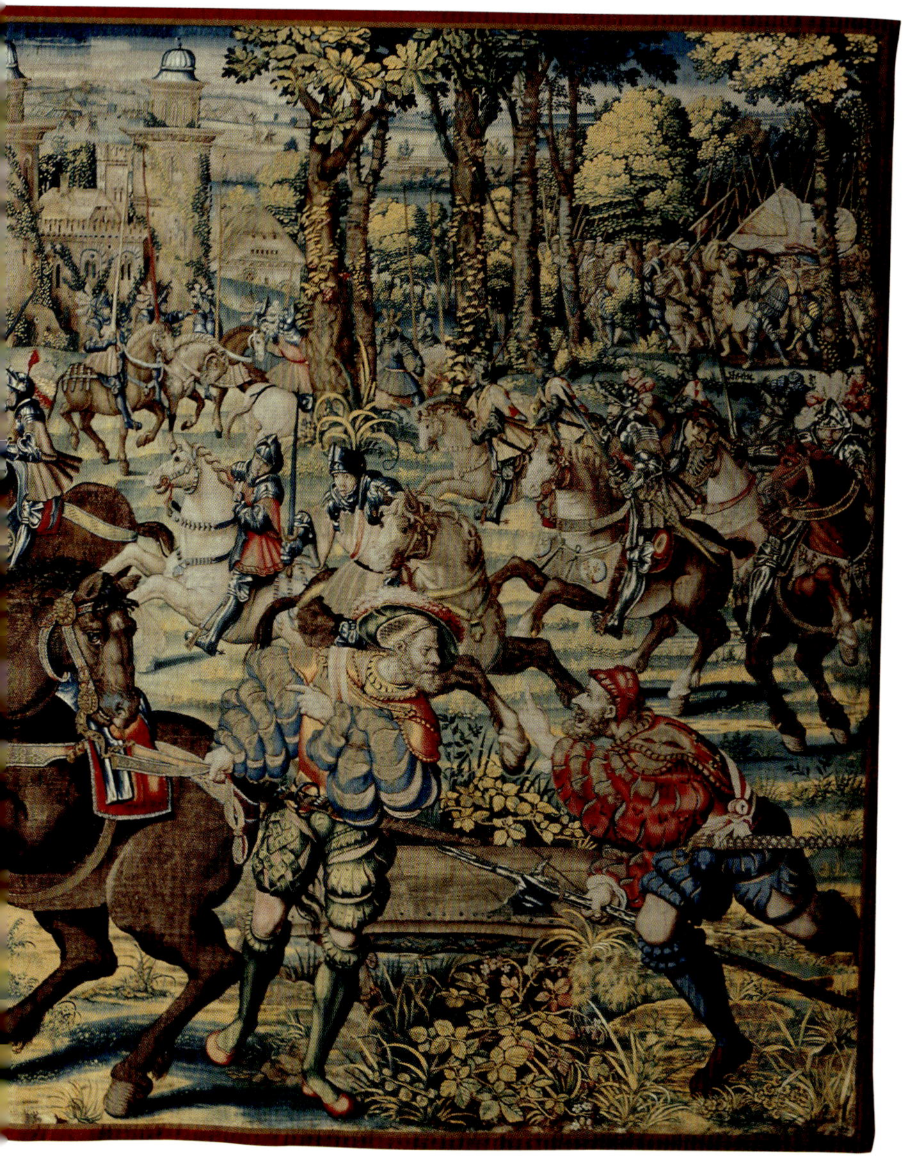

the merchants obtained a deposition from Mostinck to attest to their good character. His authority as a judge was established on the basis that he had been the officer responsible for Henry VIII's tapestry collection for the preceding twelve years, a period that approximately coincides with the date of his appointment in 1529. According to the deposition, Henry's collection was larger than that of any Christian king, or at least as large, both in quality and number.[63] Having established his credentials, the deposition states that during this period Mostinck had not encountered any evidence of the deceitful practices of which the merchants were accused.[64]

Taken in conjunction with the stated function of his office when his grant was renewed in 1537, the implication of this deposition is that Mostinck must have played an important role in Henry VIII's tapestry purchases in the preceding years. We can speculate that during the period 1529–37 Mostinck spent much of his time in the Netherlands, inspecting prospective purchases and developing and supervising commissions. And if Mostinck was working directly with the merchants and workshops in the Netherlands, it would also explain why so little documentation has survived of his activity, because the Brussels tapestry guild records were lost in a fire that destroyed the guildhall in 1690. It is probably no coincidence that two of the enterprises named in the deposition, those of Dermoyen and Kempeneer, are known to have owned the cartoons for various series whose inception can be dated to the 1530s on stylistic grounds and of which weavings can be identified in the 1547 inventory of Henry's tapestries.

Tapestry Purchases in the Early 1530s

So what sort of tapestries might Mostinck have been acquiring for Henry during the 1530s? This was a period of artistic and stylistic development as Netherlandish designers continued to respond to the innovations of the Raphael school cartoons. The success of Bernaert van Orley's designs of the mid-1520s resulted in a series of more ambitious commissions from the Habsburg court circle.[65] The most groundbreaking was that undertaken for the States General of Brabant sometime around 1527 for a set of tapestries depicting the *Battle of Pavia*. This revolutionary set was completed by 1531, the year in which it was presented to Charles V. The seven scenes illustrated a chronology of the events of the battle, including life-size portraits of many of the protagonists and carefully observed visualizations of the topography of the town of Pavia and the surrounding countryside (fig. 11.9).[66] The development of the designs and execution of the portraits must have required

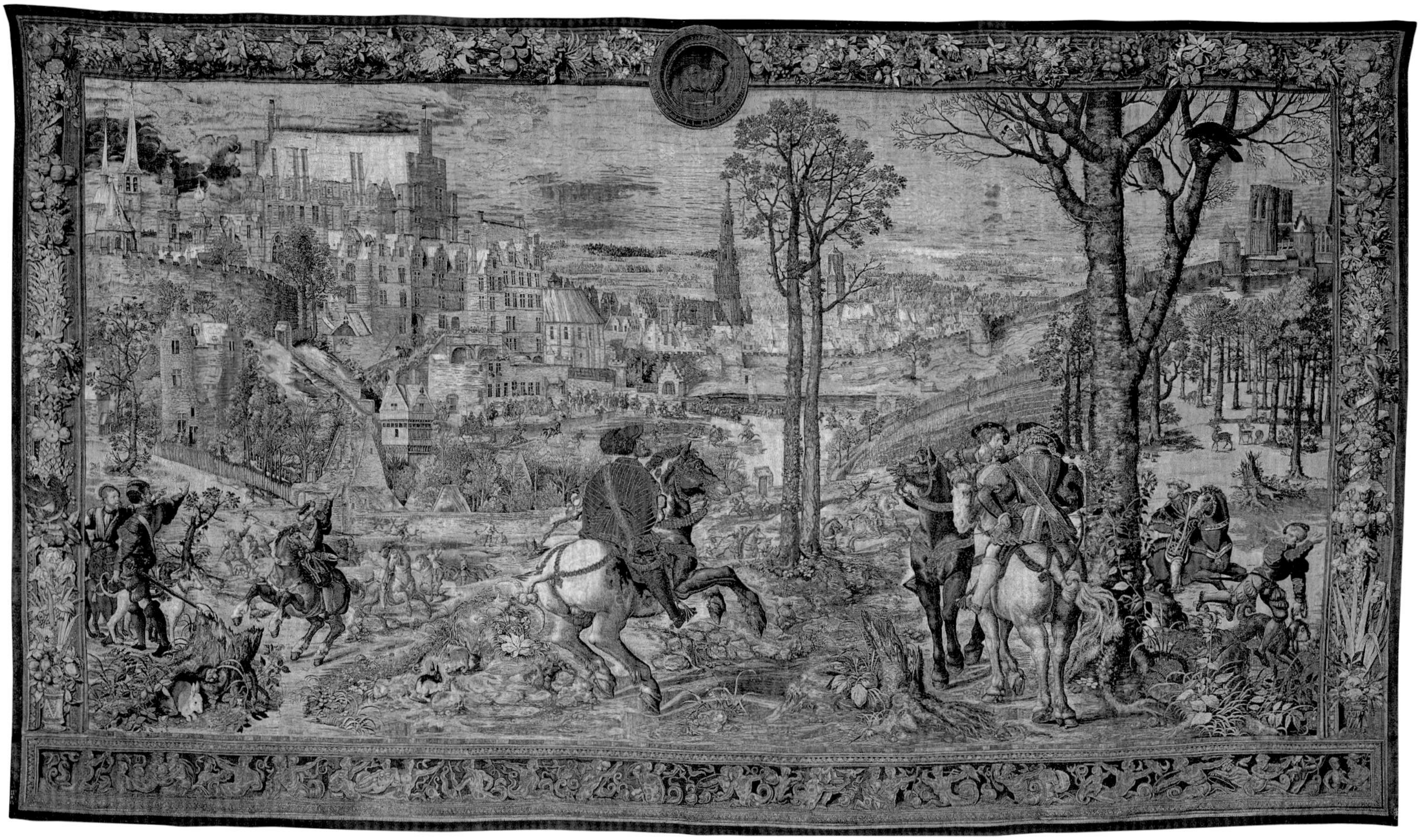

11.10 *March* from the *Hunts of Maximilian.* Tapestry designed by Bernaert van Orley, woven in the Dermoyen workshop, Brussels, ca. 1531–33. Wool, silk, and gilt-metal-wrapped thread, 440 x 750 cm. Musée du Louvre, Paris

considerable collaboration between Van Orley and members of Charles V's entourage. At the time they were conceived and woven, these designs were the largest and most ambitious attempts at figurative verisimilitude that had been undertaken north of the Alps.

By the date the *Pavia* set was completed, a second, equally revolutionary design by Van Orley must also have been on the looms, the so-called *Hunts of Maximilian* (figs. 11.10, 11.11).[67] This represented members of the Habsburg court, including Charles V and his sister Mary of Hungary, hunting and feasting in recognizable locations in and around Brussels. Where the *Pavia* set represented the Habsburgs victorious at war, the *Hunts* was a celebration of the peace, prosperity, and good governance that their regime had brought to the Netherlands, as represented by the figures of King Modus and Queen Ratio—the fictional authors of a fifteenth-century hunting treatise—who appear in the final tapestry of the set, enthroned in the ducal palace in Brussels. Again, the choice of subject matter and recording of locations and portraits must have required lengthy involvement on the part of the Habsburg household.

The style that Van Orley developed in the 1520s was to influence tapestry design for the following thirty years, but it was not a rigid formula. Tapestry production of the 1530s was characterized by innovation and experiment, as Netherlandish designers balanced the requirements of narrative structure, verisimilitude, and decorative values. The result was a period in which several design trends coexisted and cross-fertilized in the leading ateliers of Brussels and Antwerp. Besides his work for the Habsburg court, Van Orley began producing designs commissioned by such Brussels merchants as Willem de Kempeneer of which one, the *Story of Jacob,* will shortly be the subject of discussion. In these, he retreated from the ambitious realism of the *Pavia* and *Hunts* series to a more traditional blend of decorative elements and multiple narrative.[68] Meanwhile, his contemporaries developed his innovations in a variety of directions. Most notable of these was Pieter

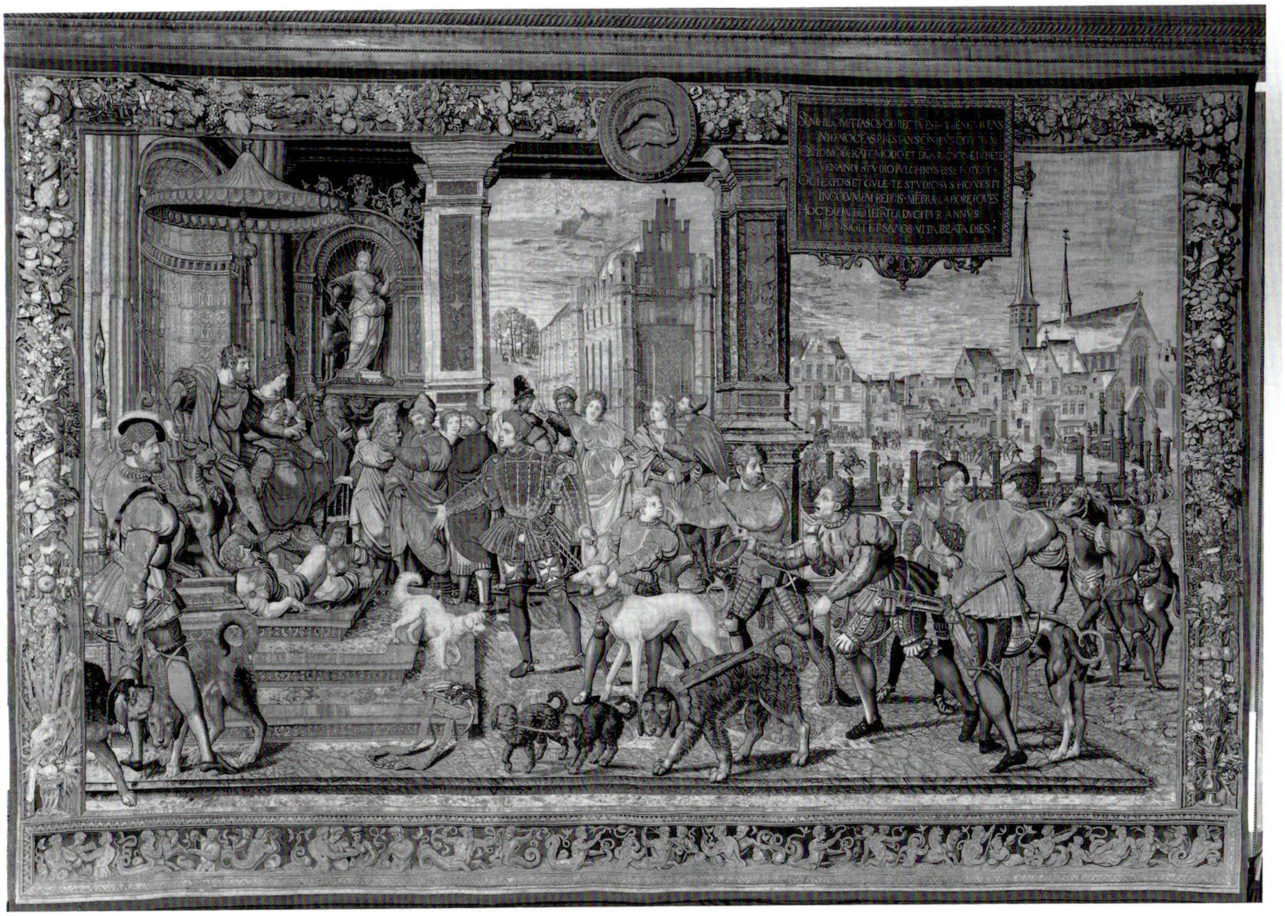

11.11 *February* from the *Hunts of Maximilian*. Tapestry designed by Bernaert van Orley, woven in the Dermoyen workshop, Brussels, ca. 1530. Wool, silk, and gilt-metal-wrapped thread, 440 x 648 cm. Musée du Louvre, Paris

Coecke. From around 1530, Coecke's designs incorporate startling viewpoints and ambitious atmospheric effects, as exemplified by the design series of the *Story of Saint Paul,* of which Francis I acquired the first weaving in 1532 and Henry a set in the late 1530s, and the *Seven Deadly Sins,* of which Henry acquired a set sometime in 1535–36.[69] During the late 1520s and 1530s, new Italian designs with an increasing element of "maniera" also continued to arrive in Brussels from artists working at both the Italian and French courts, for example, the *Scipio* series already mentioned, providing an ongoing source of inspiration to Flemish tapestry designers.

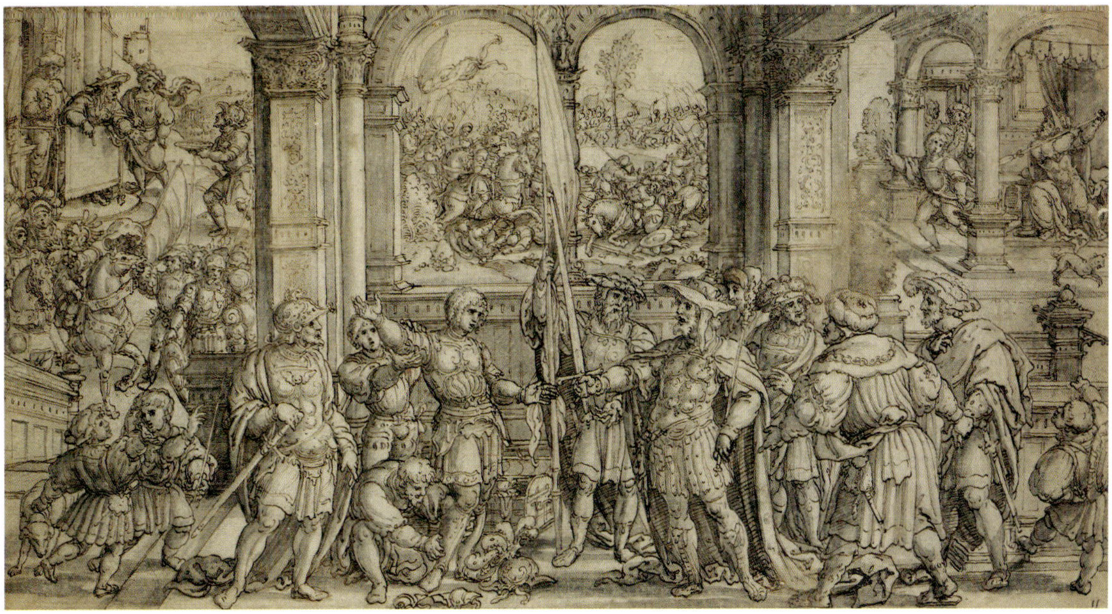

11.12 *Saul Arming David,* one of a set of *Story of David* tapestry designs attributed to Pieter Coecke van Aelst, ca. 1528–30. Pen and brown ink and gray wash, 23.1 x 41.9 cm. British Museum, London

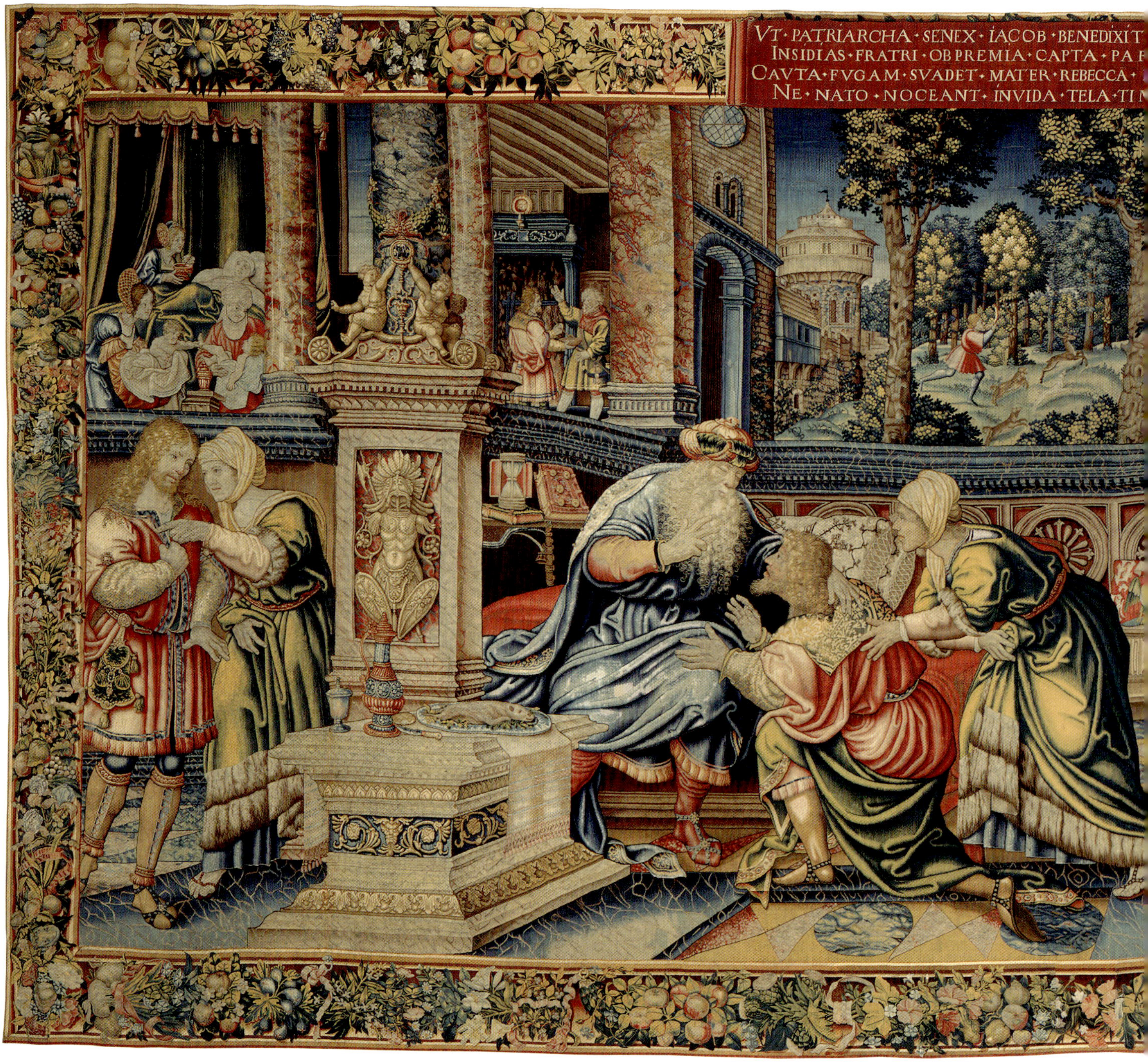

11.13 *The Blessing of Esau* from a set of the *Story of Jacob*. Tapestry designed by Bernaert van Orley, woven in the workshop of Willem de Kempeneer, Brussels, before 1539. Wool and silk, 424 x 680 cm. Musées Royaux d'Art et d'Histoire, Brussels

How rapidly these stylistic innovations and developments were reflected in the English royal collection is difficult to determine because of the paucity of purchase documentation, but some basic conclusions can be drawn. As noted, evidence that large numbers of tapestries were acquired during the 1530s, by purchase as well as appropriation, is suggested by the number of tapestries recorded in the 1547 inventory that can be identified with design series originating in the 1530s. Judging by these, Henry's purchases during these years continued to focus on series by Flemish artists, and

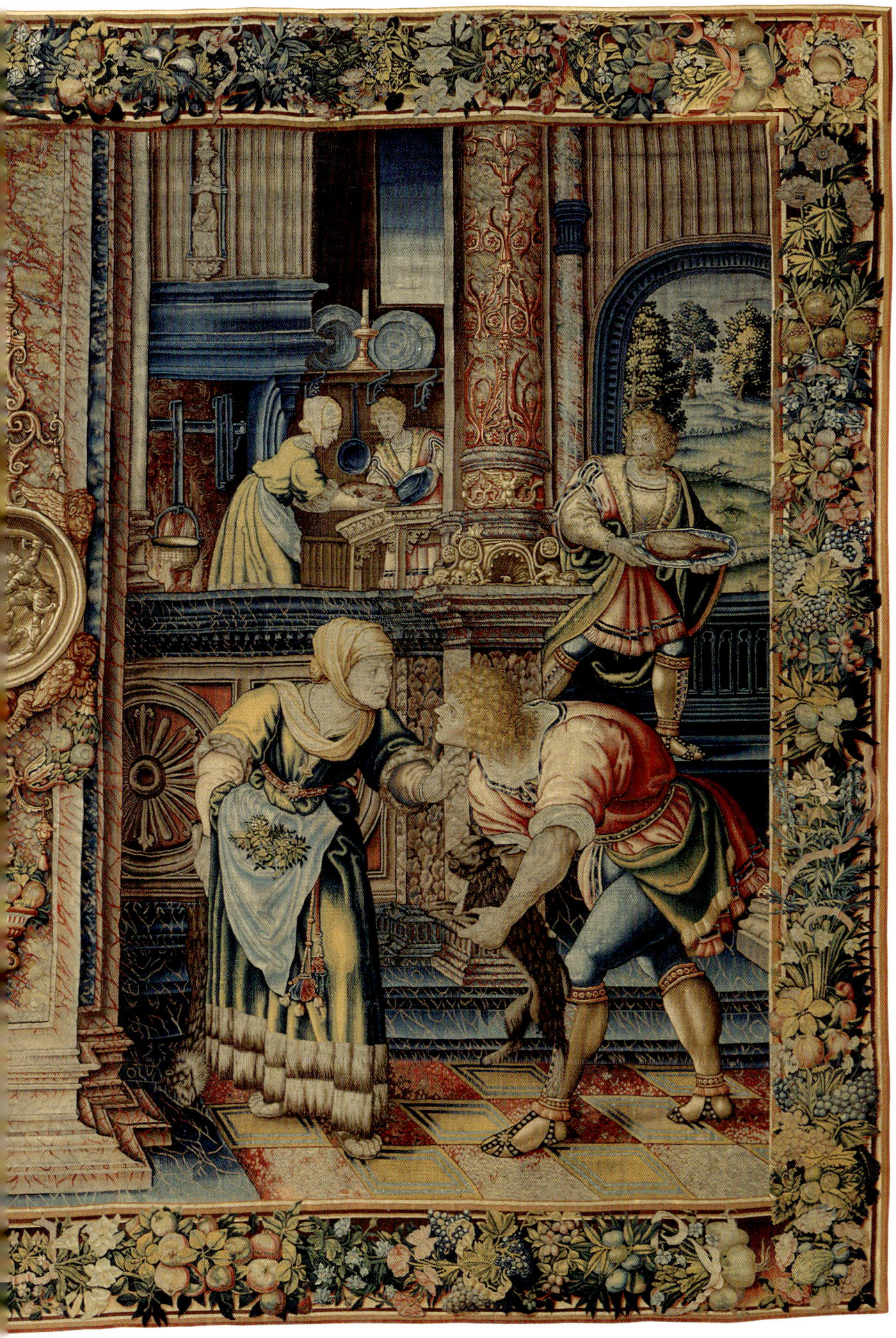

no designs by Italian artists can be identified in the English royal collection until the early 1540s. Equally, Henry does appear to have acquired the first weavings of some of the most important design series created by Flemish artists in the early to mid-1530s, which implies that, at this date, he was interested in the subject matter and iconography of the sets that he acquired rather than their artistic character or style as an end in itself.

For example, it is tempting to suggest that the "arras" set of *Job* on which the royal arras maker worked in 1530–31 may have been a new acquisition that was being lined at this date. The *Job* set is not identified in the 1547 inventory, but evidence that it survived in the collection is provided by written records of repairs to various pieces by the royal arras maker in later years.[70] Nothing more is known of the design, but one can certainly imagine Henry identifying himself with this subject. According to the Old Testament, Job was the innocent victim of God's wager with Satan that Job would not lose his faith whatever adversity inflicted upon him. Fulfilling God's expectations of him, Job remained steadfast despite great misfortunes before he was eventually restored to health and prosperity. This paradigm of trial and eventual reward held an obvious appeal for Henry as he labored to extricate himself from his marriage to Katherine.

The identity is also unknown of the eight-piece *David* set on which the royal arras maker was working at the same time as the *Job* set, but considering the number of pieces mentioned in the set and the likelihood that it was a recent delivery, it may have been a weaving of a design series for which five preparatory drawings survive at the British Museum (fig. 11.12) and of which six tapestries have survived at Burgos Cathedral, one of which incorporates a fragment from a seventh panel.[71] One of the British Museum drawings carries a contemporary inscription, "peeter Cooke van Alste." Another also carries an inscription that has been read as MD31, presumably for 1531. Although the

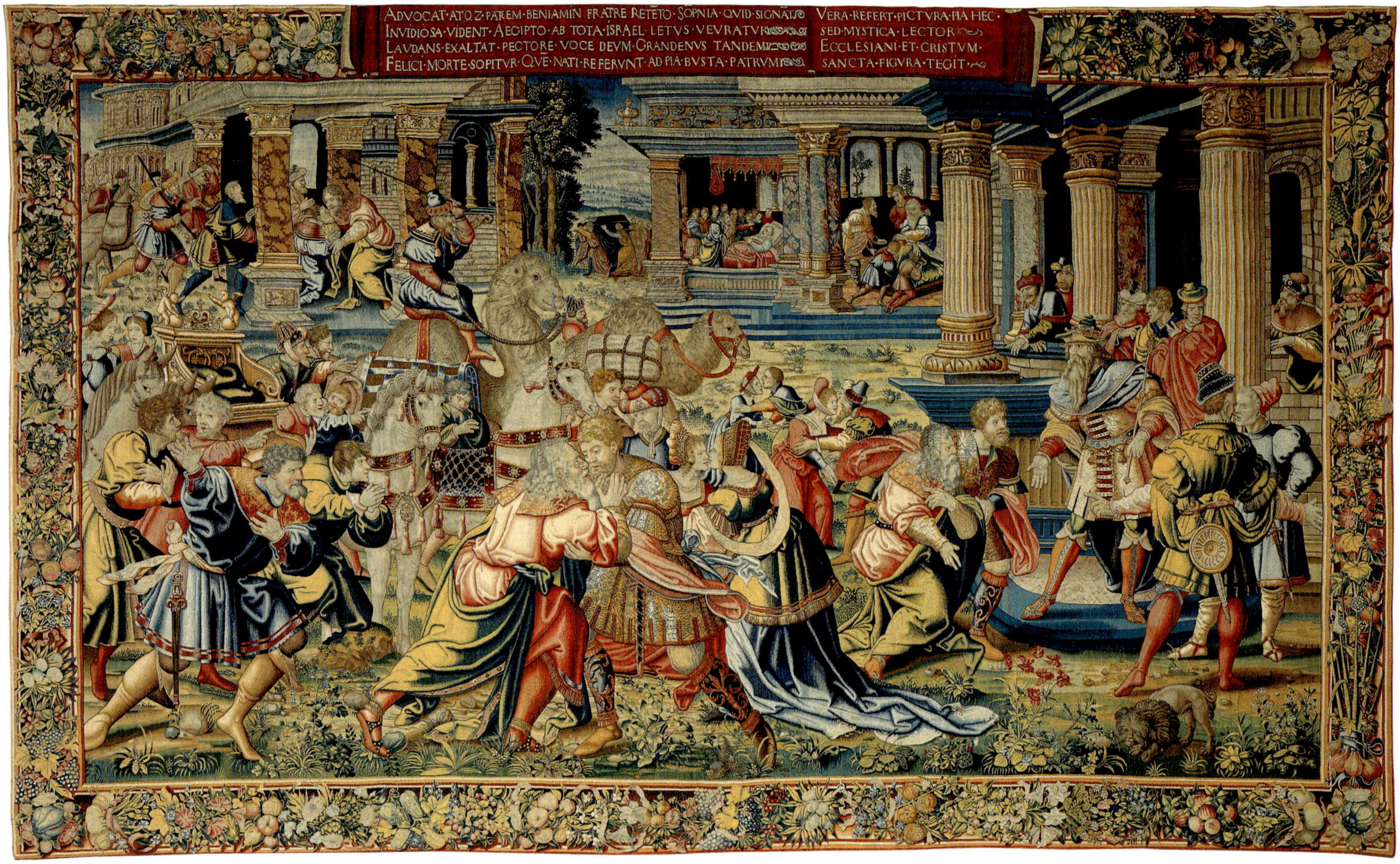

11.14 *Jacob Reunited with Esau* from a set of the *Story of Jacob*. Tapestry designed by Bernaert van Orley, woven in the workshop of Willem de Kempeneer, Brussels, before 1539. Wool and silk, 424 x 680 cm. Musées Royaux d'Art et d'Histoire, Brussels

date and attribution are open to discussion, the style of the *David* designs is close to that of the *Romulus and Remus* series that Henry had purchased in 1529, with solid figures posed in elaborate but rather whimsical "classical" architectural settings. The rhetorical gestures of the figures reflect the influence of the Raphael cartoons, although the proportions betray the artist's lack of anatomical training, and this would certainly be consistent with a design conceived by Coecke in the late 1520s under the influence of Van Orley's response to the Raphael designs. On the basis of the British Museum drawings and the Burgos tapestries, seven subjects can be identified: Samuel anointing David, the death of Goliath, the triumph of David, Saul arming David along with a battle between the Philistines and the Israelites, the marriage of David to Michal, David and Abigail, and the campaign against Rabbah. Although the set in Burgos is known to have included only seven tapestries, an eighth design, evidently from the same design series, was recently acquired by the Musée de la Renaissance in Écouen. This panel shows David presented with booty from Rabbah by his victorious generals.[72] Although the link between this eight-piece design series and the eight-piece set documented in Henry VIII's collection in 1531 must remain tentative, the style, dating, and the number of panels in the series certainly make it a strong likelihood.

The Story of Jacob

Although the character of the *Job* and *David* sets is debatable, we are on firmer ground with a ten-piece set of the *Story of Jacob* that was also probably acquired in the early 1530s. The set was recorded at Whitehall in the 1547 inventory,[73] and its dimensions indicate that it was a weaving from a series designed by Bernaert van Orley and his workshop, of which a complete set survives at the Musées Royaux d'Art et d'Histoire, Brussels (figs. 11.13, 11.14, and detail opposite p. 201). The measurements of the Brussels set have been altered by damage and modern conservation—including the loss of the right-hand side of what was originally the widest panel—but they are close enough to those of the Henrician set for there to be no question that both were made from the same cartoons.[74] The Burrell Collection owns a duplicate, from an otherwise lost set, of one of the scenes, *Jacob Meets Rachel,* which includes the section with their subsequent marriage, now missing from the Brussels set. Its width, twenty-six feet, is the same as the widest panel recorded in Henry's set (fig. 11.15).[75]

The *Jacob* series is of interest from a stylistic point of view because it provided the narrative formula that was to characterize much Netherlandish tapestry production for the next thirty years. In place of the panoramic scenes of a single moment of time that marked the *Pavia* and *Hunts of Maximilian* sets, here Van Orley returned to the more traditional device of using architectural and landscape features to separate the elements of a multiple narrative. The subjects appear to have been selected to focus on moments of psychological insight and dramatic impact and to establish a sense of suspenseful anticipation as the viewer moves from one episode to the next.[76] Although the architectural divisions that separate the scenes include Renaissance motifs, they stem from an earlier Netherlandish design tradition, providing rich, decorative filling between the individual sections of the narrative. At the same time, the vividly realized muscular figures occupying stagelike interiors rendered in realistic perspective clearly recall the compositional formula of Raphael's *Acts of the Apostles.*

The series portrays the main events in the life of Jacob, from the circumstances in which he obtained the blessing of his father, Isaac, in place of his older brother, Esau (see fig. 11.13), through the events of his marriage to Rachel, his servitude to Laban, the eventual departure from Laban, the journey during which God gave Jacob the name Israel, the reconciliation with Esau, the sale of Joseph by his brothers, Joseph's subsequent return from Egypt and reunion with Jacob, and finally the death of the patriarch, surrounded by his sons, the leaders of the twelve tribes of Israel. The tapestries all carry Latin inscriptions that provide a brief summary of the events depicted. In addition, the last piece carries a second inscription that invites the onlooker to consider Jacob as an embodiment of the Church.

In view of the resonance between the subject of the 1528 *David* purchase and the circumstances in which Henry then found himself, the question arises as to whether the *Jacob* series may also have been intended as an allegory for the English king. That Henry was a second son certainly provides one point of obvious comparison with Jacob, second son of Isaac, while the patriarch's role in fathering the twelve sons who would become the heads of the twelve tribes of Israel would have been a flattering comparison for the king's dynastic ambitions. Considering the steps that Henry was taking in the early 1530s to establish himself as the head of the English church and separate himself from the Church of Rome, the notion that the patriarch was to be identified with the Church also would have had a rich resonance for Henry's new vision of himself as the spiritual leader of his people; by this reading, Laban, with his reluctance to release Jacob, thus becomes the pope.

Although the lack of evidence for the circumstances in which the *Jacob* set arrived in the Tudor collection impedes further investigation, the possibility that the set may have been conceived with Henry in mind is raised by the fact that the cartoons belonged to Willem de Kempeneer, one of the merchants on whose behalf Mostinck testified in 1539. This fact can be inferred from a document witnessed before an Antwerp notary in 1534 whereby Kempeneer agreed to sell a wool and silk set of ten *Jacob* tapestries to the Antwerp merchant Joris Vezeleer, along with another, gold-woven set of the *Story of Iphiginia.* In addition, the *Jacob* set now at the Musées Royaux carries Kempeneer's mark on several tapestries.[77] The *Iphiginia* set is probably to be identified with that subsequently recorded in the inventory of Francis I's tapestries, but it is conceivable that the *Jacob* set was

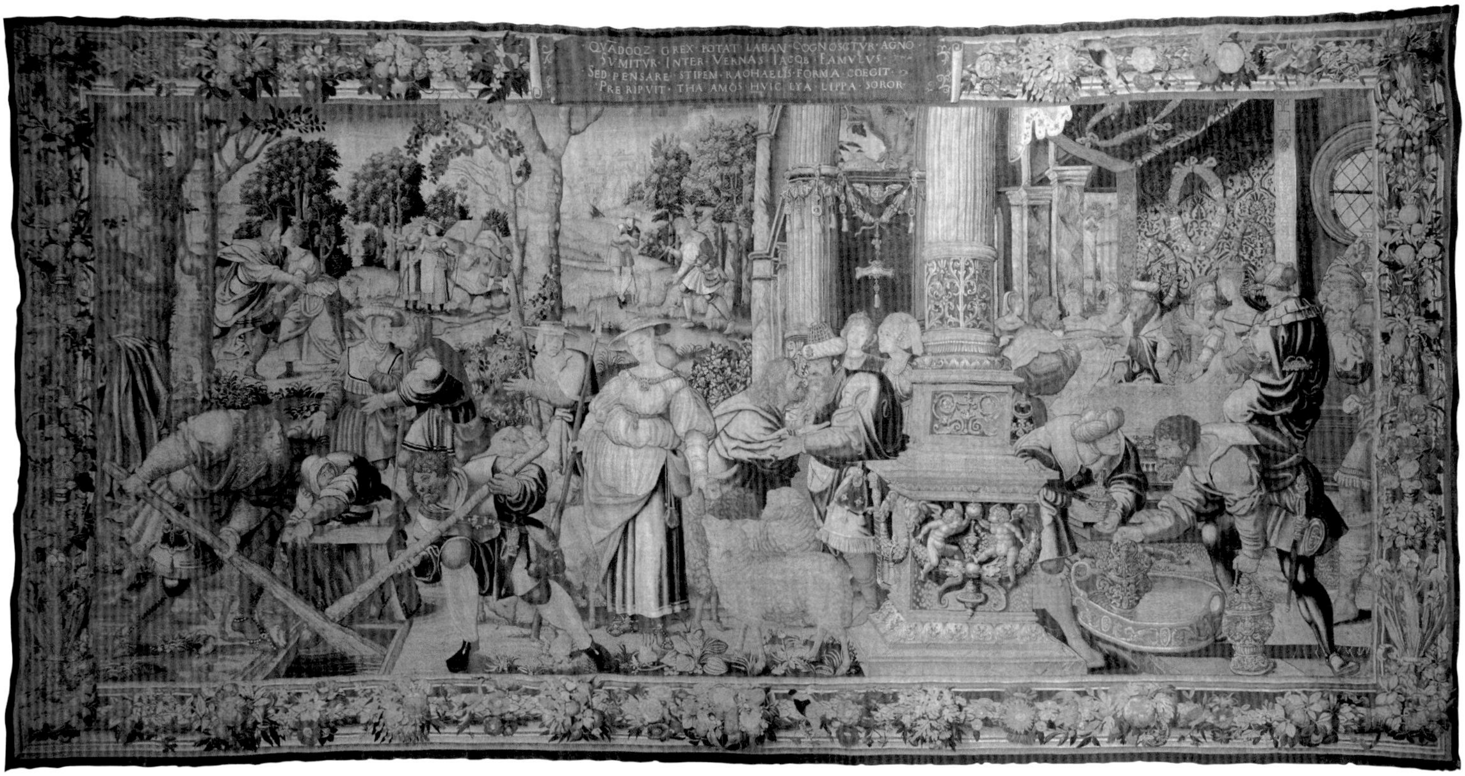

11.15 *Jacob Meets Rachel and Jacob at Rachel's House* from a set of the *Story of Jacob*. Tapestry designed by Bernaert van Orley, woven in the workshop of Willem de Kempeneer, Brussels, ca. 1535–40. Wool and silk, 441 x 792 cm. The Burrell Collection, Glasgow

destined for the Tudor court. According to the 1534 document, the *Jacob* set was as yet unfinished, but if the set in question was the first edition of the series, this would suggest a conception date sometime in 1532, a period in which the subject would have been especially suggestive for Henry, when his anticipated marriage to Anne had renewed his hopes of soon having a male heir and when he was in the process of establishing himself as the head of the English church.

The *Jacob* series was highly successful, and Kempeneer's workshops produced a number of weavings during the late 1530s and 1540s.[78] Nonetheless, even though this suggests that Kempeneer initiated the designs himself and owned the cartoons outright, without any obligation to an originating patron, it is certainly possible that the design was conceived with the English king in mind as a potential patron. As we will see, a similar process of anticipation appears to have underpinned the development of at least two other very large series that Kempeneer developed around 1540, a *Story of Caesar* and a *Story of Abraham*. In both cases, the subjects had strong resonances with Henry's perception of himself, and in both cases Henry appears to have purchased the first weaving of the series.[79]

The Seven Deadly Sins

Another notable purchase of the mid-1530s whose subject is of particular interest in the context in which it was acquired is an "arras" set of the *Seven Deadly Sins*. Its arrival in the English royal collection can be established with moderate precision because the Great Wardrobe accounts for the year Michaelmas 1535 to Michaelmas 1536 include a payment to the king's tailors for lining seven "new" pieces of this subject.[80] Subsequent evidence suggests that this set was one of the most expensive purchased by Henry during the mid-1530s. It was listed among the contents of the Tower Wardrobe in the 1547 inventory, and it was still there one hundred years later at the time of the Commonwealth sale, when it received the high valuation of £2,430.[81] Reserved for Cromwell's use, the set survived in the royal collection and underwent extensive repairs in 1696. Five pieces were subsequently hung at Saint James's Palace in 1710, while one or two pieces were sent to

Hampton Court for the state apartments at some point before 1730.[82] The fate of those at Saint James's is unknown, but one of the Hampton Court panels continued to hang in the nineteenth century in the Presence Chamber, where it was among the furnishings illustrated in the watercolor of that room made by James Stephanoff for William Henry Pyne's 1819 publication, the *History of the Royal Residences* (see fig. 19.9).[83] Enough of the tapestry is visible to allow identification with a piece that survived at Hampton Court until the late nineteenth century, subsequently entered the London trade, and is now in the Pierpont Morgan Library, New York (fig. 11.16).[84] Depicting *Avarice,* the tapestry originates from a seven-piece series whose appearance is known from duplicate weavings now at the Kunsthistorisches Museum, Vienna (figs. 11.17, 11.18), and the Spanish royal collection.[85]

As these surviving sets reveal, the *Seven Deadly Sins* series recast the long-standing medieval fascination with the psychomachia in the Renaissance guise of a sequence of triumphs. Each panel depicts the progress of one of the Seven Deadly Sins, who are represented as winged females sitting on a triumphal car, accompanied by appropriate exemplary figures, in a deep landscape with views of distant cities. The series is unique among sixteenth-century tapestries in that a manuscript description of the complex iconography survives in Madrid.[86] Although this is a mid-sixteenth-century text rather than an original scheme, it provides important information, including the statement that "maistre pierre van aelst paintre d'anvers" conceived the designs and plan ("patrons et ordonnances"). The attribution to Coecke is supported by the close analogy between the style of the compositions, especially the contorted and frenetic figures, the fiery atmospheric effects, and the wide landscapes with distant cityscapes, and Coecke's contemporary work in both tapestry and other figurative media. A tour de force of imagination, the series has long been recognized as one of Coecke's masterpieces in the tapestry medium.

Although the surviving panel at the Pierpont Morgan Library is faded and tarnished, it includes gilt-metallic thread and evidently belonged to a set of the highest quality. Other than Henry's, the earliest documented set is

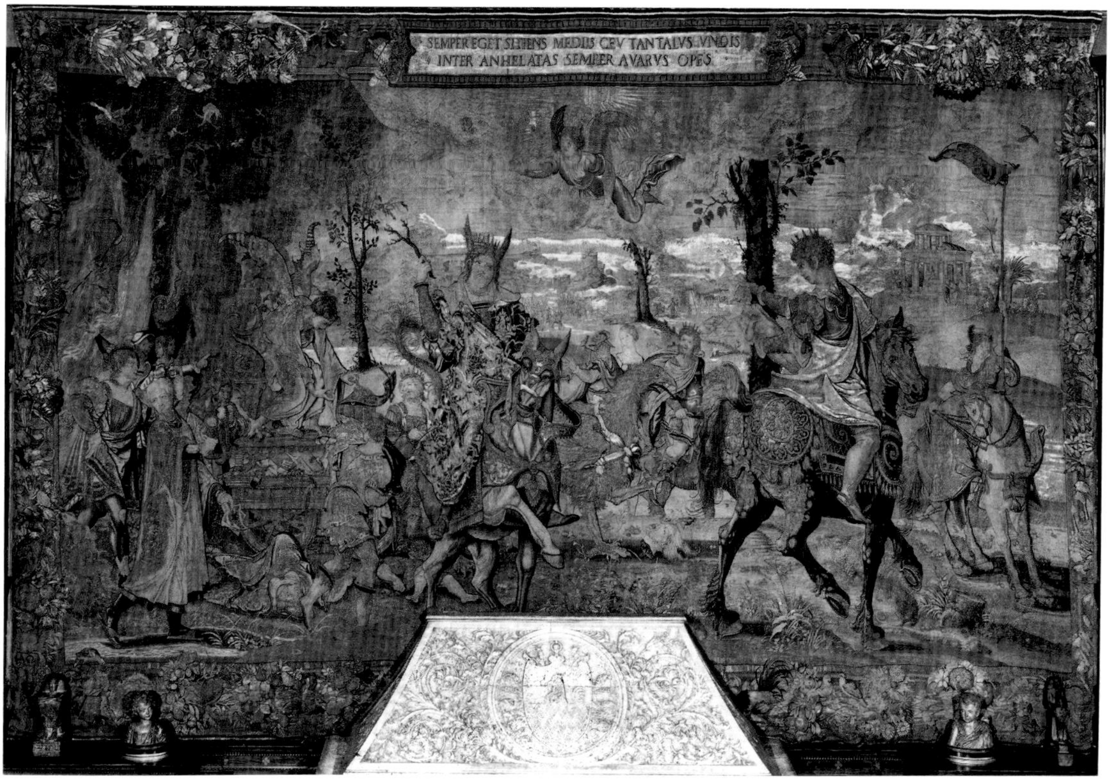

11.16 *The Triumph of Avarice* from Henry VIII's set of the *Seven Deadly Sins.* Tapestry design by Pieter Coecke van Aelst, ca. 1534, woven in Brussels, ca. 1534–36. Wool, silk, and gilt-metal-wrapped thread, 475 x 739 cm. The Pierpont Morgan Library, New York

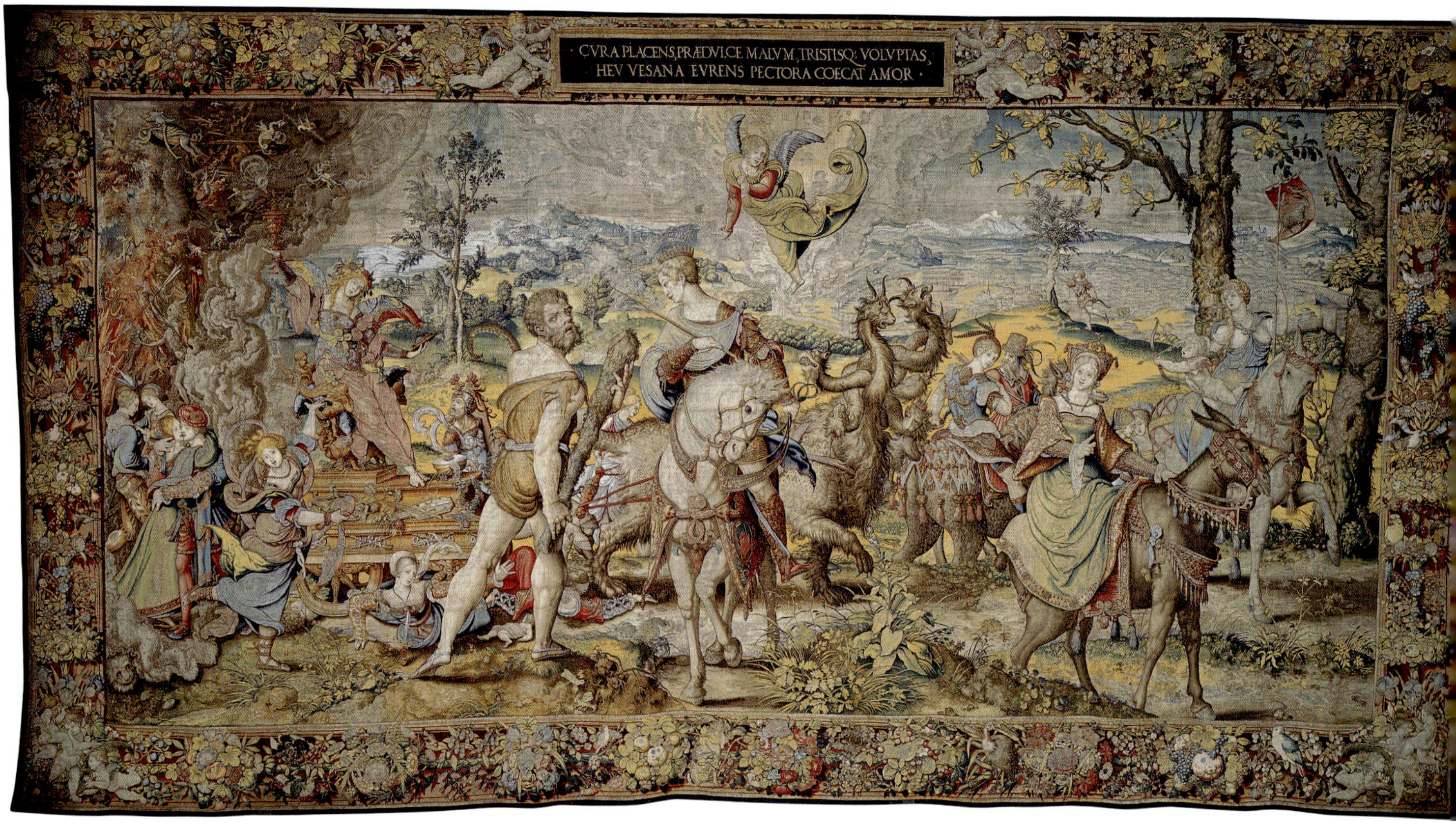

11.17 *The Triumph of Lust* from a seven-piece set of the *Seven Deadly Sins*. Tapestry designed by Pieter Coecke van Aelst, woven by the workshop of Willem de Pannemaker, Brussels, ca. 1542–44. Wool, silk, and gilt-metal-wrapped thread, 459 x 832 cm. Patrimonio Nacional, Madrid

that purchased by Mary of Hungary in 1544 from the Antwerp merchant Pieter van de Walle, but it has often been assumed that the series was conceived around 1537, the putative date inscribed on a drawing reproducing part of the scene of Pride (now at the Städelsches Kunstinstitut, Frankfurt am Main).[87] However, evidence that a set of this subject was delivered to the English court sometime between Michaelmas 1535 and Michaelmas 1536 indicates that the conception of the series must now be dated some years earlier, in late 1533 or early 1534. The set that was lined for Henry in 1535–36 was unquestionably the Coecke design, since the 1547 inventory only lists one set with this subject and this number of pieces. In light of this evidence, it therefore seems likely that Henry's ensemble was the first weaving of this design.

The interesting thing about the acquisition of this set sometime in 1535–36 is that it thus arrived at the Tudor court while Henry was in a state of introspection and emotional upheaval to which the theme of the tapestries must have seemed especially pertinent. The cause of Henry's discontent at this time was Anne Boleyn's continuing failure to provide him with a male heir and the development in his mind of a self-righteous feeling that he had somehow been bewitched or duped by her false charms. His dissatisfaction had been developing over a period of about two years, stemming from the fact that, after all the trouble he had gone through to marry her, the child she bore him in September 1533 was another girl, not the male heir that he so desired. This disappointment had been compounded by Anne's subsequent miscarriage in August 1534, an all-too-familiar echo of his previous wife's failures. When Henry began to court other women again is a matter of debate, and the tradition that he was already unfaithful during Anne's pregnancy in 1533 may be based on a misdated document.[88] Equally, his frustration after Anne's miscarriage in 1534 is well established, and by that September he was known in court circles to be having an affair. According to the Spanish ambassador Chapuis, he had "renewed and in-

11.18 Detail of fig. 11.17

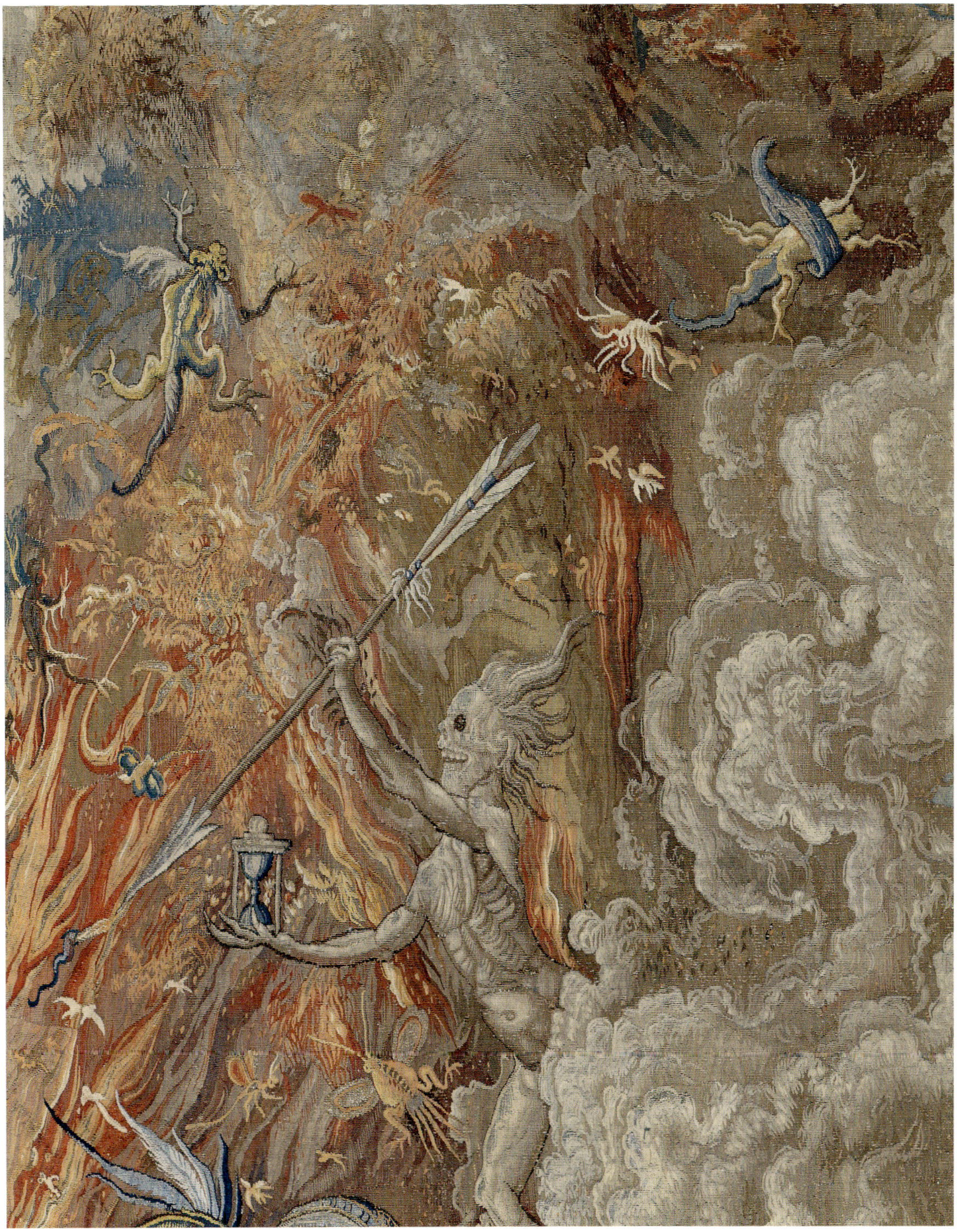

creased the love that he had previously towards another very beautiful maid of honor."[89] The identity of this woman is unknown, but by the following February he had transferred his affections to Mary (Madge) Shelton and was making little secret of his boredom with Anne. According to one observer, he was "tired to satiety" of her, and court factions opposed to Anne's influence wasted no time in providing him with alternative attractions. Jane Seymour (fig. 11.19) seems to have come to his attention in the summer of 1534, and his interest in her had become a cause of concern to Anne by the middle of the following year. The character of the early relationship is a matter of conjecture, but there is no evidence that his behavior was public knowledge until February 1536, at which point rumors began to circulate that he was

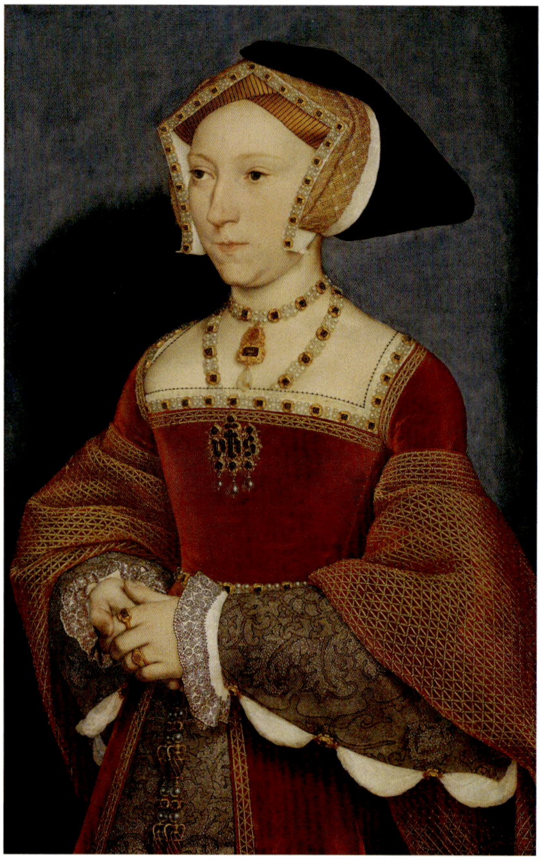

11.19 *Jane Seymour* by Hans Holbein the Younger, ca. 1536. Oil on panel, 65.4 x 40.7 cm. Kunsthistorisches Museum, Vienna

courting Jane. Two significant events in the previous month spurred Henry's more public ardor. First, Katherine of Aragon had died on January 7, 1536, so the woman whom many people still considered his true wife was finally dead. Second, Anne, who had at least been pregnant again, miscarried a male fetus on January 29, her second miscarriage since Elizabeth's birth. Henry's frustrations boiled over. Chapuis records that on the day Henry received this news, he stated that he had been seduced into marriage by witchcraft and that he would have no more children with Anne.[90] The stage was set for her removal, and on May 2 she was arrested on trumped-up charges of infidelity and incest. Subsequent events leave little doubt as to Henry's underlying motivation. Brought to trial immediately, Anne was condemned to death on May 15 and executed on May 19. Henry became formally betrothed to Jane the following day and married her on May 30. Four days later Jane was declared queen.

In this context, the purchase of such an expensive set of tapestries depicting the Vices who dupe and mislead Mankind is singular, at the very least. Was the set purchased to substantiate Henry's perception of himself as a woeful sinner who had now seen the error of his ways? And if so, was this purchase an opportunistic acquisition of a design that had been created as a speculative venture by a Flemish merchant? Or was it the consequence of a long-term project that had been developed in consultation with Henry or some of his advisers? Answers to these questions must be tentative, but the fact that Henry's set is the earliest documented weaving of the design, combined with the fact that it was richly woven with gold thread, suggest that the weaving was likely to have been commissioned by Henry rather than undertaken as a speculative venture. Whether the design was also undertaken for Henry is less certain. Allowing some twenty-four to thirty months for the preparation of the designs, the painting of the cartoons, and the weaving of the set, we might posit a conception date for the series sometime in late 1533 or early 1534, when Henry's earliest doubts about his marriage to Anne could have been developing but when, equally, there was still every reason to hope that Anne would in time produce a male heir. Although it seems unlikely that Henry himself would have conceived of such a series so early in his marriage to Anne, it is certainly possible that the designs may have been created in response to wishful speculation by one of the court factions who disliked Anne and who, emboldened by the outcome of her first pregnancy, may have hoped that a time might soon come when such a meditation on the wages of sin might have a new relevance to Henry's self-image. Whatever the circumstances in which the set was conceived, the delivery between Michaelmas 1535 and Michaelmas 1536 was extremely opportune. The tapestries provided a broad sweep of historical and mythological precedent in which to contextualize the sinful nature of Anne Boleyn and her lovers, as Henry, like the hero of a morality play, turned himself back toward the path of righteousness and his third marriage.

Marriage to Jane Seymour and Birth of Prince Edward

Henry's third marriage, to Jane Seymour, while undoubtedly a love match on his side, was essentially motivated by his continuing desire for a male heir. Jane's future might have been as brief as Anne's had she not been successful in this goal, especially when additional pressure had been added to Henry's dynastic burden by the death of Henry Fitzroy, duke of Richmond, on July 20, 1536, and thus an end to the possibility that Fitzroy might have succeeded him. Fortunately for Jane, the early months of the marriage evidently went well, and by the end of the year Jane was featuring prominently in public ceremonies. The year ended on a festive note with the reception of the Habsburg ambassador in London on December 23, 1536. According to a contemporary witness, "Yesterday the king and Queen, with all the dukes and lords and the Emperor's ambassador, rode through London and were honourably received. Such a sight has not been seen since the emperor was here. The streets were hanged with arras and cloth of gold."[91]

Jane's fortunes rose even higher in early 1537 when her pregnancy was announced to general celebration. Hall records that a "Te Deum" was sung on May 27 in Saint Paul's Cathedral to celebrate the event, with all the senior members of the court and the city in attendance in their finest livery. Finally, on October 12, after a difficult labor, she was delivered of the son for whom Henry had waited so many years. The birth coincided with Saint Edward's day, and the newborn was christened with that name on October 15. A contemporary description reflects the traditional character of the decorative provisions: "the going to the churche beganne at the princes lodging conveyed through the Counsell chamber to the gallery leading through the kinges great chambre. And so through the hall, and the ijnd court to the gallery that goeth to the Chapell. Standing all the way torches borne by the kinges servantes, and other noble mens servants, and all that way banyers wher no walls be and richly hanged and framed with rushes."[92] Once again, one longs for a Great Wardrobe list detailing the tapestries that were to be hung for this momentous occasion, but no such record has survived. We can only conjecture as to the play that may have been made between antique tapestries depicting mythological and historical forebears like Brutus and Saint Edward and newer tapestries celebrating Tudor virtues.

Edward's birth and christening were followed in short order by the death of Jane, who had suffered cruelly in the birth and received little of the rest that she needed to recover. She died on October 24, throwing Henry into a state of genuine mourning that he maintained into 1538. In due course he was to recover his spirits, and among the many projects that he engendered later in 1538 and early 1539 was a sequence of major tapestry commissions, some undoubtedly related to the birth of Edward. But before we consider these developments, we need to look further at the impact of the Reformation on the tapestry collection and Henry's artistic patronage and at the question as to why Henry did not commission tapestries relating to the momentous events of these years with subject matter of a more overt Reformist character.

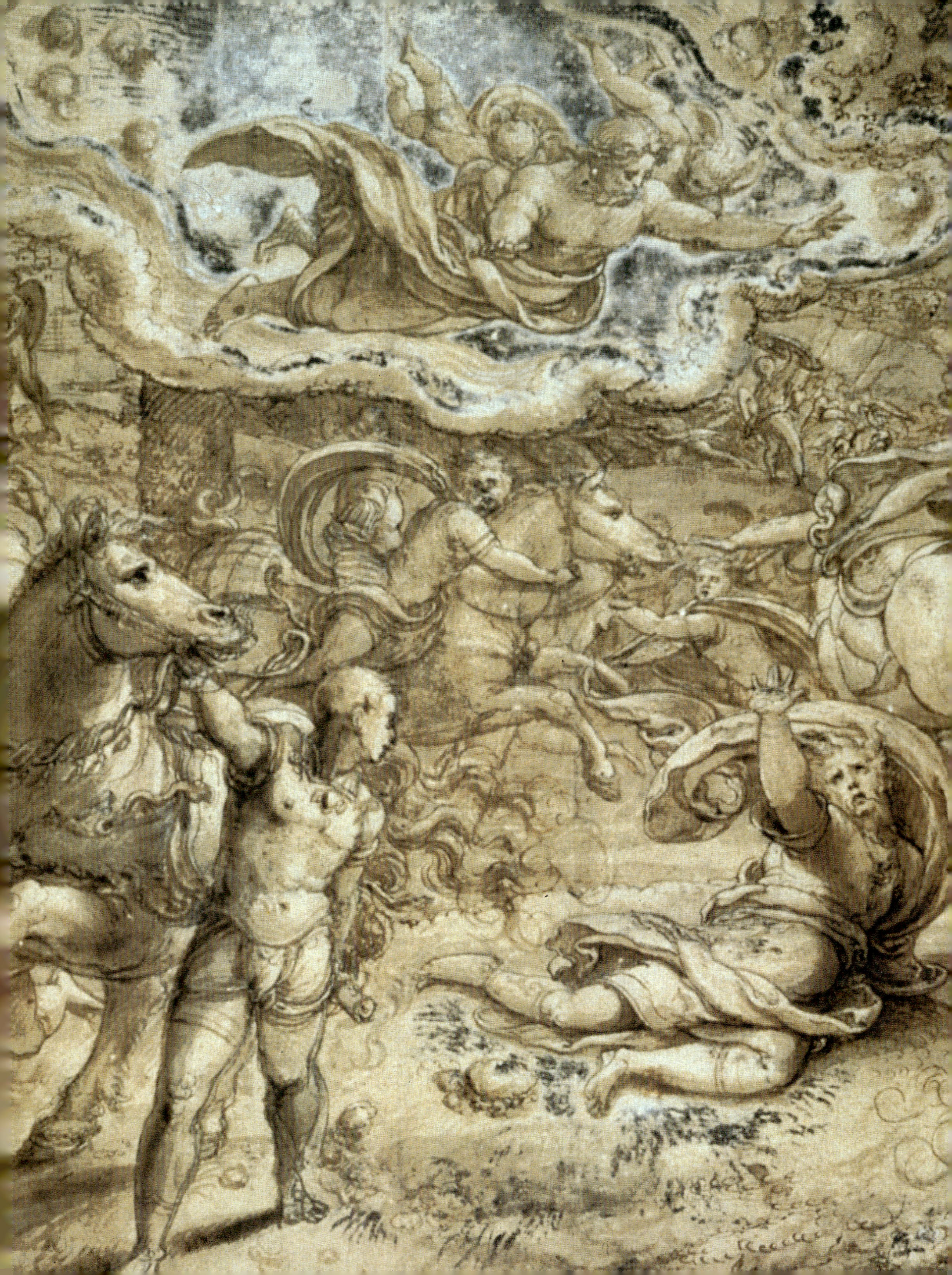

CHAPTER 12

The Impact of the Reformation on the Royal Tapestry Collection

Art and Politics at the Tudor Court during the 1530s

Earlier discussion indicated that in 1528 Henry purchased a hugely expensive set of *David* tapestries because the subject resonated strongly with how he perceived his own situation. We have also seen that other acquisitions during the early to mid-1530s may have been motivated by similar reasons, including an "arras" set of *Job*, documented in the collection by 1531, a very fine set of *Jacob* tapestries, probably purchased sometime in 1534–35, and an "arras" set of the *Seven Deadly Sins*, which was delivered to the court sometime between September 1535 and September 1536. During the late 1530s and early 1540s, this pattern of acquisition was repeated with expensive sets whose subjects, predominantly religious, provided role models that Henry considered to be especially apposite to his circumstances.

This activity raises a number of questions. Given the large sums that Henry was investing in these tapestries and the enormity of the events taking place in the 1530s, why did religious subject matter continue to play such an important part in Henry's purchases, rather than any more overt antipapal or biographical imagery? And how involved were Henry and his advisers in choosing and developing these series? To answer these questions adequately, we need to contextualize these purchases by comparison with Henry's use of other written and visual media to promote his interests during the 1530s.

As Tudor historians have long recognized, the stream of publications either from government-employed pens or disseminated by the king's printer during the 1530s, and the range of styles they display, from complex documents couched in legalistic terms to shorter dialogues incorporating persuasive and accessible language, provide evidence of a consistent intention by Henry and his advisers to use the written word to sway the opinion of a wide populace in favor of the king's divorce and subsequent doctrinal reforms.[1] As of 1534 and the Act of Supremacy, the texts of sermons that were preached by the king's license suggest a similar intent to promote an official message to a broad audience.[2] During the early 1530s much of this written material was legalistic in tone, drawing on historical and biblical precedent. On one hand Henry's advisers looked to the pseudohistoric traditions of the English royal descent, embodied in early English and French chronicles and romances such as Geoffrey of Monmouth's *Historia regum Britannicae*. These were scoured for evidence to support claims of native imperium, and the pseudohistory figured significantly in the manuscript *Collectanea satis copiosa, ex sacris scriptis et authoritatibus Catholicus de regia et ecclesiastica potestat*, a synthesis of historical and legal precedent compiled for Henry by Edward Foxe, the royal almoner, in 1529–30 to demonstrate the independence of the king's sphere of influence from that of the papacy.[3] Henry scrutinized this text, annotating it in at least forty-six places and underlining and scoring it in many others.[4] Three years later, the pseudohistory received more widespread distribution in Polydore Vergil's *Anglica historia*, which had been completed in 1513 but whose publication had been delayed until 1533 because of

Detail of fig. 12.12

12.1 *Henry VIII* by Hans Holbein the Younger, ca. 1536. Oil on panel, 28 x 20 cm. Thyssen-Bornemisza Collection, Madrid

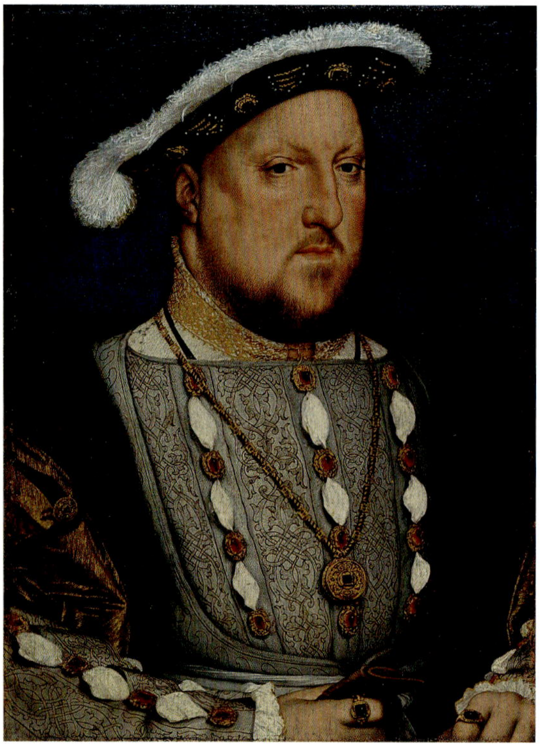

Vergil's reluctance to include the Arthur story as part of the English dynasty.[5] The following year, the weight of "evidence" presented in the *Collectanea* provided the basis for the opening statement of the Act in Restraint of Appeals to Rome, Henry's decisive repudiation of papal supremacy in England: "Where by divers sundry old authentic histories and chronicles it is manifestly declared and expressed that this realm of England is an empire."[6]

The second resource on which Henry's advisers drew was the Bible. Initially this was quarried for precedents that would provide ammunition for the king's divorce case, an effort exemplified by the Old and New Testament figures cited in the manuscript *Collectanea satis copiosa* and the 1531 publication *Determinations of the most famous and most excellent universities....*[7] The *Collectanea* cites Old Testament texts to demonstrate that the authority of the kings of Israel derived directly from God without any spiritual intercessor and that, as such, they were judges by Divine Law, who put down abuses of worship and reformed the clergy. For example, King Hezekiah is cited for destroying the bronze serpent that Moses had set up at God's command because it had now become an article of idolatry. The gloss adds that if a king can abrogate what had once been ordained by God, how much greater is his power over mere human precepts. King Jehosaphat is also cited because he led the people of Israel back from apostasy by appointing judges in each city to exercise the judgment of God.[8] These and other precedents were subsequently recycled in texts published by Henry's propagandists, as for example Edward Foxe's *De vera differentia regiae potestatis et ecclesiasticae, et quae sit ipsa veritas ac virtus utriusque,* a reformulated version of the *Collectanea,* published by Thomas Berthelet in 1534, and Stephen Gardiner's *De vera obedientia oratio,* published by Berthelet in 1535. In the latter, following argument that Saint Paul preached obedience to Caesar, Gardiner justified Henry's supremacy with an argument based on the identification between Henry and the scriptural precedents of the godly Hebrew kings such as Solomon and Hezekiah.[9]

While these propagandistic publications were essentially legalistic in tone, they also encouraged a more personalized and panegyric form of identification between Henry and the Old Testament patriarchs. This is exemplified by a manuscript of Clément Marot's *Sermon du bon pasteur et du mauvais,* drawn up by the author for Anne Boleyn in about 1533. This incorporated various changes from the printed text designed to flatter the royal couple, including a reference to Henry VIII as a second Ezekiel, sent by heaven to reform abuses.[10] Similarly, Henry Parker's *Exposition and declaration of the psalme, "Deus ultionum Dominus...,"* prepared as a manuscript in 1534 and published in 1539, praised Henry as a modern King David delivering England from the pope, the great Goliath, and as a second Moses leading England, a new Israel, out of bondage.[11]

To what extent did the Tudor court use the visual arts to substantiate the claims that were being made for Henry in written materials? This question has been the subject of considerable discussion in recent years. Early-twentieth-century commentators tended to regard Tudor artists as having little purpose other than to please the king's whims, but during the second half of the century historians increasingly applied the terminology of modern public relations and propaganda in seeking to discern a political purpose to Tudor court art during the Reformation. In the 1960s it was suggested that Henry's patronage of Holbein (fig. 12.1) was part of an attempt to promote a triumphant image of sacral kingship in support of his goals.[12] Various historians have taken this argument even further, suggesting that the Tudor monarchs were highly self-conscious about their image and that the radical administrative and religious changes instituted during the 1530s were consolidated by a carefully orchestrated image-making operation that encompassed paintings, frescoes, and prints.[13]

Critical response to this line of argument has been mixed, and subsequent studies have argued for caution in the application of modern notions of propaganda to the Tudor court.[14] The most forceful of these revisionist challenges has contended that assumptions regarding the dissemination of readily comprehensible propaganda images to a broad audience are specious and that the only genuinely ubiquitous form of propaganda during the Tudor reign was the widespread display of the royal coat of arms.[15] Cautioned by this revisionist lead, the most recent analyses have taken a more nuanced approach, seeking to focus on the context in which the purportedly propagandistic images of the reign were produced and on the audiences by whom they would have been seen.[16] The most striking conclusion that emerges from these studies is the relatively small number of painted and printed images produced by the Tudor court that did have any political content. Analysis of the inventories of Henry's collection reveals that only a handful of the three hundred or so oil paintings he owned can be identified as having overtly antipapal imagery of the kind exemplified by Girolamo da Treviso's *Four Evangelists Stoning the Pope* (fig. 12.2), which was painted in the early 1540s.[17] Indeed, the vast majority of the paintings were portraits. The small scale of the few propagandistic canvases and their location within the royal palaces would have ensured that they were seen by a limited number of people. Nor is there any evidence that such images were more widely disseminated in printed form.

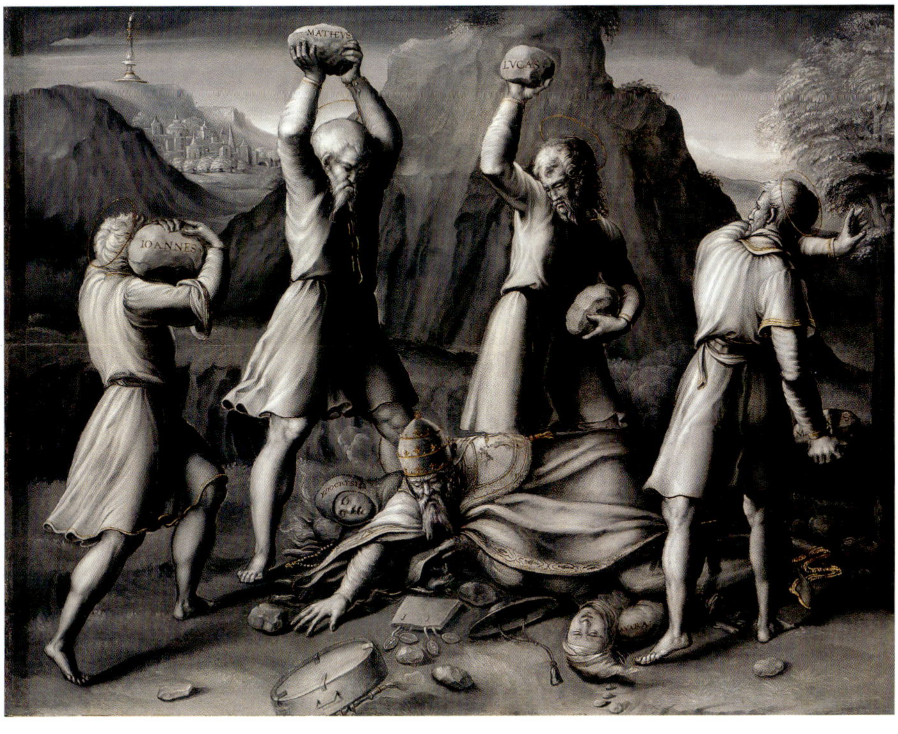

12.2 *The Four Evangelists Stoning the Pope* by Girolamo da Treviso the Younger, ca. 1540. Oil on panel, 68 x 84.4 cm. The Royal Collection

Contextual analysis also reveals the limits of even the most overtly propagandistic images created for Henry during the 1530s. For example, although we know nothing of the appearance of the fresco of Henry's coronation that was painted in the gallery at Whitehall in 1531–32,[18] its location cannot have allowed it to have been seen by many people, even if its imagery was in some way indicative of the claims for native imperium that were now being made so stridently on Henry's behalf. Much the same can be said of Holbein's dynastic portrait of Henry, Jane Seymour, and his parents, painted in the Privy Chamber at Whitehall in the mid-1530s. This was destroyed in the Whitehall Palace fire of 1698, but its appearance is known from Holbein's cartoon for the figure of Henry and from a seventeenth-century copy of the entire fresco by Remigius van Leemput (fig. 12.3).[19] Although the central Latin inscription certainly contains an explicit reference to Henry's repudiation of the papacy, the notion that it would have had a dramatic propagandistic impact has been challenged on the

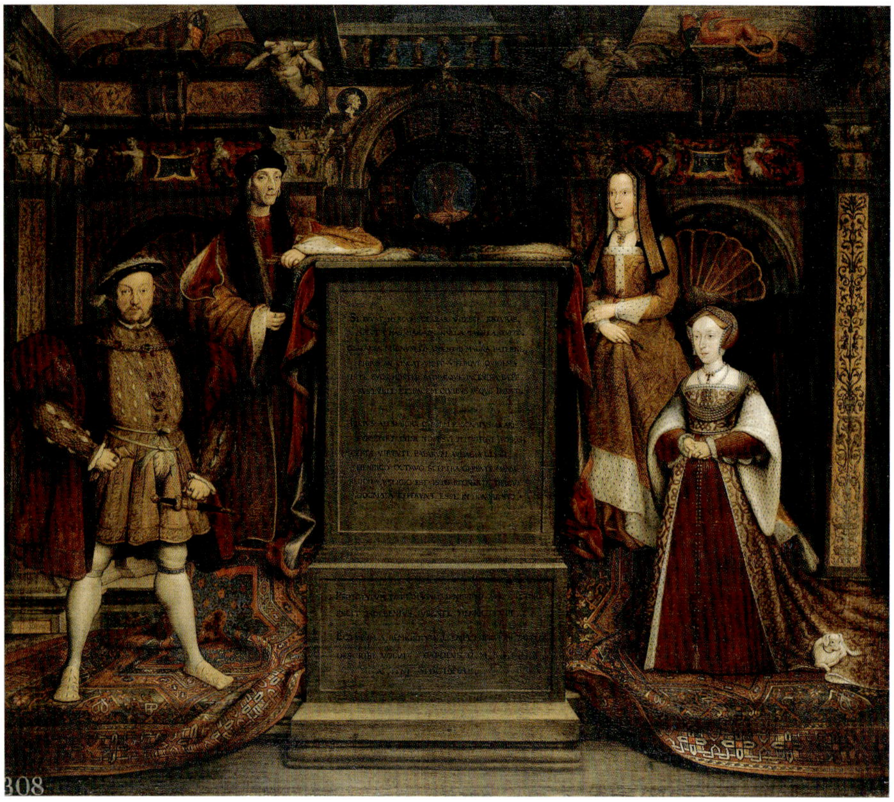

12.3 *The Whitehall Mural (Henry VII, Elizabeth of York, Henry VIII, and Jane Seymour)*, a copy by Remigius van Leemput after Hans Holbein the Younger, 1667. Oil on canvas, 88.9 x 98.7 cm. The Royal Collection

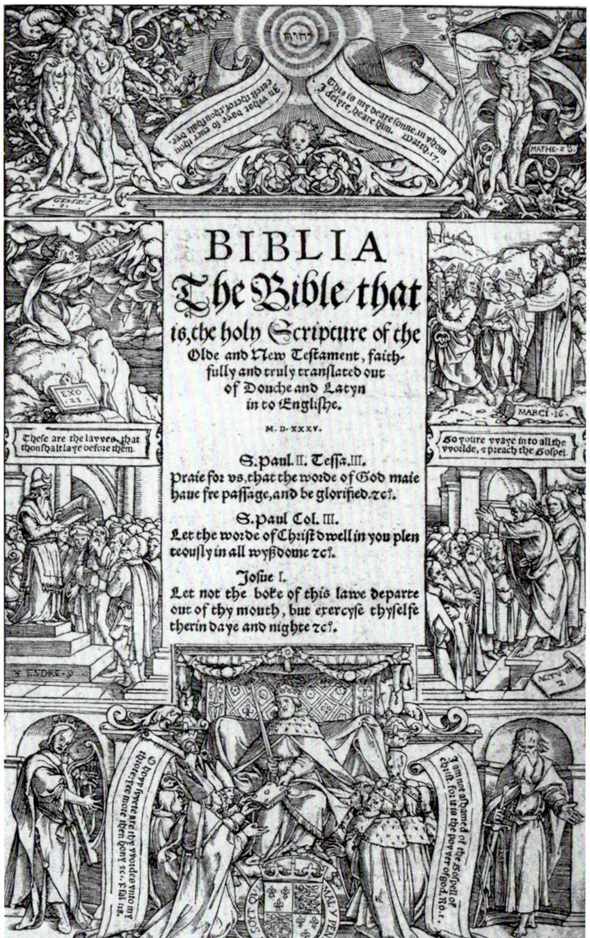

12.4 Title page of the Coverdale Bible, by Hans Holbein the Younger, ca. 1535. Woodcut, 31.5 x 18.2 cm. British Library, London

grounds that it would have been seen only by a privileged few.[20] To some extent this argument can be countered with the observation that this was not, of course, an era of universal suffrage and that the opinions Henry would have been most eager to influence were those of the key members of the nobility, clergy, and city, who were all regularly present at court. Nonetheless, the fact remains that the two Whitehall frescoes hardly constitute overwhelming evidence for a centralized program to use the figurative arts to promote the Reformation. Similarly, the suggestion that Holbein's famous portrayal of Henry was promoted by the court as an "approved" image in painting and engraving, analogous to the manner in which images of Queen Elizabeth were circulated in the 1580s and 1590s, is also not supported by the evidence. It is notably absent from the cover plate of the Great Bible, the one truly propagandistic image of Henry's reign that was certainly created at the king's order for widespread distribution in printed form. Generally speaking, surviving portraits of Henry VIII show that there was no concerted effort to promote a single image at the expense of less flattering portrayals.[21] Furthermore, dynastic portraits that can be linked to royal patronage, such as the Hampton Court group portrait of Henry, Mary, Edward, and Jane Seymour (see fig. 17.6), are lacking in any antipapal propaganda. Again, there is no evidence that images like this were spread to a wider audience in printed form.

Yet if the extant paintings and frescoes created for Henry during the 1530s provide little support for the notion of a centralized propaganda campaign, contextual study does, nonetheless, reveal how the imagery of a number of pieces reflected Henry's identification of himself with certain religious role models in an increasingly personal way. This development can be traced in four works that have often been cited as evidence for the purported "propaganda" campaign: the title page of the Coverdale Bible of October 1535; Holbein's portrayal of Solomon and Sheba of the mid- to late 1530s; the Psalter presented to Henry by Jean Mallard sometime in the late 1530s; and the

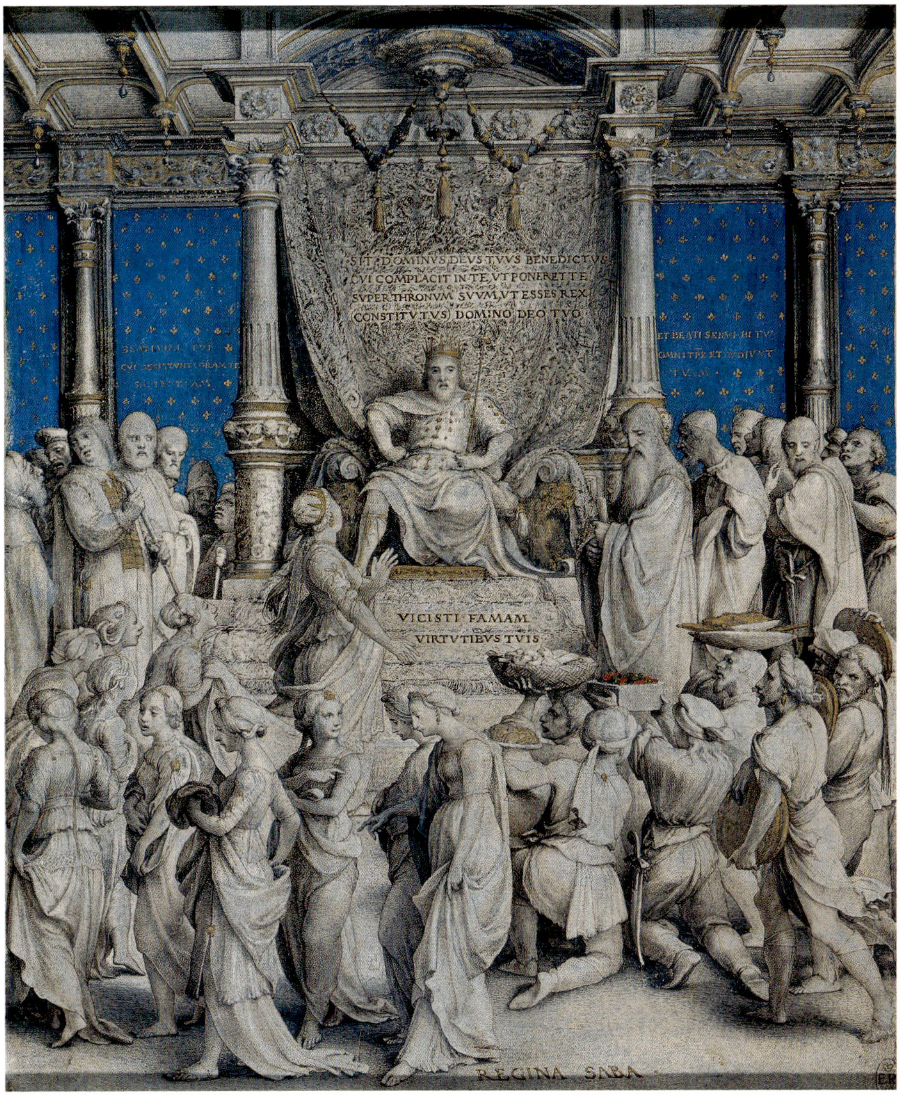

12.5 *Solomon and the Queen of Sheba* by Hans Holbein the Younger, ca. 1535–40. Pen and ink with watercolor, body color, and gold paint on vellum, 22.7 x 18.3 cm. The Royal Library, Windsor Castle

title page of the Great Bible published in 1539.

In the first of these (fig. 12.4), Henry is shown as the successor to a line of Old Testament patriarchs and New Testament apostles, all of whom had played a key role in preaching God's word. Below scenes of appropriate Old Testament role models, Henry hands a copy of the Bible to his clergy, flanked by King David and Saint Paul. Although it was not authorized and cannot be taken as an officially sanctioned image, the fact that the title page was executed by Holbein, with the probable knowledge of Cromwell, suggests that whoever conceived the design must have known that this recasting of the traditional book presentation concept would appeal to the king's taste.[22]

Holbein's painting of *Solomon and the Queen of Sheba* presents an interesting conceptual development (fig. 12.5). Where the Coverdale Bible showed Henry flanked by appropriate antecedent figures, the inscription on the painting conflates Henry with Solomon as God's elected ruler, and Solomon's features are close to Henry's.[23] The conflation of Henry with Solomon is interesting in that it parallels the shift that was also taking place in the written texts of the period, away from legalistic comparisons toward a more personal form of identification. If, as seems most likely, this portrayal was conceived as a New Year's Day gift, then it confirms the extent to which this process of identification between the king and certain prototypes was already established in contemporary court perception of the king. That such comparisons were pleasing to Henry is corroborated by the illustrations in the Psalter created for him by Jean Mallard in the late 1530s, in which King David is depicted with Henry's features (figs. 12.6, 12.7). The intense degree to which Henry identified with David is reflected by the annotations and scorings that he made in this text.[24]

The title page of the Great Bible of 1539 (fig. 12.8) provides a further variation on Henry's identification with patriarchal role models. Henry is represented in the upper right corner of the plate, kneeling on a hillside with his crown in front of him, in direct communication with God. Comparisons and analogies have been discarded in favor of an image in which Henry is shown, quite literally, as a prophet to his own people. Below, he hands the Bible to his clergy and nobility who, in turn, communicate the word to the general populace, who respond with cries of "Vivat Rex" and "God Save the King."[25] The idiosyncratic nature of the whole program suggests that it may have been dictated by the king himself.

In summary, contextual analyses of the paintings and engravings produced by and for Henry during the 1530s provide little evidence of any centralized campaign to promote the goals of the Reformation. Instead, they reveal the increasingly personal way in which Henry identified himself with certain religious role models in the course of the 1530s as he became

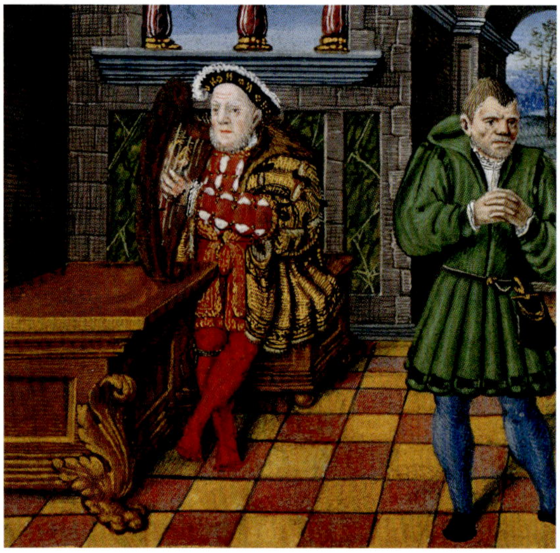

12.6 *Henry VIII as David* from the Psalter of Henry VIII. Bodycolor on vellum, 20.5 x 14 cm. British Library, London (Royal Ms 2 A XVI)

ever more autocratic and delusional about his status as God's chosen leader. In view of the extent to which the written word was used for disseminating Reformation propaganda, the lack of evidence for greater use of the visual arts is somewhat surprising, but that appears to be the case on the basis of the visual evidence treated by previous historians. Of course, as the reader of this study will now anticipate, the answer to this conundrum lies not in the paintings and engravings on which prior commentators have focused but in the royal tapestry collection.[26]

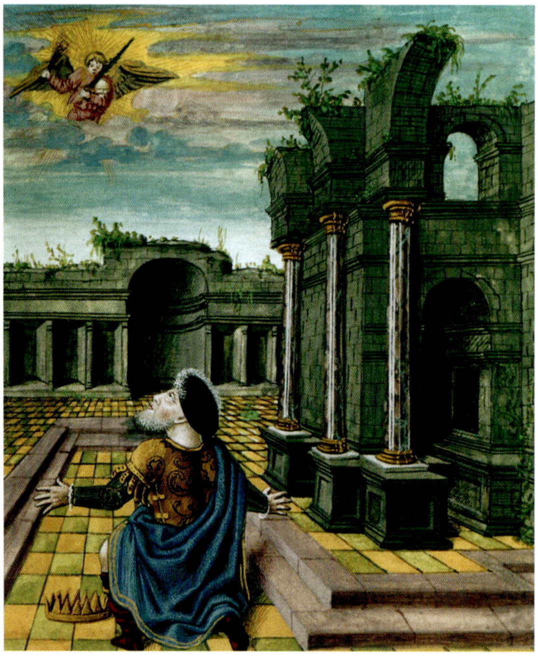

12.7 *Henry VIII as the Penitent David* from the Psalter of Henry VIII. Bodycolor on vellum, 20.5 x 14 cm. British Library, London (Royal Ms 2 A XVI)

At first sight, there is little obvious evidence that Henry used tapestry as a tool of propaganda or persuasion during the Reformation years. The 1547 inventory records few tapestries or borders with Henry's arms, and none of Henry's documented or assumed purchases are readily identifiable as celebrations of the Tudor dynasty, the events of the Reformation, or Henry's political or military achievements. Should we conclude from this that he was unaware or uninterested in the potential that tapestry provided for political display? Considering the historic and contemporary Continental precedent for the propagandistic use of tapestry and the enormous sums that Henry was investing in the medium, this seems highly unlikely. So what is the explanation for his apparent lack of initiative in this respect? Why were so few armorial tapestries added to the collection during Henry's reign, and why are there no images of Henry as the head of the English church, Henry as the defender of the faith, or Henry as the vanquisher of the papacy?

The answers to these questions are relatively simple. Regarding the lack of armorials, one factor that would have militated against the inclusion of armorial components in new tapestries from the 1520s was that, as of this date, many of the more elaborate tapestry series had borders that had been conceived as an integral part of the whole design. Almost all of the important sets in the collections of Francis I and Charles V also lacked devices identifying the patron.[27] And the likely explanation for the lack of armorial tapestry commissions from Henry VIII during this period is the relative ease with which he could now obtain embroidered armorial hangings from professional embroiderers working at the direction of the Great Wardrobe.[28] The visual elements of heraldic displays were easy to reproduce in embroidery, and the characteristics peculiar to embroidery were highly appropriate for armorial hangings as they could be embellished with raised work and precious stones to create a rich, three-dimensional surface, like those displayed in the apartment prepared for Francis I at Calais in

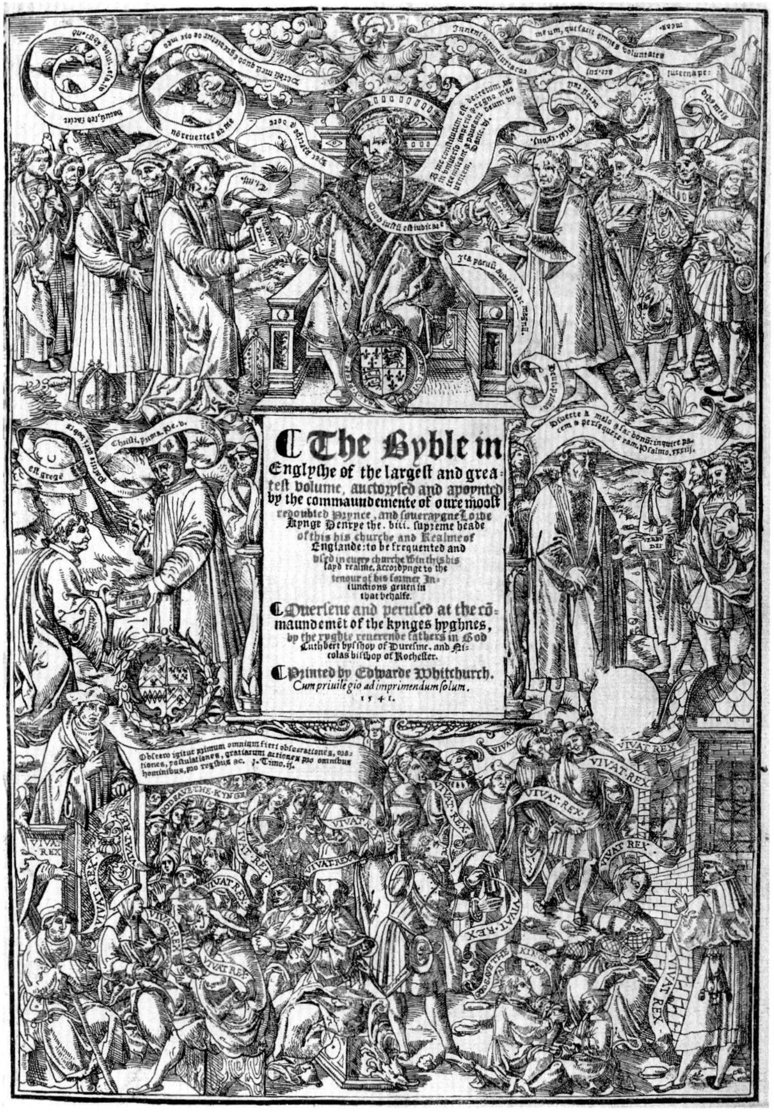

12.8 Title page of the Great Bible, 1539. 35.5 x 24 cm. The Royal Library, Windsor Castle

1532. By 1547 the collection included many such ensembles and cloths of estate.[29] None of these survive, but an impression of their richness is conveyed by the canopies depicted behind Henry in paintings like the Barber-Surgeons' portrait and the Hampton Court dynastic portrait (fig. 12.9, see also fig. 17.6).

The explanation for the lack of commissions portraying Henry as a Reformation hero is equally logical. The issue that would have focused Henry's thoughts on such propagandistic exercises, his desire to obtain a divorce from Katherine, brought him into conflict with the Habsburg court because Katherine was Charles V's aunt. The subsequent break with Rome and events of the English Reformation were wholly antipathetic to Charles's familial loyalties, political policies, and religious beliefs. It is therefore almost certain that Charles would have opposed the production of tapestries in Flemish workshops that carried iconographic schemes overtly supportive of Henry's cause. It can hardly be coincidental that all of the dynastic tapestries produced in Brussels from the 1520s featured members of the Habsburg court or their allies as, for example, the *Nassau Genealogy,* a portrait series of that family executed around 1530, or the *Spheres* tapestries executed for the Portuguese king around the same date.[30] Francis I's tapestry collection was also devoid of overtly propagandistic subject matter with the exception of one allegorical set of tapestries, a trompe l'oeil imitation of the painted and stucco gallery created for him at Fontainebleau by Rosso Fiorentino and Primaticcio (fig. 12.10). Significantly, that set was woven in a workshop created specifically for this purpose at Fontainebleau, providing circumstantial evidence that such explicit subject matter could not be commissioned from Brussels.[31] Fear of Charles's reaction was no theoretical issue for the Flemish weaving community. Bernaert van Orley and several of the leading master weavers and atelier directors had been prosecuted in 1527 for their Reformist sympathies.[32] Many received stiff fines, and it seems unlikely that any would have risked further trouble for Henry's sake during the charged climate of the early Reformation.[33]

In this context, it is interesting to note that one tapestry does have imagery celebrating Henry VIII and the Reformation, the exception that proves the rule. This little-known panel, now at Nether Winchendon House near Aylesbury (fig. 12.11), depicts Henry sitting in state, holding the orb and scepter, flanked to his right by peers and to his left by clergy.[34] A scroll next to Henry's head carries the inscription "Predicate evangelium omni creatur[ae]" (Preach the Gospel to every creature). A bearded figure wearing the Order of the Garter and carrying a rod of office stands in the left foreground, while a kneeling bishop occupies the right. The bearded figure is almost certainly John, Lord Russell, who was made a knight of the garter in 1539 and became lord privy seal in

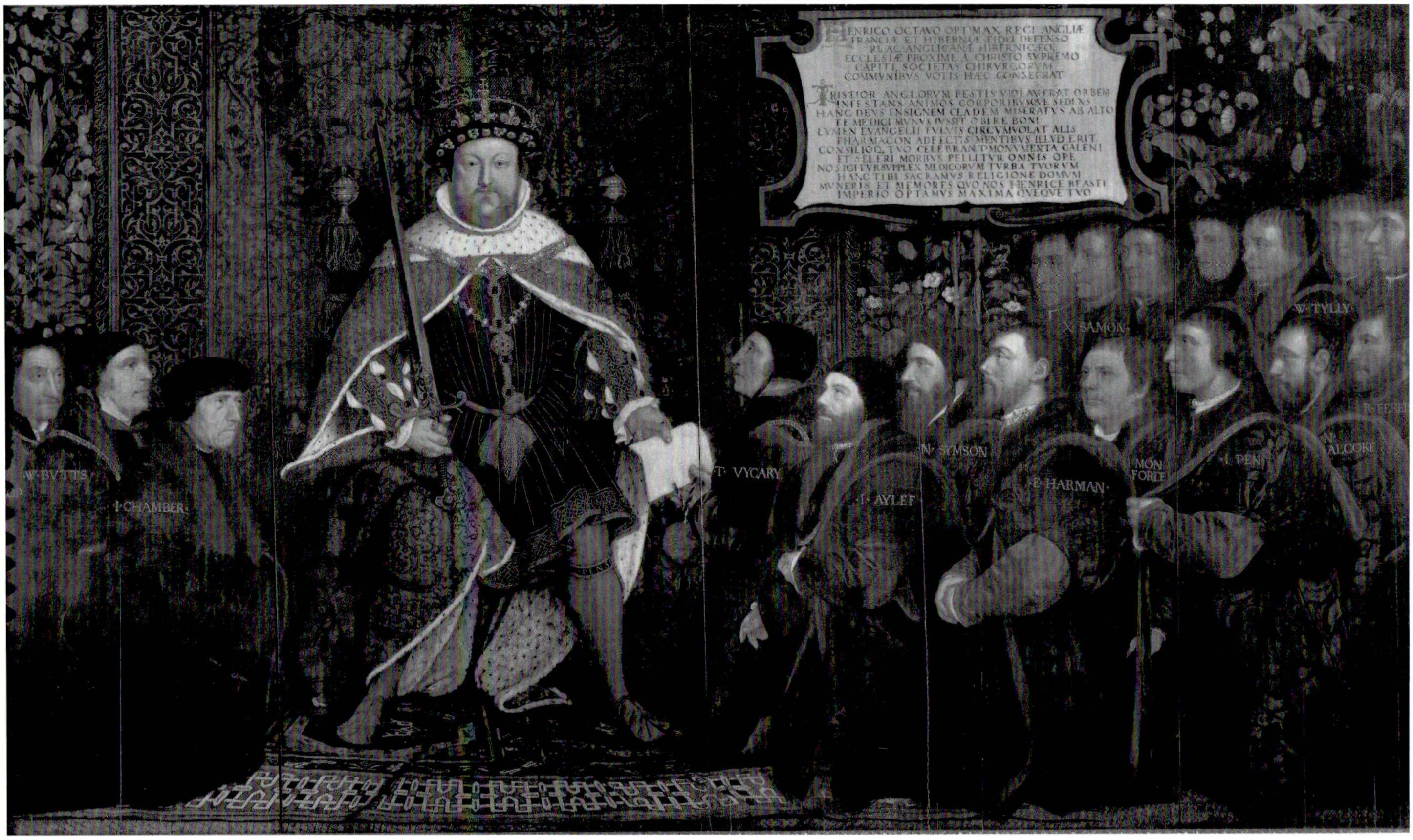

12.9 *Henry VIII Granting the Charter to the Barber-Surgeons' Company* by Hans Holbein the Younger, ca. 1541. Oil and tempera on panel, 180.3 x 312.4 cm. Barber-Surgeons' Hall, London

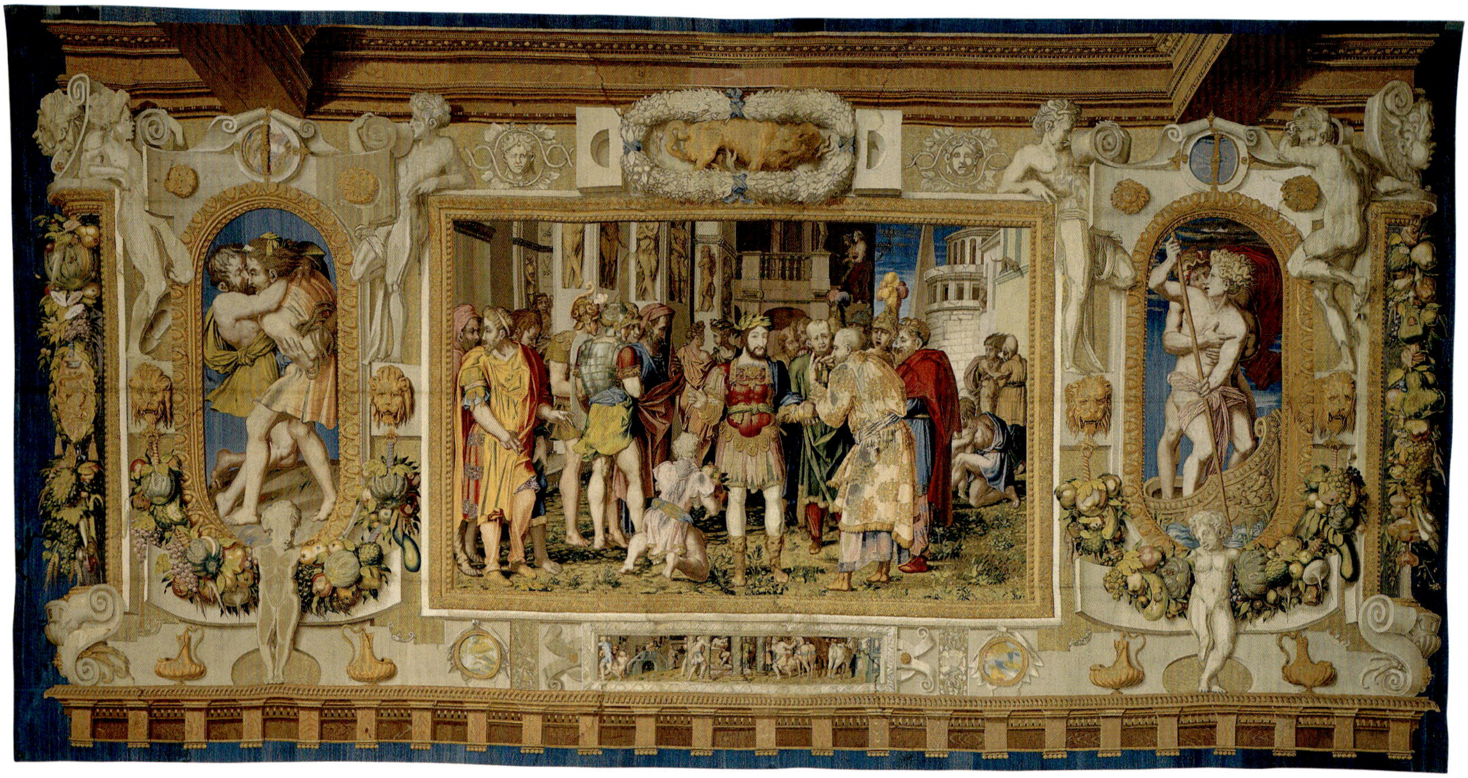

12.10 *The Unity of the State* from a six-piece set known as the *Gallery of Francis I*. Tapestry designed by Claude Baudouin and others after Rosso Fiorentino and Francesco Primaticcio, ca. 1539. Woven at Fontainebleau between 1540 and 1547. Wool, silk, and gilt-metal-wrapped thread, 330 x 620 cm. Kunsthistorisches Museum, Vienna

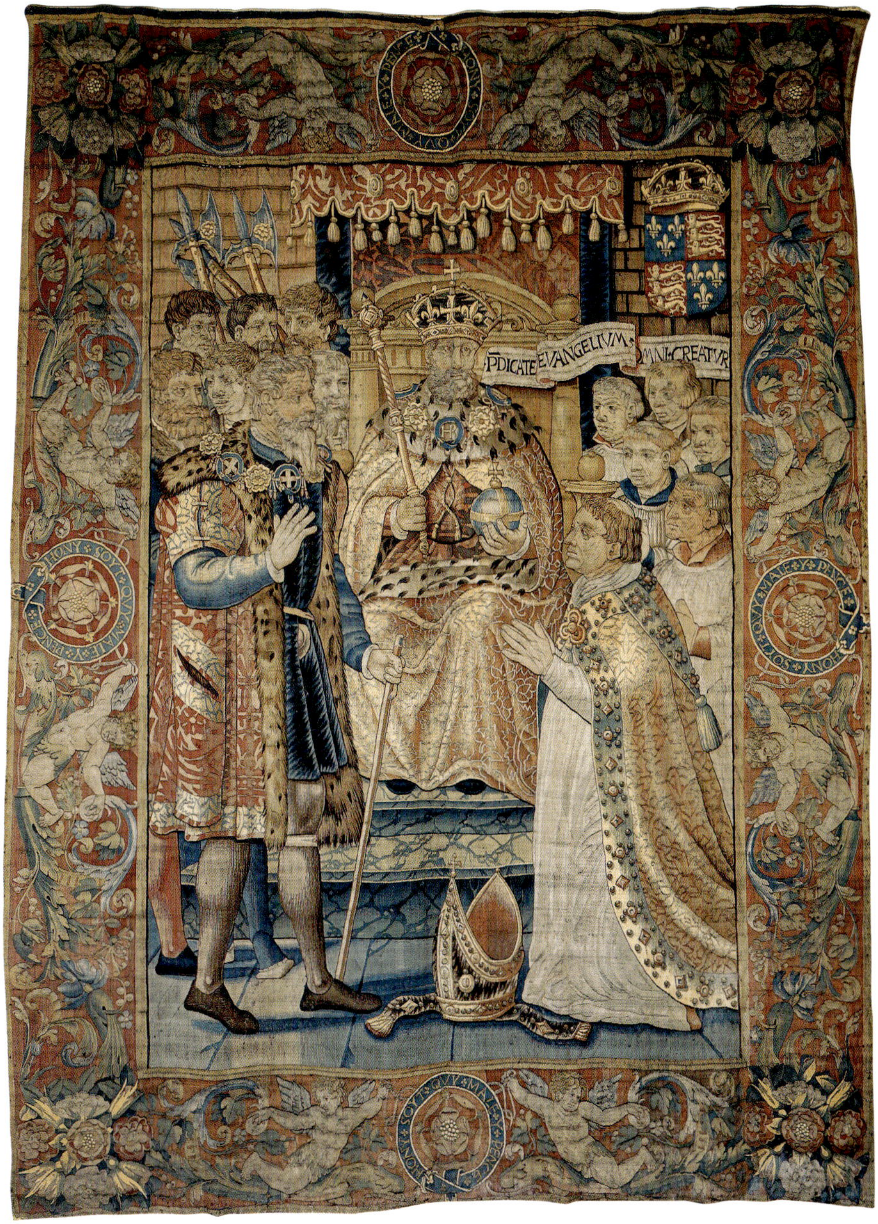

12.11 *Henry VIII with John, Lord Russell, and Archbishop Cranmer.* Tapestry woven in the Southern Netherlands or England, ca. 1539–45. Wool and silk, 335 x 244 cm. Nether Winchendon House, Aylesbury

December 1542, while the bishop must be intended as a representation of Cranmer. The date of weaving is unknown, but stylistically the piece appears to date from the mid-1540s. No tapestry of this subject appears in the 1547 inventory, which suggests that it was not a royal commission. In view of the prominent position occupied by Lord Russell, the repetition of the Order of the Garter in all four borders of the tapestry, and the fact that the house in which the tapestry survives was once in Russell's possession, it seems likely that he commissioned the tapestry, perhaps as a celebration of his appointment as lord privy seal.[35] As such, the tapestry provides further evidence of an awareness among members of the English court as to the potential of the tapestry medium for "political" portrayal. In view of Russell's high office and proximity to the king, that circle must have included the king. In this context, it is therefore even more interesting to note the rather coarse character of the design and weave, both of which suggest that this panel was made in a provincial workshop rather than in Brussels, the source of Henry's high-quality tapestries. Interestingly, the border of this panel is very similar to one that appears on a number of tapestries produced in Enghien during the 1530s and 1540s, which might even suggest that this panel was made by workers under the supervision of Jan Mostinck, the royal arras maker, who was born in Enghien and may have maintained contacts with workshops there.[36]

Yet if Henry was unable to commission overtly political or propagandistic tapestries from the high-quality workshops in Brussels, the character of the most expensive sets he acquired in the late 1530s and early 1540s is remarkably consistent. Most of them featured Old Testament patriarchs or New Testament apostles. Considering the evidence from contemporary written and visual material that Henry increasingly identified himself with these religious figures during the 1530s and the likelihood, discussed above, that earlier purchases such as the 1528 *David* set were also acquired because of the resonance of the subject to his situation, it seems probable that these later purchases reflected a similar intent. Investigation of this issue is complicated by the lack of evidence regarding when the vast majority of Henry's tapestry acquisitions entered the collection. However, in the case of the very expensive sets where the date of acquisition can be identified with certainty, analysis of the context in which they arrived at the court does, indeed, support the notion that they were acquired because the subjects provided role models that were especially significant to Henry in the context of the Reformation. These sets will form the subject of individual studies below and in the following two chapters.

The Story of Saint Paul

The earliest of the major acquisitions of the last decade of Henry's reign that can be identified is a *Story of Saint Paul*. When this arrived at the Tudor court can be established with some precision because the Great Wardrobe account for the year Michaelmas 1538 to Michaelmas 1539 records payment to the king's tailors for lining "xi" pieces of "Arras novum" of the "Actibus Apostolum."[37] The possibility that this was a reference to a set woven from the Raphael *Acts of the Apostles* cartoons can be discounted because, although Henry was to acquire a set of that design, written records show that it was not delivered and lined until 1542. Instead, the 1538–39 reference can be equated with a nine-piece, gold-woven set of *Saint Paul* listed in the Hampton Court inventory in 1547.[38] The fact that the Great Wardrobe account cites eleven pieces, not nine, must result from a scribal error. The account is a copy of a long tally of charges, and since the number is written in Roman numerals, it seems likely that the scribe mistakenly put the "i" after the "x" rather than before it.

Although Henry's *Paul* set disappeared in the eighteenth century, documentary evidence suggests that it was an exceptionally fine weaving. At the Commonwealth sale following Charles I's execution it was valued at £3,065, identifying it as one of the ten most costly sets in the collection, and it subsequently served in the redecoration of Windsor Castle for Charles II in the 1670s.[39] It was still there in the 1770s, when it was mentioned in a contemporary guide to the palace.[40] Although we have no visual record of its appearance, the documented dimensions of the set, and the details of the description from 1770, allow us to determine that it was an edition of a well-known design series of which several whole or partial sets have survived in Madrid, Vienna, and elsewhere.[41] The series comprised nine scenes depicting the principal events from Saint Paul's life, as narrated in the Acts of the Apostles, chapters 7–28 (figs. 12.12–12.14 and detail opposite p. 229). The set is attributed to Pieter Coecke on stylistic grounds, and its conception has traditionally been dated to ca. 1534. However, evidence that a seven-piece set of this theme was purchased by Francis I in 1532, with subjects corresponding to seven of the scenes in the Coecke set, indicates that the design may have been conceived some years earlier than previously thought. Although three scenes have subjects in common with the Raphael *Acts of the Apostles,* the stronger influence appears to have been the *Deeds of Scipio* by Giulio Romano and Gianfrancesco Penni. With its dynamic figures, unusual angles of viewpoint, and its attention to details of setting and costume, the *Paul*

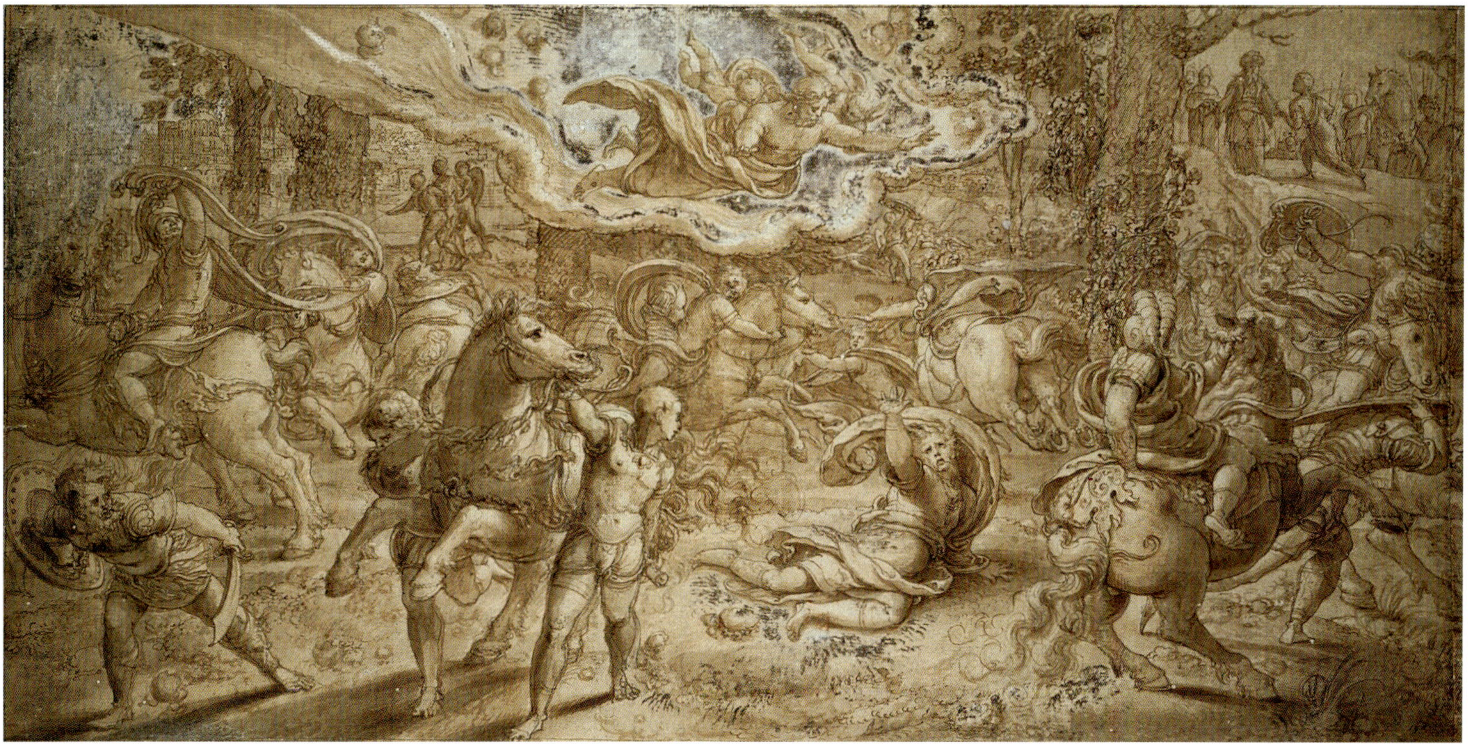

12.12 *The Conversion of Saul* by Pieter Coecke van Aelst, ca. 1529–30. Modello for the tapestry in the *Story of Saint Paul*. Pen with brown wash and white heightening on paper, 25.8 x 41.5 cm. Victoria and Albert Museum, London

design represents an extraordinary tour de force by Coecke.

Why would Henry have wanted to pay for such a rich set of Saint Paul in the late 1530s? The question takes us back to the heart of Reformation politics. The events of the early 1530s provided the opportunity for the advancement at the English court of a number of courtiers sympathetic to Lutheran ideas. Paul was an attractive figure for the Protestant movement because of his evangelical activity and the emphasis of his teaching on direct communication with God. Henry probably got his first serious exposure to Paul's work from Anne Boleyn, whose Reformist tendencies are a matter of record and who is known to have made public demonstration of her interest in Paul's epistles from the dedication that Loys de Brun wrote for a treatise on letter writing that he presented to Anne on New Year's Day, 1530.[42] With the repudiation of the papacy and the Act of Supremacy in November 1534, Paul became an especially resonant figure for English Reformers because he provided an alternative to Petrine supremacy. Similarly, his emphasis on Christ's teaching that one rendered to Caesar what was Caesar's and to God what was God's was a crucial dictum in Henry's efforts to repudiate papal jurisdiction.[43] For the more ardent Reformers he was also a prototype for the evangelical role in which they wished to cast Henry. As such, Paul featured prominently on the title page of the Coverdale Bible, flanking Henry along with King David. Although this was not an officially sanctioned image, the fact that it was executed by Holbein with the probable knowledge of Henry's chancellor Thomas Cromwell, himself a staunch Reformer, suggests that whoever conceived the design must have known that it would appeal to the king's taste.[44] With Cromwell's injunction of 1538 that a vernacular Bible should be placed in every parish church, the Act of Six Articles of 1539, and the publication of the Great Bible the same year, Henry effectively fulfilled the hopes of this radical Protestant faction, at least for a time.[45]

The acquisition of such a rich set of *Saint Paul* in this context can hardly have been coincidental. Assuming that the set would have taken at least two years to weave, we can posit a commission sometime between the end of 1536 and the end of 1537, exactly when discussions were taking place regarding dissemination of a vernacular translation of the Bible. The

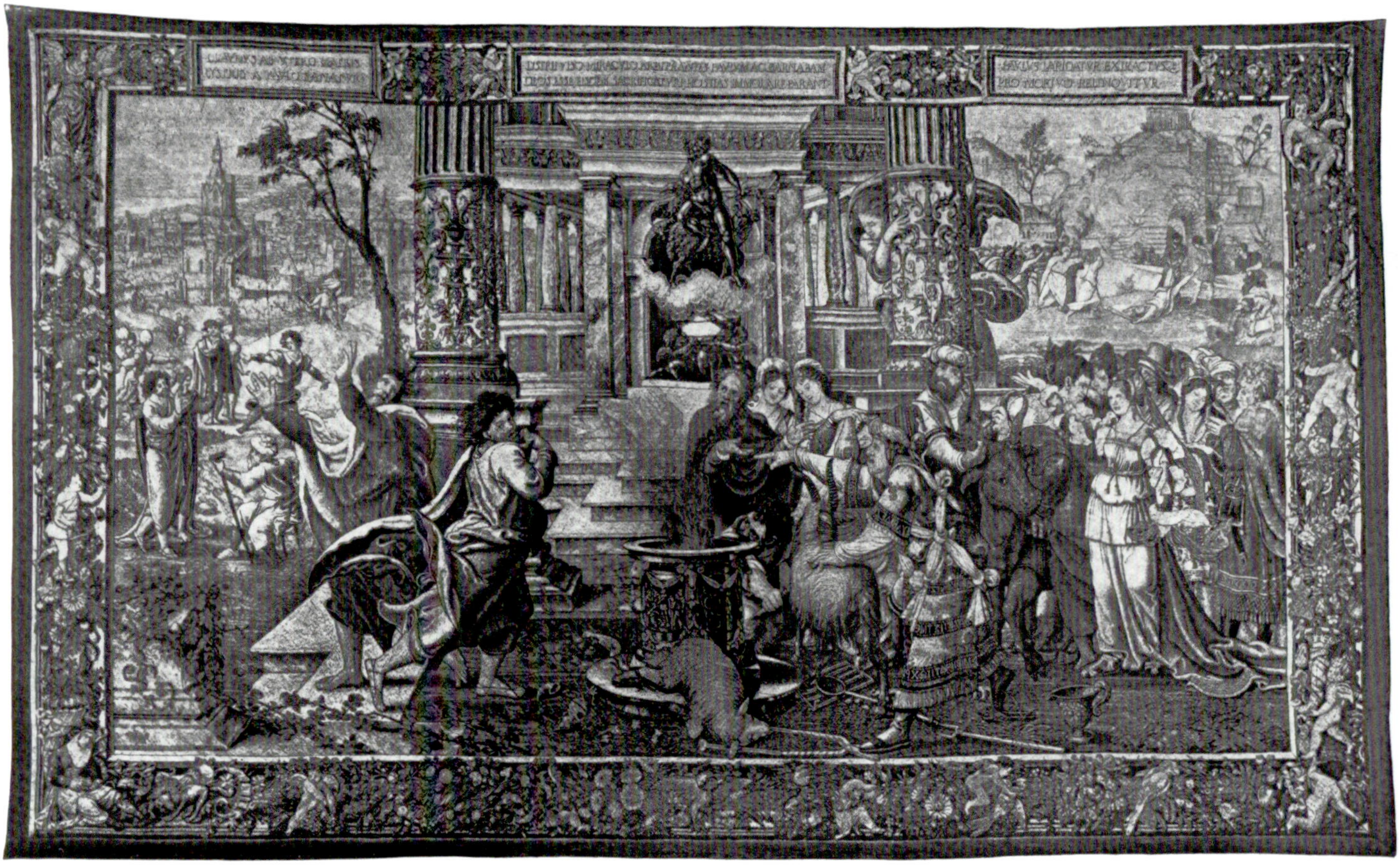

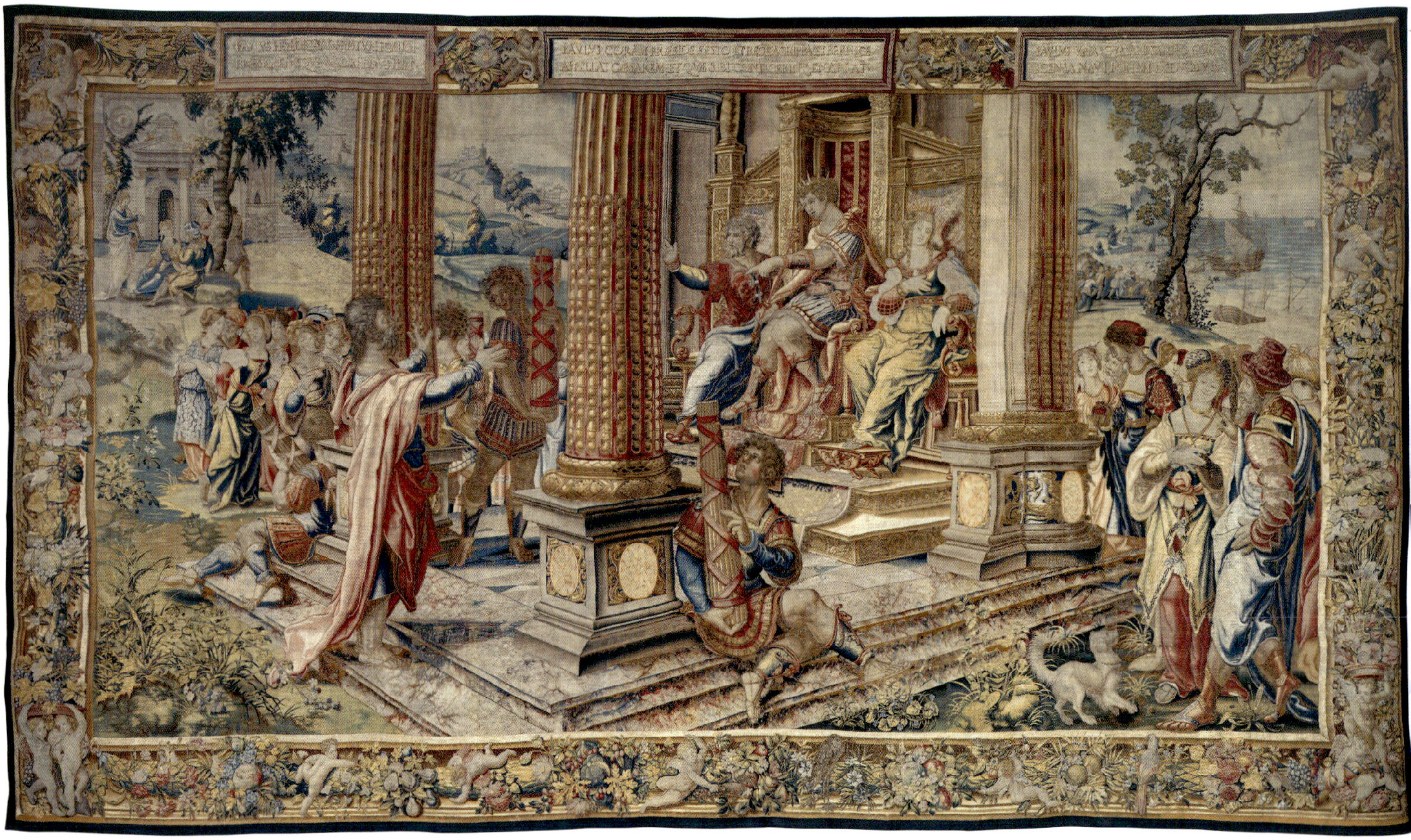

Opposite, top:
12.13 *The Sacrifice at Lystra and Other Episodes from the Life of Saint Paul* from a set of the *Story of Saint Paul.* Tapestry design by Pieter Coecke van Aelst, ca. 1530. Woven in Brussels, ca. 1540. Wool and silk, 425 x 680 cm. Schloss Friedrichshof, Kronberg

Opposite, bottom:
12.14 *Saint Paul Defending Himself before Agrippa and Other Episodes from the Life of Saint Paul* from a set of the *Story of Saint Paul.* Tapestry design by Pieter Coecke van Aelst, woven in a Brussels workshop, ca. 1540–45. Wool and silk, 370 x 700 cm. Institute of Arts, Detroit

process by which the commission was engendered remains a matter of speculation. As we have seen, the first weaving of the design was probably made for Francis I in the early 1530s and may even have been a topic of conversation between Francis and Henry during their meeting at Boulogne in 1532. Thereafter, the cartoons of the series presumably remained in the hands of the Antwerp or Brussels merchant who had commissioned them from Pieter Coecke. Given the close links that existed between the Antwerp merchant community and the Reformist thinkers at the English court, it was presumably through these channels that Henry or his advisers were introduced to the designs. Interestingly, Francis's set included only seven scenes, where Henry's included nine, so it is possible that two were specifically added for him, but in the absence of documentary evidence we can only speculate what these may have been. Whatever the case, the recurrent citation of Saint Paul as a role model for Henry in texts and sermons generated by the court during the mid- to late 1530s, provides circumstantial evidence that the purchase of this set was motivated by an intention to celebrate the parallel between Paul, the main propagator of Christ's teachings, and Henry, the latter-day evangelist who was responsible for introducing the Great Bible to every church in the country.

The *Paul* set was just the first of a number of highly expensive tapestries that Henry was to acquire during the later years of his reign, all but one with religious subject matter, but before we consider these other sets, something should be said about another aspect of the Reformation that had considerable import for the royal tapestry collection, the confiscation of secular and religious properties that occurred during the 1530s.

Tapestry Appropriations from Secular Collections during the Reformation

The dramatic reforms that Henry implemented during the early 1530s provoked considerable resistance among certain sectors of the court and the population as a whole. Between 1532 and 1540, around 880 English subjects were charged with treason, and of these, 308 were executed. Although many of these unfortunate souls were of low social status and wealth, thirty-four were individuals involved with court politics, of whom twenty were executed.[46] A side effect of this persecution was that the properties and collections of the attainted parties, including their tapestries, were absorbed into the royal collection, and many items deriving from confiscated properties can be identified in the 1547 inventory.

One of the earliest victims of this wave of persecutions was Gerald Fitzgerald, earl of Kildare, who in 1534 was summoned to London from Ireland to face charges of treason. He died that September while in detention at the Tower. An inventory of his wardrobe goods at Maynooth records thirty-four pieces of tapestry comprising six sets, of which two were said to be "fyne tapistre" and one was described as "old aras," as well as an old bed of "fine tapistrye."[47] In the same year, John Fisher, bishop of Rochester and relentless opponent of the royal divorce, was committed to the Tower for his refusal to swear the oath of compliance in entirety, and he was eventually executed there on June 22, 1535. An inventory of his goods taken earlier on April 27, 1534, "being in the said house to the use of the king," lists hangings of old "arras" in the hall, two pieces of tapestry in the chapel, five pieces of old green verdure in the parlor, and various other hangings of say and painted cloth.[48]

The following year, 1536, the swift events associated with the fall and execution of Anne Boleyn and her supposed lovers provided another windfall, this time from the possessions of Sir Henry Norris. An inventory of May 3 records goods delivered from Norris's residences at Parland, Kew, and Greenwich to the custody of Edmund Harman of the Wardrobe. Again, while the majority of these were hangings of say, several sets of tapestry were also listed, including one of *Octavian,* presumably depicting the history of the first Roman emperor of that name, another of verdures with beasts and trees, as well as several unidentified sets, table and cupboard carpets, some wrought with the king's arms, roses, and fleurs-de-lis, and twenty-eight cushions of "satin figure tapestry" wrought with Norris's arms.[49] In passing it is to be noted that another of those charged with adultery with the queen, and tried at the same time as Norris, was William Brereton, who had acted as intermediary for the Hanse merchant Edward Smytting in the sale of the rich *Passion* set to Henry during the late 1520s.

Another property and its furnishings that accrued to the Crown in 1537 were those at the Hackney residence of Henry Percy, sixth earl of Northumberland, who had the misfortune to have been associated with Anne Boleyn shortly before Henry became interested in her. According to Cavendish, Wolsey was closely involved in the process of extricating Percy, by threat, from whatever agreement he had with Anne, and he was quickly married off to Mary Talbot, daughter of the earl of Shrewsbury, to get him out of the way. This episode was said to be the root of Anne's hatred for Wolsey.[50] Percy succeeded to the family title and estates in 1527, but his relationship with his family deteriorated to such an extent that, lacking children of his own, he made a grant of his estates to the king in June 1537, shortly before his death, on account of the "debylytery and unnaturalness" of his kin.[51] The 1534 inventory of Northumberland's goods at his Hackney residence listed some fifty or so tapestries, including three small pieces of fine "arras," seven pieces of "counterfeit arras" of *Atalanta,* six pieces of *Venus,* six of the story of *Aeneas,* twenty-six pieces of fine verdures, some of "park-work" and some with roses, and another eleven pieces of a coarser type with beasts and fowls, as well as various carpets.[52]

Further properties also accrued to the Crown owing to the charges that Cromwell brought against the White Rose faction in late 1538. Cromwell had been watching Reginald Pole's family carefully since 1536 when Pole, a distant relation of the Tudors, had made his attack on the king's divorce and royal supremacy from the safety of the Continent. Pope Paul III made Pole a cardinal in 1536, and in the following years he was closely involved with plots against the English king. Armed with the confession of Geoffrey Pole, who turned king's evidence to save his own skin, Cromwell struck in late 1538 with charges against Lord Montague (Henry Pole) and his circle.[53] No inventories for the possessions of Montague or of Sir Edward Neville have survived, but precedent suggests that the properties of all three would have been forfeit. This was certainly the case with the possessions of Montague's mother, Margaret Pole, countess of Salisbury, which were seized for the king in November, as evidenced by an inventory of her possessions at Warblington House, Hampshire.[54] Similarly, an inventory of another of those accused in the Pole conspiracy, Henry Courtenay, marquis of Exeter and earl of Devonshire, also committed to the Tower in November 1538 and executed on December 9, records the goods at his residences in London and elsewhere, including a set of seven tapestries of *Hunting and Hawking,* another nine pieces of "parkwork," as well as three tapestry counterpoints, and various cupboard and window carpets and tapestries.[55] The accusations and charges resulting from this first round of arrests and executions led to a further act of attainder the following February. Among those listed was Sir Adrian Fortescue, a distant relation of Anne Boleyn, who was executed the following July. An inventory of his goods (February 18, 1539) lists hangings that, as usual, appear to have been subsumed into the royal collection.[56] Another victim of this round of arrests was Henry's former favorite and master of the horse, Sir Nicholas Carew, who was arrested in early 1539 and executed on March 8, 1539. Carew's main residence of Beddington Place, Surrey, is among those whose contents are listed in detail in the 1547 inventory, when approximately forty-five tapestries and verdures were listed. One of these was described as "oone peace of Arras with Sir Nicholas Carowis half picture sett in waynescot."[57]

Thomas Cromwell and the Dissolution of the Monasteries

If the possessions of attainted courtiers provided a significant source of tapestries to the royal collection during the 1530s, in numbers if not in quality, another aspect of the Reformation that was to affect the collection significantly was the dissolution of the monasteries. In part, this was because Henry's agents were instructed to inform him about any furnishings that might be appropriate for his use, including tapestries. More important, the enormous sums of money generated by the dissolution appreciably increased the ambition and scale of Henry's tapestry commissions during the late 1530s and 1540s.

The key architect of the dissolution was Thomas Cromwell (fig. 12.15), and in this context it is interesting to note how extensively, following his ascent to power, he too began to collect tapestries. The relatively modest character of his possessions at the start of his court career is reflected by an inventory taken at his house in Austin Friars, London, in June 1527. The contents were similar to those recorded in the properties of other prosperous merchants and court officers of the day and included one border of "arras" work, "with a picture of Occupation and Idleness," and one new tapestry counterpane. All the other hangings were of say or stained canvas.[58] That these few tapestries were considered among the objects of greatest value is reflected by a will Cromwell drafted in 1529 in which his "best coverlet of tapestry and quilt of yellow Turkey satin" were bequeathed to his son.[59] Evidence that Cromwell was already seeking to expand his collection is provided by a note of 1528 in which the correspondent informed him about various objects in a property at Felixstowe, including "old hangings, of little value, of the life of Job."[60] (In view of this dismissive valuation, it seems unlikely that this set was related to the eight "arras" hangings of the same subject on which the royal arras maker worked in 1530–31 and that were subsequently carefully repaired later in the sixteenth century.) By this date

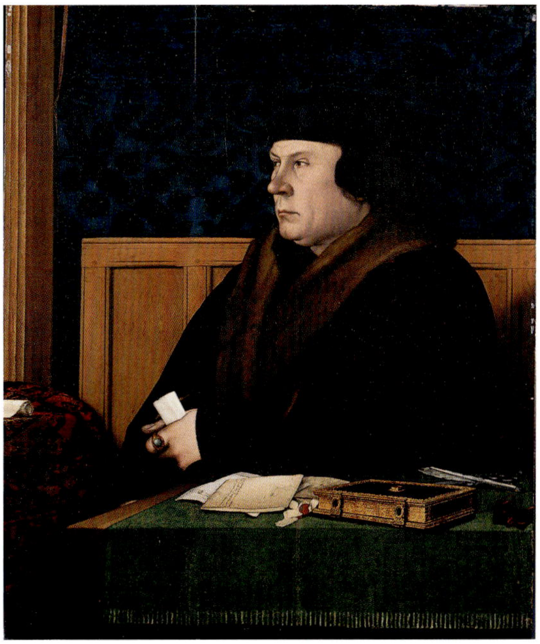

12.15 *Thomas Cromwell* by Hans Holbein the Younger, 1542–43. Oil on panel, 78.4 x 64.4 cm. The Frick Collection, New York

Cromwell must also have been commissioning tapestries from Continental sources, as indicated by a letter of 1530 in which John Williamson informed Cromwell that he has "fetched home the piece of arras and paid the maker."[61]

The caliber of Cromwell's collection changed radically during the next five years, with his promotion to the Privy Council in 1531 and subsequent appointments as chancellor of the Exchequer in 1533 and king's secretary in 1534. The financial benefits he received in these offices allowed him to purchase the sizeable building in Austin Friars that Giovanni Cavalcanti and his merchant colleagues had previously occupied.[62] Cromwell evidently undertook some repair and expansion to this property, and in August 1535 Thomas Thacker, a member of his household, reported that "the roofs thereof are framing with all speed; your lodgings trimmed with windows, glass and hangings—a goodly place in my opinion."[63] What these hangings were is unrecorded. The only named set of tapestries for which we have documentation at this time is a purchase he made in November 1539 through Richard Gresham for thirteen "hangings of verdures with waterflowers," at a cost of 2s. 2d. per ell.[64]

Given his position at court, Cromwell was well placed to exploit the same channels through which Henry was acquiring tapestries. Indeed, evidence that he was also involved in acquiring tapestries on behalf of the king is indicated by a letter of March 14, 1538, from John Hutton, the English agent in Brussels, to Sir Thomas Wriothesley, mentioning that he has written to Cromwell regarding the "rich hanging of arras which Hobbie has seen."[65] This must have been Sir Philip Hoby, gentleman usher and politician, who was then in Brussels with Hans Holbein, who had traveled there to make a portrait of Christina of Denmark, duchess of Milan, for Henry VIII. Hoby was a sophisticated patron of the arts, and his will of 1559 mentions a number of hangings.[66] Given Cromwell's close commitment to the advancement of the Reformation cause in England, and considering the close contacts that he enjoyed with merchants who were active in the Netherlands, he could well have played a part in determining the character of some of Henry's grandest acquisitions of the late 1530s. In particular, it seems reasonable to conjecture that he may have been involved in, or influenced, the purchase of the *Story of Saint Paul* that was delivered in 1538–39.

Any purchases that Cromwell did make may also have been supplemented by appropriations. As the principal agent of Henry's Reformation it was to Cromwell that the commissioners reported regarding the religious institutions under investigation. The circumstances of these confiscations are well known. The Act of Supremacy in 1534 confirmed the king's right of visitation in his capacity as supreme head of the Church and empowered him to carry through the religious reforms that he intended. Early in 1535 Henry appointed Cromwell as his vicar general with a commission to hold a visitation of the churches, monasteries, and clergy. The *Valor Ecclesiasticus,* a survey of the wealth of the English church, was compiled in 1535, and in early 1536 a dissolution statute permitted the suppression of all monastic houses with an annual income of less than £200, unless they were licensed to continue.

By autumn of that year the dissolution was well under way, and contemporary documents provide a vivid impression of the goods that Cromwell's agents proceeded to seize for the king's use. However, although the dissolution was to yield enormous financial benefits for the Crown, the number of tapestries accrued from this process cannot have been as large as that from private individuals. Tapestry was an expensive commodity, and few of the smaller houses would have had the financial resources to make such purchases. For example, an inventory of goods at the Abbey of Tilty, Essex, drawn up in early 1536 includes only hangings of painted cloth and red say.[67] Similarly, the inventory of Austin Friars, Shrewsbury, of 1538 records only a stained cloth before the altar in the chapel and old stained cloths and hangings in the chambers.[68] That of Austin Friars, Ludlow, taken in the same period, records six old stained altar cloths in the choir.[69] In other cases, no textile hangings are recorded. Of course, there were exceptions. An inventory of June 6, 1536, recording goods delivered by the abbot of Beeleigh, Essex, to the king's commissioners, mentions a number of tapestries along with articles of furniture in the different chambers. Similarly, an inventory taken at White Friars in Ludlow in 1538 records an old cloth of "arras" in the sacristy and say hangings in the prior's chamber.[70] In some cases, houses had been endowed or gifted valuable textiles by wealthy patrons, such as at the Nunnery of Minster in Sheppey, Kent, where on March 27, 1536, the commissioners listed two hangings of verdures with the arms of the Norwoods hanging on either side of the choir and four small tapestries with the same arms for the kneeling stools in the Lady Chapel, along with hangings of green say in the prioress's chamber.[71]

As the dissolution spread to larger institutions, the pickings became richer, and it is evident from the commissioners' correspondence that they did find tapestries suitable for the king in a number of instances. For example, on October 29, 1538, Dr. John London sent Cromwell a report regarding the ownership of nine pieces of "arras" in the choir of Austin Friars at Northampton, valued at £12, that had been reserved for the king's use.[72] The following September, Thomas Moyle wrote from Reading Abbey to inform Cromwell that, "As we were to certify what stuff were meet for the king; there is a chamber hanged with meetly good tapestry which would hang a mean little chamber in the king's house, and this is all the household stuff meet to be reserved. There is a chamber hung with six pieces of verdure with fountains, but the ends are foul and greasy. The other hangings are of say and other coarse things. . . . In the church are eight goodly pieces of tapestry, but of no depth."[73] Proportionally speaking, however, few of the many Reformation inventories refer to tapestries, although several mention cloth hangings of low value. On the basis of this evidence, it seems probable that the dissolution of the monasteries may have yielded between one and two hundred tapestries to the royal collection but that few would have been of especially high quality.

Wardrobe Provisions for the Expanding Tapestry Collection

As we have seen, the royal tapestries were divided by tradition between standing wardrobes at the most important palaces, where they were among the furnishings under the direct supervision of the palace keepers. This practice continued unbroken during Henry VIII's reign. The Household Ordinances of 1526 provide names of the keepers at the palaces at that date, and subsequent changes are reflected by the introductory sections of each of the palace wardrobes in the 1547 inventory.[74]

As a number of recent studies have revealed, Henry's reign reflects a period of transition for the royal household from an essentially itinerant body that carried much of its wealth and furnishings on its travels to one that traveled frequently among a group of permanently furnished palaces along the Thames Valley.[75] On average, Henry moved about fifty times a year, peaking at eighty-one times in 1541, the year he traveled to York to meet King James V of Scotland. The huge volumes of precious furnishings that the Crown owned by the mid-1530s, inherited, purchased, and appropriated, only encouraged the development of more permanent collections at the key palaces. At his accession Henry inherited twelve royal palaces and buildings with standing wardrobes at Richmond, Westminster, Windsor, and possibly Nottingham Castle. By the time he died, he had increased the number of royal properties to about fifty-five, with standing wardrobes at sixteen palaces. Works accounts and archaeological research suggest that at the greater palaces the wardrobe stuffs were often divided among several storage areas: the king's wardrobe of the beds, the queen's wardrobe of the beds, and the main standing wardrobe. Several of these standing wardrobes were expanded during the 1530s, and new ones were provided in some of the lesser palaces. A new standing wardrobe was constructed at Greenwich in 1533, while a two-story structure for the same purpose was built at Hampton Court in 1536. One had also been built at Whitehall by 1547.[76] The 1547 inventory records the contents of standing wardrobes at all the greater houses: Greenwich, Whitehall, Hampton Court, Oatlands, Windsor, Woodstock, The More, Richmond, and Newhall. In addition, standing wardrobes were also maintained at Nonsuch, Beddington, and Nottingham. These wardrobes were fitted with cupboards and storage racks. At Greenwich the wardrobe had "long presses ffor the kynges arres, grett carpetts, cussions and hangyngs," as well as "vii newe ladders made as well for the wardroppe to hang up clothes of Arras." One of the Greenwich wardrobes was fifty feet in length, a reflection of the number and size of many of the tapestries in the collection.[77] Measures were evidently taken to ensure that the hangings were kept in a climate that would deter mold, and a number of wardrobe accounts list payments for fuel to heat the various wardrobes.[78] Evidently, these problems were not limited to the wardrobes, as indicated by a payment to a tallow chandler called John Parker, who supplied eight earthenware pans for burning charcoal to Whitehall Palace for use "in the Kynges lodgynges the qwhyense and the Gallarysse of the same for the dryng of the moyster of the hangynges there."[79]

The terms under which the wardrobe keepers were responsible for the objects in their care can be characterized by an inventory of the Windsor Wardrobe, completed on March 26, 1539. According to the preamble, this palace had formerly been in the custody of Robert Little, deceased, and its contents were now delivered by his wife to William Tildesley, the new keeper. The transaction took place in the presence of John Morrison, gentleman usher, and Josias Joskyn, clerk of the Great Wardrobe, who had been sent to Windsor to make a view of the wardrobe contents, draw up a new inventory, and take "deferences as shold appear lakking in thendenture of the said Robert Litle"—that is, to note any discrepancies between the collection as it had been inventoried when it was placed under Little's jurisdiction and as it now existed.[80] The resulting inventory was drawn up in duplicate. One copy was signed by Tildesley and taken as a record by Joskyn, while the second was signed by Joskyn and kept at Windsor by Tildesley. The task of checking the furnishings against the old inventory, now lost, took four days, as evidenced by a payment to the wardrobe officers made the following month.[81] These details are typical of those given for other inventories surviving from this and subsequent periods.[82] In each case, the keeper was entrusted, by indenture, with a body of furnishings of which he kept one list and of which the Great Wardrobe kept another. The French court followed an analogous practice.[83]

Apart from the detailed inventories drawn up on the transfer of responsibility from one keeper to another, there appear to have been periodic "views" of the collection as a whole, in which records were updated and at which those furnishings no longer deemed appropriate for the king's service were discarded. The character of these reviews and the perquisites they provided to more senior courtiers is suggested by a letter written to Lady Lisle in the late 1530s by her agent, John Hussee, who was trying to obtain suitable furnishings and tapestries for the Lisles to take to Calais. Hussee comments: "You shall not need to attempt buying any carpets out of the Wardrobe. There is no good to be done till the view be taken, which passeth not once in thirty years, and then the lord Chamberlain and the head officers have the best stuff, and the worst remains for the mean and inferior officers."[84]

A view of sorts seems to have taken place during the early 1540s, as several individual palace inventories survive from these years, apparently part of a larger sequence that was not related to specific changes of personnel or responsibility and that therefore may have been instigated by the considerable expansion of the collection in the previous decade. In 1540 Roland Rugely, yeoman of the Wardrobe, Josias Joskyn, clerk, and two other officers were paid for traveling to Greenwich for six days and taking a view of the wardrobe stuff there at 2s. a day each. After this Joskyn and David Vincent, another officer of the Wardrobe, traveled to Hampton Court, where they spent another eleven days, "making up their books of the view of the said Wardrobe stuff and measuring of the stuff."[85] Neither inventory survives, but subsequent inventories from other palaces are extant. These include one taken in May 1540 of the wardrobe stuff at Westminster (that is, Whitehall), "unappointed" and in the custody of Anthony Denny, groom of the stool,[86] and another of the wardrobe stuff delivered into the hands of Denny, on April 24, 1542, in his capacity as keeper of Whitehall Palace, with additions recording deliveries after that date.[87] A third records the goods at Windsor in the keeping of William Tildesley, "particulerly surveid viewed and geven in charge in due order unto the said William by the kinges comaundement by Nichas Bristowe his highnes Clerk" in February 1543.[88] Like the Whitehall inventory of 1542, this includes addenda listing subsequent receipts, with marginal notes detailing later disbursements.

The rigor with which the Wardrobe officers were held accountable for the objects in their keeping is suggested by the painstaking detail with which the inventories were drawn up, often with the precious textiles measured to the nearest half nail, or about an inch. A further insight is provided by the difficulty that the Lisles experienced in their efforts to borrow furnishings from the Great Wardrobe. On February 3, 1537, Geoffrey Wolfet, clerk of the king's closet, informed Lisle that "John Keyn lately moved me in my lady's name touching one of the king's traverses with other ornaments for an alter.... I cannot spare one parcel without making the king privy thereto, except the one vestment of new rich tissue, which serveth for every day, with other cloths and balkyn."[89]

The Removing Wardrobes

In addition to the standing wardrobes located at the greater palaces, the Great Wardrobe continued to provide "removing wardrobes" for key members of the royal family. At the time of the 1547 inventory the Removing Wardrobe of the king, presumably Edward at this date, included fifty-six figurative tapestries comprising six sets—*Hercules, Lady Fame, Charlemagne,* "Turques," and two heraldic ensembles—and another fifty-one pieces of verdure comprising five sets.[90] No indication of quality is given in this section of the inventory, but it seems probable that these would have been high-quality hangings. A smaller number of high-quality religious tapestries were also in the keeping of the clerk of the closet, as evidenced by two indentures between Richard Rawson, chaplain and clerk of the king's closet, his predecessor Geoffrey Wren, and Sir Henry Wyatt, master of the jewels. These list the plate and stuff in Rawson's keeping, including two rich "arras" altar frontals of the *Three Kings,* three others of "Our Lady," one of *The Three Kings and the Crucifix,* a piece of "arras" of the *Passion,* and two "arras" altar frontals of the *Assumption* and the *Salutation,* with images of Saint John the Baptist and Saint John the Evangelist.[91]

Analogous provisions were made for Prince Edward in the year following his birth. In July 1538 Josias Joskyn, clerk of the Great Wardrobe, and Lancelot Aldeforde, a groom of the same, received payment for ten days' work with servants and horses, "furnishing Prince Edward's house with Wardrobe stuff and fetching stuff from Newhall for the purpose."[92] New purchases were made in the following year. Andrew Windsor's Great Wardrobe account for the year to Michaelmas 1539 records payment to William Lynton for sixteen verdures "vocat blome flowers," containing 488 ells (274 square yards) for the dressing chamber of Prince Edward at a cost of £69 8s. 4d.; another unidentified set of eight pieces containing 397 ells (223 square yards) for the prince's "Camera magna," costing £165 8s. 4d.; and another of seven pieces of "Tapistrye meilior," or better tapestry, containing 418 ells (235 square yards) for the chamber of presence, costing £232 6s. 8d.[93] The value of these sets thus varied in a ratio of 1 : 2.4 : 3.3, which evidently reflected a progression in physical quality and appearance.[94] Other purchases for the prince in this period are reflected by an entry in an inventory taken at Whitehall in 1540 for a "newe bed of riche aras called my lorde prince his bed which was brought of peter van de wall," and by another for six verdure cushions with the prince's arms, listed among deliveries of "new made stuff" in the 1542 Whitehall inventory.[95] Pieter van de Walle was a rich Antwerp merchant who in 1539 had been granted a safe conduct to import luxury goods to London, with the proviso that the king should have the first viewing and choice. His role as a purveyor of tapestries will be considered further below.

Nothing more is known of the bed supplied by Van de Walle, but it is probably to be identified with a gold-woven tapestry bed purchased from the Commonwealth sale by Cardinal Mazarin in 1654. According to Mazarin's agent, Antoine de Bordeaux, the tapestry represented a landscape and was designed by Hans Holbein.[96] The subsequent fate of the ensemble is unknown, so de Bordeaux's connoisseurship, heavy-handed at the best of times, cannot be verified. Although no evidence has survived to substantiate the intriguing possibility that

Holbein may have produced tapestry designs for Henry, he certainly made designs for a variety of other royal jewels and decorative objects, and his linear style would have been ideally suited to the tapestry medium.[97]

The subjects of the other early purchases and disbursements on behalf of the prince are unrecorded, but some at least presumably survived among the sets listed in the wardrobe allocated to him at Durham Place in the 1547 inventory.[98] In total, 106 tapestries are cited, seventy-seven with figurative subjects. Another twenty-one were verdures deriving from six different groups, and eight were tapestry counterpoints. The collection included only three "arras" panels, depicting the *Three Estates,* a subject that, in the context of the Reformation, had presumably been chosen to celebrate the absolute sovereignty of the Tudor dynasty over all three estates, including the Church. No evidence survives to indicate whether this was an antique tapestry that had been divided into shorter sections or a modern tapestry purchased by Henry, but that it was an antique is suggested by the representation of this subject in tapestry during the mid-fifteenth century and not in later production.

Several other sets in the Prince's Wardrobe can also be identified as dating from the late fifteenth century. The most impressive of these ensembles were the eight-piece *Story of Thebes* purchased by Edward IV and four pieces of the *Story of Troy,* possibly duplicates of the Grenier *Trojan War* set purchased in 1488; those in the Prince's Wardrobe were all about one foot shorter than those in the set purchased by Henry VII. Another notable ensemble was a six-piece set of the *City of Ladies,* the same exemplary subject formerly recorded in Princess Mary's Wardrobe, probably dating from the early sixteenth century. Many of the other panels depicted Old Testament subjects, including three panels of *Nebuchadnezzar,* single panels of *Zachariah, Ahasuerus,* and *Solomon,* four of *Jacob,* and three of the Old Testament prophet *Balaam.* There were also eleven panels of coarse tapestry of the *Prodigal Son.* Devotional panels included three pieces of the *Passion* and another of the *Annunciation.* Another large panel depicted the "*Dome*" (sic), presumably the "Doom" or Last Judgment. There were also several sets depicting hunting, one of "*Moryans*" (Moors), and five ensembles of verdures.

As will be readily evident from this summary, the selection of tapestries for the prince was evidently determined to a large extent by a desire to provide "exemplary" subject matter, either in the deeds of the heroes of old, notably those of the classical world rather than of Carolingian legend, or models of virtue drawn from the Old and New Testaments. As we have seen, similar selections had been made in earlier years for Princess Mary and the duke of Richmond. The humanistic notion of the educational potential of images, celebrated by Elyot's Governour of 1531, had recently been recast by Henry and his advisers in the *Ten Articles,* promulgated in 1536, which permitted images as "representers of vertue and good example" and as "the kendelers and stirrers of men's myndes, [to] make men ofte to remembre and lamente theyr synnes and offences, especiallye the ymages of Christ and our lady."[99] The extent to which Henry was involved in the selection of tapestries for Edward is open to discussion, but as we shall see, the educational intention underlying their choice would manifest itself even more markedly in the major tapestry commissions that Henry was to make in the next three or four years.

Quite apart from the provisions made for members of the royal family, lesser allocations were also made on an occasional basis for ambassadors, dignitaries, and members of Henry's own court. For example, in a letter of December 30, 1538, the French ambassador Castillon reported to the duke of Montmorency that following his arrival in London, the king had lodged him at Bridewell Palace and had sent him appropriate tapestry and furniture.[100]

PART V

The Great Sets of the Last Decade

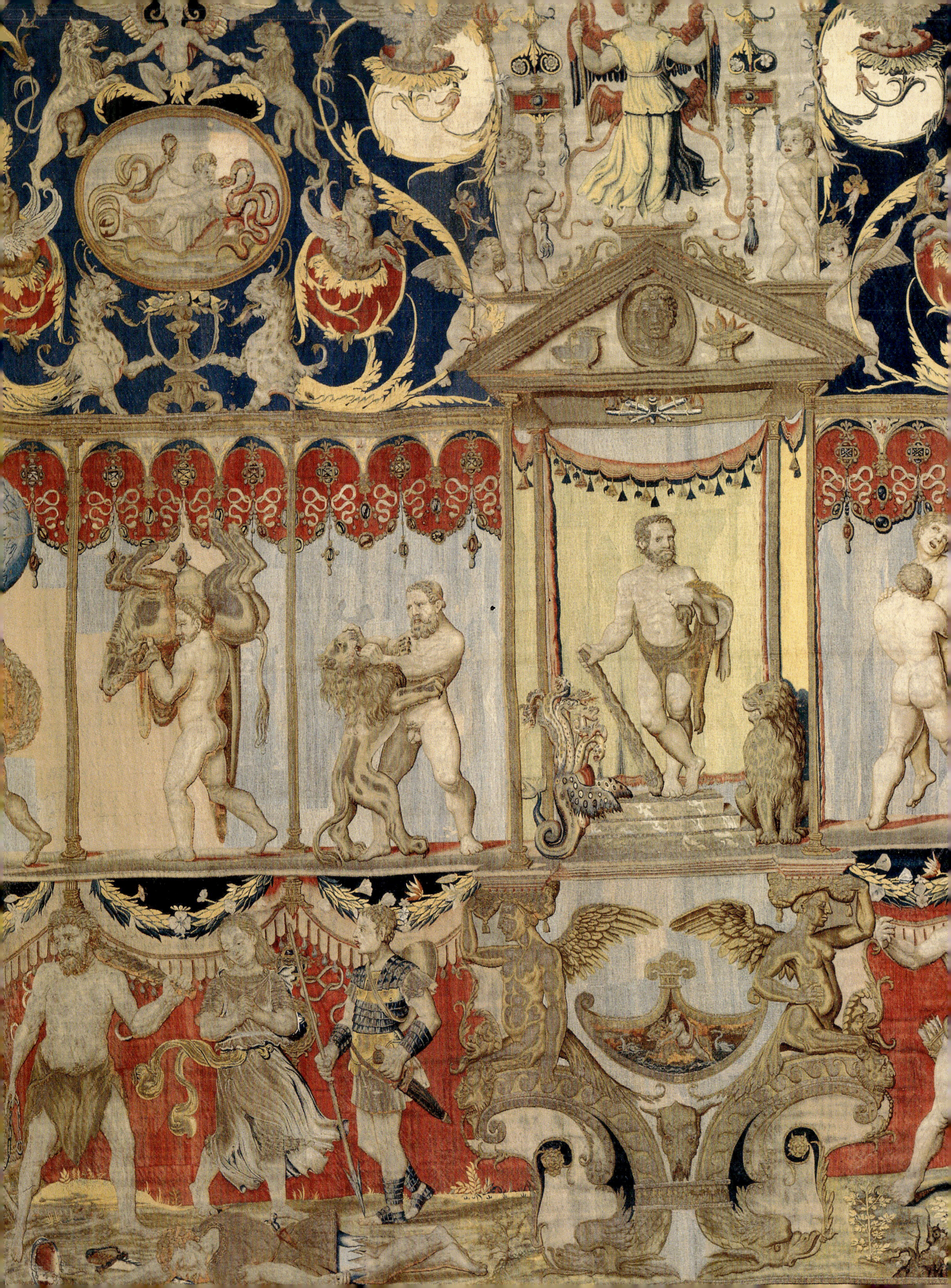

CHAPTER 13

The Profits of the Dissolution and New Purchases, 1538–1542

"The king, who in former years has been solitary and pensive, now gives himself up to amusement"

While confiscations from the properties of attainted courtiers and dissolved religious institutions yielded a significant volume of tapestries to the royal collection during the mid- to late 1530s, the collection also continued to grow through acquisitions made by the king and officers of the Great Wardrobe. Indeed, the years between 1538 and 1547 were marked by purchases of unprecedented scale and magnificence.

The most important factor underlying this heightened level of investment was the new funding available to Henry through the dissolution of the monasteries. Between 1536 and 1540, 536 monasteries and religious bodies were dissolved, yielding a profit to the Crown of some £1.3 million that was channeled through the Court of Augmentations. The second factor that undoubtedly played a part in Henry's patronage during the late 1530s was his state of mind. This was a period of recovery for Henry following the trials, literal and psychological, of the previous ten years. He had lost his latest wife, but he now had the male heir for whom he had waited so long and the main legislative elements of the Reformation had been completed. Although civil unrest remained a matter of grave concern, the collapse of the Pilgrimage of Grace (a rising of Roman Catholics in northern England) and the execution of the ringleaders in 1537 ushered in a new period of calm and consolidation, allowing Henry to turn his considerable energies to other matters. Foremost among these was the enlargement and improvement of various royal palaces, particularly Hampton Court and Whitehall Palace (see figs. 13.3, 13.13). Although the scope of these building projects, especially those at Hampton Court, is well documented by the Works accounts, the records are silent about the furnishings envisaged as part of them. Yet circumstantial evidence indicates that, quite naturally, the furnishings were an integral component of these ambitious projects, proportionate to their scale and splendor.

The character of Henry's renewed interest in the arts at this period is suggested by a letter drafted in June 1539 by Charles de Marillac, the French ambassador. In this he reported that "the king, who in former years has been solitary and pensive, now gives himself up to amusement.... He evidently delights now in painting and embroidery having sent men to France, Flanders, Italy and elsewhere for masters of this art, and also for musicians and other ministers of pastime. All his people think this is a sign of his desire to marry if he should find an agreeable match."[1] Marillac was, of course, prescient, and Henry's advisers were already scouting for a new bride for Henry among the Germanic states as an insurance against the alliance that had recently emerged between Francis I and Charles V, who, it was feared, might join forces against England. Holbein had undertaken several journeys to the Continent during the previous year to portray prospective brides, and it was during August 1539 that he famously traveled to the court of Cleves to paint Anne of Cleves.[2] But in this context the part of Marillac's report that is of especial interest are the words regarding Henry's "delight" in embroidery and

Detail of fig. 13.18

sending abroad for masters of the art. Given that Henry already had a team of capable embroiderers attached to the Great Wardrobe, it is possible that Marillac's words in fact related to Henry's renewed interest in tapestry. Certainly, it must have been during 1539 and 1540 that Henry placed commissions for a number of very costly sets that were eventually delivered to the Tudor court between 1542 and 1544. Circumstantial evidence indicates that during the same period the English court continued to purchase large numbers of moderate-quality tapestries through a variety of channels.

Sources and Agents

No accounts for the Privy Purse survive between 1532 and 1542, but sizeable sums continued to be paid to Sir Anthony Denny (fig. 13.1) throughout the 1530s, both from the Chamber and from various other sources such as the Exchequer, the Court of First Fruits and Tenths, established in 1535, and the Court of Augmentations, established in 1536.[3] When Denny presented his accounts following Henry's death, he declared receipts of £243,387 between 1542 and 1547, approximately £50,000 per year, which had been dispensed at the king's oral command.[4] Much of this expenditure had been for luxury goods, and two very expensive tapestry sets are specifically listed. It is conceivable that other tapestry payments may also have been concealed within the large sums that Denny dispensed to merchants who are previously known to have supplied Henry with tapestries.

Other purchases may have been funded directly from the Court of First Fruits and Tenths and the Court of Augmentations. The accounts of the former include at least one specific tapestry transaction, a payment of £630 in 1536 by John Gostwick, the treasurer, to John Longegraunt (sic), merchant of Flanders, for "arras" and three diamond rings.[5] Since the same merchant had also delivered gold rings and arras to Henry when he married Anne Boleyn, it is tempting to speculate that the hangings supplied on this occasion may have been intended for Jane Seymour. Although this is the only tapestry transaction specifically noted in the Court of First Fruits and Tenths, surviving accounts for both funds include large payments to merchants known to have supplied tapestries to Henry at other times.[6] For example, in June 1540, Richard Gresham received payment of £1,716 13s. 4d. "for certeyne stuf bought by him and delivered to the kinges use as by a warrant therof made"; in February 1542, £1,107 6s. 6d. for "certeyn velvets, damasks and sattens"; and in March 1542, £800 for velvet, damasks, and satins.[7]

One figure who seems to have played a lesser role in royal purchases than hitherto was Jan Mostinck, the royal arras maker. His assumption of responsibility in 1537 for running the tapestry repair workshop in the Great Wardrobe would have kept him in London to a greater degree than before, and although we do not know the date of his birth, Mostinck was certainly getting on in age by this date. When he was appointed in 1529 he was described as having previously been the tapestry man to Margaret Beaufort, who had died in 1509, twenty years before. The census of aliens living in London in 1540 indicates that his workshop was in the parish of Saint Martin in the Fields in Westminster, that he was then employing five workers, and that his goods were valued at £60.[8] In December 1541 he received a grant of denization as well as a

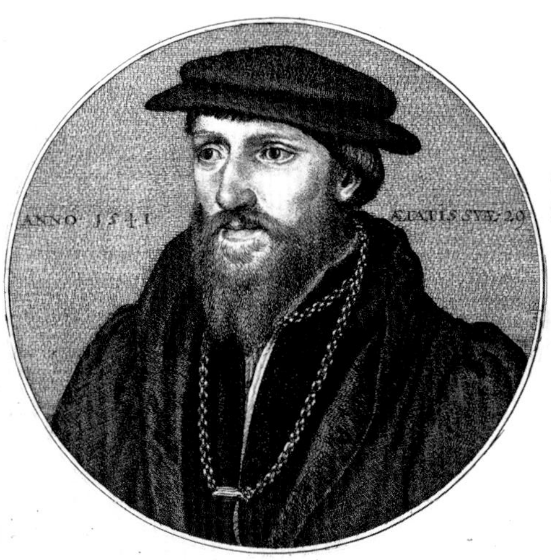

13.1 *Sir Anthony Denny*. Etching by Wenceslaus Hollar, ca. 1647, after lost original of 1541 by Hans Holbein the Younger. 13.3 x 10.8 cm. British Museum, London

13.2 *View of Antwerp*, ca. 1518–40. Oil on panel, 108 x 183 cm. National Scheepvaartmuseum, Antwerp

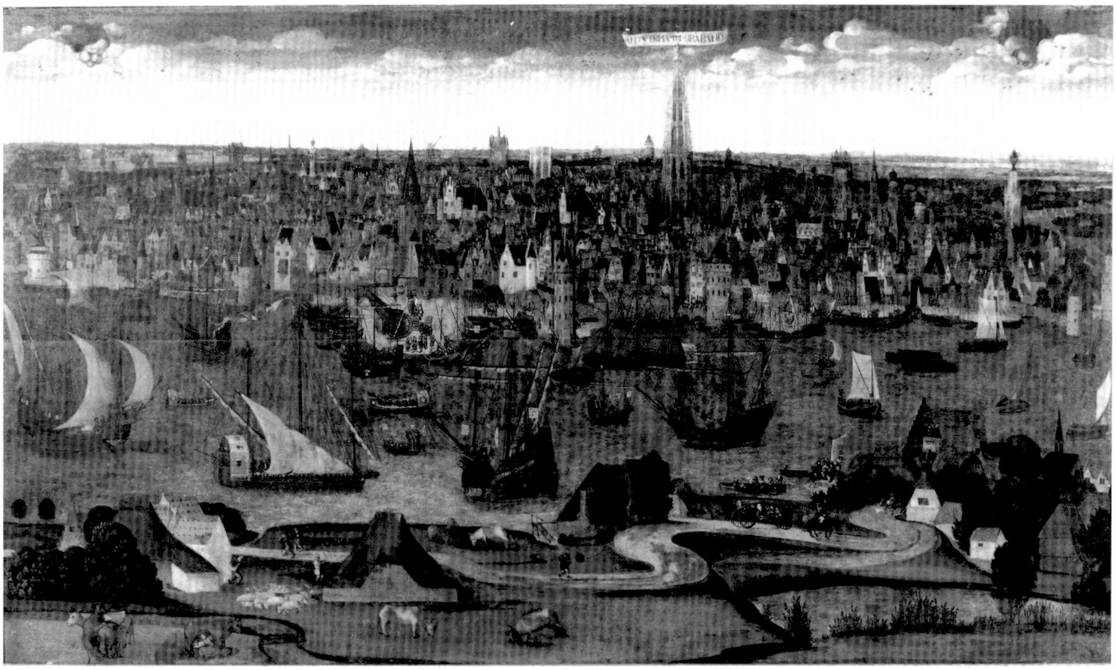

license to have six journeymen or covenanted servants, not being denizens, born in parts beyond the sea, in his service.[9] But Mostinck's health may have been failing, because in December a John Bukke, "arras maker," a native of the emperor's dominions, also received denization and a grant of the reversion of the office of the king's chief arras maker after the present incumbent, and Mostinck was dead by early 1542.[10] According to the initiating warrant for Bukke's grant, signed by the stamp by William Clerc in September 1541, it was issued at the suit of Lord Sir John Saint John.[11] Bukke was not to enjoy the office for long because in July 1542 a further grant was issued to Cornelius Mostinck, son of John, to be the king's "arras maker" and repairer of his cloths of arras and tapestry, "vice John Buck, deceased, with 12d. a day from Easter last."[12] In this case the appointment was said to be at the suit of John Penne, groom of the Privy Chamber and the king's barber.[13] A subsequent Great Wardrobe account for 1545–46 duly records payment to the "arras makers" for repairs to sixty-two tapestries, with the payment for repair materials being received by Cornelius Mostinck.[14]

The foregoing evidence suggests that if Mostinck did act as a tapestry agent for Henry during the early and mid-1530s, the importance of this role waned after 1537. This may explain why it is that from this period more documents survive for tapestry transactions that were conducted through other means. For example, an indication that Henry's Continental agents were on the lookout for appropriate goods in the marketplace is provided by the letter, mentioned above (p. 244), that John Hutton, the English agent in Brussels, sent Sir Thomas Wriothesley on March 14, 1538. Hutton had reserved two hundred ells (approx. 113 square yards) of "goodly tapestry" at a cost of 9s. per ell, which was of such quality that "there hath not been bought this 20 year any so good for the price." He also told Wriothesley that he had written to Cromwell in regard to a rich hanging of "arras" that Sir Philip Hoby had seen and advised him to further its purchase.[15] In view of the implied cost (£90), and Wriothesley's proximity to the king at this time, it seems probable that Henry was the intended patron. This is the only evidence of Hutton acting as a tapestry adviser for the English court, but the statement that he had also written to Cromwell with regard to another hanging suggests that this was not the first such engagement.[16] Based in Antwerp (fig. 13.2), Hutton was ideally placed to observe the activities of the major cartoon and tapestry

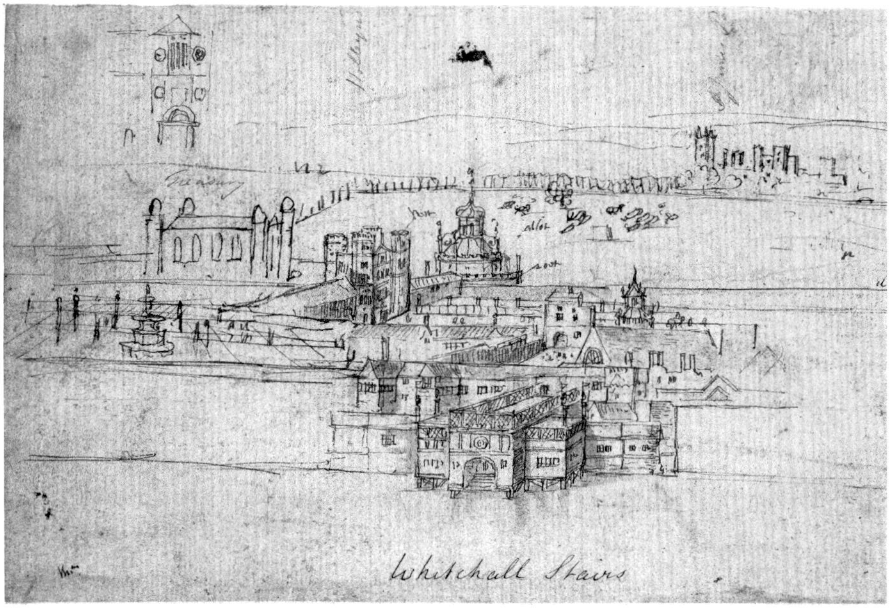

13.3 *Whitehall Palace from the East (Riverside)* by A. van den Wyngaerde, ca. 1558. Pen and ink, 15.3 x 27.4 cm. Ashmolean Museum, Oxford

workshops, and his contacts with Netherlandish and Continental merchants in Brussels would have provided him with information about new designs and commissions. When Hutton died in Antwerp in September 1538, his wife was left with debts of £600, which included £300 for tapestries and other luxury goods.[17] The inventory of Hutton's possessions lists only relatively inexpensive hangings, so it is likely that these costs had been incurred in purchases made for the king or other courtiers.[18] Following Hutton's death, Stephen Vaughan, a close friend of Thomas Cromwell, succeeded him as governor of the Merchant Adventurers and Henry's ambassador in the Low Countries.[19] During the following years Vaughan spent much time in Brussels and Antwerp, negotiating loans on the Bourse and acting as an agent in a variety of transactions on the king's behalf. As such, he may also have played a role in acquiring tapestries for Henry and his circle.

It is conceivable that Hutton's death may have been one of the factors that resulted in Henry turning to another source of supply the following year. In 1539 Pieter van de Walle, a merchant and jeweler of Antwerp, was given a grant of safe conduct for him and his agents to come to England from time to time, importing a miscellany of goods, the "jewels, &c. to be brought to the king before sale, that he may have first choice of them."[20] Like several of his rich Antwerp peers, Van de Walle played an important role in the Netherlandish tapestry industry during the 1540s, evidently owning a number of tapestry cartoons. In 1544 he supplied a set of the *Seven Deadly Sins* to Maria of Hungary, and in 1550 his son, Jan van de Walle, supplied a set of the *Story of Romulus and Remus* to Prince Philip of Spain. The following year, Jan also supplied a set of the *Story of the Creation* to Duke Cosimo de' Medici in Florence.[21]

Evidence that Pieter was in contact with Henry VIII from at least April 1539 suggests that it was his association with the English court that established his stature in the tapestry field. As already noted, he provided the rich "arras" bed for Prince Edward that was recorded at Whitehall in 1540.[22] And according to the 1547 inventory, he was responsible for supplying a four-piece set of the *Story of Romulus and Remus* listed toward the end of the Hampton Court section of the inventory, indicating that it been a recent addition to the palace holdings.[23] The identification and character of this set will be considered below. Although these are the only tapestry purchases to which Van de Walle is linked by documentation, he probably supplied other high-quality sets to Henry during the late 1530s and early 1540s. He evidently enjoyed a close relationship with the English court, brokering substantial deals for jewelry and other commodities and on occasion acting as a middleman between Henry and the Fuggers.

The Character of the New Acquisitions

Although the purchase records cited above are fragmentary, further information about tapestry acquisitions during the late 1530s and early 1540s can be gleaned from the inventories of the royal palaces that were taken between 1539 and 1542. Some of these describe particular tapestries as "new" or mention the merchant from whom they were purchased. For example, the 1539 Windsor inventory refers to eleven tapestries of "new stuff" of *Hawking and Hunting* and another two of the *Story of David*.[24] The 1540 Whitehall inventory is especially interesting in this respect because in addition to the prince's new "arras" bed, it includes a section titled "hangings of new tapestry" in which eight sets or partial sets of figurative tapestry are listed.[25] These included the *Story of Meleager,* the *Sabines, Virtue,* the *Story of Ruth,* two sets of *Hawking and Hunting,* the *Story of the King of "Surrey"*—probably a set of the *Story of Cyrus*—and two pieces of the *Seven Deadly Sins,* not to be confused with the gold-woven set of the same subject that was lined in 1535–36 and was listed at the Tower in the 1547 inventory. In several cases, such as the sets of the *King of Surrey, Ruth,* and the *Sins,* only two or three panels were listed in 1540, whereas more pieces were listed in the subsequent 1542 inventory.[26] This may imply that the pieces listed in the 1540 inventory were the initial deliveries of sets then under production. Considering that these sets were probably purchased to provide decorations for the royal apartments created at Whitehall during the 1530s, the balance between classical history and mythology, religious, exemplary, and genre subjects, provides an interesting reflection of taste at the Tudor court.

Two at least of these sets can be identified with moderate certainty, the *Cyrus* set and the *Sabines.* Cyrus was a popular subject in Flemish tapestry during the second quarter of the sixteenth century. In this case, the dimensions of the set suggest that it was woven from the same cartoons as a design series of which the most complete set survives in Boston (fig. 13.4).[27] Dating from the mid- to late 1530s, the design was evidently executed by an artist of moderate talent working under the influence of Van Orley. It portrays rather wooden figures clothed in contemporary costume in schematic landscapes. As such, it contrasts markedly in character and style with the *Sabines* set. Here, the unusual subject and dimensions of the tapestries indicate that Henry's set was woven from a design series of which a six-piece set was once in the French royal collection—destroyed after the Revolution—and of which several fragmentary sets survive (fig. 13.5).[28] Traditionally attributed to Giulio Romano, the designs were more probably created by an artist who was familiar with Romano's work.

13.4 *King Astyages Commands Harpagos to Kill Cyrus* from a set of the *Story of Cyrus.* Tapestry woven in the Southern Netherlands, probably Brussels, ca. 1530–40. Wool and silk, 419 x 601 cm. Isabella Stewart Gardner Museum, Boston

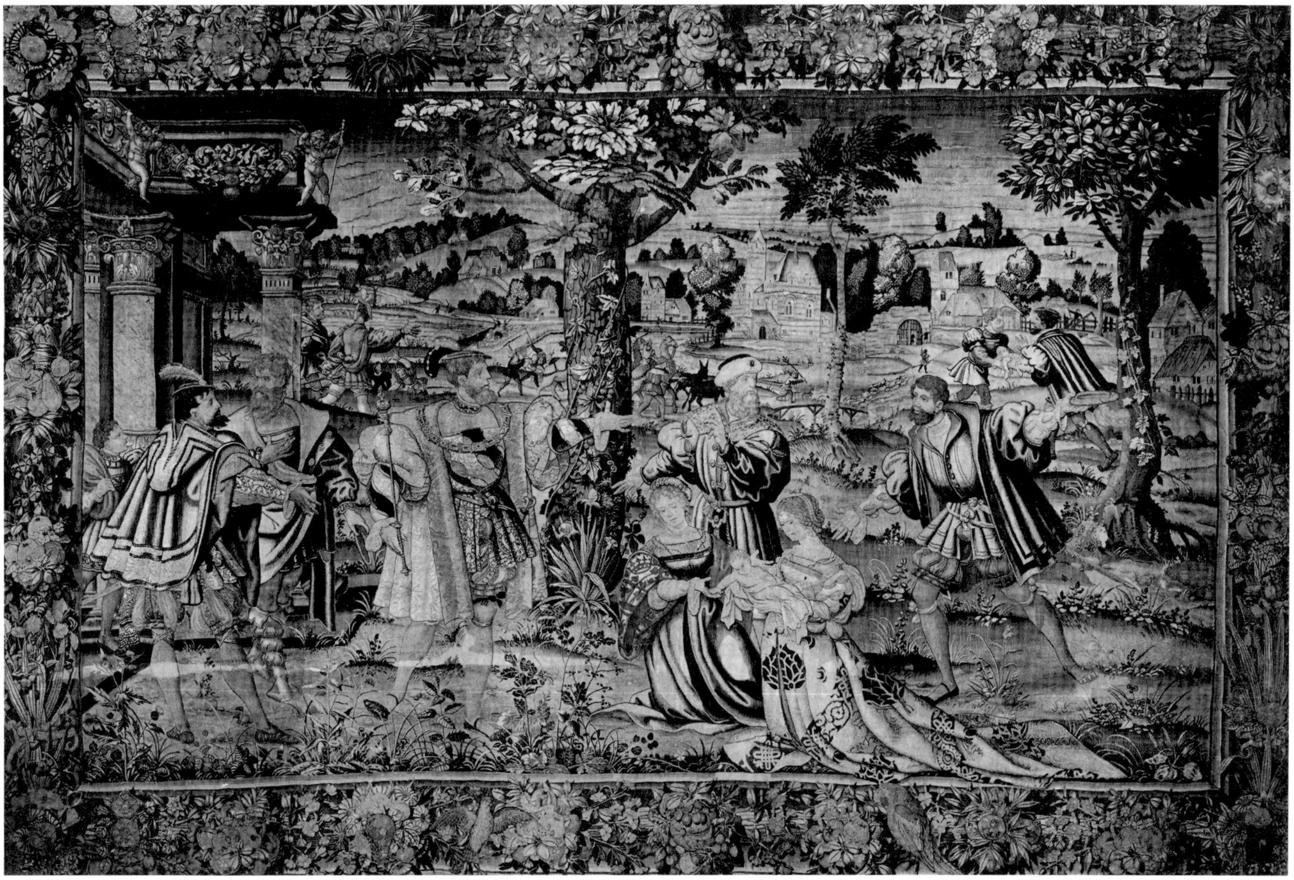

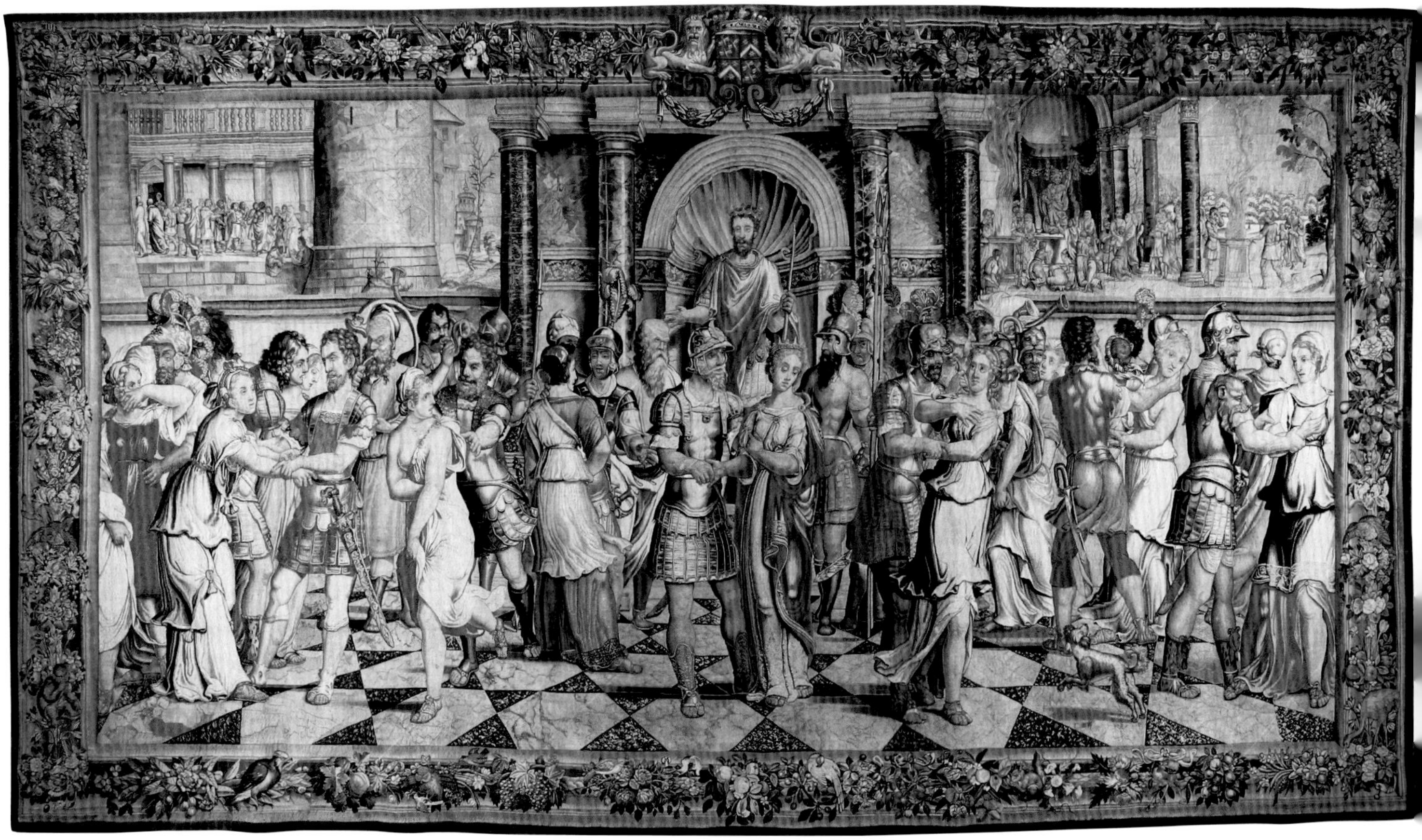

13.5 *The Abduction of the Sabine Women* from a set of the *Story of the Sabines*. Tapestry design by an artist from the circle of Giulio Romano, woven in Brussels, ca. 1535–40. Wool and silk, 340 x 600 cm. Château d'Azay-le-Ferron

The series is of note for the effort that the artist made to provide an accurate rendering of historic costume and appropriately "classical" settings. Taken together, the *Cyrus* and *Sabines* sets suggest Henry's taste for classical subjects and display the range of artistic styles and material quality in which such subjects were being produced in Brussels workshops. Irrespective of questions of style, it is to be noted that the context for which these tapestries were delivered, new apartments created at Whitehall for both the king and queen, raises the possibility that the sets featuring embodiments of female virtue, the *Story of Ruth* and the *Story of the Sabines,* may have been intended for the royal consort's apartments, while those embodying male qualities of heroism and virtue, the *Story of Meleager* and the *Story of Cyrus,* may have been intended for the king's apartments.[29]

Another set of tapestries listed in the 1540 Whitehall inventory that must have been a recent delivery was a twelve-piece "arras" set of the *Twelve Months*. By 1547 this had been moved to the Tower Wardrobe, where it probably remained until the Commonwealth sale, after which its fate is unknown. Its appearance can be deduced, however, on the evidence of duplicates of this series that were woven at the Mortlake manufactory during the early 1620s. This workshop, established by James I in 1619 with Flemish weavers who were brought to London in great secrecy, was dependent on sixteenth-century models in the early years of production before an artist was specifically assigned to the workshop in 1626.[30] One of the first two series developed at Mortlake was a twelve-piece set of the *Months,* which was copied from a sixteenth-century set in the royal collection. The finest and earliest Mortlake example is now at the Palazzo Bianco in Genoa (fig. 13.6).[31] The borders are a seventeenth-century addition to the design, but the main fields show all the characteristics of having been conceived by an artist working in Bernaert van Orley's circle, sometime in the mid-1530s. The scenes depict a mixture of genre and courtly figures in an Arcadian vision of country life.

Regarding the other figurative sets, it is interesting to note that the new tapestries at both Windsor and Whitehall included scenes of *Hawking and Hunting*. Such scenes had long been popular, but the genre had received new impetus with the creation of Van Orley's so-called *Hunts of Maximilian,* woven between 1530 and 1533, which included realistic portrayals of recognizable members of the Habsburg family and court in exquisitely detailed settings in and around Brussels (see figs. 11.10, 11.11).[32] The cartoons for the Habsburg series were certainly used more than once; a second set was exported to Constantinople in 1533 in the hope of a sale to Süleyman the Magnificent. The venture was unsuccessful, and the fate of that second set is unknown. A single piece duplicating the month of *February* survives in fragmentary form in the Spanish royal collection, while an adapted version of this subject with figures in antique costume appeared in the art market in the 1950s.[33] The Van Orley cartoons stimulated the development of a variety of other hunting series in the late 1530s and 1540s that portrayed hunters in naturalistic forest settings. Some were of high quality, as evidenced by a single piece, now at Hever Castle, Kent, depicting hunters in a livery of white and red (fig. 13.7).[34] Other derivations were more basic, incorporating simplified figures and landscapes, like the isolated piece in the collection of the Detroit Institute of Arts (fig. 13.8).[35] Yet others depicted smaller figures, and were thus less costly to weave, in generalized woodland settings.[36] We can conjecture that any hunting tapestries purchased late in Henry's reign are likely to have reflected these stylistic developments.

Besides the new figurative tapestries, the 1540 Whitehall inventory also itemizes thirty-six "newe hanginges of verdures" from seven ensembles of varying quality. One set was described as being of "small flowers" and another of "the best sorte with water flowers." The others were all of "brode bloomes." These descriptions and relative numbers reflect the changes taking place in the design of verdure tapestries during the second quarter of the sixteenth century as the millefleurs genre developed toward ever more naturalistic representations of flowers and foliage under the influence of new interests in naturalism, the study of botany, and the importation of exotic plants from the New World.[37] Two

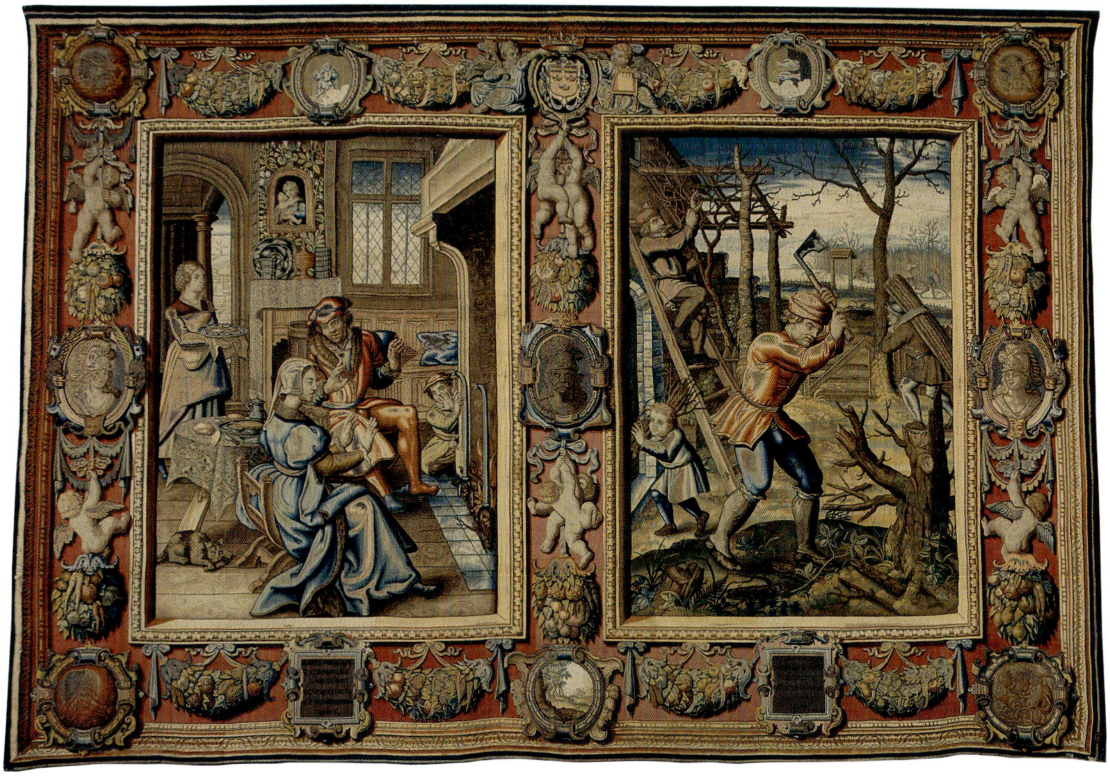

13.6 *January and February* from a set of the *Months*. Tapestry woven at the Mortlake manufactory, ca. 1625, the main fields copied from a 16th-c. design. Wool and silk, 330 x 475 cm. Palazzo Bianco, Genoa

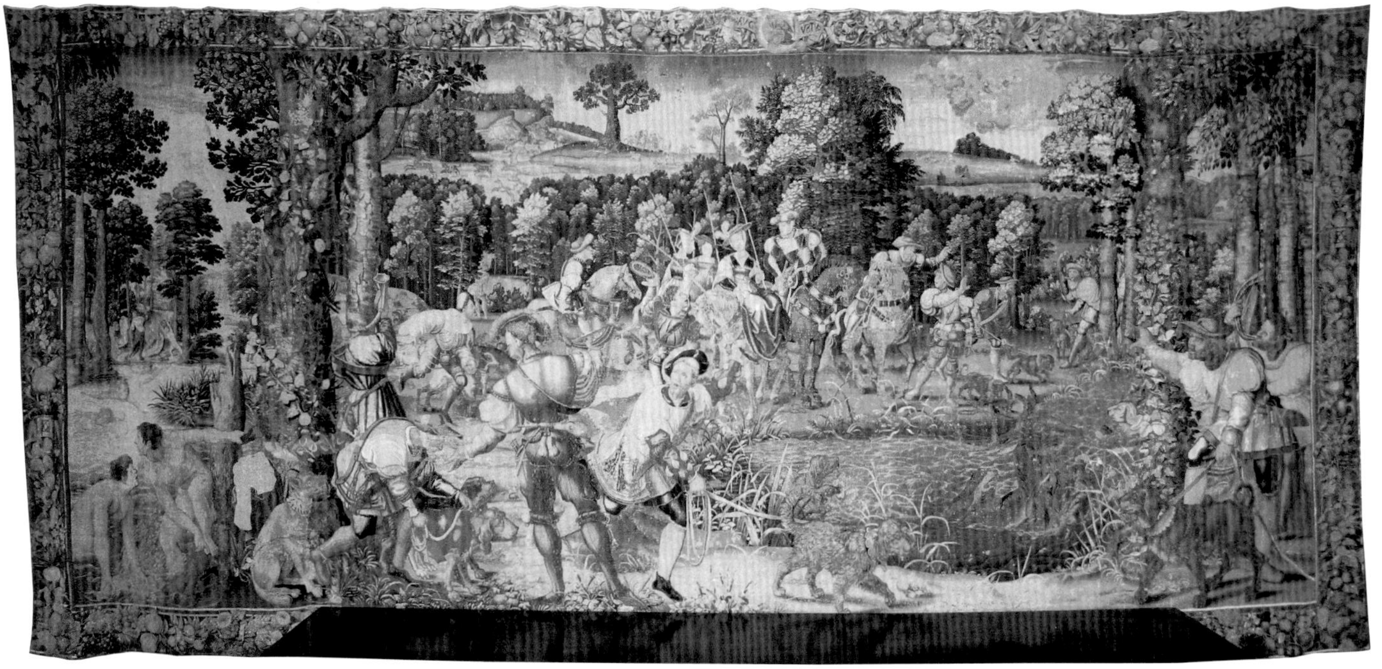

13.7 *The Stag Hunt*. Tapestry woven in Brussels, ca. 1535. Wool and silk, 310 x 725 cm. Hever Castle, Kent

principal types of verdure can be identified in this period, although each was the subject of many variants and permutations. The first, which enjoyed success during the 1520s and 1530s, was essentially a development from the traditional millefleur type and depicted lush grounds of naturalistic reeds, lilies, and water flowers. Those pieces that the 1547 inventory describes as with "water-flowers" were presumably like this.[38] While some of the extant examples carry Brussels marks, a number also carry the Enghien town mark.[39] The second type that enjoyed great popularity during the second third of the century depicted dense thickets of serrated acanthus fronds, often with large flowers, populated with beasts or birds, sometimes with architectural elements (fig. 13.9).[40] The majority of the verdures that the 1547 inventory describes as of the "broad bloom" probably fall into this group. The many extant examples indicate that they must have been produced in large numbers, and this must have been the predominant type purchased by Henry after 1530.

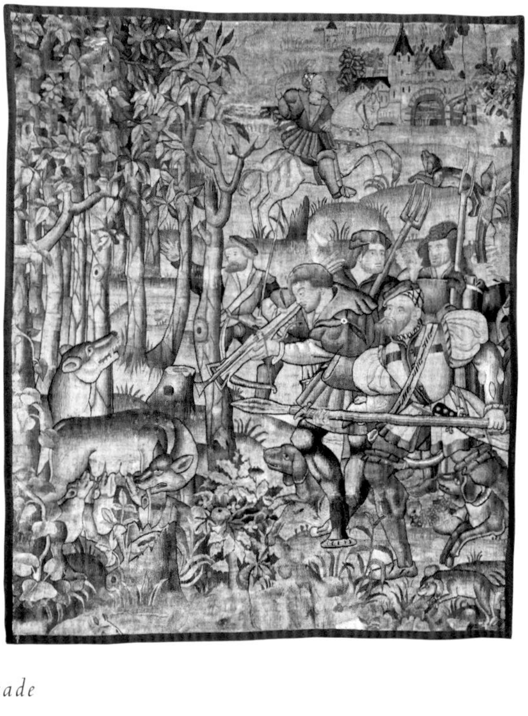

13.8 *The Wolf Hunt* (fragment). Tapestry woven in the Southern Netherlands, ca. 1530–40. Wool and silk, 258 x 210 cm. Institute of Arts, Detroit

The glimpse of "new" tapestries provided by the 1540 Whitehall inventory may be typical of similar acquisitions made during the late 1530s and 1540s for other royal palaces. For example, the 1547 inventory lists a nine-piece set of the *Story of Venus and Cupid* at Hampton Court, whose dimensions coincide closely with the dimensions of a design series of which a partial set from Mary of Hungary's collection survives in the Spanish royal collection (fig. 13.10).[41] Representing an eclectic mix of scenes featuring *Venus and Cupid*, the designs date from the late 1530s. The figural and landscape style typify the moderate-quality mythological tapestries that were produced in Brussels from the late 1530s. Although they are hardly of great

13.9 *Large-Leaf Verdure*. Tapestry woven in the Southern Netherlands, ca. 1540–50. Wool and silk, 300 x 333 cm. Bunratty Castle (Co. Cork)

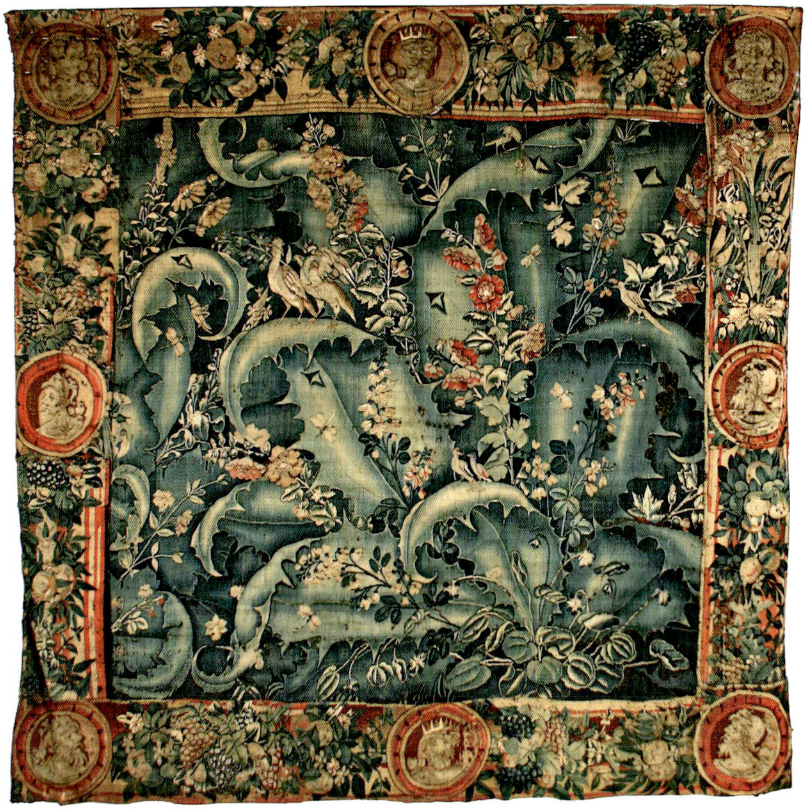

13.10 *The Adoration of Venus* from the *Story of Venus and Cupid*. Tapestry woven in Brussels, ca. 1535–45. Wool and silk, 408 x 591 cm. Palacio Real, Madrid

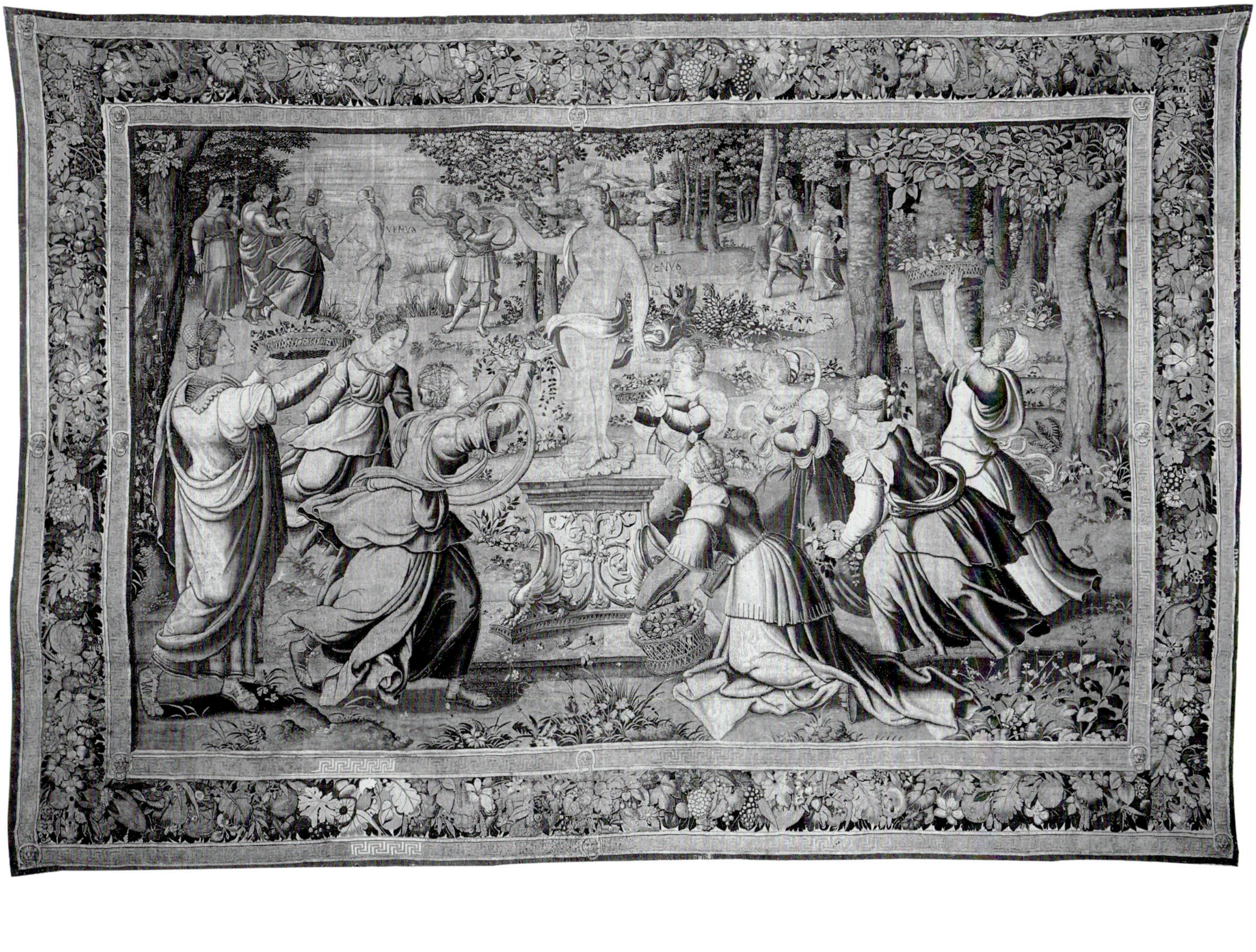

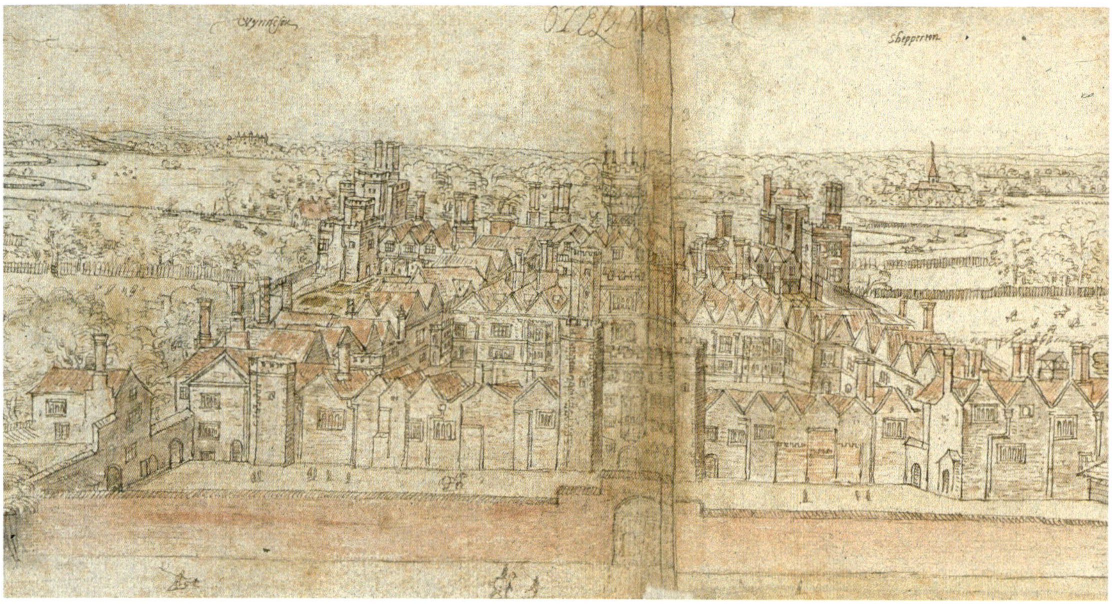

13.11 *Oatlands, Surrey* (detail) by A. van den Wyngaerde, 1559. Pen and brown ink and watercolors over black chalk, 11.9 x 118.3 cm. Ashmolean Museum, Oxford

artistic merit, sets such as these must have played an important part in familiarizing Tudor audiences with classical subject matter.

Henry's Marriage to Anne of Cleves

The foregoing evidence provides an idea of the sort of tapestries that the Tudor court acquired during the late 1530s. Great Wardrobe records reveal that the officers responsible for moving and hanging the royal tapestries were extremely busy during these years.[42] Accounts relating to the visit of the embassy from the duke of Cleves in October 1539 are typical. These detail payments to John Norris with five yeomen and four grooms for four days' work preparing lodgings at Hampton Court for the ambassadors in September; to David Vincent for riding from Windsor to Greenwich and the Tower of London with his men, to "fet[ch] stuff to make ready for the ambassadors at Windsor," four days' work, and riding from thence to Greenwich, the Tower, Westminster, and Richmond, for stuff to make Hampton Court ready for the same ambassadors; and to Walter Vaughan with three yeoman and three grooms, for preparing the college of Windsor.[43]

In advance of his marriage to Anne, Henry rebuilt and refurbished the manor of Oatlands (fig. 13.11), a sizeable residence that he acquired by exchange in December 1537.[44] Some of the furnishings were provided from Parlaunt, Henry Norris's home at Langley Marish, Buckinghamshire, that Henry acquired in May 1536. These included a tapestry carpet "wrought with the kinges armes" that Norris had received as a perquisite when he was the keeper of the Greenwich Wardrobe.[45] By 1547 there were almost four hundred tapestries at Oatlands, most of them sets of hunting and verdure. Although many may have been brought in from other palace wardrobes, the sheer number suggests that a portion may have resulted from the sort of block order that the Great Wardrobe undertook for Newhall in 1516. The subjects of the narrative sets would certainly have been appropriate for a palace that the king was preparing to receive a new bride who might bear him more sons, including sets of *Cupid*, the *Prodigal Son*, *Solomon*, and *Hercules*.

In the event, Henry's marriage to Anne of Cleves (fig. 13.12) was doomed from the moment he set eyes on her, but he felt obliged to go through with the ceremony for the sake of form. One of the first people to whom he confided his disappointment with her plain appearance and manner was Sir Anthony Denny, who enjoyed a close friendship with Henry during the last decade of the king's life.[46] As quickly as possible, Henry divested himself of Anne. Order was given that she was to receive the manors of Richmond and Blechingly, as well as hangings, plate, furniture, and money for her household until her income was sufficient.[47] No inventory of the tapestries has survived, but annual wages for her household officers included £6 13s. 4d. for "Tilman Tappessier."[48] Oatlands was to get its moment of glory when it served as the setting for Henry's marriage to Catherine Howard on July 28, 1540.

Another outcome of the disastrous marriage to Anne of Cleves was that it precipitated the fall of Thomas Cromwell, who had been so instrumental in pressing the Reformation in England and in the development of the tapestry collection in various ways during the late 1530s. As with other attainted courtiers, Cromwell's possessions were appropriated by the Crown. No inventory of his tapestries has survived, but the 1547 royal inventory lists two "arras" tapestries at the Tower that were both specified as "late the Lorde Cromewelles," one of "our ladye hir sonne and another woman having a peare in hir hand," and the other of the "roote of Jessey."[49] The large dimensions of the *Jesse* tapestry suggest that it may have been a fifteenth-century piece. Whether Cromwell had received this as a perquisite from the Crown or whether he had acquired it from another source is uncertain. The devotional panel sounds similar in description to a number of pieces that date from the first two decades of the sixteenth century. Although these are the only tapestries specified as from Cromwell's collection, they may have been part of a larger number.

The foregoing discussion has indicated the character of tapestry acquisition and usage by the court during the late 1530s and the very early 1540s. The full splendor of the tapestry collection as it then existed was mustered for another extravagant display in the summer of 1541. The event that occasioned this preparation was the meeting with King James V of Scotland planned for September 1541. Henry departed from London on June 30, with five thousand horses and a thousand soldiers. The meeting was supposed to take place at the old Abbey of Saint Mary at York, and Marillac reported to Francis I that the preparations were occupying twelve hundred to fifteen hundred men working night and day: "Besides he has brought from London his richest tapestry, plate and dress."[50] Henry's intention was to provide an overwhelming display of power and magnificence to reinforce his standing in the potentially rebellious northern provinces.[51] James V had an interesting tapestry collection in his own right, so the summit would have been sumptuous, but in the event, James failed to show up, so Henry hurried home on September 29.[52] Unsurprisingly, this diplomatic fiasco was not commemorated in detailed descriptions, so we can only guess at the nature of the tapestries taken north by Henry. Splendid as they undoubtedly were, they were soon to be cast into the shade by the arrival of new purchases, several of which must have been commissioned during the previous two or three years. It is to discussion of these sets that we now turn.

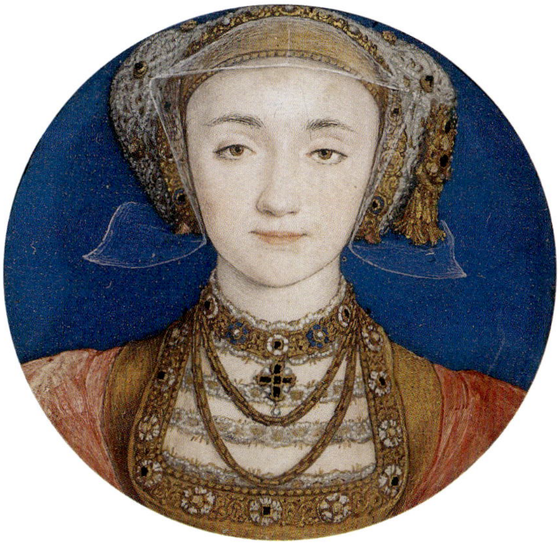

13.12 *Anne of Cleves* by Hans Holbein the Younger, ca. 1539. Bodycolor on vellum, 4.5 x 4.5 cm. Victoria and Albert Museum, London

The Acts of the Apostles

During the last seven years of his reign, Henry purchased a number of extremely costly tapestry sets that provided the standing wardrobes at Whitehall (fig. 13.13) and Hampton Court, his most important palaces, with hangings that were as rich, or richer, than anything owned by any of his Continental peers. In some cases, these tapestries were reweavings from designs that had been created for an earlier patron. In

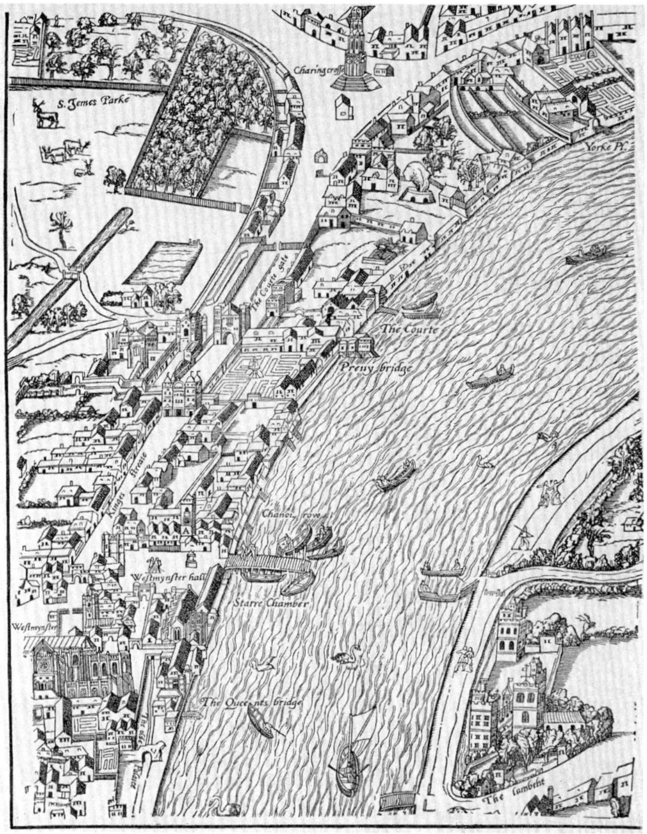

13.13 Copperplate map of London (detail) showing Whitehall Palace, ca. 1561–66. The Museum of London

others, they appear to have been the first weavings of the designs. But in all cases, the subjects seem to have been carefully chosen for their relevance to Henry's interests. The arrival of four of these sets can be ascertained with relative precision, two in the summer of 1542 and two sometime between September 1543 and September 1544. The subjects and design of these sets, and the context in which they were delivered, provide a key to understanding Henry's artistic preoccupations and tastes during the final decade of his reign.

The first two of the documented deliveries are recorded by the inventory of furnishings for which Sir Anthony Denny, keeper of Whitehall Palace, assumed responsibility on April 24, 1542. Among the valuable textiles and tapestries were two pieces "of Arras of the history of Thacts of thapostles" and another two "of hangings of Arras of thistory of Antiques." A marginal annotation records that all four were lined on November 3 of the same year, "wherof they doo not holde their contents afore charged in this booke and for that cause the contents of them be corrected." Annotations in the inventory indicate that because of the lining the tapestries were each reduced in length by about three inches.[53] The care with which these changes are noted indicates the reliability of the measurements in the Henrician inventories, at least where the more expensive tapestries are concerned.

No mention is made in the inventory of other *Acts* or *Antiques* tapestries. However, the following pages list furnishings that arrived at Whitehall after the compilation of the inventory, including a delivery of "Stuff new made by the king his highness comaundement," on November 3, 1542. This comprised several sets of tapestry including "seven peces of hangings of arras of thacts of the appostells lyned thorought with canvas" and "fyve peces of hanginges of Arras wrought with Antiques lined throughout with canvas." A marginal note records that these twelve pieces were purchased from "John Baptist Gualterote," merchant of Florence, in June 1542.[54] Gualteroti was one of a family of rich Florentine merchants who had been based in Antwerp since the beginning of the sixteenth century and who played a leading role in the Netherlandish spice trade.[55] This is the first evidence that he supplied tapestries to Henry VIII, but, since much of the Netherlandish tapestry industry was controlled by financiers who underwrote the advance costs of materials and wages, his involvement is unsurprising.[56] With the date at which the inventory was compiled providing a terminus ante quem, it appears that Gualteroti must have supplied the first two pairs of tapestries to Whitehall Palace sometime before April 1542, but not much earlier than that, since otherwise they would have been lined by then. The main part of the sets were then delivered in June 1542, and they were presumably all sent to the king's tailors together, since the date at which the earlier arrivals were lined coincides with that at which Denny took receipt of the main part of both sets at Whitehall. Further purchase information is added by the declaration of account that Denny presented on September 4, 1547, regarding disbursements he had made between April 22, 1541, and January 28, 1547. This mentions various large payments to merchants for precious textiles, including one of £2,325 15s. 6d. to "John Baptiste Galterott for two peces [sets] of Riche Arras thone of the Actes of Thappostelles and thother of Antiques."[57] At a price of £2 2s. per ell, and a total cost of more than £1,100 apiece, these sets were among the most expensive of Henry's documented acquisitions, ranking in price with the *Story of David* purchased in 1528.

Identification of these sets is straightforward because both are well documented. Following the execution of Charles I the *Acts* set was sold in October 1650 to Robert Houghton, leader of one of the fourteen syndicates that acquired large numbers of royal artworks. Shortly thereafter it was resold for £3,599 to the Spanish ambassador in London, Don Alonso de Cárdenas, who was acting on behalf of Don Luis Mendez de Haro, marqués del Carpio.[58] By 1662 it had passed into the collection of the duke of Alba, where it remained until 1823 when it was purchased by the British consul in Catalonia, a Mr. Tupper, who brought the set back to England. It was exhibited in London and the Midlands before being acquired for the Kaiser Friedrich Museum in Berlin in 1844 and is assumed to have been destroyed in Berlin in 1945. Fortunately, photographs of the set had been made before its disappearance.[59]

As these photographs reveal (figs. 13.14–13.16), the set was a duplicate of the famous set depicting scenes from the lives of Saint Peter and Saint Paul that was made for Pope Leo X in the late 1510s in the Brussels workshop of Pieter van Aelst from cartoons by Raphael and his assistants (see fig. 10.12). As noted in the discussion of Netherlandish tapestry design in the 1520s and 1530s, the *Acts* were groundbreaking, embodying the first full-scale application to the tapestry medium of the heightened realism that Raphael had developed over the previous years in the Vatican Stanze frescoes. Framed by a faux porphyry border, the dramas depicted in the main scenes appeared to be taking place in a space that was immediately adjacent to the seated congregation. The immediacy of the scenes was heightened by the focus of the design

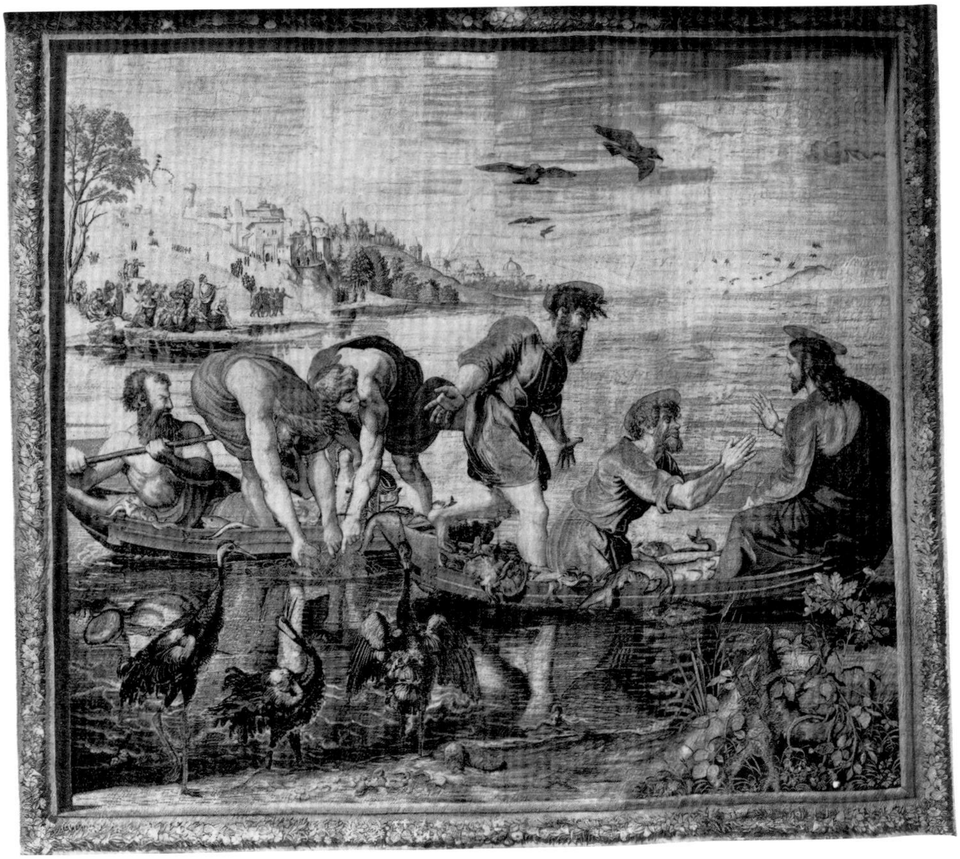

13.14 *The Miraculous Draft of Fishes* from Henry VIII's set of the *Acts of the Apostles*. Unidentified Brussels workshop after a cartoon by Raphael, ca. 1540–42. Wool, silk, and gilt-metal-wrapped thread, 389 x 442 cm (after removal of outer borders). Current location unidentified, formerly Kaiser Friedrich Museum, Berlin

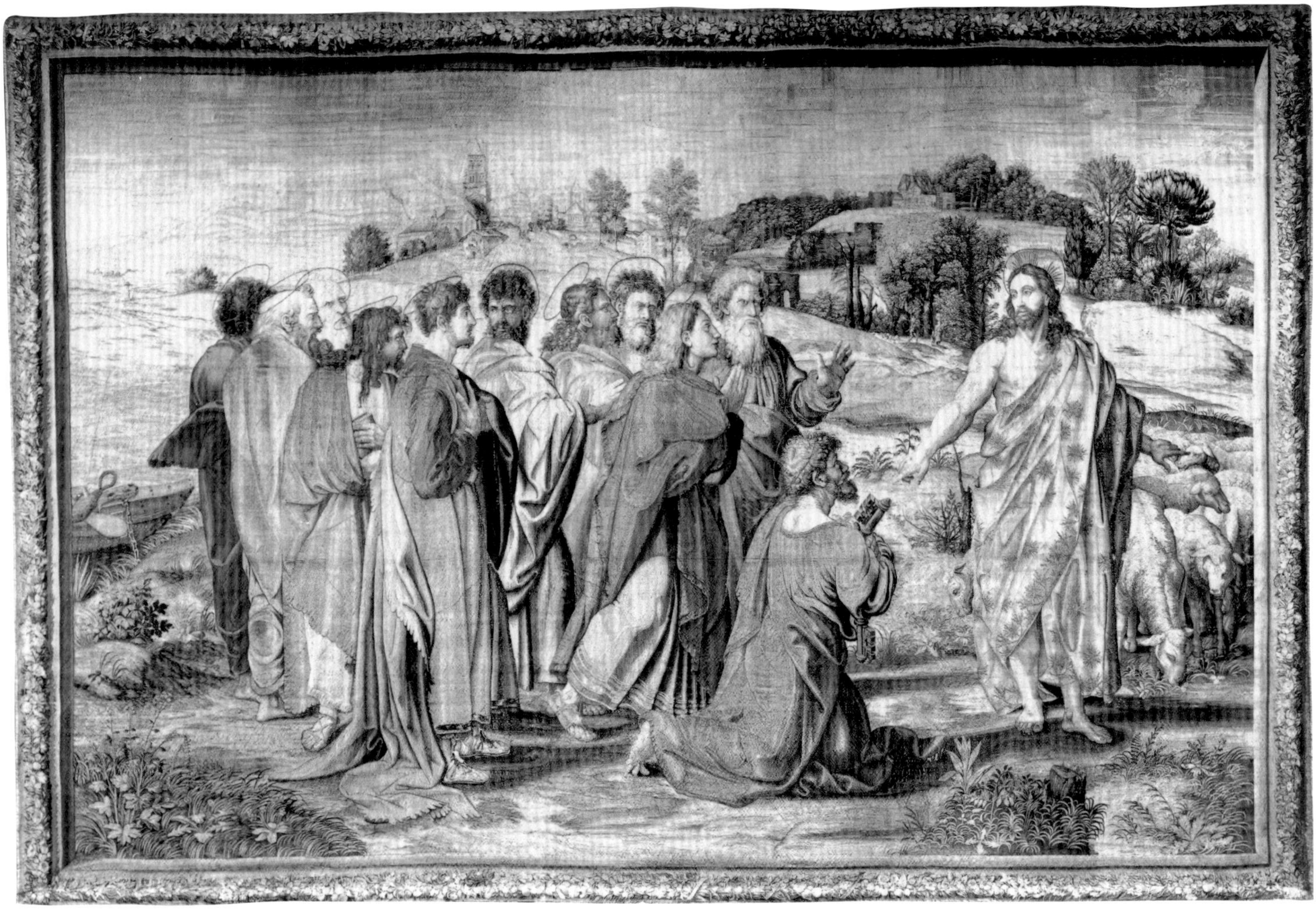

13.15 *The Charge to Peter* from Henry VIII's set of the *Acts of the Apostles*. Unidentified Brussels workshop after a cartoon by Raphael, ca. 1540–42. Wool, silk, and gilt-metal-wrapped thread, 386 x 566 cm (after removal of outer borders). Current location unidentified, formerly Kaiser Friedrich Museum, Berlin

on the expressions, physiognomy, and rhetorical gestures of the principal figures, rather than on extraneous detail. The costumes and architecture were based on ancient models, and the landscapes were the most thoughtful representations of the antique world yet undertaken.

The content of the series was no less carefully considered. Commissioned within the first two years of Leo's pontificate, the conception of the Raphael tapestries fell in a period when Leo was most actively using the arts to celebrate papal authority and to project his own status.[60] The spiritual importance of the Sistine Chapel for which the tapestries were intended, the artistic precedents embodied there, and the elite and sophisticated character of the audience in that venue ensured that the planning of the scheme received careful attention, as reflected by the deliberation with which the subjects and iconography were chosen.[61] The preeminence of the Catholic Church was based on its joint foundation by Peter and Paul and its consecration through their joint martyrdom in Rome.[62] Papal authority derived primarily from Peter's appointment as Christ's vicar on earth. Leo's tapestries celebrated this legacy by focusing on key episodes from the lives of the two apostles. The tapestries thus provided a celebration of the doctrine of the apostolic succession and, by implication, of the present incumbent, as suggested by one scene in particular, the so-called *Charge to Peter*, in which, following the Gospel of Saint Matthew (16:15–19), Christ entrusts Peter with the keys to the Kingdom of Heaven (see fig. 13.15).[63]

The implicit celebration of Leo was reinforced in the papal set by the borders, of which the bottom part emulated a frieze with some sections depicting scenes from the life of Saint Paul and others, scenes from Leo's life before

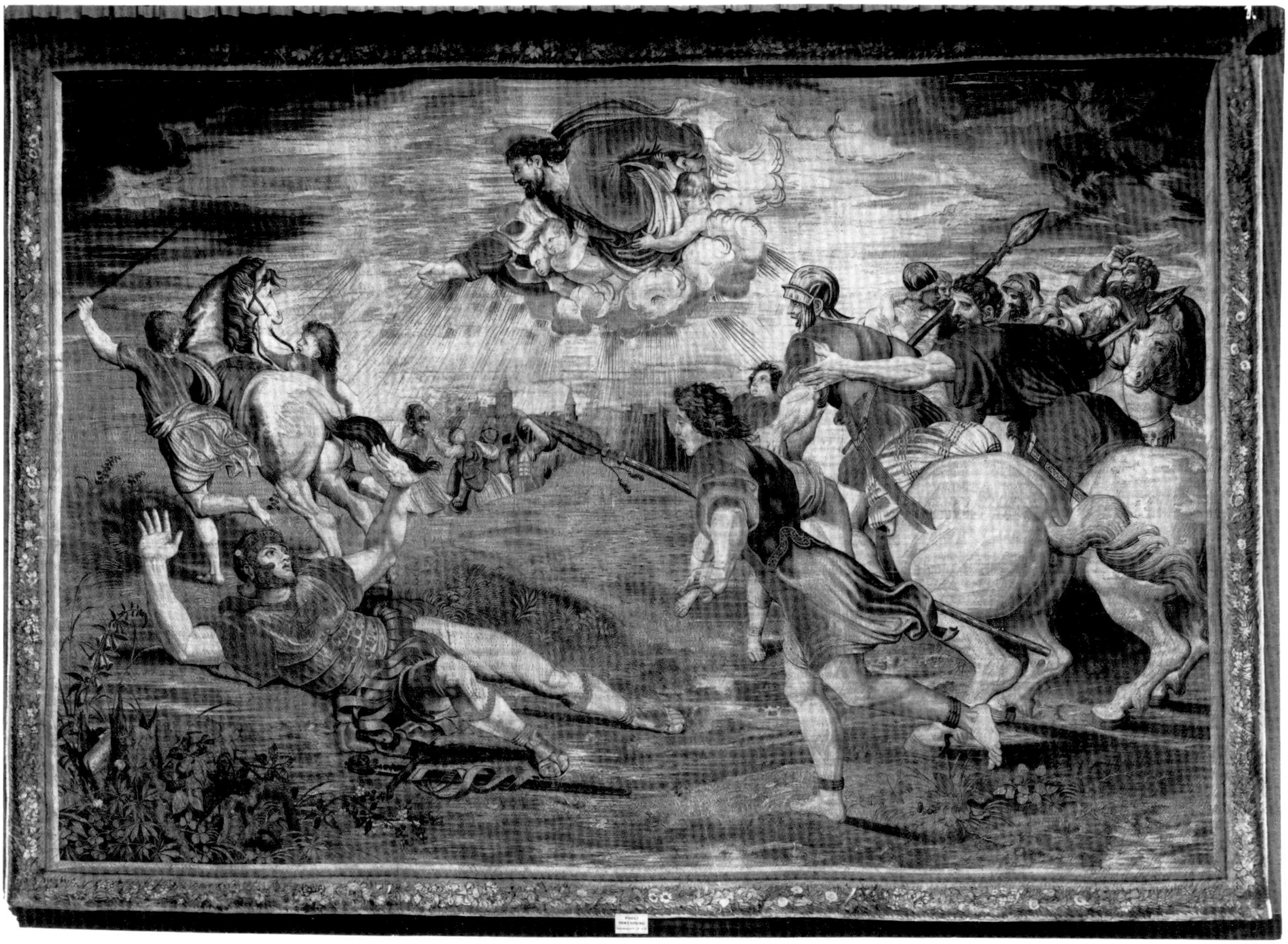

13.16 *The Conversion of Saul* from Henry VIII's set of the *Acts of the Apostles*. Unidentified Brussels workshop after a cartoon by Raphael, ca. 1540–42. Wool, silk, and gilt metal-wrapped thread, 396 x 556 cm (after removal of outer borders). Current location unidentified, formerly Kaiser Friedrich Museum, Berlin

his election. The vertical borders depicted the Seven Liberal Arts, the Seven Virtues, the Hours, the Seasons, the Elements, and the Labors of Hercules. The iconography of these vertical borders has been obscured because of the loss of some sections following the sack of Rome in 1527, but the main theme appears to be the triumph of *Virtú* over *Occasio*, a message that resonates with the cycle of events from the patron's life depicted in the lower borders.[64] The figure of Hercules was included because, according to contemporary exegetical texts such as Aegidius of Viterbo's *Historia viginti saeculorum* (1515–18), he was the first Tuscan hero to carry the "insignia leonis."[65] The border design was thus an "exemplum virtutis," a sophisticated celebration of Leo's Christian virtues framed in terms of classical models.

The photographs of Henry's lost set reveal that, like the duplicate set that Francis I purchased in the early 1530s, it did not include the scene of *Paul Escaping from Prison*, almost certainly because this narrow panel was considered unnecessary outside the context of the Sistine Chapel, where it had filled a space adjacent to the choir balcony. Other than this, the photographs show that the main scenes of Henry's tapestries reproduced Raphael's cartoons as they had been woven in Leo's set, including a strip of landscape above the heads of the apostles in the scene of the *Charge to Peter* that had not been included in the original cartoon. Equally, Henry's tapestries also incorporated a number of minor design adaptations that appear in two other mid-sixteenth-century sets, one made for Cardinal Ercole Gonzaga in about 1550, the other made for an unidentified member of the Habsburg family and now in the Spanish royal collection (fig. 13.17). These variations indicate that

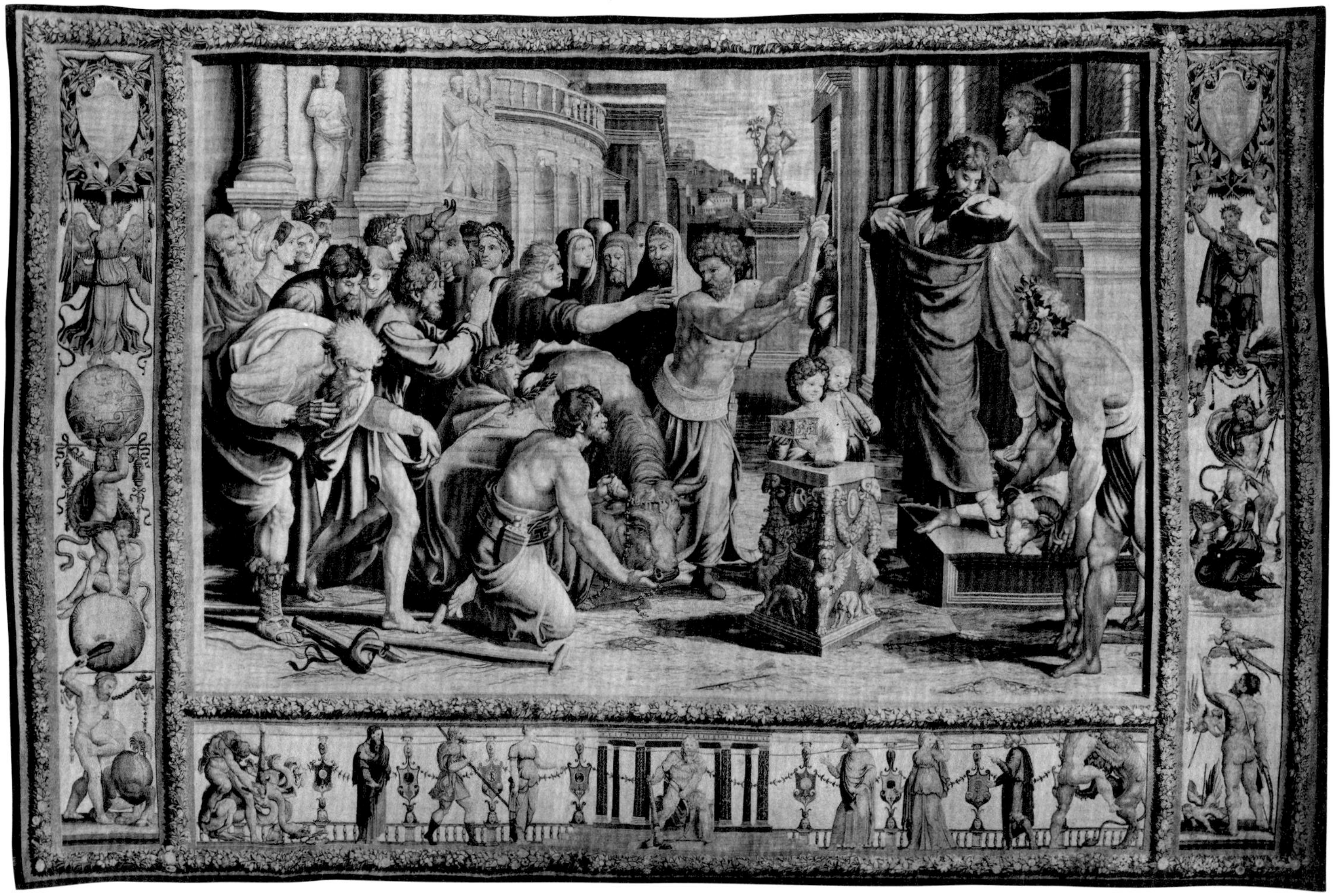

13.17 *The Sacrifice at Lystra* from the *Acts of the Apostles*. Tapestry designed by Raphael, woven in Brussels, ca. 1550. Wool and silk, 495 x 621 cm. Patrimonio Nacional, Madrid

Henry's set was the third weaving of this design, postdating the set made for Francis in the early 1530s (a fact that can be established on documentary grounds) but predating those in Madrid and Mantua.

The most significant difference between Henry's set and that in Rome appeared in the borders. When Henry's set reappeared in the nineteenth century it was simply bordered with a floral band, which led earlier commentators to assume that this was its original appearance.[66] However, analysis of the dimensions provided by the Tudor and Commonwealth sale inventories reveals that the dimensions of Henry's set were very close to those of the duplicate sets that survive in Mantua and Madrid.[67] Both the Mantua and Madrid sets have wide lateral borders like those on the original tapestries made for Leo X, but these are separated from the main scenes by bands of flowers rather than the trompe l'oeil porphyry frames that surround the Leonine set. More significantly, in place of the faux relief with scenes of the lives of Saint Paul and Leo that occupied the lower border of the original set, these later versions depict mythological and allegorical figures that are probably intended to embody an allegorical meditation on the benefits of good government. As the first known re-edition of the *Acts* series was made for Francis I in 1533, and because one of the later borders depicted Hercules as Eloquence (see fig. 13.17), a figure associated with Francis in court panegyric by French humanists—in contrast to the Libyan Hercules associated with Charles V—it has been suggested that these variant borders were designed for the French king in the early 1530s.[68] Visual confirmation that Henry's set was also woven with these variant borders is provided by the photographs taken before their destruction. Like the Mantua and Madrid sets, Henry's set was surrounded by floral bands, and the photographs show that these originally continued beyond the edges of the tapestries as they survived in recent times. We can therefore conclude that the figurative part of the borders of Henry's set were removed at some date after it left the royal collection and that the Mantua and Madrid sets thus provide a reliable indication of the appearance of Henry's tapestries in their original form. In passing it is to be noted that the loss of the borders on Henry's set explains why they did not carry Brussels marks, a lack that led earlier commentators to make the erroneous assumption that they had been woven before 1528, the year when it became obligatory for all Brussels tapestries to carry the town mark.

The Antiques

Identification of the *Antiques* set that Henry acquired at the same time as the *Acts* is straightforward because two pieces survive in the royal collection today (figs. i.3, 13.18, 13.19, and details opposite pp. ix, 251). As these demonstrate, the set was also woven from a design series commissioned by Leo X from the Raphael workshop sometime during the late 1510s.[69] The papal set disappeared in the late eighteenth century, but its appearance can be reconstructed on the basis of sixteenth-century weavings; the two pieces from Henry's collection and three from a mid-sixteenth-century set now in Paris (fig. 13.20); and copies of the

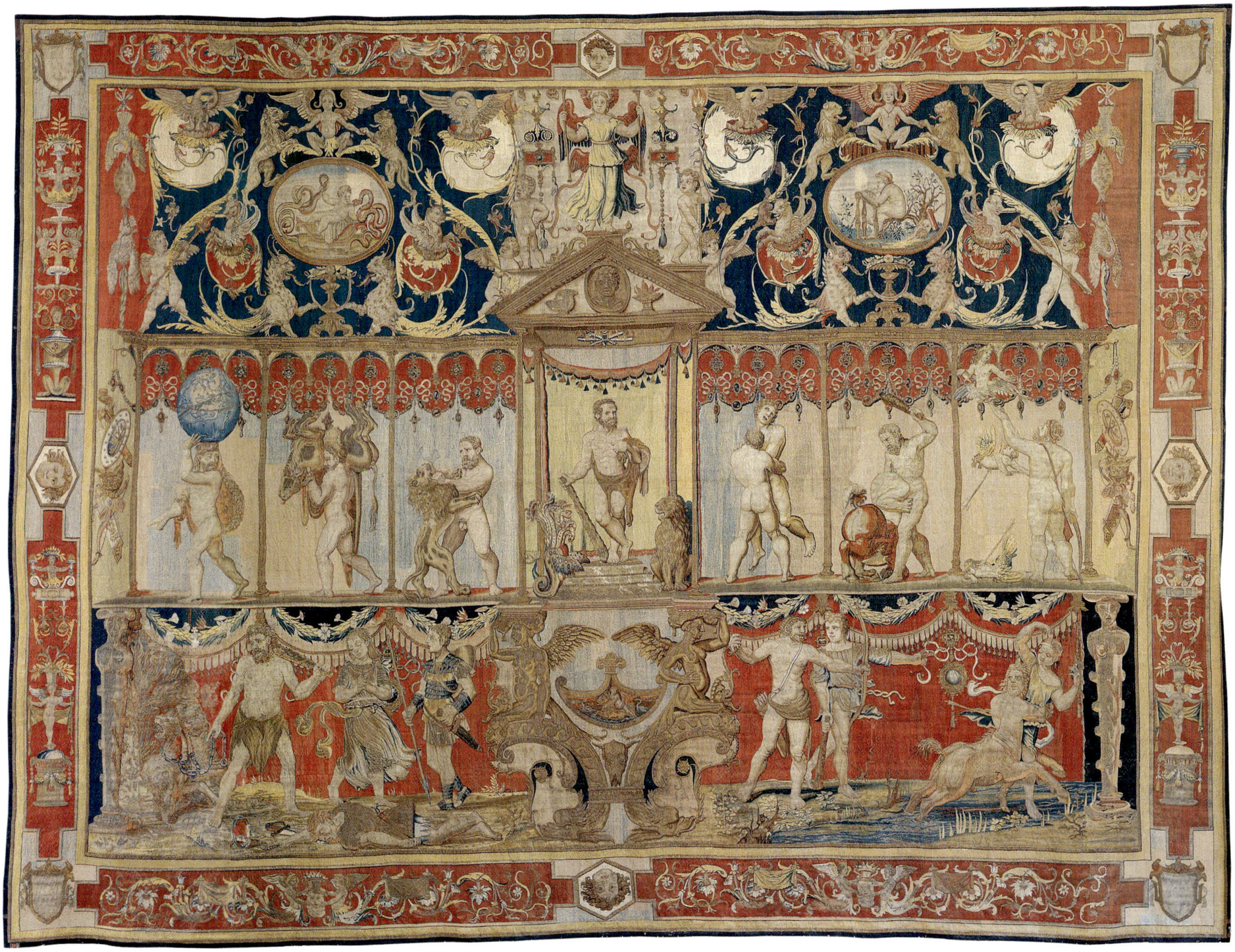

13.18 *The Triumph of Hercules* from Henry VIII's *Antiques* set (now known as the *Triumphs of the Gods*). Unidentified Brussels workshop after a design attributed to Giovanni Francesco Penni and Giovanni da Udine, ca. 1517–20, woven in Brussels, ca. 1540–42. Wool, silk, and gilt-metal-wrapped thread, 480 x 632 cm. Hampton Court Palace

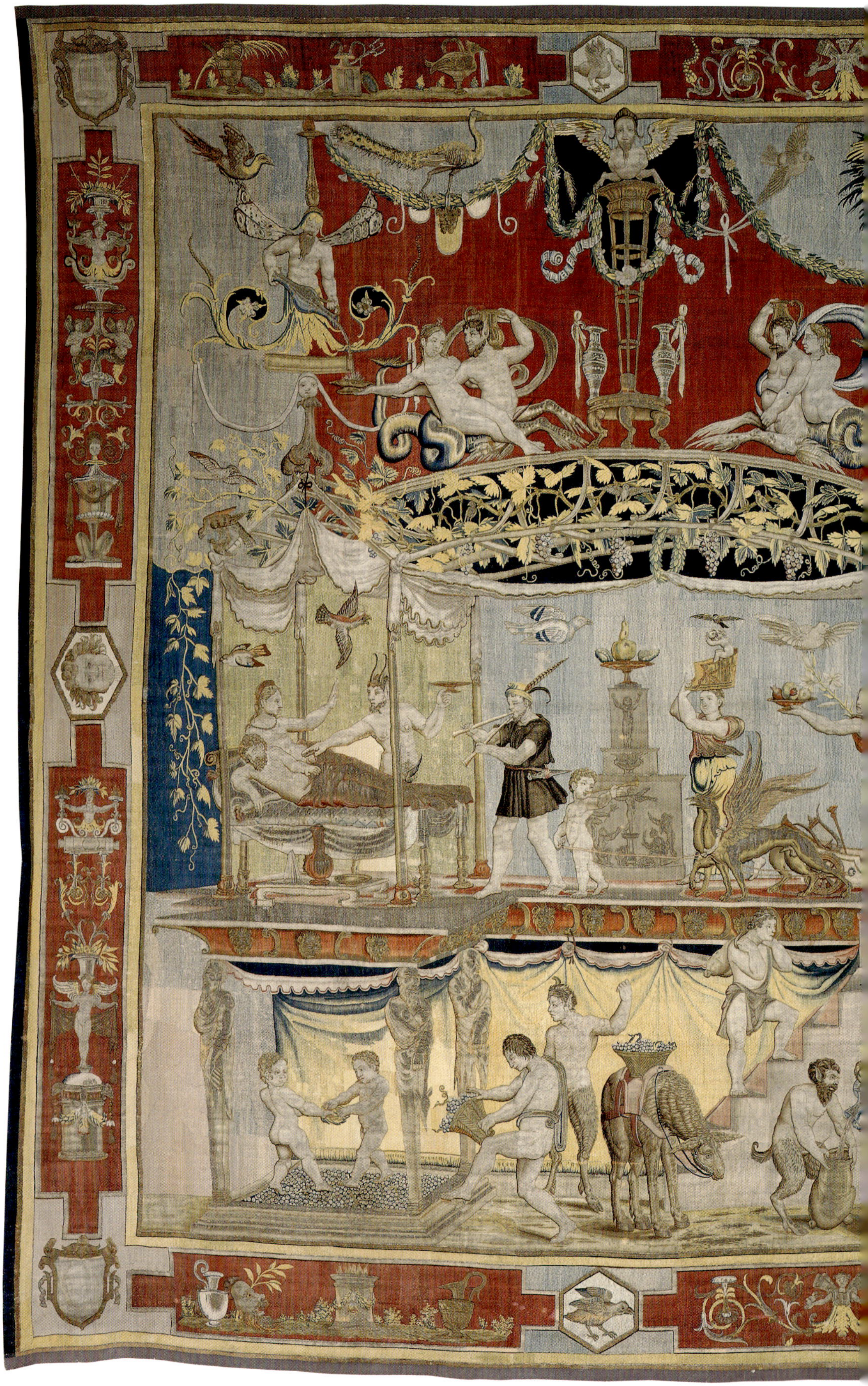

13.19 *The Triumph of Bacchus* from Henry VIII's *Antiques* set (now known as the *Triumphs of the Gods*). Unidentified Brussels workshop after a design attributed to Giovanni Francesco Penni and Giovanni da Udine, ca. 1517–20, woven in Brussels, ca. 1540–42. Wool, silk, and gilt-metal-wrapped thread, 475 x 745 cm. Hampton Court Palace

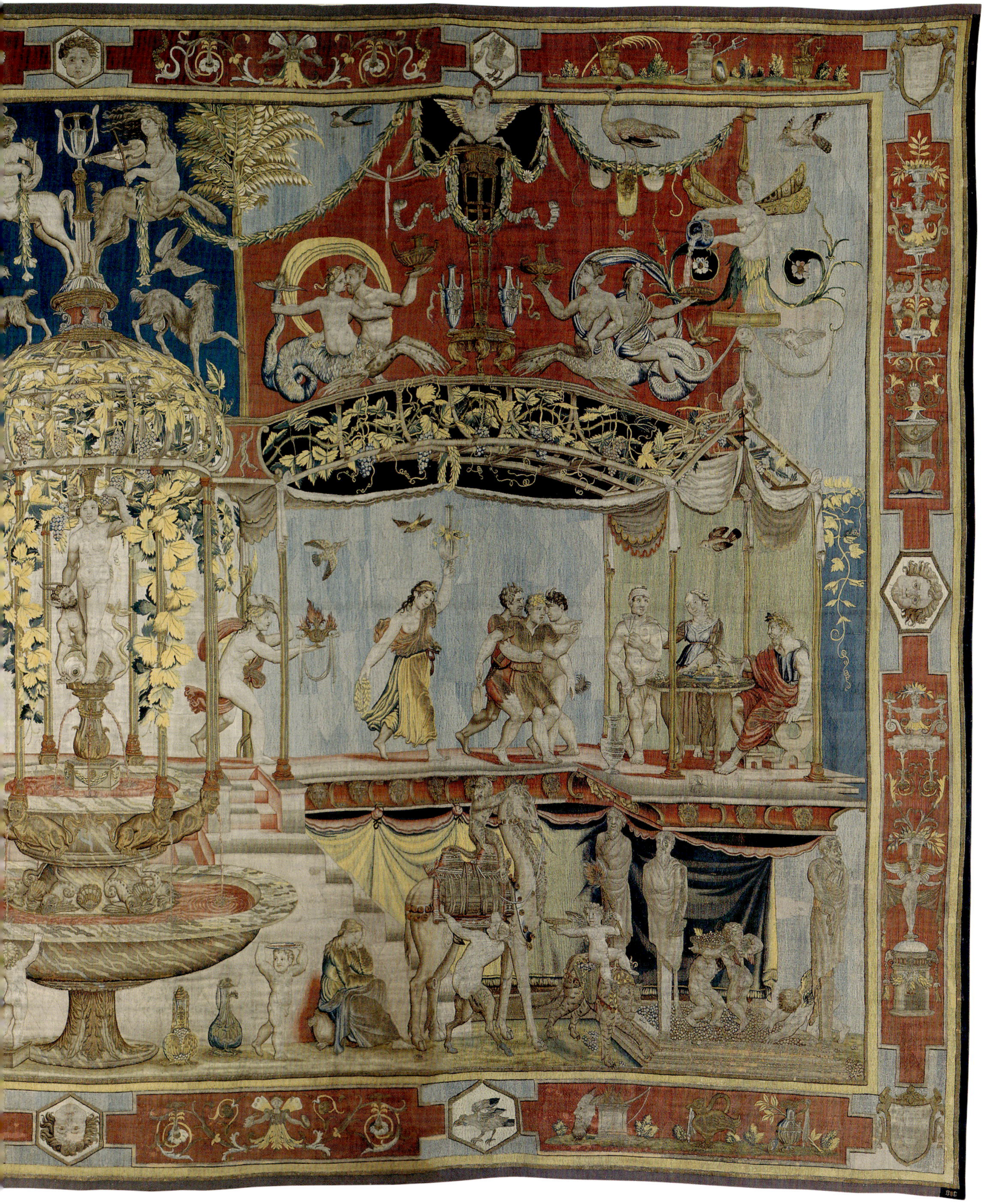

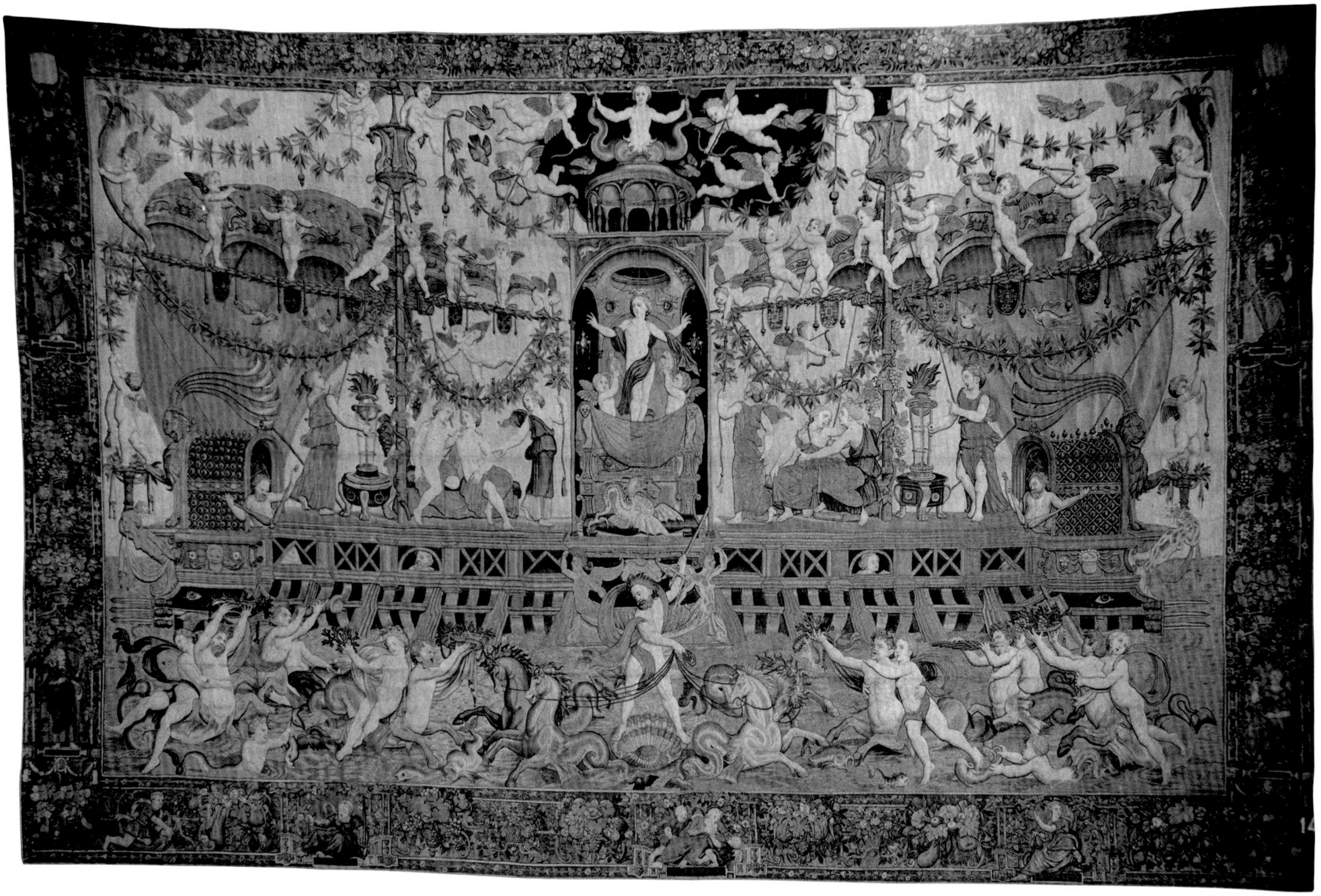

13.20 *The Triumph of Venus* from the *Triumphs of the Gods*. Tapestry design attributed to Giovanni Francesco Penni and Giovanni da Udine, ca. 1517–20, woven in the workshop of Frans Geubels, Brussels, ca. 1560. Wool and silk, 501 x 739 cm. Mobilier National, Paris

entire set made for Louis XIV in the seventeenth century. Each tapestry featured a classical god or personification within "grotesque" decorations. The subjects of the complete series can be identified as the Triumphs of Apollo, Bacchus, Hercules, Minerva, Mars, Venus, Faith among the Virtues, and Grammar among the Liberal Arts.[70] Interestingly, where Leo's set included eight panels, Henry's included only seven, and it is possible that one of the original designs had been consciously omitted.

Stylistically, the concept of the series was almost as innovative as the *Acts*, being the first in which grotesque elements were applied as an allover decorative formula. Many of the figures portrayed in the tapestries are directly inspired by antique models. Giorgio Vasari records that the designs were by Giovanni da Udine, but it is not known who painted the cartoons. Considering the style of the final designs, as represented by surviving tapestries, it seems most likely that they were executed in Rome by Giovanni, with the assistance of other Raphael collaborators such as Giovanni Francesco Penni, Giulio Romano, and Perino del Vaga. Like Leo's other commissions, the first set of the designs, known as the *Grotesques of Leo X* in Vatican inventories, were almost certainly woven in the workshop of Pieter van Aelst. The *Triumph of Bacchus* panel from Henry's set carries the Brussels mark in the lower selvage. In addition, Henry's *Triumph of Hercules* tapestry carries an incomplete merchant or weaver's mark that may belong to the workshop of Guillaume (Willem) and Jean Dermoyen (or Van der Moyen).[71] As noted earlier, the Dermoyens were among the merchant weavers on whose behalf Mostinck had testified in 1539. Circumstantial support for the possibility that Henry's *Acts* were also woven in the Dermoyen workshop is provided by the fact that payment for the set of the *Acts* that Francis I made in

1534 was made to Cornelie de Rameline, an agent who acted for the Brussels merchants Daniel and Antoon Bombergen and Willem Dermoyen.[72]

Like the *Acts,* Leo's *Grotesques* had a strong political theme. As we have seen, the vignettes of Hercules in the lateral borders of Leo's *Acts* suggest that this scheme was designed as an allegorical celebration of his pontificate. Several of those Hercules vignettes reappear in the main field of the *Grotesques* panel devoted to the *Triumph of Hercules,* and although the iconography of this series awaits detailed study, it seems likely that it also encompassed an allegory of the achievements of Leo's reign and a celebration of the new era of spiritual and intellectual harmony that it had produced, as epitomized by the scenes of the *Ascendancy of Faith among the Virtues* and the *Ascendancy of Grammar among the Liberal Arts.*[73]

Knowledge of the two sets that Gualteroti delivered to the Tudor court in the summer and fall of 1542 raises the question as to why Henry would have wanted to spend so much money to acquire these designs at this time. In comparison to the tapestries he had purchased in previous years, the *Acts* and *Antiques* sets are remarkable for two reasons. First, as will be readily apparent, they provided a very large and splendid embodiment of the style that Raphael had developed in Rome during the 1510s. Although the influence of this style had manifested itself in Netherlandish tapestry design through the work of Bernaert van Orley and Pieter Coecke, examples of whose work were certainly being acquired by Henry from the late 1520s, the *Acts* and *Antiques* commissions are the first in which Henry is known to have purchased such overtly "Italianate" designs. The second interesting aspect about Henry's choice is that both embodied such overt celebrations of Leo X's papacy. To what extent was Henry aware of such aesthetic and political issues?

In seeking answers to these questions, it is instructive to consider the context in which the tapestries were acquired. The sets were delivered to Whitehall Palace in 1542 and had presumably been commissioned at least two years before.[74] Whitehall was Henry's main palace in central London, but at this time it was a hodgepodge of brick buildings, lacking architectural uniformity. In an attempt to remedy this situation, extensive rebuilding and redecoration were undertaken in the early 1540s, including the construction of a new banqueting house and an outside loggia decorated with "antique" devices (fig. 13.21).[75] The interior decorations involved a number of Continental artists and craftsmen, of whom the leading spirit was almost certainly an Italian called Nicholas Bellin of Modena, who may have worked with Giulio Romano in Mantua in the late 1520s and certainly worked at Fontainebleau with Rosso and Primaticcio between 1532 and 1537.[76] Bellin

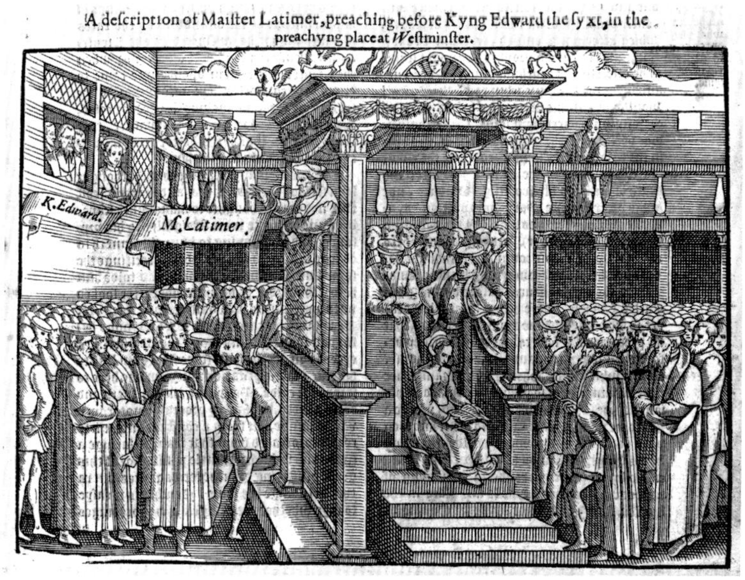

13.21 *The Preaching Place at Whitehall Palace* from John Foxe's *Acts and Monuments* (1563)

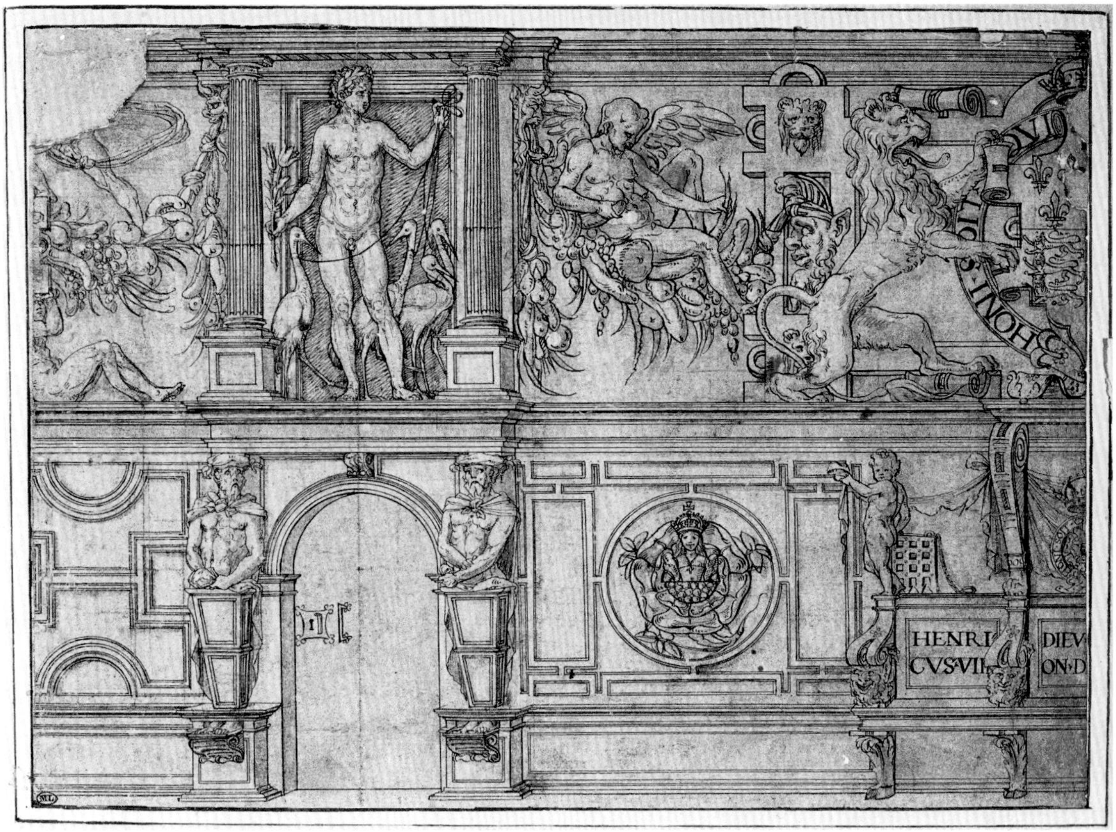

13.22 Design for an Interior with the Arms of Henry VIII attributed to Nicholas Bellin of Modena, ca. 1545. Pen and ink, 20.5 x 27.5 cm. Musée du Louvre, Paris

relocated to London in 1537, and his skills were sufficiently valued for Francis to ask for his return, but Henry refused on the grounds that Bellin was an Italian subject. Bellin is recorded working at Whitehall as a painter and designer of stucco in 1540, and between 1541 and 1545 he was primarily responsible for designing and overseeing the production of the stucco decorations for Nonsuch. None of Bellin's work for Whitehall has survived, but its character can be inferred from various sources, of which the most explicit is an anonymous design for plasterwork with the arms of Henry VIII and Catherine Parr (fig. 13.22).[77] Dating from between 1543 and 1546, this design reveals how closely Bellin's work for Henry was related to that at Fontainebleau, embodying a flamboyantly mannerist style.

The 1542 inventory does not specify the location for which the two new tapestry sets were intended within the palace. However, a possible clue is provided by Henry Peacham's reminiscence in *The Compleat Gentlemen* (1622) of "those stately hangings of Arras, containing the History of Saint Paul out of the Acts," which "long since you might have seene in the banquetting house at White-hall."[78] Since we know that a new banqueting house was built at Whitehall during 1540–41—that is, just before the delivery of the tapestries—this statement indicates that the tapestries were linked with the modernization taking place in the early 1540s.

Yet if the Italianate style of the *Acts* and *Antiques* designs played a part in their selection for Whitehall, the question remains as to whether Henry was aware of the extent to which the tapestries had been conceived as a celebration of papal power. Considering how much Henry's life had been dominated by conflict with the papacy during the 1530s, why did he choose these designs, particularly one that was conceived as a celebration of the apostolic succession from Saint Peter to the pope, which he was now rejecting? The answer to this question must lie in the character of Henry's other expensive tapestry purchases during the late 1530s and early 1540s and his self-identification with religious role models. In particular, evidence that Henry had purchased a very expensive set of the *Story of Saint Paul* in 1538–39, just at the time that he was licensing the translation of the Great Bible, provides a new context for understanding his decision to commission a set of the Raphael *Acts of the Apostles* sometime around 1540. The *Saint Paul* set had been assigned to Hampton Court, which had been greatly extended and rebuilt during the 1530s as an enormous entertainment complex. With the acquisition of the *Acts* set, Henry now had at Whitehall an equally grand set to project an image of himself as a latter-day evangelist. The notion that the iconography of the papal set may have been problematic to Henry, particularly the scene of the *Charge to Peter,* is to misunderstand how intensively Henry and his circle had considered this very question. Raphael's design conflated two scriptural sources to celebrate Christ's selection of Peter as his successor: the Gospel of Saint Matthew (16:15–19), which records the moment when Christ appeared to his disciples after the Resurrection and told Peter, "I will give unto thee the keys of the Kingdom of Heaven," and the Gospel of Saint John (21:1–17), when Christ appeared to seven disciples and told Peter to "Feed my sheep." The conflation of these two scenes was clearly intended to celebrate Peter above the other apostles.[79] But for English Reformists, Christ's injunction was addressed to the disciples in general. This point was specifically discussed in treatises by Henry's propagandists, respectively Edward Foxe's *De vera differentia regiae potestatis et ecclesiasticae...* (1534) and Stephen Gardiner's *De vera obedientia* (1535).[80] According to Foxe, "Where ... our lord doth geve unto Peter this power of binding and lowsing of a trewth it is not to be doubted ... but in Peter which bare the figure of the church it was geven unto all thapostles ... all bysshoppes and preestes have equall auchtoryte with Peter."[81] This typifies the defenses presented by Henry's propagandists in texts and sermons during the 1530s. The notion that Christ's charge was to the apostles in general is given explicit visual expression in one of the vignettes on the title page of the Coverdale Bible, in which all the disciples are shown carrying keys to the Kingdom of Heaven (fig. 12.4). Thus, by the time the *Acts* tapestries were delivered in 1542, Henry and his courtiers would have been so used to interpreting the *Charge to Peter* as a general injunction to all the apostles that this detail was probably not nearly as problematic as might first appear to a modern audience.

An analogous argument applies to the *Antiques* set. In the absence of any overt reference to Leo, there was no reason that Henry could not equally enjoy the associative reading that the designs invited between Henry and the classical deities, particularly Hercules. After all, the use of Hercules as a role model was hardly unique to the papal court. European patrons had been commissioning sets of tapestries depicting Hercules for more than a century, and there were several old sets of this subject in the English royal collection. Henry himself had dressed up as Hercules when he met with Francis I at Guines in 1520. Nonetheless, the selection of the *Grotesques* set for Whitehall in the early 1540s is especially interesting because there is evidence that the comparison with Hercules had attained new currency for Henry at this time. A set of *Hercules* tapestries was among a delivery of new tapestries made to Whitehall by William Lok in February 1544.[82] Although the acquisition may reflect no more than Henry's continuing interest in this classical theme, evidence that the subject had new metaphorical relevance in the post-Reformation context is provided by the preface to Sir Anthony Cope's translation of Livy's *History of Hannibal and Scipio,* published in 1544, which compares Henry to Hercules and Rome to the Hydra.[83]

Further evidence of the renewed significance of Hercules for Henry is provided by the didactic scheme that Nicholas Bellin created on the facades of the interior courtyard and the exterior walls at Nonsuch. The interior courtyard was faced with stucco panels arranged in three tiers. On the basis of sixteenth-century descriptions it appears that the lower tier on the king's side of the courtyard depicted the Feats of Hercules, while those on the queen's side depicted the Liberal Arts and Sciences

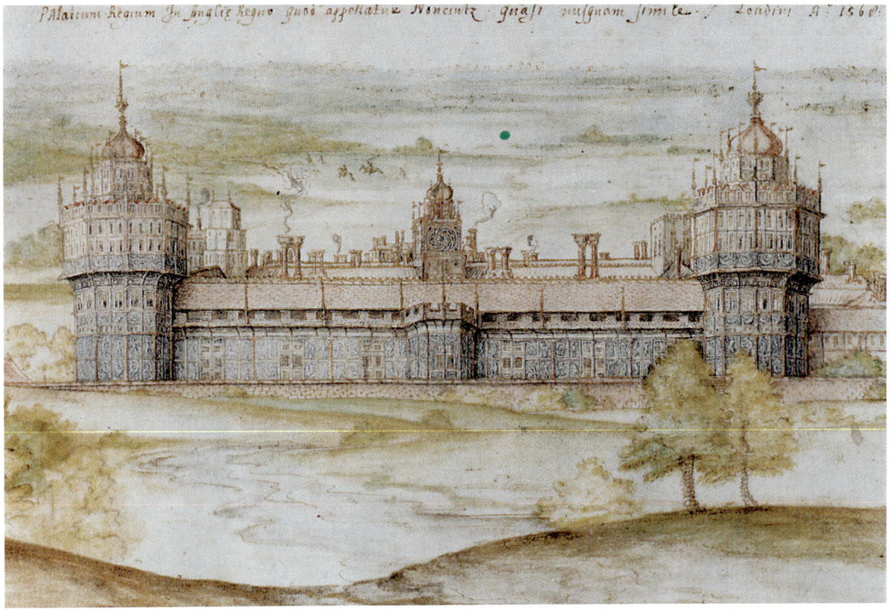

13.23 *Nonsuch Palace from the South* by Joris Hoefnagel, 1568. Pen and ink and colored wash on paper, 21.6 x 32.5 cm. Private collection

and the Virtues. The middle tier depicted the male and female pagan gods, arranged respectively on the king's and queen's sides, and the upper tier represented the twenty-four caesars.[84] No description survives of the stuccoes on the exterior facade, but evidence that these may have replicated those on the interior is provided by watercolors of the palace painted in 1568 by Joris Hoefnagel (figs. 13.23, 13.24).[85] Although these depictions are schematic, some of the scenes on the south facade on the king's side of the house also appear to feature the Labors of Hercules, with large figures occupying the complete space of the stucco panel, much as they occupy the architectural frames in the vignettes of the *Acts* borders and in the central field of *The Triumph of Hercules*. The iconographic program of the Nonsuch stuccoes is not fully documented, but it evidently embodied a classicized celebration of the virtues and arts and the path to Honor in a scheme that was, at the very least, similar in tone to that of the *Grotesques* tapestries. Given the closeness in date of the delivery of the *Grotesques* tapestries to the execution of the stuccoes at Nonsuch, it seems likely that a knowledge of the tapestry designs influenced, even determined, the iconography and appearance of some of the stucco panels.

The *Acts* and *Antiques* may thus have appealed to Henry both for their sophisticated Italianate style and for the coincidence of their subject matter to Henry's post-Reformation self-image. The question remains as to why he chose to commission these particular designs sometime around 1540. As we have seen, Francis had acquired a set of the *Acts* as early as 1533, but there is no evidence to suggest that this example spurred Henry to develop an interest in Italian designs during the 1530s. So why should they have appealed to him seven years later around 1540? The probable answer surely lies in the role played by Nicolas Bellin. As Bellin had worked at Fontainebleau throughout the period of Francis's most active tapestry patronage, he must have arrived at the English court with a keen sense of the merits of the tapestry designs then available. Indeed, the possibility that Bellin worked with Giulio Romano in the late 1520s raises the prospect that he may have had a firsthand account of the tapestry projects of the Raphael workshop. Either way, he would have been uniquely placed to provide Henry with information about the original Leonine tapestries and the variant borders created for Francis's duplicate set. Bellin's involvement in Henry's commission for the *Acts* and *Antiques* set and his understanding of the underlying iconography of the designs would also explain the echoes of that iconography in the decorations that he created for the facade of Nonsuch Palace between 1541 and 1545.

In summary, the circumstances in which Henry acquired sets of the *Acts of the Apostles* and the Leonine *Grotesques* suggests that these commissions were stimulated by both iconographic and aesthetic motivations. The designs had been created as the crowning celebration of papal power under Leo X from designs by the leading Roman artist of the day. Twenty years later, when Henry was promoting his own status as apostle to his own people, and also concerned to decorate Whitehall Palace in the most up-to-date Continental style, he acquired duplicate weavings of these designs. Adaptations that had already been undertaken to the *Acts* borders on behalf of Francis enabled Henry to reinterpret the papal iconography to

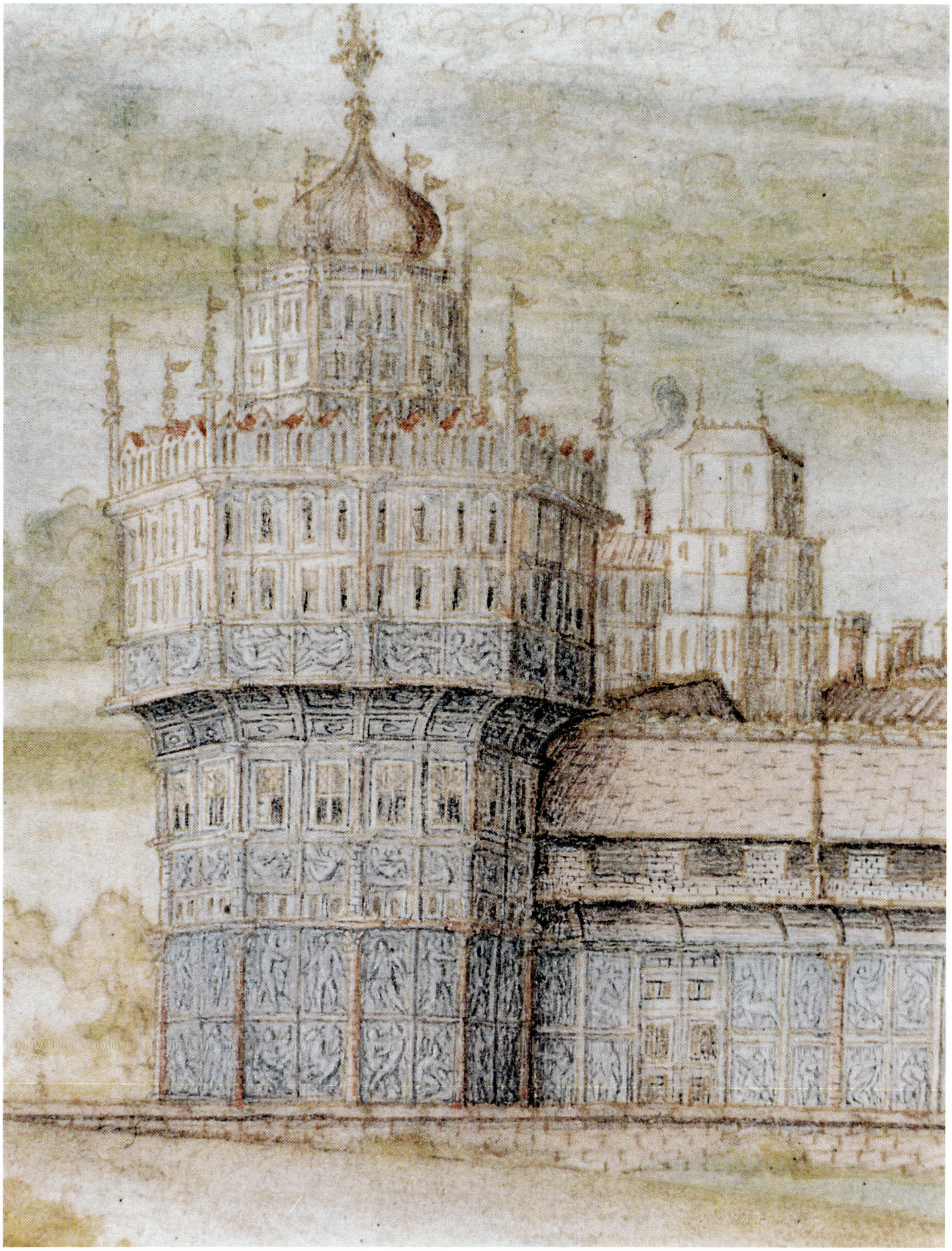

13.24 Detail of fig. 13.23

his own purposes, while the knowledge that these designs were originally created for the papal court must have provided a strong resonance for Henry and his circle. In effect, Henry had appropriated and transferred the splendor and trappings of apostolic succession from the papal palace in Rome to his own palace at Westminster, the visual focus of the Tudor court in London. Henry's acquisition of these designs thus represents the most remarkable example of cultural appropriation that took place during his reign, a subversion of papal imagery and style to aggrandize his status as head of the English church.

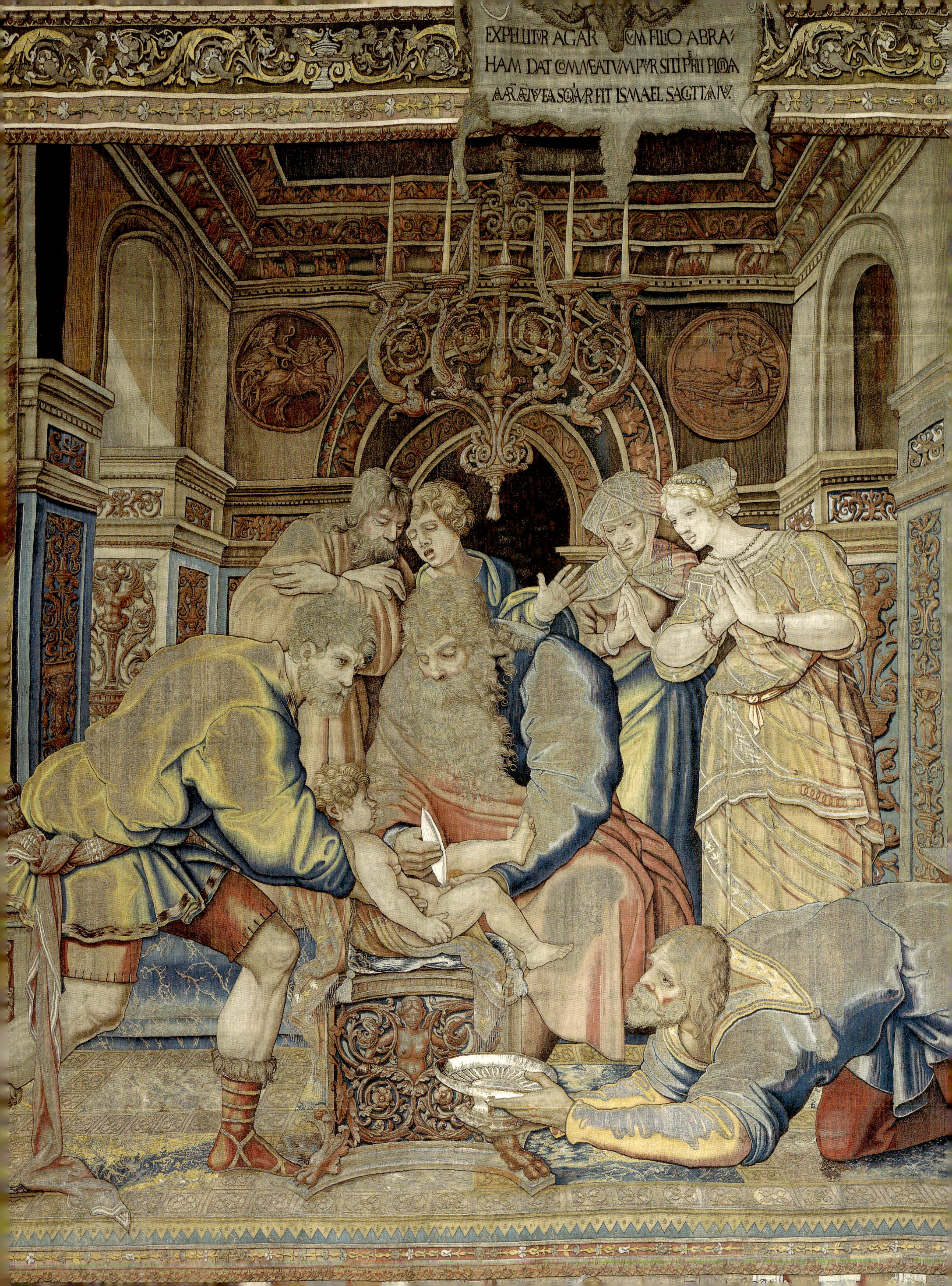
EXPELLITVR AGAR CVM FILIO ABRA
HAM DAT COMMEATVM PVER SITI PERIT PLORA

CHAPTER 14

The *Story of Caesar* and the *Story of Abraham*

The account of the Great Wardrobe for the year Michaelmas 1543–44 documents the arrival in London of the second pair of very expensive tapestry sets. It records a charge by the king's tailor for lining two named sets, of "Augusto Cesere" and of the *Story of Abraham*, each of ten pieces.[1] It is possible that they had been delivered slightly earlier, but even if they were, their arrival cannot have predated their lining by much because the style of the designs suggest that they were conceived ca. 1539–40 at the earliest. Analogy with other new acquisitions during this period suggests that tapestries were lined almost as soon as they were delivered, and allowance for the time in which they were woven must also be made, at least eighteen to twenty-four months for sets of such size and quality.

The Story of Caesar

Although the *Caesar* set has not survived, documentary evidence indicates that it was the second most valuable in the collection. Described as a ten-piece set of "newe Arras" in the 1547 inventory, its richness is revealed by the astonishing appraisal of £5,022 that it received at the Commonwealth sale.[2] Subsequently, it was among the sets that were reserved for Cromwell's use, ensuring its survival in the royal collection.[3] Four pieces were hung in the Privy Chamber at Kensington Palace for William III during the 1690s, and they remained in use there until the early nineteenth century, after which their fate, and that of the six pieces that had remained in storage at Hampton Court, is unknown. Fortunately, two pieces are visible in a watercolor of Queen Caroline's Drawing Room at Kensington Palace made by Charles Wild for Pyne's *Royal Residences* (see fig. 19.7). Although the tapestries are covered by paintings, enough of the lower border of the foreground tapestry can be seen to identify Henry's set as a weaving from a design series of which a single piece from a duplicate set survives at the Vatican (fig. 14.1). The upper left corner of the tapestry depicts Artemidorus attempting to warn Caesar of the plot against him, and the main scene shows the assassination of Caesar. The inscription in the upper cartouche emphasizes that Caesar failed to read the message that might have saved him.[4] The Vatican tapestry is dated 1549, presumably the date of weaving. Although the rest of this set is lost and no other mid-sixteenth-century weavings of this series are known, an impression of the complete ensemble can be deduced from late-sixteenth- and seventeenth-century tapestries that were woven from second- and third-generation cartoons that copied the original designs, albeit with variations of scale and detail. In turn, these later weavings allow the identification of an original modello for one scene and an original cartoon fragment from another.[5]

In conjunction with archival references to the Vatican set and to other lost sets, we can deduce that the first-generation *Caesar* designs represented key events in Caesar's career, including the *Battle of Germania* (sic); *Caesar Breaking into the Treasury; Caesar Crossing the Rubicon;* the *Battle of Pharsalia;* the *Assassination of Pompey;*

Detail of fig. 14.10

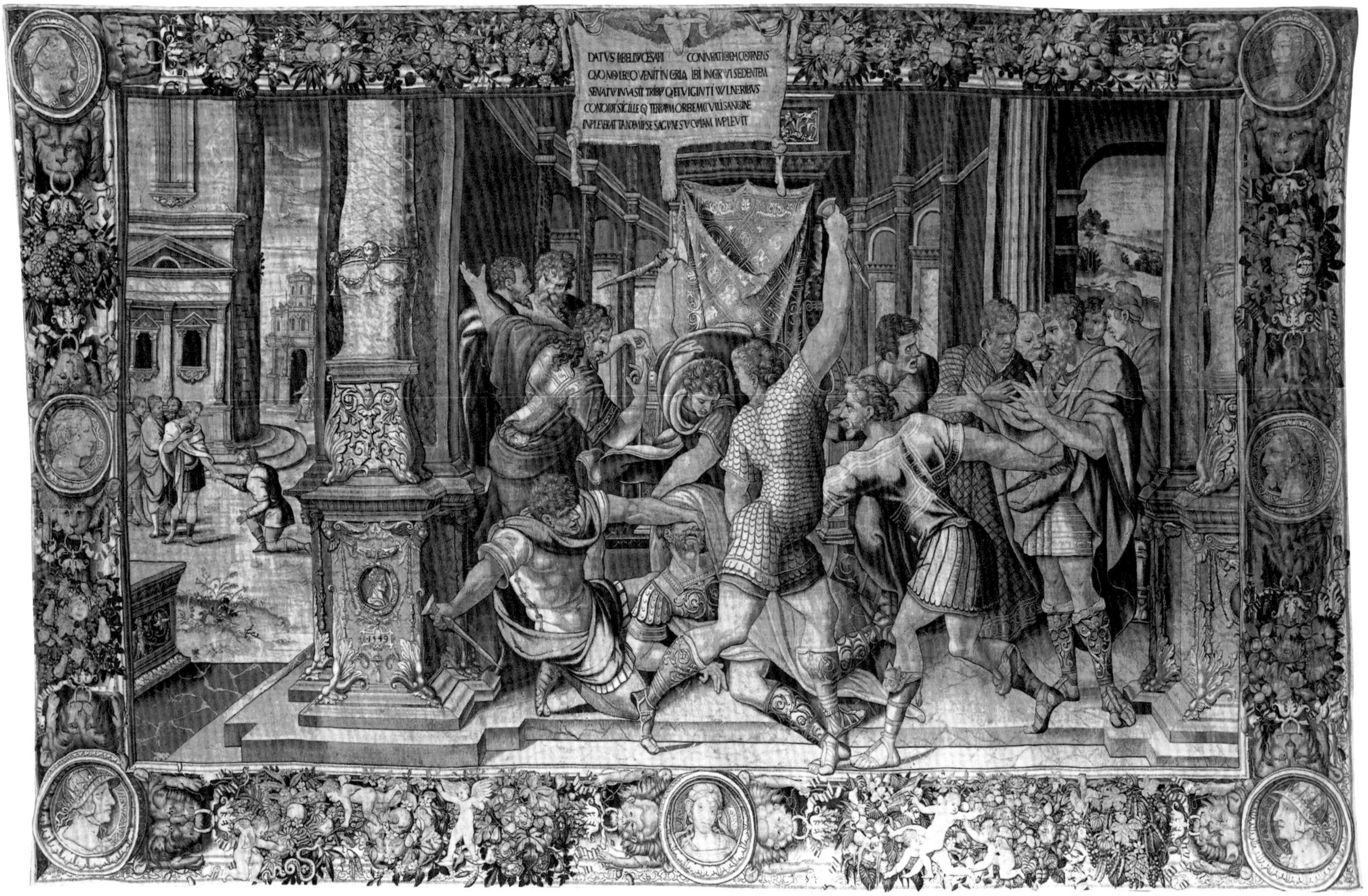

14.1 *The Assassination of Caesar* from a set of the *Story of Caesar*. Tapestry design by Pieter Coecke van Aelst and workshop, woven in Brussels, dated 1549. Wool and silk, 495 x 710 cm. Vatican Museums, Vatican City

Spurina Predicting Caesar's Fate; and the *Assassination of Caesar*.[6] The style of the Vatican tapestry, with dramatic figures depicted in exaggerated *contrapposto* in an elaborate architectural setting, suggests that the design may have been conceived by Pieter Coecke, an attribution that is also supported by the draftsmanship of the modello.[7] The Vatican tapestry is unmarked, but the border is identical with that on a *Story of Abraham* tapestry now at the château of Chambord that carries the mark of the Brussels merchant, Willem de Kempeneer, and we may therefore suppose that Kempeneer owned the *Caesar* cartoons and supplied Henry's set. Kempeneer's mark also appears on the *Abraham* set that was delivered to the Tudor court at the same time. He evidently sold a number of other sets of the *Caesar* design during the 1540s, but nothing indicates an earlier weaving than Henry's, so we can assume that Henry's was probably the first.

Why would Henry have wanted to commission this subject at this date? As a brilliant military and political tactician Caesar was a flattering comparison for any Renaissance prince, and several instances might be cited to illustrate the currency of the analogy for other contemporary patrons. For example, a translation of Caesar's *De bello Gallico,* commissioned for Francis I in 1519, starts with a dialogue in which Caesar addresses the French king as "Roy liberal & pacifique vray heritier de ma gloire" and contains an illumination of the two conversing in the Forest of Fontainebleau.[8] That the comparison continued to be congenial to the French king is shown in a drawing by the Italian artist Primaticcio that dates from the early 1540s and depicts Francis as Caesar.[9] The subject was of equal interest to Charles V, who included the *De bello Gallico* among his most favored reading matter and used it as a model for his memoirs.[10] However, there is no evidence to indicate that either Francis or Charles owned tapestry sets of this series or any other design of this subject.

Henry, on the other hand, manifestly aspired to imperial status in a variety of ways. In contrast to the peaceful policies pursued by his father, his reign began and closed with military campaigns against France, in both of which he was personally involved. During the early 1540s, when the *Caesar* set was commissioned, military and political adventures in Wales, Scotland, Ireland, and France may have appeared to Henry and his subjects as stages in the development of an empire-like sphere of influence, reminiscent of that of Caesar.[11] However, the comparison with Caesar possessed still more fundamental meaning for Henry. As discussed above in the context of Reformation propaganda, the notion that a king was emperor in his own kingdom had long been current in the rhetoric of medieval legal argument, but it became a crucial issue for Henry during the 1530s, as his frustration with the pope's intransigence over the royal divorce spurred him to reexamine his relationship to the papacy and that between the Church in England and the Church of Rome. England's subsequent break with Rome was justified largely by the argument that as emperor in his own realm, Henry, and not the pope, was the head of the English church. Recent research has traced the origins of this Caesaropapist position, and though it evidently only reached its full development in the 1530s, Henry had believed from early in his reign that the English monarchy was endowed with imperial status.[12] As the debate over the royal divorce became increasingly complex during 1529 and 1530, the concept of imperium became more central to Henry's cause, as reflected in the *Collectanea satis copiosa,* the manuscript synthesis of historical and legal precedent that Henry's propagandists drew up in 1530 to articulate the independence of his sphere of influence from that of the papacy. The theme reached its fruition in the preamble to the Act in Restraint of Appeals to Rome of 1533, in which the statement that "this realm of England is an Empire" became the keystone for an assertion of Henry's secular and spiritual supremacy in England. The same premise formed the basis for the Act of Supremacy of 1534.

In view of the central role that the Caesaropapist argument played in English politics during the 1530s, Henry's motive in purchasing a set of *Caesar* tapestries must have been to celebrate and affirm the parallels between himself and the Roman ruler, the primary exponent of the absolute authority that he now claimed for himself. If that was the case, the question then arises as to whether some or all of the episodes might have been chosen to emphasize particular aspects of Caesar's virtues and, by implication, those of Henry. Because the subjects of the first-generation designs are not fully established, answers to this question must be tentative, but scenes of military prowess and victory would, of course, have been flattering by association. The subject of Caesar breaking into the treasury to fund his campaign against Pompey must have struck a chord with Henry, in light of the benefits that he had gained from the dissolution of the monasteries over the previous eight years, allowing the purchase of this expensive tapestry set among others. Yet, if the subjects of the set had been chosen with specific relevance to Henry, it is odd that it should have included a scene of Caesar's assassination with an inscription that placed such an emphasis on his failure to prevent his own death. After all, Henry and his propagandists could have chosen another exponent of imperial and military prowess who was not assassinated by his former friends and supporters.

Various explanations need consideration. First, Henry's version of the *Assassination of Caesar* may have carried a variant inscription with a more positive content, as does a surviving second-generation version of the design.[13] Alternatively, it is conceivable that the inclusion of the *Assassination* scene in Henry's set, seemingly incongruous, may have come about because the series was conceived as a speculative venture by Kempeneer, without prior discussion of all the subjects with any specific patron. This would be analogous to the sequence of

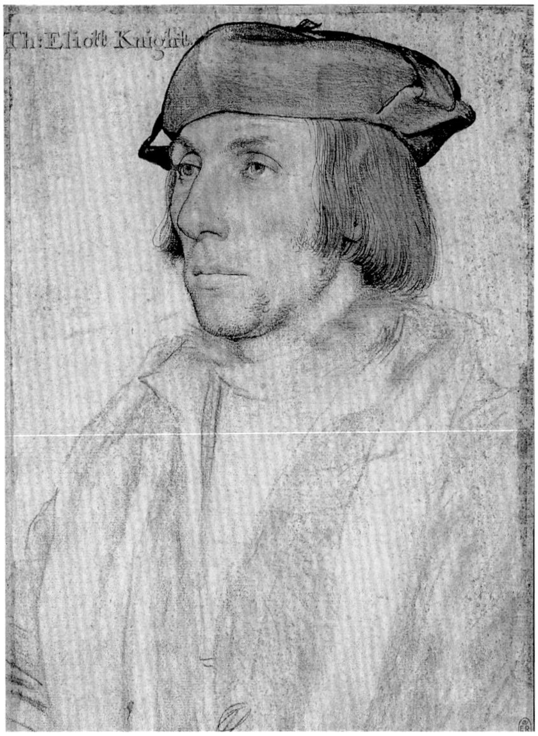

14.2 *Sir Thomas Elyot* by Hans Holbein the Younger, ca. 1531–34. Colored chalks, white bodycolor, and black ink on pink prepared paper, 28.4 x 20.5 cm. The Royal Collection

events that preceded Francis I's commission for the *Story of Scipio* in 1532, when the king ordered the set after he was shown three completed pieces.[14] Similarly, Henry could have been involved in the development of some aspects of the set, but the set as delivered might have included certain less pertinent scenes, simply because they had already been designed or woven before he decided to purchase it.

The third and most likely explanation, however, may be that the moralizing element of this scene enhanced its appeal to Henry, for although Caesar's early career exemplified military genius and both private and public virtues, his fate provided a textbook demonstration of the pitfalls of power, for both ruler and subjects alike. Caesar was one of the most frequently cited figures in the educational treatise *The Boke named the Governour,* written by Thomas Elyot (fig. 14.2) and published at Henry's wish in 1531, when the king confidently expected that Anne Boleyn would shortly bear him a son. Elyot considered this exact dichotomy between achievement and weakness. On one hand, Elyot cited Caesar as an example of the perfect pattern of industry and achievement, and he recommended Caesar's commentaries as appropriate reading for "princes of this realme of Englande and their Consailours" because "therof maye be taken necessarye instructions concernynge the warres, agayne the Irisshe men or Scottes: who be of the same rudenes and wilde disposition, that the Suises and Britons were in the time of Cesar."[15] At the same time, Elyot cited Caesar as a case study of the tyrannical ruler brought down by his own failings, in particular the fact that he neglected the counsel of his advisers: "Thus Caesar by omittinge his olde affabilitie dyd incende his next frendes and companions to sle hym."[16] "Affability," the quality of being open to the advice of one's subjects, is a principal quality of leadership that Elyot celebrates in the *Governour.*[17] It is to be noted that it is exactly this flaw, not listening to the advice of one's loyal counselors, that is emphasized within the tapestry depicting Caesar's assassination, both by the scene at the left, which shows Artemidorus trying to warn Caesar of the danger awaiting him, and by the inscription above.

Considering the central role that Caesar plays in Elyot's text and the emphasis that Elyot placed on this weakness, it is surely significant that this failing was also the subject of the last scene of the *Caesar* tapestries. The heir for whom Henry had waited for so long had been produced by Jane Seymour in 1537. The commission for the *Caesar* tapestries must therefore have been placed when Prince Edward was three or four (fig. 14.3), just when Henry would have been concerned with his education and was, in all likelihood, rereading Elyot's treatise. And proof that Caesar was very much in Henry's mind as a role model for Edward is provided by the elaborate speculum principis that was being executed in stucco and slate on the interior and exterior facings at Nonsuch Palace under the direction of Nicholas Bellin while the *Caesar* tapestries were being woven. As noted, the facade of the inner courtyard was arranged in three tiers, the lower register depicting the Feats of Hercules, the Virtues, and the Liberal Arts, the middle section the pagan gods, and the upper tier, a cycle of portrait busts of the twenty-four caesars.[18]

The purchase of the *Caesar* set and the appearance of the Caesars in an overtly exemplary scheme in the Nonsuch stuccoes can hardly be coincidental. We can therefore speculate that the purchase must have been motivated, at least in part, by Henry's wish to provide a speculum principis for Edward and the Tudor court. As we will see, a similar intent appears to have dictated the form of the allegorical borders surrounding the *Abraham* tapestries that were delivered at the same time.

Again, this begs the question of whether the *Caesar* design was conceived for Henry. Because his set seems to have been the *editio princeps* of the series, this is a possibility. But the obvious appeal of Caesar as a role model for other patrons prevents us from asserting anything more than that. Caesar was an obvious comparison for any Renaissance prince, and although there is no evidence that Francis I and Charles V owned sets of this design, an awareness of their interest in the subject may have given Kempeneer confidence in commissioning the designs as an entrepreneurial exercise. And while the coincidence of the subject of the last tapestry with that of Elyot's text is intriguing, it should be remembered that Elyot, writing ten years earlier, was articulating a well-established European tradition. In this respect it may be telling that there is no evidence that the *Caesar* series included the invasion of England, a subject that one would have expected if Henry and his advisers had conceived the scheme. As with the *Saint Paul* series, it therefore seems more probable that the design was commissioned as a speculative venture, possibly by Kempeneer, albeit with Henry in mind as the likely patron. This does not preclude the possibility that Henry's advisers could have played some part in the final determination of particular subjects for the set, perhaps in response to modelli sent via the numerous contacts that existed between the Tudor court and the Antwerp and Brussels merchant community.

14.3 *The Young Edward VI* by Hans Holbein the Younger, ca. 1539. Oil on canvas, 57 x 44 cm. National Gallery of Art, Washington

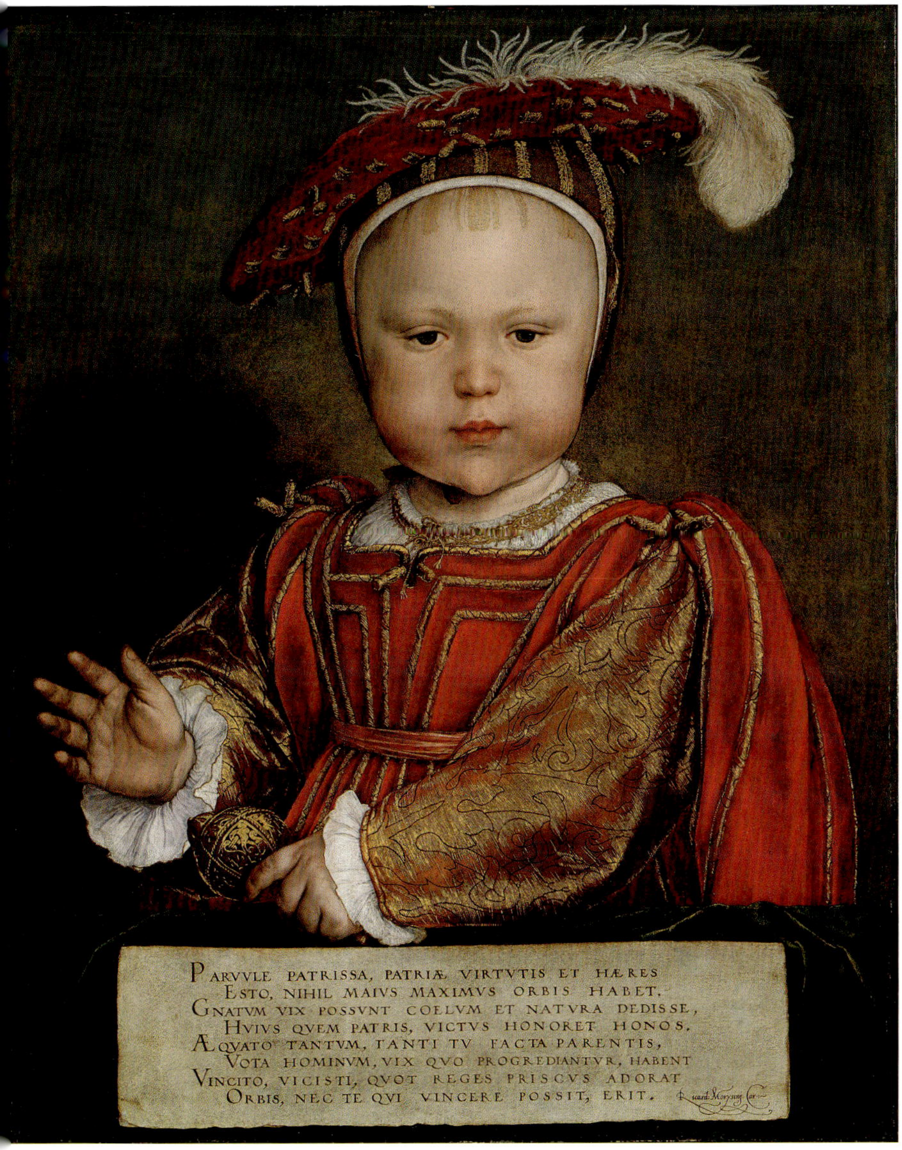

Whether or not the design was conceived for Henry, his motives in commissioning a very fine weaving of this design seem clear: first, to provide a celebration, by proxy, of the imperial values that he was now claiming for himself; second, to provide a speculum principis for Prince Edward and the Tudor court. Of course, the advantage of framing the *Caesar* story within a didactic context was that it asserted Henry's moral superiority to the subject, allowing him to share the positive associations while distancing himself from the less flattering analogies of his imperial forebear.

The Story of Abraham

The *Story of Abraham* delivered at the same time as the *Story of Caesar* was unquestionably Henry's most expensive tapestry acquisition.[19] At the time of the Commonwealth sale it was valued at £8,260, twice the price of all but one set in the collection—the *Caesar* set—and vastly more than most of the tapestries and old master paintings.[20] Remarkably, the set still hangs at Hampton Court Palace (see figs. i.1, 14.4–14.16). At a total length of about eighty-eight yards and a height of just over five yards, it is certainly the most impressive sixteenth-century set to survive in Britain. With its large percentage of silk and high content of gilt-metallic thread, it is also among the most lavish sets produced in Brussels during the sixteenth century.

Several of the tapestries carry the Brussels town mark and that of Willem de Kempeneer.[21] But no documentation relating to its purchase has yet emerged, and until recently the earliest known reference to the set was that of the 1547 inventory, in which it is described as "newe."[22] Evidence that the *Abraham* and *Caesar* sets were lined sometime between Michaelmas 1543 and Michaelmas 1544, and had thus been delivered during this period, allows us to define the context of this commission with greater exactitude.[23] A set of this figurative complexity and technical fineness would have taken at least two to three years to weave, so weaving must have begun between fall 1541 and fall 1542, if not earlier. In turn, the conception of the series and the execution of the full-scale cartoons must have taken place sometime during 1540 to 1541 at the latest.

Further confirmation of Henry's interest in Abraham at the time the tapestries were delivered is provided by a contemporary Chamber "receipt and issue" book. Among the rewards distributed to Henry VIII's courtiers and servants on New Year's Day, 1544, there is a payment of 6s. 8d. to a "Nicholas Modena that brought the king a story of Abraham."[24] The artist in question must have been Nicholas Bellin of Modena, whose major role at Whitehall and Nonsuch has already been discussed, but the character of the *Story of Abraham* that he gave to Henry remains a mystery. It could have been a painted work that has since been lost, in which case the payment confirms that the subject was likely to be one in which Henry was interested at this time. However, in view of the possible role that Bellin may have played in the purchase of the *Acts* and *Antiques* sets, and in light of the coincidence of this reward with the period in which the *Abraham* tapestries arrived at the English court, it is also possible that the "story" related in one way or another to this set, whether Bellin was involved in the literal delivery itself, or whether this was a reference to the modelli, or some related visual key to the borders or overall iconography. One way or another, Bellin's reward may indicate that the *Abraham* tapestries had been delivered to the Tudor court before the end of 1543.

Chronology of the Hampton Court Abraham *Set and Other Early Weavings*

Evidence that the Hampton Court *Abraham* tapestries were delivered to Henry between Michaelmas 1543 and Michaelmas 1544 raises the question as to the relation between this set and other weavings of the same design. The *Abraham* series enjoyed considerable success during the second half of the sixteenth century, and at least six duplicate sets are known. The earliest appears to have been that acquired by Bertran de la Cueva, third duke of Albuquerque, sometime during the 1540s.[25] This may have been the set that was displayed in the Brussels town hall at a banquet held for Prince Philip of Spain by the Brussels authorities on May 5, 1549.[26] Albuquerque's set was purchased from his descendents by Philip III of Spain, and seven panels survive today in the collection of the Patrimonio Nacional, Madrid.[27] These are almost identical with those at Hampton Court, but minor variations in some details show that the cartoons from which this set was woven had been altered, establishing that it was woven after Henry VIII's set.[28] The same is true of another mid-sixteenth-century weaving now in Vienna, in which further changes of design indicate that it postdated both the Hampton Court and Madrid sets.[29] All three sets carry the mark of Willem de Kempeneer. That in Vienna also carries two other marks, one unidentified, the other generally attributed to Pieter van Aelst the younger, who emerged as an important merchant in the Brussels tapestry industry during the 1540s and 1550s.[30] In addition to the foregoing, at least three other sixteenth-century sets survive, but all can be dated later than the Hampton Court set on the basis of variations within the main field of the design resulting from repairs or adaptations made to the cartoons before they were woven.

The lack of archival or visual evidence for an *Abraham* set predating Henry's is not in itself definitive evidence that his was the first. After all, an earlier weaving may simply have been lost. However, few patrons could have afforded such an enormous set, and no evidence has yet emerged from written records relating to the other great collections of the day to indicate a prior weaving of this design. Two further pieces of circumstantial evidence suggest that the Hampton Court set was the editio princeps. First, as with the *Caesar* tapestries, the style of the *Abraham* design indicates that it could not have been conceived much before 1540. Henry's set therefore appears to have been woven almost as soon as the design was conceived. Second, there is the quality of Henry's set. In contrast to other surviving sets, which are woven in wool and silk alone, Henry's set is extraordinarily rich, heavily laden with gilt-metallic thread in both the main fields and the borders. In the borders, the metallic wefts are carried across three warps at a time, in groups of three, to give an additionally rich, basket-weave effect.[31] Although this may reflect no more than that Henry ordered a particularly sumptuous weaving of an existing design, it is also fairly likely that the first weaving of such a major series would have been of high quality. The almost continuous exposure of the tapestries since 1699 has resulted in significant fading of the colors and tarnishing of the metallic threads, but an impression of the rich appearance of the tapestries when they were new is provided by the reverse sides (fig. 14.12).

The Designer of the Abraham *Series*

The design has been variously attributed to Bernaert van Orley and Michiel Coxcie. More recently it has been suggested that the cartoons were executed by the Antwerp workshop of Pieter Coecke, possibly in part after an initial scheme by Van Orley, who died in 1541.[32] Coecke's reputation as a tapestry designer has largely depended on designs that he produced during the 1530s, such as the *Story of Saint Paul,* the *Seven Deadly Sins,* and the *Story of Joshua.* Yet there is strong evidence that he continued to produce tapestry designs and cartoons during the 1540s: the Antwerp authorities specifically rewarded him for establishing a tapestry cartoon workshop in Antwerp at the beginning of the decade, and he aided Jan Vermeyen in completing the *Conquest of Tunis* cartoons in the late 1540s.[33] Attribution of the *Abraham* designs is dependent on stylistic links with Coecke's earlier tapestry designs as well as his later engraved and painted work. The situation is confused by the fact that several of the figures and architectural elements resemble those in stained glass designs executed by Van Orley for the Cathedral of Saint Gudule in Brussels during the late 1530s. The likely explanation for this is provided by the fate of the Saint Gudule project, which was awarded to Michiel Coxcie after Van Orley's death, but not before Coecke had also made a bid for the project, as evidenced by an unexecuted window design in his hand.[34] Evidence that a similar competition may have taken place in regard to the *Abraham* project, but with Coecke winning the contract, is provided by a modello, apparently in Coxcie's hand, for a scene of *Abraham Meeting Melchizedek,* in which the principal figures are close to those in the tapestry of this subject. The style of the completed tapestry designs are unrelated to Coxcie's other work, indicating that he was not successful in this bid, but the fact that the principal figures of Coxcie's drawing reappear in the tapestry design suggests that both Coxcie and Coecke were drawing, in part, on an earlier, uncompleted project by Van Orley. Although the final answer to this question awaits the discovery of new archival evidence, the possibility that Coecke produced the *Caesar* and *Abraham* designs in Antwerp, the hub of Netherlandish trade relations with London, would be logical if, as suggested below, the design was conceived

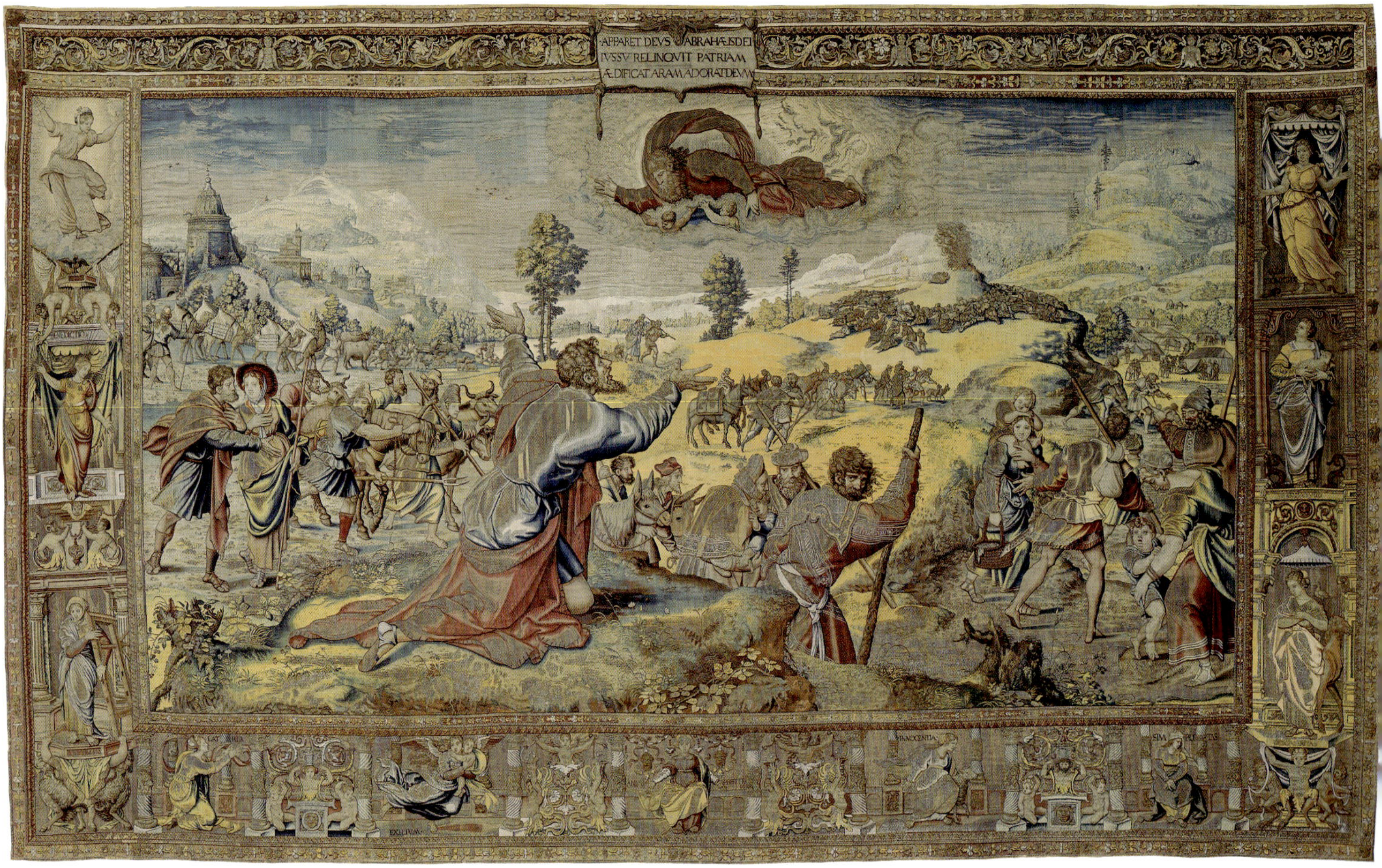

14.4 *God Commands Abraham to Lead the Israelites into Canaan* from a ten-piece set of the *Story of Abraham*. Tapestry design attributed to Pieter Coecke van Aelst, woven in the workshop of Willem de Kempeneer, Brussels, ca. 1541–43. Wool, silk, and gilt-metal-wrapped thread, 482 x 779 cm. Hampton Court Palace

at the prompting of the English court or in anticipation that it would appeal to Henry's interests.

Iconography of the Abraham *Series*

The *Story of Abraham* comprises ten scenes depicting the principal events of Abraham's life, as narrated in Genesis, chapters 12 through 24, especially those pertaining to his role as the founder of the Hebrew nation and the continuation of God's covenant with Abraham through his son, Isaac. Each scene is surrounded by a wide, elaborate border, divided by architectural niches and decorative elements into a series of compartments filled by allegorical and symbolic figures, each identified by a Latin inscription, three in each vertical border and five in each lower border. Eighty-four personifications are featured, some several times though never in the same form, giving a total of 110 figures. From a structural point of view the figures and fanciful settings derive their inspiration from the borders of Raphael's *Acts of the Apostles*, but the *Abraham* borders represent a distinct iconographic departure. In the Raphael designs the figures in the lateral borders evoked a broader humanistic framework, but they were essentially incidental to the main narrative. In contrast, the *Abraham* personifications serve a more idiosyncratic purpose. The exact significance and relationship of the figures is not always readily apparent because the representations include cardinal virtues, classical gods, and abstract personifications, and there does not appear to be a rigorous logic to the order of their depiction. It is clear, however, that some symbolize the primary event or theme of the scene, others personify either the virtues that the protagonists exemplify in those circumstances or the opposing vices, and yet others symbolize the consequences of practicing those virtues or vices. Taken as an ensemble, the presence of these figures enriches the main scenes by encouraging the viewer to consider the subject not just in terms of a narrative but in the context of a broader moral spectrum. Although there was a long tradition for the use of tapestry as a medium for didactic schemes, the *Abraham* tapestries are the first in which the borders appear to have been designed as an integral part of that program. Considering the enormous investment that the set represented and its significance within Henry's tapestry acquisitions, the complex iconography of the set requires special attention.

The first scene depicts the moment at which God appears to Abraham and tells him to lead the Israelites into Canaan, promising to bless him and his people as narrated in Genesis 12:1–8 (fig. 14.4 and detail opposite title page). Several border figures encapsulate the main events of the scene, *Apparition, Worship, Exile,* and *Blessing*. Others provide a meditation on the qualities that distinguished Abraham as the recipient of God's covenant: *Obedience, Willingness of the Spirit, Innocence, Candor, Meekness,* and *Gentleness*.[35]

The second, third, and fourth tapestries all depict scenes that relate to Abraham's relationship with other figures of authority. The second focuses on the return of Sarah by the Pharaoh following his discovery that she was Abraham's wife, not his sister, as he had been led to believe (Gen. 12:15–20; fig. 14.5). The border figure of *Vengeance* relates to the plagues visited by God on the Pharaoh, while Sarah's beauty is evoked, somewhat incongruously, by *Venus*. Other figures celebrate the noble behavior of the Pharaoh: *Remorse, Alacrity, Restitution, Promise, Trust,* and the implied opposite to this behavior, *Rape*. Those at the top of the left border point up the contrast between the Poverty of the Hebrew travelers and the *Magnificence* ("Luxus") of the Pharaoh's gifts to Abraham.

The separation of Lot and Abraham to prevent further fighting among their tribesmen (Gen. 13:8–9) is illustrated in the third scene (fig. 14.6). Here, the main themes are suggested by the figures of *Dispute, Discretion, Division, Separation, Friendship,* and *Approbation*. The rest of the figures broaden this general theme by invoking the rewards of the harmonious relationship between Abraham and Lot: *Abundance, Repose, Peace,* and *Concord*.

Abraham's victory over the Elamites following their defeat and capture of Lot, and the hospitality and blessing that he received from

14.5 *The Return of Sarah by the Egyptians* from a ten-piece set of the *Story of Abraham*. Tapestry design attributed to Pieter Coecke van Aelst, woven in the workshop of Willem de Kempeneer, Brussels, ca. 1541–43. Wool, silk, and gilt-metal-wrapped thread, 482 x 939 cm. Hampton Court Palace

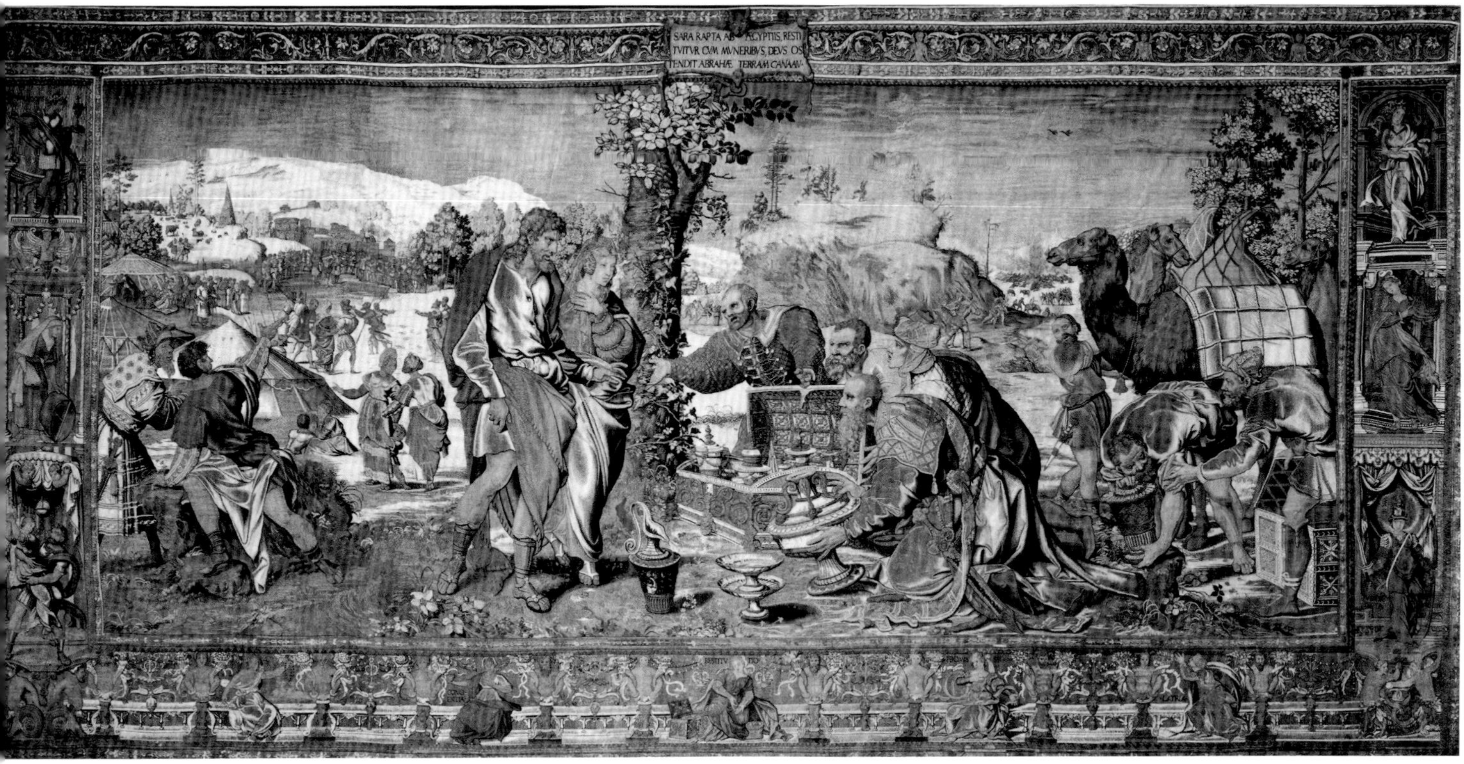

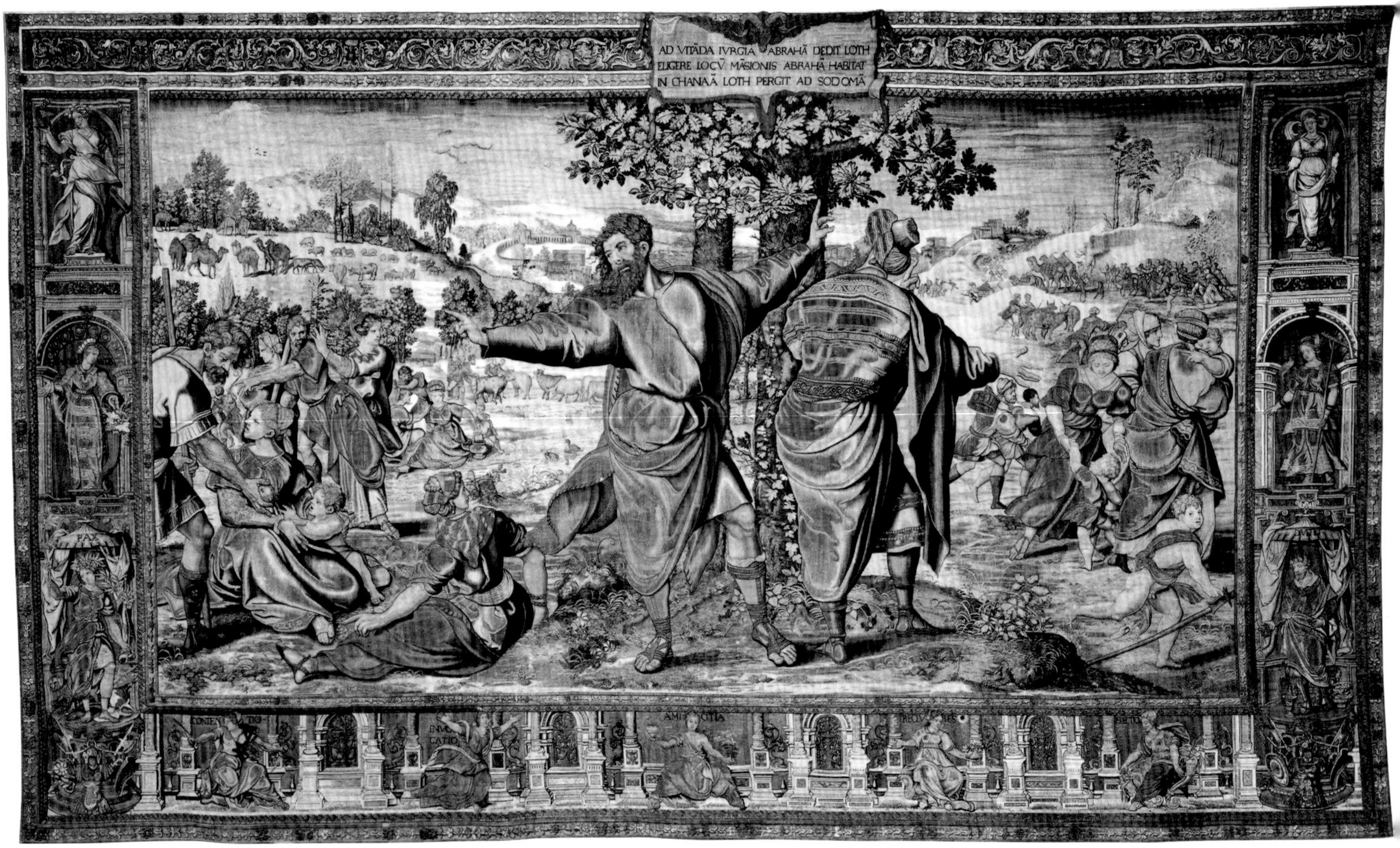

14.6 *The Separation of Abraham and Lot* from a ten-piece set of the *Story of Abraham*. Tapestry design attributed to Pieter Coecke van Aelst, woven in the workshop of Willem de Kempeneer, Brussels, ca. 1541–43. Wool, silk, and gilt-metal-wrapped thread, 487 x 792 cm. Hampton Court Palace

Melchizedek, the king and high priest of Salem (Gen. 14:15–20), provides the subject of the fourth panel (fig. 14.7). Here, the border figures contrast the Elamites' behavior, *Violence, Pillage, Battle,* and *Tyranny,* with that of Abraham and Melchizedek, *Kindness, Peace,* and *Brotherly Love.* Abraham's prowess as a leader in war and peace is celebrated by figures representing *Victory, Good Reputation,* and *Honor* (fig. 14.8). The appearance of these last figures is of especial note as these accolades were celebrated as the pinnacle of achievement for European rulers by the contemporary speculum principis treatises. The presence of these personifications places the narrative in the context of a wider meditation on tyranny and honorable rule.

The fifth scene relates again to Abraham's relationship with God. The main scene depicts God, here shown as the Trinity, appearing to Abraham to tell him that he would receive a son and to warn him of the destruction of Sodom and Gomorra. The escape of Lot and his daughters appears in the background (Gen. 18: 2–33; fig. 14.9). Several of the border figures encapsulate key points of the narrative; "Risus," Sarah's scorn at the notion that she would bear a child at her age; "Trinitas," the form in which God appeared to Abraham; *Hospitality,* as offered by Abraham to the Trinity; and *Vengeance,* enacted on the sinners of Sodom and Gomorrah. *Entreaty* and *Candor* emphasize the qualities that Abraham demonstrated by pleading on behalf of the innocent citizens. The consequence of this appeal is reflected in the personifications of the right border, *Promise* and *Mercy.*

The sixth and seventh tapestries turn the focus on Abraham's son, Isaac. The sixth represents the circumcision of Isaac, the visual symbol of the continuation of God's covenant with Abraham through his son, and the expulsion of Hagar and Ishmael, Hagar's son by Abraham (Gen. 18:1–21; fig. 14.10 and detail opposite p. 277). Here, personifications of *Fecundity, Contempt,* and *Jealousy* relate to Sarah and Hagar's mutual dislike, while others reflect

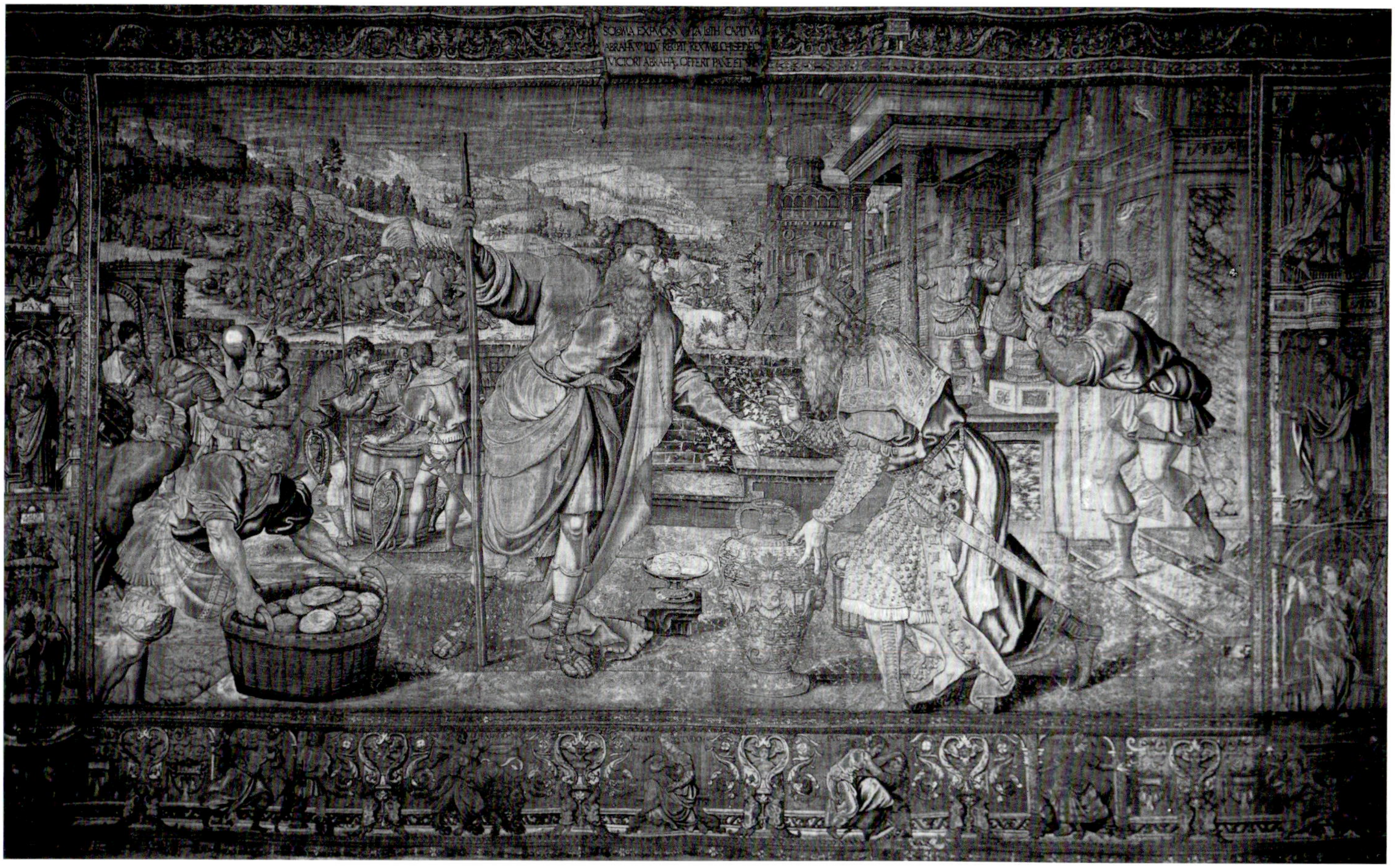

14.7 *The Meeting of Abraham and Melchizedek* from a ten-piece set of the *Story of Abraham*. Tapestry design attributed to Pieter Coecke van Aelst, woven in the workshop of Willem de Kempeneer, Brussels, ca. 1541–43. Wool, silk, and gilt-metal-wrapped thread, 480 x 779 cm. Hampton Court Palace

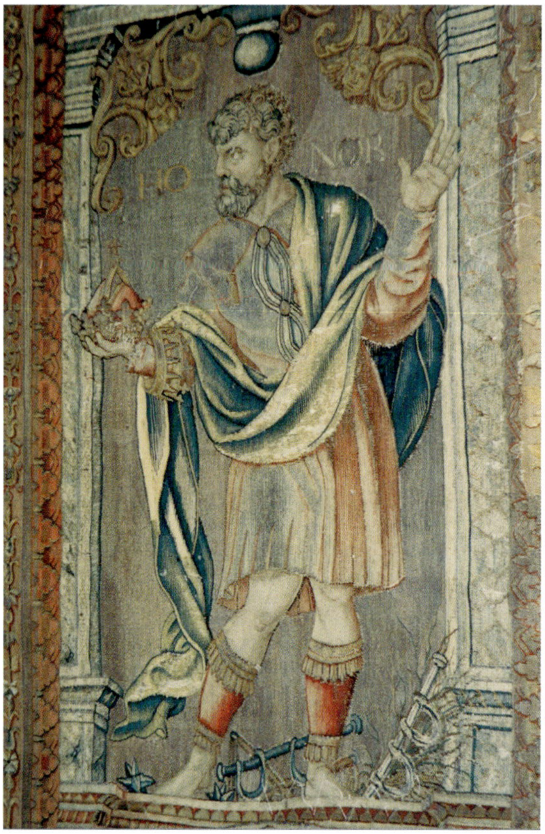

14.8 Detail of fig. 14.7 showing "Honor"

Hagar's fate: *Flight, Despair, Consolation, Pity,* and *Obedience*. "Vita Silvestris" (*Life in the Wild*) defines Ishmael's fortune following his expulsion, while "Liber Pater" (*Free Fatherhood*) presumably relates to Abraham's polygamous rights as a patriarch.

Abraham's intention to sacrifice Isaac, according to God's command (Gen. 22:5–18), provides the subject of the seventh scene of the set (figs. 14.11, 14.12). Here, the border figures continue the theme of obedience to God, representing *Steadfastness, Witness, Faith, Candor, Obedience, Willingness of the Spirit, Sacrifice, Promise, Hope,* and *Blessing*. As in the narrative, the prevalent theme is that of trust and obedience—Abraham to God, and Isaac to his father.

The eighth scene illustrates Abraham purchasing the Field of Ephron as a burial site for Sarah and, ultimately, himself (Gen. 23:10–16; fig. 14.13 and detail opposite p. 335). In this case, border figures of *Time, Age, Death, Complaint,* and *Lament* broaden the subject into a contemplation on the transience of life, while others suggest

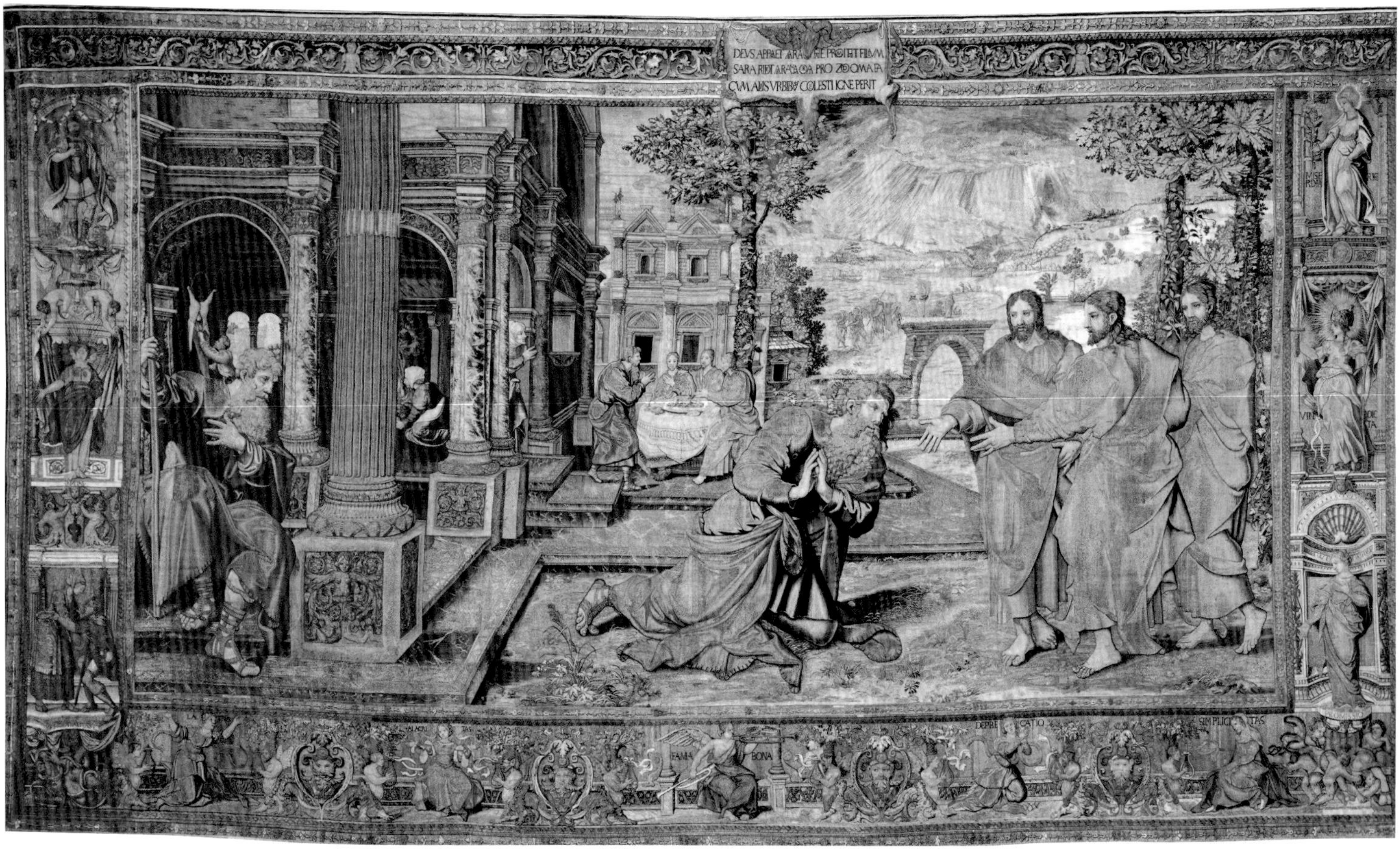

14.9 *God Appears to Abraham* from a ten-piece set of the *Story of Abraham*. Tapestry design attributed to Pieter Coecke van Aelst, woven in the workshop of Willem de Kempeneer, Brussels, ca. 1541–43. Wool, silk, and gilt-metal-wrapped thread, 477 x 883 cm. Hampton Court Palace

the means by which the Christian prince transcended mortality; *Hope, Gloria* (fig. 14.14), *Judgment, Resurrection,* and *Immortality*. Again, the use of the figure of *Gloria* (Fame) in this context, rather than personifications of the Christian virtues, places the scheme firmly within the speculum principis tradition.

Where the first eight tapestries focus on the leadership and faith which distinguished Abraham as a ruler and chosen recipient of God's covenant, the two final scenes turn the focus on Abraham's faithful servant, Eliezer. The ninth tapestry depicts the oath and departure of Eliezer in his search for a suitable wife for Isaac (Gen. 24:1–10; fig. 14.15). The personifications of the left border relate to the nature of his charge, *Inquiry, Bridesman,* and *Virginity*. Those of the lower and right borders emphasize the manner in which he honored Abraham's command: *Acceptance, Promise, Promptness, Faithfulness, Willingness of the Spirit,* and *Obedience*. Finally, the tenth scene celebrates the moment when Eliezer recognized the qualities for which he was searching in Rebekah (Gen. 24:15–18; fig. 14.16 and details opposite pp. 317, 347). Most of the personifications again refer to how Eliezer performed his undertaking: *Prudence, Devout Man, Avowal, Circumspection,* and *Diligence*. Others suggest the qualities embodied by Rebekah: *Care, Ceres* (the classical goddess, signifying fecundity), *Liberality,* and *Purity*.

In summary, while the order of the border personifications does not follow a strict program, and while their relationships to one another are not always clear, the general purpose is readily evident. First and foremost, they invite the viewer to consider the narrative as a meditation on Abraham's secular and religious virtues and, in the final scenes, the qualities embodied by a dutiful son, a faithful servant, and a virtuous wife. Second, they relate these qualities to the concepts of Fame and Honor, which were held up as the pinnacle of achievement for European rulers by the speculum principis tradition and which had been celebrated in various tapestry series, most notably the *Honors* set made for Charles V during the early 1520s. Although the *Abraham* scheme is more haphazard than that of the *Honors,* there can be no doubt of the comparable import of its program.

Discussion of the iconography of the *Abraham* set raises the question as to why during the early 1540s Henry wanted to spend what must have been an enormous sum of money on a didactic set of tapestries celebrating the Old Testament patriarch Abraham. In light of the discussion in previous chapters, the answer now seems obvious. As we have seen, Old and New Testament role models had played an important part in the imagery associated with Henry since the 1520s, in both the private and public spheres. Such self-identification must also have determined this commission. Abraham, founder of the Hebrew nation and first of the great patriarchs, was the Old Testament model most congenial for Henry as he sought to establish a new Church of England centered on the Tudor dynasty. Chosen for a covenant with God, Abraham served as a prototype for the exalted role that the increasingly delusional king was now asserting for himself: he was the consecrated king of England, the spiritual and secular leader of his people. The analogy would have been additionally appealing in the late 1530s and early 1540s because, with the birth of Prince Edward in 1537, Henry finally had an heir, just as Genesis established Abraham's undisputed succession through Isaac. The borders of the *Abraham* tapestries expanded the analogies between Abraham and Henry, Isaac and Edward, into a broader affirmation of the moral values embodied by the Tudor kingship.

The Conception of the Abraham *Series*

In view of the scale and complexity of the *Abraham* designs and the resonance of the patriarchal analogy to Henry and Edward, we must ask whether the series was conceived and designed at Henry's request. As we have seen, Henry had purchased a number of expensive tapestry sets depicting Old Testament patriarchs and New Testament apostles during the late 1520s and 1530s, but no documentary evidence has survived to indicate that these were woven from custom-made designs. Where visual evidence of their appearance has survived, they were evidently duplicates of designs that were also purchased by other patrons. Does the richness of the *Abraham* set and the significance of the subject for Henry at the time it was acquired suggest that this case was different?

Henry certainly held no monopoly on biblical analogies, and the subject of the *Abraham* set would have been equally resonant for any king or prince hoping to ensure the continuation of his line, including Henry's rivals, Francis I and Charles V, both of whom had male heirs by the early 1540s. Abraham does not seem to have been a common theme in the iconography associated with either the French or Habsburg courts, but he was not totally neglected. For example, records of the triumphal entry made by Prince Philip of Spain into various Flemish towns in 1549–50 reveal that biblical patriarchs and their sons, including Abraham and Isaac, were a theme of the installations created to mark the event.[36] Nonetheless, the likelihood that the Abraham design might have been conceived at the behest of Francis, Charles, or any of the other great magnates of the day, rather than Henry, can be discounted on the grounds that Henry does appear to have owned the first weaving of the set and that no *Abraham* set is recorded in the collections of his rivals.

In the absence of any documentary evidence or written program, are there any telling details of iconography within the main scenes or the borders that provide a clue to link the design to the Tudor court? Taking the main fields first, a case could be made that, quite apart from the appeal of the continuation of God's covenant with Abraham in the person of his son, several individual scenes may have had a pointed meaning for the Tudor court. For example, in the fourth scene, the image of Melchizedek, the high priest of the church, blessing and providing succor to Abraham, must have been pleasing for Henry in the context of the subservience he was now demanding from the sen-

Overleaf:
14.10 *The Circumcision of Isaac and the Expulsion of Hagar and Ishmael* from a ten-piece set of the *Story of Abraham.* Tapestry design attributed to Pieter Coecke van Aelst, woven in the workshop of Willem de Kempeneer, Brussels, ca. 1541–43. Wool, silk, and gilt-metal-wrapped thread, 482 x 805 cm. Hampton Court Palace

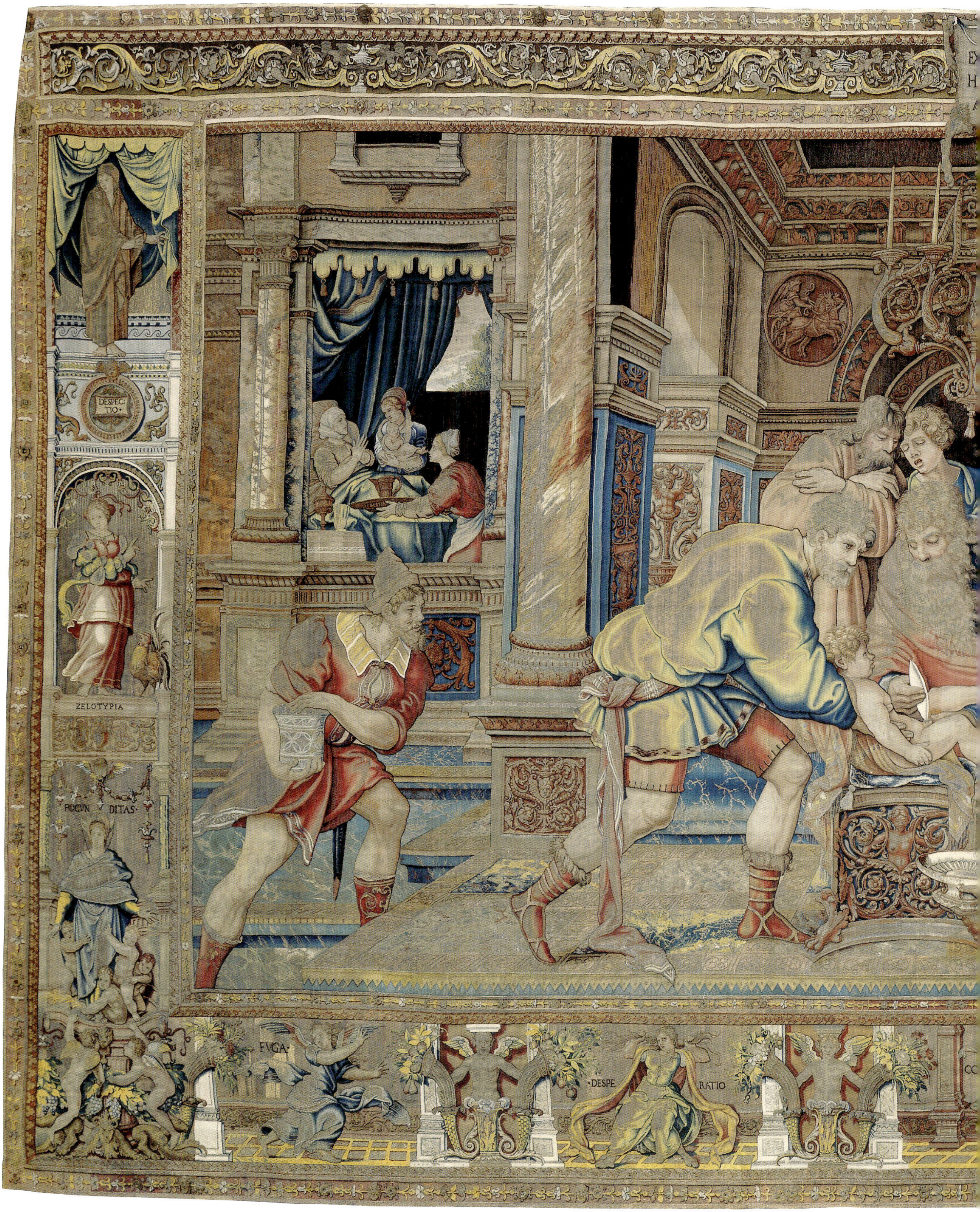
DESPEC TIO
ZELOTYPIA
FVGA
DESPE RATIO

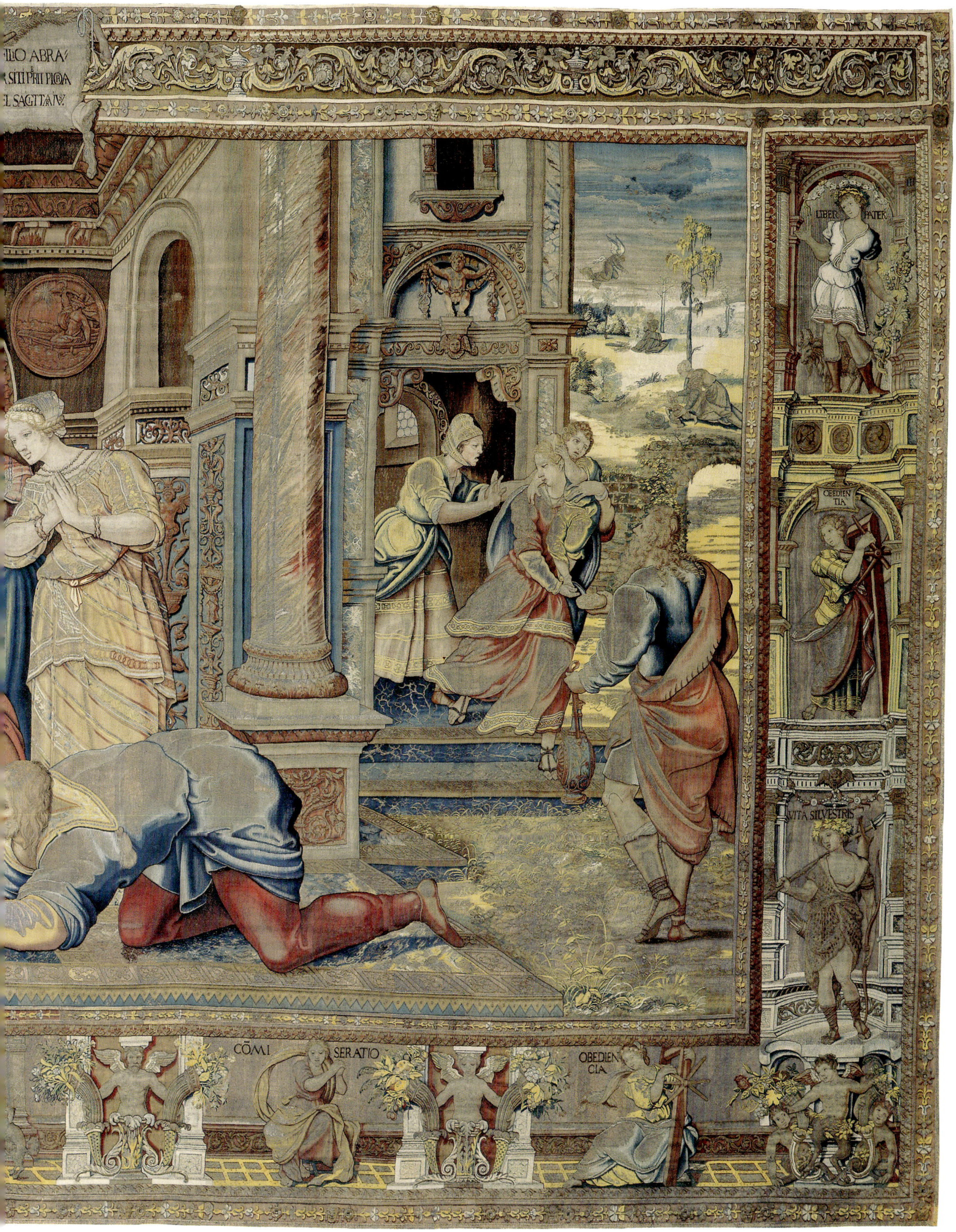
LIBER PATER
OBEDIEN TIA
VITA SILVESTRIS
CŌMI SERATIO
OBEDIEN CIA

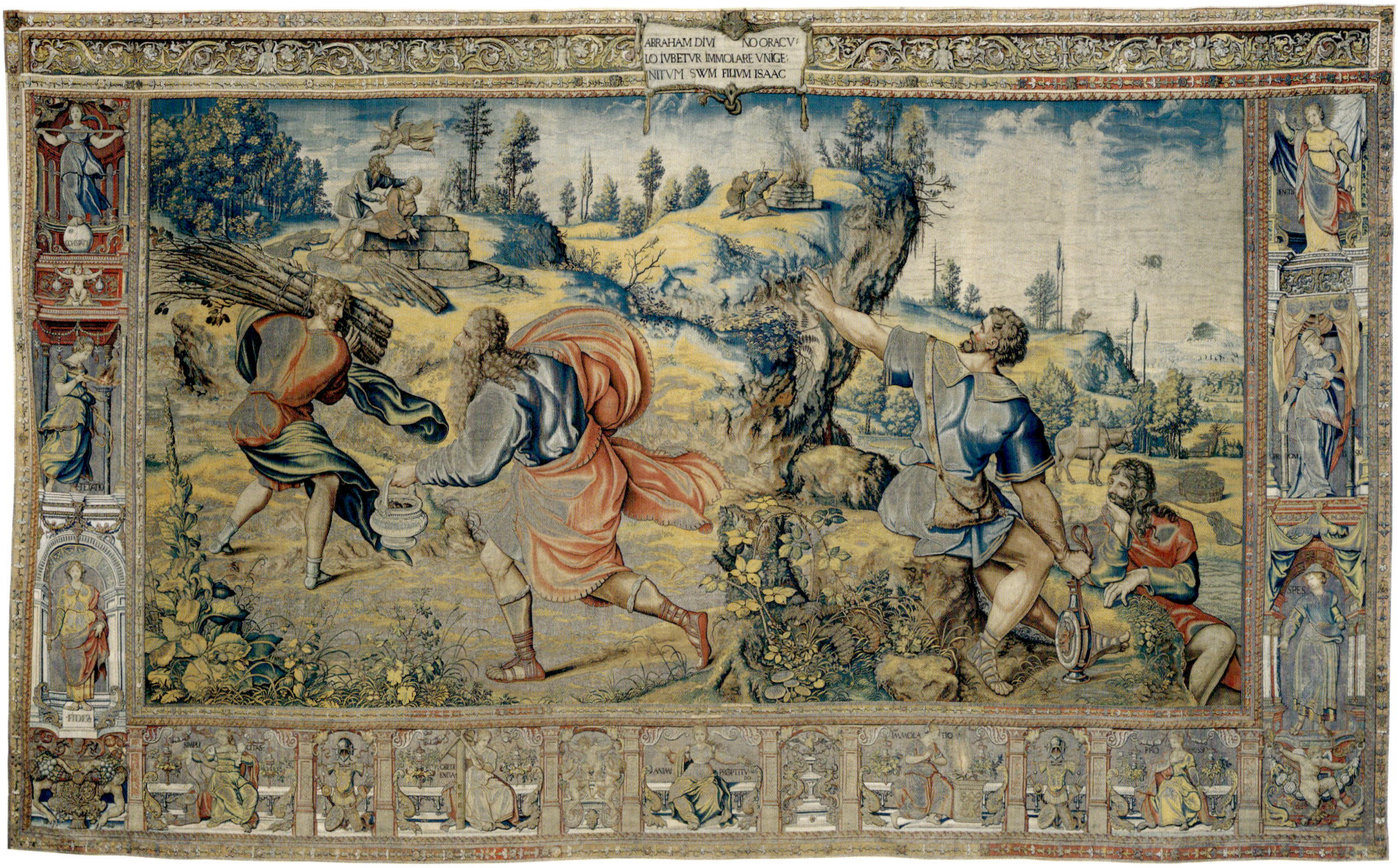

14.11 *The Sacrifice of Isaac* from a ten-piece set of the *Story of Abraham*. Tapestry design attributed to Pieter Coecke van Aelst, woven in the workshop of Willem de Kempeneer, Brussels, ca. 1541–43. Wool, silk, and gilt-metal-wrapped thread, 488 x 792 cm. Hampton Court Palace

14.12 Reverse of 14.11

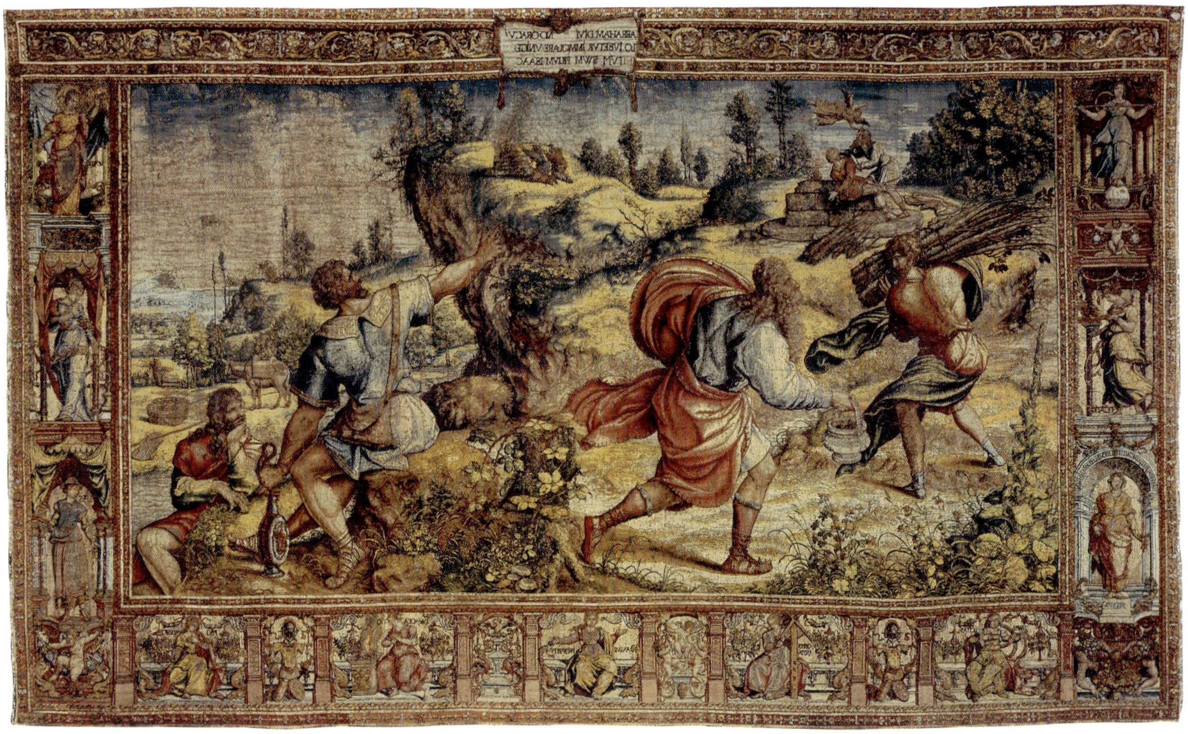

ior clergy of the Church of England. In the sixth scene, the rejection of Hagar and the first-born child, Ishmael, in favor of a legitimate successor, Isaac, may have been pregnant with meaning for Henry and his courtiers in regard to the predicament of Princess Mary following the birth of Prince Edward. The eighth scene, depicting Abraham purchasing the Field of Ephron as a burial place for himself and his wife, may have chimed with plans that Henry was then making for his own elaborate tomb. And in view of Henry's failing health from the late 1530s and the possibility that he would die before Edward reached his majority, the demonstration of Eliezer's loyalty in the final panels of the series must have been a model that Henry hoped his senior councillors would heed. Yet, if these parallels are noteworthy, they are also subjective. A range of comparable analogies might be constructed between the *Abraham* narrative and the lives of other contemporary patrons, so the possible relevance of these scenes to the Tudor court can hardly be presented as certain evidence that the designs were created for Henry.

What then of the borders? Considering the number of personifications that are depicted, one might suspect that here at least insignia or iconographic details would indicate a link with a particular patron, but this is not the case. The most idiosyncratic details that stand out are the imperial crowns worn by *Honor* and *Gloria* in the fourth and eighth panels (see figs. 14.8, 14.14), but although it could be suggested that this indicates a link to the Habsburg court, the fact that Henry was also claiming imperial status for himself from 1533 undermines that argument. Indeed, the absence of any other attributes or insignia, apart from these crowns, might itself be turned into an argument in favor of the possibility that the set was conceived for Henry. As has already been suggested, the overt rivalry between the Tudor and Habsburg courts ensured that no Brussels artist or tapestry merchant was likely to create tapestries explicitly supportive of Henry's re-

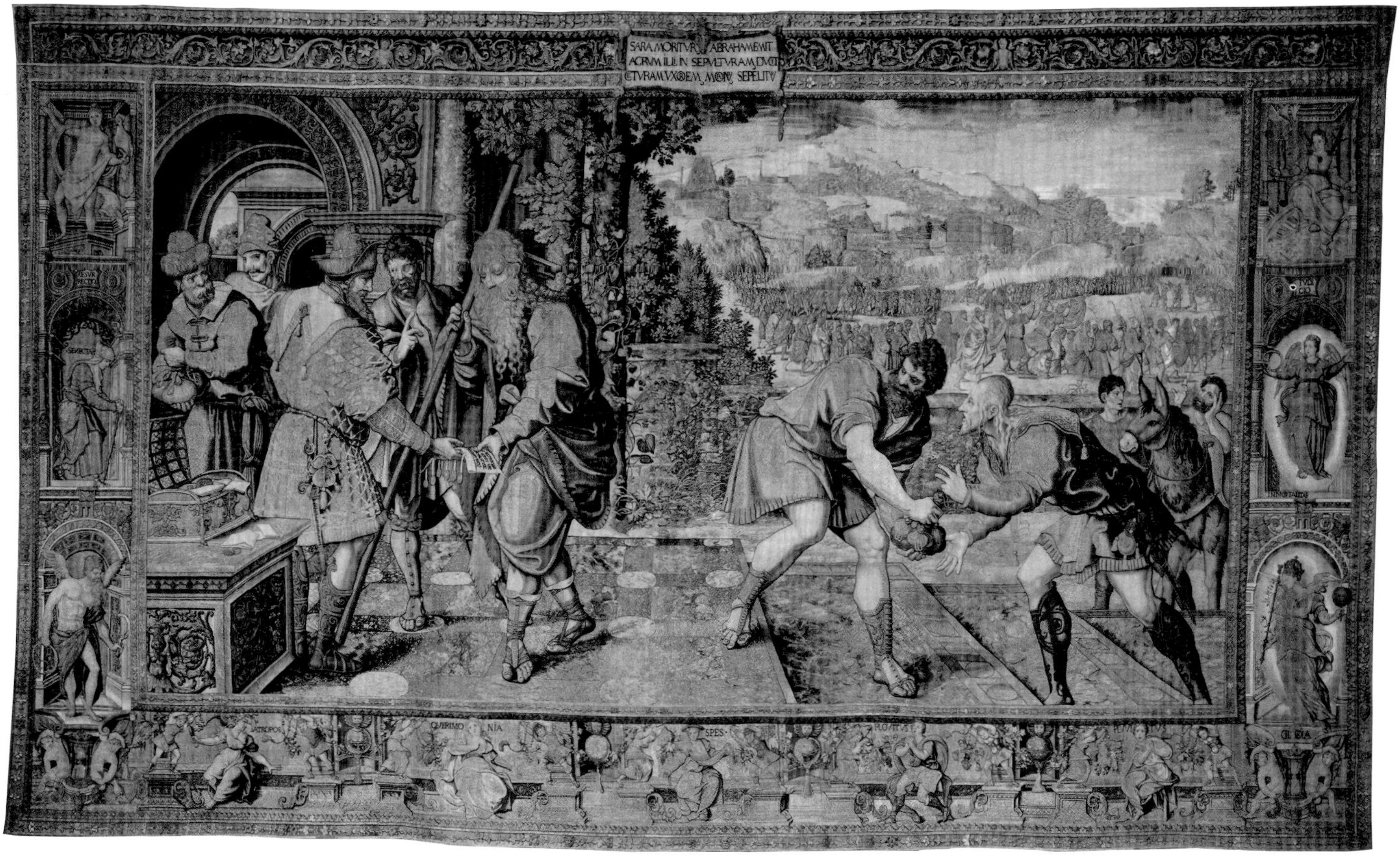

14.13 *Abraham Purchases the Field of Ephron* from a ten-piece set of the *Story of Abraham*. Tapestry design attributed to Pieter Coecke van Aelst, woven in the workshop of Willem de Kempeneer, Brussels, ca. 1541–43. Wool, silk, and gilt-metal-wrapped thread, 490 x 769 cm. Hampton Court Palace

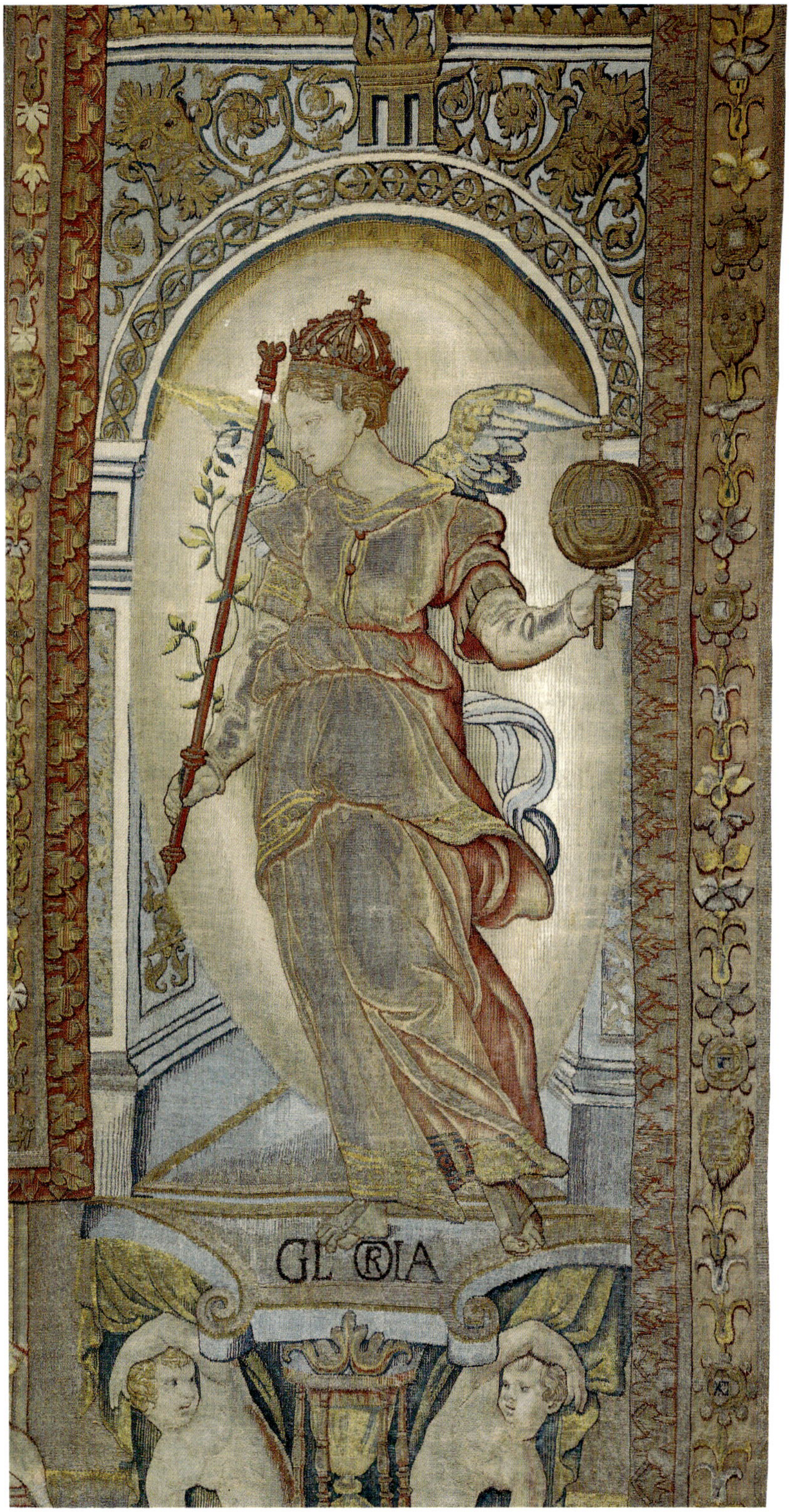

14.14 Detail of fig. 14.13 showing "Gloria"

formist agenda, especially since leading members of the Brussels community had already been subjected to religious persecution in relation to the Lutheran preacher Claes van der Elst in 1527.[37] Nonetheless, the generic nature of the personifications, coupled with the lack of firm evidence that Henry commissioned other bespoke designs, indicates that caution must be exercised before any such conclusion is drawn in this case.

If the attributes with which the personifications are depicted provide no evidence of a particular patron, does the choice of figures provide any clue? Is there anything idiosyncratic that relates the program of the borders to other contemporary schemes at the Tudor court? In this respect the most immediate comparison is with the complex speculum principis undertaken at Nonsuch in the early 1540s. Unfortunately, we know too little about the details of this scheme to make any definitive comparisons, but on the basis of later descriptions it seems that whereas the lost Nonsuch stuccos also involved a plethora of exemplary figures, the humanist pantheon it embodied had more in common with the deities and virtues represented in the *Antiques* tapestries than with the idiosyncratic selection of personifications represented in the *Abraham* borders.[38] More intriguing is the comparison provided by Elyot's didactic *Boke Named the Governour,* which does include discussion of a number of the qualities that appear as personifications in the *Abraham* borders. For example, Elyot devotes sections of his book to discussion of "amicitia" (friendship) and "mansuetudo" (gentleness), both of which appear as personifications in the borders, while his consideration of the importance of being true to one's word is paralleled by the figure of "adiuratio" (avowal) in the tenth panel.[39] Similarly, although there is no literal representation of another of Elyot's preoccupations, "affability"—the virtue of being open and available to the advice of honest counsel—the subject is celebrated in the subject and personifications of the fifth panel, Abraham's plea to God on behalf of the innocent of Sodom.[40] Another potential link between Elyot and the tapestry scheme is provided by the fact that a significant number of the personifications that appear in the *Abraham* borders are listed in a *Dictionary* that Elyot published in 1538. This, the first substantive Latin-English dictionary to be published, includes definitions that correspond to seventy of the

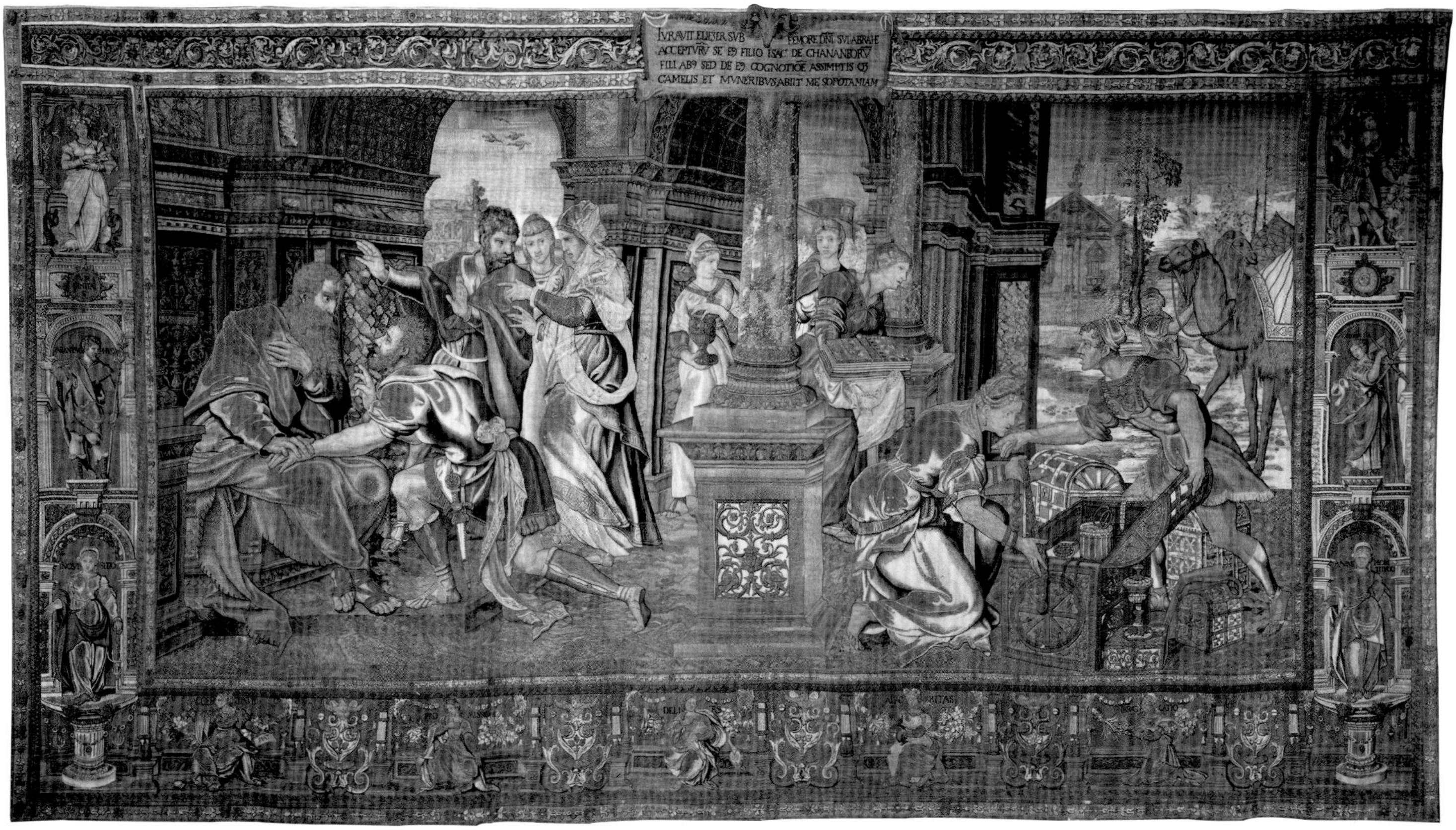

14.15 *The Oath and Departure of Eliezer* from a ten-piece set of the *Story of Abraham.* Tapestry design attributed to Pieter Coecke van Aelst, woven in the workshop of Willem de Kempeneer, Brussels, ca. 1541–43. Wool, silk, and gilt-metal-wrapped thread, 487 x 853 cm. Hampton Court Palace

eighty-four personifications that appear in the borders. In order to write this dictionary, Elyot was granted access to Henry VIII's library, through the intercession of Thomas Cromwell, Sir Anthony Denny, and William Tildesley, the king's librarian.[41]

Although these coincidences provide tantalizing evidence of a common mode of thought between one of the leading humanists at Henry's court and the person who devised the *Abraham* scheme, it must be noted that the parallel between the issues discussed in the text of *The Boke Named the Governour* and the border program of the tapestry series is not so close as to provide a definitive link. Several themes that Elyot discusses are not dealt with in the tapestry borders, and the borders also introduce a range of virtues that are not mentioned by Elyot. While the inclusion by Elyot in his *Dictionary* of so many personifications that also appear in the *Abraham* borders is intriguing, it seems most likely that this is a reflection of the common humanist sources on which he, and the devisor of the tapestry series, were drawing. Elyot's *Dictionary* was not unique, and he is known to have copied a number of his definitions from Robert Estienne's *Dictionarium Latinogallicum,* which was published in Paris a few months earlier.[42] Comparison between the two reveals that Estienne's work includes definitions that correspond to sixty-four of the personifications that appear in the tapestry borders. Although Elyot's *Dictionary* thus includes six terms that are not included by Estienne, the number is not sufficiently large, nor is the character of the additional entries sufficiently distinctive, to substantiate a direct link between Elyot and the *Abraham* borders.[43] The likelihood of Elyot's involvement in this scheme is also questionable because he was out of favor with Henry by the late 1530s. In short, although the content and character of the innovative *Abraham* border scheme may well have been stimulated by the availability of Elyot's and Estienne's dictionaries from 1538, analysis of these works does not provide evidence for the locale in which the *Abraham* series was initiated.

In summary, lacking any documentary, iconographic, or stylistic evidence that would

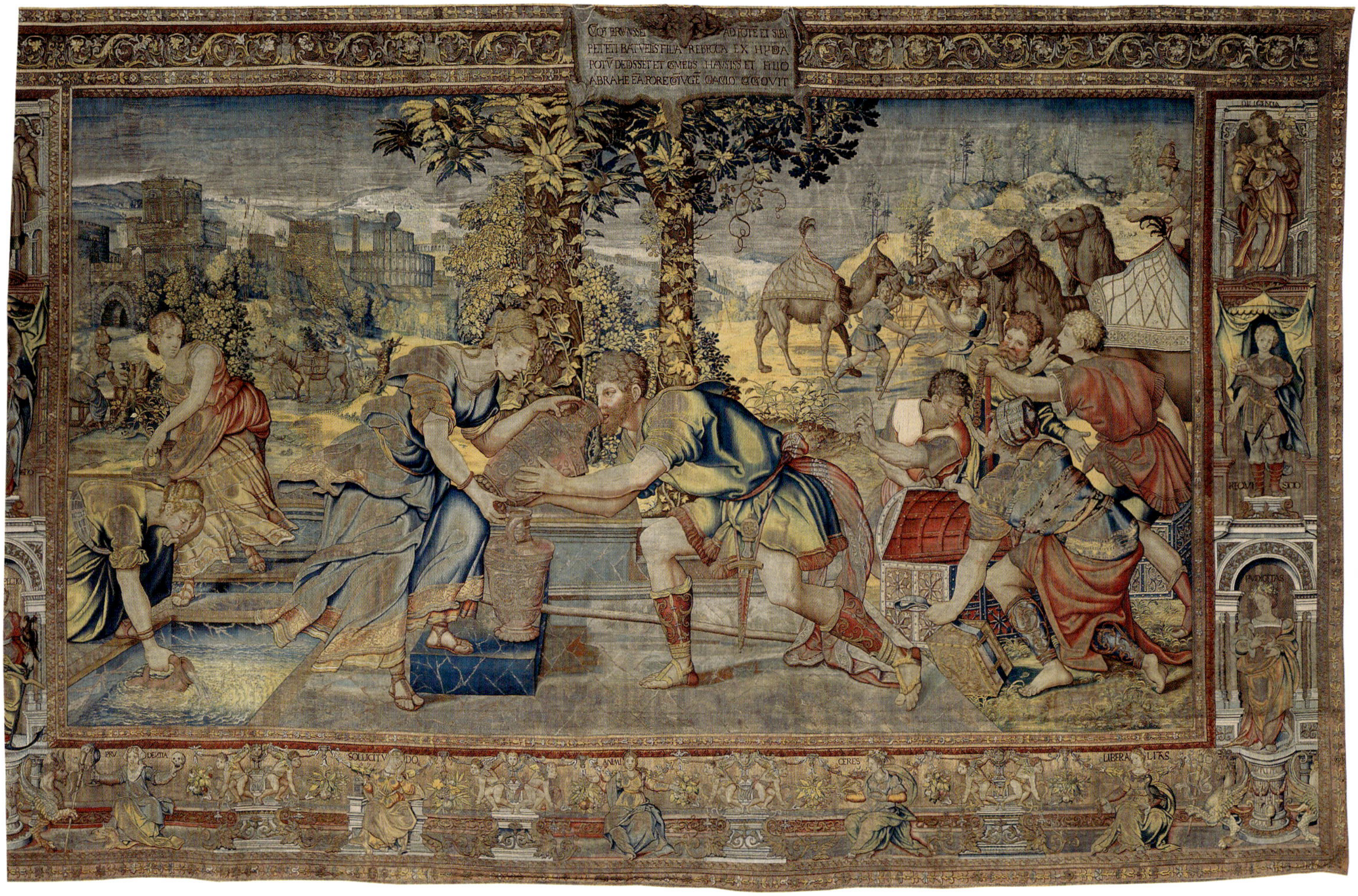

14.16 *Eliezer and Rebekah at the Well* from a ten-piece set of the *Story of Abraham*. Tapestry design attributed to Pieter Coecke van Aelst, woven in the workshop of Willem de Kempeneer, Brussels, ca. 1541–43. Wool, silk, and gilt-metal-wrapped thread, 477 x 777 cm. Hampton Court Palace

allow us to link the initiation of the *Abraham* series to the Tudor court with absolute certainty, it seems prudent to reserve judgment on the circumstances in which it was conceived. As we have seen, its subject, like that of the *Caesar* series, would have had a broad appeal, and Kempeneer could have commissioned the design in the knowledge that he would be likely to find a client, first and foremost, at the English court, but that it would also appeal to one of Henry's Continental rivals. Kempeneer certainly seems to have been one of the most entrepreneurial Brussels tapestry merchants during the 1530s and early 1540s, owning the cartoons for several large design series that were not linked with any particular originating patron.[44] And if he owned the *Abraham* cartoons outright, without any prior obligation to an initial patron, this would certainly explain why he was able to use them to make duplicate copies of the design so soon after production of the first weaving for Henry.

This scenario does not, however, rule out the possibility that the design may have been fashioned, at least in part, in response to prompting from the English court. Kempeneer enjoyed close links with the community of Antwerp merchants, many of whom dealt directly with Henry's leading advisers. A still more direct link with Henry's court is indicated by the documented relationship with Henry's arras maker, evidenced by Mostinck's deposition when Kempeneer was accused of fraudulent practices in 1539. Thus it seems plausible that Kempeneer had an intimate knowledge of the sorts of designs and subjects that would appeal to the English king and that he commissioned the designs based on this knowledge. Moreover, the evident link between Kempeneer and Mostinck makes it possible that full-scale cartoons for the *Abraham* series may have been developed after the English king had commissioned weavings of these designs, perhaps on the basis of modelli that had been shown to him. And if that were the case, then it is certainly possible that the king and his advisers might have been involved in the choice of some, if not all, of the subjects of the main fields and the personifications in the allegorical borders. Although the idea that the designs developed from some such intercourse is speculative, it is certainly supported by the parallels between these subjects and the rhetoric employed by Henry and the Reformation movement.

Even though the exact process whereby the *Abraham* set was conceived remains in question, the date at which the set entered the English royal collection, the relevance of the subject matter to Henry at that time, and the extraordinary richness and scale of the tapestries leave little doubt that it was intended to celebrate and promote the parallels between Abraham and Henry, and the continuation in the person of his son, Prince Edward, of the virtues that Henry embodied. As such, this acquisition, like that of the *Caesar* set and other Old and New Testament subjects acquired by Henry during the 1530s and 1540s, provide definitive evidence of steps taken by Henry and his advisers to use the visual imagery of the tapestry medium to promote and celebrate particular ideas and associations in the arena of the Tudor court.

Intended Location

For what forum was the *Abraham* set intended? It was first inventoried at Hampton Court in 1547, and it has remained there ever since. Hampton Court was undergoing major development during the late 1530s and early 1540s. If it was commissioned for this palace, the only room that could have accommodated the set as a whole was the great hall, built during the mid-1530s, and the tapestries do indeed fit snugly beneath the windows. Assuming that the tapestries may have been hung edge to edge and draped back around doorways, rather than placed at either side, it is conceivable that the entire set may have been intended to hang in the great hall on ceremonial occasions, or in the sequence of state rooms, now destroyed, that led from the hall to the presence chamber. In addition, it is also possible that when the set was commissioned, Henry had another, grander setting in mind. The *Abraham* tapestries were hung in Westminster Abbey in 1685 for the coronation of James II (see fig. 19.4), and there is some evidence that the disposition of tapestries on this occasion reflected a long-standing tradition.[45] Because the Stuart kings are known to have followed the precedent and even to have actively emulated practices associated with state events during the Tudor era, it is possible that the *Abraham* tapestries may have been hung in this location for sixteenth-century coronations as well.[46] Unfortunately, the documentary evidence is incomplete for the sixteenth-century coronations, and there is no record of the tapestries that were used for those of Edward VI or Mary. Descriptions of the decorations of Elizabeth I's coronation mention that the abbey was hung with the *Acts of the Apostles* and scenes from Genesis, and it is conceivable that the latter may have included the *Abraham* tapestries.[47] While this argument is tenuous, the resonance of the subject matter and the extreme richness of the set certainly support the possibility that Henry may, from the first, have envisaged the *Abraham* set not only as a central element in the decorations for his own state ceremonies but also as the future backdrop to the coronation of his son.

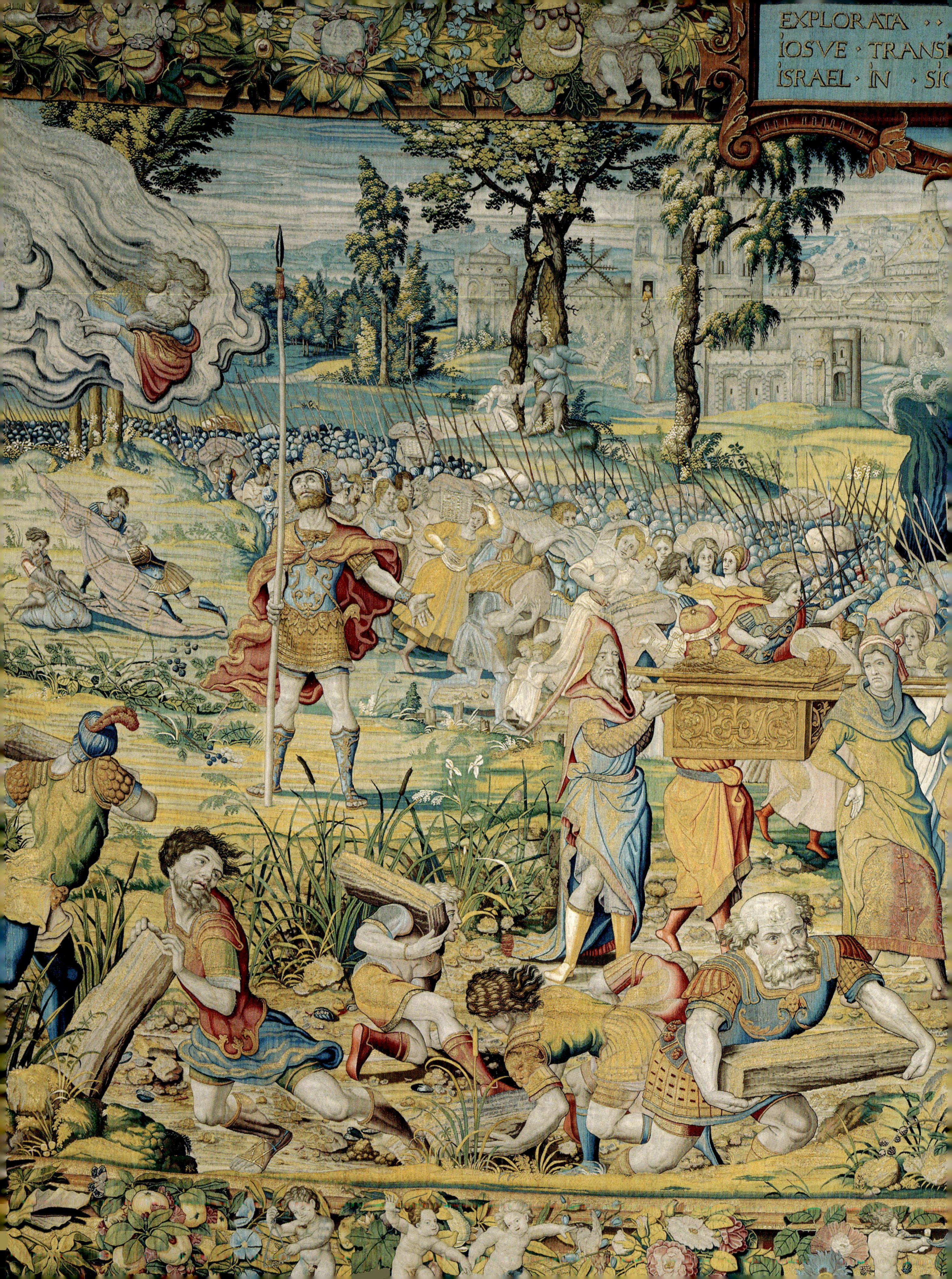
EXPLORATA
IOSVE · TRANS
ISRAEL · IN · SIC

CHAPTER 15

Purchases and Appropriations, 1543–1547

Antwerp Agents and Merchants

The *Acts, Grotesques, Caesar,* and *Abraham* sets have received special attention because of their artistic and iconographic interest and because the context in which they were acquired can be identified with some precision. Nonetheless, they were evidently just part of a larger number of high-quality tapestries purchased by Henry during the last five years of his reign. Although many of these acquisitions are as poorly documented as those of previous decades, how they were obtained can be deduced by a handful of archival references, while key acquisitions can be identified from the 1547 inventory and subsequent documentation.

The most valuable transactions were handled through the rich London and Antwerp merchants who had played such an important part in previous years. For example, Pieter van de Walle continued to receive large payments for supplying a range of goods to the court. Evidence that these included tapestry is provided by the 1547 inventory, which mentions four pieces of "arras" of the *Story of Romulus and Remus* "bought of Petre van dvall merchaunt."[1] This set was listed toward the end of the Hampton Court inventory, indicating that it had been a recent addition to that wardrobe. It is possible that it was for this set that Van de Walle received payment of £1,000 in February 1547, further to a warrant signed by Henry the previous August.[2] From 1545, immense sums were also delivered, via merchants such as Richard Gresham or Anthony Bonvisi, to Stephen Vaughan, Henry's agent in Brussels, to settle the "king's debts" in the Netherlands. Although these payments related largely to provisions for the campaign in France, they may also have included sums for gold-woven tapestries.[3] That Vaughan was involved, on occasion, in sourcing artworks for Henry is indicated by a watercolor of a pendant that the Fuggers wanted to sell to Henry and that Vaughan sent to William Paget in 1546.[4]

Other Antwerp merchants who may have supplied Henry during these years are identified by a deposition of 1549, signed by four merchants on behalf of a Jerome Crieckelman, who had been imprisoned in the Antwerp Steen for unknown reasons. The signatories were Pieter van de Walle, Jehan Baptiste Gualteroti, Joseph Mostaert, and Jacques Hoevenagel, all said to be merchants resident in Antwerp. According to the deposition, the merchants had used Crieckelman on many occasions to transport rich jewels, silver vessels, tapestries, and other merchandise from Antwerp to London. As their agent, Crieckleman was licensed by Henry VIII to import these goods into England without paying customs.[5]

Another Antwerp merchant who also supplied Henry with at least one set of tapestries in the last year of his reign is identified by a list of documents signed by the stamp in 1546. These include an obligation of £20,000 to "Erasmus Sketes" for shipments of grain and munitions, a passport to the same, and a license for him to bring in "arras" and jewelry.[6] Subsequently, another list of documents signed by the stamp in September 1546 includes the "discharge of custom" for certain "arras" bought of "Erasmus Sketes."[7] No further

Detail of fig. 15.1

details are given, but the 1547 inventory mentions a set of the *Story of Tobias* at Hampton Court, "bought of Erasmus Skotte."[8] Erasmus Schets was one of the richest merchants and bankers in Antwerp, having risen to prominence during the 1520s. He specialized in the trade of precious metals, a field in which he competed, and on occasion associated, with the Fuggers, and he lent huge sums of money to the Habsburg government. Besides being a major figure in the financial world, he was also a notable humanist. He maintained an extensive correspondence with Desiderius Erasmus and succeeded Pieter Gillis as the transfer agent for English annuities of that revered intellectual. During the 1540s Schets also played an important role as an entrepreneur and underwriter to the Flemish tapestry industry. Apart from the tapestries he supplied to Henry, he also sold Mary of Hungary a set of the *Story of Scipio* in 1544, a composite of the design series purchased by Francis I in the early 1530s (see fig. 11.7); and a *Story of Tobias* in 1547, a duplicate of that purchased by Henry (see fig. 15.3). Schets's status during this period is indicated by the fact that in 1545 he entertained Charles V at the fine house he had built for himself in Antwerp.[9]

These Antwerp merchants played a large part in supplying the most magnificent of Henry's later tapestry purchases, but they did not command a monopoly over royal commissions. Evidence that English merchants also supplied tapestries to the Crown comes from the consignment, already mentioned, by William Lok to Whitehall Palace in February 1544. According to an addendum to the 1542 Whitehall inventory, these tapestries were subsequently returned to Sir Anthony Denny on April 24, having been lined. The delivery comprised six tapestries of *Hercules,* eight of the *Prodigal Son,* and three sets of verdure of the "brode blome."[10] During the same period, large payments continued to be made from the Court of Augmentations to such figures as Richard Gresham, as evidenced by a payment of £576 9s. 10d. Gresham received in July 1544 for rich damasks and satins.[11] Although none of the abbreviated citations associated with such payments mention tapestry, it is certainly conceivable that tapestries were among the luxury goods that Gresham continued to source for the Crown.

The foregoing evidence provides an indication of the degree to which rich merchants continued to supply Henry with high-quality tapestries until shortly before his death. The character of these goods can be established on the basis of the 1547 inventory, in which a number of pieces are described as "newe" or can otherwise be identified as recent acquisitions. Generally speaking, two marked tendencies are apparent. First, Henry continued to invest very large sums in tapestries depicting religious role models. The size of these ensembles indicates that, like the *Saint Paul, Acts,* and *Abraham* sets, they were for display in the largest reception rooms of the palaces to which they were assigned and that, like those, they were intended to substantiate Henry's post-Reformation status as head of the English church. The second, equally apparent, tendency is that Henry also acquired a number of high-quality sets with subjects drawn from classical mythology and history. The dimensions and subjects of these sets, particularly the mythological subjects, suggest that they were selected for use in Henry's private apartments.

The Story of Joshua

The most significant of the new religious sets were deposited at Hampton Court. The tapestry section in the 1547 inventory for this palace starts with the largest and finest tapestries. The first entries, described as "newe arras," included the ten-piece set of *Abraham,* the ten-piece set of *Caesar,* the nine-piece set of *Saint Paul,* and a ten-piece set of *Joshua.*[12] As we have seen, "newe" was a relative term, since the *Saint Paul* set had been in the collection since 1539, while the *Abraham* and *Caesar* sets were acquired in 1543–44 at the latest. It is therefore possible that the *Joshua* set had been acquired some years before, and this likelihood is heightened by the fact that the *Tobias* set that

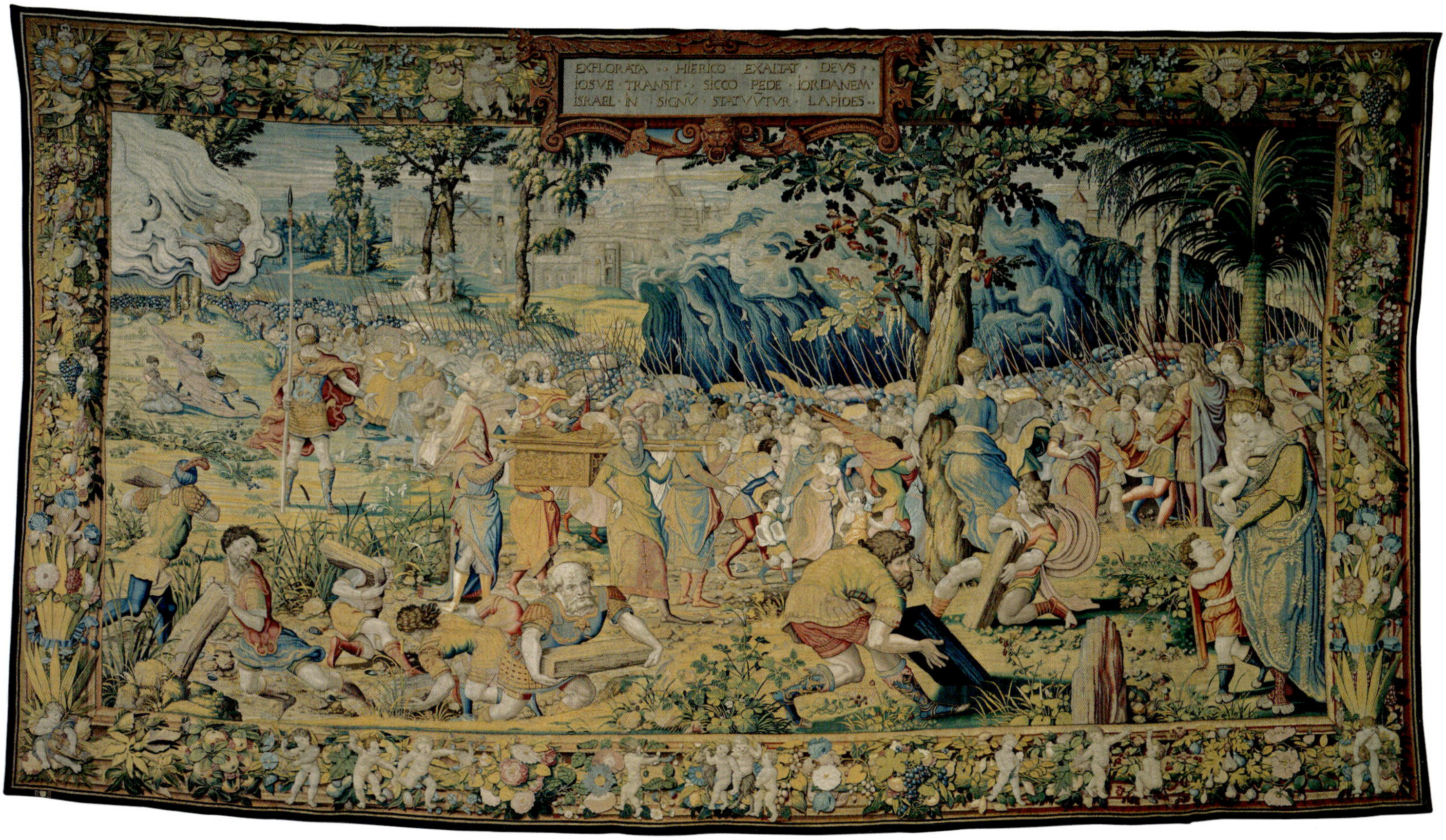

15.1 *The Crossing of the River Jordan* from an eight-piece set of the *Story of Joshua*. Tapestry designed by Pieter Coecke van Aelst, woven in the Dermoyen workshop, Brussels, ca. 1542–44. Wool, silk, and gilt-metal-wrapped thread, 448 x 830 cm. Kunsthistorisches Museum, Vienna

Schets supplied in late 1546 is listed separately at the end of the inventory. As with the other grand sets at Hampton Court, the identity of the *Joshua* set can be established on the basis of subsequent evidence. That it was one of the most splendid sets in the collection is shown by the appraisal of £3,399 placed on it at the time of the Commonwealth sale.[13] Reserved for Cromwell, the set continued in use at Hampton Court and Windsor Castle until 1693, when it was repaired for William III's new state apartments at Hampton Court.[14] Part of the set was then hung in the King's Bedchamber, where it remained for much of the eighteenth century and where it was recorded in such contemporary guides as George Bickham's *Deliciae Britannicae* (1742).[15] Other pieces were hung in the state bedchamber prepared in the 1710s for the Prince of Wales in the east wing, subsequently known as the Queen's Bedchamber, where they survived in the early nineteenth century and where they were illustrated in a watercolor of this room prepared by Richard Cattermole for William Henry Pyne's *Royal Residences* (see fig. 19.8).[16] The tapestries were removed in 1841, and their subsequent fate is unknown.[17]

In view of the rarity of Joshua as a subject in high-quality, mid-sixteenth-century tapestries it would have been logical to speculate that Henry's set was woven from the same cartoons as those used for an eight-piece set purchased by Francis I in 1539, now lost, and another eight-piece set purchased by Mary of Hungary in 1544. The last of these survives today in the Kunsthistorisches Museum in Vienna (figs. 15.1 and detail opposite p. 299) and is woven from designs that are attributed on stylistic grounds to Pieter Coecke.[18] The set depicts key events in the life of the patriarch, with the main narrative focusing on his succession to Moses and the completion of the Israelites' journey to the Promised Land. The problem with the assumption that Henry's ten-piece set was woven from the same cartoons as Mary of Hungary's set is that none of the eight Vienna tapestries correspond to the design of the one piece that can be seen clearly in Cattermole's watercolor of the Queen's Bedchamber at Hampton Court. However, a solution to this

15.2 *Joshua Dividing Israel among the Tribes* from a set of the *Story of Joshua* (detail). Tapestry woven in Brussels, ca. 1620, after a 16th-c. design by Pieter Coecke van Aelst. Wool and silk, dimensions unidentified. Present location unidentified

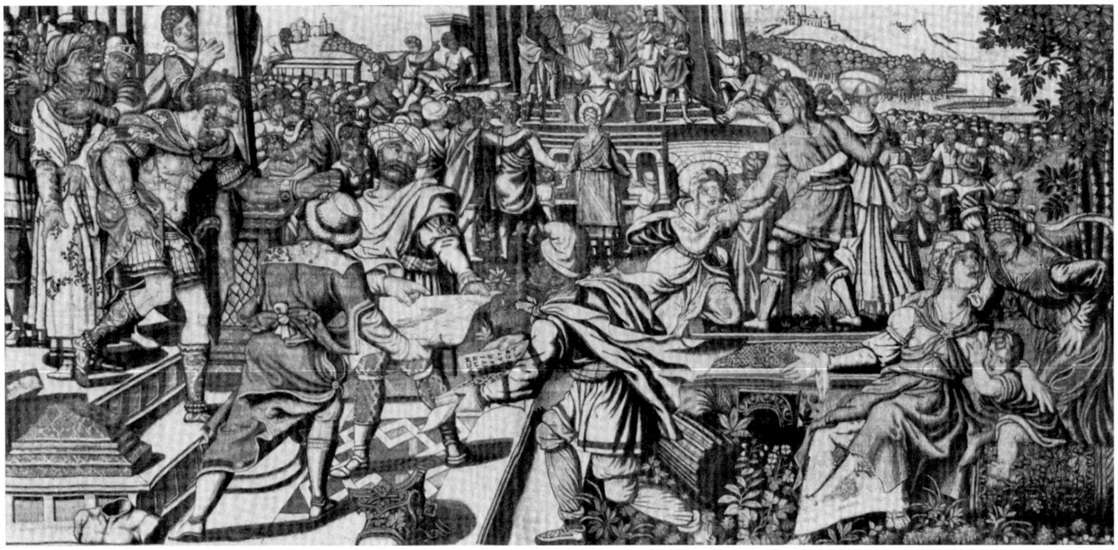

riddle is provided by a seventeenth-century tapestry, present location unknown, that does correspond to Cattermole's illustration (fig. 15.2) and that shows an unidentified warrior in the foreground looking at a map and, in the background, some sort of assembly.[19] Although this later piece was a relatively coarse weaving, it appears to have been based on a sixteenth-century design that was closely related to the style of Pieter Coecke's *Joshua* tapestries. In particular, the principal male figure wears similar armor and carries a sword identical to that with which Joshua is portrayed in the Vienna tapestries. Because so many sixteenth-century designs were copied in the seventeenth century, the visual evidence of this later tapestry, in conjunction with the known subjects of the Vienna pieces, suggests that the sixteenth-century cartoon on which it was based must have depicted Joshua dividing Israel among the tribes (Joshua 18:6), a subject not included in the Vienna series. If this assumption is correct and the set hanging at Hampton Court was indeed woven from the same cartoons as the Vienna set, then it appears that this was one of two scenes included in Henry's set but not in those of Francis I and Mary of Hungary.

The circumstances in which Henry's *Joshua* set was commissioned remain unknown, but there can be little doubt that the underlying intention of this purchase was to emphasize the parallel between Henry and Joshua, who, along with Abraham and Moses, played such a crucial role in the foundation of the Hebrew nation, just as Henry was now reestablishing the English church and state. The fact that Henry's set included a scene of the division of Israel among the tribes that was not included elsewhere is of note because the authority implied in Joshua's division of Israel must have provided Henry with a reassuring image of control over the future, as he considered how best to ensure a smooth transfer of power to his young son in the volatile political atmosphere of the Tudor court.

The design of the Coecke *Joshua* series had been conceived by 1537 at the latest, because Francis I acquired his eight-piece set in 1539. Considering that the theme was more in character with the religious series that Henry was acquiring during the 1530s and early 1540s, rather than the more mannerist designs and esoteric subject matter associated with Francis's patronage at this time, it is possible that the design was in fact conceived with Henry in mind, whether or not he purchased the first weaving. Equally, since we know that Henry committed large sums of money to tapestry purchases from around 1538–39, it is equally possible that the set may have been commissioned around this time from an existing design and delivered to the Tudor court sometime between 1540 and 1543, along with the two additional designs of *Caesar* and *Abraham*.

The Story of Tobias

The *Tobias* set supplied by Schets may have been the last of the great patriarchal series that Henry acquired. Assuming that it was indeed the subject of the license issued to Schets in July 1546, then Henry's set may be identical with one in which Schets purchased a part share from the Brussels merchant-weaver Balthazar van Vlierden at some point before March 21, 1546 (when Van Vlierden sold his interest in the rest of the set to the merchant-weaver Frans Thonis).[20] The set remained in the royal collection into the seventeenth century, and at the time of the Commonwealth sale it was appraised at £3,409, one of the most valuable sets in the collection.[21] Reserved from sale, it continued to be recorded among the Hampton Court goods until the early eighteenth century, when the set was cleaned and repaired before the use of five pieces at Saint James's Palace.[22] The subsequent fate of those tapestries is unknown, but a single piece of the set had been hung in the First Presence Chamber at Hampton Court sometime before 1785, when it was mentioned in a contemporary guide.[23] It continued to hang there into the nineteenth century, when it was one of four tapestries depicted in the room in another watercolor prepared by James Stephanoff for Pyne's *Royal Residences* (see fig. 19.9). Although it is almost totally covered by a painting, the distinctive winged figure at the left allows it to be identified with a tapestry still at Hampton Court today (fig. 15.3). On the basis of this surviving panel, the lost set can be identified as a weaving of a design series of which a fragmentary set, purchased by Mary of Hungary, survives today in the Spanish royal collection (fig. 15.4).[24] Written records show that Mary's set was also purchased from Schets and that the first payment was made on June 21, 1547, postdating the acquisition of Henry's set.[25] No other weaving of this set has yet been identified, so we are once again presented with the possibility that Henry may have owned the first weaving of this series.

The designer has not been identified. Stylistically, the figures are less refined than those of

15.3 *Tobias Presents Raphael to His Father Tobit* from a set of the *Story of Tobias.* Tapestry woven in Brussels, ca. 1545. Wool, silk, and gilt-metal-wrapped thread, 452 x 600 cm. Hampton Court Palace

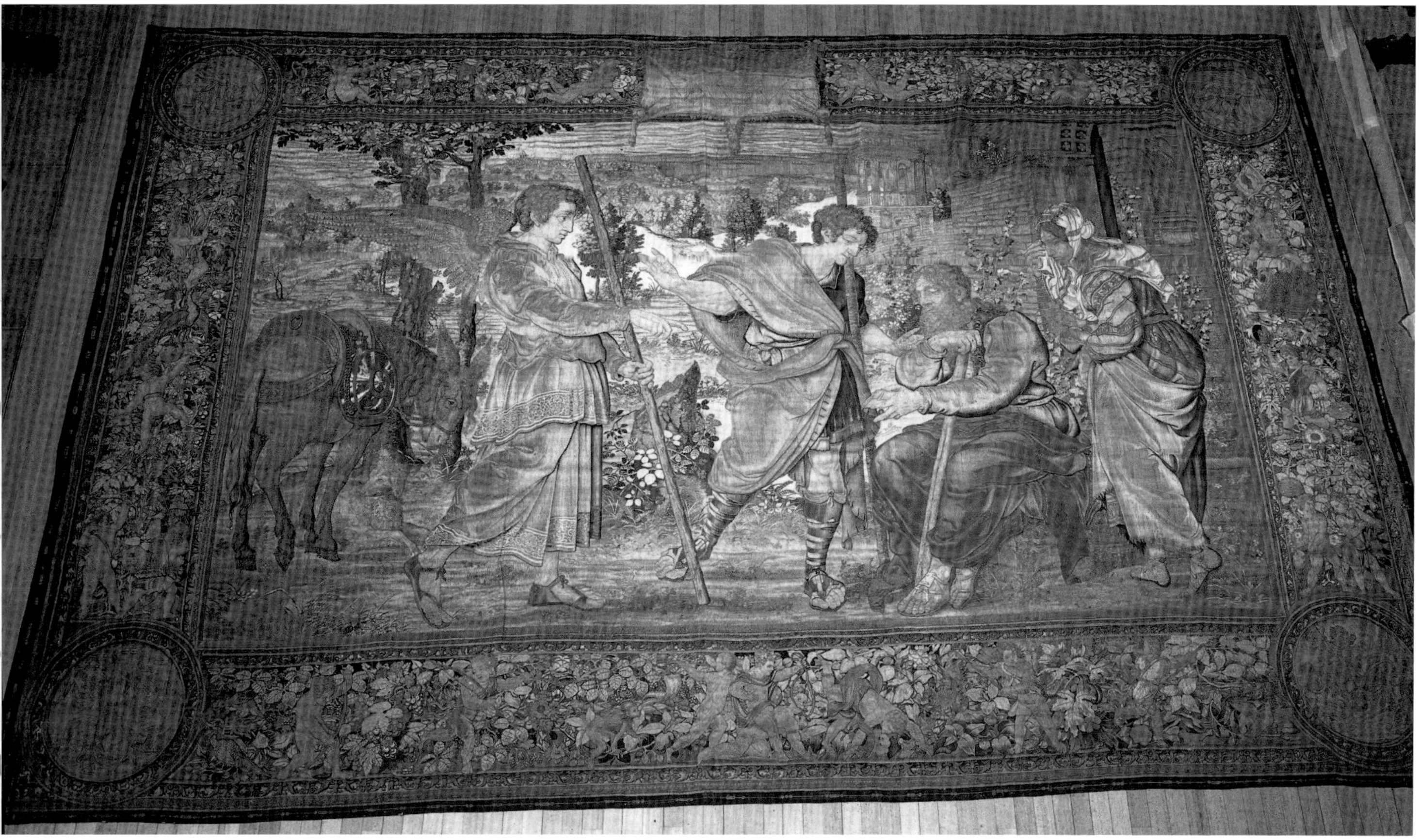

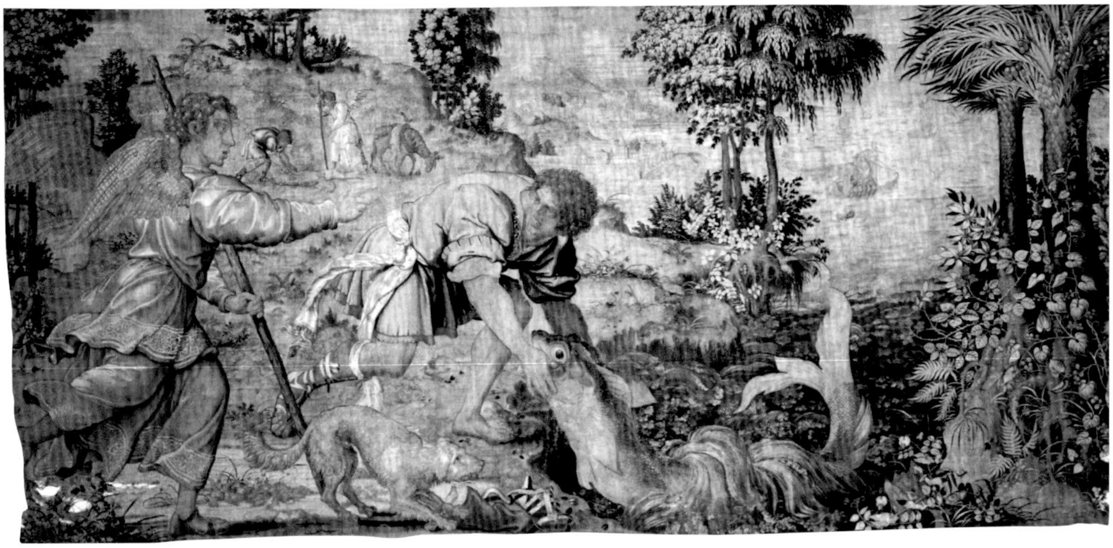

15.4 *Tobias Catches the Fish* (fragment) from a set of the *Story of Tobias*. Tapestry woven in Brussels, ca. 1545–47. Wool and silk, 440 x 710 cm. Palacio Real, Madrid

Coecke's oeuvre and less idealized than those of Michiel Coxcie. The closer resemblance is to a *Story of Samson,* said to have been designed for Henry II of France but never executed because of that king's death in 1559, and known only from seventeenth-century weavings based on the original sixteenth-century cartoons. According to an early-seventeenth-century description of the *Samson* series, it was designed by one "Gillio Mechelaon di Malines," of whom nothing else is known.[26]

The *Tobias* series focuses on the well-known story of Tobit of Nineveh, who, like Job, suffered ill fortune and the affliction of blindness before God answered his prayers. The tapestries depict the journey of his son Tobias to Media to collect a debt, in the company of the angel Raphael, whom God had sent to guide him. When Tobias is attacked by a large fish while bathing, Raphael instructs him to keep the gall, heart, and liver because they make good medicine (see fig. 15.4). In Media he meets Sarah, who has prayed for death because she is possessed by the Devil, with the consequence that she has had seven unsuccessful marriages. At Raphael's direction, Tobias uses the fish's heart and liver to exorcise Sarah, whom he then marries. Together they return to Nineveh, where Tobias uses the fish's gallbladder to cure his father's blindness.

Although the context in which this design was conceived is unknown, the subject evidently had several resonances that would have appealed to Henry, particularly the theme of resignation to the will of God, God's intercession on behalf of the faithful, childlessness as a curse, the devotion of a son to his aging father, and the succession of that son. As such it seems clear that, once again, this purchase was intended to celebrate the parallel between Old Testament prototypes and the Tudor succession: Tobit and Tobias, Henry and Edward.

Other Religious Subjects Acquired during the Mid-1540s

Even though the *Joshua* and *Tobias* sets stand out because of their high material quality and the prominent manner of their listing in the 1547 inventory, they were just part of a larger number of Old Testament subjects Henry purchased in the 1540s. The sheer number of such subjects listed in the 1547 inventory is arresting—at least sixty ensembles of two or more pieces, totaling about three hundred tapestries—and though many of these were certainly inherited or appropriated, Henry and his agents clearly had continued to buy medium-quality tapestries of such subjects in addition to gold-woven sets. Circumstantial evidence of at least one other patriarchal set that must have been acquired in the 1540s, a *Story of Solomon,* is provided by two Mortlake tapestries dating from the early 1620s, now at Easton Neston, Northamptonshire (fig. 15.5). These depict scenes of Solomon and Sheba and carry the arms of George Villiers, duke of Buckingham, in the upper borders. As already noted, the Mortlake manufactory copied a number of "old master" tapestry sets from Henry VIII's collection during the first years of its production, and although the borders of these two tapestries are seventeenth century in style, the main field appears to be based on a prototype conceived in the early 1540s.[27] The figures are close in character to those of the *Abraham* series, but the compositions lack the grace of conception of that series, which indicates that the designs and cartoons may have been produced by an artist working in Pieter Coecke's circle rather than the master himself.

The foregoing evidence suggests that Henry's palaces were adorned with imagery of the Old Testament patriarchs. Proof that apostolic comparisons also continued to appeal to his taste is provided by the Great Wardrobe account for 1545–46, which shows that nine new pieces of the *Story of Paul* were lined by the king's tailors in this year, along with other tapestries for Greenwich.[28] This nine-piece set is subsequently listed in the Greenwich inventory as tapestry, indicating that in contrast to the gold-woven set delivered in 1538–39 and subsequently listed at Hampton Court, it was woven in wool and silk alone. Though it was thus a less splendid weaving than that at Hampton Court, it is nonetheless of note that Henry should have chosen to commission a second set of this design for Greenwich Palace seven or eight years after the delivery of the first. It is conceivable that a single panel now at Schloss Friedrichshof, Kronberg (see fig. 12.13) originates from this second *Paul* set. Friedrichshof was built for Empress Friedrich III, Queen Victoria's oldest daughter, Victoria of Saxe-Coburg Gotha, and still contains furnishings and works of art that she took to Germany, including a number of tapestries and paintings, formerly in the English royal collection.

15.5 *The Queen of Sheba Arrives at the Court of King Solomon* from a set of the *Story of King Solomon*. Tapestry woven at the Mortlake manufactory, ca. 1625, the main field copied from a mid-16th-c. tapestry by an unidentified Flemish artist. Wool and silk. Easton Neston (Northamptonshire)

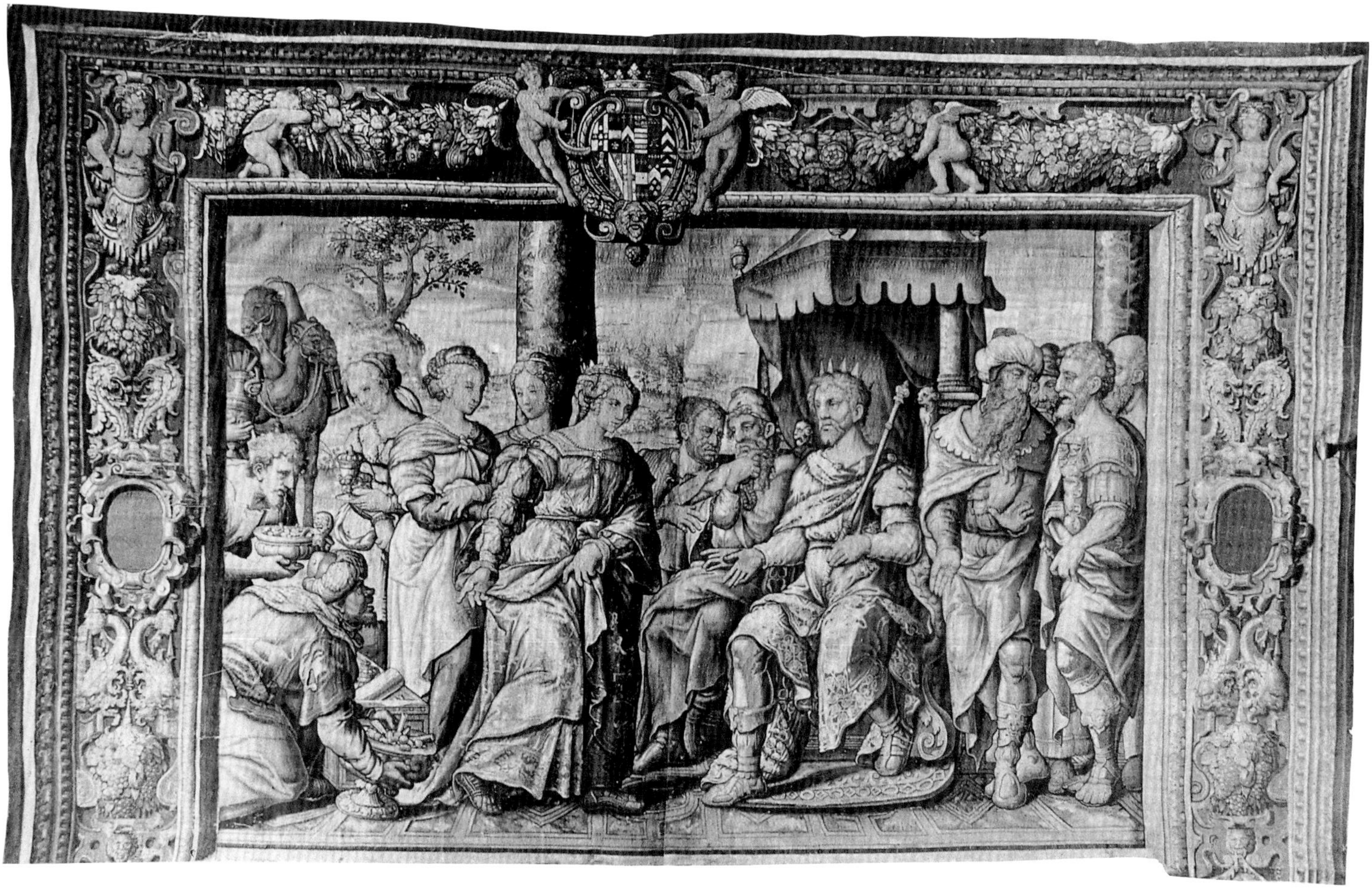

It is to be noted that in the 1547 inventory, the dimensions of the Greenwich *Saint Paul* set are specified in Flemish ells rather than yards, much as Wolsey's recent purchases from Gresham had been listed in his 1522 inventory, perhaps reflecting the use of dimensions marked on the linings. By analogy, four other sets listed near the *Saint Paul* set in the 1547 Greenwich inventory for which the dimensions were also provided in Flemish ells may also have been very recent acquisitions. These included eight pieces of the *Prodigal Son,* fifteen of the *Story of David,* eight pieces of the *Passion,* and seven pieces of verdure.

Purchases with Classical Subjects

The scale and splendor of the religious subjects deposited at Hampton Court indicate that they were purchased to equip the large reception rooms at this palace with a seamless display of patriarchal and apostolic imagery. Hampton Court had been rebuilt during the late 1530s and early 1540s as an enormous entertainment complex for the grandest receptions and banquets of the day, and it seems unquestionable that these tapestries were purchased to celebrate and reinforce parallels between religious role models and Henry in the eyes of the wider court and visiting dignitaries. During the same period, however, the purchases made for Henry's private apartments were of a markedly different character, concentrating more on scenes of classical mythology.

The Story of Romulus and Remus

One of the most beautiful and striking of these must have been the four-piece *Romulus and Remus* set also purchased for Hampton Court. According to the 1547 inventory it was supplied by Van de Walle, and because it was listed toward the end of the inventory, it seems likely that it was a recent addition. It survived in the royal collection until the Commonwealth sale, when it was sold to a consortium led by a draper called John Geere.[29] In turn, it is almost certainly to be identified with a four-piece *Romulus and Remus* set documented among goods purchased by Don Alonso de Cárdenas, Spanish ambassador in London, on behalf of Don Luis Mendez de Haro, marqués del Carpio.[30] Shipped to Spain in 1654, the set then vanishes from the records, but its appearance can be suggested on the basis of its size and supplier. Charles V's son, Philip (later Philip II), is known to have purchased a gold-woven, four-piece set of *Romulus and Remus* in 1550 from a "Juan Vandebela," or Jan van de Walle, son of Pieter, of which six fragments survive today, two in the Spanish royal collection and four elsewhere (fig. 15.6).[31] These fragments have evidently been cut from longer, frieze-like panels, each of which must have depicted two or three narrative scenes. The appearance of another four scenes can be deduced from a second-generation version of the design, now in Vienna, in which each scene is woven as a separate tapestry.[32] Assuming that Philip's four panels included about ten scenes in all and that each would have had a surface area roughly equivalent to those of the surviving fragments, we can calculate that Philip's set was of a similar size to that purchased by Henry. Both sets were supplied by members of the Van de Walle family, so it seems likely that they were woven from the same cartoons. Again, this identification raises the possibility that Henry may have possessed the earliest documented example of another of the most attractive design series of the day.

As we have seen, Henry had purchased another four-piece set of *Romulus and Remus* tapestries from Richard Gresham in 1529, woven from designs by Van Orley or an artist in his circle. This later series can be attributed to designs by Michiel Coxcie on the basis of the idealized figures and classical architecture featured in the scenes. Coxcie is known to have resided and worked during the 1530s in Rome, where he copied and absorbed the figural style of Michelangelo and the Raphael school, whose models he was to reproduce, sometimes verbatim, in his subsequent work.[33] In this case, the muscular and youthful figures of Romulus and Remus, and their antique armor, carry many

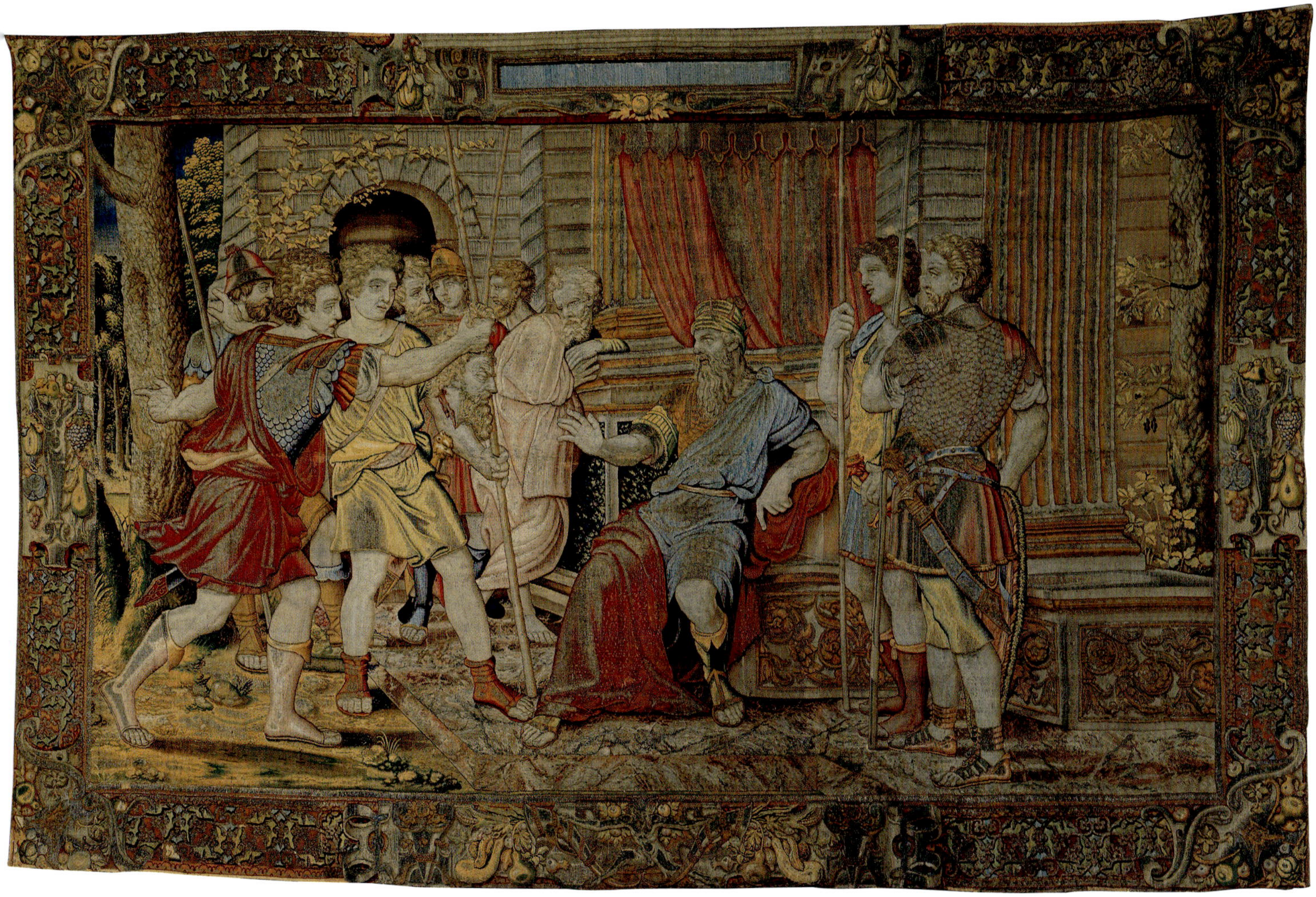

15.6 *Romulus Reveals the Head of Numitor to Amulius* from a set of the *Story of Romulus and Remus*. Tapestry design by Michiel Coxcie, woven in the workshop of Willem de Pannemaker, Brussels, ca. 1540–45. Wool, silk, and gilt-metal-wrapped thread, 210 x 310 cm. Private collection, London

echoes of figures executed by Raphael and his collaborators in the Vatican Stanze. As with the earlier *Romulus* series, the narrative focuses on the key events in the lives of the heroes and the foundation of Rome. The idiosyncratic dimensions of the set, with wide panels of moderate height, suggests that the series was designed to be set in paneling in a room of specific dimensions.

The Story of Vulcan and Venus *and the* Story of Paris and Helen

The *Romulus and Remus* designs provided a marked contrast to the religious acquisitions made for Hampton Court, perhaps indicative of a choice for the decoration of more private apartments. A similar tendency is apparent in purchases made for Whitehall Palace during the same period. The 1547 inventory of goods at Whitehall specifically describes two sets as "new": one of the *Story of Vulcan, Mars, and Venus*, the other of the *Story of Helen and Paris*.[34] The character of the latter is unknown, but the former can be identified with certainty, providing a fascinating insight into the motives that may have led Henry to acquire these two famous classical love stories.

The *Vulcan and Venus* set was sold from the royal collection at the time of the Commonwealth sale, but its appearance can be deduced from reproductions made at Mortlake during the early 1620s, where it was the first design that the manufactory copied and wove (fig. 15.7).[35] These reproductions reveal that the Mortlake cartoons were copied from a sixteenth-century series of which a five-piece set survives at Biltmore House, Asheville, North Carolina (fig. 15.8). The identity of the designer is unknown. The set depicts episodes from the story of

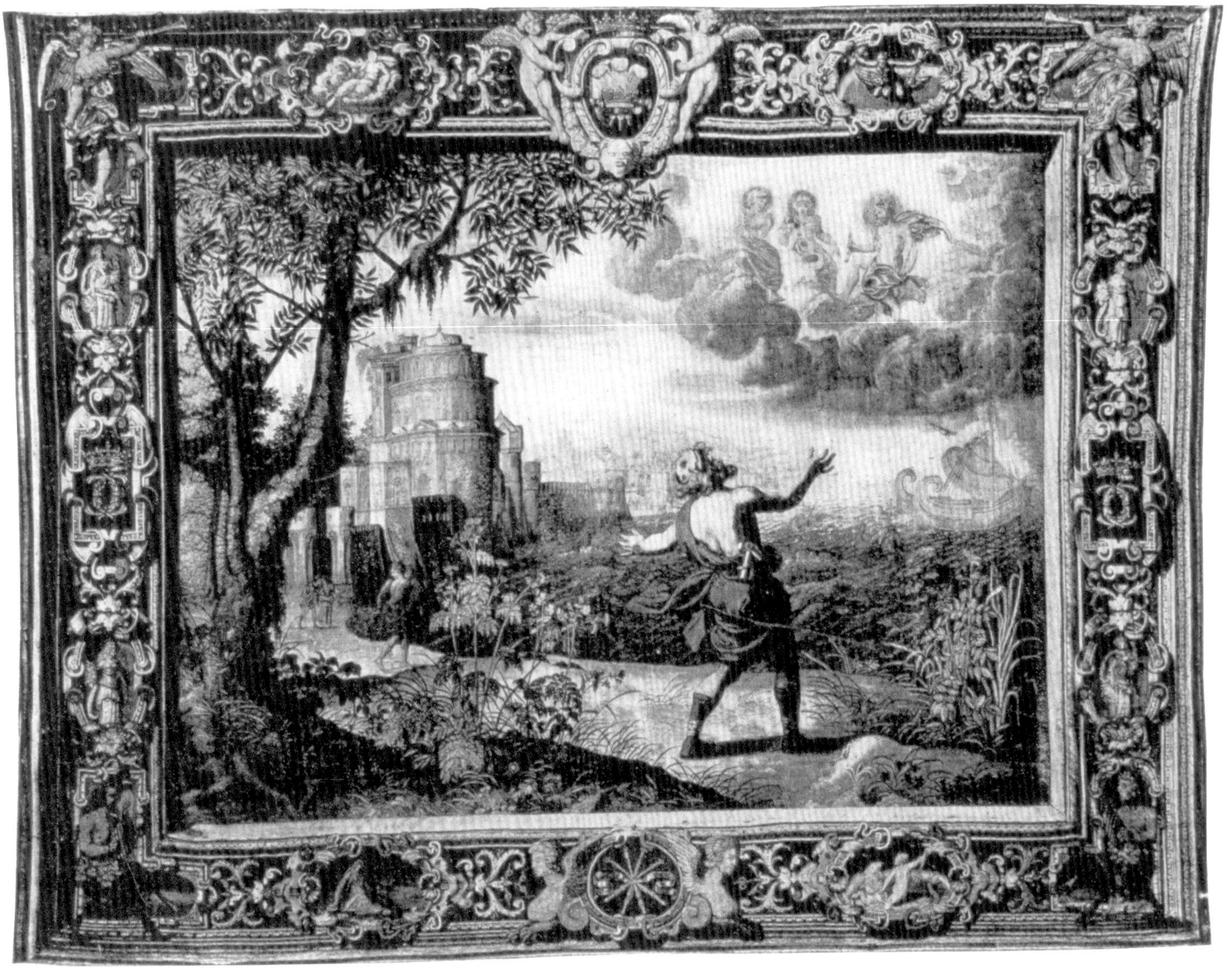

15.7 *The Complaint of Vulcan* from a set of the *Story of Vulcan and Venus.* Tapestry woven at the Mortlake manufactory, ca. 1625, after a 16th-c. design. Wool, silk, and gilt-metal-wrapped thread, 455 x 557 cm. Private collection, London

Venus's affair with Mars, Vulcan's discovery of their infidelity, Vulcan's capture of the lovers, as narrated in Ovid's *Metamorphoses,* and the additional subject of Neptune interceding for the lovers taken from the *Odyssey*. It has been suggested that the Biltmore set may be that once in Henry's collection, but this is uncertain because it contains metallic thread, whereas Henry's set was described as "tapestry" in the 1547 inventory, not "arras," indicating that it did not. Either way, there can be no doubt that Henry had a weaving made from the same cartoons as the Biltmore tapestries. The subjects of the two lost scenes can also be deduced from later Mortlake weavings.[36]

Further light on the context in which Henry obtained this set is given by a letter sent to Cosimo de' Medici on May 23, 1545, by his ambassador to the imperial court, Giovan Battista Ricasoli, bishop of Cortona.[37] Written from Antwerp, this describes a seven-piece set of *Vulcan* that Ricasoli had seen and thought Cosimo might wish to buy. The set was woven with silk but no metallic thread, and the dimensions correspond to those of the set recorded as new in Henry's inventory two years later. In the event, Cosimo de' Medici did not purchase the set, so it is possible that Henry's set was that which Ricasoli had seen in April 1545 or an earlier weaving. This would suggest that it had been woven as a speculative venture for the unidentified Antwerp merchant whose mark appears on the Biltmore tapestries.[38] It is conceivable that Henry's set was the editio princeps since no evidence has yet emerged of an earlier weaving.[39]

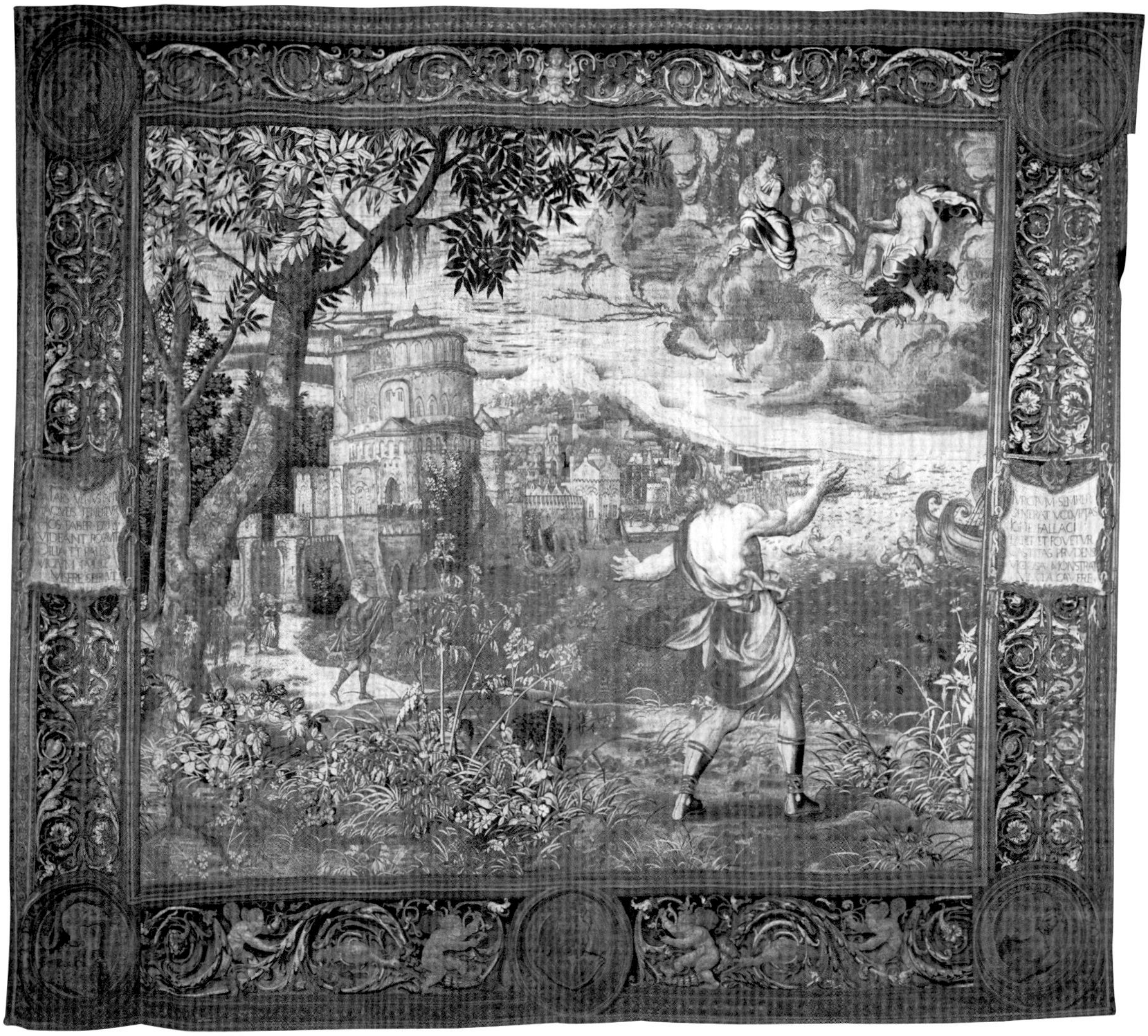

15.8 *The Complaint of Vulcan* from a set of the *Story of Vulcan and Venus.* Tapestry woven in Brussels, ca. 1545. Wool and silk, 437 x 522 cm. Biltmore House, Asheville, NC

The foregoing details suggest that Henry was not involved in the conception of the design, but the subject of the infidelity of Venus is intriguing in the context of Henry's recent marital experience. Catherine Howard, with whom he had been infatuated from the summer of 1540—they were married at the end of July—was accused of infidelity one year later on October 31, 1541. Following his initial disbelief and distress, Henry responded with predictable fury, and Catherine was executed on February 13, 1542. In these circumstances, the themes of infidelity and betrayed love must have been extremely poignant for Henry during the following months, and the moralizing inscriptions that appear in the cartouches in the lateral borders of the *Vulcan and Venus* set are in the same spirit as the passages that he scored and marked in his personal Psalter and in his Book of Proverbs.[40] That accompanying the scene of Vulcan forging and spreading the net in which the lovers are to be caught is typical: "Love and beauty are treacherous phantoms, by which are ensnared the minds of fools, whom never-fading passion, though thrice indulged, cannot sate."[41] It is therefore tempting to speculate that Henry felt drawn to this subject as a reflection on the trials and tribulations of his own affairs of the heart.

Although we have no evidence for the appearance of the *Paris and Helen* set that was also recorded as new at Whitehall, it seems reasonable to propose that, in the circumstances, this other classical tale of the destructive power of love may have appealed to Henry for similar reasons.

Other Subjects Drawn from Classical History and Mythology

The *Romulus and Remus* and *Vulcan and Venus* sets are the most easily identified of Henry's later acquisitions with subjects drawn from classical mythology, but the 1547 inventory suggests that they may have been just part of a larger number of similar purchases. As we have seen, Hercules was evidently a resonant classical role model for Henry from the late 1530s, and a set of this subject was delivered to Whitehall Palace by William Lok in 1544. The number of *Hercules* sets listed in the 1547 inventory indicates that this was just one of a number that he acquired during his reign. Although the appearance of the 1544 delivery is no better known than that of any other of the *Hercules* sets purchased by Henry, we can speculate that he would almost certainly have acquired a version of the design series that Willem Dermoyen provided to Mary of Hungary in 1535, of which part survives in the Spanish royal collection (fig. 15.9).[42] The artist is unidentified, but he was evidently one of the leading designers of the day because his hand is recognizable in other contemporary designs.[43] This series enjoyed immense success and was rewoven and copied many times in the course of the following thirty years both in Brussels and in other centers such as Oudenaarde.

Greenwich Palace may also have been provided with new sets depicting classical subjects in Henry's final years. The 1547 inventory lists

15.9 *The Battle of Hercules and Anteus* from a set of the *Story of Hercules*. Tapestry woven in workshop of Jan Gheteels, Brussels, ca. 1540. Wool and silk, 362 x 403 cm. Palacio Real, Madrid

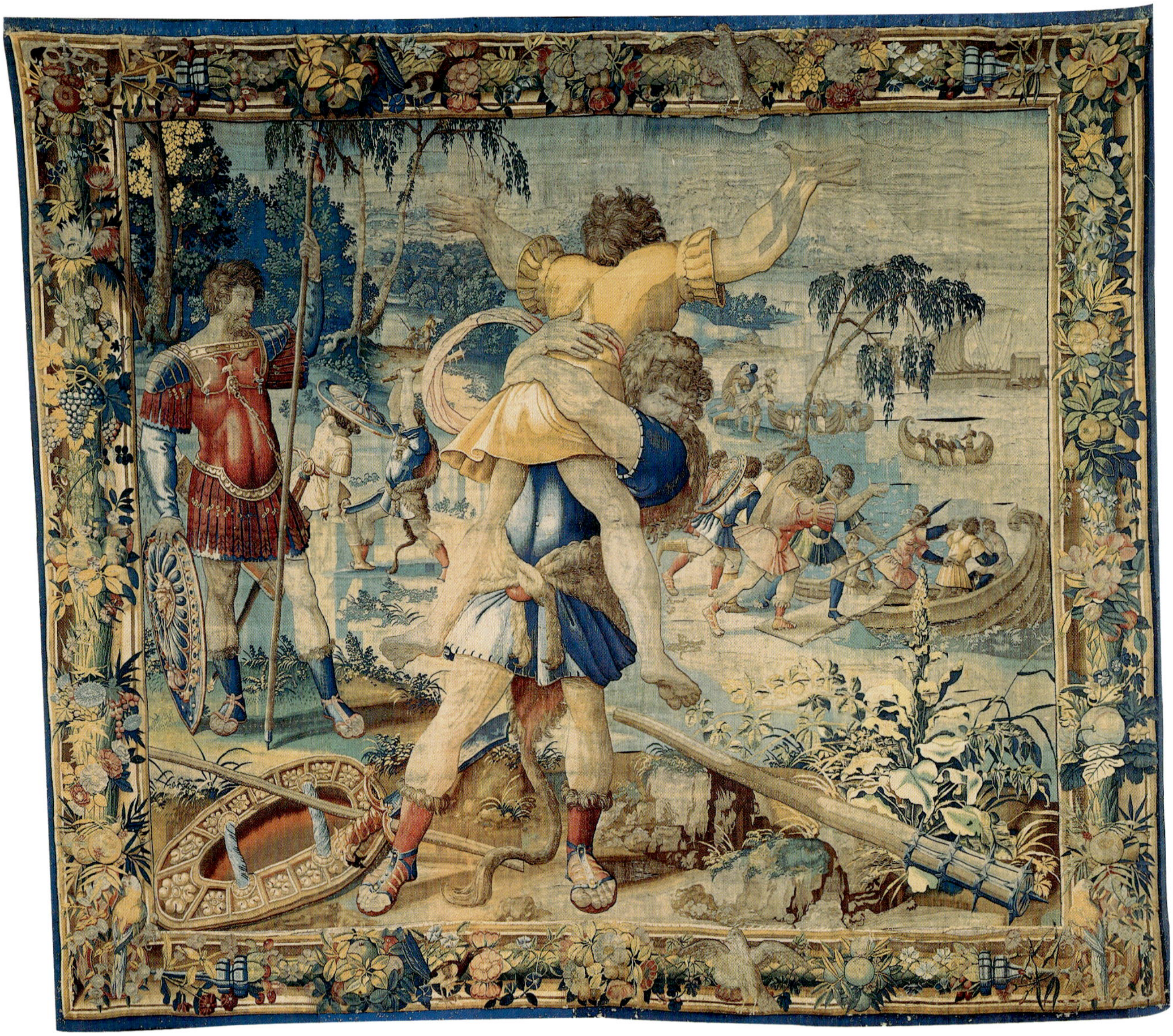

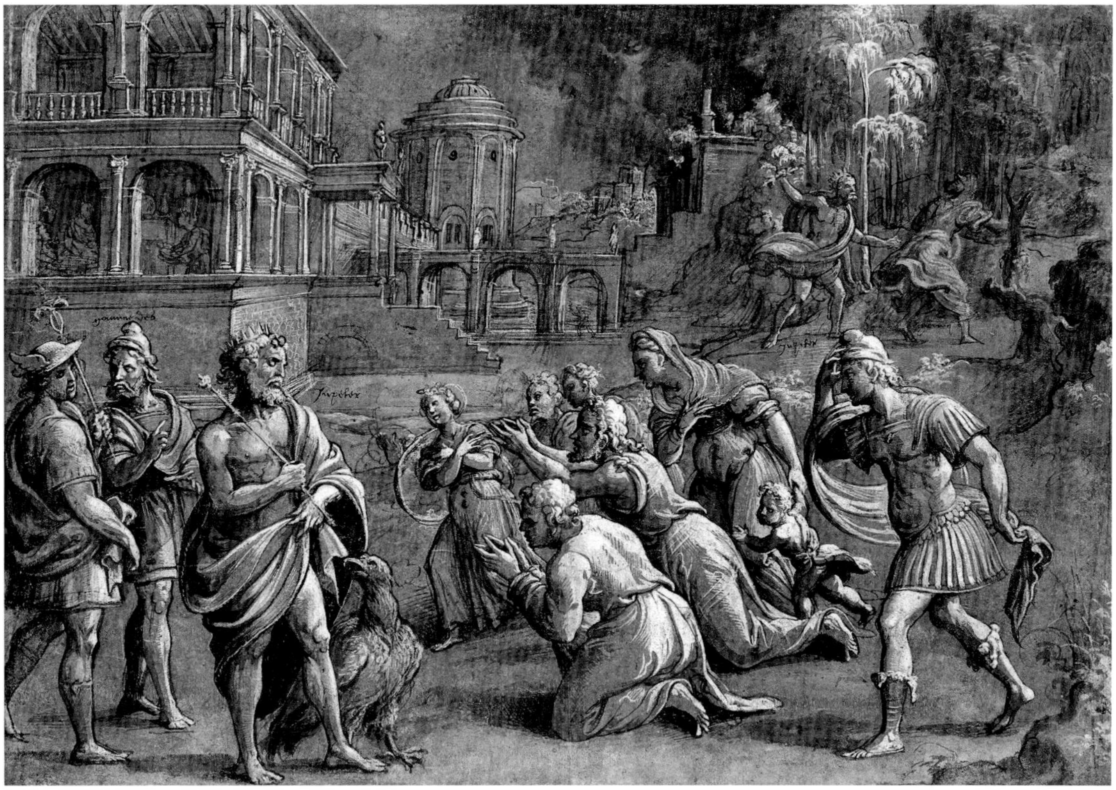

15.10 *Scenes from the Story of Jupiter.* Tapestry design by an unidentified Flemish artist, ca. 1535. Pen and brown ink and wash, heightened with white, gold, and touches of red, over black chalk, 28.8 x 39.4 cm. Location unidentified (Sotheby's, London, July 11, 2001, lot 36)

a six-piece "arras" set of *Meleager* at Greenwich, but since some of the finest of tapestries listed at Greenwich appear to have been supplied during the late 1510s and 1520s, it has already been suggested that this may have been an edition of a series conceived sometime between 1515 and 1520s, of which a single piece survives in the Toledo (Ohio) Museum of Art.[44] The 1547 Greenwich inventory also lists a six-piece set of *Hannibal* whose origin is uncertain and whose identification is additionally impeded by the lack of recorded measurements. This may have been a reduced version of the Giulio Romano–Giovanni Francesco Penni design series of which the first weaving was made for Francis I during the early 1530s.[45] Adapted versions of part of the Romano series were certainly made for several Continental patrons, including one that Erasmus Schets supplied to Mary of Hungary in the late 1540s.[46] However, the Romano–Penni series is largely focused on Scipio, rather than Hannibal, so it is more likely that the Greenwich set was an early weaving of a design series of which a six-piece set has survived at Zamora Cathedral.[47] The designs appear to have been conceived in the early 1540s by an artist who was subsequently responsible for a number of classical history series.

Discussion of the character of Henry's *Hannibal* series takes us into speculative territory, since it is equally possible that the set may have been an older, unrelated weaving of this subject. Two other equally speculative identifications also require mention because of their potential significance. The first was also of classical subject matter, a seven-piece set of the *Story of Jupiter* recorded at Richmond.[48] Most of the tapestries listed at Richmond in the 1547 inventory appear to have dated from Henry VII's reign or earlier, but the *Jupiter* set stands out for several reasons. Although it appears to have been tapestry rather than "arras," it is listed first in the inventory, suggesting that it had a certain importance within the collection as a whole. The width dimensions vary from eight and a half yards to four yards, which might be explained if it was a very large, old tapestry that had been cut up. Equally, it may also reflect that this was a set that was made with specific dimensions for a particular chamber, and the possibility that this set resulted

15.11 Two tapestries from a set of the *Fates*. Tapestry design by Bernaert van Orley or circle, woven in Brussels, ca. 1535–40. Wool and silk. Castle Ashby, Northamptonshire

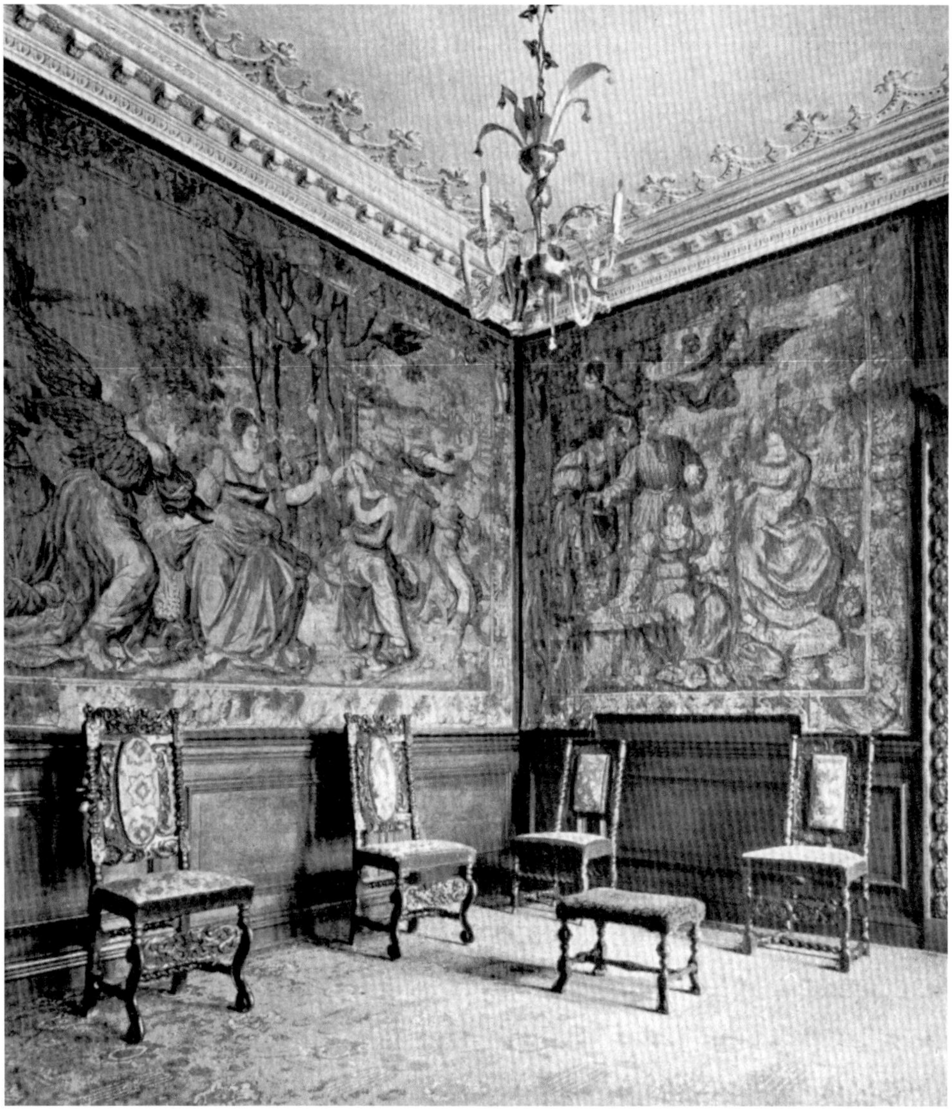

from a commission by Henry VIII, rather than one of his predecessors, is supported by the rarity of Jupiter as a subject in its own right in tapestry sets made before the second quarter of the sixteenth century. A highly distinctive set of this subject was designed by Perino del Vaga for Andrea Doria in the early 1530s, which featured scenes of Jupiter coupling with his various paramours in an elaborate allegory of divine love and imperial power, with Jupiter standing for both God and Charles V.[49] The set made for Doria appears to have been unique because the cartoons were returned to Genoa with the tapestries, but the exercise stimulated a Flemish treatment of this subject in the mid-1530s, of which various pieces appeared in the trade, along with a preparatory sketch for one of the pieces (fig. 15.10).[50] The design, by an unidentified artist in the circle of Van Orley, is closely related in style to a number of series produced in Brussels during the mid-1530s, such as the *Story of Venus,* of which Henry acquired a set in the late 1530s (see above). It is therefore possible that the *Jupiter* set at Richmond may have been a weaving of this design. It is to be noted that the 1547 inventory also lists an "arras" tapestry of *Jupiter and Juno* at the Tower, whose date and appearance are unknown.

The other enigmatic classical subject listed in the 1547 inventory was a three-piece "arras" set of the "three fatall Ladies of Destenye," or the Three Fates.[51] A single tapestry with a depiction of the *Three Fates* on a millefleur ground dating from about 1500 survives at the Victoria and Albert Museum, and the Hampton Court set may have been analogous to this design.[52]

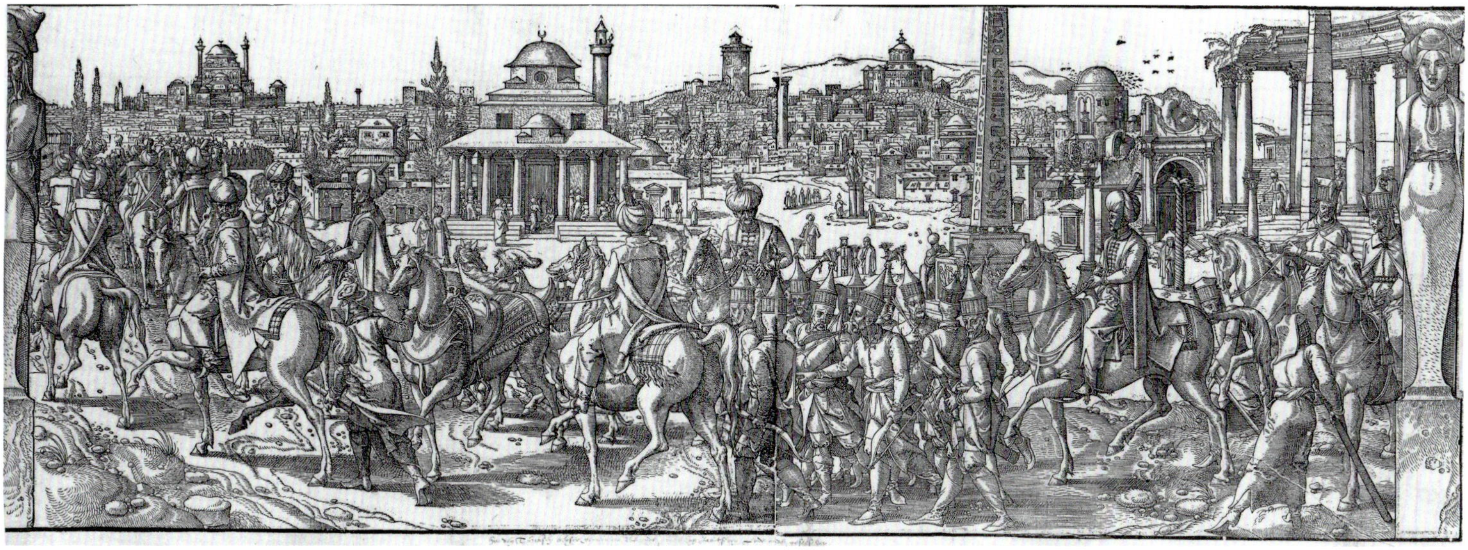

15.12 *Procession of Sultan Süleyman through the Atmeidan* from the *Customs and Fashions of the Turks*. Pieter Coecke van Aelst, 1553. Woodcut, 29.5 x 83.2 cm. The Metropolitan Museum of Art, New York

But since the entry for this set appears in the inventory immediately before those for other "arras" sets that Henry acquired in the late 1530s and early 1540s, it seems more likely that the set was a recent acquisition. A possible identification is suggested by an oral tradition associated with a gold-woven set of the *Fates* that dates from the late 1530s and is now at Castle Ashby. This fragmentary and unpublished set is said to have been given to the earl of Northampton by Queen Elizabeth.[53] Study is now impeded because the surviving tapestries—two complete tapestries and two fragments—are obstructed by large and heavy items of furniture, but a photograph published in the early twentieth century reveals that the two complete panels depict the Fates weaving and cutting the thread of time, with symbols of the Months in the sky above (fig. 15.11). Although faded and damaged, the tapestries are of high quality, woven with silk and metallic thread, from a cartoon in the style of Bernaert van Orley.

One other possible late purchase requires brief mention. Among tapestries listed by the 1547 inventory in the King's Removing Wardrobe was a six-piece set of "Turques." Unfortunately, no dimensions are recorded to provide any further clues to the identity of this set,[54] but it may have been based on designs made by Pieter Coecke following his visit to Constantinople in the early 1530s. It has been remarked that the format of Coecke's engravings, *Customs and Fashions of the Turks* (fig. 15.12), published by his wife after his death in 1553, is close to that of the tapestry designs he produced during the late 1530s, particularly the *Story of Joshua* series. It is therefore conceivable that the *Customs and Fashions* designs had, indeed, first been devised as modelli for a set of tapestries.[55] If that was the case, it would then be plausible to suggest that Henry may have owned a set of this design, particularly since he owned weavings of all of Coecke's other major tapestry designs. Circumstantial support for this possibility is provided by a description of the decorations at

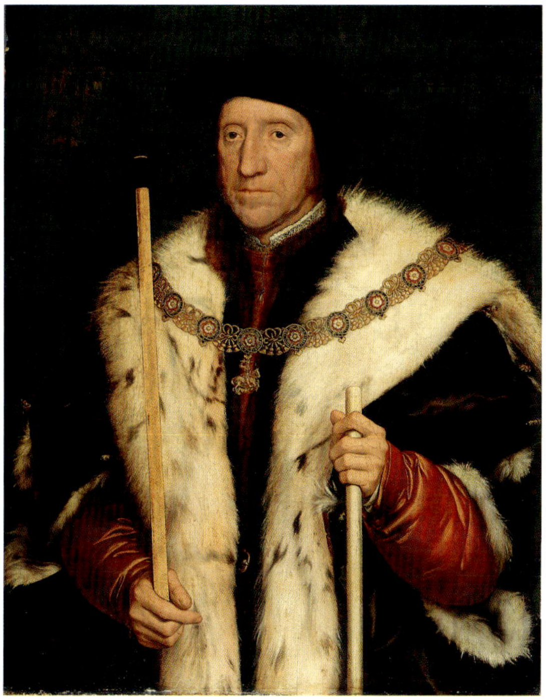

15.13 *Thomas Howard, Third Duke of Norfolk*, by Hans Holbein the Younger, 1539. Oil on panel, 80.3 x 61.6 cm. The Royal Collection

Hampton Court written in 1598 by Paul Hentzer. According to this, "All the other rooms, being very numerous, are adorned with tapestry of gold, silver and velvet, in some of which were history pieces; in others, Turkish and American dresses, all extremely natural."[56] In the absence of further evidence, however, it would be unwise to base too much weight on this description, which might have applied equally to several other design series, such as the so-called Morians, or Moors, probably acquired by Wolsey two decades earlier, some of which were still located at Hampton Court in 1659 (see below).

Final Appropriations

Although Henry's health was failing fast by late 1546, the tapestry collection continued to grow through appropriations resultant from the power struggle around the dying king. The principal victims of this maneuvering, Henry Howard, earl of Surrey, and his father, Thomas Howard, third duke of Norfolk (fig. 15.13), were accused of treason and committed to the Tower in December 1546. Surrey was executed on January 21, 1547, but the duke's life was saved by the king's timely death on the day that the act of his attainder was passed. He remained in the Tower throughout Edward's reign, and most of his valuable goods were appropriated for the Crown, as evidenced by the inventory of possessions drawn up at the time of his attainder. This lists 185 tapestries at Kenninghall alone, comprising some twenty or so sets of "arras" (thirty pieces), counterfeit arras (twenty-five pieces), tapestry (approximately ninety pieces) and verdure (approximately forty pieces).[57] According to annotations made to the inventory in the fifth year of Edward's reign, twenty-seven of these tapestries had been delivered to the king's use, seventy-five had been delivered to Princess Mary, fifty were to be sold, and about twelve pieces had been given to the duchess of Norfolk. That the 1547 inventory includes at least some of these pieces is demonstrated by the presence of six verdures "chequered with red and tawney" with the late Duke of Norfolk's arms in the middle at Nonsuch.[58] The description and dimensions correspond precisely with tapestries recorded at Kenninghall in 1546, which had been "delivered to Ed. Pigeon to the kinges Ma.ties use by Sir John Gates knight." Evidence of the lengths to which the Wardrobe officers would go in order to implement confiscations is given by the fate of another thirty or so tapestries that the inventory lists as belonging to the earl of Surrey in Boulogne and at the property of Saint Leonard's by Norwich. According to marginal annotations, these had been mortgaged to a Norwich merchant, and despite the enormous number of tapestries present in the royal collection by this date, Sir John Gate paid the merchant in order to redeem the tapestries "to his Maj. Use."[59]

PART VI

The 1547 Inventory

TAPESTRY IN PLACE

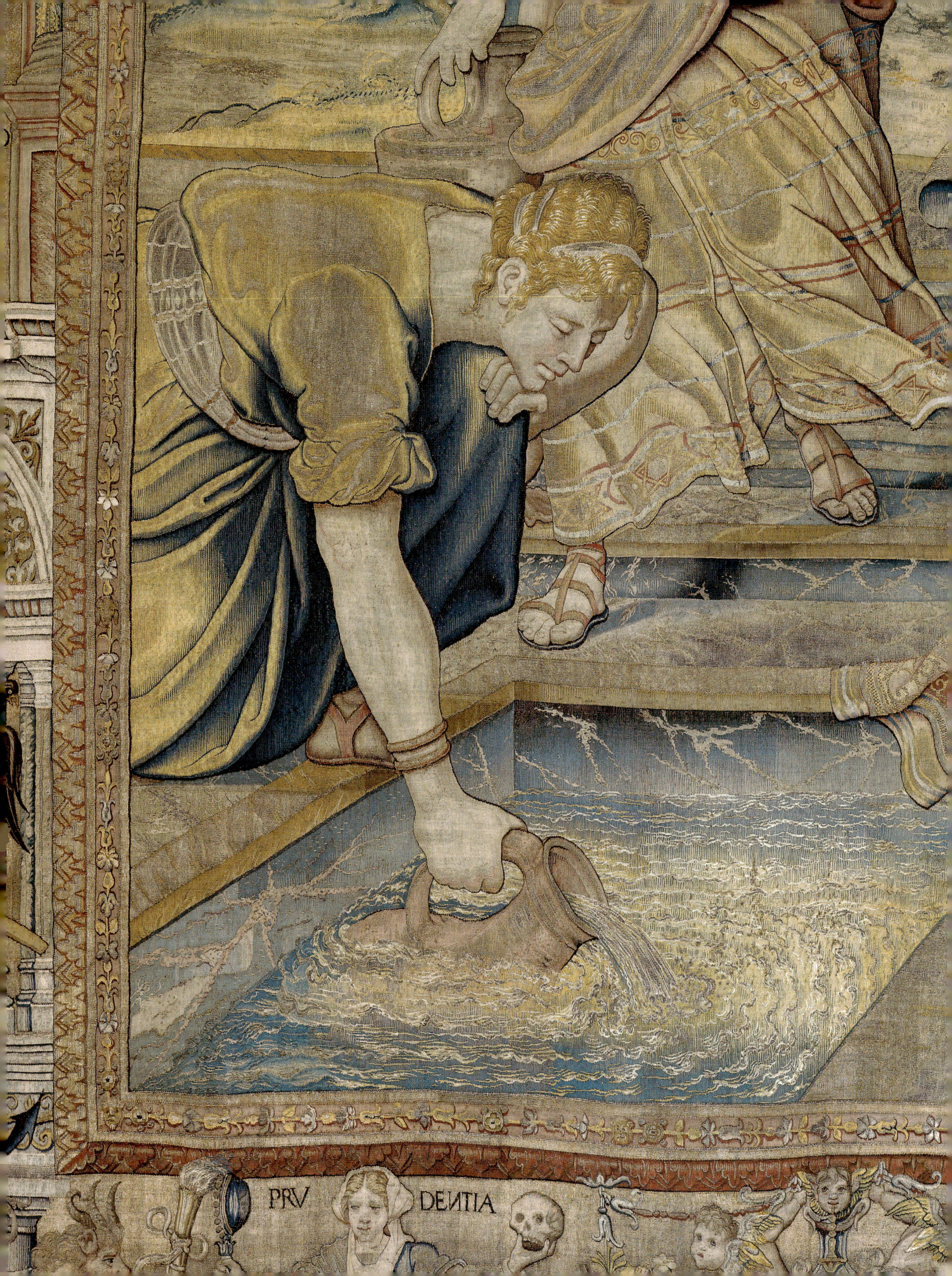
PRU DENTIA

CHAPTER 16

The Disposition and Typology of the Collection in 1547

Henry died on January 27, 1547. In a meeting held shortly after his death, the Privy Council decided not to sell objects from the royal collection to pay for legacies and other related expenses because the royal possessions were a crucial component in representing the wealth and power of England and their sale would imply weakness abroad.[1] But it was not until almost eight months after Henry's death on September 14, 1547, that letters patent were issued under the great seal for a complete inventory of the royal possessions to be compiled. This commission resulted in a series of smaller inventories relating to various aspects of the royal collections that were then bound in two large books that survive today in the Society of Antiquaries and the British Library and that have recently been the subject of a complete transcription and much study.[2] With close to eighteen thousand entries detailing approximately fifty thousand items, these volumes provide a unique picture of the royal possessions and works of art at the end of Henry's reign. Although the inventory has been central to the identification of many of the sets discussed in previous chapters, it deserves special consideration at this point, because it is the key to a final analysis of Henry's taste and motivation as a tapestry patron. In particular, it provides crucial information regarding the disposition of the tapestries, old and new, the typological character of the collection as a whole, and its material richness.

Disposition of the Collection

Henry had inherited twelve palaces and houses. By the time he died, he owned about fifty-five, with standing wardrobes maintained at sixteen of them. According to the 1547 inventory, the tapestries were divided among fourteen of these palaces and lesser residences and four removing wardrobes. Each tapestry is identified by subject or a brief description, and in almost every case the dimensions are also provided, measured to the nearest half "nail" (about an inch). As noted in the Introduction, excluding the hangings of embroidery and other precious textiles, the inventory details a total of about 2,450 tapestry wall hangings, including three hundred sets of three of more pieces.[3] In addition, the inventory also lists about 320 miscellaneous furnishing tapestries, mostly window pieces and counterpoints, giving a combined total of about 2,770 tapestry items.

With a few exceptions, the inventories for each palace wardrobe divided the tapestries according to quality and, to a lesser extent, usage, with the "arras" hangings distinguished from the tapestry hangings, and verdures also listed separately. Like the other items listed by the 1547 inventory, none of the tapestry items were valued because the inventory was not compiled for the purposes of a sale, but the officers responsible for making the inventories were, by and large, punctilious in making the distinction between "arras" and tapestry. For example, the Woodstock inventory includes one item described as a "piece of old Arras named in tholde booke but Tapistre" and another as a "verye olde pece of tapestrie mencioned in tholde booke for Arras."[4] The distinction observed in Wolsey's inventory between "arras," "counterfeit arras," and tapestry is not followed in the 1547 inventory, and all Wolsey's "counterfeit arras" hangings that

Detail of fig. 14.16

can be recognized are now listed as tapestry. The reason for this shift is probably simple. In Wolsey's inventory, which included only a relatively small proportion of "arras" tapestries, the important distinction was between those woven with silk and those woven in wool alone. By contrast, in Henry's collection, which numbered more than 330 "arras" tapestries, the crucial qualitative distinction was between those woven with and without gold thread.

None of the inventories for the main royal residences specify locations for the tapestries, but while some of the old or coarser pieces may have been used with considerable freedom because they were too faded or damaged to have much worth, and although the large "arras" sets at the Tower may have been used ad hoc in a variety of locations, a significant proportion of the rest of the collection was probably associated with specific locations either by design or by tradition. This assumption is based on analogy with Wolsey's purchases, many of which were for particular locations (not that these were all maintained under Henry), and by evidence relating to the royal collection itself. For example, as detailed above, before he left for the Netherlands in 1516, James Chapell traveled to Newhall to measure the rooms for which he was purchasing tapestries. Similarly, the tapestries supplied for the duke of Richmond in 1525 were intended for distinct chambers, as were those supplied for Prince Edward in 1538–39.[5] A few years later, the Great Wardrobe accounts for 1543–44 record payment to the tailors for lining twelve pieces of "good tapestry for the king's private apartment" at Hampton Court.[6] Yet none of these locations are mentioned in subsequent inventories. Two of the few entries in the 1547 inventory that do mention locations occur in the Greenwich section, where one tapestry was described as "a pece for the Gallerye at the neyther ende of the halle" and another group of twenty-five were said to be "parcell of the peces provided for the longe gallery towardes the Fryers at Richemounte."[7] But again, no mention is made in the Richmond section of the inventory to corresponding pieces for the gallery in question. Rather than assuming that these Greenwich tapestries were among the only site-specific items in the collection, it seems better to assume that their locations were recorded because they were not hanging in their accustomed position. It is unclear why the officers responsible for the 1547 inventory did not give location information, but this may have been perceived as an irrelevance in the context of an inventory whose main purpose was to assess the holdings of the collection.

In passing, it is interesting to note that this reference to tapestries intended for the long gallery at Richmond is indicative of a broader trend. Much has been written about the development of the gallery as an architectural feature of the grand houses of the early sixteenth century, providing a space for retreat, contemplation, and play. Similarly, historians of British patronage have written at length about the Elizabethan vogue for displaying sequences of portraits of famous personages in galleries.[8] But an aspect of this development that has gone largely unremarked is that the main decorative component of the grand galleries of the sixteenth century were the tapestries with which they were hung. The earliest evidence of this vogue dates from 1517, when Henry purchased "arras" tapestries for the gallery at Greenwich in 1517. Shortly thereafter, Wolsey ordered sets of tapestry for his galleries at York Place and Hampton Court. Subsequent citations in the various royal inventories suggest that this became a widespread practice. In 1535, the gallery at Hackney was hung with fourteen pieces of "counterfeit arras," and in addition to the items cited above in relation to Richmond, the 1547 inventory refers to ten verdures "that dyd hange in the quenes galerye."[9] In short, it seems that an important factor in the development of the galleries of the day was the opportunity they provided for the display of the owner's finest tapestry hangings.

Another issue that the inventory does not elucidate is the extent to which Henry's palaces were stripped of their hangings following the departure of the court. The finest pieces were certainly kept in storage and only brought out for more important events. Whether pieces of more moderate quality hung on a quotidian basis is unclear, but in view of the large numbers of tapestries recorded by the 1547 inventory it is certainly possible that this was the case, at least toward the end of the reign, a situation that would have been analogous to the decoration of Wolsey's palaces with old and secondhand tapestries on "inferior days."[10] Indeed, many of the moderate-quality tapestries listed in the inventory were presumably hanging in situ when the inventory was compiled. Although we therefore lack evidence as to what tapestries were hanging and where, and which were in storage, the inventory nonetheless provides a fascinating record of the division of the collection among the palaces in 1547 and the basis for some general conclusions about the character of the decorations at each.

Windsor and Richmond

Perhaps unsurprisingly, most of the older tapestries remained at the medieval palaces with which they had been long associated by tradition. This was particularly the case with Windsor (fig. 16.1). Still essentially a relatively uncomfortable medieval castle, this was primarily used in the summer months for hunting. The collection here was small in proportion to those at Whitehall and Hampton Court, numbering only one hundred panels.[11] However, these comprised some of the finest antique "arras" hangings in the collection, including the *Trinity and the Assumption of the Virgin* and the *"Sepulchre of our lorde,"* probably to be identified with panels given to Richard II by Philip the Bold, and the six rich panels of *Attorney* that, as suggested above, may have been the remnants of the *Jousts of Saint Denis* set taken from the French royal collection in the 1420s by the duke of Bedford. That was certainly the origin of the cloth of estate, comprising a celure and tester, of "King Clovis of France with fleur de lys." Other early-fifteenth-century "arras" panels included three of *Charlemagne,* two of *Mountalbon,* probably also from a Charlemagne series, and another panel of "youth cities and Townes." "Arras" sets of *Esther and Ahasuerus* and the *Siege of Jerusalem* can be identified as having been

16.1 *Bird's-eye view of Windsor Castle from the South-East* by Wenceslaus Hollar. Published in Elias Ashmole's *The institution, laws and ceremonies of the most noble Order of the Garter,* London, 1672

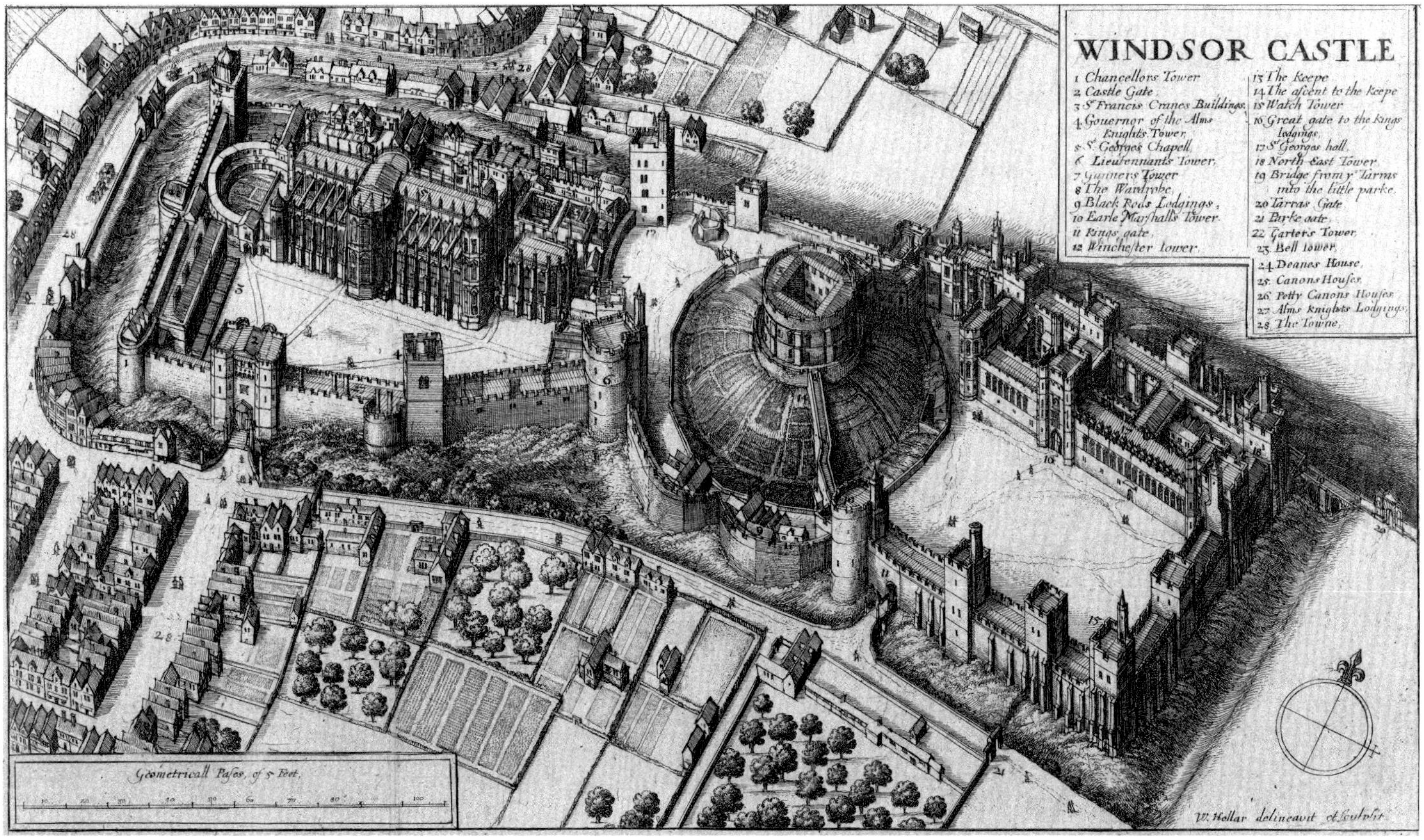

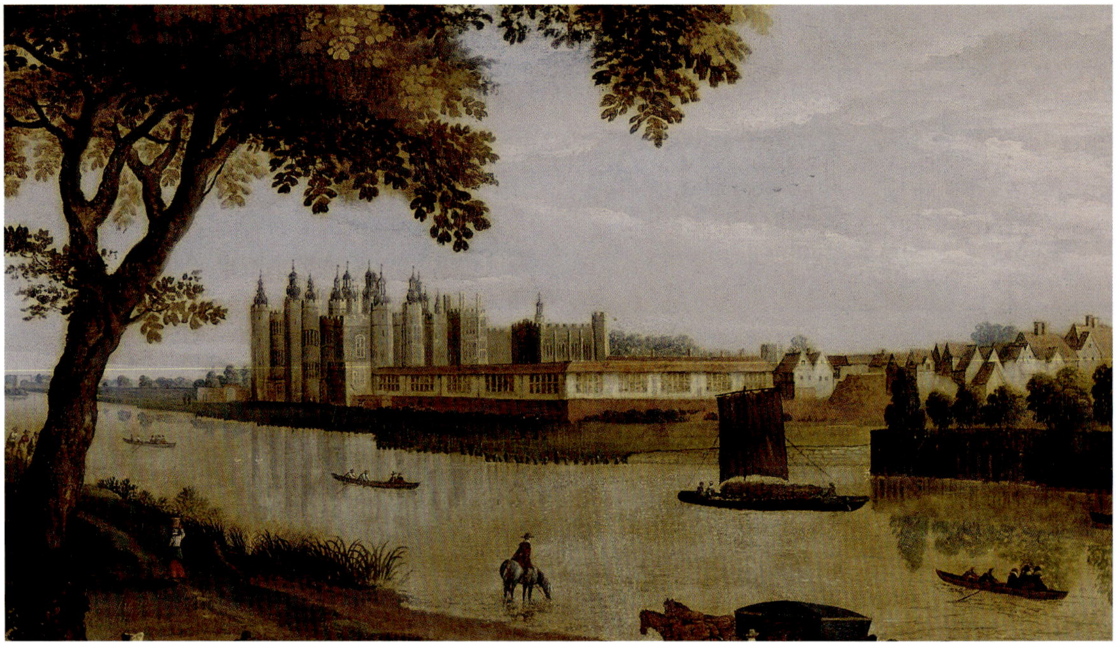

16.2 *Richmond Palace from the South* (detail) by an unidentified 17th-c. artist. Oil on canvas, 151 x 304 cm. The Fitzwilliam Museum, Cambridge

supplied to Edward IV and Henry VII by Pasquier Grenier. Regarding the tapestries, most of the storiated sets were also defined as old, including six panels of *David* and the Grenier *Trojan War* set. The most modern ensemble at Windsor was of the *Triumphs,* possibly part of the fine Petrarchan set acquired by Wolsey in 1520. The absence of any more modern pieces at Windsor suggests that, by a combination of heritage and choice, the castle was hung with older tapestries that accentuated its atmosphere of age and tradition.

While the Windsor Wardrobe contained the most archaic of the hangings, those at Richmond (fig. 16.2) were also predominantly antique, but the material quality of the tapestries was lower, for only eight of the 190 or so hangings were described as "arras."[12] This perhaps reflects the lesser use that Henry made of Richmond during his later reign; during the first twenty years of his reign he stayed there more than fifty times, but only six times during the 1530s and 1540s. The "arras" hangings included several pieces that probably dated from the early fifteenth century, including two pieces of "Cressent," two of *Bevis of Hampton* and single panels of the *Root of Jesse, Nebuchadnezzar,* and the *Siege of Jerusalem.* A wide "arras" panel of the

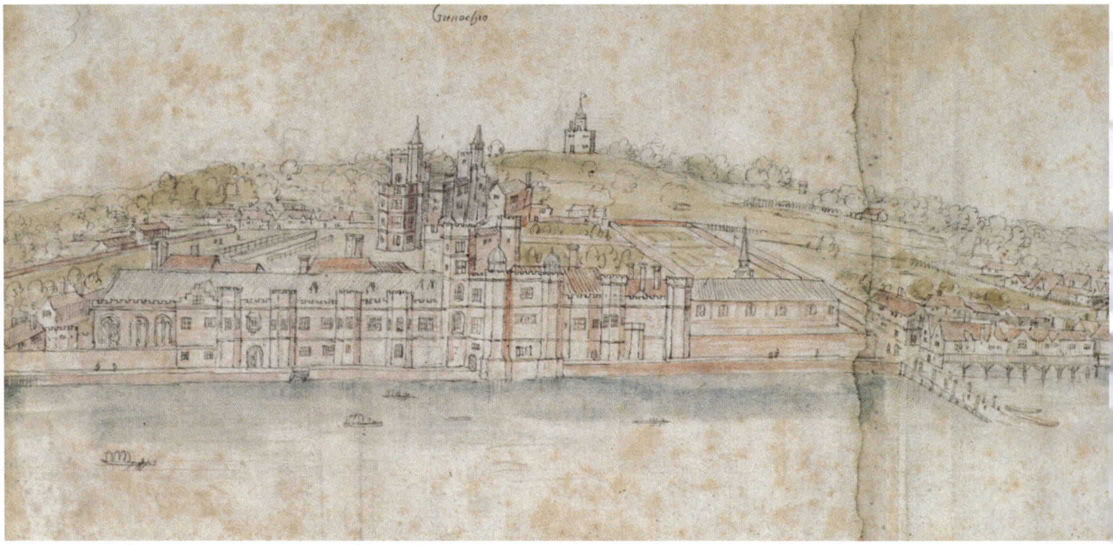

16.3 *Greenwich Palace from the North Bank of the Thames* (detail) by A. van den Wyngaerde, 1558. Pen and brown ink and watercolor over black chalk, 29.4 x 120.6 cm. Ashmolean Museum, Oxford

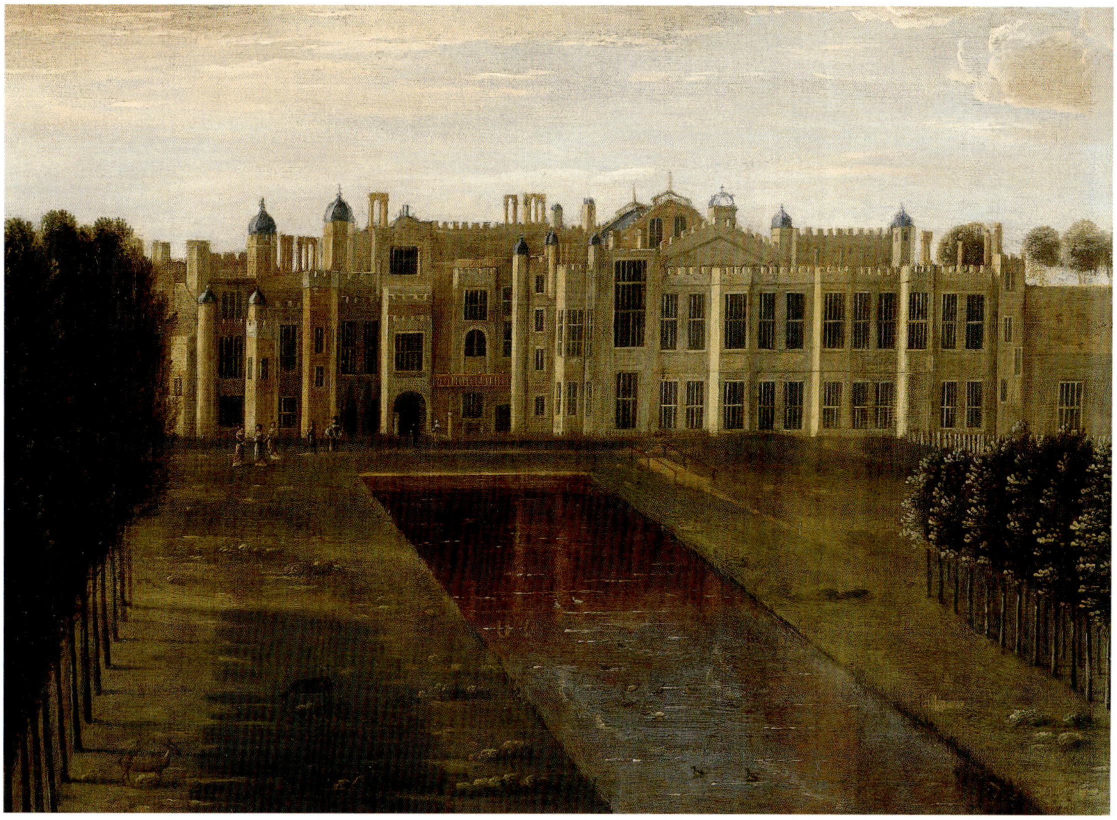

16.4 *Hampton Court Palace from the East* (detail) by Hendrick Danckerts, ca. 1665. Oil on canvas, 102.5 x 99.7 cm. The Royal Collection

Story of Trajan had similar dimensions to the Bern tapestry of this subject and can thus be dated to the third quarter of the fifteenth century. Some of the tapestries were similarly antique, including early- and mid-fifteenth-century panels of the *Transfiguration,* the *Combat of Virtue and Vice,* the *Old Law,* and the *Bishop of Rome and the Emperor.* The numerical majority of the tapestry sets at Richmond depicted scenes of hawking and hunting and verdure. Narrative sets included the *Story of Brutus,* probably acquired by Edward IV. The most enigmatic set at Richmond was the seven-piece *Story of Jupiter,* with widths ranging from eight and a half yards to four yards, suggesting that it had been made for a specific location. As noted above, it is uncertain whether this was an antique set or a more recent acquisition by Henry VIII.

Greenwich, Hampton Court, Whitehall, and the Tower

Where the majority of the hangings at Windsor and Richmond were medieval in character, those at the other main residences reflected a greater mix of old and new, with the valuable new tapestries deposited at the palaces of greatest importance. The wardrobe at Greenwich (fig. 16.3), Henry's birthplace and favorite palace for much of his reign, included two hundred or so tapestries, of which twenty-seven were "arras."[13] These included antique celure and tester panels of *Youth* that hung in the great hall and presumably belonged to the same ensemble of which one wall hanging remained at Windsor. More recent acquisitions included the sets of *Saint John* and *David* purchased from Pieter van Aelst in 1517 and/or 1520 and six "arras" pieces of *Meleager,* probably an acquisition of the 1510s or 1520s. The tapestries also included a number of old sets such as six panels of "greate hawking," and more recent acquisitions such as the *Romulus and Remus* set purchased from Gresham in 1529 and the *Saint Paul, Prodigal Son, David,* and *Passion* sets acquired in the late 1540s.

Hampton Court, Henry's main entertainment complex (fig. 16.4), was the most magnificently furnished of all the residential palaces, with approximately 430 hangings.[14] Of these, about 120 were "arras," deriving from more than twenty sets, while the tapestries numbered over two hundred panels from more than thirty-two sets. There were also about sixty verdure tapestries and about fifty furnishing panels. The "arras" tapestries included a number of fifteenth-century celure and tester ensembles, several of which had passed through Wolsey's collection as royal perquisites. In addition, there were several antique ensembles that had evidently been relocated to Hampton Court after it came to Henry's possession. These included the ten-piece set with heraldic devices of Charles VI, taken from the French royal collection by the duke of Bedford in the 1420s, and six pieces of the *Beatitudes* that had originally been one long panel measuring twenty-four yards in width. The *Beatitudes* is not identifiable in earlier inventories but presumably depicted images of the blessed citizens of the Kingdom of Heaven, as described by Christ in his Sermon on the Mount. The "arras" panels of *Henry VII Defeating Richard III* and the putative Tudor marriage panel were now also located at Hampton Court, as was the eleven-piece *Old and New Law,* probably acquired during Henry VII's reign.

Of more recent origin, many of Wolsey's best tapestries also remained at Hampton Court, including five of the *Triumphs* he had purchased and about fifteen Old Testament sets equipped with borders of his coat of arms. In all likelihood, these sets continued in use in the rooms he built around the inner and outer courtyards. The most impressive hangings at Hampton Court were the enormous "arras" sets that Henry purchased during the late 1530s and early 1540s for the new great hall and state rooms constructed during those years, namely those of *Paul, Joshua, Abraham,* and *Caesar*. And last, as already noted, the latest additions to Hampton Court included the "arras" sets of *Romulus and Remus* and *Tobias* provided by, respectively, Pieter van de Walle and Erasmus Schets.

The size of the collection and, literally, of many of the sets at Hampton Court, reflects how extensively Henry had expanded the palace, already large by the end of Wolsey's tenure, as a center for the grandest court entertainments during the 1530s. Between 1533 and 1538, enormous new ranges of apartments had been constructed west of Wolsey's Fountain Court, providing parallel royal apartments for the king and queen.[15] These expansions provide the likely explanation for the relocation of many antique textiles from Windsor to Hampton Court during the mid-1530s, as well as the subsequent commissions that came to fruition with the *Saint Paul, Joshua, Abraham, Caesar, Tobias,* and *Romulus and Remus* "arras" sets.

In contrast to Hampton Court, Whitehall, or the new palace of Westminster (see figs. 13.3, 13.13), Henry's main residence in central London, was more constricted by the scale of its historic buildings, which explains the lesser number of large "arras" hangings at this location. The number was additionally depleted in 1547 because the *Acts* and *Antiques* sets were relocated to the Tower Wardrobe following Edward's accession. The reason for this transfer is undocumented, but it may reflect the fact that these sets were particularly associated with parts of the palace occupied by Henry until his death. The Whitehall inventory lists thirty-seven "arras" tapestries and approximately two hundred figurative tapestries.[16] About half of the "arras" hangings were of relatively small dimension and featured devotional subjects suitable for use as altar frontals or antependia. Several of Wolsey's "arras" panels can be recognized, including his two panels of *Saint Jerome* and his two "arras" panels of the *Justice of Trajan*. Of greater size were five "arras" panels of *David,* perhaps to be identified with the purchase made by Henry in spring 1520.

The tapestry hangings at Whitehall also reflected the varied history of the collection.[17] Large panels of *Honor* and the *Governor,* both measuring seventeen yards in width, can be identified as of early-fifteenth-century origin, while eight panels of *Hector* may also have dated from this period. Other sets originated from Wolsey's ownership of the palace, including two ensembles of *Triumphs,* one of the *Nine Worthies,* a large set of twenty pieces of

Joseph, and another twelve of *Christ and Mary.* It seems likely that these would have remained in association with areas built by Wolsey during the late 1510s. Regarding Henry's purchases, a ten-piece set of *Jacob* can be identified as a weaving of the Van Orley design of this subject and, thus, as an acquisition made in the early to mid-1530s. The new sets of tapestry provided for Henry in the late 1530s are all readily identifiable toward the end of the 1547 inventory, including those of *Vulcan and Venus, Helen and Paris, Meleager,* the *Sabines,* the *Seven Virtues, Ruth,* the *King of Surrey* (sic), the *Story of the Prodigal Son, Sin and Virtue,* and *Hercules.* These presumably formed the decorations of rooms and apartments redecorated for Henry at Whitehall during the late 1530s and early 1540s.

As just noted, the *Acts* and *Antiques* sets were relocated to the Tower Wardrobe following Henry's death, where they joined a deposit of the finest tapestries in the collection. Indeed, the Tower (see fig. 18.6) was to remain the main repository for the Great Wardrobe until the Commonwealth sale a century later. Approximately 170 tapestries are recorded at this location, of which just over one hundred were defined as "arras."[18] These included both antique and modern pieces. Among the antique tapestries were two large panels of *Saint George,* one of which may have been identical with that first recorded in the collection of the duke of Gloucester in the late fourteenth century and the other the panel purchased by Henry VI in 1444. There were also panels described as the *Eight Kings* and the *Ten Kings of France,* the *Eight Kings* perhaps one of the genealogical tapestries purchased by Richard II, the *Ten Kings* perhaps the "Twelve peers" first recorded in Henry IV's collection in 1413. Large "arras" sets of *Samson* and the *Boucherons* (woodcutters) may have dated from Edward IV's reign, as was certainly the case with a large panel of "Roses and Suns" defined as made for Edward IV. The older "arras" pieces also included a large panel of *Herkinbald* of similar dimensions to the Bern *Justice of Trajan and Herkinbald* (the dimensions were different from those listed at Richmond, so this was evidently a second rich piece of the same subject).[19] More recent acquisitions included the nine-piece, gold-ground verdure purchased from Pieter van Aelst in 1519–20, the ten-piece *David* purchased from Gresham in 1528, the four-piece Van Orley *Passion* of ca. 1528, the *Seven Deadly Sins* acquired in 1535–36, the *Twelve Months* of the late 1530s, and the *Acts* and *Antiques* of 1542. The extent to which the "arras" sets at the Tower were considered moveable properties is revealed by the thirty-nine canvas bags in which "to putte fyne Arras" also listed among the wardrobe contents. Evidently, these were to protect the hangings during transportation.[20]

Other Suburban and Provincial Palaces and Residences

Although the most important tapestries in the collection were located at Windsor, Richmond, Greenwich, Hampton Court, Whitehall, and the Tower, a significant number were located at the lesser palaces that Henry had inherited, or those that had been outfitted or built for him in his reign. As we have seen, Henry's most northernmost residence, Nottingham Castle, had been prepared with tapestries in 1511, and a small but interesting collection of about fifty tapestries remained there in 1547.[21] These included three early-fifteenth-century panels of "Charlemagne of Amys and Amilis," probably deriving from Richard II's collection, and other early-fifteenth-century panels depicting *Solomon, Abraham,* and the *Story of the Trojan War.*

Woodstock, the popular destination for royal hunting parties during the fifteenth and early sixteenth centuries, had declined in significance during Henry's reign and that probably explains the relatively small collection of seventy tapestries located there.[22] These included six "arras" panels all apparently dating from the early fifteenth century, including two of *Charlemagne,* two of knights jousting, made from a single large panel that had been cut in two, and a very wide panel of the *Crucifixion and the Assumption of the Virgin.* With the exception of one set of *Moses,* almost all the other tapestry hangings depicted hunting and genre subjects,

16.5 *Nonsuch Palace from the North-West* (detail) by an unidentified artist, ca. 1620. Oil on panel, 152 x 302.5 cm. The Fitzwilliam Museum, Cambridge

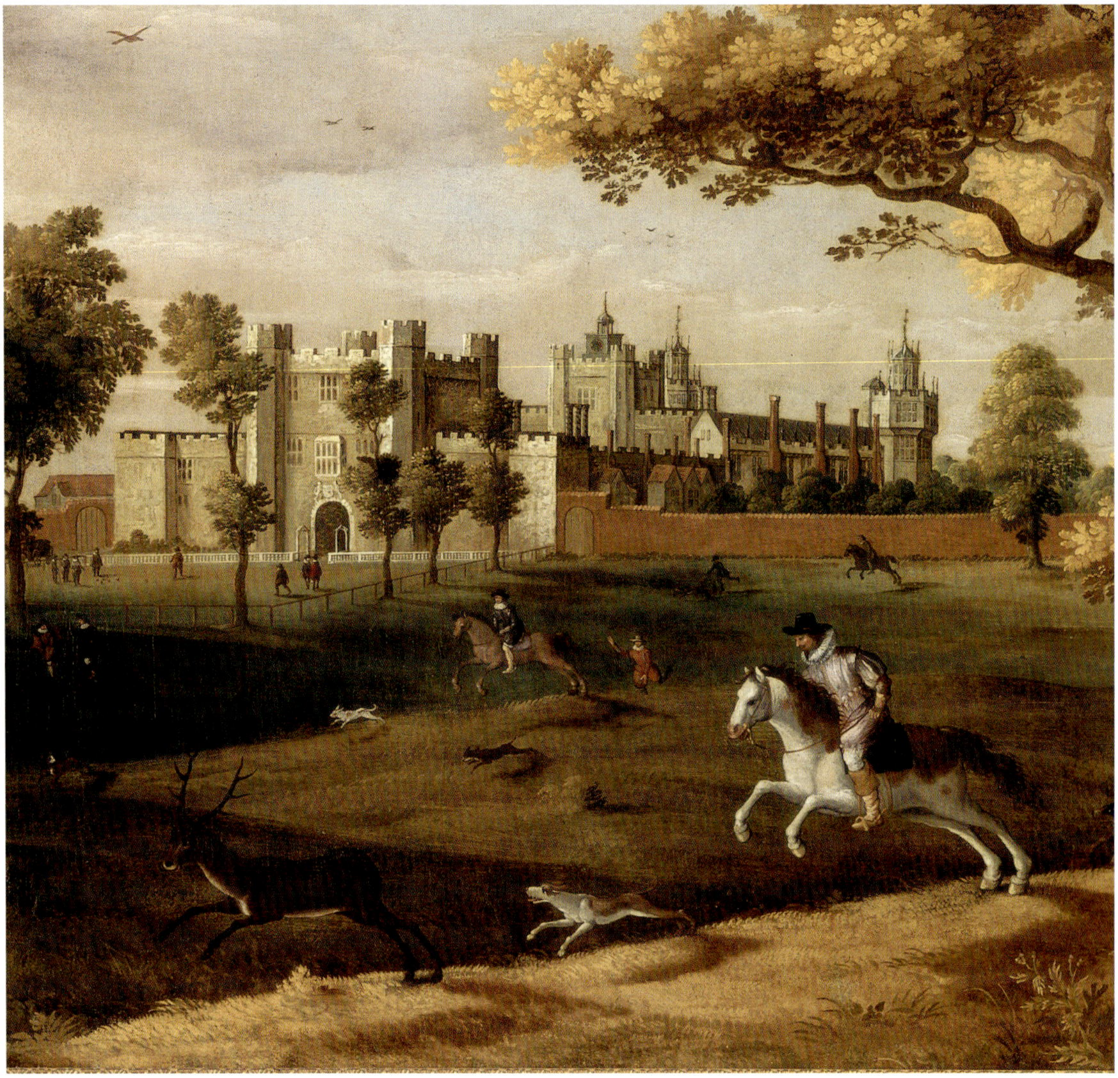

appropriate to the principal function of the palace. More than half of the tapestries at Woodstock were verdures.

Oatlands, prepared during the late 1530s in anticipation of the arrival of Anne of Cleves, was abundantly equipped with moderate-quality tapestries, much as Newhall had been back in the late 1520s. Indeed, many of the tapestries at Oatlands may have come from Newhall, which, at the time of the 1547 inventory, had been entirely stripped of its tapestry hangings. The inventory lists approximately four hundred tapestries of a predominantly decorative character, with a large proportion comprising hunting scenes and verdures.[23] Only about ten of the fifty or so sets listed depicted narrative subjects. These included a large ensemble of more than twenty tapestries of the *Prodigal Son*, a set of *Cupid*, one of *Solomon*, two ensembles of *Joseph and Jacob*, and a twelve-piece set of *Hercules*.

In contrast to Oatlands, the other major construction project of the later years of Henry's reign, Nonsuch Palace (fig. 16.5; see also figs. 13.23, 13.24), had relatively few tapestries, probably a reflection of the palace's small size and its interior plasterwork decorations, which must have limited the space available for tapestry displays.[24] More than two-thirds of the eighty tapestries listed at Nonsuch were verdures. Only two "arras" panels were listed there, one a small devotional panel of the *Passion*, the other an old piece of unspecified subject. Although unidentified, the fact that this panel had been chosen for display at this location suggests that it may have been a piece of historic or iconographic significance to Henry. One other item of note at Nonsuch was a small cupboard carpet of tapestry with "a Quenes hed and this scrypture by it Quene Katheryne of Englonde."[25] Considering the location and the fact that this object must have been introduced during the 1540s, it seems probable that this must have been a portrayal of Catherine Parr, perhaps created as a New Year's Day gift by the royal arras maker.

Several other residences listed in the 1547 inventory had come to Henry through appropriation, and the tapestries at these locations appear to have been those with which they were already equipped. The More, for example, was decorated with approximately 150 tapestries, of which more than two-thirds came from Wolsey's collection. Many still carried his coat of arms and had evidently been relocated from Hampton Court and Whitehall after the compilation of the 1522 inventory.[26] Only four antique "arras" panels were listed there, one of *Charlemagne,* two of "duke Brye," presumably identical with the large panel of the Duke of Bry and "Gyaunte Orible" listed in Wolsey's inventory twenty-five years before, and one from the early-fifteenth-century ensemble depicting birds with the "banners of tharmes of Englonde about ther neckes." As at Hampton Court, several of these can be identified as having passed through Wolsey's hands as perquisites. This may also have been the origin of the most intriguing of the tapestries at The More, a four-piece set of *Arthur* of which nothing more is known.

Small tapestry collections were also listed at Beddington, confiscated from Sir Nicholas Carew in 1539—approximately forty-five tapestries—and the manor of Saint John's in Clerkenwell, the former monastic property of the Knights of Saint John of Jerusalem—three pieces of unidentified old "arras" and about forty-five tapestries.[27]

The Removing Wardrobes

Brief mention should also be made of the four removing wardrobes recorded by the 1547 inventory. The first of these was that attendant on King Edward when he was prince and has already been the subject of discussion. It included just over one hundred tapestries of which only one ensemble, the *Three Estates,* was specified as "arras."[28] All the rest were tapestries and verdures. The storiated tapestries included a number of large, single panels whose dimensions and subjects indicate that they were of fifteenth-century origin, including the *Dome* (sic), the *Salutation of the Virgin,* and the *City of Peace.* The Prince's Wardrobe also included at least two sets that dated from the time of Edward IV and Henry VII, namely, the eight-piece *Story of Thebes* purchased by Edward IV, now said to be in very poor condition, and four panels of the *Story of Troy* whose dimensions suggest that they were duplicates of, but not identical to, the set purchased by Henry VII and then at Windsor. The Prince's Wardrobe also included a six-piece set of the *City of Ladies.*

The second removing wardrobe detailed in the 1547 inventory is specified as "the Guarderobe attendaunt at the Courte uppon the kinges moste Roiall parsonne."[29] Given the date of the inventory, this personage was probably Edward, as one would expect anything to do with Henry to be identified as the property of the "late king" (which is not to say that several of the sets listed in this wardrobe may not formerly have been in the removing wardrobe attendant on Henry). This supposition is supported by the fact that the wardrobe did not include any of the religious subjects that were so closely associated with Henry by the end of his reign. Four sets of narrative hangings are specified, respectively, *Hercules, Lady Fame, Charlemagne,* and "Turques." Two other tapestry sets depicted heraldic matter. The wardrobe also included five sets of verdure hangings and thirty-eight tapestry counterpoints.

Regarding the wardrobes designated for Princess Mary and Princess Elizabeth, these were both said to have been delivered after the death of Henry VIII, and as such, it is in these categories that there may be some duplication with tapestries listed in other sections of the inventory. Equally, annotations in the inventory of the duke of Norfolk indicate that many of his best sets were delivered to Princess Mary's Wardrobe in 1547, and this appears to be the origin of a significant portion of the verdures and moderate-quality items subsequently listed there. At any rate, Mary's Wardrobe consisted of one hundred tapestries, including eight ensembles of narrative tapestry.[30] Those responsible for compiling the inventory were unsure of the subjects, relying instead on brief descriptions that are inadequate to provide modern identifications. The largest ensemble in her wardrobe depicted a religious allegory of apocalyptic character.

Finally, the wardrobe provided to Princess Elizabeth comprised about 115 tapestries, including two sets of narrative subjects depicting *Hercules* and *Triumphs*.[31] All the other tapestries supplied to Elizabeth depicted genre and hunting scenes or verdures.

Typological Analysis of the Royal Tapestry Collection in 1547

The 1547 inventory provides fascinating evidence of the physical disposition of the collection at Henry's death, but the information it provides about the typology of the collection is no less interesting. Analysis reveals that by 1547 approximately a third of the collection, 860 tapestries, were verdures of various kinds and age. These comprised 630 wall hangings, 120 counterpoints, and 110 miscellaneous furnishing tapestries. A further two hundred or so wall hangings depicted genre and hunting scenes. As we have seen in previous discussion, such hangings were traditionally used in rooms and apartments intended for informal and private use, or rooms of lesser social status, although there were certainly exceptions to this rule, such as the "arras" "Boucherons" that Henry inherited and the gold-ground verdure he purchased from Pieter van Aelst in 1519–20. Generally speaking, however, the majority of the tapestries of this kind acquired during Henry's reign were likely purchased by wardrobe officers for relatively quotidian use.

Of the remaining twelve hundred or so storiated wall hangings in the collection, approximately half, 530 pieces, represented religious subjects.

Of these, about three hundred depicted Old Testament themes. These comprised about sixty ensembles of two or more pieces of which approximately half were from Wolsey's collection. Of the sixty-seven "arras" tapestries in the Old Testament category, Henry purchased at least fifty, including three *David* sets and the *Abraham, Joshua,* and *Tobias* sets. Henry's interest in David was especially evident. Besides the three "arras" sets of the subject that he purchased in 1517, 1520, and 1528, and a pair of antique "arras" panels of *David and Absolom,* seven other tapestry sets, comprising seventy tapestries in total, were specifically identified as of the *Story of David*. Of the other religious role models represented in the collection, the most common were Jacob and/or Joseph (ten sets), Samuel and Saul (seventeen tapestries from various ensembles), Solomon (twenty-eight tapestries from at least six ensembles), and Esther (twenty-five tapestries from seven sets).

Scenes from the New Testament or the lives of the saints featured in 230 tapestries. Forty panels, many of them single devotional pieces, depicted the Virgin and infancy of Christ, while approximately seventy-five depicted *Passion* subjects. These categories included a high proportion of "arras" tapestries. About ten sets, comprising some fifty or so tapestries, featured narratives based on the lives of the saints, including the "arras" sets of *John,* the *Acts of the Apostles* and *Paul,* certainly purchased by Henry. About ten sets of tapestry depicted the *Story of the Prodigal Son*.

If religious subjects accounted for approximately half of the storiated tapestries in the collection, classical subjects also accounted for a significant portion. Approximately seventeen sets, comprising about 110 hangings, depicted classical histories or historical legend. Six of these, some forty tapestries, were concerned with the Trojan War. None were of "arras," and only one, the *Paris and Helen* set, was certainly purchased by Henry. In contrast, of the nine sets representing subjects related to Roman history, most were purchased by Henry VIII, including the "arras" *Dido and Aeneas, Romulus and Remus,* and *Caesar* sets and the tapestry sets of *Romulus and Remus* and the *Sabines.* Other subjects drawn from classical history that can possibly be identified as acquisitions made during Henry's reign included sets of *Octavian, Hannibal,* and, certainly a Henrician purchase, *Cyrus.*

Besides his taste for classical history, Henry evidently had considerable interest in subjects drawn from classical mythology. Approximately 120 tapestries from about twenty sets depicted subjects drawn from classical mythology (this number excludes subjects drawn from the *Iliad* and *Aeniad,* already included in the Trojan War and foundation of Rome categories mentioned above). While a number of these certainly dated from the fifteenth century, more than two-thirds were acquisitions of Henry's reign. Of these, two sets, a *Story of Meleager* (Greenwich) and the *Antiques,* were "arras," the first probably and the second certainly purchased by Henry. By far the most popular theme was *Hercules,* represented by nine sets, comprising about fifty-four tapestries. As we have seen, classical subjects also formed a significant proportion of the new tapestries delivered to Whitehall during the late 1530s and early 1540s, including subjects such as *Meleager* and *Vulcan and Venus.*

Henry's interest in classical history and mythology and the purchases he made of such subjects stand in contrast to the lack of additions in the category of medieval histories and romances that had formed such an important part of the subject matter of the royal collection during the fourteenth and fifteenth centuries. French history or legend, predominantly of Charlemagne, featured in about twenty-five "arras" and tapestry panels, all of which appear to have dated from the fifteenth century. Although both Buckingham and Wolsey acquired sets of the *Nine Worthies,* this was not a subject Henry himself purchased. English legend featured only in a number of older, large "arras" panels, such as the *Eight Kings* and a pair of *Bevis of Hampton,* and two tapestry sets, one of *Brutus* and one of *Arthur.* Again, with the exception of Henry VII's dynastic panels, all the others appear to have been of fifteenth- or very early sixteenth-century origin. Although Henry made no investment in sets of these subjects, the antique pieces evidently continued to enjoy considerable prestige.

The allegorical subjects that made up such an important part of the canon of fifteenth- and early-sixteenth-century taste, particularly those featuring Vices and Virtues, also seem to have maintained their significance during Henry's reign. About 180 of Henry's tapestries, fifty of them "arras," depicted allegorical subjects. At least half the "arras" pieces were of fifteenth-century origin, and several evidently continued to play an important role in court iconography, both in the context of the residential palaces and the wardrobes appointed to the royal children. Henry's key identifiable acquisitions were the "arras" sets of the *Three Fates,* the *Twelve Months,* and the *Seven Deadly Sins.* In addition, allegorical tapestries of the *Seven Virtues* and *Sin and Virtue* were certainly purchased for Whitehall during the late 1530s.

Last, it should be noted that the 1547 inventory lists only approximately thirty tapestries deriving from sets with heraldic or emblematic devices, and about two-thirds of these dated from the fifteenth or early sixteenth centuries. As already noted in the context of the work of the royal arras maker, the explanation for the relatively small number of heraldic tapestries in the collection is the ease with which such hangings could be prepared by the embroiderers attached to the Royal Wardrobe.

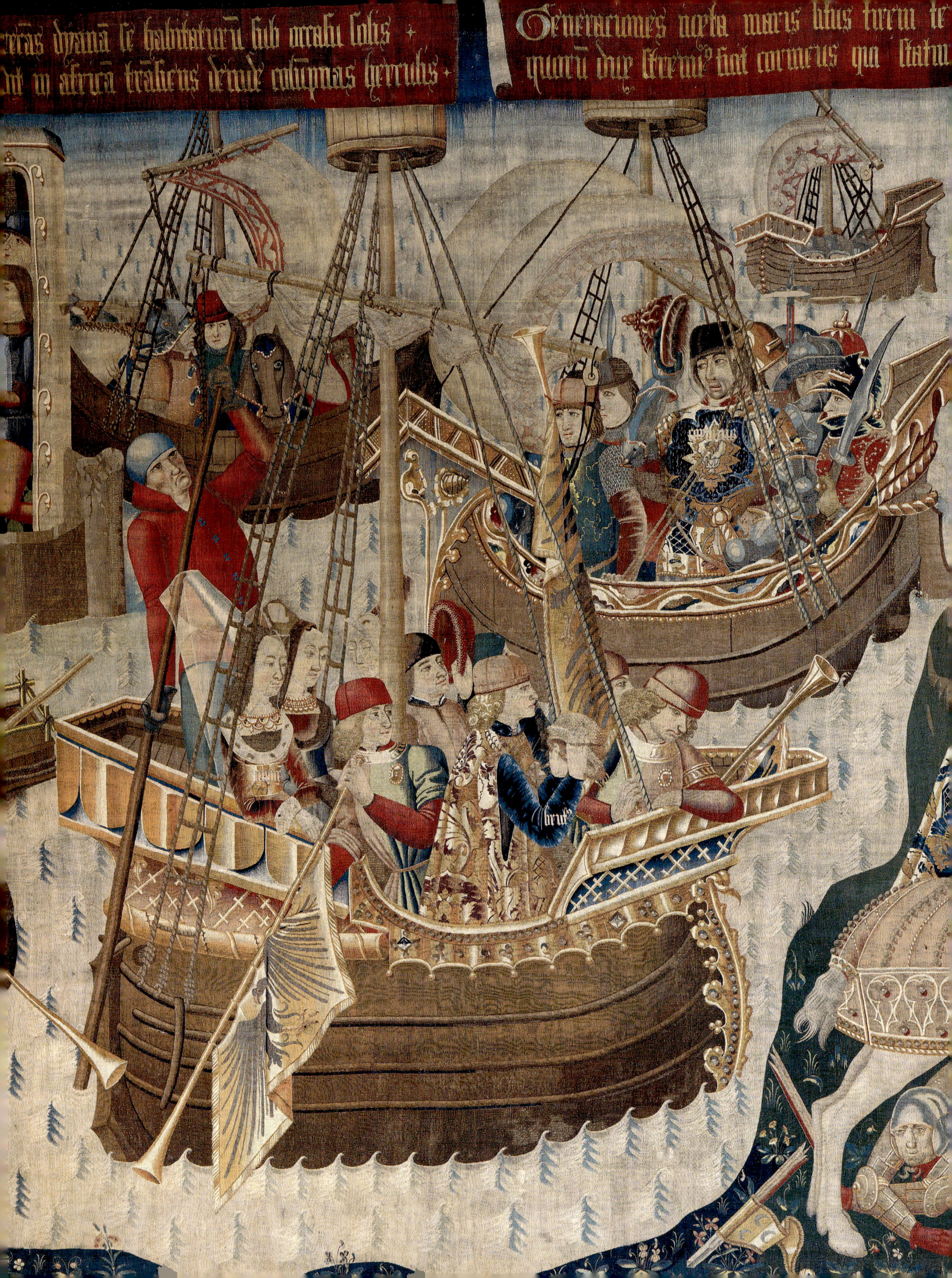

CHAPTER 17

Taste and Perception

Detail of fig. 3.14

Appreciation and Status of the Older Tapestries

As the foregoing survey suggests, one of the most striking issues that emerges from the 1547 inventory is how extensively older hangings continued to provide the main decorations at Windsor and Richmond, with some especially historic items being located at Greenwich, Whitehall, Hampton Court, and the Tower. These were not, of course, the faded, fragmentary objects that survive today from the fourteenth and fifteenth centuries. Frequent usage undoubtedly took a heavy toll, particularly if the tapestries were exposed to bright sunshine or excessive smoke. Equally, many of the finer pieces that were used only for special occasions and had been carefully repaired may still have been in relatively good condition. After all, even the items dating from Richard II's reign would have been only 160 years old. In this respect, an enlightening comparison is provided by tapestries woven at the Gobelins workshop in Paris in the 1840s—an equivalent distance in time for today's audience, most of which survive in good condition and color. Of even greater interest in this respect are the tapestries woven by William Morris's Merton Abbey workshop in the 1880s, 125 years ago at the time of writing, where the natural dyes used were studiously similar to those available in the fifteenth century. Here again, most of the surviving pieces retain their original color and beauty. We can therefore assume that many of the rich ensembles made for Henry's Yorkist and Lancastrian forebears or appropriated from the French royal collection may have been in at least moderate condition. Some sets made for Edward IV and Henry VII may have suffered almost no color loss at all, and their metallic thread may have retained much of its original luster. Thus, the range of old-fashioned styles these hangings embodied must have provided a striking contribution to the character of the Tudor palaces and a marked contrast to the more illusionistic weavings that became available during Henry's reign.

How were these older textiles valued and appreciated? Assessment of this question is impeded by the lack of written observations on the matter, but evidence that they did enjoy considerable prestige can be deduced from various sources. For a start, although no explicit record of Henry VIII's personal taste for the antique tapestries survives, their continuing use in all the principal palaces, including Hampton Court, to which they must have been transferred after the palace came into Henry's hands at Wolsey's fall and in response to the large building program of the mid-1530s, provides adequate grounds for such an assumption, as does the fact that the royal arras maker was regularly paid for repairs to such pieces. For example, the *Trojan War* tapestries (see figs. 4.3, 17.1) were extensively repaired as late as 1538–39.[1] This practice was analogous with that followed by the Habsburg court in Brussels, where the surviving highlights of the Burgundian tapestry collection were carefully tended and repaired during the first decades of the sixteenth century. Further evidence of the prestige associated with antique hangings is provided by the inquiry that Wolsey directed to Sellier in 1517 regarding the availability of tapestries of an

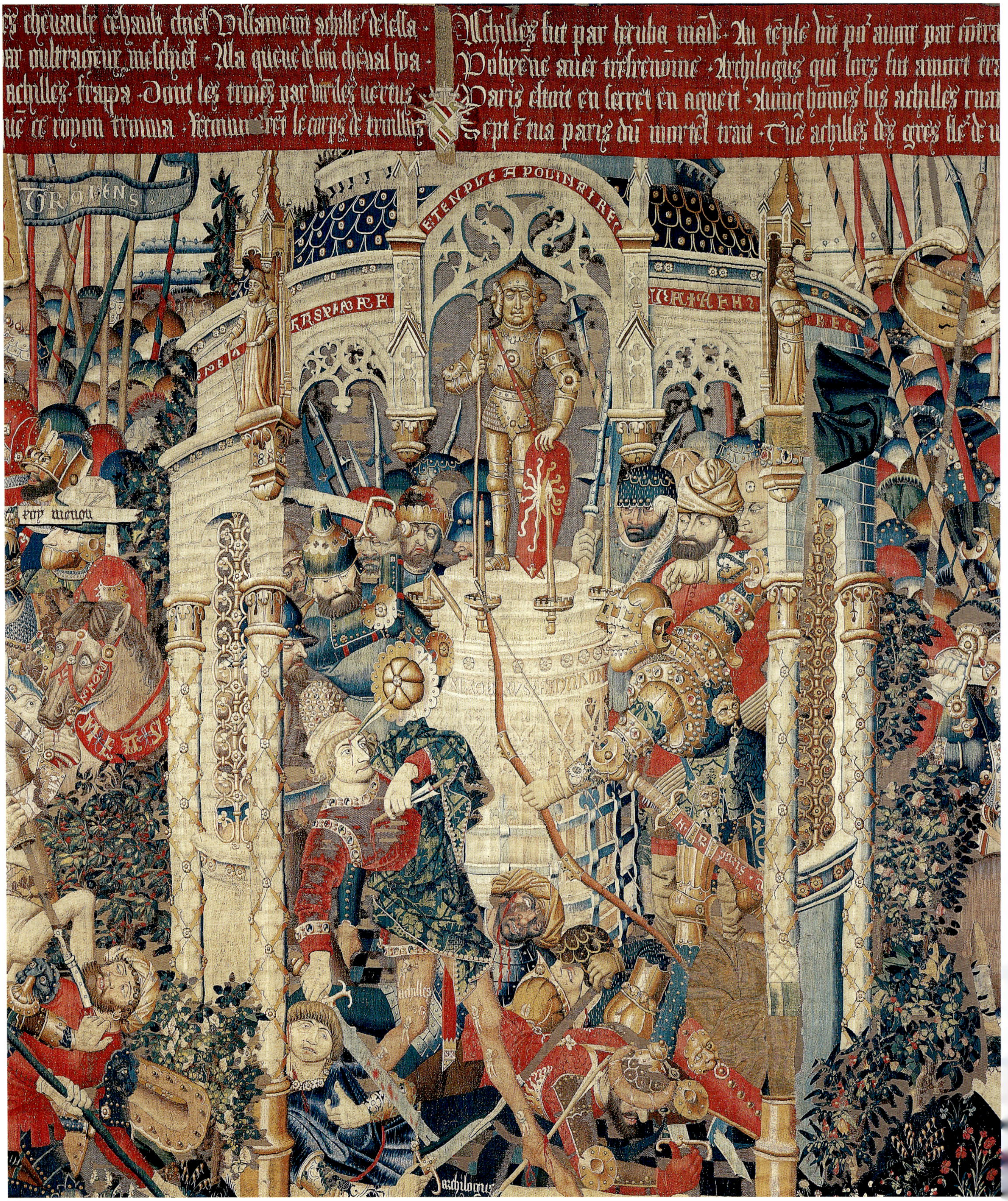
TROIENS
achilles
archilogus

17.1 *The Death of Troilus, Achilles, and Paris* (detail) from an eleven-piece set of the *Story of the Trojan War*. Tapestry woven in the Southern Netherlands, probably Tournai, ca. 1480–90. Wool and silk, 481 x 942 cm. Museo Catedralicio, Zamora

older style. As we have seen, the 1522 inventory of Wolsey's collection lists a number of antique tapestries, some of which evidently originated from the royal collection. Thomas Cromwell also owned an enormous fifteenth-century tapestry of the "Rote of Jessey," again almost certainly a perquisite of his office.[2]

Underlying such efforts we can assume a variety of motivations. Aside from the intrinsic value of those pieces containing metallic thread and appreciation of the skill and artistry with which they were made, another major factor must have been the associations they carried, whether in terms of specific iconography or simply by virtue of their age and provenance. Circumstantial evidence that certain pieces may have been linked with particular court events is provided by a tradition that continued during the reign of Charles I, whereby the *Saint George* tapestries deposited at the Tower were regularly taken to Windsor for use at the annual celebrations associated with the Order of the Garter. Given the ritualistic nature of Stuart court ceremonies, it seems probable that such practices had Tudor antecedents.

More generally, many of the old tapestries evidently held rich associations in exactly the same way that antiques "enhance" a stately residence today. For Wolsey and Cromwell, both self-made men in an age when power resided in the hands of dynastic noble families, the primary motivation to obtain older tapestries may have been a wish to acquire the trappings that their peers would have inherited as a matter of course. But the associative value of antique tapestries would have been no less relevant for Henry VIII. We have already seen how the cathedral church at Calais was decorated with antique armorial tapestries from the collection of Charles VI for the meeting between Henry VII and Philip the Handsome in 1506, perhaps an allusion to the historic English claim to the French throne, and certainly a reminder of past glory. A similar intent to link the Tudor court with the past must have motivated the display of the antique hangings and the rich bed known as "Hugh Dyke's bed" at the christening of one of Henry VII's children or, more than thirty years later, the transference of ancient "arras" hangings from the Windsor Wardrobe to that at Hampton Court, once it had come into Henry VIII's possession.

Another reflection of the status of the older hangings is provided by the accounts of visitors to Windsor in the late sixteenth century. Several of these mention the continuing display of the *Clovis* tapestry from the ensemble that the duke of Bedford took from the French royal collection in the 1420s. The details provided by Thomas Platter are especially interesting. Presumably based on what he was told by his guide, Platter records that the French had frequently tried to repurchase the *Clovis* tapestry "because it was so old and beautiful and depicts the French genealogy," but they had been refused at any price.[3] Although it might be argued that this was simply a manifestation of the nationalistic pride of the Elizabethan era, it seems reasonable to suppose that the same sentiments would have been current during the reign of Henry VIII, if not more so. After all, with the exception of the Crown jewels and the royal palaces themselves, the older hangings were the most striking visual component of the Tudor kings' inheritance. Because Henry's reign opened and closed with war against the French, the physical presence of trophies from the campaigns of Henry V must have been resonant indeed.

In this context, it is of note that a desire to relate the Tudor monarchy to a glorious past seems to have played an important part in determining the character of Henry VIII's artistic patronage during the Reformation period at exactly the time that major decisions were being made about the disposition of tapestries within various palaces. The most striking example of this is provided by the great hall at Hampton Court (see figs. i.1, 19.10), constructed with a traditional hammer beam roof in the early 1530s, albeit with a veneer of Renaissance ornament. This enormous edifice, built long after the date at which halls were the focal point of the royal household, was evidently intended to articulate continuity between medieval traditions of hospitality, splendor, and magnificence and ongoing Tudor practice.[4] The fact that such an ambitious project was undertaken in a self-consciously traditional style reveals the varied and sophisticated nature of the motives underlying Henry's patronage and provides a useful context for understanding the continuing use of the inherited tapestries during his later reign. It is interesting to note the presence of at least one enormous antique tapestry even at Nonsuch in 1547, the most modern and stylish of Henry's palaces.[5]

In summary, although we lack any explicit written record of sixteenth-century appreciation of fifteenth-century tapestries, it is evident that they continued to play an important part in the visual culture of the Tudor court, providing an atmosphere of venerable antiquity and traditional splendor both in the older palaces and at certain key points in the newer palaces or during important state events.

Trends in Taste during Henry VIII's Reign

The inventory provides fascinating information about the disposition of the older tapestries within the royal palaces. It also gives a valuable overview of the trends that governed the choice and use of tapestries acquired during Henry VIII's reign. As revealed in previous discussion, many of the royal tapestries, particularly those of moderate quality, were purchased by agents acting on the king's behalf. Equally, because of the enormous cost of high-quality tapestries, Henry must have been involved in decisions pertaining to those acquisitions. The proportionate representation of particular themes in the low- and high-quality hangings therefore provides valuable evidence about the nature of acquisition by the officers of the Great Wardrobe and by Henry himself. Two main trends emerge from this evidence, the first regarding the expensive tapestries in which Henry invested for public display, the second regarding the tapestries that he purchased for more personal spaces.

Religious Role Models and Public Display

The 1547 inventory confirms the deductions made in preceding chapters about Henry's investment in rich "arras" sets depicting role models relevant to his circumstances as he perceived them, particularly religious role models. The inventory also reveals that these themes formed the subject of a sizeable proportion of the medium-quality tapestries in the collection. Although Henry or his officers did not purchase all of these pieces, the disposition of tapestries recorded by the inventory suggests that even when the tapestries were appropriated, the selection process involved in deciding which tapestries to take from particular collections, or which sets to assign to the more important residences, was determined by a preference for religious subjects. In effect, all of the key palaces were equipped with sets of the *Story of David* and, to a lesser extent, the *Stories of Jacob and Joseph* and *Solomon*, indicating how closely these subjects were connected in court culture with the Tudor dynasty. Similarly, the number of *Esther* sets suggests that a similar process may have been pursued in relation to Henry's wives and daughters, while the number of sets of the *Prodigal Son*, several of which were certainly acquired during the last decade of Henry's reign, suggests the development of a similar link between this theme and the young prince. Although such typological association was hardly novel or sophisticated, the Tudor court is remarkable in the sheer number of such tapestries and the extent to which these analogies were reinforced in almost every palace and residence by sets of varying age and style.

The largest and most valuable "arras" sets depicting these religious role models were distributed in a manner that suggests an intention, by the end of the reign, to ensure that all of the key palaces were equipped with imagery appropriate to Henry's vision of himself as both patriarch of, and apostle to, his people. Greenwich was already equipped with the rich "arras" *David* set purchased in 1517. As we have seen, during the mid-1540s, a set of *Saint Paul* was purchased for this palace. Whitehall had

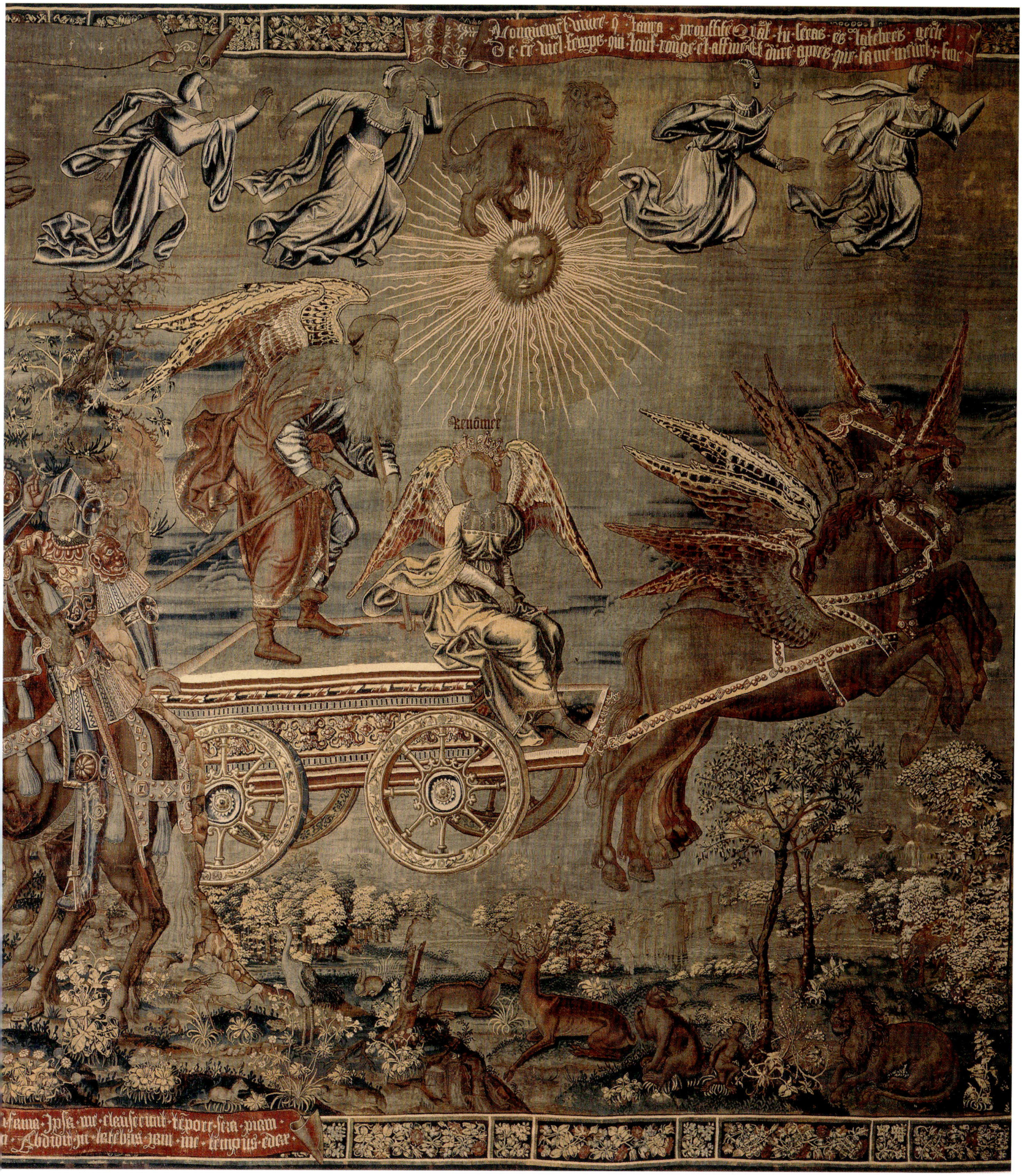

17.2 *Time Overcoming Fame* (detail) from a set of the *Triumphs of Petrarch*. Tapestry woven in the Southern Netherlands, probably Brussels, ca. 1515–20. Wool and silk, 427 x 810 cm. Hampton Court Palace

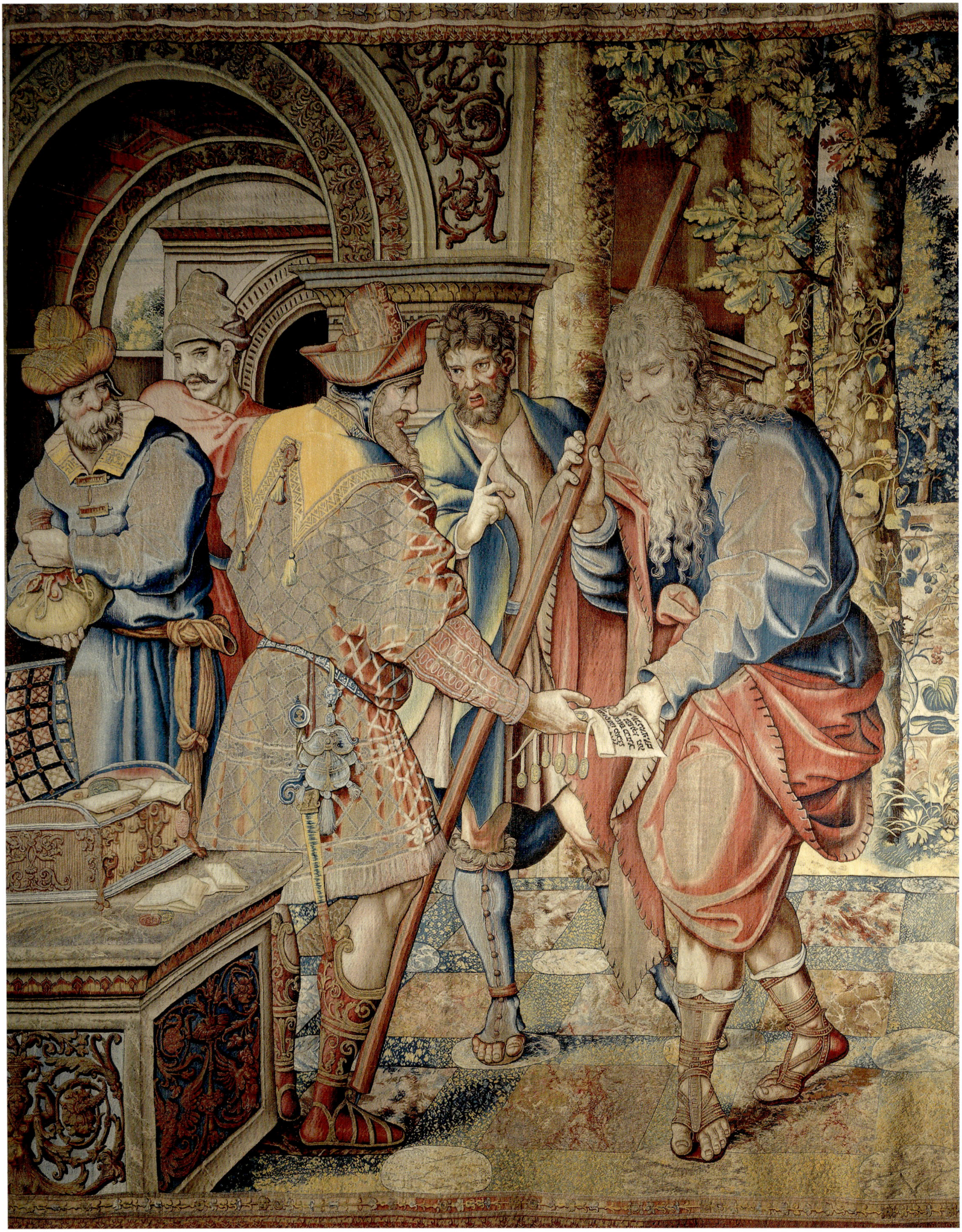

17.3 Detail of fig. 14.13

the *David* set purchased in 1519–20 and, during the mid-1540s, received the *Acts* and *Antiques* sets. Hampton Court was evidently the best equipped of all of the palaces, appropriately so, in view of its function as the focus of Tudor court entertainment and ceremony. The new state apartments created in the 1530s and 1540s provided the largest wall space of any of Henry's palaces in which to display rich tapestries, and it must have been for these that the *Saint Paul, Joshua, Abraham* (fig. 17.3), and *Caesar* sets were bought.

As will be readily apparent, all of Henry's grandest purchases of the late 1530s and early 1540s were of religious role models, with the exception of the *Caesar* and *Antiques* sets.

Henry evidently identified with these prototypes on a personal basis, yet the sheer scale of these sets and the huge investment they represented indicate that they were acquired for more than the king's enjoyment. Their size ensured that they could have been displayed in entirety only in large halls, reception rooms, processional routes, and public spaces. Similarly, their quality suggests that they would have been displayed only for ceremonial occasions. It therefore seems reasonable to suppose that they were acquired with the intention of promoting the associations that were so meaningful for Henry, and for his advisers, in the arena of the Tudor court. The fact that there is little evidence regarding the use of paintings and drawings to perform a similar function, with the exception of the title page of the Great Bible, is almost certainly misleading and should not be used as the basis for a similar inference in regard to tapestry. As the largest, most impressive, and most costly figurative art form available to him, tapestry rather than painting or sculpture was the logical choice for Henry to celebrate his vision of his transcendent role. It was in tapestry rather than in any other figurative media that we find a parallel to the analogies and comparisons that are so familiar in the written propaganda of the day.

Does the acquisition of tapestry sets with an identifiable political purpose constitute evidence of Tudor court propaganda in the modern sense? The ad hoc manner in which several sets were woven from existing cartoon series, the varying content of the sets, and the relatively limited audience that would have seen the tapestries, either at court or in more public spaces on state occasions, scarcely corresponds to our modern sense of the word. Equally, the underlying intent of these commissions seems to have been relatively consistent, to project and reinforce Henry's vision of his role as the current embodiment of a great tradition of divinely sanctioned rulers and communicators of God's word. Similarly, even though the audience who would have been exposed to these tapestries represented a small percentage of the population, this was hardly an era of universal suffrage. The reins of power and influence were vested in the nobility, clergy, and merchant class concentrated in the City of London. The leading members of these three estates were all regularly attendant at court and, of course, for ceremonies of state. Thus, insofar as the acquisitions had an underlying persuasive intent, they would certainly have been seen by the significant political body of the nation. As such, they must have contributed to the intellectual climate that created the Reformed Church in England.

Classical Role Models in More Private Apartments

The inventory reflects Henry's and his officers' intent to associate the Tudor dynasty with religious role models, especially in the large "arras" sets that would have been displayed for special occasions, yet it also confirms how much classical heroes continued to appeal to Henry's taste, particularly in the context of his private apartments. The founders of Rome and the imperial line evidently held special appeal. Henry had inherited sets depicting the Trojan Wars, Brutus, and the ancient origins of Rome, and during his own reign he complemented these cycles with one or possibly two sets of the *Story of Aeneas* and two sets of *Romulus and Remus*. The idiosyncratic measurements of the *Dido and Aeneas* set supplied in the early 1530s suggests that it was made for one of the king's private closets, while the four-piece *Romulus and Remus* set purchased in 1529 and subsequently located at Greenwich was also of a size that would have suited a large chamber rather than a great hall. Several of the classical subjects supplied for Whitehall in the late 1530s had unusual dimensions, suggesting that they also were supplied for particular rooms in the palace. And the dimensions of the *Romulus and Remus* set supplied by Pieter van de Walle in the mid-1540s for Hampton Court were especially uncommon, comprising four long thin panels, which were presumably intended to hang within a paneled framework. Another set that invites comment in this respect is the *Story of Jupiter* recorded at Richmond. Although this set was not, indubitably, Henry's purchase, the subject suggests that it dated from his reign, and the dimensions again indicate that it had been custom made, or adapted, for a specific room.

The other figure from classical legend who evidently figured large in Henry's acquisitions during the 1530s and 1540s was Hercules. Hercules had long been a popular subject in tapestry design, and several of the sets of this subject listed in the 1547 inventory may have been purchased by Henry's forebears. Nonetheless, the number of sets listed in 1547 indicates that Henry had a particular interest in this theme, which had probably been stimulated by Renaissance glosses on Hercules as an embodiment of Christian virtues. As we have seen, two new sets were delivered to Whitehall in, or around, 1540 and 1544, and Hercules was a key figure in the *Antiques* set purchased in 1542. A set of this subject was also included in the King's Removing Wardrobe.

In short, the evidence suggests that many of the classical histories and mythologies supplied for Henry from the 1520s onward were intended for his more private chambers, in contrast to the religious subjects that were purchased for more public display. The question of whether there was any stylistic distinction between tapestries purchased for public and private consumption will be considered below.

Perception and Appreciation of the Tapestry Medium

For much of the twentieth century, historians characterized Tudor taste as being focused on the richness and intricacy of the object, with the assumption that gold, opulence, color, and visual complexity were the order of the day. The underlying implication is that Henry and his circle were somewhat brash and undiscriminating in their artistic patronage. The first and most striking fact that emerges from consideration of the tapestry collection is that such assumptions were based largely on the sense that the Tudor court was some sort of a figurative backwater because the painting collection was relatively modest and uninteresting in comparison to those of Henry's Continental peers. Study of the tapestry collection reveals the extent to which this assumption is based on an anachronistic twentieth-century notion of the status of the figurative arts, in which painting is assumed to be primary. For the Tudor audience, particularly the king, the modern valuation placed on painted images over woven images is a reversal of the criteria that existed in the early sixteenth century. For Henry, a figurative image woven in silk and gold was more valuable than a painted image, sometimes by a factor of hundreds of pounds. Thus, the twentieth-century distinction between woven and painted images is largely irrelevant in considering the arts at the Tudor court.

The consequence of this misconception is that the importance accorded to painting rather than tapestry in modern studies of this period has resulted in a fundamental misrepresentation of the visual culture of the courts of Henry VII and Henry VIII. As this book demonstrates, tapestry was the predominant figurative art form, both in terms of the surface area that it covered and in terms of the cost and effort expended in obtaining, displaying, and maintaining the collection. Nothing makes this point more clearly than the inventories, taken in the 1540s, of paintings belonging to Henry VIII and Edward VI. These list about three hundred paintings, most of them portraits, as opposed to more than twenty-five hundred tapestries listed in the 1547 inventory.[6] Even if we exclude the coarse and essentially decorative tapestries from this comparison, it is clear that fine-quality tapestry played a much more important role as a source of figurative images than any other medium to which the Tudor courtiers were exposed by prints, manuscripts, paintings, or frescoes. One just has to think how different our sense of Tudor court art would have been if those tapestries had been painted in oil or fresco to realize the extent to which an accurate history of figurative art at the Henrician court has yet to be written.

How, then, can we characterize the aesthetic sensibility of Henry and his courtiers? The evidence is ambiguous because there was no written tradition to record contemporary responses to works of art, whether painted or woven. Evidently, we should not conclude from this that artistic achievement was not appreciated. The number of portraits commissioned from Holbein and the number of major projects assigned to Nicholas Bellin demonstrate clearly that their work was highly regarded. But in the absence of any self-conscious culture of written connoisseurship, it seems probable that their work was essentially valued in terms of craftsmanship: Holbein for the skill with which he captured appearances, Bellin for the complexity and richness of his inventions. The preoccupation with individual artistic genius that developed in Italy during the opening decades of the sixteenth century, subsequently codified by Vasari's hagiographic *Vitae,* and the concomitant preoccupation with issues of authorship and attribution were not to influence English royal patronage to any major extent until Charles I's reign.

In the case of tapestry, the notion of artistry was further obscured because the point of contact with the patron was often the rich merchant who underwrote the production of the series. And beyond him lay the complex collaborative process involved in tapestry production, with the initiating artists providing modelli, the cartoonists turning those into full-scale cartoons, and the weavers interpreting those cartoons. Indeed, these factors continue to present problems to a modern audience. This is not to say that sophisticated Continental patrons did not appreciate tapestry as an artistic medium as well as one of magnificence and suggestion. During the 1520s, 1530s, and 1540s, there is abundant evidence of Italian patrons commissioning leading artists of the day to design tapestry series that were evidently prized for their artistry as well as their iconographic content.[7] Closer to home, Francis I evidently saw tapestry as a medium in which he could obtain the work of the great Italian artists he so admired, as shown by his commissions for the Raphael *Acts of the Apostles* and the Romano *Story of Scipio* sets. Perhaps most intriguing in this respect was his commission in the early 1540s for a set of tapestries that reproduced, with some variations, the complex allegorical celebration of his reign that had been rendered in stucco and fresco in the grand gallery at Fontainebleau by Rosso and Primaticcio. As already noted, this set was woven in a workshop established at Fontainebleau, not Brussels, providing further evidence that it was not possible for rivals of Charles V to commission overtly propagandistic works from the Brussels workshops.

Does anything suggest that Henry VIII shared this sophisticated perception of tapestry as a medium of artistry as well as of iconographic display? Judging by the purchases in which he was probably involved, it seems that his consistent motivation in purchasing expensive tapestries was to obtain sets that provided resonant role models to his own position. No evidence survives to indicate that he sourced new designs from artists in his entourage, although this may simply reflect the partial nature of the documentation. Even in the case of the Raphael workshop *Acts* and *Antiques,* the circumstances in which these sets were acquired suggest that they were purchased first and foremost because they provided role models that conformed to Henry's sense of his status as head of the English church, a latter-day Saint Paul spreading the Christian message to his people, a Christian Hercules laboring to overcome the challenges in his path.

Should we conclude from this that Henry was indifferent to the artistic quality of the tapestries or to the extraordinary stylistic and iconographic development that characterized the medium in his lifetime? Answers to this question must be tentative, but given the extent to which tapestry was the traditional art form for the richest and most powerful European rulers, and given the enormous investment that Henry made in the medium from early in his reign, it seems certain that it was the subject of considerable discussion in which questions of design must have figured. Wolsey was notoriously interested in tapestry at the time when he was Henry's closest aide and adviser, and it must have been the subject of mutual discussion between the two men, ranging from shared amusement in the interpolation of their portraits in Wolsey's *Triumphs of Petrarch* (see figs. 8.4, 8.7–8.10, 17.2) to the more serious business of commissioning tapestries that reinforced the arguments that Henry was propounding to support his case for a divorce from Katherine of Aragon. Similarly, although no record survives of Henry discussing tapestry with Francis at Guines in 1520 or at Boulogne in 1532, we know that the English tapestries were particularly splendid at the first event and that the French tapestries were remarkable at the second. Moreover, we know from a contemporary Venetian account of 1533 that Francis was inordinately proud of the tapestries that had been displayed for Henry the previous year. Similarly, we know that many of the licenses granted to merchants to import luxury goods ensured that Henry received first view of their wares, occasions on which he must have been exposed to some sort of "sales pitch." Moreover, Henry's major commissions of the late 1530s and 1540s must have been attended by considerable discussion, at the point of conception, order, and reception.

Although these elements hardly constitute concrete evidence, they are redolent of a culture in which tapestry was the subject of discussion and appreciation, and it seems highly unlikely that such discourse could have taken place without mentioning the artistry of the medium. Thus, it seems reasonable to suppose that the extraordinary advances made by Raphael, Van Orley, Pieter Coecke, and Michiel Coxcie, among others, would indeed have been recognized and appreciated, particularly after the arrival of Nicholas Bellin from the French court. As discussed above, Bellin probably played an influential role in the circumstances that led Henry to purchase the duplicate sets of the *Acts* and the *Antiques,* and he may have also played a part in the *Abraham* and *Caesar* commissions, as evidenced by the enigmatic account in the 1543 list of New Year's Day gifts, when he received a reward for bringing Henry a "Story of Abraham." Considering that Bellin may have worked at Mantua with Giulio Romano, one of the key collaborators in the Raphael workshop tapestry designs, and that he had then certainly worked at Fontainebleau with Primaticcio, who had been involved in the development of the *Scipio* series, it seems unlikely that he would not have discussed Italian artists and Italian tapestry designs with Henry and his advisers. Assuming that Henry's sets of the *Acts* and *Antiques* may have taken two years or so to weave from the date of commission, it seems more than likely that conversations with Bellin in the year or two after his arrival at the English court precipitated Henry's commission for these sets. Thus, regardless of Henry's earlier sensitivity to questions of taste and aesthetics, there is a strong probability that by the late 1530s he was aware of developments in Italianate art and the prestige attached to the work of masters like Raphael and Giulio and that this was the background to his own commissions to Bellin, among others.

In this respect, one characteristic of Henry's acquisitions is of especial note. As we have seen, during the second half of his reign, Henry's purchases for public display seem to have concentrated, by and large, on religious role models, whereas those he acquired for more private spaces tended to feature classical heroes. It is therefore interesting that, on the basis of the sets in his collection that can be identified with extant designs, it seems true to say that the majority of the religious subjects Henry purchased tended toward a slightly more elaborate and traditional Flemish style, whereas some, at least, of the classical sets were designed in more Italianate styles. For example, the style of the *David* set purchased in 1528 was unquestionably conservative, with its linear, crowded composition, whereas the *Romulus and Remus* set purchased the following year reflected a Flemish artist's response to Raphael's *Acts of the Apostles* designs. During the 1540s, the High Renaissance *Acts* and *Antiques* sets were designated for Whitehall, probably for chambers specifically associated with the king, whereas the *Paul, Joshua, Abraham,* and *Caesar* sets, conceived in a more Flemish mannerist style, were allocated to Hampton Court. And although those rich elaborate designs were intended for display in the state apartments, Henry acquired the *Romulus and Remus* set by the Romanist Michiel Coxcie for his more private chambers. Though this evidence is hardly conclusive—after all, Henry may simply have been buying what was available—it does open up the possibility that Henry felt that the grand style of Van Orley and Coecke was appropriate for the tapestries purchased for public display but that he was open to a more modern Italianate style for sets intended for his own use.

Whatever Henry's personal sophistication in respect to the aesthetics of the tapestry medium, there can be no question of the overall contribution that the collection made to the visual culture of the Tudor court. It was the

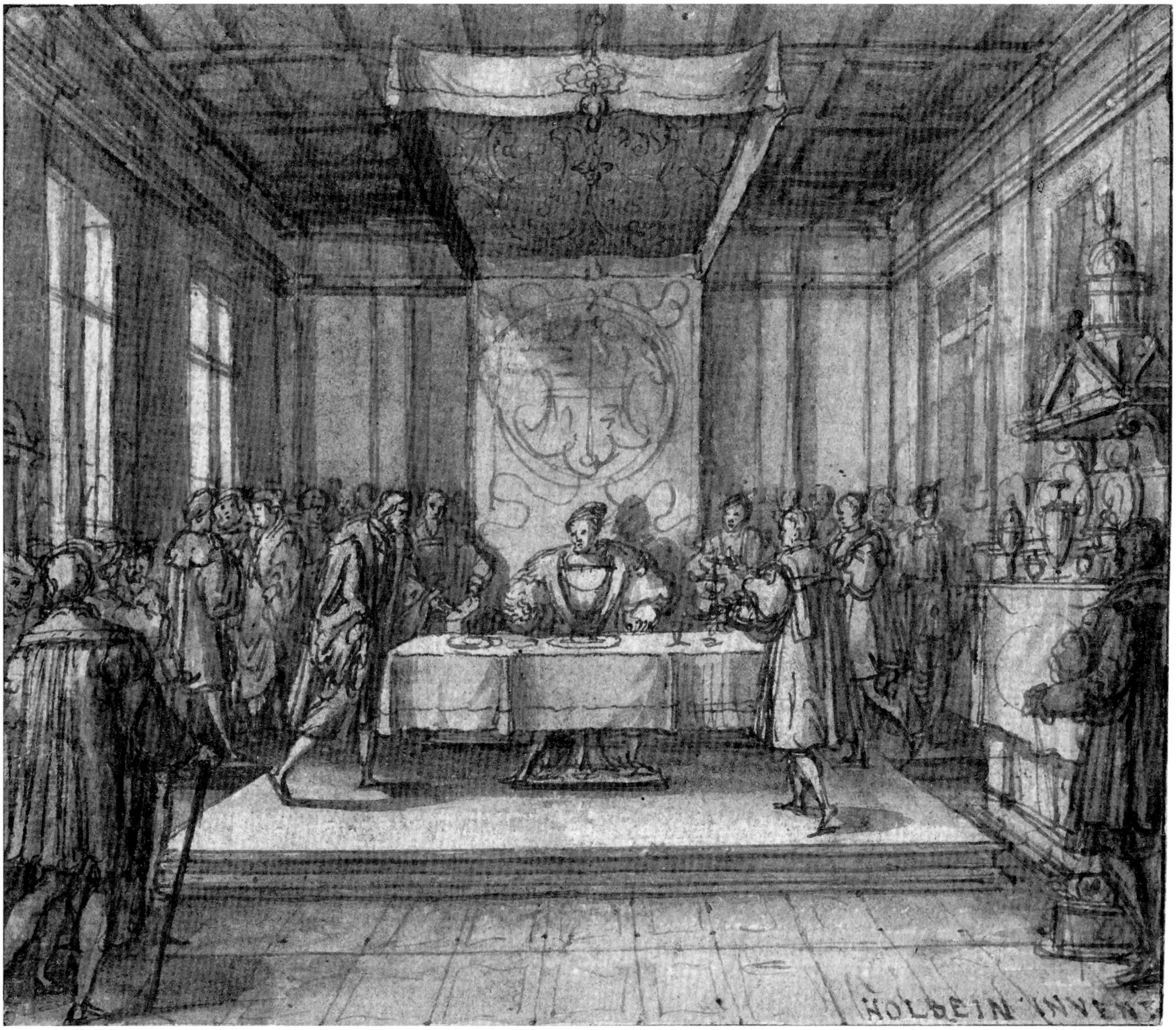

17.4 *Henry VIII Dining in His Privy Chamber* by an unidentified artist, ca. 1540. Pen and brown ink with gray wash, 9.5 x 11.1 cm. British Museum, London

17.5 *Henry VIII Enthroned,* from John Foxe's *Acts and Monuments* (1563)

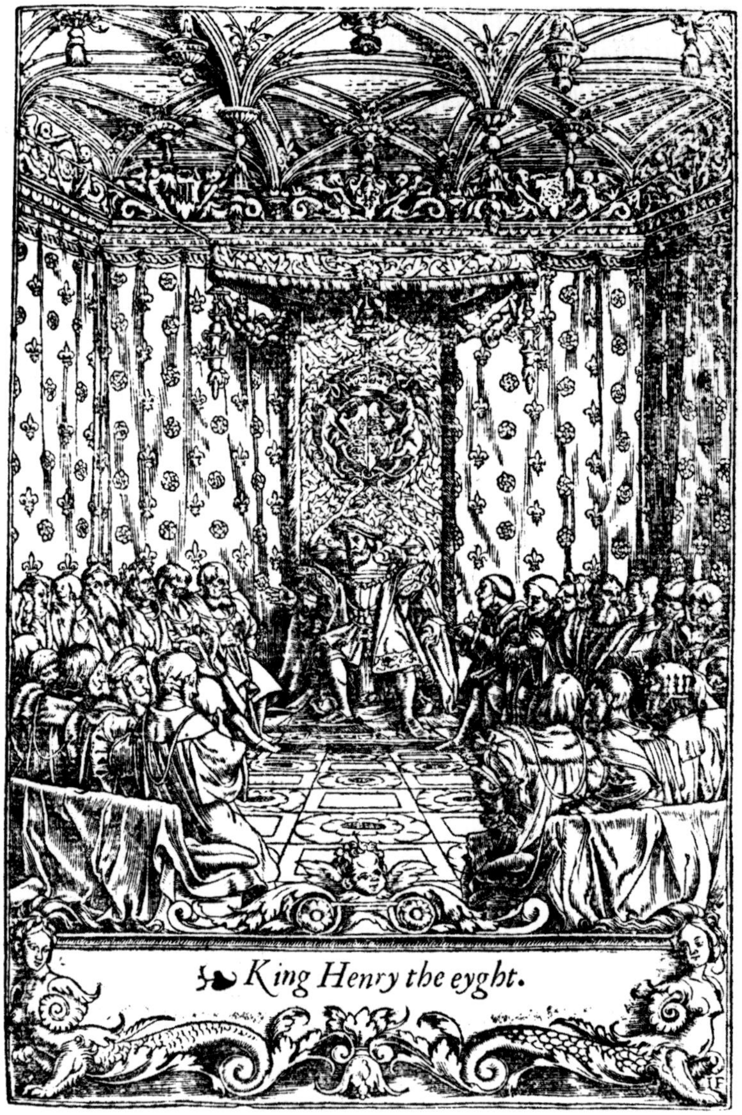

ubiquitous figurative art form, providing a broad spectrum of style and subject matter that has been almost entirely neglected in modern studies. It was through tapestry, far more than paintings and engravings, that Henry and his court received, on one hand, continuing exposure to the myths, legends, and artistic style of their medieval ancestors and, on the other, their first and most impressive exposure to High Renaissance aesthetics.

How "Magnificent" Was Henry's Tapestry Collection?

The final question that the 1547 inventory illuminates is how truly splendid was the Tudor tapestry collection. As we have seen, Henry maintained practices well established during his father's reign, the tapestry collection being deployed in a theatrical manner to maximize the impression of magnificence. The best tapestries were reserved for special occasions, and both at such times and in daily life it was common practice to use tapestries of varying quality to give visual expression to the hierarchy of state rooms leading to the presence chamber with its throne and canopy of state (figs. 17.4–17.6). Contemporary chronicles and descriptions duly record the magnificence of the royal tapestries. Invariably they are described as "rich," "with gold," and "costly." Evidently, perception of the magnificence of the collection depended above all on the material quality of the tapestries. However, with the loss of the majority of the collection and in the absence of detailed purchase accounts, the

Opposite:
17.6 *The Family of Henry VIII* (detail) by an unidentified artist, ca. 1545. Oil on canvas, 141 x 357 cm. The Royal Collection

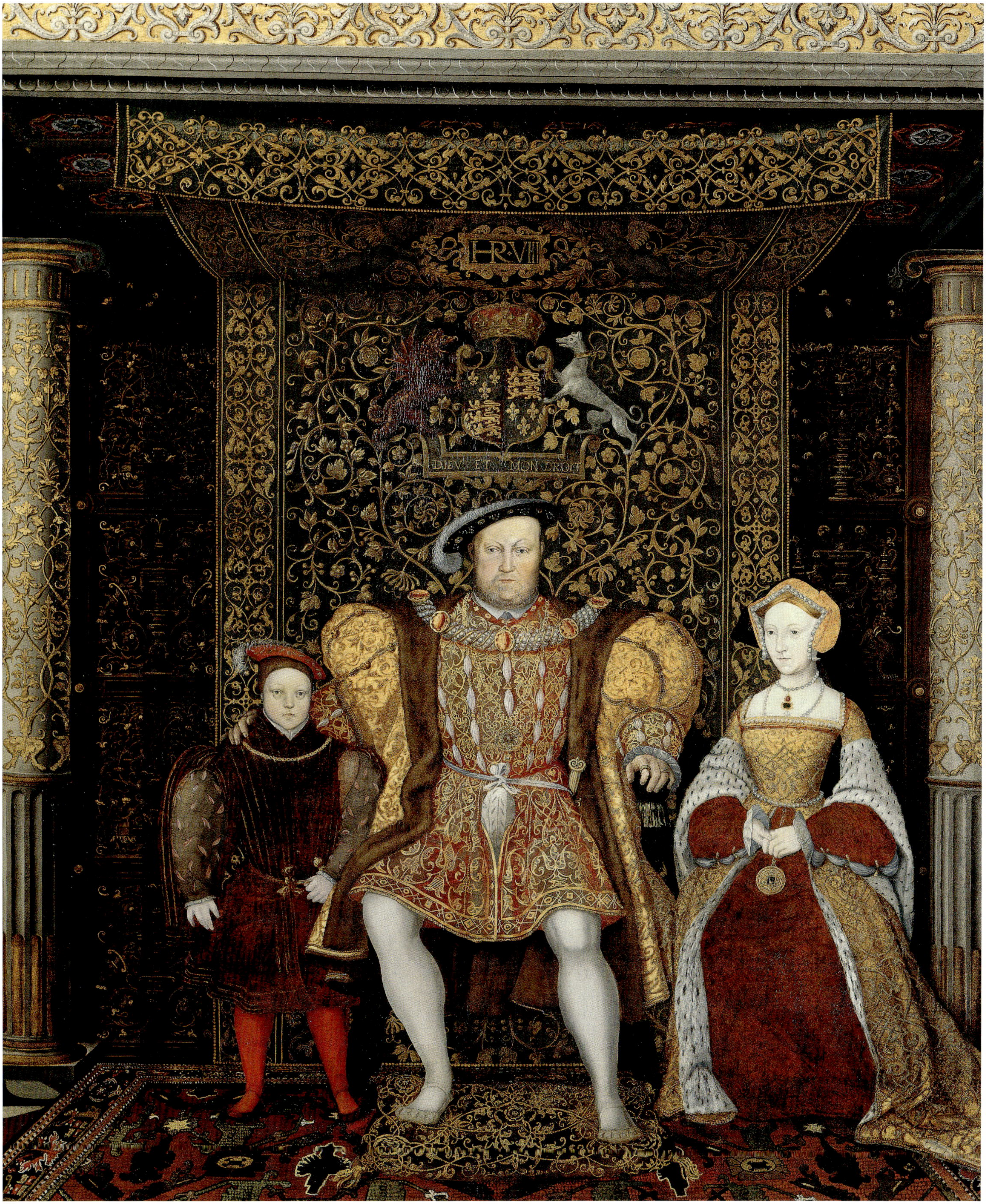
HR·VIII
DIEV ET MON DROIT

repetitive nature of many contemporary descriptions encourages a somewhat skeptical reading of the reported magnificence. Just how impressive was the collection?

One rule-of-thumb answer is provided by the number of tapestries woven with gilt-metallic thread. The 1547 inventory lists forty-one sets of "arras" ranging in number from three to ten pieces, along with another eleven pairs and sixty-four individual pieces, giving a combined total of about 330 "arras" tapestries. The subjects and locations of as many as a third of these indicate that they may have been inherited or appropriated, but documentary or comparative evidence suggests that Henry was responsible for purchasing, at the least, "arras" sets of the following subjects: the *Story of David* (1517), the *Story of Saint John* (1517), the *Story of David* (1520), the gold-ground *Verdure* (1520), the *Story of David* (1528), the *Passion* (1528–29), the *Story of Aeneas* (early 1530s), the *Seven Deadly Sins* (ca. 1535–36), the *Story of Saint Paul* (1538–39), the *Twelve Months* (ca. 1540), the *Acts of the Apostles* (1542), the *Antiques* (1542), the *Story of Abraham* (1543–44), the *Story of Caesar* (1543–44), the *Story of Joshua* (early 1540s), the *Story of Romulus and Remus* (1545–46), and the *Story of Tobias* (1546?). In addition, he was also almost certainly responsible for purchasing other "arras" sets and individual panels, especially devotional panels, listed by the 1547 inventory whose date of acquisition is unknown, to say nothing of the many large, high-grade tapestry sets bought during his reign.

How rare and valuable would these "arras" tapestries have appeared to a Tudor audience? The imprecision of the contemporary use of terms like "arras" and tapestry in contexts other than the royal collection impedes conclusive answers, but analysis of contemporary collections does indicate that nobody but the king owned "arras" tapestries in any quantity. The largest identifiable group in a collection other than that of the Crown is that recorded in Wolsey's collection in 1522, which included about forty "arras" pieces.[8] Yet of these, half were components for three state beds that must have been acquired as perquisites from the royal collection, and most of the others were devotional pieces of small dimensions. Elsewhere, the number of "arras" tapestries in contemporary collections was considerably lower. The earl of Oxford's inventory taken in 1513 lists about ten pieces of "arras," most of which appear to have been of considerable age and may also have been acquired as perquisites, in a collection whose finest pieces are generally defined as "counterfeit arras."[9] The duke of Buckingham purchased gold-woven tapestries in 1512, and we can assume that these entered the royal collection after his execution, but only two "arras" pieces with his arms are listed in the 1547 royal inventory.[10] The duke of Norfolk's collection at Framlingham in 1524 was composed entirely of "counterfeit arras," tapestry, and verdure.[11] The inventory of Henry Percy, sixth earl of Northumberland, taken at his residence in Hackney in January 1534 lists only three small pieces of "fine arras" in a collection of about sixty tapestries.[12] Thomas Cromwell owned at least two "arras" tapestries that passed to the king after his execution, one a small devotional piece, the other a large antique piece.[13] The inventory of Lord Sandys taken at The Vyne in 1541 lists only one old piece of "arras" in a collection that is otherwise notable for sets of new tapestry with borders of "antickes" and Sandys's arms.[14] Finally, the inventory taken at Kenninghall in 1546 after the attainder of the duke of Norfolk and the earl of Surrey refers to several sets of "arras" tapestry, but since a number appear to be identical with pieces described as "counterfeit arras" in the earlier Framlingham inventory, the use of the term in this context is not a reliable indication, in this instance, of tapestries woven with gilt-metal. It is conceivable that only one piece, a small devotional panel described as "very fine arras," may actually have included such thread.[15] As this thumbnail sketch suggests, there is little evidence for the extensive presence of gilt-woven tapestries in any native collections other than that of the king, and it seems safe to assume that the majority of the finest tapestries in the collections of leading courtiers were woven with wool and silk, as in the case of Wolsey. Even these were the exception rather than the rule, most being woven exclusively in wool.

If comparison with contemporary collections provides a general sense of the exceptional nature of Henry's "arras" tapestries for an English audience, is it possible to focus this issue in terms of overall value? How did the cost of these sets compare to contemporary incomes and material prices? In answering this question it is interesting to look again at the contemporary Port Books of Rates. As discussed above in Chapter 5, tapestry was among a range of commodities listed with their nominal values in the Port Books of Rates as an aid to the assessment of import duties by customs officers. The 1507 Book of Rates, which listed three different grades of tapestry, but not gold-woven tapestry, was reissued first in 1532 and then, in expanded form, in 1545 and 1550. By the mid-sixteenth century the list had developed into a printed handbook, but because the nominal values had not changed despite the inflation of the previous fifty years, they bore little relation to the real value of the goods to which they referred. In 1552 the commission of the king's courts of revenue took steps to update the figures, and revised books were issued in 1558 and again in 1562. An expanded version appeared in 1582, which remained current until a new evaluation was issued in 1604.[16] The 1558 version is of particular interest here because it confirms the proportional variation of price between the different grades of tapestry then available. Five categories are listed. The cheapest tapestry was now "Tappestry of Heare course" at 8d. per ell, while the inclusion of wool or "caddas" increased the price to 1s. and 2s., respectively. Tapestries with silk were estimated at 3s. 4d. per ell. The most expensive category was that of "Tappestry with Golde called Arras," valued at 40s. per ell.[17] It therefore appears that the value of different grades of tapestry had remained relatively consistent since the early sixteenth century—with a proportional cost differential of 1 : 2 : 3.3 : 50—the cheapest wool tapestry being valued at about 1s. per ell, and the most expensive gold-woven tapestry at about 40s. per ell.[18] These comparative figures are supported by documentation relating to Henry's purchases. For example, the set of *Months* purchased from Richard Gresham in 1528 cost 2s. per ell and was therefore presumably woven in good-quality wool, whereas the gold-woven ten-piece *David* purchased at the same time cost 41s. per ell.[19] In 1528 Smytting hoped that the king would pay £3 per ell for his expensive four-piece *Passion* set, but he had to settle for £2 per ell in 1529.[20] Thirteen years later Henry's high-quality sets of the *Acts of the Apostles* and the *Antiques* were purchased for a total cost of £2,325 15s. 6d.[21] If both sets were valued at the same rate, then the dimensions provided by the 1547 inventory indicate that they were valued at £2 2s. per ell.

Lest it be argued that the large sums paid for these sets may have been exceptional, similar costs can be deduced for the other large "arras" sets in Henry's collection. Multiplying the surface area of the richest sets, as calculated from the 1547 dimensions, by the value of £2 per ell for "arras" tapestry, approximate costs can be calculated as follows: £768 for the gold-ground *Verdure* first recorded at Guines in 1520; £416 and £1,017 for the *Months* and *Deadly Sins* sets listed at the Tower in 1547; and £1,060 for the *Tobias,* £1,130 for the *Joshua,* £1,262 for the *Paul,* £1,502 for the *Caesar,* and £1,694 for the *Abraham* sets, recorded as "newe" at Hampton Court in 1547. In fact, the cost of some of the Hampton Court sets may have been higher, because the Commonwealth inventories one hundred years later suggest that they were particularly valuable. While the ten-piece *David* set, the *Antiques* set, and the *Saint Paul* set were valued at £4, £5, and £5 per ell, respectively, the Commonwealth officers valued the *Joshua* set at about £6 15s., the *Tobias* and *Caesar* sets at £7, and the *Abraham* set at £10 per ell.[22] Although these valuations may, in part, have reflected the condition of the sets, comparison between the surviving tapestries at Hampton Court confirms that the *Antiques* have a lower gilt-metal thread content than the *Tobias* and *Abraham* tapestries. The *Abraham* set is especially rich, with the ground of the borders being woven throughout in gilt-metal thread. These figures are conjectural, but they certainly suggest the magnitude of the sums that Henry must have disbursed for these magnificent tapestries. It is, of course, no coincidence that the largest and finest were acquired when the royal coffers were benefiting from the dissolution of the monasteries.

Comparison with contemporary incomes reveals the size of these figures relative to contemporary incomes. Modern analysis of the data compiled by government officers for the subsidy assessment of 1534 shows that the median income for the thirty-nine noble families assessed at that date was £921. The increase of £120 over the median of the 1523–24 assessments can probably be accounted for by efforts to make the 1534 survey as accurate as possible.[23] The *Valor Ecclesiasticus* taken in 1535 shows that the median income of the bishops was £1,050.[24] Legally, any freeholder with an income over £40 was eligible to take up knighthood, and an annual income of between £20 and £40 was an approximate threshold of gentility.[25] Ninety percent of the population lived on an income below £20 a year.[26] The king's tapestry expenditure is especially striking in comparison to the salaries and expenses of the artists on whose work evaluation of Tudor visual culture has largely depended. Gerard Horenbout and Holbein received annual salaries from the crown of £33 6s. and £30, respectively, while skilled artisans like the master mason, the royal tailor, and the royal arras maker received salaries of approximately £20 per year. Laborers received about 6d. per day (approximately £8 per year).[27] The cost of the "arras" sets were equally significant in proportion to real estate and building expenses.[28] As will be readily apparent, the enormous gilt-woven tapestry sets were among the most expensive commodities of the day, a prerogative of the king simply by virtue of their inordinate cost. In a culture in which there was no literary tradition for recording aesthetic responses to works of art, it is no surprise that again and again it is the value and splendor of the tapestries that are noted. We can conclude that contemporary descriptions of the "magnificence" of the collection were deserved.

PART VII

Use and Dispersal of the Collection from 1547 to the Present Day

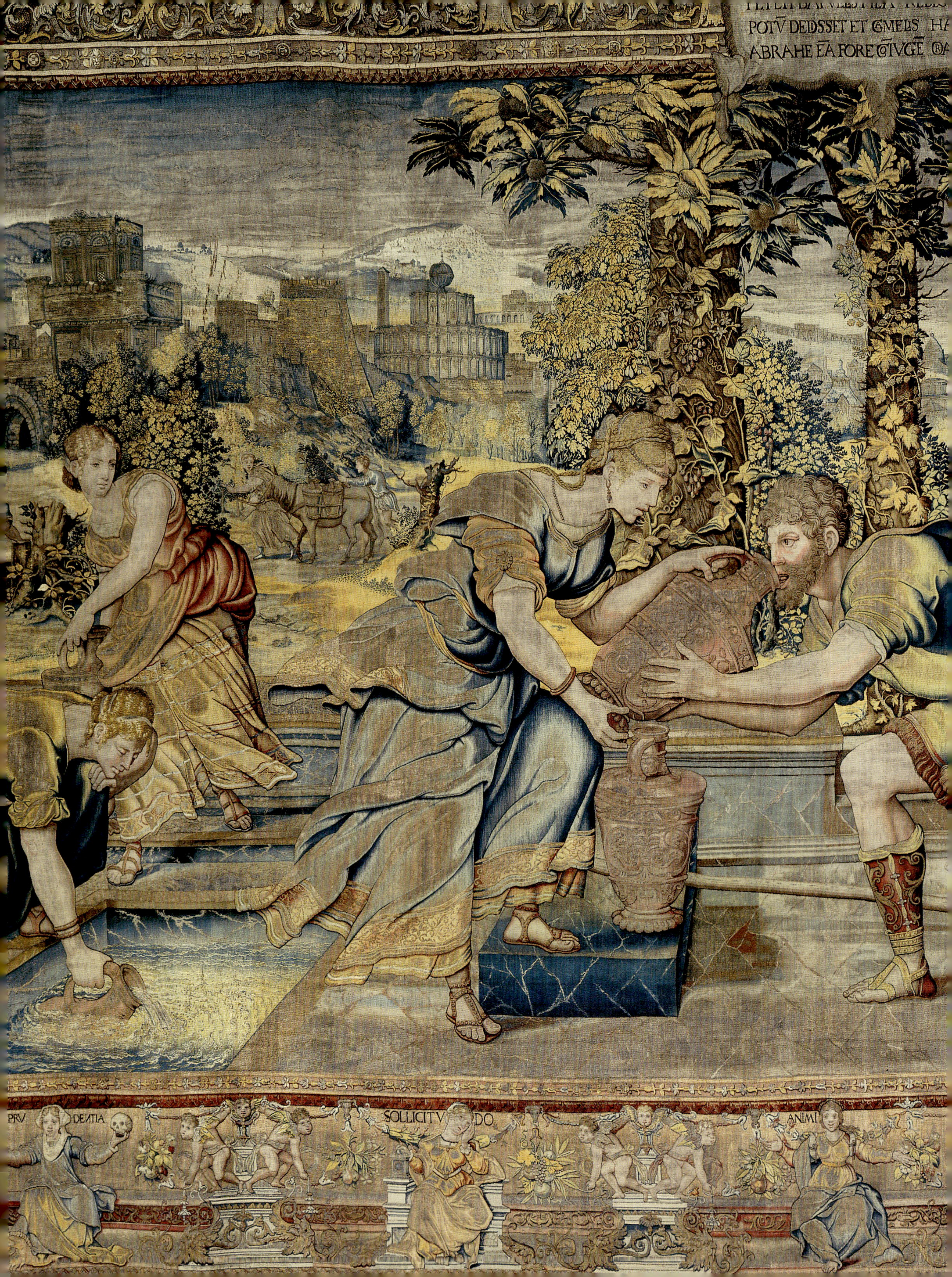
POTŪ DEDISSET ET CAMELIS
ABRAHE ĒA FORE CŌIVGĒ
PRVDENTIA
SOLLICITVDO
ANIMI

CHAPTER 18

The History of the Tudor Collection, 1547–1659

The Use of the Tudor Tapestries under Edward VI, Mary I, and Elizabeth I

How did the enormous tapestry collection recorded by the 1547 inventory disappear so completely from sight that it is barely mentioned in cultural and artistic histories of the Tudor court? The following two chapters attempt to answer this question by providing an overview of the subsequent usage, valuation, and dispersal of the collection. Tapestry certainly remained a key component of court decoration and splendor for almost two centuries after Henry's death, and many of the traditions of display and usage established during the Tudor era continued until the early eighteenth century. But the continuity of court traditions took place against a background of shifting tastes and fashions, and over the years the tapestry collection was diminished both in a literal sense by loss and dispersal and in a conceptual sense by the steady diminution of the status of tapestry as an art form. The process was long and gradual.

Following traditional practice, the streets of London were hung with tapestry and "arras" for the coronation of Edward VI (fig. 18.1), and an eyewitness account records that the choir of Westminster Abbey was "very richly hung with Cloath of Arras." During the following years, the public appearances of the young prince continued to be staged against a backdrop of Henry VIII's tapestries and precious textiles (fig. 18.2), and we can assume that these would have been selected to emphasize his lineage and status as the anointed Tudor king. But while several descriptions, including Edward's own diary, mention rich tapestry displays at particular grand events, they are uninformative about the subjects.

Although traditions of use continued unbroken following Henry's death, the expansion of the collection was an altogether different story. After three decades of exponential growth, acquisitions now ground to a near standstill. Edward was a nine-year-old minor under the control of appointed guardians, and although it is conceivable that a small number of purchases may have been made by Edward's guardians in his name, the collection was already so full of sets whose subjects might be displayed to suggest flattering analogies that there can have been little incentive to undertake major initiatives in this respect. Nonetheless, the English court remained an obvious target for speculative ventures, as evidenced by a grant issued in 1553 to the Antwerp merchant Cornelius de Vader, who had "caused to be made a riche and costely hanging of tapystry of the story of the prodygall sonne." De Vader was allowed to import the tapestry specially to show King Edward and to take it out of the realm if not sold, without paying custom or subsidy, provided that "caution" was given at the port of entry for payment in the event of the tapestry being sold or "otherwise uttered to the king or any other person in the realm."[1]

Edward's premature death on July 6, 1553, ensured that he exerted minimal impact on the tapestry collection, and much the same can be said of his elder sister Mary, who was crowned queen on October 1, 1554. Her reign was inaugurated with the usual splendid preparations, and her coronation took place against a back-

Detail of fig. 14.16

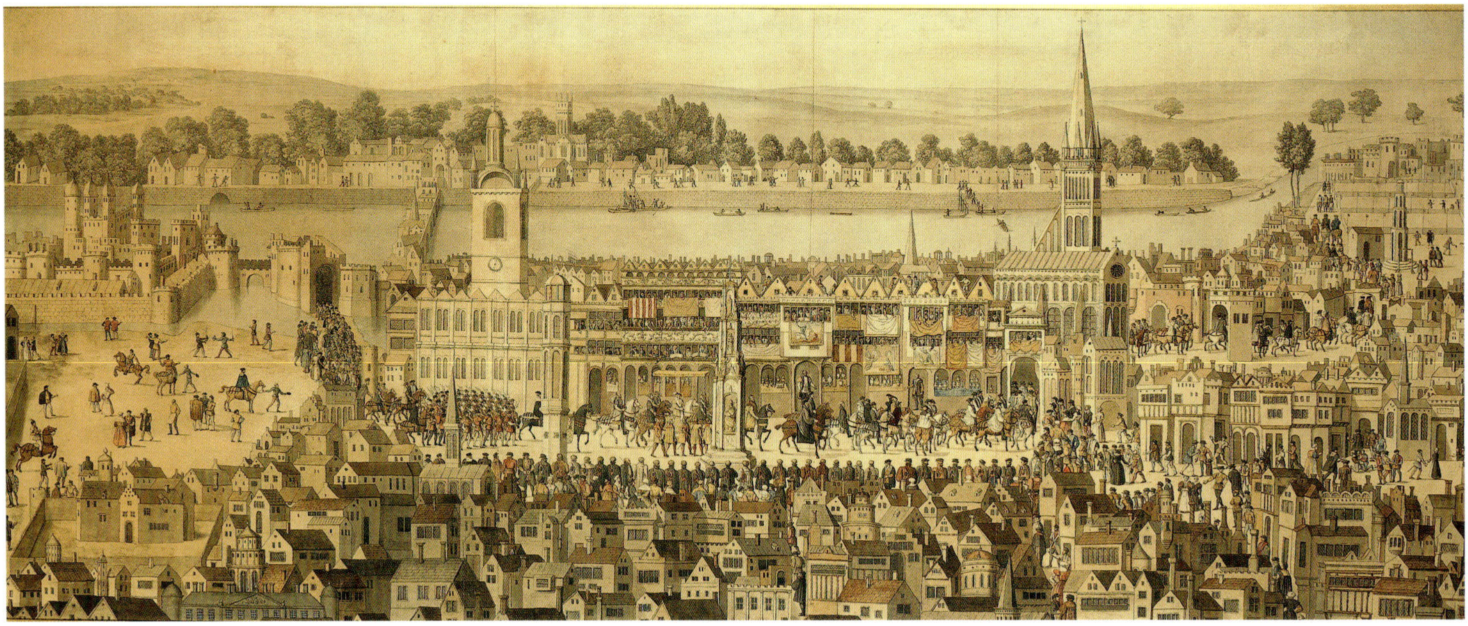

18.1 Copy by Samuel Hieronymous Grimm after the *Coronation Procession of Edward VI* by an unidentified artist (from the Cowdray House mural), 1785. Drawing on paper, 75.4 x 152.2 cm. Society of Antiquaries, London

drop of tapestries at Westminster Abbey, where the choir was hung with "arras" and the parliament chamber was "richly hung."[2] But the turbulent circumstances of her brief reign, roiled as it was by efforts to reverse the English Reformation and reintroduce Catholicism as the state religion, were not conducive to the long-term planning that major tapestry commissions required. In the context of this study, however, it is interesting to note that Mary's husband, Philip of Spain, was heir to the greatest Continental tapestry collection of the day, and their marriage did expose the English court to at least one part of that collection. On June 20, 1554, Sir John Mason, the English ambassador to the court of Charles V, wrote from Brussels to inform Mary that a set of tapestries depicting the *Conquest of Tunis* was being transported to England for the marriage. He noted that the set is "one of the fairest pieces of work that has been made in these times." Had he known, he might also have noted that it was the most expensive work of art commissioned by Charles during his reign. The twelve-piece set was an epic visualization of Charles's campaign to Tunis in 1535 (fig. 18.3). The designs were by the artist Jan Vermeyen, who had accompanied Charles on the campaign, and weaving was undertaken between 1548 and 1554. In the event, the tapestries were not hung in Winchester Cathedral as tradition claims, perhaps because the subject was considered to be too overt a celebration of Spanish power at this extremely sensitive moment in English dynastic history. They

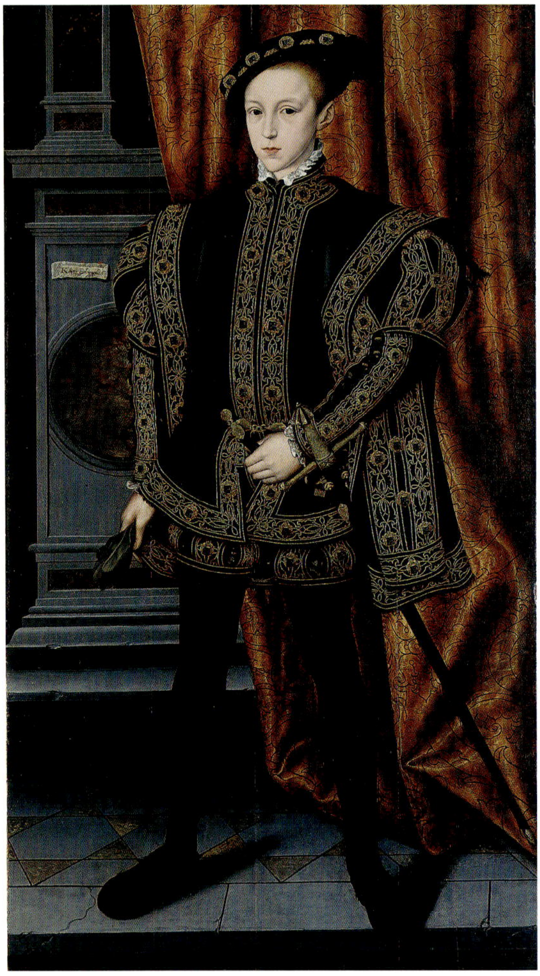

18.2 *Edward VI* attributed to William Stretes, ca. 1550. Oil on panel, 167 x 90.8 cm. The Royal Collection

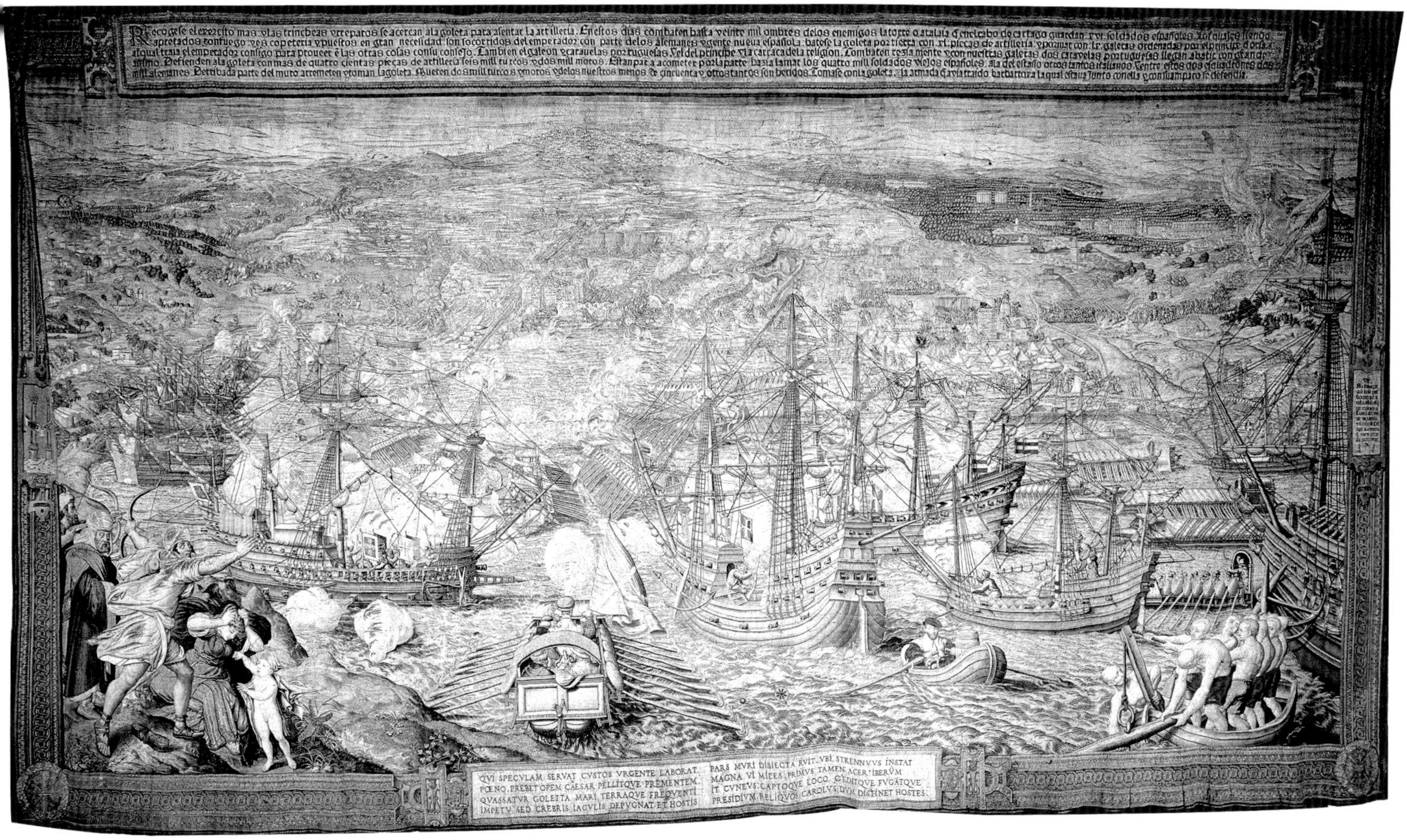

18.3 *The Battle at Goleta* from a twelve-piece set of the *Conquest of Tunis*. Tapestry designed by Jan Vermeyen, woven in the workshop of Willem de Pannemaker, Brussels, ca. 1549–54. Wool, silk, and gilt-metal-wrapped thread, 525 x 920 cm. Palacio Real, Madrid

were, however, displayed at Whitehall Palace for Philip and Mary's entrance to London, an imposing demonstration of Spanish might, now that the wedding had been celebrated.[3]

The spectacle of Mary and Philip's wedding was the highlight of their relationship, and the period of intimacy between the two monarchs was too short for Philip to have exerted any discernible influence on Mary as a patron of the medium. Indeed, it is conceivable that the influence ran the other way. Following his sojourn in England, where he would have been surrounded at every turn by Henry's finest hangings, Philip was to emerge as one of the most significant tapestry patrons of the late 1550s and 1560s, commissioning sets such as the *Story of Noah* and the *Apocalypse*.[4] The appropriation of such messianic and apocalyptic subject matter by Philip is allied more closely with the imagery of Henry's key commissions than the iconography of the collection that Philip inherited from his own father, Charles V (fig. 18.4).

The brief and troubled reigns of Edward and Mary stand in marked contrast to that of their younger sister, Elizabeth, who, in the course of her forty-five years as queen, reasserted the stability of her father's rule and ensured the effective completion of the English Reformation. The Henrician tapestries were deployed from the moment of Elizabeth's accession. A contemporary account records that on the occasion of her coronation, Westminster Abbey was hung with tapestries of the *Acts of the Apostles* and scenes from Genesis, while the "chambers" were hung with the *Story of Caesar and Pompey*.[5] The *Acts* were evidently the Raphael set delivered to Henry in 1542. The Genesis tapestries almost certainly included the *Abraham* tapestries, which were displayed in this location for coronations of the Stuart kings in the seventeenth century. The imagery of this set, with its celebration of the transference of God's covenant from Abraham to his son, Isaac, was especially resonant in the context of the coronation and the celebration it embodied of the succession of divine kingship from one monarch to another. The *Caesar* tapestries were also hung in Westminster Hall

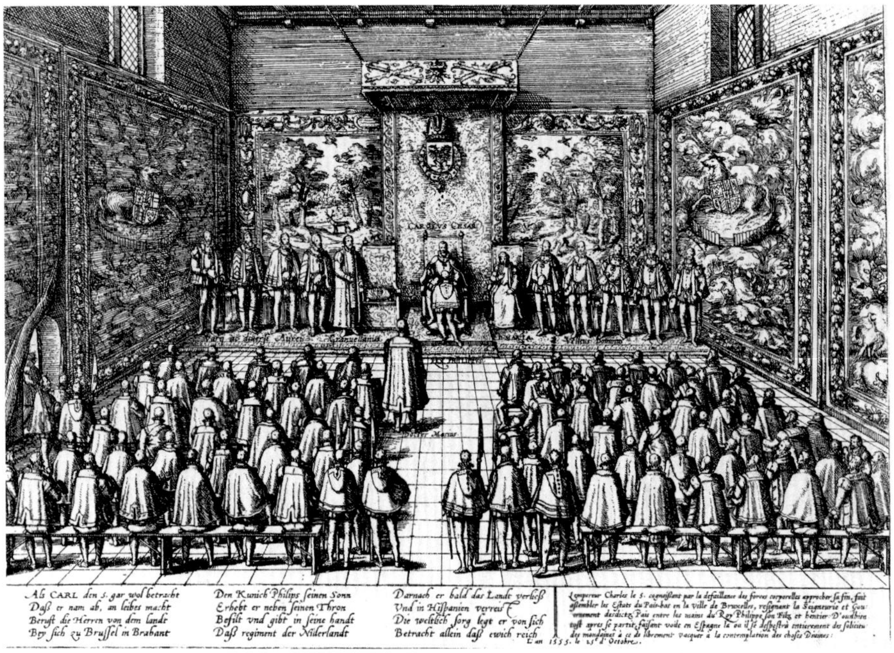

18.4 *The Abdication of Charles V* from *Events in the History of the Netherlands, France, Germany, and England between 1535 and 1608.* Later impression of an engraving by Frans Hogenberg, ca. 1558. 19.8 x 27.3 cm. The Metropolitan Museum of Art, New York

for James II's coronation in 1685, so the brief details provided by this account may hint at the origins of a practice that continued well into the late seventeenth century.

Whether Elizabeth commissioned new tapestries is uncertain, but with a collection of the size that she inherited there was no practical need for expansion. She was at the center of a circle of nobles and courtiers who, at her encouragement, expended enormous sums of money on new palaces and the tapestries to decorate them, many of which survive today. Most notable of these were the tapestries commemorating the *Defeat of the Spanish Armada,* which were commissioned by Charles Howard, the lord high admiral, and woven in Delft between 1592 and 1598 (fig. 18.5). A telling insight to Elizabeth's attitude to such works is provided by a contemporary account of her visit to Howard's estate in 1602: "The Lord Admiral's feasting the Queen had nothing extraordinary, neither were his presents so precious as was expected, being only a whole suite of apparel, wheras it was thought he would have bestowed his rich hangings of all the fights with the Spanish Armada in eighty-eight."[6] The set was subsequently purchased from Howard's descendants by James I and eventually hung in the House of Lords at Cromwell's orders during the Commonwealth. Generally speaking, however, it seems that Elizabeth was content to continue living in the stately splendor of her father's palaces, which, as years passed, provided a constant reminder to her subjects of her Tudor lineage and regal authority. The lord chamberlain's records certainly indicate that the inherited collection was carefully repaired throughout her reign.[7]

Evidence of the continuing display of the historic hangings in the royal palaces at the end

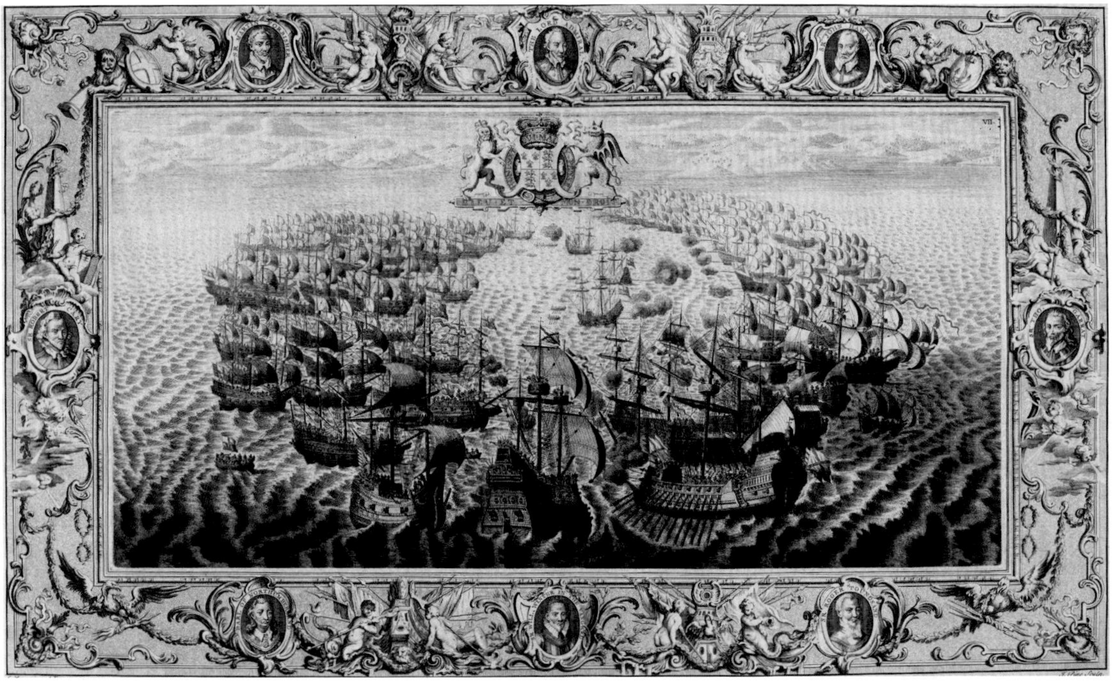

18.5 *The English Send Burning Ships against the Armada off Calais.* Engraving after a Delft tapestry of this subject from John Pine's *The Tapestry Hangings of The House of Lords . . .* (London, 1739). The borders are Pine's invention.

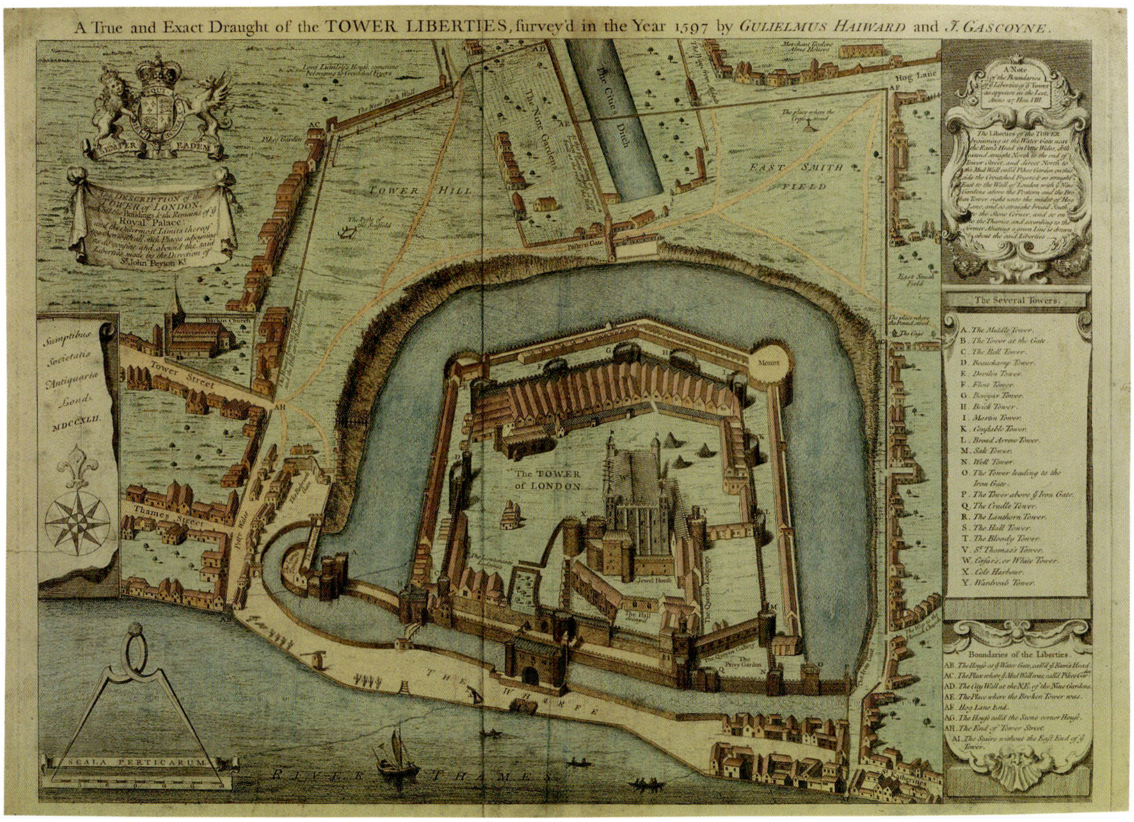

18.6 *The Tower of London in 1597* from G. Hayward and J. Gascoyne, *A True and Exact Draught of the Tower Liberties* (London, 1597). The Royal Library, Windsor Castle

of the sixteenth century is provided by the accounts of visiting dignitaries and tourists between the 1580s and the mid-1610s. The Tower (fig. 18.6) remained the main Great Wardrobe depot, and several accounts record the mix of treasures stored there. That of Paul Hentzer, a lawyer from Brandenburg, in 1598 is typical: "Upon entering, we were obliged to leave our swords at the gate and deliver them to the guard. When we were introduced, we were shown about 100 pieces of arras belonging to the crown, made of gold, silver and silk; several saddles covered with velvet of different colors; an immense quantity of bed-furniture, such as canopies and the like, some of them most richly ornamented with pearl; some royal dresses so extremely magnificent, as to raise any one's admiration at the sums they must have cost."[8] The following year, Thomas Platter received a similar tour. Having viewed the contents of the Tower Wardrobe, he was shown into another room with "a very ancient tapestry which had been in this castle some five hundred years. The history embroidered on it showed a king's daughter disguised as a man in peasant clothes piling up wood; this tapestry was very fine and large; here we gave the fifth gratuity."[9] Tips were evidently a crucial element of these visits.

At Windsor the tourists marveled at the richness and age of the hangings and beds, foremost among which was the cloth of state with King Clovis of France that had been looted from the French in the 1420s. Several detailed accounts of this antique survive, of which the most detailed was Platter's, quoted above. Platter's guide at Windsor was the "castle overseer," so his account presumably reflects the common veneration of this object. It is certainly remarkable for the detailed description of the tapestry, perhaps a hint of a broader proto-antiquarian veneration associated with such objects.[10] Similarly appreciative comments on the antiques were made by Philip Julius, duke of Stettin-Pomerania, on the occasion of his visit to Windsor in 1602. Besides the French canopy "said to be eight hundred years old," Julius noted another antique bed "in which the red and white roses, after many long wars, were united by friendly marriage."[11]

Other visitors recorded rich tapestries at Greenwich and Theobalds, but Hampton

Court inspired the greatest praise. Indeed, the palace was evidently the highlight of such tours, in terms of both the scale and splendor of the palace and the richness of its contents. For example, in 1592 Friedrich, duke of Wurttemberg, commented: "In short, all the apartments and rooms in this immensely large structure are hung with rich tapestry, of pure gold and fine silk, so exceedingly beautiful and royally ornamented that it would hardly be possible to find more magnificent things of the kind in any other palace."[12] And as noted in Chapter 15, Paul Hentzner made similar comments when he visited Hampton Court in 1598.[13] Although these descriptions evidently refer to the large-figure tapestries purchased by Henry in the 1530s and 1540s, Hentzner also noted the presence in the hall of tapestry with "negroes riding upon elephants," probably a set depicting European explorers in the New World of the kind produced in Tournai during the 1510s and 1520s. Further evidence that "pre-Renaissance" style tapestries continued to be displayed in older sections of the palace comes from the 1610 account of the duke of Saxe-Weimer, who after noting the beauty and splendor of the *Abraham* and *Tobias* tapestries, recorded a set of "the history of the Creation of the World," in which "the Deity is always represented as three old persons in Episcopal habits, with crowns on their heads and scepters in their hands."[14] This description almost certainly relates to a weaving of the *Redemption of Man* design, but it is uncertain whether this was the gold-ground set putatively purchased by Henry VII or the wool and silk weaving bought by Wolsey, of which part had been located at The More in 1547. By the time of the Commonwealth sale in 1650, the gold-ground set was located at Richmond Palace (see below).

Because so many of the tourists visiting Hampton Court during these years record seeing the *Abraham, Tobias,* and *Caesar* tapestries, the question arises as to whether these sets were now hanging permanently. The evidence is ambiguous. In 1585, Samuel Kiechel recorded that "the royal treasures and tapestries are kept only in that palace in which for the time being the Queen resides; when she removes to another, everything is taken away, and only the bare walls remain standing."[15] Similarly, writing in 1598, Hentzner described being shown a chamber in which were stored "several excessively rich tapestries, which are hung up when the Queen gives audience to foreign ambassadors."[16] The following year, Platter recorded being shown a room, "containing many fine royal beds, also numerous canopies and royal chairs all very lavish and ornate; and the walls everywhere were hung with extremely costly tapestries worked with gold, silver and silk, so life-like that one might take the people and plants for real."[17] The room was evidently one of the wardrobe chambers in which some of the finest tapestries had been hung for the amazement of visiting dignitaries and, no doubt, the enrichment of the resident wardrobe officer. Nonetheless, at the time of Hentzner's visit the king and queen's state apartments were also hung with rich tapestry. Similarly, Platter recorded tapestries from the *Story of Caesar* and the *Story of Tobias* in the king's apartments and the *Story of Caesar* and the *Story of Abraham* in the queen's apartments. Of the *Abraham* set he commented that it was thought "to be the finest and most artistic in England."[18] Such observations support the notion that Hampton Court may have been maintained as a sort of Tudor showpiece during Elizabeth's later years, a constant celebration of the grandeur of her father's reign and of the legitimacy and foundation of her achievements.[19] This would explain the information provided in 1602 by the duke of Stettin-Pomerania, who wrote that "the decorations consisted entirely of tapestries exquisitely wrought in good gold-thread and best silk, that not easily will such be found anywhere in such quantities as in this place; the common linen ones are generally hung over those of higher value."[20] Whether the finest tapestries were hanging semipermanently in Elizabeth's later years or whether the surviving accounts simply reflect that visitors made the effort to visit Hampton Court when the queen was in residence, the accounts all concur in suggesting that great care was taken with the finest tapestries. Subsequent testimony tends to confirm how rarely they were exposed. At the time of the Commonwealth sale in 1650, Cardinal Mazarin's agent informed him that the *Abraham* set was "fort bien conservée, n'ayant jamais servi que dans les jours des cérémonies" (very well conserved, having never been used except for feast days).[21] In contrast, it seems likely that many of the older, lower-grade tapestries were hung semipermanently at this date.

Here it should be noted that although the best of Henry's sets continued to play an important role in the decoration of the royal palaces, a process of gradual dispersal must have been occurring from shortly after his death, through the perquisites attendant on the monarch's death and coronation. According to tradition, the lord chamberlain could claim the furnishings of the sovereign's apartment at the time of death, while the lord great chamberlain was allowed to claim those of the rooms in which the monarch stayed on the eve of the coronation.[22] Although precise details are lacking for the Tudor period, both claims appear to have been established by the sixteenth century.[23] It also seems to have been regular practice for the royal wardrobes to be subjected to periodic "views" every twenty to thirty years, when certain courtiers had their choice of objects deemed to be too old and worn for royal use.[24] How extensively the royal tapestries were depleted by this process is hard to ascertain because of the difficulty of identifying and then tracing them in contemporary inventories. But an impression of the gradual dispersal is provided by the appearance of tapestries with Wolsey's armorials in the inventories of three noblemen in the sixteenth and seventeenth centuries. The 1561 inventory of William Herbert, earl of Pembroke, lists twenty-eight "hangings of the Cardinalles hatte"; that taken in 1614 at the death of Henry Howard, earl of Northampton, lists five pieces of "Bruxels worke garnished in the border with Cardinall Wolsey his armes"; and the 1622 inventory of Cossey House, once the home of Anne of Cleves and given by Queen Mary to Sir Henry Jerningham, records "Three pieces of hangings with the Cardinals Hat."[25]

The Use of Historic Tapestries under James I and Charles I

Although perquisites and gifts depleted the collection in the second half of the sixteenth century, the vast majority of the finest tapestries survived in royal hands at the opening of the seventeenth century and continued to play a major part in court ceremony during the reigns of James I and his son, Charles I. Like their Elizabethan forebears, the Jacobean courtiers were keen patrons of the Netherlandish workshops, and the continuing valuation of tapestry as the principle medium of courtly magnificence undoubtedly contributed to the formation of the Mortlake tapestry manufactory in 1619. This was established by James under the direction of Sir Francis Crane, secretary and friend of Charles, Prince of Wales.[26]

Lacking a skilled tapestry designer in its early days, the first Mortlake products were copied from Henrician sets, a reflection of the esteem in which these older designs continued to be held. The models chosen included the *Months, Vulcan and Venus, Solomon and Sheba,* and the *Playing Boys.*[27] It is uncertain whether the model for the last of these, the *Boys,* was one of Henry's acquisition, since the design was conceived for Ercole Gonzaga in about 1545. This may be one of the few sets that can be identified as entering the collection after Henry's death. In each case, the sixteenth-century designs were carefully reproduced, but the borders were woven from new designs provided by artists working for the Stuart court. At the same time, agents working on behalf of Charles and Crane sought to acquire old cartoons on the Continent. Their greatest coup was the purchase in 1623 of seven of the original *Acts of the Apostles* cartoons painted by the Raphael workshop. Copies of these cartoons were made by Francis Clein, the artist associated with the Mortlake manufactory from 1626, and several high-quality sets and individual panels of this design were woven for Charles and his courtiers,

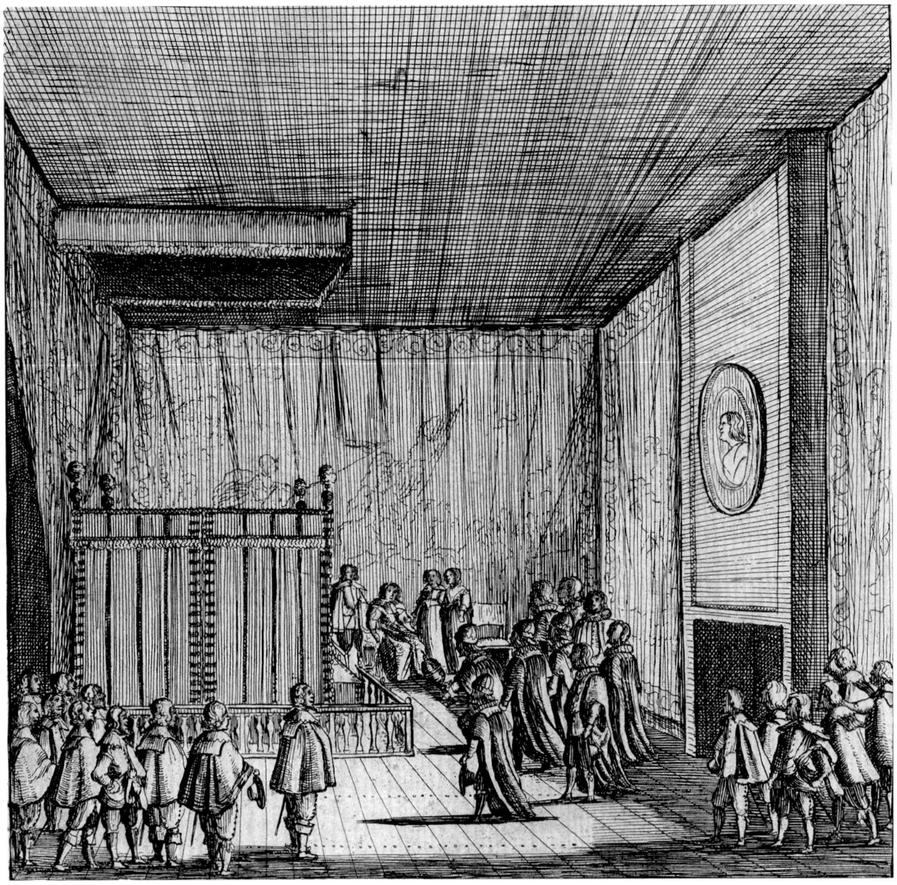

18.7 *Marie de' Medici Holding Court at Saint James's Palace during Her Visit to the English Court in 1638.* British Museum, London (Mm3-19)

some with complex allegorical borders.[28] It is interesting to note that among the works of art in Charles's Cabinet Room there was a book explaining the "Poeticall invention" of the borders of the "Ax of the Apostles," which had been bought by the king and copied by the Records office.[29] Whether this was a key to the borders of the Henrician set or the more recent Clein designs is unclear, but either way, it shows that complex tapestry iconography remained a subject of erudition and connoisseurship.

Charles spent large sums on Mortlake tapestries, but contemporary records show that the inherited collection continued to play a central role in court ceremony. Many of the finest Henrician tapestries, beds, and textiles were left in situ at Hampton Court, whose Tudor character seems to have been assiduously maintained during Charles's reign.[30] Carefully husbanded because of their value, quality, and scale, the older hangings were regularly used for occasions of state throughout Charles I's reign, as shown by documents relating to the lord chamberlain's office, which records numerous royal warrants requesting the delivery of tapestries from one royal wardrobe to another for special events.[31] As the most splendid tapestries at Hampton Court, the *Abraham* tapestries were in particular demand. For example, they were taken up to Whitehall to provide decorations for the solemnization of the peace with Spain in December 1630, the celebration of Saint George's Feast in April 1635, the reception of the Moroccan ambassador in November 1637, and the reception of the Spanish ambassador in 1640.[32]

Judging by the warrants recording such transfers, certain antique tapestries were associated with particular sites on particular occasions. For example, two tapestries of *Saint George* were regularly brought from Windsor to Whitehall, along with the *Abraham* tapestries and some of the *Tobias* tapestries, for the celebration of Saint George's Day.[33] Another rich set that continued in regular ceremonial use was the gold-ground *Verdure,* which was used especially in association with Henrietta Maria, wife of Charles I, in the context of the rooms prepared for the various royal births during the 1630s. It also featured prominently in the rooms prepared for her mother, Marie de' Medici, when she visited London in 1638 (fig. 18.7).[34] The official description of Marie's visit, published the following year, provides vivid testimony of the continuing use of old and new tapestries in proximity and the esteem in which the older hangings were held. The *Verdure* was hung in the Presence Chamber, and the eulogistic description records that "the flowers of the spring were so well and naturally depicted by the pencil of the needle, that one might easily persuade oneself that the artisan who made that tapestry had originally been a gardener, and thereby having his imagination always filled with different sorts of flowers which he had formerly sown, he had very happily planted them anew in this work, since they seemed here blown with the same beauty as in the parterres."[35]

The continuing use of the finest antique tapestries and the addition of new Mortlake tapestries to the collection coincided with the ongoing gradual dispersal of lesser hangings. In part this was through ad hoc decoration requirements at other palaces, as evidenced, for example, by the warrant issued to the Hampton Court Wardrobe in October 1631 to deliver a set of *Venus and Cupid* and "20 peeces more of ordinary Hangings" for his Majesty's service at Saint James's Palace.[36]

The Commonwealth Sale

The next and most dramatic stage in the depletion of the collection was precipitated by the Civil War and the sale of royal goods held by the Commonwealth government. The main events of the sale are well documented. Following the execution of Charles I on January 30, 1649, the Council of State directed that the collections of the late king, the queen, and the Prince of Wales should be sold to pay the royal debts. A group of trustees was appointed to inventory and value the objects and to present lists to the Council of State so that some goods might be reserved for the use of the State before the sale of the rest at Somerset House. The necessary Act of Parliament passed on July 4, 1649, and inventories and valuations were drawn up over the next six months. The sale of works of art was under way by the end of the year.

The Commonwealth inventory provides an extraordinary overview of the royal tapestry collection as it existed in the early 1650s, comparable in significance to that made one hundred years before, after Henry's death. Most of the fine tapestries were in storage in the various palace wardrobes, but many of the lesser pieces had been appropriated to decorate the apartments of government officers, particularly at Whitehall Palace. Visiting Hampton Court in 1652, Lodewijk Huygens commented that "the furniture had all been removed, except for the tapestries which had been behind the good ones to protect them from the damp of the walls. They said that in the time of the king there had been some splendid ones."[37]

In total, the inventories list more than sixteen hundred tapestries. Of these, more than a thousand dated from the sixteenth century, the surviving part of the enormous collection amassed under Henry VIII. The rest originated from purchases made by Charles I, mostly from the Mortlake manufactory.[38] Although the dimensions are less precise than those given in the 1547 inventory, and though the distinctions of "arras" and tapestry are not recorded, an indication of the quality of the various hangings is provided by their appraisals. The valuations placed on the paintings largely reflected their market value, which had been stimulated during the second quarter of the seventeenth century by the strong competition between English and Continental collectors. It was a different story with the tapestries. These appear to have been appraised in a very summary manner according to their condition, the quality of the material they included, and their surface area, regardless of their age, provenance, or artistic merit. Generally speaking, unless a set contained gilt-metal-wrapped thread or was exceptionally large, most were appraised in the region of between £20 and

£30, considerably below their replacement value. Older fragments and individual pieces fared worse. Many of the fifteenth-century tapestries that survived at Windsor Castle and Richmond Palace were valued at derisory figures. The antique cloth of state depicting the *Story of Clovis* that had been a tourist attraction at Windsor Castle for so many years was valued at just £2. The highest valuation for a fifteenth-century set was the £366 placed on the *Story of the Trojan War* that Henry VII purchased in 1488. Sixteenth-century tapestries fared little better. Many of the gold-woven devotional panels that had formed some of the most precious pieces in Wolsey's collection were valued at only £1 or £2. In this case, part of the problem was the subject matter, which was considered "Popish," although the Commonwealth officers recognized that there would be a market for such works abroad. The large set of the *Triumphs of Petrarch* that survives today at Hampton Court was valued at just £166.

A striking contrast to these low appraisals was provided by about twenty sets of very high-quality tapestry that, because of their size and condition and the large amount of metallic thread they included, were valued far in excess of any other works of art in the collection. About a third of these rich sets had been made at Mortlake for Charles I, but the others had been purchased by Henry VIII, including the *Story of Abraham,* which received the highest valuation of the whole collection at £8,260. Other sixteenth-century "arras" sets that received high appraisals included the *Redemption of Man* (£1,877), the gold-ground *Verdure* (£2,292), the sets (or set) of *David* that had been purchased in 1517 and 1520 (£1,072 and £994), the *David* set purchased in 1528 (£2,544), the *Seven Deadly Sins* (£2,430), the *Antiques* (£2,437), the *Acts of the Apostles* (£4,429), and the stories of *Joshua* (£3,399), *Tobias* (£3,409), *Saint Paul* (£3,065), and *Julius Caesar* (£5,022).[39]

The sale of works of art began in late 1649, but the response was less rewarding than the Council of State had hoped, and although initial sales allowed payments to be made to some of the neediest creditors, by May 1650, there were still more than nine hundred outstanding claims. The committee responsible for the sale therefore decided to apportion works of art to the creditors in lieu of payment. To facilitate this process, many of the creditors divided themselves into syndicates, and the dispersal of goods to these "dividends" took place in October 1651. The process had an immediate impact on the fate of the tapestry collection. Just over one hundred tapestries were sold in 1649, and another two hundred or so were sold by May 1650. With the dispersal to the dividends in late 1651, more than six hundred were turned over to the creditors, most of whom had little interest in the tapestries other than to sell them as quickly as possible. The sale included some of the finest sets in the collection, such as the ten-piece *Story of David* that Henry VIII had purchased in 1528 from Richard Gresham. During the same period, a number of tapestry sets were also removed from their historic homes for the use of members of Parliament, as reflected by documents in the state papers. For example, five *Triumphs* and seven pieces of the *Siege of Jerusalem* were removed from Windsor in 1651.[40]

Acquisitions by Foreign Collectors

By early 1652, almost a thousand tapestries had been transferred into private hands, and it was from individual dealers, or the representatives of the dividends, that the agents of foreign collectors like Cardinal Mazarin and Don Luis Mendez de Haro, Philip IV's *valido,* subsequently made many of their purchases. These agents had been circling like hawks for some time already.[41] In a letter of May 16, 1650, the French agent in London informed Cardinal Mazarin that he had seen his Spanish counterpart, Don Alonso de Cárdenas, at Somerset House, where "il se fit monstrer toutes les tapisseries et fut fort long temps a voir les tableaux dont il fit prendre des notes, il en a desja acheté plusieurs" (he was shown all the tapestries and took a long time to inspect the paintings about which he made notes, he has already purchased many). Cárdenas's standing in London had been precarious from both a

18.8 *Cardinal Mazarin in His Palace,* 1659. Engraving by Robert Nanteuil and Pierre van Schuppen. Bibliothèque Nationale de France, Paris

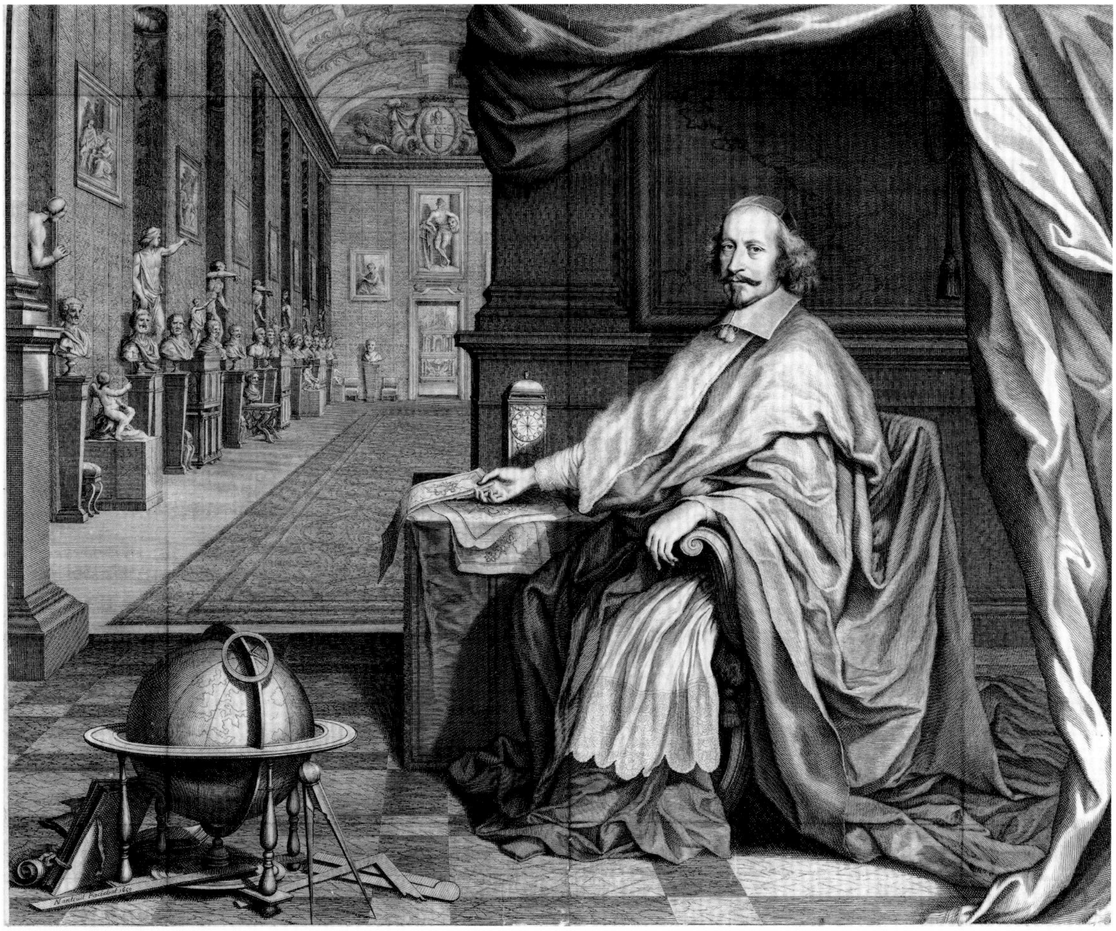

political and a financial point of view throughout 1649 and early 1650, but these problems were removed in October, when he received full diplomatic credentials from Philip IV. In contrast, the French agent was asked to leave England shortly thereafter because he lacked the appropriate credentials from Louis XIV. The Spanish ambassador's main source of competition was thus removed at a time when there were literally hundreds of tapestries on the market, and he clearly profited from this opportunity to buy some of the finest, both for de Haro and for his own use. His purchases for de Haro included the set of gold-ground *Verdure* tapestries that Henry had bought from Pieter van Aelst for the meeting with Francis I at Guines in 1520 and the set of the *Acts of the Apostles* purchased in 1542. (The *Verdure* set was subsequently destroyed in a fire at the Alcazar in the eighteenth century. The *Acts* passed into the collection of the duke of Alba, from which it was eventually sold in 1823.) Thus, because of the rupture of diplomatic relations between the Commonwealth government and the French crown, a crucial period passed during which French collectors lacked the opportunity afforded to the Spanish ambassador. In addition, the most active French tapestry collector of the period, Cardinal Mazarin, must have been largely preoccupied with other matters, for this was when he was temporarily exiled from Paris because of the Fronde. However, with his return to the capital in February 1653, and the arrival of his agent, Antoine de Bordeaux in London from the beginning of that year, Mazarin was again in a position to benefit from the sale of Charles's tapestries, and he evidently sought to make up for lost time as rapidly as possible.

Much information has survived about the tapestry collection that Mazarin (fig. 18.8) developed and the numerous and complex deals into which he entered with various Continental dealers, owners, and manufacturers.[42] The most famous sets he owned were the so-called *Grand Scipio,* woven for the maréchal de

Saint-André about 1550 and the so-called *Hunts of Maximilian* that he acquired along with other tapestries from the duc de Guise.[43] The opportunity that the sale of the English royal tapestries afforded was clearly not one that Mazarin was going to miss. De Bordeaux's correspondence with Mazarin shows that he had been instructed to find particular tapestries that would complete sets that were available on the Continent and to search out other pieces of high quality and value.[44] The speed with which a large portion of the goods allotted to the dividends had already been resold is reflected by the difficulty that de Bordeaux experienced in finding appropriate tapestries. In April de Bordeaux informed Mazarin that he had located five tapestries of *David* corresponding to others that Mazarin had purchased from the commandeur Souvré, perhaps confirming the suggestion made above, that the two groups of *David* tapestries listed at Greenwich and Whitehall were related. From that point on, de Bordeaux's correspondence is peppered with references to tapestries he had seen or heard about and hoped to buy or had already bought. From the summer of 1653 he was evidently in regular contact with the government trustees who were responsible for selling the tapestries. On August 11, he was shown some of the finest pieces that remained in the collection, including the *Abraham* set of which he reported that "tous ceux qui ont vu celle d'Abraham l'estiment la plus belle quie fust en Angleterre" (everyone who has seen that of Abraham judges it the most beautiful in England).[45] Although the sale was temporarily halted because of a government investigation into the trustees operating the sale, several of his subsequent letters refer to the possible purchase of this set. Mazarin had been disappointed that Henry's set of the *Acts of the Apostles* had already been sold to the Spanish ambassador, and he now urged de Bordeaux to obtain the *Abraham* set at the best price possible, but definitely not to let it get away.[46] In the event, both that set and all the other tapestries that remained in the collection were reserved for the use of Oliver Cromwell when he was appointed lord protector in late 1653. Though this meant that Mazarin had no hope of acquiring any more tapestries directly from the royal collection, de Bordeaux's correspondence and the inventories of Mazarin's possessions taken in 1653 and 1661 show that he mopped up a substantial number of the royal tapestries that had continued to circulate in the English market.

Some of these may have been purchased even before de Bordeaux arrived in London. The inventory of Mazarin's goods that Colbert began to compile in late 1653 lists six sets of tapestry that can be identified as products of the Mortlake manufactory, several of which came from the collection of the earl of Pembroke rather than the British royal collection. All were described as "fabrique d'Angleterre." In addition, the Mazarin inventories also record approximately fifty other tapestries, some in sets and some individual pieces, which were also said to be "fabrique d'Angleterre" but for which no analogous Mortlake designs are known. Several were evidently of high quality, woven with silk and gold, and many were described as old, or as having designs by "Lucas" or Dürer, generic identifications applied somewhat indiscriminately in the inventories of the time to early-sixteenth-century tapestries. No evidence has survived of any sizeable figurative tapestry industry in England before the Mortlake manufactory, and there is absolutely no evidence of any high-quality production there during the sixteenth century. In contrast, the description of several of these tapestries is analogous with surviving early-sixteenth-century Flemish tapestries. For example, the 1653 inventory of Mazarin's collection lists one tapestry that was said to represent the miracle of the two drowned infants. The idiosyncratic subject matter and dimensions allow it to be identified as a weaving of the *Justice of Trajan* of which, as discussed above (pp. 140–41), a gold-woven example had formerly existed in Wolsey's collection, possibly to be identified with that later at Knole and now at the Museum of Fine Arts in Boston. The piece listed in Mazarin's collection did not contain gold thread, and such an example sur-

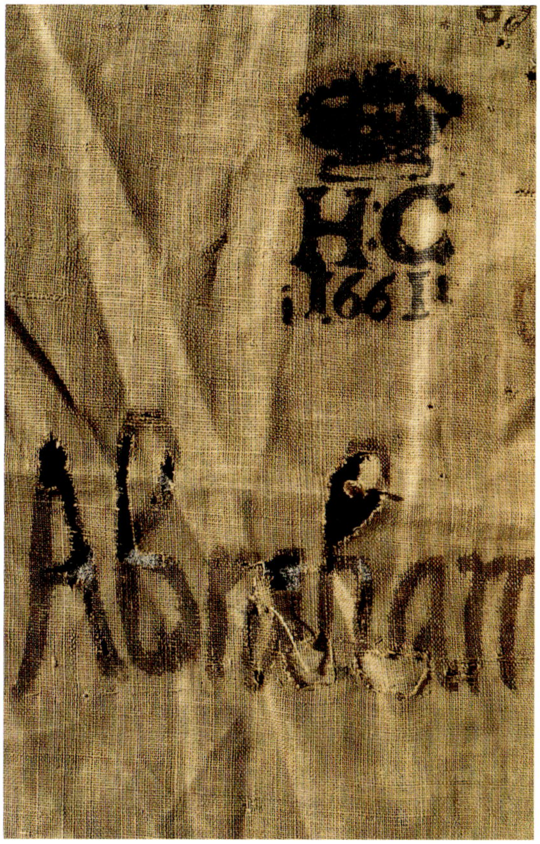

18.9 17th-c. label on the lining of one of the *Story of Abraham* tapestries at Hampton Court

vives today in the Norton Simon Collection. Whether this second weaving of the design also came from the English royal collection is uncertain. As noted above (p. 85), the description of another tapestry listed in the 1661 inventory, also said to be "fabrique d'Angleterre," allows it to be identified with the so-called *Glorification of Christ,* now at the National Gallery in Washington (see fig. 4.18), whose provenance from the Mazarin collection is well established.

Both of these tapestries are generally accepted as having been woven in Brussels in the early sixteenth century, so the question arises as to why these and so many other Flemish tapestries were described as "fabrique d'Angleterre" in Mazarin's inventory. The probable answer is that they had been purchased in London, or were known to stem from the English royal collection, and that the officers responsible for compiling Mazarin's inventory assumed that they had been made in England because they did not carry any weaver or town marks, which did not become compulsory until 1528 for Brussels tapestries and 1544 for those made in other Netherlandish centers.[47] In view of the evident quality of the Mortlake tapestries whose English origin was undisputed, the assumption that many of the older tapestries from the royal collection were also English is understandable. The mistake may have been compounded by markings on the backs of the tapestries from the royal collection. According to regulations instituted in 1630 to safeguard Great Wardrobe property, any hanging removed from a royal palace to the Great Wardrobe for repairs was to be brought in with its original lining and a "label of parchment sowed to the same which the clerk of his Majesty's wardrobe's has subscribed therunto significing of the charge of what house or wardrobe the same stuff is."[48] Whether this was a new regulation or the reiteration of an existing practice is uncertain, but if it was the latter, it might explain the number of tapestries that are listed in the 1547 inventory as "marked with letter." Although no linings are extant from before the 1660s on tapestries in the royal collection, those linings that survive from later in the century are marked with the subject and height of the tapestry and a stamp with the royal cipher, as exemplified by the linings on one of the *Abraham* tapestries now at Hampton Court (fig. 18.9) and one of the *Diogenes* tapestries now at Holyrood House.[49] In the absence of any marks of origin on pre-1528 Brussels tapestries, it therefore seems that Mazarin's wardrobe officers interpreted such markings as an indication of the English origin of many of the tapestries that they were cataloguing. Similar assumptions appear to have been made in regard to sixteenth-century Netherlandish tapestries from the English royal collection in a number of other French collections.

On the basis of this evidence, we can therefore speculate that Mazarin's collection included at least fifty pre-1528 Flemish tapestries from the English royal collection. These were just a part of his purchases from this source, as revealed by de Bordeaux's correspondence, which mentions the acquisition of other sets identified as "Brussels" in the 1653 and 1661 inventories. We can thus appreciate the significant part that the sale of the royal goods played in the formation of Mazarin's collection.

Mazarin was the French collector who benefited most from the dispersal of the English royal tapestry collection, but his peers also availed themselves of the opportunity to purchase tapestries either in London or via French merchants. For example, several of the sets listed in the 1661 inventory of Nicholas Fouquet's tapestry collection were said to be "fabrique d'Angleterre" or were so described later, when they passed into Louis XIV's collection. These included a panel of *Saint Luke Painting the Virgin* of similar dimensions to the piece of this subject now in the Louvre. Many of the tapestries from Mazarin's and Fouquet's collections were purchased or appropriated by Louis XIV and are recorded in the various inventories of the French royal collection. By this means, the French royal collection was enriched with several sets of the finest Mortlake tapestry and many of the "fabrique d'Angleterre" pieces listed in Mazarin's and Fouquet's inventories.

Fouquet was not the only member of his family to profit from the sale. His brother Francis, archbishop of Narbonne, is known to have left a ten-piece set of the *Redemption of Man* to the Chapter of Saint-Just in February 1673 of which one piece survives today in Narbonne Cathedral (see figs. 4.19, 5.2). While parts of at least seven sets of this design series survive, this is the only example that includes gold thread. Given the rarity of gold-woven sets of this design and the evidence that a gold-woven set of this design was in the English royal collection until the Commonwealth sale and that shortly thereafter a gold-woven set appears in the Fouquet collection, it seems logical to deduce that they were one and the same.

In view of the large numbers of tapestries dispersed from the English royal collection in the early 1650s we must assume that those discussed so far may have been only a small part of the number that eventually found their way onto the French market. The taste for tapestry manifested by Mazarin and Fouquet was not exceptional and it remained a subject of keen interest for the nobility and the rich. In 1656 the marquis de Louvois, Louis XIV's war minister, commented that his "curiosité était pour les tapisseries" (interest was for tapestries).[50] At his death in 1685 he owned more than forty sets of tapestry, including a number described as "fabrique d'Angleterre" that may once have belonged to the English royal collection. Another notable patron of the French court, Jean-Baptiste Colbert, also owned tapestries described in this way.[51] Nor was this interest restricted to the nobility. In 1656 Gilles Renard, a French politician whose agent had been in competition with de Bordeaux in London, sold the *Life of Christ* tapestries that had been donated to Canterbury Cathedral in 1511 to the cathedral of Aix-en-Provence, where part of the set survives today.[52] Physical evidence of the dispersal of other tapestries with English provenances is provided by numerous identifiable pieces in modern collections, including several Tudor pieces. As discussed above in the context of Wolsey's patronage, Sens Cathedral has a tapestry of *Judith and Holofernes* with the cardinal's arms in the top border. Another fragment with Wolsey's arms is at the Musée Lécuyer, Saint Quentin, in this case deriving from a set of the *Story of Tobias*. The Musée Lécuyer also has a tapestry depicting a scene from the *Story of Saint John the Baptist* whose dimensions and subject correspond to a panel described in the inventory of Wolsey's collection. Although it does not have Wolsey's arms, it is stylistically similar to tapestries still at Hampton Court. Other sets from both the royal and courtier collections were dispersed even further afield. The Mortlake set of the *Months,* originally carrying the arms of John Williams, lord keeper and bishop of Lincoln, now covered over with those of the de Franchi family, had arrived in Genoa before 1650, when it was mentioned in the will of Giovanni Andrea de Franchi.[53] A similar fate appears to have befallen the fine-quality *Triumphs of Petrarch* set with portraits of Cardinal Wolsey and Henry VIII. This was also in Genoa by the late 1650s.[54]

The Discontinuation of the Sale and Reservations for Cromwell

While connoisseurs like Mazarin and the Spanish ambassador managed to purchase some of the finest sets, the sheer cost of the best, which far exceeded the value placed on even the rarest and most important old master paintings, ensured that negotiations regarding their sale were protracted.[55] Further dispersal was delayed by the investigation into the trustees in charge of the sale. In this way a number of the most valuable, including the Hampton Court *Abraham* and *Tobias* sets, were unsold when Cromwell was elected lord protector, at which point the sale was discontinued and the remaining goods were reserved for him.[56] An inventory taken at Cromwell's death in 1659 records the disposition of the tapestries that had been appropriated for his use at Hampton Court. Interestingly, several of the "pre-Renaissance" sets were hanging in prominent positions at this time, confirming their continuing use and significance. These included nine pieces of the *Old and New Law,* or the *Redemption of Man* set, in the Privy Chamber, which was evidently from Wolsey's set because the gold-woven set formerly at Richmond had been sold by this date; five pieces of the "Morians" in the Withdrawing Room; and three pieces of *Triumphs* in the late king's Presence Chamber. Later Henrician tapestries included five pieces of the *Antiques* in the "Rich Bedchamber" and the *Seven Deadly Sins* in the Paradise Room. The other two *Antiques* panels were in the late king's Withdrawing Room, while five of the *Tobias* panels hung in the late king's Privy Chamber.[57]

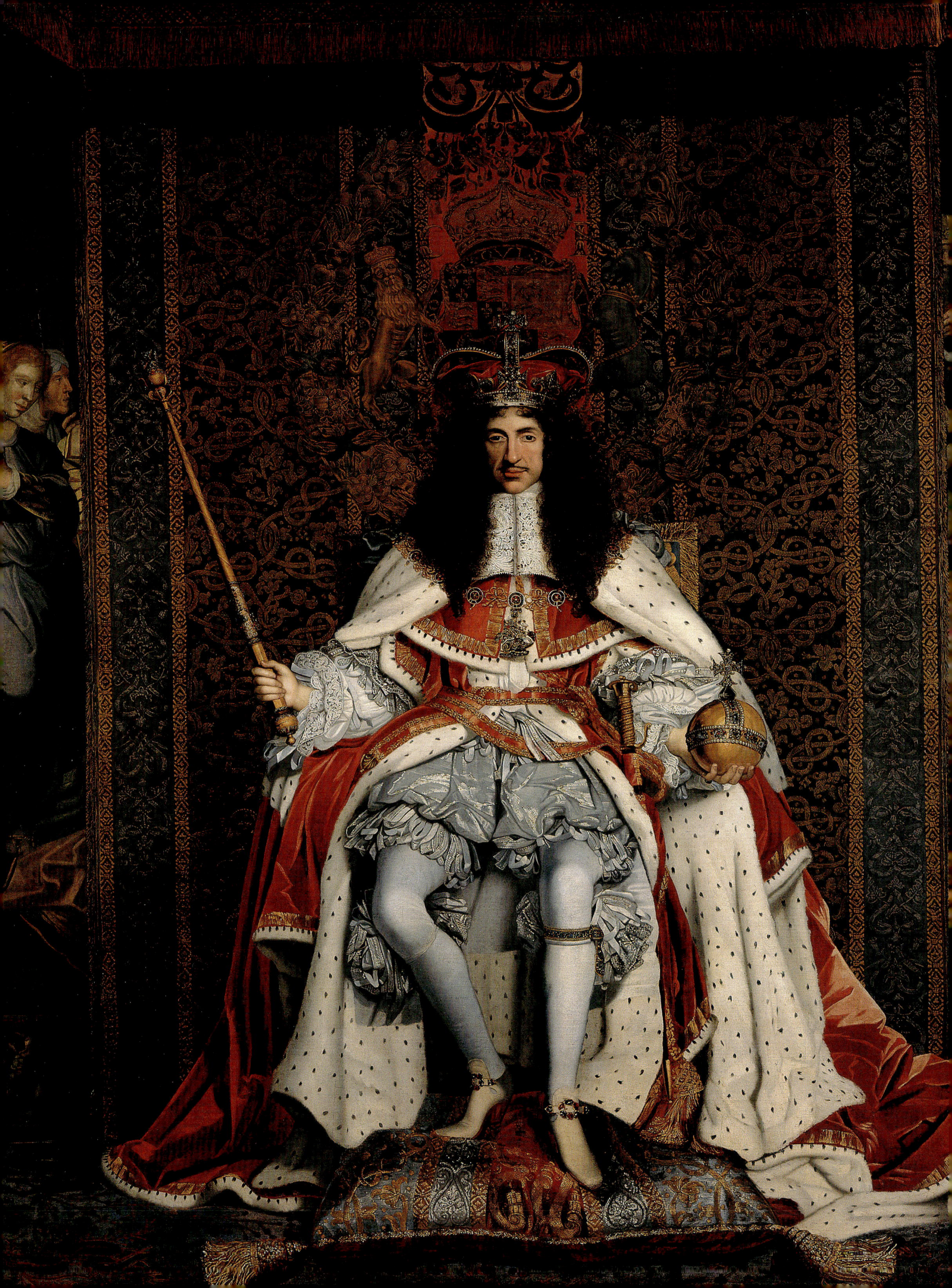

CHAPTER 19

The History of the Tudor Collection from 1660 to the Present Day

The Use of the Tudor Tapestries under Charles II and James II

The election of Cromwell as lord protector in December 1653 and the discontinuation of the Commonwealth sale so that appropriate furnishings might be allocated for his residences ensured the survival of a significant portion of the grandest Henrician tapestries in the collection when Charles II (fig. 19.1) was restored to the throne in 1660. In the following years efforts were made to buy back some of the other pieces that had remained in England, but these were few.[1] Despite the turbulent events of the previous two decades, the structure of the royal household pertaining to the palace furnishings remained relatively unchanged after the Restoration, and the lord chamberlain's papers show that the depleted tapestry collection continued to play as important a role in royal magnificence as it had done before the Civil War.[2]

Before Charles II's coronation, the Great Wardrobe purchased four mid-sixteenth-century *Abraham* tapestries for display in Westminster Abbey, of which fragments survive there today.[3] These duplicated the design of four of the panels at Hampton Court with the crucial difference that although they are finely woven in wool and silk, they lack gilt-metallic thread. The reason for purchasing duplicates when the original set was available at Hampton Court is unclear, as is the provenance of the duplicates. But the fact that this Henrician design was particularly sought out for the coronation proceedings suggests how strongly the iconography was associated by tradition with this ceremony.[4]

19.1 *Portrait of Charles II* by John Michael Wright, ca. 1660. Oil on canvas, 283.2 x 225.4 cm. The Royal Collection

Charles II's reign was coterminous with that of Louis XIV, the most ambitious tapestry patron since the age of Henry VIII, Charles V, and Francis I. Acting on his behalf, Jean-Baptiste Colbert amalgamated various Paris tapestry workshops at the Gobelins site in 1662 under the direction of the royal artist Charles Le Brun. During the subsequent three decades Louis invested enormous sums of money in allegorical, mythological, and historical tapestries to celebrate and aggrandize his kingship (figs. 19.2, 19.3). Following this example, tapestry remained the traditional form of regal magnificence and figurative decoration at all the European courts, despite the parallel rise of interest in old master and contemporary painting. Evidence that Charles may have wished to emulate Louis's example is provided by his appointment of Ralph Montagu, master of the horse for Queen Catherine's household and ambassador extraordinary to the French court, as head of the Great Wardrobe in 1672 and by the fact that Montagu took over the premises and equipment of the old Mortlake tapestry manufactory in 1674.[5] However, the financial and political restrictions under which the British monarchy now labored prevented the realization of any ambitious purchases or commissions and ensured a continuing dependence on the inherited tapestry collection.

The scale and disposition of the collection during Charles II's reign is recorded by an inventory taken in 1676.[6] As this reveals, the fifteenth-century tapestries seem to have remained together at Windsor, presumably by weight of tradition and the suitability of their style to the ancient building. The most notable

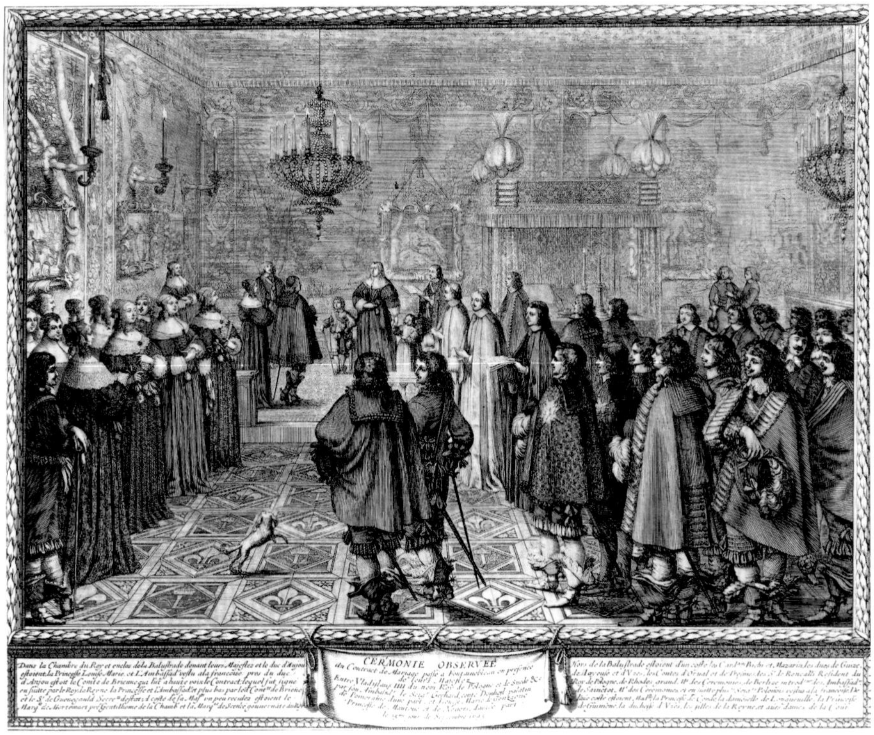

19.2 *Ceremony of the Contract of Marriage between Vladislas IV, King of Poland, and Louise Marie Gonzaga, Princess of Mantua, at Fontainebleau* by Abraham Bosse, 1645. Etching, 27.1 x 33.1 cm. The Metropolitan Museum of Art, New York

of these antiques were now the nine pieces of the *Siege of Jerusalem,* seven pieces of *Charlemagne,* six pieces of the *Story of the Trojan War,* four of *Vineyards,* and eight pieces of *Triumphs.* All were described as "old" or "very old." The *Siege of Jerusalem* and *Charlemagne* sets had always been described as "arras" in earlier inventories, but the relatively low valuations placed on them at the Commonwealth sale suggests that they were now faded and worn. Both are described as tapestry in the 1676 and subsequent inventories, an indication of the erosion of traditional distinctions following the Restoration.

While the fifteenth-century tapestries largely remained at Windsor, the Henrician tapestries traditionally allocated to Hampton Court had been returned to that wardrobe, along with other tapestries, once Wolsey's, also associated with the palace, such as the *Old and New Law* set, three pieces of the *Triumphs of Petrarch,* others of the *Nine Worthies,* and various Old Testament subjects with Wolsey's arms in the borders.[7] The gold-woven *Seven Deadly Sins* and *Antiques* sets had been returned to the Tower, but along with the *Spanish Armada* set these were now the only tapestries listed there. The removing wardrobes at other former Tudor residences such as Greenwich, Oatlands, and Theobalds were now defunct, but a number of tapestries listed in the Whitehall Removing Wardrobe were identified as originating from these palaces.[8] Identification of tapestries listed in the 1547 inventory and those at Whitehall is difficult because of the mingling of old and new sets there. But the survival of a number of Henrician sets is suggested by designations such as "old stuffe" or "very old," and a few of the more idiosyncratic subjects can certainly be identified as deriving from the Tudor collection, such as the "very Old Tapestry Hangings of the Rape of the Sabeans."[9] Most of the older sets listed in the Whitehall Standing and Removing Wardrobes were of moderate and indifferent quality, and only one Henrician "arras" set was listed there, the five pieces of *Aeneas.* Several new English and Flemish sets had been added to the collection since the Restoration, and these were dispersed among Windsor, Hampton Court, and Whitehall, but all were described as tapestry, a reflection of the Crown's limited financial resources in comparison to its French counterpart.

A visual hint of the role played by antique tapestries during Charles's reign is provided by a portrait painted in the early 1660s by John Michael Wright (see fig. 19.1). This shows the king in front of an armorial cloth of honor that is placed before a tapestry. Enough of the tapestry is visible for it to be identified as the *Birth of Romulus and Remus* from the *Romulus and Remus* set purchased by Henry VIII from Richard Gresham in 1529. In 1676 this set was listed among the holdings of the Standing Wardrobe at Whitehall, and according to an annotation in the inventory it was hanging in the banqueting house, so this may be where the portrait was executed.[10] Although the use of this moderate-quality set reflects the continuing presence of old tapestries in the decoration of the court, it also suggests that the traditional dramatization of the hierarchy of the state rooms with hangings of ever increasing richness had fallen into abeyance because of the lack of appropriate high-quality tapestries at each palace.

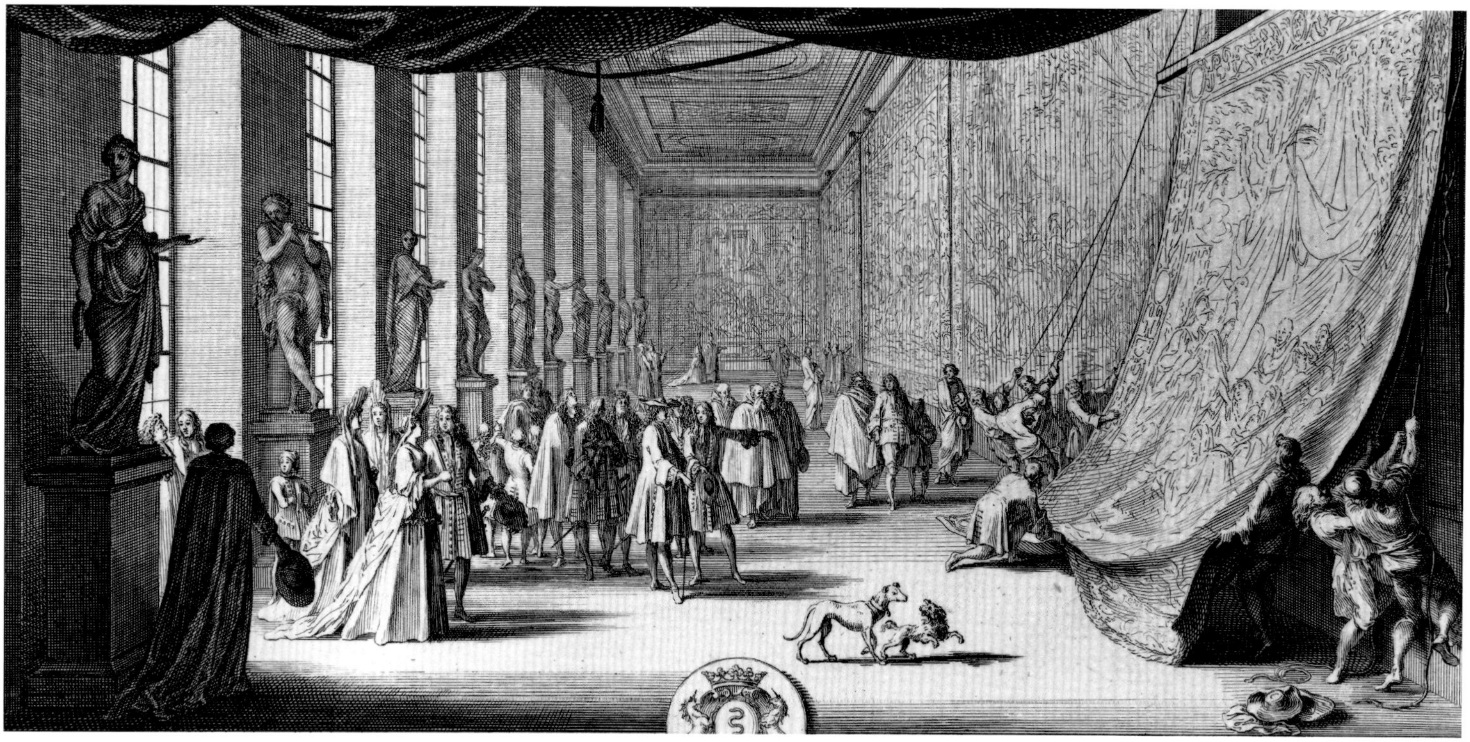

19.3 *The Visit of Colbert de Villacerf to the Gobelins* by Sébastien Le Clerc, ca. 1691–99. Engraving, 14.4 x 23.7 cm. The Metropolitan Museum of Art, New York

As in the decades before the Civil War, the lord chamberlain continued to requisition major sets from one palace for use in another for important occasions. For example, a number of fifteenth-century sets were brought from Windsor to Whitehall to provide suitable decorations for the celebrations of Saint George's feast in April 1667, including the *Siege of Jerusalem, Story of the Trojan War,* and *Triumphs* sets. The same ensembles were also provided to the Houses of Parliament in September 1672.[11] But in the context of the royal palaces, Henry VIII's gold-woven tapestries continued to make the greatest contribution to court grandeur. Indeed, the restricted financial circumstances that characterized the post-Restoration monarchy seem to have precipitated a change in how the finest tapestries were used. From Charles II's reign many of these sets were hung more permanently, often behind paintings, sconces, and light brackets. For example, the state apartments prepared for Charles II at Windsor in July 1678 were decorated in part with Henrician tapestries. The King's Presence Chamber was hung with a set of *Hezekiah,* which had been described as new in the Commonwealth inventory,[12] and the Privy Chamber was hung with a set of Mortlake *Months.* But the Withdrawing Room and King's Bedchamber were hung with tapestries from Henry's *Saint Paul* set. The Queen's Presence Chamber was hung with Henry's *Antiques,* and her Privy Chamber and Withdrawing Room with the *Joshua* set. The long room next to these was hung with the *Seven Deadly Sins.* New tapestries of the *Months* and *Seasons* were eventually supplied for the King's and Queen's Bedchambers.[13] The long-term display of Henrician sets embodied by this installation was to set the tone for subsequent monarchs.

The historic tapestries played a major part in the decorations prepared for the coronation of James II in 1685. The lord chamberlain directed the keeper of the Great Wardrobe to provide Westminster with the "same Hangings and furniture which was furnished in every place at the Coronation of his late Majesty of blessed memory [Charles II]." These included the *Caesar* and *Joshua* tapestries for Westminster Hall and various other antique sets for other key chambers. The only deviation from the arrangements of 1660 were those for the abbey itself, where it was stipulated that the Hampton Court *Abraham* tapestries were to be hung about the altar and in Saint Edward's Chapel, rather than the duplicate pieces used

19.4 *The Coronation of James II.* Engraving from Francis Sandford's *The History of the Coronation of the Most High, Most Mighty, and Most Excellent Monarch, James II . . .* (1687). 44.5 x 29.8 cm. The Metropolitan Museum of Art, New York

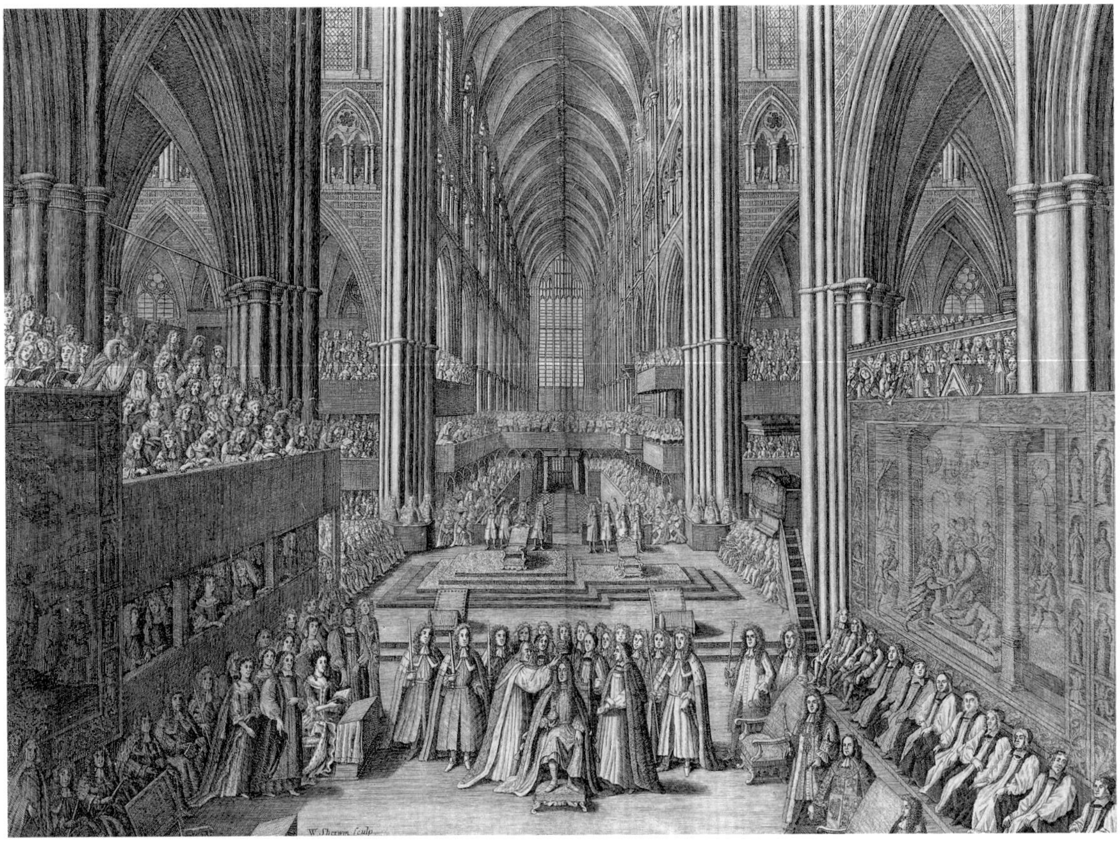

in 1660, and several pieces of the *Abraham* set appear in the engravings made to commemorate the event (fig. 19.4).[14] Most notably, the *Circumcision of Isaac* can be identified next to the high altar, a selection that must have been made to emphasize the continuity of the royal line. Several of the tapestry sets supplied to Westminster on this occasion seem to have remained on permanent display thereafter.

Where the 1676 inventory provided dimensions for each tapestry in each set, the inventory taken in 1688, the last year of James II's reign, is more summary, with sets identified only by title, number of pieces, and height.[15] Generally speaking, the disposition of 1676 remained largely unaltered, although the Windsor *Jerusalem* and *Trojan War* tapestries were now in the custody of the Whitehall Wardrobe, presumably because they were on display at Westminster, while the *Antiques* and *Deadly Sins* formerly at the Tower are now listed at Windsor, as were the *Joshua* set and part of the *Saint Paul* set from Hampton Court. Evidently, many of the older moderate-quality sets were on their last legs, and this is made explicit by descriptions of several sets at Hampton Court. For example, nine pieces of *Esther and Ahasuerus* with inscriptions in the upper borders were described as "very old and past service," while ten pieces of *Hawking and Hunting* were said to be "very course and old and unserviceable."[16]

The Use of the Tudor Tapestries under William III and Queen Anne

Following his accession, William III (r. 1689–1702) ordered a number of new sets of tapestry from Brussels workshops.[17] But the limited financial circumstances by which he, too, was restrained ensured that he followed and developed the practice that Charles II had initiated, hanging antique tapestries more permanently in the main rooms of his palaces to give them an appropriate regal and traditional atmosphere.[18] When the new state apartments at Hampton Court, designed by Sir Christopher Wren, were nearing completion in March 1693, order was given for the cleaning and repair of the *Abraham* and *Joshua* tapestries.[19] Initial prepa-

19.5 Engraving by Simon Gribelin (1720) showing *Acts of Apostles* cartoons hanging in the Cartoon Gallery at Hampton Court

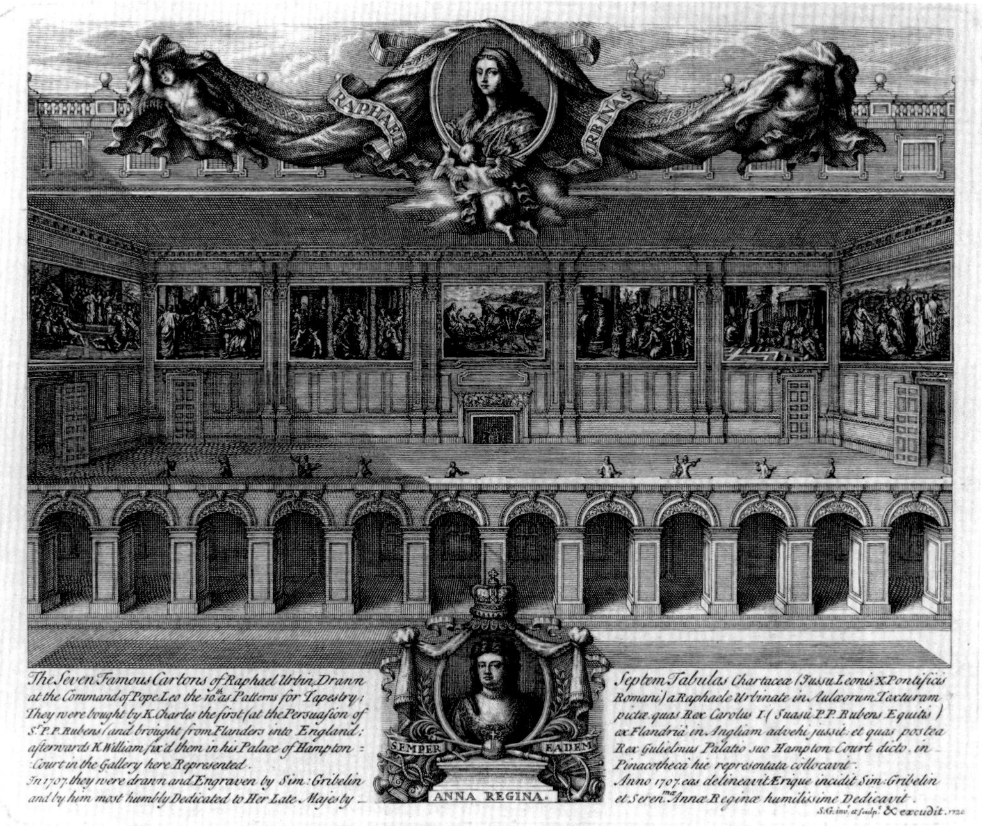

ration of the apartments was abandoned after the death of Queen Mary in 1694, but when the king's apartments were eventually completed for William in 1699, they were decorated with these sets. A number of other sixteenth-century pieces were also used, including the *Triumph of Hercules* from the *Antiques* and the *Triumph of Lust* from the *Deadly Sins*.[20] This selection must have been made because both tapestries featured Hercules, a role model invoked for William III by various decorative schemes at Hampton Court, such as the grisaille roundels in the Wren court and Antonio Verrio's allegorical painting in the staircase leading to the King's State Apartments. In the case of the *Lust* panel it was an infelicitous choice, because Hercules qualified for inclusion in the scene not as an antetype but as a victim. According to legend, he fathered fifty-two children by the fifty daughters of King Thestius. As such, the selection reflects the superficial understanding of the iconography of the tapestry by the Great Wardrobe officers. That the court audience was equally uncritical is reflected by the fact that this tapestry was still hanging in the Presence Chamber more than a hundred years later.

The decorative scheme at Hampton Court appears to have survived Queen Anne's accession without alteration, for although tapestries were sent to London from both Windsor and Hampton Court for the coronation, an order survives instructing that they be replaced in their previous positions afterward, and when Celia Fiennes visited the palace early in Anne's reign, she noted tapestries in several of the king's rooms.[21] Although she does not list any subjects, circumstantial evidence that the *Abraham* set remained the key component of the display is provided by a Great Wardrobe bill of 1713 that records repairs to eight of "Michael Angelo's Abraham and the Old Testament at Hampton Court" in the previous year. The same account also includes a charge by the upholsterer for taking down "all the tapestry hangings in our apartment at Hampton Court and fitting them to the places and putting them up again."[22] The bill also included a charge for six thousand tacks and two thousand penny nails, so there can be little question of the relative permanence of such installations. The attribution of the design to Michelangelo is intriguing. Assuming that it was current a decade or so before, a subsidiary motive in the selection of the *Abraham* tapestries may have been an intention to bring the work of this Renaissance master into proximity with that of Raphael, whose *Acts of the Apostles* cartoons were now displayed in the Cartoon Gallery that Wren created parallel to the King's State Apartments (fig. 19.5).[23]

The furnishings at Hampton Court were especially grand, but they set the tone for tapestry usage in the other palaces equipped during William's reign. According to an inventory of the royal tapestries taken in 1695, panels from the Hampton Court *Caesar* set were then on display at Windsor in the King's Withdrawing Room and the Queen's Privy Chamber, while panels from the *Saint Paul* set were hung in the Queen's Presence Chamber. More private rooms were hung with plain or figured damask.[24] Following Mary's death, some of the *Caesar* panels were reassigned to the King's Drawing Room at Kensington Palace, later known as Queen Caroline's Drawing Room (see fig. 19.7), where they provided a grandiose contrast to the contemporary *Chinoiseries* and *Teniers* genre tapestries that were purchased from London workshops for the more informal and private chambers.[25]

A similar practice was followed under Queen Anne. When Saint James's Palace was refurbished for Anne in 1703–4, five of the Hampton Court *Tobias* tapestries were provided for one of the state apartments, along with a variety of Flemish and English sets of more recent origin. At Somerset House, redecorated in 1707–8, the state apartments were similarly equipped; the Guard Chamber with a set of *Hercules,* probably one of Henry's sets; the Presence Chamber with a Mortlake set of *Vulcan and Venus,* copied from a Henrician model; the Privy Chamber with another Mortlake set of *Hero and Leander;* the Drawing Room with five of Henry's *Antiques* set; and the Bedchamber with a Mortlake set of the *Triumph of Julius Caesar,* copied from Andrea Mantegna's famous paintings.[26] Again, these large-figure tapestries contrasted to the more decorative character of the private apartments.

Between the early 1690s and the late 1710s, the wardrobe accounts provide extensive details of the cleaning and repair of numerous tapestries, many of which dated from the Tudor era. For example, in 1695–96, John Vanderbank, the royal arras maker from 1689 to 1720, was paid a total of £1,896 9s. for repairs to approximately fifteen sets of tapestry. This sum included £128 10s. for cleaning and mending the *Deadly Sins* set and £256 10s. for similar work on the seven *Antiques* tapestries. The latter charge included 105 ells of new selvage edge and "patterns and draughts [designs] to work after to mend the defective parts of the said hangings." In the same year, he also received £39 for repairs to three tapestries of *Charlemagne* from Windsor and £64 15s. for repairs to the Whitehall *Romulus and Remus* set, two other sets that dated from the late medieval and Tudor eras.

The number of tapestries repaired in 1695–96 was high but not exceptional, and it reflects the careful maintenance of the collection at this time. The extensive character of many of the repairs, often involving new selvage edges and the reweaving of sections that had been damaged, shows that the tapestries were being maintained as serviceable hangings, regardless of whether they were valued as antiques or works of art. Indeed, it is clear that neither William nor Anne, or any of the Great Wardrobe officers working for them, had qualms about cutting or extending historic tapestries as necessary to fit them, like wallpaper, to the dimensions of the chambers in which they were used. For example, when the *Trojan War* and *Romulus and Remus* tapestries were hung permanently at Westminster sometime around 1690, they were cut and folded back around various architectural features and doorways (see below). And in 1703–4, Henry's *Dido and Aeneas* tapestries had sections of modern weaving added to two panels, so that the whole set was of uniform height, for use in an unidentified location.[27] Evidently the historic tapestries were still regarded with respect, but they were now considered above all as furnishings, to be used and adapted as appropriate.

During these years the collection continued to be subject to gradual attrition. The dispersal of older, damaged pieces is typified by a warrant issued in October 1693 from the lord chamberlain's office to James Marriott, keeper of the Hampton Court Wardrobe, to dispose of various pieces of furniture and "Tenne peices of old Tapestry hangings of severall suites" as he saw fit, to avoid rot and moths affecting the other goods in the wardrobe.[28] The dispersal of more valuable objects to senior court officers also took its toll on the collection. For example, at some point in the 1690s Charles Sackville, sixth earl of Dorset, received valuable silver furniture, a state bed, and a set of tapestries made in London either as a gift or as a perquisite in his capacity as lord chamberlain following the death of Queen Mary. These furnishings all survive at Knole today. As mentioned earlier, until the early twentieth century the Sackville collection included a number of early sixteenth-century Netherlandish tapestries that corresponded closely to the subjects and dimensions of pieces listed in the collections of Wolsey and Henry VIII, so these, too, may well have come from the royal collection as gifts or perquisites.

The respectful but uninformed attention paid to the royal tapestries during the early eighteenth century is reflected by contemporary guides to the royal palaces. One of the earliest of these, James Beeverell's *Les Delices de la Grand Bretagne et de l'Irlande* (1707), states that the Hampton Court apartments were "richemont meubles, ornez de magnifiques tapisseries et de bons tableaux de plusieurs habiles Peintres" (richly furnished, decorated with magnificent tapestries and good paintings by many talented painters).[29] Three years later, the author of *Le Guide de Londres dedié aux Voyageurs Etrangers* commented on the fine tapestries at Whitehall, Kensington—where one must not forget to "graisser le main de la Gardienne" (grease the hand of the guardian—that is, tip him)—and Windsor, where the apartments were very rich as much for the rare paintings as for the rich tapestries.[30] Not everyone was so impressed. The diary by Zacharias Conrad von Uffenback, relating to his visit to London in 1710, remarks in disdainful fashion on the tapestries that the *Guide de Londres* extolled. Regarding the tapestries in the Painted Chamber at Westminster, he wrote, "There are some uncommonly ugly and worn tapestries hung there." The comments he made of the *Armada* tapestries are especially interesting: "The Tapistry accounted the finest in Europe . . . now looks so wretched and tarnished with smoke that neither gold nor silver, colours nor figures can be recognized. All the same it is curious on account of the intrinsic value of the gold and silver with which it is lavishly worked, and of the story of the invincible Spanish Armada."[31]

Von Uffenback's comments relating to the extreme dirtiness of the tapestries draws attention to the physical circumstances of their display and the soot and smoke to which they must have been exposed from coal fires. This must explain why from the 1670s, when many of the tapestries were exposed permanently, many sets were cleaned and repaired every twenty to thirty years, sometimes more often. Unfortunately, the method by which the cleaning was undertaken may itself have been destructive. Typically the tapestries were sprinkled with wet bread crumbs, which were then swept across the face of the tapestry with brooms.[32] Although the damp crumbs would have extracted some dirt, much as an eraser lifts graphite from a paper surface, the abrasion of the bristles against the delicate silk and gilt-metallic wefts must account for the extreme deterioration of the gold thread on the small number of tapestries that have survived from the English royal collection.

The Use of the Tudor Tapestries under George I and George II

The practice established by Charles II and followed by William and Anne, whereby antique tapestries, particularly the Henrician "Romanist" sets, were hung permanently in the various royal state apartments to establish a suitably august atmosphere, was to continue through much of the next century. When the Queen's State Apartments at Hampton Court were decorated for George, Prince of Wales, in the late 1710s, the remaining pieces of Henry's *Joshua* tapestries were hung in the state bedchamber along with a selection of other large figure tapestries of more recent origin in the other state rooms.[33] Panels from the Henrician *Story of Tobias* may also have been used on this occasion; hangings of this subject were recorded in the Prince of Wales's Presence Chamber by 1742.[34] Although the Brussels workshops were continuing to produce history and mythological subjects, there is no evidence that George I or his son made any effort to purchase such sets at this time.

The arrangement of antique and modern tapestries in the state apartments of Hampton Court, Windsor, Kensington, Saint James's, and Somerset House was to remain relatively stable for much of the next fifty years. The Great Wardrobe accounts record the ongoing care and treatment that the tapestries received during the reigns of George I and George II. For example, those at Hampton Court were subjected to extensive campaigns, including some rearrangement, in 1730–31, 1732–33, and 1736–37, and during these campaigns a total of fifty-four tapestries were cleaned and mended.[35] It was probably during the first of these campaigns, instigated by the need to refresh and refurbish Hampton Court for George II, that a set of early-eighteenth-century *Story of Alexander* tapestries were hung in the Queen's Gallery. These had probably been purchased by the king from the auction of the possessions of William, first earl of Cadogan, in February 1717.[36] The bright colors of this set must have provided a strong contrast to the more muted and faded tones of the *Joshua* tapestries in the adjacent bedchamber.

Similar campaigns are documented at other royal palaces. The tapestries at Somerset House were cleaned and repaired in 1732–33,[37] and extensive work to repair and clean the tapestries at Saint James's was undertaken between 1740 and 1748.[38] From the 1720s the written records relating to these repairs refer to the tapestries in an increasingly summary fashion, and individual sets are rarely distinguished by name. This was evidently a manifestation of the way that the great historic sets, previously treated with some reverence as individual artistic entities, were now perceived as generic historic furnishings. There is no documentary evidence to suggest that the early-sixteenth-century "pre-Renaissance"-style tapestries played a part in the state apartments of any of the palaces, but judging by the faded and soiled nature of the extant pieces, they, too, probably remained on display, presumably in association with Tudor sections of Windsor, Whitehall, and Hampton Court. This supposition is supported by the extensive reweaving visible in some of the *Triumphs of Petrarch* panels, similar in material and discoloration to those on the Hampton Court *Dido and Aeneas* tapestries, which, as noted, were repaired and rewoven by John Vanderbank's workshop in 1703–4.

The Use of the Tudor Tapestries under George III, George IV, William IV, and Queen Victoria

The disposition of the historic tapestries in the royal palaces becomes even more difficult to trace during the late eighteenth and early nineteenth centuries. In part this is because of the lack of detail regarding specific tapestries in the Great Wardrobe records from around 1720 and in part because traditional practices and accounting procedures were altered in the mid-1740s. The office of royal arras maker seems to have fallen into abeyance, and work on the interior furnishings of the palaces was now contracted out to various upholsterers. In addition, from the 1760s accounts for work on the palaces were submitted to the Office of Works, rather than the lord chamberlain's office, and the tapestries are infrequently mentioned. By and large they seem to have been regarded as part of the historic fabric of the palaces rather than as movable works of art.

An insight into the respectful but wholly uninformed way in which the tapestries were now considered by their royal owners, the palace staff, and visitors to the palaces, is provided by George Bickham's *Deliciae Britannicae, or the Curiosities of Hampton Court and Windsor Castle Delineated,* published in 1742. Describing what must have been the *Triumph of Bacchus* and *Triumph of Hercules* panels from the *Antiques,* then in the King's Presence Chamber at Hampton Court, Bickham wrote, "The Room is hung with rich old Tapestry, that has no particular Story wrought in it; but Landscape-Work, with the Figures of Nymphs, Fawns, Satyrs, Neriedes Ec."[39] Of the tapestries in the Second Presence Chamber, the *Triumph of Lust* and the *Triumph of Avarice* from the *Seven Deadly Sins,* he wrote, "The hangings of this Room are very antient Tapestry, but very rich, the Lights being all Gold, and the Shadows Silk; the Subject of those on the left is Hercules and the Hydra; and those on the Right is Midas with his Asses Ears."[40] Evidently, the broader iconographic schemes to which these panels originally belonged were long since forgotten. Elsewhere, Bickham recognized the subjects of some of the *Abraham, Joshua,* and *Tobias* tapestries but commented only on their richness. Indeed, the only set that drew more extensive commentary was the *Story of Alexander* in the Queen's Gallery, for which he identified each of the subjects and reported the tradition of its origin: "bought from Flanders by General Cadogan, and purchas'd at a common Auction at a Price far inferior to their intrinsick Value."[41] Then, as now, it was sometimes easier to enthuse a general audience about the financial value of an object than its aesthetic merits.

Subsequent guides, such as *London and its Environs Described* (1761) and Henry Chamberlain's *A New and Compleat History and Survey of the Cities of London and Westminster . . .* (1770), closely followed Bickham's descriptions of the Hampton Court tapestries, in some cases repeating his descriptions word for word. Accounts of tapestries in palaces other than Hampton Court were as ill informed and inconsistent as those for Hampton Court. For example, *London and its Environs* mentioned a *Diana* tapestry and a *Teniers* scene at Kensington Palace but made no mention of the *Caesar* tapestries that certainly remained in the Presence Chamber at that date.[42] In the state apartments at Windsor, the same guide noted various seventeenth-century tapestries of the *Months* and *Seasons* woven in London and Brussels. Of another set in the Queen's Audience Chamber, it reported that the tapestry was "made at Coblentz in Germany and presented to King Henry VIII."[43] This attribution is patently wrong if, as seems probable, the tapestries in this room were still the *Saint Paul* set hung there during William and Mary's reign.

Chamberlain's guide of 1770 largely followed the wording of the earlier guides, although it adds some detail about the tapestries at Windsor, noting "tapestry representing some religious ceremonies of the jews" in the King's Audience Chamber and tapestry of the *Story of Queen Athaliah* in the King's Presence Chamber, both perhaps part of the *Hezekiah* set listed there in the late seventeenth century, which may, in fact, have been a set representing scenes from the Old Testament Book of Kings. Chamberlain repeats the enigmatic attribution of the tapestry in the Queen's Audience Chamber to Coblentz, and then adds that the tapestry in the Presence Chamber "represents the history of the beheading of Saint Paul, and the persecution of the primitive Christians," allowing us to identify it as one of the pieces of Henry VIII's set.[44] Evidently, much of the tapestry decorations from William and Mary's reign were still in place.

In the late eighteenth and early nineteenth centuries the historic tapestries were most vulnerable to abuse and destruction. During the 1760s and 1770s a tapestry room was still a fashionable component of the grandest houses, whether antique or modern, and the Gobelins Manufactory enjoyed a series of orders for decorative en suite tapestry chambers from designs by François Boucher for various houses designed by Robert Adam.[45] Nonetheless, tapestry was no longer the prestigious and ubiquitous medium of display that it had been in the past, and George III seems to have had no interest in it whatsoever, being much more interested in painting. The grandiose displays

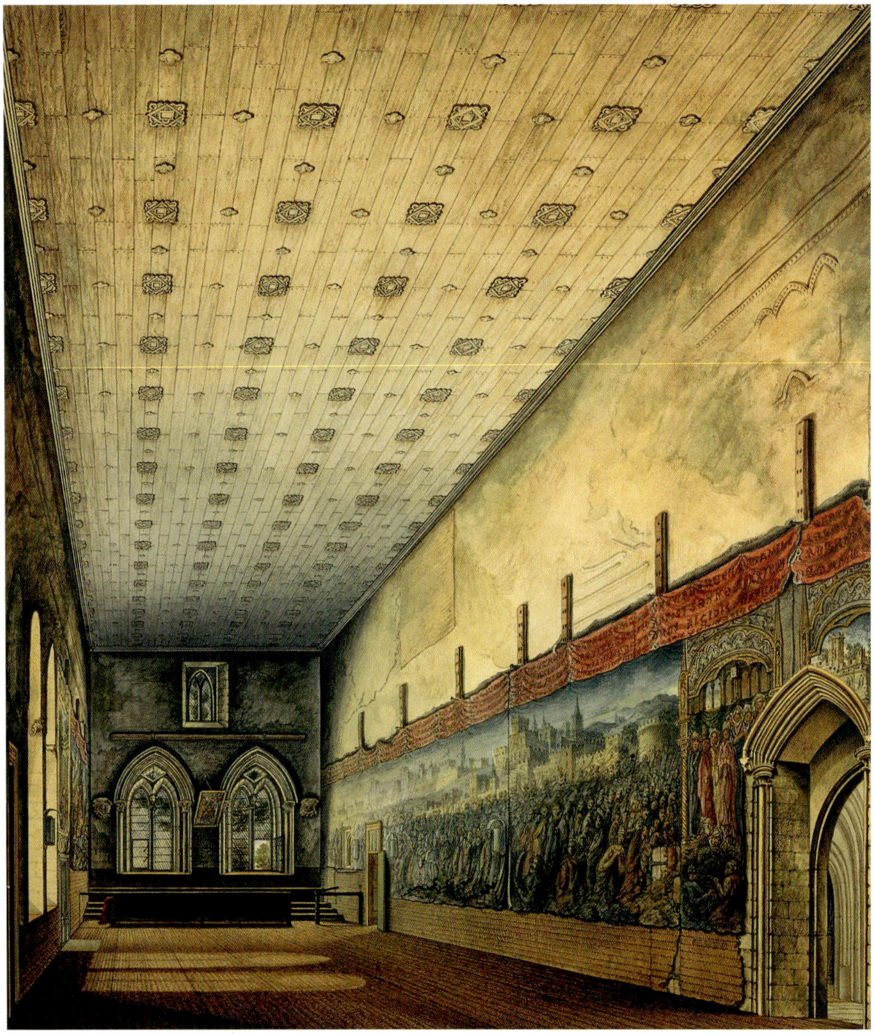

19.6 *The Painted Chamber at Westminster Palace* by William Capon, 1799. Watercolor. Although extremely stylized in this representation, the tapestries hung in this room can be identified from other sources as panels from Henry VII's *Story of the Trojan War*. Society of Antiquaries, London

at Hampton Court probably survived his reign thanks to the fact that he never used the palace as a residence. But elsewhere it was a different story, and it was during George III's reign that many of the historic tapestries that had survived so long on the walls of the royal palaces begin to disappear. Details of this process are mostly sketchy, but the fate of the tapestries at Somerset House is probably typical. These appear to have been sold or shredded for their gold content before the building was destroyed in 1775. Joseph Moser, nephew of the first keeper of the Royal Academy, accompanied Sir William Chambers on his survey of Old Somerset House before its demolition and some years later recorded his impressions in the *European Magazine* (1802). "With respect to the gold and silver which were worked in the borders and other parts of the tapestries with which the royal apartments were, even within my remembraunce, hung, it had been carefully picked out while those rooms were used as a barracks. Some very elegant landscapes, beautifully woven in tapestry, adorned the library of the Royal Academy until the dissolution of the building."[46] While the landscape tapestries may have been preserved at the dissolution of the building, he noted that other old tapestries were sold to brokers for derisory prices. Several went to a man called Walker, one of which was a large panel from a set of *Haman and Mordecai,* thus a scene from the story of *Esther and Ahasuerus,* perhaps that formerly at Hampton Court, "expressed in the habits of the fifteenth or sixteenth century" and bearing an inscription of a dozen lines in old French. Measuring between fifteen and twenty feet in length, this panel was exhibited at Walker's shop in Harp Alley, with a price of one and a half guineas.[47]

Further evidence of the emergence of a nascent antiquarian interest in historic tapestries and, equally, the relative lack of interest in the subject by those classes of society that had traditionally purchased and used tapestries, is reflected by the fate of various Tudor tapestries at the Houses of Parliament during the early nineteenth century. As noted, various sets had been delivered to Westminster (old) Palace in the 1690s, of which the most famous were the *Armada* tapestries, pictured and described in a dedicated publication by the herald John Pine in 1739 (see fig. 18.5).[48] In addition, a handful of other tapestries continued to adorn other chambers (fig. 19.6), and some of these were the subject of study by the antiquary John Carter (1748–1817). Carter made drawings of two sets in the Painted Chamber (see fig. 4.2) and the Prince's Chamber (see figs. 10.18, 10.20). He also published a series of descriptions of these tapestries in a sequence of articles in the *Gentleman's Magazine*.[49] On the strength of these drawings and descriptions, the sets can be identified with certainty. Those in the Painted Chamber were the remnants of Henry VII's *Story of the Trojan War,* while those in the Painted Chamber came from the *Story of Romulus and Remus* purchased by Henry VIII from Richard Gresham in 1529. Both had been cut and adapted to fit around various architectural features and were in a sad state of repair. Carter was unaware of the subjects of either set but recorded that the main figure in one scene, now identifiable as the *Birth of Romulus and Remus,* resembled Henry VIII. On his drawing of this subject he labeled this figure "Henry VIII" and noted that the scene was "said to be The Birth of Queen Elizabeth." His articles appealed for the preservation of these sets, not so much as works of art, but for the information they provided about historic costume and manners. In the event, his appeal fell on deaf ears. The *Trojan War* tapestries were taken down and sold in 1820 to a man called Yarnold and the *Romulus and Remus* tapestries had also been removed and sold before the Prince's Chamber was demolished in 1823. The subsequent fate of these ensembles is unknown with the exception of the *Romulus and Remus* fragment that appeared in the art market in the 1980s in a worn and faded state (see fig. 10.19).

The display of tapestries in the state apartments at the other palaces continued through much of the reigns of George III and George IV, as reflected by contemporary printed guides to Hampton Court and the subsequent visual evidence of the first extensively illustrated history of the palaces, Pyne's *Royal Residences,* published in 1819.[50] Besides the aquatint illustrations accompanying this three-volume work, the original preparatory watercolors survive today in the royal collection. Pyne's text describes tapestries in several of the state apartments at Hampton Court, including the *Joshua* set in both the King's and Queen's Bedchambers, but he mentions tapestries only in passing in a handful of locations at the other palaces. Nonetheless, the illustrations accompanying the descriptions of other palaces show tapestries in several interiors, inevitably hidden behind dense displays of paintings. In some cases, enough of the tapestry is visible for identification to be made with pieces whose installation in these locations is documented more than one hundred years before. This is the case with the *Caesar* tapestries in the Presence Chamber at Kensington Palace (fig. 19.7) and the

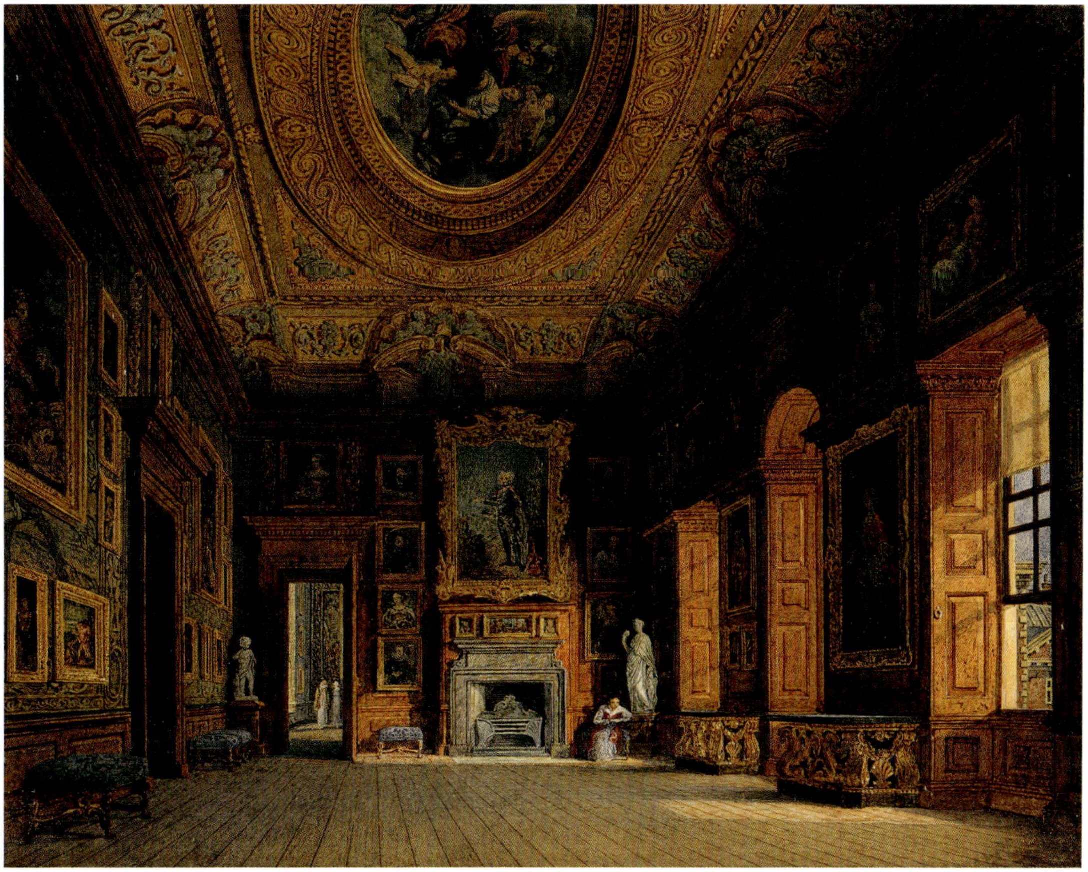

19.7 *Queen Caroline's Drawing Room, Kensington Palace,* ca. 1819, by Charles Wild (1781–1835). Watercolor, 20.3 x 25.1 cm. The Royal Library, Windsor Castle

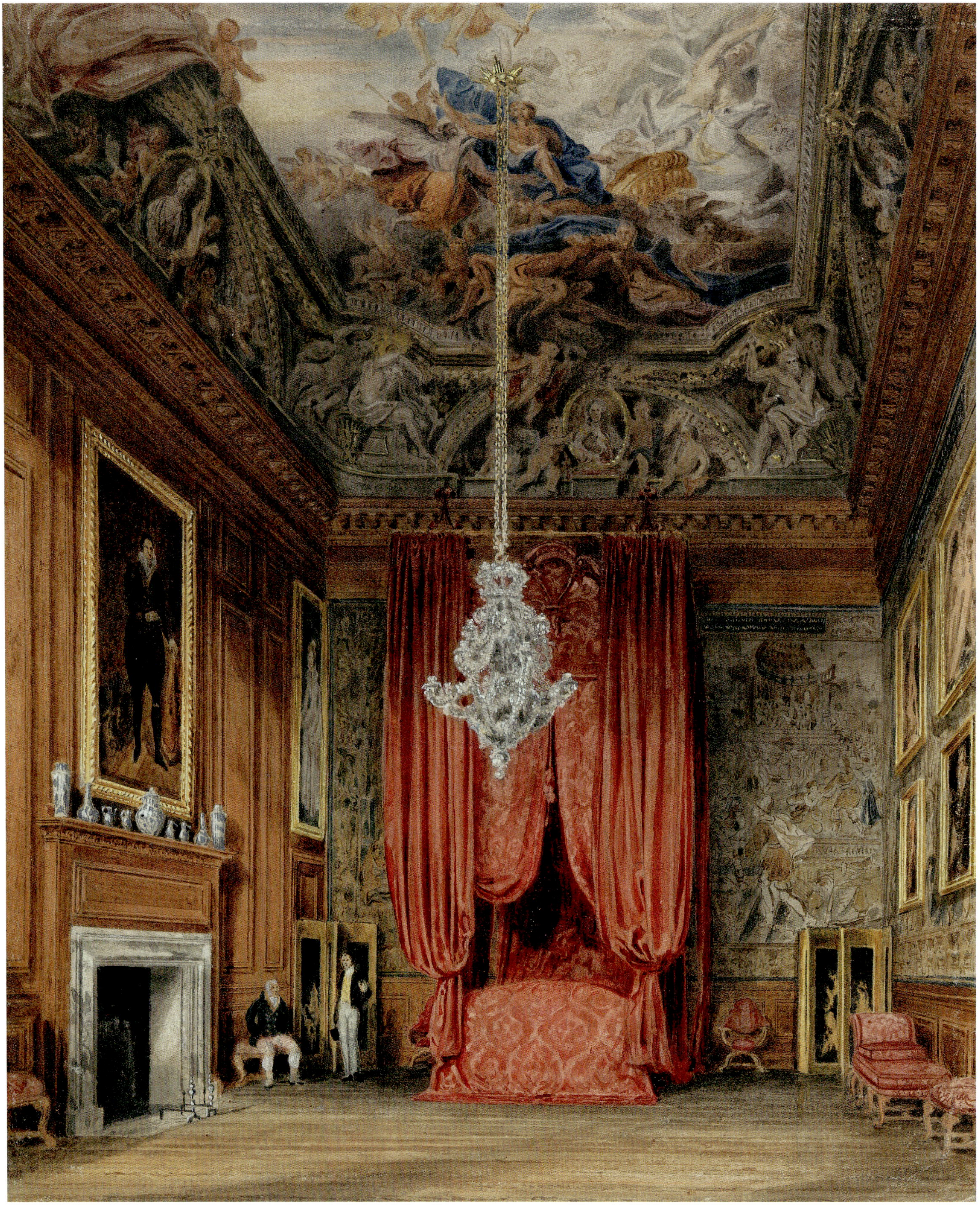

19.8 *The Queen's State Bedchamber at Hampton Court* by R. Cattermole, ca. 1819. Watercolor. The walls are hung with three of Henry VIII's *Joshua* tapestries. The Royal Library, Windsor Castle

19.9 *The First Presence Chamber at Hampton Court* (now known as the King's Presence Chamber) by J. Stephanoff, ca. 1819. Watercolor. The Royal Library, Windsor Castle

Abraham and *Joshua* tapestries at Hampton Court (figs. 19.8, 19.9)

Although a number of the historic tapestries had survived in the older state apartments at Hampton Court and Kensington by virtue of neglect, they were largely excluded from those areas of the palaces that were redecorated for George IV. Carlton House was the first royal residence in which tapestry played absolutely no part in the decorations. When the state apartments were rebuilt at Windsor in the 1820s, tapestry was selected as the appropriate decorative medium for several of the state apartments, but in place of historic items from the existing collection, eighteenth-century Gobelins tapestries, formerly in the French royal collection, were purchased from a Continental dealer.[51] The bright colors of these "modern" weavings and the luster of the gilt paneling in which they were installed must have provided a striking contrast to the faded hangings at the other royal palaces. The fate of the historic tapestries that had previously decorated the Windsor state apartments is unrecorded.

The introduction of new tapestries at Windsor seems to have hastened the removal of antique hangings elsewhere, and between 1820 and 1840 the majority of the historic tapestries that had survived in the various royal residences were largely removed. In some cases the motivation was to replace the tired appearance of existing state apartments with something more appropriate to the pomp and circumstance of a court that was becoming the focus of the largest industrial empire in the world. In others it was to provide apartments with more modern and congenial decorations. In the case of Hampton Court, the change was instigated by the decision to turn the palace into a repository where the public could view part of the royal collection of paintings. But the result of these changes was the same, with

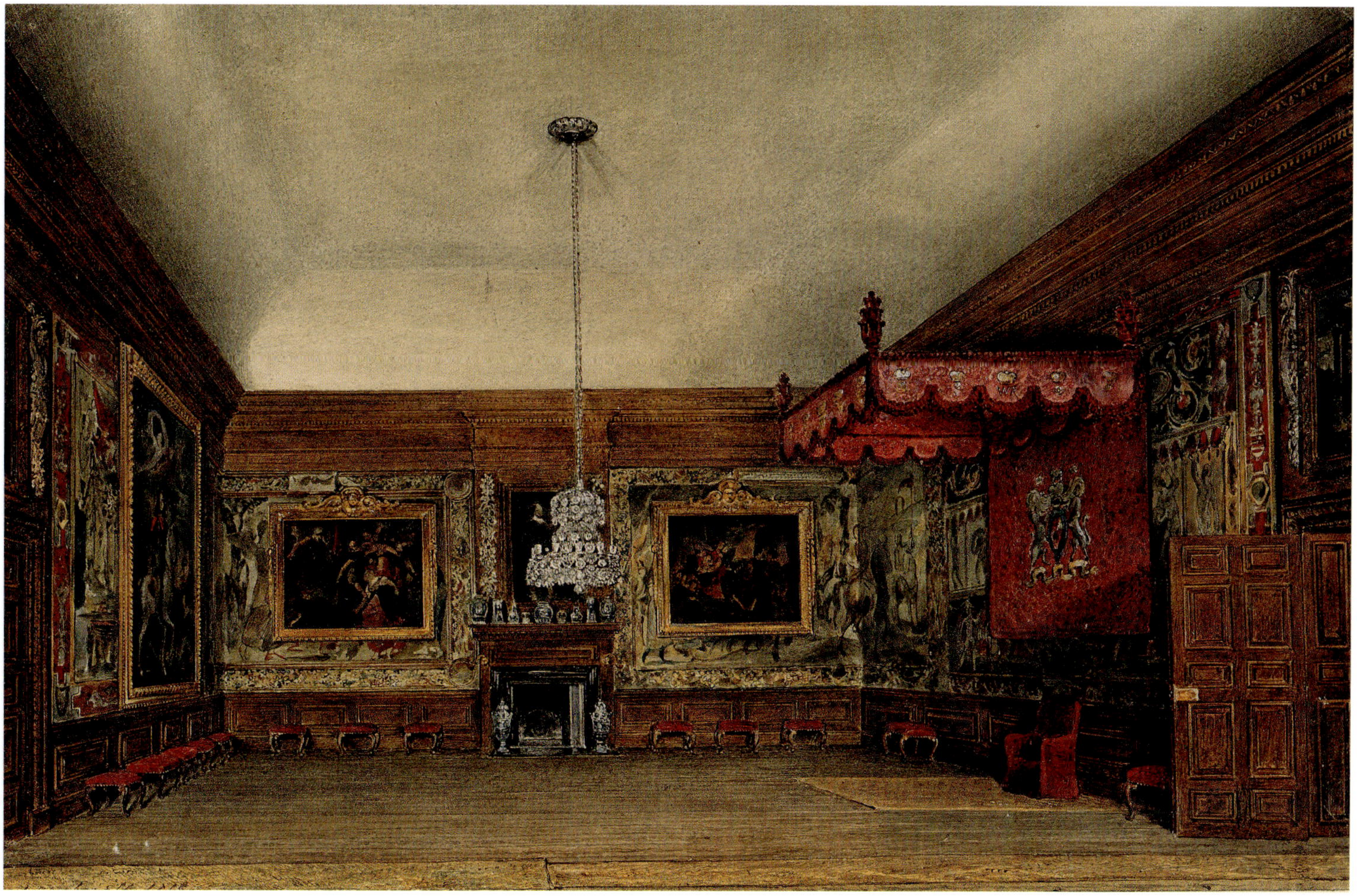

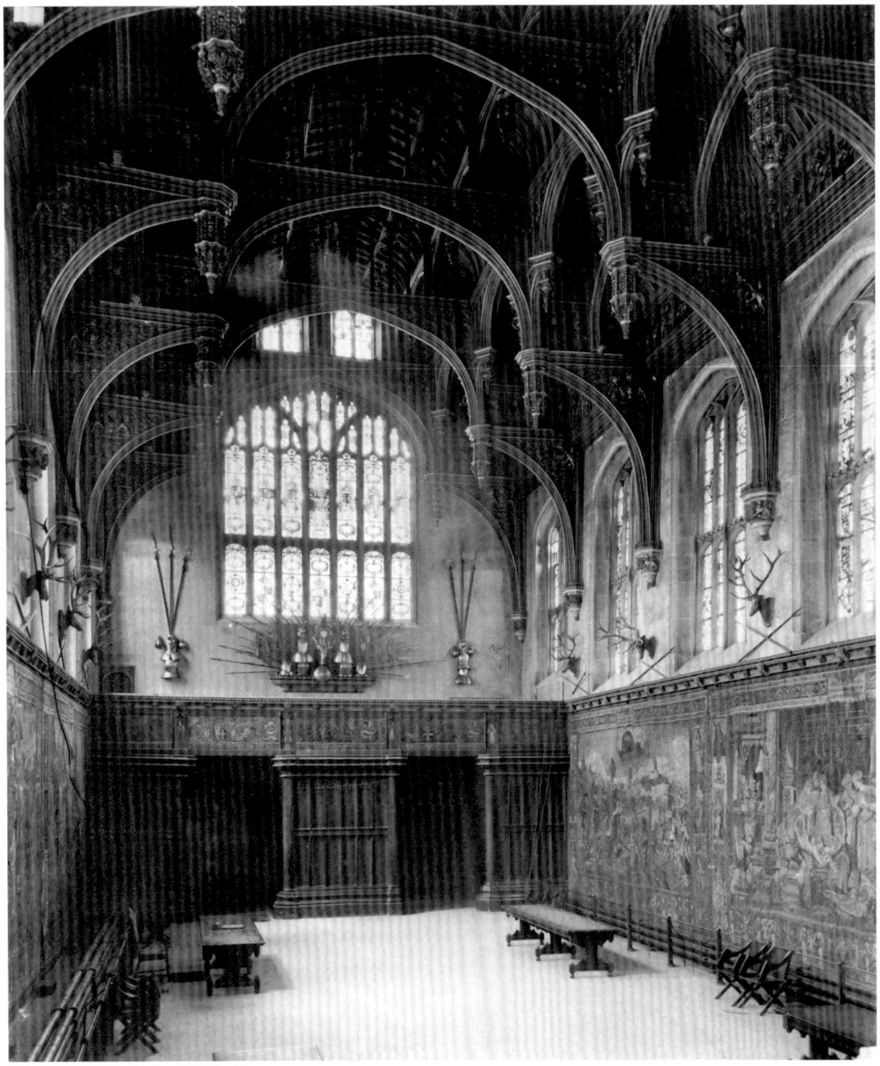

19.10 The great hall at Hampton Court after construction of the paneling and screen in the 19th c.

many of the most important antique tapestries being removed from locations in which they had hung since the reign of William III. Most have subsequently disappeared, and the circumstances of their disappearance remain obscure. Some tapestries were evidently distributed to Queen Victoria's children along with other royal furnishings. This accounts for a number of tapestries now at Schloss Friedrichshof, Kronberg, which were among the furnishings taken to Germany by Victoria's eldest daughter, Princess Victoria, when she married the Prussian emperor Friedrich III. This group includes an armorial made for William III and a sixteenth-century *Saint Paul* tapestry that may have formed part of the set purchased by Henry VIII for Greenwich in 1544 (see fig. 12.13).[52] Evidence that tapestries were also divided among other members of the royal family comes from the fate of the *Triumph of Lust* panel, from Henry VIII's *Seven Deadly Sins,* which survived in the Hampton Court Presence Chamber as late as 1819. This appeared in the art market in the early twentieth century, and an internal inquiry by the lord chamberlain's office revealed that it was one of a number of objects embezzled by a Hampton Court housekeeper from an apartment that was being used to store objects belonging to one of Victoria's other daughters.[53]

These examples hint at the fate of a small number of the royal tapestries; others, such as the *Joshua* and *Caesar* sets, disappeared without trace some time after they were illustrated in Pyne's *Royal Residences.* Their probable fate is all too easy to guess. Almost all of the gold-woven sixteenth-century tapestries in the French royal collection were burned by the French revolutionary government during the late 1790s in an effort to extract the gold thread they contained. Subsequently, this practice seems to have spread through Europe. For example, many of the gold-woven tapestries made for Leo X, including the Raphael workshop *Grotesques* and *Giochi di putti,* disappear from papal records around 1800, and it seems that they, too, were destroyed in this period, perhaps after Rome was occupied by Napoleonic troops. Although no official records of the destruction of tapestries from the English royal collection have come to light, the disappearance of so many rich pieces during the second quarter of the nineteenth century, combined with the knowledge that, forty years before, the gold thread had been picked out of the tapestries that adorned Somerset House, suggests that these tapestries may have shared a similar fate, whether through official or unofficial channels.

It is unclear why the *Story of Abraham,* the *Triumphs of Bacchus* and *Hercules,* and a single panel of the *Tobias* set survived at Hampton Court, but it may be because they continued to hang in place at the time that the palace, no longer used by the Crown, was opened to the general public and thus to public scrutiny. Many of the Crown paintings had been transferred to Hampton Court from Kensington on

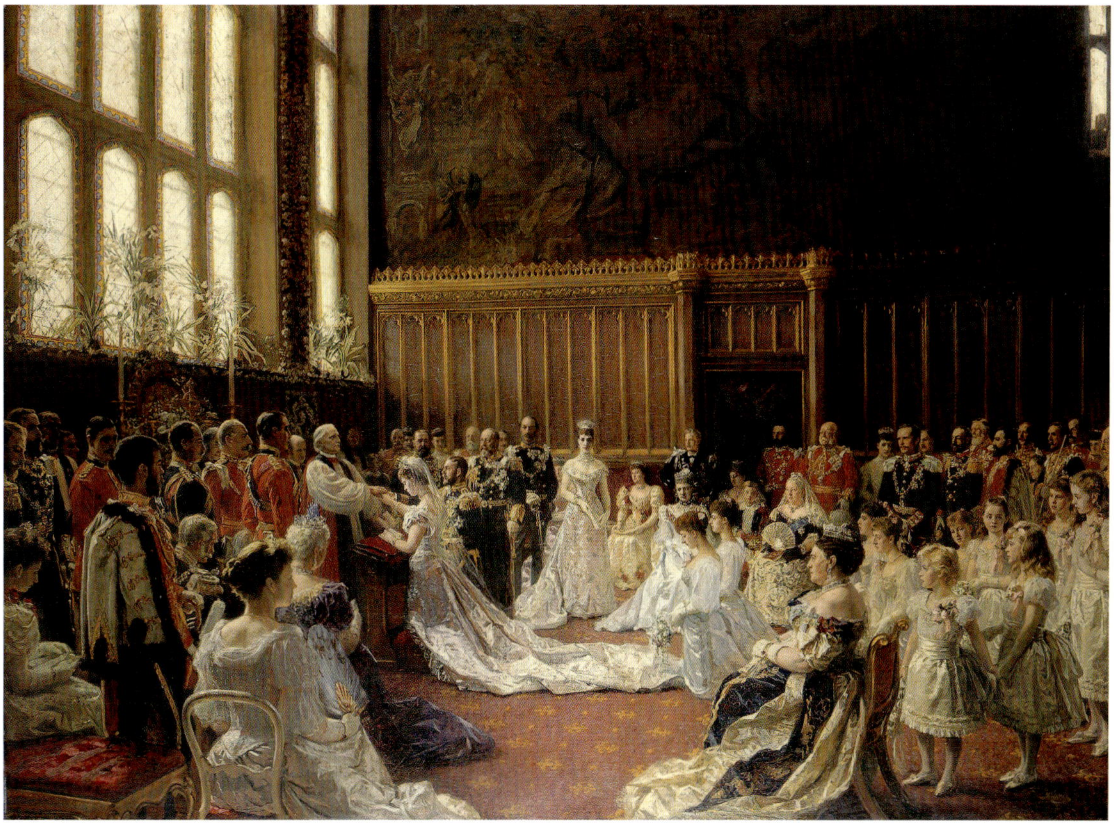

19.11 *The Marriage of George, Duke of York, 6 July 1893,* by Laurits Regner Tuxen, 1894. Oil on canvas, 169.5 x 229.9 cm. The Royal Collection

the orders of George IV, and during the late 1830s the decision was taken to use the palace as a public gallery for part of the royal painting collection.[54] Several of the most important Henrician tapestries historically associated with the palace were still hanging in the King's State Apartments at this time. With the opening of the palace to the public, the *Triumphs* and possibly also the *Tobias* panel were dispatched to Buckingham Palace, where they remained until 1864, after which they were returned to Hampton Court until removal to Windsor in 1901.[55] The *Abraham* set was kept at Hampton Court. Two were hung in the Public Dining Room, six others in the great hall in paneling that was specially built to receive them at the direction of Edward Jesse, the deputy surveyor (fig. 19.10).[56] It was in this location that they were described with great admiration by Jesse in 1842: "the walls are covered with Tapestry of such excellent design, and of such costliness of material, that it may be safely asserted that its parallel does not exist in Europe at this time."[57] The two panels from the Public Dining Room were subsequently moved to the Royal Chapel at Saint James's Palace (fig. 19.11), where they remained until 1893.[58]

Jesse also expressed great admiration for the early pieces displayed in the "Presence Chamber, commonly called Wolsey's withdrawing room," extolling their interest both as part of the original palace decorations and as examples of "Gothic design." Noting that they ignored the rules of perspective and propriety of costume, he opined, "Yet for all these drawbacks, these tapestries possess qualities which the real artist and connoisseur will immediately recognize as worthy of study and attention."[59] In contrast, he dismissed the once-esteemed, early-eighteenth-century Brussels *Alexander* set with the comment that it was "now too faded to attract any interest or attention."[60]

In 1859, Henry Cole, director of the South Kensington Museum—now the Victoria and Albert Museum—drew attention to the sorry plight of some of the Hampton Court tapestries in a privately published pamphlet entitled *Some Thoughts on Hampton Court Palace*. In this he noted that since many royal pictures were transferred to Hampton Court from Kensington

Palace, it had been little more than a storehouse. "The Tapestries forming the original decoration of the walls, as in the Queen's gallery and elsewhere, have been covered up, and the pictures hung almost at haphazard. In some cases the pictures have been actually nailed to the tapestries." He argued that the palace would be much more attractive if restored as much as possible to its original state of decoration: "In many rooms this could be done by simply taking down the battens and faded calico which conceal the tapestry. The tapestries themselves would be much more interesting to the public than the present incongruous arrangement of pictures."[61] Part of Cole's motivation in penning these reflections seems to have been the hope of transferring a number of key works of art to the South Kensington Museum, a goal that was rewarded with the transference of the Raphael *Acts of the Apostles* cartoons in April 1865. Although Cole was unsuccessful in winning any of the Hampton Court tapestries for his museum, he did stimulate a rearrangement of the galleries and the removal of the linen and paintings that had obscured the *Alexander* tapestries in the Queen's Gallery.[62]

During the following decades the Hampton Court tapestries became the focus of greater attention, benefiting in part from the revived interest in historic tapestry stimulated by the creation of the short-lived Royal Windsor Manufactory (1876–90) and the production of William Morris's Merton Abbey tapestry workshop in the 1880s and 1890s, and in part from the attention being paid to historic tapestry at the South Kensington Museum, which was making its first purchases of medieval tapestries at the urging of William Morris.[63] A catalyst to further action was provided by a fire that destroyed part of Hampton Court in 1882. Following an inspection of the damage, Alan Cole reported that the tapestries in the Watching Chamber were "fragmentary… begrimed and badly treated." Public concern was sufficient for a question to be raised in Parliament, which was reported in the *Times*. John Robinson, now the surveyor of the royal paintings, replied with a cautious letter: "Considering that most of the tapestries at Hampton Court are very ancient and that they must now be regarded as curious relics of antiquity rather than decorative furniture, I do not think that any attempt should be made to renovate or systematically 'restore' them, but that whatever is done should be confined to arresting further decay and disintegration."[64]

Following further inspection of the tapestries by experts from South Kensington, a conservation program was instituted in 1885 with modest government funding. This work, which involved consolidation of the tapestries, was undertaken in a workshop set up at Hampton Court. Thirteen needlewomen were employed to mend thirty-seven tapestries for a sum of £400, extended with a further £200 in 1886. Thereafter government funding again dried up, and a request for a further £200 in 1887 was refused.[65]

Though administrative action and care was thus still a stop-start affair, the long period of neglect for the early tapestries was clearly lifting, and after a period of more than two hundred years in which they are barely identifiable in court records, the pre-Renaissance pieces suddenly reemerge in sharper focus as various authors sang their praises in guide books created for the public. Ernest Law devoted a chapter of his study of Hampton Court during Tudor times to the historic documentation and extant pieces of Cardinal Wolsey's tapestry collection.[66] But the highlight of the collection remained the *Abraham* tapestries. In 1893, the two panels that had been displayed in the Queen's Chapel at Saint James's Palace were also returned to Hampton Court.[67]

Elsewhere, the developing market for historic art and furnishings during the first half of the nineteenth century resulted in the reemergence of a number of Henrician tapestries, although the reception and interest in these pieces was initially sporadic, as exemplified by the fate of Henry's *Acts of the Apostles* set. This was purchased from the duke of Alba in 1823 by the British consul in Catalonia, a Mr. Tupper. It was exhibited in London in the following year, and according to the German artist Johann David Passavant, it was "offered to the King at a very high price, and the purchase was never concluded."[68] Subsequently the set was exhibited again in London in 1838 and then in Manchester, but when the owner failed to find a purchaser in England, the set was acquired for the Kaiser Friedrich Museum in 1844.[69]

Other Henrician sets fared better in the following years, but their provenance from the English royal collection passed unrecognized until recently. In 1847 the French Ministry of State purchased from a Genoese dealer the ten-piece set of the *Story of David* that can almost certainly be identified with that purchased by Henry in 1528. (One of the prized possessions of the Cluny Museum, it remained on display until 1938 but was not reinstalled thereafter because of the postwar decision to present the salle de Thermes as a Roman ruin. The set therefore remained in storage until a sequence of international exhibitions in the 1970s. It was transferred to the Musée de la Renaissance at Écouen Château in 1980.)[70] A notable tapestry sale of the 1870s was that of the Berwick and Alba collection, held in Paris in April 1877, which included a number of very high quality sixteenth-century tapestries, including three of the four Van Orley *Passion* set acquired by Henry in the late 1520s. The fourth panel appeared in the Robert Lehman collection early in the twentieth century. During the same period the Victoria and Albert Museum purchased the three *Triumph of Petrarch* panels, identified above as from the set made for Wolsey in 1520, from a Genoese collection. During the 1890s and early 1900s, the burgeoning market in America for European works of art also played its part in the further distribution of surviving fragments of the English royal collection. J. Pierpont Morgan purchased all of the pre-Renaissance tapestries from the Sackville collection at Knole in 1912, now dispersed among various American museums.[71] Morgan was also the buyer for the Henrician *Triumph of Avarice* that had hung in the Presence Chamber at Hampton Court and is now in the Pierpont Morgan Library in New York (see fig. 11.16).[72]

19.12 Tapestries being repaired at Hampton Court by workers from the William Morris Tapestry Company in the 1920s

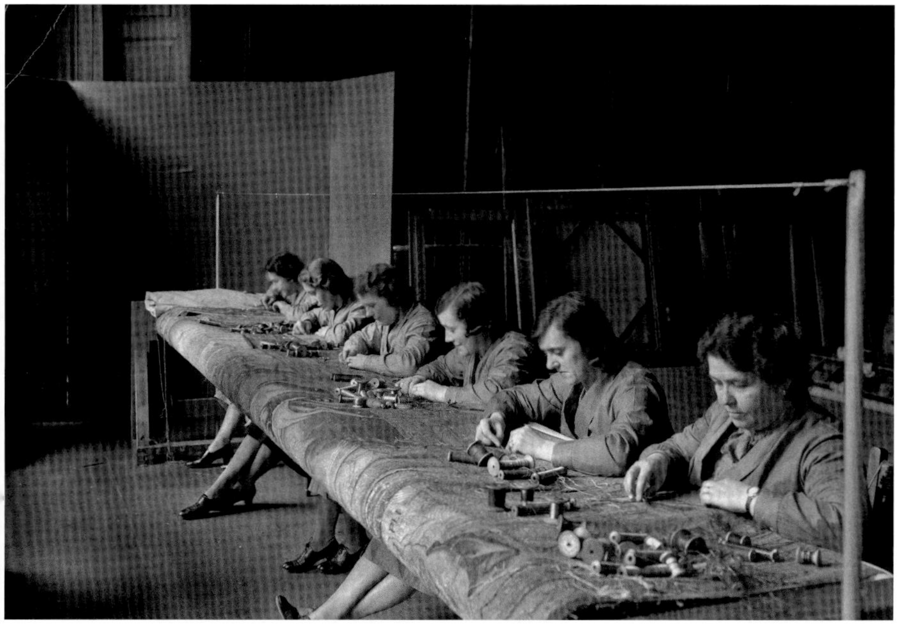

From 1901 to the Present Day

The scholarly and commercial attention paid to historic tapestries during the late nineteenth century stimulated further work in the opening years of the twentieth century. The prestige of the Hampton Court tapestries was contextualized through two publications by W. G. Thomson that appeared in 1906 and 1914, respectively the first survey of tapestry history and the first study of English tapestry patronage and production to have been published in English.[73] The Hampton Court tapestry collection was enhanced in 1905 by the gift of Baron d'Erlanger to the Crown of a set of early-seventeenth-century Brussels tapestries of the *Acts of the Apostles*. These were installed in the Cartoon Gallery and the Queen's State Apartment. In 1919 the so-called "Anglesey" panel from Wolsey's set of the *Redemption of Man* was also acquired for the nation through a fund subscribed by the Exchequer and the National Art Collections Fund (see fig. 7.6).

One consequence of this continuing attention was a renewed effort to consolidate the condition of the surviving tapestries. In April 1912 the Crown convened a supervisory committee to oversee a comprehensive conservation program of the Hampton Court tapestries.

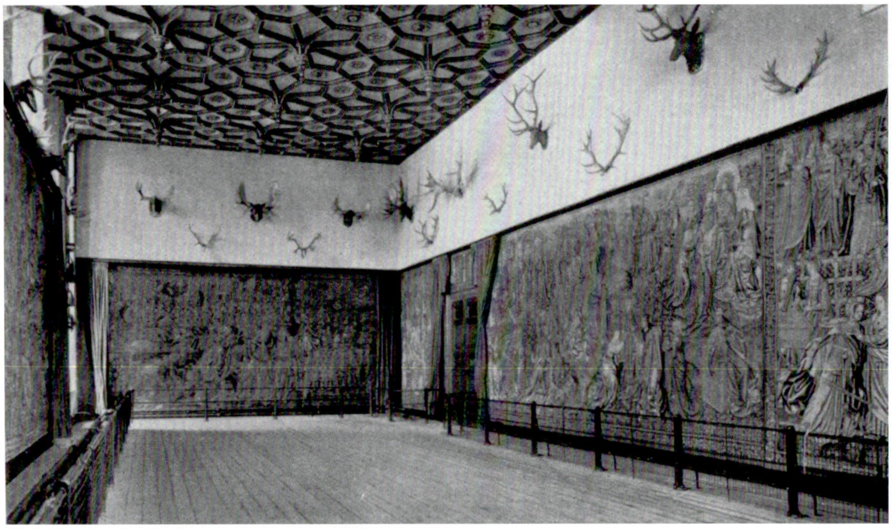

19.13 Tapestries hanging in the Great Watching Chamber at Hampton Court in the late 1920s with protective curtains

The early-sixteenth-century pieces were the first to be treated, undergoing cleaning and conservation work at Hampton Court from weavers of what was now called the William Morris Tapestry Company, under the direction of H. C. Marillier (fig. 19.12).[74] During the 1920s, the installation in which these tapestries were incorporated included protective curtains, a measure sadly lacking today (figs. 19.13, 19.14).[75]

It was also during the 1920s that the *Abraham* set was reunited and photographed at the Victoria and Albert Museum before being returned to Hampton Court.

Further light on the comparative importance of the tapestries was provided by the research undertaken by Marillier, which was published in 1931 in a catalogue devoted to the Hampton Court tapestries (revised 1951, second revision 1962). After work on the "pre-Renaissance" tapestries had been completed, work began on the *Abraham* tapestries in 1932. This was interrupted temporarily when the Morris Company enterprise was forced into liquidation in 1940, but responsibility for the workshop was taken over by the Board of Works, and by 1972 all but one of the *Abraham* tapestries had been completed by this newly created body, now known as the Textile Conservation Studio.[76] At the time of writing, the last panel, the *Meeting of Abraham and Melchizedek*, is still under conservation.

Following the fire at Hampton Court in March 1986 and the creation of the Historic

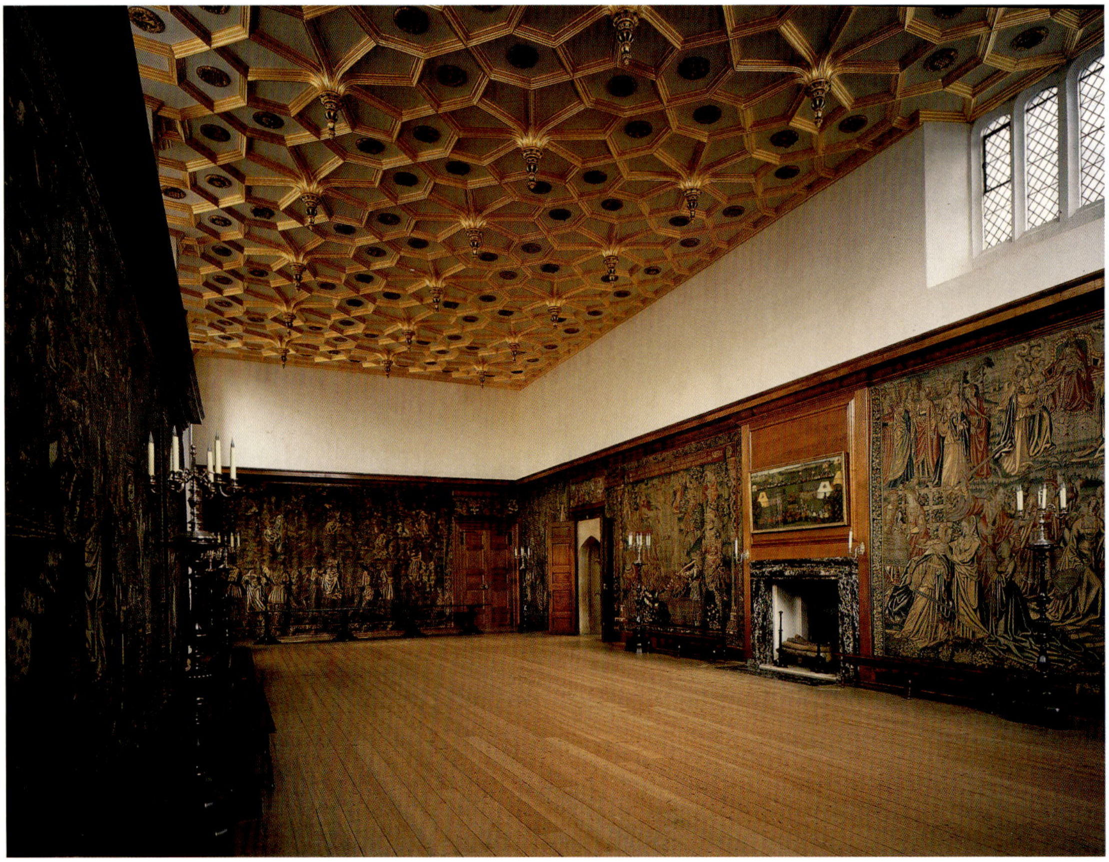

19.14 The Great Watching Chamber in the 1980s hung with tapestries from the *Triumphs of Petrarch* and *Redemption of Man* sets

Opposite:
19.15 The King's Privy Chamber at Hampton Court Palace, hung with one of the *Story of Abraham* tapestries

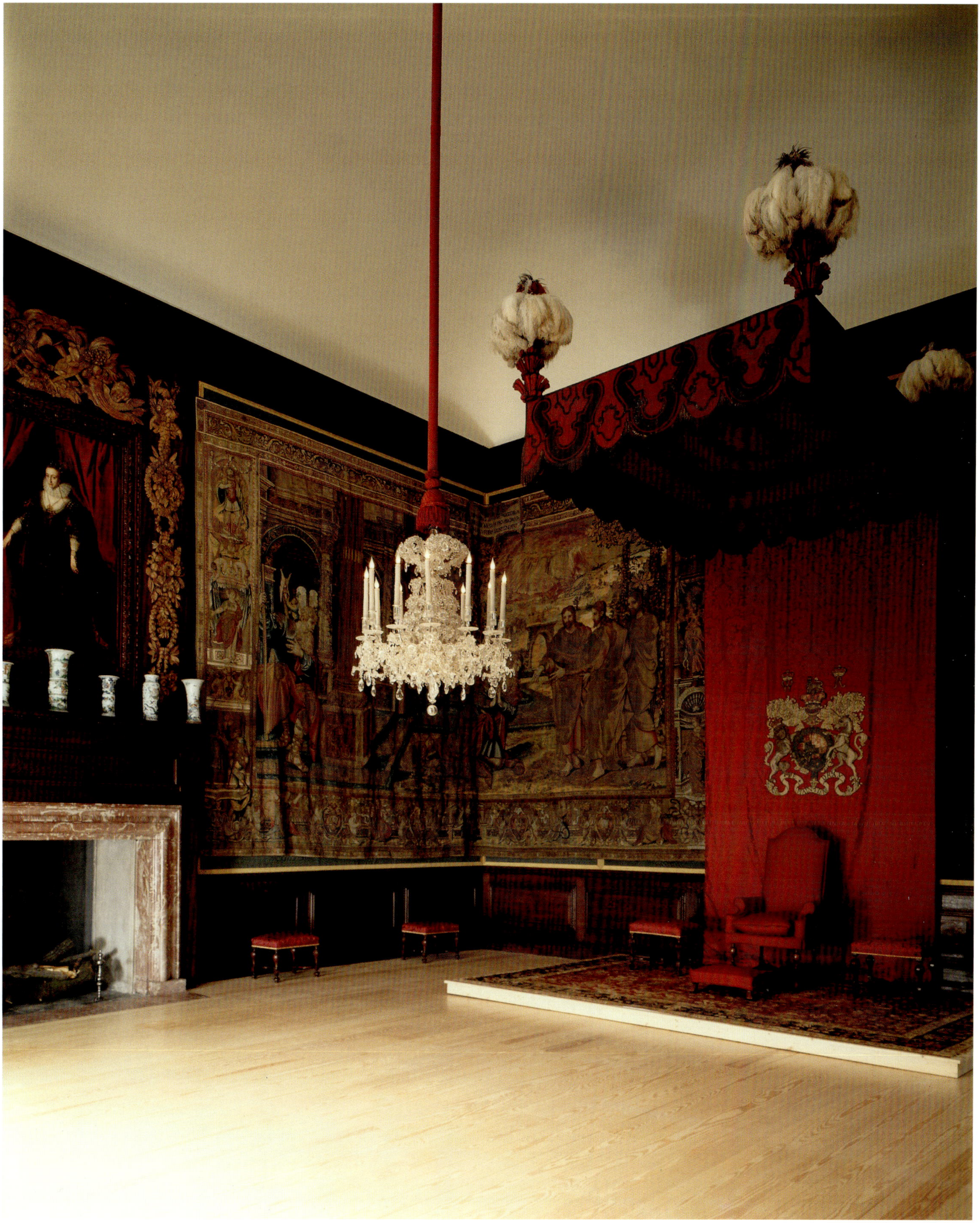

Royal Palaces Agency, various research projects were undertaken in the late 1980s to establish the character of the decorations that had been installed in the King's and Queen's State Apartments during the late seventeenth and early eighteenth centuries.[77] As part of this work, I was commissioned to undertake a study of the tapestries used in the King's State Apartments for William III. Besides establishing the central role that the *Abraham* tapestries had played in the William III scheme, my research resulted in the rediscovery of the *Tobias* and *Antiques* tapestries, which had remained in storage at Windsor since the opening years of the twentieth century. On the basis of this work, some of the *Abraham* tapestries and the two *Antiques* were reinstalled in the King's State Apartments (fig. 19.15). This installation continues to the present day, a testament to the past splendor of the Henrician tapestry collection. Nonetheless, serious questions remain about the long-term care and preservation of these precious textile relics.[78] It is to be hoped that this book will help to reinforce the rarity and historic significance of this depleted collection and to focus attention on the need for long-term preventative care that will ensure its preservation for future generations.

Abbreviations

BL	British Library
CSP Ven.	R. Brown et al., eds., *Calendar of State Papers and Manuscripts Relating to English Affairs Existing in the Archives and Collections of Venice,* 18 vols. (London, 1864–1912)
DNB	*Dictionary of National Biography* (Oxford, 1973)
GC	A. Thomas and I. Thornley, eds., *The Great Chronicle of London* (London, 1938)
GDA	*Grove Dictionary of Art* (London, 1996)
Harl. 599	BL Ms Harleian 599 (Inventory of Cardinal Wolsey's goods taken in the early 1520s)
Harl. 1419	BL Ms Harleian 1419 (Inventory of Henry VIII's possessions taken after his death in 1547, vol. 2)
HKW	H. Colvin, ed., *History of the King's Works,* 6 vols. (London, 1963–73)
LP	J. Brewer and R. Brodie, eds., *Letters and Papers, Foreign and Domestic, of the Reign of Henry VIII, 1509–1547,* 21 vols. (London, 1862–1932)
Marillier Catalogue	London, Victoria and Albert Museum, Textile Department Ms, *Marillier Manuscript Tapestry Catalogue,* 50 vols.
ODNB	*Oxford Dictionary of National Biography,* 60 vols. (Oxford, 2004)
TNA	The National Archives, Kew; formerly known as the Public Record Office (PRO)
Rotuli Parliamentorum	*Rotuli Parliamentorum; ut et Petitiones et Placita in Parliamento tempore, 1278–1532,* vol. 4, ed. J. Strachey et al. (London, 1773), 229–41

All other works are cited by author and date of publication

Notes

Introduction

1. "Ende dat de zelve Co. Mat. heeft meer tapitzeryen (ten minste wel alsoo vele) dan ennich kerstilic Coninck." Denucé 1936, 18–19.
2. Society of Antiquaries Ms. 129; Harl. 1419. Both inventories are transcribed in Starkey, ed., 1998.
3. Guiffrey 1885, 1:293–374.
4. In approximate date order these are as follows: one tapestry from a larger set of the *Story of Hercules,* ca. 1510–15 (inv. no. 1058); two tapestries from a four-piece set historically known as the *Seven Deadly Sins,* ca. 1515–20 (inv. nos. 1036, 1034); two panels from a ten-piece set of the *Redemption of Man,* ca. 1515–20 (inv. nos. 1035, 1088); one tapestry with a court scene from an unidentified allegorical set, ca. 1515–20 (inv. no. 1030); four tapestries, including one duplicate, from a six-piece set of the *Triumphs of Petrarch,* ca. 1515–20 (inv. nos. 1031–33); one tapestry known as the "Gryphon Allegory" from a larger set of the *Path to Honor,* ca. 1520 (inv. no. 1046); five pieces from a set of the *Story of Dido and Aeneas,* ca. 1530 (inv. nos. 1041–45); ten tapestries of the *History of Abraham,* ca. 1540-43 (inv. nos. 1001–10); two tapestries from a seven-piece set known as the *Antiques,* ca. 1540-42; and one tapestry from an eight-piece set of the *History of Tobias,* ca. 1545. The collection also includes five armorial strips, three with Cardinal Wolsey's arms and two with those of Henry VIII. For details, see Marillier 1962; T. Campbell 1994, 22–31; T. Campbell 1996a, 73–138; and T. Campbell 1996d, 69–78.
5. For nineteenth-century literature on tapestry production and patronage, see Guiffrey 1904, esp. 55–56, for Britain. For the first survey of Wolsey's patronage, see Law 1885–91, 1:57–68. For the first discussion of Henry VIII's collection, see Müntz 1890.
6. W. Thomson 1906, 263–78; W. Thomson 1914, 34–41.
7. W. Thomson 1906, 258–63.
8. W. Thomson 1930, 239–61; W. Thomson 1973, 241–60. The 1930 revision includes speculation about the English origin of various tapestries in the collection, refuted below. The 1973 revision includes additional references to the collection derived from the calendar of the Letters and Papers of Henry VIII's reign.
9. Auerbach 1954, 38.
10. For a bibliography on figurative art of the period, see Ford, ed., 1989, 337–43.
11. Marillier 1932; Marillier 1951; Marillier 1962.
12. D. King in Edwards et al., 1956, 101–6; Wood 1965, 402–4.
13. Russell 1969, 43–44, 47.
14. Kipling 1977, 61; Kipling 1981, 137–44.
15. See Bibliography for details.
16. A first essay on this subject was undertaken by Christine Adams in an M.Phil. diss. (Adams 1982) that analyzed Henry VIII's tapestry collection on the basis of Thomson's publication of the 1547 inventory. This work was limited by its dependence on the secondary literature and lack of knowledge of contemporary tapestry production.
17. T. Campbell 1995–96, 29–50, esp. 32–37.
18. For extensive discussion of the technical process of weaving, see Tabard 1978.
19. Campbell in New York 2002, 41–48.
20. Delmarcel in Balis et al. 1993, 43–44.
21. T. Campbell 1995–96, 32–33; T. Campbell 1999, 200–204.

Chapter 1. The Royal Tapestry Collection before 1399

1. Wilckens 1991, 262–67.
2. For the origins of early medieval tapestry production, see Lestocquoy 1978; Salet 1988; Joubert 1993, 24–28; and Cavallo 1993, 61–65.
3. Stapleton 1836, 333.
4. Ibid., 343.
5. Ibid., 344.
6. Wilson in Gordon, Monnas, and Elam, eds., 1997, 45, 281n56.
7. Palgrave 1836, 239–40, 246–47; McKendrick 1995, 56–57n47.
8. W. Thomson 1906, 76–79.
9. Consitt 1933, 69, 71.
10. Göbel 1933–34, 152–54; Evans 1949, 92–93; McKendrick 1995, 55n32; Crowfoot, Pritchard, and Staniland 2001, 69–70. For Edward III's involvement with the wool trade, see Lloyd 1977, 144–224.
11. Nichols 1780, 128; McKendrick 1995, 55n32. For the Scrope tapestries, see Murray 1992.
12. Arnold 1988, 163–65.
13. Nichols 1780, 60; Wilson in Gordon, Monnas, and Elam, eds., 1997, 281n55.
14. TNA E 361/5/1 rot. 1, rot. 3; McKendrick 1995, 56n47.
15. Legg and Hope, 1902, 96–97.
16. Cavallo 1993, 84–93.
17. Nichols 1780, 73.
18. Jubinal 1840, 25–28; Labarte 1879, 62–66.
19. Ledos 1889; Joubert 1981.
20. Dehaisnes 1886, 842–47; Winter 1976, 134–59.
21. Prost 1889–90; Guiffrey, ed., 1894–96, 2:206–24.
22. Lestocquoy 1978; Joubert 1990, 602.
23. For convenient guides to medieval romances, see Lacy, ed., 1986, and Gerritsen and van Melle, eds., 1998.
24. Cailleteau et al. 1987.
25. Winter 1976, 134–59; Joubert 1990.
26. Winter 1976, 152; Brassat 1992, 164.
27. Guiffrey 1911, 29–30.
28. Froissart 1857, 2:188.
29 Dillon and Hope 1897.
30. Ibid., 289.
31. Campbell in New York 2002, 29–32.
32. Pinchart 1885, 11.
33. McKendrick 1995, 45, 54n15.
34. Dehaisnes 1886, 697; Prost and Prost 1902–13, 2:599, 604.
35. Dehaisnes 1886, 709.
36. Ibid., 710.
37. Ibid., 737.
38. McKendrick 1995, 49.
39. TNA E 101/403/19 no. 67. Published with inaccuracies by W. Thomson 1906, 99–100. For the context, see Wilson in Gordon, Monnas, and Elam, eds., 1997, 281n55.
40. *Rotuli Parliamentorum* 1773, 229–41.
41. McKendrick 1991, 46.
42. McKendrick 1995, 54n15.
43. TNA E 361/6/2 m. 1; *Rotuli Parliamentorum* 1773, 238, 241; McKendrick 1995, 56n45.
44. Dillon and Hope 1897, 288; TNA E 101/403/19 no. 67. One or both of the Charlemagne tapestries can also be identified in the 1422 inventory; *Rotuli Parliamentorum* 1773, 235, 238.
45. McKendrick 1995, 58n71.
46. TNA E 361/6/2 m. 1.
47. *Calendar of Inquisitions Miscellaneous* 1963, 169–72; McKendrick 1991, 46n22; McKendrick 1995, 58n70.
48. Dugdale 1675, 1:237–38.
49. McKendrick 1988, 190–92; McKendrick 1991, 46n22; McKendrick 1995, 56n44.
50. TNA E 361/5/7; McKendrick 1995, 49, 57n50.
51. Monnas in Gordon, Monnas, and Elam, eds., 325–26n44.
52. TNA E 101/403/19 no. 67; Thomson 1906, 99–100.
53. The 1399 list identifies this panel only as "Cipro," but a Wardrobe list of 1413 provides the additional information that it showed the king of Cyprus.
54. For contemporary Continental collections, see Lestocquoy 1978, esp. 134–37.
55. Pinchart 1885, 15; Dehaisnes 1886, 908.
56. Dehaisnes 1886, 844–46.
57. Goodman and Gillespie, eds., 1999, esp. essays by Saul and Schieferle.
58. Barron in ibid., 138.
59. Monnas in Gordon, Monnas, and Elam, eds., 1997, 165–77, esp. 172.
60. S. Mitchell in Gordon, Monnas, and Elam, eds., 1997.
61. The hooks from which the tapestries hung were probably removed when internal masonry

was renewed in the nineteenth century; Wilson in ibid., 45, 281n55.
62. Gordon, Monnas, and Elam, eds., 1997.
63. Monnas in ibid., 172.
64. Ibid., 325–26n44.
65. Guiffrey, ed., 1894–96, 2:209–10.
66. *Rotuli Parliamentorum* 1773, 232; McKendrick 1995, 49–50, 57n61.
67. For discussion of these various tapestries and further bibliography, see Stucky-Schürer 1972, 49–85.
68. Wilckens 1991, 270–72.
69. Turin 1952, 14–15.

Chapter 2. The Royal Tapestry Collection, 1399–1461

1. Nichols 1780, 156; Nicolas 1826, 141.
2. TNA E 361/6, rot. 8v (where the list of tapestries in the Wardrobe and the list of tapestries in the keeping of John Stout appear in close proximity); TNA E 101/406/15 duplicates the first of these lists.
3. The 1413 list states that the *Peers* panel was woven with gold thread, but the 1422 inventory specifies that it was not (*Rotuli Parliamentorum* 1773, 229). The explanation for this discrepancy is unclear.
4. Montfaucon 1731, 74–75 and pl. 19; Winter 1976, 154–55; L. Campbell 1990, 44, 46, 249n24.
5. *Rotuli Parliamentorum* 1773, 238.
6. Gold is not mentioned in the 1413 list but is specified in that of 1422; TNA E 361/6, rot. 8v; *Rotuli Parliamentorum* 1773, 235.
7. *Rotuli Parliamentorum* 1773, 230.
8. Cavallo 1993, 94–124.
9. Meiss 1974, 63–64.
10. Stucky-Schürer 1972, 85–104; Joubert in Joubert, Lefébure, and Bertrand 1995, esp. 44–47.
11. Pinchart 1885, 19–20.
12. Ibid., 18; McKendrick 1995, 45, 54–55n17.
13. Pinchart 1885, 19.
14. *Rotuli Parliamentorum* 1773, 229–41.
15. Ibid., 235, 238, 232.
16. Ibid., 230, 232, 234.
17. Ibid., 233, 234.
18. Ibid., respectively, 234, 238, 230, 233.
19. Cavallo 1993, 148–55.
20. *Rotuli Parliamentorum* 1773, 230, 232, 233, 234.
21. Lestocquoy 1978, 49–51, 54.
22. Wingfield-Digby and Hefford 1971; Wingfield-Digby and Hefford 1980, 12–14.
23. *Rotuli Parliamentorum* 1773, 230, 234.
24. Ibid., 239, 240, 241.
25. Ibid., 230, 233, 241.
26. McKendrick 1995, 57–58n65.
27. McKendrick 1991, 48.
28. Strong and Strong 1981, 94.
29. TNA E 101/408/2; McKendrick 1995, 49, 50, 58n75.
30. Stratford 1993, 3–8, 61.
31. Ibid., 73–83.
32. Guiffrey 1878–85, 15–16.
33. Guiffrey 1887.
34. Stratford 1993, 86–89.
35. Ibid., 108–9.
36. Griffiths 1998, 217–25.
37. Guenée and Lehoux 1968, 62–70.
38. Stratford 1993, 21–54.
39. Ibid., 83, 224–25.
40. Ibid., 45–46, 429–30ff.
41. Cavallo 1993, 174–89.
42. Stratford 1993, 88–89.
43. Ibid., 20, 26.
44. Ibid., 73, 87–89, 226.
45. Ibid., 87, 89.
46. Harl. 1419, fols. 209, 300v; Starkey, ed., 1998, nos. 11969, 13069; McKendrick 1995, 57n60.
47. Platter 1937, 214–15, 239; Platter 1968, 2:847.
48. Stratford 1993, 89. For the context, see Griffiths 1998, 482–92.
49. Stratford 1993, 84–85, 225, 351–53.
50. Harl. 1419, fols. 298–98v; Starkey, ed., 1998, nos. 13047, 13049. For the repairs, see TNA E 101/415/7, fol. 11, and E 101/416/3, fol. 30v.
51. Stratford 1993, 78n33, 272.
52. McKendrick 1995, 48, 51.
53. Tafur 1926, 199. For Bruges as a center of tapestry trade, see E. Duverger in Bruges 1987, 35–52, and Campbell in New York 2002, 37.
54. Lestocquoy 1978, 39–66, esp. 51–53; Campbell in New York 2002, 32.
55. Tafur 1926, 201–2.
56. Historical Manuscripts Commission 1881; Goodall 2001, 18–19, 281–91.
57. Rapp Buri and Stucky-Schürer 2001, 41–70.
58. Goodall 2001, 325n7.
59. Rapp Buri and Stucky-Schürer 2001, 259–65.
60. Campbell in New York 2002, 88.
61. Goodall 2001, 18–19.
62. Harl. 599, fol. 8v; Campbell 1995, 109–10; Cleland 2007.
63. TNA E 101/409/12, fols. 21v, 35; McKendrick 1995, 55n33.
64. TNA E 101/409/12, fol. 22; McKendrick 1987, 521n5.
65. McKendrick 1995, 57n56.
66. Ibid., 50, 57n62.
67. Guiffrey 1911, 28.
68. Eton College Archives COLL/INV/4 (1465 indenture of the college's goods delivered to Saint George's, including "ii pese of tappestry werke on the sides of the high awter; ii peses of tappestry werke on the rode lofte"). For the return of these tapestries, see audit rolls for 1467–68 and 1470–71; Eton College Archives 61/AR/C/2, memb. 5; ibid., 61/BD/C/6, memb. 9; James 1920, 403; and Scofield 1923, 2:436–37.
69. Harl. 1419, fol. 347r; Starkey, ed., 1998, no. 13523.
70. Batlle Huguet 1946, 15–25; Rapp Buri and Stucky-Schürer 2001, 361, 372.
71. Smith 1979, 335–36.
72. Harl. 1419, fol. 298v; Starkey, ed., 1998, no. 13051.
73. Harl. 1419, fol. 364; Starkey, ed., 1998, no. 13750.
74. Harl. 1419, fols. 318, 328: Starkey, ed., 1998, nos. 13239, 13334.
75. Turin 1952, 19–20; Crick-Kuntziger [1958], 17–19; Asselberghs in Tournai 1967, 25–27; Wingfield-Digby and Hefford 1980, 18–19.
76. *Calendar of the Patent Rolls* 1909, 471.
77. Amyot 1827, 257–73.
78. McKendrick 1995, 51. For the argument that the panel depicted the Siege of Falerii, and discussion of the relevance of this subject to Fastolf's attempts to restore his reputation during the 1430s and 1440s, see Hawkyard 2005, 59–60.

Chapter 3. The Royal Tapestry Collection under Edward IV, 1461–1483

1. Smith 1979; Smith 1989; Ainsworth in New York 1998, 24; Campbell in New York 2002, 17–18.
2. Laborde 1849–52, 2:267–75; Smith 1979, 334.
3. Vaughan 1973, 206; Smith 1979, 335–36.
4. Smith 1989.
5. Chastellain 1863–66, 4:93–94.
6. Brussels 1967.
7. Rapp Buri and Stucky-Schürer 1998; Rapp Buri and Stucky-Schürer 2001, 230–45.
8. McKendrick 1988.
9. Paris 1981, 35–38, nos. 11a–d; Brassat 1992, 164–66.
10. Brassat 1992, 68–69.
11. Guiffrey 1878–85, 66–69; Cavallo 1993, 29.
12. Ross 1997, 261–62.
13. TNA E 404/73/3, nos. 73a, 73b; E 403/839, entry for Feb. 20, 1468; McKendrick 1987, 521, 522, 524.
14. McKendrick 1987, 521, 521n10.
15. Ross 1997, 262.
16. Ibid., 99–101; McKendrick 1987, 522n10.
17. Lestocquoy 1978, 71–80; McKendrick in GDA, vol. 13, 1996, 634; Campbell in New York 2002, 33–34ff.
18. Soil 1892, 24, 213, 376–77.
19. Smith 1979, 339–41.
20. Lestocquoy 1978, 73, 82, 100.
21. Soil 1892, 316; Morelowski 1936.
22. Soil 1892, 210, 316.
23. Campbell in New York 2002, 32–34.
24. McKendrick 1987, 521, 522.
25. Rapp Buri and Stucky-Schürer 2001, 221–29.
26. Deuchler 1984; Rapp Buri and Stucky-Schürer 2001, 114–43.
27. Harl. 599, fol. 8; Campbell 1996a, 122. Harl. 1419, fol. 209v; Starkey, ed., 1998, no. 11974.
28. BL Add. Ms 30367, fol. 26; Harl. 1419, fol. 7v; Starkey, ed., 1998, no. 9006.
29. Weightman 1989, 30–60.
30. Franke 1998, 48–49.
31. Haynin, 2:25–28; Franke 1991, 53–60; Franke 2005, 156–60.
32. Rapp Buri and Stucky-Schürer 2001, 266–79.
33. Franke 1995; Franke 1998, 60–72.
34. GC, 215.
35. For discussion of the extent to which this anecdote has generated misleading assumptions about Henry VI and his court in earlier years, see Starkey 1999.
36. Fortescue 1885, 125.
37. Starkey 1999.
38. Myers 1959, 13–34; Ross 1997, 260.
39. Vaughan 2002, 163–64; Rapp Buri and Stucky-Schürer 2001, 338–40.
40. HKW 1963, 1:198–99, 241, 425, 472; Ross 1997, 275–76.

41. Weightman 1989, 98.
42. McKendrick 1995, 49, 57n56.
43. Backhouse 1987, 29–30; Kren in Los Angeles 2003, nos. 25, 41.
44. J. Duverger in Bruges 1987, 44–45.
45. Backhouse 1987, 23–32.
46. McKendrick 1994, 160.
47. Ibid., esp. 158–59, 165.
48. Backhouse 1987, 24.
49. TNA E 404/76/4/135; Backhouse 1987, 27; McKendrick 1994, 161–66.
50. McKendrick 1987, 522, 524.
51. TNA E 404/76/4, nos. 41, 43, 49, 95, 99, 122, 123; for the issues, TNA E 403/845, entries for Aug. 26, 1478, and Jan. 26, 1479.
52. BL Royal Ms 7F. XIV, fol. 127.
53. Allan 1979, 172–73, 189nn3, 4.
54. BL Harleian Ms 7353; Ross 1997, 300–301.
55. TNA E 404/77/1, no. 25; McKendrick 1987, 524.
56. Donnet 1896, 272; Duverger 1971.
57. BL Harleian Ms 4780, fols. 11, 29, 32, 35; Nicolas 1830, 117, 118, 120, 132, 134, 141–42.
58. Weightman 1989, 209–12.
59. TNA E 404/77/1, no. 43.
60. McKendrick 1987, 522–24.
61. J. Junquera in Tournai, Brussels, Madrid 1985, 147–49; Asselberghs 1999, 223–37.
62. TNA E 404/77/3, no. 44; McKendrick 1987, 522–24.
63. Harl. 1419, fol. 385; Starkey, ed., 1998, no. 14043; Vallodolid, Medina del Campo, Ávila 2004, 396–97.
64. McKendrick 1987, 523n35.
65. Harl. 1419, fol. 343v; Starkey, ed., 1998, no. 13494.
66. Torra de Arana et al., 1985, 91–98.
67. Göbel states that Charles the Bold acquired a set of *Brutus* tapestries in 1469, but the basis of this claim is uncertain; Göbel 1923, 1:92.
68. Anglo 1992, 41–44.
69. Philadelphia Free Library, Lewis E201; Philadelphia 2001, 228–32. For the heraldry, see http://www.library.phila.gov/medieval/lewis_e201/banners.html.
70. Starkey 1999.
71. Myers 1959, 120.
72. Thurley 1993, 74.
73. Ross 1997, 272.
74. Ibid., 220.
75. Kingsford, ed., 1913, 386.
76. Rozmital 1957, 46–47.
77. Croyland Chronicle 1684, 559; Ross 1997, 277.

Chapter 4. Tapestry Acquisitions under Henry VII

1. Lestocquoy 1978, 32, 37; Göbel 1928, 1:348.
2. For tapestry usage at the court of Charles VIII, see Guiffrey 1878, 33, 67, 68, 83; Göbel 1928, pt. 1, 26, 260–62; and Brassat 1992, 164–66.
3. For surviving and documented sets, see Weigert 2004a, 121–69, and Weigert 2004b.
4. W. Campbell 1877, 2:25–26.
5. Leland 1970, 4:204.
6. Ibid., 220.
7. Calculated at 2d. per day, his costs from Aug. 22, 1486, to Feb. 2, 1487, totaled 27s. 2d.; W. Campbell 1877, 2:167–68.
8. For general discussion of Henry's income and expenditure, see Chrimes 1972, 125–26, 216–18, and Grummitt 1999. The main source of information for Henry VII's purchases are the books of payments maintained by John Heron, treasurer of the Chamber, of which the following survive: TNA E 101/414/6, fols. 1–91 (1495–97); TNA E 101/414/16, fols. 1–78 (1497–99); TNA E 101/415/3 (1499–1502); BL Add. Ms 59899, fols. 1–101 (1502–1505); BL Add. Ms 21480, fols. 2–32 (1505); and TNA E 36/214, fols. 7–351 (1505–1509). These can be supplemented with partial transcriptions made by the antiquary Craven Ord of other books, now lost, from the period 1491–95; BL Add. Ms 7099, of which extracts were published in Bentley 1831. Additional information is provided by Wardrobe accounts and warrants to the Exchequer and the keeper of the Great Wardrobe; TNA E 101/412/16–101/416/6. Warrants from the Privy Office to the Exchequer of the Receipt during Henry VII's reign are included in the sequence TNA E 404/79–86.
9. W. Campbell 1877, 2:34.
10. TNA PSO 2/3/s.n.; W. Campbell 1877, 2:280–81.
11. TNA E 101/413/1; W. Campbell 1877, 2:487–88.
12. Harl. 1419, fol. 299r; Starkey, ed., 1998, no. 13053.
13. McKendrick 1991, 57, 61.
14. The largest group, on which identification of Henry VII's set depends, is at the Victoria and Albert Museum, Prints and Drawings Department, E2225-1924 to E2245-1924. For details of other drawings belonging to the Society of Antiquaries and the British Museum, see McKendrick 1991, 59–60.
15. McKendrick 1991; Cavallo 1993, 243–46.
16. Paris, Musée du Louvre, Cabinet de Dessins, R.F. 2140–47; Lugt 1968, 17–19; McKendrick 1991, 63, 70–73.
17. McKendrick 1991, 49–50.
18. Ibid., 80–81.
19. Wingfield-Digby and Hefford 1980, 14–19.
20. McKendrick 1991, 43, 68–69.
21. Ibid., 78–79.
22. Campbell in New York 2002, 89.
23. McKendrick 1991, 51–55, 58.
24. Ibid., 77.
25. Campbell in New York 2002, 31–32, 47–48, 64.
26. TNA E 101/415/7, no. 5.
27. Harl. 1419, fol. 298; Starkey, ed., 1998, no. 13045. Another single piece was at Richmond, probably to be identified with the panel recorded in Richard II's collection; Harl. 1419, fol. 346v; Starkey, ed., 1998, no. 13519.
28. For the 1675–76 inventory, see TNA LC 5/86 (Windsor section).
29. Souchal in Paris 1973, 61–65; Blazy et al. 1996, 16–18; Cavallo 1993, 198–209; Forti Grazzini 2003, 23–33.
30. Forti Grazzini 2003, 34–39.
31. TNA E 404/80, no. 147; W. Campbell 1877, 393.
32. Gómez-Martinez and Chillón Sampedro 1925, 51–53, pl. 3; Asselberghs 1999, 354–56.
33. Harl. 1419, fol. 298v; Starkey, ed., 1998, no. 13050.
34. Torra de Arana et al. 1985, 46–47, 99–121; Delmarcel 1999, 60–63; Franke 1998.
35. TNA E 404/81/3.
36. GC, 286.
37. Harl. 1419, fol. 7; Starkey, ed., 1998, no. 9003.
38. GC, 251. For the palace, see Thurley 1993, 27–32.
39. Kipling 1990, 71–73.
40. TNA E 101/416/16, fol. 26v.
41. TNA E 404/82.
42. TNA E 101/414/16, fol. 64v.
43. Ibid., fol. 72.
44. Campbell in New York 2002, 35–36, 131–38.
45. Schneebalg-Perelman 1969, 279–323 ; Delmarcel 1990, 25–28; Delmarcel in Mechelen 2000, 13–15; Campbell in New York 2002, 131–33ff.
46. Campbell in New York 2002, 133.
47. On Apr. 1, 1498, a payment of £18 14s. to "Pet. Venyngham" for 102 Flemish ells (57½ square yards) of "arras" at 3s. 8d. per ell; BL Add. Ms 7099, 46. On May 8, two further payments, one for £29 3s. 4d. for 175 Flemish ells (98 square yards) of "verdoures" at 3s. 4d. per ell, the other of £113 16s. 6d. for 590½ ells (332 square yards) of tapestry at 3s. per ell and 101 ells (56½ square yards) of "counterpoynt" at 5s. the ell; TNA E 101/414/16, fol. 26.
48. TNA E 101/415/3, fol. 37.
49. *Calendar of the Close Rolls* 1963, 2:16 no. 43.
50. A fragmentary account of the Treasurer of the Chamber for the years 1504–5, includes an entry in regard to "Petro van Enghen tapysere et lodowico de fava." This is barely legible, but it relates to a sum of £600, the same as that mentioned in the recognizance of November 1500; TNA E 101/415/16, fol. 26. Other large payments to De la Fava, unrelated to tapestry, recorded on fols. 13, 15.
51. Schneebalg-Perelman 1969, 320–21.
52. TNA E 101/415/3, fol. 58.
53. TNA E 404/84.
54. Raine 1879–94, 2:311.
55. Anglo 1992, esp. 28, 35, 130.
56. Monnas 1987, 1989.
57. Cavallo 1993, 275–76; McKendrick 1995, 43.
58. TNA E 101/415/7, fol. 111.
59. Kendrick 1904–5, 490, 495; T. Thomson 1915, 20–22; Chitty 1932, 14–16; Asselberghs in Tournai 1970, no. 5.
60. Kendrick (1904–5, 495) identified the device as that of King Arthur, while T. Thomson (1915, 20–22) suggested it was that of the ancient kings of England. Chitty (1932, 15) identified it as that of "Belimawr or Belinus, King of Wales," and this was followed by Asselberghs (Tournai 1970, no. 5). For King Arthur's shield device and heraldry, see Scot-Giles 1964–65, 333, and Lacy, ed., 1986, 278–81.
61. Recorded in inventories of 1505 and 1510; respectively, Saint John's College, Cambridge, D91.24.1, fol. 3, and D102.19, fol. 3.
62. Harl. 1419, fols. 217–17v; Starkey, ed., 1998, nos. 12026, 12028.
63. Millar 1972, 158–59.

64. BL Harleian Ms 4898, fol. 238v, transcribed in W. Thomson 1930, 149, 317. The dimensions are not given in Millar 1972, 158–59, which is based on PRO LR2/124, fol. 98. See also Harl. Ms. 7352, fol. 94.
65. Cosnac 1884, 402–3; Michel 1999, 447. The traditional identification between Henry VII's dynastic panels and the early-sixteenth-century tapestries now at Magdalen College, Oxford (Kipling 1981, 144), can be dismissed because the former were designated as "arras" in the 1547 and Commonwealth inventories and were thus almost certainly woven with gold, whereas the Magdalen tapestries are coarse in both design and materials. In addition, the subject of one of the Magdalen hangings can be identified as *David Watching Bathsheba at the Fountain,* suggesting that others also show scenes from this story (Warren 1928).
66. The putative link between Henry VII's dynastic "arras" tapestries and a fragmentary piece, formerly at Lyme Regis (Thomson 1930, 150 and facing pl.), can be dismissed because the surviving piece does not contain metallic thread. A more probable identification of the subject of the Lyme Regis tapestry is provided by an almost identical piece sold at Christie's, London (Oct. 1, 1998, lot 242). In this, the male figure is identified as Jacob by a prominent inscription on his chest.
67. Kendrick 1924, 83–89; McGrory 2003, 103–6.
68. McGrory 2003, 71–77.
69. Anglo 1969, 35–43; McGrory 2003, 101–2.
70. Wauters 1878, 48–49; Campbell in New York 2002, 133–35.
71. Campbell in New York 2002, 135–36.
72. Souchal in Paris 1973, 176–80.
73. For the description in Mazarin's inventory, see Cosnac 1884, 400 no. 1735. For the probability that this panel derived from the English royal collection via the Commonwealth sale, see T. Campbell 1999, 195, and Michel 1999, 447. If the Mazarin tapestry did originate in the English royal collection, then it may have been one of two "arras" tapestries described as *Christ Sitting in Judgement* recorded at Richmond in the Commonwealth inventory; Millar 1972, 207.
74. For Mazarin's acquisitions from the Crown, see Cosnac 1884; Schnapper 1994, 192–96; and Michel 1999, 210–13, 216–17, 438–58.
75. Harl. 1419, fols. 210–10v; Starkey, ed., 1998, no. 11979. The 1547 inventory lists the set as tapestry rather than "arras," but confirmation that it did include gold thread is provided by the high valuation it received at the Commonwealth sale.
76. For tourist descriptions, see Ramssla 1734, 296, and Rye 1865, 167. For the Commonwealth inventory, see Millar 1972, 207.
77. Souchal in Paris 1973, 208–9, 213.
78. Cavallo 1993, 428–37.
79. Wingfield-Digby and Hefford 1980, cat. no. 9, 21.
80. For coarse millefleur tapestries, see Joubert 1987, 188–89. For high-quality examples, see Cavallo 1993, 502–5, and Adelson 1994, 105–15.
81. Harl. 1419, fol. 433v; Starkey, ed., 1998, no. 15207.

Chapter 5. Tapestry Usage under Henry VII

1. Hayward 1998a, 21.
2. For example, a warrant of Mar. 26, 1487, requests the delivery of two verdure counterpoints and one of tapestry, to the Wardrobe of the Queen's Beds (TNA E 101/412/20, no. 19). Subsequently, the accounts for the eighteen months to Michelmas 1488 record the receipt of fifteen counterpoints of tapestry and nine counterpoints of verdure, while those for the years 1493–95 record the receipt of seventeen verdure and tapestry counterpoints (TNA E 101/413/1; W. Campbell 1877, 2:487–88; TNA E 101/413/10).
3. W. Campbell 1877, 2:282. Elizabeth of York's expenses in 1502 include payments to her wardrobe officers for the transport and provision of tapestries; Nicolas 1830, 53–54.
4. Nichols 1863, 2.
5. Sutton and Hammond 1983, 66–70.
6. W. Campbell 1873, 1:259, 405, 406; Bakes's wage incorrectly transcribed in Thomson 1906, 171 (and subsequent editions), as "4d. a year." The annual payment of £24 6s. 8d. is confirmed by a list of warrants issued under the royal seal during the first seven years of Henry's reign; TNA E 407/6/137, 3rd parchment.
7. Lovekyn received 12d. per day, and £5 per year for life for a house in the City of London; W. Campbell 1873, 1:535.
8. For Bakes's predecessors, see McKendrick 1995, 56n33. Kipling 1981, 139–40, mistakenly claims that this was a new office.
9. Van der Strete received the office of royal arras maker (also referred to as that of "stragulatoris") with the usual wages of 12d. per day, "as John Bakes late our arasmaker had"; *Calendar of the Patent Rolls* 1976, 2:278, and TNA E 404/84.
10. Three of these extended accounts survive for the years 1498–99, 1503–4, and 1504–6, providing evidence of the labor costs and materials used by the arras maker and those under his direction; respectively, TNA E 36/209, E 101/415/10, and E 101/416/3.
11. TNA E 101/415/7, fol. 5.
12. Ibid., fol. 111.
13. Ibid.
14. Ibid., fol. 91; E 101/415/10, fols. 27–28.
15. TNA E 101/415/7, fol. 98.
16. Devon 1837, 393; McKendrick 1995, 55–56n33.
17. Margaret's trousseau also included a state bed and cloth of honor, both with armorials and heraldic devices, two altar cloths, and a set of vestments; TNA E 101/415/7, fol. 111.
18. TNA E 101/416/3, fol. 30v.
19. Various closely related manuscripts survive of which the earliest, compiled about 1491–93, appears to be BL Add. Ms 38174; transcribed in Grose and Astle 1807–9, 1:296–341. As Starkey 1999 demonstrates, this was based in part on an earlier Lancastrian text. Details regarding royal deliveries and christenings are repeated in BL Harleian Ms 6079, transcribed in Leland 1970, 4:179–84. These new directives were promulgated by the "Articles ordained by King Henry VII for the Regulation of His Household," issued in December 1493; transcribed in *Collection of Ordinances and Regulations* 1790, 109–33. For analysis of these various sources, see Staniland 1987, esp. 298–99, and Starkey 1999.
20. Leland 1970, 4:179; Grose and Astle 1807–9, 1:304, 305, 333.
21. Grose and Astle 1807–9, 1:305, 337.
22. Leland 1970, 4:249.
23. Gay 1887, 1:774.
24. Leland 1970, 256.
25. Stratford 1993, 409–10.
26. For detailed discussion of the Port Book of Rates, see the extended introduction to the 1582 Book of Rates given in Willan 1962. The 1507 version is published in Gras 1918.
27. Gras 1918, 704.
28. Luxury goods imported on behalf of the king were exempt from tax. For example, see Henry VII's letter to Richard Fox, bishop of Exeter and keeper of the Privy Seal, regarding his 1488 purchase of the *Story of Troy* set and other tapestries; W. Campbell 1877, 2:280–81.
29. T. Campbell 1995, 33.
30. Ibid., 29–50, esp. 32–37.
31. Ibid. My analysis did overlook one useful citation in the 1547 inventory, the description of a tapestry at Woodstock as "one peice of tapestrie of hawkinge & huntinge lyned with canvas mencyoned in tholde booke to be countefeit Arras" (Harl. 1419, fol. 319; Starkey ed., 1998, no. 13249). This provides further support for my argument that "counterfeit arras" was a form of tapestry, not a textile that imitated tapestry.
32. BL Cotton Vespasian c. xii, fols. 236ff.; quoted in Gairdner 1858, 285.
33. For the context, see Chrimes 1972, 291–92, 294.
34. Nichols 1846, 54–60.
35. Kingsford 1921, 39–54.
36. Hope 1915, 275–348.
37. Harl. 1419, fol. 6v; Starkey, ed., 1998, nos. 8995, 8996.
38. Ridgard 1985, 129–58.
39. Anglo 1969, 10–46.
40. For full details, see Leland 1970, 4:187–201, and Anglo 1969, 21–35.
41. Anglo 1969.
42. Gairdner 1858, 307ff.; Hommel 1959, 246.
43. TNA E 101/415/3, fol. 24.
44. Nichols 1846, 50.
45. Grose and Astle 1807–9, 2:284–85; Kipling 1990, 39–40.
46. Grose and Astle 1807–9, 2:290; Kipling 1990, 45.
47. Grose and Astle 1807–9, 2:315; Kipling 1990, 72.
48. Kipling 1990, 72, 160.
49. Grose and Astle 1807–9, 2:315; Kipling 1990, 160.
50. Grose and Astle 1807–9, 2:316; Kipling 1990, 73.

Chapter 6. Henry VIII: Purchases and Use of Tapestry, 1509–1519

1. Inventories of Margaret Beaufort's tapestries and household goods survive at Saint John's

College, Cambridge, dating from October 1505, March 1509, August 1509, September 1509, and a slightly later undated list. That of 1505 has been calendared in Cooper 1973, 178–214. For John de Vere's collection, see Hope 1915; for Thomas Howard, see Ridgard, ed., 1985. Warham and Fox both made specific mention of tapestries in their wills; respectively, Nichols and Bruce 1863, 23, and Allen and Allen 1929, 169–70.
2. GC, 340.
3. For tapestries belonging to the Ironmongers by 1489, the Mercers by 1495, and the Merchant Taylors by the end of the century, see McKendrick 1995, 51, 59nn91–94. For tapestries commissioned by the Goldsmiths' Company during the reign of Henry VIII, see Unwin 1966, 179.
4. Hall 1904, 1:5.
5. Ibid., 10.
6. Ibid., 24.
7. Ibid., 26.
8. Ibid., 27.
9. Weir 2001, 139–40.
10. D. Kraak in M. Russell et al. 1990, 166–69.
11. Christie's, London, Jan. 13, 1993, lot 243.
12. T. Campbell 1996a, 101, 112. For discussion of perquisites at Knole, see Jackson-Stops 1977, 1620–22, and Beard 1997.
13. Biriukova 1965, 28, pls. 107–16.
14. For Tudor court finance, see W. Richardson 1952 and Loades 1987, 74–83. For the King's Book of Payments, 1509–1521, see TNA E 36/214, E 36/215, E 360/216 (calendared in LP 2, pt. 2:1441–80, and 3, pt. 2:1533–45). For tapestry references in the Treasurer of the Chamber's accounts for 1528–30, see TNA E 101/420/11 (calendared in LP 5:304–17).
15. Hayward 1998a, 62–63.
16. Thus, in the first year of the reign Van der Strete was paid 60s. for fifteen "tappets," perhaps made in his own workshop, for windows at the Tower; TNA E 36/215, fol. 43; LP 2, pt. 2:1444. During the same period, Rauf Jenet, yeoman of the Wardrobe, purchased various textiles, including six "new counterpoints of good green verdure of wool, each to contain 30 Flemish ells,", and another six of twenty-four Flemish ells; TNA E 101/417/3. In September 1512 we find Jenet making a more substantial purchase of "verdours and tapestry" from an Anne Harpesfield. On this occasion, the price of £86 14s. was paid from the Treasury of the Chamber; TNA E 36/215, fol. 203; LP 2, pt. 2:1458. Harpesfield seems to have been a London-based supplier of luxury textiles. The 1526 will of William Lord Willoughby also refers to hangings of tapestry "which I bought of Harpesfeld"; Lincoln Record Office, 2 Anc. 3/A/41, n. 9.
17. LP 1, pt. 1:no. 357 (2).
18. Marillier 1962, 26 and pl. 20.
19. Latham 1904–9, 2:319–27; Burrell coll., inv. nos. 46/134–39. A seventh appeared in the trade in 1967; Sotheby's, London, Dec. 8, 1967; Boccara 1971, 44–45.
20. LP 1:no. 218 (16). The ordinances for the Royal Household promulgated by Wolsey in January 1526 confirm the wages for various royal servants and cite "Cornelius van de Strete, arras maker" at a wage of £18 5s.; LP 4:no. 1939 (12). This was the same as that received by Thomas Foster, comptroller of the works, and William Vertue, master mason.
21. TNA E 101/417/4, fols. 42v, 43, 43v.
22. BL Egerton Ms 3025, fols. 27–28.
23. Percy 1905, 384–85; Hayward 1998a, 157.
24. Hefford 1979.
25. LP 2:1068; Hall 1904, 1:65.
26. Hall 1904, 1:72.
27. Ibid., 83.
28. Campbell in New York 2002, 139–40, 288–92; Franke 2005, 160–64.
29. LP 1:no. 2302.
30. Cruickshank 1990, 127; LP 1:no. 2375.
31. For discussion of tapestries produced at Tournai in the late fifteenth and early sixteenth centuries, respectively, see Tournai 1967; Tournai 1968; and Campbell in New York 2002, 140–41.
32. LP 1:no. 2391; Cruickshank 1971, 11.
33. Cruickshank 1971, 18; Soil 1891, 42, 258, 401.
34. Soil 1892. 41–42, 257–59, 264, 398–402.
35. Ibid., 173–74; Campbell 1995, esp. 45–47.
36. Hinds, ed., 1912, no. 660.
37. Weir 2001, 179–80.
38. LP 2:no. 1573.
39. Hall 1904, 1:163.
40. LP 2:no. 4362.
41. TNA E 36/215, fol. 320; LP 2, pt. 2:1465.
42. TNA E 101/417/2, no. 146.
43. Hall 1904, 1:124.
44. TNA SP 1/230, fol. 246; LP 1, pt. 2:no. 3272.
45. According to this bill, Van der Strete had now received £495 from Sir John Dance "by a bill of exchange made with John Cavalcante factor of Phylippe Calthorpe," and £173 14s. through William Copeland, leaving £39 4s. 8d. outstanding. According to a final annotation, John Dance paid the outstanding sum on Sept. 24, 1514; TNA E 101/56/10 file 6, no. 217; calendared in LP 1, pt. 2:no. 3614 (217).
46. For this and what follows, see Sicca 2002, 164–69; Sicca 2006.
47. It also included two sumptuous sets of cloth of gold embroidered with heraldic devices and various other beds and furnishings; TNA PROB 31/8/137, fol. 77v.
48. Hall 1904, 1:163.
49. HKW 4, pt. 2:172; Thurley 1993, 44–45.
50. TNA E 101/622/31.
51. In November 1518 William Holyngworth was paid £31 4s. 2d. for lining "arras" at Newhall; TNA E 36/216, fol. 47; LP 2, pt. 2:1480.
52. It is not possible to identify any of the hangings in the 1547 inventory because only a handful of counterpoints remained at Newhall by that date. Some hangings may have been redistributed when the manor was taken from Princess Mary in 1533 and granted to Lord Rochford, Anne Boleyn's brother. Others were taken from Newhall to furnish Prince Edward's residence in 1538; LP 13, pt. 2:no. 1280.
53. For examples, see Tournai 1970, nos. 20–26; Cavallo 1993, 36–38, 359–72, 488–501, 574–85; and Joubert 1987, 168–77, 186–87.
54. Quoted from Weir 2001, 22, 37.
55. TNA E 36/215, fol. 366; LP 2, pt. 2:1467.
56. Thurley 1993, 40–44.
57. TNA E 36/215, fol. 552; LP 2, pt. 2:1476.
58. Interestingly, when Van Aelst got into financial difficulties in the early 1520s, he mortgaged five tapestries of *David* and two of *John the Baptist* to the Munich bankers Ligsalz and Shrenk; Strieder 1930, 34–35.
59. TNA E 36/215, fol. 533; LP 2, pt. 2:1476. For construction at Greenwich, see Thurley 1993, 48.
60. Millar 1972, 358.
61. Crick-Kuntziger 1944, 9–11.
62. Crick-Kuntziger 1936; Steppe 1976a, 215–17; Mechelen 2000, 14.
63. TNA E 36/216, fol. 64; LP 3, pt. 2:1534.
64. Thurley 1993, 45–46.
65. LP 3, pt. 2:1534. No further sales to the Crown by Gerard Smytting are recorded, but evidence of his continuing activity as a supplier of tapestries to the court circle is provided by the fact that in 1523 he sued Wolsey for money owed to him for tapestries purchased by Thomas Ruthal, bishop of Durham; T. Campbell 1996a, 87n55.
66. Heal 1980, 65, 72; Cornwall 1988, 143–44; Foister 2004, 97.
67. Miller 1955, 18.
68. For comparisons, see Loades in Greenwich 1991, 174, and Thurley 1993, 44, 52, 58.
69. Harl. 1419, fol. 37v; Starkey, ed., 1998, no. 9264. For the Toledo tapestry, see Onghena 1974, 13–14.
70. T. Campbell 1999, 173–74.
71. For extensive discussion of classical subject matter listed by the 1547 inventory and possible identifications, see ibid., 159–67, 173–77.
72. For Henry's religious orthodoxy at this date, see Scarisbrick 1968, 110–13, and Weir 2001, 134–35.
73. Campbell in New York 2002, 291–92.
74. Harl. 1419, fol. 217v; Starkey, ed., 1998, nos. 12027, 12029.
75. For examples, see Cavallo 1993, 334–46, esp. figs. 121, 123, and no. 23.
76. Cleland, in press.
77. Hayward 1998a, 67–69.

Chapter 7. Cardinal Wolsey's Tapestry Patronage, 1509–1519

1. T. Campbell 1996a.
2. Thurley in Gunn and Lindley, eds., 1991, 76–77; Thurley 1993, 40–44.
3. Foister 1981, 273–82.
4. For choir hangings of tapestry and other precious materials in English cathedrals in the early sixteenth century, see the following: for Winchester, Strype 1812, 2:712; for Canterbury, Legg and Hope 1902, 163, 164, 168ff.; for Exeter, Oliver 1861, 325–30, esp. 328; for Saint Paul's, Walters 1939, 85; for Salisbury, Dodsworth 1914, 232; for York Minster, Raine, ed., 1859, 227.
5. Aix-en-Provence 1977; Toulouse, Aix-en-Provence, Caen 2004, 102–11.
6. Raine 1879–94, 3:358.
7. Nichols and Bruce 1863, 23; Allen and Allen

1929, 169–70; LP 6:no. 625.
8. Soil 1891, 259; Cruickshank 1971, 143–87.
9. Cruickshank 1969, 45.
10. Cavendish 1959, 15; LP 5:no. 6075, (17) and (18).
11. Chambers 1965, 129–30; LP 1:no. 3261.
12. LP 1:nos. 3495, 3963; Chambers 1965, 140.
13. Harl. 599, fols. 8v, 18v; T. Campbell 1996a, 123, 129.
14. LP 2:no. 1153.
15. B. M. 1834, 47.
16. Thurley in Gunn and Lindley 1991, 76–102.
17. Ibid., 84–85.
18. Ibid., 87–91; Thurley 2003, 16–26.
19. LP 2:no. 336; Cruickshank 1971, 143ff.
20. BL Cotton Calig. E.1, 144; LP 2:no. 852.
21. Harl. 599, fols. 13–15; T. Campbell 1996a, 126–27.
22. Harl. 599, fol. 13; T. Campbell 1996a, 126. For examples and bibliography, see Wingfield-Digby and Hefford 1980, 30–32, and Gentil Quina 1998. For contemporary collections and interest in exotica, see Steppe and Delmarcel 1974, 41, 52nn78–85.
23. *Condemnation de Banquet* 1980.
24. T. Campbell 1996a, 101.
25. LP 2:nos. 1153, 3605.
26. Campbell in New York 2002, 168–74.
27. BL Cotton Calig. VI. D, 316–17; LP 2:no. 3206.
28. Cruikshank 1971.
29. Soil 1891, 399; Delmarcel and E. Duverger in Bruges 1987, 44–46, 63.
30. For Scellier in England, see LP 2, pt. 2:no. 2820. For Brandon's tapestries, see LP 2:no. 2826, and Soil 1891, 257, 400–401.
31. For the Netherlandish trade fairs, see Ewing 1990, 558–84.
32. For the date of Scellier's death, see LP 2, pt. 2:nos. 3550, 3720.
33. Harl. 599, 2v–4v; T. Campbell 1996a, 119–21.
34. Hampton Court inv. no. 1035, known as *The Deadly Sins,* and no. 1088, known as the "Anglesey" tapestry; Marillier 1931, 12–14, and pl. 5; Marillier 1962, 13–17, pls. 11, 12. The "Anglesey" was acquired by the marquis of Anglesey in 1912. Its association with the Hampton Court panel is assumed by the fact that at this time it carried an armorial strip with Henry VIII's arms similar to those that survive at Hampton Court; Marillier 1931, 12. The association of the so-called *Deadly Sins* panel with Hampton Court is presumed to be unbroken.
35. Harl. 599, fols. 2–4; T. Campbell 1996a, 120–21.
36. The *Judith and Holofernes* and *Ruth* tapestries were joined when they were first identified at Sens Cathedral in the late nineteenth century; Müntz 1906, 97–115. They are now separated.
37. Harl. 599, fols. 3–3v; T. Campbell 1996a, 120.
38. J. Duverger 1957–58, 9–15.
39. Harl. 599, fol. 4; T. Campbell 1996a, 120.
40. D. Campbell 1980, 133.
41. Weil-Garris and d'Amico 1980, esp. 58–63, 113n97.
42. Ibid., 45–68, for original text and translation.
43. For discussion of whether the layout of Hampton Court was influenced by Cortesi's work, see Foyle 2002 and Thurley 2003, 404n18.
44. R. Brown. ed., 1854, 2:314. For the context of this report and the lengths to which Wolsey would go to obtain high-quality furnishings, see D. King 1985, 49–52.
45. Cavendish 1959, 69–70. For Wolsey's plate, see Glanville 1991, 131–48, esp. 135.
46. Harl. 599, fols. 6–8v; T. Campbell 1996a, 121–23.
47. Harl. 599, fol. 8v; T. Campbell 1996a, 123. For the Bern panel, see Rapp Buri and Stucky-Schürer 2001, 41–70. With a recorded length of fourteen yards, Wolsey's panel would have been over two yards longer than the Bern panel, suggesting that the cartoon had been adapted for this particular weaving.
48. Cleland 2007.
49. Harl. 599, fols. 6–7; T. Campbell 1996a, 121–22.
50. Harl. 599, fol. 6v; T. Campbell 1996a, 122. Wolsey owned two *Saint Jerome* panels, one measuring 1 by 1½ yards, the other 1⅜ by 1¾ yards. The dimensions of the latter are close to those of a panel sold at Sotheby's, London, Dec. 13, 1974, lot 220, which was woven with silk and a high proportion of metal thread, as Wolsey's "arras" panel of this subject would also have been. Other high-quality small panels of *Jerome* survive in the Spanish royal collection and the Decorative Arts Museum, Paris, but the dimensions of these are larger than those of Wolsey's panels; see Junquera de Vega and Herrero Carretero 1986, 33, and Arras 1969, cat. 27.
51. Harl. 599, fol. 6; T. Campbell 1996a, 121. For the Knole panel, see Cavallo 1967, 89–91, where the subject is misidentified as *Saint Claude.* For the correct identification, see Delmarcel in Brussels 1976, 246–51. For a duplicate panel woven without gold thread at the Norton Simon Museum, see D. King 1976, 232–37.
52. A worn panel of this subject, of similar style to the Boston Trajan panel but lacking gold thread, was sold at Parke Bernet Galleries, New York, May 7–8, 1971, lot 225.
53. Gunn and Lindley 1991, 16–17.

Chapter 8. The Field of Cloth of Gold

1. For the context, preparations, and events of this meeting, see J. G. Russell 1969.
2. Caley 1827, 177–78.
3. Ibid., 179; LP 3:no. 704.
4. LP 3:nos. 919, 333.
5. TNA E 36/216, 168; LP 3, pt. 2:1539.
6. TNA E 36/216, 180; LP 3, pt.2:1541.
7. For full details, see J. G. Russell 1969, 37–46.
8. Letter from Gioan Joachino; CSP Ven., 3:41.
9. Hall 1904, 1:191–92.
10. For Sanuto, see CSP Ven., 3:54; for Donado to Giovanni Francesco Gritti, ibid., 3:64–65.
11. "Tapezarie atacate d'a oro e de seta historiata de la Creatione de l'homo, tutto el Testamento vechio e il Nove, e fra le altre cose li è David quando fece amazare Uria e li tolse Betesabe che pareno vivi"; Bamforth and Dupèbe 1991, 222, lines 79–84.
12. Gasparo Spinelli, Venetian secretary in London, to his brother in Venice, May 7, 1527; CSP Ven., 4:57, no. 105.
13. T. Richardson 2002.
14. Harl. 1419, fol. 6; Starkey, ed., 1998, no. 8990.
15. Harl. 1419, fol. 37; Starkey, ed., 1998, no. 9260.
16. Harl. 1419, fol. 64v; Starkey, ed., 1998, no. 9700.
17. Millar, ed., 1972, 4, 331, 362; T. Campbell 1996b, 126, 138n27.
18. Millar, ed., 1972, 55, 73; T. Campbell 1996b, 131.
19. TNA LR 2/124, fol. 1, 17; Millar 1972, 55, 73. The group formerly at Greenwich measured 11, 11, 11, 12, and 10 by 6½ ells, the other 12, 11, 11, 8, and 9 by 6½ ells. If the measurements of the two groups are combined and translated into meters in decreasing order of size, they are as follows: 8.23, 8.23, 7.54, 7.54, 7.54, 7.54, 7.54, 6.85, 6.17, 5.48. This putative set would therefore have been narrower than the Écouen set by the following amounts (in meters); −0.09, −0.06, −0.61, −0.6, −0.50, −0.47, +0.28, −0.29, −0.12, −0.43.
20. CSP Ven., 3:20.
21. Harl. 1419, fol. 5v; Starkey, ed., 1998, no. 8989.
22. Millar, ed., 1972, 4.
23. Loomie 1989, 261, 264–65n42.
24. Rowlands 1985, 78, pls. 117–19; Foister 2004, 65–67.
25. Baldass 1920, pls. 62–64 (series 33).
26. CSP Ven., 3:76.
27. Harl. 1419, fol. 128; Starkey, ed. 1998, no. 12033; Hayward 1998a, 66.
28. Hall 1904, 1:195.
29. Ibid., 1:214–15.
30. Campbell in New York 2002, 143–44.
31. The following is based on T. Campbell 2004, pts. 1 and 2.
32. For this and what follows on the origin of the design, see ibid., pt. 1.
33. For reconstruction of the entire series and discussion of the design and iconography, see ibid., 376–84.
34. Ibid., 385.
35. Harl. 599, fol. 14v; T. Campbell 1996a, 127; T. Campbell 2004, pt. 2, 602–4.
36. Harl. 599, fol. 2; T. Campbell 1996a, 119; T. Campbell 2004, pt. 2, 602ff.
37. T. Campbell 2004, pt. 2, 604–5.
38. Ibid., 608.
39. Ibid., 604–7.
40. J. G. Russell 1969, 16; Weir 2001, 219, 225, 228.
41. TNA E 101/417/6, no. 7.

Chapter 9. The Patronage of Cardinal Wolsey and Henry VIII in the Early 1520s

1. DNB 1973, 8:582–85; Bindoff 1982, 2:248–50; ONDB 2004, 760–64.
2. TNA SP 1/21, 112, dated Oct. 14, 1520; Ellis 1846, 234; LP 3:no. 1021.
3. Harl. 599, fols. 9–9v, 10–11v; T. Campbell 1996a, 123–24, 124–26.
4. Harl. 599, fols. 10, 10v; Campbell 1996a, 124. For the Musée Lécuyer panel, see Duverger 1957–58, 9–15.
5. Harl. 599, fol. 11v; T. Campbell 1996a, 125. The subject is confirmed by the 1547 inventory, which lists "three peces of tapestrie of Emalike Malaon and Ruthe havinge the said borders [Wolsey's arms]," at The More; Harl.

1419, fol. 329; Starkey ed., 1998, no. 13344.
6. Harl. 599, fol. 9; T. Campbell 1996a, 109, 123.
7. Steppe 1976b, 100–117.
8. For comparison, see the inventory of Edmund Dudley, taken at his London residence in 1509, *Archaeologia* 21 (1921): 39–42; that of Lord Darcy, taken in 1519, TNA SP 1/21, fols. 65–71 (calendared in LP 3:no. 1001); that of Lord Monteagle taken at Hornby in 1523, LP 3, pt. 2:no. 2968; and that of Sir Henry Guildford taken at his London residence and Leeds Castle, Kent, in 1532, *Archaeologia Cantiana* 15 (1883): 282–385 (calendared in LP 5:no. 1064).
9. Hope 1915; Ridgard 1985, 129–58.
10. Scattergood 1983, *Collyn Clout,* lines 940–79.
11. CSP Ven., 4:303. For this misleading dating, see LP 5:no. 6148, where the inventory is associated with material from 1530.
12. For the dating, see King 1985, 41, and T. Campbell 1996a, 84–85n45.
13. For Wolsey's building at The More, see Thurley in Gunn and Lindley 1991, 91–93.
14. Harl. 599, fols. 5, 12, 14v, 19; T. Campbell 1996a, 121, 125–27, 130.
15. Harl. 599, fol. 13; T. Campbell 1996a, 126. These tapestries can be identified with those described as "Certayn storres called Rolles" whose subjects are described in the inventory taken at Cawood after Wolsey's death; TNA E 36/171, fol. 6v; T. Campbell 1996a, 131.
16. Harl. 599, fol. 15; T. Campbell 1996a, 127.
17. Harl. 599, fols. 19v, 21v; T. Campbell 1996a, 130–31; Gwyn 1990, 279, 301.
18. For the Bramshill panels, see Marillier 1931, 7; Tipping 1927, 380, 381; and Hussey 1923. Sold at Sotheby's, London, Mar. 13, 1931, these were acquired by French and Company, New York, who restored and rearranged the panel with the inscription (French and Company Archive, Getty Resource Center, Santa Monica, stock no. 38025 C, neg. no. 16585). This panel is now in the Burrell Collection, inv. no. 46/117. Fragments of the second panel were sold at Parke Bernet Galleries, New York, Nov. 25–26, 1949, lots 306, 307. For the Warsaw panel, a duplicate of the central section of the second Bramshill panel, which was formerly in the Bernheimer collection and was sold at Christie's, London, June 11, 1931, lot 6, see Poznan 1971, cat. 1.
19. For the circumstances and validity of these charges, see Ives in Gunn and Lindley 1991, esp. 298.
20. Thurley 2003, 27–29.
21. Harl. 599, fol. 12; T. Campbell 1996a, 126.
22. Marillier 1962, 23–24 and pl. 27. The dimensions do not match exactly to those given in the inventory, but the difference, about one foot in height and length, is within the margin that might be allowed for mismeasurement when the inventory entry was made and/or subsequent shrinkage.
23. Junquera de Vega and Herrero Carretero 1986, 22–25 (ser. 5); Delmarcel 1977c, 72–74; Delmarcel 1979, esp. 161–62.
24. Harl. 599, fol. 7; T. Campbell 1996a, 122.
25. Cavendish 1959, 19, 20.
26. Harl. 599, fol. 19; T. Campbell 1996a, 130.
27. Harl. 599, fol. 16; T. Campbell 1996a, 127.
28. Harl. 599, fol. 18v; T. Campbell 1996a, 129–30.
29. Cavendish 1959, 68.
30. Ibid., 69.
31. Ellis 1846, 1:237; LP 3:no. 1114.
32. Kingsford 1921, 39–54.
33. Harl. 1419, fol. 237v; Starkey, ed., 1998, no. 12174.
34. W. Thomson 1973, 144–46. Much information about tapestry patronage of the Scottish kings in the late fifteenth and early sixteenth centuries is cited in the *Calendar of Scottish State Papers.*
35. For Thornbury, see Howard 1987, 57–58, 221n33; for Penshurst, ibid., 208.
36. For Buckingham's household, see Rawcliffe 1978, esp. 94.
37. Doehaerd 1962–63: 233 no. 3752.
38. LP 3, pt. 1:no. 1285, 503.
39. Harris 1986, 171.
40. BL Add. Ms 36542, fols. 104–5; LP 3, pt. 2:1578, no. 21.
41. LP 3:no. 3375 (5); for the repairs, TNA E 101/421/16, fol. 38v.
42. Harl. 1419, fol. 6v; Starkey, ed., 1998, no. 8995.
43. Two years later a lesser collection came to the Crown from Lady Agnes Hungerford, attainted for murder in 1523. An inventory of possessions at her property records hangings of say, "paned" in red and green, in the hall and chapel, but the three main chambers of the house were hung with suites of "arras" of which one was new, with matching counterpoints, celors, and testers, totaling twenty or so hangings. In addition, the inventory records four fine "arras" cushions "with royses," as well as sundry table carpets and counterpoints; TNA SP 1/27, fols. 83–86; LP 3:no. 2861.
44. Hall 1904, 1:246.
45. Ibid., 1:255; CSP Ven., 3:236 no. 466.
46. Hall 1904, 1:255.
47. For full discussion, see Delmarcel's monographic catalogue, Mechelen 2000.
48. Campbell in New York 2002, 181–84.
49. For discussion of these series, see Campbell in New York 2002, 225–45ff.
50. LP 3:no. 2214. For this question, see Sicca 2002, 170.
51. Sicca 2002, 170–71; Sicca 2006.
52. Sicca 2002, 172–73.
53. Ibid., 179, 188–97.
54. TNA LC 9/51, fol. 130v; E 36/224, fol. 63.
55. TNA SP 1/19, fols. 150–51; LP 3:no. 580. For Mary's accommodation, see Thurley 1993, 78–79.
56. TNA SP 1/28, fols. 242–43; LP 3:no. 3375 (4).
57. TNA SP 1/28, fol. 244; LP 3:no. 3375 (5). For Princess Mary's household servants, including yeomen and grooms of the Wardrobe of Beds, see LP 4:no. 1577.
58. For the tradition, see Walker 1996, 99–100.
59. Erasmus 1936, 145.
60. Rude, ed., 1992, 119; see also 194.
61. Weir 2001, 255. For the accommodation provided for Richmond, see Thurley 1993, 81.
62. TNA SP 1/35, fols. 209, 210v; LP 4:nos. 1514, 1530.
63. LP 5:no. 2063 (2).
64. BM Royal Ms 7F. XIV, fols. 94v–96; LP 11:no. 163; Nichols 1855.
65. For duplicate weavings, see Steppe and Delmarcel 1974; Delmarcel in Mechelen 2000, 37–41.
66. Weir 2001, 239–40.
67. Grose and Astle 1807–9, 2:184–207.
68. Weir 2001, 96–100.
69. Grose and Astle 1807–9, 2:190.
70. Ibid., 203.
71. Ibid., 202.
72. Ibid., 186–87.
73. Ibid., 205.
74. Foister 2004, 121–28.
75. CSP Ven., 4:no. 105 (p. 57).
76. Hall 1904, 2:88.
77. Ibid., 2:108.

Chapter 10. Royal Patronage in the Late 1520s

1. TNA E 101/420/11, fol. 5v; LP 5:304.
2. Harl. 1419, fol. 6; Starkey, ed., 1998, no. 8990.
3. There is a slight discrepancy between the dimensions recorded for the 1547 set and those of these three dispersed groups. This could have arisen if the borders of the tapestries had been folded back to accommodate them to a particular setting or if a mistake was made in the recording of the measurements in the Commonwealth inventory. For full discussion, see T. Campbell 1996b, 126.
4. For full details of the identification between the set purchased in 1528 and the design of the set that survives at Écouen, see ibid., 121–40.
5. For David as a role model for medieval kingship, see Delmarcel 1977b, 134.
6. Tudor-Craig 1989, 183–205, esp. 191.
7. Ibid., 191–92.
8. Harl. 1419, fols. 6, 28, 37, 38v, 64v, 211v–12, 218v, 260v, 299v, 329v.
9. Delmarcel 1977b, 134–35 and n16.
10. Delmarcel 1977a, 250–59; Mechelen 2000.
11. Salet 1980, 105. For how quickly the Brussels ateliers produced high-quality tapestries, see Delmarcel in Balis et al. 1993, 43–44.
12. For the breakdown of Henry's marriage to Katherine and the development of his relationship with Anne Boleyn, see Ives 1988, 99–110. For the broader political context, see Bernard 2005, 1–50.
13. Ives gives the terminus post quem as June 1525 on the grounds that this was when Henry created Henry Fitzroy duke of Richmond; Ives 1988, 100.
14. Tudor-Craig 1989; King 1994.
15. Elton 1972, 180–81.
16. Nicholson 1977, 5–6.
17. For discussion that assumes a date of design in the late 1510s as well as that the design includes some elements referring to the Burgundian/Habsburg court, see Delmarcel 1977b, 143–49.
18. Campbell in New York 2002, 187–203.
19. Ibid., 225–29.
20. Ibid., 229–33.
21. Ibid., 237–41.
22. Ibid., 287–303.
23. Ives 1976, 76–81; T. Campbell 1996a, 87.
24. LP 4:no. 979 (1).
25. According to a letter from Smytting to Brereton, the king refused to pay £3 10s. per "stike"

(ell). Smytting would therefore lose £100, but rather than take them out of the realm again, he would offer them at 5 marks per ell; LP 4:no. 979 (2).

26. The Treasurer of the Chamber accounts record payment of £251 5s. to Herman Hullesmann, merchant of the Hanse by warrant of December 22, for "three fyne peces of arras of the passion of Christ, wroght with silk, silver and gold," 83¾ ells long, at £3 per ell; TNA E 101/420/11, fol. 12v. LP 5:306–7 mistakenly gives the price as £201 5s.
27. The Treasurer of the Chamber accounts record a payment of £81 to "Edw. Smeking" and Robert Cockes on Nov. 13, 1529, for 27 ells (15.21 square yards) of "arras" of silver and gold of the story of Christ's Passion. In view of the dimensions and cost (£3 per ell), this tapestry was evidently the fourth piece of the set; TNA E 101/420/11, fol. 64v; LP 5:317.
28. Thurley 2003, 41.
29. Ives 1986, 164.
30. Harl. 1419, fol. 6; Starkey, ed., 1998, no. 8992. Translated into meters and arranged in decreasing order of size, this set measured (H x L): 3.54 x 3.66, 3.54 x 3.59, 3.54 x 3.54, and 3.54 x 3.54.
31. J. Brown 1994, 69, 71–72, 75–76, 79, 95, 97.
32. Burke 1984, app.:157. Using the 1547 inventory as the basis for calculation, Henry's set measured 107 square ells. The extant Alba tapestries have a total surface area of just under 108 ells.
33. Burke 1984, 1:126, and app.:188–90.
34. Campbell 1996d, 70.
35. *Collection de S. A. Le Duc de Berwick et d'Albe* 1877, lots 5–7. Ainsworth in New York 2002, 303–21.
36. Standen 1985, 1:65–73; Ainsworth in New York 2002, 304–9.
37. The Alba set measurements are as follows (H x L): *Last Supper,* 3.63 x 3.51; *Christ in the Garden of Gethsemane,* 3.69 x 3.58; *Christ Carrying the Cross,* 3.45 x 3.45; and *The Crucifixion,* 3.64 x 3.54. Allowing for shrinkage and replacement of the border edges, these dimensions are close enough to those of Henry's set to support the possibility that the two sets were one and the same.
38. Delmarcel 1992b, 127–60.
39. Junquera de Vega and Herrero Carretero 1986, 1:306–7.
40. T. Campbell 1998b, 42–50.
41. TNA E 101/420/11, fol. 47; LP 5:313.
42. Harl. 1419, fol. 38; Starkey, ed., 1998, no. 9278.
43. For full details, see T. Campbell 1998b.
44. Wegner 1973, 24–25; Campbell in New York 2002, 295–96.
45. Popham 1932, 22–23 and pls. 6, 7; T. Campbell 1998b, 49.
46. Ibid., 47.
47. Junquera de Vega and Herrero Carretero 1986, 1:93–99 (ser. 14); G. Delmarcel in Amsterdam 1993, 64–91.
48. Scarisbrick 1968, 21–40, 424–57; Guy 1986, 151–76; Guy 1995, 36–37.
49. Hayward 1998a, 15.

Chapter 11. The Royal Divorce and the Break with Rome

1. Hall 1904, 2:150. For payment to Thomas Garton for preparing the Parliament Chamber, see LP 5:311.
2. Bernard 2005, 37.
3. Cavendish 1959, 98–99. For the context, see Ives in Gunn and Lindley 1991, 286ff. For Wolsey's symbolic gift of his palaces and possessions to the king in 1525, see Thurley in ibid., 90–91.
4. LP 5:nos. 6017, 6214.
5. Cavendish 1959, 122.
6. Hall 1904, 2:174.
7. LP 5:no. 6748 no. 15. For new building work at Southwell and Cawood, see Thurley in Gunn and Lindley 1991, 78–79.
8. TNA E 36/171, fols. 9v, 10; T. Campbell 1996a, 133–34.
9. TNA E 36/171; T. Campbell 1996a, 131–34.
10. For example, the sets of *Certayn storres called Rolles* and the *Passion* [TNA E 36/171, fols. 6v, 7v–8; T. Campbell 1996a, 131–33] correspond to sets recorded in the "counterfeit arras and tapestry somewhat worne" category in the earlier inventory [Harl. 599, fols. 13, 13v; T. Campbell 1996a, 126], while panels of "ii aungells holding the sacrement" and "christe beyting merchaunts owt off the temple" [TNA E 36/171, fols. 8, 8v; T. Campbell 1996a, 132–33] correspond to pieces recorded in the "old hangings of counterfeit arras and tapestry" category [Harl. 599, fol. 18; T. Campbell 1996a, 129].
11. For the Treasurer of the Chamber's accounts, 1528–30, see TNA E 101/420/11 (calendared in LP 5:304–17); for the Privy Purse, see Nicolas 1827.
12. TNA E 101/420/11, fol. 36; LP 5:311.
13. DNB 1909, 12:93; ODNB 2004, 34:331–32.
14. Quoted from Hayward 1998a, 64.
15. Nicolas 1827, 59.
16. Ibid., 215; LP 5:758.
17. LP 5:759.
18. Hayward 2004, 1:3.
19. Hayward 1998a, 86.
20. TNA SP 1/76, fol. 119; LP 6:no. 535.
21. Harl. 1419, fol. 63v; Starkey, ed., 1998, no. 9691. For the dimensions of the five extant tapestries, see Marillier 1962, 25–26. Allowing for the fact that two of the narrow panels have had an additional section added at the top, the dimensions given in the 1547 inventory and those of the surviving panels are close enough to suggest that they are one and the same.
22. The attribution by Wayment 1968 of the design to Adrien van den Houte is unconvincing.
23. TNA LC 5/44, 227.
24. Tanner 1993.
25. Starkey 1985, 76–77.
26. Ives 1986, 22–46.
27. Campbell in New York 2002, 143–44.
28. Cox-Rearick 1995, 365–66.
29. Ibid., 366–67.
30. Ibid.
31. Lefébure 1993, 81–87; Cox-Rearick 1995, 377–83; Campbell in New York 2002, 341–48.
32. Campbell in New York 2002, 341–49.
33. "Quatre pièces de tapisseries principales, qui sont des victoires de Scipion l'Afriquain, fait de haute-lisse, tout de fil d'or et de fil de soye, ces personnages les mieux faits et au naturel qu'on pourroit faire, et n'est possible à paintre du monde des faire mieux sur tableaux de bois; et dit on que l'aune en couste cinquante escus"; Cox-Rearick 1995, 381, 470n158.
34. Ibid., 377; also T. Campbell 1996c, 443n46.
35. Delmarcel in C. Brown and Delmarcel with Lorenzoni 1996, 151–57.
36. Hall 1904, 2:218–19.
37. Ibid.
38. LP 6:no. 396.
39. Hall 1904, 2:230; LP 6:no. 601.
40. Hall 1904, 2:236.
41. Ibid., 2:242; LP 6:no. 1111.
42. TNA E 101/417/3, no. 104; Hayward 1998a, 161.
43. Thurley 2003, 55–58.
44. BM Royal Ms 7F. XIV, fols. 126–27.
45. Richardson 1952, 419–22; Loades 1987, 80.
46. TNA LC9/51, fols. 176, 183v.
47. LP 5:no. 5243 (20).
48. Denucé 1936, 19. For Enghien tapestries, see Delmarcel 1980.
49. Delmarcel 1999, 168.
50. LP 5:no. 5234 (12).
51. Ibid., 311.
52. Granted by patent, Jan. 12, 1529; LP 5:no. 6654 (23).
53. LP 8:no. 634 (3).
54. See T. Campbell 1999, app. 1, for summary of accounts for the years 1530–31, 1531–32, 1533–34, and 1535–36. All refer to the workers as "arras makers" with the exception of that for 1531–32, which uses the term "arras menders."
55. TNA E 101/420/14, n.p.
56. TNA E 101/421/3.
57. TNA E 101/421/16, fol. 38v.
58. TNA E 315/455, fol. 40.
59. TNA C 66/671, m. 9; LP 12:no. 795 (22).
60. TNA LC 9/51, fols. 274–74v; E 315/456, fols. 47v–48.
61. *Victoria County History of Middlesex* 12 (August 2004).
62. Like Mostinck's predecessors, both subsequent holders of this office, Thomas White in 1557 and William Hyckes in 1569, were appointed merely to repair the king's tapestries and arras.
63. Denucé 1936, 18–19.
64. Ibid. For the context, see Schneebalg-Perelman 1961, 191–210.
65. Campbell in New York 2002, 292–300.
66. Buchanan in New York 2002, 321–28.
67. Balis et al. 1993; Delmarcel in New York 2002, 329–38.
68. Campbell in New York 2002, 300–303.
69. Ibid., 379–85.
70. *Job* hangings were repaired in 1561–62 (one piece from the Queen's Wardrobe of the Robes), 1577–78 (two pieces, described as tapestry, from the Queen's Wardrobe of the Robes at Windsor), and 1586–87 (one piece, described as tapestry, from the Wardrobe of the Robes); respectively TNA AO 3/1106 anno 3–4, AO 3/1109, anno 19–20, and LC 9/78 fol. 41v.
71. Popham 1932, 21–23 and pls. 6, 7; Beauvois-Faure 1969.

72. Oursel 1999.
73. Harl. 1419, fol. 65v–66; Starkey, ed., 1998, no. 9712. This entry is immediately followed by a list of nine "other" pieces of *Jacob*, but these originated from the large group of *Jacob and Joseph* tapestries acquired by Wolsey for the Whitehall gallery, of which twenty more pieces with his arms are also listed; Harl. 1419, fols. 66, 66v; Starkey, ed., 1998, nos. 9713, 9719.
74. Converted to meters and in decreasing order of size, the dimensions (H x L) of Henry's set were as follows: 8 x 3.89, 7.32 x 4.34, 7.32 x 4.11, 6.63 x 4.11, 6.4 x 4.11, 6.4 x 3.66, 6.17 x 4.34, 6.17 x 4.11, 6.17 x 4.11, 5.49 x 4.11. Those of the Brussels set are: 6.88 x 4.25, 6.8 x 4.24, 6.8 x 4.3, 6.76 x 4.3, 6.75 x 4.33, 6.7 x 4.2, 6.26 x 4.23, 6.15 x 4.3, 6.1 x 4.3, and 6.1 x 4.28.
75. Christie's, London, June 30, 1925, lot 29; now Burrell Collection (inv. no. 46/110). Although the Burrell piece is taller than Henry's panel by about eighteen inches, this may reflect a mismeasurement in the 1547 inventory, since its height conforms with the average height of other pieces in Henry's set.
76. Ainsworth 1982, 161–63.
77. Crick Kuntziger 1954. For the weaver's mark, see Joos 1985, 61–73.
78. A single piece of the *Reconciliation of Jacob and Esau* appeared in the trade in the 1990s, for which see Galerie Chevalier [trade cat.], Paris, 1997. An unpublished fragment of the *Departure of Jacob* is at Penshurst Castle. Six pieces of a reduced set are in the Uffizi collection, for which see Berti et al. 1979, 1050–53. Finally, four pieces from a variant design series, based in part on the Van Orley design, are in the collection of the Fine Arts Museums of San Francisco, for which see Bennett 1992, 111–21.
79. One final detail worth noting is that the set now in Brussels comes from a building in Bologna that belonged to descendants of Wolsey's nemesis, Cardinal Campeggio, and it has therefore been suggested that it was acquired by him. This suggestion remains unproven, but if it were the case, it provides a tantalizing link between this series and one of the key personalities involved in papal efforts to prevent Henry's break from Rome.
80. TNA E 315/455, fol. 40.
81. Harl. 1419, fol. 6; Starkey, ed., 1998, no. 8991; Millar 1972, 4–5.
82. TNA LC 9/280 no. 66, fols. 380v and ff.; TNA LC 5/45, 144.
83. T. Campbell 1994, 26–27.
84. Ibid., 30n41.
85. Schloss Halbturn 1981, esp. 83–99.
86. National Library, Madrid, Ms. no. 6015; transcribed in ibid., 91–99.
87. Marlier 1966, 332, 334; Schloss Halbturn 1981, 60–62, 84.
88. For conflicting interpretations of the evidence, see Ives 1986, 238–45, and Weir 2001, 347, 359, 368. Although Weir's interpretation may be partly based on an erroneous dating of Chapuys's letter regarding Henry's involvement with the unidentified maid of honor, Ives's interpretation of Henry's extramarital interests as a question of chivalric, rather than sexual, attention, seems a prudish interpretation of the evidence.
89. Ives 1986, 241–42.
90. Ibid., 343; Weir 2001, 370.
91. Letter from Richard Lee to Lisle; LP 11:no. 1358.
92. BM Egerton 985, fols. 61v, 63v, quoted from Adams 1982, 94.

Chapter 12. The Impact of the Reformation on the Royal Tapestry Collection

1. Elton 1972, 171–216; String 1996, 22–34.
2. Elton 1972, 188–90; String 1996, 34–45.
3. BL Cleopatra E.VI, fols. 16–135. For the authorship, see Nicholson 1977, esp. 82–90, 114–19.
4. Nicholson 1977, 112–13.
5. Koebner 1953; Turquet 1983, 115–16; String 1996, 20–21.
6. Guy 1986, 156–63; Anglo 1992, 55–56.
7. Guy 1986, 156–63; String 1996, 23–26.
8. Nicholson 1977, 81–90.
9. String 1996, 41.
10. M. Dowling in Greenwich 1991, 109–10.
11. King 1994, 87.
12. R. Strong 1967, esp. 6–10.
13. Hampton Court 1993, jacket and 24–25.
14. Anglo 1992, 3.
15. Ibid., esp. 19, 28–39, 130.
16. String 1996; Walker 1996, 72–99.
17. In 1547, the Treviso painting was located in the long gallery at Hampton Court; Starkey, ed., 1998, no. 12321. At that time, the only other painting in the collection with explicit anti-papal imagery was at Westminster in an unspecified location. It was described as follows: "a Table with the picture of the kynge henrye theight standinge upon a Myter with three crownes havinge a Sarpent withe seven headdes commynge oute of it and havinge a sworde in his hande wherin is written Verbum Dei"; ibid., no. 10632. For full details of Henry VIII's paintings, see ibid., esp. 237–40, 287–89, 384–85. For discussion, see String 1996, 118–23, and Foister 2004, esp. 80–81, 85–87, 122–23, 150–51.
18. Auerbach 1954, 12, 13.
19. Foister 2004, 175–91.
20. Hampton Court 1993, 29; Foister 2004, 178–79.
21. Walker 1996, 75–80; Foister 2004, 191–94.
22. String 1996, 101–6; Walker 1996, 85–88; Foister 2004, 159–63.
23. String 1996, 77–80; Walker 1996, 89–92; Foister 2004, 152–54.
24. Tudor-Craig 1989, 183–205; King 1994, 83–85 (and 90n12 for the problematic dating of this manuscript).
25. String 1996, 106–18; Walker 1996, 92–93.
26. Walker 1996, 104, 117n32.
27. Some tapestries may have had embroidered armorials attached that have since been lost or removed. For example, the Hampton Court *Antiques* have blank escutcheons in the corners that once may have been covered. In other cases, such armorials may have intentionally been removed. Any that incorporated allusions to Katherine of Aragon, Anne Boleyn, Anne of Cleves, or Catherine Howard may have been excised within Henry's lifetime. Although no documentary evidence of this has survived, analogy with the removal of heraldic devices from stained glass windows suggests how rigorously such changes were undertaken; see Wayment in Greenwich 1991, 30–31, and Anglo 1993, 36–38.
28. S. Levey is preparing an article on the tailors and embroiderers working for Henry VIII. For the predecessors and successors of these Tudor craftsmen, see Sutton and Hammond 1983, 63–64; Arnold 1988, 177–92; and Wardle 1995, 144, 147–54.
29. Starkey, ed., 1998.
30. For the *Nassau Genealogy*, see Fock 1969, 1–28; for the *Spheres*, see New York 1991, 54–67.
31. Campbell in New York 2002, 465–68ff.
32. For the trial, see J. Duverger 1977, 221–27. For the context, see Boon 1992, xxvi–xxix.
33. For a drawing with a satire of the Catholic Church, previously thought to have been the modello for a tapestry, see Boon 1992, xxvi–xxix. This identifies the drawing as a copy from a contemporary painting by a follower of Bernaert van Orley.
34. Oswald 1960, 986–89.
35. The BL preserves a three-volume illuminated version of the Great Bible that appears to have been presented to Henry in 1542. In this, the figure of Cromwell that appeared in the original woodcut was replaced with that of Lord Russell in a position analogous to that in which he appears in the tapestry; see String 1996, 113–16.
36. Hefford 2002, 43–46.
37. TNA E 101/423/10 fol. 74.
38. Harl. 1419, fol. 208; Starkey, ed., 1998, no. 11964.
39. Millar 1972, 158.
40. Chamberlain 1770, 656, 658.
41. Bauer in Schloss Halbturn 1981, 37–53; Campbell in New York 2002, 380–81, 406–10.
42. Dowling in Greenwich 1991, 107; Weir 2001, 302–3.
43. For examples of the use of Saint Paul in contemporary sermons and written court propaganda, see String 1996, 35–41, 105.
44. Ibid., 101–6; Walker 1996, 85–88.
45. Weir 2001, 418.
46. Elton 1972, 388–90.
47. TNA SP 1/86, fols. 185–86; LP 7:no. 1382.
48. LP 7:no. 557.
49. LP 10:nos. 794, 1240.
50. Ives 1986, 77–79.
51. ONDB 2004, 43:717–20.
52. LP 7:no. 106.
53. Weir 2001, 416–17.
54. LP 13, pt. 2:no. 838.
55. TNA SP 1/134, fol. 139; LP 13, pt. 1:no. 1365, 13, pt. 2:no. 754.
56. LP 14, pt. 1:no. 317.
57. Harl. 1419, fol. 380; Starkey, ed., 1998, no. 13985.
58. LP 5:no. 3197.
59. Ibid., no. 5772.
60. Ibid., no. 5145.
61. Ibid., no. 6223.

62. Sicca 2002, 176–77.
63. LP 9:n. 66.
64. LP 14, pt. 2:no. 555.
65. TNA SP 1/130, fol. 53; LP 13:no. 508.
66. Foister 2004, 100–101, 200.
67. LP 10:no. 408.
68. LP 13, pt. 2:no. 88 (2).
69. Ibid., no. 171 (2).
70. LP 11:App. no. 1; LP 13, no. 2:no. 171 (4).
71. LP 10:no. 562.
72. LP 13, pt. 2:n. 791.
73. LP 14, pt. 2: no. 136.
74. LP 4:no. 1939 (9). Subsequent changes are reflected by the names given in the 1547 inventory; Harl. 1419. For the responsibilities and status of the keepers, see Thurley 1993, 83, and Hayward 1998a, 90, 132–54.
75. Hayward 1998a, 81–82, 193.
76. Thurley 1993, 74.
77. BL Add. Ms 10109, fol. 60v; Thurley 1993, 75; Hayward 1998a. 160, 184.
78. Hayward 1998a, 184.
79. Bodleian Library English History b 192/1, unfolioed section between fols. 58–59; Hayward 1998a, 156.
80. BL Add. Ms 10602, fol. 2; LP 14, pt. 1:no. 607.
81. *King's Payments in 1539,* LP 14, pt. 2:no. 781, 305.
82. Hayward 1998a, esp. 17–18, 29–30.
83. See Schneebalg-Perelman 1971 for comparison.
84. LP 14, pt. 1:no. 1145.
85. LP 16:no. 380, fol. 119b.
86. BL Royal Ms 7C. XVI.
87. TNA E 315/160; transcribed and analyzed in Hayward 2004.
88. BL Add. Ms 30367.
89. LP 12, pt. 1:no. 329.
90. Harl. 1419, fols. 394–94v; Starkey, ed., 1998, 354–55. Most of these sets had been repaired and relined in 1545–46; TNA E 351/3025.
91. LP 5:no. 3085.
92. LP 13, pt. 2:no. 1280.
93. TNA E 315/456, fol. 31.
94. Ibid.
95. BL Royal Ms 7C. XVI, fol. 61; TNA E 315/160, fol. 121.
96. Cosnac 1885, 222.
97. Greenwich 1991, 127, 135.
98. Harl. 1419, fols. 383–86, 391; Starkey, ed., 1998, 353–55.
99. String 1996, 86.
100. LP 13, pt. 2:no. 1162.

Chapter 13. Purchases, 1538–1542

1. LP 14, pt. 1:no. 1092.
2. Foister 2004, 200.
3. Richardson 1952, 327, 422.
4. Ibid., 422; Loades 1987, 82–83.
5. TNA SP 1/106, fol. 69; LP 11:no. 381.
6. Richardson 1952, 326–40.
7. Respectively, TNA E 315/249, fol. 47v, E 315/250, fol. 55, and E 315/252.
8. Hefford in Delmarcel, ed., 2002, 43–44.
9. The grant described him as "John Mustyng, the king's stragulator," commonly called "our aresmaker," a native of the emperor's dominions; LP 16:no. 1488 (2); Page 1893, 176.
10. Granted Oct. 3, 1545, delivered Dec. 10, 1545; LP 20, pt. 2:no. 1068 (23).
11. LP 20, pt. 2:no. 418 (64).
12. Granted June 6, 1546, delivered July 14, 1546; LP 21, pt. 1:no. 1383 (53).
13. LP 21, pt. 1:no. 1165 (15).
14. TNA E 351/3025.
15. TNA SP 1/130, fol. 53; LP 13, pt. 2:no. 791. The latter incorrectly gives the figure as 900 ells.
16. Further evidence for such activity is provided by the will of William Lord Willoughby, dated May 4, 1526. This includes "my hanginges of counterfeit arras which I bought of the rent master in Flanders of the Story of Gressel"; Lincoln Record Office, 2 Anc. 3/A/41.
17. LP 13, pt. 2:no. 426.
18. Ibid., no. 286 (2).
19. ODNB 2004 56:201–3.
20. LP 14, pt. 1:no. 904 (24). For a grant in July 1547 to John Lange and his son, merchant jewelers of Paris, see *Calendar of the Patent Rolls* 1925–26, 5:399. For a similar grant of 1550 to Bartholomew Compagny, a Florentine merchant, see ibid., 3:208.
21. For the *Seven Deadly Sins* supplied to Maria of Hungary, see Schloss Halbturn 1981, 84–85. For the *Romulus and Remus* set, see Junquera de Vega and Herrero Carretero 1986, 1:140–42 (ser. 20), and Buchanan 1999, 133; for the *Creation* set, see Meoni 1989.
22. BL Royal Ms 7C. XVI fol. 61; LP 15:no. 686.
23. Harl. 1419, fol. 218; Starkey, ed., 1998, no. 12032.
24. BL Add. Ms 10602, fol. 4.
25. BL Royal Ms 7C. XVI, fols. 62.
26. TNA E 315/160, fols. 7v–8.
27. Cavallo 1986, 48–55.
28. For the documentation, see Paris 1965, 37–38; for surviving pieces, see Asselberghs 1971a, 16, and Franses 1986, 18–22. For attribution of the design, see Delmarcel in C. Brown and Delmarcel with Lorenzoni 1996, 202–4, 205n11.
29. Although the identity of the *Meleager* series remains a matter of conjecture, several design series from this era are documented, at least in part. A fine-quality "Brussels"-style piece dating from about 1520 is now at the Toledo (Ohio) Museum of Art; Onghena 1974, 13–14, and above, chap. 6, p. 123. Two fragments from a later set, dating from ca. 1535–40 and probably woven in Brussels, have appeared separately at New York, American Art Association/Anderson Galleries, Mar. 12–13, 1937, lot 375, and Paris, Hotel Drouot, salles 5 et 6, Oct. 13, 1980, lot. 59. Finally, a high-quality design, of Meleager killing the Calydonian boar, dating from ca. 1540, appeared at auction, Parke Bernet Galleries, New York, Dec. 6–7, 1940, lot 142.
30. W. Thomson 1930, 277–94; Hefford 1999.
31. Tagliaferro 1981, 80–83, 92, and fig. 12-23.
32. Balis et al. 1993.
33. Delmarcel in ibid., 39–40; Junquera de Vega and Herrero Carretero 1986, 1:313; Parke Bernet Galleries, New York, Dec. 5–6, 1952, lot 387.
34. Sold Galerie Georges Petit, Paris, Dec. 8–10, 1902, lot 310; Balis in Balis et al. 1993, 74.
35. Tournai 1970, no. 26.
36. For an example dating from the late 1530s, see Hotel Drouot, Paris, Mar. 17, 1943, lot 135.
37. Wingfield-Digby and Hefford 1980, 54; Franses 2005.
38. Harl. 1419, fols. 119, 254v; Starkey, ed., 1998, nos. 10546, 12564.
39. The Louvre owns an unpublished set with the Brussels mark and that of Willem de Pannemaker's workshop; inv. nos. OAR 35–41. For Enghien examples, see Delmarcel 1980, 46–49.
40. For examples, see Delmarcel 1980, cat. 15–17, 42–45; Wingfield-Digby 1980, cat. no. 68–72, 54–56; Standen 1985, cat. no. 24, 174–79; Cavallo 1993, cat. no. 52, 600–607; and Adelson 1994, 116–21.
41. Harl. 1419, fol. 217v; Starkey, ed., 1998, no. 12030. For the set in the Spanish royal collection, see Junquera de Vega and Herrero Carretero 1986, 1:297–303. For a seventh scene of *Venus and Cupid Lamenting the Death of Adonis,* see Asselberghs 1974, 25 and pl. 12. Six other pieces from this design series survive at North Mimms Park. For illustrations, see Christie's, North Mimms Park sale, Sept. 24–26, 1979, lots 496–98.
42. For 1539, see LP 14, pt. 2:no. 781, 313, 315; for 1540, LP 16:no. 380, fols. 132b, 142, 142b, 147; for 1541, LP 16:no. 1489; for 1542, LP 17:no. 880 (p. 477).
43. LP 14, pt. 2:no. 781, 315.
44. Thurley 1993, 60–65.
45. Hayward 1998a, 95.
46. Weir 2001, 430, 435.
47. LP 15:no. 899 (4) and (5).
48. Ibid., no. 937. Wardrobe officers were paid for preparing furnishings for Anne in July; LP 16:no. 380 (fol. 142b).
49. Harl. 1419, fol. 8; Starkey, ed., 1998, nos. 9015, 9016. See also BL Add. Ms 30367, fol. 28.
50. LP 16:no. 1183. See Scarisbrick 1968, 427–28, for the context.
51. Weir 2001, 450–51.
52. For inventories of the Scottish royal tapestries taken in 1539 and 1561, see T. Thomson 1885, 31, 49–51, 103–4, and J. Robertson 1863, 20–21, 36–40.
53. TNA E 315/160, fol. 7v; Campbell 1996d, 73; Hayward 2004, 2:nos. 196, 197.
54. TNA E 315/160, fol. 122v; Campbell 1996d, 73; Hayward 2004, 2:nos. 3334, 3335.
55. For the Gualteroti family, see Denucé 1934, 11–17.
56. Buchanan 1992, 380–84.
57. BL Lansdowne Charter 14.
58. For the sale to Houghton, see Millar 1972, 5. For the resale, see J. Brown 1986, 211, 299n69. For the context of the resale, see Loomie 1989, 257–67. Loomie incorrectly states that the set was burnt at the Alcázar; ibid., 264n41.
59. The *Charge to Peter* and *Conversion of Saul* were published by Kumsch 1914, pl. 16. The rest of the set, with the exception of the *Conversion of Saul,* were published in Grimm 1941, pls. 274–77. A set of photographs survives in the Hunter archive in the Getty Resource Collections.
60. Jones and Penny 1983, 147–54.
61. Shearman 1972, 90; Shearman 1988, 202–7.
62. Shearman 1972, 61nn95, 96.
63. For full discussion of the *Acts* series and further bibliography, see Campbell in New York

2002, 187–203.
64. Shearman 1972, 89.
65. Ibid., 15nn87, 89; Campbell in New York 2002, 194–95.
66. Shearman 1972, 144. The dimensions of the tapestries as they survived in the early nineteenth century are given in feet and inches in Trull 1840, 24–46.
67. Millar 1972, 5; see T. Campbell 1996d, 74–75, for analysis of the dimensions.
68. Delmarcel in C. Brown and Delmarcel with Lorenzoni 1996, 151–55.
69. Campbell in New York 2002, 225–29, 246–52.
70. Forti Grazzini 1994, 378–79.
71. Campbell 1996d, 76–78.
72. Laborde 1877–80, 2:372; *Collection des ordonnances des rois de France, 1877–1908*, 7:31, no. 28674. Cox-Rearick 1996, 376–77.
73. Campbell in New York 2002, 228–29, 250–51; Karafel, in press.
74. T. Campbell 1996d, 73–74.
75. For the building at Westminster during the early 1540s, see Thurley 1993, 58–60, 107–8, 217, and Thurley 1999, 52–64. For the banqueting house, see Biddle 1966, 113.
76. Biddle 1966, 107–8.
77. For this attribution, see ibid., 119, and Béguin 1970, 9–14.
78. Peacham 1622, 137.
79. Campbell in New York 2002, 194, 204–10.
80. Nicholson 1977, 62–63.
81. Stafford 1548, fols. xiib–xiiia, xvb; Nicholson 1977, 61.
82. TNA E 315/160, fol. 130.
83. Turquet 1983, 230.
84. Ibid., 52–63.
85. Turquet 1983, 66–73; Biddle 1984.

Chapter 14. The Story of Caesar *and the* Story of Abraham

1. TNA E 101/423/10, fol. 74.
2. Harl. 1419, fol. 208v; Starkey, ed., 1998, no. 11967.
3. Millar 1972, 158.
4. "Datus libellus Cesari conjurationem continens / Quo non lecto venit in curia ibi in curuli sedentem / Senatus invasit tribus qs et viginti vulneribus / Conodit sic ille qu terarum orbem civili sanguine." (The note containing the conspiracy is given to Caesar but without reading it he goes to the Senate House where, as he is seated on the throne of the Senate, a crowd invades and dispatches him with twenty wounds, and thus this man, who had showered the entire earth with the blood of citizens, in the end floods the Senate House with his own blood.")
5. For reconstruction of the *Caesar* series, see T. Campbell 1998a.
6. Ibid., 2–29.
7. In my initial reconstruction of the *Caesar* set, I tentatively related it to drawings that Nicole Dacos has attributed to the Florentine painter, Leonard Thiry (Dacos 1996a, 1996b). In the absence of any firm evidence that Thiry had anything to do with tapestry design, I now consider that attribution inappropriate and that the *Caesar* series was almost certainly a product of Pieter Coecke's Antwerp workshop; Campbell in New York 2002, 383–84. Dacos 2005 adds nothing to the argument except further unsubstantiated claims on behalf of Thiry.
8. Backhouse in Greenwich 1991, 87; Cox-Rearick 1996, 5–6.
9. Cox-Rearick 1996, 21, 23.
10. Fernández Alvarez 1975, 180.
11. Scarisbrick 1968, 21–40, 424–57.
12. For details, see T. Campbell 1998a, 34–35.
13. For this panel, whose current location is unknown, see ibid., 56. The inscription of this adapted design reads: "Caeditur in patrum consessu Caesar inique / Sed volat in superas spiritus ipse domos" (Caesar is felled, murdered unjustly in the assembly of the Patricians, but his spirit flies to the heavenly mansions).
14. Campbell in New York 2002, 347–48.
15. Rude, ed., 1992, 52.
16. Ibid., 126.
17. Ibid., 123.
18. Turquet 1983, esp. 85–118, 322–31, for the cycle of twenty-four Caesars.
19. The following text is partly based on T. Campbell 2003.
20. Millar 1972, 158.
21. The mark was erroneously identified as that of Willem de Pannemaker by Marillier 1962, 7, a mistake that has been perpetuated in much of the literature relating to Hampton Court. For correct identification of the mark, see Calberg and Pauwels 1961, 112–13. For Kempeneer, see Schneebalg-Perelman in Szablowski, ed., 1972, 418–19. See also Campbell in New York 2002, 278, 300–302, 421, 423.
22. Harl. 1419, fol. 208v; Starkey, ed., 1998, no. 11966; T. Campbell 2003, 82n14.
23. TNA E 101/423/10, fol. 74.
24. BL Add. Ms 59900, Chamber Receipt and Issue book of Henry VIII, Michaelmas 1543–Michaelmas 1544, fol. 72v.
25. Rodriguez Villa 1883, 22.
26. Jacquot 1960, 445, 451; Calvete de Estrella 1873–74, 2:184.
27. Junquera de Vega and Herrero Carretero 1986, 1:206–13; T. Campbell 2003, 61.
28. For discussion of the chronology of the various weavings, see T. Campbell 2003, 62.
29. This carries the cardinal's hat and armorials of Charles de Lorraine-Vaudémont, which dates his ownership between 1561 and 1587, but the arms are a later addition. Baldass 1920, 2:1–5 (ser. 2), pls. 21–30.
30. For these marks, see Birk 1883, 216–17. For Pieter van Aelst the younger, see Delmarcel 1992a.
31. Bauer in Vienna 1983, 13, states that the Vienna *Abraham* set is woven with gold, but in private correspondence the author has since informed me that this was an error and that the Vienna set does not contain metallic thread.
32. Campbell in New York 2002, 422–23.
33. Ibid., 382–91.
34. Ibid., 422–23; T. Campbell 2003, 62–64.
35. For a complete list and identification of the border figures, see T. Campbell 2003, 79–80.
36. For Philip's triumphal entries, and further bibliography, see Jacquot 1960, 445, 451.
37. Campbell in New York 2002, 278, 279, 421.
38. Turquet 1983.
39. For Elyot on promises, see Rude 1992, 199.
40. Ibid., 103, 123, 149.
41. Hayward 1998a, 114.
42. For Elyot's dependence on Estienne, see Starnes 1954, 51–52.
43. Personifications that are defined in Elyot, but not Estienne, include Latria, Paranymphus, Atropos, Adiuratio, and Ceres.
44. Schneebalg-Perelman in Szablowski, ed., 1972; Campbell in New York 2002, 278, 300–301.
45. Sandford 1687, 24.
46. For example, in May 1630 Charles I directed the clerk of the Great Wardrobe to "certiffye ye presidents of the times of k. Henry VII & H. VIII touching ye lying in of Queenes & provisions for christening of the king's children"; TNA LC 5/132, 188.
47. CSP Ven., 7:16.

Chapter 15. Purchases and Appropriations, 1543–1547

1. Harl. 1419, fol. 218; Starkey, ed., 1998, no. 12032.
2. TNA E 315/256, fol. 91v.
3. For examples comprising many thousands of pounds, for which no further details are given, see TNA E 315/253, fols. 60v, 61; E 351/254, fols. 78v, 84v, 85; and E 315/255, fol. 106v, 107.
4. LP 21, pt. 1:no. 127; Hayward 1998a, 143; ODNB 2004 56:201–3.
5. "Ils ont par diverses fois porte de la ville d'anvers plusieurs bagues et riches Joyaux avecq piereries, vasseles dargent et tapisserien et autres manieres de marchand"; Antwerp record office, *Minutes du notaire S'Hertogen Sr.*, vol. 5, *1549–1551* (N.2074); Donnet 1896, 330.
6. TNA SP 4/1, July 1546, no. 73–76; LP 21, pt. 1:no. 1382 (73–76).
7. TNA SP 4/1 Sept. 1546, no. 6; LP 21, pt. 2:no. 199 (6).
8. Harl. 1419, fols. 217v–218; Starkey, ed., 1998, no. 12031.
9. For biography and bibliography, see "Erasmus Schets of Maastricht" in Bietenholz, ed., 1985–87, 3:220–21. For his tapestry sales to Maria of Hungary, see Utrecht 1994, 295. For the context, see Buchanan 1992, 380–84.
10. TNA E 315/160, fol. 130.
11. TNA E 315/253, fol. 55v.
12. Harl. 1419, fol. 208–208v; Starkey ed., 1998, 268–69.
13. Millar 1972, 158.
14. TNA LC 5/69, 58, no. 40; T. Campbell 1994, 22–24.
15. Bickham 1742, 52.
16. T. Campbell 1994, 24–25, 30n23.
17. TNA LC Work Series 1/25, order dated Aug. 26, 1841.
18. For Francis I's set, see Schneebalg-Perelman 1971, 289, no. 280. For the Habsburg set, see

Bauer in Schloss Halbturn 1981, 19–32.
19. T. Campbell 1994, 22–23, 25–26.
20. Donnet 1896, 281. Donnet gives the surface area of the *Tobias* set in question as 540 square ells. In contrast, Henry's set measured approximately 940 square ells (based on the dimensions given by the 1547 inventory). This disparity may reflect a misreading of the document or the portion of the set that Thonis purchased at this date.
21. Millar 1972, 158.
22. For the 1695 inventory, see TNA LC 5/87, HC section, 1. For the repairs, see TNA LC 5/70, 206, and LC 5/44, fol. 244.
23. Knight 1785, 5. For full details, see T. Campbell 1994, 28.
24. Junquera de Vega and Herrero Carretero 1986, 1:241–47 (ser. 34).
25. E. Duverger 1958, 14n51; J. Duverger 1972, 724n50; Buchanan 1992, 382n13.
26. Bandera 1987, 75–93.
27. Hefford 1999, 96–99.
28. TNA E 351/3025.
29. Harl. 1419, fol. 218; Starkey, ed., 1998, no. 12032; Millar 1972, 164.
30. Burke 1984, app.:doc. 3.2, 154.
31. Junquera de Vega and Herrero Carretero 1986, 1:140–42 (ser. 20); Mahl 1965, 30–32; Christie's, New York, Nov. 22, 1980, lot 276. Two related tapestries, possibly from the same set, have also reappeared in recent years: *The Rape of Rhea Silvia by Mars* belongs to the Treuhand Verwaltung von Kulturgut, Munich (control list 8.11.1961), and is now in the German Embassy, London; *Romulus and Remus Brought before Amulius* was sold at Sotheby's, London, May 19, 1995, lot 8.
32. Mahl 1965, 7–40.
33. Campbell in New York 2002, 394–402.
34. Harl. 1419, fol. 68; Starkey, ed., 1998, nos. 9729, 9730.
35. Siple 1938, 212–20; Siple 1939, 268–78; Hefford 1999, 91–98.
36. Hefford 1999, 93–95.
37. Adelson 1985, 6, 15.
38. For the mark, an "R" with dots resembling a flower, see Siple 1938, 220.
39. For a set in the Swedish royal collection by 1553, see Böttiger 1895–98, 4:13.
40. Tudor-Craig 1989; J. King 1989, 79–80; Weir 2001, 457.
41. Translation from Siple 1938, 218.
42. Junquera de Vega and Herrero Carretero 1986, 1:155–62 (ser. 23); Delmarcel and Van Tichelen 1994, 53–60.
43. For example, a *Story of Aeneas* series conceived in the mid- to late 1530s, for which see Junquera de Vega and Herrero Carretero 1986, 1:325–32.
44. *Artes Textiles* 8 (1974): pl. 3. See above, p. 123.
45. Harl. 1419, fol. 37v; Starkey, ed., 1998, no. 9273.
46. Lefèbure 1993, 81–87; Campbell in New York 2002, 349.
47. Gómez Martinez and Chillón Sampedro 1925, 93–101; Asselberghs 1971a.
48. Harl. 1419, fol. 343; Starkey, ed., 1998, no. 13492.
49. Campbell in New York 2002, 352–57.
50. "Old Master Drawings including the Castle Howard Michelangelo," Sotheby's, London, July 11, 2001, lot 36.
51. Harl. 1419, fol. 207v; Starkey, ed., 1998, no. 11963.
52. Wingfield-Digby and Hefford 1980, 39–40.
53. Tipping 1927, 174.
54. Harl. 1419, fol. 394; Starkey, ed., 1998, no. 14134.
55. For Coecke's trip, see Delmarcel in Balis et al. 1993, 40–41.
56. Walpole 1757, 79.
57. TNA LR 2/115.
58. Harl. 1419, fols. 280v–281; Starkey, ed., 1998, no. 12880.
59. TNA LR 2/115, fols. 70v–72v.

Chapter 16. The Disposition and Typology of the Collection in 1547

1. Hayward 1998a, 18–20.
2. Society of Antiquaries 129; BL Harl. 1419. Transcribed in Starkey, ed., 1998.
3. These numbers are based on my own transcription of the inventory and vary from those of Thomson's transcription, which omits various items.
4. Harl. 1419, fols. 318, 318v; Starkey, ed., 1998, nos. 13242, 13245.
5. TNA E 315/456, fol. 31.
6. TNA E 101/423/10, fol. 74.
7. Harl. 1419, fol. 38; Starkey, ed., 1998, nos. 9277, 9280.
8. Howard 1987, 116–19; Strong 1969, 43–50.
9. Hayward 1998a, 111–12.
10. Harl. 599, fol. 19; T. Campbell 1996a, 130.
11. Harl. 1419, fols. 298–300; Starkey, ed., 1998, 310–11.
12. Harl. 1419, fols. 343–47; Starkey, ed., 1998, 333–35.
13. Harl. 1419, fols. 37–39; Starkey, ed., 1998, 195–97.
14. Harl. 1419, fols. 207v–220; Starkey, ed., 1998, 268–74.
15. Thurley 2003, 54–70.
16. Harl. 1419, fols. 63–64v; Starkey, ed., 1998, 207.
17. Harl. 1419, fols. 64v–69; Starkey, ed., 1998, 207–9.
18. Harl. 1419, fols. 5v–181; Starkey, ed., 1998, 180–81.
19. Harl. 1419, fols. 7v, 346v; Starkey, ed., 1998, nos. 9011, 13520.
20. Harl. 1419, fol. 10; Starkey, ed., 1998, no. 9034.
21. Harl. 1419, fols. 364–65v; Starkey, ed., 1998, 343–44.
22. Harl. 1419, fols. 318–20; Starkey, ed. 1998, 321–22.
23. Harl. 1419, fols. 254–61v; Starkey, ed. 1998, 292–95.
24. Harl. 1419, fols. 280–81v; Starkey, ed., 1998, 302–3.
25. Harl. 1419, fol. 281; Starkey, ed., 1998, no. 12883.
26. Harl. 1419, fols. 328–31; Starkey, ed., 1998, 326–27.
27. Harl. 1419, fols. 368–72, 373–76; Starkey, ed., 1998, 344–46, 346–47.
28. Harl. 1419, fols. 383–86v; Starkey, ed., 1998, 350–51.
29. Harl. 1419, fols. 394–94v; Starkey, ed., 1998, 354.
30. Harl. 1419, fols. 433–34; Starkey, ed., 1998, 376–77.
31. Harl. 1419, fols. 440–41v; Starkey, ed., 1998, 381.

Chapter 17. Taste and Perception

1. TNA E 315/456, fol. 47.
2. Harl. 1419, fol. 8; Starkey, ed., 1998, no. 9016.
3. For this, see Thomas Platter's account in Clare 1937, 214–15.
4. Howarth 1997, 14–15.
5. Harl. 1419, fol. 280v; Starkey, ed., 1998, no. 12879.
6. Shaw 1937; Starkey, ed., 1998.
7. Campbell in New York 2002, 187–203, 225–45, 341–63, 483–505ff.
8. T. Campbell 1996a, 109–12.
9. Hope 1915, 275–348.
10. Harl. 1419, fol. 6v; Starkey, ed., 1998, nos. 8995, 8996.
11. Ridgard 1985, 129–58.
12. LP 7:no. 106.
13. Harl. 1419, fol. 8; Starkey, ed., 1998, nos. 9015, 9016.
14. Chute 1888, 21, 24, 144–62.
15. TNA LR 2/115, fols. 12–59.
16. Willan 1962.
17. Ibid., 60.
18. T. Campbell 1995, 33.
19. T. Campbell 1996b, 125, 138n21.
20. T. Campbell 1996a, 87; see above, pp. 190–95.
21. BL Lansdowne Charter 14.
22. For the valuation of the *David* set, see T. Campbell 1996b, 126, 138n27. For the other sets, see Millar 1972, 5, 158–59.
23. Miller 1955, 18, 26.
24. Heal 1980, 72.
25. Cornwall 1988, 8–14.
26. Ibid., 27–29.
27. For Holbein and Horenbout, see L. Campbell and Foister 1986, 722, and Foister 2004, 22–23. For skilled artisans associated with the court, see the 1526 Royal Household Ordinance, calendared in LP 4:no. 1939.
28. For comparisons, see Loades in Greenwich 1991, 174, and Thurley 1993, 44, 52, 58.

Chapter 18. The History of the Tudor Collection, 1547–1659

1. *Calendar of the Patent Rolls* 1925–26, 5:150.
2. Knighton, ed., 1998, 11, 12.
3. Samson 1999, 208–9.
4. Junquera de Vega and Herrero Carretero 1986, 1:54–62, 268–72. Also Buchanan in New York 2002, 435–40.
5. CSP Ven., 7:16.
6. Brassat 1989, 175–76.
7. For wardrobe accounts detailing tapestries repaired by the royal arras maker during

Elizabeth's reign, see TNA LC 9/52–93 and AO 3/1106–22. My thanks to Hilary Turner for sharing her transcriptions of these documents with me.
8. Rye 1865, 207n42.
9. Platter 1937, 162.
10. Ibid., 213–15, 239.
11. Bulow, ed., 1892, 5.
12. Rye 1865, 18.
13. Ibid., 203n38.
14. Ibid., 167.
15. Ibid., 89.
16. Walpole 1757, 81.
17. Platter 1937, 201.
18. Ibid., 201–3.
19. Thurley 2003, 99–103.
20. Bulow, ed., 1892, 53.
21. Cosnac 1884, 186.
22. Roberts 1989, esp. 61–62.
23. For example, see the items received by John de Vere at Henry VII's coronation in his capacity as lord chamberlain in Hope 1915.
24. See above, p. 246.
25. Victoria and Albert Museum L.30-1982, fol. 93; Shirley 1869, 355, 359; Historical Manuscripts Commission 1885, app., pt. 4:163–64.
26. W. Thomson 1930, 277–94; Hefford 1999.
27. Hefford 1999.
28. Shearman 1972, 145–48; Hefford in ODNB 2004, 12:12–14.
29. Van der Doort 1960, 126; Mitchell 1971, 197.
30. Thurley 2003, 112–13.
31. TNA LC 5/132–35 passim.
32. TNA LC 5/132, fol. 216; LC 5/134, fols. 56, 203, 384.
33. TNA LC 5/132, fol. 356; LC 5/134, fols. 56, 438.
34. TNA LC 5/132, fols. 269, 273; LC 5/134, fol. 313.
35. La Serre 1639, 89.
36. TNA LC 5/132, fol. 269.
37. Huygens 1982, 134.
38. This estimate is based on a comparison of the 1547 inventory and that of the Commonwealth sale.
39. Millar 1972, 4, 5, 55, 73, 158, 207, 331, 362.
40. W. Thomson 1930, 351.
41. Michel 1999, 200–213.
42. Ibid.
43. Ibid., 281–84.
44. Ibid., 210–13.
45. Cosnac 1884, 199; also 180, 182, 184, 194, 197.
46. Ibid., 194.
47. Michel 1999, 442, comes to a similar conclusion but fails to appreciate the full significance of this misapprehension in his analysis of Mazarin's tapestry collection, mistakenly identifying many sixteenth-century tapestries as English manufacture, rather than of English origin.
48. TNA E36/234, fol. 2r; Hayward 1998a, 145.
49. Swain 1988, 16.
50. Schnapper 1994, 376.
51. Macon 1913, 250.
52. Schnapper 1994, 187.
53. Hefford 1999, 92.
54. T. Campbell 2004, pt. 2, 608.
55. Millar 1972; Cosnac 1884.
56. Historical Manuscripts Commission 1879, 91–92; Millar 1972.
57. Law 1885–91, 2:277–308; Thurley 2003, 126–28.

Chapter 19. The History of the Tudor Collection from 1660 to the Present Day

1. Historical Manuscripts Commission 1879, 88–89; Millar 1972, xxi–xxii; Gleissner 1994.
2. For the period 1660–90, see esp. TNA LC 5/137–150.
3. T. Campbell 2003, 59–60.
4. TNA LC 5/137, fol. 23.
5. W. Thomson 1930, 300–304.
6. TNA LC 5/86.
7. Ibid.
8. Ibid., fols. 1–22.
9. Ibid., fol. 20.
10. Ibid., fol. 2.
11. TNA LC 5/138, fol. 267.
12. Millar 1972, 74.
13. Watson n.d.: Ms. Transcription from Lord Chamberlain's papers, for warrant of July 15, 1678.
14. Sandford 1687, 24; T. Campbell 1998b, 50n13.
15. BL Harleian Ms 1890 (hereafter Harl. 1890).
16. Harl. 1890, fols. 19, 19v.
17. Wauters 1878, 269–71.
18. For the disposition of tapestries before 1695, see the 1676, 1688, and 1695 inventories of royal tapestries; respectively, TNA LC 5/86; Harl. 1890, and TNA LC 5/87 (the latter is summarized in W. Thomson 1930, 364–68).
19. T. Campbell 1994.
20. Ibid., 27–28.
21. Fiennes 1947, 354–56.
22. TNA LC 9/285, 26n46; LC 5/45, fols. 249, 256.
23. For discussion of the cartoons and their use in the Cartoon Gallery, which ran parallel to the King's State Apartments, see Shearman 1972, 148–51.
24. TNA LC 5/87.
25. TNA LC 5/69, 30v; LC 5/44, 245v; T. Campbell 1998a, 2–3.
26. TNA LC 5/45, 20, 25, 26.
27. TNA LC 5/44, fol. 227.
28. TNA LC 5/151, fols. 277–79.
29. Beeverell 1707, 4:871.
30. Colsoni 1710, 6, 25, 29, 53.
31. Uffenbach 1934, 74.
32. Hefford 1979.
33. TNA LC 9/390, fol. 36v; T. Campbell 1994, 24–25; Thurley 2003, 246–47.
34. Bickham 1742, 89.
35. TNA LC 5/47, fols. 159–59v; LC 9/288, fol. 69v [1730–31]; LC 5/47, fol. 221 [1732–33]; LC 5/48, fol. 21v; LC 9/289, fol. 144v [1736–37].
36. Thurley 2003, 280–81.
37. TNA LC 5/47, 221.
38. TNA LC 9/290, 3v, 34, 118v, 136, 160, 191.
39. Bickham 1742, 32.
40. Ibid., 44.
41. Ibid., 57–81.
42. Dodsley 1761, 3:268–72. The *Diana* tapestry was actually a Gobelins or Brussels *Hunt of the Caledonian Boar* after Le Brun.
43. Dodsley 1761, 3:334.
44. Chamberlain 1770, 656, 658.
45. Standen 1985, 1:385–401.
46. HKW , 5:267.
47. Whitley 1928, 275.
48. Pine 1739.
49. *Gentleman's Magazine* 69 (1799): 661–62; 70 (1800):301–2, 423–25, 527–29, 624–26, 628–29, 712.
50. Bickham 1742; *London and its environs . . .* 1761; Chamberlain 1770; Knight 1785; Knight 1799; Pyne 1819.
51. Cust 1917.
52. The Friedrichshof tapestry does not include gold thread and so cannot be identified with the "arras" set of this subject hung at Windsor in the 1680s.
53. Campbell 1994, 30n41.
54. Thurley 2003, 310–12, 317–21.
55. Laking 1905, 91–93.
56. Thurley 2003, 294–95.
57. Jesse 1842, 24.
58. Ibid., 24–30; Cole 1861, 23–28, 45–46. The pieces at Saint James's Palace were the fourth and tenth of the set, *The Meeting of Abraham and Melchizedek* and *Eliezer and Rebekah at the Well.* For the Tuxen painting of the marriage of George, duke of York, in which the latter appears in the background, see Millar 1992, cat. no. 789.
59. Jesse 1842, 31–32.
60. Ibid., 69.
61. Cole 1859, 1–2.
62. Thurley 2003, 312–13; Band in Lennard and Hayward 2005, 25.
63. Wingfield-Digby and Hefford 1980, 6–7.
64. Band in Lennard and Hayward 2005, 25, 27.
65. Ibid., 25.
66. Law 1885–91, 1:57–71.
67. Thurley 2003, 316.
68. Passavant 1836, 1:92.
69. Shearman 1972, 143.
70. Salet 1980, 12; T. Campbell 1996b, 121, 136.
71. Ricci 1913.
72. Campbell 1994, 26–27.
73. W. Thomson 1906; W. Thomson 1914.
74. Marillier 1931, 7; Thurley 2003, 388–89; Band in Lennard and Hayward 2005, 25.
75. As illustrated in Keate 1932, pl. opp. 46.
76. Band in Lennard and Hayward 2005, 25–26.
77. For full discussion of the restoration, see Thurley 2003, 383–98.
78. Band in Lennard and Hayward 2005, 25–27.

Glossary

armorial Tapestry with a heraldic device as the principle motif, often against a decorative or millefleur ground

arras Term used in court circles from ca. 1500 to describe a high-quality tapestry woven with gilt-metal-wrapped thread

cartoon Full-scale colored version of the intended design that weavers copy during weaving. Generally painted on linen until the late fifteenth century. From the early sixteenth century on, cartoons were painted mostly in body color on paper.

celure Canopy for a bed or throne

chamber Set of en suite tapestries or textiles, sometimes with matching bed or throne components

coster Used to describe large wall hangings in the fourteenth century

counterfeit arras Used in English court circles, ca. 1500–1530, to describe a high-quality tapestry with a preponderance of silk in the highlights

counterpoint Bedcover

dorser Hanging, sometimes of tapestry, to go behind the throne or bed at the focal point of a room

ell Many tapestries listed in English documents of the fifteenth and sixteenth centuries are measured in "Flemish ells," sometimes also called "stikks," a unit of length that was calculated in England as 27 inches (68.58 cm) (Connor 1987, 95). This was slightly shorter than the length attributed to the Brabant ell on the Continent in subsequent periods, equivalent to 69.5 cm (Machabey 1962, 56, 74, 75). I have not come across any instance in which tapestries are recorded in English ells (45 inches: 114.3 cm).

gold thread Thread in which a silk core is wrapped with a fine filament of gilt-metal thread

hachure Fine triangle of color used by the weaver to transition from one area of color to another

halling Used in fourteenth-century documents to describe a large tapestry or set of tapestries for a large chamber

high-warp loom Loom in which the warp threads are arranged vertically

loom Structure on which tapestries are woven

low-warp loom Loom in which the warp threads are arranged horizontally

millefleurs Tapestry in which a significant portion of the ground is covered by floral motifs

modello Preliminary design from which the larger cartoon is developed

nail Linear measurement equivalent to about 2¼ inches often used in Tudor inventories

say Fine woolen cloth

selvage Edge of tapestry

shed Small space between even and odd warp threads through which the weaver passes the weft

sorting Used in many sixteenth-century documents to describe miscellaneous tapestries, often of lower value

stikk See *ell,* above

tapestry Type of figurative textile woven by hand on a loom

tester Canopy above a bed or throne

verdure Used in many fifteenth- and sixteenth-century English documents to describe tapestries in which the ground was predominantly of floral motifs (that is, the type often now known as millefleurs)

warp Plain thread(s) between which the colored weft threads are interlaced at a right angle to create the tapestry

weft Colored thread of wool, silk, or gilt-metal-wrapped thread that the weaver interlaces with the plain warp thread to create the tapestry design

Bibliography

FREQUENTLY CITED DOCUMENTARY SOURCES

BL Add. Ms 10602 Inventory of Windsor Standing Wardrobe (March 1539).

BL Add. Ms 30367 Wardrobe stuff at Windsor (February 1543, with annotations made in 1562) and the Tower (1547)

BL Harleian Ms 599 Inventory of Cardinal Wolsey's goods taken in early 1520s

BL Harleian Ms 1419 Second volume of inventory of Henry VIII's goods commissioned in 1547

BL Harleian Ms 1890 1688 Inventory of royal tapestries

BL Royal Ms 7F. XIV Posthumous inventory of Catherine of Aragon's goods (February 1535)

BL Royal Ms 7F. XIV Posthumous inventory of the Duke of Richmond's goods (July 1536)

BL Royal Ms 7C. XVI Wardrobe stuff "unappointed" at Westminster (May 1540)

TNA E 36/171 Posthumous inventory of Wolsey's goods at Cawood Castle (1530)

TNA E 101 Exchequer accounts, including miscellaneous Great Wardrobe documents

TNA E 101/403/19 no. 67 List of Richard II's tapestries (1399)

TNA E 101/406/15 Wardrobe account for 1413, including lists of tapestries

TNA E 101/408/2 List of tapestries and textiles purchased by Henry VI from Henry V's executors

TNA E 315/160 Goods at Westminster in keeping of Sir Anthony Denny, with subsequent deliveries (April 1542–47)

TNA E 361/5/1 Posthumous inventory of Edward III's tapestries (1377)

TNA E 361/6 rot. 8 Wardrobe account for first year of Henry V's reign, including a list of royal tapestries and another of those entrusted to John Stout by patent

TNA E 403 Issue Rolls of the Exchequer of Receipt

TNA E 404 Warrants for Issues from Privy Seal office to Exchequer of Receipt

TNA LC 5/86 1675 Inventory of royal tapestries

TNA LC 5/87 1695 Inventory of royal tapestries

TNA PSO 1 Initiating warrants from the Signet Office to that of the Privy Seal

BOOKS AND PERIODICALS

Ackerman, P. 1933. *Tapestry: The Mirror of Civilisation.* New York.

Adams, C. 1982. "Henry VIII's Tapestry Collection." M.Phil. diss., Courtauld Institute, London University.

Adelson, C. 1985. "Documents for the Foundation of Tapestry Weaving under Cosimo I de' Medici." In A. Morrogh, ed., *Renaissance Studies in Honor of Craig Hugh Smyth*, 2:3–17. Villa I Tatti, 7. Florence.

———. 1990. *The Tapestry Patronage of Cosimo I de' Medici, 1545–1553.* 4 vols. in 2. Ph.D. diss., New York University; Microfilm, Ann Arbor, MI.

———. 1994. *European Tapestry in the Minneapolis Institute of Arts.* Minneapolis.

Ainsworth, M. 1982. *Bernart van Orley as a Designer of Tapestry.* Ph.D. diss., Yale University; Microfilm, Ann Arbor, MI.

Aix-en-Provence 1977. *Les tapisseries de la Vie du Christ et da la Vierge d'Aix-en-Provence.* Exh. cat. (Musée des Tapisseries).

Allan, A. 1979. "Yorkist Propaganda: Pedigree, Prophecy and the 'British History' in the Reign of Edward IV." In C. Ross, ed., *Patronage, Pedigree and Power in Later Medieval England*, 171–92. Gloucester.

Allen, P., and H. Allen. 1929. *Letters of Richard Fox, 1486–1527.* Oxford.

Amsterdam 1993. *Golden Weavings: Flemish Tapestries of the Spanish Crown.* Exh. cat. by Guy Delmarcel et al. (Gaspard de Wit Foundation). Mechelen.

Amyot, T. 1827. "Inventory of Effects Formerly Belonging to Sir John Fastolfe." *Archaeologia* 21:257–63.

Anglo, S. 1969. *Spectacle, Pageantry, and Early Tudor Policy.* Oxford.

———. 1992. *Images of Tudor Kingship.* London.

Arnold, J. 1988. *Queen Elizabeth's Wardrobe Unlock'd: The Inventories of the Wardrobe of Robes . . . .* Leeds.

Arras 1969. *Légende dorée de la tapisserie du Moyen Âge à nos jours.* Exh. cat. (Musée Arras).

Asselberghs, J.-P. 1970. "Les tapisseries tournaisiennes de la Guerre de Troie." *Revue Belge d'Archéologie et d'Histoire de l'Art* 39:93–182.

———. 1971a. "François Geubels et le tapissier bruxellois de l'histoire d'Hannibal." *Revue des Archéologues et Historiens d'Art de Louvain* 4:165–74.

———. 1971b. "Tapisseries de choeur des XVe et XVIe siècles." In Tournai 1971, 9–27.

———. 1974. *Les tapisseries flamandes aux États-Unis d'Amérique.* Brussels.

———. 1999. *Los tapices flamencos de la catedral de Zamora.* Ed. S. Samaniego Hidalgo. Salamanca.

Auerbach, E. 1954. *Tudor Artists.* London.

Backhouse, J. 1987. "Founders of the Royal Library: Edward IV and Henry VII as Collectors of Illuminated Manuscripts." In Williams, ed., 1987, 23–42.

Baldass, L. 1920. *Die Wiener Gobelinssammlung.* 3 vols. Vienna.

Balis, A., et al. 1993. *Les chasses de Maximilien.* Paris.

Bamforth, S., and J. Dupèbe. 1991. "Francisci Francorum Regis et Henrici Anglorum Colloquium." *Renaissance Studies* 5, nos. 1–2:app. 4, 220–24.

Band, J. 2005. "The Survival of Henry VIII's History of Abraham Tapestries: An Account of How They Were Perceived, Used and Treated over the Centuries." In Lennard and Hayward, eds., 2005, 20–27.

Bandera, L. 1987. "Gillio Mechelaon di Malines: Una proposta per i cartoni delle Storie di Sansone." In *Arazzi per la cattedrale di Cremona*, 75–93. Exh. cat. (Santa Maria della Pietà, Cremona). Milan.

Barbier de Montault, X. 1878. "Inventaire descriptif des tapisseries de haute-lisse conservées à Rome." *Mémoires de l'Académie des Sciences, Lettres et Arts d'Arras*, 2nd ser., 10:175–284.

Batlle Huguet, P. 1946. *Los tapices de la catedral primada de Tarragona.* Tarragona.

Beard, G. 1997. *Upholsterers and Interior Furnishing in England, 1530–1840.* New Haven and London.

Beauvois-Faure, L. 1969. "Een nieuwe reeks met de geschiedenis van David naar een ontwerp van Barend van Orley." In *De bloeitijd van de Vlaamse tapijtkunst* 1969, 29–39.

Beer, R. 1891. "Acten, Regesten und Inventaren aus dem Archivo General zu Simancas." *Jahrbuch der Kunsthistorischen Sammlungen des Allerhöchsten Kaiserhauses* 12:158–64.

Beeverell, J. 1707. *Les Delices de la Grand Bretagne et de l'Irlande.* 5 vols. Leiden.

Béguin, S. 1970. "À propos d'un dessin de Nicolas da Modena recémment acquis par le Louvre." *La Revue du Louvre* 20, pt. 1:9–14.

Belgrano, L. T. 1875. *Della vita privata Genovesi.* Genoa.

Beltramo Ceppi, C., and N. Confuorto, eds. 1980. *Firenze e la Toscana dei Medici nell'Europa del cinquecento; Palazzo Vecchio: Committenza e collezionismo medicei.* Florence.

Bennett, A. 1976/1992. *Five Centuries of Tapestry from the Fine Arts Museums of San Francisco.* San Francisco. [Rev. ed., 1992.]

——— et al. 1979. *Acts of the Tapestry Symposium; November 1976.* San Francisco.

Bentley, S. 1831. *Excerpta Historica, or Illustrations of English History.* London.

Bernard, G. 2005. *The King's Reformation: Henry VIII and the Remaking of the English Church.* New Haven and London.

Berti, L., et al. 1979. *Gli Uffizi: Catalogo generale.* Florence.

Bertolotti, A. 1880. *Artisti Belgi ed Olandesi a Roma nel secoli XVI e XVII.* Florence.

Bickham, G. 1742. *Deliciae Britannicae or, the Curiosities of Hampton Court and Windsor Castle Delineated.* London.

Biddle, M. 1966. "Nicholas Bellin of Modena: An Italian Artificer at the Courts of Francis I and Henry VIII." *Journal of the British Archaeological Association*, 3rd ser., 29:106–21.

———. 1984. "The Stuccoes of Nonsuch." *Burlington Magazine* 126 (July):411–17.

———, et al. 2000. *King Arthur's Round Table: An Archaeological Investigation*. Woodbridge.

Bietenholz, P., ed. 1985–87. *Contemporaries of Erasmus: A Biographical Register of Renaissance and Reformation*. 3 vols. Toronto.

Bindoff, S. 1982. *The House of Commons, 1509–1558*. 3 vols. London.

Biriukova, N. 1965. *The Hermitage, Leningrad: Gothic and Renaissance Tapestries*. London.

Birk, E. Ritter von. 1883–84. "Inventar der im Besitz des Allerhöchsten Kaiserhauses befindlichen Niederlanden Tapeten und Gobelins." *Jahrbuch der Kunsthistorischen Sammlungen des Allerhöchsten Kaiserhauses* 1:213–48, 2:167–220.

Blazy, G., et al. 1996. *Catalogue des tapisseries: Musée des Tissus, Musée des Arts Décoratifs*. Lyon.

B. M. 1834. "Lease of the Manor of Hampton Court to Cardinal Wolsey." *Gentleman's Magazine* 104, pt. 1:45–47.

Boccara, D. 1971. *Les belles heures de la tapisserie*. Zug.

Boccardo, P. 1983–85. "Fonti d'archivio per una storia degli arazzi a Genova." *Studi di Storia delle Arti* 5:113–31.

Bonnet-Laborderie, P. 1982. *Les tapisseries de la cathédrale de Beauvais*. Beauvais.

Boon, K. 1992. *The Netherlandish and German Drawings of the Fifteenth and Sixteenth Centuries of the Frits Lugt Collection*. 3 vols. Paris.

Böttiger, J. 1895–98. *Svenska statens samling af väfda tapeter: Historik och beskrifvande förteckning*. 4 vols. Stockholm.

Brassat, W. 1992. *Tapisserien und Politik, Funktionen, Kontexte und Rezeption eines repräsentativen Mediums*. Berlin.

Brewer, J. N. 1816. *The Beauties of England and Wales: Or Original Delineation, Topographical, Historical and Descriptive of Each County*. Vol. 10, *Middlesex*, pt. 4, 469–74. London.

Brewer, J. S. 1867. *Calendar of the Carew Manuscripts Preserved . . . at Lambeth, 1515–1574*. London.

Brosens, K., ed. 2003. *Flemish Tapestry in European and American Collections: Studies in Honour of Guy Delmarcel*. Turnhout.

Brown, C., and G. Delmarcel with A. Lorenzoni. 1996. *Tapestries for the Courts of Federico II, Ercole, and Ferrante Gonzaga, 1522–63*. Seattle, WA.

Brown, J. 1986. *Velázquez, Painter and Courtier*. New Haven and London.

———. 1994. *Kings and Connoisseurs: Collecting Art in Seventeenth-Century Europe*. Princeton, NJ.

Brown, R., ed. 1854. *S. Giustinian: 1515–19; Four Years at the Court of Henry VIII*. 2 vols. London.

———. 1862–1912. *Calendar of State Papers and Manuscripts Relating to English Affairs Existing in the Archives and Collections of Venice*. 18 vols. London.

Bruges 1987. *Bruges et la tapisserie*. Exh. cat. by G. Delmarcel and E. Duverger (Musée Gruuthuse and Musée Memling).

Brussels 1967. *La librairie de Philippe le Bon*. Exh. cat. ed. by G. Dogaer and M. Debae (Bibliothèque Royale Albert Ier).

Brussels 1976. *Tapisseries bruxelloises de la pré-Renaissance*. Exh. cat. by G. Delmarcel et al. (Musées Royaux d'Art et d'Histoire).

Brussels 1995. *Fiamminghi a Roma, 1508–1608*. Exh. cat. ed. A.-C. de Liedekerke (Palais des Beaux-Arts).

Buchanan, I. 1992. "Designers, Weavers and Entrepreneurs: Sixteenth-Century Flemish Tapestries in the Patrimonio Nacional." *Burlington Magazine* 134 (June):380–84.

Buenos Aires, 1965. *Arte flamenco en las colecciones argentinas*. Exh. cat. (Museo Nacional de Arte Decorativo).

Bulow, G. von, ed. 1892. *Diary of the Journey of Philip Julius, Duke of Stettin-Pomerania, through England in the year 1602*. London.

Burke, M. 1984. *Private Collections of Italian Art in Seventeenth-Century Spain*. 3 vols. Ph.D. diss., New York University; Microfilm, Ann Arbor, MI.

Cailleteau, J., et al. 1987. *La tenture de l'Apocalypse d'Angers*. 2nd ed. Cahiers de l'Inventaire, 4. Nantes.

Calberg, M., and H. Pauwels. 1961. "Découverte de la marque du tapissier sur la tenture de l'histoire de Jacob." *Bulletin des Musées Royaux d'Art et d'Histoire* 33:112–13.

Calendar of Inquisitions Miscellaneous. 1963. *Calendar of Inquisitions Miscellaneous (Chancery) Preserved in the Public Record Office*. Vol. 6, *1392–1399*. London.

Calendar of the Close Rolls. 1955–63. *Calendar of the Close Rolls. Henry VII: 1500–1509*. 2 vols. London.

Calendar of the Patent Rolls. 1909. *Calendar of the Patent Rolls Preserved in the Public Record Office. Henry VI*. Vol. 5, *1446–1452*. London.

———. 1925–26. *Calendar of the Patent Rolls Preserved in the Public Record Office. Edward VI*. 5 vols. London, 1925–26.

———. 1976. *Calendar of the Patent Rolls Preserved in the Public Record Office. Henry VII*. 2 vols. London.

Caley, J. 1827. "Two Papers Relating to the Interview between Henry the Eighth and Francis the First of France." *Archaeologia* 21:176–85.

Calvete de Estrella, J. C. 1873–74. *Le très-heureux voyage fait par [. . .] Don Philippe, fils du grand empereur Charles-Quint, depuis l'Espagne jusqu'à ses domaines de la Basse-Allemagne . . . .* Trans. J.-J. Petit. 5 vols. Société des Bibliophiles de Belgique, 7, 10, 11, 15, 16. Brussels.

Campbell, D. 1980. "English Foreign Policy, 1509–1521." Ph.D. diss., Cambridge University.

Campbell, L. 1976. "The Art Market in the Southern Netherlands in the Fifteenth Century." *Burlington Magazine* 118 (April):188–98.

———. 1990. *Renaissance Portraits: European Portrait-Painting in the Fourteenth, Fifteenth, and Sixteenth Centuries*. New Haven and London.

Campbell, L., and S. Foister. 1986. "Gerard, Lucas and Susanna Horenbout." *Burlington Magazine* 128 (October):719–27.

Campbell, T. 1989. "Report on the Tapestries Hung in the Hampton Court State Apartments in the First Half of the Eighteenth Century." Ms. Historic Royal Palaces Agency, Hampton Court.

———. 1994. "William III and the 'Triumph of Lust': The Tapestries Hung in the King's State Apartments in 1699." *Apollo* 140 (August):22–31.

———. 1995–96. "Tapestry Quality in Tudor England: Problems of Terminology." *Studies in the Decorative Arts* 3 (Fall–Winter):29–50.

———. 1996a. "Cardinal Wolsey's Tapestry Collection." *Antiquaries Journal* 76 (December):73–137.

———. 1996b. "Henry VIII and the Château of Écouen *History of David and Bathsheba* Tapestries." *Gazette des Beaux-Arts*, 6th ser., 128 (October):121–40.

———. 1996c. "Pope Leo X's Consistorial 'letto de paramento' and the Boughton House Cartoons." *Burlington Magazine* 138 (July):436–45.

———. 1996d. "School of Raphael Tapestries in the Collection of Henry VIII." *Burlington Magazine* 138 (February):69–78.

———. 1998a. "New Light on a Set of *History of Julius Caesar* Tapestries in Henry VIII's Collection." *Studies in the Decorative Arts* 5 (Spring–Summer):2–39.

———. 1998b. "Romulus and Remus Tapestries in the Collection of Henry VIII." *Apollo* 147 (June):42–50.

———. 1999. "The English Royal Tapestry Collection, 1485–1547." Ph.D. diss., Courtauld Institute, London University.

———. 2003. "The *Story of Abraham* Tapestries at Hampton Court Palace." In Brosens, ed., 2003, 59–86.

———. 2004. "New Evidence on 'Triumphs of Petrarch' Tapestries in the Early Sixteenth Century. Part I: The French Court." *Burlington Magazine* 146 (June):376–85; "Part II: The English Court" (September):602–8.

Campbell, W. 1873–77. *Materials for a History of the Reign of Henry VII*. 2 vols. London.

Carley, J. 2000. *The Libraries of King Henry VIII*. London.

Carter, J. 1800. *Gentleman's Magazine* 70 (July–December): 628–29.

Casali, L., et al. 1993. *Gli arazzi della Battaglia di Pavia nel Museo di Capodimonte a Napoli*. Pavia.

Castelnuovo, E., ed. 1990. *Gli arazzi del cardinale: Bernardo Cles e il Ciclo della Passione di Pieter van Aelst*. Storia dell'arte e della cultura. Trent.

Cavallo, A. 1967. *Tapestries of Europe and Colonial Peru in the Museum of Fine Arts, Boston*. 2 vols. Boston.

———. 1993. *Medieval Tapestries in The Metropolitan Museum of Art*. New York.

Cavendish, G. 1959. *The Life and Death of Cardinal Wolsey*. Ed. R. Sylvester. Early English Text Society, 243. London.

Chamberlain, H. 1770. *A New and Compleat History and Survey of the Cities of London and Westminster . . . from the Earliest Accounts, to the Beginning of the Year 1770*. London.

Chambers, D. S. 1965. *Cardinal Bainbridge in the Court of Rome, 1509–1514*. London.

Chastellain, G. 1863–66. *Oeuvres de Georges Chastellain*. Ed. J. M. B. Constantin, Baron Kervyn de Lettenhove. 8 vols. Brussels.

Chicago 1975. *Raiment for the Lord's Service: A Thousand Years of Western Vestments*. Exh. cat. by C. Mayer-Thurman (Art Institute of Chicago).

Chitty, H. 1932. *Medieval Sculptures at Winchester College*. Oxford.
Chrimes, S. 1972. *Henry VII*. London.
Christie, A. 1938. *English Medieval Embroidery*. Oxford.
Chute, C. 1888. *A History of the Vyne*. Winchester.
Cleland, E. 2007. "An Exemplum Justitiae and the Price of Treason: How the Legend of Herkinbald Reached Henry VIII's Collection." In R. Marks, ed., *Gothic: Art for England, 1400–1547; Proceedings of the Conference, Victoria and Albert Museum, London, 21–23 November 2003*. London.
———. In press. "'. . . The blood of the grape': Tapestries as Tools of Private Devotion during the Renaissance." *Bulletin of the Metropolitan Museum of Art*.
Cole, H. 1859. *Some Thoughts on Hampton Court Palace*. London.
——— (pseud. Felix Summerly). 1861. *A Handbook for the Architecture, Tapestries, Paintings, Gardens and Grounds of Hampton Court*. London. Orig. publ. 1841.
Collection de S. A. Le Duc de Berwick et d'Albe. 1877. *Collection de S. A. Le Duc de Berwick et d'Albe: Tableaux par Velazquez, Murillo, Rubens: 75 Tapisseries de Premier Ordre . . . .* Hotel Drouot, salles nos. 8 et 9, Paris, April 7–20, 1877.
Collection des ordonnances des rois de France. 1887–1908. *Collection des ordonnances des rois de France: Catalogue des actes de François I*. 10 vols. Paris.
Collection of Ordinances and Regulations. 1790. *Collection of Ordinances and Regulations for the Government of the Royal Household*. London.
Colsoni, F. 1710. *Le Guide de Londres dedié aux Voyageurs Etrangers*. 3rd ed. London.
Como 1986. *Arazzi del cinquecento a Como*. Exh. cat. by N. Forti Grazzini (Como Cathedral).
Condemnation de Banquet. 1980. *Les tapisseries de la Condemnation de Banquet*. Guide, Musée Lorrain, Nancy.
Connor, R. 1987. *The Weights and Measures of England*. London.
Consitt, F. 1933. *The London Weavers' Company*. Vol. 1. London.
Cooper, C. 1973. *Memoir of Lady Margaret*. Cambridge.
Cordellier, D., and B. Py. 1992. *Raphäel, son atelier, ses copistes*. Musée du Louvre, Cabinet des Dessins. Inventaire général des dessins italiens, 5. Paris.
Cornwall, J. 1988. *Wealth and Society in Early Sixteenth Century England*. London.
Cortés Hernández, S. 1982. *Dos series de tapices flamencos en el Museo de Santa Cruz de Toledo*. Madrid.
Cosnac, G.-J. 1884. *Les richesses du Palais Mazarin*. Paris.
Cox-Rearick, J. 1996. *The Collection of Francis I: Royal Treasures*. Antwerp.
Crawford, A., ed. 1992. *The Household Books of John Howard, Duke of Norfolk, 1462–1471, 1481–1483*. Stroud.
Crick-Kuntziger, M. 1936. "Eine unveröffentlichte Wandteppichfolge von Peter van Edinghen, genannt van Aelst." *Pantheon* 17:193–98.
———. 1944. *Les tapisseries de L'Hôtel de Ville de Bruxelles*. Antwerp.
———. 1954. *Le tenture de l'Histoire de Jacob d'après Bernard van Orley*. Académie Royale d'Archéologie de Belgique. Antwerp.
———. [1958]. *Musées royaux d'art et d'histoire de Bruxelles: Catalogue des tapisseries (XIVe au XVIIIe siècle)*. Brussels.
Crowfoot, E., F. Pritchard, and K. Staniland. 2001. *Textiles and Clothing, c. 1150–c. 1450*. Medieval Finds from Excavations in London, 4. Woodbridge.
Croyland Chronicle. 1684. "Historiae Croylandensis Continuatio." In W. Fulman, ed., *Rerum Anglicarum Scriptores Veterum*, 449–592. Oxford.
Cruickshank, C. 1969. *Army Royal: Henry VIII's Invasion of France*. Oxford.
———. 1971. *The English Occupation of Tournai, 1513–1519*. Oxford.
Cust, L. 1917. "Notes on Pictures and Works of Art in the Royal Collections, XXXVII: The Gobelins Tapestries, Part I." *Burlington Magazine* 30 (January):16–18; "Part II" (February):59–65.
Dacos, N. 1980. "Tommaso Vincidor: Un élève de Raphaël aux Pays-Bas." In *Relations artistiques entre les Pays-Bas et l'Italie à la Renaissance: Études dédiées à Suzanne Sulzberger*, 61–99. Études d'histoire de l'art, 4. Brussels.
———. 1987. "Raphael et les Pays-Bas: L'école de Bruxelles." In M. Sambucco Hamoud and M. Letizia Strocchi, eds., *Studi su Raffaello, Atti del Congresso internazionale di studi, Urbino and Florence, April 6–14 1984*, 611–23. Urbino.
———. 1996a. "Léonard Thiry de Belges, peintre excellent: De Bruxelles à Fontainebleau en passant par Rome." *Gazette des Beaux-Arts*, 6th ser., 127 (May–June):199–212.
———. 1996b. "Léonard Thiry des Belges, peintre excellent: De Fontainebleau à Bruxelles." *Gazette des Beaux-Arts*, 6th ser., 128 (July–August):21–36.
———. 2005. "Pour Léonard Thiry, pour les Romanistes: Une question de méthode." In N. Dacos and C. Dulière, eds., *Italia Belgica*, 111–35. Turnhout.
Davidson, B. 1988. "The *Furti di Giove* Tapestries Designed by Perino del Vaga for Andrea Doria." *Art Bulletin* 70 (September):424–50.
De bloeitijd van de Vlaamse tapijtkunst. 1969. *De bloeitijd van de Vlaamse tapijtkunst / L'âge d'or de la tapisserie flamande: International colloquium, May 23–25, 1961*. Brussels, 1969.
Dehaisnes, C. 1886. *Documents et extraits divers concernant l'histoire de l'art dans la Flandre, l'Artois et le Hainaut avant le XVe siècle*. 2 vols. Lille.
Delmarcel, G. 1976. "La légende d'Herkenbald et la justice de l'empereur Trajan: Notice iconographique." In Brussels 1976, 246–51.
———. 1977a. "The Dynastic Iconography of the Brussels Tapestries 'Los Honores' (1520–1525)." In *Actas del XXIII Congreso internacional de Historia del Arte*. Vol. 2, *España entre el Mediterráneo y el Atlántico*, 250–59. Granada.
———. 1977b. "De wandtapijten met de geschiedenis van David en Betsabee." *Bulletin des Musées Royaux d'Art et d'Histoire*, 6th ser., 49:143–50.
———. 1977c. "Présence de Boccace dans la tapisserie flamande des XVe et XVIe siècles." In Gilbert Tournoy, ed., *Boccaccio in Europe*, 67–90. *Proceedings of the Boccaccio Conference, Louvain, December 1975*. Symbolae Facultatis Litterarum et Philosophiae Lovaniensis, ser. A, 4. Louvain.
———. 1979. "The *Triumph of the Seven Virtues* and Related Brussels Tapestries of the Early Renaissance." In Bennett et al., 1979, 155–69.
———. 1980. *Tapisseries anciennes d'Enghien*. Mons.
———. 1981. "La Vie de la Vierge: Deux nouvelles tapisseries du cardinal Erard de la Marck." In Maurits Smeyers, ed., *Archivum Artis Lovaniense: Bijdragen tot de geschiedenis van de kunst der Nederlanden, opgedragen aan Prof. Em Dr. J. K. Steppe*, 225–38. Louvain.
———. 1982. "L'auteur ou les auteurs en tapisserie: Quelques réflexions critiques." In *Le dessin sous-jacent dans la peinture*, 43–48. Colloque IV, Louvain-la-Neuve.
———. 1990. "Gli arazzi de Bruxelles all'epoca della serie della Passione di Trento e l'atelier di Pieter van Aelst." In Castelnuovo 1990, 19–33.
———. 1992a. "Aelst, Pieter van (d.j.)." In *Saur: Allgemeines Künstler-Lexicon*, 1:440. Munich.
———. 1992b. "De Passietapijten van Margareta van Oostenrijk (ca. 1518–1524)." *Revue Belge d'Archéologie et d'Histoire de l'Art* 61:127–60.
———. 1993. "Tissage." In Balis et al. 1993, 38–45.
———. 1999. *Flemish Tapestry from the Fifteenth to the Eighteenth Century*. Trans. A. Weir. Tielt. Paris.
———, ed. 2002. *Flemish Tapestry Weavers Abroad: Emigration and the Founding of Manufactories in Europe*. Proceedings of the International Conference, Mechelen, October 2–3, 2000. Leiden.
Delmarcel, G., and C. Dumortier. 1986. "Cornelis de Ronde, wandtapijtwever te Brussel." *Revue Belge d'Archéologie et d'Histoire de l'Art* 55:41–67.
Delmarcel, G., and I. van Tichelen. 1994. "La tapisserie des Pays-Bas Meridionaux sous l'Ancien Régime." In *Les fresques mobiles du Nord: Tapisseries de nos régions, XVI–XX siècles*. Exh. cat. (Hessenhuis). Antwerp.
De Mendonça, M. 1983. *Inventário de tapeçarias existentes em museus e palácios nacionais*. Lisbon.
Denucé, J. 1932. *The Antwerp Art-Galleries: Inventories of the Art Collections in Antwerp in the Sixteenth and Seventeenth Centuries*. Historical Sources for the Study of Flemish Art. 2. Antwerp.
———. 1934. *Italiaansche koopmangeslachten te Antwerpen in de XVIe–XVIIIe eeuwen*. De wettenschappelijke bibliotheck. Amsterdam.
———. 1936. *Antwerp Art-Tapestry and Trade*. Historical Sources for the Study of Flemish Art, 4. Antwerp.
De Smedt, R., et al. 1993. *Michel Coxcie, pictor regis (1499–1592): Internationaal colloquium, Mechelen, 5 en 6 juni 1992*. Mechelen.
D'Essling, Prince d', and E. Müntz. 1902. *Pétrarque: Ses études d'art, son influence sur les artistes . . . l'Illustration de ses écrits . . . .* Paris.
De Strobel, A. M. 1989. *Le arazzerie romane dal XVII al XIX secolo*. Quaderni di storia dell'arte, 22. Rome.
Deuchler, F. 1984. *Der Tausandblumenteppich aus der Burgunderbeute: Ein Abbild des Paradieses / La millefleurs du butin de Bourgogne: Une image du paradis*. Zurich.

Devon, F. 1837. *Issues of the Exchequer, Henry III to Henry VI, from the Pell Records.* London.
Dillon, Viscount, and W. St. John Hope. 1897. "Inventory of the Goods and Chattels Belonging to Thomas, Duke of Gloucester . . . ." *Archaeological Journal* 54:275–91.
Dodsley, R., and J. Dodsley. 1761. *London and its environs described* . . . . 6 vols. London.
Dodsworth, W. 1914. *An Historical Account of the Episcopal See and Cathedral Church of Sarum or Salisbury.* Salisbury.
Doehaerd, R. 1962-63. *Études anversoises: Documents sur le commerce international à Anvers.* 3 vols. Antwerp.
Donnet, F. 1896. "Documents pour servir à l'histoire des ateliers de tapisserie de Bruxelles, Audenaarde, Anvers etc., jusqu'a la fin du XVIIe siècle." *Annales de la Société Royale d'Archéologie de Bruxelles* 10:269–335, 349–52.
Dugdale, W. 1675. *The Baronage of England, or An Historical Account of the Lives and most Memorable Actions of Our English Nobility* . . . . 2 vols. London.
Duverger, E. 1969. "Tapijtwerk uit het atelier van Frans Geubels." In *De bloeitijd van de Vlaamse tapijtkunst* 1969, 91–204.
———. 1993. "De Brusselse stadspatroonschilder voor de tapijtkunst Michiel van Cocxyen (ca. 1497–1592): Een inleidende studie." In De Smedt et al. 1993, 161–92.
Duverger, J. 1957–58. "Vlaams legwerk te Saint-Quentin." *Artes Textiles* 4:3–18.
———. 1977. "Lutherse predicatie te Brussel en het proces tegen een aantal kunstenaars (april-juni 1527)." *Wetenschappelijke Tijdingen* 36:221–28.
Edwards, R., et al. 1956. *The Tudor Period, 1500–1603.* London.
Ellis, H. 1846. *Original Letters Illustrative of English History.* 3rd ser. 4 vols. London.
Elton, G. 1972. *Policy and Police: The Enforcement of the Reformation in the Age of Thomas Cromwell.* Cambridge.
Erasmus, D. 1936. *The Education of a Christian Prince.* Ed. L. Born. New York.
Erkelens, A. 1962. *Wandtapijten 1 / Tapestries 1: Late Gotiek en vroege Renaissance.* Facetten der verzameling, 2nd ser. 2, 4, Rijksmuseen. Amsterdam.
Erlande-Brandenburg, A. 1973. "Les tapisseries de François d'Angoulême." *Bulletin de la Société de l'Histoire de l'Art Français,* 19–31.
Evans, J. 1949. *English Art, 1307–1461.* Oxford.
Ewing, D. 1990. "Marketing Art in Antwerp, 1460–1560: Our Lady's *Pand.*" *Art Bulletin* 72 (December):558–84.
Farmer, J. 1981. *Bernard van Orley of Brussels.* 2 vols. Ph.D. diss., Princeton University; Microfilm, Ann Arbor, MI.
———. 1994. "How One Workshop Worked: Bernard van Orley's Atelier in Early Sixteenth-Century Brussels." In G. T. Clark et al., eds., *A Tribute to Robert A. Koch: Studies in the Northern Renaissance,* 21–53. Princeton, NJ.
Fenaille, M. 1903. *État général des tapisseries de la Manufacture des Gobelins . . . 1600–1900.* Vol. 2, *Période Louis XIV, 1662–1699.* Paris.
Fermor, S. 1996. *The Raphael Tapestry Cartoons: Narrative, Decoration, Design.* London.
Fernández Alvarez, M. 1975. *Charles V: Elected Emperor and Hereditary Ruler.* London.
Fock, C. 1969. "Nieuws over de tapijten, bekend als de Nassause Genealogie." *Oud Holland* 84:1–28.
Foister, S. 1981. "Paintings and Other Works of Art in Sixteenth-Century English Inventories." *Burlington Magazine* 123 (May):273–82.
———. 2004. *Holbein and England.* New Haven and London.
Ford, B., ed. 1989. *The Cambridge Guide to the Arts in Britain.* Vol. 3, *Renaissance and Reformation.* Cambridge.
Fortescue, J. 1885. *The Governance of England: Otherwise Called the Difference between an Absolute and a Limited Monarchy.* Ed. C. Plummer. Oxford.
Forti Grazzini, N. 1982. *L'arazzo ferrarese.* Milan.
———. 1989. "Arazzi." In *Giulio Romano,* 486. Exh. cat. (Palazzo del Te). Mantua.
———. 1991. "Precisazioni sugli arazzi delle 'Storie di Salomone.'" In *Le storie di Salomone e altre opere d'arte novaresi,* 57–89. Novara da Scoprire, 3. Novara.
———. 1994. *Gli arazzi.* 2 vols. Il patrimonio artistico del Quirinale. Rome.
———. 2003. *Gli arazzi della Fondazione Giorgio Cini.* Venice.
Fox, A., and J. Guy. 1986. *Reassessing the Henrician Age: Humanism, Politics and Reform, 1500–1550.* Oxford.
Foyle, J. 2002. "A Reconstruction of Thomas Wolsey's Great Hall at Hampton Court." *Architectural History* 45:128–58.
Franke, B. 1995. "Charles le Téméraire, nouvel Assuérus." *Le Pays Lorrain* 76, no. 4 (October–December):291–93.
———. 1998. *Assuerus und Esther am Burgunderhof: Zur Rezeption des Buches Esther in den Niederlanden (1450 bis 1530).* Berlin.
———. 2005. "Female Role Models in Tapestries." In D. Eichberger, ed., *Women of Distinction: Margaret of York, Margaret of Austria,* 155–66. Mechelen.
Franses, S. 1986. *European Tapestries, 1450–1750: A Catalogue of Recent Acquisitions.* London.
Friedländer, M. 1917. "Pieter Coecke van Alost." *Jahrbuch der Königlich Preussischen Kunstsammlungen* 38:73–94.
Froissart, J. 1857. *Chronicles of England, France, Spain and the Adjoining Countries from the Latter Part of the Reign of Edward II to the Coronation of Henry IV.* 2 vols. Trans. T. Johnes. London.
Gairdner, J. 1858. *Memorials of King Henry VII.* London.
———. 1861–63. *Letters and Papers Illustrative of the Reigns of Richard III and Henry VII.* London.
———. 1895. "'The Spousells' of the Princess Mary, Daughter of Henry VII to Charles Prince of Castille A.D. 1508." *Camden Miscellany* 9.
———. 1904. *The Paston Letters, A.D. 1422–1509.* 6 vols. London.
Gasquet, D. 1906. *Henry VIII and the English Monasteries.* London.
Gay, V. 1887. *Glossaire archéologique du Moyen Âge et de la Renaissance.* Paris.
Gentil Quina, M. 1998. *A maniera de Portugal e da India: Una serie de tapeçaria quinhentista.* Lisbon.
Gerritsen, W., and A. van Melle, eds. 1998. *A Dictionary of Medieval Heroes: Characters in Medieval Narrative Traditions and Their Afterlife in Literature, Theatre and the Visual Arts.* Trans. T. Guest. Woodbridge.
Ghent 1955. *Charles-Quint et son temps.* Exh. cat. (Musée des Beaux-Arts, Ghent). Brussels.
Ghent 1987. *Tapisseries flamandes du château du Wawel à Cracovie et d'autres collections européennes / Vlaamse wandtapijten uit de Wawelburcht te Krakau en uit andere Europese verzamelingen.* Exh. cat. by. G. Delmarcel et al. (Sint-Pietersabdij).
Glanville, P. 1991. "Cardinal Wolsey and the Goldsmiths." In Gunn and Lindley 1991, 131–48.
Gleissner, S. 1994. "Reassembling a Royal Art Collection for the Restored King of Great Britain." *Journal of the History of Collections* 6:103–15.
Göbel, H. 1923. *Wandteppiche.* Band 1: *Die Niederlande.* 2 vols. Leipzig.
———. 1928. *Wandteppiche.* Band 2: *Die romanischen Länder.* 2 vols. Leipzig.
———. 1933–34. *Wandteppiche.* Band 3: *Die germanischen und slawischen Länder.* 2 vols. Berlin.
Gómez Martinez, A., and B. Chillón Sampedro. 1925. *Los tapices de la catedral de Zamora.* Zamora.
Goodall, J. 2001. *God's House at Ewelme: Life and Devotion in a Fifteenth-Century Almshouse.* Aldershot.
Goodman, A., and J. Gillespie, eds. 1999. *Richard II: The Art of Kingship.* Oxford.
Gordon, D., L. Monnas, and C. Elam, eds. 1997. *The Regal Image of Richard II and the Wilton Diptych.* London.
Gras, N. 1918. *The Early English Customs System.* Cambridge, MA.
Greenwich 1991. *Henry VIII: A European Court in England.* Exh. cat. ed. by D. Starkey (National Maritime Museum, Greenwich). London.
Griffiths, R. 1998. *The Reign of King Henry VI.* 2nd ed. Stroud.
Grimm, H. 1941. *Raffael.* Berlin.
Grodecki, C. 1985. *Architecture—vitrerie—menuiserie—tapisserie—jardins.* Documents du Minutier central des notaires de Paris. *Histoire de l'art au XVIe siècle (1540–1600).* Vol. 1. Paris.
Groos, G. 1981. *The Diary of Baron Waldstein: A Traveller in Elizabethan England.* London.
Grose, F., and T. Astle. 1807–9. *The Antiquaries Repertory.* 4 vols. London.
Grummitt, D. 1999. "Henry VII, Chamber Finance and the 'New Monarch': Some New Evidence." *Historical Research* 72, no. 179 (October):229–43.
Guenée, B., and F. Lehoux. 1968. *Les entrées royals françaises de 1328 à 1515.* Paris.
Guiffrey, J. 1878–85. *Tapisseries françaises.* Pt. 1 of Jules Guiffrey, Eugène Müntz, and Alexandre Pinchart, *Histoire générale de la tapisserie.* Paris.
———. 1885. *Inventaire général du mobilier de la couronne sous Louis XIV (1663–1715).* 2 vols. Paris.
———. 1887. "Inventaire des tapisseries du roi Charles VI, vendues par les Anglais en 1422." *Bibliothèque de l'École des Chartes* 48:59–110, 396–444.

———. 1904. *Bibliographie critique de la tapisserie dans les différents pays de l'Europe depuis ses origines jusqu'à nos jours.* Paris.

———. 1911. *Les tapisseries du XIIe à la fin du XVIe siècle.* Histoire générale des arts appliqués à l'industrie, 6. Paris.

———. 1913. *Inventaire descriptif et méthodique des tapisseries du Garde-Meuble.* Inventaire général des richesses d'art de la France, 4. Paris.

———, ed. 1894–96. *Inventaires de Jean, duc de Berry (1401–1416).* 2 vols. Paris.

Gunn, S., and P. Lindley, eds. 1991. *Cardinal Wolsey: Church, State and Art.* Cambridge.

Guy, J. 1986. "Thomas Cromwell and the Intellectual Origins of the Henrician Revolution." In Fox and Guy 1986, 151–78.

———. 1995. "Thomas Wolsey, Thomas Cromwell and the Reform of Henrician Government." In MacCulloch 1995, 35–58.

Gwyn, P. 1990. *The King's Cardinal: The Rise and Fall of Cardinal Wolsey.* London.

Hall, E. 1809. *Chronicle* [1548]. London.

———. 1904. *Henry VIII.* 2 vols. C. Whibley, ed., *The Lives of the Kings.* London.

Hampton Court 1993. *Henry VIII: Images of a Tudor King.* Exh. cat. by C. Lloyd and S. Thurley (Hampton Court Palace). London.

Harris, B. 1986. *Edward Stafford: Third Duke of Buckingham, 1478–1521.* Stanford, CA.

Hawkyard, A. 2005. "Sir John Fastolf's 'Gret Mansion by me late edified': Caister Castle, Norfolk." In L. Clark, ed., *The Fifteenth Century.* Vol. 5, *"Of Mice and Men": Image, Belief and Regulation in Late Medieval England,* 39–66. London.

Haynin, J. de. 1905–6. *Mémoires, 1465–77.* Ed. D. Brouwers. Liège.

Hayward, M. 1997. "The Packing and Transportation of the Goods of Henry VIII, with Particular Reference to the 1547 Inventory." *Costume* 31:8–15.

———. 1998a. "The Possessions of Henry VIII: A Study of the Inventories." Ph.D. diss., London University.

———. 1998b. "Repositories of Splendour: Henry VIII's Wardrobes of the Robes and Beds." *Textile History* 29:134–56.

———. 2004. *The 1542 Inventory of Whitehall: The Palace and Its Keeper.* 2 vols. London.

Hazard, M. 1987. "'Order gave each thing view': 'Shows, pageants and sights of honour' in King Henry VIII." *Word and Image* 3, no. 1:95–103.

Heal, F. 1980. *Of Prelates and Princes: A Study of the Economic and Social Position of the Tudor Episcopacy.* Cambridge.

Hefford, W. 1979. "Bread, Brushes and Brooms: Aspects of Tapestry Restoration in England, 1660–1760." In Bennet et al. 1979, 65–78.

———. 1992. "Ralph Montagu's Tapestries." In T. Murdoch, ed., *Boughton House: The English Versailles,* 96–107. London.

———. 1999. "The Duke of Buckingham's Mortlake Tapestries of 1623." *Bulletin du CIETA* 76:90–103.

———. 2002. "Flemish Tapestry Weavers in England: 1550–1775." In G. Delmarcel, ed., 2002, 43–62.

Henschel, G. 1884–87. *Glossarium mediae et infimae latinatis.* 10 vols. Niort.

Hinds, A., ed. 1912. *Calendar of State Papers and Manuscripts Existing in the Archives and Collections of Milan.* London.

Historical Manuscripts Commission. 1879. *Seventh Report.* Pt. 1. London.

———. 1881. *Eighth Report.* App., pt. 1. London.

———. 1885. *Tenth Report.* App., pt. 4. London.

Hommel, L. 1959. *Marguerite d'York, ou la duchesse Junon.* Paris.

Hope, W. St. John. 1915. "The Last Testament and Inventory of John de Veer, 13th Earl of Oxford." *Archaeologia* 66:275–348.

Horn, H. 1989. *Jan Cornelisz Vermeyen, Painter of Charles V, and His "Conquest of Tunis": Paintings, Etchings, Drawings, Cartoons and Tapestries.* 2 vols. Doornspijk.

Howard, M. 1987. *The Early Tudor Country House: Architecture and Politics, 1490–1550.* London.

Howarth, D. 1997. *Images of Rule: Art and Politics in the English Renaissance, 1485–1649.* Los Angeles.

Hussey, C. 1923. "Bramshill, Hampshire IV." *Country Life,* June 23, 891–93.

Huygens, L. 1982. *The English Journal, 1651–1652.* Ed. and trans. A. Bachrach and R. Collmer. Leiden.

"Inventory of the Goods of Edmund Dudley." 1921. *Archaeologia* 21:39–42.

Ives, E. 1976. "Letters and Accounts of William Brereton of Malpas." *Lancashire and Cheshire Record Society* 116.

———. 1988. *Anne Boleyn.* Oxford, 1988.

———. 1991. "The Fall of Wolsey." In Gunn and Lindley 1991, 286–315.

Jackson-Stops, G. 1977. "Purchases and Perquisites: The Sixth Earl of Dorset's Furniture at Knole." *Country Life,* June 9, 1620–22.

Jacquot, J., ed. 1960. "Panorama des fêtes et cérémonies du règne: Évolution des thèmes et des styles." In *Fêtes et cérémonies au temps de Charles Quint,* 413–91. IIe Congrès de l'Association internationale des historiens de la Renaissance, 2nd sec., Brussels, Antwerp, Ghent, and Liège, September 2–7, 1957. Collection Le choeur des Muses. Paris.

James, M. 1920. "Chapel Inventories." *Etoniana* 26 (September):401–8.

Jesse, E. 1842. *A Summer's Day at Hampton Court.* London.

Jones, M., and M. Underwood. 1992. *The King's Mother: Lady Margaret Beaufort, Countess of Richmond and Derby.* Cambridge.

Jones, R., and N. Penny. 1983. *Raphael.* New Haven and London.

Joos, B. 1985. "De wandtapijten met de Geschiedenis van Jakob: Een verborgen signatuur van Bernart van Orley." *Bulletin des Musées Royaux d'Art et d'Histoire* 56:61–73.

Joubert, F. 1981. "L'Apocalypse d'Angers et les débuts de la tapisserie historiée." *Bulletin Monumental* 139:125–40.

———. 1987. *La tapisserie médiévale au Musée de Cluny.* Paris.

———. 1990. "Les 'tapissiers' de Philippe le Hardi." In *Artistes, artisans et production artistique au Moyen Âge.* Vol. 3, *Fabrication et consummation de l'oeuvre,* 601–8. Colloque International, Centre National de la Recherche Scientifique, Université de Rennes II, Haute-Bretagne, May 2–6, 1983. Paris.

———. 1993. *La tapisserie.* Typologie des sources du Moyen Âge occidental, 67. Turnhout.

Joubert, F., A. Lefébure, and P.-F. Bertrand. 1995. *Histoire de la tapisserie en Europe, du Moyen Âge à nos jours.* Paris.

Jubinal, A. 1840. *Recherches sur l'usage et l'origine des tapisseries à personages dites historiées, depuis l'antiquité jusqu'au 16e siècle inclusivement.* Paris.

Junquera de Vega, P., and C. Herrero Carretero. 1986. *Catálogo de tapices del Patrimonio Nacional.* Vol. 1, *Siglo XVI.* Madrid.

Karafel, L. Forthcoming. "Mythology and Metamorphoses: Raphael's Woven Grotesques for the Vatican Palace." Ph.D. diss. in progress, Institute of Fine Arts, New York.

Keate, E. 1932. *Hampton Court Palace: A Short Popular Guide to the Palace and Gardens.* London.

Kendrick, A. 1904–5. "Tapestry at Winchester College." *Burlington Magazine* 6:490, 495.

———. 1924. "The Coventry Tapestry." *Burlington Magazine* 44:83–89.

King, D. 1976. "Tapestries from France and Flanders." *Connoisseur* 192 (November):232–37.

———. 1985. "The Carpet Collection of Cardinal Wolsey." *Oriental Carpet Textile Studies* 1:41–54.

———. 1989. "Tapestries and Other Hangings." In MacGregor 1989, 308–14.

King, J. 1989. *Tudor Royal Iconography: Literature and Art in an Age of Religious Crisis.* Princeton Essays on the Arts. Princeton, NJ.

———. 1994. "Henry VIII as David: The King's Image and Reformation Politics." In P. Herman, ed., *Rethinking the Henrician Era,* 78–91. Urbana, IL.

Kingsford, C. 1921. "Inventory of the Goods of Edmund Dudley." *Archaeologia* 71:17–54.

———, ed. 1913. "The Record of Bluemantle Pursuivant, 1471–1472." In *English Historical Literature in the Fifteenth Century,* 379–88. Oxford.

Kipling, G. 1977. *The Triumph of Honour: Burgundian Origins of the English Renaissance.* The Hague.

———. 1981. "Henry VII and the Origins of Tudor Patronage." In G. Lytle and S. Orgel, eds., *Patronage in the Renaissance,* 137–44. Princeton, NJ.

———. 1990. *The Receyt of the Ladie Kateryne.* Oxford.

Knight, C. 1785. *Les Delices des Chateaux Royaux, or a Pocket Comparison to the Royal Palaces of Windsor, Kensington, Kew and Hampton Court.* Windsor. 2nd ed., Windsor, 1799.

Knighton, C., ed. 1998. *Calendar of State Papers Domestic Series of the Reign of Mary I, 1553–1558.* Rev. ed. London.

Koebner, R. 1953. "'The imperial crown of this realm': Henry VIII, Constantine the Great and Polydore Vergil." *Bulletin of the Institute of Historical Research* 26:29–52.

Kumsch, E. 1914. *Die Apostel-Geschichte: Eine Folge von Wandteppichen nach Entwürfen von Raffael Santi.* Dresden.

Kurath, H., ed. 1954. *Middle English Dictionary.* Ann Arbor, MI.

Labarte, J. 1879. *Inventaire du mobilier de Charles V, roi de France.* Collection de documents inédits sur l'histoire de France, 3rd ser., Archéologie. Paris.

Laborde, L., Marquis de. 1849–52. *Les ducs de Bourgogne: Études sur les lettres, les arts et l'industrie pendant le XVe siècle et plus particulièrement dans les Pays-Bas et le duché de Bourgogne.* 3 vols. Ed. Jules Guiffrey. Paris.

———. 1877–80. *Les comptes des bâtiments du roi (1528–1571), suivi de documents inédits sur les châteaux royaux et les beaux-arts au XIV siècle.* 2 vols. Ed. Jules Guiffrey. Paris.

Lacy, N., ed. 1986. *The Arthurian Encyclopedia.* New York.

Laking, G. 1905. *The Furniture of Windsor Castle.* London.

La Serre, J.-P. 1639. *Histoire de l'entrée de la Reyne Mère du Roy Très-Chrestien dans la Grande-Bretagne.* London.

Latham, C. 1904–9. *In English Homes.* 3 vols. London.

Law, E. 1885–91. *History of Hampton Court Palace in Tudor Times.* 3 vols. London.

Ledos, G. 1889. "Fragment de l'inventaire des joyaux de Louis Ier, duc d'Anjou." *Bibliothèque de l'École des Chartes* 50:168–79.

Lefébure, A. 1993. "La tenture de 'L'Histoire de Scipion': Un nouveau regard." *Revue du Louvre* 43 (December):81–87.

Legg, J. W., and W. H. St. John Hope. 1902. *Inventories of Christchurch, Canterbury: With Historical and Typographical Introductions and Illustrative Documents.* London.

Leland, J. 1970. *Antiquarii de rebus Britannnicus collectanea.* Ed. Thomas Hearne. London. Orig. publ. London, 1774.

Lennard, F., and M. Hayward. 2005. *Tapestry Conservation: Principles and Practice.* Oxford.

Lestocquoy, J. 1978. *Deux siècles de l'histoire de la tapisserie (1300–1500): Paris, Arras, Lille, Tournai, Bruxelles.* Mémoires de la Commission Départementale des Monuments Historiques du Pas-de-Calais, 19. Arras.

Letters and Papers, 1862–1932. *Letters and Papers, Foreign and Domestic, of the Reign of Henry VIII.* Ed. J. S. Brewer et al. 21 vols. London.

Lloyd, T. 1977. *The English Wool Trade in the Middle Ages.* London.

Loades, D. 1987. *The Tudor Court.* Totowa, NJ.

London 1963. *Opus Anglicanum: English Medieval Embroidery.* Exh. cat. by Donald King (Victoria and Albert Museum).

London 1975. *Treasures from the Burrell Collection.* Exh. cat. (Hayward Gallery).

Loomie, A. 1989. "New Light on the Spanish Ambassador's Purchases from Charles I's Collection 1649–53." *Journal of the Warburg and Courtauld Institutes* 52:257–67.

Los Angeles 2003. *Illuminating the Renaissance: The Triumph of Flemish Manuscript Painting in Europe.* Exh. cat. by Thomas Kren and Scot McKendrick (J. Paul Getty Museum).

Lunsingh-Scheurleer, Th.-H. 1960–62. "Documents on the Furnishing of Kensington House." *Walpole Society* 38:15–58.

MacCulloch, D., ed. 1995. *The Reign of Henry VIII: Politics, Policy and Piety.* London.

MacGregor, A., ed. 1989. *The Late King's Goods: Collections, Possessions and Patronage of Charles I in the Light of the Commonwealth Sale Inventories.* London.

Machabey, A. 1962. *La métrologie dans les musées de province et sa contribution à l'histoire des poids et mesures en France depuis le troisième siècle.* Paris.

Macon, M. 1913. "Les tapisseries de Colbert." *Archives de l'Art Français,* n.s., 7:248–54.

Mahl, E. 1965. "Die Romulus und Remus-Folgen der Tapisseriensammlung des Kunsthistorisches Museums." *Jahrbuch der Kunsthistorischen Sammlungen in Wien* 61:7–40.

Mandach, A. von. 1987. *Der Trajan- und Herkinbald-Teppich: Die Entdeckung einen internationalen Portraitgalerie des 15. Jahrhunderts.* Bern.

Mander, K. van. 1980. *Het Schilder-Boeck.* Reprint ed. 2 vols., Documents of Art and Architectural History, ser. 1, 2. New York. Orig. publ. Haarlem, 1604.

Marcombe, D. 1987. *The Last Principality: Politics, Religion and Society in the Bishopric of Durham, 1494–1660.* Nottingham.

Marillier, H. C. 1931 / 1951 / 1962. *The Tapestries at Hampton Court Palace.* London. [Rev. ed., 1951; 2nd rev. ed., 1962.]

Marlier, G. 1966. *La Renaissance flamande: Pierre Coeck d'Alost.* Brussels.

McGrory, D. 2003. *A History of Coventry.* Chichester.

McKendrick, S. 1987. "Edward IV: An English Royal Collector of Netherlandish Tapestry." *Burlington Magazine* 129 (August):521–24.

———. 1988. "Classical Mythology and Ancient History in Works of Art at the Courts of France, Burgundy and England (1364–1500)." Ph.D. diss., Courtauld Institute, London University.

———. 1990. "La Grande Histoire Cesar and the Manuscripts of Edward IV." *English Manuscript Studies, 1100–1700* 2:109–38.

———. 1991. "The *Great History of Troy:* A Reassessment of the Development of a Secular Theme in Late Medieval Art." *Journal of the Warburg and Courtauld Institutes* 54:43–82.

———. 1994. "The Romuléon and the Manuscripts of Edward IV." In N. Rogers, ed., *England in the Fifteenth Century,* 149–69. *Proceedings of the 1992 Harlaxton Symposium.* Stamford, CT.

———. 1995. "Tapestries from the Low Countries in England during the Fifteenth Century." In C. Barron and N. Saul, ed., *England and the Low Countries in the Late Middle Ages,* 43–60. New York.

Mechelen 2000. *Los Honores: Flemish Tapestries for the Emperor Charles V.* Exh. cat. by Guy Delmarcel (Cultureel Centrum Antoon Spinoy, Mechelen). Antwerp.

Meiss, M. 1974. *French Painting in the Time of Jean de Berry: The Limbourgs and Their Contemporaries.* With contributions by S. Dunlap Smith and E. Home Beatson. 2 vols. New York.

Meoni, L. 1989. "Gli arazzieri delle 'Storie della Creazione' medicee." *Bollettino d'Arte,* 6th ser., 6, 74 (November–December):57–66.

Michel, P. 1999. *Mazarin, prince des collectionneurs.* Paris.

Michelant, M. 1872. "Inventaire des joyaux, ornements d'église, vaisselles, tapisseries, livres, tableaux, etc., de Charles Quint dressé à Bruxelles au mois de mai 1536." *Bulletin de la Commission Royale d'Histoire,* 3rd ser., 13:199–368.

Millar, O. 1992. *The Victorian Pictures in the Collection of Her Majesty the Queen.* 2 vols. Cambridge.

———, ed. 1972. "The Inventories and Valuations of the King's Goods, 1649–1651." *Walpole Society,* 43. London.

Miller, H. 1955. "Subsidy Assessments of the Peerage in the Sixteenth Century." *Bulletin of the Institute of Historical Research* 28:15–34.

Mitchell, M. 1971. "Works of Art from Rome for Henry VIII." *Journal of the Warburg and Courtauld Institutes* 34:197–200.

Mitchell, S. 1997. "Richard II: Kingship and the Cult of Saints." In Gordon, Monnas, and Elam 1997, 115–24.

Monnas, L. 1987. "The Vestments of Henry VII at Stonyhurst College: Cloth of Gold Woven to Shape." *Bulletin du CIETA* 65:69–80.

———. 1989. "New Documents for the Vestments of Henry VII at Stonyhurst College." *Burlington Magazine* 131:355–59.

Montfaucon, R. P. Dom B. de. 1731. *Les monuments de la monarchie françoise.* Vol. 3. Paris.

Morelowski, M. 1936. "Le tapissier Pasquier Grenier et l'église Saint-Quentin à Tournai." *Revue Belge d'Archéologie et d'Histoire de l'Art* 6:203–21.

Morris, C., ed. 1947. *The Journeys of Celia Fiennes.* London.

Müntz, E. 1878–85. *Histoire de la tapisserie en Italie, en Allemagne, en Angleterre, en Espagne, en Danemark, en Hongrie, en Pologne, en Russie et en Turquie.* Pt. 2 of Jules Guiffrey, Eugène Müntz, and Alexandre Pinchart, *Histoire général de la tapisserie.* Paris.

———. 1890. "Les tapisseries de Westminster sous Henri VIII." *Archives des Arts,* 55–67.

———. 1906. "Les tapisseries du Cardinal Wolsey et l'histoire de Judith à la cathédrale de Sens." *Notes d'Art et d'Archéologie, Revue de la Société de Saint-Jean* 18:97–115.

Murray, H. 1992. "The Scrope Tapestries." *Yorkshire Archaeological Journal* 64:145–56.

Myers, A. 1959. *The Household of Edward IV: The Black Book and the Ordinance of 1478.* Manchester.

New York 1991. *Resplendence of the Spanish Monarchy: Renaissance Tapestries and Armor from the Patrimonio Nacional.* Exh. cat. by C. Herrero Carretero et al. (The Metropolitan Museum of Art).

New York 1998. *From Van Eyck to Bruegel: Early Netherlandish Painting in The Metropolitan Museum of Art.* Exh. cat. by M. Ainsworth and K. Christiansen (The Metropolitan Museum of Art).

New York 2002. *Tapestry in the Renaissance: Art and Magnificence.* Exh. cat. by T. Campbell et al. (The Metropolitan Museum of Art).

New York 2005. *Giant Leaf Tapestries of the Renaissance, 1500–1600.* Exh. cat. by S. Franses (S. Franses Gallery, New York). London.

Nichols [I], J. G. 1780. *A Collection of all the Wills Known to be Extant of the Kings and Queens of England . . . .* London.

Nichols [II], J. G. 1846. *Chronicle of Calais in the Reigns of Henry VII and Henry VIII.* London.

———. 1855. "Inventories of the Wardrobes, Plate, Chapel Stuff &c. of Henry Fitzroy, Duke of Richmond, and Katherine, Princess Dowager." *Camden Miscellany III,* 61. London.

Nichols, J. G., and J. Bruce. 1863. *Wills from Doctor's Commons: A Selection from the Wills of Eminent Persons, 1495–1695*. Camden Society, 83. London.

Nicholson, G. 1977. "The Nature and Function of Historical Argument in the Henrician Reformation." Ph.D. diss., Cambridge University.

Nicolas, N. H. 1826. *Testamenta Vetusta: Being Illustrations from Wills, of Manners, Customs, and c. as well as of the Descents and Possessions of Many Distinguished Families; From the Reign of Henry the Second to the Accession of Queen Elizabeth*. London.

———. 1827. *The Privy Purse Expenses of King Henry the Eighth from November 1529–December 1532*. London.

———. 1830. *Privy Purse Expenses of Elizabeth of York: Wardrobe Accounts of Edward IV*. London.

———, ed. 1834–37. *Proceedings and Ordinances of the Privy Council of England, 1386–1542*. 7 vols. London.

Nordenfalk, C. 1966. "Queen Christina's Roman Collection of Tapestries." In M. Von Platten, ed., *Analecta Reginensia 1, Queen Christina of Sweden: Documents and Studies*, 266–95. Stockholm.

Odescalchi, L. n.d. *Inventario e descrizzione di tutti gli arazzi posseduti dallagia fù maestà della Regina Cristina di Svezzia . . . e posseduti presentamente dall'altezza del Signor Principe D. Livio Odescalchi, duca di Bracciano* . . . . Rome.

Oliver, G. 1861. *Lives of the Bishops of Exeter*. Exeter.

Onghena, M. 1974. "Vlaamse Wandtapijten in het Stadhuis te Middelburg (Zeeland)." *Artes Textiles* 8:3–28.

Oswald, A. 1960. "Nether Winchendon, Buckinghamshire—II." *Country Life*, March 5, 986–89.

Oursel, H. 1999. "David se fait présenter le butin des Ammonites" [note of purchase]. *Revue du Louvre* (June):84–85.

Page, W. 1893. *Aliens in England, 1509–1603: Letters of Denization and Acts of Naturalisation*. Huguenot Society of London, 8. London.

Palgrave, F. 1836. *The Antient Kalenders and Inventories of the Treasury of His Majesty's Exchequer*. Vol. 3. London.

Paris 1965. *Le XVIe siècle européen: Tapisseries*. Exh. cat. by G. Viatte (Mobilier National).

Paris 1973. *Chefs-d'oeuvre de la tapisserie du XIVe au XVIe siècle*. Exh. cat. by G. Souchal (Grand Palais).

Paris 1981. *Jean Fouquet: Catalogue*. Exh. cat. by N. Reynaud (Musée du Louvre).

Paris 1994. *Le dessin en France au XVIe siècle: Dessins et miniatures des collections de l'École des Beaux-Arts*. Exh. cat. ed. by E. Brugerolles (École Nationale Supérieure des Beaux-Arts).

Parker, J. 1853. *Some Account of Domestic Architecture in England*. Vol. 2, *From Edward I to Richard II*. Oxford.

———. 1859. *Some Account of Domestic Architecture in England*. Vol. 3, pts. 1 and 2, *From Richard II to Henry VIII*. Oxford.

Parry, L. 1983. *William Morris Textiles*. New York.

Passavant, J. 1836. *A Tour of a German Artist in England*. London.

Peacham, H. 1622. *The Compleat Gentleman*. London.

Percy, H. 1905. *The Regulations and Establishment of the Household of Henry Algernon Percy the Fifth Earl of Northumberland at His Castles of Wressle and Leckonfield in Yorkshire*. London.

Philadelphia 2001. *Leaves of Gold: Treasures of Manuscript Illumination from Philadelphia Collections*. Exh. cat. ed. by J. Tanis and J. Thompson (Philadelphia Museum of Art).

Philobiblon Society. 1861. *Inventaire de tous les meubles du Cardinal Mazarin, dressé en 1653* . . . . London.

Pinchart, A. 1885. *Tapisseries flamandes*. Pt. 3 of Jules Guiffrey, Eugène Müntz, and Alexandre Pinchart, *Histoire générale de la tapisserie*. Paris, 1878–85.

Pine, J. 1739. *The Tapestry Hangings of The House of Lords: Representing the Several Engagements Between the English and Spanish Fleets, in the Ever Memorable Year MDLXXXVIII* . . . . London.

Platter, T. 1937. *Thomas Platter's Travels in England, 1599*. Ed. and trans. C. Williams. London.

———. 1968. *Beschreibung der Reisen durch Frankreich, Spanien, England und die Niederlande, 1595–1600*. 2 vols. Ed. R. Keiser. Basel.

Pollard, A. 1913. *The Reign of Henry VII from Contemporary Sources*. London.

Popham, A. 1932. *Catalogue of Drawings by Dutch and Flemish Artists Preserved in the Department of Prints and Drawings in the British Museum*. Vol. 5, *Dutch and Flemish Drawings of the Fifteenth and Sixteenth Centuries*. London.

Poznan 1971. *Gobeliny zachodnio-europejskie w zbiorach polskich XVI–XVIIIw*. Exh. cat. (Muzeum Narodowe W Poznaniu).

Prost, B. 1889–90. "Les tapisseries du duc de Berry." *Archives Historiques, Artistiques et Littéraires* 1:385–92.

Prost, B., and H. Prost. 1902–13. *Inventaires mobiliers et extraits des comptes des ducs de Bourgogne de la maison de Valois (1363–1477)*. 2 vols. Paris.

Public Record Office. 1963. *Lists and Indexes, no. XXXV: List of Various Accounts and Documents . . . Formerly Preserved in the Exchequer* . . . . Reprint ed. New York.

Pyne, W. 1819. *History of the Royal Residences* . . . . London.

Raine, J., ed. 1859. *The Fabric Rolls of York Minster*. Surtees Society, 35. London.

———. 1879–94. *The Church of York and Its Archbishops*. 3 vols. London.

Ramssla, N. von. 1734. *Beschreibung der Reise . . . herzog von Sachsen Weimer Johann Ernstder Jungere genandt in Frankreich, Engeland und Niederland (1613–1614)*. Lubec.

Rapp Buri, A., and M. Stucky-Schürer. 1998. "Alexandre le Grand et l'art de la tapisserie du XVe siècle." *Revue de l'Art* 119, pt. 1:21–32.

———. 2001. *Burgundische Tapisserien*. Munich.

Rawcliffe, C. 1978. *The Staffords, Earls of Stafford and Dukes of Buckingham 1394–1521*. Cambridge.

Ricci, S. de. 1913. *Catalogue of Twenty Renaissance Tapestries from the J. Pierpont Morgan Collection*. Paris.

Richardson, T. 2002. *The Armour and Arms of Henry VIII*. Leeds.

Richardson, W. 1952. *Tudor Chamber Administration, 1485–1547*. Baton Rouge, LA.

Ridgard, J., ed. 1985. "Inventory, Framlingham Castle, 28th May 1524." In *Medieval Framlingham: Select Documents, 1270–1524*, 129–58. Suffolk Record Society, 27. Woodbridge.

Roberts, H. 1989. "Royal Thrones, 1760–1840." *Furniture History* 25:61–85.

Robertson, J. 1863. *Inventaires de la Royne Descosse, douairière de France: Catalogue of the Jewels, Dresses, Furniture, Books and Paintings of Mary Queen of Scots*. Edinburgh.

Robertson, S. 1883. "Leeds Castle: Inventory." *Archaeologia Cantiana* 15:382–85.

Rodriguez Villa, A. 1883. "Inventario del moviliario, alhajas, ropas, armeria y otros efectos del Excelentisimo Señor D. Beltran de la Cueva, tercer duque de Albuquerque; A. 1560." *Revista de Archivos, Bibliotecas y Museos* 9:19–104. Madrid.

Rogers, P. 1988. "The Armada Tapestries in the House of Lords." *Royal Society of Arts Journal* 136:731–35.

Rome 1984. *Aspetti dell'arte a Roma prima e dopo Raffaello*. Exh. cat. (Palazzo Venezia).

Ross, C. 1997. *Edward IV*. Rev. ed. New Haven and London.

Rotuli Parliamentorum. 1773. *Rotuli Parliamentorum; ut et Petitiones et Placita in Parliamento tempore 1278–1532*. Vol. 4, *1773*, 229–41. Ed. J. Strachey et al. London.

Rowlands, J. 1985. *Holbein: The Paintings of Hans Holbein the Younger*. Oxford.

Rozmital, L. von. 1957. *The Travels of Leo of Rozmital*. Trans. and ed. M. Letts. Hakluyt Society, 2nd ser., 108. London.

Rude, D., ed. 1992. *A Critical Edition of Sir Thomas Elyot's "The Boke named the Governour."* New York.

Russell, J. G. 1969. *The Field of Cloth of Gold: Men and Manners in 1520*. London.

Russell, M., et al. 1990. *Paintings and Textiles of the Bass Museum of Art*. Miami.

Rye, W. 1865. *England as Seen by Foreigners in the Days of Elizabeth and James I Comprising Translations of the Journals of the Two Dukes of Wurtemberg in 1592 and 1610* . . . . London.

Saintenoy, P. 1921. "Les tapisseries de la cour de Bruxelles sous Charles V." *Annales de la Société Royale d'Archéologie de Bruxelles* 30:5–31.

———. 1934. "Les arts et les artistes à la cour de Bruxelles." *Académie Royale de Belgique; Classe des Beaux-Arts; Mémoires*, 2nd ser., 2, no. 3; 5th ser., no. 1. Brussels.

Salet, F. 1980. *David et Bethsabée: Château d'Écouen*. Paris.

———. 1988. "Remarques sur le vocabulaire ancien de la tapisserie." *Bulletin Monumental* 146:211–29.

Samson, A. 1999. "The Marriage of Philip of Habsburg and Mary Tudor and Anti-Spanish Sentiment in England: Political Economies and Culture, 1553–1557." Ph.D. diss., London University.

Sandford, F. 1687. *The History of the Coronation of . . . James II . . . and of His Royal Consort Queen Mary . . . with an Exact Account of the Several Preparations* . . . . London.

Saul, N. 1999. "The Kingship of Richard II." In Goodman and Gillespie 1999, 37–58.

Scarisbrick, J. 1968. *Henry VIII*. London.

Scattergood, J., ed. 1983. *John Skelton: The Complete English Poems*. Harmondsworth.

Scheifele, E. 1999. "Richard II and the Visual Arts." In Goodman and Gillespie 1999, 255–71.

Schloss Halbturn 1981. *Tapisserien der Renaissance nach Entwürfen von Pieter Coecke van Aelst.* Exh. cat. by J.-K. Steppe and R. Bauer (Schloss Halbturn). Eisenstadt.
Schnapper, A. 1994. *Curieux du grand siècle: Collections et collectionneurs dans la France du XVIIe siècle.* Vol. 2, *Oeuvres d'art.* Paris.
Schneebalg-Perelman, S. 1956–61. "'La retouchage' dans la tapisserie bruxelloise ou les origines de l'édit impérial de 1544." *Annales de la Société Royale d'Archéologie de Bruxelles* 50:191–202.
———. 1969. "Un grand tapissier bruxellois: Pierre d'Enghien dit Pierre van Aelst." In *De bloeitijd van de Vlaamse tapijtkunst,* 279–323.
———. 1971. "Richesses du garde-meuble parisien de François Ier: Inventaires inédits de 1542 et 1551." *Gazette des Beaux-Arts,* 6th ser., 78 (November):253–304.
Schofield, R. 2004. *Taxation under the Early Tudors, 1485–1547.* Oxford.
Scofield, C. L. 1923. *The Life and Reign of Edward the Fourth.* 2 vols. London.
Scot-Giles, C. 1964–65. "Some Arthurian Coats of Arms." *Coat of Arms* 8:332–39.
Shaw, W., ed. 1937. *Three Inventories of the Years 1542, 1547 and 1549–50 of Pictures in the Collections of Henry VIII and Edward VI.* London.
Shearman, J. 1972. *Raphael's Cartoons in the Collection of Her Majesty the Queen, and the Tapestries of the Sistine Chapel.* London.
Shirley, E. 1869. "An Inventory of the Effects of Henry Howard, K.G., Earl of Northampton, Taken on his Death in 1614, Together with a Transcript of His Will." *Archaeologia* 42:347–78.
Sicca, C. 2002. "Consumption and Trade of Art between Italy and England in the First Half of the Sixteenth Century: The London House of the Bardi and Cavalcanti Company." *Renaissance Studies* 16, no. 2 (June):163–202.
———. 2006. "Pawns of International Finance and Politics: Florentine Sculptors at the Court of Henry VIII." *Renaissance Studies* 20, no. 1 (February):1–34.
Siple, E. 1938. "A Flemish Set of Venus and Vulcan Tapestries: I. Their Origin and Design." *Burlington Magazine* 73 (November):212–21.
———. 1939. "A Flemish Set of Venus and Vulcan Tapestries: II. Their Influence on English Tapestry Design." *Burlington Magazine* 74 (June):268–78.
Smith, J. C. 1979. "The Artistic Patronage of Philip the Good, Duke of Burgundy (1419–1467)." 2 vols. Ph.D. diss., Columbia University.
———. 1989. "Portable Propaganda: Tapestries as Princely Metaphors at the Courts of Philip the Good and Charles the Bold." *Art Journal* 48 (Summer):123–29.
Soil, E. 1892. *Les tapisseries de Tournai: Les tapissiers et les hautelisseurs de cette ville.* Tournai.
Souchal, G. 1968. "La tenture de David et la Bible." *Gazette des Beaux Arts,* 6th ser., 71 (January):17–32.
———. 1972. "La tenture de David du Musée de Cluny." *Revue du Louvre et des Musées de France* 22, no. 1:43–50.
Spencer-Longhurst, P. 1993. *The Barber Institute of Fine Arts: Handbook.* Birmingham.
Stack, L., et al. 1993. *Conservation Research: Studies of Fifteenth- to Nineteenth-Century Tapestry.* Studies in the History of Art, 42, Monograph Series 2. Washington, DC.
Stafford, Henry, Lord. 1548. *The true dyfferens betwen the regall power and the Ecclesiastical power.* London.
Standen, E. A. 1985. *European Post-Medieval Tapestries and Related Hangings in The Metropolitan Museum of Art.* 2 vols. New York.
Staniland, K. 1987. "Royal Entry into the World." In Williams, ed., 1987, 297–314.
Stapleton, T. 1836. "A Brief Summary of the Wardrobe Accounts of the Tenth, Eleventh and Fourteenth years of King Edward the Second." *Archaeologia* 26:318–45.
Starkey, D. 1985. *The Reign of Henry VIII: Personalities and Politics.* London.
———. 1999. "Henry VI's Old Blue Gown: The English Court under the Lancastrians and Yorkists." *Court Historian* 4, no. 1 (April):1–28.
———, ed. 1998. *The Inventory of King Henry VIII: Society of Antiquaries MS 129 and British Library Harley 1419. The Transcript.* London.
Starnes, De Witt T. 1954. *Renaissance Dictionaries: English-Latin and Latin-English.* Austin, TX.
Steppe, J.-K. 1976a. "Inscriptions décoratives contenant des signatures et des mentions du lieu d'origine sur des tapisseries bruxelloises de la fin du XVe et du début du XVIe siècle." In Brussels 1976, 193–230.
———. 1976b. "Le triomphe des Vertus sur les Vices." In Brussels 1976, 100–117.
Steppe, J.-K., and G. Delmarcel. 1974. "Les tapisseries du cardinal Erard de la Marck, prince-évêque de Liège." *Revue de l'Art* 25:35–54.
Stratford, J. 1993. *The Bedford Inventories: The Worldly Goods of John, Duke of Bedford, Regent of France (1389–1435).* London.
Strieder, J. 1930. *Aus Antwerpener Notariatsarchiven.* Stuttgart.
String, T. 1996. *Henry VIII and the Art of the Royal Supremacy.* Ph.D. diss., University of Texas, Austin; Microfilm, Ann Arbor, MI.
Strong, P., and F. Strong. 1981. "The Last Will and Codicils of Henry V." *English Historical Review* 96:79–102.
Strong, R. 1967. *Holbein and Henry VIII.* London.
———. 1969. *The English Icon: Elizabethan and Jacobean Portraiture.* London.
Strype, J. 1812. *Memorials of Thomas Cranmer, Sometime Lord Archbishop of Canterbury.* 2 vols. Oxford.
Stucky-Schürer, M. 1972. *Die Passionsteppiche von San Marco in Venedig: Ihr Verhältnis zur Bildwirkerei in Paris und Arras im 14. und 15. Jahrhundert.* Bern.
Sutton, A., and P. Hammond. 1983. *The Coronation of Richard III: The Extant Documents.* Gloucester.
Swain, M. 1988. *Tapestries and Textiles at the Palace of Holyroodhouse in The Royal Collection.* London.
Szablowski, J., ed. 1972. *The Flemish Tapestries at Wawel Castle in Cracow: Treasures of King Sigismund Augustus Jagiello.* Antwerp.
Tabard, F. 1978. "The Weaver's Art." In P. Verlet et al., *The Book of Tapestry: History and Technique,* 188–224. New York.
Tafur, P. 1926. *Pero Tafur: Travels and Adventures, 1435–1439.* Trans. and ed. M. Letts. London.
Tagliaferro, L. 1981. "Per venticinque arazzi 'genovesi.'" *Bollettino dei Musei Civici Genovesi* 3, no. 7–9 (January–December):69–127.
Tanner, M. 1993. *The Last Descendant of Aeneas: The Habsburgs and the Mythic Image of the Emperor.* New Haven and London, 1993.
Thomson, T. 1815. *A Collection of Inventories and Other Records of the Royal Wardrobe and Jewelhouse, and of the Artillery and Munitoun in Some of the Royal Castles (1488–1606).* Edinburgh.
Thomson, W. G. 1906 / 1930 / 1973. *A History of Tapestry from the Earliest Times until the Present Day.* London. 2nd rev., London, 1930. 3rd rev., Wakefield, 1973.
———. 1914. *Tapestry Weaving in England from the Earliest Times to the End of the Eighteenth Century.* London.
Thurley, S. 1988. "Henry VIII and the Building of Hampton Court: A Reconstruction of the Tudor Palace." *Architectural History* 31:1–51.
———. 1991. "The Domestic Building Works of Cardinal Wolsey." In Gunn and Lindley 1991, 76–102.
———. 1993. *The Royal Palaces of Tudor England: Architecture and Court Life, 1460–1547.* New Haven and London.
———. 1999. *Whitehall Palace: An Architectural History of the Royal Apartments, 1240–1698.* New Haven and London.
———. 2003. *Hampton Court: A Social and Architectural History.* New Haven and London.
Tipping, H. 1927. *English Homes: Period III.* Vol. 2, *Late Tudor and Early Stuart, 1558–1649.* London.
Torra de Arana, E., et al. 1985. *Los tapices de la Seo de Zaragoza.* Saragossa.
Toulouse, Aix-en-Provence, Caen 2004. *Saints de choeurs: Tapisseries du Moyen Âge et de la Renaissance.* Exh cat. by Catherine Arminjon et al. (Toulouse, Ensemble conventuel des Jacobins; Aix-en-Provence, Musée des Tapisseries; Caen, Musée de Normandie). Milan.
Tournai 1967. *La tapisserie tournaisienne au XVe siècle.* Exh. cat. by J.-P. Asselberghs (Musée d'Histoire et d'Archéologie).
Tournai 1968. *La tapisserie tournaisienne au XVIe siècle.* Exh. cat. by J.-P. Asselberghs (Musée d'Histoire et d'Archéologie).
Tournai 1970. *Tapisseries héraldiques et de la vie quotidienne.* Exh. cat. by J.-P. Asselberghs (Musée d'Histoire et d'Archéologie).
Tournai 1971. *Tapisseries et laitons de choeur XVe et XVIe siècles.* Exh. cat. by J.-P. Asselberghs et al. (cathédrale Notre-Dame de Tournai).
Tournai, Brussels, Madrid 1985. *Tapisserie de Tournai en Espagne: La tapisserie bruxelloise en Espagne au XVI siècle.* Exh. cat. by E. Duverger et al. (Tournai, Brussels). Madrid.
Tout, T. 1920–33. *Chapters in the Administrative History of Medieval England: The Wardrobe, the Chamber and the Small Seals.* 6 vols. Manchester.
Trull, W. 1840. *Raphael Vindicated by a Comparison between the Original Tapestries of Leo X and the Cartoons at Hampton Court.* London.
Tudor-Craig, P. 1989. "Henry VIII and King David." In Daniel Williams, ed., *Early Tudor England:*

Proceedings of the 1987 Harlaxton Symposium, 183–205. Woodbridge.
Turin 1952. *Arazzi e tappeti antichi*. Exh. cat. by F. Mercedes Viale and V. Viale (Palazzo Madama).
Turquet, J. "The Inner Court of Nonsuch Palace." Ph.D. diss., Courtauld Institute, London University, 1983.
Uffenbach, Z. von. 1934. *London in 1710: From the Travels of Zacharias Conrad von Uffenbach*. Trans. and ed. W. Quarrel and M. Mare. London.
Unwin, G. 1966. *The Gilds and Companies of London*. London.
Utrecht 1994. *Maria van Hongarije: Koningin tussen keizers en kunstenaars, 1505–1558*. Exh. cat. ed. B. van den Boogert and J. Kerkhoff (Rijksmuseum Het Catherijneconvent, Utrecht, Noodbrabants Museum, 's-Hertogenbosch). Zwolle.
Valladolid, Medina del Campo, and Ávila. 2004. *Isabel la Católica: La magnificencia de un reinado*. Exh. cat. by E. García et al. (Valladolid, Monasterio de Nuestra Señora de Prado; Medina del Campo, Colegiata de San Antolín; Ávila, Madrigal de las Altas Torres and Monasterio de Nuestra Señora de Gracia).
Van der Doort, A. 1960. "Catalogue of the Collections of Charles I." Ed. Oliver Millar. *Walpole Society* 37 (1958–60). Glasgow.
Vandormael, H. 1988. *Château de Gaasbeek*. Brussels.
Van Tichelen, I., and G. Delmarcel. 1993. "Marks and Signatures on Ancient Flemish Tapestries: A Methodological Contribution." In Stack et al. 1993, 57–69.
Vaughan, R. 1973 / 2002. *Charles the Bold*. London. 2nd ed. with intro. by W. Paravicini, Woodbridge, 2002.
Vienna 1983. *Tapisserien im Zeichen der Kunst Raffaels*. Exh. cat. by Rotraud Bauer (Reitschule der Hofstallungen, Messepalast).
Vignau-Wilberg, T. 1995. *Von Cranach bis Beckmann: 70 Jahre "Vereinigung der Freunde."* Munich.
Walker, G. 1991. "Cardinal Wolsey and the Satirists: The Case of Godly Queen Hester Re-opened." In Gunn and Lindley 1991, 239–60.
———. 1996. *Persuasive Fictions: Faction, Faith and Political Culture in the Reign of Henry VIII*. Aldershot.
Walpole, H. 1757. *A Journey into England by Paul Hentzner in the Year 1598*. Strawberry Hill.
Walters, H. 1939. *London Churches at the Reformation*. London.
Wardle, P. 1995. "The King's Embroiderer: Edmund Harrison (1590–1667)." *Textile History* 26 no. 2:139–84.
Warren, H. 1928. "Magdalen College, Oxford: IV. The President's Lodgings." *Country Life* 64, November 3, 618–21.
Watson, A. n.d. "Extracts from Warrants of the Lord Chamberlain's Department: Furnishing of the Royal Palaces." Victoria and Albert Museum Ms. 86.GG.9.
Wauters, A. 1878. *Les tapisseries bruxelloises*. Brussels.
Wayment, H. 1968. "A Rediscovered Master: Adrien van den Houte (c. 1459–1521) and the Malines/ Brussels School, II: Adrian van den Houte as a Tapestry Designer." *Oud Holland* 83:71–94.
Wegner, W. 1973. *Die niederländischen Handzeichnungen des 15.–18. Jahrhunderts*. 2 vols. Kataloge der Staatlichen Graphischen Sammlung München, 1. Berlin.
Weigert, L. 1994. *Weaving Sacred Stories: Narratives of Saints in French Choir Tapestry*. Ph.D. diss., Northwestern University; Microfilm, Ann Arbor, MI.
———. 2004a. "Les tentures de choeur des églises françaises du Moyen Âge à la Renaissance." In Toulouse, Aix-en-Provence, Caen 2004, 16–39.
———. 2004b. *Weaving Sacred Stories: French Choir Tapestries and the Performance of Clerical Identity*. Ithaca, NY.
Weightman, C. 1989. *Margaret of York, Duchess of Burgundy, 1446–1503*. London.
Weil-Garris, K., and J. d'Amico. 1980. "The Renaissance Cardinal's Ideal Palace: A Chapter from Cortesi's 'De Cardinalatu.'" In H. Millon, ed., *Studies in Italian Art and Architecture: Fifteenth through Eighteenth Centuries*, 45–124. Memoirs of the American Academy in Rome, 35. Rome.
Weir, A. 2001. *Henry VIII: King and Court*. London.
Whitley, W. 1928. *Artists and Their Friends in England, 1700–1799*. London.
Wilckens, L. von. 1991. *Die textilen Kunste von der Spätantike vis um 1500*. Munich.
Willan, T. 1962. *A Tudor Book of Rates*. Manchester.
Williams, D., ed. 1987. *England in the Fifteenth Century: Proceedings of the 1986 Harlaxton Symposium*. Woodbridge.
Wingfield-Digby, G., assisted by W. Hefford. 1971. *The Devonshire Hunting Tapestries*. London.
———. 1980. *The Tapestry Collection, Medieval and Renaissance*. Victoria and Albert Museum, London.
Winter, P. de. 1976. *The Patronage of Philippe Le Hardi, Duke of Burgundy (1364–1404)*. Ph.D. diss., New York University, 1976; Microfilm, Ann Arbor, MI.
———. 1985. *La bibliothèque de Philippe le Hardi, duc de Bourgogne (1364–1404)*. Paris.
Wood, M. 1965. *The English Mediaeval House*. London.
Zupko, R. 1981. *Italian Weights and Measures from the Middle Ages to the Nineteenth Century*. Memoirs of the American Philosophical Society, 145.

Index

Italic page numbers refer to illustrations

Illustration Credits

Restoration funded by Aéroports de Paris. RMN & Aéroports de Paris. Photo: De Wit Royal Manufacturers, 10.1, 10.2, 10.5, 10.6, 10.7, 10.8, 10.9, 10.10; Alinari Archive, Florence, 4.6; By permission of Anova Books Company Limited, 19.10; Médiathèque d'Arras ms.no.266, 8.12; Ashmolean Museum, Oxford, 4.9, 6.13, 13.3, 13.11, 16.3; Collection of the Bass Museum of Art, Gift of John and Johanna Bass, 6.4; Bayerische Staatsbibliothek München, Cod.gall.6, 3.4; Bernisches Historisches Museum, 2.16, 3.6; © Robert Spencer Bernard, Photograph by Bruce White, 12.11; Bibliothèque nationale de France, 3.3, 8.5, 8.6, 18.8; © Bibliothèque publique et universitaire, Geneva, Switzerland, 2.12; © Martin Biddle, 13.23, 13.24; Courtesy of Biltmore Estate Asheville, N.C. © The Biltmore Co., 15.8; © British Library Board. All Rights Reserved (Add Ms.18850), 2.13; © British Library Board. All Rights Reserved (C.132.h.46), 12.4; © British Library Board. All Rights Reserved (MS Harl.4380), 1.14, 1.15; © British Library Board. All Rights Reserved (MS Royal 2 A XVI), 12.6, 12.7; © British Library Board. All Rights Reserved (MS Royal 14 EIV), 1.7; © British Library Board. All Rights Reserved (MS Royal 17 F II), 3.9; © British Library Board. All Rights Reserved (MS Royal 19 E V), 3.12; Copyright the Trustees of The British Museum, 11.12, 13.1, 17.4, 18.7; Brussels Stadhuis/ Hôtel de Ville, 6.16; Cabildo Metropolitano de Zaragoza, 2.8, 3.14, 4.8, 5.3; Caixa Geral de Depósitos (Lisbon), 7.2; Castle Ashby, 15.11; Cathédral Saint-Just, Narbonne, Photographs by Bruce White, 4.19, 5.2; Genoa, Civiche Collezioni (P.B.1903). Photo: Centro di documentazione per la storia, l'arte et l'immagine di Genova / Paolo Repetto, 3.2; Ayuntamiento de Madrid, Colección Municipal Dispersa, 3.11, 4.7; © College of Arms, 6.3; The Berger Collection at the Denver Art Museum, 6.1; Gift of K. T. Keller. Photograph © 1984 The Detroit Institute of Arts, 13.8; Founders Society Purchase. Photo: De Wit Royal Manufacturers. © 2004 The Detroit Institute of Arts, 12.14; Reproduced by permission of English Heritage, MNR, 1.8, 9.11, 19.12; Fine Arts Museums of San Francisco, Gift of The William Randolph Hearst Foundation, 54.14.4, 4.2; Reproduction by permission of the Syndics of the Fitzwilliam Museum, Cambridge, 16.2, 16.5; Franses Tapestry Archive, London, 10.19, 15.6; By permission of The Free Library of Philadelphia, 3.15; © The Frick Collection, New York, 12.15; © Germanisches Nationalmuseum, Nürnberg, 1.13; Hunter Archive, Getty Research Institute, 13.14, 13.15, 13.16; © Glasgow City Council (Museums), 2.19, 6.7, 9.7, 11.15; © Guildhall Library, City of London, 13.13; Reproduced by kind permission of Haddon Hall, 4.13; Domschatzverwaltung, Halberstadt, 1.1; With permission from Lord Hesketh, 5.5; © Hever Castle, 4.12, 13.7; © Historic Royal Palaces, 8.7, 9.1, 13.21, 15.3, 17.2, 17.5, 18.6, 19.5, 19.9, 19.13, 19.14, 19.15; Institut de France—Paris, Musée Jacquemart-André, 10.15; © Iparmıvészeti Múzeum, Budapest, 10.13; Isabella Stewart Gardner Museum, Boston, 2.18, 13.4; © Kunsthistorisches Museum, Wien, 3.1, 8.3, 11.19, 12.10, 15.1; Photo F. Lauginie, 13.5; The Master and Fellows, Magdalene College, Cambridge, 9.10; The Metropolitan Museum of Art, Bequest of Susan Dwight Bliss, 1966 (67.55.1010), Image © 2006 The Metropolitan Museum of Art, 8.2; The Metropolitan Museum of Art, The Cloisters Collection, 1959 (59.85), Photograph © The Metropolitan Museum of Art, 2.2; The Metropolitan Museum of Art, Harris Brisbane Dick Fund, 1928, Photograph © The Metropolitan Museum of Art, 15.12; The Metropolitan Museum of Art, Harris Brisbane Dick Fund, 1930 (inv.30.54.32), Photograph © The Metropolitan Museum of Art, 19.2; The Metropolitan Museum of Art, Harris Brisbane Dick Fund, 1953 (inv.53.6.2617), Photograph © The Metropolitan Museum of Art, 19.3; The Metropolitan Museum of Art, Harris Brisbane Dick Fund, 1943 (inv.43.95), Photograph © The Metropolitan Museum of Art, 19.4; The Metropolitan Museum of Art, The Robert Lehman Collection 1975, 1975.1.1915, 10.16; The Metropolitan Museum of Art, Gift of Harriet Barnes Pratt, in memory of her husband Harold Irving Pratt (1877–1939), 1949 (45.76), Photograph © 1981 The Metropolitan Museum of Art, 2.7; The Metropolitan Museum of Art, Gift of John D. Rockefeller, Jr., 1947 (47.101.1), Photograph © 1985 The Metropolitan Museum of Art, 2.2; The Metropolitan Museum of Art, Rogers Fund, 1909 (09.137.2) Photograph © 1990 The Metropolitan Museum of Art, 2.14; The Metropolitan Museum of Art, Rogers Fund, 1946 (46.175), Photograph © The Metropolitan Museum of Art, 1.3; The Metropolitan Museum of Art, Photograph: Bruce Schwarz, 1.4, 1.5, 1.6, 1.7; The Metropolitan Museum of Art, The Elisha Whittelsey Collection, The Elisha Whittelsey Fund (inv.59.570.200[11]), Photograph © The Metropolitan Museum of Art, 18.4; Paris, Collection du Mobilier National. Cliché du Mobilier National, 13.2; Collection Musée Antoine Lécuyer, Saint-Quentin, France. Photographie du Musée Antoine Lécuyer, Saint-Quentin, France, 7.8, 9.2; Les Arts Décoratifs. Musée des Arts décoratifs, Paris. Photos Laurent Sully Jaulmes. All rights reserved, 2.4, 3.13; Cliché Musées de Sens, J.-P. Elie, 7.7, 9.3; © Musée des Tissus et des Arts Décoratifs. Photo de Studio Basset, 4.5; Assessorato ai Musei Politiche Culturali e Spettacolo del Comune di Padova, 1.11; © Museo Catedralicio, Zamora, Photographs by Bruce White, 3.10, 4.3, 5.4, 17.1; Segovia, Museo de Tapices, Palacio de San Ildefonso. Inv. PN. S./5. Photograph by Bruce White. © 1991 The Metropolitan Museum of Art, 9.12; © Museo Thyssen-Bornemisza, Madrid, 12.1; Photograph © 2007 Museum of Fine Arts, Boston, 7.3, 7.13; Nationaal Scheepvaart Museum, Antwerp, 13.2; © The National Gallery, London, 1.9; Andrew W. Mellon Collection, Image © 2006 Board of Trustees, National Gallery of Art, Washington, 14.3; Widener Collection, Image © 2006 Board of Trustees, National Gallery of Art, Washington, 1.9, 4.18, 10.14, 10.17; © National Portrait Gallery, London, 4.1, 8.11, 10.11, 11.1; Madrid, Palacio Real (Inv. PN. S.26/5), Photograph by Bruce White. © 1991 The Metropolitan Museum of Art, 11.7; Palazzo Bianco Genoa, 13.6; © Patrimonio Nacional, 6.14, 6.15, 6.19, 6.20, 9.9, 11.17, 11.18, 13.10, 13.12, 13.17, 18.3; © Pierre Peeters, 1.12; The Pierpont Morgan Library, New York, 11.16; Per gentile concessione della Fototeca della Soprintendenza Speciale per il Polo Mussale napoletano, 11.9; Private Collection, 9.14; Image Bernard Renoux © CMN, Paris, 1.5, 1.6; © Photos RMN, 1.4, 2.3, 2.5, 4.4, 5.1, 6.10, 6.11, 7.1, 11.5, 11.8, 11.10, 11.11, 13.22; The Board of Trustees of The Royal Armouries, 10.3, 10.4; The Royal Collection © 2006, Her Majesty Queen Elizabeth II, Photograph: The Author, 14.8, 18.9; The Royal Collection © 2006, Her Majesty Queen Elizabeth II, 2.9, 3.7, 3.8, 4.10, 4.16, 6.8, 7.5, 7.6, 7.9, 7.10, 7.11, 8.1, 8.13, 9.8, 9.13, 11.2, 11.3, 11.4, 12.2, 12.3, 12.5, 12.8, 14.2, 14.5, 14.6, 14.7, 14.9, 14.15, 15.13, 16.1, 16.4, 17.6, 18.2, 19.1, 19.7, 19.8, 19.9, 19.11, 14.12; The Royal Collection © 2006, Her Majesty Queen Elizabeth II. Photograph: Bruce White, 1.1, 1.3, 1.8, 6.6, 6.22, 9.4, 9.5, 13.18, 13.19, 14.4, 14.10, 14.11, 14.13, 14.16, 17.3, pp. ii, viii, 346; © Royal Museums of Art and History—Brussels, 1.10, 2.21, 3.5, 6.9, 6.21, 7.4, 9.6, 11.13, 11.14; By permission of the Master and Fellows of St. John's College, Cambridge, 6.2; Saint Mary's Hall, Coventry, 4.17; Schloss Friedrichshof 12.13; © Shannon Heritage 2006, 13.9; Fürstlich Hohenzollernschen Sammlung Sigmaringen, 6.17; By permission of the Society of Antiquaries of London, 18.1, 19.6; By courtesy of the Society of Jesus, London, 4.11; By courtesy of Sotheby's Picture Library, London, 6.12, 7.12; Kupferstich-Kabinett, Staatliche Kunstsammlungen Dresden, 2.15; The State Hermitage Museum, St. Petersburg, 6.5; © Tarragona Cathedral, Photographs by Bruce White, 2.20; Toledo Museum of Art, Purchased with funds from the Libbey Endowment Gift of Edward Drummond Libbey, 1928.204, 6.18; Courtesy of the Vatican Museums, 13.14, 14.1; Photo Vatican Museums, 11.6; © V&A Images / Victoria and Albert Museum, 1.2, 2.6, 2.11, 4.2, 8.4, 8.8, 10.18, 10.20, 12.12, 13.12;; Photographs by Richard Shorter, reproduced by kind permission of the Warden and Scholars of Winchester College, 4.14; Courtesy of the Worshipful Company of Barbers, 12.9; Reproduced by kind permission of the Dean and Chapter of York, 1.2.

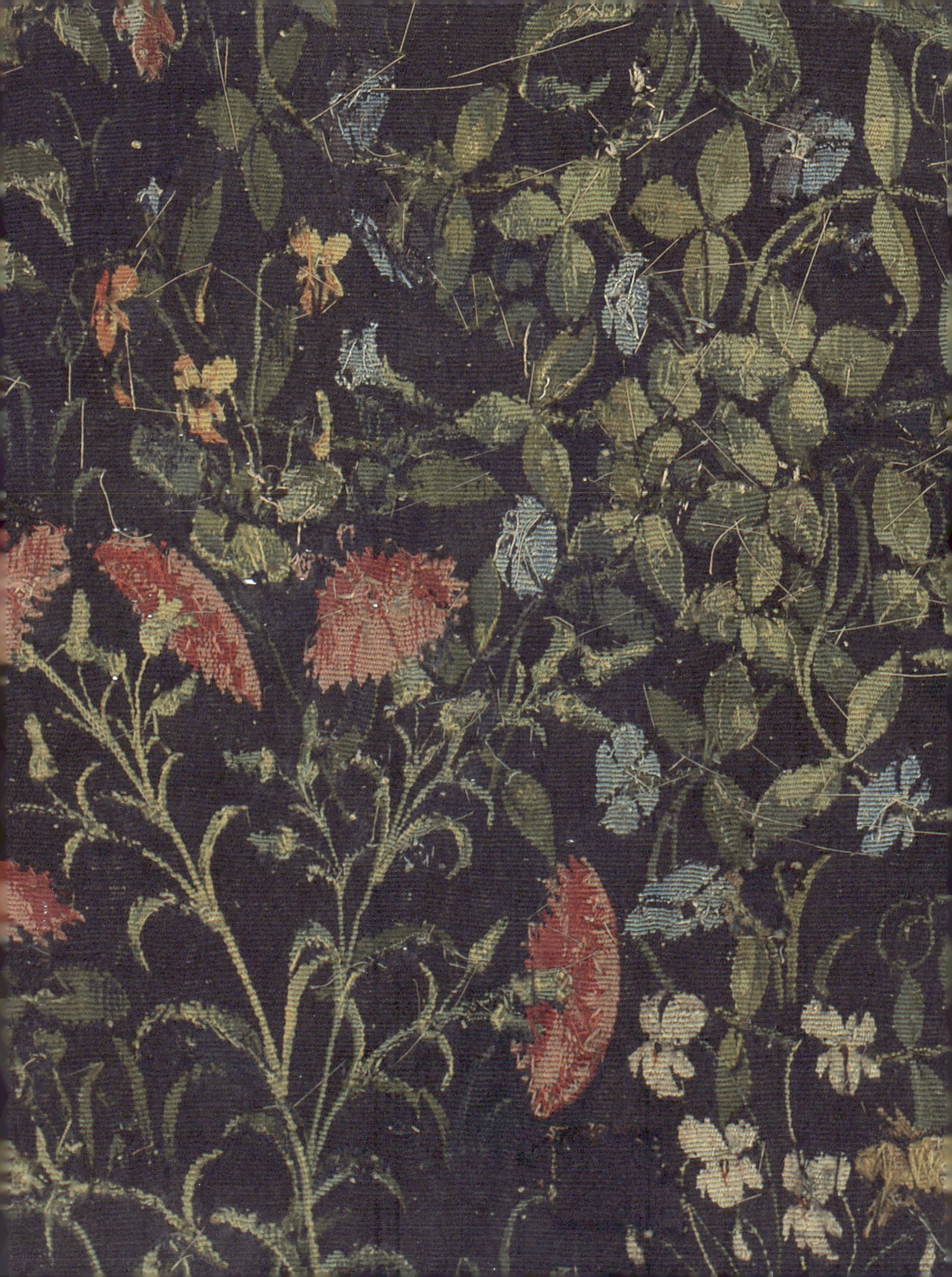